Library of America, a nonprofit organization,
champions our nation's cultural heritage
by publishing America's greatest writing in
authoritative new editions and providing resources
for readers to explore this rich, living legacy.

ALBERT MURRAY

ALBERT MURRAY

COLLECTED ESSAYS & MEMOIRS

The Omni-Americans
South to a Very Old Place
The Hero and the Blues
Stomping the Blues
The Blue Devils of Nada
From the Briarpatch File
Other Writings

Henry Louis Gates Jr.
and Paul Devlin, *editors*

THE LIBRARY OF AMERICA

South to a Very Old Place copyright © 1971 by Albert Murray. *The Hero
and the Blues* copyright © 1973 by Albert Murray. *The Blue Devils of Nada*
copyright © 1996 by Albert Murray. Published by arrangement with Vintage
Anchor Publishing, an imprint of The Knopf Doubleday Publishing Group, a
division of Penguin Random House LLC.

The Omni-Americans copyright © 1970 by Albert Murray. *Stomping the Blues*
copyright © 1976 by Albert Murray. *From the Briarpatch File* copyright ©
2001 by Albert Murray. "'The Problem' Is Not Just Black and White," *Life*,
July 3, 1964, copyright © 1964 by Albert Murray. "U.S. Negroes and U.S.
Jews: No Cause for Alarm," copyright © 2016 by The Albert Murray Trust.
"'Soul': Thirty-two Meanings Not in Your Dictionary," *Book World*, June 23,
1968, copyright © 1968 by Albert Murray. "'Stone': Definition and Usage,"
Book World, April 20, 1969, copyright © 1969 by Albert Murray, "Two Na-
tions? Only Two?" *American Heritage*, December 1994, copyright © 1994
by Albert Murray. "Bearden in Theory and Ritual," from *Romare Bearden in
Black-and-White: Photomontage Projections 1964*, by Gail Gelburd and Thelma
Golden (New York: Whitney Museum of American Art, 1997), copyright ©
1997 by Albert Murray. Published by arrangement with The Albert Murray
Trust and The Wylie Agency LLC.

"Three Omni-American Artists" and "Jazz: Notes Toward a Definition,"
from *Murray Talks Music: Albert Murray on Jazz and Blues*, edited by Paul
Devlin (University of Minnesota Press, 2016), copyright © 2016 by the
Regents of the University of Minnesota. Published by arrangement with the
University of Minnesota Press.

This paper meets the requirements of
ANSI/NISO Z39.48–1992 (Permanence of Paper).

Distributed to the trade in the United States
by Penguin Random House Inc.
and in Canada by Penguin Random House Canada Ltd.

Library of Congress Control Number: 2016934861
ISBN 978–1–59853–503–7

First Printing
The Library of America—284

Manufactured in the United States of America

Albert Murray:
Collected Essays & Memoirs
is published with support from

Charlie Davidson
Futhermore / J. M. Kaplan Fund
Crystal McCrary and Raymond J. McGuire
Stephen and Mary Beth Daniel
Jazz at Lincoln Center
Lewis and Kristin Jones
Henry and Celia McGee
Larry Miller
Douglas E. Schoen
Joyce and George Wein Foundation
&
Dr. Benjamin F. Payton,
in gratitude to the faculty of Tuskegee University
for Albert Murray's stellar undergraduate education.

Contents

THE OMNI-AMERICANS

Some Alternatives
to the Folklore
of White Supremacy

To my wife Mozelle Menefee Murray
and for our daughter Michele,
a stage to dance on and
also some shoulders to stand on

The individual stands in opposition to society, but he is nourished by it. And it is far less important to know what differentiates him than what nourishes him. Like the genius, the individual is valuable for what there is within him. . . . Every psychological life is an exchange, and the fundamental problem of the living individual is knowing upon what he intends to feed.

—André Malraux

CONTENTS

5

Introduction

IN A GENERAL SENSE perhaps all statements are also counter-statements. Even the simplest pronouncements, for example, whether of measurable fact or of a point of view, are also assertions to contradict something that is assumed to be otherwise. Perhaps even the most objective descriptions, definitions, and formulations (as well as being implicit protestations against subjectivity, imprecision, and fantasy) are in effect counter-actions against the void of the undefined, unformulated, and confusing. It may be, then, that such opening remarks as are found in the forewords to books are really answers before the questions; nay, replies, retorts, and refutations to exceptions that are not only bound to be taken but in a sense already have been.

In the same general sense statements may also be restatements. For instance, on close inspection, affirmation for one thing not only is an inevitable negation of something else but may also be a revision and extension. Seldom does unanimity stop with a simple yes or no. A concurring *yes*, that is to say, is not only a dissenting *no* to a different set of *yes*es but may also be a modification or adaptation that rephrases an implicit, perhaps unrecognized, question.

Even the most casual personal introductions are counter-statements of a sort. Names exist to counteract confusion of identity—*and intention*—in the first place. Thus even as an author, for example, tells you his name he declares his position (and involves himself in opposition!). Any name will do, of course, even the illiterate X designed as His Mark, for instance.

Nor are chance extensions of, or chance associations with, or puns upon any name without functional significance. (Martin Luther King *was* a Martin Luther, a reformer in rebellion against orthodoxy.) For example, at a time when an ever increasing number of writers seems to mistake the jargon of social science for insight into the nature and condition of man, if the name of a brown-skin U.S. Negro student of fiction and Americana reminds a few readers, by whatever chance, of Gilbert Murray, the great English author of *The Rise of the Greek*

Epic and *Five Stages of Greek Religion*, and suggests, no matter how remotely, that the study of ritual might be a means of coming to terms with some of the ambiguities of human nature and conduct that may be outside the scope of current survey methodology, such an association might not be far from the intentions of that brown-skin student. If the juxtaposition further suggests to those who, perhaps unwittingly, have oversubscribed to social science, that interpretations of human behavior in the raw require at least as much respect for the complexity of human motives as the interpretation of a poem or play or a story, well, perhaps one might not even need to bother with saying anything other than one's name. But at the risk of being overly explanatory, let me be definite about the statements, counter-statements, restatements that have gone into the making of *The Omni-Americans*, a book, whose very title is intended as no small counter-statement.

II

The essays, commentaries, and reviews out of which *The Omni-Americans* has been built, are all intended as counter-statements and restatements in the generic sense. Their most general significance should be suggested by the title. To race-oriented propagandists, whether white or black, the title of course makes no sense: they would have things be otherwise. But the United States is in actuality not a nation of black people and white people. It is a nation of multicolored people. There are white Americans so to speak and black Americans. But any fool can see that the white people are not really white, and that black people are not black. They are all interrelated one way or another. Thus the title *The Omni-Americans* is among other things an attempt to restate the problem formulated by the *Report of the National Advisory Commission on Civil Disorders* by suggesting that the present domestic conflict and upheaval grows out of the fact that in spite of their common destiny and deeper interests, the people of the United States are being misled by misinformation to insist on *exaggerating* their ethnic differences. The problem is not the existence of ethnic differences, as is so often assumed, but the intrusion of such differences into areas where they do not belong. Ethnic

differences are the very essence of cultural diversity and national creativity.

In the context of the so-called national dialogue on the nature
and implications of black experience, the counter-statements of
The Omni-Americans are specifically forensic in intent. Each,
that is to say, was written in an effort to make, so to speak, an
affirmative rebuttal to negative allegations and conclusions
about some aspects of Negro life in the United States. As a
result they become not only somewhat argumentative from
time to time, but also, and quite deliberately, polemical. Unlike
the standard polemics of black American protest, however,
they are immediately concerned not so much with political
injustice as such as with inaccuracies and misconceptions that
contribute to and even rationalize injustice. They question and
dispute the reliability, validity, and comprehensiveness of information. They challenge and restate the issues. They suggest
alternative points of view, and they seek to provide *a basis for
action* which is compatible with those facts that in instances
when Negroes are not involved are generally assumed to represent the universal element in all human nature.

In directing themselves toward action, these polemics, one
would hope, are to be distinguished from the polemics of
moral outcry, such for instance as are found in the well-known
works of Richard Wright and James Baldwin, two of the most
powerful exponents of protest/accusation since the days of
Émile Zola. The work of these writers (who will be the subject
for further examination) seems to be designed to make those
toward whom it is directed—i.e., white racists—feel guilty and
fearful: white man, listen—or be damned. Take heed and mend
your sinful ways because if you don't, I foresee fire and brimstone next time and believe me, you're going to get just what
you deserve!

Producing guilt may or may not be fine, but stimulating intelligent action is better. And intelligent action always needs to
have its way paved by a practical estimate of the situation. The
immediate objective of the polemics in *The Omni-Americans* is
to expose the incompetence and consequent impracticality of
people who are regarded as intellectuals but are guided by racial bias rather than reason based on scholarly insight. *How is it
that you white people who otherwise seem to be so knowledgeable*

and competent are suddenly so obtuse about something that is as obvious as the fact that human nature is no less complex and fascinating for being encased in dark skin? Don't you know that the direction of such stupidity is just the kind of general confusion that will destroy all of us? Don't you even know that prisoners sleep better than jailors? Get wise. As of now you are working against your own interest as much as that of your black compatriots! Furthermore, to the extent that your misdefinitions are picked up by Negroes, you are only aggravating the problem. This just simply is not the time for the politics of unexamined slogans.

The prime target of these polemics is the professional observer/reporter (that major vehicle of the nation's information, alas) who relies on the so-called findings and all-too-inclusive extrapolations of social science survey technicians for their sense of the world. The bias of *The Omni-Americans* is distinctly proliterary. It represents the dramatic sense of life as against the terminological abstractions and categories derived from laboratory procedures. Its interests, however, are not those of a literary sensibility at odds with scientific method. Not by any means. On the contrary, a major charge of the argument advanced here is that most social science survey findings are not scientific enough. They violate one's common everyday breeze-tasting sense of life precisely because they do not meet the standards of validity, reliability, and comprehensiveness that the best scientists have always insisted on. As a result they provide neither a truly practical sociology of the so-called black community nor a dependable psychology of black behavior.

At any rate, the counter-formulations posed in *The Omni-Americans* are expressions of a sensibility structured, no matter how imperfectly, by science as well as literature. They are submitted as antidotes against the pernicious effects of a technological enthusiasm inadequately counter-balanced by a literary sense of the ambiguities and absurdities inherent in all human experience. To the literary sensibility, which is geared not to categorical jargon but to such universal patterns of human behavior as emerge from stories of suspenseful trials and instructive errors, the problems created by the misapplication of data are no less social than intellectual.

The overenthusiastic use of the highly specialized concepts

of clinical psychology to define social conditions that are obviously beyond the controlled observation of the laboratory (and to do so without having established a "criterion" for normal limits) results in oversimplification. Like the glib pseudo-terminological use of such clichés as the ghetto, minority group, middle class Negro, and so on, it can never do justice to the facts of life. And as in the courtroom, doing justice to people goes hand in hand with doing justice to the evidence involved in their case.

The Omni-Americans is based in large measure on the assumption that since the negative aspects of black experience are constantly being overpublicized (and to little purpose except to obscure the positive), justice to U.S. Negroes, not only as American citizens but also as the fascinating human beings that they so obviously are, is best served by suggesting some of the affirmative implications of their history and culture. After all, someone must at least begin to try to do justice to what U.S. Negroes *like* about being black and to what they *like* about being *Americans*. Otherwise justice can hardly be done to the incontestable fact that not only do they choose to live rather than commit suicide, but that, poverty and injustice notwithstanding, far from simply struggling in despair, they live with gusto and a sense of elegance that has always been downright enviable.

But then perhaps only works of fiction on the scale of Tolstoy, Joyce, and Thomas Mann can truly do justice to the enduring humanity of U.S. Negroes, people who, for instance, can say of their oppressors, "Yeah, we got our troubles all right. But still and all, if white folks could be black for just one Saturday night they wouldn't never want to be white folks no more!" By which is not implied that white people necessarily should give up any wealth and power—but after all, the overwhelming majority of white people are neither wealthy nor powerful!

Maybe black assets are so seldom mentioned in books by most other U.S. Negro writers because such things are simply taken for granted. Underlying every allegation of *The Omni-Americans*, however, is the frank contention that the time for accentuating the positive and eliminating the negative is long overdue. This case for the affirmative is presented in three parts.

Part One, which consists of the title essay, begins with a discussion of the so-called question of black identity in terms of the cultural dynamics involved in the formation of the national character of the United States as a whole; moves on to an indictment of those theorists and social welfare technicians whose statistics-oriented interpretations of black experience add up to what functions as a folklore of white supremacy and a fakelore of black pathology; and concludes with a review, intended as a stimulus and rudimentary orientation for more extensive investigation and development by scholars and creative writers alike, of the actualities and potentialities of black American experience as such elements are reflected in the blues idiom, one of the art styles most characteristic of U.S. Negro self-expression.

All of the reviews, articles, and pop-off exercises in Part Two, "The Illusive Black Image," were specifically intended as nonfiction counter-sketches, as it were—or indeed as sketch page erasures of images that were unlikenesses. (This material was written on various occasions between 1964 and 1969, and in some instances has been revised and expanded for inclusion here.) Together the selections are meant to define a continuing concern with the ways in which writers who are advertised as scholars produce social science fictions instead of scientific information—and how writers who are advertised as storytellers and artists produce pseudo-scientific social theories.

The reflections on black studies, black consciousness, and black heritage in Part Three represent extensions and applications of an assumption that is implicit in the definition of the Omni-American, that the function of education in the United States is to develop citizens who are fully oriented to cultural diversity—and are not hung up on race.

III

When issues engage widespread public attention, the so-called national dialogue becomes more of a verbal free for all than a formally (or informally) structured debate. As in a battle royal, everybody is out to get in his own punchline. In such a context, the literary intellectual or would-be intellectual assumes responsibilities and takes prerogatives somewhat similar to those of a piano player in a jam session. His relationship to the argument's overall frame of reference is very much like the relationship of the piano player to the chordal structure and progression of the piece of music being used as the basis for improvisation. Of all the musicians in a jam session, it is most likely the piano player who provides the point of reference in the score. He is not necessarily the best musician in the session, but his approach, like that of the apprentice to literature, is necessarily comprehensive. Thus he is not only authorized but obligated to remind the other participants what the musical "discussion" is about. Indeed, the most self-effacing accompanist did as much for Bessie Smith and for Coleman Hawkins.

These are the obligations assumed here. That few writers are likely to be able to exert the definitive authority of a Duke Ellington (who, the reader will see, is a hero of this book) is only too obvious. Nevertheless, once taking a position at the keyboard, even the novice on his first gig is required by the very nature of his responsibility to forget that he is not Duke Ellington. In any case, no matter what else he may be, the literary piano player is a would-be arranger-composer and maestro of discussions, who finds himself calling the soloists home in spite of himself. Sometimes he may even rap a knuckle here and there (almost as if he were also old Professor "Clinkscales"—which he definitely is not), but only in interest of the total sound and in accordance with his reading of the score, which of course is far from infallible but at least reaches for a sense of the whole.

In the context of a national dialogue, perhaps the only authorization required for "putting in your little two cents worth" is the constitutional provision for free speech. Moreover, the basis for the presumptions of dissent and counter-statement is the same as for popping off: the merest hint or suspicion that outrage is being committed against one's conception of actuality.

As for intellectual or scholarly authority, perhaps it is better never to claim more than one's ideas as expressed can make self-evident. By the same token, no more will be conceded to the opposition than, say, a Negro athlete would allow an opponent who has a Ph.D. in physical education from Harvard or Yale. There is simply too little difference between official certification and media promotion as things now stand.

Uptown Manhattan, 1969

PART I

The Omni-Americans

The Omni-Americans

In the prelude to *Joseph and His Brothers*, Thomas Mann, whose awareness of context as a space-time continuum was as functional as it was comprehensive, refers to the historical background of things as being a bottomless well. He then goes on to suggest that it is bottomless indeed if what one has in mind is the background of mankind, which he describes as being a "riddling essence" encompassing one's own "normally unsatisfied" but quite "abnormally wretched" existence. The mystery of the bottomlessness past, he points out, not only includes one's own mystery but is in fact the beginning as well as the end of all inquiries and is thus also the mystery that gives immediacy to all statements and significance to all human endeavor.

According to Mann, a bottomless or formless quality is the essential nature of the space-time continuum of human experience. The deeper one probes into the background of mankind, the further the earliest foundations of culture recede into vagueness and myth. Moreover, as Lord Raglan corroborates in *The Hero: A Study of Tradition, Myth and Drama*, recent foundations have a way of receding in much the same manner. In any case, the ultimate sources of derivation almost always tend to defy scientific verification.

Nonetheless, writes Mann in a passage which suggests that the whole of history itself is largely mythological, "There may exist provisional origins, which practically and in fact form the first beginnings of the particular tradition held by a given community, folk or communion of faith; and memory, though sufficiently instructed that the depths have not actually been plumbed, yet nationally may find reassurance in some prehistoric period of time, and personally and historically speaking, come to rest there." As did the memory of Joseph himself, for instance, who for his part, as Mann goes to some lengths to show, regarded a certain occurrence in Babylonia as the beginning of all things, that is, of all that mattered to him—or more precisely, since such reassurance, whether national or personal, is always likely to be interwoven with strategic considerations, all that really mattered as an operational frame of reference. "In such wise," Mann adds later in his prelude, "are formed those beginnings, those time-coulisses of the past where memory may pause and find a hold whereon to base its personal history." And hence its national myths and symbols.

In other words, how far back into the past one goes in order to establish the beginnings of one's own tradition or cultural idiom is not only relative but even at best is also, on close inspection, very likely to be downright arbitrary and quite in accordance with some specific functional combination of desirable skills and attitudes in terms of which one wishes to project oneself. Thus there are some (many of whom are the makers of schoolbooks) who mark the beginnings of the American tradition from the time of the landings of the first Europeans in the Western Hemisphere, if not from the birth of Christopher Columbus (who never even saw the mainland). There are others for whom the settling of Virginia marked the official as well as the mythological birth of the nation. For still others it is as if nothing of significance happened before the landing of the *Mayflower*. And other "original beginnings" have been located in the Boston Tea Party, the Battle of Bunker Hill, the signing of the Declaration of Independence, the Constitutional Convention at Philadelphia. So it goes depending upon the orientation of the historian.

Constance Rourke (author of *American Humor: A Study of the National Character* and *The Roots of American Culture*), unlike many such historians, assumed quite accurately that there were "time-coulisses" in the pre-Columbian past that were relevant to the understanding of the American experience. Of the Boston Tea Party, for example, she wrote that "it may well be a question whether the participants enjoyed more dumping the tea in the harbor or masquerading in war paint and feathers with brandished tomahawks." "On the frontier," she goes on to say, "the whites had adopted Indian dress and used Indian weapons, among other things, keeping the names of villages, for instance, even when the original inhabitants had been ruthlessly expelled."

Nor did Constance Rourke overlook the Negro elements
that have long been so deeply embedded in what she refers to
as the "national character." "The Negro," she writes in a reference to a visit by a European to the America of 1795, "was to
be seen everywhere in the South and in the new Southwest, on
small farms and great plantations, on roads and levees. He was
often an all but equal member of many a pioneering expedi-
tion. He became, in short, a dominant figure in spite of his
condition, and commanded a definite portraiture." What is
more, Rourke's acclaimed scholarly investigations of the origin
and development of black face minstrels did not lead her to
confuse elements of the national character with the folklore of
white supremacy. Quite the contrary, her image of The American is a composite that is part Yankee, part backwoodsman
and Indian, and part Negro. In tracing this composite, she was
not unaware of the profound implications of *homo Americanus*
as a vernacular adaptation, modification, and extension of
homo Europaeus, whom Paul Valéry once described as a combination of ancient Greek, ancient Roman, and Judeo-Christian.

The three interwoven figures in the native fabric loomed
large, Constance Rourke explains, "not because they represented any considerable numbers in the population but because something in the nature of each induced an irresistible
response. Each had been a wanderer over the lands, the Negro
a forced and unwilling wanderer. Each in a fashion of his own
had broken bonds, the Yankee in the initial revolt against the
parent civilization, the backwoodsman in revolt against all civilization, the Negro in a revolt which was cryptic and submerged
but which nonetheless made a perceptible outline." Such figures,
she goes on, were the embodiment of a deepseated "mood of
disseverance, carrying the popular fancy further and further
from any fixed or traditional heritage. *Their comedy, their irreverent wisdom, their sudden changes and adroit adaptations provided emblems for a pioneer people who required resilience as a
prime trait.*" (Italics added.)

So wrote Constance Rourke, whose richly informed observations on the texture of life in the United States seem to have
exercised no significant influence on the so-called findings of
the current crop of social science survey technicians. Nor is

there any compelling evidence that her influence has been re-markably stronger among historians and literary intellectuals—most of whom, it turns out, are no less oriented to the folklore of white supremacy than are politicians. Nevertheless, so did she delineate the image and pattern of *homo Americanus*, and thus did she locate the taproots of contemporary style, and so in the process define "all that matters" in the national charac-ter. And however provisional as an historical coulisse or even a geographical coulisse, such is the composite wellspring from which the mainstream of American tradition derives.

Whence also, and no less directly or inevitably, is derived the U.S. Negro idiom, for all its distinctive nuances. There is, of course, no question at all that the ultimate source of the dance-orientation so central to the life style of most contem-porary U.S. Negroes lies somewhere in the uncharted reaches of some region of prehistoric Africa. But for all immediate practical purposes, the blues tradition, a tradition of confron-tation and improvisation—that is, to use Rourke's word, of "resilience"—is indigenous to the United States, along with the Yankee tradition and that of the backwoodsman.

Thus, though recognizing that the depths, which after all are bottomless, have not actually been plumbed, there is no truly urgent reason to trace the origin of U.S. Negro style and manner any farther back in time than the arrival of a Dutch ship of war in Virginia with a cargo of twenty black captives for sale in 1619—if indeed that far. Negroes definitely were reluc-tant immigrants to the new world, but in view of the life they had experienced in the land of their origin, they could hardly have regarded it as a stronghold of individual freedom and limitless opportunity. Nor could they have been unmindful of the obvious fact that Africans "back home" were as actively engaged in the slave trade as were the Europeans and Ameri-cans. Many contemporary Americans, both black and white, obviously assume that the slave runners simply landed their ships and overpowered the helpless natives at will. Such was not the usual case at all. For the most part, such entrepreneurs bartered for "Black Ivory" much the same as for elephant tusks. "The whites," Negro historian Benjamin Quarles points out, "did not go into the interior to procure slaves; this they left to the Africans themselves. Spurred on by the desire for

European goods, one tribe raided another, seized whatever captives it could and marched them in coffles with leather thongs around their necks to coastal trading centers."

It is all too true that Negroes unlike the Yankee and the backwoodsman were slaves whose legal status was that of property. But it is also true—and as things have turned out, even more significant—that they were slaves *who were living in the presence of more human freedom and individual opportunity than they or anybody else had ever seen before.* That the *conception* of being a free man in America was infinitely richer than any notion of individuality in the Africa of that period goes without saying.

That this conception was perceived by the black slaves is shown by their history as Americans. The fugitive slave, for instance, was culturally speaking certainly an American, and a magnificent one at that. His basic urge to escape was, of course, only human—as was his willingness to risk the odds; but the tactics he employed as well as the objectives he was seeking were *American* not African. In his objectives, he certainly does not seem to have been motivated by any overwhelming nostalgia for tribal life. The slaves who absconded to fight for the British during the Revolutionary War were no less inspired by *American* ideas than those who fought for the colonies: the liberation that the white people wanted from the British the black people wanted from white people. As for the tactics of the fugitive slaves, the Underground Railroad was not only an innovation, it was also an *extension* of the American quest for democracy brought to its highest level of epic heroism. Nobody tried to sabotage the *Mayflower*. There was no bounty on the heads of its captain, crew, or voyagers as was the case with all conductors, station masters, and passengers on the northbound freedom train. Given the differences in circumstances, equipment, and, above all, motives, the legendary exploits of white U.S. backwoodsmen, keelboatmen, and prairie schoonermen, for example, became relatively *safe* when one sets them beside the breathtaking escapes of the fugitive slave beating his way south to Florida, west to the Indians, and north to far away Canada through swamp and town alike seeking *freedom*—nobody was chasing Daniel Boone!

Or to take another area of American experience. The pioneer

spirit of American womanhood is widely eulogized. But at no time in the history of the Republic has such womanhood ever attained a higher level of excellence than in the indomitable heroism of a runaway slave named Harriet Tubman, who "kidnapped" more than three hundred of her fellowmen out of bondage, and of whom William H. Seward once said, "a nobler, higher spirit, or a truer, seldom dwells in human form." Harriet Tubman was, like Sojourner Truth, already a legend in her time. Ralph Waldo Emerson, Bronson Alcott, and Horace Mann, among numerous others of that golden era of national synthesis, immediately and eagerly acknowledged what the dynamics of racial oneupmanship have obscured for so many succeeding students of American civilization: Tubman was not only an American legend; she also added a necessary, even if still misapprehended, dimension to the national mythology.

Another example. In such an epochal figure as that of the mulatto fugitive, abolitionist, and statesman named Frederick Douglass, contemporary American Negroes can find all the fundamental reassurance as to their identity and mission as Americans that the Joseph of Thomas Mann found in the Man from Ur Kashdim. Indeed, not even such justly canonized Founding Fathers as Benjamin Franklin and Thomas Jefferson represent a more splendid image and pattern for the contemporary American citizenship of anyone. On balance not even Abraham Lincoln was a more heroic embodiment of the American as a self-made man. After all, Lincoln like Franklin and Jefferson was born free.

Not just the advantages of birth but also some aspects of his thought, rank Lincoln lower than Douglass. It was Lincoln who described the United States as man's last best hope on earth. It was also Abraham Lincoln who stated the case against secessionism most eloquently. But on the question of what to do about Negroes when they became free men, the Great Emancipator, who was not untainted with racism withal, and who was soft on segregation, was not above becoming involved with schemes to colonize American Negroes in Africa and South America. Needless to say, no such obscene compromise ever tempted Frederick Douglass, who incidentally did not hesitate to let the President know that Negroes were here to stay.

For all this, Lincoln himself did not allow the archetypal heroism of Frederick Douglass to go unremarked. The Reverend John Eaton, who arranged one of their several interviews, later reported that Lincoln had declared "that considering the condition from which he had risen and obstacles he had overcome, and the position to which he had attained that he [Lincoln] regarded him [Douglass] as one of the most meritorious men, if not the most meritorious man in the United States."

Thus, in the second and third quarters of nineteenth century America, Negroes can find adequate historical as well as mythological documentation for "all that really matters" in the establishment of their national identity. Not that they need to do so to meet any official requirements whatsoever. After all, such is the process by which Americans are made that immigrants, for instance, need trace their roots no further back in either time or space than Ellis Island. *By the very act of arrival*, they emerge from the bottomless depths and enter the same stream of American tradition as those who landed at Plymouth. In the very act of making their way through customs, they begin the process of becoming, as Constance Rourke would put it, part Yankee, part backwoodsman and Indian—and part Negro!

No one can deny that in the process many somewhat white immigrants who were so unjustly despised elsewhere not only discover a social, political, and economic value in white skin that they were never able to enjoy before but also become color-poisoned bigots. Indeed, an amazing number of such immigrants seem only too happy to have the people of the United States regard themselves as a nation of two races. (Only two!) Many who readily and rightly oppose such antagonistic categories as Gentile and Jew, gleefully seize upon such designations as the White People and the Black People. But even as they struggle and finagle to become all-white (by playing up their color similarities and playing down their cultural differences), they inevitably acquire basic American characteristics—which is to say, Omni-American—that are part Negro and part Indian.

The bitterness of outraged black militants against such people is altogether appropriate even if sometimes excessive. The militants' own insight into the pragmatic implications of the heritage of black people in America, however, is often only one-dimensional. Indeed, sometimes it seems as if they are more impressed by the white propaganda designed to deny their very existence than by the black actuality that not only motivates but also sustains them. In any case, when they speak of their own native land as being the White Man's country, they concede too much to the self-inflating estimates of others. They capitulate too easily to a con game which their ancestors never fell for, and they surrender their birthright to the propagandists of white supremacy, as if it were of no value whatsoever, as if one could exercise the right of redress without first claiming one's constitutional identity as citizen!

White Anglo-Saxon Protestants do in fact dominate the power mechanisms of the United States. Nevertheless, no American whose involvement with the question of identity goes beyond the sterile category of race can afford to overlook another fact that is no less essential to his fundamental sense of nationality no matter how much white folklore is concocted to obscure it: Identity is best defined in terms of culture, and the culture of the nation over which the white Anglo-Saxon power elite exercises such exclusive political, economic, and social control is not all-white by any measurement ever devised. *American culture, even in its most rigidly segregated precincts, is patently and irrevocably composite. It is, regardless of all the hysterical protestations of those who would have it otherwise, incontestably mulatto.* Indeed, for all their traditional antagonisms and obvious differences, the so-called black and so-called white people of the United States resemble nobody else in the world so much as they resemble each other. And what is more, even their most extreme and violent polarities represent nothing so much as the natural history of pluralism in an open society.

WHITE NORMS FOR BLACK DEVIATION

No other inhabitants of the United States have ever been subjected to the economic, social, legal, and political outrages that have been and continue to be committed against Negroes. Not even the Indians have been more casually exploited and more shamelessly excluded from many of the benefits of the material wealth of the nation. The overall social status of

Negroes is such that even though the overwhelming majority are native born to multi-generation American parents, they do not enjoy many of the public services, normal considerations, and common privileges that are taken for granted not only by the most lowly of immigrants even before they become eligible for naturalization but also by the most questionable foreign visitors, even those from enemy countries.

The average law-abiding Negro citizen is constantly being denied such legal safeguards as are readily extended to the most notorious criminals, not to mention prisoners of war. It is a fact, for example, that Negro pilots of the 332nd Fighter Group who were captured during World War II preferred the treatment they received from the Nazis to that which they had endured at the hands of their fellow countrymen in Alabama, whose solicitude of German internees was beyond reproach! Qualified citizens of no other democratic nation in the world encounter more deviousness or nearly as much outright antagonism and violence when they attempt to participate in the routine process of local, state, and federal government.

Nor do Americans who are guilty of such atrocious behavior hesitate to add insult to injury. The very opposite is the rule. They hasten to *exaggerate* the damage they have perpetrated in the images of black depravity they advertise on every possible occasion and through every available medium. These images —which naive Negro spokesmen given to moral outcry seize upon as evidence of the need for reform—are all too obvious extensions of the process of degradation by other means, and have always functioned as an indispensable element in the vicious cycle that perpetuates white supremacy through the systematic exploitation of black people.

The negative image, for example, now permits decent white people to find satisfaction in the so-called norms—which would not exist but for the exploitation and exclusion of black people. These creatures, the logic-tight cycle begins, being non-white (the *negative* of white) are *less* than white, and being less than white are less than *normal* as human beings and are therefore exploitable; and having been rendered even *less* human as a result of exploitation, are thus *further* exploitable because less than human, and so on. (It is not at all unusual for some arrivistes to make casual references to Negroes as being unassimilable.)*

The cycle is no less vicious because philanthropy sometimes blurs its machinations. Indeed, American welfare programs for Negroes (and often for others too) increase the debasement they are supposed to ameliorate. Except in extremely unusual instances, the assistance afforded Negroes by philanthropic and governmental rehabilitation programs alike is not much more than a choice between contemptuous oppression and condescending benevolence. Not since the Reconstruction have there been any significant rehabilitation measures designed to accelerate the movement of Negroes toward equality. (The Reconstruction, of course, ultimately became the biggest betrayal in the history of the nation, but even so, no subsequent programs have approached, for one example, the achievements of the Freedman's Bureau.) In fact, even the best of the programs now in operation are more slapdash substitutions for justice and equality than anything else—and at worse, they are downright insidious.

The point is not simply rhetorical. In New York City, for example, the HARYOU-Act Program was ostensibly initiated as a measure to accelerate the movement of Harlem youth into the mainstream of national activity. But what its built-in racism has actually stimulated is a greater sense of alienation. HARYOU is a so-called community development program that bunches young Negroes even closer together in Harlem and provides even less contact with other areas of the city than they *normally* have. It also encourages them to think not like the many-generation Americans—which they are—who have as great a stake in this country as anybody else, but like Afro-Americans. As a consequence of such programs, many Negroes who once proceeded in terms of the very concrete and immediate problem of coming to grips with themselves as native-born Americans, now seem to feel that because they are black (which most are not!) they must begin by establishing some symbolic identification with Africa, mistaking a continent for a nation as native-born "Africans" seldom do. But the riots

*A closer look at the uses and meanings of *non-white* is taken in a later essay, "Oneupmanship in Colorful America."

across the nation since the summer of 1964 suggest that the self-segregation that seems so implicit in black racism is far less likely to lead to voluntary separatism than to a compression of resentment that explodes in violent rebellion.

The operating monograph for HARYOU, Kenneth Clark's *Youth in the Ghetto: A Study of the Consequences of Powerlessness and a Blueprint for Change*, is a monument to social science nonsense and nonsensibility. It demonstrates again that other Americans, including most American social scientists, don't mind one bit what unfounded conclusions you draw about U.S. Negroes, or how flimsy and questionable your statistics, or how wild your conjectures, so long as they reflect degradation. And anybody who thinks this statement is too strong, should try giving *positive* reasons for, say, Andrew Brimmer, General Davis, Carl Stokes, John Johnson, and see if most social scientists don't insist on *negative* ones, nor will their insistence be based on any celebration of the dynamics of antagonistic cooperation.

Another kind of "help" provided Negroes is exemplified in most of the plans and programs for the rehabilitation of places like Harlem and Watts. Such efforts begin with studies that find such places are "ghettos" which suffer as a result of being somehow blocked away from the rest of New York and Los Angeles. Every failing of man and beast is attributed to the inhabitants of such places; *and then the programs promptly institute measures that could only have been designed to lock the inhabitants even further away from the center of things.* Suddenly, programing experts begin discussing ways to make Harlem and Watts *self-sufficient.* Nobody ever explains why Harlem should be self-sufficient but Inwood not. In concocting such plans, no social scientists seem to remember anything at all about the natural principles of centralization that underlie the existence of garment districts, financial districts, theater districts, shopping districts, manufacturing complexes, and so on. For some reason, when it comes to Negroes, the planners seem to forget all about the desirability of keeping residential areas free of commercial congestion.

But ill-conceived and condescending benevolence seems to be the way of American welfare-ism when dealing with Negroes. It is all of a piece with the exasperating convolutions of an immense number of social science theorists and survey technicians who, consciously or not, proceed on assumptions equivalent to those which underlie the rationalizations of intentional white supremacy and black subjugation. Moreover, not only are the so-called findings of most social science surveyors of Negro life almost always compatible with the allegations of the outright segregationist—that is, to those who regard Negroes as human *assets* so long as they are kept in subservience— they are also completely consistent with the conceptions of the technicians who regard Negroes as *liabilities* that must be reduced, not in accordance with any profound and compelling commitment to equal opportunities for human fulfillment but rather in the interest of domestic tranquility.

The statistics and profiles of most contemporary social science surveys also serve to confirm the negative impressions about Negroes that the great mass of "uninvolved" white people have formed from folklore and the mass media.

What such universal concurrence actually reflects, however, is far less indicative of the alleged objectivity, comprehensiveness, validity, and reliability of the methodology employed than of its preoccupation with the documentation of black shortcomings. There are, to be sure, many social science theorists who question and reject the motives of the segregationist. But few seem to find it necessary to register any insistent dissent to his assessment of Negroes as being generally backward —except perhaps to disavow any suggestion that such backwardness is inherent in black racial origins. (Of course no contemporary American social science theorist and technician of any professional standing would endorse racism in any form!) And yet no other survey makers in the world seem to have a greater compulsion to catalogue human behavior in terms of racial categories.

The widely publicized document that became known as the Moynihan Report (*The Negro Family: The Case for National Action*) is a notorious example of the use of the social science survey as a propaganda vehicle to promote a negative image of Negro life in the United States. It has all the superficial trappings of an objective monograph of scientific research and has been readily accepted by far too many editors and teachers across the nation as if it were the final word on U.S. Negro behavior. Many white journalists and newspaper readers now presume to explain the conduct of Negroes in the United States in terms of the structure of Negro family life as described by Moynihan. And yet Moynihan did not initiate his research project as a comprehensive study of family life at all. He set out to compile such data as would advertise Negro family life in the worst possible light in order to make, as he insists even in his title, "The Case for National Action."

In these terms, the report certainly has not achieved its purpose. The sensational nationwide attention the report has generated has not been in response to the case it makes for action. Not even the most generous do-gooders have made very much of that. Some black wailing-wall polemicists have in their usual quasi-literate intellectual bankruptcy grab-bagged it as "useful to the cause." But to most white people, sympathetic and antagonistic alike, it has become the newest scientific explanation of white supremacy and thus the current justification of the status quo.

Moynihan insists that his intentions were the best, and perhaps they were. But the fact remains that at a time when Negroes were not only demanding *freedom now* as never before but were beginning to get it, Moynihan issued a quasi-scientific pamphlet that declares on the flimsiest evidence *that they are not yet ready for freedom*! At a time when Negroes are demanding freedom as a *constitutional right*, the Moynihan Report is saying, in effect, that those who have been exploiting Negroes for years should now, upon being shown his statistics, become *benevolent* enough to set up a nationwide welfare program for them. *Not once does he cite any Negro assets that white people might find more attractive than black subservience.* Good intentions notwithstanding, Moynihan's arbitrary interpretations make a far stronger case for the Negro equivalent of Indian reservations than for Desegregation Now.

The source of this document, strange to say, was not the Department of Health, Education, and Welfare but the Department of Labor. Yet the report does not concern itself at all with any of the extremely urgent labor problems that Negroes are forever complaining about, and it includes no data on the extent of noncompliance with local, state, and federal policies and laws against racial exclusion in employment. What it cites are numerous figures on illegitimate Negro children, broken homes, lack of education, crime, narcotics addiction, and so on. It charts Negro unemployment, but not once does it suggest national action to crack down on discrimination against Negroes by labor unions. Instead, it insists that massive federal action must be initiated to correct the matriarchal structure of the Negro family!

Even if one takes this point at face value, nowhere does Moynihan explain what is innately detrimental about matriarchies. In point of fact, there is nothing anywhere in the report that indicates that Moynihan knows anything at all either about matriarchies in general or about the actual texture of Negro family relationships in particular. And if his sophomoric theories about father figures were not being applied to black people, they would no doubt be laughed out of any snap course in undergraduate psychology. They most certainly would be questioned by any reasonably alert student of history and literature. Was Elizabethan or Victorian England a matriarchy? What about the Israel of Golda Meir? No father figure ranks above that of epic hero, and yet how many epic heroes issue from conventional families?

As for Moynihan's glib but predictably popular notions about the emasculation of the Negro male, not only do they have all the earmarks of the white American male's well-known historical trait of castrating black males by any means but the report's own statistics on illegitimate births among Negroes would seem to contradict any neat theories about the cycle of black female dominance at the very outset. For if males are generally emasculated and the women are well-established matriarchs, it is very curious, to say the least, that it is the women who get stuck with the illegitimate children and most of the problems of raising them while the men run loose. There was a time when you could bag Negro males for being diseased rapists. Moynihan now represents them in terms of complete emasculation and, as his figures on child-birth show, prodigious promiscuity at the same time.

The fact of the matter is that Moynihan's figures provide for more evidence of male exploitation of females than of females henpecking males. Instead of the alleged cycle of illegitimacy-matriarchy and male emasculation by females, which adds up to further illegitimacy, the problem of Negro family instability might more accurately be defined as a cycle of illegitimacy, matriarchy, and female victimization by gallivanting males who refuse to or cannot assume the conventional domestic responsibilities of husbands and fathers. In any case, anybody who knows anything at all about Negro women knows very well that what they complain about is not the lack of masculine authority among Negro men either as husbands or as father figures but the lack of employment and the lack of interest in conventional domestic stability. *Black women, who seem to be more aware of the instability of the white family than apparently is Moynihan, are forever referring wistfully to the white woman's ability to make the white man pay and pay and pay!*

But then if Negro males were as thoroughly emasculated as the Moynihan consensus insists they are, there would be no current racial crisis. White people would not feel so hysterically insecure about the resentment of those whom they are convinced have lost their manhood. White men would not feel that they needed a lynch *mob* to take revenge on *one* uppity Negro. White policemen would not go berserk at the slightest sign of black resistance. White teachers in Harlem would be able to handle Negro pupils at least as well as the great majority of Negro teachers have always handled them elsewhere. Nor would white people ever have felt the need to enact or defend any laws against interracial marriages.

Further, though images of black masculinity may simply be invisible to Moynihan, it does not follow that they are also nonexistent for Negroes themselves. Thus, while white supremacists were responding to Uncle Toms, Old Black Joes, and Stepin Fetchits, Negroes were celebrating John Henry, Stagolee, Jack Johnson, and Joe Louis. While white people promote wailing-wall spokesmen, black people are committed to numerous "unknown" local leaders. For all his rhetorical resonance, the late great Reverend Martin Luther King was much more highly regarded among Negroes when he *did* more and *talked* less, not that they didn't love the way he talked. The mass media provide unheard of publicity for empty-handed black hot-air militants but the truth is that while Negroes obviously enjoy making white people nervous, they much prefer to keep them guessing.

The Moynihan Report is the stuff of which the folklore of white supremacy is made, and providing such stuff is the role that the social science technicians and theorists all too often play in the extension of black degradation through the systematic oversimplification of black tribulations. There was a time when the white supremacist ideologized his conduct in terms of the divine rightness of the status quo: "If the good Lord had intended all people to be equal, he would have made everybody the same." In the current age of liberal enlightenment, however, even some of the most reactionary segregationists gear their prejudices to the methodology of scientific research. The situation now is that the contemporary folklore of racism in the United States is derived from social science surveys in which white norms and black deviations are tantamount to white well being and black pathology.

That most social science technicians may be entirely unaware of the major role they play in the propagation of such folklore can be readily conceded. But the fact that they remain oblivious to the application of the material that they assemble neither reduces the degree of their involvement nor mitigates the distortion, oversimplification, and confusion that they aid and abet. As a matter of fact, their innocence, which is not altogether unlike that of certain ever so nonviolent munitions experts, allows them to function with a routine detachment that is even more deadly than deliberate underhanded manipulation of facts, figures, and interpretations. The forthright white supremacist, after all, must often contend with matters of conscience, if only to rationalize them away (which accounts for much of his need for folklore in the first place). The unwitting survey technician has no such problem. Believing himself to be free of ulterior motives, he assumes that his studies are disinterested.

As even the most casual examination of his actual point of departure and his customary procedures will reveal, however, such a technician's innocence is not nearly so innocent as it is intellectually irresponsible. Nor should his lack of concern with consequences be mistaken for scientific objectivity. When the technician undertakes any research project without having become thoroughly familiar with its practical context and with the implications of his underlying thesis, his action does not represent the spirit of scientific inquiry at all. *It is the very embodiment of traditional piety.* And it permits him to substantiate the insidious speculations and malevolent preconceptions of the white status quo as readily as it allows him to do anything else.

Ordinarily American intellectuals, like those elsewhere, are profoundly preoccupied with the abnormally wretched predicament of contemporary Western man in general. Ideas derived from Karl Marx (who was convinced over a hundred years ago that modern white society was so hopelessly corrupt that its only cure was violent revolution) like those derived from Sigmund Freud (who came to view the personality structure of contemporary European man as a tangle of pathology) occupy a central position in all intellectual and cultural deliberations. Furthermore, almost every significant work of art of the twentieth century contains some explicit and often comprehensive indictment of the shortcomings of contemporary society and the inadequacies of contemporary man. There is very little indeed in the texture of the existence reflected in *The Waste Land*, "The Hollow Men", *The Great Gatsby*, *The Sun Also Rises*, or *U.S.A.*, that anybody can interpret as a glorification of white excellence in the United States. And matters are hardly improved by including such masterworks of contemporary Europe as *Ulysses*, *The Magic Mountain*, and *The Castle*.

As soon as any issue involving Negroes arises, however, most American social science theorists and technicians, the majority of whom are nothing if not Marx-Freud oriented, seem compelled to proceed as if Negroes have only to conform more closely to the behavior norms of the self-same white American middle class that writers like Theodore Dreiser, Sinclair Lewis, and Sherwood Anderson had already dissected and rejected long before the left wing political establishment of the nineteen thirties made it fashionable for even the average undergraduate to do so. Somehow or other, the minute the social science technician becomes aware of Negroes having fun "stomping at the Savoy" and enjoying luxuries (of say, Cadillacs) in spite of bad housing and low incomes and injustice, he begins to insist that they should cut out the apathy and escapism and join the all-American rat race—blithely ignoring the fact that there are in almost every Negro community domestic servants and relatives and friends of domestic servants who often have infinitely more first-hand experience with and inside information concerning the social structure and existential texture of white "middle class" life in the United States than is likely to be represented in any survey. In fact, it may well be that few psychiatrists have either more intimate contact with or more functional understanding of the effects suffered by white people from trying to keep up with the Joneses—or with the whims of Madison Avenue.

Some of the omissions and self-contradictions of white norm/black deviation folklore reveal the most appalling intellectual hypocrisy. Whereas the rate of illegitimate births among Negroes is represented as being catastrophic, for instance, the implications of the fantastically lucrative abortion racket among white Americans is conveniently overlooked—as are the procedures that deliberately obscure the rate of white illegitimacy. When the "high rate of crime" among Negroes is featured as cause for alarm, the universally conceded anti-Negro double standards of most white police, judges, and juries somehow become irrelevant! At that point, they apply only a single standard. When problems of drug addiction are under consideration, the very same Harlem that otherwise is always assumed to be suffering from the most abject poverty immediately becomes the main market for the multi-million dollar international cash-and-carry trade in narcotics. (References to crime can hardly explain this last inconsistency—not even if surveys could show that one half of Harlem burglarized the other half every night.)

The Moynihan Report, which insists that Negro men are victims of a matriarchal family structure, makes no mention at all of the incontestable fact that aggressiveness of white American women is such that they are regarded as veritable amazons not only in the Orient but also by many Europeans and not a few people at home. But then the Moynihan Report also implies without so much as a blush that all of the repressions, frustrations, and neuroses of the white Organization Man add up to an enviable patriarchal father image rather than the frightened insomniac, bootlicking conformist, "The Square," which even those who are too illiterate to read the "Maggie and Jiggs" and "Dagwood" comic strips can see in the movies and on television. Shades of father Jack Lemmon and Tony Randall.

Similarly those white Americans who express such urgent concern when the reading test scores of Harlem school children do not conform to white-established norms seem to forget that some Negroes know very well that all the banality and bad taste on television and the best seller lists comes from and is produced for those same norm-calibrated whites. But Sancho Panza was far from being the last man of the people who had to go along with the pedantic foolishness of cliché-nourished bookworms. Nobody in his right mind would ever seriously recommend illiteracy as a protection against brainwashing, to be sure; but still and all it may well have been his illiterate immunity from the jargon of the fashion magazines that enabled the little boy in Grimms' fairytale to see that the emperor's fancy new clothes were nothing more than his birthday suit.

There may or may not be something to be said for being an unenthusiastic black sheep in a school system that emphasizes conformity to the point of producing a nation of jargon-and-cliché-oriented white sheep. Nevertheless, one factor that is always either overlooked or obscured in all interpretations of the low academic performance of Negro pupils is the possibility of their *resistance* to the self-same white norms that they are being rated by. What some white teachers refer to as being the *apathy* of Negro pupils, competent black teachers are likely to describe as lack of interest and motivation. Black teachers know very well that *when there is genuine Negro interest there is seldom any complaint about Negro ability.* And yet most social science technicians persistently interpret low Negro test scores not in terms of the lack of incentive but in terms of a historic and comprehensive *cultural deprivation.*

But then nowhere are the omissions and contradictions of white norm/black deviation folklore more operative than in matters of formal education. Indeed, the establishment of the notion of a so-called "culture gap" seems to have been the ultimate function of norm lore from the outset. By ignoring the most fundamental definitions of anthropology and archaeology along with the most essential implications of the humanities, the contemporary American social science technician substitutes academic subject matter for culture. He then misrepresents deficiencies in formal technical training as cultural deprivation, a very neat trick indeed.

Such is the procedure that enables the folklore technician to provide statistical evidence as proof to show that Negroes are not like other Americans. But why is it that no widely publicized social science surveys ever measure conformity and deviation in terms of norms of citizenship, which are based on the national ideals as established by the Declaration of Independence and the Constitution? The Constitution not only expresses principles of conduct that are valid for mankind as a whole; *it is also the ultimate official source for definitions of desirable and undesirable American behavior.*

The major emphasis in the large surveys is never placed on the failure of white Americans to measure up to the standards of the Constitution. The primary attention repeatedly is focused on Negroes as victims. Again and again the assumption of the surveys is that slavery and oppression have made Negroes *inferior* to other Americans and hence less American. This is true even of such a relatively fair-minded study as *An American Dilemma.*

In point of fact, however, slavery and oppression may well have made black people more human and more American while it has made white people less human and less American. Anyway, Negroes have as much reason to think so as to think otherwise. It is the political behavior of black activists, not that of norm-calibrated Americans, that best represents the spirit of such constitutional norm-ideals as freedom, justice, equality, fair representation, and democratic processes. Black Americans, not Americans devoted to whiteness, exemplify the open disposition toward change, diversity, unsettled situations, new structures and experience, that are prerequisite to the highest level of citizenship. Black not white or even somewhat white Americans display the greatest willingness to adjust to the obvious consequences of those contemporary innovations in communication and transportation facilities whose networks have in effect shrunk the world to one pluralistic community in which the most diverse people are now neighbors. It is Negroes, not the median of the white population, who act as if the United States is such a world in miniature. It is the nonconforming Negro who now acts like the true descendent of the Founding Fathers—who cries, "Give me liberty or give me death," and who regards taxation without representation as tyranny. It is the norm-oriented white American who becomes the rednecked progeny of the Red Coats, and yells, "Disperse, ye rebels." It is the white American who, in the name of law and order, now sanctions measures (including the stock piling of armor piercing weapons to be used against American citizens) that are more in keeping with the objectives of a police state than those of an open society.

There is little reason why Negroes should not regard contemporary social science theory and technique with anything except the most unrelenting suspicion. There is, come to think of it, no truly compelling reason at all why Negoes should not regard the use of the social science statistical survey as the most elaborate fraud of modern times. In any event, they should never forget that the group in power is always likely to use every means at its disposal to create the impression that it deserves to be where it is. And it is not above suggesting that those who have been excluded have only themselves to blame.

PALEFACE FABLES, BROWNSKIN PEOPLE

It seems altogether likely that white people in the United States will continue to reassure themselves with black images derived from the folklore of white supremacy and the fakelore of black pathology so long as segregation enables them to ignore the actualities. They can afford such self-indulgence only because they carefully avoid circumstances that would require a confrontation with their own contradictions. Not having to suffer the normal consequences of sloppy thinking, they can blithely obscure any number of omissions and misinterpretations with no trouble at all. They can explain them away with terminology and statistical razzle-dazzle. They can treat the most ridiculous self-refutation as if it were a moot question; and of course they can simply shut off discussion by changing the subject.

The self-conception in terms of which most Negroes have actually lived and moved, and had their personal being for all these years, however, has always been, as they say, something else again. Perhaps self-indulgence causes white people to overlook the most obvious fact in the world: Negroes are neither figments of bigoted imaginations nor academic abstractions. They are flesh-and-blood organisms and not only do they possess consciousness, they also enjoy self-awareness. They are, that is to say, purposeful human beings whose existence is motivated by their own self-centered interests.

There are, no one should be surprised to find, a number of prominent Negro spokesmen and black ideologists of welfareism who employ, repeat, and even extend the imagery of white supremacy. In most instances, they appear to have been far more thoroughly victimized by the current popularity of social science than by the system of oppression itself. In any case, what they say about how Negroes have been damaged by slavery and oppression is almost always restricted by Marxian and Freudian dialectics. But what many of them do often evokes nothing so much as the irrepressible spirit of '76— without so much rag tag and bobtail to be sure: the Negro revolution is certainly one of the most fashion conscious uprisings of all times. (Even the protest hair-dos, to the extent that they are protest, are geared to high fashion, often misguided, no doubt, and sometimes disastrous, but high fashion nonetheless.)

The nature of Negro moral outcry polemics, it should also be remembered, is now such that the most glibly self-confident and even the most smugly chauvinistic black spokesmen and leaders readily and frequently refer to themselves as being fear-ridden, emasculated, and without self-respect. No wonder white Americans continue to be so shocked and disoriented by the intensification of the civil rights struggle. Instead of relying on what is now known about the nature of social uprisings, white Americans keep allowing themselves to expect the theoretical Sambo promised, as it were, by Stanley M. Elkins in *Slavery: A Problem in American Institutional and Intellectual Life*, implicitly confirmed by the pronouncements of Kenneth Clark in *Dark Ghetto*, and conceded by so much self-deprecating rhetoric. But what these same white Americans keep running up against is such bewildering, outrageous, and (to some of them) terrifying behavior as the intransigent determination of leaders like Charles Evers in Mississippi; the mockery and high camp of media types like H. Rap Brown on all networks; and people like those in Watts, Newark, and Detroit, who respond to the murderous hysteria of white police and national guardsmen with a defiance that is often as derisive as it is deepseated.

The compulsions nourished by the folklore of white supremacy seem to be such that white Americans are as yet unable to realize that they themselves are obviously far more impressed by their own show of brute force than black insurgents ever seem to be. They still do not seem to realize that what they actually see on television during all of the demonstrations and, as the saying goes, civil disruptions is not a herd of wall-eyed black natives cringing before white authority. What they see are heavily armed, outraged, and slaughter-prone white policemen and soldiers smoldering with rage and itching to perpetrate a massacre, confronting Negroes who are behaving not only as if the whole situation were a farce and a carnival but who also have time to grant television interviews in which there is as much snap-course social science jargon as street-corner hip talk: "Like it's either upward mobility, or burn, baby, burn!" As one character in *For Whom the Bell Tolls* who, shaking his head, kept saying of the Spanish during the Civil War, "What a people!" Indeed, as Negroes are forever saying in delighted puzzlement of each other, "My pee-pul, *my people.* Ain't nothing *like* 'em. Man, when you talking about *us,* you talking about something *else.*"

On the other hand, perhaps it is easy enough to see why so many white Americans who are more puzzled than delighted are always so eager to cite quotations from books like *Black Rage* and *Dark Ghetto.* When *Dark Ghetto,* a good example of how a book by a black writer may represent a point of view toward black experience which is essentially white, insists that slavery and oppression have reduced Negroes to such a tangle of pathology that all black American behavior is in effect only a pathetic manifestation of black cowardice, self-hatred, escapism, and self-destructiveness, these white Americans evidently assume its author is corroborating their own notions of black inferiority. Many treat *Dark Ghetto,* which in point of fact reveals very little if any meaningful, first-hand contact with any black community in the United States, as if it were an official document. As yet not one white social science theoretician or survey technician of national prestige has made any significant public outcry against the fact that a document whose statistics are at times clearly ridiculous and whose central assumptions and embarrassingly sloppy conclusions make a travesty of scientific methodology is by way of becoming a veritable handbook of race relations in some parts of the country. But then, not very many Negro social science technicians have come forth to take issue with *Dark Ghetto* either. Not even those ever so prideful black nationalist spokesmen who otherwise display so much suspicion about becoming victims of brainwashing (whitewashing) and who express so much militant concern about improving "the black man's image in America," seem in the least aware of the fact that almost every chapter of *Dark Ghetto* not only supports the stereotypes that Negroes have always been extremely sensitive about, but also provides a quasi-scientific refutation of the very elements of Negro American history upon which contemporary Negro leaders must build.

Dark Ghetto, which is strong on political indictment but, as will be seen, weak on psychological insight, represents Negroes as substandard human beings who subsist in a sick community. Its image of Harlem is, in effect, that of an urban pit writhing with derelicts. According to the impression the author creates (even if his figures do not), black despair has driven most of its inhabitants either to crime, narcotics addiction, prostitution, and the like, or to obsessive imitations of something which he calls "the white man's society." "Few if any Negroes," he goes so far as to claim, "ever lose that sense of shame [of being dark skinned] and self-hatred." "The obsession with whiteness," he adds later, "continues past childhood and into adulthood. *It stays with the Negro all his life.*" (Italics added.) It is extremely difficult to believe that the evidence that *Dark Ghetto* presents in support of such a sweeping generalization would meet the scientific standards of, say, Talcott Parsons, who cannot fail to note that Clark's overestimation of white well being is almost worshipful. *Dark Ghetto* actually indicts Negroes for having a low suicide rate. It also confuses the personal motives of homicide with the socialized motives leading to warfare. It is all part of the game for a polemicist to denounce a murderer for not being a soldier, but just how scientific is it for a psychologist to do so?

The emphasis on black wretchedness in *Dark Ghetto* easily exceeds that in most of the books written by *white racists to justify segregation*. And yet Gunnar Myrdal, for instance, does not regard its author as a man who hates both himself and other Negroes for being black. Myrdal seems quite certain that Clark is an ideologist of social welfare measures much like himself. In the foreword to *Dark Ghetto*, Myrdal describes the author as being "desperately anxious that the ugly facts of life in the Negro ghetto become really known to the ruling majority." But Myrdal, who is anything but a de Tocqueville, then ever so hastily equates "the balanced view" with *false objectivity* (!) and so implies that *ugly* facts are more important and more useful than *plain* or even *beautiful* facts, not to mention *comprehensive* facts.

But thus have wailing-wall spokesmen almost always confused the politics of philanthropy with the *real politik* of municipal, state, and national government. The exaggeration of black suffering or "putting on the poor mouth" may be a time-hallowed means for obtaining benevolent handouts, but it is hardly the best method of developing rugged political power. In fact, many of the white politicians who back stop-gap poverty appropriations bills do so because they assume that this is the surest and smoothest way of delaying active and equitable participation in the power mechanisms.

Social science folklore-oriented black ideologists of welfare appropriations are seldom guilty of deliberate duplicity. They simply do not realize that their one-sided featuring of black pathology might frighten white Americans into an easier tolerance of anti-Negro police tactics. They really think that their exaggerations will gain white sympathy for black grievances. As incredibly naive as it may sound—and in point of fact is— they seem to think their emphasis on black mistreatment will make comfort-seeking but easily rattled white people react charitably to black threats and disruptions. Thus, when the author of *Dark Ghetto* came out for the integration of Manhattan schools, he overlooked the fact that he was trying to browbeat "powerful" white people into intermingling their norm-secure children with Negroes whom he himself had described as powerless hoodlums, addicts, and prostitutes. No thinking person really expects white people to do such a thing, certainly not if they accept the findings of books like *Dark Ghetto*. (There is good reason to believe that Clark is sincerely appalled by the current trend toward "black separatism." But when he takes militant separatists to task, he seems to forget that a book like *Dark Ghetto* gives them no alternative except militant self-pity!)

Many welfare spokesmen engage in such wholesale debasements of the image of their fellow Negroes not because they want to sell them out, for their commitment to social betterment is as unquestionably sincere as the form it takes is politically infantile. They do so because somehow or other neither their common understanding nor their formal education has yet to come to terms with that which the folk wisdom of the fugitive slave and the Reconstruction freedman took for granted long ago: *The Declaration of Independence and the Constitution are the social, economic, and political heritage of all Americans.*

Unfortunately, it seems that such spokesmen, like most other Americans, have been conditioned by school systems and communications media that have overpromoted the methodology and the categories of social science at the expense of the more comprehensive wisdom of the humanities and the arts—leaving thereby their sense of context deficient. In any case, they appear to have become so fascinated by pretentious terminology and easy oversimplifications that they no longer remember what experience is really like. If so, perhaps it is only natural that they no longer realize how complicated human life is, even at its least troubled and freest. Which, of course, means that they are not likely to realize how rich and exciting its possibilities are either. And yet such people, who confuse metaphorical ghettos with real ones, are often regarded as expert planners and programers! They are not. They are polemicists, and often third-rate polemicists at that. Or worse. Their propaganda is often more useful to the other side than to their own.

The obsessive preoccupation of the white people of the United States with the folklore of white supremacy makes one thing all too obvious: *White Americans do not take the privileged status of white people for granted. They work at it.* They pretend that it is natural to their social inheritance. So would they impress others and so perhaps do they reassure themselves, somewhat. But in reality they leave little to nature, and what they inherit is the full-time obligation to keep up social appearances without ever seeming to do so. As with all other forms of oneupmanship, however, nothing is more clearly indicative of the depth of their watchful concern than is their never quite casual indifference.

In other words, beneath the ever so carefully structured surface of solipsistic complacency and seemingly thoughtless condescension, there is almost always the anxiety of a people who live in unrelieved anticipation of disaster. For, people who really feel secure in their status just simply do not expend all of the time and energy, not to mention the ingenuity, that white colonialists have always been convinced is necessary to "keep Negroes in their place." There is no denying that as a result of constant practice, some white smugness becomes quite habitual. But that is not all the same thing as becoming natural; and in truth, as Negro slaves found out long ago, the vaguest hint of black hostility is more than enough to throw the most arrogant white Americans into a frenzy of trigger-happy paranoia. Some white Americans seem to regard every hostile black remark as if it were an official declaration of war.

After all, white people in the United States are not simply explaining anti-Negro atrocities of police by attributing them, as they seem ever so eager to do, to high-handed inhumanity and moral callousness. When white people wink away the hot-headed murder of a fourteen year old Harlem schoolboy by an experienced, six foot, white New York policeman, or excuse a Los Angeles patrolman for the instant execution of a cantankerous but unarmed black husband for running traffic signals en route with his pregnant wife to the maternity hospital, it seems clear that they do so out of a sympathy born of their own very simple human terror at the prospect of having to confront an angry Negro on "equal" terms! Over a century and a quarter after Nat Turner's revolt, even the most highly certified white American intellectuals reviewing William Styron's *Nat Turner*—which will be examined in some detail later—still insist that such a black thrust forward toward freedom could only have been a form of fantasy, if not insanity. They still seem to find *comfort* in the fact that more than two hundred unarmed Negro slaves were killed in retaliation for the liquidation of less than sixty white slavocrats. Also, whenever the possibility of anti-white violence is mentioned, white intellectuals (whose conception of military demography, incidentally, is not only obsolete but tribal) keep reminding everybody that white people enjoy a ten-to-one population majority. *But they keep acting as if such odds were not enough.*

Norm deviation folklore, mass media images, and wailing-wall polemicism notwithstanding, Negroes have always lived in full, even if somewhat inarticulate, awareness of the fact that whenever there are circumstances which suggest the possibility of black and white person-to-person or group-to-group confrontation, to say nothing of antagonism, white Americans almost always react as if they have only the highest regard for black capacity and potential. Most police forces seem to feel that they cannot handle black disorders without super weapons! Negroes have always noted with wry satisfaction that white Americans rarely if ever display even the slightest condescension or disdain in such situations. They beef-up the police force, organize rifle clubs and combat schools, stockpile arms and incendiary tanks.

But then, regardless of the obsequious rhetoric of so many of their outcry-oriented spokesmen, only the most inattentive Negroes have ever really assumed that white Americans have been unmindful of black Americans as human beings the consequences of whose self-interest is something to be reckoned with. As so much of their secretiveness goes to show, most Negroes have always suspected that white Americans only *pretend* to be misinformed about black motives and aspirations. Nor is their traditional black distrust of white people ever likely to permit many Negroes to accept anybody else's dehumanized images of black people. So far as most Negroes are concerned, the so-called problems of the Black Image have always been a matter of calculated misrepresentation. Much goes to show that the so-called problem of black identity is essentially a problem of bad publicity. Time and again it turns out that when Negro spokesmen refer to the lack of black identity, they are really complaining about the lack of public recognition, appreciation, and acclaim.

In any case, most Negroes are not likely to believe that white

Americans do not really know that there is an obvious difference between the drive to acquire more of the material benefits of the United States and the desire to be white. Consistent with their own traditional secretiveness and idiomatic abstruseness, they concede that white people could only be confused about many Negro motives and hence do not appreciate a great number of nuances in Negro style and manner. But they are also consistent when they accuse the same white Americans of being dishonest about what they really do know and how they actually do feel about Negroes.

Most Negroes, far from believing that white Americans have only the lowest opinion of black Americans, are forever revealing the fact that they are firmly convinced that even those white people of wealth and power spend a highly significant amount of time emulating Negroes while pretending not to. No conviction is more indicative of Negro self-esteem, the appreciation Negroes have for other Negroes, or the ambivalence of which their response to white Americans is seldom free. Nor does anything contradict all of the current pseudo-psychiatric nonsense about black self-hatred and self-rejection more profoundly than the arrogant bitterness with which Negroes complain that ruthless, mechanically efficient, but essentially provincial white Americans prosper on pale dilutions and hopelessly square commercial vulgarizations of the music of the Negro idiom. The catalogue of elements that make up the so-called mainstream of American culture but which Negroes claim were appropriated from the Negro idiom is endless. And of course, what is significant is not the accuracy of the enumeration but rather what the existence of such a belief reveals about how Negroes really feel about white "supremacy."

Nowhere, incidentally, do the curious notions about Negro "self-hatred" and "group hatred" become more preposterous than when race-oriented psychopolitical technicians and theorists insist on drawing sweeping pathological inferences from fads in fashions and cosmetics. Seldom do "scientists" show such an exasperating tendency to draw such far-reaching conclusions from such "evidence." *Dark Ghetto*, as might be expected, provides a good example. "The preoccupation of many Negroes with hair straighteners, skin bleaches and the like," runs one wrong-headed passage, "illustrates this tragic aspect of American racial prejudice—Negroes have come to believe in their own inferiority."

But the book makes nothing whatsoever of the traditional and undisguised *contempt* that Southern Negroes have always displayed toward "poor white trash." *Dark Ghetto* manages somehow to ignore the implications of Negro distaste for almost every aspect of the hillbilly life-style; it doesn't even hint at the self-regard implicit in the seething resentment that Northern Negroes have always felt because the system permits so many white immigrants whom Negroes regard as being the European equivalent of rednecks to get ahead of Negroes who are clearly more deserving. *Dark Ghetto* makes no mention at all of the black *snobbishness* so explicit in the epithet *ofay*, which is not only a condemnation of whiteness as being synonymous with "square" but is also accepted as such by countless "middle class" white Northerners as being justifiably contemptuous. Almost any Negro seems to feel that he can call any white person square and get away with it.

The implications of fashion fads are anything but as simple as the typical one-dimensional conjectures in works such as *Dark Ghetto* would make them out to be. To begin with, dark-skinned Negroes, it should be obvious to anyone interested in such matters, do not apply skin bleaches to all parts of their bodies as white people anoint themselves with suntan oil. Such bleaching agents as *Nadinola* and *Black and White* normally come in two-ounce containers and frequently last for months because they are used primarily to remove facial splotches. But who knows! Perhaps some determined race-oriented psychologizer will interpret this as a form of schizophrenia, white faces or masks but black bodies. That sort of thing. It makes, as they say, jolly good theory but no more tenable than the one that could be made from the symbolic self-mutilation involved in the nose jobs that are so popular among many Jewish Americans, who as any Negro country club dishwasher knows, already have white skin, straight hair, status employment, and even wealth.

As for the hair styles of Negro women, perhaps the best thing to do is to leave all female head decorations to the fashion magazines. It does seem, however, that Negro women can often do things with wigs and hair colors that could hardly have been dreamed of by the white people who manufacture them and who, by the way, did not originally design them for Negroes.

Incidentally, a number of "natural texture" promoters notwithstanding, in African culture there is much less emphasis on naturalness than on design and stylization. Traditional African sculpture, for example, is not representational but abstract. And certainly no one regards ornamental face and body cicatrices, filed teeth, Ubangi lip extensions, the wearing of nose rings, and so on, as accentuations of the natural. Indeed, the marvelous masks, the prevalence of mask-like makeup, and the exuberant inventiveness found in the personal adornments of tribe after tribe would seem to indicate that the African ancestors of U.S. Negroes have hardly ever been so excited about "The Natural Look" as the editors of *Vogue* and *Harper's Bazaar* become from time to time. And of course one can only guess what the self-hatred specialists will make of evidence that indicates not only that some Africans have always gone in for wigs (and blond wigs at that) but that others were also slicking their hair down with mud and other ingenious pomades including cow dung long before white Europeans arrived as agents of oppression. (The chances are that Africans were extending their human characteristics by appropriating such animal features as they admired—say, like Richard the Lion Hearted, or the Detroit Lions.)

With male hair styles, perhaps what is most often overlooked by those who insist that the Negro man's process or conk is an imitation of the straight-haired, pale-faced "oppressor," is the fact that those Negro men who are clearly most interested in integration and assimilation, who have gone to interracial schools, who work in integrated employment, live in interracial communities and whose speech and dress (whether naturally or deliberately) most closely resembles that of the so-called white middle class, *seldom if ever have processed hair.* Indeed they have always been the major opponents of the process. On the other hand, those who do—and there never has been a time when the majority did—are almost always unmistakably Negro-idiom oriented.

Survey technicians who take the time to do the necessary historical research will probably find that the conk was much more directly influenced by the dark-, sleek- (or wavy-) haired Latin type dandy than by the pale- (or ruddy-) faced, straight- (or shaggy-) mopped Anglo-Saxon of the power elite. Modish Negro men seem to feel closer affinity with the "dark and handsome" movie smoothies who go at least as far back as Rudolph Valentino and the young George Raft, than with the lighter all-American squares like Gary Cooper and James Stewart. Nor should careful research fail to take into account the completely "normal" influence of curly-headed mulatto-type relatives, friends, and heroes, who are admired and imitated not simply because they resemble the "oppressors" but for any number of other reasons that are no less operative among other people than among U.S. Negroes.

But perhaps of even greater immediate relevance to current questions of identity and Negro self-regard is the likelihood that truly insightful students of culture will upon reflection come to concede that no matter what its origins were, the conk has long become a U.S. Negro "thing," and that therefore a young man sporting a Sugar Ray Robinson or Nat "King" Cole process, say in the mid-fifties, was not copying someone who was trying to be like white people but rather copying a very special Negro whom he rated above *all* other people in the world. When pop singer James Brown switched from his patent-leather glossy coiffure to Brillo, he made a number of statements about black identity and pride, but those who followed him already knew precisely who he was all the time as well as what he represented, and they were already as proud of him as they could possibly be.

Actually, when most Negroes who have not been "faked out" by social science jive artists see a conk, they are almost certain to assume the person wearing it is either in show business or identifies with Negroes in the world of show business—which, of course, includes stylish prizefight promoters, gamblers, pimps, racketeers, and so on. For most Negroes the process goes with certain manners in clothes, speech, music, and even movement, which are anything but ofay oriented.

Processed hair, in other words, implies no less emphasis on black identity than the *au naturel*, Afro-Brillo. Nor should the role of show business in the development of the current natural texture fad be forgotten either. In fact, to do so would be to omit a key element in the *American* image-making process. For just as certain popular post-bop musicians have given beards chic status among certain black hipsters, so had the neo–Paul Robeson image of Harry Belafonte and Sidney Poitier begun to popularize the so-called natural texture-do, which the bop era had already initiated among hipsters long before the promoters of *negritude* began trying to philosophize it or the late Malcolm X to politicalize it.

The truth is, as Negro beauticians (who are mainly hair dressers) are forever reminding their customers, some people look marvelous in wigs while others are every bit as stunning when processed and still others are equally as wonderful looking with the Afro-Brillo. (Some of course are just fine looking in any style and some, alas, are not.) Thus, perhaps the most realistic thing to point out about Negro hair styles—as about styles in general—is the altogether fascinating fact that in contemporary America the cosmetics and fashions industries have so expanded the possibilities of makeup and make believe that all questions of image and identity are now matters of some personal choice for all Americans of all racial derivations. If you don't like the hair texture or hair color you were born with, you can now buy what you like on installment plan if necessary.

But even more fundamental and no less obvious is another fact which the racism that underlies most discussions about American identity almost always obscures: In spite of the seemingly hypnotic spell that updated versions of the Huck Finn or Norman Rockwell plug-ugly and the shirt collar ad Anglo-Saxon and Gibson girl images exercise over so many self-effacing, assimilation-bent European immigrants, *there is no standard melting pot mold for the American Image. The only official national image is the eagle.* There never has been a standard image, and currently, for all the emphasis on norms, nothing seems to change more than the points of conformity. Meanwhile, although they are most often referred to (even by many of their own spokesmen) as if they were all jet black natives only recently arrived from the dark land of Africa, U.S. Negroes represent a composite of all images. No other segment of the population of the United States encompasses more of the nation's limitless variety, whether in physical appearance or in behavior. Indeed, perhaps the most significant and scientifically supportable observation to be made about native-born U.S. Negroes as a *race* is that they may well be by way of becoming a new racial (i.e., physical) type, perhaps the only one that is truly indigenous, so to speak to contemporary North America. But this is just an aside: as stated before *race* is hardly as useful as an index to human motives as is culture.

As for behavior or life style, no other people in the land have as yet evolved a characteristic idiom that reflects a more open, robust, and affirmative disposition toward diversity and change. Nor is any other idiom more smoothly geared to open-minded improvisation. Moreover, never has improvisation been more conditioned by esthetic values—or at the same time been more indicative of the fundamental openness that is the necessary predisposition for all scientific exploration! Improvisation after all is experimentation.

When such improvisation as typifies Negro music, dance, language, religion, sports, fashions, general bearing and deportment, and even food preparation is considered from the Negro point of view, there is seldom, if ever, any serious doubt about how Negroes feel about themselves or about what they accept or reject of white people. They regard themselves not as the substandard, abnormal *non-white* people of American social science surveys and the news media, but rather as if they were, so to speak, fundamental *extensions* of contemporary possibilities.

That much of the blackest frustration grows out of being excluded goes without saying, but much of it also comes from having to witness others making a mess of something you are convinced you can do better. The white press notwithstanding, Negroes do *not* regard successful Negroes as proof that black people can do as well as white people; they regard them as proof that given only half a chance black people can do better than most white people who have had all the advantages. *Arrogant? Oh, but yes! The topic is self-esteem.*

The whole world defers to the supremacy of American political and economic power mechanisms. Negro attitudes toward the so-called white cultural establishment, however, are entirely consistent with the pragmatic improvisational irreverence that most Negroes display toward so many other established patterns and values. As a result, many things that most other Americans seem to accept as models for reverence and emulation, Negroes, not unlike jam session–oriented musicians, use mainly as points of departure. Even when Negroes set out to make literal imitations of white people, they often seem to find it impossible not to add their own dimensions.

THE BLUES IDIOM AND THE MAINSTREAM

The creation of an art style is, as most anthropologists would no doubt agree, a major cultural achievement. In fact, it is perhaps the highest as well as the most comprehensive fulfillment of culture; for an art style, after all, reflects nothing so much as the ultimate synthesis and refinement of a life style.

Art is by definition a process of stylization; and what it stylizes is experience. What it objectifies, embodies, abstracts, expresses, and symbolizes is a sense of life. Accordingly, what is represented in the music, dance, painting, sculpture, literature, and architecture of a given group of people in a particular time, place, and circumstance is a conception of the essential nature and purpose of human existence itself. More specifically, an art style is the assimilation in terms of which a given community, folk, or communion of faith embodies its basic attitudes toward experience.

And this is not all. Of its very nature, an art style is also the essence of experience itself, in both the historical and sensory implications of the word. It is an attitude, description, and interpretation in action—or rather, perhaps most often, in reaction. For needless to say, action is seldom gratuitous or unmotivated. Not only does it take place *in* a situation, it also takes place *in response to* a situation.

Kenneth Burke has equated stylization with strategy. To extend the military metaphor, one can say stylization is the estimate become maneuver. In such a frame of reference, style is not only insight but disposition and gesture, not only calculation and estimation become execution (as in engineering), but also motive and estimation become method and occupation. It is a way of sizing up the world, and so, ultimately, and beyond all else, a mode and medium of survival.

In current social science usage, the concept of "survival

technique" has somehow become confused with technology and restricted to matters of food, clothing, and shelter. (Incidentally, the most transparent fallacy of almost all white norm/ black deviation folklore is its exaggeration of the *cultural* implications of the control by white people of the production and distribution of the creature comforts required for subsistence in the Temperate Zone.) Human survival, however, involves much more than biological prolongation. The human organism must be nourished and secured against destruction, to be sure, but what makes man human is style. Hence the crucial significance of art in the study of human behavior: *All human effort beyond the lowest level of the struggle for animal subsistence is motivated by the need to live in style.*

Certainly the struggle for political and social liberty is nothing if not a quest for freedom to choose one's own way or style of life. Moreover, it should be equally as obvious that there can be no such thing as human dignity and nobility without a consummate, definitive style, pattern, or archetypal image. Economic interpretations of history notwithstanding, what activates revolutions is not destitution (which most often leads only to petty thievery and the like) but intolerable systems and methods—intolerable styles of life.

Most Americans know very well that the blues genre which in its most elaborate extensions includes elements of the spirituals, gospel music, folk song, chants, hollers, popular ditties, plus much of what goes into symphonic and even operatic composition, is the basic and definitive musical idiom of native-born U.S. Negroes. But few if any students of America seem either to understand or even to have any serious curiosity about the relationship of art style to Negro life style. None seems to consider the blues idiom a major cultural achievement. Not even those writers who have referred to it as being perhaps the only truly American innovation in contemporary artistic expression seem able to concede it any more significance than of some vague minor potential not unlike that of some exotic spice.

As for the contemporary American social survey statistician, his interests seem never to extend beyond social pathology and the need for revolutionary political reform or community rehabilitation. Seldom do any of his all too comprehensive evaluations of Negro cultural phenomena reflect either anthropological insight into the dynamics of ritual or stylization, or even a rudimentary appreciation of the functional role of esthetics. What the blues represent in his view of things is a crude, simpleminded expression of frustration and despair. Thus, so far as he is concerned, swinging the blues achieves only an essentially pathetic therapeutic compensation for the bleak social and economic circumstances of black people in the United States.

Obviously most American social survey technicians see no connection at all in this context between swinging the blues and the fact that the pronounced emphasis on rhythm-oriented improvisation in U.S. Negro creative expression is derived from dance-oriented antecedents in African culture (although in other contexts, everyone is quick to talk about the African roots of this and that). But worse still they are thus also oblivious to the fact that the same basic improvisational stylization (with its special but unmistakable overtones of what Johan Huizinga, discussing man as *homo ludens*, refers to as the play element in all cultures) applies to positive as well as to negative situations. As a result, they consistently misconstrue what is really the dynamics of confrontation for the mechanics of withdrawal, escape, and relief!

The blues ballad is a good example of what the blues are about. Almost always relating a story of frustration, it could hardly be described as a device for avoiding the unpleasant facts of Negro life in America. On the contrary, it is a very specific and highly effective vehicle, the obvious purpose of which is to make Negroes acknowledge the essentially tenuous nature of all human existence.

The sense of well being that always goes with swinging the blues is generated, as anyone familiar with Negro dance halls knows, not by obscuring or denying the existence of the ugly dimensions of human nature, circumstances, and conduct, but rather through the full, sharp, and inescapable awareness of them. One blues ballad after another informs and keeps reminding Negro dance couples (engaged, as are all dance couples, in ritual courtship) of the complications and contradictions upon which romances are contingent: *Now, don't be coming to*

*me with your head all knotty and your nose all snotty; if you don't
know what you doing you better ask somebody.*

As an art form, the blues idiom by its very nature goes beyond the objective of making human existence bearable physically or psychologically. The most elementary and hence the
least dispensable objective of all serious artistic expression,
whether aboriginal or sophisticated, is to make human existence *meaningful.* Man's primary concern with life is to make
it as significant as possible, and the blues are part of this effort.

The definitive statement of the epistemological assumptions
that underlie the blues idiom may well be the colloquial title
and opening declaration of one of Duke Ellington's best-known
dance tunes from the mid-thirties: "It Don't Mean a Thing if
It Ain't Got That Swing." In any case, when the Negro musician or dancer swings the blues, he is fulfilling the same fundamental existential requirement that determines the mission of
the poet, the priest, and the medicine man. He is making an
affirmative and hence exemplary and heroic response to that
which André Malraux describes as *la condition humaine.* Ex-
temporizing in response to the exigencies of the situation in
which he finds himself, he is confronting, acknowledging, and
contending with the infernal absurdities and ever-impending
frustrations inherent in the nature of all existence *by playing
with the possibilities that are also there.* Thus does man the
player become man the stylizer and by the same token the hu-
manizer of chaos; and thus does play become ritual, ceremony,
and art; and thus also does the dance-beat improvisation of
experience in the blues idiom become survival technique, esthetic equipment for living, and a central element in the dynamics of U.S. Negro life style.

When the typical Negro dance orchestra plays the blues, it is
also *playing with* the blues. When it swings, jumps, hops,
stomps, bounces, drags, shuffles, rocks, and so on, its manner
not only represents a swinging-the-blues attitude toward the
"bad news" that comes with the facts of life, it also exemplifies
and generates a riffing-the-blues disposition toward the "rough
times" that beset all human existence.

The blues-idiom dancer like the solo instrumentalist turns
disjunctures into continuities. He is not disconcerted by intru-
sions, lapses, shifts in rhythm, intensification of tempo, for

instance; but is inspired by them to higher and richer levels of improvisation. As a matter of fact (and as the colloquial sense of the word suggests), the "break" in the blues idiom provides the dancer his greatest opportunity—which, at the same time, is also his most heroic challenge and his moment of greatest jeopardy.

But then, impromptu heroism such as is required only of the most agile of storybook protagonists, is precisely what the blues tradition has evolved to condition Negroes to regard as *normal procedure*! Nor is any other attitude towards experience more appropriate to the ever-shifting circumstances of all Americans or more consistent with the predicament of man in the contemporary world at large. Indeed, the blues idiom represents a major American innovation of universal signifi-cance and potential because it fulfills, among other things, precisely that fundamental function that Constance Rourke ascribes to the comedy, the irreverent wisdom, the sudden changes and adroit adaptations she found in the folk genre of the Yankee-backwoodsman-Negro of the era of Andrew Jack-son. It provides "emblems for a pioneer people who require resilience as a prime trait."

Obviously those who are conditioned by the folklore of white supremacy would have it otherwise. They insist that po-litical powerlessness and economic exclusion can lead only to cultural deprivation. One unmistakable objective of white norm/black deviation survey data is to show how far outside the mainstream of American culture Negroes are. Another may well be to insinuate that they are unassimilable. The blues idiom, however, represents the most comprehensive and the most profound assimilation. It is the product of a sensibility that is completely compatible with the *human* imperatives of modern times and American life. Many white composers, unlike most white social technicians, are already aware of the ease with which the blues idiom sound track can be extended from the cotton fields and the railroad through megalopolis and into outer space.

So far, incredible as it may be, no Negro leader seems to have made any extensive political use of the so-called survival tech-niques and idiomatic equipment for living that the blues tradi-tion has partly evolved in response to slavery and oppression.

Even more incredible is the fact that most Negro leaders, spokesmen, and social technicians seem singularly unaware of the possibility of doing so. (There are many spokesmen whose fear of being stigmatized as primitive is so hysterical that they reject out of hand any suggestion that U.S. Negro life style is geared to dance-beat improvisation. As far as they are concerned, such a conception is inseparable from the racism behind the old notion that all Negroes have natural rhythm.) In any case, the riff-playing or vernacular inventiveness that is so fundamental to the way Negroes react otherwise is conspicuously absent from their political behavior. In other situations they play by ear, but for some curious reason they seem to think that political problems must be solved by the book, which in most instances only a few seem to have read and not that many have digested.

No self-respecting Negro musician would ever be guilty of following the stock arrangements of white song writers as precisely as Negro leaders adhere to the Tin Pan Alley programs of white social technicians! Nor is bravado an adequate substitute for efficiency. Nor should riff-style be confused with the jive-time capers of second-rate con-men. White squares are always being "taken" by such small-time hustlers—but only for peanuts!

Part of the political failure of most Negro leaders, spokesmen, and even social technicians is that they really have been addressing themselves all these years to moral issues and not the actualities of local, state, and national power. Perhaps as more of them become more deeply and intimately involved with the practical requirements of government in action and hence more personally familiar with the chord structure and progression of official maneuvers, the extension of the riff-style into politics is inevitable. Perhaps when this happens even the young black radicals will move beyond their present academic reverence for radicalism per se and begin playing improvisations on the gospels of Marx, Mao, Guevara, and Fanon. Perhaps even they will begin to realize that when great Negro musicians like Armstrong, Basie, Ellington, Parker play by ear, they do so not because they cannot read the score but rather because in the very process of mastering it they have found it inadequate for their purposes. Nor should it be forgotten that they often find their own scores inadequate. (Harold Cruse's *The Crisis of the Negro Intellectual* represents a heroic attempt of one Negro writer to establish his own context and perspectives.)

As yet, however, most Negro social technicians seem unable to realize that the civil rights movement has now entered a stage that requires them to shift their primary emphasis from protest to practical politics. Such an obvious cultural lag may grow out of the fact that the most widely publicized black spokesmen are preachers, heads of organizations sponsored by white liberals, and student idealists, for all of whom a preference for moral outcry over the dirty business of wheeling and dealing with political machines is only natural.

Meanwhile, it is no less natural, or at least predictable, that Negroes in general continue to function in terms of extensions and elaborations that enabled their ancestors not only to endure slavery but also to sustain an unexcelled sense of human worth and possibility in the process. In spite of the restrictions and atrocities of the plantation system, the personal and social intercourse among slaves was so fabulous in the richness of its human fellowship, humor, esthetic inventiveness, and high spirits that the masters—who, ironically, lived in constant fear of black uprisings—could only pretend to shrug it off as childishness! It was not infantilism, however, that girded fugitive slaves for the ordeals of the Underground Railroad and conditioned so many of them to become productive and responsible citizens and men of their time as rapidly as the means became accessible and white resistance would allow.

Nor is it otherwise for contemporary Negroes. It is not cultural lag that creates the major obstacle for those who migrate from the farms and small towns of the South into the industrial and commercial web of the Northern metropolis. It is racism, much of it official, that prevents them from obtaining adequate employment, decent housing, and equal protection under the law. As for their ever so widely publicized lack of preparation in, for instance, specific job skills, such deficiencies, which are hardly greater than those of thousands of white immigrants, are more than offset by Negro eagerness to receive the technical training required. Nor are Negroes from the South any less teachable than any other erstwhile peasants. For the rest, sensibilities formed in the blues tradition seem uniquely equipped to withstand the dislocation traumas that usually result from such an abrupt and radical shift in environment and mode of existence.

Indeed, someday students of machine-age culture in the United States may find that Negro slaves in the cotton field had already begun confronting and evolving esthetic solutions for the problems of assembly line regimentation, depersonalization, and collectivization. After all, the so-called Industrial Revolution had as much to do with the way personnel was used as with machinery as such. In any event, Harlem and Detroit Negroes, for example, are neither terrified by the intricacies of contemporary technology nor overwhelmed by the magnitude of megalopolis. On the contrary, they seize every opportunity to get into the swing of things, almost always contributing vitality and new dimensions of elegance when they succeed.

It is also possible that the time will come when students of U.S. life styles will regard the so-called abnormal structure of the Negro family not as the national liability that the Moynihan Report depicts but as a positive force! They may find that it is an institution with a structure that has always been remarkably consistent and compatible with the structure of modern society, and produces personalities whose rugged flexibility is oriented to cope with the fragmented nature of contemporary experience. Further investigation may discover that the actual family of many contemporary Negroes, like that of plantation slaves, is the neighborhood. Much goes to show that among U.S. Negroes parental authority and responsibility have always been shared by neighborhood uncles and aunts of whom sometimes none are blood relatives. *White Southerners were not the only people who benefited from the magnanimity of the black mammy.* Nor have all Negroes been as inattentive to the worldly wit and wisdom of Uncle Remus as most of the current crop of civil rights spokesmen seem to have been.

The cultural deprivation from which Negroes in general suffer is not their own but rather the deprivation that makes for the incredible provincialism of those white social science technicians (and their Negro protégés), who when they report their observations and assessments of Negro life, invariably *celebrate* the very features of American life that the greatest artists and intellectuals have always found most highly questionable if not downright objectionable. But come to think of it, what usually seems to matter most in all findings and evaluations made by American social science survey technicians are indices of material affluence and power. In fact, sometimes it seems that even the most comprehensive social science assessments are predicated upon some indefinite but ruthlessly functional theology involving the worship of wealth and force. In any case, it almost always turns out that whoever has acquired money and power—by any means whatsoever—is assumed to be blessed with everything else, including the holiest moral disposition, the richest sense of humor, creative genius, and impeccable taste.

Of course the mechanics (or machinations) of white supremacy permit white Americans in general to presume themselves the natural heirs and assignees to a median legacy of such qualities. But for the rest, so barbarous is the anthropological value system to which contemporary American social science seems to be geared that so far as the technicians who survey Negro communities are concerned people without affluence and power are only creature-like beings whose humanity is measured in terms of their potential to accumulate material goods and exercise force with arrogance.

Alas, not even the most fundamental human value that democratic societies are specifically designed to guarantee seems to count for very much once such technicians become involved with Negroes. On the contrary, far from revealing any significant preoccupation with or even appreciation for personal freedom and self-realization in any intrinsic sense, the technicians now proceed in an alarming number of instances as if statistical measurements of central tendencies—for all that they may have been initiated in the interest of programing the greatest good for the greatest number—have become a means of justifying an ever increasing standardization, regimentation, and conformity. In so doing, they tend to condemn the very elements in U.S. Negro life style that other non-totalitarian cultures seek and celebrate: its orientation to elastic individuality, for one, and its esthetic receptivity, and its unique blend of warmth, sensitivity, nonsense, vitality, and elegance.

There is, as no man of good will would ever dispute, everything to be said for the high priority that most Negro leaders and spokesmen have always placed on emergency measures to counteract poverty, exclusion, and injustice. But in giving so much emphasis to the moral aspects of the case, they often seem to neglect the fundamental nature of the hardheaded pragmatism that underlies so much American behavior. Sometimes Americans are disposed to fair play and sometimes they are not. But they almost always invest their time, money, and enthusiasm in assets with promise, not liabilities. Even those who become involved in salvage operations have been sold on *inherent potential.*

There should never be any relaxation of the pressure for national fair play. But even so it may well be that more emphasis on the discovery, development, and assimilation of things that the so-called black community may contribute to the welfare of other Americans (who are not nearly so well off as advertised) may make the best sales pitch for the cause of black people precisely because it will offer investment possibilities that will best serve the immediate as well as the long term interests of the entire Republic. The so-called population explosion does not alter the fact that there never has been a time when the United States did not need all of the human ingenuity it could muster.

Nor are the people who evolved the blues idiom likely to restrict their ingenuity to the proliferation of technological innovations. As would be entirely consistent with their tradition or life style, they are far more likely to regard all mechanical devices as truly significant and useful only to the extent that such devices contribute to the art of living, the art, that is to say, of human enjoyment—without which there can be no such thing as human fulfillment no matter how rich the nation's natural resources or how refined its technology.

PART II

The Illusive Black Image

Introduction

PROVIDING THE AMERICAN PUBLIC with images of black experience has become over the past decade a major source of income and public and sometimes academic status for both the survey technicians who are oriented to tabloid journalism and the tabloid journalists who spout the jargonistic conjectures of social science survey technicians. While the quest for the illusive black image may never provide the sort of dependable data that can be of practical significance to the well being of the total national community, it already seems to have created a new job category: the Two-Finger Pig-Latin Swahili Expert, an image technician who files survey-safari reports on Ghettoland, U.S.A.

This new and very special type of white or somewhat white hunter is an American not an African phenomenon. He makes survey data safaris into the deep, dark, torrid-zone interior of the Eight Ball. He is regarded as an expert on U.S. jungle manners and mores, but his natives are no longer referred to as savages. They are "culturally deprived [i.e., non-white!] minorities." And the natives are no longer thought of as cannibals who eat *other* people. As now reported, they are people who spend most of their time eating *their own hearts out* (and being generally self-destructive) because they are not white.

The self-styled, publicly proclaimed friendship of this very special white hunter for U.S. Negroes, whom he has recently taken to calling the blacks in the old white African manner (but also with overtones of Jean Genet's *Les Nègres*), is quite like the friendship of his prototype in Kenya in that it seldom extends beyond the requirements of the safari. When he brags that, "Malcolm X said I was one of the few whites he . . ."; or that "Eldridge Cleaver accepted me and said . . .", he is really taking care of several bits of the very urgent business of self-promotion at once: (1) He is consolidating his one-up status over those base-camp white people (who subsidize his reports because they are interested in reading about Negroes but are terrified at the mere notion of entering the Eight Ball) and also over other white reporters; (2) he is up-grading his credentials and bargaining power with white editors and publishers; and (3) he is making a public presentation of his black passport to such Eight Ball tribal chiefs as might figure in future safari assignments.

The Two-Finger Swahili Reporter and Image Collector never makes it clear as to which Eight Ball creatures are the natives and which are the animals. He is out to get them all into his black notebag of white supremacy folklore anyway. This section considers some of these image collectors and their techniques—and some of the literary counterparts of both— and the realities they are trying to capture. It begins with a short look (so as to set the focus) at one of the realities, Harlem, and at one of its images, the so-called ghetto, and then turns to techniques, collectors, and other reports and "students" of U.S. Negro life.

Image and Unlikeness in Harlem

M ASS MEDIA IMAGES of contemporary Harlem reveal only a part of the actual texture of the lives of the people who inhabit that vast, richly varied, infinitely complex, and endlessly fascinating area of uptown Manhattan. Those who create such images almost always restrict themselves to documenting the pathological. Thus not only do they almost always proceed in terms of the liabilities of Harlem but what they record more often than not also leaves the entirely incredible but somehow widely accepted impression that there are no negotiable assets of any immediate significance there at all.

But not only do the human resources of Harlem exceed the liabilities, even the existing material assets and possibilities do. There are thousands of rundown, poverty-ridden, vermin-infested tenements in Harlem which have long been unfit for human habitation and which are not only overpriced but also overcrowded. But even so, far from being one sprawling and teeming network of endless shambles, Harlem is an industry-free, ideally situated residential area with broad avenues and well-planned streets, and the convenience of its transportation facilities is unexcelled by any other residential community in Manhattan. Nor do many other areas match the charm and elegance of its architecture. (Some of the least interesting buildings in Harlem, such as those in Delano Village near where the Savoy used to be, were constructed comparatively recently. They provide modest urgently needed comfort but little else.)

There may or may not be such a thing as a Moynihan Report image finder, a *Dark Ghetto* image finder, and so on, but there most certainly are focused viewpoints that exclude almost everything except that which substantiates Moynihan's Victorian notions about broken homes, Clark's (self-excepted) descriptions of black powerlessness and black self-hatred, and various pop art constructions of juvenile delinquency and

This article, which first appeared in *The Urban Review*, was written to accompany a group of fine photographs by Fred McDarrah.

uptown camp. But what is there to see if one lifts away these blinders?

Much has been made of the Harlem dweller's response to rats, discrimination, and poverty (but no more, incidentally, than Richard Wright made of Bigger Thomas' response to the same rats and the same discrimination and poverty in the Chicago of *Native Son*). What most observers almost always seem to be unaware of for some strange reason, however, is the incontestable fact that Negroes in Harlem, like those elsewhere, also respond to beauty, style, and elegance—even as their wonderful ancestors found delight in the magnolias and honeysuckles, the crepe myrtles and cape jasmines, the terrain, the fabulous thickets, woodland streams, and verdant hillsides, the gourd vines and trellis work near the cabins, the graceful lines of plantation mansions and even the deep richness of the soil they tilled during the darkest and most oppressive days of slavery.

It is true that most people in Harlem have little interest for articles in, say, *Vogue* or *House Beautiful* about the grillwork on wrought iron gates, the ornamental griffins, period-piece bay windows, splendid archways, and charming courtyards to be found in the area. But after all, there are other and perhaps better ways of responding to such things. One can assimilate them, for instance, and simply live in terms of them, which is largely what they were made for in the first place. Obviously, there is much to be said for the conscious cultivation and extension of taste, but there is also something to be said for the functional reaction to artistic design (and honeysuckles) as normal elements of human existence. And there is, of course, also quite a bit to be said against fastidiousness and academic pretentiousness. (Not that Harlem can't use all the art history it can get.)

As James Weldon Johnson noted years ago, not very many New Yorkers in other parts of town seem to have as much involvement with their immediate neighborhoods as do the people of Harlem. Nor is the Harlemite's involvement a mark of oppression. It is a mark of openness. Most other New Yorkers seem to spend so much of their time hustling from one interior to another that they don't ever seem to see very much of their affluent and antiseptic neighborhoods except on the run, and they seem to see even less of the neighbors whose status locations they pay such high rents to share. On the other hand, weather permitting, the sidewalks and the brownstone doorways and steps of most of the streets of Harlem always hum and buzz with people in familiar contact with other people. The need for better housing and more adequate community services in Harlem is a national scandal, but what many Harlemites do with what they have is often marvelous all the same.

The life style of Harlem Negroes of all levels, in fact, goes with the very best esthetic features not only of Harlem but of New York at large. Harlem Negroes do not act like the culturally deprived people of the statistical surveys but like cosmopolites. Many may be indigent but few are square. They walk and even stand like people who are elegance-oriented. They talk like people who are eloquence-oriented. They dress like people who like high fashion and like to be surrounded by fine architecture. The average good barber shop and tailor shop in Harlem is geared to a level of sartorial sophistication that is required only from the best elsewhere. There is no telling what outside image makers think of the amount of formal wear sold and rented in Harlem, but one thing it suggests is that many of the social affairs sponsored by Harlemites scintillate. Not even the worst dressers in Harlem are indifferent to high fashion. They are overcommitted to it!

It is very curious indeed that at a time when Harlem Negroes encounter fewer restrictions, exercise more political power, earn more money, and have more involvements elsewhere than ever before, media reporters (following a writer like Clark) describe them as denizens of a ghetto, who are all but completely ostracized from the mainstream of American life—which media reporters refer to as the white world. The term ghetto does not apply to Harlem, if indeed it applies to any segregated housing area in the United States. Perhaps it applies to this or that Chinatown. It *does not* and *never has* applied to segregated areas where U.S. Negroes live. The overwhelming majority of the residents of Harlem, along with most other native-born U.S. Negroes, are part-white Anglo-Saxon Protestants, and Southern at that, with all the racial as well as cultural ramifications that this implies. Harlem contains a vast network of slum areas which are an ambitious social worker's absolute delight, but Harlem itself is no ghetto at all. No matter how rotten with racial bigotry the New York housing situation is, it is grossly misleading to imply in any way that the daily involvements, interests, and aspirations of Negroes are thereby restricted to the so-called black community.

Harlem Negroes are New Yorkers. (The mainstream is not white but mulatto.) Harlemites have their special cultural distinctions, as do New Yorkers who live in the Bronx, Queens, Greenwich Village and so on, but a Harlem Negro looking down Fifth Avenue from Mt. Morris Park is not nearly so cut off from the center of things as the word "ghetto" implies. He is looking toward midtown and downtown, where most people in Harlem work, and he feels as intimately involved with Macy's, Gimbels, Saks, and Bloomingdale's as his income and his credit card will allow. He, like most people in Harlem, is also aware that midtown is, among other things, Lena Horne at the Waldorf, Ella Fitzgerald at the Royal Box, Diahann Carroll at the Plaza, Jackie Wilson at the Copa, Count Basie at the Riverboat, and a wide choice of Negro prizefight champions and basketball players at Madison Square Garden. Nor is Leontyne without uptown followers—and competitors. The Harlem Negro knows very well that there are uptown lawyers and judges in the downtown courts, and that the Manhattan Borough President is almost always a Negro. After all, he probably helped to put him (or her) there. Segregation in New York is bad enough, but it just isn't what it used to be. The national headquarters of the NAACP is at 57th Street on Broadway, and the office of the NAACP Legal Defense Fund is at Columbus Circle.

But what useful purpose is really served by confusing segregated housing in the U.S. with the way Jewish life was separated from the gentile world in the days of the old ghettos? After all, in addition to physical segregation, the real ghettos also represented profound differences in religion, language, food customs, and were even geared to a different calendar. It is grossly misleading to suggest that segregated housing anywhere in the United States represents a cultural distance that is in any way at all comparable to the one that separated a Jewish ghetto from the life styles of various European countries.

Duke Ellington, whose music encompasses at least as much of the flesh and blood reality of life in the United States as do books like *An American Dilemma*, was well aware of the widespread hunger and filth and crime and political frustration in Harlem as long ago as when he wrote "Harlem Airshaft" (he had already written "The Mooch"), and so was William Strayhorn when he wrote "Take the A Train." But Ellington and Strayhorn and most of the other Harlem musicians, including the old rent party piano players, were—and still are—also aware of something else: that Harlem for all its liabilities generates an atmosphere that stimulates people-to-people good times which are second to none anywhere in the world. (Life in Paris is better celebrated in story but not in song and dance.)

The music of Harlem makes people all over the world want to dance. It makes the rich, the poor, the powerful and weak alike clap their hands and tap their foot in celebration of the sheerest joy of human existence itself. Not only that, but it disposes them toward affirmation and continuity even as, with the blues, it reminds them of their infernal complexity. (Incidentally, musicians and athletes are far more numerous, more symbolic, and more influential in Harlem than are the criminals and addicts.)

Images of Harlem that could have been derived only from the current fad in psychopolitical gossip about Negro self-hatred, only serve to charge an atmosphere already at the point of explosion. The system of racial exclusion in employment forces most people in Harlem to function far below their minimum potential even as it enables recently arrived white immigrants with no better qualifications than Harlemites to exceed their wildest dreams. Not even the most degenerate rituals of the South are more infuriating to multigeneration U.S. Negroes than the pompous impertinence of those European refugees who were admitted to the U.S. on preferential quotas, who benefit by preferential treatment because of the color system, and who then presume to make condescending insinuations about the lack of initiative, self-help, and self-pride among Negroes.

Meanwhile the least that is required of those who would help Harlem achieve its aspirations (some of which may very well be higher than many of those held in the most self-satisfied

and self-restricted white communities and which are, if anything, even better for the nation at large than for Negroes) is
that they disentangle themselves from the folklore of condescension and approach the people of Harlem with the attitude
that good photographers seem to take when they aim their
cameras at the streets and the buildings.

Oneupmanship in Colorful America

ONE WAY OF NOT SEEING U.S. Negroes for what they are is to call them non-white. But the mystery is that when people define Negroes this way, as do especially those people who are given to reading and quoting the behavioral sciences, it is extremely difficult to know for sure whether they are being incredibly naive or deliberately so—or both. It is easy enough, however, to see that such people, whatever their avowed commitments, are very much involved, knowingly or not, in at least one version of the all-seasons game of U.S. color oneupmanship.

The indications are unmistakable. One American classifies another as non-white. He does so with a straight white face to indicate that such a classification is the most obvious, objective, and scientific thing in the world. However, if the second American, whose face may be every bit as white as the first American's or not quite as black as the ace of spades, classifies the first as non-Negro, the first immediately becomes apoplectic white and then red-white. Then he smiles. But it is a serious smile, and it gives the whole grim game away. Because it is also a powerful smile, and he does his best to make it as powerful as the power structure itself. It is an establishment smile, of the sort that tolerates the likes of Black Muslims and other news media types, but behind it is all the vicious compassion the one who suddenly and unexpectedly has been upped has for the audacious, the unthinkable, and the pathetically outrageous.

The implications of this by now classic but somewhat unsportsmanlike game are even less mistakable. In spite of all the well-known honestly admitted, widely lamented, all too human, and of course self-declared shortcomings of those who, as it were, are yes-white, am-white, is- and are-white, those who are classified as non-white are somehow, as has been noted, all too naturally assumed to be non-this, non-that, and non-the-other. Thus are all the fundamental assumptions of white supremacy and segregation represented in a word, in one key hyphenated and hyphenating word.

One hears endless talk and sees much hand wringing and

71

head shaking about the problem of race and racism in America, most of it by people who always confuse race with culture. But the real key to understanding the actual dynamics of segregation in the United States is not *race* and certainly not culture as the social sciences would define it and have it, but COLOR. When your yes-am-is-are-white U.S. citizen says non-white, he has said it all and given away the game. What he forgets, however, and much too easily, is the fact that, as the self-chosen model from which the non-white variant is a bad departure, he himself, more often than not, is self-identified, self-certified, and self-elected. He also forgets that he is self-esteemed—and for the most part only self-esteemed. Or does he ever really forget this? *What is the U.S. system of segregation if not institutionalized paranoia?*

As for U.S. Negroes being non-white, nothing could be further from scientific accuracy. Indeed, no classification was ever less accurate. By any definition of race, even the most makeshift legal one, most native-born U.S. Negroes, far from being non-white, are in fact part-white. They are also by any meaningful definition of culture, part-Anglo-Saxon, and they are overwhelmingly Protestant. And not only are they more often than not Southerners, they tend to be Southern aristocrats! (Aristocratic is the only word for their basic orientation to sports, style, leisure, luxury, and even money and power. In such matters, seldom are they middle class; many may be ignorant but few are that square. Poor often, but *poor whites* never: what with all those yard children for relatives, they were one up on the poor white even during the days of slavery.)

None of this is really news. It is really quite obvious, at some level of consciousness, even to the most casual observer. And yet it is perhaps the second most persistently overlooked flesh-and-blood fact of everyday life in the United States. The first of course is the all but unmentionable but equally undeniable fact that an infinite and ever-increasing but forever hidden number of assumed white Anglo-Saxon Protestants are among other parts part-Negro. Off-white and not-very-white Negroes seem to know more about this than anybody else. (They always knew, for instance, which assumed-white movie stars used to be Negroes, and they have said all along that Jackie Robinson was not the first Negro to play major league baseball, only the first dark one.)

There is no need to make any claims for any of this or to stake any claims on it. Nor is there any reason, the mail-order psychoanalysts to the contrary, to feel any special pride, shame, or confusion about any of it. It is a fact, and it is incontrovertible, even by law. It exists both in men's hearts and in their genes, although it is most "marketable" when it shows white in their faces. It exists for something, for nothing, or for everything, but whatever, it is just the sort of demographic detail that characterizes an open society.

Nevertheless, color gamesmanship is as American as apple pie, credit cards, the Ku Klux Klan, Miami Beach, peroxide blondes, sun lamps, and suntan lotions. And it finds expression in many ways. Many be-white, passing-for-white, or occasional-white Americans sport the deepest tans for the express purpose of emphasizing the primordial extremeness of their whiteness, a whiteness not one degree less white than the whiteness of Herman Melville's white whale. And of course not-very-white Negroes are always suspicious of those assumed-white people who make compulsive complaints about getting sunburned and those who are forever referring to how ghastly and ghostly pale they always get in mid-winter.

Political, social, and economic colormanship or rather colorlessmanship, requires other techniques. Some of them are amusing, but some are without any humor whatsoever. The key to everything is the people who belong to the all-white establishment. These are yes-am-is-are (or assumed-) white Anglo-Saxon Protestants, or, for short, yes-Wasps. Some of these have blood that is said to be blue. This means that one of their ancestors might have been a blue-eyed tennis player on the *Mayflower* or might have been a convicted base stealer released to Oglethorpe in Georgia or might have been the blue-eyed illegitimate son of some blue-eyed somebody well off enough in England to stake him to forty acres and a mule in Colonial Virginia. Such blueblood can be certified several shades bluer if subsequent ancestors engaged in the slave trade or owned slaves, and another shade of blue is added for any lingering guilt about this last, provided the guilt be philanthropic. The ironic thing about the establishment, however, is that your yes-Wasp has more part-white, off-white, and assumed-not-white blood relatives than everybody else.

Be that as it may, your yes-Wasps make up the am-white establishment. They determine color validity and color symbols. All other Americans gear their color machinations to the yes-Wasp system.

Now, your sheet-white Anglo-Saxon Protestant, or sheet-Wasp, regards his identification with the yes-Wasp establishment as a matter much too serious for gamesmanship of any kind. It is a matter that is not only sacred to him, it is his one and only reason for being. He shakes and trembles at the very thought of his sheetness. It is so sacred indeed that it must be ritualized with flaming crosses and human sacrifices. But it is still gamesmanship, a gory game of up-black-man-ship.

Currently, of course, there are the increasing number whose colormanship comes in the guise of what is called "social science." The one place U.S. Negroes have always found themselves most rigidly segregated is not in the inner sanctum of the is-white family but in the insistent categories of behavioral science surveys, studies, and statistics. It was none other than social science that contributed the "non-white" category to the modern American vocabulary in the first place—and this, despite the fact that there is no scientific method by which one can establish that a measurable percentage of any given trait or given number of traits, racial or otherwise, makes some people only part-white and others all-white. As things stand now nobody really knows which person has how much of what. And if you cannot determine who is all-white, it is perhaps a bit unscientific to claim that you already know who is non-white. But social scientists seem not to have given this simple line of reasoning much thought.

The key question to ask a social scientist is why he fools with these categories in the first place. Ask him that. Why does the social scientist make so many studies about the differences between yes-whites and non-whites? Why does he want to know so much about these two? Why is the need for information about the *differences* between yes-whites and non-whites so much more urgent than information about the differences between, say, U.S. Christians and U.S. non-Christians; U.S. Germans and U.S. Scandinavians; U.S. Irish Catholics and U.S. Italian Catholics; U.S. synagogue Jews and U.S. non-synagogue Jews; or, say, native-born U.S. Negroes and West Indian-born U.S. Negroes. Yes-whites apparently assume that all these yes-white/non-white surveys are made in the interest of behavioral science. Alleged non-whites assume that they are a matter of color politics and blackman-outmanship.

But still and all your social science oneupman is always right in there, and he has some significant results to show for his highly subsidized efforts: *Many book reading Negroes read social science and nothing else.* They read all those negative things about themselves, wrapped in all that educated terminology, and become convinced for the first time that to be non-white is to be inferior after all.

But that is only half of it. The minute they accept the idea of white supremacy, they proceed to become more be-white than everybody else! Which of course is easy enough, what with social science providing a yes-white checklist which contains nothing that anybody didn't already know. So what really happens? Nobody was ever more devoted to white middle class norms than social science Negroes! But luckily they are few. And in recent months, many of these have taken to acting like middle class Africans.

There are, of course, people who are white, and there are those who are not, and some of both live in the United States, and of course there are many differences between them. That is not the point. The point is that social science as an intellectual discipline has yet to deal with those differences in suitable terms, many of which have much more to do with esthetics than with science. And as for equality—it is a scandal that one must raise this point again and again—who needs social science to say who is equal and who is not? This is the issue that was solved some time ago by the Declaration of Independence and the Constitution.

There are many other U.S. color techniques and technicians. But no such technicians are more worthy of note than the not altogether or somewhat white liberal Intellectual, that watchdog of the do-good establishment. He is almost always a self-advertised revolutionary or radical of some kind, although most of the time his Marxism, Freudianism, or Reichianism gets so mixed up, it is hard to say whether he is really interested in world revolution or world revenge (or as some one has said, even sex revenge), but that is another game. Whatever his motives and purposes, most of the methods he uses in the color game involve the use of intellectual confusion—and even intellectual chaos. This complicates matters all right, but there are times when it is not at all difficult to see that the confusion is designed to ingratiate the not-altogether white with the yes-white establishment, at the (incidental?) expense of the al- leged non-white.

For instance: the yes-Wasp knows very well that most U.S. Negroes are part-Wasp. He pretends to ignore it and confronted with the fact, he hysterically denies it, and of course, he abso- lutely refuses to think about how many assumed-yes-Wasps are part-Negro. But he knows all this because he brought it all about.

And although he was in Europe or somewhere (sometimes China or Japan) when it all happened, your not-altogether white intellectual is having none of that, and in he moves with commentary after commentary, and reams of scholarly propa- ganda reassuring everybody that nothing of the sort ever hap- pened or ever could have happened, and he invents the black ghetto or ebony chinatown or muslim medina to prove it. Thus the U.S. Negro becomes the all-black dweller in the all-black ghetto and the somewhat white, one-time immigrant, now full-time expert on blackness becomes simply (but not quite purely) white!

Among all other U.S. color gamesmen, the liberal intellec- tual is the one who insists most urgently on being accepted as the U.S. Negro's very best yes-white friend. Sometimes he even comes begging forgiveness for the slave trade, which his peasant ancestors (well, they may have been seamen) had very little to do with indeed. It is hard to say whether all this goes to show that he has no sense of humor and irony at all, or that he has far too much.

But what always seems to get overlooked in all the color- prestidigitation is the fact that the United States goes right on being an open society. Not yet open in enough ways, to be sure, but open enough to make future improvements always likely. And perhaps this is another practical way of looking at the U.S. Negro side of the black rebellion, as many alarmed but intransigent people call the civil rights movement. Negroes are already integrated in many long standing but unacknowledged ways, but they are not yet desegregated nearly enough in some other ways, especially in some bread and butter ways that they feel are their natural due—as flesh and blood members of the great American family.

The Illusive Black Middle Class

PERHAPS THE MOST ILLUSIVE of all black images is that of the so-called middle class Negro. Safari technicians are forever accusing their brown-skin peers and betters of being Middle Class, insinuating thereby that because such Negroes are literate and employed they are somehow not only betrayers of their black fellow men but also traitors to blackness. Moreover, the safari theoretician almost always seems to visualize middle class Negroes as being lighter-skinned, that is to say, whiter than "the real Negro" (the black Blacks!) so much so in fact that when he actually finds himself in the presence of a very dark Negro who displays professional competence and is well to do, the ghetto safari expert seems compelled either to regard him as a pretentious black-face comedian or simply to ignore what is happening and insist that here is another pathetic black victim in need of white charity.

But nowhere is the sneaky hostility of some friendly white ghettologists, and their antagonism to the Negro middle class, more transparent than when they become involved in what amounts to the promotion of a black intramural class struggle. Only such a sinister objective could induce the pseudo-academic publicity the ghettologists have given to the off-the-cuff Marxist notion that there is a historical basis for such a struggle in the house slave/field slave structure of the plantation system.

Students of life in the antebellum South agree that there was indeed such a thing as a plantation hierarchy and that field hands as a rule were at the foot of the scale. Historians also agree that the domestic servants, such as the butlers, maids, nurses, and cooks, enjoyed certain "advantages" by living in the master's household. But some highly publicized contemporary historians seem to forget that there was also a "class" of skilled and semi-skilled artisans who were neither house slaves nor field slaves.

In *From Slavery to Freedom*, black historian John Hope Franklin writes about the functional class structure of slavery as follows:

In 1850 there were 400,000 slaves living in urban communities. It may be assumed that not only a majority of these were
engaged in non-agricultural pursuits, but that their number
was augmented by those plantation slaves whose owners hired
them out to townspeople. There is no way of knowing how
many such slaves were hired out, but there must have been
thousands, especially in the period between the harvest and the
new planting. It was in the non-agricultural pursuits that the
slaves displayed the greatest variety of talent and training. Many
plantations had their slave carpenters, masons and mechanics;
but the skilled slaves were to be most frequently found in
towns. Indeed, a large number of town slaves possessed some
kind of skill. In the Charleston census of 1848, for example,
there were more slave carpenters than there were free Negroes
and whites. The same was true of slave coopers. In addition,
there were slave tailors, shoe makers, cabinet makers, painters,
plasterers, seamstresses and the like. Many owners realized the
wisdom of training their slaves in the trades, for their earning
power would be greatly enhanced; and if the slave was ever
offered for sale he would perhaps bring twice as much as a field
hand of similar age would bring.

But then some Class Struggle–prone historians seem to
proceed from an oversimplified hypothesis of slavery rather
than from historical documentation in the first place. The following description in *Life and Labor in the Old South* by conservative old U. B. Phillips (perhaps the most famous apologist
for slavery), provides much more accurate information about
the circumstances of slavery than does the image evoked by
the misguided house Negro/field Negro dialecticians: "At all
times in the South as a whole *perhaps half* [italics added] of the
slaves were owned or hired in units of twenty or less, which
were too small for the full plantation order, and perhaps half of
this half were on mere farms or in town employment, rather as
'help' than as a distinct laboring force. Many small planters'
sons and virtually all the farmers in person worked alongside
any field hands they might possess; and indoor tasks were par-
celed among the women and girls white and black." The point
is, anyone who talks in terms of two antagonistic "classes"
among American Negro slaves is talking incorrect theory not
fact.

Not even the long-standing, widespread employment of the present-day HNIC—Head Negro (mispronounced Southern style) in Charge—who derives from the figure in charge of the black compound in the temporary absence of the white boss-man, can be used in support of the pseudo-Marxist house slave/field slave hypothesis. For the HNIC is most often likely to be (as was his forerunner) a man not from the big house but from the compound itself. (Contrary to the cliché image, the domestic slave, whose position was not hereditary by the way, was admired, envied, emulated, and respected by less favorably placed slaves, but the domestic did not automatically exercise the authority of a black overseer over field hands. Nor is there reason to believe that he placed the master's interests above the liberation of his fellow bondsmen. There were Judases as well as snobs among the domestics to be sure; but as a general rule, the house slave seems to have brought infinitely more tactical information *from* the big house to the cabins than any information about subversive plans he ever took back.) The HNIC, then as now, is a man of the people become black foreman, black strawboss.

Perhaps the most important thing to remember about the HNIC is that he is selected by white people. Nor should it be forgotten that he may often be selected primarily because he *symbolizes* militancy. Part of his job is to be tough, and of course he may brag about what he is going to do to whitey. But consistent with his main function as black foreman, which is to keep Negroes in line, his physical acts of violence are most often committed not against *white* people but against *black* people! It is seldom the loudmouth spokesman who tees off on whitey. The cool non-leaders do that. Remember who triggered the "riots" in Watts, Newark, Detroit, and elsewhere.

The main objective of the HNIC is obviously *to be in charge*. Currently there are those who are status quo conservatives, those who are welfare gradualists, those who are syndicate-controlled cynics, others who are verbal rebels and others who are one vague type of left-wing revolutionary or another. Some HNICs are outright separatists and some are not. But desegregation in any form is a threat to the very existence of the HNIC, whatever the type. It is pretty hard to control a black student who takes all that education jive seriously enough to become an engineer, earn, say,

$35,000 a year, move his family out of a tenement district and into a more comfortable suburban subdivision—so you accuse him of being a deserter to the cause! A charge which is seldom brought against dropouts, dope addicts and murderers!

And naturally the friendly white theoretician agrees. A main part of *his* job seems to be to support the White Man's Black Man by building up the image of the HNIC as the Black Man's White Man! The white dialectician loves black revolutionary rhetoric and TV side-show heroics, but black revolutionary action scares the hell out of him. So much so that he spends much of his time staving it off by trying to convince "the real Negroes" that all black achievement is really a token dispensation from the all-powerful, all-white power structure. Regardless of what is said, however, it is extremely difficult to believe that white athletes, for instance, *permitted* Willie Mays, Bob Gibson, Big O, and O. J. Simpson to become superstars; or that the white people of Massachusetts are so charitably disposed towards Negroes that they elected a Negro senator in order to placate black militants in Roxbury—not to mention the citizens in the South Side of Chicago!

In all of this nonsense about black good guys and bad guys—in their varying shades of militancy and class origin and status—what is most often forgotten is the nature of the problem. *So far as white people are concerned, the most revolutionary, radical, and devastating action any U.S. Negro can engage in is to compete with other Americans for status, employment, total social equality, and basic political power.* Even more obvious (one would have assumed) is the fact that it is the so-called middle class Negro (or Negro with so-called middle class aspirations) who represents the most fearsome revolutionary threat to the white status quo. White Americans are forever expressing their concern about the poverty and ignorance of the black "masses" and about crime in the streets. But they know very well that the police are not really worried about the essentially routine transgressions of the poor and the ignorant. Nobody knows better than the police that there is all the difference in the world between the random violence of individuals during an upheaval and, what is not characteristic of the poor and the ignorant, the tactics and strategies of revolutionary activists.

Attentive students of the actual dynamics of modern revolution realize that revolts are seldom initiated by the so-called masses. They are engineered by the disgruntled "middle class" ideologists who know how to inspire and organize (and manipulate) the masses. Such was certainly the case in the American, French, and Russian revolutions, and it is also the case in the civil rights struggle. The highly literate college-oriented young people of SNCC, CORE, SCLC have seldom been any less "middle class" than the good gray NAACP—which, incidentally, probably has more grass roots members and activities than any other civil rights organization of national scope—and the spruce, buttoned-down Urban League.

Not only is it the so-called middle class Negro who challenges the status quo in schools, housing, voting practices, and so on, he is also the one who is most likely to challenge total social structures and value systems. Black proletarians do not seem to embrace radical doctrines or become members of such mass revolutionary organizations as the Communist party any more readily than do theory-oriented black "middle class" types. And certainly the black masses don't go around theorizing about culture, identity, hair texture, and the like (while sticking with *Vogue* and *Apparel Arts* on most other details!). To the extent that the so-called black masses become involved in such matters, they seem most likely to be following the fashions of the day which have been popularized if not initiated by the so-called middle class whom they seem to admire and emulate much more than they envy. The one thing they don't tolerate from successful Negroes is arrogance. Adam Clayton Powell is arrogant toward white people and other successful Negroes not the masses of black people.

It should not be at all difficult for students of social power to see the dynamics of the so-called middle class at work in the civil rights movement over the past decade. Thurgood Marshall for example was every bit as "middle class" when he was winning epoch-making decisions, as when he penetrated the most exclusive power sanctum of all, the U.S. Supreme Court. The Reverend Doctor Martin Luther King (who as clergyman was really an aristocrat) would certainly qualify as middle class by the cliché standards of most white reporters, and no black leader in the history of the United States developed a greater and more active and trustful following among the black "masses" in all sections of the nation. Malcolm X, whose role as spokesman and leader was also geared to the inherently elite status of clergyman, first came to national attention, not as a hustling criminal but rather as the most articulate intellectual of the Black Muslim movement. Moreover, his phenomenal prominence, which is not to say power, went hand in hand with his increasing preoccupation with books, theories, and college lectures, as well as dialogs with TV intellectuals, who as a rule are nothing if not "middle class" oriented. During his actual lifetime, however, Malcolm X was never able to exercise either the institutional power or the widespread mass influence of such "middle class" activists as James Farmer, Robert Moses, Floyd McKissick, and Stokely Carmichael. Dedicated man that he was, Malcolm was on the scene during a number of historic confrontations, but the "masses" on such occasions had been mobilized and the contentions had been defined, not by Muslims but by SNCC, CORE, SCLC, or the NAACP.

It is also worth noting that many of the most vocal of Malcolm's present-day followers were not old enough to be active when he was alive. The heroic influence that he exercises over them has most likely been through his posthumous *Autobiography*, a book whose collaborator was a "middle class" professional, a magazine writer, and a book that was edited, published, and promoted by the avant garde–oriented (!) Grove Press. Further, although the young people seem to forget it, *they* themselves are book reading, theory-oriented, "middle class" student-types. They are not the food, clothing, and shelter-oriented black masses. Nor would the masses want them to be. The masses want leaders who are educated as well as trustworthy. Nor do the black masses regard "middle income" Negroes as tokens. They regard them as people who got the breaks—or who were able to make the most of the breaks.

All this is so much news to most white reporters who, when they concern themselves with U.S. Negroes, seem to blind themselves wilfully to the obvious fact that no matter how lowly the birth of a leader, any man automatically becomes upper class when he becomes a leader because he automatically becomes a member of the power elite. If Whitney Young and Adam Clayton Powell are middle class, who is above them? If Eldridge Cleaver is lower class, what then is the class status of the Ivy League and *Ramparts* magazine types who follow and look *up* to him? In point of fact, top Negro leaders enjoy functional as well as protocol rank far superior to that of most of the white Americans who are ever so much richer but whose social power is either only local or regional, or of a lower order.

Perhaps the supreme irony is the fact that white reporters always seem to be taken in by precisely those so-called middle class Negroes who actually do exploit black causes for personal gain. But such black operators, who are loud-mouthed and poor-mouthed by turns, are nothing if not pros at their trade. They know very well that manipulating condescending but unhip white reporters is the first step towards the do-good-foundation budgets and the appropriations committees of the federal government, which is where the real con game begins. To such black con artists the reporter is as incidental as is the Black Cause. (No special skill is needed to be such an artist. All you have to do nowadays is put on a costume and pretend to be a racist.)

But then the class struggle hypothesis of black experience ignores what should be the most obvious weakness of the class structure approach to American society: social science has never been able to establish a meaningful cut-off point between class levels. Certainly income is not a reliable index to class status among U.S. Negroes. (A large income is not a primary requirement for membership in black organizations that carry the highest social prestige.) Nor is residence a dependable key, for many Negroes who are exceptional in every other respect, who are leaders, educators, people of highly refined taste, of high standing in the arts and so on, earn middling incomes and reside in mid-range or even welfare-range buildings and neighborhoods because of discrimination in employment and housing. And in many cases, their conduct as well as their outlook is infinitely more comparable to the white upper or elite class than to the essentially mediocre middle class white people of the statistical surveys.

Nor is education a valid index. After all, many white journal-ists and survey technicians tend to regard any brown-skin or light-skinned American who speaks grammatically and enunci-ates carefully as educated and therefore middle class. But is Claude (Manchild) Brown of Howard and Rutgers middle class? If not, why not? And if so, is he more or less middle class than, say, the eloquent James Baldwin of no college, or than Richard Wright of no high school? What about the semi-literate parents who live on a Connecticut estate with their son, a wealthy electronics engineer whom they put through M.I.T. by working as menials? Where do they fit into the class structure with reference to, say, a very articulate brown-skin welfare officer, a Columbia M.A., the son of a highly successful Harlem doctor, who for the past ten years has been residing in a labor union housing project on the Lower East Side of Manhattan with his Jewish wife (by whom he has two children) and her widowed mother, a former semi-skilled garment district worker who speaks with a heavy Warsaw ghetto accent?

Is being a public figure an adequate index? If so, is rich folk singer Harry Belafonte more middle class than millionaire "soul" singer James Brown? Is Ray Charles more middle class than the conductor of the glee club at Yazoo City high school? Is Stokely Carmichael more middle class than Muhammad Ali? What about such well-known public figures as O. J. Simpson, Willie Mays, Sidney Poitier, LeRoi Jones, Robert Hooks, and, oh yes, Leontyne Price? Where do they stand or fall status-wise beside Jervis Anderson, Harold Cruse, Martin Kilson, Archie Epps, and the editorial board of *Freedomways* magazine?

But finally is not the term "black middle class" or "black bourgeoisie" now used more often as a political epithet than as an objective sociological category? Can specific people actually be classified as middle class in accordance with any existing scientific yardstick? Perhaps *black elite* would be a more accurately comprehensive and less contradictory term. The people it suggests are no less illusive to be sure, but that is exactly the point. The status or rather the *influence* of such people is too mobile and is based on too many different things to be easily and precisely defined in terms of class dialectics. In any case, the term *black elite* will allow black polemicists as well as white Eight Ball experts to place Eldridge Cleaver beside Julian Bond without contradicting themselves and confusing their readers.

As for those militant, and in truth somewhat envious, black rhetoricians who (to the delight of white do-gooders and do-badders alike) accuse affluent black inhabitants of the "integrated" suburbs of having deserted the cause, they should take a more careful look. The minute a Negro moves into any integrated situation in the U.S. he becomes blacker than ever before. Ever so friendly white suburbanites almost always insist that their black neighbors identify themselves as a part of black suffering everywhere. White integrationists are far more likely to condemn and reject their clean-cut, professionally competent black neighbors for not being black enough than to congratulate or simply accept them for not being problems. "Man," said one middle-aged black resident of Westchester County, a man who has spent his whole life working for better Negro education, job opportunities, and civil rights, "you go to one of those parties and fail to show the proper enthusiasm for Malcolm, Rap, and Cleaver, and then some ofay millionaire and his wife will call you an Uncle Tom to your face! And you know who will back them up? Almost every establishment editor present. Man, it's getting so that if you don't go in there pissing and moaning and making threats, they'll call you a moderate and drop your butt fifty times faster than Malcolm ever would. You got to cuss them out, or you're out of it, buddy. But damn, man, the minute you sound off, you realize that they've tricked you into scat singing and buck dancing for them; because there they are, all crowding around, like watching you masturbate, like they are ready to clap their hands and yell, 'Go, man, go. Get hot, man.' But Goddamnit, you know what they really want you to be? A blind man with a guitar!"

Two Case Histories

WHAT FOLLOWS ARE COMMENTS on two books that purport to be personal memoirs but which in fact are much closer to being social science case histories and which have more to do with the fakelore of black pathology than with the texture of everyday experience. Black actuality is no less illusive in these and similar case histories than in the statistical surveys that some readers obviously assume such histories corroborate.

CLAUDE BROWN'S SOUL FOR WHITE FOLKS

Being black is not enough to make anybody an authority on U.S. Negroes, any more than being white has ever qualified anybody as an expert on the ways of U.S. white people. It simply does not follow that being white enables a Southern sheriff, for instance, even a fairly literate one, to explain U.S. foreign policy, air power, automation, the atonality of Charles Ives, the imagery of Wallace Stevens, abstract expressionism, or even the love life of Marilyn Monroe.

If it did, then it would also follow that the oldest and blackest Negro around would be the most reliable source of information about Africa, slavery, Reconstruction politics, the pathological effects of oppression, the tactics and strategies of civil rights organizations, the blues, championship sports competition, and the symbolic function of the stud horse principle (and the quest for the earth dark womb!) in interracial sexual relationships.

Neither does it follow that because somebody lives or even works in the garment district, he has authentic inside information on the labor problems of the needle trades. Nor does it follow that the best diagnostician at Bellevue is somebody who has personally suffered the most serious diseases.

Nothing in the world could be more obvious. And yet this seems to be precisely the sort of thing that no longer goes without saying. A book like Claude Brown's *Manchild in the Promised Land* (The Macmillan Co., 1965), for example, is recommended all-around as if it were a profound, knowledgeable, and even comprehensive account of life in Harlem because its author is a Negro who grew up there and had a rough time doing so. An astonishing number of book reviewers and U.S. social critics actually insist that *Manchild* reveals what it is really like to be a Negro.

It does no such thing. It tells them absolutely nothing about Willie the Lion Smith, Sugar Ray Robinson, Adam Clayton Powell, Constance Baker Motley, the chief of maintenance at Lenox Terrace, the barman at Smalls Paradise, the society editor of the *Amsterdam News*, and so on. There's hardly anything in the book about how it feels to help run the most complicated transport system in the world—which is what quite a few New York Negroes do. As a matter of fact *Manchild* (a title that probably makes some white people think they know how chitterlings and collard greens taste), like so many other books written for white people by Negroes, is so full of the fashionable assumptions of the social sciences that little of what its young author has to reveal about what it is like to be one very special Harlem Negro named Claude Brown really represents his own insights. Perhaps one of the most significant things this book actually reveals is how difficult it is to be a serious writer when you've been interviewed, advised, rehabilitated, and structured by social workers, liberals, and other do-gooders year after year.

Many U.S. social critics or whatever they are, seem to be every bit as innocent as those newsmen and opinion-surveyors who interview the man-in-the-street but never catch onto the obvious fact that the man-in-the-street mostly knows what he reads in newspapers, hears on the radio, and sees on TV. And even when he knows more, he is likely to express only what he thinks will grind his own special ax or will make him appear especially informed (and in this, he is not unlike the average U.S. college student).

Thus do so many samples of ordinary public opinion turn out to be so many big fat jokes on the gullability of both the opinion-surveyor and the reader of surveys. But perhaps the most outrageous joke of all is the one on the reporter who doesn't recognize his own half-dashed news item when it is fed back to him by some Negro standing on Lenox Avenue or sitting in a hamburger joint in the Watts section of Los Angeles. And more exasperating than outrageous is the fantastic number of sociologists and psychologists who go out and allow themselves to get sucked in on their own conjectures and rumors!

When a U.S. Negro, whether his name be Martin Luther King, James Farmer, Whitney Young, slum dweller 45, or narcotics case 46, begins talking in terms of the ghetto, culturally deprived minorities, disadvantaged youth, middle class norms, upward mobility, self-rejection, alienation and so on, you are listening to a very pretentious and confused American displaying his stylish vocabulary—and very little else. There was a time, one likes to think, when any ordinary reporter could spot the difference between sidewalk savvy and newsstand erudition. But perhaps there were not so many newsstands in those days. Or perhaps there was just more common sense.

Personal experience, one hastens to concede, is a fundamental element in all writing. It is indispensable. But so are several other elements. Personal experience is a very fine thing to have indeed, the richer the better, but what one is able to make of it in a book is something else again. This is likely to be determined by one's sensibility, one's imagination, one's perspective, the depth and keenness of one's insights, one's linguistic precision and eloquence. The would-be writer's complexion, his street address, and police record can never really make up for the absence of any of these.

Only to the extent that Claude Brown, James Baldwin, James Joyce, Wright Morris, or anybody else has a rich enough awareness of many things other than his complexion, street address, and police record is he as a writer likely to be able to reveal very much about himself that one can't come by just as easily from his case history. Indeed, if these things are all that a writer knows, what he is most apt to produce is precisely a personal case history, and one of limited documentary value at that. The fact that somebody assures you that the incidents in a book really happened in the flesh does not add to the credibility or validity of the book. It is more often than not only an excuse for bad writing.

But then this whole thing about somebody revealing what it is really like to be black has long since gotten out of hand anyway. Not even the autobiography of Sigmund Freud reveals what it is really like to be Jewish, for instance. Nor do the memoirs of, say, J. William Fulbright reveal what it is really like to be a white Southerner. Does anybody actually believe that, say, Mary McCarthy reveals what it is really like to be a U.S. white woman, or even a Vassar girl?

It is all but impossible for one to imagine a U.S. Negro, no matter how substandard his formal educational background, telling anybody white or black that any one book reveals what it is really like to be a white man. Nevertheless a white Negro like Norman Mailer, a part-time Negro like Nat Hentoff, a non-Negro like Norman Podhoretz, and a non-Jewish New York know-it-all like Tom Wolfe, the trick typist from Virginia by way of Yale, have all engaged in promoting *Manchild* as the raw truth and excusing its shortcomings, as if the raw truth didn't require just as much writing skill as the refined granulated or confectionalized truth.

It sounds like the old jazz situation all over again. *White reporters write about jazz for other white people.* Although most jazzologists and record liner scholars can't even pat their feet in the presence of Negroes without embarrassment, they write about the Negro idiom in U.S. music as if U.S. Negro readers don't exist. (Which incidentally goes to show the difference between most white jazz *reporters* and white jazz *musicians.* During a rehearsal for the Newport Jazz Festival several years ago, a white piano player complained that his white trumpet player was not swinging enough on a certain up-tempo blues number. Aghast, the white trumpet player turned and coolly looked the white piano player up and down and then replied, "And how would *you* know?" They stood glaring at each other, and then suddenly they both realized that the veteran Negro bass player was waiting, somewhat impatiently, for them to get the hell on with the rehearsal. Both turned without another word and resumed their playing positions and nodded for *him* to give the downbeat.)

Perhaps the white negrologists could learn something about intellectual and artistic sincerity as well as American culture from the more serious white jazz musicians. These jazzmen sound as if being closely interrelated with Negroes were the most natural thing in the world. Unlike the white negrologist (not to mention the white writer, who rarely endows black people with dreams and heroic aspirations that in any way approach his own), white jazz musicians eagerly embrace certain Negroes not only as kindred spirits but also as ancestral figures indispensable to their sense of purpose and to their sense of romance, sophistication, and elegance as well. Negroes like Duke Ellington, Louis Armstrong, Bessie Smith, Billie Holiday, Chick Webb, Coleman Hawkins, and others too numerous to enumerate, inspire white Americans like Woody Herman, Gerry Mulligan, and countless others to their own richest sense of self-hood and to their highest levels of achievement. As for the white jazzologist, he is forever celebrating the authenticity of this or that white musician, but he never seems to realize how you get that way.

Young Brown himself, it must be said, seems to have a much clearer conception of the practical significance of his first and somewhat less than brilliant book than do most of his downtown boosters and admirers. He is, no doubt, delighted at how famous it is making him, astonished at all the easy money, and he also hopes quite frankly that all the publicity will add up to the kind of usable popularity that will bring him political power.

Brown may well outgrow the autobiographical social science fiction of *Manchild in the Promised Land*. Some day he will probably be able to see just how superficial all of those welfare department assumptions really are—and maybe at that time he will also begin to understand why so many U.S. Negroes with much more wisdom than they're usually given credit for, don't put too much stock in books as such although they have the greatest respect in the world for the kind of education and training that "qualifies" other people and may someday qualify them to exercise so much power.

And if he follows his announced intention and enters Harlem politics one day, Brown is almost certain to outgrow the role of the black boy who tells white folks dirty stories about Negroes. The mass-media-made Negro spokesman is one thing, but a duly elected representative is something quite different indeed. No Negro media-spokesman really needs to be anything more than a very special kind of entertainer who uses charts, graphs, and monographs as his stage props. All he ever has to do is keep his gossip obscene and irrelevant enough, his rumors ridiculous enough, and then pretend (with a militancy nice enough) to be upset about the miserable plight of his white-ridden or his black-ridden "brothers," and he can make himself a fairly sizable income and keep himself in a limelight of sorts as long as this kind of thing pleases enough white people enough.

The Harlem politician, however, like most other vote seekers elsewhere, must please his constituents. He just flatly cannot afford to waste his time representing the precious misconceptions of self-righteous non-resident kibitzers. They can write all the contemptuous editorials they want to so long as the people in his district think he is taking care of business. Once Brown enters politics he will no doubt discover very soon that Harlem voters have their own notions about how they want to be represented. Outsiders refuse to believe this, in spite of the fact that Congressman Adam Clayton Powell has a twenty-odd year re-election record to prove it. But then, as any con artist knows very well, outsiders always prefer social science fiction to the black and white, flesh and blood facts of everyday life among U.S. Negroes—in Harlem or elsewhere.

GORDON PARKS OUT OF FOCUS

Gordon Parks, as is well known and seldom disputed, least of all by his peers, is one of the finest photographers in the world. He is also, any way you look at it, a very remarkable man. He is indeed, one delights to say, the kind of well-rounded twentieth century human being the best U.S. schools have been trying to turn out for all these years. He is well adjusted, as they say in the seminars on developmental psychology, exceptional in his chosen profession, well above average in a number of others, and has a high potential in still others. In fact, it is hard to imagine him below average in anything he really puts his mind to.

Parks also has the kind of personal style, cosmopolitan taste, beautiful manners, charming wit, and sophisticated connections that not even the most exclusive schools catering to the richest and most ambitious families can guarantee. And as if all that were not enough, he is also solidly grounded in the kind of all-round efficiency that only the self-made man can fall back on when the going really begins to get rough.

As a matter of fact, Gordon Parks not only updates most of the old Horatio Alger success stories; he also up-ends most of the superficial nonsense about those marks of oppression one encounters in print everywhere these days—some of which, one is scandalized to say, his own writing is not always free of. And finally, not the least fabulous thing about this remarkable man of so many parts is the fact that for all his already widely recognized accomplishments, he is at fifty-plus even more promising than he was at nineteen. Few characteristics are more representative of life in the United States.

Parks has been a member of the photographic staff of *Life* magazine for some twenty years. During this time he has done photographic essays on subjects that have taken him into almost every region on the globe. Today he is a contributing photographer, which is just about as "in" one can get to be in that field. No photographers on any staff anywhere get more choice assignments, are better paid, and have their work more expertly showcased, taken more seriously, or distributed more widely.

He has also done outstanding pictures, both artistic and commercial, for a number of the leading fashion magazines, including *Vogue* and *Harper's Bazaar*. And not only has work by him been included in most of the major exhibitions representing photography as a fine art, there was an outstanding one-man show in the gallery on the ground floor of the Time-Life Building. It was called "The Works of Gordon Parks: Images, Words, Music," and outside, facing Sixth Avenue at 50th Street, there was a dramatic newsprint shot which shows him to be a strikingly handsome and dashingly romantic U.S. Negro man of action. Inside, in addition to the arresting excellence of the photography itself, one was immediately impressed by the extraordinary range of interest that the subject matter revealed. There were studies that captured the mobility of Alexander Calder's sculpture, portraits of women of wealth and fashion, compositions that blended old paintings with still life objects, abstract color études comparable to good contemporary painting, landscapes, skyscapes, seascapes, natural studies, sporting events, and so on. Among the fine black and white enlargements, which included selections from a documentary study-in-depth of a South American family and a wide variety of shots taken on news assignments, was one smoggy and sooty Harlem rooftop panorama which might have been the work of a Manhattan Piranesi.

In addition to the photography, there was music. His piano concerto, which had a premiere with some fanfare in Venice in 1952, was used as the background sound track for the show. One heard nothing that reflected the composer's early years as a honky tonk piano player; instead of Kansas City for getting with it, what one heard was rather like Honegger for the Darkroom. However, it sounded thoroughly professional, if a bit ofay when one thought of Count Basie.

There were also words, galley proofs, and copies of his books. During the past several years, Parks has become a part-time writer. A number of his articles have appeared in *Life*, and in 1963 he published a novel about early adolescence in the Midwest. One also learned that Parks was planning to make a motion picture based on this novel, *The Learning Tree*. Meanwhile his current book is *A Choice of Weapons* (Harper & Row, 1966).

Some of the sequences of *The Learning Tree* were written with professional competence, and from time to time, there are some details that are expertly rendered. But on the whole, it must be said, one was left with the impression that the author was really much more interested in turning out a fictionalized memoir to illustrate the "meaning" of certain experiences of his own childhood than in telling a story about Newt Winger, the book's young hero, and his friends and competitors, who have such wonderfully nostalgic names as Beansy, Jappy, Earl, Marcus, and Skunk.

A Choice of Weapons is a nonfiction memoir, which begins in a sense where *The Learning Tree* ends. There is a prologue, but the story begins in Kansas with the death of Parks' mother when he was sixteen. It covers his coming of age in Minnesota in the nineteen thirties, his struggle to put himself through high school, his experiences as busboy, dining car waiter, basketball player, piano player, song writer, and Civilian Conservation Corps worker. It also relates his adventures in and around pool rooms, bars, whorehouses, and flop houses; his travels to Chicago, the far West, New York; and there are accounts of his early marriage and family life and of how he came to be a photographer. The book ends with him returning to Harlem after having been promised and then denied an overseas assignment as a combat cameraman with the all-Negro 332nd Fighter Group during World War II.

Given the author's subsequent success in his line of work, *A Choice of Weapons* is a newsworthy book. It is also, given the action it encompasses, an occasionally interesting book. But on balance, it is not really in itself a very good book. Sometimes, for all the details that are supposed to tell it like it really is, it is not even a very convincing one. Not, one hastens to add, because one questions the accuracy of the facts but because unfortunately they too often are so artificially structured that they just simply do not ring true enough.

To begin with, the book does not "sound" at all like Gordon Parks talks, walks, looks, and certainly not the way he operates. Parks, as his career suggests, is a man who has always been on easier terms with the everyday world than are most other people. The *facts* in his narrative make this clear enough. One has only to remember how well he handled himself and maintained his personal integrity and his ambitions throughout all the difficulties of his first days in Minnesota, to say nothing of the days that followed. But his insistent interpretations are often so stilted and self-conscious that, more often than not, they project a false naiveté on the one hand and a totally uncharacteristic pretentiousness on the other. His sentiments upon hearing the news of Pearl Harbor, for instance, are so noble that they would put Douglas MacArthur himself to shame. "Self-concern at such a time was petty, I told myself, but I could not still my anxiety." Man, how you sound!

Gordon Parks functions easily enough in almost any situation almost anywhere in the world. He can get along very well in the slums or in the most elegant drawing rooms. A street fight doesn't faze him, and neither does an occasion of state. He is hip in a crap game, cool at the swankiest race tracks, gone in the world of high fashion, with it in the world of the intellectuals, a pro in Hollywood, cagey in the political capitals, smooth on the dance floor, and canny in combat. He tools on land, by sea, and in the air, as they used to say during World War II. But *A Choice of Weapons* seems deliberately designed to read like the story of a very lucky little black boy who somehow or other did not become a social problem but rather has made an astonishing breakthrough into the great wide wonderful white world of milk and money—has made it but not quite, or something like that.

Most of the time the author of *A Choice of Weapons* is so busy trying to show that his actions are conditioned by a background of U.S. Negro experience that he becomes confused and misleading not only about the nature of his own life and the lives of other U.S. Negroes but also about the nature of human motives as such. Sometimes, in fact, *A Choice of Weapons* reads for all the world as if Gordon Parks, a classic U.S. son of a gun if there ever was one, is trying to pass himself off as the son of social science fiction, Flash Gordon, the upward mobile kid from the (segregated) twilight zone of inner space!

Yes. *Of course* his actions are conditioned by the experience of his U.S. Negro background. What the hell else is he going to operate out of? Even when he is applying some esthetic insight which he learned roaming alone through the Chicago Art Institute, he is responding out of it. The trouble is that his conception of U.S. Negro experience, in this book at any rate, tends to be more abstract than real. He just simply will not let enough of the encounters stand on their own, without commentary; and ironically, like most U.S. Negro writers these days, he seems most convinced that he is laying on the heroic complications when he is only piling up the academic oversimplifications.

The background experiences of U.S. Negroes is a rich source of many things. But many people insist that it is only the source of frustration and crime, degradation, emasculation, and self-hatred. But then most of these people are headlong do-gooders who, for all their good will, are too hopelessly superficial to realize that all human circumstances are the source of these very same things. That is just too much for them to think about. Nevertheless, it is patently ridiculous to assume that there is automatically more frustration and crime in a segregated slum area than there is in power politics or high finance. Nor is there necessarily more personal compensation in Scarsdale than Lenox Terrace, not if neurotic behavior is any indication!

The background experience of U.S. Negroes includes all of

the negative things that go with racism and segregation; but it also includes all of the challenging circumstances that make for ambition, integrity, and transcendent achievement. And anyway, nobody who is really and truly interested in the perpetually fascinating mystery of human motive and conduct is ever likely to ignore the fact that many of the non-Negroes who infest Greenwich Village, the Bowery, and the narcotics dens of the Upper West Side often come from a background of freedom and even wealth and power. Nor will anyone with a reliable sense of human potential ever fail to realize that an obviously well-heeled and cultivated U.S. Negro sitting in a Paris café speaking charming French to a countess may well be operating out of a background of an Alabama cotton picker who once averted his eyes (or pretended to) every time a barefooted red-headed, red-neck girl spoke to him. It should be no news to anyone that a large number of the smoothest city slickers come from the country. That many U.S. Negroes have never lived anywhere except the city should be no news either.

And of course, any truly serious student of American culture should know that segregation for all its brutal restrictions never has blocked U.S. Negroes off from the essential influences of the public school system. Nor has it screened them against the educational fallout from the mass media. Thus, in spite of all the substandard test scores, anybody who assumes that the average white U.S. schoolboy is really closer to the classics, for instance, than the average U.S. Negro schoolboy is either talking about the relative percentage of literary snobs or is simply kidding himself. A white schoolboy *may* be persuaded to bone up and pass a formal exam on, say, metaphysical poetry, but that doesn't actually mean that he gives a damn about it. A Negro boy, on the other hand, might well have a genuine feeling for the blues, which certainly represent an indigenous "substitute" for certified high-culture poetry.

One assumes, of course, that Gordon Parks is well aware of all this. At any rate he operates with it, and he tries very hard to show its relevance to his development. But unfortunately he does not succeed very well. Thus he has not done himself justice in *A Choice of Weapons*. The result is that sometimes it is as if he himself doesn't quite know what to make of what he has in fact *already* made of himself.

Nevertheless, many people who are otherwise extremely careful about the books they rate noteworthy may not only make a fuss over this one but will be prepared to give all kinds of essentially sentimental excuses for its obvious shortcomings. And one suspects that many will be doing so because Gordon Parks is a successful U.S. Negro and because everybody is for encouraging the Negro this year. This is a hell of a reason to excuse anybody for not writing well enough. But then many of these people never did expect to see a poor little black boy write as well as Parks already does.

But white supremacists will be white supremacists, it seems, some without ever actually becoming aware of it. But they are. These "friendly" ones are the benevolent white supremacists, who are forever forgiving Negroes for something. As a matter of fact many are all too eager to forgive all sorts of sins that Negroes were never guilty of in the first place. And there are, to be sure, those doubly innocent U.S. Negroes who actually accept such totally irrelevant forgiveness—and then go around fuming about the crocodilia they put up with from white folks.

Gordon Parks is not that kind. He is never very likely to accept anybody else's excuses for anything he has ever flubbed. This is why he got where he is today, as the Southern Negro high school principals say. And in this he is not unlike the U.S. Negro prizefighter. Nobody ever heard of a Negro fighter excusing himself for a poor showing in the ring because he comes from a low income family and never got enough to eat. And one reason a fighter knows better than to try to pull this kind of old thin stuff is that there are too many other hungry Negro fighters (many of them fatherless—anti-matriarchists please note) winning championships.

The makers of sentimental excuses always seem to overlook the most obvious facts of everyday life. Nothing, for example, could be more obvious than the fact that anybody who has a life that merits an autobiography has had to overcome one sort of obstacle or another, just one hog ass thing *after* the other, as the saying goes. Thus, when one refers to Gordon Parks as having had an unpromising beginning and reports that his life has been beset with obstructions, one is really only indicating that Parks' life has the makings of a good story. Everybody knows that there can be heroes without walls and dragons. But people who substitute psychological or psychiatric theory for experience go right on pretending and perhaps even believing that nobody ever actually survives any adventure or reaches the enchanted castle.

There are others whose confusion about all this even leads them to write as if no one can enjoy a spring rainscape unless he also has the right to vote, a passionate night of love unless he has executive status, or even a succulent prime steak unless he has a seat on the New York Stock Exchange—even though he has the price of the bill of fare.

When one says that there was little in his early environment to indicate that young Gordon Parks would someday grow up to become such a magnificent photographer, one should also remember that there could hardly have been more in the environment of young Mathew Brady either. And furthermore, if becoming a member of the photographic in-crowd of *Life* magazine represents a very special breakthrough for Negro Gordon Parks, it is no less a breakthrough for every other in-crowd member and not one bit less special. One has only to remember all the unsegregated white boys squinting into view finders all over the country and dreaming of taking pictures for *Life*. It is, when one stops and thinks about it, absolutely impossible for Negro Gordon Parks to be more gratified by his progress than non-Negro Carl Mydans is by his or non-Anglo-Saxon Mark Kauffman is by his.

Gordon Parks is aware of all this also, and there is every reason to assume that he is aware of a good many other things as well. But he has been unable to get them into sharp enough focus in *A Choice of Weapons*. Thus this book, like *The Learning Tree*, cannot be ranked beside his best photography. One wishes that Parks had worked closer to the theme suggested by the highly evocative title and had made more of the implications of the storybook hero forging his sword. This may even have given all of the insistent political overtones a much deeper resonance. But perhaps in the actual process of recording the events involved he found the military metaphor too restrictive, or perhaps, as often happens, the title came afterwards. In any case, a camera is not only a magic weapon to be used against chaos. In the hands of someone as gifted as Gordon Parks, it becomes something even better, something that works miracles with form and gives both insight and delight.

Who That Say, What Dat, Every Time Us Do That?

A WELL-KNOWN NEW YORK NEWSPAPER PUNDIT, a somewhat reconstructed but sometimes sentimental Southerner out of Virginia through Maryland, once wrote that he had never met a Negro who didn't trust white people too much and that he had met very few who really understood what white people were really doing to them. This is perhaps all too true of far too many of the Negroes this well-meaning but sometimes condescending white maverick's maverick has actually met or allows himself to remember ever having met. Nevertheless, one cannot help wondering about the company he keeps.

There are, after all, Negroes, and still other Negroes, not all of them naive, nice nonentities, non compos mentis—or even non-white. There are, to be sure, many who give little evidence that they have any understanding of anything, except how to survive by hook or by crook; and not a few of these are the ones publicized by the mass media as leaders and spokesmen. Sometimes, however, it is hard to tell whether the mass media establishment regard some of them as leaders or as disguised replacements for Amos and Andy and Lawyer Calhoun.

But there always have been many others who not only have always understood all too well what other people have been doing to them all these years, but have also been doing a few things of their own on their own in the meantime. These others are part of that enduring U.S. tradition of self-control, wisdom, courage, and commitment to human freedom and individual fulfillment, which few other native traditions, in this country or elsewhere can equal and none excel—and of which the Underground Railroad was a part. For a long time the tradition has also been represented by the educational, inspirational, and political role of the Southern Negro doctor. People who are more interested in highly tenuous theories of social class than in everyday Negro life have long ignored and denied the key role of the Negro doctor as community leader. But Southern Negro educators (another overlooked type) cannot, nor can any grass roots worker in the civil rights movement.

It is incredible that none of the mature, knowledgeable or just plain shrewd Negroes one sees not only surviving but also laughing about it seems to have made any significant impression on the white intellectuals of these nothing if not academic times—perhaps least of all on those most given to explaining the meaning and mysteries of black experience, which many usually confuse either with *bleak* experience or *psychedelic* experience.

An ever increasing number of U.S. intellectuals these days seems absolutely convinced that all knowledge and certainly all guidelines for the perplexed are found only in books, and that all wisdom comes engraved in sacred terminology with reverent references to other books, especially those based on the gospels of Karl Marx and Sigmund Freud. But it is a mistake to assume that people have no knowledge or understanding of their circumstances because their reactions may not be conventional or because their verbalization does not fit neatly into somebody else's value system or some commonly accepted highfalutin frame of reference.

No Negro intellectual who really keeps his eyes and ears open at home, on the street, and in the barber shop and then goes on to college, is likely to underestimate the accuracy of the insights of other American Negroes, no matter how many formal intellectual disciplines he himself may master. Nor are most black people unaware of another completely obvious phenomenon: They themselves may be essentially *invisible* to most other people, but a whole lot of other people are in turn all too *transparent* to the black people all around them everywhere every day.

It is also a mistake to forget that there are always those people who are not going to tell other people what they really think about anything. They just do not trust other people that much. There is also, one should not forget, something to be said for the *prudence* of a domestic servant, a day laborer, or even a managing editor who does not reveal that he knows something crooked is going on and who does not tell his boss what he really thinks of him—and it would hardly make sense to tell the boss's friends and spies. Neither should one forget that there are also those people who find out that other people will believe anything, and so they tell them anything, *anything at all.*

Perhaps it has been extremely difficult for many Northern-born Negroes to realize what their white liberal friends have been doing to them behind all those interracial handshakes and brotherhood smiles. Only recently have they begun to realize the extent of the double dealing. But although some Southern Negroes have also been confused by Northern do-gooders from time to time and some for a long time were overimpressed with Northern Negro tales about unsegregated buses and hamburgers, many have always realized what Southern white people—solid, moderate, or extreme—were up to. They have always been on to Southern courthouse hoaxes, and white gentlemen's shady agreements. Sharecroppers, for instance, have never really been fooled by all that phony book-keeping. Trapped, to be sure, but fooled by no means. And, of course, everybody knows what all those laws against intermarriage, as the saying goes, are all about. Since they hardly ever see anybody being put in jail about all those mulatto children, Southern Negroes know very well that those laws are never intended to be used against race mixing, or commingling, as the white preachers sometimes say. Everybody has always known that these laws are really against shotgun weddings, *as nobody ever says*!

There just simply never was a time when most U.S. Negroes trusted any white people too much or did not really understand what was going on. The captive Africans, who never had trusted any enemies to begin with, certainly had no illusions at all about the white slave traders. The only thing that really surprised them about it all, so one old barber shop version goes, was that these Europeans, who were clearly the most savage foes any Africans had ever encountered, did not intend to eat them. Some comb and scissors historians trace all of that wonderfully complicated U.S. Negro laughter and mockery back to that realization. There is absolutely no evidence, however, that U.S. Negroes have ever lost their suspicions about other things.

Perhaps the New York news prophet has allowed himself to be misled by his contacts with too many social science Negroes. These Negroes often seem to regard themselves as The-Black-Man's-New-York-Intellectuals because they read monographs subsidized by the philanthropic foundations and know all about footnotes, bibliographies, and cross references (but who, unlike real New York intellectuals, who are truly people of the book, also regard themselves as down to earth pragmatists because they read only earthy fiction and have no interest in any art that goes beyond fashionable entertainment). And then there are the social workers, a breed slightly apart, who often seem to regard themselves as The-Black-Man's-White-People (or Middle Class Establishment, as it were), but who more often than not are themselves regarded by other Negroes as being The-White-Man's Negroes, or Strawboss Negroes.

It should be easy enough for no-nonsense newsmen, or anybody else for that matter, to spot both these types at interracial confabs, their natural habitat. Both speak with a profoundly pretentious sense of long-standing cultural deprivation and a fairly generously underwritten commitment to moral outrage. The social science type on one side of the drawing room usually smiles at *his* white interracialists and says something like, "Do you dig Odetta?" in a carefully decontaminated Ivy-accented voice. (*He* digs Joan Baez!) Also for the benefit of *his* white people he responds to any statement by other Negroes with, "Define your terminology." On the other side of the room the welfare or power structure type either nods his head murmuring, "Progress," or shakes it sadly, muttering, "No progress," with just the right overtones of black militancy to make *his* white folks feel safely hip. When he wants to shake them up, he looks away, shrugs his shoulders, and refers to "Moll-com" (Malcolm X) as if to an old billiards drinking friend. When either one of these types says, "Now we are getting down to the nitty gritty," he does not mean the basic human implications of the social issues under discussion. He means money for a welfare project.

As American as they are, neither of these apple pie people represents the complex mass of U.S. Negroes, not to be confused with The Negro. Both types, for example, are forever referring to white middle class norms as if they were talking about the greatest good for the greatest number. But most other Negroes, whether down-home or up here, know all about the "squareness" and mediocrity of those norms and the hypocrisy of middle class values.

After all, integrated or not, Negroes have always been in a position to observe almost everything that has been doing and undoing in this country. Other people always seem to forget it, but Negroes are almost always behind the scenes, whether they are on camera or not. And for inside news, no U.S. press club could ever really compare with the good old Negro barber shop (and beauty parlors) where all the old doormen, waiters, pullman porters, valets, chauffeurs, ex–shoe shine boys (and maids and cooks) go to swap lies and to signify about the state of the nation.

Most Negroes have always had enough inside information about the history of this great hit-and-miss republic to know that other people have been deliberately writing Negroes out of the history books, even as the same people permitted newly arrived immigrants to write themselves in. Even the social science and welfare elite know this (but unfortunately all they seem to be able to do about it is to suggest that black history be taught to black people who already know it—or to pretend that U.S. Negroes are all descendents of African kings, queens, and Hottentot potentates). Other U.S. Negroes, however, realize that as long as white Americans are misinformed about the actualities, the history of the United States is going to cause even more confusion among white citizens than among black ones.

Sentimental friends and self-styled benefactors of The Cause were flabbergasted when so many Negroes went along with the nomination of Lyndon Johnson for the vice-presidency. Negroes themselves, however, had been saying all along that if they ever found a Southern politician (politician, mind you, not liberal) who really felt concerned about what white people have been doing to Negroes, they would finally have somebody in the White House who would really try to do something about it. On the other hand, they have seldom felt that any Northern political humanitarians really *could* feel bad enough about it. And besides, they also know only too well that many Northerners turn up trying to become honorary Confederate drummers or something. Negro voters and political bird watchers had some hopes for FDR and JFK, felt stuck with Ike, are still philosophical about Truman; *but they put their money on LBJ*—and were somewhat saddened to find how many of their Northern liberal friends insisted that LBJ's civil rights record counts for nothing and that Negroes should *hate* him because of his blunders in Vietnam. Many suspected that much of the opposition to Johnson's foreign policy was really another sneaky Northern backlash trick to weaken his *domestic* policy!

The mass media may continue to give a lot of wrongheaded publicity to a few noisy, headline hunting–hype artists, but many U.S. Negroes know that the people who are really being taken in are not always black and exploited but perhaps most often white and sometimes rich and powerful. With all due respect to overzealous police surveillance and researchers at Harvard, Yale, and the Lemberg Center for the Study of Violence, one must remind people like that nice if somewhat proprietary newsman that they probably meet very few *white* people who do not trust all *Negroes* too much and hardly any who even begin to understand what *Negroes* are really doing to *them* and making them do to themselves. At this very moment, for instance, Negroes have thrown the whole white world, as the saying goes, into a state of shock, confusion, and almost suicidal exasperation with a simple little black magic trick like insisting that the Constitution is really nothing more or less than the Golden Rule. The best white minds, as the IQ experts say, are having trouble figuring that one out! And yet there are intellectuals who still insist that power and intelligence go hand in hand. Perhaps such is the case. But there are at least a few Negroes who have their own ideas about the keys to the handcuffs. These have always insisted that while white supremacy may sometimes be devious, it is not really predicated upon intelligence but on ruthlessness.

A Clutch of Social Science Fiction Fiction

ONLY A FEW American writers since the twenties have been
able to create fiction with implications beyond the most
obvious and tiresome of the clichés derived from social science. Even the most existentialistic and psychedelic avant-
garde experimentalists seem as often as not to be circumscribed
by assumptions that are essentially only Marxian or Freudian.
Moreover, most book reviewers, no less than American readers
in general, now seem to regard fiction as being little more than
a very special extension of the social science case history.

Unlike the stories and novels of Hemingway, Fitzgerald, and
Faulkner, which, like those of Melville, Mark Twain, and Henry
James, embody the writer's insight into the poetic and dramatic dimensions of the human situation (man's aspirations
and his possibilities), those of more recent American writers
frequently read like interim research reports and position papers. Indeed, what most American fiction seems to represent
these days is not so much the writer's actual sense of life as
some theory of life to which he is giving functional allegiance,
not so much his complex individual sensitivity to the actual
texture of human experience as his intellectual reaction to
ideas *about* experience.

Fiction about Negroes offers an obvious example. Instead of
the imaginative writer's response to the infinitely fascinating
mysteries, contradictions, and possibilities of human existence,
what fiction about U.S. Negroes almost always expresses is
some very highly specialized and extremely narrow psycho-
political theory about American *Negro* existence. And what is
even worse, these are the theories that, for the most part, only
add up to the same old bigoted assumptions that underlie the
doctrine of white supremacy.

Accordingly, although Negro life in the United States has
always been the incarnation of the "very essence of adventure
and romance" (Henrietta Buckmaster's phrase), most often
fiction about it is specifically concocted as a documentation of
U.S. Negro wretchedness. Seldom do American writers celebrate U.S. Negroes as heroes in fiction. There was William

Faulkner, to be sure, who created Lucas Beauchamp, Dilsey, Sam Fathers, and Ned William McCaslin, but the best most other white American writers seem to be able to do by the Negro is show that he deserves economic and political assistance. Nor do many U.S. Negro writers do any better. (But that is another story—one about wailing-wall polemics.)

Here are three reviews of novels which deal with the subject of U.S. Negroes in various mixes of social science and fiction. The novels range from middlebrow ladies' entertainment to very serious efforts at fictional re-creation indeed.

STAR-CROSSED MELODRAMA

Perhaps the most significant thing about *Five Smooth Stones* (Crown, 1966), a first novel by Ann Fairbairn, is the fact that it represents a consistent and positive attitude toward the so-called U.S. Negro middle class. The author does not confuse middle income Negroes with white Americans who represent the middle class "norms" of the statistical surveys, and she avoids most of the other usual condescending clichés about educated middle and upper income Negroes. By and large she seems much more concerned with creating people who have human interest and historical resonance than with forcing some theory of class conflict into the interpretation of the behavior of people who make up what is perhaps the most open and intimately interrelated social class structure in the United States.

The career of her hero is nothing if not a testimony to the fluid nature of Negro life in America. David Champlin, who was born in poverty and segregation in New Orleans during the Depression, grows up with ever extending horizons of aspiration, graduates with honors from an integrated college in the Midwest, finishes Harvard Law School, becomes successful in his profession, and moves with assurance in the integrated social circles of Boston and London without ever losing contact with any area of Negro life he has ever known. Moreover, the higher he rises, the more his respect for the rich humanity of his "uneducated" grandfather increases. There are scientific studies and surveys, usually based on over-simplifications, that would have it otherwise, but in this case at least, it is the subjective observations of the fiction writer that come closest to the complexity of actuality.

Still, *Five Smooth Stones* has some curious inconsistencies in its treatment of Negro subject matter. In spite of the author's obvious personal and intellectual freedom from bigoted thinking, she is given to an exasperatingly sloppy overemphasis on race as a social category. Time and again as the omniscient narrator, she uses such expressions as "people of his own race," "one of his own race," "she was of his own race," when "Negroes," "Negro," and "she was a Negro" would be smoother as well as more accurate. And besides, her book demonstrates at every turn how Negroes are racially *interwoven* with other Americans. That U.S. Negroes make up a very distinct sociopolitical group with discernable cultural features peculiar to itself goes without saying, but by no ethnological definition or measurements are they a *race*.

Also Ann Fairbairn is all for intermarriage, as the saying goes, and illustrates her case in terms that are as human as you please. And her conception of the hero's grandfather reveals a rare understanding and magnificent feeling for the role of the older generation Negro as a source of "faith and courage." And yet the minute she has to consider Negroes in terms of "social problems," she becomes as cliché-ridden as a survey technician, and her writing degenerates to the level of the most irresponsible tabloid journalism. She obviously thinks she is making a big fat plea for social rehabilitation when she has one of her most dedicated do-gooders describe the Negroes of the Chicago South Side, East Philadelphia, Watts, and Harlem as being "gangsters at ten, addicts at fourteen, killers at seventeen and dead inside at twenty." But the best that can be said for such glib nonsense is that it reflects an incredibly stupid approach to polemics. It should take a certified imbecile less than fifteen seconds to realize that if the main problem of Negro children in Harlem and Watts is that they are gangsters, addicts, and killers, there would be no overcrowded classrooms and no serious agitation for school desegregation in these places. In fact, there would be no Northern civil rights movement at all! And besides, the Negro youths who are most troublesome to white people these days are not the hoodlums but the social reformers!

In many ways, then, *Five Smooth Stones* is another book of social science fiction despite its virtues. It has implications of an epic and overtones of tragedy, but it never gets beyond the platitudes of melodrama, which just might be the literary fate of such fiction at best. In any event, *Five Smooth Stones* is a melodrama with an unhappy ending. The good guy, in this instance, is David, who has the nicest and most humane white friends and benefactors in the world. The bad guys are the ugly, snarling segregationists and the sneaky reactionaries. The great chase, of course, is the civil rights movement. And the girl the good guy gets is Sara, an apple pie of a white girl, who, as tiny as she is, just has too much of the pioneer spirit of her ancestors in her to be restricted by the kind of people who would not want their sisters and daughters "to marry one." The climax, however, is only as American as a hysterical mob of white backlashers and a Mississippi redneck with a sniper's rifle. But the momentum for constructive nonviolent social action is there, and Negroes are bound to show up better on social science surveys hereafter.

Without denying any of David's obvious and often charming differences, the author of *Five Smooth Stones* can accept a Negro hero as being as American as anyone else. The author of *Mojo Hand* (Simon & Schuster, 1966), Jane Phillips, cannot. Not only does she insist that middle income Negroes are as dull and as square as she finds or imagines the white middle class to be, she even gives them pale faces and goes on to portray a mulatto girl as if she were really only a white girl who is fascinated by folk Negroes, gin, awkward language in general, and foul-mouthed repetitiousness in particular. Eunice, the unlikely heroine, has all the earmarks of an overromantic unhip ofay beatnik who is hooked on folk music as a form of "escape." Everything she does betrays her identity to the reader if not to the other characters in the book, who after all are as unlikely as she is. She says, does, and is interested in all the wrong things for the wrong reasons.

The story line of *Mojo Hand*, although not easy to follow, is as simple as it is unconvincing. Eunice hears a folk blues record by a guitar player named Blacksnake, falls in love with him and Art and "real" life, leaves her cotillion-oriented (wow!) middle class mulatto parents in California, sets out for Louisiana with a guitar on her knee looking for Blacksnake. She finds him and the blues, the blues as defined in ofay jazz mags—that is, she talks nasty, does low down, gets pregnant, and so becomes a "real person" among "real people" instead of being a paleface imitation of life. Which gets pretty close to condemning Constance Baker Motley as a phony because she finished law school instead of going on the road with, say, T-Bone Walker. But then, look at all the confusion caused by white people who mistake Congressman Adam Clayton Powell for good old Cab Calloway of the Cotton Club days. One loud Hi-de Hi-de Hi-de-ho and most of Powell's troubles with "the white world" would probably vanish overnight.

Neither *Five Smooth Stones* nor *Mojo Hand* should be confused with literature. As for *Mojo Hand*, it is a fiasco from the very outset and can be dismissed and forgotten as if it never happened. That its young author would rather be a novelist than a social science expert is somehow clear enough; but as yet her conception of the art of fiction is as aboriginal as that of certain widely patronized Negro literary figures who have yet to realize that banal sayings, slang anecdotes, dirty remarks, and bad song lyrics do not become literature simply because they are published in book form.

As for *Five Smooth Stones*, it seldom rises above the comfortable sentiments of the middle brow ladies' magazines and the TV serials. As fictional journalism, however, it is a fascinating and insightful behind-the-scenes account of some of the personal tribulations interwoven with the public political struggles of the civil rights movement. But even so, except where her key characters are involved, the author, like most other writers, shows little understanding and appreciation of what the Southern Negro's extremely complicated resistance to provocation really means. Thus, she not only oversimplifies and misrepresents it as fear, but also in the process she in effect de-emphasizes white insecurity-become-hysterical by treating it as if it were only high-handed callous brutality.

Whether or not *Five Smooth Stones* becomes the best-seller its publishers are hoping for, it seems definitely headed for most social science reading lists. And the author is not very likely to object in either case. It is obvious that she set out to write a popular star-crossed civil rights romance, a plea for good citizenship and a Black Primer for White Folks, all in one. What she seems to have forgotten, however, is the fact that, for those who do not already agree with you, fiction is most compelling as propaganda not when it is used primarily as an aspic for the ideas behind the writer's commitment to a cause but when the narration is compelling.

WARREN MILLER AND HIS BLACK FACE VAUDEVILLE*

Warren Miller is much too slick and much too superficial for his work to be mistaken as serious fiction. But you never know for sure. What with book promotion being what it is these days and what with his subject matter being life in Harlem, his very slapdash slickness may actually be the means by which he may yet slide into some highly important position as a very special expert on Negro Matters. All too often it happens.

One of his books, *The Cool World*, has already been made into a deadly serious avant garde propaganda film, which has been generally dismissed as Art but praised as realistic documentation. It is no more realistic than the book itself, which was much more concerned about being cute about everything than about being accurate about anything. But so it goes, and it should surprise no one in Harlem if the mass media elect Warren Miller number one U.S. white Negro. So it went back in the days of the king of jazz and the king of swing and so it could go again. As a matter of fact, James Baldwin—who, by the way, knows much more about the goings on in Greenwich Village, Saint-Germain-des-Prés, and even Saint-Tropez than he is ever likely to know about Harlem, who certainly knows infinitely more about the guerrilla warfare of New York intellectuals than he has ever actually known about uptown street gangs, and whose scintillating prose style is much closer to Oscar Wilde than to the vernacular of Harlem—has called *The Cool World*, "One of the finest novels about Harlem that has ever come my way." Stuff.

The Cool World is not only not fine, it is hardly a novel at all. Whatever his literary potential may be otherwise, when Warren

*This essay was written in 1964, before Warren Miller's death. It is printed here without changes.

Miller writes about Negroes and Harlem, he immediately becomes a second-rate blackface comedian, an opportunistic
clown cutting topical capers for the entertainment of, as they
say in Amagansett, the "white world" (*shitman get hot man
stay cool man shitman soul man shitman*). Many white Americans have always gone for this kind of old razzmatazz, and
they still pay well for it. And, of course, there are also those
ever so smooth Negro con artists who operate in the sad, fuzzy
world of the white U.S. liberal, and who will allow themselves
to be sprayed with this kind of you-know-what just to prove
how tolerant Negroes are, or how superior they are to it. One
well-known NAACP bigwig, for instance, used to have one of
those Aunt Jemima memo boards hanging in his kitchen
during open house just to prove how sophisticated he was! He
ain't. He something else. He white folks number one Negro
mispronounced as Baldwin does it when referring to himself
on TV.

Those who insist on working their way through the everlasting coyness of the language that screens *The Cool World* will
not find themselves in a landscape created by an imaginative
novelist. They will find a series of patently contrived situations
hastily derived from the currently fashionable generalizations
of the so-called social sciences. They will find themselves in the
prefabricated world of the up to date social worker, a newspaper stage-set with crudely carved ebony and mahogany
puppets moving their lips in a snazzy jazzy tempo while an
inept ventriloquist mouths overworked Marxist and psychiatric
clichés disguised as the untutored wisdom of the curbstones:

> Hurst live in a cellar an dont know whut the world all about.
> He dont know the world run by crooks pushers and hood from
> top to bottom. In the white houses an in the vegetable stores
> on the corners all of them got big hands in the pie. Its no world
> to be nice in . . .
> Harrison slam his book shut. It go Thuck. He stand up and
> go to the window an look out. He say to the window. "They
> make us live like animals. Is it any wonder then that some of
> us act like animals an some of us become animals. The fantastic
> thing is how few of us succum to their idea of us." An he went
> on like that standing there at the window not looking at us
> lookin out at Harlem.

And so on.

This kind of language is supposed to project the sensibility of fourteen year old Duke Custis, the first-person narrator protagonist, whose great ambition is to keep a pistol and become the absolute ruler of his gang. This boy's existence is represented as being so circumscribed that he has no significant awareness of the rich diversity of life about him in Harlem, to say nothing of life in New York at large. Nor does his sensibility reflect any meaningful contact with the contents of radio programs, movies, TV, magazines, or even comic books. His conception of space travel is that of an idiot. But Luann, the gang's teenage prostitute, takes the cake. She doesn't even know about the subway! What ever happened to the good old A train, so long familiar to every Negro cotton picker arriving from Alabama?

Now if a writer cannot, will not, or at any rate doesn't identify with his characters, he is not likely to write truly about life as he actually knows it. Certainly he cannot condescend to his characters and at the same time expect his readers to believe in them. The fact is, Warren Miller simply cannot imagine himself as Duke Custis. Much has been made of the fact that Miller is a white man who lived in Harlem for five years. This is all very well, but as a writer he seems unable to imagine himself living in Harlem as a Negro for five minutes.

The Harlem described by Warren Miller could never produce a James Baldwin. Thus Baldwin's endorsement of *The Cool World* would seem exaggerated to say the least. (But there is a curious consistency operating here. For the Harlem described by James Baldwin himself could not possibly produce a James Baldwin either.)

II

The Cool World was a slapdash job. It was also slapstick, but one is not certain how much of the clowning was really intentional. *The Siege of Harlem* (McGraw-Hill, 1964) is also slapdash, and here the slapstick is all too intentional. It is a minstrel show in which the writer comes pumping on stage doing a saggy bottomed, tangle footed buck and wing in the guise of Joel Chandler Harris, which he ain't; and he ain't no

Octavus Roy Cohen either. Neither is he any Roark Bradford, however he may yearn for them good old green fried chicken pastures.

Here you find Uncle Remus uptown telling bedtime Amos and Andy war stories to a group of children who have such side splitting musical comedy names as M'boya, Jomo, N'Krumah, Ahmad, Shabad, and such like. Harlem has become a nation within New York City, has nationalized the numbers racket, and there are such hilarious vaudeville landmarks as Station WEB Du Bois, checkpoint Frederick Douglass, the Black House, and so on. No need to catalogue the cornballisms. Not even the best comedians at the Apollo Theatre can bring stuff this thin to life. Not even the great Pigmeat Markham can make this stuff stack. (Not that you can't still make yourself a fortune by putting on a costume and conning the media into advertising you as a politicized Father Divine. After all, media people, who are nothing if not "committed" regard that as being far more "relevant" than such "razzmatazz" as "Stompin' at the Savoy.")

So much for *The Siege of Harlem*, unless somebody turns it into a TV spectacular. In color yet. But whenever you complain about how some white writer misrepresents Negro life, somebody always wants to know if you think it is possible for any white person to write accurately about any Negroes. The question almost always has racist implications, but the real issue is not racial but cultural. Of course it is possible. Why shouldn't it be possible? If Ernest Hemingway could write good stories about Italy, France, Spain, and Cuba, and if numerous other writers can produce outstanding books about people who lived not only in distant lands but in distant times, why the hell shouldn't a white writer be able to do an excellent book about contemporary Harlem?

The same question comes up when you complain about the inauthenticity of most white jazz musicians. Can a white man really play Negro music? Of course he can. If he is a good enough musician and respects the medium as he would any other art form. If he develops the same familiarity with its idiomatic nuances, the same love of it, and humility before it as the good Negro musician does. Why not? But certainly not if he is really ambivalent about it. Not if he hangs around with it for a while and then withdraws and allows himself to become a "white hope." Not if he allows his publicity to convince him that he is superior to the masters he knows damn well he is still plagiarizing.

Of course white writers can write well about Negroes. Some of William Faulkner's very finest characters are Negroes. And of course white writers are just as free to have as much fun with Negro characters as with any other. Most of Faulkner's Negroes in *The Reivers* are very funny indeed. But Warren Miller's feeble attempts at ridicule only expose his own provincialism, which he sadly mistakes for a superior sophistication. Routine Negro comics do a better job of spoofing the civil rights movement every night.

For one thing, Miller just doesn't seem to be able to resist the all-American temptation to put Negroes in their place by reducing them to stereotypes. Joel Chandler Harris was certainly no great shakes as a writer, but doggone my cats if his talking animals aren't infinitely more human than any character in either *The Cool World* or *The Siege of Harlem*.

Nevertheless, Negroes would do well to keep an eye cocked on Warren Miller, slapdash, slapstick, and all. With your white Negro anything is possible. Say if the sequel to *The Siege of Harlem* is another mirthful matinee piece called *Porgy and Bess Stomping at the Savoy and the Walls Come Tumbling Down*, and then this very same Warren Miller grows a beard or something, goes serious and slaps together still another one about how once upon a time a boy in Boston heard a record nightmare by Artie Shaw and became an expert on jazz and the jazz life and had a cotton field romance with a Negro girl and became an expert on Negro sex life as it really is and then was befriended one night by a Negro hipster and became an expert on the narcotic life as it really is and went on to spout a steady stream of magazine articles explaining the civil rights movement as it really is, this very same Warren Miller could very easily be mistaken as a very genuine and understanding friend of Negroes. The trouble is that the Indians used to have friends like that. And look what happened to the Indians. They now live in ghettos. Or is it Casbahs? As Jelly Roll Morton or somebody said: *If you see dear Mrs. Equitone tell her I bring the horoscope myself: one must be so careful these days.*

WILLIAM STYRON AND HIS TROUBLESOME PROPERTY

The most fundamental shortcoming of almost all fiction written by white Americans about their black fellow countrymen is
also almost always the most obvious. It is, given the deepseated
racism of most Americans, also the most predictable. In almost
every instance, the white American writer starts out either unable or unwilling to bring himself to make a truly intimate and
profoundly personal identification with the black protagonist
whose heroism he himself has chosen to delineate and whose
sense of life he has elected to impersonate, if not emulate.

In fact, there are times when the emotional distance between
the white writer and his black subject matter becomes so great
that it seems like an act of deliberation or even calculation—as
if what really matters most were not the fabulous self-extensions
and enhancements inherent in the storyteller's magic of make
believe but rather the writer's own petty provincialisms and
preoccupations with social status. Such writers often behave as
if the slightest notion of a black compatriot as a storybook
hero compels them to equate the strongest Negroes with the
most helpless. Or so it seems.

William Styron remarked several years ago that even so great
a novelist as William Faulkner created Negro characters who,
although marvelously drawn, were *observed* rather than *lived*.
Even Faulkner, wrote Styron in "This Quiet Dust," an article
for *Harper's* magazine (April 1965), "hesitated to think
Negro." Styron was also moved to point out that not even
Dilsey, who, as he concedes, comes so richly alive in *The Sound
and the Fury*, is created from what he calls a sense of withinness. At the last moment, he insists, "Faulkner draws back, and
it is no mere happenstance that Dilsey alone among the four
central figures from whose points of view the story is told is
seen from the outside rather than from that intensely inner
vantage point, the interior monologue."

It was also William Styron, the author of *Lie Down in Darkness*, *The Long March*, and *Set This House on Fire*, and hence a
writer to be reckoned with, who contended, not without some
deeply felt passion, that it had become the moral imperative of
every white Southerner to break down the old law (which requires the denial of the most obvious of all Southern entangle-

ments) and come to know Negroes. Nor was the fact that Styron himself comes from a lower middle class Tidewater Virginia background likely to strike most Negroes as being either surprising or even curious. On the contrary, many Negroes have long since come to feel that more forthright involvement can almost always be expected from reconstructed or even partially reconstructed Southerners than from any other white people in the United States.

Whatever degree of liberal fellowship the reconstructed Southerner has been able to attain—according to a number of Negroes who are anything but naive or sentimental about such matters—is thoroughgoing and dependable precisely because it is something achieved rather than received. The Northern liberal may or may not back up his protestations with action. But the Southerner's first liberal *remark* is likely to be a bridge burning action in itself. Thus, his statements are often a reliable index to the actual extent of his commitment. Or so many Negroes would have it, and there is the best of Robert Penn Warren, C. Vann Woodward, Ramsey Clark, and yes, Lyndon Johnson to bear them out.

In *The Confessions of Nat Turner* (Random House, 1967), however, Negroes will find very little evidence of the reconstruction many may have felt they had reason to anticipate. The very news that a writer of Styron's talent and determination had undertaken a novel about a Negro whose greatness is a matter of historical record (no matter how smudged) was itself cause enough for high hopes. But even better was the fact that a white Southerner had felt a moral imperative to go all the way and tell the story as his own. Those Negro intellectuals who keep check on such things were downright enthusiastic in their endorsement. Even the black nationalists who place race above literature were at least willing to wait and see. After all, Negritude, as the mulatto exponents of Afro-Americanisimus are wont to say, is only a state of mind, and of course there's that old saying about "room for many more." And besides, as black barber shop politicians were quick to acknowledge, it is infinitely more useful to The Cause for a William Styron to become Nat Turner than for Benny Goodman to become Jimmie Noone or for Stan Getz to become a paleface Lester Young, or numerous others to become Miles Davis and Charlie Parker.

But what Negroes will find in Styron's "confessions" is much the same old failure of sensibility that plagues most other fiction about black people. They will find a Nat Turner, that is to say, that many white people may accept at a safe distance but hardly one with whom Negroes will easily identify. The Nat Turner whom Southern Negro school children celebrate (or used to) in pageants during Negro History Week was a magnificent forefather enshrined in the national pantheon beside the greatest heroes of the Republic. There is an old song which goes:

> Well you can be milk-white and just as rich as cream
> And buy a solid gold carriage with a four-horse team
> But you caint keep the world from movering round
> Or stop old Nat Turner from gaining ground

These folk lyrics are about a dedicated man who did far more than declaim great phrases (later to become national clichés) about taxation without representation, liberty or death, and the times that try men's souls. He was, like all epic heroes, a special breed of man who had given his last full measure of devotion to liberation and dignity.

What Southern Negroes will find in Styron's version, alas, is not the black man's homeric Negro but a white man's Negro (specifically, Mister Stanley M. Elkins') Sambo—a Nat Turner, that is to say, who has been emasculated and reduced to fit all too snugly into a personality structure based on highly questionable and essentially irrelevant conjectures about servility (to which Styron has added a neo-Reichean hypothesis about the correlation between sex repression and revolutionary leadership). Instead of the man of meditation who fasted and prayed to become the Moses of his people, the good shepherd who left a legacy of activism to American ministers which was never more operative than at present, both black and white men of the gospel will find here a black man who really wants to marry somebody's white sister—a man with a sex hangup who goes out into the wilderness to meditate only to get a simple thing like freedom all but hopelessly confused with masturbation while having fantasies about white women.

Ironically, in spite of Styron's expressed intention to get deeper inside his Negro hero than Faulkner did, he seems somehow to have begun by overlooking the fact that the *Negro* conception of Nat Turner was already geared to the dynamics of ritual and myth and hence to literature. In any event, his own seems to have been restricted to such assumptions as underlie sociopolitical science and hence the melodramatic success story. Thus, the Nat Turner who nourished the hopes of Negroes is a tragic hero who symbolizes the human spirit victorious in defeat. Whereas Styron has been able to concede him only "a kind of triumph"—a sort of social science B-plus for effort—for almost succeeding. As if the definition of success were suddenly limited to the consummation of a revolution (which would have annihilated all of Styron's great grandparents) and thus as if heroism were being measured only in terms of its concrete military contribution to the class struggle. (To concede a "kind of triumph" to Robert E. Lee is readily understandable and appropriate. Lee fought on the wrong side and became the biggest loser in the nation's history. But he also became one of the nation's greatest symbols of dignity in defeat.)

But then "This Quiet Dust" shows Styron, who ordinarily is anything but a dialectical materialist, falling into the trap of establishing a Marxist context at the very outset, misled perhaps by too many one-sided historians. Styron *disagrees* with Marxist historian Herbert Aptheker. But he does not reject Aptheker's frame of reference. Aptheker seems to be seeking revolutionary potential. Styron is talking about a failed potential of the same kind. Anyway, he seems to have begun by accepting the old pro-slavery image of white brutality and black docility recently resurrected by historian Elkins, the father of Samboism, in the interest of his own Marx-Freud or psychopolitical theory of black castration. Negro students are likely to find it absolutely incredible that a would-be soul brother could so fail to appreciate what "troublesome property" their ancestors were as to write, as Styron does, that for two hundred and fifty years slavery was "singularly free of organized uprisings, plots and rebellions." Compare this with the non-Marxist view of U. B. Phillips (in *Life and Labor in the Old South*): "The advertising columns of the newspapers bustled with notices of runaways; and no plantation record which has come to my hand is without mention of them."

Styron's failure of sensibility, because of which the best he has been able to do by his own choice of a darling protagonist is to make him a somewhat queer exception to black emasculation, is due at least in part to an overexposure to untenable historical information. After all, Elkins, perhaps too impressed by Nazi cold bloodedness, oversells the psychological damage of oppression on Negroes while making next to nothing of what the never relaxed preoccupation with black codes, fugitive slave laws, patrol systems, and disciplinary cruelty did to white people. The slave owners and drivers like many present-day police were not simply high-handed and callous, they were mostly always on the edge of hysteria from the fear of black uprisings.

Perhaps what on balance is almost certain to strike many Negroes as the pathetic rather than the heroic quality of the action in *The Confessions* also comes from not relying on Negro folk heritage. To Styron the story of Turner's insurrection is not an exemplary endeavor (ending with Nat in jail, echoing, say, Prometheus bound) but only a historical irony, "a decisive factor in the ultimate triumph of the pro-slavery forces."

It so happens, however, that the Nat Turner of Negro folklore is not only a figure ready-made for bards, gleemen, and dramatists but is also one that stands up well under careful documentation. He is, for example, also the Nat Turner of so scholarly a historian as Kenneth Stampp, for whom Turner's forty-eight-hour feat was "an event which produced in the South something resembling a mass trauma, from which the whites had not recovered three decades later. The danger that other Nat Turners might emerge, that even more serious insurrections might someday occur, became an enduring concern as long as the peculiar institution survived. Pro-slavery writers boldly asserted that Southerners did not fear their slaves—but fear of rebellion, sometimes vague, sometimes acute, was with them always."

Now, reviewers who have seized upon white post-insurrection atrocities as a precedent for an inevitable and overwhelming defeat of black militants by the white backlash have not only allowed their need for historical reassurance to becloud the actual historical significance of valid literary implications, but could only have done so by neglecting their homework in

U.S. history in the process. "The shock of Nat Turner caused Southerners to take preventive measures," Stampp reports, "but these," he adds, "never eliminated their apprehension *or the actual danger*. [Italics added.] Hardly a year passed without some kind of alarming disturbance somewhere in the South. When no real conspiracy existed, wild rumors often agitated the whites and at times came close to creating an insurrection panic."

The fact is, slavery survived for only thirty-two years more. Emancipation was proclaimed in 1863. Moreover, almost every major figure of the Civil War was already alive at the time of Nat Turner's rebellion. Lincoln himself was twenty-two years old and a flatboatman about to enter politics. Grant was nine. Sherman was eleven. Jefferson Davis, twenty-three, and Robert E. Lee, twenty-four, were both officers already out of West Point. Frederick Douglass was fourteen. Harriet Tubman was eight. William Lloyd Garrison was twenty-six, and Harriet Beecher Stowe was twenty!

As for such a statement as, "Ask any Negro if he is prepared to kill a white man and if he says yes, you may be sure that he is indulging in the sheerest brag," which Styron puts into the mouth of Nat Turner, it would have been regarded as the sheerest nonsense by precisely those Confederate soldiers who defeated the Union's black regiment (the Massachusetts 54th), led by the splendid young white colonel, Robert Shaw, Harvard '60, in the Battle of Fort Wagner. But speaking of ironies, for a scene that at best has only a questionable basis in fact Styron has invented a white Major who, while counter-attacking Turner with integrated forces, says, "That's the spirit boys . . . fire away lads." Which should remind Negroes of nothing so much as Colonel Shaw's dying exhortation to his Negro troops, "Onward boys."

That William Styron is a novelist who is capable of extraordinary self-extension is obvious to anyone who is familiar with the effects he achieved with the interior monologue of Peyton, the central female character of *Lie Down in Darkness*. Nevertheless, he may have done better to use another or perhaps even several different points of view for *The Confessions of Nat Turner*. The withinness of the first-person narration, after all, is not necessarily the best way to tell a story. As the in-character speculations of white Southern types, some of Styron's misconceptions may have come off as brilliant, creative details. As the thoughts of Nat Turner they will probably strike most Negroes as ridiculous. It is hard to believe that either the author of Uncle Remus or William Faulkner could ever have written, "The life of a little nigger child is dull beyond recounting," to say nothing of presenting it as the conception of a Negro, certainly not one who has reached page 138 of a highly poetic 428 page confession.

The moral imperative to know Negroes does not necessarily require other people to "think Negro." But storytellers who would do so must in effect be able to sing the spirituals and/or swing the blues (as, for example, Stephen Vincent Benét did in his story "Freedom's a Hard-Bought Thing"). A narrator who is properly tuned in on what underlies the spirituals would hardly allow the kind of vile language in the presence of a man of God like Nat Turner that a Harlem poolroom hoodlum would not tolerate in the presence of any known minister.

As for swinging the blues, the affirmative beat of which is always geared to the rugged facts of life, if you run Schillinger exercises instead of riffing down-home, you only *think* you're swinging. Which, of course, also applies to any Negro writer who assumes that "black consciousness" is only a matter of *saying* you're black while writing about black experience.

James Baldwin, Protest Fiction, and the Blues Tradition

NOT SO VERY LONG AGO, as these things are reckoned in the annals of human letters, James Baldwin, then a promising young Greenwich Village intellectual from Harlem, wrote an article for *Partisan Review* (June 1949) about *Uncle Tom's Cabin*. It was called "Everybody's Protest Novel," and what made it especially significant was the fact that in it Baldwin, a Negro whose personal commitment to militant social and political action was unquestionable, seemed to be firmly and completely, if somewhat hastily, rejecting social protest in fiction as bad art, a mirror of confusion, dishonesty, and panic, as sentimental fantasy connecting nowhere with reality.

He stated that the avowed aim of such fiction was to bring greater freedom to the oppressed. But he was unenthusiastic about this lofty purpose in itself, nor did he share the then current optimism about the effectiveness of books produced by those committed to it. In fact, he was convinced that "novels of oppression written by Negroes . . . actually reinforce . . . the principles which activate the oppression they decry."

Baldwin overstated his case, of course, but many serious students of American literature were very much impressed by what they thought all of this implied about his own ambitions as a writer. They assumed that more than anything else he was stating his own personal objections to the narrowness of propaganda fiction as such. They assumed that whatever else was intended, his statements about Harriet Beecher Stowe represented his own esthetic orientation. It is easy to see why. "She was," he wrote, "not so much a novelist as an impassioned pamphleteer; her book was not intended to do anything more than prove that slavery was wrong; was, in fact, perfectly horrible. This makes material for a pamphlet but it is hardly enough for a novel. . . ."

At this time Baldwin seemed very much concerned about the fact that he was living in an over-mechanized civilization which overlooked, denied, and evaded man's complexity, treated him as a time-saving invention, a deplorable conundrum to be explained by science. Protest fiction, he felt, was a part of all this, a formula created "to find a lie more palatable than the truth." But as for himself, he was seeking himself and the power to free himself not in the mechanical formulas and in causes, but within what he called a "web of ambiguity, paradox, hunger, danger, and darkness." It was the power of revelation, he declared, that was "the business of the novelist, this journey toward a more vast reality which must take precedence over all other claims."

He then went on to indict *Uncle Tom's Cabin* for, among other things, its self-righteous sentimentality and its senseless and unmotivated brutality, including a theological terror of blackness and damnation. He also called it the prototype of the American protest novel, and in the process he described the hero of Richard Wright's *Native Son*, the most celebrated protest novel of the day, as Uncle Tom's descendant, an exactly opposite portrait perhaps but flesh of Tom's flesh. But then Wright himself had called the people of his previous book by its title, *Uncle Tom's Children*. There was no argument on that score. There was, however, or so it seemed at the time, a more fundamental conflict. Richard Wright seemed to represent the very qualities in fiction that James Baldwin deplored most heatedly.

In fact, the very attempt of fiction such as Wright's to improve the conditions of life was regarded by Baldwin at that time as a betrayal of life. The tragedy of the hero of *Native Son*, he wrote, was not that he was cold, hungry, black or American but that he has accepted a theology that denies him life, "that he admits the possibility of his being subhuman and feels constrained therefore to battle for his humanity." Baldwin then concluded his article as follows: "The failure of the protest novel lies in its rejection of life, the human being, the denial of his beauty, dread, power, in its insistence that it is his categorization alone which is real and which cannot be transcended."

Some two years later, Baldwin, then a very special young U.S. expatriate from Greenwich Village and the streets of Harlem living in Paris among other U.S. expatriates from Greenwich Village, the Ivy League, the Big Ten, and even the genteel South, and among Africans mostly from the French colonies, and not far from the French existentialists, continued his by then much admired remarks about protest fiction. In another article, "Many Thousands Gone," also for *Partisan Review* (November–December 1951), he took *Native Son* to task again. A necessary dimension had been cut away, he said at one point, because the other Negroes in the story are seen only from Bigger Thomas' limited point of view, "this dimension being the relationship that Negroes bear to one another, that depth of involvement and unspoken recognition of shared experience which creates a way of life."

He also characterized the climate of *Native Son* as one of anarchy and unmotivated and unapprehended disaster; "and it is this climate common to most Negro protest novels," he went on, "which has led us all to believe that in Negro life there exists no tradition, no field of manners, no possibility of ritual intercourse, such as may, for example, sustain the Jew even after he has left his father's house." And then came the following highly suggestive statement: "But the fact is not that the Negro has no tradition, but that there has as yet arrived no sensibility sufficiently profound and tough to make this tradition articulate."

At the time the implications seemed unmistakable. It was assumed by almost everybody concerned about such matters, that all this was still another indication that here was a young writer-in-progress whose single passion was to give his own fiction greater human depth and richer historical reverberation than he had found in any of the novels he mentioned.

Overlooked in all of the enthusiasm, however, was the astonishing fact that in addition to *Uncle Tom's Cabin* and *Native Son*, Baldwin had mentioned only *Gentleman's Agreement*, *The Postman Always Rings Twice*, *Kingsblood Royal* and *If He Hollers Let Him Go* (!), and had alluded to *The Sound and the Fury*, one of the outstanding achievements of modern fiction, only to protest an alleged racial discrimination. But perhaps this was deliberately overlooked. After all it was the assumed promise that really mattered. The means of fulfillment could always be evolved in the process. At any rate, it is not erudition as such that counts in a novelist.

Or isn't it? At least for something? As a matter of fact the very same paragraph in which Baldwin declared the existence of an as yet unrealistically articulated Negro tradition, contains a significant clue to his subsequent difficulties and confusions as a serious writer and the clue concerns a matter of erudition. "For a tradition," he continued, "expresses, after all, *nothing more* than the long and painful experience of a people; it comes out of the battle waged to maintain their integrity or, to put it more simply, out of their struggle to survive." (Italics added.) And then in the next sentence he added the following observation: ". . . when we speak of the Jewish tradition, we are speaking of centuries of exile and persecution, of the strength which endured and the sensibility which discovered in it the high possibility of the moral victory."

All of which is utterly confusing. Baldwin doesn't mention a single Jewish novel that would justify such a statement. And no wonder. Whatever else the great Jewish tradition in literature represents, it not only represents protest, it is *characterized* by a great deal of protest as such. But then perhaps Baldwin had built-in his confusion at the very outset. A tradition involves *much* more than the long and painful experiences of a people. The modern Jewish tradition, which someone has referred to as an instantly erectable wailing wall, may well represent centuries of exile and persecution, but it also represents much more. As did the ancient Greek and Roman traditions. As do the modern French and English traditions.

As for the tradition of U.S. Negroes, Baldwin may or may not realize that he is making a fundamental statement about it when he says that it is only in music that the Negro in America has been able to tell his story. Actually this story is also told in folktales and lore, sayings, jokes, and various other forms. Nonetheless, music does contain the most comprehensive rendering of the complexities of the American Negro experience. Whatever the reason, very few U.S. Negro writers (or painters, for example) rank in range and achievement beside musicians like Louis Armstrong, Scott Joplin, or even Charlie Parker, not to mention the great Kansas City stylists and Duke Ellington.

But it should be clear that what U.S. Negro musicians express represents far more than the fact that American black folks been 'buked and been scorned and nobody know de trouble dey seen. Distinctive as it is, U.S. Negro music, like U.S. Negro life, is, after all, or rather first of all, also inseparable from life in the United States at large. Thus, as an art form it is a direct product of the U.S. Negro sensibility, but it is a by-product, so to speak, of all the cultural elements that brought that sensibility into being in the first place. The spirituals, for example, always expressed more than a proletarian reaction to poor pay and bad working conditions. They did reflect life on the plantation and the effects of political bondage; but they were also a profound and universally moving expression of Protestant Christianity, interwoven with New England Puritanism, and frontier elements, American aspirations in general and many other things, including an active physical existence and a rich, robust, and highly imaginative conception of life itself.

As for the blues, they affirm not only U.S. Negro life in all of its arbitrary complexities and not only life in America in all of its infinite confusions, they affirm life and humanity itself in the very process of confronting failures and existentialistic absurdities. The spirit of the blues moves in the opposite direction from ashes and sackcloth, self-pity, self-hatred, and suicide. As a matter of fact the dirtiest, meanest, and most low-down blues are not only not depressing, they function like an instantaneous aphrodisiac! And there are also significant implications of affirmation inherent in the basic fact that U.S. Negro music has always been a part of a great tradition of dance and physical labor.

All of which (and more) would seem to be of immediate and fundamental interest to any serious student of American culture, to say nothing of a serious writer of American fiction. And yet James Baldwin, for all his understandable dissatisfaction with the thinness of Richard Wright's characters and situations, and for all his fine, youthful arrogance about a sensibility sufficiently profound and tough to make the Negro tradition articulate, has never written in terms of any of the sustaining actualities of that tradition in any of his own stories.

Instead, he has relied more and more on the abstract categories of social research and less and less on the poetic insights of the creative artist. So much so that the very characteristics of protest fiction which he once deplored in the work of

Harriet Beecher Stowe and Richard Wright now seem to be his stock in trade; they are in any case the things he is now world famous for. His best-selling novel *Another Country*, for instance, reflects very little of the rich, complex, and ambivalent sensibility of the novelist, very little indeed, no more than does the polemical essay *The Fire Next Time*. What it actually reflects in this connection, is the author's involvement with oversimplified library and laboratory theories and conjectures about the negative effects of racial oppression.

And like *Native Son*, it does so for a very good reason. It was designed to serve a very worthy cause, the cause of greater political, social, and economic freedom and opportunity for Negroes in the United States. And the current civil rights movement has profited from his recent books and his position as a public figure in many very tangible ways. In fact, he has become one of the best known heroes of the Negro revolution, a citizen spokesman, as eloquent in his own way as was citizen polemicist Tom Paine in the Revolution of '76, a major achievement in itself.

Polemics, however, are not likely to be epics. They are likely to be pamphlets, even when they are disguised as stories and plays. Thus, ironically enough, Baldwin's historical role in the civil rights struggle has also been all but indistinguishable from the one played by Harriet Beecher Stowe in the Civil War. And with some of the same exasperating confusion. For in spite of what he once declared about near paranoiac novels of oppression actually reinforcing the principles that activate the conditions they decry, he himself has found it expedient in his work to degrade U.S. Negro life to the level of the sub-human in the very process of pleading the Negro's humanity—something he once said one had only to accept!

Baldwin writes about Harlem, for example, with an evangelical sense of moral outrage, and his declarations on this subject are said to have stirred the conscience of the nation. But he never really accounts for the tradition that supports Harlem's hard headed faith in democracy, its muscular Christianity, its cultural flexibility, nor does he account for its universally celebrated commitment to elegance in motion, to colorful speech idioms, to high style, not only in personal deportment but even in the handling of mechanical devices. Intentionally or not, much of what he says implicitly denies the very existence of Harlem's fantastically knowing satire, its profound awareness and rejection of so much that is essentially ridiculous in downtown doings. Sometimes he writes as if he had never heard the comedians at the Apollo Theatre. Life in Harlem is the very stuff of romance and fiction, even as was life in Chaucer's England, Cervantes' Spain, Rabelais' France.

But what Baldwin writes about is not really life in Harlem. He writes about the economic and social conditions in Harlem, the material *plight* of Harlem. But far from writing in terms of a U.S. Negro tradition, he confuses everything with Jewish tradition and writes about life in a black ghetto! In point of fact, James Baldwin, like most native-born U.S. Negroes, is probably a part-white Anglo-Saxon Protestant of Southern derivation. Sometimes he likes to say that he comes from a long line of field hands (and maybe a Texas sheriff or so, too), but he often writes as if he were really a black, brown, or beige New York Jewish intellectual of immigrant parents. On these occasions, there is very little to indicate that the spellbinding power of much of his polemical eloquence really comes out of his background as a boy-preacher in a Harlem storefront church.

A serious novelist, like all other good citizens, should, needless to say, support worthy political causes; but that he should distort his work to do so is another matter altogether. In "Everybody's Protest Novel," Baldwin strongly implied that protest and distortion were inseparable, that protest fiction insists on false categories, rejects life, decries the beauty and power of human beings. But are these generalizations necessarily so? One has to think only of the basic and very clear-cut element of protest in all of the fiction of James Joyce. And among other outstanding novels of the twentieth century alone, what of *The Sun Also Rises, Light in August, The Magic Mountain, The Castle,* or, for that matter, *The Great Gatsby*? (The element of social protest as such underlies as much of the action in the upper middle class world of *The Great Gatsby* as it does in the revolutionary proletarian milieu of André Malraux's *Man's Fate.*)

Nor is the element of propaganda in itself necessarily detrimental. The advertisement of alleged values is a fundamental aspect of all literature, as is the damnation of all that would jeopardize or destroy what is held to be of value. In this sense, Henry James, of all people, produced some of the best propaganda ever written. There is no doubt in anybody's mind that the author of *The Ambassadors* and *The Turn of the Screw* was for goodness and against evil, and he made a convincing case for his position; but he did not oversimplify the virtues of his heroes, the vices of his villains, the complexity of their situation, or the ambiguity of their motives.

But perhaps Baldwin had in mind political propaganda as such, which of its very nature almost always tends to gear itself to expedient means and immediate action. Perhaps this does create very special problems for the artist. Perhaps it leads him in spite of himself to oversimplify all situations in terms of the remedial program to which he is committed, and of course this could easily involve him in the kind of writing that produces election campaign slogans and advertising copy for cure-all medicines. But in these terms, political propaganda contains no *unique* dangers. Propaganda that oversimplifies life in terms of faith, hope, charity or romantic love produces a distortion of reality which is every bit as misleading.

Nevertheless, there are many reasons why it is all but impossible for a serious writer of fiction to engage his craft as such in a political cause, no matter how worthy, without violating his very special integrity as an artist in some serious way. All of these reasons are complicated and some may seem downright questionable, but perhaps none is more important than the fact that, as well-meaning as he may be, the truly serious novelist has what almost amounts to an ambivalence toward the human predicament. Alarming as such ambivalence may seem, it is really fundamental to his open-minded search for the essential truth of human experience.

There is first of all the serious novelist's complex awareness of the burdensome but sobering fact that there is some goodness in bad people however bad they are, and some badness or at least some flaw or weakness in good people however dear. In fact, sometimes the artist comes pretty close to being politically suspect; because on the one hand he is always proclaiming his love for mankind and on the other he is forever giving the devil his due!

And then there is a crucial ambivalence in his eternal and even infernal involvement with the ironies of *antagonistic cooperation*! He is all for achieving the good society, the salubrious situation, the excellent environment. But at the same time he insists that the beautiful community does not automatically produce either beautiful people who stay good or sweetness and light that lasts forever afterwards. Not only this, but he actually seems to be more excited about the fact that sorry situations, ugly communities, trying circumstances, and impossible environments, along with whatever else they do, *of their very nature* produce not only good people but incomparable *heroes* who come from the awful darkness but bring sweetness and light.

Perhaps it is in the nature of things that activists, whether young or middle-aged, will have little patience with such intellectual checks and balances. Nevertheless, the serious apprentice to the art of fiction can never afford to dispense with them.

II

For several years before Baldwin's articles, Richard Wright was a famous U.S. Negro expatriate living in Paris among the most famous French existentialists, who then were having a field day protesting against U.S. can goods, refrigerators, automobiles, and most of all U.S. dollars in the hands of U.S. citizens. Wright, who seemed to regard himself as, so to speak, U.S. Negro-in-residence, gave them additional U.S. absurdities and atrocities to protest about. He also liked to function as American political pundit for the African colonials along the boulevards and around the old Latin Quarter.

He was by way of becoming something of an existentialist himself, but he was still given to ripping red hot pages of accusations from his outraged and smoldering typewriter and angrily flinging them all the way back across the Atlantic and into the guilt ridden lap of America. During this time, he also flung one such book at the guilt ridden face of pagan Spain and two or three at the guilt ridden face of white folks everywhere.

It was bad enough that the fiction Wright began to turn out during this time was even worse than that of Jean-Paul Sartre (which was really going some, by the way); much more important is the fact that for all the down-home signifying and uptown sassiness he put Sartre and Simone de Beauvoir hip to, or maybe precisely because of it, he was unable to keep the ever square but news prone Mister Sartre, the world's fastest academic hip-shooter, from being sucked in on the politically benevolent racist notions of *negritude*, an all but hopelessly confused theory or doctrine of international Negroism—or is it black nationalist internationalism?

At any rate, negritude, notion or doctrine, not only tends to mistake tradition (or cultural inheritance) for racial inheritance (or racial mysticism), it also encourages the kind of esthetic nonsense that has involved an alarming and increasing number of young and not so young U.S. Negroes in programs, movements, and organizations that can only make it even more difficult for them to realize the infinite potential of the black dimensions of the *American* tradition.

Most of the programs for the promotion of what sometimes is called the "black arts" are more political than anything else, and naively political at that. Many so-called Black Artists identify themselves not with the United States but with Africa, which is political naiveté coupled with an incredible disregard for the dynamics of socio-cultural evolution. Politically naive also is their amusing disregard for the national boundaries on the continent of Africa. Americans that they are, they seem to be forever confusing the countries of Africa with the states of the United States. And if this is pan-Africanism, then how naive can you get?

Some of the black arts affiliates are anti-American, anti-American white folks, that is. At least they pretend to be, some belligerently so. But so far, what they intend to accomplish either in government or the arts is not very clear. So far it has only added up to a whole lot of black anarchy, which of course is considered to be a legitimate enough objective by some ideologies, and not for such pseudo-sanguinary/pseudo-nasty esthetic reasons as may be bragged about during some obscene intellectual seance in some Greenwich Village night club where the speakers say another four-letter word when they really mean spit and confuse blood with strawberry Kool-Aid.

Whatever their objectives and however political, every last one of the so-called black arts movements seems to be commercially oriented toward white American audiences above all others; and curiously enough not one is seriously considered to be subversive. Far from it. As a matter of fact, most of the promotions, encouragement, and financial underwriting which is not smuggled in from abroad comes from devoted white patrons. But that is a very special story in itself, as is the fact that for his own perverse reasons both personal and political, the U.S. white who involves himself in these activities seems to regard the whole thing as some new fashionable outrageous but very safe game in which he is not so much rejected as envied and not so much ignored as wooed! Roughly perhaps, but he seems to like it like that.

In some ways, it all seems like one of those boring acts from one of those third rate but ever clever clown shows by the grand old off-Broadway darling of the beatniks and Susan Sontag's campfire girls, Jean Genet, the French scatologist whom J.-P. Sartre calls a modern saint! Indeed, for all its homemade overtones of Uncle Tom's chillun scandalizing Miss Ann and Mister Charley in front of company, most of the pretentiously aggressive racism in the black arts movement in New York, seems to come from the Genet play that has been translated as *The Blacks*. (Incidentally, the French title of this play is not *Les Noirs* but rather *Les Nègres*, which to U.S. Negroes usually means something else altogether!)

In other ways, however, one is also reminded of some of the less political but by no means less naive capers that characterized so much of the so-called Negro renaissance back in the nineteen twenties. This New Negro movement, as it was sometimes called, was also a black arts movement encouraged and supported by white people. The positive role played by the renaissance in the development of black artist self-consciousness is not simply to be conceded but celebrated. *The New Negro*, Alain Locke's anthology of the movement, is still an outstanding landmark in the history of black American expression. But to the extent that the renaissance was influenced by decadent white esthetes who confused black U.S. peasants with jungle aborigines, it also encouraged and subsidized more primitive abandon between the Hudson and Harlem rivers in uptown Manhattan than ever existed near the Congo. In fact, actual primitive life is nothing if not formal. Primitive behavior is the very opposite of wild abandon. It conforms to taboos. Abandon, like bad manners and crime, is not inherent in the restrictions of primitive discipline by any means. It is rather one of those natural products of the freedom and individuality that comes with what is called civilization. It is the super-civilized avant garde bohemian, not the superstition-ridden savage, who is forever and ever in wild eyed, hot-collar, soap-box, street-marching or window-breaking rebellion against all sorts of restrictions—some of them purely imaginary.

The current black arts movement, like the one before it, is nothing if not avant garde, ersatz tiger noises underneath the bamboo tree boom boom and all. But the avant garde sort of thing is not exclusive to the cognoscenti these days. It also makes sensational news copy for the New York dailies, *Time*, *Life*, *Look*, *Newsweek*, NBC-TV, CBS, and ABC. Some of it gets staged through the angelic efforts of New York theatrical matrons, some of them female. Some of it gets printed by the big, fat publishing firms; and some of it comes out on Columbia and RCA Victor records.

Meanwhile, one can only hope that in spite of the popularity of negritude in some circles at the moment, there are also U.S. Negro writers whose literary insights will enable them to do much more than turn out shrill, defensive, and predictable counter-propaganda against the doctrine of white supremacy, as important as this propaganda is. Their literary insights should also enable these writers to realize that they have as much responsibility for representing the mainstream of U.S. life as anybody else. It is always open season on the truth, and there never was a time when one had to be white to take a shot at it.

Indeed, if there is one thing that all U.S. Negroes think they know about American literature it is that white writers seldom deal with the realities of American experience. Negroes think they know far too much about the everyday doings of the white people around them to be taken in by the phony bedtime stories in most of the books and magazines, in spite of the fact that most white people seem to allow themselves to be taken in by them. Black people think they know quite a bit about how this and much more happens. One can only hope they learn how to get into fiction some of what they really know and how they truly feel, rather than what somebody tells them they are supposed to know and how somebody tells them they're supposed to feel.

Many white writers go on year after year turning out book after solipsistic book in which they pretend that the world is white. In this they go hand in hand with most U.S. journalists, photographers, and motion picture producers. But any U.S. Negro sharecropper surrounded by a field of snow white cotton knows better than that. And he knows that the world is not black either. He knows that the only color the world has is the color of infinity. Whatever that color may be. This particular sort of U.S. Negro knows very well that the white man, for all his relative political and economic power, is not free. Perhaps not many Negroes have read *The Waste Land*, but this particular one has heard the blues, and some of them really are about Miss Ann and Mr. Charley. But he is not cheered by the fix they're in; he is sobered by it—as his great great grandfather was sobered by the spirituals that sometimes whispered *nobody knows the trouble I seen when I seen what was really happening in the* BIG HOUSE. No wonder great great grandpa took religious salvation so seriously.

And yet your negritude promoter, for all his bamboo boom boom jive, often gives the impression that he is out to paint the world black only because he believes it's white and that white is really all right but he's going to change it out of spite! But who knows? Perhaps this is only a part of the political fakery involved in this kind of confidence game. How *could* one know? Your negritude promoter sometimes also identifies himself with the most militant integrationists!

Thus does the American species of negritude bring itself by a commodious vicus of recirculation back to protest fiction and Marxist environs. Whereupon enter the old effeterati, now become the politerati, doing an ofay version of the one-butt shuffle to the fading but still audible strains of the old nineteen thirties dialectical boogie woogie.

These white friends of the Negro, that is to say, friends and friends-in-print of Negro Causes (or is it the Negro Cause?), are very sincere in many ways, and they have done much good in some ways. But they have also done and continue to do untold harm in a number of perhaps unrecognized but very fundamental ways. They encourage inferior standards and values by accepting or pretending to accept shoddy and immature workmanship. They sanction inadequate education by going along with what they know, if they know anything, is intellectual rubbish and esthetic nonsense. And furthermore, only the most snobbish and most self-indulgent condescension would permit them to tolerate so much arrogant stupidity and subversive irresponsibility.

It is about time U.S. Negro writers realized that whether or not these particular white friends themselves have any literary taste and maturity (and one wonders), they do not assume that Negro writers have any. Nor do they assume that Negro writers have any major literary ambitions. They seem to assume that for Negroes literature is simply incidental to protest. And it is about time Negro writers began to wonder why. It is about time they started asking themselves why these people are happiest when Negroes are moaning and groaning about black troubles and miseries. It is undeniable that these friends also tolerate and seem to enjoy being insulted, accused, bullied or baldwinized from time to time, but that is another one of those stories about choosing one's own punishment.

And it should also be remembered that these people never show real enthusiasm for the affirmative elements in U.S. Negro life. Quite the contrary. These are the self-same people who insist on explaining away qualities such as tough-minded forbearance and faith, compassion, musical expressiveness, and even physical coordination as being marks of oppression or even embarrassing evidence of racial inferiority.

U.S. writers and would-be writers who have any valid literary ambitions whatsoever obviously cannot afford to allow themselves to be overimpressed by the alleged superiority of the academic or professional background of their white-friends-in-print. Only people who have learned nothing at all from literary biography and have no fundamental understanding of the ironies involved in the creative process itself would hold, as these people so often do, that Negroes will be able to write first rate novels *only after* all oppression is removed, *only after* such time as Negroes no longer feel alienated from the mainstream of U.S. life.

What could be more misleading? Writers have always thrived

on oppression, poverty, alienation, and the like. Feodor Dostoevski, for example, was very poor, much oppressed, and in addition to all sorts of other personal problems, he was epileptic. He was certainly alienated. He was imprisoned; and one time he came within minutes of being officially lynched. But he wrote good books. Because he liked good books. Because his mind and imagination functioned in terms of good books. Even in jail. A writer who is oriented toward good books will at least try to write good books. But the sad fact is that there is very little to show that very many U.S. Negro writers have ever actually tried to write major novels.

There is certainly justification for some doubts and even suspicions about the *literary* value of the white-friends-of-the-Negro-Cause. One can only doubt that they know how art comes into being—or suspect that they know only too well. But be that as it may. They *could provide* a literary atmosphere in which Negroes would become oriented toward major works of art. But they do not. They do something else altogether. They actually discourage interest in art by overemphasizing and oversubsidizing the social sciences and by insinuating that Negroes who are interested in great art are not really interested in the everyday problems and realities of life. They accuse them of trying to escape the rigors of oppression by fleeing to the Ivory Tower, as if to say great art is for later, when and if you get to be as human as white folks. Right now your "thing" is to tell it like it is, which means show your ass!

None of this is intended as any excuse for U.S. Negroes themselves. Many things may be segregated, but great books and great ideas are not. Not really. Not even the Ku Klux Klan has shown any great concern because a Negro was sitting somewhere in a quiet corner reading Goethe or Thomas Mann. (They are much too busy seeing to it that the white pupils get the trade schools first!) No, the argument here is only to indicate the literary quality of the Negro's white well wishers. But to make a long story short, all you have to do is compare the kind of encouragement given by the typical white literary patron with the aspirations of the managers and promoters of Negro prizefighters. Financial double dealing aside, the backers of Negro boxers are out to produce champions of the world.

It is about time all U.S. Negroes took a closer look at all their friends-of-the-cause. To be conned by such self-styled good will as is usual with so many of these cheap-note aristocrats is not only to invite contempt and not only to encourage it, but also to deserve it.

III

Ralph Ellison wrote an article about Richard Wright which was published in the *Antioch Review* in the summer of 1945. This was four years before James Baldwin came to write "Everybody's Protest Novel" and some six before he was to do "Many Thousands Gone." Baldwin, as has been seen, was sharply critical of Wright, who incidentally was an old personal friend and onetime benefactor. Ellison, also an old personal friend, was generous almost to a fault.

So much so that when Wright encountered him shortly afterwards all Wright could do was shake his head in pleased bewilderment, somewhat, one imagines, as the tunesmith of *Body and Soul* must have done upon meeting Coleman Hawkins; and all he could say was almost exactly what one imagines the tunesmith would have said: "Man, you went much further than the book. Much further." (He himself was not to go even as far again.)

All Ellison, a former trumpet player and student of music composition, could do was shake his head in turn and smile reassuringly and reply, "Well, what you wrote made it possible for me to say what I said about it. All I was trying to do was use what you put there. All I was trying to do was play a few riffs on your tune. It was your tune. I just hope I didn't embarrass you. I just hope I did it justice." He did it more than justice.

Ellison's article was a commentary on *Black Boy*. This autobiographical record of Wright's childhood and youth employed all the techniques of fiction and was obviously intended to be a literary work of art as well as a personal document. Ellison called it "Richard Wright's Blues," and his remarks did go far beyond the book itself. They included what the book itself stated, and as in all really perceptive literary criticism, they suggested what was also represented, symbolized, ritualized.

Richard Wright, in spite of the shifts in his formal political affiliations, was always essentially a Marxist thinker. It is true that he maintained, and no doubt believed, that Marxism was only a starting point for Negro writers; and he himself was certainly the kind of intellectual who realized that Negro folklore had important literary significance. He also had a very extensive knowledge of world history and cultures, of ideas as such, and of contemporary world literature. But although his wide intellectual interests, so much broader than those of most other U.S. Negro writers, were a very active part of his everyday writing equipment, he remained primarily a Marxist. He read Eliot, Stein, Joyce, Proust, Hemingway, Gorky, Nexø, and most of the others, and he used much of what he learned, but he was almost always restricted by the provincial limitations of dialectical materialism. He used Freud, for example, primarily to score Marxian points; and even his later involvement with existentialism seemed to have political revolution as its basic motive.

Ellison was very much aware of the comprehensive range of Wright's intellectual and literary background, and in passing he suggested parallels between *Black Boy* and Nehru's *Toward Freedom*, Joyce's *Portrait of the Artist as a Young Man*, Dostoevski's *House of the Dead*, Rousseau's *Confessions*, and Yeats' *Autobiography*. But what impressed him most was that, knowingly or not, Wright had written a book that was in essence a literary equivalent to the blues.

> The blues [Ellison wrote] is an impulse to keep the painful details and episodes of a brutal experience alive in one's aching consciousness, to finger its jagged grain, and to transcend it, not by the consolation of philosophy but by squeezing from it a near-tragic, near-comic lyricism. As a form, the blues is an autobiographical chronicle of personal catastrophe expressed lyrically. And certainly Wright's early childhood was crammed with catastrophic incidents. In a few short years his father deserted his mother, he knew intense hunger, he became a drunkard begging drinks from black stevedores in Memphis saloons; he had to flee Arkansas, where an uncle was lynched; he was forced to live with a fanatically religious grandmother in an atmosphere of constant bickering; he was lodged in an orphan asylum; he observed the suffering of his mother, who became a

permanent invalid, while fighting off the blows of the poverty-stricken relatives with whom he had to live; he was cheated, beaten and kicked off jobs by white employees who disliked his eagerness to learn a trade; and to these objective circumstances must be added the subjective fact that Wright, with his sensitivity, extreme shyness and intelligence, was a problem child who rejected his family and was by them rejected.

Thus along with the themes, equivalent descriptions of milieu and the perspectives to be found in Joyce, Nehru, Dostoevski, George Moore and Rousseau, *Black Boy* is filled with blues-tempered echoes of railroad trains, the names of Southern towns and cities, estrangements, fights and flights, deaths and disappointments, charged with physical and spiritual hungers and pain. And like a blues sung by such an artist as Bessie Smith, its lyrical prose evokes the paradoxical, almost surreal image of a black boy singing lustily as he probes his own grievous wound.

"Their attraction" he added, referring again to the blues near the end of the article, "lies in this, that they at once express both the agony of life and the possibility of conquering it through sheer toughness of spirit. They fall short of tragedy only in that they provide no solution, offer no scapegoat but the self."

Baldwin, who made no mention of *Black Boy* or of Ellison's commentary when he wrote about the Negro tradition and the Negro sensibility in "Many Thousands Gone," once stated in an address at the New School in New York that as a writer he had modeled himself on none of the white American writers, not even Hemingway or Faulkner, but on black musicians, black dancers, and so on, even on black whores (or did one hear right?), and of all most assuredly on the blues singers. He then spoke lovingly about Billie Holiday and lamented the current personal and legal difficulties of Ray Charles.

But Baldwin's Broadway play, *Blues for Mister Charlie* (1964), had very little if anything to do with the blues. It fills the stage with a highly stylized group of energetic and militant self-righteous Negroes hollering and screaming and cussing and accusing and talking out of school and under other folks' clothes, and threatening to raise hell and all that, but generally feeling as sorry for themselves as if they had all just come from reading *An American Dilemma*, *The Mark of Oppression*, and most of the "liberal" magazines. There is an up tempo beat which *could* go with a classic Kansas City shout, but what comes out sounds more like the reds than the blues.

Baldwin's criticism of *Native Son* was essentially valid. The people, the situations, and the motivation in that quasi-realistic novel were more than oversimplified. They were exaggerated by an overemphasis on protest as such and by a very specific kind of political protest at that. Oversimplification in these terms does lead almost inevitably to false positions based on false assumptions about human nature itself. Every story whatever its immediate purpose is a story about being man on earth. This is the basis of its universality, the fundamental interest and sense of identification it generates in other people.

If you ignore this and reduce man's whole story to a series of sensational but superficial news items and editorial complaints and accusations, blaming all the bad things that happen to your characters on racial bigotry, you imply that people are primarily concerned with only certain political and social absolutes. You imply that these absolutes are the sine qua non of all human fulfillment. And you also imply that there are people who possess these political and social absolutes, and that these people are on better terms with the world as such and are consequently better people. In other words, no matter how noble your mission, when you oversimplify the reasons why a poor or an oppressed man lies, cheats, steals, betrays, hates, murders, or becomes an alcoholic or addict, you imply that well-to-do, rich, and powerful people don't do these things. *But they do.*

Baldwin in his essays on Wright seemed sensitive to this sort of embarrassment. He accused Wright of trying "to redeem a symbolical monster in social terms," and he spoke of the truth as implying "a devotion to the human being, his freedom and fulfillment; freedom which cannot be legislated, fulfillment which cannot be charted." He also seemed firmly convinced that categories were not real and that man "was not, after all, merely a member of a society or a group"—but "something *resolutely indefinable, unpredictable.*" (Italics added.)

These seemed like the assumptions of a writer who is interested in literature. Assumptions like these underlie all of the world's great stories. The unpredictable is the very stuff of storytelling. It is the very stuff of dramatic power, suspense, thrills, escapades, resolutions; the very stuff of fears, hopes, quests, achievements. It is the very stuff of the human condition.

That a sophisticated intellectual like Richard Wright knew all of this goes without question. But he chose to operate within the framework of his basic political commitment. This was an unfortunate choice. But in spite of his arbitrarily circumscribed point of view, he wrote a number of things that were politically useful, and there were also times, especially in certain parts of *Uncle Tom's Children* and *Black Boy*, when the universal literary values of his work automatically went beyond the material objectives of political ideology.

Now, Baldwin in effect began his literary career by rejecting Wright's achievements as being inadequate and also dangerous. The grounds for his rejection generally seemed solid enough. And he seemed to promise not only something different but something more.

So far he has not fulfilled that promise. The only thing really different about Baldwin's work to date has been his special interest in themes related to the so-called sexual revolution. And this is different only from Wright; it is not at all different from a lot of other writers these days, all of them white. Otherwise, Richard Wright is the author that James Baldwin the novelist, playwright, and spokesman resembles more than any other, including Harriet Beecher Stowe.

Baldwin once complained about the climate of anarchy and unmotivated and unapprehended disaster in *Native Son*. But in his own recent novel, *Another Country*, he seems to think this sort of climate has some profound, absurd, existentialist significance. It does not. Wright's existentialism, such as it was, had led to the same mistake in *The Outsider*, which Baldwin had already spotted in *Native Son*.

Both Baldwin and Wright seem to have overlooked the rich possibilities available to them in the blues tradition. Both profess great pride in Negroes, but in practice seem to rate the theories and abstract formulations of French existentialism over the infinitely richer wisdom of the blues. Both, like most other intellectuals (and/or most of the social scientists), seem to have missed what should be one of the most obvious implications of the blues tradition: *It is the product of the most complicated culture, and therefore the most complicated sensibility in the modern world.*

The United States has all of the complexities of all the other nations in the world, and also many of its own which most other nations are either not yet advanced enough or powerful enough to have. And in all these areas of U.S. life one finds Negroes. They are always reacting to what is happening and their reactions become elements in the blues tradition. Racial snobbishness and U.S. provincialism and deference to things European keep many Americans from realizing it, but the most old-fashioned elements in the blues tradition are often avant garde by the artistic standards of most other countries in the world. Europeans seem to appreciate this better than most Americans.

Somehow or other James Baldwin and Richard Wright seem to have missed the literary possibilities suggested by this. Ralph Ellison has not. He went beyond Richard Wright in the very process of commenting on *Black Boy*, and he went beyond every other American writer of his generation when he wrote his first novel. The possibilities he had talked about in "Richard Wright's Blues" were demonstrated most convincingly when he published *Invisible Man*, probably the most mature first novel, American or whatever, since *Buddenbrooks*. (It was certainly more mature both in craftsmanship and in vision than *This Side of Paradise*. And, of course, Hemingway's first was not *The Sun Also Rises* but *Torrents of Spring*, and Faulkner's was *Soldiers' Pay*!)

Invisible Man was *par excellence* the literary extension of the blues. It was as if Ellison had taken an everyday twelve bar blues tune (by a man from down South sitting in a manhole up North in New York singing and signifying about how he got there) and scored it for full orchestra. This was indeed something different and something more than run of the mill U.S. fiction. It had new dimensions of rhetorical resonance (based on lying and signifying). It employed a startlingly effective fusion of narrative realism and surrealism; and it achieved a unique but compelling combination of the naturalistic, the ridiculous, and the downright hallucinatory.

It was a first rate novel, a blues odyssey, a tall tale about the fantastic misadventures of one American Negro, and at the same time a prototypical story about being not only a twentieth century American but also a twentieth century man, the Negro's obvious predicament symbolizing everybody's essential predicament. And like the blues, and echoing the irrepressibility of America itself, it ended on a note of promise, ironic and ambiguous perhaps, but a note of promise still. The blues with no aid from existentialism have always known that there were no clear-cut solutions for the human situation.

Invisible Man was mainstream American writing in the same sense that U.S. Negro music is mainstream. In spite of his status as an entertainer, or sometimes perhaps as a direct result of it, the Negro jazz musician, representing the very spirit of American life itself, has, it seems, always been oriented to something different and something more. And there is much that all U.S. writers can learn from him about working with American experience in esthetic forms that are vernacular and sophisticated at the same time, particularly and peculiarly American and universally contemporary at the same time.

In terms of cultural assimilation, the blues idiom at its best is Omni-American precisely because it sounds as if it knows the truth about all the other music in the world and is looking for something better. Perhaps someday one will be able to say the same thing about American fiction. Black writers can do much to bring about that day, and there is every reason why they should. They will not do so as long as they mistake the illusions of social science for actuality.

PART III

Getting It Together

Identity, Diversity, and the Mainstream

A SHORT HISTORY OF BLACK SELF-CONSCIOUSNESS

The preoccupation with symbols and rituals of black consciousness currently so noticeable among so many civil rights activists and passivists alike is frequently misrepresented as an entirely new development. Some of the slogans and gestures may be new; and it well may be that never before have any Americans insisted in giving such revolutionary significance to a new fashion in *hair texture*. (Once and for all, how much culture and identity can you get from hair texture?) But in most other respects, the present wave of interest in self-definition and self-determination is not an innovation but a resurgence of the exuberant self-delight that characterized the so-called Harlem Renaissance or New Negro movement no longer ago than the nineteen twenties.

The New Negro movement was very specifically concerned with black identity and black heritage. Nor was it unresponsive to social and political matters. But its most significant achievements were in literature and the arts rather than in the area of social revolution. Its outstanding writers included James Weldon Johnson, Alain Locke, Walter White, Claude McKay, Countee Cullen, Rudolph Fisher, Langston Hughes, Jean Toomer, and Arna Bontemps. The artists included Aaron Douglas, Palmer Hayden, Richmond Barthé, and Augusta Savage, and there were "black conscious" performers and entertainers beyond number.

And how can even the most casual student of black culture in the United States not take note of the fact that the decade of the nineteen twenties is still known as the Jazz Age? It was from the Negro musician, not from a white writer named F. Scott Fitzgerald, that this title was derived. The nineteen twenties was the first great hey-day of the jazz- or blues-idiom musician. The music of King Oliver, Bessie Smith, W. C. Handy, Louis Armstrong, Jelly Roll Morton, James P. Johnson, and hundreds of others was impressing an affirmative consciousness of blackness not only upon other Negroes and upon white Americans, but upon the world at large as never before.

Perhaps the most magnificent synthesis, historical continuity and esthetic extension of all of the best elements of the New Negro period are to be found in the music of the Duke Ellington orchestra. No other institution in the United States represents a more deliberate and more persistent effort to come to terms with black heritage as it relates to the ever shifting complexities of contemporary life. Nor has Ellington simply clung to traditional folk forms. Culture hero that he is, he has not only confronted every esthetic challenge of his times, but has grown ever greater in the process. (Someday, Ellington may well come to be regarded as the Frederick Douglass of most black artists. He is already regarded as such by most musicians.)

During the depression of the nineteen thirties, the cultural emphasis generated by the New Negro movement gave way to a direct and very urgent concern with abstract economic theory and a general politicalization of all issues. In consequence (in part at least) black consciousness as such seems to have been de-emphasized in the interests of the polemics of class struggle dialectics, and black culture was redefined in accordance with the integration-oriented policies of friendly but paternalistic white liberals, left wing intellectuals, Communist party organizers, and other do-gooders and supporters of black causes of that period. Blackness as a cultural identity was all but replaced by blackness as an economic and political identity—or condition, plight, and blight. U.S. Negroes, that is to say, were in effect, no longer regarded as black people. They were now the Black Proletariat, the poor, the oppressed, the downtrodden minority. Sometimes, as a matter of fact, it was as if white left wing intellectuals had deliberately confused cultural issues with questions of race. In any case, there came a time (which is not yet passed) when it was not at all unusual for paternalistic white friends of black sufferers to condemn any manifestations of interest in black culture as a medium for identity as racism and separatism. By this time, many white friends even refused to concede that the blues was unique to U.S. Negro life style. Suddenly, music was just music and just as suddenly, non-Negro Benny Goodman, not Louis Armstrong, Fletcher Henderson, Count Basie, or Duke Ellington, was King of Swing, and Gene Krupa, not Chick Webb or Jo Jones, was their dyed-in-the-blue rhythm man. Moreover, they knighted Benny Goodman himself as a big fat liberal because he was nice enough to permit Negroes like Teddy Wilson, Lionel Hampton, and Charlie Christian to perform on the same stage with white "jazz musicians."

Perhaps the most comprehensive example of the post–New Negro attitude toward black experience is found—some current ideologists of blackness will be surprised to learn—in the fiction of Richard Wright, precisely because of its deficiencies. At times, as has been seen, it was as if Wright, who had every reason to know better, regarded Negroes not as acquaintances and relatives to be identified against a very complex cultural background, but rather as human problems struggling to become people. Sometimes Wright also gave the impression that he felt that the writer's basic function was to politicalize everything. Time and again he depersonalized the personalities as well as the motives and even the environment of his characters —in the interest (so far as one can tell) of revolutionary political theory. Few will deny that the social objectives behind Wright's theories were of the very highest order. But neither can it be denied that such theories contributed very little to the promotion of black identity in the sense in which it is being approached by the young people of today. Such theories, in fact, are most likely to lead to an oversimplification of the whole question of identity by their overemphasis on class as if it were the main clue to motives and manners. This, in any case, is where the theories led Wright. In *Black Power*, he seems to have found it easier to identify with Africa as a land of class brothers than as the homeland of some of his most important cultural antecedents.

In the fiction of Richard Wright, many of the same elements of black experience that were so fascinating to Negro writers of the renaissance period, and which the great Negro musicians have never ceased to celebrate (or to be inspired by), are subordinated to political conjecture. Some evidence of Wright's negative regard for the "black consciousness" of the nineteen twenties may be found in his essay "Blue Print for Negro Writing." He wrote there: "Today the question is: Shall Negro

writing be for the masses, moulding the lives and consciousness of those masses towards new goals, *or shall it continue
begging the question of the Negro's humanity.*" (Italics added.)
Then several paragraphs later: "There is a Negro church, a
Negro press, a Negro social world, a Negro sporting world, a
Negro business world, a Negro school system, Negro professions; in short, a Negro way of life in America. The Negro
people did not ask for this, and deep down, though they express themselves through their institutions and adhere to this
special way of life, *they do not want it now. This special existence
was forced upon them from without by lynch ropes, bayonet and
mob rule.* They accepted these negative conditions with the
inevitability of a tree which must live or perish in whatever soil
it finds itself." (Italics added.)

Perhaps this attitude, which is very much the same as that of
self-inflated white welfare workers, accounts at least in part for
the fact that the identity of Bigger Thomas, the protagonist of
Native Son, is more political than black. In any case, as Wright
depicts him, such soul brother characteristics as Bigger pos-
sesses have much less to do with a total complex life style than
with Wright's rather academic conception of the similarity of
black violence to the behavior of rats in a maze. Bigger, as
Wright makes clear enough in "How 'Bigger' Was Born," an
article published in *The Saturday Review of Literature*, is a political symbol, really a parable figure in a political sermon about
the revolutionary implications of the oppression of black
Americans.

Thus, those who are seriously interested in the actual texture
of life in the Chicago of Bigger Thomas (how it felt to be
among Negroes, to walk along a South Side street, to sit in a
bar, to be in love, etc.) would do well to supplement reading
Native Son with a dozen or so recordings of Earl Hines' great
Grand Terrace orchestra. Indeed, students of black heritage
will find it highly rewarding to compare the images that Richard Wright felt were representative of black experience in the
nineteen thirties and forties with the music to which black
style was literally geared. Despite the fact that the musician has
long occupied the position of supreme artist for U.S. Negroes,
Wright almost always wrote as if he were totally unrelated to

what Count Basie, Jimmie Lunceford, Fats Waller, Lionel Hampton, Louis Jordan, and others were saying about black experience during his day. At a time when Wright was making such statements as, "I thought of the essential bleakness of black life in America . . ." and ". . . I brooded on the cultural barrenness of black life . . ." Duke Ellington, whose audiences were larger than ever and whose orchestra had greater range than ever, was creating "Concerto for Cootie," "Cotton Tail," "Jack the Bear," "Portrait of the Lion," "Bojangles," "Jump for Joy," "In a Mellow Tone," "Sepia Panorama," "Harlem Airshaft," "Ko-Ko"; and for his first concert at Carnegie Hall, that citadel of white European identity, was attempting to make a comprehensive, affirmative statement about black heritage and identity in "Black, Brown, and Beige."

What with all the high pressure propaganda about the brotherhood of man and all the promises of one world (as opposed to the traditional self-aggrandizing nationalistic, or tribalistic, states), the trend away from any special positive emphasis on black consciousness per se continued during World War II and the first years of the United Nations.

Negroes were no less concerned about their rights as American citizens during all this time, to be sure. They made the double "V" sign and worked for victory over fascism abroad and victory over segregation and second class citizenship at home. In point of historical fact, it is the wartime generation that is most responsible for the accelerated activism that has come to be known as the Civil Rights Movement or the Negro Revolution. Nevertheless, that generation, whose leaders by and large were derived directly from the same intellectual environment that had produced Richard Wright, placed little emphasis on black consciousness and black culture. Perhaps the universal prominence of Ellington, Basie, Dizzy Gillespie, and Charlie Parker meant that the crucial role of black consciousness was simply being taken for granted. But the point is that spokesmen did not articulate issues in terms of it.

Given the differences between Ralph Ellison and Richard Wright on the blues idiom, it is not surprising that Ellison's novel, *Invisible Man*, published in 1952, addressed itself in an entirely different manner to the problem of black identity, black heritage, and black consciousness. The protagonist of *Invisible Man*, who becomes politically involved (much the same as Richard Wright or Angelo Herndon did), is a metaphorical ghost in spite of the fact that he has the most obvious physical features. White people see him not as an individual person, but as a problem. In a sense, he is even more invisible to himself. As Ellison once said, "The major flaw in the hero's character is his unquestioning willingness to do what is required of him by others as a way to success, and this was the specific form of his 'innocence.' He goes where he is told to go; he does what he is told to do; he does not even choose his Brotherhood name. It is chosen for him and he accepts it."

The climax of *Invisible Man* is, in itself, a highly significant statement about self-definition. The hero, as if to foreshadow the somewhat more flamboyant gestures of some of the young activists of the nineteen sixties, disengages himself from the ever so integrated but never quite desegregated Brotherhood and goes underground to hibernate and meditate on the relationship of identity to reality.

In view of the troubles of the invisible man, there is no wonder that some older students of black identity have a number of misgivings about Eldridge Cleaver. At first they thought (or hoped) that he was the Invisible Kid coming back up out of his hole and making the scene as a cool stalking Black Panther, using the Constitution like a Mississippi gambler with a deck of cards. So they edged forward waiting for him to start riffing on all the stuff he had learned from Rinehart and Ras the Exhorter, and had been down there getting "together." And then they discovered that not only was he a member of the *Ramparts* magazine brotherhood, but had chosen to define himself largely in terms of the pseudo-existential esthetique du nastiness of Norman Mailer, who confuses militant characteristics with bad niggeristics precisely because he wouldn't know a real bad Negro until one happened to him. That such a promising, young intellectual as Eldridge Cleaver would allow himself to be faked out one inch by the essentially frivolous notions of a jive-time fayboy playboy—to whom the essence of black experience seems to be the Saturday night spree, and to whom jazz is the music of orgasm—instead of utilizing the immensely superior insightfulness of the blues, is enough to scandalize any chicken-shack piano player who ever read a book by Mickey Spillane.

The point of course is not that there is anything inherently wrong about being influenced by white writers. What black writer isn't? The point is that bad taste in white intellectuals is something that black leaders and spokesmen can least afford. Whether white people, including the philanthropic foundations, can afford their customary taste for black hype artists remains to be seen. The fact that Cleaver rejects counter-racism is commendable. But who the hell needs a brown-skinned Norman Mailer?

The current campaign to stimulate greater academic interest in black studies represents a resurgence of appreciation for the black components of American culture. Such campaigns have been a long time coming. Some completely sincere but misinformed campaigners, however, are not nearly as constructive as they so obviously intend to be. They wish to establish a historical context of black achievement. But they often proceed as if respectable traditions of black heroism exist only outside the United States. Yet few glories that they may find to identify with in ancestral Africa are likely to be more directly significant or more immediately applicable than the legacy of courage and devotion to human dignity and freedom that they leave so largely unclaimed at home.

Not that the African past is unimportant. On the contrary, it represents a heritage that merits the most careful and enthusiastic study. But certainly not primarily in the interest of *race* pride, as those who have been overconditioned by the psycho-political folklore of white supremacy insist. And the danger exists that even the slightest emphasis on race pride leads all too easily to what Arthur Schomburg quite accurately labeled "puerile controversy and petty braggadocio."

Schomburg, for whom the famous Schomburg Collection of Negro Literature and History in Harlem is named, placed the fundamental relevance of African culture in clear perspective back in 1925. The following statement from "The Negro Digs Up His Past," which Schomburg contributed to Alain Locke's *The New Negro*, is as applicable to the black studies programs of today as to the Negro renaissance of the nineteen twenties. "Of course," he goes on to say, after having rejected the excesses of black counter-racism, "the racial motive remains legitimately compatible with scientific method and aim. The work our race students now regard as important, they undertake very naturally to overcome, in part, certain handicaps of disparagement and omission too well known to particularize. But they do so *not merely that we may not wrongfully be deprived of the spiritual nourishment of our cultural past, but also that the full story of human collaboration and interdependence may be told and realized.*" (Italics added.) Nor was Schomburg alone in this view. Such major U.S. Negro historians and scholars as Carter G. Woodson, Benjamin Brawley, Charles Wesley, W. E. B. Du Bois, James Weldon Johnson, Benjamin Quarles, and John Hope Franklin, have always regarded a knowledge of Africa as being basic to an adequate understanding of America —so that "the full story of human collaboration and interdependence may be told and realized."

THE ROLE OF THE PRE-AMERICAN PAST

Many Americans of African (and part-African) ancestry who are forever complaining, mostly in the vaguest of generalities, and almost always with more emotion than intellectual conviction, that their black captive forefathers were stripped of their native culture by white Americans often seem to have a conception of culture that is more abstract, romantic, and in truth, pretentious than functional. Neither African nor American culture seems ever to have been, as most polemicists perhaps unwittingly assume, a static system of racial conventions and ornaments. Culture of its very essence is a dynamic, ever accommodating, ever accumulating, ever assimilating environmental phenomenon, whose components (technologies, rituals, and artifacts) are emphasized, de-emphasized, or discarded primarily in accordance with pragmatic environmental requirements, which of course are both physical and intellectual or spiritual.

There is, to be sure, such a thing as the destruction of specific cultural configurations by barbarians and vandals. But even so, time and again history reveals examples of barbarian conquerors becoming modified and sometimes even dominated by key elements of the culture of the very same people they have suppressed politically and economically. In other words, cultural continuity seems to be a matter of competition and endurance in which the fittest elements survive regardless of the social status of those who evolved them. Those rituals and technologies that tend to survive population transplanta-tion seem to do so because they are essentially compatible to and fundamentally useful in changed circumstances. So, for example, the traditional African disposition to refine all move-ment into dance-like elegance survived in the United States as work rhythms (and playful syncopation) in spite of the fact that African rituals were prohibited and the ceremonial drums were taken away. On the other hand, the medicine man was forcibly replaced by the minister and the doctor—and he has met or is meeting the same fate in Africa!

As for those white American immigrants who faced no slave system and so presumably were not stripped of their "culture," in point of fact they were still stripped by the necessities of pi-oneer readjustment. Needless to say, they were not stripped altogether—but neither were the black chattel bondsmen. If the African in America was unable to remain an African to the extent that he may have chosen to do so, neither were very many Europeans able to remain Europeans even though they were able to construct exact duplicates of European architec-ture in Virginia and Maryland—and to the extent that they did remain Europeans, they often were out of practical touch with life around them. Nothing can be more obvious than the fact that for most practical everyday intents and purposes almost all non-English-speaking immigrants were stripped of their native tongue. Nor are French, German, Spanish, and Italian taught in American schools in interest of ethnic identity and pride. They are taught primarily as tools for research. In any case, that the black man was the victim of brutal treatment goes without saying, but how much of his African culture he would have or could have kept intact had he come over as a free set-tler is a question that should be discussed against the fact that the pressure on "free white Americans" to conform is (as non-Protestants, for example, know very well) greater than is generally admitted. The question of African survival should also be discussed in full awareness of the fact that the dynamics of American culture are such that the average American citizen is a cultural pluralist.

II

Many black New Yorkers seem to be insisting on their loss of African culture not so much because they actually feel deprived of it but because they have somehow allowed themselves to be theorized into imitating and competing with white and somewhat white immigrants whose circumstances are not really analogous. There is, for instance, much theorizing by the Jewish friends, sweethearts, spouses, and colleagues of black New Yorkers about the importance of a Jewish ancestral homeland—but no one has as yet demonstrated that U.S. Jews are in any practical sense better off since the establishment of the vest pocket state of Israel, as marvelous as that little nation has turned out to be—nor has it been shown that the fall of Lumumba, Tshombe, or Nkrumah added to the problems of black Americans.

It is not Jewish culture as such that accounts for the noteworthy academic performance of Jewish pupils—which performance seems to impress black New Yorkers no end. Rather it is much more likely to be the traditional Jewish cultural *orientation* to the written word as the basis of formalized and routinized education. Indeed, so far as specific cultural details are concerned, a significant number of outstanding American Jewish intellectuals appear to represent Germany to a far greater extent than they represent the Middle East.

The definitive academic conditioning or intellectual "occupational psychosis" or mental orientation of the American Jewish intellectual, scientist, technician, and even journalist seems to have been derived largely from the tradition of the Talmudic scholar, that inimitable master of research and midrash. In any case, it is the Talmudic scholar's traditional orientation to painstaking documentation which appears to be most functional. What sustains the fine Jewish student, that is to say, is neither Hebrew nor Yiddish, nor specific precepts from the synagogue, but rather his overall conditioning to (or attitude toward) written communication and linguistic discipline, plus a respect for prescribed procedures.

The Afro-American tradition, on the other hand, is largely oral rather than written. Even its music is likely to be transmitted largely through auditory means rather than by notation even when both pupil and teacher are musically literate. The great Jewish conductors, concert-masters, and virtuosi, by contrast, proceed very much as if they were Talmudic scholars with scores and instruments. Indeed, Euro-Americans in general are Talmudic scholars in the sense that they tend to read and talk about such musical qualities as, say, dissonance, cacophony, atonality, and so on perhaps nearly as much as they listen to or perform music that contains these characteristics. Afro-American performers and listeners alike tend to proceed directly in terms of onomatopoeia.

In his very perceptive books, *Made in America* and *A Beer Can by the Highway*, John A. Kouwenhoven, whose observations on the nature of America belong beside those of Constance Rourke, states that contemporary American culture is the result of the conflict or interaction of two traditions in the United States over the years. He called one the learned or academic and the other the vernacular, or folk or native. This distinction is a particularly useful one in the present context. The learned or documentary orientation to experience is of its very nature essentially conservative and even antiquarian. In traditions that are essentially learned, even revolutionary action is likely to be based almost as much on the documentation and analysis of past revolutions as upon the urgencies of a current predicament. Literacy, that is to say, is always indispensable to such a cultural orientation or life style.

Americans from Africa, however, are not derived from a life style that has been, or indeed has even needed to be, as concerned with preserving and transmitting the past per se as Europeans have been. Not that the past was considered entirely forgettable. Far from it. But the African concept of time and continuity (or of permanence and change) seems to have been different, and certainly the concept of history, heritage, and documentation was different. (Afro-Americans, of course, came neither from Egypt nor from the famous Lost Cities.) It is hardly surprising if African conceptions of education were also different.

In all events, it is not only possible but highly probable that the "cultural dislocation trauma" suffered by Africans transported to frontier America was considerably less than European-oriented polemicists imagine, precisely because the African's native orientation to culture was less static or structured than they assume, precisely, that is to say, because the African may have been geared to improvisation rather than piety, for all the taboos he had lived in terms of. The fact that these taboos were not codified in writing may have contributed to a sense of freedom, once he was beyond the "pale."

But perhaps most important of all, it should never be forgotten that nothing is more important to man's survival as a human being than is his flexibility, his adaptability, his talent for accommodating himself to adverse circumstances. Perhaps it is a one-dimensional and essentially snobbish conception of culture which prevents some black- and white-oriented polemicists from realizing that there is probably more to be said for the riff-style life style that Negroes have developed in response to the adverse circumstances of their lives in the United States, than can be said for the culture they were so brutally stripped of. And, besides, look at what actually happened to the Africans who remained at home with their culture intact. Some "African bag" polemicists cop out at this point. But contemporary African leaders, spokesmen, and intellectuals do not. They are the first to explain that they were invaded and colonized by *Europeans*—and by European technology, upon which they are now more dependent than they ever were before. Nor do African officials hesitate to send as many students as possible to Europe and to segregationist America. Not to become white, but to enable the students to extend themselves in terms of the culture of the world at large.

Perhaps it is also pretentiousness that prevents some psycho-political theorists from realizing that just as "Talmudic scholarship" applied to technology may account for the ability of Jewish and other literate peoples to survive and thrive in alien cultures all over the world, including South Africa, so may riff-style flexibility and an open disposition towards the vernacular underlie the incomparable endurance of black soulfulness or humanity.

There is, nevertheless, as much to be said for the vernacular tradition as for the learned tradition—and as Kouwenhoven's investigations suggest, even more to be said for the interaction of the two. At the advent of the phonograph, to take an example from recent cultural history, the typical U.S. Negro musician, not unlike his African ancestors, was clearly more interested in playing and enjoying music than in *recording* it for posterity. As a matter of fact, many Afro-Americans in general still tend to regard phonograph recordings more as current duplications (soon to be discarded as out of date) which enable them to reach more people simultaneously than as permanent documents. Euro-Americans, on the other hand, started record collections and archives, which eventually came to include the music of black Americans. Thus, it is the Euro-American whose tradition of scholarship and research has provided at least the rudiments of a source of musicological data that black historians and students in quest of musical heritage may someday make the most of.

Similarly, it is African creativity that has produced in African art one of the most marvelous achievements of the human imagination. But, as every art dealer knows, it is the Europeans who have been most interested in preserving it, and its fantastic value on the world art market is geared not to the valuation made by Africans but to the valuation of galleries and museums in Europe and America. Further, such are the practical realities that African scholars, artists, and art dealers seem far more interested in what white European and American art dealers and museum directors think about African culture than what Harlem polemicists think.

When outraged Afro-Americans indict those whose bigotry is the cause of the omissions, distortions, the wholesale falsification and outright suppression of information about black people of the United States, the merits of their case are beyond question. Indeed, the deliberate debasement of the black image has been so viciously systematic and often times so exasperatingly casual that the scope of white malevolence is hard to exaggerate.

The absence of readily available documentary materials in Africa on the history and culture of the peoples of that continent, however, can hardly be blamed on the vandalism of slave traders and certainly not entirely upon the ruthless disregard by European colonials for African culture. Though some missionaries were Huns of a sort, the British Museum, the Musée de l'Homme, and the American Museum of Natural History contain impressive evidence that not all Europeans were set on obliterating African history or denying the significance of its culture. The fact of the matter is that white archaeologists and anthropologists have been instrumental in stimulating contemporary Africans to develop a European-type concern with the documentation and glorification of the past—and glorification of the present for posterity.

It is quite true that conventional European histories of the world have largely ignored African achievements. But what of histories of the world written by Africans down through the years? Were all of these destroyed by European barbarians, or did they never exist? The chances are that those African peoples for whom there is little or no "autobiographical" record conceived of time, reckoned time, and dealt with the passage of time in ways that, as suggested earlier, belonged to an orientation that was essentially different from that of most of the peoples of Europe. It is not impossible that some African cultures were as profoundly conditioned by the vanity of vanities as was the preacher in Ecclesiastes —or as the traveler in Shelley's "Ozymandias."

That U.S. Negroes should enjoy the privilege of introducing additional African elements, including new fashion accents, ornaments, and trinkets, into the pluralistic culture of the United States not only goes without saying but, as the ads in *Ebony*, *Jet*, and the black weeklies suggest, give as big a boost to black business as to black vanity. Nevertheless, those who are so deeply and fervently concerned about the status of black culture and the prestige of black studies are likely to be motivated by forces and precedents that are not nearly so African as European or Euro-Talmudic, as it were. Thus, it is all too true that the "Americanization" process that captive Africans were forced to undergo stripped them of many of the native accoutrements that they held most dear and wished to retain. But it was also a process of Americanization that has now equipped and *disposed* them not only to reclaim and update the heritage of black Africa but also to utilize the multicolored heritage of all mankind of all the ages.

Black Pride in Mobile, Alabama

MORE OFTEN THAN NOT—or so it seems—when black New Yorkers get going on television about black identity, black pride, black heritage, and the need for what many now call black studies, they speak as if the Schomburg Collection (which many white students of Negro culture know is located in the very heart of Harlem) were either nonexistent or off-limits to black people. They make sweeping statements that suggest that they are really only shucking for the networks (and the foundations, to be sure) or are completely unaware of the pioneering, even if sometimes somewhat less than comprehensive, work of historians like Carter G. Woodson and Benjamin Brawley. They sound as if they never heard of the Association for the Study of Negro Life and History, which has been publishing the *Journal of Negro History* since 1916 and the *Negro History Bulletin* since 1937.

Some black polemicists are forever complaining that white historians have been omitting and deliberately suppressing important facts about Negro achievement, and justification for their outrage is overwhelming. But for some reason they themselves seldom if ever make even the slightest mention of the work of Negro historians like Rayford Logan, John Hope Franklin, and Benjamin Quarles, three contemporary scholars of the highest professional standing who have devoted long careers to correcting the historical perspectives on U.S. Negro life. Some may make vague references to Du Bois (or even to E. Franklin Frazier whose sociopolitical view of Negro heritage was emphatically negative!). Otherwise, those most likely to be mentioned or even quoted are Malcolm X and Marcus Garvey, both of whom were spokesmen of high purpose who aspired to be activists rather than historians, research specialists, and survey technicians. Both inspired black pride in thousands of their followers, but neither had either the time or the means to engage in primary research on U.S. Negroes, to say nothing of archaeological, anthropological, or philological research on the infinitely varied black peoples and civilizations of Africa.

But then so many of the most militant black polemicists

appear to have swallowed the assumptions and conclusions of precisely those writers who, like Frazier, describe the black American experience as adding up to little more than a legacy of degradation and despair—writers whose concern for the welfare of black people may be beyond reproach but whose opinion or esteem for them is often so low that it moves beyond condescension to contempt! As a result you often hear some of the most scandalous statements about black people repeated by the same black militants who complain loudest about the negative regard in which black people are held. This, in any case, too often tends to be the story in New York.

It is not quite the same down-home. For example, Mobile, Alabama.

II

In conversation and particularly in meetings and open forums, your Southern Negro civil rights spokesmen and activists are likely to make liberal use of many of the slogans and generalities about black identity, black pride, and black heritage heard everywhere in the North these days. So much so, as a matter of fact, that an inattentive outside observer could easily forget where he is. Indeed, unless he remains alert, a native-born Southerner who has been away a number of years might also do the same thing; for when the subject turns to black consciousness, even the traditional barber shop bull session, which used to be anything but academic, has begun to sound somewhat like a Northern campus caucus of television-oriented black power panelists doing their thing for the six o'clock report.

So much so that after a while you realize that you are the TV, and they're talking not with you and to you but at you and into you and seeing themselves zooming close as the titles breeze upward. So much so that you almost expect them to pause, not for your reply or the next question, but for the commercial.

When they finally get down to the specifics of programing, however, black Mobilians (who are really mostly various shades of brown and beige) are likely to formulate social, economic, political, and educational objectives that are significantly different from those that have recently been turned into such sensational news copy elsewhere.

When they get down to specifics they forget about television for a while and see you as yourself again or whoever they remember you as having been or whomever it pleases them to think you have become. Then they talk to you man to man, Negro to fellow-man, homefolks to our boy back down home from up the country and homefolks to homefolks about other folks elsewhere—but not without doing a little chicken butt signifying in the process either: "Now of course you folks up North, you folks up in New York, y'all in Yuyorick . . ." That is an indispensable part of the ritual. Establishes perspective. Adds proper (and anticipated) dimension of down-home ambivalence.

Then old home week can begin: "*Well, I'm for the brother everywhere because we all members in this mess together, you know what I mean. But man, some of these new Northern kiddies ain't nothing but new style white folks you-know-what. You dig? And don't know it. That's the killing part about it. All that big mouth talk about whities and honkies and that. Man, most of the time that ain't nothing but exactly what the man want to hear so he can have an excuse to do anything he want to. O.K. Remember them cattle prods? They didn't really hurt nobody, right? But they got Bull Connor and Al Lingo into all kinds of trouble because everybody all over the country was talking about what an outrageous thing that was, remember? So the man goes and finds him somebody to go on TV and start bragging about Negroes getting up rifle clubs. But who you reckon manufactured all the rifles in the goddam world and who know the serial number on every rifle in the USA. Look, we were finally getting white folks so even them poor sap suckers from back up in the hills were getting careful about how they were saying Neegrow. No more of that Nigra stuff, know what I mean? So they find somebody to get up there and say Negro is ugly because it's white talk and black is beautiful because they just found out. So now white folks up North out talking about blacks like the old slave traders, talking about blacks, coloreds, and whites like down in South Africa . . . Johnny Come Blackly, you know what I mean? Johnny come blacker than thou. But I will say this much. They finally found a way to make some of these high yallers want to give up blow-hair for clinker tops. Man, I saw a peola down here from Harlem or Philly or somewhere wearing a reverse conk. Now that's a switch. At least for a while. Man, they got some of them yaller cats up there on TV carrying on like they blacker than everybody else. You seen that stuff? Hell, they got them so you got to be looking dead at a cat to tell what color he is these days. You hear some Northern-talking cat coming on like he the ace of spades and you look up and he as white as a Scandinavian snowbird. You know what Malcolm X's nickname was? Red, Deetroit Red. Of course, me I'm just a dark-skinned Frenchman with some African ways and some African in the right places myself."*

Currently the most newsworthy of the civil rights groups in Mobile is NOW (Neighborhood Organized Workers), and Christmas 1968 it organized a Black Christmas boycott. Whatever the boycott's merits and shortcomings, its objectives were not secession but desegregation. Those who organized it were far more concerned with getting greater black participation in all of the economic and political affairs of their city than with black symbolism, nationalistic or otherwise. There are overtones of black nationalism, of course, and some black retailers always profit during such times. But as for what some New Yorkers now call "black community control" and "black community development," when black Mobilians talk about where it's at, they are referring to city hall, the city fathers, the industrial/commercial complex, and the like. According to members of NOW, unless you exercise significant influence over municipal funds and policies (they may or may not say the "establishment" or the "white power structure"), black power slogans just help to create black communities that will be far more like colonies than the metaphysical ghettos Northern spokesmen complain about.

Specifics cited by a key member of NOW are typical of those black Mobilians most actively involved in desegregation: "*For one thing we intend to get more of our people on the city payroll. We are due a share of all that. Take for example two guys going around reading water meters and things like that. You don't need much education and training for that. No reason in the world why one of them can't be black, and there are thousands of jobs like that. You see that fine new Municipal Auditorium and Arena? Well, they have some black maintenance and security people in there, but you see we think we ought to have black folks in the box office and on the staff, some committeemen and on the board of directors too. We're not boycotting that place to get a black branch, that's crazy, look how long it took them to get this one, and they've been controlling all the money like you know, since forever. That doesn't make any sense at all. That's the one and we don't need but one, and it's supposed to be as much ours as anybody else's."*

In general when you talk to militants down South about defense, they are less given to making ill-tempered threats about burning down everything in sight than to expressing a level-headed determination to use counterforce against certain traditional white methods of intimidation used by terrorist elements in the Ku Klux Klan and other white supremacy groups.

As for having a movie-style "shoot out with the lawmen," not many black Mobilians seem particularly impressed with what has been reported about the performance record of black Northerners during such showdowns over the past few years. Most were impressed with the so-called riots in Watts, Newark, and Detroit, but not with the fire power of the black communities involved and certainly not with the accuracy of the sniper fire. They are convinced that the riots did a lot of good and moved the struggle into another phase and onto another level. But much of the talk in the North about "violent confrontation" makes them somewhat uneasy because references to Che Guevara and quotations from Mao and the speculations of Frantz Fanon strike them as being more bookish than relevant and in any case they doubt the tactical wisdom of provoking an enemy who is not only armed to the teeth but is also already on the edge of hysteria. Some admit that an old Southern superstition about people who go around making the loudest threats do not follow up big talk with action also makes them uneasy. "Look," said more than one, "if you really getting ready to do something to somebody, it just don't make sense to tip them off, man." But that is only down-home superstition, of course.

Nevertheless, most black Mobilians seem to feel that the most practical way of striking back at police brutality is through NOW-style policies. Meanwhile should a gundown situation arise, it is the typical black Southerner, more than a few

Mobilians insisted, not the typical Harlemite, whose traditional intimate personal experience with weapons is most likely to pay off in terms of dependable marksmanship. "Because you see harassment is all right for pinning down police for a while. You can do that with firecrackers; but before long they going to start checking and find you ain't hurting nobody. But, man, all this is crazy anyhow. All that wolfing and now y'all got gun control worse than ever."

As for the impact of local chapters of violence-oriented militants, said one peppery Mobilian, an old poker player, who used to be a baseball umpire: "*OK, so I'm impressed with what some of them might do to somebody like me and you if they catch us in the dark or something, but hell ain't nothing new about that. You can always do something dirty to another one of your people that you don't like and get away with it because the law don't care and white people don't care. But I bet you they don't jump no cat that's really in cahoots with the white folks. Take like up there in Harlem. OK, y'all always talking about cleaning up the black community, but I bet a fat man the last ones you start messing with is them very cats that's pushing junk for the white mob, you see my point? Because that's the white mob's nigger, you see what I mean? Well, just take around here. They jump up and bomb a black man's business like that cat's liquor store the other night, but I ain't heard a thing about them hitting on none of them cracker stores downtown.*" (Who bombed the store at issue is actually not clear. White Mobilians on TV tried their best to make that particular bombing look like the work of NOW, while many Negroes including some members of NOW were not so sure that the whole thing hadn't been planned and executed by white people.)

III

In general, black Mobilians are considerably less polemical than New Yorkers on the subject of black heritage. But after all, black teachers in Mobile, like perhaps most others throughout most of the South, have been observing Negro History Week (the week in February that includes Lincoln's and Frederick Douglass's birthdays) for decades. It must be said that Alabama teachers have been incredibly apathetic about the ridiculous materials on black people in the textbook on Alabama history. But on the other hand their libraries have always tried to promote and spread interest in black publications of all kinds, and everybody is quick to point out that books like Woodson's *The Negro in Our History*, Brawley's *Negro Builders and Heroes*, and John Hope Franklin's *From Slavery to Freedom* have been used as standard references in Negro schools and colleges throughout the South all along.

Actually there never was a time when Southern Negro colleges were not aspiring to be the so-called Black University serving the special needs of black American youth. Thirty-odd years ago, for instance, when the generation of parents and grandparents now in their fifties were college age, almost every campus had teachers, scholars, or historic figures in residence who were widely known and honored for the role they played in matters relating to black heritage. At Howard, for example, there were Kelly Miller, Alain Locke, and Sterling Brown; at Tuskegee there was Monroe N. Work heading a Department of Records and Research and editing the *Negro Year Book*; at Atlanta University there were Du Bois and later Ira De A. Reid; at Fisk there were James Weldon Johnson and Charles S. Johnson, and so on.

Anyway, when involved Mobilians get down to specifics about black heritage they are likely to begin not with self-rejection but rather by saying that the special displays and programs of Negro History Week were never enough to remedy the omissions and distortions in the books used in regular courses in history and social studies. Then, in response to inquiries about offerings presently under consideration at the local school board, they summarize as follows: They do not want black heritage courses to be either extracurricular or elective. They not only want them required but required of all pupils. They do not want them restricted to "black" schools or to black pupils in "white" schools because they are convinced that white pupils need such studies even more urgently than Negroes—who in truth already absorb at least a smattering of black heritage from *Ebony*, *Jet*, and other national Negro publications. As some of them see it, the problem of improving the Black Image has as much to do with teaching white school children to honor Denmark Vesey and Nat Turner as with anything else.

Then, because they are thinking and talking like teachers and supervisors and not like TV spokesmen, they begin speculating about what will really happen when the actual classwork begins and there is not so much publicity. So they start remembering how students respond to assignments and, being teachers, they also know how precious student enthusiasm always is, but, being experienced teachers and in some instances parents to boot, they know enough about it not to exaggerate its significance. Nor do they confuse the emotional response to statements about black pride at political rallies with the academic motivation that comes from genuine historical curiosity. So they come back to specifics for school board policy. Perhaps the current emphasis will generate greater historical curiosity among larger numbers of black students (and white ones too), but meanwhile now is the time to add missing black dimensions to existing courses. Now is the time to revise and update existing text materials, no little job in itself.

As for race pride as such, there are those who think it is a good thing which has nothing to do with racism. But some others are not so sure. Some flatly reject it as a highly questionable educational objective. Others see it as representing a regression toward social provincialism and political chauvinism, of which they feel the U.S. has far too much already. Still others point out that the most urgent problems facing U.S. Negroes just simply do not have very much to do with any demonstrated lack of black pride. To them all the television talk about blackness is mostly a misuse of valuable time and mostly adds up to a misdirection of valuable energies; and they frankly doubt whether those who are doing it have any practical standards by which to calculate what degree of black pride must be developed (and by what means and through what measurable stages) before Negroes can get the hell on with the business of employment, housing, and equal protection under the law.

Nor do many of the so-called brothers on the street, on the block, and in the barber shop disagree: "*Now look, you know good and well color ain't what Rockefeller is proud of. Hell, the only time you ever hear real big white folks bragging about the color of their skin is when they got a good deep tan. You know what Rockefeller is proud of? All that money and power. And you know what Wallace and all the rest of them proud of? The same thing. Hell, anybody get up there on TV talking about Negroes don't have no pride ain't talking about no Negroes I know. Because you see, sometimes I think the whole trouble is we got too much pride. And I say we don't need to be getting no louder and prouder because what I want to see is more of our young folks getting smarter and when you got that you don't have to be up there bragging about it. Because as soon as you start carrying on like that I got to start worrying about how come you so loud because if you really proud you supposed to be cooling it. You see what I mean? Because then I got to start asking myself if you really believe it. And now I'm going to tell you something else. Black is beautifuler than ever, but them A&P specials are kinda pretty too, and ain't no flies on Sears Roebuck. Goddam it, everywhere you turn somebody talking about black, black, black. Hell, me I want to talk about the goddam stock market report, I want to talk about all them calculating machines and stuff. Black my behind. Hell, I'm old fashioned. Any joker come calling me black better make damn sure he blacker than me."*

And after all, the Indians never had any shortage of red pride. Their red identity was unmistakable and their sense of red heritage had long since become a part of their religion. But they needed more than a legacy of bow and arrow confidence and barebacked courage. They had every right to be proud of their hair as well as their feathers and buckskin and so on, but they did not have any factories and merchant fleets to be proud of. In other words, redskin pride was never any problem. The war drums took care of that business very well. Perhaps even too well, because they hopped up a number of young braves to the point where they were only too willing to risk dying for the cause without understanding the complexity of the issues. The redskin troops were magnificent. But the combat plans were out of date. *Nobody in the councils of war knew enough about world history, world geography, and demography.* The failure to understand the connection between the paleface invaders and the people on the other side of the Atlantic was disastrous. Nor was paleface pride a decisive factor since the terrified white colonists were able to offset their insecurity and lack of dignity with, among other things, superior technology.

But when qualified Negro or so-called black teachers and supervisors in New York get closer to the specifics of curriculum construction, they do not often confuse the stimulation of black pride with the refinement and extension of historical insight either. Nor do they mistake themselves as television spokesmen simply because the news media might choose to create the impression that anybody making statements about black studies is a fully qualified expert in the field of education. Most seem to go along with the black consciousness campaign as an activist tactic; and more often than not they also approve of black militancy despite the fact that some of it violates their sense of scholarly integrity (philosophically shrugging off gross oversimplification and wild exaggeration as the dues you pay for long overdue revolutionary change). But even so they also know how easy it is for self-pride to degenerate into self-inflation, empty arrogance, and chauvinism; so they want good news that meets the highest tests of reliability. They want courses in history and culture that will improve everybody's perspective on the universality of human experience and will enrich everybody's sense of context and identity.

The main difficulty, however, is the fact that black teachers in New York have less authority in such matters than do their colleagues in the South. In Mobile, those from the so-called black community who exercise most influence on school board policies relating to black heritage or the "black dimension" of American culture are likely to be teachers and principals, not all-purpose spokesmen and overnight experts. Perhaps in time the same will be true in New York. But as of now, black professionals in education in New York seem to enjoy less scholarly prestige among top school officials and other powerful white-friends-of-black-causes than the very same black students who otherwise are considered to be suffering from the gravest academic deficiencies and who paradoxically are complaining precisely because they are inadequately trained. Indeed, it is not at all unusual for white New Yorkers to allow themselves to be instructed in language usage, history, anthropology, economics, and even clinical psychology by students that they themselves rate substandard, and then presume to instruct their black professional equals and betters on the whys, wherefores, and needs of black experience.

That legendary Southern Negro refugee who used to brag that he'd rather be a lamp post in Harlem than the mayor of Mobile was probably not a school teacher—or maybe the lamp post was where the action was in those days. Anyway, as any black Mobilian old enough to remember will readily confirm, educators down-home would have regarded such empty-headed arrogance with contempt at least as far back as thirty or forty years ago. As brutal as conditions in Alabama were back during the depression of the nineteen thirties, nobody could have conceived of white Mobilians ignoring the advice of a dedicated professional like Benjamin F. Baker, then the principal of Mobile County Training School, or of Ella Grant of the Prichard School, for that of semi-literate bull session experts and para-literate adolescent intellectuals. And black parents did not accuse teachers like B. F. Baker or Miss Ella of being Uncle Toms or white folks' Negroes either—for the simple reason that they were not.

Black Studies and the Aims of Education

As LITTLE as it has been noted by the experts, the petitions for courses in black history and culture now being pushed by Negro students across the nation may actually be as much a repudiation of the content and point of view of existing offerings in the social sciences as they are a protest against anything else. In fact, such petitions, which frequently sound like ultimatums, may even be the direct and natural, if not the inevitable, result of the all but exclusive emphasis that so many schools and most of the media have been placing on the so-called findings of the socio-economic research technicians. In any case, the slogans now being chanted by the insistent young petitioners represent an unmistakable refutation of the most popular academic and generally social scientific assumptions about the nature of black experience—all that misery and ugliness—in the United States.

What student activists are now proclaiming is that black is beautiful and that it is beautiful to be black but that bigoted white historians and vicious white image makers in general have been distorting the beauties and denying the glories of blackness all these years. In other words, what the students are demanding are not more courses in the origin, development, and extent of black wretchedness. On the contrary, they first of all expect to find in the courses they are demanding historical clues to the pathological condition of white Americans. Their frequent references to the sickness, insecurity, and brutality of white Americans make that clear. Further, all the catch phrases about black identity, black power, and black pride make it even clearer that they expect the history they are demanding to reveal a magnificent, hither-to sneakily obscured tradition of black heroism and misattributed achievement.

Such a basic and comprehensive student rejection of social science–oriented interpretations of black culture as being mostly an accumulated legacy of shame and sorrow is, however, far more implicit than deliberate. It has much more to do with the inevitable, or at least the probable, consequences of the petitions than with any premeditation or calculation, much less any speculation based on specific investigation, documentation, and insight. It may actually even be more incidental than intuitive. But the result is likely to entail a significant shift in academic emphasis nevertheless, and such a shift will not necessarily be less valid or less revolutionary for not having been derived from a more precise intellectual formulation.

But perhaps there would be less confusion if it were. There is, after all, quite a lot to be said for knowing as much as possible about what you are involved in and what it is likely to encompass sooner or later. Certainly the basic intentions of black students are for the most part beyond reproach. Yet it may be that because they are unable to spot the intellectual shortcomings inherent in current social science formulations of crucial issues, they frequently become lost in a maze of terminological nonsense. They also often seem totally unaware of the possibility that at best the academic categories may not only be an inadequate source of information (not to mention wisdom), but at worst, so far as U.S. Negroes are concerned, may be downright vicious in effect, if not by design.

For example, it is hard to say whether psycho-political theoreticians who define what is obviously and quite specifically *political* behavior based on political awareness (developing among U.S. Negroes as a result of the civil rights movement) as if it were the development of black *manhood*, are being vicious or just plain stupid. To mistake new-found *insight* and *technique* for new-found *courage* is to misunderstand the very nature of human motivation. Surely there is a significant difference between cautious hesitation (because you don't know what you're doing) and cowardice (because you jest nat'l born scared).

At any rate, many so-called black militants often seem to be over-responding to white norm/black deviation survey data-oriented conjectures and doubletalk precisely because they are unprepared to identify it as the pseudo-scientific folklore of white supremacy it so frequently is. And by doing so they are likely to be reinforcing the very same condescending and contemptuous white attitudes toward black experience to which they are so vociferously opposed. Perhaps even worse, they encumber themselves with those irrelevant theoretical and sometimes completely phony issues and highly questionable

abstractions such as race pride, black identity, black consciousness, black art, black beauty, and the like, instead of striking
directly at more concrete problems.

*If U.S. Negroes don't already have self-pride and didn't know
black, brown, beige, and freckles, and sometimes even m'riny is
beautiful, why do they always sound so good, so warm, and even
cuss better than everybody else? Why do they dress so jivy and look
so foxy, standing like you better know it in spite of yourself? If
black people haven't always known how beautiful black is, why
have they always been walking, prancing like they'd rather be
dancing, and dancing like everybody else is a wall-flower or
something? If Louis Armstrong doesn't know he has black beauty
to spare how come he can create more beauty while clowning than
them other people can giving all they got? How come a hardboiled
cat like Johnny Hodges got so much tenderness and elegance left
over? And what's Coleman Hawkins doing turning the blues
into such finespun glass, and what were Dizzy Gillespie and
Yardbird Parker doing all them acrobatic curlicue lyrics about?
How come Count Basie and Lionel Hampton think they can
make a hillbilly jump, stomp, and rock—and almost do it? Why
does everybody take it for granted that Duke Ellington can wipe
out anybody anywhere, anytime he wants to?*

*And if black people have such low self-regard, why the hell are
they forever laughing at everybody else? How come as soon as they
get something desegregated so many of them feel so at home that
they subject to try to take it over by sheer bullshit (which they
would never try in an all-black situation)? How come they're
forever talking as if superstars like Willie Mays, Jim Brown,
Oscar Robertson, and even Leontyne Price come a dime a dozen
in the black community? And if they really feel so stupid, how
come a third-rate Harlem hipster is always so certain he got him
a square as soon as he spots an Ivy League white boy in a non-
academic situation?*

Rhetoric of black militancy aside, what Negroes are obviously concerned, resentful, angry, and increasingly violent
about is not too little identity or beauty or pride but too much
exclusion from the power mechanisms and resources of the
nation at large, including the publicity mechanisms which
should acknowledge and advertise black as being beautiful and
as American as blackberry jam. Most Negroes know very well

that their main problem is exclusion from equal protection under the law, exclusion from equal job opportunities, exclusion from adequate housing and public services, and exclusion from the technical training required not for subsistence on a black reservation but for affluence in an automated space age society.

There is good reason to believe that it is precisely because they are all but hopelessly overimpressed by the folklore of white supremacy and the fakelore of black pathology that so many young (and not so young) Negroes are now becoming so ensnarled in ill-digested and conflicting ideologies of blackness, blackmanship, and blackman spokesmanship. And the result is that some are beginning to embrace concepts of black communities, black states, and even black nations, concepts that are not only much closer to the racism of past centuries than to cultural nationalism but that are also based on notions about economics that are so utterly outmoded it would be generous to call them tribal.

Any number of black spokesmen who should know better have become so exhilarated with visions of a black millennium that they seemingly completely forget that secession has been tried and found unfeasible. Save your confederate money boys—the antique rates gonna rise again. White suburbanites are only moving to the outskirts of town, they're not seceding from the stock exchange, or even A&P. Nor do many rhetorical separatists seem to have investigated, or even to have heard anything at all about, life on the Indian reservations. But then neither do many seem to bother themselves in the least about such establishment-oriented nuisances as monetary stability, balance of payments, public utilities, public health facilities, social security, food and drug regulations, not to mention heavy industry, tariff, tax assessment and collection; not even a whisper about automobile tags and drivers licenses. The corporate structure of contemporary life in the United States is just simply not something you can ignore or verbalize out of existence because black is beautiful. But there are those who are talking as if they just might overthrow the whole power structure any day now and begin all over black, though as yet they have not knocked off a single bigoted labor union—just so the establishment will get the message.

When the courses in "black heritage" actually get under way (and the current emphasis on white norm/black deviate folklore is placed in proper perspective) and black students really begin to zero in on black civilizations, black kingdoms and heroes, the chances are that they are also going to find out something else: most revolutions, liberation movements, and slave rebellions, like most attempts at prison breaks, fail—not because each was betrayed by "Uncle Toms" (incidentally, Miss Harriet Beecher Stowe's Uncle Tom was not a traitor to the cause), but mostly because they were inadequately planned and inadequately timed. Attentive students of black history will also find that many of the most celebrated black rulers were able to maintain themselves in power precisely because they knew how to fake would-be rebels out of position, and into a rhetorical bag. In other words, power structures, whether white or black, do not just curl up and die because the rebel cause is impeccable. You'd better believe that many times when they seem to be giving in they are really sucking you in. Some forms of permissiveness are devastating.

The quasi-scientific rhetoric of liberation goes over very big at rallies, nonviolent demonstrations, folk festivals, and on TV, and of course these things are very much a part, and a very useful part, of every contemporary freedom movement. Nevertheless, a man who is actually involved in a prison break can ill afford to risk precious time on purely theoretical barriers when there are so many real and unmistakable ones to overcome. Thus, when black militants at Ivy League colleges begin agitating for separate areas and exclusive courses and facilities, perhaps their parents may be pardoned for questioning whether they are spearheading a drive to freedom or misdefining and hence misdirecting themselves and their efforts back into the warden's stronghold.

Certainly U.S. Negro parents have earned some right to be skeptical about any gesture that suggests separatism, no matter how you rationalize it. Especially when those making it begin by admitting that they do not know very much about what has gone on before. One of the duties of black parents and elders who respect the obligations that *they* inherited from *their* parents is to see to it that nobody comes along and either loud-talks or fancy-talks black people into the worst trap of all: self-constriction, and even self-enslavement, through self-hypnotic verbalism. That's the bag white Southerners have been trying to put black folks in ever since emancipation. The black studies department of the University of Alabama, for example, has had black facilities and black instructors for years—located in Montgomery, 100 comfortable miles away from Tuscaloosa. In other words, people like Miss Autherine Lucy (who is now a parent) have had something to say about separate tables—but who remembers that kind of historical detail? (Yes, and what will the five year olds of today think of dashikis fifteen years from now?)

As for what Africans have been thinking of them all along, here's what Tom Mboya, Kenya's late Minister of Economic Development and Planning, writing in the *New York Times Magazine*, had to say: "[Some black Americans] think that to identify with Africa one should wear a shaggy beard or a piece of cloth on one's head or a cheap garment on one's body. I find here a complete misunderstanding of what African culture really means. An African walks barefoot or wears sandals made of old tires not because it is his culture but because he lives in poverty. We live in mud and wattle huts and buy cheap Hong Kong fabrics not because it is part of our culture, but because these are conditions imposed on us today by poverty and by limitations in technical, educational, and other resources."

II

The lack of intellectual coherence on the part of young people from whose ranks the black intellectuals, technicians, spokesmen, and leaders are expected is cause for some uneasiness and at times even some exasperation but not for alarm. For the very fact that black students are petitioning for courses in history is significant evidence that they feel the need for a larger and more consistent view of things. Historical research is in itself a quest for a basis for consistency, a benchmark for further explorations.

But the atmosphere of crisis that has been generated by the confusion among some of the white Americans who control the "education establishment" *is* cause not only for alarm but for red alert and hot pursuit. For, as with so many of the white people who encourage and subsidize so much bad art among black writers, they either do not know what education is, or they know only too well.

After all, since when did students ever love existing courses of study? Since when were they not on the lookout for snap courses, preferably ungraded ones. Since when didn't they doubt the practical relevance of classroom procedures—particularly when the assignments involve hard work. Haven't students always wondered what the comma splice and quadratic equations have to do with English, Irish, German—or especially American identity? Since when didn't students ridicule teachers as being out of touch with what was really happening in the streets? And since when were students not right at least some of the time? As somebody in Harlem said not long ago, "Hell, even a stopped clock has correct time twice a day." Since when didn't students overstate their case? Why not see how far you can push things? Especially when all you need is a few black enameled clichés because you know the authorities are only going to try to match you with their own, and then give up and call in the police and then feel rotten about it. Why not?

A petition for courses in black heritage is essentially only a request for a more comprehensive approach to the American heritage. There is no reason in the world why an appeal for more comprehensive instruction should be cause for administration hysteria, or why the prospect of new historical dimensions should trigger pandemonium in the community of scholars. Ordinarily, scholars welcome opportunities for new research. Ordinarily, intellectuals would be only too eager to establish new perspectives on some area of the American experience. And needless to say, whatever in the African past is valid for black Americans is of immediate and fundamental significance to other Americans. Cultural values have universal relevance, as witness the benefits Europeans derived through Picasso, Braque, Klee, et al., from African sculpture alone.

It is the responsibility of school administrators and course of study technicians to separate the sense from the nonsense in all requests and proposals no matter what color the source. Curriculum experts who cannot make practical distinctions between vague opportunistic generalities and insightful observations about the basic educational values of newly suggested subject matter have no business formulating course objectives and projecting student outcomes in the first place. When a petition demands, for example, that courses be made more relevant to the black community, school officials must be able to make certain that such courses are no less relevant to computer and space age technology. It is also their responsibility to remind certain petitioners that for people who maintain excellent surveillance of secret nuclear explosions in the remote areas of the Soviet Union and can evaluate the heartbeat of astronauts orbiting the moon, it is a very simple matter indeed to monitor and control black enclaves on the other side of the dining hall, the other side of the campus, or the other side of town. (Certain kinds of privacy are a thing of the past.)

Technical specialization aside, the fundamental objective of American education must be to produce, as it were, fifty-dimensional citizens—people whose open dispositions are compatible with contemporary innovations in communication and transportation and who are therefore able to live in terms of the resources of each one of the fifty United States.

Negro parents, for their part, have every right to expect and even require white instructors to be open minded enough about black students, so that when confronted by one sporting an Afro-natch hair-do (which might really be more Polynesian than African) and/or a dashiki (often of cloth made in Holland for the Dutch East Indies and the African trade), the white instructor will neither condescend to the black student nor cop-out before him, but will check him out (as the lynx-eyed old Dr. W. E. B. Du Bois or the late great Charles Houston, mentor of Justice Marshall, might have done) to determine if he is for real or just shucking on the latest kick. A black or honey-brown student with his head buried in a book by Frantz Fanon, Che Guevara, Malcolm X, or Eldridge Cleaver may be searching for intellectual equipment for modern living, or then again he may only be gathering quotations against the day when at last his call comes to go on David Susskind's vaudeville hour. It is the educator's job to be able to relate current books to many other books.

After all, good instructors had been capitalizing on student interests long before John Dewey put teacher training colleges hep to progressive education or the pupil-centered classroom.

Thus, student requests for courses in black heritage, including African history, should be met because such courses also provide instructors additional opportunities to develop a richer perspective on the world-at-large for all students. But instructors should also be alert and knowledgeable enough to realize that some of the answers that black students in Northern cities are seeking may also be in the history of white immigration. And to know that not a few of the problems of the contemporary South are the direct outgrowth of unresolved issues of the Reconstruction era. In other words, the practical extensions are a matter of imaginative classroom procedure. Dewey never promised that the permissiveness of progressive education would make the instructor's work any easier. He claimed only that it could make learning easier, and more effective. Pupil-interest exploitation instruction is no snap; it is rather an unending challenge to the teacher's ingenuity. And though teaching may employ scientific method, it is not a science. It is an art, a fine art.

III

Some school authorities seem not to understand that continuity through change is precisely what tradition and therefore education (the continuous restructuring of experience) is all about. Instead, they are inclined to view the question of black studies primarily as another instance of generation conflict. But they miss a point that the nation has every right to assume its intellectuals and educators would be the first to understand: Students asking for courses in history, literature, and art may be quite obviously, even if not specifically, at issue with existing academic categories, but they are hardly rejecting their elders, at least not all of them. On the contrary, they are returning to older and even ancient generations for ancestral guidance, that background and point of departure, that equipment for flexible living that the social science–oriented *present* has failed to provide.

In any case, school authorities should be able to see the so-called generation gap for the pop media concoction that it is. In the first place, the notion of a generation gap as now used implies that there are only two generations. But since grandfather and mother are still very much around (indeed, and still running things) that makes three, and baby brother and sister make at least four! Certainly school officials whose daily involvements include the federal government as well as the nursery school cannot proceed as if there were only two generations on the scene at one time. Furthermore, wherever a gap does exist, it is not the older people but the younger ones who must be most concerned with closing it. After all, it is not the youngsters who are engineering the space age but their elders, and they are moving on. The youngsters have to get with it because they are the ones who are going to be stuck with it. When the older man tells the young man in the film *The Graduate* to check into plastics, he really is trying to put him hip to something. You cannot ignore plastics just because black is beautiful and wants to be powerful, and white being powerful is eager to be beautiful. When the older woman seduces the young man, she may well be a witch, of a sexy sort. But she is hardly a square, and she may also be initiating him into the complexity and ambiguity of contemporary actuality. In spite of the soap opera ending of *The Graduate*, present-day young people really do not have the option to go back to the days when Mickey Rooney was good old clean cut Andy Hardy.

Perhaps it would not be a bad idea for a few generation-oriented school authorities to reconsider some of the implications of *Goodbye, Mr. Chips*, the novel or the (old) movie. Mister Chips lived to see too many generations come and go to hang himself up worrying about the gaps between them. Yes, yes. Of course he was somewhat out of touch with the latest slang (and stuff), but he made up for it with charm and by doing his own thing. So he did manage to put students in touch with some of the wisdom of the ages. And he fully understood that young men always have to find their own way by trial and error.

On the other hand, activist instructors whose support for black student struggles goes beyond the old-fashioned white liberal sentimentalism about "helping those poor kids" must realize that it is not enough to say: "Those black militants are trying to tell us something." Instructors should be able to tell students something. Historians can do much to teach young revolutionaries what the dynamics of revolution actually involve.

Competent historians will not permit students to be misled by bombastic platitudes about the masses and "the real people" or the "average" black man, but will point out that the student's own responsibility lies precisely in the fact that he is trying to be better than average, and that revolutions are not really made by angry mobs thrashing about in all directions but by enlightened charismatic leaders, and that rebellions succeed when such leaders are technically proficient enough to select the most vulnerable targets and apply the most practical tactics and weapons. Who else is supposed to clarify such things if not teachers and intellectuals? By the same token, nobody was ever the agent of more black confusion than those white instructors who are always so eager to help black drop-outs, addicts, and criminals, but who (perhaps for some extremely peculiar reason) seem compelled to regard the very students who wish to educate themselves about the world at large as being black people no longer! As if those who presume to speak for black people and certainly those who opt to lead them did not owe it to their followers to know as much as possible about the world in all its ramifications.

As long as black students are allowed to ignore those fundamental intellectual disciplines and those broad sources of information that will enable them to question and evaluate the basic assumptions underlying all of the policies and programs being formulated for black communities (whether by black leaders or others) they are very likely to continue to entangle themselves in conflicting clichés. And as things now stand these clichés are likely to be inseparable from the pseudo-scientific folklore of white supremacy, no matter how revolutionary those using them think themselves to be.

Regardless of intentions and of degrees of urgency, the physical no less than the verbal responses of people who are insufficiently historical in orientation are likely to turn out to be more hysterical and irrelevant than truly purposeful, truly pragmatic, accurate, appropriate, and either immediately or ultimately effective. A gamble or calculated risk, it should be remembered, is a matter not of impulse but of the most comprehensive deliberation possible in the circumstances.

Finally, as for the so-called generation gap, the eternal as well as the most immediate problem underlying the formulation of the aims of education and the establishment of specific courses of study and subject matter credits, whether for nations or tribes, is the problem of continuity: not whether elders can adjust to the changes being wrought by younger people but whether the young people can acquire the information and insight necessary to survival. Indeed not the least among the actualities that all young revolutionaries must come to terms with is the very real possibility that theirs may be that fool-headed generation that might blow the whole shebang, kit and keboodle, and be that terminal generation that, as history shows, all nations and cultures great and small decay into. Anyway, the question of endurance comes before that of surpassing. The old saying that begins, youth must be served, should end, but so alas must the fullness of time.

Epilogue
Situation Normal: All Fouled Up

In the fall of 1966, the editors of Partisan Review *invited a number of writers, including the author, to participate in a symposium called "What's Happening to America."* SNAFU *was accepted, processed as far as the corrected galley proofs, and was then not printed for lack of space. Since the author never got around to pasting it up as a piece of Harlem storefront graffiti (and couldn't in any case decide which storefront had the greatest* Partisan Review *readership), it is printed here as an epilogue which picks up a number of themes in this book and as a not quite outdated uptown memo which includes something more than the usual platitudes about conditions inside the Eight Ball.*

There never was a time when the United States was not deeply ensnarled in a moral and political crisis. Warren G. Harding felt that the nation did not need heroics but healing during his administration: "not nostrums but normalcy; not revolution but restoration; not surgery but serenity." But Harding's understanding of the essential nature of U.S. life was easily as questionable as his vocabulary—or perhaps he was an ex-radical suffering battle fatigue. At any rate, there was no "normalcy" before the Revolutionary War, and what with the War of 1812, the question of slavery, and westward expansion, there was none before the Civil War. Unsettled Reconstruction problems have only increased in complexity, and the normal state of the nation since the Spanish-American War has been that of one critical situation overlapping another. Thousands have escaped oppression and extermination elsewhere and found relative security here, but many basic constitutional issues have never been settled. Crucial constitutional amendments have yet to be forcefully applied. Nevertheless, the specific questions about which *PR* expresses anxiety are urgent and require comment.

1. Presidential elections seem as valid as ever. Whether Elijah Muhammad, Norman Mailer, George-Lurleen Wallace, William

Buckley Jr., or Martin Luther King is in the White House makes all the difference in the world. JFK was a man of much broader scope and nobler sentiment than most people expected, but only after the assassination did the landslide majority begin to like him like Ike. The system didn't force Ike to do very much and couldn't force JFK to do more than Congress allowed. As for LBJ and the quest for consensus, he is accused on all sides: of going too far in Vietnam, too fast on civil rights; of being too good at compromise, and too arrogant in his use of power.

2. The problem of inflation is very serious indeed, and, so far as one can tell, probably grows out of seemingly irreconcilable conflicts between agricultural interests and those of labor and industry. There is also the role that advertising now plays in production, not to mention the coming of automation. But the intellectual, whether literary or all-purpose, seldom knows any more about inflation than about foreign policy, military strategy, fall-out, air pollution or water fluoridation. Such things concern him, to be sure, and he is bound to have personal opinions about them. His picket slogans, however, should be consistent with the limitations of his information.

3. Not everyone agrees that there is a split between the administration and U.S. intellectuals. Nor is there general concurrence as to who is and who is not an intellectual. Perhaps as good a guideline as any is a remark by the narrator of *The Walnut Trees of Altenburg*. "I know now," he says, "that an intellectual is not only a man to whom books are necessary, he is also any man whose reasoning, however elementary it may be, affects and directs his life." Definitive or not, it is a viable conception, and it is also comprehensive enough to include McGeorge Bundy, Nicholas Katzenbach, Maxwell Taylor, and John K. Jessup, as well as George F. Kennan, Hans Morgenthau, and Irving Howe. Moreover, it excludes those who, for all their involvement with books and ideas, are essentially sentimental, and among these of course, there are liberals and radicals along with conservatives and reactionaries.

A split between any U.S. administration and some liberals and most radicals is not only predictable, it is healthy. Much of the current dissent, however, seems to be degenerating into petulance. This is self-defeating, for as criticism becomes more hostile than reasonable, the administration is only likely to harden itself against it—or ignore it.

4. Most white Americans are obviously and often all too unconsciously committed to White Anglo-Saxon Protestant supremacy. The narcissism implied by such widely used terms as *non-white* and *assimilation* (not to be confused with desegregation or integration) is as unmistakable as it is casual. The findings and categories of social science are as irrelevant to the civil rights of native-born U.S. Negroes as to those of ignorant hillbillies and newly arrived immigrants. But somehow most white Americans seem to feel that white-oriented statistical surveys indicate whether or not Negroes are eligible for things that the Constitution already guarantees. The Department of Labor, for instance, issues the highly questionable Moynihan Report which explains the problem of Negro status in terms of the abnormal structure of Negro family life at a time when Negroes themselves are conducting nationwide demonstrations and riots against *segregation* in education and housing, *discrimination* in employment, and police *racism*!

On principle, white liberals and radicals give or "grant" sympathetic assistance to the civil rights movement, to be sure; but few Negroes are convinced that this indicates a comprehensive commitment to equality or even represents a truly intimate intellectual involvement with the fundamental issues of citizenship in an open, pluralistic society. Indeed the most serious as well as the most universal Negro indictment against the so-called liberal and radical writers is that at bottom they are as white-oriented as the mass media journalists. Even some U.S. Jewish intellectuals seem to regard Wasps as the chosen people. It is not at all unusual for second generation Jewish writers to refer to native-born multi-generation U.S. Negroes (most of whom it so happens, are part-white) as a non-white, *unassimilable* minority. Unassimilable with whom? Is Norman Podhoretz more assimilated than Count Basie?

What U.S. Negroes themselves want, it should be easy enough to see, is their share of the material benefits of U.S. life—*and they intend to upset enough smugness to get it.* For the rest, they are far more ambivalent about the so-called white world than white people seem able to realize. Nor is this simply a matter of sociopolitical action. What Louis Armstrong has been doing to popular songs all these years is an infinitely more accurate index to fundamental U.S. Negro attitudes towards "white culture" than are some of the embarrassingly superficial and contradictory gestures of alienation currently so popular among some black nationalists and "Afro-Zionists."

5. Perhaps current foreign policies will enable the U.S. to muddle through as Britain used to do, and perhaps not. Meanwhile the drift and confusion seem likely to continue not so much because the administration is so obstinate but because no one has come forth with any truly compelling and practicable alternatives. Few people are more obviously opposed to current policies than Senator William Fulbright, for instance, who not only has expressed solemn doubts and made pointed insinuations but has also conducted televised Senate hearings to air the nation's motives and has certainly been receptive to ideas critical of the present course of affairs. Neither the administration, Congress, nor the public, however, seem convinced that there is a workable Fulbright Alternative. Former Ambassador George F. Kennan suggests that the nation can disengage itself from some of its foreign involvements, and even allow some of its "allies" to go communist, without doing any serious damage to its power or moral prestige; and there is every evidence that he is as competent and responsible as he is bold. But Kennan's general guidelines for deescalation in Vietnam are not geared to evacuation but to defense perimeters. And there is no Kennan Alternative either.

Those who suggest that U.S. foreign policy is becoming an adjunct to military power seem to imply that military power exists as an end in itself. It does not. It is an instrument of national interest. And as materialistic as national interests always are, those of the U.S. are largely modified by moral considerations. Indeed, administration involvement with the moral clichés of internationalism (derived from liberal and radical ideas of the nineteen thirties) is probably as great a source of current confusion as anything else. At any rate, the nation's moral stance is not necessarily hypocritical simply because the President must always be less than candid about American material interest in "good" and "bad" wars alike.

6. At the present time not even the most open of institutions adequately represent the magnificent diversity that U.S. communication and transportation facilities make accessible to the average citizen. It is entirely possible, however, for artists and intellectuals to synthesize images and concepts that will be revolutionary enough to destroy existing restrictions (which are often mistaken for sophistication). When that happens U.S. education will fulfill its unique potential and produce The Truly Representative Contemporary Man. Perhaps every serious writer proceeds on the assumption that a sufficiently vernacular and revolutionary image can be created to initiate a millennium during his generation.

7. The impression of young people that one gets from the mass media is not at all promising, but mass media reports are not geared to accuracy or responsibility but to sensationalism. Perhaps some young people are as frivolous as ads encourage them to be; but most, as ever, are no doubt primarily concerned with growing up. Far too many college students now seem to substitute social science methodology for the discipline of the humanities, but most young Americans show very fine prospects nonetheless, and the current crisis is probably good for them. The civil rights movement, for instance, reveals thousands of young U.S. Negroes (to whom fouled-up situations have always been normal) who display an open disposition to new ideas and experiences and a sense of responsible adventure which if not yet properly celebrated is already being emulated.

SOUTH TO
A VERY OLD PLACE

For my wife
MOZELLE
who, honeysuckle-fairytale downhome girl
that she is, was, as the old folks used to say,
born knowing

(Stoop) if you are abcedminded, to this claybook, what curios of signs (please stoop), in this allaphbed! Can you rede (since We and Thou had it out already) its world? It is the same told of all. Many. Miscegenations upon miscegenations.

JAMES JOYCE
Finnegans Wake

But lo, the world hath many centres, one for each created being, and about each one it lieth in its own circle. Thou standest but an ell from me, yet about thee lieth a universe whose centre I am not but thou art. . . . And I, on the other hand, stand in the centre of mine. For our universes are not far from each other so that they do not touch; rather hath God pushed them and interwoven them deep into each other, so that you . . . do indeed journey quite independently and according to your own ends, whither you will, but besides that you are the means and tool, in our interwovenness, that I arrive at my goal.

THOMAS MANN
Joseph in Egypt

The true ancestral line is not necessarily a straight or continuous one.

W. H. AUDEN
Journal of an Airman

Not everything in this book is meant to be taken literally. Some names have been changed, some not.

CONTENTS

New York

TALL TALE BLUE OVER MOBILE BAY IN HARLEM

Y OU CAN TAKE the "A" train uptown from Forty-second Street in midtown Manhattan and be there in less than ten minutes. There is a stop at Fifty-ninth Street beneath the traffic circle which commemorates Christopher Columbus who once set out for destinations east on compass bearings west. But after that as often as not there are only six more express minutes to go. Then you are pulling into the IND station at 125th Street and St. Nicholas Avenue, and you are that many more miles north from Mobile, Alabama, but you are also, for better or worse, back among homefolks no matter what part of the old country you come from.

But then, going back home has probably always had as much if not more to do with people as with landmarks and place names and locations on maps and mileage charts anyway. Not that home is not a place, for even in its most abstract implications it is precisely the very oldest place in the world. But even so, it is somewhere you are likely to find yourself remembering your way back to far more often than it is ever possible to go by conventional transportation. In any case, such is the fundamental interrelationship of recollection and make-believe with all journeys and locations that anywhere people do certain things in a certain way can be home. The way certain very special uptown Manhattan people talk and the way some of them walk, for instance, makes them homefolks. So whoever says you can't go home again, when you are for so many intents and purposes back whenever or wherever somebody or something makes you feel that way.

There is also the "D" train which you can take from Forty-second Street over on Sixth Avenue, because that way you still come into the "A" train route at Columbus Circle. Or you can take Number Two or Number Three on the IRT, and the uptown Avenue will be Lenox, and if you get off at 125th Street you walk west to the old Theresa Hotel corner at Seventh, the Apollo near Eighth, and Frank's Chop House, on over toward

St. Nicholas. At the 135th Street IRT stop you come out at the northwest corner of Lenox Terrace, and you are also at the new Harlem Hospital. From there, which is only a few steps from the AME Church that used to be the old Lincoln Theatre, you walk east to Riverton, Lincoln, and the water. But for the Schomburg Library, the YMCA poolroom, and Smalls Paradise, you walk west toward the hill and CCNY.

Sometimes, of course, all you need to do is hear pianos and trumpets and trombones talking, in any part of town or anywhere else for that matter. Or sometimes it will be pianos and saxophones talking and bass fiddles walking; and you are all the way back even before you have time to realize how far away you are supposed to have gone, even before you become aware of even the slightest impulse to remember how much of it you thought perhaps you had long since forgotten.

Sometimes it can be downhome church organs secularized to Kansas City four-four in a neighborhood cocktail lounge. It can be a Count Basie sonata suggesting blue steel locomotives on northbound railroad tracks (as "Dogging Around" did that summer after college). It can be any number of ensemble riffs and solo licks that also go with barbershops and shoeshine parlors; with cigar smoke and the smell and taste of seal-fresh whiskey; with baseball scores and barbecue pits and beer-seasoned chicken-shack tables; with skillets of sizzling mullets or bream or golden crisp oysters plus grits and butter; and with such white potato salads and such sweet potato pies as only downhome folks remember from picnics and association time camp meetings. Or it can even be a stage show at the Apollo Theatre which sometimes rocks like a church during revival time. It can be the jukebox evangelism of some third-rate but fad-successful soul singer (so-called) that carries you back not only to Alabama boyhood Sundays with sermons followed by dasher-turned ice cream, but also to off-campus hillside roadside beer joints and Alabama pine-needle breezes.

So naturally it can also be Lenox Avenue storefront churches, whether somewhat sedate or downright sanctified. Or it can be the big league uptown temples along and off Seventh Avenue: such as, say, Big Bethel, Mother Zion, Metropolitan, Abyssinian Baptist, where on the good days Adam Clayton Powell, for all his northern-boy upbringing, sounds like Buddy Bolden calling his flock.

None of which is to suggest—not even for one sentimental flicker of an instant—that being back is always the same as being where you wish to be. For such is the definitive nature of all homes, hometowns, and hometown people that even the most joyous of homecoming festivities are always interwoven with a return to that very old sometimes almost forgotten but ever so easily alerted trouble spot deep inside your innermost being, whoever you are and wherever you are back from.

For where else if not the old home place, despite all its prototypical comforts, is the original of all haunted houses and abodes of the booger man? Indeed, was even the cradle only a goochie-goochie cove of good-fairy cobwebs entirely devoid of hobgoblin shadows; or was it not also the primordial place of boo-boo badness and doo-doo-in-diapers as well?

Once back you are among the very oldest of good old best of all good friends, to be sure, but are you not also just as likely to be once again back in the very midst of some snarled-up situation from which you have always wanted to be long gone forever?

And where else did you ever in all your born days encounter so much arrogant ignorance coupled with such derisive mockery and hey-you who-you crosstalk? Where else except in this or that Harlem are you almost always in danger of getting kicked out of a liquor store for instance for browsing too casually in the wine section. Where else except among homefolks is that sort of thing most likely to tab you not as an expense-account gourmet-come-lately but a degenerate wino? Or something worse.

But still and all and still in all and still withal if there are (as no doubt there have always been) some parts of Harlem where even such thugs and footpads as inhabited the London of Charles Dickens would probably find themselves more often mooched and mugged than mooching and mugging so are there at least one thousand plus one other parts and parcels also. Not to mention such browngirl eyes as somehow can always make even the smoggiest New York City skies seem tall tale blue over Mobile Bay.

Naturally there are those who not only allege but actually insist that there can only be ghetto skies and pathological eyes in Harlem and for whom blues tales are never tall but only lowdown dirty and shameful. But no better for them. They don't know what they're missing. Or don't they? For oh how their pale toes itch to twinkle as much to the steel blue percussion as to all the good-time moans and the finger-snapping grunts and groans in Billy Strayhorn's ellington-conjugated nostalgia.

New Haven

DEPOSITION FOR TWO AT YALE

*Y*OU CAN ALSO GO *south from midtown Manhattan by taking another northbound train from Forty-second Street: one going up beneath and then above Park Avenue. Take the Yankee Clipper, for instance, or the Merchants Limited, or the Bay State Special. But this time you keep on past 125th Street. This time you roll on across the Harlem River and continue on through the Bronx and that part of suburbia to Connecticut. Then one hour and maybe fifteen, maybe twenty, maybe thirty or thirty-five minutes later you are that many more statute miles further north from Mobile than Lenox Terrace, but you are also pulling into New Haven, where Yale has some very special downhome dimensions indeed these days. Nor are all of them derived from Yankee-shrewd concessions to militant civil rights rhetoric. There is Robert Penn Warren and there is C. Vann Woodward.*

Because yes as seldom as such things are ever mentioned with longing, whing ding-doodle banjos and twang-nosed-talking—Jim-Crow-walking guitars and barnyard saw-fiddle music or any hints thereof even on a TV soundtrack can also take you back as rapidly as anything else. Even from Lenox Terrace. Because, after all, like it or not, or concede it or not, long before it became your boy-blue stamping ground the old country had already been old man whicker-bill's buckskin camping ground, back when it was still Indian territory.

So, what with somebody forever forgetting to turn the radio off, you are carried back almost as often by such ragtime rooty-toot trumpets as used to talk confederate bugle talk above the two-beat razzmatazz of knock-down drag-out Saturday night roadhouses and moss-point casinos back when the best bootleg whiskey came from the sheriff's private stock. Yes there are also Harlem airshaft reverberations of all that too. So also such slow-dragging circus-tiger vibrato trombones as not only used to but still do tailgate such magnolia sundown sadness as is fit to test the patience of even the most gracious-seeming evil-tempered cooks and waiters

201

and bellboys who ever shucked, stuffed, and took care of business on
any steamboat or in any steamboat-gothic hotel—who could and still
do endure it but not without badmouthing it to hell in the process:
"Man ain't no goddam wonder so many of them people don't like
nobody. Hump-the-goddam-hump dancing like that some of these
sommiches bound to start whooping and hollering for somebody's
blood and balls. Man, that music ain't getting nothing together."

Anyway all of that is also part and parcel of something else to
which you are always returning without even going as far back
south from Lenox Terrace as 110th Street: that interior benchmark
site where things are still very much the same as they once were
when you used to squint one of your whicker-bill-mocking eyes
and stiffen the weather-beaten whicker-billness of your neck not
only as if it were red-devil tootletoddle red but also as if it were
wrinkled and stringy from too much tobacco chewing and so
much white shirt-and-collar-and-tie wearing; standing with one
foot forward and your whicker-bill elbows stuck out skinny, holding your back and shoulders as if you were just about to break
into old man whicker-bill Charley Comesaw's bony butt, high in-
step strut as soon as the billygoat fiddles started sawing—that
crackerjack gesture, however, being the whole joke, because as far
as you were concerned just about the only white man who really
knew how to strut his stuff walking back in those days was not
anybody anywhere in and around or even near Mobile, Alabama.
It was a western cowboy. It was the one and only Tom Mix walking neither pasty-faced nor red-necked but bowlegged; and then
standing not like a flat-assed cracker deputy but hip-cocked and
pointy-toed, with his thumbs hooked into his low-riding two-gun
cartridge belt, his silk neckerchief knotted to one side, the angle of
his ten-gallon western cowboy hat as sporty as a flashy-fingered
piano player's gambling-hall fedora.

Nor did many things ever strike you as being more laughable
than coming back down into the Saturday afternoon daylight of
the Prichard, Alabama, main street from the fabulous peanut-
gallery darkness of King's Palace Theatre and seeing Prichard,
Alabama, white boys trying to act like Tom Mix (or Buck Jones
or Fred Thomson or Ken Maynard)—and only looking more like
whicker-bill peckerwoods than ever. How could Prichard, Alabama, peckerwoods ever know what Tom Mix was all about?

All the same, all of them and all of that and more are no less

warp and woof of what home on the outskirts of Mobile, Alabama, was also very much about. Which specifically includes all
that which somebody who could easily have been one of your up-
north uncles or cousins Remus was talking about when he said to
Quentin Compson: "You're right, they're fine folks. But you can't
live with them"; which no doubt was the same situation on which
some of the old heads by the fireside were musing when they used to
come to the end of some story about somebody being in trouble,
and mutter: "You got to know how to handle them; you got to
outthink them, you got to stay one jump ahead of them"; but
which so far as any number of others, old and young, yourself included, were concerned was a very good reason to un-ass the area.
Not simply in flight, escape and hence abdication, however, but
also in exploration, quest, and even conquest.

    One snatch of either whingding or rooty-toot and even as you
sit looking at the midtown Manhattan skyline from 132nd Street,
looking south as you once did from the northward outskirts of
Mobile, you are also back in the old spyglass place seeing all of
them and that once more. But in better perspective, in proper
complexity and with proper awareness of the ambiguity and ultimate obscurity of not just black and white motives down home but
of all human motivation everywhere. Because after all that instantaneous, popeyed, no-matter-how-fleeting-expression of drawing-
room outrage you register at the impropriety of all that old
narrow-nosed, shaggyheaded blue-eyed talk when you hear it
outside the South is perhaps as much an expression of kinship as of
aginship whether you can admit it or not. Because if one part of
your reaction is supercilious another is quite obviously interwoven
with nothing so much as having to witness homefolks cutting a
"country hog" in town, among strangers. Interwoven with something else also: a grudging admiration in spite of yourself because
suddenly you also have to realize that if such talk did cut a hog,
the scandal was either intentional or was likely to become defiantly so as soon as there was any hint that the hog cutting was
being noted.

    So, with however much ambivalence, yes them too: and besides
sometimes what they represent as much as anything else is an old
familiar difference and even a similar otherness, which is sometimes, especially in situations outside the South, even familiar
when other: "Man goddamn where the hell these white folks come

*from? Man, these some of your goddamn white folks? Man, who
the goddamn hell white folks these?"*

*And no less for all the trouble so many of them represent either.
Because wherever and whenever downhome tales tall or otherwise
are told, some of the very best are always about all of that too, and
there is as much bragging about the extent and intensity of the
obstacles, the conflicts, and the showdowns as about anything else,
probably more (certainly more than either propriety or hipness
will permit about any poon-tang conquest, for instance): "Man,
you ain't seen no bad-assed crackers like them bad-assed crackers
we had down my way. Man, I'm talking about some mean and
gentlemen I mean some sure enough mean-ass peckerwoods. I'm
talking about some hoojers so goddamn mean and evil they
breathe like rattlesnakes. Man, hell, what you talking about is
just some old pore-assed white-assed damn trash. I'm talking
about some bad-assed peckerwoods, and you better believe it. You
ain't never in your born days seen no bad-assed crackers like them
bad-assed crackers we had where I come from. You know them
crackers around Bay Minette, Alabama, and on down toward
Flomaton and into that old pineywoods country down in North
Florida; you know how bad them dried-up-assed rosum-chewing
squint-eyed crackers looking like they always sighting down a gun
barrel at you, used to be out around Leakesville, Missippi, and all
out through in there? Sheeeet, man, them old crackers ain't nothing to these old goddamn crackers I'm talking about!"*

*Yes alas and alas, the also and also of all them and that all of
that, plus much more; and furthermore "what clashes here of wills
gen wonts," which is to say shaggyheads versus woollyheads much
the same, alas, as if they were still "oystrygods gagging fishygods"
has never been any less familiar than all the rest and best of it.*

———

The one that Robert Penn Warren looks and walks and talks
like is not old man Whicker-Bill Comesaw, but Red Scarbor-
ough in the old Texaco filling station out on old Telegraph
Road. As for C. Vann Woodward, whing-ding fiddle talk and
Jim-Crow walk or not, he is the spitting image of the old Life
and Casualty Insurance man (or maybe it was Tennessee Life and
Casualty or the Industrial Benefit man), whose Willys-Knight

you used to snag as if it were a gas-driven L&N switch engine. Anyway, anytime anybody from downhome sees you with either one of them and cocks an ear, popping or cutting his eyes (mostly without changing expression) and waits for you to answer whose is this one and what kind and whose that one, you can say: Filling Station Red. But from Kentucky this time, remembering the smell of the Texaco gas pumps and the inner-tube patching, remembering the free air hose and the old wooden grease rack with the galvanized oil tub, and also remembering the football games on the Atwater Kent radio.

Or in the case of Woodward you can say: Tennessee Life; but from somewhere out in Arkansas this time, remembering how easy it used to be to hobo on dirt-road switch engines, what with spare tires on the back like life preservers—and how easy it was also because he mostly pretended not to see you, and if nobody in the neighborhood spotted you he wouldn't say what he always said until he was ready to pick up speed because he was coming to where the macadam began. And of course you also remember how much fun it also was mocking him in your best whicker-bill twang-nosed throat-locked soda-cracker voice as he pulled on away and out of earshot, you and whoever was with you that particular day saying not, "All right now y'all scat off there now" but: "Say now by Gyard, git the hell and skedaddle offen that durn tyar dang bust you little possums. Dang bust you little possums. Dang bust you little possums. Dang bust you little possums." Which was really what old man Lee G. Heatherton from the grocery store always used to say when you snagged the back of the delivery wagon.

You can say that's all right about whing-ding guitars and Jim-Crow fiddles this time because this one turned out to be the kind who at a time when most students of life in the United States seem to think that cultural assimilation should be measured in terms of Reading Test scores, can say: "The ironic thing about these two great hyphenate minorities, the Southern Americans and the Negro Americans, confronting each other on their native soil for three and a half centuries, is the degree to which they have shaped each other's destiny, determined each other's isolation, shared and molded a common culture. It is in fact impossible to imagine the one without the

other and quite futile"—he might, for the benefit of not a
few social-science–oriented New York intellectuals, have said
"perverse"—"to try"; who in the very same article has written
in part: "Two thirds of all the Negroes now living in the North
and West were born and raised in the South. They constitute a
tremendous Southern impact on the North. Within a few years
many of our largest non-Southern cities will be predominantly
Negro in population. The North in fact is confronted with a
Southern invasion vaster by far than the one General Lee threatened. Under the skin the new invaders are Southern too, even
to the second and third generation of them . . . if they can
preserve their Southern heritage of endurance, courage and
grace under pressure, their country will be better for it. . . ."

You can say: It is C. Vann Woodward, not Beard, Morison,
Commager, Nevins, nor even Aptheker and certainly not
Genovese (nor, alas, John Hope Franklin either, though he has
other glories) who so far as I know has made a special point of
saying and reiterating: "I am prepared to maintain . . . that
so far as culture is concerned, all Americans are part-Negro.
Some are more so than others, of course, but the essential
qualification is not color or race." Not to mention also making
a point to add: "When I say all Americans, unlike Crèvecœur,
I include Afro-Americans. THEY ARE PART NEGRO, BUT
ONLY PART." Nor is the "only" a slur on the African part—
nor is he likely to hold much brief for those who suggest that
the white part of the so-called half-breed and mulatto is the
part that spoils things. No, the point he makes is that "Negroes
are not white people disguised beneath dark skins and Cauca-
sians are not black people beneath white skins. . . ."

Not that there aren't other Woodward formulations that you
find somewhat, well, questionable: For instance, in the very
same magazine article in which he defines downhome Negroes
as quintessentially Southern he suddenly gets going on the
so-called Negro Middle Class and turns into a social-welfare
polemicist right before your scandalized eyes. Saying such completely un-Southern things as, "While the small, mobile, trained
middle class has been moving up, the great mass of Negro
workers has been stagnating or, relative to white workers, losing
ground." Jolly good Big Daddy Moynihan nonviolent war on
poverty jive. But would C. Vann Woodward the historian draw

the same comprehensive inference from a statement to the effect that the great mass of American colonists were not moving up at a rate equal to that of the small mobile trained class that included Thomas Jefferson, George Washington, and James Madison? Isn't that small trained elite precisely the class that keeps the historians in business? Or is Woodward going to give up biography at its age-old literary best for statistics at its politically opportunistic worst? You doubt it. As well you should, for was it not Woodward himself who called upon the historian to abandon false analogies with the natural sciences?

Nor do you feel that fellow Southerner Woodward, as highly as you mostly recommend him, has given proper attention to the question of Negroes and Immigrants. Not that he has ignored the subject. He has some significant things to say about Immigration as such. But when he describes U.S. Negroes as "unneeded and unwanted" he is, to your exasperation, being as soft on the implications of white European immigration as any white supremacist you ever saw in your life. And besides, you have every reason to believe that Woodward, the very embodiment of Southern memory, knows that the Civil War was fought precisely because Negroes were the most wanted laborers in the history of Western civilization, and that he also knows therefore that just as Africans had been trained and conditioned to plantation work they no doubt would have been retrained also to fulfill the requirements of late nineteenth- and early twentieth-century industrialization, but for the influx of white immigrants on preferential quotas. What the hell was Booker T. Washington so concerned about in that Atlanta Compromise speech if not what the immigration of hungry white Europeans would do to the black freedmen? What if not white European immigrant labor was he talking to white Americans about when he not only advised but implored them to "Let down your bucket where you are"?

When Woodward permits himself to say that Negroes were unneeded and unwanted he is, to put it mildly, indulging in polemical abstraction. On the other hand, to point out that white Europeans were permitted to come over here and take jobs which in any other country would have gone first to native-born citizens is to state a historical fact of crucial significance to the present state of the nation's health.

For all that, however, it is C. Vann Woodward (the old life-insurance collector who used to stand in the front yard with one Stacy Adamsed foot propped on the second step scribbling in the policy book) you think about as often as any other historian when you think about new perspectives for American experience. For not only was it the old neatly dressed soft-voiced and not unkindly policyman from Emory in Atlanta, not some Ivy League liberal, who places the Reconstruction sell-out in the context of a national racism geared to imperialism, it is this same downhome white fellow who wrote: "National myths, American myths have proved far more sacrosanct and inviolate than Southern myths. Millions of European immigrants of diverse cultural backgrounds have sought and found identity in them. . . . European ethnic groups with traditions far more ancient and distinctive than those of the South have eagerly divested themselves of their cultural heritage in order to conform."

It was also this same downhome-raised historian who, with a discernment conspicuously missing in even the best northern historians and reporters, wrote: "The separatists and nationalists have had their native American leaders. But I am more impressed with the association of extremist doctrines of separatism with Caribbean and West Indian leaders and origins going back to Edward W. Blyden of St. Thomas, who swept the South in the nineties, and other worthies including Marcus Garvey of Jamaica and all their mystique of just how black you had to be to be a Negro." On the other hand most northern reporters seem to cling to the old assumption that all Negroes are the same—or should be.

One specific reason for coming to Yale this time is to get his downhome reaction to all of the up-north cocktail-party glibness about the alleged historical differences and natural antagonisms between the descendants of the so-called field Negroes and house Negroes. Because a few misguided TV outspokesmen and consequently a number of white northern journalists are by way of propagating another one of those Elkins type theories of black experience that, to paraphrase Woodward himself, almost make you "despair of history as a path to wisdom."

You have come to this veritable citadel of Yankeedom to see if it is possible to share with him and with Robert Penn Warren something which both he and Robert Penn Warren have claimed as an essential part of the heritage of all post-Confederate downhome folks, "black and white": that "*instinctive fear—that the massiveness of experience, the concreteness of life will be violated: the fear of abstraction.*"

So you sit there in his Sterling Library office looking at him looking almost exactly like the old life and casualty man of your Mobile, Alabama, boyhood, looking precisely as if while you were growing up to go to Mobile County Training School and Tuskegee and so on, he had collected enough policy money to go on off to Emory in Atlanta and then to Columbia and Oxford. This time your response to the whicker-bill otherness of his Arkansas bearing and manner is to remember a scene between Joanna Burden and Joe Christmas in *Light in August*, a scene you have been playing your own changes on ever since you first read it and discussed it with Jug Hamilton at Tuskegee thirty years ago: *Kneel*, you look at him thinking, *I don't ask it. Kneel. Not to me. Not to God. Not to me for forgiveness. Not before God in repentance, which is what Miss Joanna, the liberal do-gooder, who was pregnant, wanted. Not for your grandfathers and the plantations. Not for your father's generation and the Klan. To the facts of life. It is not me that asks it. Remember that. All I ask is that you respect the massiveness of experience, the concreteness of Southern life. All I ask is that you remember what you really know, not what some goddam Yankee polemicist expects all crackers to feel. Man, just consider this: Even old Ulrich B. Phillips (whom shit on) comes closer to the texture of life in bondage as described by my grandparents and yours too than all that Sambo Elkins jive you once gave such a generous blurb to.*

And his response to your question about slave categories is the one you had every reason to expect from a man who has no excuse for not knowing exactly where the old plantations were, where the big houses (some of which were not very big at all) were, where the slave quarters (which were far from always being compounds) were; a man who didn't have to go to Emory and certainly not to Columbia and Oxford to find out who worked precisely where and for how many hours a day and what the daily menu as well as the inventory of the commissary was; a man who like William Faulkner not only knows who owned whose grandparents but also, as little as it is mentioned outside Faulkner, whose blood brothers and sisters and cousins are whose.

"I remember *some* of them from my childhood," he says as unhurriedly as a cracker-barrel stick whittler, "and as you know this goes back some sixty years, when there were quite a few still around." He pauses, whittling. Then: "Yes, my father had dealings with them. We never thought of them like that." Then whittles his metaphorical stick on into an account of the House Slave/Field Slave Dialectic as it is currently being expounded, "by one of my colleagues, a Negro, here at Yale," treating each detail as if it had the challenging insightfulness of Max Weber or Thorstein Veblen. Then he whittles (or cleans and stuffs his metaphorical pipe some more) and adds: "He is quite taken with it. But I have serious doubts about its validity."

It is not a very long visit. There is not really enough stick-whittling time to get into some of the other questions you had in mind, questions, for instance, about whether slaveowners regarded the word "Negro" as being more opprobrious than the word "black," a word whose overwhelming connotations of the negative even the terrifying (the unknown, the mysterious, and death itself—being, incidentally, a universal color of mourning) are by no means limited to references to African-derived Americans. After all, what is largely at issue in the current Afro-Negro-Black controversy over what African-derived Americans should now be called is the white master's usage. As for yourself, you grew up under the impression that white people felt that "Negro" (but not "negress," which is another story like "jewess") was not only a far more respectable term than "black," which always smacked of cargoes, but was actually too dignified to be pronounced correctly—or to be capitalized. It took years of civil-rights protest to get certain national publications to capitalize the word Negro.

Meanwhile, every comment he has made on what you do have time to talk about will stand up very well indeed in all of the best barbershops you have ever known. *So him too. Because if somebody who may be a brownskin Yale student, a brownskin Yale professor, or even a brownskin Yale waiter happens to see you standing there shaking hands and hears the barnyard fiddles in his voice, and just by looking once and a half asks if he is a pretty good one: "Whose is this one? who's vouching this time?" you can smile back nodding without nodding with your eyes saying yes, one of mine, so to speak, me. Yes, better than pretty good, one of the very best around and getting better all the time—and without anybody really checking on him yet. But don't take my word. Check him out for yourself. Read what he writes. Nor is it necessary to begin with* The Strange Career of Jim Crow. *Either* Tom Watson, Agrarian Rebel, The Origins of the New South *or* The Burden of Southern History *will do just fine.*

You sit in Silliman College, Yale, chatting with Robert Penn Warren, poet, novelist, critic, and coauthor of first-rate textbooks for American College English. But what you keep thinking about is the old Telegraph Road which runs (or rather as you remember it used to run) north out of Mobile from St. Joseph Street crossing the Three Mile Creek turn bridge by a cluster of booms, sawmills, and planer mills and going upgrade by Joe Kentz's store past Greer's Hill to Plateau; then crossing the old Magazine Point streetcar line by the Red Brick Drugstore and the white folks' baseball diamond; going to Chickasaw and the shipyards. Because every time you see Robert Penn Warren, whom you have encountered casually and cordially over the past several years and whose nickname is in fact Red as it damn well should be, you remember somebody else named Red: Telegraph Road Red.

So you think: Telegraph Red. Filling Station Red. But not the one who went on to maybe Alabama Poly or Alabama Crimson Tide and maybe the Rose Bowl and afterwards on to cowboy pictures—or maybe came back with his big crimson "A" sweater with the triple sleeve stripes and had his own superservice station and then a chain of them and then became maybe sheriff or maybe commissioner of something. The spitting image yes; but a book-reading Filling Station Red from Guthrie, Kentucky, who went on to Vanderbilt and California and Yale and the Oxford of Rhodes Scholars; a book-reading, book-writing Telegraph Red, some of whose best stories create an atmosphere which almost always goes with memories of pale-face dinner-jacket saxophones and whiskey ruddy trombones tailgating stars falling on downtown

Mobile, Alabama, department stores, stars trailing an aroma of peanut and popcorn vendors and five-and-dime perfume counters and sporting-goods leather; twilight neon stars hovering above Mobile, Alabama, Coca-Cola fountains (for white people only), especially people whose friends and associates may have been Jerry Calhoun and Sue Murdock and some of the Boss's entourage in All the King's Men. *But perhaps most of all the rainbow of stars falling around Slim Sarrett browsing in Hammel's book corner with a Clark Gable foreign correspondent's raincoat over his shoulders, and naturally these are the same ones above the Mobile Press Register Building, where inky-fingered Jack Burden sits sipping sour mash and typing after-hours poetry.*

Of course you don't say meanwhile it was really old then cherub plump Louis Armstrong who could really make stars fall like confetti—not in the ballroom of the Battle House of those days to be sure but in Gomez Auditorium out on Davis Avenue. You don't say only old Louie could really make all rivers lazy and make it cozy and cuddly time Down South all over the world. Nor do you say meanwhile we had not only taken over as our very own old Hoagy Carmichael's ever so ofay "Stardust" but had also made it the brownskin dress-parade anthem that went with midnight tinsel much the same as the sound of James Weldon and J. Rosamond Johnson's "Lift Every Voice" used to go with the sepia-tinted pictures of Negro Builders and Heroes on the wall of the old coal stove plus mucilage-scented library at Mobile County Training School. You don't say anything at all about that. But you will always remember the pulsing, guitar-sweetened beat of Victory Dance music, celebrating the MCTS Whippets (and later Tuskegee Golden Tigers) in mufti. *Because there was always a dance afterwards, no matter what kind of contest. Success means being dressed to the nines with stone fox on your arm. As in the balls in* War and Peace, *for instance. But Tolstoy had no Satchmo to sprinkle that kind of stardust in the Russian sour mash. Not that the Russians were ever short on great musicians (whose music sometimes sounds like the very best of the old spirituals). But they didn't sprinkle that kind of stardust; and they didn't play and sing "Chinatown my Chinatown" and "I'm Confessing" and "I Surrender Dear" and "Wrap Your Troubles in Dreams," not like that.*

You don't say Telegraph Red but you think: *Filling Station Red become triple-threat man of letters, who knows what makes a poem or a story tick exactly like old Telegraph Red the master mechanic—who never saw an engine he couldn't tune to purr like a sewing machine. Who used to come blasting by road-testing somebody's motorcycle, used to go hop-skipping somebody's motorboat up and down the Mobile River between Three Mile Creek and the Chickasabogue, old Baling Wire Red who also used to come rattling over in a Tailspin Tommy biplane and then circle back up to Chickasaw barnstorming between the AT&N and Bay Poplar.*

Of course you don't say anything about road-testing and sour-mash tasting as such. But you do mention a very special old place long familiar to both of you, a book-reader's place called the world of William Faulkner. Then you say: "By the way I brought along a kind of jackleg poem for you, a kind of bootleg poem, if you know what I mean, some jackleg bootleg poetry about that world as now viewed from Lenox Terrace" (thinking also: A kind of shade tree T. S. Eliot poem, a kind of baling wire Ezra Pound Canto, a kind of tin-lizzy "Occasional" after Auden).

Then as you read it as a vamp of blues-idiom piano riffs, a vamp of railroad-guitar riffs, he listens, ear cocked as if with the timing light in one hand and the screwdriver in the other, as if poke-checking the firing order, as if checking and adjusting the carburetor. You read on, thinking: Keep that sour-assed mash moving, horse. Downhome boys got to do better than just hang in there, got to do even better than hang in there together. Maybe downhome boys got to be the ones to point out that if everybody in the nation was just brimming with love for mankind it still wouldn't be enough to circumvent man's fate.

At one point you also say: "One of the things I've been meaning to ask about is the old Fugitive Poets of Nashville. I mean about the origin of the name." And the account he gives is of course literary history of the first order. And the "fugitive" metaphor is valid as far as it goes. But the thing is that so far as you are concerned it didn't really go very far. Not when your idea of the fugitive as ancestral hero is derived from the runaway slave. Not when you remember some of the almost blues-idiom type changes old Faulkner was able to play on the theme of the black runaway, runagate and even renegade in such stories as "Red Leaves," "Was" and "The Bear." Not when you remember Cue in Stephen Vincent Benét's story called "Freedom's a Hard-Bought Thing." Putting the young Allen Tate, the young Donald Davidson, and cavalier old John Crowe Ransom in the same base-running, ground-gaining, broken-field razzle-dazzle league with Frederick Douglass and Harriet Tubman was like trying to bootleg George Plimpton into the same lineup with Willie Mays, O. J. Simpson, and Oscar Robertson—as a regular! But you don't say paper fugitives; you ask where the white Southern fugitives of Nashville imagined themselves fleeing to. And it turns out that they were fleeing not so much to as from. "'We flee,' I think it went," he says remembering, "'many things.' Let's see, 'but nothing so much,' yes nothing—we can look this up—'nothing so much as the old South, the old Brahmins. . . .'" He goes on remembering and recounting, and it turns out that the fugitives actually fled mostly into the homes of certain very special people in Nashville. He recalls that in addition to the stimulation and encouragement of a few of the instructors at Vanderbilt there were several Jewish businessmen of literary taste in whose homes the white make-believe fugitives found a European atmosphere of arts and letters and even further encouragement and patronage. He mentions names like the Starr brothers, Frank, Hirsch; and as he talks your mind leaps forward to the old *Southern Review*, the old *Sewanee Review* and Ransom's old *Kenyon Review* which you used to read at Tuskegee and used to wonder why they also carried some of the same Jewish writers who wrote for such Eastern liberal and left-wing magazines as *Partisan Review, Nation, New Republic*. But you don't go into that either. But you think: "*Midrash.*" *Maybe Stanley Edgar Hyman could have claimed that certain WASPS were sneaking the Talmudic Scholar's Midrash back in there and calling it the New Criticism! The Americanization of the Midrash. But then old Stanley whose Midrashes are geared to the dynamics of a WASP named Kenneth Burke says: "You don't have to be Jewish . . ."*

You don't ask Warren any point-blank questions about the sociopolitical folklore of the white supremacy of Elkins. His current thinking on such lore is, you feel, adequately reflected in the response he makes to your question about the phony issue of house slaves versus field slaves, a response you are delighted to find entirely consistent with your expectations of a downhome white boy whom you respect as a poet, a novelist, and student not only of Southern history and culture but of mankind.

"The wrongs of slavery," he says, "are beyond words, simply beyond words. No question about that, and there is no way that any of it can be excused. No way. It was an awful thing, just awful, a terrible thing. But another thing to remember, and now this you always have to remember. Always. And of course this is the horror of it, too: that it was also a human thing, institution—not to say humane—a system made up of human beings, and in such a system—any system—where what is involved is human beings, every possible, every imaginable, every *imaginable* combination of human social relationship is likely to exist. *And did exist.* Now that's what it was."

Could exist, and did exist. As described to a great extent in *Band of Angels*, for instance, and made much more apparent than in William Styron's *The Confessions of Nat Turner*. But you don't go into that either, not even to say that most reviewers seemed to have missed that aspect of it. *That could exist and did exist.* "As almost always in Faulkner." You do say that, remembering Sutpen's Hundred, in *Absalom, Absalom!*; remembering Uncle Buck and Uncle Buddy in *Go Down, Moses*.

Later on you also think: but then Faulkner, unlike Thomas Wolfe, the boy from the hill country, had the memories of a white boy in whose Mississippi Aunt Hagar was Caroline Barr become Dilsey and Earth Mother of the Compsons. The literary heritage of William Faulkner included not only books (which big word-thirsty Thomas Wolfe gulped down as if each was the last jug of good corn whiskey in the world) but also a very attentive Mississippi white boy's legacy of outrageous black wit and wisdom from local Uncles Remus beyond number; and sometimes, as in *Absalom, Absalom!*, he could write out of a background that was so richly informed by them that it was almost as if he had even done his book reading like a brownskin downhome schoolboy doing his homework in the barbershop. Because whatever else *Absalom, Absalom!* is it may also be read in outline as just such a Mississippi white boy's brownskin barbershop version of *Moby-Dick*: in which Thomas Sutpen pursues the whiteness of white sons almost precisely as if he were an Appalachian Ahab, only to become inextricably ensnarled with Uncle Remus's Tar Baby disguised this time as a mulatto in Haiti.

Not that William Faulkner didn't have his own confederate hangups. Not that this same William Faulkner couldn't on occasion get himself all worked up as if to mount up for still another Johnny Reb cavalry charge up some long-lost ridge from time to time *"when it is still not yet two o'clock on that July afternoon in 1863, the brigades are in position behind the rail fence, the guns are loaded and ready in the woods and the furled flags are already loosened to break out and Pickett himself with his long oiled ringlets and his hat in one hand probably and his sword in the other looking up the hill waiting for Longstreet to give the word and it's all in the balance."*

But even so it was still this same William Faulkner who probably could have best made even Thomas Wolfe come to appreciate how when you take the "A" train for Harlem you are heading north but also south and home again. Because the voice in which William Faulkner told his downhome yarns may have been ever so much closer to the Scotch-Irish-Gothic-Greek and Latin of Mississippi courthouse square gossip of old man Whicker-bill Charley Comesaw than the railroad-blue-steel-guitar-plus-rawhide-and-patent-leather idiom Uncle Remus used in the barbershop. Still the best of his yarns not only acknowledge Aunt Hagar and Uncle Remus but also celebrate them as the homefolks most likely not only to endure but to prevail. Nor was his point that the meek shall inherit the earth. His point was that no man could inherit the earth, that the only thing worth inheriting is humanity.

At another point you say: "Speaking of some of the things black and white Southerners share by virtue of growing up in the South, things of cultural or of anthropological significance, things shared in spite of the politics of racism, I guess that briarpatch metaphor behind the title of your piece in *I'll Take My Stand* is something we both got from Uncle Remus in one way or another."

To which he says: "Yes, it was certainly there in the air, all right," and remembers writing the article in England. But you are thinking about the metaphor, not the content of the essay, and you find yourself remembering a Mobile County Training School boy you haven't seen for probably twenty-five or thirty years, a very smooth very dark brown boy whose name was Marion Mayo but who used to call himself Reynard the Fox instead of Brer Rabbit but who not only walked and danced but also ran back punts tip-stepping cute papa cottontail style as if he could wear a pair of patent-leather dress shoes through any briar patch in the world without getting a single scratch on them. (Needless to say there was about as much similarity between your Remus and the one Joel Chandler Harris wrote about as there is between music as you know it and the way Stephen Foster wrote it. Though sometime old Joel's ear was not bad, not bad at all.)

"Oh no, my pleasure, my pleasure," Warren says, because you are looking at your watch to let him know that you do not intend to take up much more of his time. "No, no, my pleasure."

So the chat continues on into the late Connecticut April afternoon—during which time you make your pet point about Frederick Douglass deserving a place in the national pantheon, and before you get the words out he adds that Douglass's prose also belongs in the nineteenth-century literary canon along with that of Emerson and Thoreau—and then not only do you end up staying for dinner in the Refectory (huddling together as if under a poncho against the shower of media-glib Yankee talk around you. As if before the old Telegraph Road Atwater Kent radio, but talking not about the Crimson Tide or Beattie Feathers of the Tennessee Vols or about books but about a dedicated Tennessee bootlegger named Leroy McAfee and the art of keeping good sour mash moving). You also stay on for an informal discussion by the editor of a national magazine, followed by a party at the headmaster's.

"It will be a pleasure, my pleasure," he says, inviting you to come to see him in Fairfield soon. "It will be my pleasure."

So you come back to New York on the midnight train thinking about Old Telegraph Red. Old Filling Station Red from Telegraph Road. On whom you have been filing vouchers for years (even before you pulled down that A-minus for the one filed at NYU). Ever since back in college when you came across "The Hamlet of Thomas Wolfe" and "T. S. Stribling; A Paragraph in the History of Critical Realism" (also containing an early assessment of Faulkner as Artist) in Zabel's *Literary Opinion in America*. But it was with *All the King's Men* that you really started keeping an eye on him, because that was where you first ran into that old book-reading Filling Station Red stuff. In the sensibility of Jack Burden, the inky-fingered narrator. Then that year at NYU you finally got into *Night Rider* which you remember only vaguely, and *At Heaven's Gate* which you enjoyed because you were reading in New York and there it was again, and there was also Slim Sarrett.

Not Slim Sarrett as such but some of the extracurricular literary stuff he was cut from: "*In the library he never read a book, except the reserve or reference books which did not circulate. He checked out books and left. But one afternoon a week he spent in the periodical room, reading the current magazines. He never sat down, but stood before the shelves, his raincoat draped about his shoulders, the magazine poised in his left hand, the thumb and forefinger of his right hand holding the margin of a page, ready to flick it over when he had finished. He read with tremendous rapidity, and without hesitation in selection, working around the alphabetical shelves. When he came across an item, especially a poem, which pleased him or irritated him, he walked over to the desk of a young woman who was in charge, read the piece to her in his ordinary tone, making no concession to the sign above the desk. . . .*"

Because that was not only old book-reading, book-writing Telegraph Red himself on his way from, say, Tuscaloosa or Auburn not to murder and flight but to the *Southern Review*, the *Sewanee Review*, and the *Kenyon Review*. It was also Gerald Hamilton at Tuskegee. It was also Ralph Ellison at Tuskegee and it was also you. Because reading it in the Forty-second Street Library you could even smell the floor wax and the furniture polish in the periodicals room of Hollis Burke Frissell. You could hear the Alabama spring rain rattling the drain pipes outside the window. You could even remember exactly how the damp wisteria and freshly-mowed-lawn-scented late April/early May breeze used to feel.

Then there was also the fact that Slim Sarrett was trying to formulate a theory of poetry. That was the sort of thing you were also playing around with even then, which was also when you were reading R. P. Blackmur, Francis Fergusson, Jessie L. Weston, and Kenneth Burke and working on your M.A. thesis about symbols of sterility and fertility in *The Waste Land* and *The Sun Also Rises*: even as you made your regular weekly rounds to hear Dizzy Gillespie, Charlie Parker and young Miles Davis on Fifty-second Street; and to hear Lionel Hampton, Count Basie, and Duke Ellington wherever they were in those good old used-to-be days when you went to such midtown entertainment palaces as the Paramount, the Strand, and Warners' as much for the stage show as for the movie.

All of which was nine years before Warren came to write *Segregation: The Inner Conflict in the South*; it was fourteen before *The Legacy of the Civil War*, and eighteen before *Who Speaks for the Negro?* For the pretty-goodness of which written testimony by you exists.

TWO

Greensboro

OF HAGAR-WIT AND THE NETS
OF UNCLE WHAT-YOU-MAY-CALL-HIM

*T*HE TIME EN ROUTE *by railroad is about forty-eight hours when you are lucky enough to make all the connections as scheduled. By Greyhound it is likely to be about thirty. By Whisper-jet from La Guardia you can be there in less than four, all told. But this time you go hedge-hopping and whistlestopping by way of Greensboro and Atlanta and Tuskegee. This time also you go on further south from Mobile to New Orleans. Then you head back north by way of Greenville, the legendary levee town of catfish eaters on the ever so hithering-and-thithering Mississlippy Sloppy. Then Lenox Terrace is only two hours northeast from Memphis, Tennessee.*

The countryside you see from the limousine going into Greensboro does not remind you nearly so much of the South of Thomas Wolfe, the wild bull of New York literary china shops, as of Jonathan Daniels, of the old Raleigh *News and Observer*, the Jonathan Daniels who wrote the book *A Southerner Discovers the South*, which still stands up as one of the very best personal records of the immediate world you graduated into from college. Indeed, the physical as well as the metaphorical point of departure of *A Southerner Discovers the South* was a commencement ceremony at just such a high school as might have been your own: "The solemn student who had learned all the old phrases that were to his race all too often the parts of an old joke looked like a stupid black satyr, and the girls, whose very skins [which he also describes as taffy- and chocolate-colored] wedded voodoo and pagan, sang around him. But he looked beyond their brief, slim youngness to quotations from Lincoln and Milton, Andrew Jackson and Carlyle, Kipling and Tennyson. 'We go forth,' he said."

"So also I go forth," Daniels continues, "a trifle less confident, a little less certain of Lincoln and Milton as guides, but with an alarm clock set, a tank full of gasoline, a suitcase full of clothes, a suitcase full of books, maps and letters of introduction to the best—the very best—people . . . and into my ears like the South singing rang that whistle voice which took Handel's 'Hallelujah' into the heart of Africa and flung it back again at our South where the north man ultimately met the Negro and built what some have called a civilization. I rode to find it."

He was describing events in North Carolina. But who, after all, if not you at Mobile County Training School in Alabama had recited the following poem from Langston Hughes as the outchorus to your oratorical contest speech:

> *We have to-morrow*
> *Bright before us*
> *Like a flame*
>
> *Yesterday, a night-gone thing,*
> *A sun-down name*
>
> *And dawn to-day*
> *Broad arch above the road we came,*
> *We march!*

Who if not you and thousands of other bright-eyed "taffy- and chocolate-colored" Southern school boys and girls?—not that you or any schoolmate you ever knew was in the least unmindful of how red the ears of visiting white do-good dignitaries and stand-pat officials alike always turned hearing you put the heart of Africa plus the soul and spirit of Christianity (not unknowingly) into "The Star-Spangled Banner."

And who if not you graduated from Tuskegee four years later as aware of Jonathan Daniels as of Langston Hughes? as aware of the Montgomery *Advertiser* as of the Chicago *Defender*, as aware of Ralph McGill's Atlanta *Constitution* as of the Pittsburgh *Courier*? Who if not you with your clothes and books in your one Gladstone bag caught the bus for your first teaching job over in the Georgia that was still very much the state of Ole Gene Talmadge in spite of Ellis Arnall? Who, having read the *Nation* and the *New Republic* and suchlike including the *New Masses*, was ever more firmly convinced that his own vision was already as far beyond that of W.E.B. as that of Booker T.? Who if not you in that last prewar year of F.D.R.?

So the first thing you and Edwin Yoder, the associate editor (and editorialist even as W. J. Cash, author of *The Mind of the South*, once was) of the Greensboro *Daily News* talk about is young Jo-naythan whom you regard as being as much the son of Chapel Hill at its best as of old Joeseefus, the old Tarheel Editor; young Jo-naythan, who came out of the Chapel Hill of your then Tuskegee-based awareness of things knowing how to use social science without getting lost in pretentious abstractions; young Jo-naythan in his banker's glasses, who wrote as if he were not only as comfortable in seed stores and tobacco warehouses as in libraries and New York literary circles but could also declare that: "we Southerners are of course a mythological people . . . we are in part to blame for our legendary character . . . certainly the land called South is no realm for geographers"; who that long ago could also make the following pronouncement: "But in the South the tyrants and the plutocrats and the poor all need teaching. One of them no more than the others. All are in the warm dark, and whether they like it or not—white man, black man, big man—they are in the dark together. None will ever get to day alone."

He is now old Jo-naythan—not nearly so much in the conventional geriatric sense as in the traditional folk sense that some Southerners become old in your memory and imagination by becoming the fabulously familiar heroes (or villains) of local tall tales during their lifetime. What you actually find yourself thinking is: old *young* Jo-naythan, son of old Joseefus, the old time dimly remembered Tarheel Editor of my young manhood: old *forever young* Jo-naythan, forever young and forever full of piss and vinegar, who wrote such books as *A Southerner Discovers the South* and *A Southerner Discovers New England* as if with the typewriter propped against the dashboard, who got maybe as close to F.D.R. as Jack Burden was to the Boss in *All the King's Men* (up there in the White House with his banker's glasses and his seed- and feed-store facts and figures and his courthouse square yarns which he knew how to spin with exactly the right contemporary Southern mixture of inky-fingered journalistic hipness and immediacy and Chapel

Hill grass roots—not without the expected overtones of ante-bellum book learning and phrase turning to be sure).

The only reason you don't make the short trip over to Raleigh to meet and chat with him as Edwin Yoder can easily arrange for you to do is that Daniels, who is no longer editor but now publisher, is not there. He doesn't spend much time at the *News and Observer* any more. Nowadays he is, it seems, most often to be found at Hilton Head, his soft weather retreat off the coast of Savannah. He comes into Raleigh from time to time, but for the past several years he seems to have been spending his time mostly writing books. You remind Yoder that it is not really Jonathan Daniels himself in the flesh that you have come to make personal contact with anyway, but rather (as metaphysical as it might sound), the idea (even more than the specific ideas!) of Jonathan Daniels.

"The Jonathan Daniels fallout, man. Among the younger fellows. You know what I mean? Like yourself."

Still, it would have been nice to meet old Jo-naythan on the hoof at long last and tell him something about what his book meant to you that long ago. And you may or may not have also told him about how on your way forth from college out into the world of that South he had then so recently described in terms so specifically similar to the emphasis of certain of your courses in Social Science and Education, the Greyhound from Tuskegee had pulled into Columbus, Georgia, too late to make the connection with the Trailways bus to Blakely down in Early County, and you had by a chance but fabulously appropriate encounter met with a young road musician and had spent the night on a couch in the red-velvet-draped, tenderloin-gothic, incense-sultry sickroom of the legendary but then long since bedridden Ma Rainey.

That would have been determined by Daniels' response to what you most certainly have said about your conception of the blues as an idiom of experience-confrontation, and existential improvisation; as a frame for definition within which Uncle Remus, an artistic ancestor of Jelly Roll Morton and Louis Armstrong alike, is the spinner of such yarns and the weaver of such nets as become meshes to catch the wind, and in which Aunt Hagar, the earth-dark coziness of whose bosom is the wellspring of all mother-wit, is the supreme big mamma of those blue-steel cradles out of which endlessly rocking (and cooling it too) come all "taffy and chocolate"-colored wayfaring forth-farers.

Nor did they cling to the old promise quite as naively as some white boys might imagine. On the contrary, it was most likely to be the bright-eyed white boy himself (even one as free of the conventional Protestant ethic rat-race-ism as Young Jo-naythan), who was all too easily seduced by *Poor Richard's Almanac*, not the children of Aunt Hagar and Uncle Remus (to whom Po' Richard's Yankee Doodle pre–Horatio Alger jive about early to bed, early to rise is likely to sound like some more of old Marster's cotton-picking bullshit)!

But back to what Aunt Hagar in the old whispering blues-dive–diva timbre of Ma Rainey actually sang to the young initiate from Tuskegee: "*Your money can't pay for nothing in this house, my precious. Not in Mama's house, darling. Just go on the way you going, sweetheart, and just be careful.*" (Nor did she, or anybody else, have to remind you that from junior high school on having an education was as dangerous as it was precious, that a brownskin boy with education made white people even more uneasy than the idea of a man with a concealed weapon.) "*No, honeypie, Mama knows what you trying to do, and it takes more than a notion, more than a notion and every little bit helps. Mama just wants you to know how proud she is you come to her. Mama Gertrude always did back up her chillun and always will as long as she's got breath in this old body.*"

Nor did she have to tell you that you were supposed to strut your stuff for Mama. The way she patted your shoulder and stroked your arm said that as clearly as you for one would always remember her saying it on the stage when you were still a preschool tot on the outskirts of Mobile, Alabama, and they used to come tail-gating around on a platform truck advertising for the vaudeville. She would be wearing a shimmie-she-wabble-spangled dress and her blues-queen sequined headband and as each musician moved into the solo spot she would say, "*Yes, darling, yes, sweet Papa brownskin, now strut your brownskin stuff for Mama, Sweet Papa brownskin.*"

All mamas were always saying that to you in one way or another whatever they were talking about: "*Play the little man for Mama, Albert Lee. Just play the little man for mama. That's all right about that old booger man. You just be the little man for Mama. You just be my little Mister Buster Brown man. Mama's little Mister Buster Brown man ain't scared of no booger man and nothing else. Mama's little man ain't scared of nobody and nothing in creation—or tarnation either. Because Mama's little man is Mama's BIG man, just like him daddy that's what him is. That's exactly what him is, betchem bones. Him momom Mitchem Buttchem Bwown. Momoms itchem bittchem Mittchem Buttchem Bwown; betchem tweet bones.*" Then there was that song by Sissle and Blake, "If You've Never Been Vamped by a Brownskin You've Never Been Vamped at All."

As far as you yourself are concerned the connection between Aunt Hagar and Ma Rainey and Mama on the one hand and the Harriet of young Jo-naythan's boyhood is quite obvious. "My first guide," he declares in *A Southerner Discovers the South*, "was Harriet, yellow and wise, who could look all that the conventional Mammy was supposed to be but who possessed knowledge and interests which made childhood under her guiding a dark excitement of endless variety."

But how much connection between that profoundly intimate part of his childhood and your own would he have been prepared to acknowledge? and once that acknowledgment was made, how ready would he have been to see the contrast that you would insist on pointing out? After all, for all their seed-store sense of actuality, those Southern white boys who are lucky enough to have mammies to celebrate are forever getting so totally carried away with narcissistic sentimentality that they create the absolutely astonishing impression that black mammies existed only to love and care for *white* children. So far as every last mammy-oriented white Southerner you ever meet was concerned it was as if their black mammies cared nothing at all for their own children, not to mention their own children's children. Such white Southerners seem to take it for granted that their mammies did not think their own children were as good and as deserving as white children! Well, in all your days of awareness you'd only met a few of Aunt Hagar's children, whether black, brown, or mulatto, who couldn't tell them a thing or two about all that.

Most of the time you just let them go on because they sounded so corny and it was so easy to embarrass them. But sometimes when they kept going on and on, you had to cut in: "O.K., man. I hear you and I heard it before, and maybe I don't know what the hell your good old black-molasses sweet Mammy-madonna told you about little old chicken-butt me but I can tell you a whole lot of things she was telling me about y'all at the same time."

One thing she was always saying for example was: "*Mamma's little man ain't no little old crybaby like no little old white boy always got to have somebody petting him every time he got a little scratch on him somewhere. Mamma kissing Mamma's little man because she just want her some of that sweet old little pretty-man sugar that's what she kissing and hugging him so about.*"

Then there were the sometimes endlessly reiterated admonishments, such as: "*Boy, don't you ever let me catch you going around this house dropping your clothes and things all over the place and leaving them like you living in some kind of old pig pen or something, and you got somebody hired to pick up behind you. You ain't no little old spoiled white boy, and we ain't no white folks so lazy we got to have somebody else to help keep our house clean like folks suppose to. That's old poor white trash lying around in all that muck and mire because they can't pay nobody to keep them and their chillun clean, not us. I'm raising you to keep yourself neat and clean and looking like somebody think something of yourself. Myself I just can't sit down till this house is clean, don't care how tired and wore out I come in. I can't sleep in no filthy house. Lord it just makes my flesh crawl to see folks sitting in a dirty house. I just can't help it. I just can't stand no dirty house. I for one don't mean to raise no youngun to grow up and work his wife to death cleaning up after him.*"

And sometimes, not so much in reprimand as in gratuitous warning: "*Mind you manners, my young man. Ain't no child of mine going to be talking back at no grown folks like them little old sassy white chillun bristling and talking back up at their mammas and daddies like there ain't no God in heaven and no hell in the hereafter. Being nice and mannerable to grown folks ain't never done no youngun no harm, and you never can tell when you going to need somebody to put in a good word for you somewhere one of these days. You just remember that, my young man, when you get to feeling mannish; and keep your big talk to yourself when you around grown folks.*"

To which, when the time came, she was to add: "*Control your nature. Ain't nobody never going to make nothing out of hisself if he let his nature run away with him. Talking about your nature going to your head that's exactly when it's going to your head because that's when you ain't going to know whether you going or coming. Ain't no use in me wasting my time telling you something you ain't going to do so that's why I mean exactly what I say. I ain't said nothing about denying your manful nature. I said control your nature because that's exactly what a real man can do. That's what a woman expects a man to do. That's what a woman loves a man for doing.*"

As for what a unanimity of black mammies, Aunt Hagars, and mammas actually said, and signified when the time came to talk about white girls, more often than not it was as if the same voice were speaking through different (but not very different) masks: "*Just remember this, my young mister man, and you can forget it if you want to but I know what I'm talking about because I ain't talking about nothing I read in no book I'm talking about flesh and blood. So I'm going to tell you anyhow my young man and if you don't listen I'm here to tell you someday you'll wish you had. So you can mock my words if you want to but when one of them little old white gals say something to you I just want you to know the chance you taking. I raised many a one, and God knows I know ain't nothing in creation more selfish and deceitful than some little old spoiled white child snuggling up to you for you to tell a lie to cover up something and will turn right around and lie you in all kinds of trouble without batting an eye and then come sidling up expecting you to forgive them. That's the first thing. And another thing is you ain't nobody's playpretty to be picked up and thrown away whenever they like. Boy, do you hear what I say? I know you got sense enough to know that anybody who ain't going to help you get out of the trouble they got you into ain't no friend of yours. I know good and well you got sense enough to know that, so that's all I got to say about that and you better remember it the rest of your born days. If you don't and let them grin your neck into a rope, no better for you.*"

(As for what such mammies, mamas, and aunts said about the so-called Southern belle, obviously they didn't tell their white boys what they got around to telling you sooner or later: "*A frisky-tail gal is a frisky-tail gal, don't care how much they pay*

*for her perfume. You see them white gals sashaying around actin
all stuck up and making out like they just stepped out of a doll
house or somewhere, well I'm here to tell you they ain't no china
dolls, don't care how much powder and rouge they got on. Who
you reckon keeping that dollhouse clean, such as it is? On top of
washing and ironing them clothes and tying them ribbons and
bows. Who you reckon they mamas learned to from, and they
mamas's mama? Who you reckon the last one all of them always
come to show themselves to just before they go flouncing off somewhere to make a fool out of another one of them little old mannish
white boys all growed up putting on airs and calling hisself a
gentleman? And don't bit more know what they doing than the
man in the moon. Who you reckon the one made him learn all
them fancy manners he showing off?"*)

When William Faulkner declares as he did in the eulogy he
delivered at her funeral that his black mammy was a "fount of
authority over my conduct and of security for my physical
welfare, and of active and constant affection and love," and
that she was also "an active and constant precept for decent
behavior, from her I learned to tell the truth, to refrain from
waste, to be considerate of the weak and respectful of age,"
you don't doubt that he was deeply moved as he spoke or was
moved again every time he remembered what he said, but
being one of black mammy's taffy- and chocolate-colored boys
you could not only tell him a few things, you could also ask
him a hell of a lot of pretty embarrassing questions, beginning,
for instance, with: "Damn man, if the mammyness of blackness
or the blackness of mammyness was so magnificent and of such
crucial significance as you now claim, how come you let other
white folks disrespect and segregate her like that? How come
you didn't put yourself out just a little bit more to please her?
How can fellows like you be so enthusiastic about her and yet
so ambivalent and hesitant about her brothers and sisters?
Man, do you really think that your reciprocation was adequate?
Have you ever been tempted, if only for a moment, to take
some little taffy and chocolate child to your bosom as my Aunt
Hagar did to you? I mean, damn, man, the least y'all rich ones
could do is set up some Aunt Hagar fellowships something like
that Rhodes scholar jive."

But that is old stuff, so old that it is hardly worth a barber-shop shrug. Yet in view of all the recent New York drawing-room theoretics about black matriarchs what is passing strange is that none of the big fatheaded Marx-plus-Freud-oriented experts on black identity who are so glib about family structures and filial relationships otherwise have made absolutely nothing of the fact that white boys from the "best" Southern families have not only almost always claimed to have had black mammies but have also invariably depicted them as representing the quintessence of Motherhood! Many white Southerners go around talking about white womanhood or really about white girlhood which is to say belle-hood, but the conception of *Motherhood*, for some reason almost always comes out *black*! And yet not even those Freud-derived New York Jewish writers who are forever and ever complaining about their Yiddisher mamas have even made a second-rate joke or two about this particular characteristic of downhome goy boys.

Nevertheless what a Marx-Freud-oriented piece of Americana for, say, *Commentary* or *Dissent!* what with literary footnotes and psychopolitical cross-references and all. And besides, who knows? Such a piece might help even Norman Mailer to make up his mind as to whether he wants to be a Texan or an Irishman (say, like Big Daddy Pat Moynihan), or maybe he'll settle for being a U.S. Levi Yitzchak of Berditchev after all. But what a piece of Americana somebody like say Norman Podhoretz could make if he decided he didn't like white Southerners anymore or if he could ever figure out which New York Southerners are Compsons and which are Snopeses. Such a piece could also in classical New York Marx-Freud baroque style explore the possible connections between the so-called Mafia and the *mamma mia* dimension of the U.S. Italian experience. But seriously you can only wonder what happens to all that fancy Teachers College–plus–Bruno Bettelheim jive about the first few years of childhood being the most crucial, when the topic is the black mammy's relationship to the white child.

It is not, however, primarily for echoes of Aunt Hagar that you listen during your conversations with Edwin Yoder. You expect to pick up some overtones and reverberations, of course. But what you have actually come hoping specifically to hear interwoven with Yoder's own particular seed-store–feed-store plus court-house square plus Chapel Hill plus Oxford Rhodes scholar sensibility is not so much an Aunt Hagar as an Uncle Remus (or Uncle Remus–derived) dimension of downhome or blues-idiom orientation to the ambiguities of human actuality, an Uncle Remus–derived respect for human complexity, a Brer Rabbit–derived appreciation for human ingenuity.

But you have decided not to ask any point-blank questions about that sort of thing either, this time, not in Greensboro or anywhere else. Not only because (once again) not to have to ask is precisely the point, but also because point-blank answers and acknowledgments seldom tell you enough. Because at bottom the point is not really a matter of how Remus-conscious he is or how much specific credit he is willing to concede but rather how much Remus-type insight he brings to bear upon things as a matter of course.

So you don't ask him if he is one of Uncle Remus's white boys or whether his father or his father's father was one—and besides that is not necessarily the most direct line of inheri-tance anyway. As far as the dynamics of such inheritance go all you have to do is remember how many white musicians, for instance, have become the children of fabulous Uncle Louis Armstrong without ever fully realizing it because they simply do not know that much about how they came to be the way they are. Sometimes they get it out of the air. After all, the airways are saturated with perhaps even more of Uncle Dip-per's flushed-face white sons both legitimate and illegitimate than his short-coupled and sometimes-long-gone-a-wee-bit-further black ones.

Of course you could ask whatever became of all those little wide-eyed spellbound white boys who used to spend so much time sitting at the feet of Uncle Remus. What the hell did they ever do with all those fantastic nets to catch wisdom that he used to weave for them? You could say: "We know all about those who grew up to parlay the rhetoric into political bullshit (and bullshit mostly against black folks at that), but what about the others, the pretty-good ones who like his 'coffee- and taffy-colored' nephews knew that such nets were woven of the eternal verities?"

And incidentally you could also remind him and them of

something else: That it is European theory-oriented New York intellectuals, not courthouse-square Southerners who are most likely to mistake the concrete virtues of Uncle Remus (and Aunt Hagar) for the abstract attributes of Rousseau's "noble savage." To the white Southerner who as a little boy sat at his feet (and went fishing, hunting, and on journeys with him) and as a young man served his agricultural and technological apprenticeship under him, Uncle Remus was not only a funda-mental symbol of *time-honored authority*, he was also, as they say in New York, A FATHER FIGURE!, whose sense of complexity and whose intellectual sophistication is anything but that of a "noble savage." (Now how about some Oedipus-complex talk in a Hagar-Remus context?)

(Also few aspects of the current conflict over school deseg-regation strike you as being more ironic than the fact that mass-media commentators and white middle-income Southerners alike now seem totally unaware of the fact that the best-brought-up Southerners have always depicted Aunt Hagar and Uncle Remus to the world as the most expert preschool and elementary-school child psychologists in the history of child development. And that as soon as the poor white Southerner can afford to do so he hires the nearest thing to Uncle Remus and Aunt Hagar he can come by to bring up his children prop-erly! Nor is the irony restricted to the matter of child rearing. As soon as your ambitious poor white Southerner becomes af-fluent enough to buy a fine house, the very first thing he seems most likely to do is to bring Negroes into the inner circle of his family life. Of course he calls them his servants, or even his house niggers, but everybody knows very well that he has really hired them because they are the experts who can teach him to live in style like the white gentry from which many poor whites have been more completely excluded than most downhome Negroes have ever been.)

Actually, in the case of Edwin Yoder, you are inclined to as-sume from previous encounters—and from some of his articles —that you can use the fiction of William Faulkner as an Uncle Remus touchstone, or range finder, that all you have to do is allude to some character and situation in one of old Uncle Whicker-Bill's Yoknapatawpha yarns and listen for the Remus overtones in the feedback. But as a matter of fact you are also inclined to assume that you don't even have to do that. Because regardless of the specific nature and degree of his personal contact with the Remus dimension of the Southern experience perhaps the most distinctive feature of Yoder's bearing and presence, clean-cut fair-haired North Carolina boy good looks aside, is the twinkle which always lights up his expression whenever some topic engages him. Indeed, you like to think that it is precisely that Uncle Remus–derived twinkle (which is to say sense of humor and of the absurd—which is to say actuality, the perception thereof, at long range) that could be his best security against the nonsense, terminological and otherwise, that is too typical of so many other newsmen and editorialists these days.

So in point of fact you shouldn't have to use even Faulkner this time. All you should have to do is riff a couple of satchmo-elegant blues choruses on any subject whatsoever and then lay out for a few bars and listen for his jack teagarden rejoinder, as it were. But you go ahead and sound a faulkner chord anyhow. Because when you come down to the fundamentals of what you are really trying to do, you are really only using Uncle Remus himself as a touchstone for—or perhaps rather as a steppingstone to—the point you would like to make about the sad state of journalism these days, what with so many reporters substituting social-science theory and terminology for open-minded observation or just plain old-fashioned human interest, curiosity, and even hard-headed detective-story-type investigation. So what you go ahead and do is you point out how Faulkner, for his part, could use frank speculation and conjecture as literary devices or nets to catch the human content of time and motion: specifically, how by having Quentin Compson and Shreve McCannon talking years later at Harvard make up details about events not actually witnessed by themselves in Mississippi, Faulkner renders the essential truth of the climax of the story of Thomas Sutpen, and of Henry Sutpen and Charles Bon, the ill-fated half-brothers in *Absalom, Absalom!*

The point of course is that so many reporters mistake social-science metaphor for facts these days, without realizing that even the most precise concepts are only nets that cannot hold very much flesh-and-blood experience. Whereas the most pragmatic thing about *poetic* metaphor is that you know very well that your net cannot trap all of the experience in question. Indeed, you often feel that maybe most of it has eluded you. (Hence, such figures of speech as simile, metonymy, synecdoche, hyperbole, irony, and so on.) You readily concede that formulations generalized from scientific-research findings may be nets with a closer weave, still not only do they remain nets, but at best they trap even smaller areas of experience than literary configurations, expressly because they are necessarily in a narrower weave. As with what Kenneth Burke calls "trained incapacity," scientific insight may be more sharply focused but its field of vision is likely to be correspondingly more limited.

At one juncture, speaking of terminology as preconception you also say: "I have a thing about the way journalists misuse the word 'ghetto.' Naturally, I don't want to become a goddam nut about it; but, man, the chickenshit way they now use it, the word itself is equivalent to predefinition and prejudice. It equals prejudging, preinterpreting, preevaluating conduct from location, and not only conduct but character, personality. In other words, as I see it, inherent in the word itself is a very strong danger of overinterpreting both behavior and personality in terms of environment. You know what I mean? It's like saying, I know who you are and what you are going to do and why, because I know where you come from. Which is a lot of crap. Well, what I'm suggesting is that such journalists work from an inadequate grammar of motives. You know Kenneth Burke's work? His five key terms of dramatism: scene, act, agent, agency, and purpose? Well, what I mean is when they use 'ghetto' the way they do they are really trying to explain all action and purpose from scene alone—which just can't be done, especially when all you think you need to know about circumstance is a bunch of goddam statistics, computed to substantiate some half-assed theory."

It so happens that it is also to *Absalom, Absalom!* that Yoder has already referred in his essay "W. J. Cash After a Quarter Century" to point out that Southern literature "where one encounters directly the fetishes of family, physical place, and tradition," provides the best approach to the "mystical" side of the mind of the South. Moreover, it is in the very same allusion that he complains that communication of the Southern experience (even in such "bloody and tortured Iliads" as Faulkner's) is difficult in a highly commercialized and mobile society that has replaced ties of blood and household with "abstractions of a fairly impersonal sort."

There is then, little doubt that Yoder shares your misgivings about conclusion-jumping no less than do Robert Penn Warren and C. Vann Woodward; and as the conversation continues you become more and more impishly amused at your not altogether frivolous notion that his twinkle may be the reflection of a sense of humor inherited from an Uncle Remus–type sense of human complexity. Not that you are in the least unappreciative of the fact that some pretty good old yarns are also derived from the old Anglo-Saxon cracker-barrel pubs and coffeehouses. There is, also and also and also, you hasten to concede, his inheritance from Chaucer and Shakespeare, to name only two of an endless number. *But still and all you are prepared not only to suggest but also to insist that the downhome cracker barrel can always do with some of Uncle Remus's very special old fireside insights into the nature of the briar patch to temper some of that ever so easy and self-indulgent Confederate sentimentality that is forever at odds with what Warren calls "the fear of abstraction."*

Nevertheless you don't ask the all too obvious question—how far Edwin Yoder or any other white Southerner is prepared to go on the question of Southern heritage and identity, on the matter, that is to say, of the consequences of all those black bosoms and hearthstone uncles. Because once again, and again and again, the point is not to ask point-blank but to discover in due course. Because furthermore, in addition to any personal and local (which is to say, political) hangups that may inhibit a direct response there is also the likelihood that many are honestly unaware of the possibility that some of their whitest ancestors may have had black ancestors of one kind or another. That possibility after all is perhaps the source of at least as much obfuscation as anything else. Nor is such obfuscation limited to white Southerners.

Yet even as they concede, as not a few so readily do, that you for your part may be one of William Faulkner's brownskin book-reading sons you immediately and inevitably become by physical as well as logical extension not only one of William

Faulkner's black mammy's brownskin grandsons, but in consequence also the bright-eyed ever so Buster-Brown yard-nephew of Uncles Remus (or Bud or Doc or Mose or Ned), both numberless and timeless.

Indubitably. And in addition to being the most expert of all downhome handymen and ex-riverboat roustabouts, were not such uncles (whether of the fireside or barbershop variety) also among other things the most town-hip as well as roadwise of any chauffeur who ever Cadillacked an avenue; the most patent-leather–smooth of all old pro butlers and maître d's, the most déjà-vu confidential of all transcontinental Pullman porters, the most omniflexible and cosmopolitan of all transoceanic merchant seamen, as much at home in Joseph Conrad's Singapore as in Boston and Charleston and San Francisco? Indubitably.

So you could also always say this too: *Hey look man, the same old ever-so-easily-forgotten-to-be-partially-remembered Remus, who in the etceteralogical wisdom of his incomparable uncleness used to spin for you and all wide-eyed tell-me-tale taddy white boys such weather-worthy yarns as make such nets as can hold what is seizable of winds plus somewhat comprehensible of human motivation is not only the selfsame old uncle copper-coin-colored Bud-Doc-Mose-Ned who used to hand-take me fishing and crabbing on Three Mile Creek, who built me toy fair castles along rockabye rivers but is also the same who in the fullness of his fable-hood and in the intrinsicality of his honorificity has taught me the socialogistics of nightclub entertainers and road musicians, the psychologistics of skin-game survivors and the vernacularities of calculus and trigonometry among other unmentionable unmentionables during all my steel-blue times in rook joints and jook joints, for all the A-B-C days I spent in book joints.*

Indeed you could also point out that so far as you personally were concerned it was Uncle Bud-Doc-Mose-Ned-Remus, not Henry James, who first said: *"Boy, keep your eyes and ears open. Boy, try to be one on whom nothing is lost."*

But you don't say any of that either. Nor do you point out that it was not Magnolia Moonshine but such uncles that most likely had most often fubbed the girandoles of the most opulent post-bellum mansions of the most fortunate of fair-haired downhome white boys. Nor do you describe him as the best of all emperors of back-porch ice cream or suggest that disguised as Chick Webb or Cozy Cole or Sonny Greer or Jo Jones or Big Sid Catlett with a wooden spoon he gouged out the eyes of the crocodiles and beat the monkeys on the behind, in the Savoy ballroom.

What you do say are words to the following effect about what you insist are terminological preconceptions: Another name for the misapplication of the word "ghetto" by cliché-conditioned journalists is the Scenic Fallacy—which is also of a piece with several other commonly accepted assumptions underlying currently popular misrepresentations of black experience. There is the Sambo Fallacy, for instance, growing out of the contention that the experience of slavery and oppression has reduced U.S. Negroes to a subspecies consisting of a passel of emasculated, shuffling, driveling, head-scratching darkies. There is also the Minority-Group Psyche Fallacy which functions no doubt to reassure race-war-oriented white cowards that U.S. Negroes have a built-in sense of inferiority because they represent only one-tenth [sic!] of the population. And then there is the Self-Image Fallacy that permits white oneupmen to interpret all black American artwork as a reflection of low self-esteem.

The giveaway on the Sambo Fallacy is the all too obvious fact that white Americans have long been mostly terrified by the tales of uptown violence allegedly committed by downtown Sambos. How can all of the police-documented violence possibly issue from personality structures that are emasculated? The "political" behavior of employees vis-à-vis their supervisors just simply cannot be equated with their total makeup. (*Why is nothing ever made of the fact that to be Afro-American is to be derived at least in part from a mask-wearing tradition?*)

What exposes the Minority Psyche Fallacy is the fact that if you live in a black community the world looks black. You can't be ignorant of the world at large and overimpressed by it at the same time, and the same holds for the statistics of demography: You can't be ignorant of fractions and percentages and oppressed by your awareness of their significance at the same time. As for the self-image as self-rejection ploy, what could be more patently ridiculous than the assumption that the so-called average student's mastery of the tools of communication are such that he can express exactly what he sees and feels? Any competent language teacher knows better than that, and any art teacher knows that the language of art is not to be confused with conventional methods of communication. On the other hand, how well-informed are social scientists on what art communicates in its own terms as artistic expression? Yet, what nobody ever suggests is that black people, whether pupils or spokesmen, may misrepresent themselves, whether through incompetence or by design, or that they use a language which is beyond conventional interpretation. Whatever happened to the fact that some people speak foreign languages? Some, it must be remembered, even speak private languages.

(Later you realize that you forgot to point out to Yoder that the very use of the word "ghetto" is in itself a part of an insidious process of ghettoization, as attitudes and the course of events in Harlem during the past several years make only too obvious. And yet such is also the nature of linguistic vulgarization involved that even now the word ghetto is beginning to take on some less pejorative connotations: Hey look, Murray, it's only natural that each man sees the world from his own ghetto, McGeorge Bundy sees it from his, Senator Jake Javits sees it from his, Fulbright sees it from his, so naturally Dr. Kenneth P. Clark sees it from his just like the same thing goes for Rockefeller.

And still later there was also this:

> *Gimme a good ole ghetto man*
> *Say now goo(h)ood oho ghe-he-tow man*
> > *Cool in the summer*
> > *Mellow in the fall*
> > > *Warm me in the winter*
> > > *Hmn springtime, Lordy Lord . . .)*

Except for lunch at a restaurant down the street, a sightseeing stroll around downtown Greensboro, and brief visits to A&T College and to Bennett College, neither of which you have seen since the time you made a trip there for a conference when you were an undergraduate at Tuskegee, you spend all of your too brief North Carolina stopoff in the editorial rooms of the *Daily News*.

Then back at the airport waiting for the flight to Atlanta you amuse yourself by thinking up ways to vouch for the

indispensable smattering of the black mammy-wit you've always discerned behind Jonathan Daniels' Chapel Hill–polished
banker's glasses and the smidgen of old Uncle Ned in Edwin
Yoder's Oxford-cracker-barrel twinkle as against Thomas
Wolfe's starry-eyed, box-ankled, sweaty-palmed, drooly-lipped
eagerness to devour the whole earth raw.

But then you had already decided years ago that the thing
about Thomas Wolfe is that he never found out that the whiteness of white skin is only skin deep and that the rest is mostly
human nature and tradition or conditioned conduct. But alas,
poor Thomas Wolfe seemed to think that the whiteness of
dixie white skins was whale deep and not unlike Faulkner's
demonic Thomas Sutpen, he chased the whiteness of whiteness
like *yes* a hillbilly Ahab all his life. But he chased it on a tread-
mill, mistaking his mirror for time and the river, dashing off
books like long-winded notes to be left in bottles in the Ocean
Sea, books which read for the most part as if they were not so
much written as shouted. Maybe he was shouting for help.
Maybe for just such help as good old Aunt Hagar and wonderful old Uncle Remus might have given but for the asking.

THREE

Atlanta

SCORING POSITION, PEACHTREE STREET

*O*NE VERY SPECIFIC OBJECTIVE *of the trip back this time is to chat with a few writers and intellectuals like Edwin Yoder going about their routine everyday business in their natural Carolina, Georgia, Alabama, Louisiana, Mississippi, and maybe Tennessee habitat. Not that you've undertaken it on your own. Maybe somebody should, but you like it better the way it is. Because this way it is not you who asks anything of them. It is the editor of* Harper's *magazine. It is Willie Morris, who is himself one of them. It is Willie Morris from Yazoo City, Mississippi. It is Willie Morris who came north by way of Texas and Oxford looking for home and so is perhaps somewhat closer in some ways to the black renegades, the old underground runagates, than to the paper fugitives of Nashville, however much he may admire their high esthetic standards.*

All you did was get started on your line about Ralph McGill and Jonathan Daniels being perhaps the true ancestral figures of some of the better young Southern newspapermen today. That was back several years ago while McGill was still alive; and what Willie Morris had said then was, "And Hodding Carter." Then he had said, "Well, look, why don't you go down at our expense and see what kind of piece you can do about it?" Then later when Harper's *Going Home in America series was in the planning stage: "Why don't you make a circle down and back spending a little time visiting with some of them. We'll make the contacts with the ones you don't know already. There's also Marshall Frady and Pat Watters and Joe Cumming and Jack Nelson, in Atlanta. I think you'll find they're all pretty good old boys, and let's see, John Corry will call Ray Jenkins in Montgomery. I know young Hodding and Dave Halberstam knows them. You've met Walker Percy. Maybe he can set you up with Shelby Foote in Memphis. Why don't you go and come on back and see what you can do on that."*

So it is Willie Morris (for all his leftover white Southern schoolboy enthusiasm for Thomas Wolfe) and the point is precisely that you yourself do not have to ask it. Because so far as that goes the main thing is not how free you yourself are to make such requests (though that is not to be dismissed) but rather how free they are to volunteer that which should be as significant to them as to you in the first place.

"I think you ought to take time out and see what you can come up with. You'll probably get yourself a book out of it."

He then went on to reiterate that it didn't have to be anything at all like the usual news report. So you've decided to take the literary options. But still and all if you could bring it off, the ever so newsworthy political implications would be obvious enough; and after all doesn't anything that any black, brown, or beige person says in the United States have the most immediate political implications? No strain for that. But the overall statement would be literary—as literary, which is to say as much of a metaphorical net, as you could make it. What with everybody going in for the personal position paper these days, maybe you could vamp your way into a few of your own riffs on the old meandertale you think you can hear overtones of in "Cotton Tail," for instance, to mention only one of a thousand and one ambivalent fox-trots, in the Ellington repertory alone.

In all events you have picked up the Harper's *magazine advance against expenses and are en route south, this time not as a reporter as such and even less as an ultra gung-ho black black spokesman but rather as a Remus-derived, book-oriented downhome boy (now middle-aged) with the sort of alabama busterbrown-hip (you hope) curiosity "that implies impression that knits knowledge that finds the nameform that whets the wits that convey contacts that sweeten sensation that drives desire that adheres to attachment that dogs death that bitches birth that entails the ensuance of existentiality." If you could get enough of all that together you were pretty certain that all of the required polemics would also be there as a matter of course.*

As the flight moves along the taxiway to the Atlanta terminal in the twilight you feel some old familiar twinges of red alertness in that part of you that will never get used to not being welcome. But it is not the old downhome radar that clicks on first this time. It is the old midtown Manhattan subterfuge detector. Because what you are going to find out shortly now is whether the greatly improved Atlanta you have been hearing and reading so much about has improved only up to the point at which midtown Manhattan was back in the old not so long ago days when you first started making trips up the country—a point beyond which, incidentally, as no apartment hunter will dispute, midtown Manhattan has not gone very far as of today.

So preparatory to everything else you check with you-know-precisely-which-good-old-you-know-who: "Hey man, I'm stopping off here to see some newspaper people tomorrow and maybe the next day. Can you recommend a good downtown hotel?" (*Which is buster brown for: "Hey man, can you vouch for what these goddam old Alana peckerwoods been doing since I was through here last time?"*) You don't say price is no sweat because he has already checked out your luggage, your fly tailoring, your big-league cameras, because he does that on super-high-speed ektachrome, 160 at f stop 16, shutter speed 1/1000.

He nods toward the battery of "Instant Hotel Reservations" telephones across from the luggage-claim point.

"Take your pick."

Then he adds: "The limousine makes all the rounds—or if you want a taxi."

You tip him and he smiles an old Joe Louis unsmile and winks an old johnny hodges sir cedric hardwick–cool things-aint-what-they-used-to-be unwink.

It only takes an instant as advertised. *But the sudden activation of the radar has changed your mood. So you ride in this time thinking about New York. You are aware of the new traffic system here and the new developments including the new big-league baseball stadium but you find yourself thinking about the people who live along the route into Manhattan from JFK International, from La Guardia and from Newark, thinking: dog-ass and chicken shit:*

("Sorry, sir, that sign should have been taken down; we have no vacancies. Sorry, sir. I really am so sorry, sir.")

Then in your Peachtree Street hotel room later on you re-check the following entry from the looseleaf notebook you had begun in Lenox Terrace three weeks before: *The way people say things up north may not conjure up the piney woods and moccasin swamps and the sound of the bloodhounds and hooded huntsmen, to be sure; but neither can it be said that all you have to do is make it across the Mason-Dixon to be free at last among nice multicolored neighbors and omni-American friends. Not so long as it goes with policemen who are no less poor white or hysterical for being mostly potato-famine Irish. Not so long as it goes with rat-race-oriented European refugees become Harlem slumlords and merchants. Not so long as such un-Southern talk goes with housing and employment policies that make downhome segregationists seem like bush-league bigots.*

The fugitive slaves found out about forked tongues shortly after the Indians did. Perhaps too many of their up-north raised descendants have until recently preferred or pretended to forget it, but even during the heyday of the Underground Railroad all you had to do was meet a few abolitionists in their Yankee hometowns, in which free Negroes were even more rigidly segregated than in the South, to realize that their fine Christian zeal (not even theirs!) for black liberation did not go hand in hand with any all-consuming commitment to equality of opportunity or to any truly comprehensive conception of pluralism as the ideal for an American social order. And yet no image is more appropriate to the motto E pluribus unum than that of a mainstream fed by an infinite diversity of tributaries.

Perhaps the Yankee sound doesn't evoke bloodhounds and lynching bees because people up here don't say ugly downhome words —not out in public, anyway. They say ghetto instead of niggertown. They say minority group meaning subspecies not only of citizen but of mankind. They say culturally deprived meaning uncivilized—but here they forget that civilization has as much to do with the propagation of crime and perversion as with the refinement of propulsion, glass, aluminum, and ferroalloys.

Nor does it follow that downhome white people display a frankness which is to be preferred to Yankee hypocrisy. Not for one segregated second. It makes some things somewhat less confusing of course but the vicious clarification represented by the old White and Colored entrance signs is hardly better than the confusions of yankeedom. Furthermore, anybody who knows anything at all *about downhome white people knows only too well that they are likely to be ever so much more wrongheaded than forthright.*

What with all those mulattoes in almost everybody's family closet (and—to be devastatingly fair—perhaps sometimes in the last wills and testaments as well) and what with all those skeletons (not to mention mulatto fetuses) in the woodpile—not to mention the sneaky propaganda concocted about black backwardness, as much to mask as to excuse white savagery—who could ever fall for that old stuff and nonsense about at least knowing where you stand? Who the hell wants to stand in the center of a hysterical mob? What should be realized by now is that those old robes and hoods were really designed to cloak the Ku Kluxers from themselves— and perhaps also to permit the morning-after illusion of shedding the moral consequences of behavior whose perversity insofar as they themselves are concerned is literally unspeakable. So much for frankness in this red-faced neck of the woods.

To which you add:

Robert Penn Warren's point in Legacy of the Civil War *about the South using its defeat as the Great Alibi and the North using its victory as the basis for a Treasury of Virtue is well taken. Yet the North is infinitely less preoccupied with its Treasury than the South is with its Alibi. (Indeed, far from manifesting any enduring pride in its role as glorious liberator, the North is most likely to give the black Southerner the impression that it would just as soon forget the whole thing—what little it remembers to allow itself to remember of the whole thing. That, in any case, is the impression a black Southerner in the North is most likely to get, once he gets beyond all the welfare-oriented do-goodism.)*

That certain New York intellectuals place little emphasis on the Civil War (beyond that required to discuss the fiction of Faulkner) is easy enough to understand; for the most part their native past begins with post–Civil War immigration and that gives them another emphasis. Not that any of them hesitate to draw on the Treasury of Virtue, but in terms that have more to do with Marxian abstractions than with vernacular inheritance.

But what about the old-line Union Army–derived Yankee? How much accrued virtue does he help himself to when none of his civil-rights Blacks are in earshot, and the Southerner says: "Look what y'all done coming down here messing up our good thing and

*don't care no more for freedmen than we did for slaves?" You can
only wonder how many damnyankees would say yes we do and
we'll do it all over again.*

The next morning you stop in at the Atlanta bureau of the Los
Angeles *Times* and meet Jack Nelson, and he puts you in touch
with Joe Cumming, the Atlanta Bureau Chief of *Newsweek*
magazine, who invites you to meet him at Herren's for lunch.
It turns out that Pat Watters and Marshall Frady are out of
town, but Reese Cleghorn, formerly of the Atlanta *Journal*
and now in residence at the Southern Regional Council, will
be free sometime during the late afternoon.

You chat with Jack Nelson about Ralph McGill; about
young Julian Bond, whose uncle J. Max you once worked for
at Tuskegee. You are pleased to note that Nelson has a friendship with Bond which is intimate enough for him to pick up
the phone and call almost as casually as he called Cumming
and Cleghorn. But Bond is out of town on a lecture tour; so
you and Nelson sit and chat about Mobile and how good the
seafood is from there along the Gulf Coast drive to New Orleans; and then about the Charles Evers campaign for mayor of
Fayette, Mississippi, currently in progress. Among the first
things you had to notice upon entering his office was an EVERS
FOR MAYOR poster on the wall. On your way out Nelson nods
toward it and says, "When you get to Greenville tell young
Hod [Carter III] I got his stuff working up here."

So you are not at all surprised to find that his article about the
return of a black Mississippian from Chicago has none of the old
our-darkies-are-coming-back bullshit in it. The Los Angeles
Times of April 24 ran it under the following heading and sub:

GHETTO DRIVES NEGRO BACK TO MISSISSIPPI;
Growing Political Power, Improved Living
Conditions Preferred to Northern Slums

And it turns out that the Mississippi James Hamberlin (for
such is the young man's name) has come back to is the Fayette
of Charles Evers.

*

During lunch Joe Cummings, who is at work on one of *Newsweek*'s periodic roundup reports on the progress of the so-called black revolution, keeps shaking his head in compassionate and astonished bewilderment that he still finds such stiff white resistance to changes which he personally regards as being so obviously necessary. Indeed, even as he talks about the amount of legal and political trickery he finds some otherwise very nice people resorting to, he seems to become more and more discouraged—so much so that you begin to wonder if his compassion is not precisely the thing that is obscuring for him the obvious fact that revolutionary changes have taken place and that white resistance to such changes is unquestionably less than ever before in the history of the South. (Before the end of the year there was to be a Jewish mayor, a black deputy mayor, a black chairman of the school board.)

You say: "Man, I don't know. But I think maybe the trouble with most of the reports I've been reading is that they are not really based on the observation of change. I mean what bothers the hell out of me is that they almost always seem to be based on what is essentially only a textbook conception of something called 'revolution.' I mean most people never seem to realize that the patterns they see in, say, the French Revolution or the Russian Revolution were really superimposed later by historians. People talk about this phase and that phase of this or that historical movement but they forget that such cutoff points were determined much later by historians much the same as acts of a play are worked out by a dramatist. Some of these guys, it seems to me, sit somewhere in an armchair or a classroom reading about events which have been edited, see what I mean? edited, into movements with snappy names, and then they go out and try to write about current events as if they already know what the historical outline is. Well, man, you can't even do that about football—and a football game has an outline that is geared to a stopwatch."

As he chews on that, somewhat surprised but also obviously intrigued, you remember two points you were trying to make in a discussion with a Pulitzer Prize–winning foreign correspondent and a sportswriter one night in New York: that most war correspondents don't seem to know nearly as much about combat as sportswriters know about the games they report, and that if all you have is antiwar reporters on the one hand and chauvinistic reporters on the other the public is likely to be getting more propaganda than reliable combat information. They were talking about the so-called credibility gap and what you were trying to explain was why so far as you were concerned a news-media report was not necessarily closer to actuality than an official version. (And besides, how could there really be a credibility gap when most people already knew that you never could tell when politicians were telling the truth? They lied to get into office and they lied to stay there.) But what the two writers in New York were really concerned about was not credibility or accuracy in reporting but peace—or rather ending the war in Vietnam. They were very compassionate about that, and so were you. But the trouble was that you couldn't trust their compassion as a source of information. Moreover, wherever it involves Negroes, compassion is forever degenerating into condescension.

To Joe Cumming you say: "To people who really know the game, football is much more than touchdowns, field goals, and conversion points. The real progress report includes the first downs, the yards gained, the passes completed, and a hundred or so other details [including the area of the playing field in which most of the action takes place]. Not to mention all the stuff that adds up to morale and drive. A lot of civil-rights stuff I've been reading makes me think about the kind of sportswriter who sits up there looking right at you piling up more first downs than the other team, completing more passes for more yardage, and playing most of the game in their territory, and then goes off and builds an 'ekes out win' story on the fact that you won by the one touchdown you scored in the last quarter. Of course sometimes it is not that he doesn't know. And sometimes needless to say it is his simpleminded editor's notion of what news is, or rather what a given news story should be. Or take baseball. Imagine a sportswriter who is unable to evaluate the importance of being in a scoring position. Man, he doesn't know the game."

Later when he comes back to the Southern area progress report that he is going to have to file to *Newsweek*, you say at one point: "Let's take this chick waiting this table. Man, she's got to be fresh off of Tobacco Road or some goddam where.

So I wouldn't be at all surprised that if you followed her home and interviewed her for *Newsweek* she would express all kinds of negative sentiments about desegregation—a white girl shouldn't have to serve Negroes, and all that crap. She might not, but I wouldn't be surprised if she did. But is what she says when interviewed on desegregation as a specific issue really more significant than the way she is acting right now with me sitting right here? Look man, I'm not about to find more change in white Southern attitudes than a white Southerner like yourself will concede. Not me, man. If you say these cats are getting ready to fire on Fort Sumter again I for one am not going to dispute you. But the point is, I'm not down here to run any statistics but just to see how it feels. I'm operating on my literary radar, this time, my metaphor finder—how about that?—and you know what my goddam radar is telling me about this girl? That she is a country girl, new to the great big city of Atlanta, a young girl from the provinces, the Georgia sticks, come to seek her fortune in the big time, and she was far more concerned about getting our orders right just now than about anything else in the world. My radar indicates that the difference between her embarrassment when I had to help her spell Heineken and when you had to help her pronounce Shrimp Arnaud was nil. She was relieved and thankful. Man, what she is really worried about is some stern-eyed maître d' and some evil-assed cat back in the kitchen! That's not the whole story of course, but it is the part that most often gets left out. Well, I happen to think that attitudes just might be too tricky for the statistical survey in the first place—certainly the survey as we know it. But you know something? I'd be willing to bet that this girl isn't actually running into nearly as many desegregated situations as she had anticipated—and get this—had already prepared herself to accept when she decided to come out of the sticks. And you know something else? I just might be willing to extend that bet to cover the revolutionary emotional reconditioning of a lot of other white Southerners nowadays—in spite of some of the things they still say and still do. Man, I got my fingers crossed but I try to keep my eyes and ears open too. For instance the fact that we are sitting here, instead of somewhere out on Auburn Avenue or West Hunter in the first place. And I must say the fact that it seems to count for so little with you makes it all the more indicative of how fast some things have changed—especially when you look around this room at how people are minding their own business as if they were at the Algonquin or the Café de la Paix or somewhere and then remember how many of their ancestors are turning over in their Confederate graves. Some of whom are not even dead yet, man. Yet they know very well that being here puts me in scoring position, man, football or baseball."

Not that some of the old crossroad-store plus courthouse-square sensibility that you associate with the best white Southern writers isn't reflected in almost everything Joe Cumming says. It is there in the local details he cites reviewing some of the revolutionary/reactionary confrontations he has been observing recently, and you also hear it in the downhome quality of the questions he asks about New York.

On the question of prototypes and self-definition, however, it is not the mention of such Southern journalists as Ralph McGill and Jonathan Daniels that stimulates his most immediate and most personal response. He acknowledges their influence (along with that of Hodding Carter and a few others). But the real shock of recognition comes when you describe yourself as a writer whose nonfiction represents an effort to play literary vamps and intellectual riffs equivalent to the musical ones Duke Ellington feeds his orchestra from his piano:

"Oh hey, oh say, you too? Duke Ellington? The Duke? Oh, that man! Isn't he the greatest? Isn't he just absolutely—say, let me tell you something about me and that man. Look, let me tell you something. That was what I wanted to run away from and go up to New York for. That music. Duke Ellington. Me and another old boy back then. Man, I'm telling you, we were really going. You have all those old records? Me too. Oh man."

So then the two of you sit calling the names of Ellington records and sidemen back and forth to each other as Duke's boys almost always do whenever they encounter each other no matter where: *"Say, how about when. Remember when Cootie and Rex. How about when Tricky Sam Nanton. How about Jimmy Blanton and Ben Webster and Barney Bigard!"* All of which also brings back those marvelous times when it used to be one of the greatest thrills in the world just to be sitting in the Paramount Theatre in Times Square seeing old Ray Nance ("Oh that Ray Nance!") come bouncing down to the solo mike with Johnny and Lawrence and Harry Carney in the background as cool as an Egyptian brown-and-beige pantheon.

But you don't say, Hey, you know something, Duke Ellington was your Uncle Remus. Nor do you say, O.K. so let's hear some Duke on your next *Newsweek* gig. Because when it comes to that, how much Duke do you hear on black magazine gigs, especially from those writers who are most insistently blacker than thou?

Except for a brief visit to the Southern Regional Council to meet and chat with Reese Cleghorn, who used to work for Ralph McGill on the Atlanta *Journal*, you spend the rest of the afternoon sightseeing. Cleghorn suggests, as does Jack Nelson, that the man who knows McGill best is Eugene Patterson, now of the *Washington Post*—but actually you've decided that a McGill story requires more research than you have time to do. *Because along with your memories of his seed-store–feed-store journalistic insightfulness, there is also the image of the newly elected member of the Tuskegee Board of Trustees, sitting alone in sleepless embarrassment at the pedestal of the Booker T. Washington monument at three o'clock that morning with what was left of a bottle of something, complaining that he had less courage than "that black ex-slave up there."*

You look for the old landmarks along Peachtree Street (including Zachary's and Muse's the haberdashers which were to the Atlanta of your Tuskegee days what Fannin's was to Montgomery and Metzger's was to Mobile). Then you make your way once more to Rich's bookstore, remembering how it was when you first saw it back during the heyday of *Gone with the Wind*, which was also when Atlanta was trying to be an even older place than it was before the Sherman caper, saying gone with the wind but trying like hell to look as far as possible back beyond the so-called New South of Henry W. Grady all the same.

Then from Rich's you take the bus out to West Hunter to see Atlanta University, Morehouse, Spelman, Clark, and Morris Brown once more, remembering how the fried chicken in Ma Sutton's café used to be worth the trip in spite of the fact that the reason you used to make it was that the downtown Atlanta of those days was so goddam segregated you couldn't even use a clean rest room; remembering also that Atlanta University had also been a part of the so-called New South and that one of its finest graduates was James Weldon Johnson of the class of 1894; and that W. E. B. Du Bois during his first period there (1896–1909) had written *Souls of Black Folk* and had also initiated, according to Guy B. Johnson, the first real sociological research in the South.

You also remember how during your days at Mobile County Training School the rotogravure-sepia images of Du Bois in his satanic goatee, Booker T. Washington (close-cropped, beardless, full-lipped, and without mustache), Frederick Douglass (coin-perfect in his lion's mane), Harriet Tubman in her glorious bandanna, old knob-headed Jack Johnson with his satinsmooth shoulders and tight pants, and all the rest of them used to blend together in a sepia-bronze panorama when the student body used to stand and sing "Lift Every Voice and Sing," which was written by that same golden-brown James Weldon Johnson and his brother J. Rosamond Johnson and which everybody used to call the Negro National Anthem—but which for you was first of all the Brown American national school bell anthem (the comb your hair brush your teeth shine your shoes crease your trousers tie your tie clean your nails rub a dub stand and sit and look straight make folks proud anthem!). So far as you are concerned, not even Martin Luther King—the stamping ground of whose youngmanhood you are treading even now—could inspire his most eager followers to put as much aspiration and determination into "We Shall Overcome" as people always used to get into James Weldon and J. Rosamond Johnson's school bell song.

It is on the campus of Morehouse College not at SCLC headquarters or even at Ebenezer Baptist Church that you find yourself remembering Martin Luther King most vividly this time.

There is no accounting for miracles, to be sure—and certainly such a good man as Martin Luther King was as miraculous a phenomenon as any that ever came to pass; nevertheless, you like to think that every tangible thing about him was an altogether natural fruition of some aspect of the black Atlanta University system you had learned about during boyhood and youngmanhood in Mobile and at Tuskegee. The charismatic eloquence, for instance, which on occasion enabled him to lead his followers like an adult-oriented and politicized pied piper, was an unmistakable extension of a long-standing local tradition of first-rate pulpit oratory. Indeed, in the Atlanta in which King came to his calling, well-trained activist ministers were as plentiful as, say, big-league saxophone players were in the Kansas City of the young Charlie Parker!

But what strikes you most forcefully as you find your way around Morehouse this time is how specifically King also embodied the very highest ideals of the splendid black, brown, and beige Morehouse Man who whether Alpha, Kappa, Sigma, or Omega was forever dedicated to the proposition that for those precious few Negroes who were privileged to come by it—by whatever means—a college education was a vehicle not simply for one's own personal gain but for the uplift both social and spiritual of all of one's people. (Or at least as many as one's achievement permitted one to reach.) Indeed, even as your achievement raised you above your brothers it also made you not only responsible to but also accessible to an ever-increasing number of them. Not that the Talladega and Fisk traditions, for instance, were any less tightly geared to "service." As a matter of fact, the Hampton and Tuskegee traditions represent the epitome of grass-roots service. But still and all there was a special Morehouse "something," which was made up of many things but which was most impressive—which is not to say obvious—in the way Martin Luther King always kept his cool no matter what the situation, his Morehouse cool and his Morehouse dap. Indeed, in the clutches he reminded you of nothing so much as the Maroon Tiger coolness and "class" that coach Frank Forbes, who himself was always as unruffled as he was well-tailored, always used to require Morehouse athletes to maintain especially under the pressure of imminent defeat in championship competition. King may or may not have served an apprenticeship directly under Forbes but he represented the ultimate extension of that Morehouse something which nobody, not even the magnificent Benjamin Mays himself, imparted more effectively than did Frank Forbes—that something which used to make the Maroon Tigers look as good losing as other teams looked winning! It is not at all unthinkable that some of that played a part in enabling King to achieve nobility, even in the process of being brutalized by degenerate red-neck deputies.

At midnight you sit looking out over Atlanta from Polaris, the revolving cocktail lounge above the Regency Hyatt House, thinking of things you could have added to what you had said to Joe Cumming about measuring revolutionary change. Item: The most fundamental revolutionary changes begin not at the bottom with the so-called masses but at the very top. The place to look for such change is in the centers of power and prestige. Are there any highly qualified but erstwhile excluded people at the conference tables—where policies are made? Are there any in the restaurants, the cocktail lounges, drawing rooms, ballrooms, where the deals and achievements are celebrated? Those, as any competent student of social change should know, are the revolutionary questions. Facts and figures about unskilled and semi-skilled employment wages, housing, and schools are not necessarily indicative of revolutionary change. Social betterment, economic rehabilitation, yes, and by all means. But revolution is something else. Everybody talking about revolution don't mean it. Most media-oriented spokesmen don't even seem to know what a basic change is.

Item: To the statistician a token is something you can write off as being insignificant because it is not big enough. But when you are talking about revolutionary change, tokens and rituals are often more important than huge quantities. The old numbers game is a jolly good hustle for appropriations-oriented social workers, but Southern reactionaries are much more likely to fight about tokens than about numbers as such. Look at the fit pitched by all kinds of noncollege white people when Charlayne Hunter and Hamilton Holmes first entered the University of Georgia. But how big an uproar was and is there about the actual number of Negroes now employed in good-paying jobs at Atlanta Airport? Have any white reactionaries ever taken the trouble to count them? When you desegregate a school or a neighborhood, how many of those white people who flee would stay on upon being assured that incoming

Negroes absolutely would not exceed a fixed quota no matter how small? Maybe reactionaries operate on a more profound understanding of or intuition about the functional interrelationship of tokenism and incentive than those ever so compassionate white liberals who are forever insisting that all black people must be equal with each other. It is probably all too obvious to the reactionary that *expanding the horizons of aspiration* has as much to do with liberation as anything else. In any case when the reactionary says, "Who do you think you are, coming in here"; and says, "Let one in and before long there will be a whole slew of them"; and says, "Give one of them an inch and they'll take a mile"; he seems to know very well that expanding the horizons of aspiration is precisely what is at issue. He wants even the smallest black schoolchildren to feel that they will never make it to the top. And yet your compassion-oriented white liberal on the other hand seems entirely unaware of the possibility that when he writes off outstanding Negroes (especially those who move in circles higher than his own!) as tokens he could well be creating an effect on young people's horizons of aspiration that may be even more restrictive than segregation. After all, brutal exclusion often inspires determination, whereas the downgrading of achievement could easily lead to exasperation and cynicism. If all outstanding black men are only token dispensations whose intrinsic merits count for nothing, why should any Negro pupil be anything except a con man?

You wake up on the second morning with still another item: As for those ever so fashionably despairing black polemicists (those who are not hype-artists to begin with) who fall for such cheap white liberal bullshit, they have simply forgotten that U.S. Negroes, not unlike all other people, including Russian and Chinese Communist revolutionaries, want their leaders to enjoy all the privileges and protocol that all other leaders enjoy. Official pomp and circumstance after all is as indispensable to revolutionary power as to established power structures. The so-called masses want their great men to come among their people, yes, a thousand times yes, but they most certainly did not want men like Martin Luther King to be forced to put up with dilapidated segregated accommodations simply because the first-rate hotels wouldn't allow him to enter. What they clearly and justifiably resent is the fact that the white segregationist by his action is saying that even the finest achievement does not qualify a black man to the ordinary things any white man can take for granted. It is not at all surprising that even the black separatists became boiling mad and threatened to burn down Madison Square Garden because several (only several, mind you) Negroes were denied membership in the exclusive $25,000 a year New York Athletic Club. When the NYAC, which was sponsoring the track meet at Madison Square Garden that was the occasion of the protest, pointed to its record of helping worthy athletes, on some level of awareness the black protesters knew very well that helping Negro athletes out of the slums could never really make up for deliberately keeping their heroes from the summit.

Successful Negroes may try to outdo each other in demonstrating to The People that for all their accomplishments and acclaim they are still just folks. But, as perhaps anyone concerned enough to study such matters will no doubt discover, a leader, who is after all uncommon by nature, can only pretend to be a common man. It is sometimes necessary to project himself as a nice guy, a regular fellow and all that, but such is nature of charismatic authority that the so-called common people will not tolerate very much common behavior in their leaders—a public gesture or two, yes, but even so the minute a leader really climbs down off that pedestal the people are likely to replace their awe of his halo—with contempt for his feet of clay. The fact is, when you destroy the people's awe of the leader you also destroy their sense of security in his specialness. Nobody could be more mistaken than those black spokesmen who think that talking down will increase their mass appeal. Acting ignorant as the saying goes may impress certain pseudo-revolutionary white slummers but Negroes are likely to prefer leaders who sound technically proficient. Martin Luther King was not simply a sincere and familiar-sounding minister; he was an *educated*-sounding minister. The ever so down to the nitty-gritty speeches of Malcolm X never brought him the following during his lifetime that his smoothly edited "autobiography" has built up since his death.

*

Then as the limousine circles by the Dinkler Plaza on the way to the flight that will take you to Montgomery and the bus to Tuskegee, who do you see coming out of the Alibi Lounge as if on cue? What statistically unique, statistically insignificant, but no less symbolically overwhelming figure betokening the national status of Atlanta as now-South metropolis—in spite of the reactionary forces that produced and support Lester Maddox? Who else except Hank Aaron, looking as barbershop-sharp as Mobile, Alabama, baseball players have always looked walking that old be-sports-shirted, high-shine morning-before-the-game walk along the main drag, not only as if with Earl Hines' old Grand Terrace Band playing "Cavernism" on a jukebox in the background, but also as if they were really road band musicians in town to play a dance?

You rap on the window, but you don't say "*Hey there, Mobile. What say, home?*" All you do is rap and then wave as from the bleachers thinking: *Hey you some token, cousin.* All you do when he waves back is smile feeling every bit as good inside as you do sitting back watching a pregame warm-up or hearing Duke vamping into, say, "Laying on Mellow" preliminary to bringing on Johnny Hodges.

I see you, Mobile; I see you man, and me, I just happen to be the kind of homeboy that can smell glove leather, red mound clay, and infield grass all the way back to the days of Bo Peyton and Bancy and Tanny, who, as Chick Hamilton must have told you, was without a doubt the fanciest first baseman who ever did it. I see you, Mobile and I don't even have to mention old Satchel Paige, who is not only still around but right here in Alana to boot. I see you, Hank. Three hundred and seventy-five miles from Mobile by way of Boston and Milwaukee plus the time it took Atlanta to make it out of the bushes. What say, home?

FOUR

Tuskegee

TRIANGULATION POINT THREE FIVE THREE NINE

*T*HE OLD PLACE *you used to come into coming in from Atlanta by railroad was Chehaw, from which you used to take
the Chehaw Special on into the campus. Traveling mostly by air
nowadays however you land at either Columbus, Georgia, or
Montgomery and come in by bus or private car. The distance is
approximately the same from either point. But this time you've
chosen the thirty-eight-mile ride from Monkey Town to Skeegum-
Geegum because that way you can stop by to meet and talk with
Ray Jenkins.*

When you get to the Alabama Journal *however you find that
Ray Jenkins is expecting you but because of a story now breaking
must stick close to his desk for the next several hours. So you make
do with his offer of a brief chat on the spot, and take a raincheck
on his invitation to double back later on in the afternoon to continue over drinks somewhere. It sounds great, especially since the only
place you've ever done that sort of thing in the Cradle of the Confederacy is out at the officers' club at Air University. But the fact
is that even as you find out that he is one of McGill's literal heirs
(who sometimes used to stand in for him not only on speaking
engagements but also for writing assignments) you are already
beginning to visualize the old Greyhound ride along US 80 east
with the pecan orchards in the distance as you pull out heading
for Mount Meigs and Shorter and the once-more-ness of Macon
County.*

*On the itinerary the stopover at Tuskegee comes after Atlanta
and before Mobile. But it so happens that any bus you take to get
there from Monkey Town will be en route not from but to Atlanta.
So now, even as you let the seat back and the bus settles into the
old ever so easy to remember heavy-duty-rubber-on-open-country-
asphalt road hum that will last all the way from Prairie Farms to
the approach to Green Fork you are all too aware of the fact that
you are traveling not south toward but north by east and away*

from Mobile, even as the two-car basketball motorcade bringing the MCTS Whippets to the Regionals came that spring.

That time which was the first time ever, the route they took out of the Beel and the bay sky and moss plus cypress bayou country in the Ford and the Chevrolet was 43 north through Mount Vernon and Grove Hill and then 5 into 22 to pick up 80 out of Selma. But coming back up again in the late summer of that same year to matriculate, it was route 31 by Greyhound through Bay Minette and Evergreen and Georgiana and then 80 out of Monkey City. Mister Buster Brown college bound don't you let no-money turn you round. Mister Buster Brown from down in Mobile town. Who if not you Mister Buster Brown? Who else if not who ever Mister Buster Brown? And when else if not whenever and how else if not howsoever and ever Mister Buster Brown?

Whoever made it through grade school. Whoever and whoever and howsoever, and from that point on the details were almost always left to you. Not that you were really entirely on your own. You always knew very well that somebody was there and you also knew that it was not only mama plus papa or auntie plus uncle but also and also and also blood relations or no. But even so, such was the process by which they made sure that you were weaned that all anybody was ever really likely to say again was never anything that was any more than something about making something that amounts to something out of yourself.

What they meant when they said it was up to you was don't be the one to keep your own self down. Find out whatever and whoever it is you want to be and do your level best and you can count on somebody backing you up the best we can even when it's something ain't nobody ever even heard tell of before. Because folks don't necessarily have to be able to use all them big dictionary words to understand life. You just go on ahead and let them see you trying and they'll understand more than you might think. And anytime you don't believe it all you got to do is get up somewhere and mess up and see if they won't know it. "They'll know it all right and you'll be hurting them more than the white folks ever did or ever could."

You were the one getting the book learning so it was you who were supposed to be able to do such articulation as might be required. But the actual truth of the fabulous matter was that very

*little if any ever was. Nor (the steel-blue actuality they weaned
you on being what it was) could you, for your part, ever expect to
get away with blaming any of your own personal shortcomings
and failures on anybody else, including the white folks—least of
all the white folks: Boy, don't come telling me nothing about no
old white folks. Boy, ain't nothing you can tell me about no white
folks. Which was to say mean and evil low-down and dirty white
folks, whether outright stuck up, downright cruel—or whether
two-faced and underhanded. It was as if everybody had always
known about all that.*

*Indeed, absolutely the last thing in the world you could ever
imagine yourself or any other buster brown from Mobile County
Training School doing was coming back complaining, "Look
what they did to me." (I was going to town but they turned me
round.) Because the only one you could possibly blame anything
on, even when you did run afoul of white viciousness, was yourself.
Absolutely the only thing you could possibly come back saying even
then was: "I'm the one. That's all right about them, it's me, because I already knew exactly what to expect and I still didn't do
what I was supposed to do when the time came, that time. But
that was that time, watch me next time."*

*Mister Buster Brown Mister Buster Brown don't you let nobody
turn you round. Ain't always the white folks bust you down. As
you were by no means alone in finding out soon enough: Hey you
who you little granny-dodging snotty-nosed granny dodger you
ain't no goddam more than no goddam body else. Hey you who
you going around so stuck up like you so wise and other goddam
wise you can't talk to folks since you made it on up there in that
little old two-by-four high school?*

*Not that white people were not almost always likely to try to say
something infinitely worse. Nor was white antagonism likely to be
mostly only verbal. But nobody ever expected you to grin and bear
any more of that than your circumstances absolutely required you
to do for the time being. Which was not the case at all when it
came to some of the old henhouse stuff some neighborhood folks especially certain street corner woofers and tweeters were forever
signifying in one way or another:*

*Hey you who you how come you got to be the one running your
mouth so much and so proper-talking like don't nobody else know
nothing just because you passed a test in a book or something. Hey*

you who you let me tell you one goddam thing mister little-old-
know-so-much smart-ass goddam nigger you don't know no god-
dam more about it than no goddam body else because don't no
goddam body give a goddam shit about none of it no goddam
how. You can read all them old white folks books you want to and
you still ain't going to be nothing but another goddam nigger
just like every goddam body else. So don't come getting so goddam
bright-ass smart-ass around me goddam it like somebody supposed
to think you so much because you over there running up behind
some little old Mister goddam-ass Baker and them old hancty-butt
goddam Mobile County Training School goddam teachers.

But no matter how terrible some of them could sometimes make
it sound didn't "Hey you, who you" somehow or other still mean
who else if not you? At least some of the time? Because in spite of
the worrisome Sunday school lesson about going unto one's own
and having them receive you not, and also in spite of all of the
fireside admonitions about the kind of folks who worked against
their own folks like crabs pulling one another back into the basket
were you not always convinced that a time would come when
many if not most would be only too willing to say something else?
"That's my goddam boy up there taking care of that goddam
business. Hell, I used to kick his little old snotty-nose ass every time
he open his mouth anywhere near me. Ask him and ask him if I
didn't help make him the man he is today." (WHO THE ONE MAN
YOU THE ONE.)

As the Greyhound you've taken this time zooms on out of Sweet
Gum curve, you bring the seat back to the upright position and
begin checking your watch and calculating the arrival time
against such landmarks as you can still recognize (after seven
years this time) from there on in. But even as your mounting
anticipation sweeps you on ahead to Green Fork, the old Confed-
erate square and the taxi ride out to the campus and Dorothy
Hall, it is as if it is in the pit of your stomach and the seat of your
pants that you remember the two pop songs you kept humming
and whistling to yourself in Mobile that last summer. One went:
"I'm THRILLED/*I'm so excitingly/*THRILLED. . ./*the* SOME-
thing thing thing thing/. . ." And the other: "the ashes on the
floor/the way you'd slam the door/I miss them when the day is
through/when I sit alone and think of you/and those little things
you used to do/. . ." But it was not really the lyrics as such; it

was the way the music, which was only downtown Mobile radio music, downtown Mobile department-store perfume music, movie magazine music, went somehow with your awareness that the time had come to leave home perhaps forever. So all the way to Tuskegee that time it was also the music that went with the good-bye that Miss Somebody was all about from the very outset. Who said, Now I'm going to see. Who said so far so good, but now you on your own. Miss pre-"Blue Lou" Somebody, Miss pre-"Big John Special" Somebody, Miss pre-"Moten Swing" Somebody.

John Gerald Hamilton, who was there from Detroit, will remember what being a freshman was like that first September. Wherever old narrow-eyed, level-talking, pigeon-toed-walking Gerald Hamilton is now he is not likely to have forgotten those days, and he probably remembers that it did not rain very much in spite of two of the songs that were so popular that year. He will remember that it was not a very dry and dusty month either, that along with the late-summer blueness of the central Alabama sky there was a back-to-school breeze that felt as good to him socializing on the tennis courts, no doubt, as to you out for football on the practice field beyond the water tank.

Gerald Hamilton, whose nickname was Jug, not for Jughead but for jug of wine, as in underneath the bough, will remember the then rust-red but now silver dome of Tompkins Dining Hall, the weathered green clock tower, White Hall lawn, the Band Stand, the old Bugle Stand, and the whiteness of academic columns as you saw them through the flat preautumnal greenness of the elms lining Campus Avenue. Nor will he have forgotten the brick-red oldness of dormitories like Cassidy, Band Cottage, Thrasher, and the four Emories behind the Trade School on the Greenwood side of the campus. So he will also remember the newness of Hollis Burke Frissell Library, the Gym and Armstrong Hall which was already known as the Science Building but which at that time was also where most of the academic classes were held: Math and Physics and Dean W. T. B. Williams' office on One: Biology but mostly English, French, History, Political Science, Social Science on Two; with Three being mostly Chem labs.

Jug Hamilton, whose customary jug in those days was really a Leyden jar and whose wine was most likely to be the traditional chem-lab alcohol–plus–grapefruit-juice cocktail, will remember all of that and also what it was like in the hallways and on the stairways of Armstrong Hall between class bells in that year of *Esquire* magazine plus road musician and Hollywood-derived swankiness and also how it felt to know at last that going to college was *this*, and going to Harry V. Romm and Raphael Tisdale for Biology; to Ralph N. Davis, Jessie V. Parkhurst, and Charles G. Gomillion for Sociology; to lawyer Albert Turner for History and Political Science; to pipe-smoking chalk-throwing Hollis Price for Economics; to McCormick and his satchel and cigarette holder for Physics; to smiling but relentless Joe Fuller for Math; and to Red Davis whom freshmen were not alone in confusing with a District Attorney for Psychology, and, worse still, Tests and Measurements!

So will Andrew Walker and Cleo Belle Sharpe Walker remember those days, and so will Jack and Dick Montgomery from The Ham and Harold "The Deep" Smith from Memphis and Margaret Young from Selma (a town which once evoked the word "university" as Tuskegee evokes the word Institute) and so will Frecks Eskridge of Pittsburgh and Dennison Graine of Kalamazoo; and so will Mabel Smith and Lulu Hymes from Alana and Billy Hegwood from San Antonio; Jackson Burnside from the Bahamas; and Terresetta Glashen there all the way from Africa. As for Frank D. Godden who delivered the mail, it was as if he was already an upper classman.

They all will remember W. Henri Payne with his brownskin Frenchman's mustache whether they took French or not that year. They will remember Alphonse Heningburg and his beautiful wife. Nor will anybody have forgotten that the only way to repeat anything Dr. Carver said was to imitate him in as high a pitch as possible (adding precisely enunciated dirty words which would have horrified him: "They ask me: 'Dr. Carver what makes rubber stretch?' and I say to them quite frankly I don't cop what the fuck makes that shit act up like that, I don't dig no rubber-stretching shit. I dig peanuts, I dig potatoes"). In the case of Cap'n Neely the key word was "*boy*" with the notorious Neely vibrato; and then there was Cap'n "Now Now B-Buddy" Love.

Ralph Ellison who was there from Oklahoma City will also remember those days. But not as an invisible freshman. He must remember that particular year as an upperclassman. He will always remember buildings named for Collis P. Huntington and Russell Sage and Andrew Carnegie and John D. Rockefeller. He will remember already knowing about such outlying regions as Rockefeller Hill and Brickyard Hill and Rosenwald Heights and Eli Crossing, and when as in his novel *Invisible Man* he concocts marvelously outrageous anecdotes about a Bitch's Sabbath juke joint which, not unmindful of a book by Lewis Mumford, he calls the Golden Day he may well be riffing on things happening somewhere over in that vicinity before that September. But he will remember which autumn you mean because he was with the band in Crampton Bowl in Monkey Town for the Thanksgiving Game with Bama State and that was the year the Bama State Collegians kept taking off a riff which turned out to be related to "Mister Christopher Columbus," *with the trumpets reaching and screeching while a city-slicking Bama State broken-field runner probably named Red Fields, carrying the ball as if it were really draped over his arm like a waiter's towel kept directing his interference as if he had all the time in the world, as if saying: "Hey, you get this one here and you get that one there, and I'm taking care of these last two cotton-picking Booker T's my damn self."*

Ellison, who was not only there as a trumpet player but was also majoring in music, probably still shudders when something reminds him of the novelty song which everybody hated but kept singing that winter: "*You press the middle valve down/And the music goes round and round/Oh oh oh oh—ho ho/and it comes out here.*" But as a well-established upperclassman with an upperclassman's easy familiarity with members of the faculty he was also there to be remembered—along with Tom Campbell, Eddie Hollins, and John Hoskens; along with Laly Charlton and Thelma Bradley and Sue Whitefield, not to mention Big Shit Crawford, Catfish Smith, Bulldog Smith, Stinky Dog Redmon, not to mention King-Kong Wingo, Frankenstein Green, and the one and only Dad Moberly, who had been playing quarterback since the days of the legendary Big Ben Stevenson, the Satchel Paige of football who had obviously been the Four Horsemen plus the Galloping Ghost all in one.

Naturally Addie Stabler and Frank Watkins will remember most of this. And so will Leo Greene and Orlando Powers. Because like you they were also there on scholarship from Mobile County Training School—that being the year it was decided and declared that Tuskegee, not Talladega, not Fisk, not Morehouse or Spelman would get Mister Baker's Talented Tenth. But it is Gerald Hamilton whose memories of the first days in Room A H 202 for English 101 with young Mister Sprague, Morteza Drexel (Hamilton, Howard, Columbia), will no doubt be closest to your own. It is certainly old Jug Hamilton who will best remember the morning young Mister Sprague read from William Saroyan's *Daring Young Man on the Flying Trapeze*, to illustrate how free and natural and expressive of your own personality, your own sense of individuality, he wanted everybody's informal themes to be. Because it was old Jug Hamilton himself who was the only freshman who could stroll across to Sage Hall afterwards talking about such unMobile County Training School things as free association and stream of consciousness, mentioning such unheard of *avant-garde* writers as James Joyce, Marcel Proust, Virginia Woolf, and Gertrude Stein as casually as if they were boxers, baseball or football players, and movie stars.

It was old Jug Hamilton with whom you shared the copies of *Esquire* magazine with articles and stories by Ernest Hemingway that young Mister Sprague used to pass along; and it was with him that you play-talked not only he-said-she-said goddam hemingway talk but also finger-raised stage-eloquent Shakespearean iambic pentameter, sword-poised, hip-cocked Cyrano de Bergerac flippancy. Later on it was to be Mort Sprague himself with whom you shared the Auden and the current poems and essays of Eliot and the current Pound, and Kafka and Kierkegaard, and, best of all, Thomas Mann's *Joseph* story. (Nor did he find it in the least strange that your enthusiasm for Thomas Mann's dialectic orchestration went hand in hand with your all-consuming passion for the music of Duke Ellington and Count Basie. He said it proved you were one on whom Chaucer and Shakespeare were not lost and he began a collection of blues-idiom records of his own.)

But before you became an apprentice teacher you were a freshman and it was Gerald Hamilton, whose Sage Hall room looked out from under the eaves and across the fire escape and that part of the campus to the clay-red, pine-dotted hills and besides being the London flat of Sherlock Holmes was as old as any skylight garret in Paris, as fabulous as any workshop in the Florence of Benvenuto Cellini. Old Jug Hamilton's room was where you went when you wanted to be in a place that was as old as the world of Boccaccio or of Chaucer or of Rabelais or Cervantes; or as new and now as the illustrations in Sheldon Cheney's *Primer of Modern Art*, as Einstein and the Fourth Dimension, as the radio and as the candid-camera pages of *Coronet*—*Life* magazine was yet to be born, *The Literary Digest* was not yet dead—as old as the world of Abelard, François Villon, of D'Artagnan's Musketeer mentors; but also as new as Louis Untermeyer's updated anthologies of Modern Poetry, as streamlined and functional as the Frank Lloyd Wright plus Alexis de Seversky designs old Jug himself sometimes knocked out for his classes in Architecture.

Meanwhile you were also very much aware of the world of the novels being read for young Mister Sprague's English Four Something Something by Ralph Ellison, Trementia Birth, Letitia Woods and other book-reading upperclassmen, a world which began in the fall with *Moll Flanders* and *Clarissa Harlowe* and *Tom Jones* and included the people of Jane Austen and Thackeray and Dickens during the winter and ended in the spring quarter with the people of Thomas Hardy including Eustacia Vye, Clym Yeobright, Tess of the D'Urbervilles, and Jude the Obscure: somehow from that time on it has always seemed that Thomas Hardy's *Return of the Native* belonged to Trementia Birth and that *Jude the Obscure* belonged to Ralph Ellison. Many books still seem to be the exclusive property of old Jug Hamilton of course, but not even Villon's *Testament* or *Gargantua and Pantagruel* evoke his presence and that time more readily than Rockwell Kent's special edition of Voltaire's *Candide*.

Perhaps Gerald Hamilton, who for some reason seemed more concerned with such matters than other freshmen, will also remember a particular conversation about the relative merits of various prominent upperclassmen, the question being whether they were truly big-league academic caliber or mostly jive artists. Addie Stabler and Leo Greene will remember and so will Frank Watkins and Orlando Powers that back at MCTS from the ninth grade on the question was one of being of college timber, and of leadership fiber such as would bring credit not only to your alma mater but to all your people.

Gerald Hamilton, who may or may not remember what was said about Joe Lazenberry, for instance, or about, say, Jody Harris (who was pictured in the student handbook as an ideal cadet) but he will hardly have forgotten Sandophra Robinson and Ralph Waldo Edgar Allan Powe, or the day you checked him out as the other Ralph Waldo, the one in Music, the one who sometimes worked at the main circulation desk at the library, wearing expertly tied bow ties, first-quality sports jackets, welt-seamed contrasting slacks, black-and-white shoes, the one you had also seen in Miss Eva K. Hamlin's Art Room modeling a bust of Marie Howard.

"Hey what about that Ellison guy?"

"One Ralph Ellison?"

"You know him? Walks bouncing kinda like that guy that played Shadow in *Winterset*."

"Oh yes one knows one Ralph Waldo–type Ellison. Here from Oklahoma not without some bepuzzlement to one William L. Dawson, composer, conductor, as to one Alvin J. Neely, Registrar and Dean of Men, and to the utter exasperation of one Addie L. Long, housemother. One knows him."

"What about him?"

"Music major, student concert master as it were."

"I see he's been checking out a lot of good books."

"He reads them."

"I mean good ones like us, not just for class."

"He reads. College will not interfere with his education."

"He just finished *Seven Gothic Tales*."

"Then it is evidently readable matter."

"He checks out a lot of poetry too."

"He would."

"Not just Edna St. Vincent Millay. I mean like *Personae*, *The Waste Land*, Robinson Jeffers, and writes some."

"He would do that too."

"I was next to get *Roan Stallion* and there was a slip of paper with some free verse about life and death being two beautiful nothings."

"Ha! No *Hound of Heaven* for this one. The watchful Ellison eyes say otherwise."

"Hey, you think maybe he has read *Ulysses*?"

"He will if he hasn't."

"You think working there they might let him read that copy in that cabinet?"

"Egads, Joyce locked up, with Radclyffe Hall. *Ejoe ejoe am seel!* But back to the matter of one Ellison's commissions to poetry."

"How beautiful are these two nothings."

"Ah, my dear Vatson. Such matters run passing deep as whale shit as 'twere. Yet may the source be as unmistakable as one Cyrano de Bergerac's considerable proboscis. For aren't we all desolate because sick of an old passion?"

"Hey, you mean cherchez les on-sait-bien-quoi?"

"*Last night ah yester night betwixt her lips and mine there fell thy shadow, Cynara!* C'est toujours Cynara, quoi. And obviously I do not mean one Sue whatshername. Ah Wilderness. *Mais où sont les neiges d'antan?* Dans les pissoirs, I fear. Gone, I fear, with neither a fart nor a fizzle, comme tout les choses, comme ça! But e'en in dissolution is art served. But leave us not wax Baudelairian! For the art of which I speak serves mankind, what?"

Remembering all of that, good old Jug Hamilton, the greatest of all undergraduate pacesetters, will probably also find himself remembering a short story by Wilbur Daniel Steele and saying how beautiful with shoes: "*How beautiful are thy feet with shoes, O Prince's daughter!*" Then he may or may not, with or without blushing, also recall a jug-nursing soliloquy which went something like this: Ah but that goddam Ariadne Belle Robinson, one nut-brown wench of Birmingham, the insouciance of whose lips, hips, and shall we say what-the-fuck shall we say? the disturbingly, nay, destructively underslung proportions of whose chassis—beside one knuckle-head John Gerald Horny Ham fat sinking in the inner springs that were Paradise in this neck of the woods, enow."

The best-selling novels that everybody (of the book-reading minority) was reading that year and the next were *Anthony Adverse* and *Gone with the Wind* (and who remembers Lloyd

Douglas's *Magnificent Obsession* and *The Green Light?*); so naturally there were those to whom the old Alexander House sitting back in the roadbend just outside the campus beyond Cassidy Hall and diagonally across from Reid's filling station was Scarlett O'Hara's plantation house, Tara. For most other Tuskegeeans, however, students and local people alike, it was simply another very old ante-bellum place that was not quite far enough gone with the wind, and that they tried to ignore as if it were really a very old sometimes sensitive and very embarrassing scar. Mostly, they didn't even mention it except perhaps in giving directions. Mostly, it was almost as if they were pretending that it was completely hidden in the thickets. But it wasn't. It was framed in trees and shrubbery but it was anything but hidden. Indeed, when you were coming back from downtown Tuskegee (known then as now as Tuskegee *town*. There was and still is Tuskegee *Institute*, and there was and still is Tuskegee *town*) the old Alexander place with its octagonal tower and red roofs and fluted columns was the most impressive thing you saw. You came directly toward it and until you reached the wisteria and honeysuckle curve and could see the filling station, the cleaners, and the stretch of off-campus shops and the Chicken Shack it looked like a part of the Institute. In fact, white visitors were forever asking: *Is that his house? is that where Booker T. Washington lived? Is that The Oaks?* ("No but it is where Teddy Roosevelt stayed when he came down to visit Booker T. that time.")

Gerald Hamilton not only read and preferred the picaresque (and historic) sweep of *Anthony Adverse* to *Gone with the Wind* before you had, he was the one who pointed out that the expression "gone with the wind" was obviously derived from the third stanza of Ernest Dowson's (and his very own) "Non Sum Qualis Eram Bonae sub Regno Cynarae" and that it was of course also the inevitable reply to Villon's "Où sont les neiges d'antan?" But to him the old Alexander place was a part of the living past that so deeply concerned, haunted, nay (as he was wont to say) tormented and ensnarled one William Faulkner, then known mainly as the de caydent author of *Sanctuary*—then mostly regarded as a hard-to-read *God's Little Acre* and *Tobacco Road*—but which Jug Hamilton had already read in Detroit and for some reason referred to by its movie title, *The Story of Temple Drake*.

Bookwise, some, maybe most, of the po' whites you saw around the courthouse square in Tuskegee (*town*) were straight out of the smelly, bony-assed, whicker-bill-squinting, nasty-joke chortling world of Erskine Caldwell, the literary enfant terrible of the day, and so some were also out of *Sanctuary* and *As I Lay Dying*. But the old Alexander Place was William Faulkner's very own wisteria-scented and ever more unquiet grove; and when you were reading *Light in August* (the mississippi-dust-dry-beige Harrison Smith and Robert Haas edition with the august light woodcut on the title page) the old Alexander house, architectural details aside, was unquestionably such a place as had rooms such as the one in which Miss Joanna Burden (whose like you for one were to see every time the trustees came to sit—slumped stack-boned and yankee-rich—in chapel) tried to get Joe Christmas to kneel with her: *"Kneel," she said, "I don't ask it. It is not I who asks it."* (She knew nothing of what such kneeling evoked of the stern old McEachern of Joe Christmas's childhood saying: TAKE THE BOOK KNEEL DOWN.) She was completely unaware of what such a request triggered. *"For the last time, I don't ask it. Remember that, kneel with me."*

Not only did the thickets beyond the Alexander place become the Joe Christmas Thickets from then on, it was as if the Alexander House grounds themselves had been planted by Faulkner: *". . . for a whole week she forced him to climb into a window to come to her. He would do so and sometimes he would have to seek her about the dark house until he found her, hidden, in closets, in empty rooms, waiting, panting, her eyes in the dark glowing like the eyes of cats. Now and then he appointed trysts beneath certain shrubs about the grounds where he would find her naked, or with her clothing half torn to ribbons on her, in the wild throes of nymphomania, her body gleaming in the slow shifting from one to another of such formally erotic attitudes and gestures as a Beardsley of the time of Petronius might have drawn. She would be wild then, in the close breathing half dark without walls, with her wild hair each strand of which would seem to come alive like octopus tentacles, and her wild hands and her breathing: 'Negro! Negro! Negro!'"*

You yourself not old Jug Hamilton got *Light in August* from the Library first, but when he finished it—having, as was his habit, cut class to hole up Sherlock Holmes style with it and a jug—you had to check it out again and go back through it all over again. (It was also precisely at that time that you decided that you would read Faulkner with as much attention as you had come to give Hemingway. Incidentally, it was in Mort Sprague's October copy of *Esquire* that you and Hamilton —and perhaps upperclassman Ellison too—had read Hemingway's "Monologue to the Maestro.")

"Eh bien," he said, drawing on his Sherlockian meerschaum, "the first thing is not to confuse Joe Christmas with Peola. This guy Faulkner, whom watch, is no soap-opera slick like your Miss Fanny-assed Hurst. Listen, my good man, *Imitation of Life* is a lot of tear-jerking pulp about Peola wishing to be some cock-sucking ofay. But just look at this faulknerian mulatto—" (*Jug Hamilton was the first one to say faulknerian as in faulknerian landscape, faulknerian character and situation*). "This Joe Christmas is not ashamed of his black blood like Peola. He goes around telling people he *thinks* he's got some and he doesn't even *know* it for sure. Miscegenation—some word, what? full of pubic hair—is something very special and very fundamental on the faulknerian landscape, like incest in Greek tragedy. Forget about him saying 'nigger.' That's style, friend. Mark you. Style. Mississippi style but style. And the degeneracy and decay-dence, that's all a part of the poetry and drama, friend. Remember 'A Rose for Emily,' 'Dry September,' friend. Look, friend. One Willyam ass goddam Faulkner, peckerwood, whom I repeat *rigoureusement*, watch, can write his old Mississippi peckerwood ass off. We're talking about art, friend. ART. Faites donc attention, my good fellow, ART."

When *Absalom, Absalom!* came (abrupted!) that next year, making O'Neill's *Mourning Becomes Electra* look like a little-theater piece, the old Alexander place, which by that time had already become the homestead of the Compsons and the Sartorises (although not yet of the Edmondses and McCaslins), also became the Coldfield place and Sutpen's Hundred at the same time. Nor could many people have been much better situated than you and Gerald Hamilton and Ralph Ellison on the campus of Tuskegee not only to read and make believe but also to smell and touch the opening to Part II of *Absalom, Absalom!: "It was a summer of wisteria. The twilight was full of it and of the smell of father's cigar as they sat on the gallery after supper . . . while in the deep shaggy lawn below the veranda the fireflies blew and shifted and drifted in soft random . . ."*

Mozelle Menefee whose nickname is Moqué (a play on Moketubbe, no doubt) knows that if you had said the old Varner Place in the presence of people who really know Tuskegee they would have assumed that you were referring not to Frenchman's Bend (as in Gee's Bend) but to the grounds on part (but not all) of which stands the Institute. Those who know less local history than local affairs would have taken for granted that you were talking about a local Judge of Probate named William Varner, who was in fact a man on the order of a Sartoris or Compson rather than the father Faulkner created for Jody Varner. Mozelle Menefee, whose memory of wisteria is of deep purple falling over sleepy garden walls in a song being sung by Gwendelyn Persley on a high school assembly program, will remember that particular Varner not only because she grew up in Macon County, Alabama, but also since his is the name of the Judge of Probate on her marriage license.

But of course John Gerald Hamilton and Ralph Waldo Ellison will probably remember the old Alexander place not only because of books but also because of flesh-and-blood grandparents (pre-Hamiltons in Alabama before Detroit, pre-Ellisons in South Carolina before Oklahoma) some of whom were then still very much alive. *Because you yourself could say: This is another one of the kind Grandpa James was talking about when he was talking about the Big House. Such columns are like where he saw the old Marster and them weeping at Surrender. And you could also think: Big Mamma Gipson's smoothing iron, Big Mamma Gipson's crochet rack and quilting frame. And remember: The oldness of the book-pressed dried roses and the mildew smell of Big Mamma Gipson's humpback trunk the week after the burial.*

On the other hand, you were likely to forget that Booker T. Washington, who after all had been dead for only twenty years at that time, was of the same generation as many of these same grandparents (who, come to think of it, only needed to be between seventy-five and eighty-five). Indeed, such was that oldness of Booker T. Washington in chapel on Founders Day that next spring what with the choir singing against the background of the stained-glass windows, what with the words being spoken as if being recited from parchment scrolls, what with his monument outside among the academic cedars, that he seemed to have belonged not to any specific generation at all but to the ages—as did Abraham Lincoln and Frederick Douglass and Thomas Jefferson and Benjamin Franklin.

Even as you sat listening to them reminiscing about the daily encounters with "him," even as they said *"Mister Washington,"* *"Doctor Washington,"* as only those who had known him personally could say it, you found it all but impossible to believe that people like Dr. Carver the peanut expert who was then living in Rockefeller Hall and always walked to his laboratory out on the Ag Side (always wearing a green twig boutonniere that somehow only made him look more like an eccentric groundskeeper than the world-renowned chemurgist) was of the same day and time. It seemed absolutely fantastic that Mister Warren Logan, who had only recently retired (and for whom the new gym was named), that this same Von Rundstedt–looking Mister Warren Logan and countless others whom you saw about the city-state of a campus every day were actually older than most of the buildings and streets, even some of the oldest streets in Greenwood. That was every bit as incredible as it was to accept the incontestable fact that Mrs. Portia Pittman (whose Viennese Conservatory background Ralph Ellison remembers from the music school) was the daughter, not the great-great-great-granddaughter, of the shadowy figure of legend you know from the book *Up from Slavery.* As for Booker T. Three, who like Gerald Hamilton took classes in Architecture in Trades Building A, it was mostly as if the III stood for the number of centuries he was removed from a grandfather born in slavery—not generations. *But then such is the miraculous nature of memory and make-believe and hence the very essence of human consciousness that not only do forgetfulness and recollection go hand in hand they are in truth indispensable to each other. Thus, sometimes even in the most immediate press of circumstances and consequently for the most urgently pragmatic intents and purposes when you say ante-bellum you are not only conceiving but also functioning in terms of something antediluvian—even as perhaps most people in the United States have long since begun to think "prehistoric" when they say pre-Columbian—nor is pre-Columbian Europe conceived of by them as being less aboriginal than the Western Hemisphere before Columbus.*

Nor is such recollective forgetfulness in any fundamental sense unrelated to the reciprocal interaction of mythology and actuality in the whole question of your personal identity. For more often than not when you say: slavery time, folks back in slavery time, Grandma and Grandpa back in the olden days on the old plantation, you are neither thinking nor feeling in terms of the literal time involved. You are almost always thinking: Once upon a time. After all, isn't the oldness of Uncle Remus, who is of necessity less old than Aunt Hagar (mother of us all), every bit as ancient as the oldness of Aesop?

Such in any case was the nature of the oldness of the Booker T. Washington whose greatness you celebrated in chapel those days and whose achievements all U.S. Negroes were heirs to, and whose mistakes your own generation would correct. (The one and only Mister Baker, Benjamin F., had already given the word on that at MCTS: *"Booker T. Washington sacrificed too much to expediency. Dr. Du Bois in his up-north bitterness spends too much time complaining. The youth of today must find the golden mean."*) Not even such indefatigable chapel dodgers as Blue Collier, Jack Knight, Slam Green, and Daddy Shakehouse Duncan questioned the downright saintliness of Booker T. Washington's dedication to the Cause. There was never any doubt in many people's minds that Unka Booker meant well. Nor was it at all fashionable to accuse your ancestors of betraying you. They did the best they could against all but impossible odds and it was up to you to do better, and the question was could you do as well. Could you pick up and take it on from there?

Nevertheless the here-and-now tuskegeeness of those days (when the blue-serge cadet uniform was known as the Buka T) was also such that back on the upperclassmen's main stem of Sage Hall the noble inscription (chiseled in the stone pedestal of The Monument) which read: HE LIFTED THE VEIL OF IGNORANCE FROM HIS PEOPLE AND POINTED THE WAY TO PROGRESS THROUGH EDUCATION AND INDUSTRY had become: *"Hey lift the veil, man. Hey, man, lift the goddam veil."* Had become: *"Hey, horse, you know what the man said; Unka Buka say lift*

that shit, man, goddam!" On occasion it could also become:
"*Hey looka here old pardner, damn man; here I been drinking
muddy goddam water and sleeping in a hollow goddam log
hitchhiking my mufkin way all the goddam way from chittlin
goddam switch to get here and now I ain't going to get to help
y'all lift that chickenshit goddam veil because you gone hen-
ass-house and ain't going to help me work out this mess for old
Red goddam Davis.*" Or from somebody like the one and
only Mister Big-Goddam-Double-Jointed-Door-Rolling Door
Roller: "*Hey, damn man. Unka Buka say let down your somich-
ing bucket right where you dog-ass goddam at, cousin. Say, that's
all right about all that other shit. Say, you take care of this shit,
and, man, if I don't have this shit for Jerkins I am going to have
to go back home and tote that barge. Ha! ain't them up-north
crackers a bitch? Tote that barge! What kind of bullshit talk is
that? And old potgutted Paul Robeson up there singing it like it's
a goddam spiritual or something. Hey but come on man, let's tote
that goddam veil outa my goddam face for Jerkins' goddam* English. *Hell, man, we can't be letting Unka Buka Tee down.*"

That was also an indispensable dimension of tuskegeeness as
you knew it in those days, and so was the embers-like glow of
the radio dial in the after-curfew darkness of Sage Hall lounge
when you sat listening to Duke over the networks from Harlem: a world whose aristocracy also included Cab Calloway,
the King of Hi-de-ho; Chick Webb, the stomp master of the
Savoy. Then there was Earl Fatha Hines, from the Grand Terrace in Chicago; then Count Basie, who with a contingent of
Blue Devils had just succeeded to Bennie Moten's old Kansas
City domain. That was the world whose trumpet and vocal
proclamations and jests were dictated by Louis Armstrong and
which also included such courtiers as Jimmie Lunceford (formerly of Fisk), Don Redman (formerly of McKinney's Cotton
Pickers), Lucky Millinder, Andy Kirk, and John Kirby. It was
also a world which at that very moment was being infiltrated
by Benny Goodman with the help of Fletcher Henderson,
Edgar Sampson, Lionel Hampton, and a Tuskegee boy named
Teddy Wilson.

All that too was a part of what being there was like in those
days. And who, having known it will ever forget the tuskegeeness of The Block back then when the best fountain cokes and

milkshakes and freezes in the world were made by Alonzo White and the second best by one faculty-jiving student named Happy White? Nowhere could you go and find a more steady flow of out-of-town sharpies, athletes and big-league musicians to jive, wolf, and signify with than in and around the Drag, the Drugstore, and Bill Washington's clothing store, which was known as Harris and Washington in those days. Not even the mainstem of Sage Hall (which after all was only undergraduate stuff as much fun as it never ceased to be) was as much of a charmed circle as The Block—*especially in the Yardley's English Lavender euphoria of that postgame predance twilight time when happiness was simply being there standing not tall as ofay drug-store squares in their rolled-sleeved open-collared white shirts did, but stashed fly in the gladness of your most righteous threads, whether tweed or hard finished, hanging loose like a blue goose with, say, Lunceford's "Dream of You" on the jukebox for background, until White Hall clock chimed the hour when you would pick up the trillies for the stroll to Logan Hall.* Nor will anybody who was truly with it off campus, like say in the outlying region known as the Lion's Mouth, have forgotten that The Block was also the campus headquarters of such fabulous taxicab pundits as were named Big Pete, Rose Harris, Leroy Love, and later, perhaps even after Hamilton's and Ellison's time, good old Bones.

———

But the very special dimension of tuskegeeness you find yourself acknowledging and celebrating above all else this trip back is that post–Booker T. Washington Liberal Arts emphasis which was the very self and voice of Morteza Drexel Sprague. Not that you were ever remiss on that score, for through all the years since graduation it was always precisely to him that you returned as if homing to the official benchmark and the exact point of all post–MCTS departures: *"Say you know how it always is in the early morning of hemingway's havana with the drunks still asleep against the walls of the buildings before even the ice wagons start rumbling; well, on my way out to the outskirts for my first look at his finca I was thinking about you and old Jug Hamilton, whose favorite hemingway expression was* '*goddamn roastbif*' which I think he got from one of those early dispatches from the Spanish front, probably from Ken magazine.

"Say, you remember how it was with Hans Castorp on that long journey—'too long, indeed, for so brief a stay'—up in the Swiss Alps, well as Mozelle and Miqué and I (up there on vacation from Casablanca) were mounting the narrow-gauge train to begin the thrilling part of the journey—not to Davos Platz but to Rigi Kulm—'a steep and steady climb that never seems to come to an end'—I was telling Mozelle about how you and I used to be almost as thankful to good old Alfred A. Knopf and good old Mrs. H. T. Lowe-Porter as to his olympian eminence himself and that we were really there as much because of The Magic Mountain as anything else including third grade geography.

"Man, there we were, me and Ralph and Mozelle and Fanny and Miqué in the Venice of—hell, everybody all the way back beyond Marco Polo—and these Italian clowns were trying to hustle us for three different baggage fees between parking the car and the Grand Canal—us! Man, old Ralph said, 'Shit man, let's grab these bags ourselves—we got too many first cousins among them red caps in Penn Station to come all the way over here to get taken by a bunch of two-bit hustlers who wouldn't be able to make it above 110th Street.'"

And so it also went when you came back from hemingway's spain, and the paris not only of *The Sun Also Rises* and *The Ambassadors* but of everybody (but especially of Josephine Baker and Coleman Hawkins and Sidney Bechet and naturally of Jack Johnson, sitting at a sidewalk café sipping champagne through a straw, probably waiting for Mistinguett: "The day the news of Korea came I was sitting talking with Sidney Bechet in Rue Vaugirard and he said: 'It might still take the crackers a little while to get the point. But the day is over when one white man can come out on the gallery in his shirt sleeves with a toddy in his hand and tell the natives to cut out all that damn racket.'"

And so it was when you came back from Saroyan's California and Steinbeck's California and from London and Rome and Athens and Istanbul. And of course New York: "Man, old Ralph has some evermore outrageous stuff going in that thing he's working on. Man, wait till you see it and you'll see why he feels those Partisan Review guys are overimpressed with Kafka. We were talking about the title and he said, 'I guess I'll just have to fight *old H. G. Wells for it, and if I'm lucky, people will see how much more I'm trying to do with that metaphor—'"*

And this, when Invisible Man *won the National Book Award: "Hey, Ralph has finally met old Faulkner. Listen to what he says in this letter: '. . . Saxe Commins told me to come place my coat in his office and meet "Bill" Faulkner. So I went in and there, amid several bags, was the great man. You've heard the crap about his beat-up clothes? Well, don't believe it. He's neat as a pin. A fine cashmere sports jacket, tattersall vest, shined shoes, and fine slacks, tie correct and shirt collar rolling down! and I mean down, down' . . ."*

"Ralph says white intellectuals keep coming up and telling him that they find it difficult to refute Ras the Exhorter, and he keeps telling them that the answers to old Ras's rhetoric are right there in the book."

And of course there were reports from Hollywood: *"We had just come back to Château Marmont from the Columbia Recording Studios and Gordon Parks was there taking pictures which have yet to come out in* Life, *goddammit; anyway, Duke and Billy Strayhorn were talking about how to revoice the* Nutcracker Suite *for Ray Nance and Johnny Hodges and Lawrence Brown and Harry Carney, well you know; and they were playing back one of the tapes and Duke said: 'Hey Hey Hey no no no what is that?' And Billy said 'That's Tchaikovsky, I left that part like it was. I decided not to mess with Tchaikovsky on that point.' But Duke said 'Oh hell no, he caint do that. That's not the way to get from there to there, not for my guys. Put the sheets for that on the piano we have to fix that tonight.'"*

And this in a note jotted down in the Andover Shop on Holyoke Street off Harvard Square: *Was out at Boston College with Ralph and when old Ralph threw him a soft-voiced steely-eyed signifying question about the relationship between U.S. Negro alienation and certain missing dimensions in American history as traditionally written, old Sam Eliot Morison missed the goddam point comgoddamnpletely and come talking about maybe something happened inside Ralph over the years to make him feel less alienated!*

And among the tidbits that most certainly would have been included this time: *At a party to launch a newspaper (that didn't come off) there was old Norman Mailer disguised this*

*time not as a somewhat white Negro or a Brooklyn Texan but as
a Brendan Behan Irishman standing as if with one foot on the
bar rail, shoulders squared, pants baggy, stomach forward, elbows
gesturing "cheers me lods" with each sip. Somebody said, "Al,
you've met Norman of course"; and I said, "Yeah sure," Bogart
style; "everybody knows Podhoretz." And old Mailer gave me his
best Irish pub wink and did his José Torres bob and weave and
said, "He really is a very noyce goy, Podhoretz. A very noyce goy."
Or so it sounded to me at any rate. So, I hear, is Mailer, a very
nice Brooklyn nice guy. But he tends to confuse being a swinger
with being a swaggerer—or so it seems to a downhome uptown boy
like me—or maybe it is his admirers who do this. But you know
what always seems to get left out of the definitions of Mailer? The
fact that his capers never really suggest Ernest Hemingway as he
used to seem so eager to have people think but F. Scott Fitzgerald.
Take another look at all of his frantic emphasis on "making it"
and see if the image Mailer actually projects isn't that of the nice-
Brooklyn-boy version of F. Scott Fitzgerald* I mean *once you get
him untangled from Thomas Wolfe and Sinclair Lewis, yes, Sinclair Lewis,* and maybe Upton Sinclair too.

*As for what old Norman thinks of us in print, all I can say as
of now is that instead of taking off our balls he only wants to relieve us of our brains. He seems to like our balls even to the extent
of painting his own black.* And a few months later you would
have added: *Did you see that crap old Norman Mailer wrote
about us in* Life *magazine? He writes a whole big fat article defining himself in terms of the zodiac (Aquarius this, Aquarius
that and the other) and then turns around and declares that it is
black people who are such lunatics that they are all shook up because a white man has put his foot on the moon! Very nice guy
that Mailer or as Jimmy Baldwin says "A very sweet guy, really."
But is he ever full of adolescent gibberish about us!*

But this time your memories are mostly precisely of such previous memories. This time the acknowledgments are made not
to him but to yourself, and to those who, like Mike Rabb for
example, invariably refer to him when they talk to you anyway.
Because this time the Morteza Drexel Sprague—who at home
was the husband of Ellen and the father of Carol and then of
Billy and then of Pie, but who from the time when you first

knew him as the young Mister Sprague of English 101 and who for all the obvious differences as well as the similarities was to become the logical as well as the mythological extension of the mister benjamin f. bakerness of Mobile County Training School —is there no longer. Is gone—too soon departed—forever. Except in the memory (and knowing and believing and indeed even the breathing) of those who in the ironic nature of such things will miss him most. To you and them—the absolutely exclusive *you-ness* of his attention as he knitted his brow smoking and listening saying: *Ah-hunh! Is that so? Is . . . that . . . so?* And then saying: "*Incidentally.*" Or saying: "*Of course— and incidentally . . .*" will endure as long as the images on that fabulous Grecian Urn (in *Ideas and Forms*) which so far as his students during your time are concerned probably belonged as much to him as to John Keats.

So in mourning this time but with no less celebration even so. Because the crucial if not definitive good fortune that is yours for having been a pupil in whom he took special interest is everlasting. Because such is the comprehensive generosity that all truly great teachers radiate as much outside as inside the classroom that you will always rejoice at the mere fact that he was there when he was. Because such was the literary fallout that the mere sight of him strolling across the campus (his shoulders as square as if he had once played trumpet in a marching band—which he hadn't) almost always with a clutch of new books and current magazines in the crook of his left arm or against his lapel—or standing almost always as if the Hollis Burke Frissell Library Building were just over his shoulder in the background (even before he became Librarian) was itself enough to evoke the whole world of Art and Letters, the world of the *Saturday Review of Literature* in those days of Henry Seidel Canby followed by Bernard DeVoto; *The Nation* and the *New Republic* (of Malcolm Cowley and Edmund Wilson). In those pre–New York University–Gotham Book Mart days it was as if that were precisely the way André Malraux, for instance, smoked his cigarettes and clutched his corn bread paper magazines of culture and commitment.

And also let it be said for the benefit of all overnight paperback experts on the psychology of brainwashing and black identity that Morteza Drexel Sprague expected you to proceed in terms of the highest standards of formal scholarship among other things not because he wanted you to become a carbon copy of any white man who ever lived, not excepting Shake-speare or even Leonardo da Vinci. But because to him you were the very special vehicle through which contemporary man, and not just contemporary black man either, would in-herit the experience and insights of all recorded or decipher-able time. Because to him (as to everybody else on that all-black faculty) your political commitment to specific social causes of your own people went without saying. What after all were the immediate political implications of Beowulf, and of all epic heroism? Nor was true commitment ever a matter either of chauvinism or of xenophobia. To him as to the bards, the scops and gleemen in Fall Quarter Literature (201)—as to Mis-ter Baker at Mobile County Training School—commitment involved such epical exploits as penetrating frontiers and thereby expanding your people's horizons of aspirations. To him in those years when no public event, not even an FDR fireside chat, was of more immediate fundamental or comprehensive significance than a Joe Louis fight, there was no question whatsoever that brownskin heroism must of necessity be epical in scope. As for his own personal attitude toward white people, the question in those days was not one of unka-tomming but of sanding: being obsequious in the manner of the Japanese Sandman. "*O.K. O.K. O.K. but now answer me this. Will he sand for the man with his goddam hat in his goddam hand?*" HE WOULD NOT.

Not only will John Gerald Hamilton (*where ever is he now?*) remember the year which began that September without either pop-song rain showers or faulknerian dryness; he will no doubt also remember that morning when young Mister Sprague of English 101 came striding into class, his bearing, in memory at any rate, not unsuggestive of an ellington trumpet player named Arthur Whetsol, wearing a well-cut gray suit with an Ivy League white shirt and a maroon tie and black scotch grain wingtip shoes. Jug Hamilton, whose sleepy eyes seldom missed any details of any sort, will also remember that there was also a pack-age of Camels showing from the left bottom vest pocket. So he may also recall how carefully this young Mister Sprague, who, it so happens, was also the head of the English Department at that time, checked the roll, reading each name from the registration card, looking up saying Mister or Miss (college style!) each time, repeating the last name then the first name and middle initial and then mumbling it to himself, frowning, grandfather style, as he wrote in his temporary roster. Certainly everybody who was there from Mobile County Training School will remember one particular exchange that went something like this:

"Merry, Mister Merry. Mister Merry, Albert L. Mister Albert L. Merry. Is there a Mister . . ."

"Who? Oh me! Oh! Oh yessir. Present. Here!"

"Mister Albert L. Merry?"

"Present. I mean here. MUH-RAY: M-U-R-R-A-Y."

"Yes, Mister Merry. Thank you." Then to himself as he wrote: "Mis-ter M-U-R-R-A-Y, Merry, Al-bert L."

But it is probably good old A-plus prone Addie Stabler, who will probably remember that incident best of all because the very first thing she said in the hall after class was, "Well, how do, Mister Merry? Or is it Mister Marry? Oh, but isn't that Mister Sprague a cutie-pie? How about that little old cute Mister Sprague with his little old degree from *Hamilton* College and stuff?" Then as she zipped on to the stairway someone else passed saying: "Ronald Colman? Girl, Ronald Colman never is to see the day."

That is how you now remember the day that was the beginning of all that. But the last time you saw him was not in Tuskegee but in New York. And the time before that was also in New York. That was that time at Ralph's after the publication of *Shadow and Act* which Ralph inscribed to him as "A dedicated Dreamer in a land most strange."

Most strange indeed nowadays, Ralph: *an everso integrated faculty, but a bookstore (where The Drag used to be) featuring the folklore of white supremacy and the filthlore of black pathology!* Oh Hagar-witless alma mater!

FIVE

Mobile

MISTER BUSTER BROWN
BACK IN TELL-ME-TALE-TOWN

REARRIVED on expense account this time you take the limousine to the Battle House not so much remembering the stopover in Atlanta as continuing the interior monologue you began months ago back in Lenox Terrace. But thinking, or at least reiterating, this nevertheless: Yes, homecoming is also to a place of very old fears, some mine (perhaps most of which I outgrew growing up) but mostly theirs (which mostly they did not but maybe at last are at least beginning to).

You tell yourself that you are prepared to take things as they come, after all you are on a writing assignment this time. But even before the bellhop straightens up with your bags he anticipates and allays any such misgivings as may be related to those you had pulling into Atlanta.

"Did you have a nice flight in, sir?" he says; which sounds like nothing in the world so much as: "O.K., man, don't be coming down here getting so nervous you going to be forgetting my goddam tip now. That's all right about all that. So you desegregated. Well, good, so act like everybody else then and lay it on me heavy. Hell, you know I'm looking out for you so remember I got a family to be taking care of. And damn man it ain't your money no how."

It is now the Sheraton Battle House as in Statler and Hilton. But in the old days it was *the* Battle House as in *the* Plaza, as in *the* Waldorf-Astoria. It was *the* Battle House as in the one and only best there is, and what you always saw when somebody used to say Battle House Service or used to say Battle House Steaks (precisely as they would also say Palmer House Service or Parker House Rolls, for instance) was a grand crystal Belle Epoque–opulent dining room where millionaires in stiffly starched bibs sat (beside their bunned and corseted Gibson Girl–proper wives) holding their solid sterling forks, prongs down, and left-handed, eating plate-sized steaks that were obviously as tender and as succulent as Oysters Rockefeller.

Because when you used to hear the old saying that the Battle House was a place which, like the Pullman cars on the Pan American Limited or the Southern Pacific back in those days, was for no black folks at all and only a very few special white folks, "*A precious few white folks and no niggers at all*," what you thought about was not complexion but money, prestige, and power; fame, fortune, and finery. Because only a very few white folks were famous millionaires, and perhaps no black folks at all as yet, except maybe Dave Patton, the contractor, whose big house was out on Davis Avenue. But only as yet. And what you always said about all of that was: "*Don't tell them nothing. Don't tell them a thing. Don't tell them doodly squat.*" Because Mobile is also a place of very old horizon-blue dreams plus all the boyhood schemes that are, after all, as much a part of achievement as of disappointment.

As for the part about being a nigger, the most obvious thing about that was that you were not whicker-bill different like them old peckerwoods were, because you didn't look like that and you didn't talk and walk like that and you couldn't stand that old billy-goat saw-fiddle music. So you were not po' white trash and your ears and nose didn't turn red when you were either scared or excited or embarrassed, and no matter how dingy and ashy you got you never looked mangy and when you needed a haircut and didn't comb your hair you were nappy-headed and even pickaninny-headed but when pale-tailed, beak-nosed soda-cracker people got shaggy-headed they looked as sad as birds in molting season. On the other hand, you had to give them this much; mangy or not they would come out on a freezing morning wearing only a thin shirt, baggy ass-lapping pants and low-quarter shoes, but no hat, no coat, no undershirt, and no socks, and just hunch up a little and keep on going like a fish in an icy pond, while you were all wrapped up in coats and sweaters and still shivering. That was something! And some people used to think that maybe having hair that was that much like bird feathers meant that they could also close their pores like a duck against the freezing dampness of the swamp.

It was also obvious that when the peckerwoods said "nigger" they were doing so because they almost always felt mean and evil about being nothing but old po' white trash. So they were forever trying to low-rate you because they wanted you to think they were somebody to look up to; and naturally you low-rated them right back with names like peckernosed peckerwoods, crackers, rednecks and old hoojers—not hoosiers, but goddam shaggy-headed, razor-backed, narrow-shouldered tobacco-stained thin nose-talking hobo-smelling hoojers ("I'm a black alpaca ain't no flat-assed soda cracker").

When you were looking into the mirror you were the me of I am; and you were always Mamma's little mister misterman, Momom itchem bitchem mitchem buttchem bwown man and Pappa's big boo-boo bad gingerbread soldier boy; and in the neighborhood you were the you of whichever one of your nicknames somebody happened to like; and in school you were the you of your written name. Nothing was more obvious than all of that. Nor was it any less obvious that when somebody called himself or somebody like himself a nigger he was not talking about not being as good as white people or somebody rejected by himself because he is rejected by white people—not at all. He was talking about being different from white people all right, but ordinarily he was mainly talking about being full of the devil and stubborn to boot: as stubborn as a mule, mule-headed, contrary, willfully different, cantankerous, ornery, and even downright wrongheaded. When somebody said, "Don't make me show my nigger"—or "don't bring out the nigger in me," he was bragging about having the devil in his soul. And when somebody said that somebody else "started acting like a nigger" he was not talking about somebody acting like a coward or a clown. The word for that in those days was darky: "acting like a good old darky." When homefolks said that somebody was playing the darky they meant he was putting on an act like a blackface stage clown, either to amuse or to trick white folks. But when they said you were being an out-and-out nigger they were almost always talking about somebody refusing to conform, and their voices always carried more overtones of exasperation than of contempt: "Everybody else was all right and then here he come acting the nigger." Or: "Then all the old nigger in him commenced to come out. You know how mean and evil some of us can get to be sometime."

So what was suggested by the worst sense of the word "nigger" as used by people who applied it to themselves on occasion was an exasperatingly scandalous lack of concern about prevailing opinion, whether in matters of etiquette, of basic questions, of conventional morality, or even of group welfare: "After everybody got together and agreed how to do it, here he come acting the goddam nigger and talking about it don't have to be that way and can't nobody make him if he don't want to. Like some goddam body trying to make him—when all folks trying to do is get together." "That's what I say about niggers. Can't nobody make 'em do right when they get it in their head to do something else. And that's exactly how come the white man can keep us down like this. Because niggers too selfish and evil and suspicious and mule-headed to pull together!"

That was what the worst sense of the word was all about, not what white folks were always trying to say because what they were really talking about was really the best part no matter how bad they tried to make it sound. Because that was the part that went with being like Jack Johnson and John Henry and Railroad Bill and Stagolee all rolled in one. So of course, as nobody had to tell you but once, it was also the part you had to be most careful about: because the mere mention of one bad-assed nigger in a don't-carified mood was enough to turn a whole town full of white folks hysterical. A newspaper statement like "crazed negro [sic] last seen heading . . ." scared peckerwoods as shitless as an alarm for a wild fire or hurricane. Of course everybody always knew that the newspaper phrase "crazed negro" didn't really mean insane —or even berserk. Sometimes it didn't even mean angry, but rather determined or even simply unsmiling!

Some folks also used to declare that the reason the white folks wanted to lynch you for being a nigger was because when all was said and done they really believed that the actual source of all niggerness was between your legs. They said you were primitive because to them what was between your legs was a long black snake from the jungles of Africa, because when they said rape they said it exactly as if they were screaming snake! snake! snake! even when they were whispering it, saying it exactly as if somebody had been struck by a black snake in the thickets. Bloodhounds were for tracking niggers who knew the thickets like a black snake. When white folks called somebody a black buck nigger they were talking

Peeping Tom talk because the word they were thinking about was *fuck*, because when they said buck-fucking they were talking about doing it like the stud-horse male slaves they used to watch doing it back during the time of the old plantations.

They said black as if you were as black as the ace of spades not only when you were coffee or cookie or honey brown but even when you were high-yaller or as pale-tailed, stringy-haired as a dime-store hillbilly. Because to them it was only as if you were hiding your long black snake-writhing niggerness under your clothes while showing another color in your face, camouflaging yourself like a lizard. Nor did anything seem to confirm their suspicions about the snake rubbery blackness of your hidden niggerness more convincingly than the sight of you dancing. They always seemed to be snake-fascinated by that, even when it was somebody that everybody in your neighborhood knew couldn't really dance a lick.

But even so sometimes it was not so much a matter of terrified fascination as of out and out enjoyment and frank admiration. During the Mardi Gras season, for instance, when the dancing floats were passing Bienville Square and the shuffle-stepping marching bands, say like Papa Holman's, were jazzing it like it was supposed to be jazzed on such a festive occasion, there was always somebody saying something like: "Here they come, here they come; here come them niggers! Goddammit them niggers got that thing. By gyard them damn niggers got it and gone over everybody. By gyard you might as well give it to them, it'll be a cold day in hell before you ever see a durned old niggie and a bass drum going in contrary directions and that's for a fact."

Nevertheless when you heard them saying "boy" to somebody you always said mister to, you knew exactly what kind of old stuff they were trying to pull. They were trying to pretend that they were not afraid, making believe that they were not always a split second away from screaming for help. When they said Uncle or Auntie they were saying: You are not a nigger because I am not afraid. If you were really a nigger I would be scared to death. They were saying: You are that old now and more careful now so I don't have to be afraid anymore; because now you are a darky —a good old darky, so now my voice can be respectful, can remember the authority of reprimands that were mammy-black and the insightfulness that was uncle-black, now I can be respectful not only of age—as of death but also of something else: survival against

such odds. "By gyard, Uncle, tell me something, Uncle . . ."
Their fears of your so-called niggerness became less hysterical not
when they themselves grew up but when you grew older. Or so it
seemed back then. Anyway, all of that was an essential part of how
it felt to be a nigger back in those old days. Which was why white
folks couldn't say it without sounding hateful and apprehensive!
When some old chicken butt peckerwood says nigger this or nigger
that naturally he wants to give the impression that he is being
arrogant. But if you know anything at all about white folks his
uneasiness will be obvious enough, no matter how trigger-bad he
is reputed to be.

This time it is almost as if it is still the time before, which was
only five months ago when after an absence of fifteen years you
came back in January and found that the neighborhood that
was the center of the world as you first knew it had been razed,
completely industrialized, and enclosed in a chain-link fence
by the Scott Paper Towel Company.

"All of that is Scott now," somebody after somebody after
somebody kept shaking his head and saying then; and somebody else after somebody else repeats now.

"The old Gulf Refining Oil yard is still where it was and you
probably remember the old creosote plant down off the creek.
But just about everything else over in there is Scott. Three
Mile Creek to the Chickasabogue, L&N to the AT&N, Scott,
all Scott."

Indeed, to you at any rate, it was very much as if the fabulous old sawmill-whistle territory, the boy-blue adventure
country of your childhood memories (but which had been
known and feared back in the old ante-bellum days as Meaher's
Hummock), had been captured in your world-questing absence
by a storybook dragon disguised as a wide-sprawling, foul-
smelling, smoke-chugging factory, a not really ugly mechanical
monster now squatting along old Blacksher Mill Road as if
with an alligatorlike tail befouling Chickasabogue Swamp and
Creek—a mechanized monster who even in the preliminary
process of getting set (to gobble up most of the pine forests of
the Gulf Coast states, to turn them into Kleenex [sic!] paper

towels and toilet tissues) had as if by a scrape of a bulldozing paw wiped out most of the trees and ridges that were your first horizons. And although you knew better, it was also as if all the neighborhood people who had died since you were there last were victims of dragon claws, and as if those still alive had survived only because they had been able to scramble to safety in the slightly higher regions of Plateau and Chickasaw Terrace.

But even so you were (then as now) back in the old steel-blue jack-rabbit environs once more, and as you made the old rounds you were home again because you could still find enough of the old voices and old reminders to provide the necessary frame of reference; and after all what more did you expect and what else could you expect? Maybe when Thomas Wolfe said you can't go home again he meant because things ain't what they used to be. If so then all you have to do is remember that things never are (and never were) what they once were.

On the previous trip in addition to those you reencountered once more along the old Bay Bridge Road, along Tin Top Alley and up in Plateau after all those years since the days of Dodge Mill Road and No Man's Land and Gin's Alley, there was Valena Withers, a teacher over at Mobile County Training School. Her very presence there, even on an almost entirely rebuilt campus, was such that it instantly brought back vividly to mind the days of Mister Baker, Benjamin F. (whom everybody had long since come to revere even while he still lived as if he, and not Isaiah J. Whitley, were The Founder). Not only that, but everything she did and said was evidence of the continuity of the old mister-baker doctrine of MCTS verities. Indeed, she (whom you had known only casually in high school and had last seen not in Plateau but at Tuskegee) was a misterbaker returnee, just as in addition to whatever else you were, you and Addie Stabler and Frank Watkins and Leo Greene and Lehandy Pickett and Orlando Powers were also misterbaker-directed, nay, ordained, beknighted pathfinders and trailblazers specifically charged to seek your fortune—by which he meant the fortune of your people—elsewhere.

(It was Valena Withers who put you in contact with Noble Beasley, leader of the local civil-rights organization which at that time had the broadest appeal and was making the biggest impact on City Hall. She assumed that you'd want to talk with him not because there was any connection with MCTS—he is from another part of town and is also after your time; she assumed that for you as for her what Beasley's organization was doing was a logical updating and extension of what the local dimension of MCTS was all about back in the old days, and as far as you could make out she was right.)

It was also through Valena Withers that you reencountered Henry Williams, an MCTS graduate who teaches Welding at the Carver State Trade School. To this day you cannot place him as of those days except very vaguely by that part of his family which you remember as the Godbeaux or the God bolts. What Valena Withers knew, however, was that he was not only a welder whose knowledge of his trade included a lot of fascinating background information about the wrought-iron ornaments for which the architecture of Old Mobile has long been noted, but he is also a part-time historian whose first-hand field research and personal sense of local continuity were precisely what you were looking for but were afraid that you had come back too late to find. That was how you had come to spend one whole afternoon and part of the next day with an expert on all the old landmarks and homesteads, and early families, including not only those with names like Allen, Ellis, Fields, Keeby, and Lewis whose African grandparents came over on the old *Clotilda*, but also those named Augusta, Coleman, Edwards, Henderson, all great riverboat men during the sawmill era (which lasted all the way into the Great Depression you remember from the sixth grade).

As for what Henry Williams remembers about you there back then, according to him you were one of the all but out of sight upperclassmen about whom there were misterbaker-made legends, one of which was that the reason you had won your scholarship to college was that you were so conscientious that sometimes you had actually worked out your Algebra and Latin assignments by moonlight.

"Man, old Prof Baker would get going about you and I could just see you down there where you used to live, hitting them books with the moon over your left shoulder." At which you had laughed and said: "Boy, I'm telling you, that Mister Baker. Wasn't he something?"

"What the hell was he *talking* about, man?"

"I don't know. We did used to have to turn off the lamp when the L&N roundhouse blew. But I don't know, I might have snuck out to a streetlight or something to finish a translation for Latin. I can tell you this, it was not algebra."

But thinking about it again later and remembering the chapel-time misterbaker legends about your own upperclassmen you find yourself thinking that homecoming is also to the place of the oldest of all pedestals. *Wherever else is that rib-nudging "That's him! That's him! That's him! Here he comes! Here he is! There he goes!" dimension of acclaim, fame, publicity, or notoriety ever likely to be of more profound and of more profoundly personal significance than on the main drag of the home-town of your boyhood and youngmanhood? Not even your name in lights on Broadway (or on the cover of a magazine on a New York newsstand), not even the instant recognition by strangers, not even the satisfaction of seeing your name and image on national network television, is likely to surpass the sense of apotheosis of buttchem bwownhood you experience when the most familiar people in the world, the people you have known all your life, sud-denly look at you as if for the first time—as they do when you hit a home run (or, as in your case, save the game by striking out the last batter) as they do when you bring the house down with an inspired rebuttal, or an oration—as if to say, "Yes; man is indeed what he achieves and this is what you are making of yourself—but whoever would have thought that the little boy—the itchem bitt-chem baby boy we all knew when he was no bigger than a minute —would become if not quite our glory yet, at least a part—if only a modicum—of our hope!"*

Nor did Mister Baker or anyone else permit you or any other itchem mittchem buttchem bwown to forget the proximity of pedestals to pillories and guillotines, the contiguity of apotheosis to ostracism and disgrace. For after all, where on the other hand was failure ever likely to be more bitterly resented and ridiculed, more difficult to bear, than along that same main drag back home? *"Well, goddammit, boy, you messed up and messed us all up. Boy, you might have meant well but you sure played hell. Shit, boy, you should have been ready. Shouldn't no goddamn body have to tell you that. What the hell you doing up there messing with that stuff and ain't ready? Boy, who the goddamn hell told you to get up there? Boy, they saw your dumb ass coming. Boy, you up there flat-out shucking and them folks mean business. Boy, white folks always mean business with us. Fool, this ain't no goddam plaything unless you already the expert, and know your natural stuff like old Jack Johnson or somebody. And just remember they didn't stop until they brought him down. Folks counting on you and there you up there tearing your black ass in front of everybody and showing everybody's raggedy-butt drawers because you ain't ready. Hell, if you ain't ready yet don't be jumping up there in front of somebody else that is. Just let it alone, and stay out of the way. Boy, you too light behind. Hell, boy, you don't even know how to hold your mouth right to be grabbing hold to this stuff." (Mista Buster Brown how you going to town with your britches hanging down?)*

On the other hand of course there was also Mister Baker's absolute disdain for those who betrayed even the slightest misgivings about going places and doing things that no other homefolks were known to have gone and to have done. "Oh faint of heart. Oh weak of spirit. Oh ye of little faith! Oh jelly fish, oh Mollycoddle! Yes, many are called but few are chosen. Yes, only the pure in heart." *(Young man, you sure better start getting some glory and dignity from the common occupations of life because from the looks of these grades that's what you're going to be doing.)*

The teacher from the old blue-and-white MCTS whippet banner days you pop in on this time is Jonathan T. Gaines, now principal of Central High School on Davis Avenue not far from where Dunbar High School used to be. It is Sunday. He is at home, and he comes slipper-footing it in arching his brow in a put-on frown as if to say: "Yes, yes. So here you are as I knew you would be. Murray, Albert Murray. Well, well. And now, where is the rest of the class? Where is Addie Stabler? Where is Frank Watkins and Leo Greene and Lee Handy Pickett?" Then during the chat he keeps frowning his old tardy-bell plus binomial theorem frown as if he is still trying to make up his mind as to whether your high grade-point average along with your performance as a debater and an athlete will get you his tough-minded math prof vote when the faculty next sits in judgment as to who is college timber. Who has the caliber to carry the MCTS colors out into The World.

Completely delighted, you think: *Homecoming is to a very old MCTS atmosphere, where teachers knew exactly what playing Santa Claus was all about; and what they tried to teach was the blue-steel implications of fairy tales.* WHO IS THE QUICK BROWN FOX WHERE IS THE SALTY DOG.

Then later in the afternoon driving south along the old Spanish Trail and into the old Creole and pirate bayou country with Henry Williams you say: "About that joke about me and the books in the moonlight, man, one day I came on campus and everybody was congratulating me because the faculty had designated me Best All-Round Student for that year. Then I got to class and looked around for Kermit McAllister and found out that he had been promoted to the graduating class. Man, when I finished Tuskegee, he had finished Talladega in three years and already had his M.A. at Michigan and when I went up to Ann Arbor for a taste of grad school the only thing old Kermit still had to do for his Ph.D. in philosophy was the dissertation. So he was taking a year off to swim, chase the trillies, and read Santayana. The last time I saw him was in the Gotham Book Mart in New York. He was then an associate professor of philosophy at Howard. The last I heard of Addie Stabler she was teaching at Morehouse. I saw old Frank Watkins last in Los Angeles. I forget whether he was about to get his Ph.D. or had just gotten it, but he had some kind of math-and-physics–type job in electronics or aeronautics or something. I was out there with the Air Force at that time."

———

You make the old rounds answering the old questions and accounting for your whereabouts and involvements over the years not only as you did the last time and the time before that but also as everybody has always done it for as long as you can remember; and this time that part (which along with the old

street-corner hangouts and barbershops also includes gate
stops, yard visits, sitting porch visits and dinner-table reunions)
goes something like this: "Hey, look who's back down here from
up the country again. Ain't nobody seen him in umpteen chicken-
pecking years until last when was it, last January? February?
Last Feb, no, January. And now here he is again. Like somebody was saying I hope ain't nobody up there after him or
something. Oh, oh, excuse me. Hey-o there, New York? Unka
Hugh and Miss Mattie Murray's Albert! What say man? Used
to be little old Blister from down in the Point. Hey, you looking all right, boy. Don't be paying no mind. Hell, you a Mobile
boy, Murray. Ain't nobody nowhere, I don't care where they
come from, got no stuff for no Mobile boy unless he get up
there and forget where he come from. Hell, just remember
when you come from here you supposed go any goddam
where and make it."

"All I say is this," somebody else says winking, "just don't be
making none of them northern boots nervous by getting too
close to their white folks, especially with all the fancy book
learning you got. Man, that's the one thing they subject to run
you out from up there about—taking their white folks away
from them. Man, you might as well be messing with somebody's wife or something! Man, them northern Negroes love
their white folks, and don't you forget it."

"Especially them that always so ready to get up somewhere
talking about the black man this the black man that," somebody else continues grumbling as much to himself as to you
and the others. "Man they'll run over you getting to some old
white folks. Man, I used to know some there won't even give
you the time of day until they happen to find out that you
know some important-looking white folks."

"New York, hunh?," an old poolroom sage comes up slaps
you on the shoulder and says, "Hey, say, how about old Cleon
Jones and Tommy Agee and them up there with the Mets.
From Mobile County Training School. Putting old County on
the big-league baseball map. You see that fine brick house old
Cleon built over there not far from school? But hell, Mobile is
a baseball town, you know. Look at old Willie McCovey out
there in Frisco with the Giants, out there with Willie Mays

from right up there in The Ham. Not even to mention old Hank Aaron."

"Say, I got a glimpse of him when I stopped off in Lana the other day," you say, nodding. He goes on.

"Old Hank is something else, boy, and from Mobile all the way. Right out there in Whistler! Remember old Emmett Williams and them Hamilton boys? Mobile always has been a mean baseball town. Even before old Satchel Paige, and that was like goddam! I can still remember him with them old Satchel foots up there on the Chickasaw ball diamond forty some odd years ago throwing the stew out of a ball called the goddam fade away. . . ."

"Hey but let me tell you something else about some of them old New York City Negroes," a former MCTS upperclassman says. "Man, I remember when I was running out of there to Chicago on the New York Central back in the Depression. That was back when somebody was always hinting and whispering and winking and carrying on about the C.P., talking about the Communist Party. Man, party some stuff. Man the party them New York City Negroes I used to know were talking about was a sure enough party having a ball getting in some frantic white pants. And don't think them fay boys not doing the same thing vice versa. Man but here's the joke about that part. Them fay boys strictly out to get some ashes hauled and them supposed to be so educated boot chicks up there so busy putting on airs because they so sure they screwing their way into some high-class culture, they been had before they catch on that them fay boys think they all a bunch of cotton-patch pickaninny sluts! And, man, talking about snowing them, man all some lil old raggity-butt WPA fay boy used to have to do was take one of them to a cheap concert or a free museum or something and tell them he respect their *mind*. *Man, was I drug!*

"Man, but what I'm talking about is most of them New York Negroes didn't bit more care nothing about no Communism than they did Einstein and didn't know no more about it. I know what I'm talking about because I was hitting on a few of them fay frails my damn self and they'd leave you these pamphlets and I used to read some of them, and I tried to talk to some of them Harlem cats. Man them cats look at you like you carrying a violin case or something. But the minute they round a bunch of ofays don't nobody know nothing about it but them."

"Hey, how you doing, homes?" somebody else on another corner begins. "Up there in New York, hunh? But hell, all I got to do is look at you looking all classificational and I can see you taking care of business. You really looking good there boy. I kinda lost track of you there recently. We all remember you from over there at the school, you know. So we used to hear about you up at Skegee, and on the faculty and then you went to the Air Corps in the war. See what I mean? And then back to Skegee and then back in the service and traveling everywhere. Then I lost track and then that other time they said you were in here from New York so when I heard it this time I said, 'Hell, I remember that boy, I'm going over here and meddle him a little.' He know me. So how you doing, homes? Goddam, man. Sure good to see you."

Sometimes it also begins in a stylized falsetto exactly like this: "Hey, damn, man, they told me you were here and looking all clean, like for days. So now look here! I got to talk to you, man. So come on and get in this old struggle buggy and let's circle over by my place and say hello so the folks can see you and have a little taste and shoot the goddam shit awhile. I ain't going to hold you long and then I'll drive you anywhere else you got to go. Man, damn, I got to talk to you because I want to know what you think about some of this stuff I been thinking about. I know you might think I'm crazy like some of them say. That's all right. Just tell me what you think. Some of these folks around here, goddam. Some of them. And I say some of them, look like they think they got to latch onto everything come along because it's new. And it ain't even new. That's the killing part. It's old as all these old country-ass sideburns and bell-bottom sailor-boy pants and pinch-back used to be called jazz-back suits that come in back there right after pegtops and them box-backs. They think they getting with something so cool and all they being is ass-backwards. So all you got to do is just tell me what you think, like somebody been somewhere

and seen something and got some sense! Because some of this
stuff. Man, I'm telling you."

You go of course. You meet the folks and settle down in the
parlor. Then he continues, beginning with an eye-cutting,
elbow-nudging button-holing intimacy: "So now the first thing
is this, and like I say you might think I'm crazy too. But just
think about this for a minute":

Then in an italicized conspiratorial whisper: "*White folks
don't go around trying to make fun of us like they used to.* You
noticed that shit? Think about it. Now the minute you think
about it you got to remember when we were coming along
you couldn't do nothing without them trying to make out like
somebody so goddam ignorant that everything was always
funny as hell. Remember all that old Hambone stuff they used
to have in the papers, and all that old Stepin Fetchit and Willie
Best and Mantan Moreland stuff in the goddam movies and
that old Amos and Andy stuff on the goddam radio, all that
old Kingfish and Lightnin' and Madame Queen stuff. That's
the kind of old bullshit they used to try to pull on us, remember, and we used to see it and, hell, we knew exactly what they
were trying to do. You know that. So we went on about our
goddam business. So now my first point is this. *How come they
ain't making fun of nobody no more?* Wasn't nothing funny
about what we were doing and them sonbitches used to write
up every goddam thing like everybody talking some kind of
old handkerchief-headed dialect. My point is ain't nobody
never cut the fool like some of these clowns we got these days
and you don't see no crackers laughing. That's what I'm talking
about. You used to get somewhere and you were not about to
make no mistake because that's what they were waiting for you
to do and they would look at you buddy as much as to say,
Nigger, you done tore your barbarian ass. So you didn't get up
nowhere until you could cut the mustard. Hell, you're not
supposed to rip your drawers. Now that's what I call some
goddam black-ass pride! That's just what I'm talking about.
That's exactly what I'm talking about, cutting the goddam
mustard. We got some out-and-out fools will get up anywhere
nowdays carrying on with all them old passwords and secret
grips like old-time lodge members back when most folks
couldn't read and write. Talking about right on and tearing

right on through their BVD's to their natural booty holes!
And then talking about pride! And them crackers ain't even
cracking a goddam smile. So now, you know what I think?"

Whispering again: *"I think them goddam white folks know
exactly what they doing and they know if they start laughing and
correcting them, most of these clowns subject either to shut up or
wise up and straighten up!"*

Normal voice: "So see what I mean? You see the big difference, don't you? Look, don't nobody want nobody laughing at
us, you know me, cuz. I'm ready to kill some son of a bitch
come trying to make fun of me. So in a way it's good, but in
another way you better think about it. I say they ain't laughing
because they want us to follow the ones that's so loud and
wrong. You get my point? Because if they start laughing at
them that get up there talking all that old diaperical psychological economical bullshit they know good and well the others
won't follow them. So they don't. Man, white folks the very
ones encouraging them to be loud and wrong, man. And that's
the problem. Because, see, these fools think you can get up
there shucking and won't nobody know it—and the white man
working day and night figuring out ways to stay ahead of us.
Now am I shitting or gritting? Am I facking or just yakking?"

You say: "I know what you mean. I know exactly what you
mean." You say: "Man, sometimes I get that uneasy feeling that
rapping is getting to be the name of the whole goddam game
for more and more of us." You say: "Old-fashioned street-corner
woofing and simple-ass signifying and that's all, and then in
Harlem they go around later on bragging about what they said
and how it shook up the whiteys and broke up the meeting."

Then in an uptown-mocking voice that is part West Indian,
part New York Jewish intellectual, part Louis Armstrong, you
say: "I told them, man. You hear me telling them? You heard
me rapping. I said like this is the black communertee and black
people radicalized and tired of all this old shit from the sick,
racist establishment! You heard me. I said 'Forget it, Charley.'
I told it like it nitty-gritty fucking is, man. I said, all this old
honky shit ain't a thing but some old jive-time colonialism
versus upward mobility and black identity. I gave them whiteys
a piece of my cotton-picking mind. I said 'Black is beautiful,
baby, and you better believe it, chuck.'"

But the main purpose for making the rounds this time is to listen. And later on in another part of town somebody else says: "One thing the old folks used to worry about all the time. They were always talking about education, and saying when you got that in your head you had something couldn't nobody take away from you. But they also used to worry about bringing up a generation of educated proper-talking fools. Remember how folks used to look at you when they said that, and start talking about mother-wit and don't be putting on no airs? Well, we got the finest bunch of young'uns you going to find anywhere in this country these days, but when you look up there on TV you got to admit we got ourselves a whole lot of loudmouthed educated fools to watch out for among them too. Ain't no use in lying about it."

And somebody else says: "Now I'm just going to tell you. Now this is me and this is what I think and I been thinking about this for a long time. All right, so we the ones that got them to open up them schools to our children. That was us, and nobody else and we ain't never said nothing about letting nobody in there that wasn't qualified. Never. You know that. Never. So what do they do? I'm talking about the goddam white folks now. They come up and figure out how they can let a lot of loudmouth hustlers in there that don't belong in there. Because they know good and well these the ones ain't going to study and ain't going to let nobody else study. So that's what we got now. We send them up there to learn what them white boys learning about running the goddam world and they up there out marching and wearing all that old three-ring-circus stuff and talking about they got to study about Africa. Now what I say is if that's all they want to know they ain't got no business up there. That's what I say. Because the white man only too glad if they rather learn about Africa instead of how to run the world. I say them Africans already know about Africa, and what good is it doing them? Every time I see one he over here trying to get himself straight; and most of them hate to go back, and I don't blame them."

To which still someone else adds: "This is what I say. I say we know this white man. I say don't nobody nowhere in the world know this white man better than us, and this is the goddam white man that runs the goddam world. That's a fact, gentlemen, and ain't no disputing it. Don't nobody nowhere do nothing if this white man here don't really like it. You remember what Kennedy did to old Khrushchev that time about Cuba? Old Kennedy said, 'I'm going to tell it to you straight, pardner.' He said, 'Listen horse, cause I ain't going to tell you but once, so listen good or it's going to be your natural vodka pooting ass.' He said, 'Now I want all them goddam missiles and shit out of there by Wednesday' (or Thursday—or whenever the hell it was—) and he said, 'I want them back on them goddam boats heading in such and such a direction, and then goddammit when you get to such and such a latitude of longitude I want you to stop and peel back them tarpaulins so my badassed supersonic picture-taking jets can fly over and inspect that shit and then I want you to get your Russian ass out of my hemisphere and stay out.' That's this white man, and don't nobody mess with him, and what I'm saying is we the ones that know him inside out and been knowing him inside out. What I'm trying to say is we right here in the middle of all this stuff that everybody else in the world is trying to get next to and what these college boys got to do is get something to go with what we know about this white man. What I'm saying is he smart enough to go all the way up to the moon and we know he still ain't nothing but a square like he always was, so what these college boys got to do is get ready to take all this stuff we know and push it up to the nth degree and use it on this white man right here."

"Now you talking," somebody else continues, "now you saying something. Talking about Africa, this white man right here is the one you going to have to come up against, don't care where you go. And we already know him. Supposed to know him. Better know him. And all y'all know I been saying this for years. Every time somebody come up with some of all that old West Indian banana-boat jive about the 'block mon' I tell them, and I been saying it all these years and ain't about to bite my tongue. I tell them, ain't nobody doing nothing nowhere in Africa and nowheres else that this white man right here don't want them to do. I tell them. Every time a goddam African put a dime in a telephone, a nickel of it come right over here to this same white man. That goes for them Germans and Frenchmen and Englishmen, all of them over there and them Japs too. So you know it goes for them goddam bare-footed Africans. So when they come up to me with some of that old monkey-boat jive I tell them: All y'all want to go back to Africa, you welcome to go. Fare thee goddam well, horse, I say. But I tell you what I'm going to do. Because I know what's going to happen. I say: I'm going to get my college boys trained to go to New York City and Washington, D.C., and get next to something. Because what's going to happen is them Africans going to take one look at them goddam jive-time Zulu haircuts and them forty-dollar hand-made shoes and they going to lock your American ass up in one of them same old slave-trading jails they put our ancestors in, and they going to have you writing letters back over here to this same old dog-ass white man in the United States of America asking for money. Hey, wait. Hey, listen to this. Ain't going to let them get no further than the goddam waterfront. They go lock them up with a goddam Sears, Roebuck catalogue. I'm talking about right on the dock, man, and have them making out order blanks to Congress for Cocolas and transistors, and comic books, cow-boy boots and white side walls and helicopters and all that stuff. And you know what the goddam hell I'm going to be doing? I'm going to have *my* college boys sitting up there in Washington and Wall Street with a mean-assed rubber-assed goddam stamp saying Hell, no! Saying, forget it, cousin. Hey, because by that time with what we know we supposed to have this white man over here all faked out and off somewhere freaking out and I mean for days! And I'll bet you this much any day, we'll have this white man over here faked out long before any boots from Harlem fake any of them Africans out over yonder. You go over there trying to pull some old chicken-shit Harlem hype on them Africans and they subject to bundle your butt up and sell you to them A-rabs. Man, them Africans ain't going to never pay no boot like me and you no mind as long as they can do their little two-bit business directly with this same old white man that we already know fifty times better than any African, and I ain't leaving out no Harvard Africans."

You think about all the tourist-style trinkets so many naive U.S. black nationalists seem to think is the great art of the mother country, completely ignoring all of the art history and criticism that goes into museum acquisitions. You also think about how *shared experience* has been a far greater unifying force for so-called Black Americans than *race* as such has ever been to the peoples of Africa. It is not the racial factor of blackness as such which is crucial among Africans any more than whiteness as such kept the peace among the peoples of Europe. But all you do is shake your head laughing along with everybody else.

And what then follows you remember later as having been not unlike the leapfrogging chase chorus exchanges among musicians running down a theme on some of Lester Young's early, post-Basie, combo recordings: the soloists trading eight-, six-, and four-bar statements (nor did they lack any of old Lester's querulous coolness, nor any of his blues-based determination to blow it as he felt it and heard it regardless of what was currently hip):

"Hey, man, me, man (*One trumpetlike statement begins*), you know how come I don't be paying no mind to none of that old talk? Because they talking but I'm looking and listening too. They talking all that old Afro this and Afro that and black this and black the other and I'm right here looking at them cutting up exactly like a bunch of goddam rebel-yelling crackers cussing out the Supreme Court. If you want to know the truth, sometime when some of these TV cats get going about liberation I get the feeling the only freedom they want is the right to cuss everybody out."

"Hey!" (*this could be another trumpet, say with a parenthetical mute, or it could be an alto, or a getaway tenor*), "hey, but you know something else some of this old stuff put me in the mind of? A big old-fashioned church mess. You know what I'm talking about. Look, everybody going to church to try to save his soul and get to heaven. That's what getting religion is for and that's what the church is about. At least that's what it's supposed to be about. And that's exactly how come some old church folks the very ones make me so tired. Everybody in there because they trying save themself from torment and look like all they trying to do is trying to tell somebody else what to do and when you don't let them run your business they ready to gang up on you in some kind of old conference and black-ball you out and if it's left up to them right on into eternal fire and brimstone. You see my point? I'm talking about church members now. I'm talking about the very ones suppose to be living by the word. They the very ones always subject to come acting like they already so close to God they got the almighty power to do you some dirt. Man that's what I can't stand about all this ole brother and sister putting on they got all out in the streets these days. The very first thing I think about when somebody come up to me talking about bro is, here come another one of them old deceitful hypocrites."

"Well, now" (*this is plunger style trombone jive*), "talking about rebel-yelling crackers, I'm just going to come on out and tell you, me. Hell, if I'm going to be some old damn peckerwood, I'm going to make sure to be one that's got enough money to play it cool. Damn, that's the least I can do. Of course, you know me. I always did think like a millionaire, myself. I'm always out to make me some more money, myself."

"You and me both" (*you remember this as a baritone statement, barbershop Amen corner baritone*), "and I'm going to tell you something else. I'm going to tell you what they doing. I'm going to tell you exactly what they doing. Because they doing exactly what they always doing when they start talking all that old Mother Africa bullshit. Any time you hear them talking all that old tiger-rag jive about the black man and Mother Africa you just watch and see what the first thing they do going to be. The very first thing they going to do is start turning on one another. Man, you gonna have a much harder time getting two dozen of them cats on a boat going to Africa than they had dragging our forefathers over here. But what I'm talking about is some of these little rascals already getting up calling somebody nigger in front of white folks, and supposed to be getting college educated! Up there shucking and signifying while them white boys knocking themselves out qualifying!"

"And don't think the white man don't know what's happening, horse" (*signifying monkey trumpet, with a mute plus derby!*). "Because you see the white man is the one that knew exactly how we got our black asses brought over here in the first goddam place. Up there talking about black history. I'll tell you some goddam black-ass history. This is the kind of black history the white man studies. As soon as them Africans get mad they subject to take and sell one another to the white man. They been doing it. They been doing it, and they still do it. I keep telling these little rascals it ain't going to do no good calling yourself no African. You got be from the right tribe or whatever it is. Hell mess around an come up with the wrong tribe and that's your behind, Jim. Sheet, the man just about know all he got to do is wait, because just like you say, some of these little fools already up there denying their own folks."

"That's what I say." (*So on it goes and maybe this is a big tenor. But then all the words were there long before the instrumentation.*) "That's exactly what I say. And I ain't talking about criticizing. You got a right to criticize anybody you think doing wrong, I don't care who they is. That's for my own benefit. That's for everybody's benefit. I'm talking about denying your own folks just because you mad with them about something. That's what I'm talking about. I talking about them little fools up there denying their own mamas and papas. I bet you don't hear no young Jews up there calling their old folks kikes, and yids, and Hebes and dirty Christ-killers in front of other folks. Don't care how mad they get with one another. Them Jews got organizations to take care of that kind of old loudmouthed bullshit. Don't take my word for it. Ask New York. Tell them, New York."

"Hey wait a minute. Now this is what I say about that. I say ain't nobody going to never get nowhere disrespecting your mama and papa. I might not go to church as much as some folks but I believe in the Good Book and the Good Book say honor thy father and thy mother."

"Didn't it though. Oh but didn't it though. That thy days shall be long upon the land which the Lord thy god giveth thee. I can still hear old Elder Ravezee preaching that sermon when I was a boy."

"And don't forget old Reverend Joyful Keeby. Talking about Africa, I bet you one thing. I bet you ain't nobody going to catch nobody like Plute Keeby talking about going back to his kinfolks somewhere over in no Africa, and old Plute and them can trace their African blood right back to that old hull of the *Crowtillie* out there in the mouth of the Chickasabogue."

"Man, I want to thank you for putting that in there. I just want to thank you. I only want to thank you. I just want to thank you one time. But hey look here now—you know I thought one of y'all was going say when he said that about the boat going to Africa. I thought somebody was going to say something about them northern city boys always talking about Africa and can't even spend a weekend in the goddam country. Man, the minute them cats get off the edge of the concrete, they start crying for Harlem. Now if I'm lying come get me, cousin."

"Hey, yeah, but wait a minute I'm still talking about these little fools getting up there trying to put the badmouth on their own dear folks for the goddam white folks. That's putting your own goddam self in the goddam dozens without knowing it. You see what I'm saying? And talking about putting the cart before the horse! Man, damn! Who ever heard of the chillun putting badmouth on the old folks?"

"Thank you. I just want to thank you again. Because that's the Bible again. Talking about the sons of Ham. That's laughing at thy own daddy's drunkenness and nakedness. And that's exactly how come the Lord banished his dumb-ass ass to the goddam black-ass wilderness. And told him: Here you come all puffed up on something you read in some old book and laughing at thy father who gavest thee the very eyes thou seest with and the very tongue thou mockest him with, and don't know the first frigging thing about what that old man been through to get you where you at today!"

"Showing out for white folks. That's all I say it is, mocking your *own* folks to impress some little old white—and I'm talking about some little old *bullshit* whiteys that ain't got no more than nobody else. That's what I'm talking about. Somebody ain't into nothing with no profit at all. Somebody can't even do nothing for themselves. So you know they can't do nothing for you. But get you in more trouble than you already got."

"But now you see that's why it didn't surprise me a bit when they broke up with all them that used to be down here every summer two or three years ago. You know what I mean? If you want to help I say thank you. I say thank you very much. But don't come acting like you know more about my goddam business than I do and don't come expecting me to prove nothing to you like you better than me. Hell, ain't nobody better than me. Not if I'm the one telling it."

"That's exactly why I said what I said. I said come on, man. I said goddam. I said what the hell I'm doing wasting my goddam time proving some kind of old bullshit point to some little bullshit ofays down here on a summer vacation and sicking me on the goddam police to get some knots on my head and they can go home to papa and that fat-ass checkbook any time they want to. So here I am with a bunch of hickeys on my knuckle-ass head and they back up there bragging about how they helped me. Dig that. I said, man, what is this shit? I said man, fuck that shit."

"Hell, anytime they get a toothache Papa can send that private plane down here with his own private doctor on it."

"Yeah, you right. I see what you mean. But I wasn't talking about all of that. I was talking about them jive-time missionaries that come down here just wanting somebody to think they more than they is."

"You goddam right. Me I just don't want no bunch of eager-beaver ofays coming down here telling me what to do just because they might know how to type up a letter. That's one goddam thing I learned in the Army. Don't take no Ph.D. to know how to fill out them papers. You see what I'm talking about. If you supposed to be so goddam white I'm expecting you to put me next to something—otherwise forget it. Anybody can fill out them old papers."

"Well goddammit me, I'm talking about *all* of them. I'm talking about I don't have to be proving nothing to nobody. Unless I'm trying to get him to hire me. And you *know* I'm forced to be bullshitting him then, bullshitting them a *while*. I'm talking about our children the ones supposed to be leading this thing. Because if you don't watch out them little old ofays will have you all bogged up in some of that old Beatle shit, man."

"Hey but you know where the Beatles got that shit from. You know that's our shit they fucking up like that."

"Yeah, but damn, man that ain't what I'm talking about now. Hell, you know what I'm talking about. I'm talking about some little old chalk chick come talking about the Beatles and all that old rockabilly stuff. You suppose to put her hip. Tell her that's some old nowhere shit for days. Don't be come repeating some old psychological jive like it's deep just because you laying some little old fay broads that's oooing and aaaing over it because they read about it in a goddam magazine."

You say: "I think I know what you mean about the white kids, and yet they may be the first generation of white people who are really beginning to be uncomfortable about their heritage of racism. You have to give them that. But the goddam problem is that they are still no less condescending than their parents. I mean who the hell are they to be 'helping' somebody? How the hell would they know who to help anyway? Goddam it if they really mean business they've got to stop acting as if only the most confused, uninformed, and loudmouthed among us are for real. And everybody else is either stupid or is trying to pass for white."

"Ain't that a bitch," somebody says. "That is a *bitch*, gentlemen. That's a bitch and ahalf. I'm talking about how white folks can always come up with another kind of excuse to be against something look like it might profit us something."

But mostly you listen as if from the piano. So mostly what you say is very much like playing ellington and basie style comp chords. (Remembering also the old one which goes: if you don't play them just pat your foot while I play them.) But every so often it is also as if they have swung the microphone over to you for a four-, six-, or eight-bar bridge or solo insertion. This time somebody says: "Well, what you got to say about it there, Mister New York. Where the hell they getting all this old bullshit up there talking like their own people the ones trying to hold them back. Ain't no goddam body doing nothing but trying to make it *possible* for them. That's what the old folks did for us and mine always told me the way to thank them is do the same for the next generation and any child of mine get up there saying I ain't done my part is just a bigmouth lie and I bet he won't tell me to my face. Just let one of them dispute that to my face."

And somebody else cuts in as with a plunger-style trombone to say: "Hey, especially when you get your head bad. Man, goddam, I'd hate to see one of them little clowns forget he ain't talking to one of them simple-ass ofay reporters and jump you with your head bad. Great googly woogly!"

You say: "They don't really mean it." You say: "I don't think they realize what they're saying. The big thing with them nowadays is to sound revolutionary. Which is fine. But most of

those I've talked to tend to confuse revolution with community rehabilitation programs. A lot of them keep talking about
what they are going to do for the people of the black community, and I keep telling them that too many of them are only
sounding like a bunch of hancty social-welfare case workers,
and ofay case workers at that. Man, you go around to the Ivy
League campuses and listen to some of our kids talking all that
old blue-eagle jive and they sound like they've never been
anywhere near their own people. You know what I mean? Like,
well, when you come right down to it they sound almost exactly like a bunch of rich or passing-for-rich white kids ever so
hot to trot into the Peace Corps. You know what I mean? To
help the poor natives somewhere. What bothers me and this
really bothers the hell out of me is that they are responding to
what they read instead of what they know, and yet when you
check them out on what they read you find they haven't really
read very much."

"And got the gall to come thinking they so hip," somebody
says.

"Hip?" somebody else says, "Did you say hip? Come on,
man. How the hell they going to be hip? They ain't been
around long enough to be hip. Ain't been far enough. They
ain't been into enough. Come on man. How they going to be
hip up there showing how much they don't know every chance
they get because they ain't hip enough to cool it because
somebody *else* might know. Damn, man, the first thing about
being hip is being hip to how hip the other fellow is. Man
when you hip the first thing you know is you ain't never supposed to be playing nobody cheap just because they come
acting like they don't know what's happening. Man, the last
thing you can say for these clowns is they hip; and the way
some of them going they ain't going to live long enough to be
cool enough to be hip and subject to get a lot of other folks
messed up in the process, and just over some old loudmouth
bullshit."

Elsewhere you yourself also say, "You know what I want them
to be like? Our prizefighters. Our baseball players. Like our
basketball players. You know what I mean? Then you'll see
something. Then you'll see them riffing on history because

they know history. Riffing on politics because they know politics. One of the main things that too many spokesmen seem to forget these days is the fact you really have to know a hell of a lot about the system in order to know whether you're operating within it or outside it. What bothers me now is that they are so quick to start formulating policies before double-checking the definition of the problem. The difference between riffing and shucking is knowing the goddam fundamentals. Man, when I see one of us up at Harvard or Yale I want to be able to feel like you used to feel seeing Sugar Ray in Madison Square Garden or Big Oscar there, or Willie Mays coming to bat in an All-Star game. You know what I mean? I like to think that old Thurgood Marshall came pretty close. At one time when he opened his briefcase in the Supreme Court it was almost like Lawrence Brown and Harry Carney unpacking their horns backstage at Carnegie Hall."

Then for outchorus: "Man, if you don't know what to do with that kind of black heritage you're not likely to know what to do with any other kind either. Some of our kids now seem to think that heritage is something in a textbook, something that has to be at least a thousand years old and nine thousand miles across the sea. Something you can brag about. Some fabulous kingdoms of ancient African tyrants for liberation-committed black U.S. revolutionaries to be snobbish about! And yet few would regard themselves as antiquarians. Ordinarily, they're the last people in the world to be messing around with something that is the least bit out of date."

You also find time to sit and listen to what some of the very oldest among the old heads from the old days want to tell you about the condition of contemporary man in general and about the state of the nation's political well-being in particular. Because missing that part, which is always like coming back to the oldness of the old chimney corner even in summer, would be perhaps even worse than missing another chance to sit down to a full-course spread of old-time home cooking once more.

You never miss that part of it if you can help it, and this time (which is chinaberry-blue Maytime) one very special back porch after-supper rocking-chair session in the fig-tree-fresh, damp-clay-scented twilight which is supposed to be about the first three months of the Nixon administration turns into the following unka so-and-so monologue: "Lyndon Johnson. Lyndon Johnson. Old Lyndon Johnson. They can call him everything but a child of God as long as you please and I still say old Lyndon Johnson, faults and all. They talking about what they talking about and I'm talking about what I'm talking about. I'm talking about the same thing I always been talking about. I'm talking about us, and I say old Lyndon Johnson is the one that brought more government benefits to help us out than all the rest of them up there put together all the way back through old Abe Lincoln. I'm talking about Lyndon Johnson from down here out there in Texas. And they tell me old Lady Bird Johnson is from right here in Alabama. The Lord spared me to live to see the day folks been talking about ever since my own daddy, God rest his soul, was a boy and he used to say it back when I was a boy and old Teddy Roosevelt sent for old Bookety Washington to come up and have breakfast with him in the White House that time. Everybody got to carrying on so about that, and my daddy kept telling them over and over. He said, them northern white folks grinning in your face in public don't mean nothing but up to a certain point and beyond that point it don't mean a blessed thing. He said they generally more mannerable toward you than these old pecks down here. You got to give them that but that don't mean they don't expect you to lick up to them if you want something from them. And then they still ain't going no further than up to that point, and they ain't going that far if they got to buck up against any of these old white folks down here to do it. And I said the same thing when you yourself wasn't nothing but a little blister of a boy. When they all used to get to making such miration over old Franklin D. I said that's all right about Muscle Shoals and Three Point Two and God bless Miss Eleanor for being as nice as she is and all that, but I said both of them come from up there and I don't care how good they talk you just watch and see if they don't always manage to find some old excuse not to buck the Southern white man. Oh I ain't going to say they don't *never* buck him. I'm talking about bucking him in the favor of *us*. So anyhow this is what I got from my daddy, and his daddy ran away and fought for freedom with the Union Army, and I said you can say what you want to, and I might not be here to see it, but it's going to take one of these old Confederate bushwhackers from somewhere right down through in here to go up against these old Southern white folks when they get mad. My daddy used to say it over and over again. So when old Lyndon Johnson come along and got in there on a humble—and, boy that's the onliest way he ever coulda made it into there—I was watching with my fingers crossed because he was the first one from down in here since old Woodrow Wilson and all that old dirt he did to us—and them white folks up north not lifting a finger against him either, talking about old Woodrow Wilson. So anyhow, like I say I was watching him and the first thing I could tell was that them white folks up the way was the very ones that was satisfied that old Lyndon Johnson was going to be like old Woodrow Wilson all over again. But now here's what give the whole thing away to me. These white folks down here. Boy don't you never forget they always been the key to everything so far as we concerned. So what give it away to me was them. Because they the very first ones to realize that old Lyndon Johnson meant business when he said the time is here to do something. And didn't nobody have to tell them what that meant because they already knew he was one of them and if they made him mad he subject to do some of that old rowdy cracker cussing right back at them, and some of that old cowboy stuff to boot. When they commence to telling me about how mean he is that's when I tell them, I say that's exactly what we need, some mean old crackers on our side, for a change. That's when I commenced to feel maybe the Lord had spared me to see the day, and then the next thing you know them northern folks up there talking about you can't put no dependence in him no more. The very same ones that used to trust him when they thought he was another one of these old crooked Confederates. Now wait, I'm going to tell you what put us in that creditability gap you been reading about. Talking about the government lying to them about something. Boy the consarn government been lying to *us* every since emancipation. Now here they come talking about somebody lying! You remember that old Kennedy boy was the one started talking about getting a black man up there in the

Cabinet with him. All right now you got to give him his due
for that, but look at the way he up and went about trying to
do it. He looked over all them Cabinet jobs he already had
open and come talking about if he could just get a new one to
fill; and then he come right on out and told them who he was
going to put in there—like Congress going to be ever so
mighty glad to give him some kind of brand new extra job so he
can give it to one of us! Confound the luck, that didn't make
no sense at all to me. Then old Lyndon Johnson come along
and said he needed that same extra job. But you notice he
didn't say a thing about who he had a mind to put in there?
And naturally they don't just come right on out and ask him
because they know good and well he know how come they
didn't give it to Kennedy. So all they did was just kinda hint
around to let him know—since he was a cracker anyway. And
all old Lyndon Johnson did was wink a cracker wink at them and
change the subject. And then as soon as they give it to him he
turned right around and put the same one in there they turned
Kennedy down on, the same one! That's how Weaver got to
be the first one in there. That's why I say you got to give old
Lyndon Johnson credit. Because all he had to do was let them
know he was going to hold the line on the black man and he
could've stayed up there as long as he wanted to. All he had to
do every time one of us started acting up was just put on his
old head-whipping sheriff's hat and make out like he getting
up a posse or something, and theyd've *kept* him up there till he
got tired of it. That's why I got to give him credit don't care
who don't. Because I know what he coulda done and I remember what he did for a fact. He got up there in front of everybody and said we shall overcome. Boy that's enough to scare
white folks worse than the Indians, boy. But you know what
that put me in mind of? I'm going to tell you exactly who that
put me in the mind of. Old Big Jim Folsom on his way to
Montgomery. That first time, I'm talking about. Old Big Jim
Folsom talking about y'all come. You remember what Old Big
Jim Folsom said when they come up to him about what was he
going to do about us? Old Big Jim Folsom told them. Old Big
Jim ain't never been nothing but a Alabama redneck and never
will be, but he told them. He said what y'all always running
around scared of them for? He said, they been right here

amongst us all this time. He said, I ain't scared of them. That's exactly what he said. He said, Hell they just trying to get along the best they can. He said now a fact is a fact and they got something coming to them like other folks. He said live and let live. That's what he was talking about when he said y'all come. And that's when these Alabama peckerwoods took his credit away from him and started calling him Kissing Jim. That's what all that's about, boy.

"That's what old Lyndon Johnson kinda put me in the mind of when he got in there—old Big Jim before he went bad. Somebody come in there and told him, 'Mister President, I swear I can't find no experts that know what to do about them niggers being so lowdown and don't-carified.' Now this northern city joker wasn't talking about nothing but getting up some more of all that pick and shovel stuff from back in the days of old Franklin D. Boy, the last thing that joker want to see is a whole lot of our educated ones like you up there getting somewhere like everybody else. But that's exactly where old Lyndon Johnson stepped in. He know good and well all this northern joker trying to tell him is niggers just will be niggers as far as northern white folks is concerned. But I can just imagine him saying, 'Hell, how come ain't nobody tried this: Send me old Thurgill Marshall. He already whipped everybody that'll go before a judge with him. So cain't nobody say he ain't ready. I'm going to make him my chief lawyer for a while and then I'm going to ease him on up on the Supreme Court bench and let him help make some decisions. Then I'm going to put one up there with them millionaires on the Federal Reserve Bank to help me keep an eye on the money. I want him to be a real black one so they can't say I just put old Thurgill up there because he's damn near white! And another one over in the World Bank to look out for that. Make that one brown.' Think about that, boy. Two niggers watching white folks count money!

"Boy, Old Lyndon Johnson say, 'Before I get through I'm going to let some of my niggers get a taste of some of all this high class stuff.' That's what I'm talking about the Lord sparing me to be here. And I can imagine another one of them coming in there and saying, Now, I'm just going to have to come right on out and tell you Mister President, the big money folks up North getting nervous. And that's when I can imagine old Lyndon Johnson cutting into a big red apple with his silver-plated Wild West pocketknife and offering him a slice like a chew of Brown's Mules chewing tobacco and saying, 'You go back and tell 'em I'm from down south so I'm kinda used to having them around me. Tell 'em I feel kinda lost if ain't none of them around. Tell 'em they'll get used to them in here just like they already used to them cooking and running them elevators. But tell them they can depend on one thing. I ain't going to put nary a one in nowhere unless he ready, and if he don't cut the mustard I'll kick his black tail out of there so fast he'll be shame to even remember he was in there. Tell them they can depend on that.' Boy that's another thing about so many of them white folks up north. You tell 'em folks hungry and all they can think about is spoon-feeding somebody.

"The Lord spared me to be here to see that day. Talking about when old Lyndon laid it on them. But son, I never thought I was ever born to witness the day that followed, and I'm talking about followed before anybody could even get set to get something out of what we were just about to get up close to. Now that's another thing you got to give old Lyndon Johnson credit for, because you know good and well he must have meant business because he got too much sense about politics not to know there was bound to be some white backwash. But the thing of it all was the next thing. Because I been here all this many years and I declare before God I just couldn't believe it, and I know my daddy poor soul turned over in his grave. The next thing you know, some of our own folks up there jumping on Lyndon Johnson with both feet just like we in with the white folks against him, and all the time these old white folks down here just sitting back laughing and talking about they been knowing niggers didn't have sense enough to grab our chance if somebody gave it to them.

"So now do you see what I'm talking about, young fess? Because I said all of that there to say this here. Because you know good and well I ain't talking about what happened to old Lyndon Johnson. Old Lyndon Johnson can take care of Lyndon Johnson, ain't no doubt about that. I'm talking about what's happening to us. I'm talking about some of us up there

so busy showing out for them northern white folks we done
completely forgot what we supposed to be doing for one another. I'm talking about y'all up there doing what you doing and
here come all them old nice grinning northern white folks and
that's all right with me if they want to help out but the next
thing you know they got y'all up there doing everything they
talking about. Boy, you old enough to remember when they
come grinning down here back during the time of all that old
Scotchbug mess. Well, y'all up there putting more dependence
in them right now than anybody down here was near bout to
be putting in them back then when most people still suppose
to been still ignorant. So I said all that because I want you to
remember this. Just remember you got all your good book
learning because that's what the old folks wanted you to get
and they want you to see just how high you can go. But they
don't want you to get up there and forget your common sense
just because two or three of them people feel like grinning at
you and treating you nice. You don't have to just flat out and
insult nobody. Folks expect you to know better than that.
They come grinning to you. You grin right back at them if you
want to, that ain't nothing but manners and decency. But just
keep remembering they grinning about what they grinning
about and you grinning about what you grinning about. You
see what I'm talking about old Lyndon Johnson? Boy, I ain't
talking about no friendship. I'm talking about knowing what
to do when you got your chance to do business with a politician that ain't going to back up off these old Southern white
folks because he one of them. I'm talking about what old
Lyndon Johnson had to back up off of was the big-money
northern white folks. And now we got old Nixon. So now
the northern white man come trying to make out like he so
worried because old Nixon ain't doing enough for us. But now
you just wait and see how many of them going to buck up
against old Nixon. Just wait and see. Don't be surprised if old
Nixon don't have do more on his own than any of them old
nice grinning Northern white folks ever going to be willing to
try to force him to do. I'm talking about for us—ain't talking
about that old war over yonder. I say it still going to take somebody like old Lyndon Johnson from down around somewhere

in here and the Lord might not spare me to see that come around another 'gain but I just hope and pray that enough of y'all will know better next time."

You hope so too. And you want to believe most of what he says about white southerners like Lyndon Johnson as much as he apparently wants to believe it. (*"Some mean ass crackers on our side for a change, for whatever goddam reason."*) But even so if you were naming the "other folks" who would be the ones most likely to stick their necks farthest out for you out of a sense of moral obligation—and keep it out there even against the opposition of their "own people"—most of them would probably be Jewish. Not only that but, Air Force buddies aside, you actually found it somewhat less embarrassing to have to ask urgently needed personal favors of Jewish friends than of white southerners. Not to mention Yankee do-gooders. On the other hand you'd much rather have old Willie Morris, for instance, go on functioning in terms of his Yazoo City courthouse square sense of actuality than have him become another compassionate pop-cause-oriented, underdog-loving, petty cash–generous, tax write-off neo–Great White Father.

You hope for that too. But you do not ask even that of him, either—or of any other white Southerner, including old Lyndon Johnson himself. Because it is not something for which you ask (and make yourself beholden!). It is not something to be requested anyway; because, as old Lyndon seems to have come to realize as few others have, it is something already required of him—as much by his own personal predicament as by the state of things in the nation and the world at large.

———

Some altogether pleasant reencounters also go exactly like this: "Is this who I think it is? This ain't who I think it is. This can't be who I think it is. Boy, is this you? Boy, this ain't you! Come here and let me look at you, boy. Look at him. Boy, you something! You think you a man now don't you! Well I guess you turned out all right! They tell me you been some of everywhere and doing all right for yourself, and you sure look like it. Been all over there in Paris, France, and Rome, Italy, they tell me. And Casablanca and all out in Hollywood. And living up in New

York these days. Well go on then, Mister World Traveler, I hear you. Go on with all that old fancy stuff they probably taught you in Paris and Casablanca. That's all right with me. Just don't be up there thinking you so much, and forgetting where you got your start. Because some of these same little gals you left down here in poor little old countrified Mobile, Alabama, don't be backing up off none of them, and that goes for any of them little old clippity clopping bouncy-butt cuties up there in Harlem too. So go on, I know you down here on business and ain't got time for no foolishness but just don't be forgetting. These old Mobile girls never is to be standing still neither."

Other such reencounters begin in the same manner, and perhaps as often as not the topic is also essentially the same. For instance: "You got yourself a wife and family? How come you didn't bring your wife so folks can meet her? Now don't be coming down here leaving her up there because you done gone and married some little old white gal—unless she rich and stand for something. And I'm talking about with money's mammy. But shoot, I know you better than to come doing something like that. Your folks ain't worked themselves down to get you all that good education to be taking care of no old pore-tail white gal with. Boy, if you can't marry no white gal that's rich enough to take care of you, forget it. I know you better than that. So is your wife from somewhere down in here? Is she nice? I'm satisfied she pretty. So bring her on down here with you next time, ain't nobody going to bite her."

"I know she educated and I know good and well she pretty," echoes somebody else who was once almost as certain of her own pulchritudinous plurabilities. "Because you probably forgotten me but I remember you all right. You and Leo Greene. Neither one of y'all ain't never had much for no ordinary-looking broad to do—not in the light of day, I'm talking about. Because wait. You know something? Now, I'm going to tell you something. I said I was going to tell you this one of these days, and I am: So you know something? Sometimes you and old Leo Greene used to go around like y'all were trying to be so cute or something. Especially sometimes when somebody didn't stay on in school. But I think I can just about make you remember a few things, Mister Albert Lee Murray. I just about think I just about can."

You assure this one that you remember very well indeed. *But never as you will always have to remember somebody else who will always be Miss Somebody. Who looked like Kay Francis would have looked if Kay Francis had been sugar-plump brown like that with a shape like that and could have walked that kind of sugar-plump walk wearing bunny-rabbit bedroom mules to the store like that; somebody who said: "Not if you ain't going to stay out of the streets and promise me not to lose sight on the whole world because you finding out what that's made for, not if you ain't going right on keeping that head in them books where it belong"; who said "Lord boy you better not be letting no little old conniving gal come whining your name in your ear so she can come back whining something else soon enough unless you want to end up around here in one of these old sawmills or on the chain gang or something"; who said, "boy God knows you ain't nothing, but a child to me," and said: "Ain't nothing but a little old boy I don't want to see getting too mannish for his own good."*

But the mention of Leo Greene also makes you remember the time when Mister Baker started talking about The Ifs of Initiative Ingenuity and Integrity during the morning assembly period and went on and on about the vision and stick-to-itiveness of great men as contrasted with the self-indulgence of mediocre men (with everybody squirming and wondering) until after one o'clock; and then saying: "Who is going to lead our people into the great tomorrow if promising young men like Leo Greene and Albert Murray don't hold their talent and integrity firmly in clutch instead of riding bicycles all the way over to Cedar Grove to seduce girls on Monday of all nights. Ambition must be made of sterner stuff sterner stuff sterner stuff."

There is also time this trip to revisit some of the old downtown landmarks: and since you are already staying at the Battle House you begin in Bienville Square, *where the sound of the oldest of all wrought-iron municipal fountains immediately evokes Hernando de Soto and Ponce de León once more as it always did during your grade-school days.* (When what used to evoke Bienville and Iberville was the powdered wigs and slippers and pastel stockings of Felix Rex and his masked courtiers during Mardi Gras season.)

From the Square you cross Dauphin Street to Kress (better known as Kresses) which is not only the original of all five-and-dime stores but as such was also your actual prototype of all storybook bazaars, including the getting-place of Christmas toys. (There was a time when it was all too obvious that the route to North Pole and the toy workshop of Santa Claus was through the attic of Kresses.) This time the soda-fountain counter is no longer for whites only, and the palest of all pale-face girls are now free to smile their whing-ding service with a red-lipped perfume-counter-faced whing-ding smile at you too (in public). And say: "Coke and one burger comin' *right* up." And say: "Be anything else? Well thank you *kindly*, now." And say: "Come agayhan, now, you hear?" democratizing and howard-johnsoning you at one and the same time.

You also stand on the corner of Dauphin and Royal once more remembering how when you used to stand there in that time many years ago waiting for the trolley car, with Checker cabs and chauffeur-driven Cadillacs and Packards and Pierce-Arrows passing, when what with seeing so many different kinds of people and hearing that many different languages all around you because there were ships flying flags of all nations docked at the foot of Government Street, only a few blocks away; and what with the newsboys chanting the headlines against the background of the empire state tallness of the Van Antwerp Building you knew very well that where you stood was the crossroads of the world.

From Dauphin and Royal you also circle through Metzgers remembering adolescence as the age of Hart, Schaffner and Marx and Society Brand and Kuppenheimers plus Nunn Bush for some and Florsheim for others. The mere sight of L. Hammels and Gayfers reminds you of the time when the theme-song of every high-school Cinderella was "Sophisticated Lady." You stroll remembering and taking pictures along the waterfront and along Government Street. Then finally you have also checked by the Saenger Theatre and found not only that the old side street "Colored" entrance is now closed but also that the movie of the week is something called *Riot* starring Jim Brown (even as during your high school days it used to be Johnny Mack Brown the old Rose Bowl star).

———————

Then before you move from the vintage Mobile oldness of the Battle House to spend your last night in the newness of the refurbished Admiral Semmes, from which the next morning you are to begin the return trip to New York—by way of New Orleans, Greenville, and Memphis—there is one other side-walk reencounter: "Hey, well, if it ain't old Murray. Am I right? Albertmurray. I got you Murray. I know I got you. Albert Murray. Used to live in that shotgun house down there on the way to Dodge's old shingle mill. Had a chinaberry tree in the front yard and a red oak in the back and then some thickets. Boy when did you get back to this neck of the woods? Boy you sure ain't changed a bit have you? Say who you been pitching for since you left town, Murray?"

"Pitching?" you say, stretching your eyes like Duke does when somebody mistakes him for Cab Calloway and asks for Minnie the Moocher instead of The Mooche. "Man, the last time I pitched a baseball game was back when they were still playing up on old Plateau diamond. Where they used to hit left-field home runs across the Southern Railway crossing toward the Telegraph Road and Chickasaw Terrace. Man, you were probably there. And when they hit hard enough to right center it could go on past that tree and into Aurelia and Louise Bolden's yard."

"Boy, you used to could pitch your tail off. Hell, if you'd come along a little later you could have made it to the majors. Except damn when it comes to batting you couldn't hit a sack of balls from somebody that didn't have near bout as much stuff on it as you. Man, if you coulda hit like you used to could chunk and field. But that's right I do remember you also used to play all them schoolboy games too, like old Sonny Keeby, and stayed in school and went off to college, to Skegee. Yeah I remember now. That's right. Hey, who you coaching for, Murray? You got any of your boys up there in the big money yet?"

SIX

New Orleans, Greenville, Memphis

TWO MOVIEGOERS, SOME SHUCKING ON THE DELTA, SOME STUFF YOU GOTTA WATCH AND SOME BUSINESS TO TAKE CARE OF

*T*HE FIRST THING *about New Orleans in the old days used to be that it was the next and last southbound express stop on the L&N (and from there you took the Southern Pacific west through the cowboy country and beyond the Rocky Mountains and across the elbow cactus deserts to Los Angeles, California, the city of red-tiled stucco haciendas and of pineapple-yellow sunsets and the sad sailor-boy music of Hawaiian guitars and ukeleles).*

Another thing was whenever they used to say Nu-Awleens or Nu-Awlns or Gnawlins or Neweleens what you saw without even closing your eyes was a wide-open babylonian city of sin, a crescent seaport town of french lace wrought-iron and palmettos, of sporting-house madams, and incense-burning hoodoo madams, and coke sniffers in a part of town known as Algiers.

In Mobile, which after all was a very old French Catholic town too, the Mardi Gras season came only once a year, like Xmas. But in songs and barbershop tales it used to be as if in New Orleans (where they buried people in vaults on top of the ground and came back from the funeral with a brass band playing ragtime music) there was a carnival every night.

Then later on you came to realize that they also called it an open city for other reasons. Population-wise it was a Creole town, a rainbow city, a rainbow-crescent City of All Nationalities. Not that you ever quite got the impression that it was as wide open as San Francisco still was in the days of Jack Johnson. But not only was it by all odds the least segregated of Deep South cities, it had also been for a very long historical time much more cosmopolitan in many ways than were such schoolbook-sanctified capitals of Liberty and Justice for All as Boston and Philadelphia.

Nowadays, of course, it is open in many ways that it never was open before. So this time you put up at a premier-class hotel and

*you eat at the most famous of the French Quarter restaurants.
But not only as you did in Atlanta and Mobile and will do in
Greenville and Memphis but also as you and any number of other
ex-servicemen and expense-account travelers have long since become accustomed to doing when the budget permits. Because
you're back this time not only from uptown Manhattan and not
only from Manhattan at large but also from Rome and Athens
and Istanbul; Paris and London and Madrid; Amsterdam and
Copenhagen and elsewhere.*

*But even so, what you really wish you had enough time to find
the right people to ask about is the part of town you remember
from the old fireside sagas and barbershop chronicles about Robert
Charles and Aaron Harris and Black Benny and Lady Mary
Jack the Bear. Which is also the part of town that musicians like
Buddy Bolden and King Oliver and Papa Celestin and old loud
wolfing Jelly Roll Morton came from. Not to mention Louis
Armstrong who was already into his big-league stride even in
those days and was already hitting solid gold and liquid silver
notes higher than the Empire State Building as easily as shooting
marbles.*

*All you have time to do this trip, however, is pop into a few
nearby places (including such landmarks as you can find along
Rampart Street). Actually the main reason you are stopping over
in New Orleans this time is to make a side trip to Covington for
an afternoon visit with Walker Percy. Then one day and overnight in Greenville and one day in Memphis. Then back north by
east to The Apple. Beale Street to Lenox Avenue in astrojet shuttle
time. Then the tilted sandtable panorama you are sometimes
lucky enough to get banking and letting down into the La Guardia landing pattern. Then the skyline above FDR Drive, and
Harlem River as you see it from Hell Gate and through the lat-
ticework of Triborough Bridge. Then finally midtown in the twilight from the chinaberry seat above 132nd Street.*

———

Perhaps the most widely repeated detail about the personal life
of Walker Percy, the author of *The Moviegoer* and *The Last
Gentleman*, is the fact that as a boy he was a favorite nephew
and sometime household ward of William Alexander Percy of

the Greenville, Mississippi, Percys, perhaps best known by outsiders as the Percys of *Lanterns on the Levee,* the recollections of a delta planter's very cavalier book-reading son, namely Will Alexander himself. Nor is this sort of detail merely another bit of Deep South Society-page trivia, not in this instance. Some threadbare elements of pseudo-ante-bellum snobbishness are there to be sure; but even so the family reference is legitimized by the all but inescapable implication that William Alexander Percy, the lawyer turned poet, is precisely the "real ancestor" in whose footsteps young Walker, the doctor turned novelist, elected to follow. The uncle's influence may or may not be unmistakable, but it is nonetheless there, even if stronger in matters of style than of content. Moreover, had he lived to read *The Moviegoer* not only would the ancestral uncle have had reason to be proud, he might even have shown a wee bit of genteel envy for good measure.

Had he lived to read some of his no less cosmopolitan than Southern nephew's commentaries on Negroes and on the Civil Rights movement however, he is likely to have been somewhat bemused to say the least. Not that on occasion he himself didn't indulge in such yankee-trumping declarations as: "*Any little boy who was not raised with little Negro children might as well not have been raised at all.*" But when you got down to the question of black adults as full-fledged fellow citizens Uncle Will Alex for all his catholicity of taste and all his verse-oriented humility before man's fate, was a paternalistic old delta plantation racist to the end of his days.

Once he got going on black grown folks his incomparably fond memories of Nain, the warm, sweet-smelling, "divinely café au lait" teenage black mammy who nursed him, and of Skillet, his first boon companion and crawfish-hunting buddy, are completely superseded by such self-bullshitting snobbishness as: *"Apparently there is something peculiarly Negroid in the Negro's attitude toward and aptitude for crimes of violence. He seems to have resisted, except on the surface, our ethics and to have rejected our standards. Murder, thieving, lying, violence—I sometimes suspect the Negro doesn't regard these as crimes or sins, or even regrettable occurrences. He commits them casually with no apparent feeling of guilt. White men similarly delinquent become soiled or embittered or brutalized. Negroes are as charming after as before a crime. . . ."*

Such neo-Marse-John-isms as *"How is it possible for the white man to communicate with people* [who believe in voodoo], *whom imagination kills and fantasy makes impotent, who thieve like children and murder ungrudgingly as small boys fight?"*

And, perhaps inevitably, such traditional Deep South white ass-out hang-ups as: *"Every black buck in the south has gone or will go to Chicago, where it is not only possible but inexpensive to sleep with a white whore. Likewise there are Negro bellboys in Southern hotels frequented by white whores. . . . In former generations when the taboo was unquestioned, Southern women felt a corresponding obligation so to conduct themselves that any breach of the taboo was unthinkable."*

The context of which, of course, was: *"The Negro not having assimilated the white man's ethics, giving only lip-service to the white man's morality, must for his own peace and security accept wholeheartedly the white man's mores and taboos. And the one sacred taboo, assumed to be Southern but actually and universally Anglo-Saxon, is the untouchability of white women by Negro men."*

Then, in summary: *"I would say to the Negro: before demanding to be a white man socially and politically, learn to be a white man morally and intellectually—and to the white man, the black man is our brother, a younger brother, not adult, not disciplined, but tragic, pitiful, and lovable. Act as his brother and be patient."*

Thus old marse Will Alex, now in the cold cold clay where complexions are forgotten along with profits and losses and pecking orders. But not Walker, who in the following statement about adulthood in a letter to *Harper's* magazine sounds as if his real uncle was named not Will Alex at all but Remus or Lucas Beauchamp or Sam Fathers: *". . . as one thinks about the perennial adolescence of the American intellectual community . . . it suddenly occurs to one: maybe it is the likes of* [Ralph] *Ellison we've needed all along. That is to say, maybe the American intellectual will not grow up until the Negro intellectual shows him how."*

Nor can it be argued that uncle and nephew are closer together in their conceptions of the dynamics of social change in the South. And while medicine is no less realistic than law there is still some irony in the fact that it is Walker the erstwhile doctor, not Will Alexander the lawyer, whose political insight reflects the old down-home seed-store, feed-store plus courthouse-square sense of local actualities at its pragmatic best. As a matter of fact the following statement may well have been written by a nephew who read his books in someplace like, say, Gavin Stevens' law office in Faulkner's Jefferson, rather than in the library of old Percy house in Greenville: *"Changing men's hearts has nothing to do with it. The Negro will vote without difficulty in Mississippi as soon as those who would stop him know they will be put in jail if they try."*

So no Civil Rights catechism for Walker Percy either. Nor do you have to declare your own articles of faith. But then it is almost always likely to be the all too sympathetic northern do-gooder, not the so-called reconstructed Southerner, who invites you to join him on some social occasion only to bore the hell out of you with questions that often are as tastelessly personal as political and as fatuous as they are naive. Seldom do such Southerners as extend social invitations to you so presume upon their prerogatives as hosts, either to impress you with their liberal credentials and their philanthropic good will or to instruct you on the essential nature of blackness, the fundamental implications of black experience, and the social imperatives and political priorities of black organizations.

No, as it is easy enough to find out from relatives who work as domestics, on such occasions down South, the traditional proprieties and amenities of Big House hospitality apply no less to you than to anybody else. You are presented to the folks present (some of course may be discreetly absent); you are served good whiskey; you are shown the sights both indoors and out; and what with all the easy innuendoes of "Hey we know your folks and y'all know some of ours, don't we?" the talk is likely to be anything but condescending.

Nor will there be any such other guests as are likely to forget their best company manners. Not that you may not be running the risk of being ambushed on your way home. But not by any of the guests, though some may look the other way the next time you pass on a downtown street. But in this they are not terribly different from some of their northern betters. In any case it is in the northern not the Southern drawing room that the other guests are most likely to insist that you explain why the hell you're there instead of in Harlem.

Furthermore, as hung up about black sexuality as far too many white Southerners so obviously have been (apparently ever since the days of the stud male slave), when a white Southerner asks if a reformer wants his sister to marry a Negro the implications of his questions go beyond his traditional Peeping Tom nightmares. Because no matter what else he may be hung up on, the white Southerner is also asking if the yankee do-gooder is really prepared for—or even conscious of—some of the inevitable personal and private consequences of his ever-so bighearted public gestures in interest of social reform. *"O.K., fellow, you're so hot to trot on desegregating them schools and such, to help the underdog and the like, but what about when the black underdog suddenly begins to act like black is equal enough to be a normal part of the family? How 'bout that fellow?"*

Naturally, the Southerner has his own chickenshit reasons for putting this kind of old stuff in the game. But when the liberal crusader retorts that questions about love affairs and marriage are irrelevant to the question of open institutions in the United States the white Southerner is quite certain that the northerner is copping out. And even more certain, need-less to add, are all homefolks you've ever heard discussing such things. *Hell that's all right about the relevance why don't they just answer the simple ass damn question. Do you or don't you, would you, or wouldn't you try to stop her. Are you or aren't you as hung up on the possibility of black in-laws as Southerners—or perhaps even a little more so, since the Southerner's notorious racism is often more concerned with public decorum than with private behavior?* Somebody once declared that when you come right down to intimate personal contacts, the Southerner is likely to be lying when he says he is a racist and the north-erner is likely to be lying when he professes not to be one.

At any rate when Walker Percy, looking somewhat more like a book-reading moviegoer than a delta planter's son's nephew, calls for you at your Canal Street hotel in downtown New Orleans, your radar, which you rate second to none, registers Normal then Cordial then Welcome. And in no time at all the two of you are breezing along the blue and gray causeway across Lake Pontchartrain toward Covington, exchanging an-ecdotes about New York: the Manhattan he remembers from the time when he was a young doctor dissecting corpses at Bellevue; the one you sometimes recall not only from the Harlem in which Ralph Ellison was working on *Invisible Man*, but also from NYU, Greenwich Village, the Public Library, and the Gotham Book Mart, the New York year you always recall when you hear such records as say, "Night in Tunisia," "Ornithology" and "Yardbird Suite." Nor is the point of the exchange to illustrate the distance of his Manhattan from Harlem. It is rather for the express purpose of making a mutual acknowledgment of a downhome angle of vision and sensibility. Not that either he or you are in the least unaware of your numerous differences. But to be conscious of dissimilarities is not necessarily to be divided by them. Some self-styled color-blind white Americans who obviously assume that they must pretend to ignore differences in order to avoid conflict only add hypocrisy to already existing complications. Moreover, if some of the differences between two given people are racial, which is mostly to say a matter of several physical features, others are mostly personal; and human nature being what it is, whatever its habitat, there is always an outside chance that any two people even from opposite ends of the earth will find in each other more similarities of personal interest and emphasis upon which to build a friendship or at least a cordial acquaintanceship, than race-oriented differences to separate them into antithetical factions. Indeed, ethnocentrism notwithstanding, seldom is racial or even national identity alone enough to provide for an acquaintanceship comparable to one growing out of mutual personal interests.

In any case one fundamental assumption underlying your visit with Walker Percy as with Edwin Yoder and Joe Cumming and the rest goes without saying: Two book-oriented Southerners, one Afro-brown and one Anglo-caucasian, have at least as much to talk about as two downhome baseball players for instance, whose physical features and historical extractions are similarly different from and similarly similar to each other.

It is Ernest Hemingway not William Faulkner who provides the keynote and vamp-in this time. In reply to a casual inquiry about works-in-progress you sketch the objectives of *The Hero and the Blues*, a recently completed draft of literary notes in which you use the *nada*-conscious, ritual-oriented master craftsman as one of three primary literary touchstones for a blues-idiom-derived frame of reference, if not poetics, for the kind of fiction you are trying to write. But then aren't the preoccupations of *The Moviegoer* closer to the Faulkner of *Mosquitoes* and *The Wild Palms*, than to *Light in August* and *Absalom, Absalom!?* You for your part had placed the Faulkner of *Mosquitoes* and *Pylon* and *The Green Bough* in the context of T. S. Eliot's *The Waste Land* and Hemingway's *The Sun Also Rises*, long before the interview in which he called himself a failed poet.

Naturally you have absolutely no intention whatsoever of going into that sort of thing at such a time. Nor is there any need to do so, for such is the enthusiasm of Walker Percy's immediate response to the mention of Hemingway that by the time the new-smelling T-bird pulls into Covington your hastily sketched conception of the *Nada*-Confrontation Hero has provided a functional context within which the talk has included the existentialist notion of the absurd and the Malraux-Pascal image of man's fate. All of which, you realize later, is directly related to an aspect of southernness that C. Vann Woodward may be getting at when he refers to the northern illusion that "history is something unpleasant that happens to other people," and then declares that nothing about Southern history is conducive to the theory that the South is "the darling of divine providence."

The first sight of the house in Covington takes you back to the *petit château* you and your literary friends including James Baldwin used to ride out to visit in Mary Painter's Renault and sometimes swim near on Sunday afternoons during that first summer in Paris. There is something about its cozy scale and the somewhat formal layout of the front lawn that also evokes such undergraduate textbook names as Madame de Staël, Madame de Sévigné—or is it the bewigged and bepowdered Agnes Moorehead?

But what the moss-and-cypress setting along with the taste of the Louisiana bayou-scented air also takes you back to at the same time is the Spanish Main that you grew up hearing about and reading about. So you enter the fine drawing room thinking in terms of bayou *châteaux* instead of Big Houses and plantation houses this time. And being of precisely the same generation of moviegoers as Walker himself, part of you is naturally disposed to believe that every excellent old piece of furniture and bric-a-brac in sight was originally imported by buccaneers under the direct command of Akim Tamiroff.

For all the swashbuckling romance that the casks and cut-glass decanters of ruby port and golden madeira were so much a part of in the old technicolor sea and treasure-coast movies however, what you choose to sip this time is Tennessee bourbon (superimposing Charlton Heston's Andy Jackson at the Battle of New Orleans upon Lionel Barrymore's Old Hickory, the husband of the Gorgeous Hussy). And what you spend the rest of the bayou-soft, delta-blue afternoon sitting out in the backyard on the bayou marina landing watching the bayou water skiers and talking mostly about is fiction, Deep South fiction. About Shelby Foote, author of *Tournament, Follow Me Down*, and *Shiloh*, who is now into the third thick volume of a nonfiction narrative of the Civil War; about the late Flannery O'Connor, Eudora Welty, Carson McCullers, and Truman Capote.

Then about Robert Penn Warren and of course Faulkner. But what is said about William Faulkner this time is not simply in celebration of his considerable talent and remarkable achievement but rather to acknowledge some of the very serious esthetic problems he creates for younger Southern writers. The big thing, the two of you agree, is not to be overwhelmed by him; to profit from his achievement, which, as Hemingway once said about his own, is now in the public domain, without mistaking his special point of view as your own. "Man, Shelby and I talk about this sometimes and he says that stuff can get to be downright pernicious. With Ellison, of course, it is a different thing if you know what I mean."

About Thomas Wolfe he says at one point: "I've reread some of it and I'm afraid it doesn't . . . When I read it a long time ago . . ." Later when you mention Reynolds Price, William Goyen, Ernest J. Gaines, and Fred Chappell he adds Cormac McCarthy: "Have you read *The Orchard Keeper* and *Outer Dark*? He can write. Of course he's got his problems with Faulkner too, but I think you'll find him very interesting."

Nor is the conversation any less Southern or one bit less

fiction-oriented when you suddenly remember to ask if having spent some time in Alabama he happens to know the difference between what you used to call the mulberry bush and what you also knew as the mulberry tree. You haven't been able to find it in Rickett's compendious *Wildflowers of the Southeastern United States.*

He does know the difference. Or rather he is certain about the absolute difference in the berries. But not the names. In consequence however, back in New York, a week or so later you receive an envelope containing a leaf and the following note: "*Al, is this the leaf? If it is it's Spanish mulberry—has a purple berry. Shelby was disappointed not to see you.*" So now you remember. Because in Mobile they used to call them *French* mulberries. When you said mulberry tree you were talking about the kind of berries you eat. When you said mulberry bush you were talking about the pale purple almost tasteless kind you swished like play-buckshot.

As for the radar indications of relative freedom from traditional Confederate hang-ups, they remain consistently clear of the alert zone throughout the visit. So, for whatever a Buster Brown voucher may be worth in these media-conditioned times of so much grab-bag revolutionary gobbledegook, your response to the old often only visual question ("Whose and what kind is this one?") is that it is probably quite safe to consider Walker Percy a pretty good one too. Yes, for all that many of his most fondly cherished boyhood memories may well involve an uncle whose book jacket profile you for one imagined Sidney Poitier slapping in that highly improbable but ever so gleefully and liberalistically masochistic greenhouse incident in Norman Jewison's movie *In the Heat of the Night.*

Indeed for all that what the old Saenger Theatre peanut-gallery-derived part of you sometimes fantasizes is a scenario in which the likes of old man Will Alex is shown, lantern in hand, getting his paternalistic ass kicked from one end of the levee to the other by a cigar-smoking, golden-smiling Jack Johnson–looking jelly bean, wearing a silk candy-striped gambler's shirt with sleeve garters, a tan Kingfish derby, pegtop pants and two-toned pointy-toed shoes, it is precisely *Walker* Percy's freedom from condescension that you are inclined to vouch for first of all.

Nor for all your first-hand downhome experience of inter-racial violence do you find it altogether less urgent for him or Red Warren or Vann Woodward or Ed Yoder or Joe Cumming to be free of such northern-style tolerance as is only insidious benevolence than from traditional Southern-style hysteria. Anyway so far you have seen nothing to indicate that he is likely to exchange the agenbite of his inwit for the agit-prop of such New York City nitwits as are for a revolution of brotherhood, love, and racial separatism at the same time.

But, in the final analysis, since the primary reason that you are in contact with Walker Percy is that he is a writer whose work you consider significant, what more in all fairness (and indeed in all hard-headed calculation) can you ask of him than that he bring to all issues the same ambivalent literary sense of human complexity that characterizes *The Moviegoer*?

David L. Cohn may or may not have been the second generation carpetbagger-become-dilettante that some exasperated Tuskegeans used to insist that he had all the earmarks of. But in *God Shakes Creation*, which came out seven years before *Lanterns on the Levee* and could have been called *Darkness on the Delta*, he did strike you as being ever so eager to pass himself off as a delta planter's snobbish son. Whoever or whatever he was or fancied himself to be in the flesh, however, on paper he almost always came across as a book-reading redneck (which he wasn't either) trying to write his way into the inner sanctum sanctorum of white supremacy.

Sometimes William Alexander Percy could almost take his position in the status quo for granted. At such times he felt secure enough to indulge himself in the form of condescension known as *noblesse oblige*. But it was almost always as if Cohn were a book-reading and airs-taking "town" Snopes who had to be forever looking for new ways to convince himself that black people were inherently inferior to the white people he chose to identify with. Nowhere are the hypocrisies and pretensions that this often led to more apparent than in his statements on Topic One.

Thus: *"Wherever men have lived in the world sexual relations have existed between conqueror and conquered, invader and invaded, master and slave. It was thus that"* [so and so and so] *"and the white men of the south took Negro women as concubines during slavery and after freedom. . . . The white man of the Delta was merely writing his chapter in the long record of the white race throughout the world wherever it has come in contact with colored peoples of a simpler culture or weaker fiber."*

And yet: "*Rape is a crime shockingly abhorrent to men all over the world.*"

Now, that being the case, Cohn's chapter-writing delta white man suddenly becomes: *"A creature of conventions and inhibitions. He must consider public opinion and the force of law. Marriage, the child and the family are still basic units of the society in which he moves. His religion casts a shadow over eros."*

From which for David L. Cohn it somehow just naturally follows that "*The Negro on the other hand is sexually completely free and untrammeled. 'W'en I wants me a woman, I gets me a woman.' Sexual desire is raw and crude and strong. It is to be satisfied when and wherever it arises. It is not embroidered with roses and raptures of romantic love. It does not proceed tortuously through devious detours of flirtation but flies straight to its mark with the blind compulsion and devouring intensity of a speeding bullet.*"

So now therefore: "*The great inflexible taboo of sexual relationships in the Delta is that there shall not be under any circumstances, 'a sexual relationship between a white woman and a Negro.'*" But of course as for the sexual exploitation of black women by the conqueror and master: "*The women were on the whole willing and even eager to assume a sexual relationship with him and they were quite venal in their attitude.*"

But behold the conqueror once again: "*The white man of the Delta living among masses of Negroes overwhelmingly superior in number and well armed, fears them only in one aspect.* He does not fear bodily harm to himself, nor an armed uprising. There has never been such an uprising in the Delta. He does, however, fear sexual attacks upon his women."

Nor was old David L.'s hang-up any less central to his conception of things when *God Shakes Creation* was expanded and republished as *Where I Was Born and Raised* in 1948: "[*We*] *must acknowledge that the race question is primarily insoluble because in the conscious or unconscious minds of Southern whites it is a blood or sexual question,*" which wraps things up very nicely but not very neatly since it implies that the steady stream of Mississippi-born mulattoes has nothing to do with blood and sex.

In all events what you are as keenly aware of as anything else as you dial the *Delta Democrat Times* from the Downtowner Motel is the following background fact of everyday life and of letters in Greenville, Mississippi: this Hodding Carter, whom you will soon be meeting, not only enjoyed a very close, warm, and enduring friendship with William Alexander Percy, who was indeed his chief benefactor during the early days of the *Democrat Times*, but was only slightly less chummy with David L. Cohn to boot—in fact it was Cohn who put him in touch with Percy in the first place.

Of course, you are also no less aware or appreciative of the fact that nothing about *The Lower Mississippi, Where Main Street Meets the River* or *First Person Rural, The Angry Scar,* or anything else of his that you recall smacks either of planterly dilettantism or of carpetbagging opportunism gone to decadent racism. But then the point is not that you have ever had reason to suspect Hodding Carter of writing with forked quill. That is not the point at all. The point is that the Buster Brown alert system is properly calibrated and properly zeroed in. The point is that what really counts is the feedback from the Deep South zone you have entered now.

Meanwhile the tentative classification of Hodding Carter on your voucher scale over the years has been militant moderate, and the good part about his militancy is that when he came out for something he was willing to fight for it. But the bad part about being moderate is that it has permitted him to stomach too many unspeakable outrages both physical and intellectual over the years. Indeed, on the question of racial fair play he has sometimes come alarmingly close to equating northern hypocrisy with Southern mob violence, which is not to describe his intentions, only the implications of some of the positions he has sometimes taken with regard to the priorities and urgencies of black citizenship.

Anyway it is Hodding Carter that you have stopped off to

meet at this point and all you intend to vouch for this time is how he strikes you in person as of today.

But as things turn out, what with him not yet recovered from a recent siege of a recurring ailment, and what with young Hod, his successor at the *Delta Democrat Times*, having to rush off to do his last day bit for the Charles Evers campaign, the one you spend most of your visit talking to is not Hodding himself but his wife Betty; whose pattern on the detector system, incidentally, yields nothing whatsoever to any moviegoer's image of the Katharine Hepburn who used to go so well with Spencer Tracy in the heyday of his square-jawed, two-fisted editorship.

Hodding is there and in good enough spirits considering the state of his health, but it is Betty, who also reminds you of Rose Styron and Ralph Ellison's wife Fanny, who drives the station wagon and serves as the best of all possible writer-oriented guides on the town, the levee, the Indian mounds, and finally the Carter estate. It is also Betty who begins by saying, "So now tell us something about your assignment. Dave Halberstam just told us to expect you." So it is to her, not directly to Hodding, that you sketch your outline of the seed-store–feed-store courthouse-square dimension of Southern sensibility this time (and later she feeds it back to your complete satisfaction in introducing you first to Mrs. Jesse Brent and to Mrs. Roger Generelley).

It is also to her that you say: "Every time I suggest that the somewhat younger white Southern journalists who best represent what I mean are in a very real sense heirs to and extensions of the best qualities of such older guys as Jonathan Daniels and Ralph McGill, somebody almost always says: And Hodding Carter. So here I am stopping by to see y'all. Willie sends regards and so does Walker."

"Willie is doing a good job up there," Hodding says. "How does he like it?" ("Tell him to watch out up there," somebody elsewhere has already said, "they'll have him so he won't know whether he's going or coming.") But what he is most talkative about from time to time is local Indian history, the geography of the Mississippi River, and the delights of catfish eating. But when Betty points out examples of local progress toward desegregation he nods his approval and expresses his pleasure at the fact that it is proceeding with so little friction. As for the several books that he has under way it is Betty who says that he is writing beautifully and moving right along in spite of the fact that he is able to work only a few hours each day.

So what you come away vouching for this time is the fact that the Betty that Hodding wrote about with so much astonished affection in *Where Main Street Meets the River* is in as fine form as ever. As for Hodding himself, your one-day impression of him in person was essentially compatible with the one you had formed from his books and articles over the years, which was that for all the shortcomings inherent in the whiteness of his special Southern partisanship he was never quite as unmindful of the immediate implication of the nation's deeper interests as some of his closest personal friends so obviously were.

You keep trying but are unable to get Shelby Foote on the phone, but what you also do in the meantime is explore downtown Memphis, and have yourself a solid expense-account lunch at the Peabody Hotel wondering what the reaction of the management would be to a suggestion from, say, Willie Morris or Albert Erskine that they name a bar for William Faulkner or maybe a lounge for *Sanctuary*; wondering also how much historical fact there is in the old legend about how the social status of white Southerners on the make sometimes used to depend on whether or not the Negro headwaiter there recognized them, called their names with just the right inflection and seated them promptly or ignored them and their guests until all the best tables were occupied.

After lunch you look at the river from bluffs that Mark Twain, the apprentice riverboatman like Abe Lincoln the flatboatman before him, saw on his way down to New Orleans. Then you stroll along Beale Street, the old stamping ground of W. C. Handy, whose blues about it and about Memphis in the days of Boss Crump and about St. Louis, the metropolis up the river, represent a dimension of the national experience, character, and sensibility that not even the best fiction of Mark Twain and William Faulkner makes one adequately conscious of. In point of fact the "St. Louis Blues" is a veritable national anthem, the rendering of which probably stirs some very old interior place of more Americans than does "The Star-Spangled Banner." After all, what you feel (whether with pride or irony) when you hear "The Star-Spangled Banner" is mostly those schoolboy things that go with the flag and with the illustrations you remember from grade-school history books. But what the music of the "St. Louis Blues" evokes, whether along with brownskin goosepimples or along with pale faces and red ears, is the actual texture of American places and occasions that exist in your personal recollection. Anyway hearing "The Star-Spangled Banner" in a foreign country may or may not make most Americans downright homesick, but you are willing to bet that hearing the "St. Louis Blues" would. Nor would you have excluded the likes of William Alexander Percy and David L. Cohn.

By the time you come to the park named for him, you also remember that among the blues that W. C. Handy either composed or transcribed was also one about Aunt Hagar. Sometimes as in the recording by Louis Armstrong it was called "Aunt Hagar's Blues"; and sometimes as in "Erskine Hawkins Plays W. C. Handy for Dancing" it is called "Aunt Hagar's Children." But it is music that goes with having a downhome good time no matter what it is called. *You close your eyes remembering what Louis did with the words and how Erskine's arranger scored the music and suddenly you are all the way back to the old fireside times, when you yourself used to become one of Aunt Hagar's rawhide roustabouts anytime you wanted to and used to come up from the old steamboat landing to the good-time places along Beale Street doing that sporty patent-leather limp walk that such wide-eyed boy-scout yokels as Tom Sawyer and Huck Finn couldn't even begin to hold a candle to.*

What you see when you open your eyes again is the view of the updated downtown Memphis skyline that you get looking across Handy Park from the long-since rundown oldness of that part of Beale Street as of now. So Mister Buster Brown that you were brought up to never cease to be, what you feel is that very special old sensation of urgency that you inherited along with those whose restless struggles are at last adding up to the local civil-rights confrontations. But what you also find yourself all the more deeply engaged by is that which Beale Street symbolizes for you in spite of all the shabbiness, some of which was always there anyway: *Music for good times earned in adversity. A sound track for an affirmative life-style riffed in resilient blue steel from the least congenial of all American circumstances.*

If you could only find a way to make enough civil-rights spokesmen and leaders realize that there is an immediate and fundamental connection between all that and the sociopolitical objectives to which you and they like all other bright-eyed Misters Buster Brown—each in his own way—were eternally committed. If you could only get enough of them to consider that the rhetoric of welfare militancy currently so popular among them may only add up to an overreaction to a lot of second-rate folklore of white supremacy that is no less vicious than that of the old William Alexander Percys and David L. Cohns, for all the scientific terminology it is couched in these days. If you can only get them to see that they don't have to play themselves and the cause cheap just to make a case for safeguards and benefits that the constitution already guarantees as their birthright. You fight for such things. You don't go around putting on the poormouth about them.

Nor is the problem simply only that somebody is deliberately betraying the cause. That never has been a major part of the problem. And much goes to show that those who are quick to imply that it is are only running off at the mouth without thinking or else are trying to bootleg some old self-styled Emperor Jones stuff into the game. (Some Buster Browns do become Afro-Carib Emperors Mac Brown: "*Anybody don't do what I tell 'em is a part of my problem. Ain't nobody doing better than me but them that sold us all out to the white folks.*") Bullshit. HNIC Bullshit, Black strawboss bullshit.

No, as you have now come to see it, the primary problem is not combat security (not yet at any rate) but rather the mobilization and utilization of existing human resources. The problem is how to evolve socio-political tactics and strategies that are truly indigenous to and compatible with the dynamics of U.S. Negro life style. Because until somebody does, the so-called masses are not likely to become very deeply involved no matter how earnest your appeals—even to their self-interest.

Take the example of Martin Luther King, whose name is now also a part of Memphis. For all the justification of his theories of nonviolence that he found in Thoreau and Gandhi, it was probably the charismatic dynamics of the downhome church that most of his followers, even the white ones, many of them non-Christian, were responding to.

If you could only get enough spokesmen and leaders to consider the possibility that the dynamics inherent in the blues idiom might be extended further than King was able to take those derived from the downhome church. Not that you did not celebrate the effectiveness of King's methods, as far as they went. But as a political device they were limited as all moral outcry is bound to be limited. So what you hoped was that the blues idiom, *being of its essence a SECULAR form of existential improvisation*, could produce something better.

If you could only get a few key spokesmen and leaders to help you tee off on some of those hypocritical white do-gooders and one-up-men who misrepresent it as being something you should either outgrow or be cured of. If you could do that maybe you could also get a few of them to realize that when they confused Uncle Remus with Uncle Tom they were probably allowing themselves to be faked out by superficial political rhetoric instead of relying on their actual experience. Maybe you could even get a few to realize what they were doing when they let some third-rate con man jargonize them into denying Aunt Hagar—as if who if not Aunt Hagar is the source of all stone foxiness! *("Man, if you go to the Waldorf to see Lena Horne and don't realize that what she's riffing on is Aunt Hagar, you're wasting your money!")*

You also make your way over to Third and Vance streets and the Lorraine Motel where Martin Luther King was murdered by sniper fire (you were backstage at Carnegie Hall with Duke when the word came, brought by Jim Jensen of WCBS-TV news, this time in person, wearing a moviegoer's Burberry trench coat and shaking his head and adding "some goddam white guy and he got away"). So what you find yourself wondering about en route back to Memphis International for the final leg of the flight back to New York is whether the ill-fated Memphis Confrontations that cost King his life (and the movement its most magnetic spokesman and leader) would have turned out as badly if King and his staff men and well-wishers and assorted hangers-on had been just a little less hopeful about the impact of moral outcry as such, however massive its volume, and a good deal more alert to the political facts of life. It was, you concede, only natural for a very sincere minister and church folks and welfare-oriented activists to gear their methods to appeals to compassion. But that was the point. Just how deep into the complications of things does your commitment to the cause go? Do you love your people enough to do some dirty work in order to bring them some good? Or easier than that. Do you love your people enough to pay the necessary research dues for the cause? What did Max Weber, whose definition of politics as the use of power you were riffing on, say: Only those who realize how awful and self-destructive and so on people can be and still pay dues for the privilege of administering their affairs truly have talent for politics. Something like that. Max Weber from whom all the cocktail party chatter about charisma is probably derived via C. Wright Mills and Talcott Parsons.

Anyway one thing that was probably wrong with the Memphis Confrontation was that it was, as they say, already another ball game before Memphis. It was a new ball game as soon as they passed that voting rights bill. Maybe what was lacking was that King was too much of a Christian idealist to realize and capitalize on the fact that his downhome church-oriented nonviolence was really a form of political jujitsu. Perhaps the most subtle ever attempted in the whole history of the country. Maybe he was too nice to admit even to himself that he was really provoking the opposition to violence for the express purpose of tricking them into using their own strength against themselves; and yet what was he forever saying if not: *"Oh brothers and sisters let us now turn the other cheek with love and wait for Lyndon Johnson to follow the lead of Jack and Bobby and federalize the National Guard right out from under these crackers."*

King may not have been able to see himself in that role even if he had lived to be ninety. But there was hardly any way for any power technician to mistake what really happened at Birmingham and Selma. *They knew damn well that they couldn't be outgunned but what had happened was they had been outsmarted, outmaneuvered.* Any feed-store-seed-store courthouse-square power technician could figure that out and know what to change the game to. All they had to do was start cashing in on all that expensive exposure somebody had been providing free for any loudmouth hustler out to cop himself some cheap note, playing the black booger man waving a BB gun and striking matches in the woodpile. Once they got the jive-time war whoopers going, all they had to do was sit tight and wait for the media-oriented tom-toms and war dances, and any American crossroads-store power technician could tell you what the name of the game is and whose ball and bat it is going to be played with.

It could be called the Friend of Indians Game (in which "no-good" white men provide the Indians with just enough guns and ammo to set them on the warpath and into ambush). But it is usually called Shooting Fish in a Barrel. And the thing about it is that not only will the welfare foundations go for it; so will the ever so nonviolent Compassion Corps. All they need is reassurance that red-blooded white Americans would never actually shoot the mullet-heads once they have been tricked into the barrel. A few squeamish liberals might balk. But there will be plenty of New York intellectuals who will reason that a gas oven is not actually a gas oven until you actually light the gas.

All you need claim for blues-idiom-oriented political behavior at this point is that it is less given to self-defeating self-righteousness than is moral outcry rhetoric. All you need to point out is that when the self-righteous people you know turn to violence they seem to spend so much time justifying their right to pick up the gun that they forget to learn how to shoot, as if the rightness of the cause were in itself a functional substitute for combat readiness and combat intelligence. All you need to say is that blues-oriented people are conditioned to confront the facts of life.

As the airport-bound limousine rolls on out of the city limits what you remember is the news reports of the fiasco that the first Memphis Confrontation became. That is why there had to be a Second Memphis Confrontation. So it is also why Martin

Luther King was back in Memphis on the day he was shot. You
remember how well things had gone in Birmingham where
the political jujitsu worked well enough to zap Bull Connor
after all those legendary years. (Indeed, what you for your part
like best to remember King doing was not speaking of hopes
and dreams on the Washington Mall—as good as he was that
day—but making the rounds to all the toughest Birmingham
joints saying in so many words: *"Cool it for the cause, brothers.
Old Bull ain't going to know what hit him. Old Bull going to be
feeling them cattle prods long after they become jokes to us."*
But he couldn't make it work in Memphis either time. And
at least one reason why he couldn't was that by that time quite
a number of his troops were as preoccupied with proving to
the media that they were not a bunch of Mama's boys as with
improving their economic and political condition. Once Big
Daddy Moynihan's notorious monograph *The Negro Family*
got the ever so committed and compassionate media going on
all that matriarchy stuff King was bound to have more and
more trouble trying to get media-oriented window-breaking
warwhoopers to play it oriental-cool. Anyway, with all due respect to the fact that Martin Luther King appealed to the very
best in his followers and adversaries alike, what you find yourself hoping now is that when the next national leader appears
he will be a Hagar-endowed, Uncle Bud-Doc-Ned-Remus and
Zack-wise, blues-oriented, poker-watchful political technician
*(who will be prepared to keep the faith of such foreparents as
Frederick Douglass and Harriet Tubman among others, precisely
because he will know that the thing about political objectives is
that they require political strategy, who will know that the thing
about all strategy is that it will come to nothing without tactical
know-how. Not that he will not play the old moral-outcry jive line
for whatever it is worth, but neither will he so misguide himself by
his own propaganda as to commit his troops to any combat show-
down before giving due consideration to the all too obvious fact
that the thing about the force required to achieve military objectives is of its very nature predicated upon military control, which
is to say military discipline. Nor can the problem of insurgent
troop morale and discipline for the long grind be separated from
another problem: How do you alienate the great mass of Americans from their TV sets and the world of TV celebrities, especially*

*in as much as your own status as spokesman leader is itself likely
to be so largely dependent upon your TV ratings, since your most
obvious competition is not the ever so shadowy establishment itself
but the popular crime and western and variety programs, not to
mention the headline sports events).*

*Also, how do you alienate no-income people from the welfare sys-
tem, and how do you get enough low-income people to choose the esoteric abstractions of Apocalypse propaganda over the ad-induced
shopping sprees that are supported by an installment-plan credit
system, and are perpetuated by the built-in obsolescence of the
merchandise itself? Moreover, how do you sustain enough revolutionary momentum against a so-called Establishment that is not
nearly so monolithic and recalcitrant as it is diverse and resilient
—and is not only capable but is also very likely to riff your own
stuff right back at you manifold? ("Right on out of it.") Indeed,
how do you prevent the so-called Establishment from turning your
revolutionary slogans into its own pop promotion gimmicks—and
reducing you to a media cliché in the bargain?*

*Then there are other and still other riddlesome considerations
that perhaps nobody was ever any better qualified to wheel and
deal with than some of the quick brown, fox-crazy dog leaping
briarpatch negotiators, whom you (like any number of schoolboy
types, no doubt) have known, admired, and learned from for as
long as you can remember.*

Anyway, the more you for one think about some of the
theory-oriented leader/spokesmen who were already well on
their way to media-prominence even before Martin Luther
King's ill-fated mission to Memphis, the more you find yourself coming back to an old notion that it just might be his
pragmatic orientation to the flesh-and-blood actualities of
food, clothing, shelter, chance, and the contingencies of fellowship and romance that will best equip the blues-conditioned
leader to keep the faith of his forefathers during these electro-
media days of so much instantly amplified and conventionalized sound and furiousness. As for his own shortcomings, as of
now they are (specific technical skills aside) mostly a matter of
inadequate horizons of aspiration. In most instances all he
would have to do is realize the national (and international)
implications of his local achievements. Not that he has been
playing himself cheap because he is deficient in self-esteem. It

is rather his context of self-evaluation and appreciation that is too provincial, a matter which can be remedied with only the slightest turn of the screw, say no more than it took to get Willie Mays and Hank Aaron from the sandlots of Alabama to big-league superstardom.

As for the Ancestral Imperatives, now so frequently obscured by pretentious spokesmen overreacting to the Folklore of White Supremacy, what they require is very simple indeed: that you take care of the business at hand to the best of your ability, a business which begins, incidentally, not with historical romances about pre-American identities, but with such supermarket–city hall–monday morning matters as equal employment opportunities, equal protection under the law, equal access to civic services and living facilities, and adequate political representation.

As for the ancestral guidelines for the next national leader's conduct as a matinee idol, let him always remember at least this much about Uncle Jack the Bear: He was forever claiming to be nowhere precisely because he knew that there is all the difference in the world between being only faddish and being truly hip. *Man, ain't* NOTHING *happening, Man.*

―――――――

You decide not to give Shelby Foote one final buzz from the airport, because once there you are already out of Memphis. You are in a sense already out of the South. You are already back in the national zone (and indeed, even in the intercontinental zone) and it would not be like talking to him down home anymore. It would be almost the same as calling from New York. It wouldn't even be very much like calling long distance from Harlem. It would be more like using a booth somewhere in midtown Manhattan with somebody standing outside wondering how much longer you're going to be there.

So you say maybe next time for Shelby Foote.

Meanwhile, all ante-bellum joke twisting vouchers, identification papers, dog tags, signs, countersigns, and earmarks aside, what you come back up the country this time more concerned about than ever before is how to make more white intellectuals *not only down home but perhaps elsewhere first of all* more responsive to the fact that somebody has been keeping tab on them and their prettygoodness and godawfulness from such spyglass points as Lenox Terrace all along. Nor—for all the moral outcry rhetoric—has the field of surveillance ever really been restricted to interracial misbehavior. Indeed, the whole thing of tab keeping may well have begun with such captive African sages as passed the word on along to the young ones (whether in a whisper or by gestures and nods) that for all his high horses, Ole Marster got to put on his breeches one leg at a time just like everybody else; got to shake after number one and wipe after number two, for all his silk and satin; and for all his coaches and carriages and fine mansion, got to cry "Have Mercy" when the wagon come. Because he also got to end up six feet in the ground, and may or may not have had any more enjoyment than anybody else for all his wealth and power.

If you could only find a way to get some of *that* kind of old downhome folklore into the so-called National Dialogue about the quality of life in the United States.

Epilogue

Y ES THE *also and also of all that also; because the oldness that
you are forever going back again by one means or another to
is not only of a place and of people but also and perhaps most often
of the promises that exact the haze-blue adventuresomeness from
the brown-skinned hometown boy in us all. There must by now be
at least yes one thousand plus one or more tales all told of the underlying sameness; and whether retold by wine drinkers or beer
drinkers or bootleg-whiskey drinkers, and whether in fire circles or
by firesides, and whether in barbers' shoptalk or ten o'clock Latin
or in blue-ribbon anthologies twelve-plus years advanced, the implications of self-definition, self-celebration, and perhaps not a
little self-inflation and self-designation are nevertheless quite as
obvious in each as for all and since forever: when you talking
about somebody come from where us folks come from you talking
about somebody come from somewhere. You talking about people
been through something, you talking about somebody come out of
something.*

*And is therefore ready for something. Because self-nomination
after all has perhaps as much to do with promise and fulfillment
as with anything else; and promise and fulfillment probably have
at least as much to do with self-discipline as with anything else;
and the thing about self-discipline (which is to say dedication which
is to say commitment which is nothing if not self-obligation) is its
conditioned unforgetfulness which is perhaps as good a reason as any
why even the most frivolous-seeming good-time music of downhome-
derived people so often sounds like so much rhapsodized thunder
and syncopated lightning.*

THE HERO AND THE BLUES

CONTENTS

The Social Function of the Story Teller

S TORYBOOK IMAGES are as indispensable to the basic human processes of world comprehension and self-definition (and hence personal motivation as well as purposeful group behavior) as are the formulas of physical science or the nomenclature of the social sciences. Such basic insights as may be derived from the make-believe examples of literature are, moreover, as immediately applicable to the most urgent problems of everyday life as are "scientific" solutions.

With this premise, it might not be too much to say that the most delicately wrought short stories and the most elaborately textured novels, along with the most homespun anecdotes, parables, fables, tales, legends, and sagas, are as strongly motivated by immediate educational (which is to say moral and social) objectives as are the most elementary gestures, signs, labels, directives, and manuals of procedure. Indeed, at bottom perhaps even the most radical innovations in rhetoric and in narrative technique are best appreciated when viewed as efforts to refine the writer's unique medium of "instruction." In other words, to make the telling more effective is to make the tale more to the point, more meaningful, and in consequence, if not coincidentally, more useful. Nor is the painter or the musician any less concerned than the writer with achieving a telling effect.

Many contemporary American writers, editors, publishers, reviewers, and, alas, even teachers—and accordingly an ever increasing proportion of the general American reading public —seem to have forgotten, however, that fiction of its very nature is most germane and useful not when it restricts itself to the tactical expediencies of social and political agitation and propaganda as such, but when it performs the fundamental and universal functions of literature as a fine art, regardless of its raw material or subject matter. Moreover, literary "instruction," far from being indirect, is concomitant with artistic purpose as well as being multidimensional and comprehensive. As a matter of fact, fiction at its best may well be a more inclusive intellectual discipline than science or even philosophy. It can also function as an activating force which at times may be capable of even greater range and infinitely more evocative precision than music.

In truth, it is literature, in the primordial sense, which establishes the context for social and political action in the first place. The writer who creates stories or narrates incidents which embody the essential nature of human existence in his time not only describes the circumstances of human actuality and the emotional texture of personal experience, but also suggests commitments and endeavors which he assumes will contribute most to man's immediate welfare as well as to his ultimate fulfillment as a human being.

It is the writer as artist, not the social or political engineer or even the philosopher, who first comes to realize when the time is out of joint. It is he who determines the extent and gravity of the current human predicament, who in effect discovers and describes the hidden elements of destruction, sounds the alarm, and even (in the process of defining "the villain") designates the targets. It is the story teller working on his own terms as mythmaker (and by implication, as value maker), who defines the conflict, identifies the hero (which is to say the good man—perhaps better, the adequate man), and decides the outcome; and in doing so he not only evokes the image of possibility, but also prefigures the contingencies of a happily balanced humanity and of the Great Good Place.

Thus no matter how sincere his intention, the writer does not automatically increase the social significance and usefulness of his fiction by subordinating his own legitimate esthetic preoccupations to those of the social and political technicians. If he so subserves, he only downgrades the responsibility which he alone has inherited. He discontinues or reduces the indispensable social and political service which art alone can provide, only to do something which many competent journalists (given a functional point of view or doctrine—or a line of jive) can do as well and most good promoters can do better. Such an action on the part of a writer is every bit as regressive as that of, say, a surgeon who deserts the operating room to become a first-aid corpsman on the battlefield. It is as self-contradictory as the act of an expert on policies and programming who, under the illusion of making himself more useful, resigns a key administrative position to become a subordinate who grinds out practical campaign slogans in the advertising department of the same organization. Or, worse still, isn't it indeed much the same as giving up a position on the coaching staff to become a cheerleader? What has he done except leave defining fundamentals in terms of his own sense of life only to represent somebody else's formulas?

No truly serious or truly dedicated writer can afford to enlist in any movement except on his own terms. The risks of arrogance which he runs by insisting on such politically suspect individuality are occupational hazards against which only his integrity can protect him; and furthermore, every time he writes any story at all he runs the same risks by presuming that his own conception of heroic action (or nonheroic action) is significant enough to deserve as many readers as he hopes will buy or borrow his books. His discipline no less than his responsibility is his own in both instances. He must elect to be consistent with himself and suffer the consequences—or enjoy them!

Other people can always hold the writer accountable for everything he does, of course; but he can allow no one to tell him what to write. Not even the most expert editorial advisors can do any more than help him execute that which he himself has already conceived and designed. Nor does the social or political technician take over where the writer leaves off. The writer never ceases being concerned with human fulfillment. The programming and activating work of the engineer and technician, on the other hand, is only the means by which fiction becomes fact. Obviously it is the engineer, not the writer, who exercises the workaday authority which translates conceptions into actual social structures and institutions. But even so, in the final analysis it is the writer who determines which social and political systems and functional structures are adequate. Thus even as it was his word, which is to say his conception and image, that was the beginning because it stimulated the vision and aspiration, so is it likely to be his word which signals that end which is also another beginning. What must be remembered is that people live in terms of images which represent the fundamental conceptions embodied in their rituals and myths. In the absence of adequate images they live in terms of such compelling images (and hence rituals and myths) as are abroad at the time. Where there is no adequate vision the people perish, one might say, precisely because where there are no "good" writers there are always "bad" writers, where there are no adequate images there are always inadequate images. Yet the quality of the "serious" art of the times whether adequate or not is likely to be reflected in the popular art of the times.

Nothing else fulfills the inherently consummate intellectual or ideational function of the image-making processes so well as does literature. Not even the most exact and comprehensive scientific information about individual and group impulses, drives, motives, frustrations, repressions, releases, compensations, and sublimations is equivalent to either the personal or the general significance of the writer's singular and indispensable insight into the poetic, dramatic, or mythological dimensions and possibilities of the human situation. Nor for that matter was science in any form ever really intended to be anything more than a functional adjunct and auxiliary to the creative imagination. Technology exists within the context of ritual and myth, not vice versa.

And yet not only do many American writers now proceed as if the social science survey were an adequate extension of fiction, but some obviously assume that personalized journalism geared to the research methodology of the behavioral sciences can actually supersede the creative process in writing. Indeed, there are reviewers, critics, and teachers who suggest even now that fiction is obsolescent and that books which recall experience in terms of the psycho-socio-political-documentary image are already becoming well established as the New Genre which will provide the most adequate frame of reference for coming to terms with contemporary experience.

There are many American readers who now as much as admit that they are uncomfortable with any fictional representation of experience until they have translated each character and gesture and every sequence of action into the terminology of social science. What no writer with serious literary aspirations can afford to overlook, however, is that, far from extending the implications of the traditional categories of tragedy, comedy, and farce, the basic assumptions of contemporary American social science—most of which seem to derive from the formulations or quasi-scientific fabrications of Marx and Freud —only correspond to the oversimplifications of the melodramatic success story. Perhaps such fiction does represent a new genre, social science fiction fiction. The function it performs, however, as necessary as in its limited way it may very well be, is not that of literature but perhaps primarily that of social and political agitation and propaganda.

It was once stated with unmistakable import that only by some "miracle of development" could Ernest Hemingway manage to acquire the "Marxist imagination" of a Leon Trotsky; and Trotsky himself in a review* entitled "La Révolution Étranglée" was moved to indict André Malraux for making *The Conquerors* a work of fiction instead of a book of more accurate historical documentation. But while it is true that in theory Marxism, like Freudianism, operates on the dynamics of thesis-antithesis-synthesis as does narration, it is also all too true that in actual practice the Marx-Freud imagination of the social science oriented American writer is of its very nature likely to be restricted to the immediate implications of materialistic salvation through psycho-socio-political engineering.

The socio-political or social science fiction fiction hero, who should not be confused with the detective story hero, would achieve salvation by environmental change through revolution, whether by military or legislative measures. But predicated as it is upon scientific programs for remedial action, such a conception never acknowledges the fundamental condition of human life as being a ceaseless struggle for form against chaos, of sense against nonsense. Thus, in spite of temporary plot complications and setbacks, the normal expectation in every social science melodrama is that everything will turn out all right. In fact, last-minute aid for the social science hero can often be assumed to be as available as the nearest telephone!

Not that all social science fiction heroes are successful by any means. Some are defeated precisely because assistance does not arrive in time or at all, or because such assistance as does arrive is inadequate. Others show excellent prospects only to be

* *Nouvelle Revue Française*, April 1, 1931.

reduced to invalids by evils within the system as described in statistical surveys. Sometimes the social science fiction hero is a cripple among cripples, all products of systematic oppression, and his only function is to indict the system by displaying his wretchedness! Many Marx-Freud melodramas are specifically designed to demonstrate that the "system," the environment in a social structure, will destroy all mankind if it is not transformed. In any event, it is always the so-called system (political and economic habitat) which generates the complications in the social science plot structure. Thus since the successful social science fiction hero achieves his ends (or at least saves his skin) because he is able to outwit or beat the system, the one who fails does so only because he is deficient in scientific technique (and moral purpose, to be sure). As defined not only by Marxians and Freudians, but also by social reformers in general, all of the essential problems of humanity can either be solved or reduced to insignificance by a hero or man of good will who can apply adequate scientific insight to Public Administration and medicine.

(The assumptions underlying the behavior of the popular contemporary detective story hero are perhaps more consistent with the experience [and resulting perceptions of actuality] from which truly contemporary sensibilities are derived. Such detective story protagonists as Sam Spade, Nero Wolfe and Archie, Phillip Marlowe, and Dick Tracy also symbolize the hero as a scientist, a technician. But in this instance he is primarily a research technician. Sometimes he may take the action necessary to dispatch evil, but his essential job is to dig up evidence and provide information about the source or sources of specific evils. Once he accumulates enough evidence for an "indictment," the detective has, to all intents and purposes, completed the job he was hired to do and may collect his fee and move on to the next client. He provides existential information, not millennial salvation.)

But no writer who restricts his imagination to the assumptions and categories of social science and limits his concern to issues which are essentially political is likely to evolve a genre which fulfills the function of literature. It can be conceded readily enough that in all fiction there is perhaps no more exemplary protagonist than one who, whether he succeeds or fails otherwise, achieves a successful personal integration as a human being while engaged in action to promote the general welfare. But the writer who would create such a hero and would communicate the most immediate as well as the most comprehensive implications of such a view of human behavior must do so in terms of categories, conceptions, and dimensions of human existence which are necessarily beyond the scope and concern of the social sciences. The categories which the story teller requires, and which as an artist he can hardly afford to regard as by-products of non-literary objectives, are those of tragic and comic heroism and farce. The frame of reference within which he works is not that of the scientific research laboratory but that of literature. The dynamics by which he functions are not those of engineering but those of the epic. Indeed, much goes to show that farce, which is in a sense the anticategorical narrative category, is precisely the frame of reference which may be most compatible with the existential absurdity of contemporary actuality.

Science, of course, is an indispensable source of information for the contemporary writer. It is, furthermore, a necessary part of his highly technological environment. Thus it is also an inevitable component of his sensibility and a decisive even if often unapprehended component of his creative imagination. But science is not in itself an elemental wellspring of literature. Promoters of the Genre of the Documentary Image notwithstanding, even the most refined and precise research data are only raw materials which may or may not become literature. For whatever becomes a work of art of any kind does so as a result of an act of creation, an act of esthetic composition, an act involving the art of make-believe. Scientific "statements" or "remarks" as such, even when they are valid, reliable, and comprehensive, are not literature.

Even the unaltered found objects on exhibition in museums of contemporary art are creations. The deliberate act of selection (isolating, highlighting) is a process of transformation not essentially different from choosing, arranging, and giving relative emphasis to scenes and incidents in the composition of a story. After all, the decision to appropriate a given relic, pebble, or mechanical device was not made by a scientist in terms of archaeology, geology, or engineering, but by an artist in terms of esthetic perception.

As for the scientific research document, when it reads like fiction it does so because whoever compiled it possessed dramatic insight and employed the techniques of narrative composition. Realism in literature, after all, is only an esthetic *device*, and it is no less dependent upon craftsmanship than are the devices necessary to the concoction of fantasy. A narrative seems realistic because it was designed (and polished!) to create that effect. An unedited film or tape recording of people acting perfectly naturally is not very likely to create the effect of "slice of life" realism at all. The effect it creates might well be that of tedious unreality. The truth may often be stranger than fiction, but objective documentation is seldom as interesting and effective as skillful dramatic fabrication.

The act of documentation, then, needless to say, is not an act of literary creation. (The pseudo-document is of course a form of fiction, but that is another story.) Documentation is an act which is designed to provide systematic or scientific information. But such information, which is not always reliable but which might well add up to a Documentary Image nevertheless, is useful to the writer of fiction only insofar as it contributes to the credibility of what Susanne K. Langer has called the Dynamic Image, by which she means a perceptible form (such as created by a dance movement) that expresses the nature of human feeling. What the writer, no less than the actor, uses the factual detail and the natural gesture for is to create illusion. A story is a work of the writer's imagination. It seldom follows an actual occurrence with the step-by-step accuracy of the historical record—and even when it does, each step immediately becomes an act in a play which the story teller has contrived from the original events.

The aboriginal source of fiction, which seems to be the same as that of poetry and drama, is the song and dance ritual or *molpê*. Indeed, the art of fiction may also be regarded as a verbal equivalent to and extension of the art of composition and choreography. The story teller works with language, but even so, he is a song and dance man (a maker of *molpês*) whose fundamental objectives are extensions of those of the bard, the minstrel, and the ballad maker which, incidentally, are also those of the contemporary American blues singer. When he creates short stories and novels, the writer no less than these or the ancient Greek playwrights is composing and choreographing song and dance imitations of experience. It is by means of such imitations that he evokes the dynamic image which embodies and expresses his conception of human nature and of the meaning and purpose of human conduct.

It is also by means of such imitation that literature fulfills its function as a fundamental vehicle of information, instruction, wisdom, and moral guidance. The song and dance ritual, whatever its extensions, whether as drama, lyric poem, ode, hymn, lay, epic, ballad or blues, is not only a reenactment-creation, but also a reenactment illustration, demonstration, and initiation. Even as the short story and the novel embody and thus describe and define the world as the writer perceives it, they also serve to initiate the reader into it. When the writer *relates* a story to the reader, he literally *connects* him with what the story is about. He makes the reader aware of information which establishes a relationship between the reader and the writer's point of view, his scale of values, and his sense of human existence.

Further, the work of fiction, having been created, not only exists as an artifact in the static sense, but also functions as a performance. Each short story and each novel is, that is to say, a dance-extension performance, such as that which the blues singer gives when rendering a ballad for an audience. Thus, when the reader opens a book of fiction, his action is essentially the same as that of entering a theater and opening the curtain or switching on the projector. What he encounters is a production which has been written instead of staged or filmed; what he witnesses as he reads is the entertainment provided by performers in a theatrical fabrication—performers who exist not only to provide entertainment and amusement, however, but who may also provide specific instruction and general education; who show what happens in given circumstances and why it happens, but, perhaps most fascinating of all, how it happens.

The emotional response of the reader to his experience of a book of fiction is also a reenactment (of a reenactment!).

Moreover, the dynamics of recall, recognition, repetition, imitation, reconstruction, and recreation involved in such reader-audience reenactment are precisely those which underlie the entire educational process. The interaction of performer and audience is nothing if not that of instructor and student. As he turns page after page, following the fortunes of the storybook hero, the reader is as deeply engaged in the educative process as if he were an apprentice in a workshop. Indeed, he is an apprentice, and his workshop includes the whole range of human possibility and endeavor. His task is to learn from the example of journeymen and master craftsmen such skills as not only will enable him to avoid confusion and destruction, but also will enhance his own existence as well as that of human beings everywhere.

He is, by literal and historical as well as metaphorical extension, a dance apprentice who studies postures, gestures, movements, and positions, each one of which is a statement. The dancer taking a position (and thereby creating a landscape with figures) is also taking a stand, performing a stasimon, creating a stanza, and making a statement of definition. Making a gesture and executing a step, he is also taking action which is based on an established position or point of departure, and on a definition of circumstance, situation, and predicament. At the same time he is also taking an action which creates another situation which requires another definition which suggests further action!

The apprentice who has sufficient aptitude becomes a journeyman and eventually a master craftsman. All educational systems, formal and informal alike, seem to operate on some principle of graduation, the final stage of which is a commencement of independent individual application of the skills, knowledge, awarenesses, appreciations, and attitudes, etc. The master craftsman in any trade is, appropriately enough, one who knows the tread, which is to say the tracks which make the course or the way, the route and routine, the way to and the way to do. He is, that is to say, an erstwhile apprentice and journeyman who can execute the most intricate steps in an outstanding manner.

No master craftsman ever really learns everything about his line of endeavor, of course. Even at best his applications are still only a form of practice. He is a practician and follows his trade. The exceptional degree of expertise which he does develop, however, not only qualifies him to function on his own, but also enables him to extemporize under pressure and in the most complicated circumstances. Nor is a higher degree of erudition and skill possible, or even relevant. Improvisation, after all, is the ultimate skill. The master craftsman is one for whom knowledge and technique have become that with which he not only performs but also plays (one performs a dance as one plays music, and when one plays in a drama one is performing in a play). The master craftsman is also one who, as the hero in combat and the blues musician in a jam session, can maintain the dancer's grace under the pressure of all tempos.

The song and dance rituals which underlie tragedy, comedy, melodrama, and farce—the four standard categories of narrative literature, all extensions of the epic—not only provide conclusive evidence of the fiction writer's inherent and inescapable involvement with measures which contribute to human welfare; they also reveal the functional value of such involvement. When the writer's aspirations are truly literary, his dedication to the art of fiction is tantamount to a social commitment to human well-being and self-realization. His sense of art is inseparable from his sense of what is beneficial and what is detrimental in human existence.

When he writes in terms of the story pattern known as tragedy, for instance—which is in effect the retracing of the steps leading to destruction and which, as the name suggests, may well be the extension of the goat sacrifice song and dance or the Dance of the Scapegoat—he is performing a purification ritual in imitation of the life process itself. Indeed, according to Gilbert Murray, in *The Classical Tradition in Poetry*, "Tragedy is the enactment of the death of the Year-Spirit; and comedy is the enactment of his marriage, or rather of the Comos which accompanies his marriage. The centre of tragedy is death; the centre of comedy is a union of lovers."

Gilbert Murray then goes on as follows:

Thus Greek drama starts, not as a mere picture of ordinary life, or even of ordinary adventure, but as a re-creation, or *mimesis*, of the two most intense experiences that life affords; a re-creation of life at its highest power. The purpose of the drama was—it is generally agreed—originally magical. The marriage Comos was intended actually to produce fertility; the death-celebration was the expulsion of evil from the community, the casting out of the Old Year with its burden of decay, of the polluted, the Scapegoat, the Sin-Bearer. It is well to remember that dramatic performances were introduced into Rome in order to cure a pestilence. This occurred actually during the lifetime of Aristotle. But Aristotle himself has forgotten as completely as we have that tragedy was ever a magical rite: he treats it simply as an artistic performance, and judges it, not for any concrete effect it may have on the public health, but simply on aesthetic grounds. And this shows us that, for whatever reason it was created, drama persisted and increased because it answered to some constant need in human nature.

Several paragraphs later Murray also claims that tragedy "hides or adorns the coming 'bulk of death,' magnifies the glory of courage, the power of endurance, the splendor of self-sacrifice and self-forgetfulness, so as to make us feel, at least for the fleeting moment, that nothing is here for tears, and that death is conquered."

Perhaps the "happy ending" that is commonly associated with the story pattern of comedy does not so much suggest that death has been conquered as that life has been mastered, at least for the moment and at least to an extent which will allow for human continuity. The implications of the symbolic reenactment of the union of lovers as represented in the boy-meets-girl, boy-loses-girl, boy-gets-girl formula, for example, go beyond survival through copulation as such. Coming as it does after the hero has made his way through certain tribulations, the happy ending is in effect a most fundamental statement about the nature of security. As a direct result of his adventures it can be assumed that the hero has acquired enough practical first-hand experience to handle a passable amount of such difficulties as are inherent in the nature of things. The lessons he has learned are the very essence of security, which is to say survival. Perhaps another way of suggesting what is essentially the same thing is that the hero does not get the girl until his experience indicates that he is somewhat better prepared to assume the responsibilities of parenthood. In any case, the embrace which so often represents the happy ending is not the prelude to retirement. The happy ending, precisely like a marriage, is only the end of courtship. It is the beginning of family life—and so forth and so on!

The melodrama or adventure story, a typical climax of which is also the union of lovers, may well have been derived from rituals of purification as well as fertility. In fact, it is a story in which the union (or atonement) of lovers is predicated upon purification. But unlike the tragic hero whose problem is his own contamination (his own flaws, mistakes, choices, or whatever), or the comic hero whose problem is his naïveté, or lack of perception, the melodramatic hero of some sagas, of some medieval romances, and of the scientific success story purifies society. He overcomes his inadequacies, which are mostly technological, by following the proper instructions and acquires the magic formula which cures and saves an ailing body politic.

There are also elements of ritual purification and fruitful union in that category of narration known as farce. Indeed, the writer can transform any tragedy, comedy, or melodrama into a farce simply by changing his rhetorical tone and manner. A performer need make only the slightest change in his gestures in order to turn an act of purification into slapstick, the union of lovers into an obscene frolic, and heroic behavior into the ludicrous gesticulations and misadventures of a Don Quixote. When the actor, the dancer, or a writer like Cervantes does so, however, what he creates is perhaps not simply a subspecies of tragedy, melodrama, or even comedy, but in a sense another ritual altogether. What he actually accomplishes even when his intentions are satirical is the disintegration of tragic, comic, and melodramatic forms along with all other ideas of purposeful order, including the notion of common sense—which becomes stuff and nonsense.

Essentially, a farce, which always involves subversive intrusion, is a capricious or goat-like song and dance symbolizing disorder. As such it is a ritual reenactment not of goat sacrifice or of sacred totemic copulation but rather of the absurd and outrageous and inexorable resurgence of nature itself. It is thus in the most elemental sense a mock ritual which functions as a counter-agent of ritual. In a farce it is as if the intended

scapegoat were revolting and desecrating the purification ceremony. It is as if the goat-footed bridegroom were turning the
wedding procession into a feast of lasciviousness. Farce breaks
the spell of ritual. It counterbalances the magic which ritual
works upon the imagination. It protects human existence from
the excesses of the imagination and operates as a safeguard
against the overextension of ideas, formulations, and formalities. After all, extended far enough, even the idea of freedom
becomes a matter involving security measures and thus a justification for restrictions which exceed those that generated the
thrust toward liberation in the first place. The world is, or
should be, all too familiar with totalitarian systems which
began as freedom movements.

In ultimate effect, farce is a divine, Olympian, or cosmic
joke, and as such it is an indispensable antidote for the wisdom
of the ages. It is, that is to say, the ridiculous prank without
which no formal occasion can be viewed in proper perspective,
for as ironic as it may seem, frivolity and sensual intemperance
exercise a *moderating* influence on the holiness of holiday
sacraments—even now, when the word holiday has become a
synonym for debauchery.

On the other hand, the absurd and outrageous intrusion of
nature-in-the-raw is also that which all heroes must confront.
Such is the fate and mission of every hero in every situation,
whether he is the protagonist in a Greek drama, in a medieval
romance, or in an American blues ballad; he must recognize
that which threatens human existence and must either withstand and subdue it or be annihilated by it. In the end, of
course, it is always raw nature itself, the unconscious and irresponsible, inexorable earth in all its natural chaos which abides.
Nevertheless, the hero whose aspirations are always those of
Prometheus, but whose very seriousness makes him resemble
Don Quixote, presumes, endeavors, and somehow succeeds
even when he fails.

At bottom every hero is, like a solo dancer on an empty and
infinite stage, always the protagonist in an epic. He is, that is to
say, the representative man who pits himself against nature in
the raw (which of course is also nature-in-the-absurd, thus
making him also a buffoon in a farce, a minstrel clown cutting
capers which somehow coordinate, a whiteface or blackface

fool whose outlandish and silly statements somehow make sense out of its nonsense). In all events it is always some destructive or anti-human element in nature against which the hero contends, whether his immediate circumstances be those of tragedy, comedy, melodrama, or farce. In the typical tragedy, for instance, it is nature itself or the nature of things which generates the plot—which entraps the hero. The tragic hero, as defined here then, is actually an epic hero who falls victim to the atrocities which are inherent in the nature of things.

The comic hero thus becomes an epic protagonist whose difficulties are also inherent in the very nature of actuality. He mistakes, misinterprets, and misconstrues appearances and is misled into pandemonium, from which he narrowly extricates himself only because he begins to see things for what they actually are and can proceed not in spite of but in terms of (in the specific terms of) complexity. His story line: on his way to perform the act of union which will fructify all mankind, the comic hero, perhaps because he thinks good offices are enough, is led astray. But as a result of the adventures which follow, when he finally does make it to the sacred grove where the fertility rites are performed, he has learned enough to realize that sweet smiles and words and beautiful weather and landscapes can lend to confusion as well as happiness.

The comic situation is based on the fact that nature, or rather man's perception of it, is forever jumping out of focus. At some point in perhaps most melodramas, however, it pops back into focus, revealing a configuration of itself which is all too sharp and unmistakable. What the hero must enjoin in combat at that point, depending upon whether the story is an epic-like saga, a romance, a gothic adventure tale, a chronicle of crime and detection, or a dime novel, is a monster, usually from the depths of a pond, a swamp, or the world ocean; a dragon from the infernal bowels of the earth, a weird beast from the wilderness; or it may be and perhaps most often is a villain, a person that is to say of lowest estate, one from the most nature-like regions, from the outer edges of civilization, an outlaw from the regions beyond law and order, a gangster from the underworld. The smoothie in the penny dreadful cliff hanger is another aspect of the same narrative convention. In the end he always reveals himself to be the rawest and most brutal elements of nature in disguise. Beneath all the highly polished veneer of elegance and pretty manners which in retrospect were somewhat suspicious or at least disconcerting all along, is a senseless but murderous selfishness which makes him an all but unmistakable personification of the heartlessness, soullessness, and mindlessness of natural forces (*which in the context of farce become the invisible "blue devils" that beset the nimble-or-nothing hero at every turn*).

Thus do such esthetic considerations as types of narrative statement involve such ethical matters as categories of heroic action; and thus is the story teller's moral obligation or social commitment inherent in his craft. The art of fiction is an art of make-believe. It is therefore, and precisely by the same token, also an art of persuasion and even of propaganda. But what the story teller in his capacity as artist wants those who respond to the fortunes of the storybook hero to believe goes far beyond the credibility of any given political formulation. Even when specific political issues motivate the plot he is recounting, the story teller's point is still that of the fable underlying all drama: Once upon a time there was someone who somehow did or did not achieve that favorable, no matter how delicate, balance between essential human values on the one hand and cosmic absurdity (as well as political outrage) on the other.

The Dynamics of Heroic Action

THE REMARK which Ernest Hemingway made in *Green Hills of Africa* about writers being forged in injustice has two very functional implications which are of immediate relevance to writers—black and white—who would use the experience of black people in the United States as material for fiction. The first is obvious: Hemingway was convinced that the experience of such things as war, upheaval, poverty, and injustice were not of themselves bad for writers. On the contrary, he felt that such experience, as horrible as it is for mankind at large, could actually be of great advantage for writers. In his opinion Tolstoy, Dostoevsky, Stendhal, and Flaubert, for instance, were all better writers for having been involved in human life at the elemental level of wartime existence, revolution, exile, and so on.

Such experience, Hemingway knew only too well, involves disenchantment and alienation; but he also knew that it tests the writer's basic values, improves his perspective and objectivity. He spoke of the necessary shock to cut the "overflow of words." In "Monologue to the Maestro" he tells a young apprentice that the best early training for a writer is an unhappy childhood; and in *A Moveable Feast* he remembered his days of poverty in Paris as being good for his discipline. In replying to George Plimpton's question about writing and injustice (in an interview for *Paris Review*), he went on to say that the most essential thing for a good writer was a built-in, shockproof crap detector, which (he told Robert Manning, then of *Time* magazine in another interview) should have a manual drill and crank handle in case the machine breaks down.

The first implication of Hemingway's remark about justice thus becomes obvious as soon as one realizes that all serious writers have had a deep-seated sense of exclusion, disaffection, alienation, disillusionment, detachment, dissatisfaction, disorientation, and so on, and that this as much as anything is what makes them tick as writers.

The second implication is not so obvious at first glance. Its significance, however, extends beyond the writing process as such and into the dynamics of the blues tradition as a whole. In a sense the whole point of the blues idiom lyric is to state the facts of life. Not unlike ancient tragedy, it would have the people for whom it is composed and performed confront, acknowledge, and proceed in spite of, and even in terms of, the ugliness and meanness inherent in the human condition. It is thus a device for making the best of a bad situation.

Not by rendering capitulation tolerable, however, and certainly not by consoling those who would compromise their integrity, but—in its orientation to continuity in the face of adversity and absurdity—the blues idiom lyric is entirely consistent with the folklore and wisdom underlying the rugged endurance of the black American. In addition, or rather concomitantly, blues-idiom dance music challenges and affirms his personal equilibrium, sustains his humanity, and enables him to maintain his higher aspirations in spite of the fact that human existence is so often mostly a low-down dirty shame.

Hemingway himself, it should be understood, did not spell out any elaborate theory of cultural dynamics in this or in any other connection. Nor is there any evidence that he ever concerned himself to any great degree with comprehensive intellectual formulations as such. His intellectual discipline was the craft of fiction, and most of his nonfiction was either his special brand of personal journalism or observations which suggested practical everyday guidance for writers; and, far from thinking of any of his suggestions as the principles which in truth they are, he was much more likely to claim only that they worked for him. The excuse which he gave for publishing "Monologue to the Maestro," for example, was that some of the information it contained would have been worth the price of a copy of *Esquire* magazine to him when he was twenty-one.

Nevertheless, the image of the sword being forged is inseparable from the dynamics of antagonistic cooperation, a concept which is indispensable to any fundamental definition of heroic action, in fiction or otherwise. The fire in the forging process, like the dragon which the hero must always encounter, is of its very nature antagonistic, but it is also cooperative at the same time. For all its violence, it does not destroy the metal which becomes the sword. It functions precisely to strengthen and prepare it to hold its battle edge, even as the all but withering firedrake prepares the questing hero for subsequent trials and adventures. The function of the hammer and the anvil is to beat the sword into shape even as the most vicious challengers no less than the most cooperatively rugged sparring mates jab, clinch, and punch potential prize-fighters into championship condition.

Heroism, which like the sword is nothing if not steadfast, is measured in terms of the stress and strain it can endure and the magnitude and complexity of the obstacles it overcomes. Thus difficulties and vicissitudes which beset the potential hero on all sides not only threaten his existence and jeopardize his prospects; they also, by bringing out the best in him, serve his purpose. They make it possible for him to make something of himself. Such is the nature of every confrontation in the context of heroic action.

It is all very ironic, of course, but after all experience itself is not only ironic, it is sometimes downright absurd. Science, whether physical or social, cannot abide irony and absurdity, but there is nothing it can do about them. On the other hand, all great story tellers have always known that irony and absurdity are not only thorns in the briarpatch in which they themselves were bred and born but also precisely what literary statement is forever trying to provide adequate terms for!

Which is a very good reason indeed why promising young men in stories, as in life, do not become heroes by simply keeping their police records clean and their grade point averages high enough to qualify them for status jobs and good addresses inside the castle walls. Nice young men are the salt of society, the soul of respectability, the backbone of the nation, and their faces appear at court functions and their names are recorded on official documents. But those young men who become the heroes whose deeds merit statues, red-letter days, and epics do so by confronting and slaying dragons.

Moreover, the outlying regions, the sinister circumstances beyond statistics, *cooperate* with the hero by virtue of the very fact of and nature of their existence. They help beget real-life and storybook heroes alike, not only by generating the necessity for heroism in the first place but also by contesting its development at every stage and by furnishing the occasion for its fulfillment. Indeed, since in the final analysis the greatness of the hero can be measured only in scale with the mischief, malaise, or menace he can dispatch, the degree of cooperation is always equal to the amount of antagonism.

Everyday manifestations of this kind of cooperation are infinite. Complicated diseases, for example, wreak havoc, but they also bring out the best doctors and the best in doctors. Without exasperating legal snarls there are only ordinary inexperienced lawyers, however promising. Schools with the most difficult course requirements turn out the best trained graduates. Strict factory testing procedures guarantee dependable products. And so it goes. Nor should there be any confusion because of the elimination involved. What brings out the best also shows up the worst, a procedure as indispensable as it is paradoxical.

Much has been made of the inevitability of fate in ancient Greek mythology. But as much, if not more, can be made of the dynamics of antithesis. Greek drama has as much to do with perception through purpose and passion as with predetermination; Greek tragedy, as is well known, was concerned with catharsis, which was always the result of confrontation and struggle, and as such it was a testing, elimination, forging and proving process, designed to achieve a durable synthesis, whether of personal fibre or of common sense.

Sometimes, as in the story of Oedipus, the cooperative antagonist is all too conspicuous by his absence. All Oedipus wants is to be a nice fellow and avoid trouble, and yet his very best deeds only serve to bring him closer to the disaster he is running away from. A young man of obvious if somewhat naïve good intentions, Oedipus is not actually undone by the oracle which predicts that he will murder his father and marry his mother, but by his unwillingness to stay in Corinth and face his problems. In some ways it is as if Oedipus were essentially a social science–oriented intellectual (born centuries before the contemporary vogue) whose basic assumption is that life can be free of ambivalence, complexity, and strife. He proceeds as if there were actually environments antiseptically free from folly and safe against sin—welfare states, as it were, moderately taxed but well budgeted against social problems and therefore immune to personal conflicts.

Whatever his assumptions, his first-hand knowledge of human complexity is inadequate, and he oversimplifies his circumstances in terms of his own good intentions. But his integrity, which has not been forged in "cooperative" injustice but in loving courtly care, is not rugged enough to withstand the provocations and temptations of everyday life. Thus he is noble enough not to want to harm his father but not actually generous enough to defer to a cantankerous old stranger at the crossroads. High IQ undergrad type that he is, he can answer such academic questions as are put by Ivy League sphinxes, but he is not really hip enough to realize that he should never make love to any queen under any circumstances. He hastens to call in the experts and survey technicians to find out what is wrong with other people but never suspects that anything might be wrong with himself. He never even tries to find out why he has been walking with a limp all of his life (which incidentally, also means he doesn't even know the *meaning* of his name, which actually summarizes his biography). He is, in this, somewhat like the white American who seems unable to realize that it is the oppressor not the oppressed, whose condition is inherently and intrinsically pathological. The oppressed, after all, is faced with very real threats and hostilities outside himself. Anxiety, and even terror, are intrinsically normal responses to danger.

Oedipus, who in a sense really has no mission except to avoid trouble, begins his journey untried in the ways of mischief. Shakespeare's Prince Hal, on the other hand, becomes a worthy King Henry V because he has served an apprenticeship in the regions outlying the castle and has become wise in the ways of Falstaff and his ruffians.

The bullfight, which never ceased to fascinate Hemingway, is a ritual in which the element of antagonistic cooperation is more clear-cut and fundamental. By definition the good fighting bull is a cooperative antagonist to the extent that he provides the dangers (i.e. opportunities for risk taking) without which there can be no good matadors and therefore no *corridas* worthy of the name. In the bullfighter, Hemingway studied at close range a very special exemplification of the hero in action. Not only is the matador a volunteer who seeks out, confronts, and dispatches that which is deadly; he is also an adventurer who runs risks, takes chances, and exposes himself with such graceful disdain for his own limitations and safety that the tenacity of his courage is indistinguishable from the beauty of his personal style and manner.

Such a conception of heroism is romantic, to be sure, but after all, given the range of possibilities in human nature and conduct, so is the notion of the nobility of man. And so inevitably, whether obvious or not, are the fundamental assumptions underlying every character, situation, gesture, and story line in literature. For without the completely romantic presuppositions behind such elemental values as honor, pride, love, freedom, integrity, human fulfillment, and the like, there can be no truly meaningful definition either of tragedy or of comedy. Nor without such *idealistic* preconceptions can there be anything to be *realistic* about, to protest about, or even to be cynical about.

The unbelievably splendid conduct of the bullfighter has the same basic ritualistic function as the superhuman exploits and escapades of the epic protagonist. It affirms that which is upstanding in human nature, that which stands out against the overwhelming odds of the nonhuman and anti-human elements in the universe. The bullfighter, like the epic hero, is the beau ideal, the prototype and paradigm of the positive potential in all human behavior, and most noteworthy of all, he inspires the ordinary man, the individual, to extend himself beyond routine conceptions and achievements.

American protest fiction of the current Marx/Freud-oriented variety is essentially anti-adventure and, in effect, nonheroic. It is predicated upon assumptions which have much more to do with philanthropy than with the dynamics of antagonistic co-operation. It concerns itself not with the ironies and ambiguities of self-improvement and self-extension, not with the evaluation of the individual as protagonist, but rather with representing a world of collective victims whose survival and betterment depend not upon self-determination but upon a change of heart in their antagonists, who thereupon will cease being villains and become patrons of social welfare! It is as if such writers see human experiences in terms of melodramatic predicaments, only to substitute supplication for precisely that heroism which Marx/Freud-oriented surveys and ideologies would seem to require, for revolutions are nothing if not adventures.

Heroism, which is, among other things, another word for self-reliance, is not only the indispensable prerequisite for productive citizenship in an open society; it is also that without which no individual or community can remain free. Moreover, as no one interested in either the objectives of democratic institutions or the image of democratic man can ever afford to forget, the concept of free enterprise has as much to do with adventurous speculations and improvisations in general as with the swashbuckling economics of, say, the Robber Barons.

There may be ever so much passion and bloodshed in protest fiction. But since its blackest rage and most sanguinary confrontations are likely more often than not to be designed primarily as indictments against indifference, injustice, or brutality, rather than as examples of the obstacles which beset all quests for manhood, or rather personhood, selfhood, the just society, and everything else, such fiction belongs not to the literature that provides images which, to paraphrase André Malraux, enable men to become aware of the greatness in themselves that they might otherwise ignore. It belongs to the rhetorical category of supplication.

In effect, protest or finger-pointing fiction such as *Uncle Tom's Children* and *Native Son* addresses itself to the humanity of the dragon in the very process of depicting him as a fire-snorting monster: "Shame on you, Sir Dragon," it says in effect, "be a nice man and a good citizen." (Or is it, "Have mercy, Massa?") Indeed, in their fiction no less than in their essays, writers like Richard Wright, James Baldwin, and their imitators often seem to be appealing to the *godliness* of the dragon: "O, you who are so all powerful, let my people go." When you name the dragon the devil, as Malcolm X used to do, or pig, as Eldridge Cleaver does now, aren't you really trying to convert him by putting the bad mouth on him?

Nor is the threat a heroic weapon.

Why is it that so few moral outcry protest agitators seem to realize or even to suspect that all political establishments are always likely to have built-in devices to counteract the guilt and bad conscience which the exercise of power of its very nature entails? Aren't political establishments or administrations likely to function much the same as some U.S. business establishments that have special departments to handle complaints, while the other transactions flow on as usual?—the ever so nice smiles in the complaint department making up for the defective goods in the stockroom!

Sometimes, to be sure, a power establishment does respond with corrective action, or at least some show of corrective action. But many times it responds with crestfallen acknowledgment and little else, compensating for its crime by feeling genuinely sorry for the victim. At other times it may simply allow the discontents to blow off hot air until their sense of frustration is relieved enough or they become bored enough with themselves to settle back down into the routine. And so on it goes. Nobody was probably ever more obscenely naïve and self-defeating than certain ever so wrathful moral outcry militants who do not realize which of their accusations and threats are effective and which are simply being indulged, and who don't even seem to suspect that sometimes indulgence is all they are going to get for their efforts.

But then, contrary to any fundamental commitment to heroic action, protest fiction seems to assume that the risks involved in such action should be avoided, averted by massive official action. Over any romantic implications of shining armor the protest writer seems to prefer the humility of sackcloth and ashes. Instead of the man on horseback, it seems content to promote the man of moderation and peace—or the loud-mouthed wretch who hurls abuse at those whom he quite obviously assumes to be his betters, who stations himself and his picket-troops at some safe and convenient capital city wailing wall and beseeches or browbeats the partly deaf Olympians of the Power Structure to send official decontamination squads into his boondocks to spray the dragons away. Even when the outraged protest writer threatens damnation, it is easy for anybody to see that he is mostly only bluffing and that the real threat is in the confusion being propagated. Most dragons are well aware of the fact that when his threats materialize as violence, the protest writer is likely to be as surprised and confused as everybody else, that what he really wanted to do all along was negotiate for legislation and appropriations. Most Northern-style U.S. dragons are not at all unmindful of how easy it is to get some of the loudest protestors to settle for a few compassionate reassurances that some one is beginning to Give a Damn.

Not that anyone in his right mind should or would ever hesitate to seek and use all available tax-supported anti-dragon forces—or refuse to take every possible preventive measure. Nevertheless, it is hardly wise to proceed as if any nation or community will never need any more citizen dragon fighters who are battle-seasoned in hand-to-hand combat. For not only must there always be someone qualified to command the official anti-dragon operations, but there also must be adequate forces in being and in reserve to be mobilized and deployed.

Without such forces prayer availeth naught and the threat of damnation even less. And yet the estimates of the situation upon which most American protest fiction is based would seem to indicate that any effective resistance is impossible, except by people whose fitness is evidently based on the fact that they have never had to resist anything. Almost every gesture in recent American protest fiction seems designed to convince the reader of one thing above everything else: Dragons bring only terror and devastation. But if this is so, then the writers of protest fiction can only be agents of sheer nonsense. They are professional supplicants who are in the grotesquely pathetic position of making urgent requests which they cannot possibly believe will be honored by the enemy. And how can they believe that their threats of rebellion and revolution can be fulfilled by their dragon-withered fellow victims of the Wasteland? As any basic training NCO will tell you, it will take forever to make effective combat troops out of the sad sacks in all those statistical surveys.

On the other hand, the writer who deals with the experience of oppression in terms of the dynamics of antagonistic cooperation works in a context which includes the whole range of human motivation and possibility. Not only does such a writer regard anti-black racism, for instance, as an American-born dragon which should be destroyed, but he also regards it as something which, no matter how devastatingly sinister, can and will be destroyed because its very existence generates both the necessity and the possibility of heroic deliverance. The firedrake is an evocation to the hero, even as the very existence of dangerous big game animals was in itself a call to Hemingway's huntsmen.

The fiction writer whose imagination is essentially philanthropic, whether its orientation is to the benevolent foundations, liberal politics, Marx/Freud-utopianism, or welfare-state ideology, is likely to regard the protagonist not as an image of man the giant killer, but as the personification of a cause in need of benefactors. Such a protagonist, of course, is no hero at all. He is the underdog, and far from projecting charisma, he evokes compassion. He is an object not of inspiration, but of sympathy and even of pity.

Any storybook hero worthy of his name, however, is more often than not an object of admiration or emulation. Even when he fails, there is something in his deportment that inspires others to keep trying. Even his difficulties are considered desirable. Indeed, as every schoolboy should remember easily enough, to aspire to heroism is to wish for the adventures of Ulysses, the obstacles of Hercules, the encounters of Sir Lancelot—and so on, to the predicament of Hamlet or the poverty and isolation of Stephen Dedalus.

The implications for contemporary American writers, whether black or white, should be easy enough to grasp: Precisely as white musicians who work in the blues idiom have been simulating the tribulations of U.S. Negroes for years in order to emulate such musical heroes as Louis Armstrong, Lester Young, and Duke Ellington, and such heroines as Bessie Smith and Billie Holliday, so in fiction must readers, through their desire to imitate and emulate black storybook heroes, come to identify themselves with the disjunctures as well as the continuities of black experience as if to the idiom born. Moreover, the basis for such omni-American fiction is already in existence. Even now young white activists are beginning to regard themselves and their problems, with however much imprecision, in terms which are largely black. In any case, it may already be somewhat easier for them to project themselves as black civil rights activists than to imagine themselves as ancient Greek Argonauts, or even as early modern British seadogs and nineteenth-century

Empire builders, not to mention the Indian fighters and slave traders that some of their own American ancestors actually were—*and not so very long ago either.*

Thomas Mann, whose essay *The Coming Victory of Democracy* is one of the most compelling statements of the case for commitment in contemporary literature, once thought of himself as being a nonpolitical man. When the consummate craftsman and Olympian ironist who wrote *The Magic Mountain, Joseph and His Brothers,* and *Doctor Faustus* was an incredibly gifted younger man writing *Buddenbrooks, Tonio Kroger,* and *Death in Venice* (any one of which would qualify him as a contemporary master), he regarded art as being of its very nature separate from such everyday concerns of life as politics. Art in the bourgeois Germany of his youth, he later confessed, was assumed to exist in the very special domain of culture, which to him included music, metaphysics, psychology, a pessimistic ethic, and an individualistic idealism, and from which he "contemptuously excluded everything political."

Such assumptions did not reduce the validity of his early fiction, however, for, significantly, even as he proceeded in terms of a conception based on what he was later to regard as an artificial separation of art from life, he was preoccupied with the theme of the personal, social, and human incompleteness of the truly dedicated artist—who accepts his isolation in the Ivory Tower but also yearns for the simple and "normal" life, "the blisses of the commonplace." Mann, whose insight into the relationships between genius and pathology, between creativity and criminality, was characteristic of his distinctive and definitive irony, never overromanticized the role of the artist in society.

Nevertheless, in his longest work of nonfiction, *The Reflections of a Non-Political Man,* he insisted on the necessity for the artist to remain aloof from politics. At this time he defined democracy as the political functioning of the intellect, and he immediately rejected such functioning as a threat to culture and even to freedom. But what he meant by freedom then was moral freedom, and of the connection between moral freedom and social freedom he "understood little and cared less."

But when he came to write the foreword to *Order of the*

Day, he could look back on his *Reflections* as the extended prologue to a long series of manifestoes and attestations. The book itself, he says in the essay "Culture and Politics," has been the expression of a crisis, in response to profoundly disturbing events which had caused him to examine the question of the individual human being and the problem of humanity as a whole as never before, and he came to see that there is no clear dividing line between the intellectual and the political, that the German bourgeoisie had erred in thinking that a man of culture could remain unpolitical.

He also came to realize that culture itself stood in the greatest danger wherever and whenever it lacked interest and aptitude for the political. The nonpolitical man had equated democracy with the readiness of the intellect to be political only to condemn it. But not only did the free world spokesman recommend it in *The Coming Victory of Democracy*, he had also come to equate political behavior with human behavior. The self-exiled, world-renowned man of letters, writing "Culture and Politics" in the United States at a time when totalitarian forces had completely enslaved his homeland, could only thank his "good genius" that the anti-political inhibitions of his German upbringing had not suppressed the "feeling for democracy" which followed *The Reflections of a Non-Political Man*. "For where should I stand today," he wrote, "on what side should I be if in my conservatism I had clung to a Germany which in the end had not been saved by all its music and all its intellectualism from surrender to the lowest form of worship of power, nor from a barbarism which threatens the foundations of our Western Civilization."

The political essays and speeches in *Order of the Day* repudiate the restricted conception of the writer as artist which *The Reflections of a Non-Political Man* represented. But the effect which *Mario and the Magician*, *The Magic Mountain*, *Joseph and His Brothers*, and *Doctor Faustus* had on the earlier fiction was that of enrichment. In retrospect, the line of development from Tonio Kroger, the gifted ambivalent outsider, through Hans Castorp, the competent, ambivalent engineer, to Joseph, the fantastically endowed if still somewhat ambivalent provider, seems not only natural but irrepressible. In progress, however, it had all of the complexities involved in the dynamics of thesis, antithesis, and synthesis (complexities which only reinforce its consistency).

The antithetical crisis during which Thomas Mann progressed from esthetic isolation to social consciousness and commitment was The War and Aftermath. His response to the world-shattering events which began with the outbreak of war in 1914 led first to the defensive introspection of *The Reflections*, and then to the revelation of democracy and the realization of the nature of his involvement in mankind—and to his subsequent metamorphosis, not only into a Humanist but also into the epic poet and prophet of what he called The Coming, The New, or The Third Humanism.

The Magic Mountain, the narrative of Hans Castorp's seven-year sojourn among the living dead in the nether world of a sanitorium in the Swiss Alps, was published in 1924 and was, in addition to its other dimensions, Mann's testament of the Apocalypse. It was also his Book of the Transfiguration. Thus it is as if Mann's output through *Death in Venice* were deliberately designed to describe an antecedent state of error (or of erroneous innocence) while that which begins with *The Magic Mountain* is both the process and the embodiment of the New Enlightenment.

The introverted adventures of Hans Castorp provide adequate evidence of the difficulties involved in the self-induced metamorphosis which Mann undertook as a writer and underwent as a man. They also reveal the very special nature of the transfiguration achieved: he did not become a new man; he became a new extension of the old man, or rather, of the young man. So thoroughgoing was the self-reexamination that the result, ironically, was not so much an eradication and replacement as a synthesis. The new creature was very much the product of the old. There is much of Tonio Kroger the Artist in Joseph the Provider. Tonio has not been destroyed; he has been modified by new elements and by a more comprehensive re-combination. Incidentally, the nature of such recombination is given playful but no less profound treatment in *The Transposed Heads*, a finger exercise.

The enlistment of Thomas Mann was not a response to the pressures of recruitment. There were such pressures, of course. His situation was, in fact, not at all unlike that of Hans Castorp, who was beset at every turn by the enticements of Settembrini, Krowkowski, Hofrat Behrens, and even Claudia Chauchat and Mynheer Peeperkorn. But what Mann reacted to was the totality of his situation; thus the social conscience which he developed was consistent with the actual complexity of human nature. What Mann enlisted to serve was therefore not a political doctrine such as Marxism but a new conception of man in which political involvement is inseparable from cultural security.

What he called the New Humanism or the Third Humanism was both consistent and comprehensive. It did not flatter man by looking at him through rose-colored glasses. It was based on a hard-headed awareness of man's dark, demonic "natural" side as well as a reverence for his suprabiological spiritual worth. The new humanity would also be universal; "and it will have the artist's attitude; that is, it will recognize that the immense value and beauty of the human being lies precisely in the fact that he belongs to the two kingdoms of nature and spirit. It will realize that no romantic conflict or dualism is inherent in the fact but rather a fruitful and engaging combination of determinism and free choice, upon that it will base a love for humanity in which its pessimism and its optimism will cancel each other."

The New Humanism is at the core of everything Mann wrote from *The Magic Mountain* onward. But nowhere does it achieve a more comprehensive formulation than in the special dimensions of the image of Joseph, the hero of *Joseph and His Brothers*. It is Joseph, the seer and provider, with his fabulous fusion of poetic imagination and political skill, who is best equipped of all Mann's protagonists to confront and come to realistic terms with the problems of contemporary existence. No epic hero is without flaws, of course: there is Joseph's sometimes unmanageable egoism, and, among other things, there is (or was for a long time) also his extremely peculiar and, in truth, not altogether masculine involvement with flirting, of teasing others to the point of seduction while regarding his own chastity as sacred. But he is as well prepared as any other hero in modern fiction to function in the circumstances of the world described by André Malraux; furthermore, he is equipped (perhaps precisely by his egoism and compulsion to flirt with danger) to assume the responsibilities (or risks) of leadership in such a world.

It is easy enough to project Joseph forward into the revolutionary China of *Man's Fate* or into the beleaguered Spain of *Man's Hope*. But it is also, if anything, even easier to resurrect him as an immigrant to the contemporary United States (which on balance might well be an infinitely more complicated milieu than was Egypt during the time of the Pharaohs). Nor is it insignificant that Thomas Mann himself had become an immigrant to the United States when he wrote the episodes which define the Provider. But perhaps even more significant evidence of Joseph's contemporary immediacy is the altogether fascinating fact that the seemingly undauntable optimism which supports his flexibility no less than his tenacity of purpose makes him an excellent epic prototype for the U.S. Negro hero—who, like him, it should be remembered, was also sold into bondage.

Indeed, Afro-Americans will find that Joseph shares fundamental qualities in common with the epic hero of the blues tradition, that uniquely American context of antagonistic cooperation. Joseph goes beyond his failures in the very blues singing process of acknowledging them and admitting to himself how bad conditions are. Thus his heroic optimism is based on aspiration informed by the facts of life. It is also geared to his knowledge of strategy and his skill with such tools and weapons as happen to be available. These are the qualities which enable him to turn his misfortunes into natural benefits. At any rate, he proceeds as if each setback were really a recoil action for a greater leap forward, as if each downfall were a deliberately designed crouch for a higher elevation.

Perhaps Joseph's physical endowments are not as impressively athletic as those required for a U.S. Negro protagonist. But then the Negro hero should not be confused with the heavyweight champion of the world, either. As a matter of fact, Jack Johnson, the greatest of all heavyweight champions, fought with the agility of a middleweight. Mann makes it clear enough that the golden brown Joseph is neither too tall nor too short, but precisely the right height—which is as it should be. After all, no hero was ever as huge and as powerful as a dragon. Moreover, heroic achievements are a matter of super-natural skill, not extraordinary brawn. Indeed, it is entirely possible that heroes are tall, for instance, only in the imagination of those who need them—for in action, even the six-foot-six gladiator is a darling, beleaguered underling. In any case, the actual physical appearance of even the greatest of heroes, for all their charisma, is frequently so unimposingly average that special effort seems necessary in order to set them apart from the proverbial man in the street. It is as if the typical hero has to be borne on the shoulders of worshipful admirers, bedecked with special raiments, elevated to special platforms, and thence to thrones and ultimately to pedestals in order that he may look impressive enough to be capable of the miraculous feats of championship which he has in fact already accomplished. In all events his relatively unprepossessing physical stature only intensifies the hero's glamour and mystery, even as it humanizes and universalizes his appeal.

Nevertheless, Joseph, unlike the U.S. hero in general and the U.S. Negro hero in particular, does not exhibit any special physical dexterity and prowess along with his incomparable spiritual tenacity. Not that any hero, even Hercules, ever had as much physical strength as moral courage. Perhaps also, in spite of all his smooth talk and tantalizing ways, Joseph may strike most U.S. Blacks as being somewhat deficient in sensual gusto, if not sophistication. He is, alas, for all his good looks, not really a very extraordinary man among women. Indeed, not unlike the naïve Oedipus who compounds his troubles by making love to the wrong woman, Joseph, by attracting and then refusing the wrong one, is brought to the very brink of disaster, from which he escapes only because his errors always have a way of turning out to be blessings in disguise.

But even so, there is good reason to assume that given the necessity, Joseph, who is not only an irresistible sweet man and a first-rate stylist withal, but also a most apt desegregationist indeed, could put together the prerequisite combination of patent-leather finesse, rawhide flexibility and blue steel endurance to swing, tip, or stomp with uptown authenticity at the Savoy and in other situations as well. Nor should it be forgotten that Joseph's conduct is oriented to both choice and chance.

It is no more difficult to project the Joseph of Thomas Mann into the blues tradition than it could possibly have been to get Moses from the Old Testament into the spirituals—and, religious objectives aside, there is good reason to believe that it might be an even more rewarding undertaking. For while Negroes have been overlooking the special implications of Joseph's journey into Egypt, they have been overemphasizing the role of Moses as Messiah and grossly oversimplifying what the Exodus was really all about. Many have been teaching, preaching, singing, and signifying about Moses and the Promised Land for generations without ever making any practical or political application of the obvious fact that in U.S. terms, being half this, half that, he was a mulatto! Nor do they seem to have found anything significant in his role as lawgiver and utopian; and they seem completely oblivious to the confusion inherent in identifying with a nationalist who defines freedom and fulfillment in terms of leading his people out of the country of their actual birth and back across the sea to some exclusive territory.

Joseph, on the other hand, not only uses his inner resources and the means at hand to take advantage of the most unlikely opportunities to succeed in the circumstances in which he finds himself; he also makes himself indispensable to the welfare of the nation as a whole. Those who follow Moses are forever talking about going back home; but to Joseph, to whom being at home was as much a matter of the spirit as of real estate, anywhere he is can become the Land of Great Promise.

No one can deny to Moses, great emancipator that he was, the position as epic hero of anti-slavery movements. But neither should anyone overlook what Joseph, the riff-style improviser, did to slavery. He transcended it to such an extent that his previous "condition of servitude" became the sort of apocryphal cottonpatch-to-capital-city detail so typical of U.S. biography. Only a Horatio Alger could look at the elegantly tonsured and tailored Joseph at a function of state and believe that such a fine figure of a man was once not only a slave but a convict. As for Joseph himself, he never regarded himself as being anything other than a Prince of the Earth. He never, even in the deepest and foulest dungeons, thought of himself as an outcast, but rather, as Mann points out time and again, he saw himself as *a man set aside for a special purpose.*

The Joseph which Thomas Mann has created in *Joseph and His Brothers* represents the human being as artist and improviser. The emphasis which in the fiction of Ernest Hemingway is always placed on the skill and style of the hero is another way of making what is essentially the same literary statement. And what André Malraux declares to be the function of art indicates just how fundamental such a "statement" is. All art, he says in *The Voices of Silence* (as elsewhere), is a revolt against man's fate, against the limitations of human life itself. And the victory of each individual artist over his servitude implements the eternal victory of art over the human situation.

Not that Thomas Mann requires very much corroboration in such matters. *The Magic Mountain*, after all, is the story of the transformation of an engineer into a man who has begun to master the art of living! When Mann refers to the mundane Hans Castorp as life's delicate child or the problem child of nature, he is obviously associating and perhaps deliberately confusing Castorp's ordinary burgher sensitivity with the esthetic sensibility of an artist like Tonio Kroger. Man, he points out in *The Coming Victory of Democracy*, is not only a part of nature, he is also the means by which nature becomes aware of itself. Thus the erstwhile seemingly robust but now admittedly fragile Hans Castorp, taking stock of himself while recuperating in a sanitorium, personifies nature become conscious of itself, developing a conscience—and acquiring a sense of responsibility. Hence the obligations of heroism.

In *Order of the Day*, Mann refers to art as man's guide on the difficult path toward understanding himself. "Art is hope," he writes in the statement defining humanism, but which has no less to do with the story teller's preoccupation with the dynamics of heroism. "I do not assert that hope for the future of mankind rests upon her shoulders; rather that she is the expression of all human hope, the image and pattern of all happily balanced humanity."

THREE

The Blues and the Fable in the Flesh

ANDRÉ MALRAUX defines art as the means by which the raw
material of human experience becomes style. He contends
that stylization, whether abstract or representational, is the supreme objective of the creative process. He also maintains that
the artist derives not from nature itself but from other artists
and that the sense of life which any given artist expresses always involves an interaction with other works of art. "Never
do we find an epoch-making form built up without a struggle
with another form," he states and reiterates throughout *The
Voices of Silence*; "not one problem of the artist's vision but is
conditioned by the past." Nor does there seem as yet to be any
evidence from either archaeology or anthropology to refute
him. "Always," he writes in reference to existing examples of
prehistoric art such as the rock paintings of Rhodesia and the
cave paintings of Altamira and Lascaux, "however far we travel
back in time, we surmise other forms behind the forms which
captivate us." As for the modern folk or modern primitive art,
he points out that for all their apparent crudeness, innocence,
and assumed naturalness, such forms likewise follow conventions and traditions which it would be rash to ascribe to naïveté
alone. "The painters at our country fairs," he adds as a reminder, "know well what subjects are expected of them . . .
and what styles these call for."

Applied to the art of fiction, Malraux's description of the
dynamics of artistic creation suggests a practical point of departure which is both consistent with the history and geography of contemporary man and also commensurate with the
complexity of contemporary experience and esthetic sensibility.
Along with Malraux's conception of the museum without
walls, which may well have been derived from long existing
anthologies of world literature in the first place, this description
also provides a working context within which the contemporary
writer can come to practical terms with what is perhaps the most
fundamental issue underlying every problem of craftsmanship
involved in the actual process of literary composition: the

383

functional relevance of literary tradition to the immediate requirements of vernacular communication.

T. S. Eliot addressed himself to what he defined as the problem of tradition and the individual talent and concluded that it was necessary for the writer to live in what is not merely the present but the present moment of the past. Tradition, he held, as did Thomas Mann in his essay "Freud and the Future," is not something dead but rather that which is already living. In Eliot's sense as in Malraux's, tradition is thus as much a part of the writer's environment as anything else. "The historical sense," Eliot insisted, "compels a man to write not merely with his own generation in his bones but with a feeling that the whole of the literature of Europe from Homer and within it the whole of the literature of his own country has a simultaneous existence and composes a simultaneous order." The historical sense, which he goes on to describe as a sense of the timeless and the temporal together, is what makes a writer traditional, *but it is also what makes him* "most acutely conscious of his place in time, of his own contemporaneity."

The manner in which Eliot employed specific elements from medieval romance and ancient ritual along with fragments from literary works in *The Waste Land*, however, seems to have been as misleading to some as it has been instructive to others. Not unlike the many who were confused by James Joyce's use of ancient Greek mythology in *Ulysses*, there are those who ignore the actual style and texture of the poem and mistake as the total statement what is essentially only the point of departure. The revelation of a traditional mythological substructure of human existence is not the objective of Eliot's poem. Nor did Joyce write his novel on the assumption that the art of fiction was really a matter of pigeonholing contemporary characters and events in terms of prototypes in antiquity.

Ulysses is not a contemporary adaptation of the *Odyssey*, only an allusion to it—an arrangement, which is to say a contemporary orchestration based on the chordal structure and progression of the *Odyssey*. The creative process for Joyce, as for Eliot, was a matter of making the most of the inevitable interaction of tradition and the individual talent. He used his scholarly insights not to discover and certainly not to establish mythological parallels and equivalencies for Irish experience, but to enrich his poetic imagination. In *Ulysses* he created his own local mythological system, the "cosmic" framework of which is one day in Dublin. (Essentially the elements of classical myth in *Ulysses*, like those in *The Waste Land*, are used as historical puns—or perhaps one might even call them mnemonic devices.) What is really of most immediate significance about Molly Bloom, for instance, is not that she is the reincarnation (or modernization) of a figure or figures from classical mythology and primitive ritual (which she is of course), but that in her Joyce created a compelling image in a mythological romance of his own. Anna Livia Plurabelle in *Finnegans Wake* also echoes other voices from many other times, towns, and villages, but she herself is nothing if not a mythological figure of contemporary Ireland. She is James Joyce's Irish conception and creation of an Irish woman. She is his Irish image of all women, not simply his Irish repetition of other images in other stories. She is his complex and richly informed (but no less Irish for being universal) metaphor to represent the Irish female to end all females, his Irish womb of the world, as it were, the vernacular Irish female to end and begin again and again all males as well as females.

Joyce began (as Malraux claims all artists do) by imitating existing models, which, thanks to the printing press, represented a range as wide as all of the content in accessible libraries. Much has been made of the international essence of *A Portrait of the Artist as a Young Man*, *Ulysses*, and *Finnegans Wake*. But what the contemporary apprentice must also remember is that James Joyce, who has become for so many students of literature an archetype of the twentieth century literary cosmopolitan, always wrote out of a sensibility that became more and more sophisticated about the world at large only to become more and more Irish at the same time, even as it embraced the idea of timelessness in order to remain up to date.

Ernest Hemingway, who was no less cosmopolitan and no less sophisticated in the use which he made of tradition than were Eliot, Joyce, Malraux, or even Thomas Mann, was especially concerned about the misuse of it. The remarks he made to express his longstanding misgivings about being able to distinguish what one actually experiences from what one has been taught to respond to represent a fundamental and comprehensive protestation against the misapplication of traditional meanings. So was his reference to Thomas Wolfe's overflow of words. But on a number of occasions he also focused his attention on the problem of the writer's specific relationship to tradition as such. At one juncture in *Green Hills of Africa*, for instance, he mentions Poe as being a skillful writer, Melville as being good sometimes in spite of the rhetoric; and then he goes on to register a protest, the implications of which are temporal as well as geographical and environmental. "There are others," he points out, "who write like English colonials from an England of which they were never a part to a newer England that they were making very good men with the small, dried and excellent wisdom of Unitarians; men of letters; Quakers with a sense of humor."

He was referring to "Emerson, Hawthorne, Whittier and company. All our early classics who did not know that a new classic does not bear any resemblance to the classics that have preceded it. It can steal from anything that it is better than, anything that is not a classic, all classics do that . . . But it cannot derive from or resemble a previous classic. Also these men were gentlemen or wished to be. They were all very respectable. They did not use the words that people always have used in speech, the words that survive in language. Nor would you gather that they had bodies. They had minds, yes. Nice, dry, clean minds. . . ."

His own accent was unmistakably contemporary and unquestionably American. And yet *The Sun Also Rises*, for instance, can be read in the same timeless, international mythological-ritualistic frame of reference as *The Waste Land*. It is as accurate to refer to Jake Barnes as being a Fisher King as to say that he is an impotent expatriate. On the other hand, when he is placed in the mythological context which underlies *Ulysses*, Jake the war veteran takes on overtones of a marooned Odysseus—perhaps (but not necessarily) on the Isle of Circe. But in the end as in the beginning, just as *Ulysses* is a story about an Irishman in Dublin, so is *The Sun Also Rises* a story about an American in Paris (and Spain). So rich is the natural heritage of the writer today that such multilevels can be the resonance of a truly contemporary voice.

Essentially, questions about experimentation in the arts are also questions about the relevance of tradition. They are questions, that is to say, about the practical application of traditional elements to contemporary problem situations. Hence they are also questions about change and continuity. Indeed, they are specifically concerned with the requirements for continuation, which is to say endurance, which also is to say survival. Implicitly, experimentation is also an action taken to insure that nothing endures which is not workable; as such, far from being anti-traditional, as is often assumed, it actually serves the best interests of tradition, which, after all, is that which continues in the first place. The traditional element is precisely the one which has endured or survived from situation to situation from generation to generation. To refer to the blues idiom is to refer to an established mode, an existing context or frame of reference.

But then not only is tradition that which continues; it is also the medium by which and through which continuation occurs. It is, or so it seems in the arts at any rate, precisely that in terms of which the objectives of experimentation are defined, and against which experimental achievements are evaluated. Accordingly it is within the tradition of fiction that innovations in fiction evolve—and no matter how startling such innovations turn out to be, their effect is not to destroy fiction but to enhance and *extend* it. Perhaps a better word for experimentation as it actually functions in the arts is improvisation. In any case, it is for the writer, as for the musician in a jam session, that informal trial and error process by means of which tradition adapts itself to change, or renews itself through change. It is, that is to say, the means by which the true and tested in the traditional regenerates itself in the vernacular.

The more any art form changes, by whatever means and by whatever methods, motivations, or infusions, the more it should be able to fulfill its original function. The observations of Susanne K. Langer on the nature and purpose of art are hardly those of a reactionary. On the contrary, such books as *Philosophy in a New Key*, *Feeling and Form*, and *Problems of*

Art, like Malraux's *The Voices of Silence* and *The Metamorphosis of the Gods*, and Hemingway's *Death in the Afternoon* and *Green Hills of Africa*, not only provide a comprehensive justification for experimentation in the arts but also establish a solid point of departure for it.

"Each art," Susanne Langer writes in *Problems of Art*, in a passage which seems as applicable to fiction as to any other form, "begets a special dimension of experience that is a special kind of image of reality." She refers to this special dimension as "the primary illusion or primary apparition" and states that the arts are defined by their primary apparition and not by materials and techniques. "Painted sculpture is not a joint product of sculpture and painting at all, for what is created is sculpture, not a picture. Paint is used, but used for creating sculpture—not for painting. The fact that poetry involves sound, the normal material of music, is not what makes it comparable to music—where it is comparable."

As for obvious differences which do develop as a result of experimentation, they frequently represent extensions and refinements, but seldom do they represent fundamental changes. The difference between a simple footlog across a stream and that elaborately engineered structure of steel and concrete spanning the Hudson River does not alter the original function of a bridge at all. Perhaps (some American automobile designers notwithstanding) the original functions are more easily obscured in the arts than in engineering, but even so, sooner or later the writer will realize that even those novels which are written to show that there is no story to tell must nevertheless narrate *that* story both effectively and affectively.

New forms do evolve, of course, even as the novel may be an extension of a form which was once known as the *molpê* in Ancient Greece, and by other names elsewhere. But a novelist who creates poems or case histories is no longer a novelist. He has become a poet or a social scientist. A painter using materials and methods of photography is still a painter as long as what he is making is a painting. If what he produces is a photograph with elements of a painting, however, he has become a photographer. In its original military sense, the avant garde is an exploratory extension of the main body of troops. In the arts its advanced position has never been so much a matter of programming as of effect. It is the applicability of his technical achievement which establishes a writer as a forerunner, a path-finder, and a trailblazer, not his intentions alone, and certainly not the fact that he engages in experimentation as such. In point of fact, inasmuch as the very act of literary creation is always a matter of trial and error, literary composition is in it-self an experimental process. Writers are always trying to solve problems of rhetoric, form, style, and so on, through modifi-cations, innovations, and inventions. Experimentation is as in-dispensable to the development of the individual style of Flaubert and Henry James as to the overall or definitive style of a generation or of an epoch.

The objective of artistic experimentation, whether in the case of the individual or of an entire esthetic school or move-ment, is to develop a device with which to render the subtleties of contemporary sensibility. The maximum communication of these subtleties, however, is achieved only to the extent that rhetorical innovations become a part of the natural mode of expression of the time. The lasting results of avant-garde ex-perimentation always become inevitable-seeming parts of the grand style of the mainstream of discourse.

Perhaps every masterpiece represents the assimilation of the grand or epoch-making style (which should not be confused with grand manner or with high style). The grand style is, one might say, the comprehensive rhetorical strategy. It is, in other words, that combination of literary tactics and devices which best enables the writer to encompass or to capture the essential nature, the essential feeling of the experience of his time, place, and circumstances. It is that stylization of experience which actually comes to seem the least stylized. Maurice Grosser, the author of *The Painter's Eye*, makes an observation about the grand style in painting which is directly applicable to fiction. "These people, in Hogarth, in Reynolds, in Goya, in Copley are real," he writes. "And that is the Grand Style, for the Grand Style is no style at all. It is not a way of painting. It is only the painter's greatest subject. It is what every painter strives to paint. It is the painter's view of ultimate reality."

Whenever he was asked about the experimental aspects of his work, William Faulkner invariably answered that he was trying primarily to write about people, that he was simply trying to get the story told by one means or another. Nevertheless, *The Sound and the Fury*, *As I Lay Dying*, *Light in August*, *Absalom, Absalom!*, and *The Bear* belong among the most outstanding technical experiments in contemporary American fiction. Nor was Faulkner's experimentation as offhand as his remarks on the subject may suggest. Perhaps he did remain unconscious of much of the natural traditional influence of such writers as Balzac, Mark Twain, Melville, and possibly Henry James (whom, incidentally, he called a prig). But his awareness of the immediate functional implications of both content and technical innovations by such contemporaries as Sherwood Anderson, Joyce, Proust, and even Hemingway for his own work is unmistakable.

Nor, on balance, does he seem to have intended his remarks to be misleading; for there is much to indicate that he was not so much concerned about deprecating or disavowing his involvement with technical explorations as with keeping it in proper perspective. But perhaps his remarks were misleading in spite of all the obvious evidence in the works themselves. In any case, during the time when most of his best fiction was being published he was largely ignored by critics except for supercilious references to his southern subject matter and his compositional obscurity, both of which were regarded as Gothic, decadent, and even degenerate.

Ernest Hemingway, on the other hand (not unlike, say, Louis Armstrong in the world of music), was spotted and celebrated as a significant stylist by critics and writers alike at the very outset of his career. Indeed, the influence of certain aspects of Hemingway's technique is one of the most obvious characteristics of U.S. fiction since the nineteen twenties. Even as Armstrong's influence is evident in U.S. music from the same time forward, most contemporary readers seem to feel that description, dialogue, and narrative pace are most natural when rendered with Hemingway's functional directness. Fiction editors still celebrate the greatness of Herman Melville and Henry James, but they tend to scrutinize manuscripts through Hemingway's reading glasses, true to his influence even as the pop-ballad singers who seem most natural to contemporary American ears are likely to be those who derived (whether directly or indirectly) from Louis Armstrong.

Hemingway himself, however, was no more involved with avant-garde programs *per se* than was Faulkner. The young apprentice in *A Moveable Feast* was working out his own individual problems of craft, as was the student of bullfighting. "In writing for the newspaper," he recalled in *Death in the Afternoon*, "you told what happened and, with one trick or another, you communicated the emotion aided by the element of timeliness which gives a certain emotion to any account of something that has happened that day; but the real thing, the sequence of motion and fact which made the emotion and which would be valid in a year or ten years, or, with luck and if you stated it purely enough, always, was beyond me and I was working very hard to try to get it. . . ."

He was trying to work out his own individual problem, but his response to a *Time* magazine inquiry about the status of his personal influence in 1947 reveals his insight into the interrelationship of individual accomplishments, tradition, and continuity in one telegraphic sentence: "Hemingway influence," he replied seriously and quite objectively but not without levity, "is only a certain clarification of the language which is now in the public domain."

Nor did he mean simplification; precision, he meant, to be sure, but the clarification he was always working for was multi-dimensional. "If I could have made this enough of a book," he began in the epilogue to *Death in the Afternoon*, "it would have had everything in it." Perhaps the five Hemingway dimensions are as elusive as the figure in the carpet of Henry James, but the out-chorus rhetoric of *Death in the Afternoon* has qualities of fiction, poetry, documentation, and exposition, as well as painting and musical composition. Incidentally, he always listed painters among those from whom he learned how scenes are made, and he also included musicians among his literary forebears. Assuming, as he told George Plimpton, that what he had learned from them would be obvious, also obvious is the fact that he was trying to write fiction, not change its function.

When Faulkner was asked whether there was a conscious parallel between *As I Lay Dying* and *The Scarlet Letter*, his answer was still another revelation of the fact that his working knowledge of the dynamics of literary tradition and the comprehensive nature of the grand style was essentially the same as Hemingway's. "No," he said, "a writer don't have to consciously parallel because he robs and steals from everything he ever wrote or read or saw." He was simply writing a tour de force, and as every writer does, he took whatever he needed wherever he could find it, without any compunction and with no sense of violating any ethics or hurting anyone's feelings "because any writer feels that anyone after him is perfectly welcome to take any trick he has learned or any plot he has used. Of course we don't know just who Hawthorne took his from. Which he did—because there are so few plots to write about."

Faulkner made these remarks at the University of Virginia in 1957. Hemingway, it will be remembered, made his statement about writers stealing from other books (and the one about some writers being born only to help another writer write one sentence) in *Green Hills of Africa* in 1935. Both Hemingway and Faulkner were forever disclaiming any status as intellectuals or men of letters. Culture, Hemingway once declared, with as much insight as irreverence, was a good thing to have, like a 1/1000 map to maneuver on; Faulkner said it was all right, "but to me—I ain't interested in it." "Most writers are not literary men," he said, "they are craftsmen," and elsewhere he referred to writing his books as being "a matter of the carpenter trying to find the hammer or the axe that he thinks will do the best job."

The practical working point of all of this should be clear enough. Ernest Hemingway and William Faulkner, who on balance must be regarded as the most effective twentieth-century American avant-garde fiction writers to date, operated on essentially the same assumptions about the interreaction of tradition and the individual creative talent as did T. S. Eliot and Thomas Mann. Experimentation for them was not an effort to escape or reject the past but a confrontation of the present, or, as Eliot and Mann would have it, the present moment of the past. So far as Hemingway was concerned, all art was created by individuals. When the great individual artist arrives, he "uses everything that has been discovered or known about his art up to that point, being able to accept or reject in a time so short it seems that knowledge was born with him . . . and then the great artist goes beyond what has been done or known and makes something of his own." Even as Shakespeare once did in literature. Even as Duke Ellington has done in contemporary American music.

Indeed, the most valid aspiration as well as the most urgent necessity for any writer who truly takes the social, which is to say the ethical, function of fiction seriously is not to create something at least different if not new but rather to achieve something natural to himself and to his sense of life, namely a stylization adequate to the complexity of the experience of his time and place—and perhaps with the luck of past masters, something that is more than merely adequate. Thus does the writer make his unique and indispensable contribution to good conduct: not by creating a pop-image that illustrates what is only a "conventional" conception of a Revolutionary hero, but rather by projecting an image of man (and of human possibility) that is *intrinsically* revolutionary. Such an image is likely to be automatically at radical odds with the status quo.

All of which has more than a little to do with the literary implications of the dynamics (or natural history) of blues idiom statement *per se*: when André Malraux suggests that art should give man a sense of human grandeur, he expresses a point of view with which perhaps even the most gung-ho of activists would readily agree. But Malraux (himself a veritable prototype of the cause-oriented twentieth century writer) is also fully aware of what art not only involves but requires. "It is a revealing fact," he states in *The Voices of Silence*, "that when explaining how his vocation came to him, every great artist traces it back to the emotion he experienced at his contact with some specific work of art; a writer to the reading of a poem or novel (or perhaps a visit to the theatre); a musician to a concert he attended; a painter to a painting he once saw. Never do we hear of a man who, out of the blue, so to speak, feels a compulsion to express some scene or startling incident . . . What makes the artist is that in his youth he was more deeply moved by his visual experience of works of art than by that of the things they represent. . . ." In other words, the origin for art is likely to be art itself.

The primary subject matter of *The Voices of Silence* is painting and sculpture. But perhaps the observations which Malraux makes about what is in effect the natural history of the creative impulse may also be applied with equal force to musicians who work in the blues idiom. "Artists," Malraux goes on to say, "do not stem from their childhood, but from their conflict with the achievements of their predecessors; not from their own form-less world, but from the struggle with the form which others have imposed on life. In their youth, Michelangelo, El Greco and Rembrandt imitated; so did Raphael, Velázquez and Goya; Delacroix, Manet and Cézanne—the list is endless. Whenever we have records enabling us to trace the origins of a painter's, a sculptor's, any artist's vocation, we trace it not to a sudden uprush of emotion (suddenly given form) but to the vision, the passionate emotion, or the serenity of another artist."

Similarly, though few students of American culture seem aware of it, but as those who are truly interested in promoting "black consciousness" in literature should note, what makes a blues idiom musician is not the ability to express *raw* emotion with primitive directness, as is so often implied, but rather the mastery of elements of esthetics peculiar to U.S. Negro music. Blues musicians do not derive directly from the personal, so-cial, and political circumstances of their lives as black people in the United States. They derive most directly from styles of other musicians who play the blues and who were infinitely more interested in evoking or simulating raw emotion than in releasing it—and whose "*primitiveness*" is to be found not so much in the *directness* of their expression as in their pro-nounced emphasis on stylization. In art both agony and ecstasy are matters of stylization.

Currently popular social science conditioned interpretations notwithstanding, U.S. Negro singers, for example, are influ-enced far more directly and decisively by Bessie Smith and Louis Armstrong, among others, and by the sonorities of vari-ous downhome church rituals than by any actual personal experience of racial oppression, no matter how traumatic. In-deed, what is most characteristic of the black American life style is infinitely more closely related to an orientation to African-derived dance and work rhythms and to the rich vari-ety of music which Afro-Americans have heard in the United

States than to any collective reaction to the experiences of slavery and segregation as such.

The actual working procedures of such blues-oriented arrangers, composers, and conductors as those who provided the scores for the orchestras of Fletcher Henderson, Chick Webb, Earl Hines, Jimmie Lunceford, Count Basie, Lionel Hampton, and numerous others can hardly be explained by references to oppression or even economic exploitation. When viewed in the context of artistic creation, however, such procedures can be as immediately understood and as fully appreciated as those of the playmakers who supplied the scripts for the Elizabethan stage companies.

As a matter of fact, the Elizabethan playmaker suggests an historical frame of reference within which Duke Ellington, the most masterful of all blues idiom arranger-composers, becomes the embodiment of the contemporary artist at work. The Ellington orchestra is frequently booked for recitals in the great concert halls of the world, much the same as if it were a fifteen-piece innovation of the symphony orchestra—which in a sense it is. Nevertheless, by original design and by typical employment as well, Ellington's is still an itinerant song and dance band. Moreover, its repertory clearly reflects the fact that over the years most of its performances have been in night clubs, theaters, dance halls, and at popular music festivals. However, it is largely because of, not in spite of, such show business affiliations that the image Ellington the artist so closely resembles is that of the Elizabethan playmaker, whose productions, it must not be forgotten, also began as popular entertainment. Show business motivation underlies Ellington's construction of numbers for the special solo talents of, say, Cootie Williams, Johnny Hodges, and Ben Webster, no more nor less than it underlies Shakespeare's composition of soliloquies for the actor Burbage. This similarity is perhaps at least as important to an understanding of Ellington's esthetics as are existing psycho-political theories about black experience, by which is usually meant black misery.

But what is perhaps even more significant is that the arranger-composer, whose sense of structure and movement is in large measure derived from the small informal combo and the jam session, proceeds in terms of a tradition of improvisation which is fundamentally the same as that which Elizabethans inherited from the *commedia dell'arte*. And when, as often happens, the arranger-composer works from existing tunes as the typical Elizabethan playmaker often employed existing story lines (and as Greek dramatists made use of existing myths and legend), improvisation becomes in actuality the same process of stylization in terms of which Malraux defines all art.

When Ellington creates blues-extension concertos in which the solo instrument states, asserts, alleges, quests, requests, or only implies, while the trumpets in the background sometimes mock and sometimes concur as the "woodwinds" moan or groan in the agony and ecstasy of sensual ambivalence and the trombones chant concurrence or signify misgivings and even suspicions (which are as likely to be bawdy as plaintive) with the rhythm section attesting and affirming, he is quite obviously engaged in a process of transforming the raw experience of American Negroes into what Malraux calls style. He is also stylizing his sense of the actual texture of all human existence not only in the United States or even the contemporary world at large, but also in all places throughout the ages.

Such is the nature, as well as the scope, authority, and implications of art. And it should be just as obvious that Ellington, who is not only a genius but who after all is no less dedicated to music (and no less accomplished at it) than a Herman Melville, a Mark Twain, or even a Henry James was to fiction, is likewise no less involved with what T. S. Eliot referred to as the "objective correlative" or the "objective equivalent" to feeling. Also obvious is that he is concerned (as Susanne K. Langer in *Problems of Art* points out that all artists are concerned) with the *life of human feeling* (which is to say, how it feels to be human) beyond everything else.

But what should be, if anything, most immediately obvious of all is that for Duke Ellington himself and for the members of his orchestra, textures of human feeling exist in music in terms of arrangements and compositions which are always related to other arrangements and compositions. Accordingly, the performance of an Ellington composition is not nearly so dependent upon the personal feelings of his musicians as upon their attitude toward music and styles of other musicians. The performer's personal feelings do count for something, of course, but only insofar as he can relate them to his musical imagination and his musical technique. The feelings which incompetent arrangements and inept performances seem most likely to involve are confusion, annoyance, boredom and, mercifully, indifference.

Sooner or later those who are truly interested in the promotion of black consciousness or of a black dimension in American literature are likely to discover that "black esthetics," as the saying goes, is not as some agitprop rhetoricians seem to think, simply a matter of a group of spokesmen getting together and *deciding* and then prescribing how black experience is to be translated into poetry, drama, fiction and painting, but rather of *realizing what any raw material of any experience must undergo in order to become art.* How do you give esthetic articulation to the everyday facts of life? The problem of every writer is how to make his personal sense of experience part of the artistic tradition of mankind at large.

In other words, esthetic problems are not likely to require less esthetic insight and orientation simply because the subject matter at hand happens to be black experience. Certainly no artist can accept the suggestion that art is artless. Not even the most spontaneous-seeming folk expression is artless. No matter how crude some folk music, for example, might sound to the uninitiated, its very existence depends on a highly *conventionalized* form. Folk airs, ditties, tunes and ballads are labeled traditional precisely because they conform to well-established even if unwritten principles of composition and formal structure peculiar to a given genre or idiom which, after all, is an esthetic *system* in every essential or functional meaning of the phrase.

As for the currently popular extensions of the old downhome church-derived dance music which pop singers like James Brown, the late Otis Redding, Aretha Franklin, and Ray Charles, among others, express with such "soulful naturalness" not only is such music derived directly from other musicians (many of whom play in downhome style churches), it also undergoes countless very strictly controlled rehearsals. And it is constantly being revised and refined to suit the ear of the

arranger-conductor, a process which, by the way, is likely to
have as much to do with keeping it "roughed up," natural, and
"authentic" as with diluting it. Sooner or later those who
would serve their "commitment" through fiction must realize
that every masterpiece in literature, as in painting and music, is
testimony to the fact that at least as much esthetic technique is
required in order to "tell it like it is" as to tell it "like it ain't."
The truth may well be even more difficult to relate than it is to
find.

In any case, straining for political relevance is likely to produce the same deleterious effect on the creative process as
straining for commercial relevance. As most students of art
history will perhaps agree, chauvinism is often only another
form of the cheapest kind of commercialism.

Such is the nature of art that the only thing the creative
person is justified in straining for is his personal point of view,
and paradoxically this probably has much to do not with
straining but with learning to relax so as to discover how one
actually feels about things.

Of course, the fact that so many self-styled *engagé* writers
are so impatient to score political points is quite understandable. But the danger is that such well-intentioned impatience
may cause writers to neglect precisely those elements of their
chosen métier that would enable them to provide the most
effective esthetic basis for political statement.

There is, in other words, good reason to assume that whatever his social intentions, the writer is likely to achieve his best
(and most useful) work when his mastery of his craft is such
that he is able to play with his story, even as the musician plays
a score, even as actors play a script, even as athletes play a
game.

In general, contemporary American writers seem to regard the
epic with misgivings as strong as those which Ernest Hemingway expressed in *Death in the Afternoon* when he referred to it
as something which bad writers were in love with. Perhaps
some contemporary apprehension is a reaction to a "false epic
quality" in books such as some of those by John Dos Passos
and Thomas Wolfe. Perhaps some is related to those grandiose
movie productions, each with a super-colossal cast of thou-

sands, which are also called epics by the writers of Hollywood promotion copy. But perhaps there are also those who have come to realize, as Hemingway no doubt did, that the epic is not nearly so much a matter of intention, deliberation, and design as of comprehensive literary achievement—that stories which have become national epics, like those which have become academic classics, have done so by virtue of the nature of the response they have generated.

In any case, there is not very much evidence in contemporary fiction of any widespread preoccupation with what used to be called The Great American Novel. What the overwhelming majority of contemporary U.S. writers seem to be primarily concerned with instead, however, is The Image of the Individual. The list of American stories about the condition of the individual in the modern world is endless. Furthermore, even those writers who work in terms of the Documentary Image are primarily engaged in bringing the Individual into focus. Nobody expresses more concern about the problems of individual welfare than do writers who are oriented to the social sciences; and of course all political agitation and propaganda in the United States, that of Communists and Socialists no less than of the advocates of free enterprise, begin and end in the name of individual freedom and personal fulfillment.

But all the epic ever required was one individual in the first place. It was never contingent upon wide-screen panoramas, multitudes, or even large-scale actions. Only its implications need be comprehensive—and perhaps even they need less basis than do statistical projections. Moreover, every hero in every story is nothing if not a symbolic individual, and as such he is the Representative Man in the statistical as well as the ritualistic sense. Indeed, Kenneth Burke has suggested that the word *symbolic* may be equated with the word *statistical*! Nor can the statistician deny that his norms are intended to represent the typical.

The storybook hero, of course, is that projection or extension of the typical individual which functions, at least to some degree, as the archetypal. Indeed, no matter what else the writer may have consciously designed him to be, every storybook hero is likely to be not only archetypal but also charismatic. He is, that is to say, the writer's (local) personification of the hope, such as it is, of mankind. He is in the statistical sense a formulation of that which is a possibility and a probability. He is thus perhaps also a prediction and even a promise, and as such he may be a warning as well as an inspiration. But perhaps an ultimate function is also to make the impossible seem not only possible but imminently (which is to say presently and locally) probable.

Such at any rate is a function of charisma, and such is the basis of the hero's social usefulness. He is man's hope (as the writer finds it to be) of glory, salvation, deliverance, fulfillment, continuity, survival, or even sanity. There is no such thing as a negative hero. Nor can any storybook protagonist be a non-hero. He may be inadequate to his mission, of course, but even so he represents mankind. Not even the meek protagonist in "The Secret Life of Walter Mitty" is a nonhero. His public life is a caricature of suburban conventionality, but his secret life, which represents the most heroic intentions in the world, is the epitome of swashbuckling charisma. Nor, for all their ordinariness, are the actions and achievements of Leopold Bloom in *Ulysses* of a lower order of basic human significance than those of his Homeric prototype.

Nor is there any such thing in literature as a simple story about one individual in one time, place, and circumstance. All stories are examples of some essential aspect of human experience in general, and each is recounted precisely because what it implies has general implications. The unmistakable implication of the traditional narrative expression *Once upon a time . . .* is: "time after time in place after place such and such came to pass." The storyteller fabricates, composes, generalizes, and (if only by implication) moralizes. Human existence, he postulates, is thus and so; for example: time after time there was (and is) a man who, whose circumstances were (and are) such and such, and he did (and does) this and that, and the outcome was and is likely to be as follows. All of which goes to show what human existence is really like. Therefore, human conduct should be like this and not like that. This is good. That is bad. Do this. Avoid that.

Few things are more obvious than the fact that a novel like *Native Son*, for example, was never intended to be read as the simple case history of one atypical U.S. Negro involved in a series of unusual events which relate only to himself. Nor is *The Adventures of Augie March* or *Herzog* the case of one U.S. Jew. Nor is *All the King's Men* that of one or even two white Southerners. *Native Son* is, for all its naturalistic detail, a generalization about Black Americans' behavior as a whole, and it is based on another generalization or assumption about the nature of human nature as a whole: People who are forced to live in subhuman conditions develop subhuman traits; they react subhumanly and become bad people through no fault of their own.

That many do is cause enough for alarm, of course, but the generalization is fallacious and misleading nonetheless. *Most do not!* Many by one means or another maintain a level of conduct which is quite as normal as that of people in normal circumstances—and so achieve another glory for humanity. Moreover, not only do others develop above-normal attributes, but also much goes to show that the number of people they benefit exceeds to an overwhelming extent the number of those who are damaged or destroyed by the others who are reduced to barbarism and diabolical malevolence. One hundred poverty-ridden, oppression-maddened murderers subsisting in the slums of Chicago are certainly more than enough justification for the most urgent rehabilitation measures. But in point of actual fact one hundred slum-dwelling criminals do not affect as many people as does one single slum-dwelling shoe-shine boy who becomes a doctor, lawyer, preacher, teacher, or even a big league athlete!

The most fundamental as well as the most obvious shortcoming of Bigger Thomas as a symbolic individual U.S. Negro in *Native Son* is that he is an exaggerated oversimplification and is thus an inaccurate statistical projection of both the complexity as well as the potential of Negro life in the United States. He is not even a reliable reflection of the norms of *abnormal* U.S. Negro behavior. His story is not a sufficiently representative anecdote about either Black Americans in particular or about human nature and conduct in general. It is instead—for all the literary aspirations which Richard Wright protests from time to time in "How 'Bigger' Was Born"—mostly only a very special kind of political anecdote. It is an atrocity story, and Wright reveals as much when he relates that he designed the climax to register the "moral horror of Negro life in the United States." Wright also relates that he rejected the emotional response which his first book, *Uncle Tom's Children*, evoked from "bankers' daughters," and that he was determined to make *Native Son* "so hard and deep" that people would have to face it "without the consolation of tears," a statement which suggests (despite the validity of the intention underlying it) that his own commitment to political action may have misled him to underestimate the significance of catharsis, in spite of the emphasis which he placed on the tragic climax.

In any case, *Native Son* is not a tragedy. It is a social science–oriented melodrama with an unhappy ending. In other words, its plot complications do not represent the inscrutable "Olympian" contradictions and humiliations of human existence itself. They reflect only the man-made restrictions of an oppressive political system. They do not adequately symbolize the eternal condition of man. They simply document a very special condition of society and, what is more, they are predicated on the assumption that such conditions can be ameliorated. Such is the obvious moral of every melodrama; and of course the most insistent if not the only message of revolutionary political and social propaganda is that the dragon must be slain and the curse exorcised so that man can live happily ever afterwards. The moral of tragedy, however, like that of comedy and farce, is that the essential condition of man cannot be ameliorated, but it can be transcended, that struggle is precisely that which gives meaning to movement, that it is in the struggle that one finds oneself.

Thus Bigger Thomas is not a tragic hero but rather only a quasi-protagonist who is incapable of performing any of the traditional feats of the melodramatic hero. He does not escape from the dungeon, nor does he rescue the princess and live happily ever afterwards; and instead of removing the menace of the dragon, he himself becomes a villain. He becomes a *natural* product of his environment, only to be destroyed as an "enemy" of society. Such is the extent of Richard Wright's irony, and such is the extent of Bigger Thomas "as a meaningful and prophetic symbol."

But even so, the very title of *Native Son* implies that the story of Bigger Thomas is the representative anecdote about an archetypal Black American. This, of course, is only another way of saying that Richard Wright was no less engaged in an effort to produce a national epic than were the bards, scops, minstrels, gleemen, and ballad-makers who created, danced, and chanted *The Iliad*, *The Odyssey*, the *Chanson de Roland*, the *Nibelungenlied*, *Beowulf*, and so on. Nor do the esthetic aspirations behind the anecdotes of Homer seem to have been more epical than those behind the song and dance ceremonies of Hopi, Zuni, and Watusi tribesmen. What is created, expressed, performed, played, imitated, reproduced, reenacted, recounted, reflected, and related in each instance is an anecdote which is assumed to represent the essential nature of existence among a given folk in a given community, communion of faith, tradition, or nation; hence they are national epics.

Perhaps such narrative categories as tragedy, comedy, melodrama, and farce may be regarded as specific ritual-statements within the larger ritualistic framework of the epic. In fact, epic, in its original sense, was only another word for narration or story-telling: in this sense, any step or statement that the aboriginal song and dance man (or maker of *molpés*) made beyond the simplest, or most impulsive lyric gesture, as it were, was an epical reenactment. It was, that is to say, an anecdotal imitation of an action; and of course as such it required protagonists and antagonists. These became heroes and obstacles, and from them came heroic action. Tragedies, comedies, melodramas, and farces thus represent special kinds of anecdotes about specific categories of heroic action.

The tragic hero is a representative individual of good intentions or high aspirations who fails because of some fatal flaw within himself and because of the inscrutable ways of nature. The comic hero succeeds to the extent that he learns to live by trial and error. The melodramatic hero proceeds on the assumption that there is a magic key to success! In the narrative category of farce, as construed here, however, the hero survives and succeeds only insofar as he is nimble enough to cope with the slapstick absurdities inherent in the slapdash nature of things.

The slapstick protagonist, like the jam-session soloist, is either nimble or nothing. Moreover, of all the storybook heroes

he is perhaps the most comprehensive as well as the most sophisticated archetype of the "successful" individual. Indeed, in
a very fundamental sense he seems to begin where all other
storybook heroes end. In fact, it is as if he were born with a
functional awareness of that which it takes the others a lifetime
to learn. His aspirations and intentions are comparable to
theirs in every way, but his conception of human nature is significantly different. His definition of integrity, for instance, is
much more complicated than that of the tragic hero. Thus he
is less vulnerable to the fatal flaw of pride. Somewhat like Jacob
in Thomas Mann's *Joseph and His Brothers*, he values his mission, responsibilities, blessings, or long-range aspirations so
highly that he can withstand any embarrassment and can even
regard humiliation as a passing episode (which incidentally
gives him useful information about his adversary's pride).

Unlike the comic protagonist whose adventures are essentially
a series of initiation rituals which will enable him to live with the
fact that life is one great mystery, the slapstick hero seems to
have been oriented to the ambiguities of human experience
from the outset. Nor by his standards is the technical skill of the
melodramatic hero much more than the beginning of the all-
purpose, even if sometimes Chaplinesque, flexibility required by
the never-ending ramifications of cosmic slapdash situations.

The adventures of the contemporary detective-story hero
are often as melodramatic (or as full of theatrical suspense) as
those of the dragon slayers in the old medieval European romances. Nor is this all. The detective, not unlike the noble
knight of the quest tradition, is also a man seeking or pursuing
something. Furthermore, his success in what he has undertaken to do will result in improved living conditions, an effect
which is directly related to the elimination of some menacing
element from the landscape. Also, the detective is often depicted as something of a gallant or even as a philanderer, as
were some of his medieval forerunners.

But even so, there are differences which are perhaps significant enough to permit a composite of such detectives as Sam
Spade, Philip Marlowe, and Dick Tracy to be defined in terms
of the context of farce and the blues idiom rather than in that
of melodrama, or more specifically, social science fiction fiction
—which is to say Marx-Freud heroism. To begin with, the

detective-story hero is in quest not of the Holy Grail and salvation, but of evidence concerning the source or sources of "evil." Indeed, for all the fisticuffs and shoot-em-ups so frequently involved, the detective-story hero's quest may perhaps be more appropriately described as a research mission. As a matter of fact, the detective, as his very name suggests, is in actuality a research technician above all else. Unlike the social science fiction fiction research hero, however, who is very likely to be a Marxian-Freudian deliverer discovering or inventing some all-purpose device or magic cure, the detective is mostly concerned with clues bearing on the nature and cause of specific troubles. He regards technological devices as useful gadgets, but he is not so naïve as to expect human nature to be made any less human by them.

The obvious fact is that the detective functions in terms of a conception of science and of what scientific method and insight can and cannot accomplish that is more sophisticated than that of the Marx-Freud Knight-Errant. He employs scientific procedure with the consummate expertise of, say, the most advanced physicists. But behold, he also follows tips, plays hunches, buys scraps of data from informers or stool pigeons; and he eavesdrops as a matter of course. He is, in other words, a researcher whose openmindedness is closely geared to precisely the sort of riff-style improvisation that typifies the blues idiom sensibility.

And finally, when the contemporary detective achieves his stated objective, he has done only that, as it were. It is not assumed that his successful action has rid the environment of any such all-powerful dragons or curses as were drying up all streams and turning the whole countryside into a wasteland. He has exposed one or maybe several sources of social misfortune. But there is always another and another no less urgent assignment awaiting his return to the office. In the detective story the hero seldom gets but the briefest respite between clients and cases. He is forever being called away from his hobby, a vacation, the racetrack, or the arms of some marvelously intriguing woman because the times are out of joint once again.

In still other words, then, the detective-story hero may also be classified as a species of blues idiom hero, a *nada*-confrontation hero, which is also to say, a slapstick hero, not only because of the nature of his quest and certain characteristics of his sensibility, but also because his behavior is so compatible with his circumstances, which are nothing if not slapdash jam-session situation or predicament in the first place.

As much as has been made of the literary implications of existentialism, little if any attention seems to have been given to the comprehensive significance of farce and the slapstick hero. But then perhaps the so-called nonhero of recent avant-garde fiction (or is it avant-garde commentary?) represents an effort to describe a protagonist for cosmic slapstick situations. If so, the results leave much to be desired as an archetypal image of the contemporary individual in the United States. The so-called nonhero, after all, is not only unable to achieve any functional equilibrium in terms of the blues tradition of antagonistic cooperation; he is, alas, only a sad sack of a man for whom all situations are overwhelming. Thus where the blues-oriented slapstick or jam-session hero is ever alert and agile, as only befits one whom U.S. transportation and communication facilities have made heir to all times and places, the so-called nonhero is either a benumbed victim of circumstances or an anxious alien. (Even where he occupies the official seat of all but limitless power, he is likely to proceed as if he were an innocent stranger who has somehow or other been unjustly condemned, completely forgetting, as the blues-oriented hero would not, that guilt is inherent in man's humanity and that heroes often increase their guilt in the very process of performing good deeds!)

And yet the dynamics of farce and cosmic slapstick heroism seem to underlie much if not most of the literature of Europe and America. The gods on Mount Olympus, for example, to whom thunderbolt slinging and the manipulation of storm winds and tidal waves were no more serious than vaudevillian pie throwing, obviously regarded human existence as a farce. To them, according to the writers who depicted them, the confusions and insecurities of the ancient Greek mortals were all too often only a matter of capricious concern at best. It was not for nothing that the wily Odysseus was a picaresque hero whose nimbleness was his fortune. Nor has his survival as an archetype been inconsistent with the fundamental European conception of human actuality.

But perhaps even more curious is the fact that most contemporary U.S. intellectuals have made next to nothing of the inevitable connection between existential absurdity and the concept of antagonistic cooperation. All the same, there is no narrative tradition which is more fundamental to European and American literature. Nor is any conception of human endeavor more inherently ludicrous. It is sheer nonsense to insist that obstacles are really opportunities and that chaos is constructive! Nevertheless, most stories are irrefutable evidence that such is precisely the urgent secret which most of the great masters of fiction have always been trying to reveal.

No less obvious are the images of the world as farce in the work of such masters of contemporary fiction as André Malraux, Thomas Mann, and Ernest Hemingway. The human condition as described by Malraux is utterly absurd. For the Malraux protagonist, however, it is as if such absurdities as chaos, nature-in-the-raw, fate, and the inscrutable were simply other terms for dragon, which of course is only a romantic synonym for *requirement for heroism*. Indeed, the fiction of Malraux, far from being non-heroic, represents the world of the composite epic hero. Essentially all of Malraux's stories are anecdotes about contemporary men who are involved with primordial issues. Such, according to *The Voices of Silence*, is man's fate, but perhaps that which defines man's fate also suggests man's hope.

When in *Attitudes Toward History*, Kenneth Burke speaking of what he calls poetic categories classifies the epic (as well as the tragic and comic) in terms of a frame of acceptance (as opposed to such frames of rejection as plaints, elegies, satires, etc.) he is not talking about accepting one's sorry lot in some god-awful socio-political structure or of making one's peace with the devil. What Burke describes as a fundamental function of the epic as a poetic category can also be applied to farce as defined here, and also to the blues idiom. Indeed the blues statement is nothing if not an experience-confrontation device that enables people to begin by accepting the difficult, disappointing, chaotic, absurd, which is to say the farcical or existential facts of life. Moreover, even as it does so it also prepares or disposes people to accept the necessity for struggle.

The Joseph story of Thomas Mann is a definitive representation of the world as farce (and of man as quick-witted, nimble-footed dreamer in action). There is, to begin with, the all-inclusive absurdity inherent in the relativity of time, which is at once the container of consciousness and that which consciousness contains, the all and the nothingness of past-present-future am–isness. Then there is Jacob the hoaxer, son of Isaac; Jacob who hoaxes Esau—to get that which was already his by birthright—only to be hoaxed by Laban, by Joseph, and by The Brothers (at the time of Joseph's disappearance). Jacob's dearest bliss, like his deepest despair, is the response to a hoax.

There is also Joseph himself, whose completely fantastic career, as Thomas Mann recounts it, is one long chronicle of metaphysical dreams which become political schemes. But after all, Joseph, whose misfortune—for much of which he is personally responsible—is outrageously interwoven with his good luck, is only an extension and elaboration of the preposterous but altogether fascinating notion that Jacob was as much concerned with creating God as with serving Him. In Joseph as in Jacob, both past masters of the lunar syntax of artful fabrication, Mann has embodied yet another prototype of the contemporary writer as one whose special insight into the mysterious interrelationship of illusion and reality is as much a burden as it is a blessing.

Nothing is more curious, more challenging, or, upon reflection, more platitudinous than the assumption of Jacob and of Joseph that experience is for the most part what you are able to make it. Nor is any notion more implicitly existential or fundamental to the cosmos of Hemingway, all of the values of which were conceived (made-up, not described) in full, clear, well-lighted cognizance of the innate absurdity of all-enveloping *nada*. No hero in contemporary fiction is more acutely aware of the vanity of human wishes and endeavors than is Frederic Henry in *A Farewell to Arms*; and certainly no one, not even K, the completely lost and confused land surveyor (!) in Kafka's *The Castle*, knows better than Jake Barnes in *The Sun Also Rises* that deadpan slapstick is slapstick nonetheless. But then, as so much of his fiction suggests, Ernest Hemingway, whose response mechanisms were as sensitive to the textures of existence in the United States as to those of the contemporary world at large, was essentially a maker of blues ballad extensions.

So much is obvious if only by inference, and in addition much goes to show that the blues tradition itself is, among other things, an extension of the old American frontier tradition (which, incidentally, was always as applicable to the city and the plantation as to the wilderness, the mountains, and the plains). There is, for instance, the same seemingly inherent emphasis on rugged individual endurance. There is also the candid acknowledgment and sober acceptance of adversity as an inescapable condition of human existence—and perhaps in consequence an affirmative disposition toward all obstacles, whether urban or rural, whether political or metaphysical. In all events, the slapstick situation is the natural habitat of the blues-oriented hero—who qualifies as a frontiersman in the final analysis if only because he is a man who expects the best but is always prepared, at least emotionally when not otherwise, for the worst.

But perhaps above all else the blues-oriented hero image represents the American embodiment of the man whose concept of being able to live happily ever afterwards is most consistent with the moral of all dragon-encounters: *Improvisation is the ultimate human* (i.e., *heroic*) *endowment.* It is, indeed; and even as flexibility or the ability to swing (or to perform with grace under pressure) is the key to that unique competence which generates the self-reliance and thus the charisma of the hero, and even as infinite alertness-become-dexterity is the functional source of the magic of all master craftsmen, so may skill in the art of improvisation be that which both will enable contemporary man to be at home with his sometimes tolerable but never quite certain condition of *not* being at home in the world and will also dispose him to regard his obstacles and frustrations as well as his achievements in terms of adventure and romance.

STOMPING THE BLUES

For Mozelle and Michele

CONTENTS

ONE

The Blues as Such

---

*S*OMETIMES *you forget all about them in spite of yourself, but all too often the very first thing you realize when you wake up is that they are there again, settling in like bad weather, hovering like plague-bearing insects, swarming precisely as if they were indeed blue demons dispatched on their mission of harassment by none other than the Chief Red Devil of all devils himself; and yet perhaps as often as not it is also as if they squat obscene and vulturelike, waiting and watching you and preening themselves at the same time, their long rubbery necks writhing as if floating.*

Not that they are ever actually seen. They are always said to be blue, even as common-variety ghosts are always said to be at least somewhat gray. But being absolutely insubstantial, they are in fact completely invisible for all that everybody seems to have the distinct impression that they are always very small and not only plural but so numerous as to be numberless.

Still even as they are represented as teeming, swarming, and writhing nobody ever describes how they actually look. Because they have no image. Thus they do not appear and disappear. They are there because they have already come, and they linger somewhat as if clinging with tentacles, and they go, mostly when driven. But never soon enough. Nor do they ever seem to go far enough away even so. Once they have been there they only shift from the foreground to the background, and maybe you forget about them for the time being, but only for the time being.

All anybody ever presumes to describe with any precision is how you are likely to feel when they are present. You become afflicted as if infected by some miasma-generating microbe. You feel downhearted and uncertain. You are woebegone and anxiety-ridden. So much so that you would think that their characteristic coloration would be something suggesting the grayness of low-hanging clouds rather than blue. But in truth nobody ever seems to give that matter any thought at all, and there is even less concern about which specific shade of blue is involved. At the same time, however, nobody ever confuses anything about their behavior with the silky blueness of high and cloudless skies either.

415

They are also absolutely noiseless at all times. Their movements make no sound whatsoever. And they are evidently voiceless. They are said to speak, but only in the silent language of spirits. So even when they are quoted as if verbatim, you know the speaker is paraphrasing, because the accent and tone and even the volume and timbre are always very obvious stylizations of a voice all too obviously his own. Moreover, no matter how concrete the references, you already know very well that the statement is meant only to be taken as allegorical. (Item: When Jimmy Rushing sings, "Good morning, blues. Blues how do you do? Blues say, 'I feel all right but I come to worry you,'" the reply is given as if literal but not only is the voice still Rushing's, there is also no confusion at all when the singular I is used instead of the plural we.)

Nor do they ever seem to shock and terrify as some specters sometimes do (as often by simply vanishing and reappearing and vanishing into thin air again as by popping into uncertain view from nowhere in the first place). You know they are there only because you feel their presence in the atmosphere once more as you did the time before and the time before that; because everything, which is to say time itself, has somehow become heavy with vague but dire and disconcerting forebodings of impending frustration leading perhaps to ultimate doom. So sometimes at first it is as if you yourself have been draped with a leaden invisible net. Then you realize that you don't feel so good anymore, not because all at once you have been stricken but because a dull and unspecific ache is beginning to throb. Then sometimes you feel yourself becoming rueful, or glum, or sometimes either sullen, mean, and downright evil on the one hand or weak in the stomach and knees on the other.

Sometimes it is as if they themselves actually generate and inflict misery upon their victims much the same as pathogenic bacteria cause infection. But not always. Perhaps most often it is as if their primary purpose is to becloud your outlook by foreshadowing misfortune, and there are also times when they seem to come along with whatever the trouble is, or to issue from it not unlike the side effects that are really only the symptoms of far more serious physical ailments.

Also, as is likewise the case with many physical afflictions, sometimes you already know the cause as well as you know the symptoms. Because all too often they are back again for exactly the same reason that they came to be there the times before. Not al-

ways, to be sure. But often enough for the consideration to be automatic. Indeed it may well be that the element of déjà vu *is sometimes the source of as much anguish and hopelessness as the actual causal incident, if not more. Because it almost inevitably suggests (especially to those who have not yet come to realize that even in the best of times the blues are only at bay and are thus always somewhere in the not-too-distant background) that the mishap of the moment is but the latest episode in a string of misfortunes that are so persistent as to amount to a curse, and maybe even an ancestral curse at that.*

But no matter how they come to be there again, the main thing about them is all the botheration they bring, and your most immediate concern is how to dislodge them before the botheration degenerates into utter hopelessness. So the very first problem that it all adds up to is as specific as is the ghostlike vagueness of their very existence (which not everybody accepts as such anyway). What it requires is the primordial and ever persistent effort to purify the environment once more.

As in Oedipus Rex, *for instance, which begins with a chorus of suppliants lamenting a curse that hangs over the city-state of Thebes and beseeching the hero/king to seek out and dispatch the menace and restore good times. As in the Wasteland episode in the medieval romance of the Quest in which the knight-errant comes into a region whose inhabitants are suffering under a blight because their ruler, known as the Fisher-King, is apparently bewitched and his impotence extends not only to the housewives but also to the cattle, the fields, and even the streams. As in Shakespeare's* Hamlet, *in which the young prince is charged by the ghost of his late father to rid the kingdom of Denmark of the evil forces that dominate it.*

Also always absolutely inseparable from all such predicaments and requirements is the most fundamental of all existential imperatives: affirmation, which is to say, reaffirmation and continuity in the face of adversity. Indeed, what with the blues (whether known by that or any other name) always somewhere either in the foreground or the background, reaffirmation is precisely the contingency upon which the very survival of man as human being, however normally unsatisfied and abnormally wretched, is predicated.

No wonder Hamlet came to debate with himself whether to be or not to be. Nor was it, or is it, a question of judging whether life is or is not worth living. Not in the academic sense of Albert Camus's concern with the intrinsic absurdity of existence per se. Hamlet's was whether things are worth all the trouble and struggle. Which is also what the question is when you wake up with the blues there again, not only all around your bed but also inside your head as well, as if trying to make you wish that you were dead or had never been born.

The Blues Face to Face

SOMETIMES exposure through forthright acknowledgment of their unwelcome presence is enough to purge the immediate atmosphere, and no further confrontation is necessary. At such times they seem to vanish very much the way ghosts are said to do at the slightest indication that for all their notorious invisibility they have been discovered. There are times as a matter of fact when all it seems to take is the pronunciation (or mispronunciation) of their name with the proper overtones. Quite often not only will a few well-chosen epithets and outrageous hyperboles do the trick, but even a firmly pointed, sternly aimed finger.

Sometimes, since it is assumed that to know a name is also to be onto the game, the merest threat of revealing their diabolical identities and intentions through full-scale description is even more effective. Nor is bold and blatant misdefinition any less. Moreover when descriptions and definitions involve numbers of any kind, nothing less than instant terror is the most likely response, even when the numbers are patently phony (perhaps because the inevitable effect of enumeration and measurement is to reduce the infinity of the invisible to the finite and hence to modality, which after all is not only discernible but also controllable, and thus to mortality!).

Another form of acknowledgment and exposure is imitation, which includes mockery as well as mimickry. Because imitation, it should not be forgotten, whether with sound or by movement, is representation, which is to say reenactment, which of its very nature is obviously also the most graphic description and thus also the most specific definition. Which is bad enough. But perhaps far worse is casual mimickry, which even when it is relatively exact is an act of defiance to say the least. As for deliberately distorted mimickry, not only is it outright misrepresentation (and thus naked misidentification and misdefinition), but it is also undisguised defiance become downright mockery expressing contempt and even disdain.

Where there is bare-faced mockery the depth of the resistance goes without saying. And the same holds true in the case of malediction, or bad-mouthing, which in addition to loud-mouthing or damnation by diatribe and vilification also includes insinuation and scandalous innuendo. The main thing, whatever the form, is resistance if not hostility. Because the whole point is not to give in and let them get you down. Nor is a flamboyant display of militant determination necessarily more effective than is cool resolution. Sometimes a carefully controlled frown or even the faintest of supercilious smiles will work as much havoc as a scream or a shout.

Nor does an entirely phony show or gesture of belligerent opposition seem to carry any less impact than the real thing. It is in fact as if the difference were not even discernible. But when you come down to fundamentals, it is precisely the spirit and not the concrete substance which counts in such confrontations, for the spirit, after all, is not only what is threatened but is also the very part of you that is assumed to be most vulnerable. For what is ultimately at stake is morale, which is to say the will to persevere, the disposition to persist and perhaps prevail; and what must be avoided by all means is a failure of nerve.

There are also other counteragents. There is voodooism, for instance. Many people seem to take it completely for granted that most if not all of their troubles have been brought on by sorcery of one kind or another. Such people regard the spell of the blues as a magical curse or fix instigated by enemy conjuration. Thus even if such people describe themselves as being haunted by blue demons they think of them as coming not from the Devil or even from some natural misfortune but from some specific potion, gris-gris, jomo, charm, or talisman, which can be counteracted only with the aid of a voodoo queen or madam (or somewhat less often, a voodoo king, doctor, witchdoctor, or snakedoctor) whose powers of conjuration are superior.

Most people, however, seem to feel that you might as well try to deal directly with the blues in the first place as become ensnarled in the endless network of superstition and intimidation upon which voodooism is predicated. To them the voodoo madam and the snakedoctor are if anything even more troublesome than the blues as such. Furthermore, what is to stop the voodoo madam/doctor from replacing the existing fix with one of his or her own? Not that most people are as free of voodoo-derived, or in any case voodoolike, fetishism as they perhaps like to think, as you have only to look at all the good-luck charms and signs around you everywhere every day to realize.

Whiskey, gin, brandy, vodka, wines, and other alcoholic beverages and concoctions are also traditional antidotes, or in any case personal fortifications, against the pernicious effects of the blues. And so are narcotics. But while for many people the stimulation of liquor and/or drugs is often sufficient to get them going or sometimes even to help them through many very difficult situations, the problem for countless others is not only that such stimulation is not enough but when it subsides you are likely to find the same old blues still very much there and indeed nagging at you worse than ever, not to mention how they thrive and multiply on the nourishment of your hangover. Moreover, perhaps the most obvious of all chronic blues casualties are those who are driven to alcoholism or drug addiction—which is to say, into the vicious circle of intoxication and depression.

But of all the age-old ways of dispelling the ominous atmosphere that comes along with the blues, the one most people seem to have found to be most consistently effective all told also turns out to be essentially compatible with a great majority of the positive impulses, urges, drives, cravings, needs, desires, and hence the definitive purposes, goals, and ideals of their existence. Nor should its identification come as a surprise to sufficiently attentive students of culture and civilization, and certainly not to students of the nature and function of aesthetics. The blues counteragent that is so much a part of many people's equipment for living that they hardly ever think about it as such anymore is that artful and sometimes seemingly magical combination of idiomatic incantation and percussion that creates the dance-oriented goodtime music also known as the blues.

Hence the dance hall as temple. Hence all the ceremonially deliberate drag steps and shaking and grinding movements during, say, the old downhome Saturday Night Function, and all the sacramental strutting and swinging along with all the elegant stomping every night at such long-since-consecrated ballrooms as, say, the old Savoy, once the glory of uptown Manhattan. And hence in consequence the fundamental function of the blues musician (also known as the jazz musician), the most obvious as well as the most pragmatic mission of whose performance is not only to drive the blues away and hold them at bay at least for the time being, but also to evoke an ambiance of Dionysian revelry in the process.

Which is to say, even as such blues (or jazz) performers as the appropriately legendary Buddy Bolden, the improbable but undeniable Jelly Roll Morton, the primordially regal Bessie Smith, played their usual engagements as dance-hall, night-club, and vaudeville entertainers, they were at the same time fulfilling a central role in a ceremony that was at once a purification rite and a celebration the festive earthiness of which was tantamount to a fertility ritual.

Ballroom dances, which like house-party dances probably represent the most comprehensive elaboration and refinement of communal dancing, are of their very nature festive occasions. They are always held in celebration of something. Sometimes they celebrate victory in combat, sports, and other contests. They also celebrate achievements in business, politics, and the arts, among other things. Then there are all the traditional events, such as birthdays, marriages, graduations, and all the seasonal and official red-letter anniversaries. The difference between blues-oriented ballroom dances and the others, however, is of fundamental significance. Customarily, in keeping with the one-dimensional frivolity of the proceedings, the music for the others is light, airy, gay, conventional, in a word, anything but serious. Whereas not only do a number of blues lyrics express an urgent and unmistakable concern with defeat, disappointment, betrayal, misfortune, not excluding death; but even the most exuberant stomp rendition is likely to contain some trace of sadness as a sobering reminder that life is at bottom, for all the very best of good times, a never-ending struggle.

And yet the irrepressible joyousness, the downright exhilaration, the rapturous delight in sheer physical existence, like the elegant jocularity and hearty nonsense that are no less characteristic of blues music, are unsurpassed by any other dance music in the world. Still, the captivating elegance that always seems so entirely innate to blues-idiom dance movement is something earned in a context of antagonism. Not unlike the parade-ground-oriented sporty limp walk of the epic hero and the championship athlete, it has been achieved through the manifestation of grace under pressure such as qualifies the matador, for example, for his suit of lights and his pigtail.

But as to the matter of dispersing gloom and spreading glee, evidence in favor of the sorcery of Madam Marie Laveau, also known as the Widow Paris, the most notorious New Orleans voodoo queen, and the mojo hands of Doctor Jim Alexander, né Charles La Fountaine, also known as Indian Jim, her male counterpart, is questionable to say the very least. Testimony that the dance-beat incantation and percussion of Bessie Smith and Louis Armstrong almost always worked as advertised is universal.

THREE

The Blue Devils and the Holy Ghost

THERE ARE BLUE DEVILS, and there is also the Holy Ghost. Thus not everybody defines blues music and blues-idiom dance movements in the same terms. What the dance hall seems always to have suggested to the ministers and elders of most downhome churches, for instance, is the exact opposite of a locale for a purification ritual. To them any secular dancing place is a House of Sin and Folly, a Den of Iniquity, a Writhing Hellhole, where the weaknesses of the flesh are indulged to the ruination of the mind and body and eternal damnation of the soul. Which is also to say that all such places are also gateways to the downward path to everlasting torment in the fire and brimstone that is the certain fate of all sinners.

The vitriolic prayers and sermons against ballroom dances in general and the denunciation of the old downhome Saturday Night Function in particular express a preoccupation that amounts to obsession. By contrast, the all but total absence of any urgent concern about all of the incontestably pagan fetishism that is almost as explicit as implicit in the widespread involvement with good-luck charms, love potions, effigies, and all the other magical trinkets and devices that are so prevalent even among some regular churchgoers is nothing short of remarkable. Furthermore, for all the didactic allusions to the unrelenting opposition of the Prophets to idolatry and soothsaying in Biblical times, traditional downhome sermons by and large tend to ignore contemporary fortunetellers and voodoo madams and snakedoctors. Not so in the case of the local honkytonk and dance-hall proprietors. They are castigated weekly, often by name.

As for the Saturday Night Function being a ritual to purge the atmosphere of baleful spirits, church-oriented downhome people are likely to express a very firm conviction that such diabolical afflictions exist only in the bad conscience of the sinful in the first place. In their view such pestilential vexations are not sent from the Devil (whose earthly stock in trade is enticement), but are manifestations of the wrath of the Lord, and they are only harbingers of the miseries sinners bring upon themselves by remaining outside the almighty protection of God's Word as represented by the church.

The problem as defined from the pulpit is not the purgation of the environment, which is inherently evil, but rather the purification of yourself and fortification against temptation. Because the only salvation of your soul is through conversion, baptism, and devotion. Not that you will never feel dejected again. But not because of the blues. When church members feel downcast it is because they have somehow displeased God, in whose sight mortal flesh must always feel itself unworthy even at best. In any case, the all but impossible way to Grace is through the denial of sensual gratification, never through the Garden of Earthly Delights.

It is accordingly precisely the blues musician's capacity to generate merriment that downhome church elders have always condemned first of all. They have never taken such incantation and percussion as being anything even remotely defiant or in any way antagonistic to any demons whatsoever. On the contrary, to them it is the Devil's very own music. They have always been completely certain that it not only brings out the devilment inherent in the weakness of the flesh (born as it is in sin and shaped in iniquity), but is also a call to the Devil himself to come forth and reign on earth as in Pandemonium.

Which is not to say that the church service is without its own merriment. Along with all the solemn rituals of devotion through submissive obedience there is also a fundamental requirement for the faithful to make a joyful noise unto the everlasting Glory of God. Thus there is also good-time music that has less of a place in the regular order of devotional services than the prayers, solemn hymns and anthems, spirituals, sermons, and the Amen Corner chants and moans. Nor is it at all unusual for the hand clapping and foot shuffling plus rocking and rolling of a congregation singing chorus after medium to uptempo chorus of, say, *I Couldn't Hear Nobody Pray* or *Just a Closer Walk with Thee*, to generate paroxysms of ecstasy that exceed anything that happens in the most gutbucket-oriented of honky-tonks. On occasion the Bacchanalian music of the Saturday Night Function becomes forthrightly orgiastic, as everybody not only knows but expects. But even so, nobody is likely to compare the highly stylized intensity of the most lascivious honky-tonk dance movements with what happens when a Sunday Morning worshiper is allowed to shout until he or she begins speaking in unknown tongues because possessed by the Holy Ghost.

In point of fact, traditionally the highest praise given a blues musician has been the declaration that he can make a dance hall rock and roll like a downhome church during revival time. But then many of the elements of blues music seem to have been derived from the downhome church in the first place. After all, such is the nature of the blues musician's development that even when he or she did not begin as a church musician, he or she is likely to have been conditioned by church music from infancy to a far greater extent than by blues music as such. There are, it should be remembered, no age limits on church attendance or church music. Whereas during the childhood of all the musicians whose work now represents the classics of the idiom, blues music was considered to be so specifically adult that as a rule children were not even permitted to listen to it freely, and for the most part were absolutely forbidden to go anywhere near the festivities of the Saturday Night Function until they were of age.

In any case, not a few of the idiomatic elements now considered to be components of the definitive devices of blues musicianship were already conventions of long standing among downhome church musicians long before Buddy Bolden, Jelly Roll Morton, King Oliver, W. C. Handy, and Ma Rainey came to apply them to the dance hall. Whatever were the ultimate origins of the solo-call/ensemble-riff-response pattern, for example, the chances are that blues musicians adapted it from such church renditions as the following:

Solo-call:	*On the mountain.*
Congregation:	*I couldn't hear nobody pray.*
Solo:	*In the valley.*
Riff:	*Couldn't hear nobody.*
Solo:	*On my kneehees.*
Riff:	*Couldn't hear nobody.*
Solo:	*With my Jesus.*
Riff:	*Couldn't hear nobody.*

Solo:	*Oh, Lord.*
Riff:	*I couldn't hear nobody.*
Solo:	*Oh, Lordahawd!!!*
Riff:	*Couldn't hear nobody pray.*
Everybody:	*Way down yonder by myself*
	I couldn't hear nobody pray.

Incidentally, the primary effect of barrelhousing and ragging and jazzing is not to make honky-tonk music more intrinsically dance-oriented than church music, but to make it more secular, which is to say, more appropriate to secular circumstances, attitudes and choreography. Downhome church music (by which is meant the conventional music of southern U.S. Negro Protestants) is not of its nature fundamentally less dance-beat-oriented, it simply inspires a different mode of dance, a sacred or holy as opposed to a secular or profane movement, a difference which is sometimes a matter of very delicate nuance. Indeed, sometimes only the initiated can make the distinctions. But churchfolks are always very much aware of them, and so are blues musicians for the most part, or at least so they used to be in the old days before certain gospel-fad pop hits popularized by Ray Charles and James Brown, and Aretha Franklin, among a whole horde of others less famous but no less shameless. Back then only misguided white audiences were likely to dance to such church music as *When the Saints Go Marching In* without any sense of transgression.

In the old days to play church music as dance music used to be condemned as a sacrilege by church elders and dance-hall patrons alike. There were some exceptions, of course, and some very notable ones at that. There were the now classic renditions of *The Saints* and *Bye and Bye*, for example, by none other than Louis Armstrong himself. But Armstrong, it must be remembered, besides being a genius (to whom nothing is sacred) was also a product of the highly unconventional religious attitude that the existential bodaciousness of New Orleans post-cemetery music expresses. Even so, Armstrong almost always legitimized the iconoclasm of his secular use of sacred music with an unmistakable element of parody. Which many outsiders to the downhome church idiom seem to ignore, but which to insiders signals that Armstrong the musician, who sometimes also plays the role of Satchmo the Jester, has now donned the mask of Reverend Dippermouth the Mountebank and is by way of conducting a mock or jivetime church service, so no matter how worked up the musicians become, the deportment and the dance movements of the audience should be governed by the spirit of caricature. Even as are church-sponsored Tom Thumb weddings, in which a cast of children poke fun at the solemnity of religious marriage rites.

Thus Armstrong's use of church music in secular situations was not performed to stimulate the usual dance-hall bumps and grinds, and the same spirit of parody holds true for the mock sermons of Louis Jordan. But such is not always the case with Ray Charles. When he bootlegs *This Little Light of Mine, I'm Goin' Let It Shine* into his dance-hall version, *This Little Girl of Mine*, the assumption seems to be that the sacrilege can be nullified by sentimentality; but the effect of doing ballroom and honky-tonk steps to such music would have once struck people of both branches of the idiom as being infinitely more offensive than parody. By comparison, using the name of the Lord in vain would probably have been considered a relatively minor trespass. There is, after all, a world of difference between the way you clap your hands and pat your feet in church and the way people snap their fingers in a ballroom, even when the rhythm, tempo, and even the beat are essentially the same. Once you become a member of the church it is as if you are forbidden to make certain movements; they constitute a violation of a body that has been consecrated to God.

As a matter of fact, a majority of downhome worshipers used to have difficulty reconciling exuberant expression with religious devotion even when it was an indisputable part of a church service. Conventional downhome Baptists and Methodists, as anybody with any firsthand experience will testify, have never been quite at ease about the appropriateness of all the dithyrambic ebullience of the Sanctified or Holy Roller church. Not that they doubt the sincerity of the communicants, whose deportment outside the church is always very sanctified indeed. But what with all the jam-session-like call-and-response leapfrogging, all the upbeat drumming and on trap drums of all things, all the shimmy-shaking tambourines and free-for-all caper cuttings as if by the numbers, the ragtime overtones of a shindig have always been too much for most conventional witnesses.

As for the blues musician being an agent of affirmation and continuity in the face of adversity, hardly anything could be further from the conventional downhome churchgoer's most fundamental assumptions about the nature of things. The church is not concerned with the affirmation of life as such, which in its view is only a matter of feeble flesh to begin with. The church is committed to the eternal salvation of the soul after death, which is both final and inevitable. Human existence is only a brief sojourn in a vale of trials, troubles, and tribulations to be endured because it is the will of the Creator, whose ways are mysterious.

It is not for man to affirm the will of God, because His will is not something that a mere man can question anyway, no matter how arbitrarily adverse the circumstances. Actually, the only thing that a good church member can affirm is his faith in the Word and God's mercy, because what is forever in doubt is not life, however wretched, but your own worthiness, which is to say, steadfastness in the face of temptation.

The overall solemnity of the services of non-Sanctified downhome churches is entirely in keeping with the fact that more than anything else they are rituals of propitiation, which place primary emphasis not on joyous celebration but on prayer and sacrifice and thanksgiving. Unlike the revelers at the Saturday Night Function, the worshipers attending the Sunday Morning Service are very much concerned with guilt and with seeking forgiveness for their trespasses against the teachings of the Holy Scriptures. Accordingly what each expresses is not affirmation of life as such but rather his determination not to yield to the enticements of the fleshpots of Baal.

But the Saturday Night Function is a ritual of purification and affirmation nonetheless. Not all ceremonial occasions are solemn. Nor are defiance and contestation less fundamental to human well-being than are worship and propitiation. Indeed they seem to be precisely what such indispensably human attributes as courage, dignity, honor, nobility, and heroism are all about. André Malraux might well have been referring to the blues and the function of blues musicians when he described the human condition in terms of ever-impending chaos and declared that each victory of the artist represents a triumph of man over his fate. That he was addressing himself to fundamental implications of heroism should be clear enough.

What the blue devils of gloom and ultimate despair threaten is not the soul or the possibility of everlasting salvation after death, but the quality of everyday life on earth. Thus the most immediate problem of the blues-bedeviled person concerns his ability to cope with even the commonplace. What is at stake is a sense of well-being that is at least strong enough to enable him to meet the basic requirements of the workaday world. Accordingly, in addition to its concern with forthright confrontation and expurgation, the Saturday Night Function also consists of rituals of resilience and perseverance through improvisation in the face of capricious disjuncture.

Still, with all its component rituals that fulfill such pragmatic needs, the Saturday Night Function, unlike the Sunday Morning Service, is also something to be enjoyed solely as an end in itself. After all, beyond the good time (much, if not exactly, the same as with the experience of the work of art) there is mostly only more struggle. Between this Saturday night and the next there is Monday morning and the next work week. In any case, at the Saturday Night Function primary emphasis is placed upon aesthetics not ethics. What is good in such circumstances is the beautiful, without which there can be no good time. What counts is elegance (not only in the music and the dance movement but in the survival technology inherent in the underlying ritual as well).

Not that perhaps most Saturday Night Revelers may not hold the church in traditional reverence at the same time. Many will be present at Sunday Morning Service, sometimes with bloodshot eyes and queasy stomachs, but almost always with breaths dealcoholized at least somewhat with cinnamon, Juicy Fruit, or peppermint. Nor does it follow that those who never go do not expect a church funeral ceremony. The least that most expect is a few words by a minister at church cemetery.

FOUR

The Blues as Music

THE BLUES AS SUCH are synonymous with low spirits. Blues music is not. With all its so-called blue notes and overtones of sadness, blues music of its very nature and function is nothing if not a form of diversion. With all its preoccupation with the most disturbing aspects of life, it is something contrived specifically to be performed as entertainment. Not only is its express purpose to make people feel good, which is to say in high spirits, but in the process of doing so it is actually expected to generate a disposition that is both elegantly playful and heroic in its nonchalance.

Even when blues lyrics are about the most harrowing anxieties, hardships, and misfortunes (as they so often but by no means always are), blues music is no less appropriate to good-time situations. Even when what the instrumentation represents is the all but literal effect of the most miserable moaning and groaning, the most excruciating screaming and howling, the most pathetic sighing, sobbing, and whimpering, blues music is never presented to more enthusiastic response than at the high point of some festive occasion. Nor is it likely to dampen the spirit of merriment in the least. On the contrary, even when such representations are poorly executed they seldom fail to give the atmosphere an added dimension of down-to-earth sensuality.

That the blues as such are a sore affliction that can lead to total collapse goes without saying. But blues music regardless of its lyrics almost always induces dance movement that is the direct opposite of resignation, retreat, or defeat. Moreover, as anyone who has ever shared the fun of any blues-oriented social function should never need to be reminded, the more lowdown, dirty, and mean the music, the more instantaneously and pervasively sensual the dance gestures it engenders. As downright aphrodisiac as blues music so often becomes, however, and as notorious for violence as the reputation of blues-oriented dance-hall records has been over the years, blues-idiom merriment is not marked either by the sensual abandon of the voodoo orgy or by the ecstatic trance of a religious possession. One of its most distinctive features, conversely, is its unique combination of spontaneity, improvisation, and control. Sensual abandon is, like overindulgence in alcohol and drugs, only another kind of disintegration. Blues-idiom dance movement being always a matter of elegance is necessarily a matter of getting oneself together.

Sometimes the Blues Set in a dance program used to be referred to as the one that put the dancers, and in fact the whole event, into the alley, back out in the alley, out in the back alley, or way down in the alley. Because sometimes blues music also used to be said to come from down in the alley. Which meant that it was not only not from the drawing room (and the overextensions and overrefinements thereof), but was of its very essence the sound-equivalent of the unvarnished, or unpainted back-alley actualities of everyday flesh-and-blood experience. Hence, among other things, much of the onomatopoeia of the workaday world and at least some of the dirty tones and raggy overtones of the riffraff and the rabble.

Which by the same token is also why the Blues Set is sometimes said to be the one that gets things back down to the so-called nitty gritty, which is to say back down from the cloudlike realms of abstraction and fantasy to the bluesteel and rawhide textures of the elemental facts of the everyday struggle for existence. As a result of which the dancers (who were sometimes said to have been put in the groove) were normally expected to respond not with uneasiness and gestures of fear and trembling but with warm person-to-person intimacy that was both robust and delicate.

In short, the situation for which the blues as such are synonymous is always at least somewhat regrettable if not utterly wretched and grievous. But as preoccupied with human vulnerability as so many of its memorable lyrics have always been, and as suggestive of pain as some of its instrumentation sometimes seems to be, blues music can hardly be said to be synonymous with lamentation and commiseration. Not when the atmosphere of earthiness and the disposition to positive action it engenders are considered. And besides, sometimes the lyrics mock and signify even as they pretend to weep, and as all the finger snapping, foot tapping, and hip cocking indicate, the instrumentation may be far less concerned with agony than with ecstasy.

Which, incidentally, should make it easy enough to distinguish between blues music on the one hand and the secularized gospel music known as soul music and the rhythm-and-folk blues-oriented hillbilly music known as rock music (erstwhile ofay rock-and-roll or rockabilly) on the other. Both soul and rock make free use of idiomatic devices borrowed from blues musicians, but the so-called funky atmosphere they generate is charged with sentimentality rather than earthiness. Also, soul and rock almost always place primary emphasis on a one-dimensional earnestness that all too easily deteriorates into a whining self-pity or a highly amplified tantrum of banging and crashing and screaming and stamping that obviously has far more to do with the intensification of a mood of despair than with getting rid of any demons of gloom.

Not that there is no such thing as sorrowful blues music. But not so much as many people seem to think. Not that there have not always been some blues musicians trying to earn a living by making wretchedness a public feature. But the blind musician on the corner with his tin cup has never been the typical blues musician. Unlike Ma Rainey, Bessie Smith, Jimmy Rushing, and Big Joe Turner, whose acts were always a part if not the high point of the main event, he is at best only a sobering sideshow. On the other hand, a blind musician putting the dancers in a lowdown back-alley groove at a Saturday Night Function needs no tin cup.

Even those people who sing, play, dance to, or just listen to blues music mostly because they feel blue seem much less likely to do so in self-commiseration than because it helps them get rid of the blues. But even so, most people listen to blues music for the simple fact that it always makes them feel good. And they are just as likely to listen and dance to it when they already feel very good, because it always makes them feel even better. As for those who sing and play it, they do so not to publicize their most intimate secrets and most personal embarrassments but because Music is their profession and blues music is an idiom for which they feel they have some aesthetic affinity and technical competence. Nor are they likely to have chosen music in the first place because of some personal calamity which they feel compelled to spend the rest of their lives publishing abroad, but rather because their admiration for some older musician led to emulation. Bessie Smith, for example, owes much more to Ma Rainey than to hard luck, and she also owes not a little to the good luck that began with being born with a voice the magnificence of which, like that of Louis Armstrong's trumpet and Duke Ellington's orchestrations, no amount of adversity has yet produced in anybody else.

FIVE

Blues Music as Such

DEFINITIONS OF BLUES MUSIC in most standard American dictionaries confuse it with the blues as such. They also leave the impression that what it represents is the expression of sadness. Not one characterizes it as good-time music. Nor is there any reference whatsoever to its use as dance music. Moreover, primary emphasis is always placed on its vocal aspects, and no mention at all is made of the fact that over the years it has come to be dominated by dance-hall-oriented instrumentalists to a far greater extent than by singers.

According to the third edition of *Webster's New International Dictionary*, blues music is "a song sung or composed in a style originating among American Negroes, characterized typically by use of three-line stanzas in which the words of the second line repeat the first, expressing a mood of longing or melancholy, and marked by a continual occurrence of blue notes in melody and harmony." Which not only suggests that musicians pray the blues instead of playing them, but also limits the mood to melancholy and longing. Bessie Smith's recording of *Florida Bound Blues* which begins, "Goodbye, North; Hello, South . . ." is tinged with melancholy to be sure, but what it expresses in the main is determination (to get back down South to a good place) and in the process it becomes a paean for a good man. Determination is also stronger than the melancholy strains of her *One and Two Blues.* The regret is unmistakable, but as in *The Golden Rule, Hard Driving Papa*, and *Worn Out Papa*, the point is to get *him* told off—as the point in Jimmy Rushing's (and Count Basie's) *Goin' to Chicago* (Columbia G31224) is to get *her* told.

The entry in *Webster's* also fails to take into account such undisputed classics of the idiom as Louis Armstrong's renditions of *The Memphis Blues* and *Beale Street Blues*, in which the mood is joyous and in which instead of melancholy and longing there is low gravy mellowness. Thus Armstrong's version of *The St. Louis Blues* (RCA Victor LPM-2971) would also be precluded. The melody would qualify and so would the lyrics in part, but the actual mood of the performance in question (which is determined by the up-tempo beat plus the riff-style call-and-response choruses) would not.

The clues provided by *Webster's Collegiate*, the much more widely consulted desk-size abridgement of *Webster's New International* are of very little practical use. If blues music is, as it states, a type of song written in a characteristic key with melancholy lyrics and syncopated rhythms, then neither W. C. Handy's *The Memphis Blues* (said to be the first blues ever copyrighted) nor his *Aunt Hagar's Blues* qualifies. Neither has melancholy lyrics. (Incidentally, although Aunt Hagar herself is represented as describing blues music as melancholy, she is also quoted as saying "When my feet say dance, I just can't refuse—When I hear that melody they call the Blues.")

The *American College Dictionary* reports that blues music is melancholy in character and usually performed in slow tempo. But while this applies to any number of other kinds of music, including the spirituals, it does not apply to such standard Kansas City blues compositions as Pete Johnson's *Roll 'Em Pete* or Count Basie's *Sent for You Yesterday*, which are usually played in up-tempo.

Funk and Wagnalls Encyclopedic Dictionary echoes standard confusion of blues music with the blues as such, as does the *World Book Dictionary*, which implies that blues music is any composition played in a slow jazz rhythm as a lamentation!

The relatively new *American Heritage Dictionary* gives misrepresentations and restrictions that are as old as the rest: "A style of jazz evolved from southern American Negro secular songs and usually distinguished by slow tempos and flatted thirds and sevenths." Which again places too much emphasis upon slowness. Some blues music is most effective in a slow tempo. Some is best in a moderate tempo. Some should always be played in up-tempo. Many are no less effective in one as in another. However, it is hard to imagine either of the following traditional verses performed in anything except up-tempo:

> Well the blues jumped the rabbit and run him for a
> solid mile
> Said the blues jumped the rabbit and run him for a
> solid mile

Till the rabbit laid down and cried like a little baby
    chile.

What makes my grandma love my grandpa so
S'what makes old grandma love old grandpa so
W' he can still hoochie coochie like he did fifty
    years ago!

(Incidentally instruments can shout such stanzas to an even
greater effect than voices.)

Grove's *Dictionary of Music and Musicians* (5th edition,
1960) is generally considered by professionals and students
alike to be a long-established and highly authoritative standard
reference in the field of music. Yet its discussion of the blues as
music, written by Hugues Panassié, one of the earliest critical
experts in the field, contains perhaps as much confusion and
nonsense as facts and insights:

> The origin of the blues is unknown; they are probably of
> remote African provenance, but the form in which we know
> them today is predominantly American. They bear, in fact, very
> definitely the stigma of the yoke of slavery to which the black
> races were subjected in the U.S.A., as may be gathered from
> the note of pathos which makes them emotionally as disturbing
> as any of the world's music. Yet when Negroes sing their blues
> it is not in order to give in to sadness, but rather to find relief
> from it. That is why the blues are never sentimental, in the
> pejorative sense of the term, but on the contrary full of vitality
> that shows no mere resignation in the American Negro, but a
> protest against the sad lot that was inflicted upon him.
>
> From the technical point of view the blues are short pieces
> twelve bars in length based on an invarying harmonic sequence.
> The difference between two blues lies exclusively in the melody
> superimposed on the harmonies—and even that is often the
> same—in the words, and particularly, in each singer's individual
> performance.
>
> The outstanding melodic characteristic of the blues, and
> that of the harmony resulting from the tunes, is its tendency to
> flatten certain notes of the scale by a semitone, which have for
> that reason been called "blue notes."

It is far more accurate to say that some of the most distinctive *elements* of blues music were derived from the music of

some of the West African ancestors of U.S. Negroes than it is to imply, however obliquely, that the blues idiom itself ever existed anywhere on the continent of Africa. Nor should it be forgotten that elements quite as essential and no more dispensable were derived from the music of some of the European ancestors of U.S. Negroes.

The point, however, is that the blues idiom, whatever the source or sources of its components, is native to the United States. It is a synthesis of African and European elements, the product of an Afro-American sensibility in an American mainland situation. There is no evidence, for example, that an African musical sensibility interacting with an Italian, German, French, British, or Hungarian musical sensibility results in anything like blues music. The synthesis of European and African musical elements in the West Indies, the Caribbean, and in continental Latin America produced calypso, rhumba, the tango, the conga, mambo, and so on, but not the blues and not ragtime, and not that extension, elaboration, and refinement of blues-break riffing and improvisation which came to be known as jazz.

In point of historical fact, the use of the word *blue* (which is European to begin with) to connote an emotional state or circumstance has much more to do with light-skinned people than with dark-skinned people. Figures of speech, after all, are always likely to have been derived from concrete experience. In any event, not only is it natural for people of European pigmentation to think of themselves as literally changing colors as a result of an emotional state, but English lexicographers have found records that show that the phrase "to look blue," meaning to suffer anxiety, fear, discomfort, and low spirits, was in currency as long ago as 1550. (Incidentally, one Middle English form of the word was *bla*, which survives in the word *blae*, sometimes spelled *blah* and thought to be a colloquialism for feeling dull, bored, dispirited, but which in Middle English already referred to looking as well as feeling livid or leaden.)

On the other hand it would seem extremely unlikely that the African ancestors of U.S. Negro blues musicians were any more inclined to describe themselves as turning blue with sorrow than to say that their faces were red with embarrassment or excitement, or that they were turning green with envy. Thus the chances were that blues-oriented Afro-Americans acquired both the word and its special connotation from their Euro-American ancestors. English usage of the term blue devils to designate baleful demons has been traced back as far as 1616. Its figurative use as a metaphor for depression of spirits has been traced as far back as 1787, and its plural use as a name for apparitions seen or experienced during delirium tremens has been in use since 1822.

American usage of the blues as a term for depressed spirits, despondency, and melancholy dates, according to *The Dictionary of American English on Historical Principles*, at least as far back as 1807, when Washington Irving used the following sentence in *Salamagundi XI*: "He concluded his harangue with a sigh, and I saw that he was still under the influence of a whole legion of the blues." And no less of a national figure than Thomas Jefferson is on record as having written in 1810: "We have something of the blue devils at times."

Other instances have been documented by the *Dictionary of American English* as follows: 1820, *Western Carolinean*, 18 July, "The fact is he was but recently convalescent from a severe spell of the blues"; 1837, *Southern Literary Messenger III*, 387, "I shall have a fit of the blues if I stay here"; 1850, N. Kingsley *Diary*, 143, "Some are beginning to get the blues on most horribly"; 1866, Gregg, *Life in the Army*, "It was well for me that day that I was able to look on the brightest side of the case and avoid a severe attack of the blues"; 1871, *Scribner's Monthly* I, 489, "The Silence alone is enough to give a well man the blues"; 1883, *Harper's Magazine*, Dec., 55, "Come to me when you have the blues."

All of which suggests that blues music bears a vernacular relationship to the blues that is much if not very nearly the same as that which the spirituals bear to the Christianity of frontier America. Musicologists have indeed traced numerous rhythmic, structural, and sonic elements of the spirituals to African sources, but the fact remains that the spirituals as a specific musical idiom are both indigenous and peculiar to the religious experience of Africans transplanted to the United States. They are a product of the interaction of certain elements derived from African religious and musical sensibilities with European-derived music and religion. But this interaction only took place in the United States. Not in Africa, for all the Africans converted by European missionaries; and not in Europe, and not even in the Caribbean and Latin American countries.

Likewise, the actual historical as well as geographic circumstances, and consequently the conceptual framework in terms of which the blues as such are first perceived, defined, and then responded to by musicians and dancers is not West African, nor is it European. Nor Euro-African. It is Afro-U.S. However many demons there might have been in ancestral West Africa and however many of them may have been some ominous shade of blue, the specific rituals—if any—they gave rise to were likely to be far more closely related to voodoo ceremonies than to the Saturday Night Function. The underlying dance-beat disposition involved is obviously West African in origin, and so are the definitive stylistic elements that give the incantation and percussion—which is to say, blues music—its special idiomatic character. But even so the blues seem to have been imported to the United States from Europe, along with the Christian conception of God and the angels of Heaven and the Devil and the imps of Hell.

Hugues Panassié's description of blues music as "bearing very definitely the stigma of the yoke of slavery—as may be gathered from the note of pathos . . ." is highly questionable to say the least. To most musicologists the so-called note of pathos is largely a matter of African-derived quarter-tone or blue notes, which is to say, a matter of convention and tradition predating the importation of black slaves to the United States. Moreover, the subject matter and imagery of blues lyrics are usually nothing if not concrete and specific, and not unlike the subject matter and imagery of lyric poetry in general, they are much more preoccupied with love affairs than with such political issues as liberty, equality, and justice.

What with all the references in the spirituals to The House of Bondage, The Walls of Jericho, The Lion's Den, The Fiery Furnace, Deliverance from Old King Pharaoh, The Wilderness, The Valley of the Shadow, The Rainbow Sign, and The Promised Land, it is easy enough to associate their deeply moving sonorities with slavery and political oppression. Indeed, even the most metaphysical concerns of the spirituals often readily lend themselves to immediate political interpretation and application. Also, such is the intrinsically moral orientation of the imagery of the spirituals that no great violence is done to the essential poetic statement when references to the spiritual predicament of man are seen as reflecting his earthly plight.

But even when blues lyrics address themselves directly to negative economic, political, and judiciary circumstances, far more often than not, the main emphasis is likely to be placed on the victim's love life. The pseudo-folk lyrics currently so dear to the hearts of avant-garde night-club patrons and self-styled revolutionary revelers blame the crooked judge, but traditional folk lyrics are about the damage to a love affair. The source of the trouble that brings on the blue tormentors being addressed by Bessie Smith in *Jailhouse Blues*, *Workhouse Blues*, *House Rent Blues*, *Money Blues*, *Hard Times Blues*, and *Backwater Blues* is not perceived as the political system as such but rather almost always as some unfaithful lover. In fact in the 160 available recordings of Bessie Smith (Columbia five-album set, GP33, G30126, G30450, G30818, G31093), a few notable exceptions such as *Washwoman's Blues* and *Poor Man's Blues* notwithstanding, the preoccupation is clearly not at all with hard workmasters, cruel sheriffs, biased prosecutors, juries, and judges, but with the careless love of aggravating papas, sweet mistreaters, dirty nogooders, and spider men. Old Pharaoh in the spirituals may often stand for Ole Marster as well as the ruler of a sinful and oppressive nation; and Egyptland is often the U.S. South as well as the mundane world. But the man who imprisons the woman body-and-soul in Bessie Smith's lyrics is neither sheriff nor warden. He is the slow and easy but sometimes heartless lover.

In any case, Panassié's political emphasis is not borne out by any outstanding internal evidence of political consciousness. Therefore his characterization of blues music as "a protest against the sad lot that was inflicted on him [i.e., U.S. Negroes]" is gratuitous for all its unquestionably good intentions.

As a matter of fact, much goes to show that in the world as represented by most traditional blues lyrics, it is usually as if the political system were simply another elemental phenomenon, as much a part of the nature of things as were the inscrutable

forces personified by the Gods of Mount Olympus, which also
suggests the possibility that the source of any overtone of pathos that may be heard is likely to be more existential or even
metaphysical than political. Nor is such an eventuality in the
least inconsistent with charges made by church elders against
blues music when they accuse it of being good-time music.
The overtones they hear are mostly of frivolity.

Not that blues music is without fundamental as well as immediate political significance and applicability. But the nature
of its political dimension is not always as obvious as some promoters of folk-music-as-social-commentary seem to believe. The
political implication is inherent in the attitude toward experience that generates the blues-music counterstatement in the
first place. It is the disposition to persevere (based on a tragic,
or, better still, an epic sense of life) that blues music at its best
not only embodies but stylizes, extends, elaborates, and refines
into art. And, incidentally, such is the ambiguity of artistic
statement that there is no need to choose between the personal
implication and the social, except as the occasion requires.

As for the note of pathos that Panassié finds to be as moving
as that of any other music in the world, the element of downright sadness, forlornness, bitter deprivation, and raw anguish
is by all odds a far greater characteristic of the folk music of
white southerners than of the downhome honky-tonk Saturday Night Function and ballroom. When a hillbilly musician
or country-and-western musician plays or sings a lament, the
music is likely to reinforce the mood of melancholy and longing, but in the performance of a blues ballad the chances are
that even the most solemn words of a dirge will not only be
counterstated by the mood of earthy well-being stimulated by
the beat but may even be mocked by the jazziness of the
instrumentation.

As imprecisely as the words of so many blues lyrics are
treated in actual performance, even by the most celebrated
vocalists, beginning with Ma Rainey and Bessie Smith, and including Louis Armstrong, Jimmy Rushing, and Big Joe Turner,
they provide the most specific clues to the historical source of
the blues predicament to which they address themselves. What
blues instrumentation in fact does, often in direct contrast to
the words, is define the nature of the response to the blues

situation at hand, whatever the source. Accordingly, more often than not, even as the words of the lyrics recount a tale of woe, the instrumentation may mock, shout defiance, or voice resolution and determination.

Panassié, however, as the entry in Grove's *Dictionary* also goes on to show, is by no means unaware of the affirmative thrust of blues music. Having overstated the historical implications of what he calls the note of pathos, he states in the very next sentence that when Negroes play their blues it is not to give way to sadness, but rather to find relief from it, which he says is "why the blues are never sentimental in the pejorative sense." In his book *The Real Jazz* he puts it somewhat differently:

> It has been stated that the blues were a cry of the black man's soul under the oppression of the whites. Hence the plaintive quality, the often hopeless accent. But let us make no mistake; when a Negro sings the blues it is not to give way to sadness, it is rather to free himself of it. He has far too much optimism and too vivid a sense of life to permit himself to do otherwise. That is why the blues, in spite of their nostalgic mood, have nothing to do with whining—but rather express a confidence, a tonic sense of vitality. The Negro has no time for that sentimental, languorous tone which is the scourge of so much music. . . . Furthermore when the blues are sung in rapid rather than slow time they can assume an even joyful note.[!]

Perhaps it is overemphasis based on assumptions that are too specifically political that prevent some commentators from realizing that it may be much more to the point to speak rather of a difference of conventions between blues and hillbilly music than to characterize the latter, if only by implication, as bearing no stigma of the yoke of slavery—or as bearing a greater stigma of something else. The correlation of plaintive musical overtones with political status is not likely to be very clearcut in either case.

But then the term *stigma* can hardly do justice to the complex heritage of the experience of slavery in the United States anyway. Much is forever being made of the deleterious effects of slavery on the generations of black Americans that followed. But for some curious reason, nothing at all is ever made of the possibility that the legacy left by the enslaved ancestors of blues-oriented contemporary U.S. Negroes includes a disposition to confront the most unpromising circumstances and make the most of what little there is to go on, regardless of the odds—and not without finding delight in the process or forgetting mortality at the height of ecstasy. Still there is a lot of admittedly infectious exuberance, elegance and nonsense to be accounted for.

The entry in *A Dictionary of Americanisms on Historical Principles*, which defines blues music as "a type of mournful, haunting Negro folk song adapted and often burlesqued for use in music halls, vaudeville shows, etc.," includes two fundamental clues omitted by other standard references, only to misinterpret them and end up with the same old confusion and exclusions. But once the mood has been limited to haunting mournfulness and the level of execution to that of folk (which is to say nonprofessional or semiprofessional if not amateur) expression, it is no doubt easy enough to preclude burlesque or ridicule as perfectly normal elements of blues-idiom statement, and to imply that the music hall and the vaudeville stage are not its natural setting. Eliminated by doing so, however, are Ma Rainey, Bessie, Clara, Mamie, and Trixie Smith, Ida Cox, Jelly Roll Morton, Louis Armstrong to name a few, the best of whose work often contained elements of burlesque, mockery, and derision, and was nothing if not music hall and vaudeville along with whatever else it was.

The vaudeville circuit was as natural to Ma Rainey, the Smith queens, and Louis Armstrong as the street corner and the cheap honky-tonk were to Blind Lemon Jefferson and Robert Johnson. Nor was their music a special adaptation of folk expression. It was rather a perfectly natural historical development. It was an extension, elaboration, and refinement that was no mere embellishment but an evolution altogether consistent with the relative sophistication of the musicians involved.

That blues music began as folk expression goes without saying. Nor have the original folk-type blues musicians ever gone out of existence. But in point of historical fact, once W. C. Handy had arranged, scored and published *The Memphis Blues* (1912), *The St. Louis Blues* and *Yellow Dog Blues* (1914) and *Beale Street Blues* (1916), it was no longer possible to restrict blues music to the category of folk expression. Certainly there was nothing provincial about the musicians who were providing the instrumentation for Bessie Smith by the early 1920s when her now classic repertory was being established as a nationwide phenomenon (via phonograph records to a great extent). Clarence Williams, Fletcher Henderson, James P. Johnson, Louis Armstrong, Joe Smith, Buster Bailey, Coleman Hawkins, Charlie Green, and the rest were anything but folk performers. They were professionals with no less talent and authenticity for all the technical facility, range, and control at their command.

The entry on blues music in the *Standard Dictionary of Folklore, Mythology, and Legend* describes the poetry of the blues as the "tender, ironic, bitter, humorous, or typical expression of a deprived people"; and then goes on to catalogue the subject matter of the blues as careless love, the woman who has lost her man, the no-good woman a man can't forget, the longing to go north with train whistles in the night, floods, cyclones, jails, chain gangs, levee camps, lonesome roads, back alleys, and barrelhouses. It is a source of some wonder to find the barrelhouse, a place of merriment if there ever was one, included in a catalogue of examples of deprivation. Elsewhere the *Standard Dictionary of Folklore, Mythology, and Legend* describes it with casual condescension as cheap: "A cheap saloon of the period of about 1900 during which jazz developed, in which customers could fill their own glasses from a cask, the drip from the spigot falling into a 'gutbucket' on the floor." Not all barrelhouses were cheap, though none were very swanky. Not all permitted customers to serve themselves: but the barrel and the gutbucket are touchstones of nostalgia, not regret. The term, the entry also goes on to say, "is applied to the kind of music played in such places and especially to the rough, 'dirty' timbre of instrumental tone characteristic of this early jazz." But barrelhousing has more to do with dance rhythm than with timbre, and is associated mostly with the piano. A dirty tone on a trumpet or clarinet, for instance, is not referred to as barrel-house.

Overemphasis on the sociopolitical is evident again in such

remarks as, "Singing the blues is one way to say what would not be tolerated in speech. Chain gang bosses, for instance, will ignore comment in song about the work, the food, the misery, of the prisoners, that would bring swift reprisal if spoken, so long as the picks and hammers keep swinging to the music, the words don't matter, except to those who sing them."

Of much more practical use are such observations as follow:

> Musically, the blues are distinguished by an 8 or 12 bar structure (16 and 20 bars in later stages), by a strongly antiphonal quality, by syncopation and by polyrhythm characteristic of Negro music, by simple harmonic progressions, and by a slight flatting of the third and seventh intervals of the scale, these latter are known as "blue notes". Singers make use of subtle variations in pitch and rhythm, portamento, and a wide range of tone coloration. Certain passages may be hummed or rendered in nonsense syllables called "scat." Instrumental accompaniment (by guitar, piano, or various combinations) improvises melodic and rhythmic patterns to the singer's lead or around a solo instrument, and achieves enormous tonal variety by the use of vibrato, mutes, and ordinarily non-musical instruments such as washboards, jugs, etc.

Also to the point are the following observations on the blues lyric:

> The stanza consists typically of a statement repeated one or more times, sometimes with slight variations and a gnomic comment or response. This construction, both in the words and in the music that is molded to them, relates to earlier Negro styles of religious and work singing, with their narrative call lines and responses, and back to African singing. The "punch" lines in their frequently proverbial form, hark back to widespread African use of proverbs in song and story, and the whole song may be of a double-meaning, allusive character close to the African songs of allusion and derision.

The Random House Dictionary of the English Language defines blues music as "a song of American Negro origin, that is marked by the frequent occurrence of blue notes, and that takes the basic form, customarily improvised upon in performance, of a 12-bar chorus consisting of a 3-line stanza with the second line repeating the first . . . the genre consisting of such songs." Thus it does not make the usual mistake of confusing blues music with blues as such. But it is misleading nevertheless. Blues music is always an artful combination of incantation and percussion. It is not always song in the conventional sense of the word. Sometimes if not most times the incantation is instrumental, and while it is true that blues instrumentation is derived from voice extension, it is equally true that much vocalization is now derived from instrumentation.

In all events, defining blues music as song not only gives the lyrics more emphasis than is warranted by the way they are used in actual performance, but also contributes the assumption implicit in those misdefinitions which confuse the music with the blues as such in the first place: that what is said is more important than the way it is said. It is not. The truth is that when a singer likes the tune he is likely to proceed as if any words will do. Moreover much goes to show that only a very few of the millions of devoted admirers of Ma Rainey, Bessie Smith, Jimmy Rushing, and Big Joe Turner, for instance, can actually understand more than half the words of their lyrics as sung, not to mention the idiomatic imagery and references. Perhaps many respond to what they wish to think is being said rather than to the statement the composer wrote, but even so the chances are that most of their goose pimples and all of their finger snapping and foot tapping are produced by the sound far more often than by the meanings of the words.

SIX

Singing the Blues

As COMPELLING as so many blues lyrics so often are, and for all the apt phrases, insightful folksay, and striking imagery that blues singers have added to the national lore, the definitive element of a blues statement is not verbal. Words as such, however well chosen, are secondary to the music. What counts for most is not verbal precision (which is not to say vocal precision) but musical precision, or perhaps better still, musical nuance. Even the most casual survey of the recordings of Ma Rainey, Bessie Smith, Louis Armstrong, Jimmy Rushing, and Big Joe Turner, to say nothing of Blind Lemon Jefferson, Leadbelly, and Robert Johnson, will show that it is not at all unusual for blues lyrics of the very highest poetic quality to be mumbled, hummed, and even garbled by the outstanding performers of the idiom.

Folklore-oriented social historians (sometimes also known as compilers of oral history) and tone-deaf lexicographers—not blues musicians and Saturday night revelers—seem most inclined to ascribe primary significance to the literal content of blues lyrics. Blues singers almost always seem to be much more preoccupied with vocal subtleties than with rendering the lyrics as written. Not that any singer is ever likely to be in the least unmindful of the power of eloquence. After all, some of the blues singer's lines are likely to be even more widely quoted than the holy gospel according to the reigning evangelical spellbinders.

But all the same, the blues singer's primary concern with words is not as a conventional means of coherent communication. So long as the vocalist hits the desired notes, the essential message is not greatly impaired by mispronunciation, sloppy syntax, or even misquotation. The chances are that when in her recording of *Yellow Dog Blues*, Bessie Smith misquotes "Letters come from down in 'Bam/and everywhere that Uncle Sam has even rural delivery!/" as "And everywhere that Uncle Sam is the ruler of delivery/" the change if noted was not in the least disturbing to her listeners.

And yet the substitution substantially alters the image. Handy's was a topical reference to U.S. R.F.D. (rural free delivery), a then recent phenomenon, still in process of development in 1914. The change has no less topical overtones, but of post–World War I U.S. military might. In 1925, the time of Bessie's record, newspaper reports of U.S. Marine operations in the Caribbean made Uncle Sam seem the ruler of many far-flung places. The point, however, is that the musical authority with which she hits "and everywhere that Uncle Sam is the RULER of de . . ." overrides the distortion of the original fact. (She hits it, by the way, with exactly the same authority as a first-bench Amen Corner church sister singing: "and everywhere that God Almighty is the RULER.") She also sings "Dear Sue: Your easy rider struck this burg today/on a southbound rattler *beside* the Pullman car/" where as Handy had written: "on a southbound rattler, side door Pullman car," which is a slangy reference to riding in an empty boxcar. But once again, who really cared? Because, as the scat vocal has always illustrated beyond doubt, when the singer sounds good enough the words don't have to make any sense at all.

The concrete information contained in a blues lyric as performed is likely to be largely incidental. The essential message is usually conveyed by the music, whether vocal or instrumental. Thus regardless of how scrupulously accurate the singer's rendition of even the most powerful lyrics, that verbal statement can be contradicted and in effect canceled by any musical counterstatement. If the lyric laments but the music mocks, the statement is not one of lamentation but of mockery. If the words are negative yet the music either up-tempo or even medium or slow but earthy, the tidings are not sad but glad withal. Even when the tempo is drag-time, it is far more likely to be sensual than funereal. The words may bemoan the loss of a lover, but if the singer is also involved with such choreographic gestures as finger popping, shoulder rocking, and hip swinging all the while, the statement can hardly be considered a form of bereavement.

If blues lyrics in themselves accounted for as much as most standard dictionary definitions so obviously take for granted, the effect they create would be quite different from what it is in fact well known to be. The music would reinforce rather than counterstate the melancholy tale of woe—negative emphasis being the point at issue—and the choreography most suitable for the Saturday Night Function would also be entirely appropriate for the traditional downhome Sunday Morning Service.

Which is not at all the same as saying that blues lyrics are unimportant. They may be mumbled, jumbled, or even scat-riffed, but they play a definitive role in the fundamental ritual of purification, affirmation, and celebration nonetheless. Also, in as much as the purpose of the incantation, percussion, and dance ritual of which the lyrics are a part involves ridding the atmosphere of demons, it is only natural that some will emphasize and in effect document misery. But that is only to say that blues lyrics often address themselves to the blues as such. It is not to say that blues music is not blues music without such lyrics. If such were the case, *The St. Louis Blues*, which has melancholy words, would qualify, but, to the consternation of most working blues musicians, such universally accepted classics as *The Memphis Blues* and *Beale Street Blues*, the words of which celebrate good times and good-time places, would not.

But with or without words, so far as working blues musicians are concerned, *The Memphis Blues* and *Beale Street Blues* are performed in slow and medium tempos, while *The St. Louis Blues* may be played in any tempo, and perhaps as often as not is taken medium- to up-tempo to hot. There is Bessie Smith's slow-drag version, for example, recorded in 1925, which is performed as a conventional, albeit idiomatic, lament in which the mournful voice detailing the plight of the victim is reinforced by a tearful harmonium and is perhaps just barely counterstated by the playful elegance of Louis Armstrong's cornet obbligato. But there is also Armstrong's own bookity-bookity up-tempo solo plus riff-chorus-response instrumental version (RCA Victor LJM 1005) recorded in 1933, that moves right through counter-statement to exuberant celebration, wiping out far more gloom in the process than is suggested by the lyrics in the first place. Then there is another Armstrong version, a medium-tempo vocal recorded in the 1950s (Phillips B07038L), with Velma Middleton singing the standard lyrics fairly straight and Armstrong substituting a new set of his own, which shifts the subject from lost love to insouciant sexuality.

There is also, among other festive treatments too numerous to list, Earl Hines's boogie-woogie arrangement for piano and orchestra, which became a big popular hit in the 1940s. But then long before the heyday of boogie woogie—which, it so happens, is by functional definition blues music played eight to the bar in medium- or up-tempo over a steady bass or left hand—instrumentalists were ragging and jazzing blues choruses. W. C. Handy's band musicians are said to have begun jazzing the breaks on *The Memphis Blues* (erstwhile *Mister Crump*) on the very first performance, and there is good reason to believe that such jazzing was already a part of the stock in trade of the folk musicians whose work Handy used as his point of departure. It was by all accounts already the forte of the legendary Buddy Bolden before the turn of the century. By the way, *Bolden's Blues*, which others called *Buddy Bolden's Blues* has been dated as of 1902, some seven years before Handy's *Mister Crump*, of 1909, which he redid and renamed *The Memphis Blues* in 1912. And Jelly Roll Morton, whose orchestrated extensions, elaborations, and refinements of blues music represent achievements of far greater significance than Handy's tunes, seems to have been ragging, stomping, jazzing, and riffing everything within earshot at least as early as 1900.

In point of fact, up-tempo treatment alone is of itself enough to contradict, repudiate, and transcend lyrics far more downhearted than those of *The St. Louis Blues*. But as is also entirely consistent with the festive and affirmative nature of the traditional Saturday Night Function, and the vaudeville show too, for that matter, when *The Memphis Blues* and *Beale Street Blues* are rendered in medium or slow-drag tempo, the effect is not to negate or even diminish but rather to reiterate the goodtime-oriented message of the lyrics. Far from being incompatible with an atmosphere of enjoyment, the slow-drag tempo is, as the very notion of the fabled Easy Rider implies, a key factor operating to create that idiomatic groove of down-to-earth, person-to-person intimacy that is as inimical to gloom and doom as is the up-tempo stomp, the jump, or the shout.

Still the notion that all blues lyrics are necessarily mournful has become so deeply embedded over the years that any reference to *singing* the blues is likely to suggest the act of crying over misfortune, or moaning and groaning in misery and wretchedness, whining for sympathy over one's mean lot in life, voicing a complaint, or just plain bellyaching—infinitely more instantaneously than it ever evokes the simple concrete image of a musical performance, even of melancholy lyrics! On the other hand, when working musicians speak of playing the blues their terminology is not only consistent with what actually happens in a musical performance, but is no less applicable to the vocalist than to instrumentalists.

Blues musicians play music not only in the theatrical sense that actors play or stage a performance, but also in the general sense of playing for recreation, as when participating in games of skill. They also play in the sense of gamboling, in the sense that is to say, of fooling around or kidding around with, toying with, or otherwise having fun with. Sometimes they also improvise and in the process they elaborate, extend, and refine. But what they do in all instances involves the technical skill, imagination, talent, and eventually the taste that adds up to artifice. And of course such is the overall nature of play, which is so often a form of reenactment to begin with, that sometimes it also amounts to ritual.

By the same token, to the extent that references to singing the blues have come to suggest crying over misfortune, there is also likely to be the implication that blues music does not require artifice but is rather a species of direct emotional expression in the raw, the natural outpouring of personal anxiety and anguish, which in addition to reinforcing the old confusion of blues music with a case of blues as such, also ignores what a blues performance so obviously is. It is precisely an artful contrivance, designed for entertainment and aesthetic gratification; and its effectiveness depends on the mastery by one means or another of the fundamentals of the craft of music in general and a special sensitivity to the nuances of the idiom in particular.

When working musicians (whether they execute by ear or by score) announce that they are about to play the blues, what they most often mean is either that the next number on the program is composed in the traditional twelve-bar blues-chorus form, or that they are about to use the traditional twelve-bar chorus or stanza as the basis for improvisation. They do not mean that they are about to display their own raw emotions. They are not really going to be crying, grieving, groaning, moaning, or shouting and screaming. They mean that they are about to proceed in terms of a very specific technology of stylization.

SEVEN

Playing the Blues

SOMETIMES it all begins with the piano player vamping till ready, a vamp being an improvised introduction consisting of anything from the repetition of a chordal progression as a warm-up exercise to an improvised overture. Sometimes the vamp has already begun even before the name of the next number is given. Some singers, for instance, especially those who provide their own accompaniment on piano or guitar, use it as much as background for a running line of chatter, commentary, or mock didacticism as to set the mood and tempo for the next selection. Also, sometimes it is used to maintain the ambiance of the occasion and sometimes to change it.

Then the composition as such, which is made up of verses (optional), choruses (refrains), riffs, and breaks, begins. Some blues compositions such as Handy's *Yellow Dog Blues* have an introductory or verse section which establishes the basis for the choral refrain. Many, like Bessie Smith's *Long Old Road* and Big Joe Turner's *Piney Brown's Blues*, do not, and in practice perhaps more often than not the verse is omitted by singers as well as instrumentalists. But whether there is a vamp and/or a verse section, the main body of a blues composition consists of a series of choruses derived from the traditional three-line-stanza form. There may be as many choruses as the musician is inspired to play, unless there are such predetermined restrictions as recording space, broadcast time, or duration of a standard popular dance tune.

The traditional twelve-bar blues stanza-chorus consists of three lines of four bars each. But there are four bars of music in each line and only two bars (plus one beat) of lyric space:

	IST BAR	2ND BAR
WORDS	Going to Chicago	Sorry but I can't take you
MUSIC	*1 - 2 - 3 - 4*	*1 - 2 - 3 - 4 - 1*
	3RD BAR	4TH BAR
MUSIC	*2 - 3 - 4*	*1 - 2 - 3 - 4*

	5TH BAR	6TH BAR
WORDS	Going to Chicago	Sorry but I can't take you
MUSIC	*1 - 2 - 3 - 4*	*1 - 2 - 3 - 4 - 1*
	7TH BAR	8TH BAR
MUSIC	*2 - 3 - 4*	*1 - 2 - 3 - 4*
	9TH BAR	10TH BAR
WORDS	S'Nothing in Chicago	That a monkey woman can do
MUSIC	*1 - 2 - 3 - 4*	*1 - 2 - 3 - 4 - 1*
	11TH BAR	12TH BAR
MUSIC	*2 - 3 - 4*	*1 - 2 - 3 - 4*

Which by the way also means that there is always approximately twice as much music in a blues chorus as lyric space—even when it is a vocal chorus and the singer is performing a cappella and has to hum and/or drum his own fills.

Some choruses are refrain stanzas played by an instrumental ensemble, apparently a derivation and extension of the vocal choir. Some are played by a single instrument representing a choir. Originally a chorus, which is derived from the same root as *choreography*, was a dance and by extension a group of dancers (as it still is in musical comedies) and by further extension it also became an ensemble or a band of musicians who played for dancers. In ancient Greek drama it was the group of dancers and chanters who provided the necessary background, so to speak, for the solo performer or protagonist. Hence eventually the passages of the European oratorio which are performed by the choir, whether in unison or in polyphony, as opposed to the solo passages.

In most conventional compositions the chorus or refrain is the part that is repeated by all available voices or instruments. But sometimes musicians refer to the solos as choruses. Duke Ellington, for example, used to announce that the first chorus of his theme song would be played by the pianist (himself); then he would sit down and improvise an extended solo of any number of stanzas. Likewise the singer's solo of a blues arrangement may consist of one or several choruses but is also known as the vocal chorus.

Blues musicians also make extensive use of riff choruses. A blues riff is a brief musical phrase that is repeated, sometimes

with very subtle variations, over the length of a stanza as the
chordal pattern follows its normal progression. Sometimes the
riff chorus is used as background for the lead melody and as
choral *response* to the solo *call* line. But many arrangements are
structured largely and sometimes almost entirely of riff choruses. In Count Basie's original recording of *One O'Clock Jump*
(Decca DXSB-7170) for example, the piano begins with a brief
traditional music-hall or vaudeville vamp and a solo and is followed by a tenor-sax solo backed by a trumpet-ensemble riff.
Then comes a trombone solo over a reed-ensemble riff; and a
second tenor saxophone is backed by the trumpet ensemble
playing a different riff; and a trumpet solo is backed by another
reed-ensemble riff. Then there is a twelve-bar rhythm chorus
punctuated by solo piano riffs; and finally there is a sequence of
three more ensemble riff choruses (the trumpets and trombones
repeating a call-and-response figure over and over while the
reeds play three different unison riffs) as a climax or outchorus.

When they are effective, riffs always seem as spontaneous as
if they were improvised in the heat of performance. So much
so that riffing is sometimes regarded as being synonymous
with improvisation. But such is not always the case by any
means. Not only are riffs as much a part of some arrangements
and orchestrations as the lead melody, but many consist of
nothing more than stock phrases, quotations from some familiar melody, or even clichés that just happen to be popular at
the moment. But then in the jam session, which seems to have
been the direct source of the Kansas City riff style as featured
by Bennie Moten, Count Basie, and Andy Kirk, among others,
improvisation includes spontaneous appropriation (or inspired
allusion, which sometimes is also a form of signifying) no less
than on-the-spot invention. Moreover, as is also the case with
the best of the so-called unaltered found objects on exhibition
in some of the better avant-garde art galleries, the invention of
creative process lies not in the originality of the phrase as such,
but in the way it is used in a frame of reference!

Background or accompanimental riffs not only provide a
harmonic setting for the solo melody, but sometimes they also
function as the ensemble response to the solo call, much the
same as the Amen Corner moans and the chants of the
general-congregation reply to the solo voice of the minister

(and the prayer leader) during the Sunday Morning Service. Which is also to say that they may sometimes serve as an exhortation to the soloist. But sometimes what with all the shouting and stomping, it is also somewhat as if the ensembles were either chasing or fleeing, or otherwise contesting the soloist. At other times it is not so much like a contest as like a game of leapfrog.

Nothing is likely to seem more spontaneous than call-and-response passages, especially in live performances, where they almost always seem to grow directly out of the excitement of the moment, as if the musicians were possessed by some secular equivalent of the Holy Ghost. But as is no less the practice in the Sunday Morning Service, the responses are not only stylized (and stylized in terms of a specific idiom, to boot), but are almost always led by those who have a special competence in such devices. After all, no matter how deeply moved a musician may be, whether by personal, social, or even aesthetic circumstances, he must always play notes that fulfill the requirements of the context, a feat which presupposes far more skill and taste than raw emotion.

Obviously, such skill and taste are matters of background, experience, and idiomatic orientation. What they represent is not natural impulse but the refinement of habit, custom, and tradition become second nature, so to speak. Indeed on close inspection what was assumed to have been unpremeditated art is likely to be largely a matter of conditioned reflex, which is nothing other than the end product of discipline, or in a word, training. In any case practice is as indispensable to blues musicians as to any other kind. As a very great trumpet player, whose soulfulness was never in question, used to say, "Man, if you ain't got the chops for the dots, ain't nothing happening."

That musicians whose sense of incantation and percussion was conditioned by the blues idiom in the first place are likely to handle its peculiarities with greater ease and assurance than outsiders of comparable or even superior conventional skill should surprise no one. But that does not mean, as is so often implied, if not stated outright, that their expression is less a matter of artifice, but rather that they have had more practice with the technical peculiarities involved and have also in the normal course of things acquired what is tantamount to a more refined sensitivity to the inherent nuances.

All of which makes what is only a performance seem like a direct display of natural reflexes, because it obscures the technical effort. But blues performances are based on a mastery of a very specific technology of stylization by one means or another nonetheless. And besides, effective make-believe is the whole point of all the aesthetic technique and all the rehearsals from the outset. Nor does the authenticity of any performance of blues music depend upon the musician being true to his own private feelings. It depends upon his idiomatic ease and consistency.

Another technical device peculiar to blues music is the break, which is a very special kind of ad-lib bridge passage or cadenza-like interlude between two musical phrases that are separated by an interruption or interval in the established cadence. Customarily there may be a sharp shotlike accent and the normal or established flow of the rhythm and the melody stop, much the same as a sentence seems to halt, but only pauses at a colon. Then the gap, usually of not more than four bars, is filled in most often but not always by a solo instrument, whose statement is usually impromptu or improvised even when it is a quotation or a variation from some well-known melody. Then when the regular rhythm is picked up again (while the ensemble, if any, falls back in), it is as if you had been holding your breath.

Louis Armstrong's Hot Seven recording of *Weary Blues* (Columbia Golden Era Series CL 852)—which, by the way, expresses not weariness but a stomping exuberance—contains a number of easily identified breaks. The first follows the opening waillike ensemble chant and is filled by a clarinet. The second follows the first full chorus by the ensemble and is also filled in by the clarinet. The third, fourth, and fifth are filled in by the banjo. The sixth, seventh, and eighth are filled by the tuba; and the ninth by Armstrong himself on trumpet.

In a sense Armstrong's second solo in *Potato Head Blues* (Columbia Golden Era Series CL 852) represents a more elaborate use of the options of the break. It consists of sixteen consecutive two-bar phrases, each filling a break following a heavy beat that functions as the musical equivalent of a colon. Then there is also Duke Ellington's *C-Jam Blues* (RCA Victor

LPV 541) in which each of the five solo choruses, beginning
with Ray Nance on violin, starts out as a two-bar-break improvisation. Ellington's title *Bugle Breaks* (Jazz Society AA 502) is
quite simply a literal reference to the structure of what is one
of his versions of *Bugle Call Rag*, which he plays as if mainly to
feature four trumpet break-fills plus one by trombone and two
by a trumpet ensemble.

Break passages are far more likely to be improvised on the
spot than riff figures. But sometimes improvising on the break
is also referred to as riffing, as Armstrong does on his recording
of *Lazy River* (Columbia Golden Era Series C 854) when he
finishes scatting a break and chuckles (not unlike a painter
stepping back to admire his own brush stroke): "Boy, if I ain't
riffing this evening I hope something."

Many riffs no doubt begin as just such on-the-spot break-fill
improvisations as the one Armstrong was so pleased with. Because, as evolution of the so-called head or unwritten arrange-
ment/composition suggests, as soon as the special ones are
played they are almost always made a part of a score (written
or not) either by the player or somebody else.

Sometimes the riffs replace the original melody, or indeed
become the melodic line of an extension that may be a new
composition. Duke Ellington's *Crescendo in Blue* and *Diminuendo in Blue* sound like such an extension of *The St. Louis
Blues*, and when his arrangement for a vocal version of *The St.
Louis Blues* (RCA Victor LPM 306) is heard with the singer
out of the range of the microphone as in the recording (Pima
01 and 02) made during a performance at the Chicago Civic
Opera, November 11, 1946, then it sounds like still another
composition. Similarly, the only scrap of the melody of the
original *St. Louis Blues* in the version arranged for Dizzy Gillespie by Budd Johnson (RCA Victor LJM 1009) is Gillespie's
trumpet-solo approximation of the vocal lines: "St. Louis
woman with her diamond rings/pulls that man around by her
apron strings." The rest is mostly riff choruses plus a saxophone
solo plus the trumpet playing what amounts to a sort of mini-
concerto which, by the way, includes a bop-style break daz-
zlingly executed by Gillespie—the likes of which was matched
only by Charlie Parker.

What with recordings making them available for the most

careful study through endless repetition, break passages are also memorized, repeated, imitated, and incorporated into scores. It is not at all unusual for one musician's break to become another's riff chorus—or lead melody. The break with which King Oliver opens his cornet solo in *Snag It* (Decca Jazz Heritage Series DL 79246) seems to have been considered as being in the public domain as soon as other musicians heard it, and has been used as a Buddy Bolden–like clarion call to revelry ever since, not only by other soloists but by arrangers as well. Blues musicians across the nation spent long hours rehearsing and appropriating Armstrong's breaks on *Beau Koo Jack* (Okeh 8680) to name only one, and the same thing happened with Charlie Parker's alto break on *Night in Tunisia* (Baronet Records B 105).

In other words, when Armstrong said what he said on *Lazy River*, he knew very well whereof he spoke. A riff is a musical phrase used as a refrain chorus, background chorus, response chorus, echo chorus, and so on; and a riff tune is one constructed mainly of riff choruses; but the process of riffing (from the verb, *to riff*) refers not only to making riff phrases and playing riff choruses and substituting riffs for melodies as written, but also to improvisation in general. Thus the term *riff session* often refers to a jam session.

Among other fundamental prerequisites for playing (and playing with) blues music are such essentials of rhythmic nuance as beat and syncopation. Keeping the beat or beating time, whether by foot tapping, hand clapping, finger snapping, head rocking, or by means of the bass drum, bass fiddle, tuba, piano pedal, and so on, may seem ever so natural to the uninitiated listener, but it is a matter of very precise musicianship nevertheless. The more precise the musicianship, which is to say, the musical know-how, discipline, and skill, the more natural-seeming the beat—as natural in effect as the human pulse. One of the most precise, distinctive, and highly celebrated rhythm sections in the entire history of blues music was the so-called All American Rhythm Section (Jo Jones, drums; Walter Page, bass; Freddie Green, guitar; and Count Basie, piano) of the Count Basie Orchestra from the mid-1930s to the late 1940s. And yet the drummer not only seemed to be the most nonchalant person on hand, it was also almost always as if you felt the beat more than you actually heard it, which of course was exactly the way it should be. Sometimes, indeed it was as if Jo Jones only whispered the beat.

At the same time nonchalance was also the ultimate effect created by the flamboyant showmanship of Chick Webb. All of the stamping and sweating of Gene Krupa, a Webb-derived white drummer of the so-called Swing Era, gave the impression that he was putting himself so totally into the act of beating it out that he was possessed (for the time being) by some violent tom-tom-oriented savage force. But with Webb it was as if the breathtaking rolls, lightninglike breaks and juggler-type stick twirling were designed for the express purpose of making it appear that the drummer was not at all preoccupied with such an elementary matter as timekeeping—or that keeping musical time was so natural that he was ever so free to fool around while doing so.

Yet keeping the appropriate beat is hardly more natural to U.S. Negro musicians than it was for their drum-oriented forebears in ancestral Africa, where musicians were always required to be thoroughly trained and formally certified professionals. To the Africans from whom the dance-beat disposition of U.S. Negroes is derived, rhythm was far more a matter of discipline than of the direct expression of personal feelings. African drummers had to serve a long period of rigidly supervised apprenticeship before being entrusted with such an awesome responsibility as carrying the beat!

Nor is the process of beat, off-beat, or weak-beat accentuation known as syncopation any less a matter of competent musicianship. Used as required by the blues idiom, syncopation seems as natural as the contractions, liaisons, slurs, ellipses, and accents of a normal speaking manner. But the fact that syncopation is necessarily idiomatic means that it is a customary or stylized rather than a natural aspect of expression. Thus it can be refined, elaborated, extended, abstracted, and otherwise played with. It is, as the juxtaposition of any blues recording with any piece of conventional European music will bear out at

once, something that blues musicians play with in the sense of
making use of it as an indispensable device, as well as in the
sense of having fun.

Beat and syncopation are also a matter of taste. But what is
taste if not a matter of idiomatic preference? As in the kitchen,
taste is a sense of recipe, a sense of the most flavorful proportion of the ingredients. In music it is a sense of nuance that
defies notation in the same way as, say, a very fine downhome
cook's offhand-seeming use of a pinch of this, a touch of that,
and a smidgen of the other, confounds the follower of precisely
measured formulas. In both instances the proportions are
matters of idiomatic orientation. Thus the preference is also a
matter of conditioning which is a result of the most careful
training however informal. Indeed, in such cases the more
subtle the training, the more likely the outcome to seem like
second nature.

Still another fundamental aspect of blues musicianship that is
often mistaken as a natural phenomenon is tonal coloration. But
once again the quality of voice that notes are given in the actual
performance of blues music is, uniquely personal endowments
aside, perhaps mainly a matter of idiomatic orientation. Which is
to say that it is perhaps mostly a matter of tonal stylization derived from other performers. Before Bessie Smith there was Ma
Rainey. Before Louis Armstrong there were King Oliver and
Bunk Johnson. Before Duke Ellington there were Jelly Roll
Morton, King Oliver, and Armstrong, as well as the Harlem
Stride piano players and the Fletcher Henderson orchestra.

That timbre and vibrato are devices that Bessie Smith and
Louis Armstrong played with much the same as they played
with beat should be so obvious that it need be mentioned only
in passing, and no less obscure is the profound influence of
Bessie Smith and Louis Armstrong on the tonal coloration of
other musicians over the years. But perhaps the most clearcut
indication of the blues musician's involvement with tonal coloration is some of the accessory equipment such as wa-wa and
Harmon mutes, plungers, and aluminum, felt, and cardboard
derbies for brass; an assortment of sticks, brushes, mallets, and
various other gadgets for voicing drums; and so on. Duke Ellington's use of timbre and vibrato as orchestral devices, as well

as other extensions and refinements, made him the preeminent composer/conductor of blues music.

The tonal nuances of blues music are also a matter of singers playing with their voices as if performing on an instrument, and of instrumentalists using their brasses, woodwinds, strings, keyboards, and percussion as extensions of the human voice. Perhaps reciprocal "voicing" is inherent in the old call-and-response or voice-and-echo pattern as produced by the ratio of instrumental accompaniment space to the lyric space in the basic traditional blues stanza. But, inherent or not, the so-called scat vocal with which the singer plays instrumental music with his voice by using nonsense syllables instead of the words of a lyric is only the most patent form of vocal instrumentation. When Louis Armstrong began singing, it was very much as if he were using his voice to supplement what he had been saying with his trumpet all along—some of which was backtalk for Ma Rainey (as on *Countin' the Blues* [Milestone M 4721] for example) and Bessie Smith (as on *Reckless Blues* and *Sobbing Hearted Blues* [Columbia G 30818]). Nor was the voice of any scat singer ever played more like an instrument than that of Bessie Smith, who, as has been pointed out, could get the same musical effect with the most banal, inconsequential, and indeed *non sequitur* lyrics as with those of the highest poetic quality, which she often misquoted.

On the other hand such was the vocal orientation of Duke Ellington's genius that in addition to achieving the most highly distinctive overall instrumental orchestral sound (made up of instrumental voice extensions), he not only played his orchestra as if it were a single instrument (to an extent that cannot be claimed for any other composer or conductor) but expressed himself on it as if the three-man rhythm section, three trombones, four to six trumpets, five woodwinds (plus occasional strings) were actually the dimensions of one miraculously endowed human voice. As in the tearful hoarseness of the shouting brass ensemble in the call-and-response outchorus of *Perdido* (RCA Victor LPM 1364) for instance; the somewhat worn-out and breathless ensemble woodwinds calling or answering the flippant piano after the drum roll following the stratospheric trumpet solo in *Let the Zoomers Drool* (Fairmont FA 1007); as in the querulous mumbling mixed in with all the stridency of the first trumpet solo of *Hollywood Hangover* (Saga 6926), as in the Armstrong-like gravel tone of the main theme ensemble passages of *Blue Ramble* (Columbia C 31 27).

Such is also the nature of the craft involved in the fusion of in-cantation and percussion known as blues music that even as they play as if on extensions of human voices, blues musicians proceed at the very same time as if their strings, keyboards, brasses, and woodwinds were also extensions of talking drums, fulfilling the conventional timekeeping function while the designated rhythm section, in addition to filling its traditional role, also functions as an instrumental extension of the human voice, making vocal-type statements along with other instrumental voices.

Of course the conventional tonalities inherent in the very nature of keyboards, strings, brasses, and woodwinds are also utilized as such in the process, just as in the most representa-tional painting where paint is used as paint, brush strokes as brush strokes, while the canvas remains a canvas. Inevitably the idiomatic extensions are based squarely on the fact, or at any rate the supposition, that musicians can do certain things on instruments that cannot be done with the human voice—or with talking drums (which seem to have been used for the same reason in the first place). Nor is there likely to be much doubt that such reedmen, say, as Sidney Bechet, Coleman Hawkins, Lester Young, Johnny Hodges, Charlie Parker, and Harry Carney preferred playing saxophone to being singers—or drummers.

Nevertheless, one way for those whose ears are uninitiated to the idiom to become oriented to blues music is for them to begin by listening as if each blues composition was being played by so many talking drums, some voiced as guitars and banjos, some as pianos, trumpets, trombones, saxophones, clarinets, and so on.

Sometimes, as in *Diminuendo in Blue* and *Crescendo in Blue*, not only do the trumpets and trombones extend the shouting and hey-saying voice of the downhome church choir, but they also take the lead in doing drum work and drum talk at the same time. Nor for the most part are the terms in which any of the brasses or woodwinds speak on Count Basie's *Swinging the Blues, Time Out,* and *Panassié Stomp* (Decca DXSB 7170). And what a master drummer among drummers Louis Armstrong becomes with his trumpet and with his voice as well on *Swing That Music* (Decca Jazz Heritage Series DL 79225).

Drum talk is not only what the accompanying guitar, banjo, or piano answers or echoes the folk blues with, and not only what such singers answer and echo themselves with when they hum, beat out or otherwise furnish their own comps, fills, and frills; but it is also most likely to be what all blues singers do even as they play with their voices as if on brasses, keyboards, strings, and woodwinds. But then the use of the break as a fundamental element of blues musicianship already provides an unmistakable clue to how closely blues-idiom statement is geared to the syntax of the drummer. In any case it is a mistake for the uninitiated listener to approach blues music with the assumption that rhythm is only incidental to melody, as it tends to be in European music.

It is not enough, however, to say that blues musicians often play on their horns, their keyboards, and strings as if on drums. Nor is it enough to say that the drums are more African than European in that they keep rhythm and talk at the same time. The rhythmic emphasis of blues music is more obviously African than either the so-called blue note or the call-and-response pattern, but all the same, the actual voices of which all blues instrumentation is an extension speak primarily and definitively as well in the idiomatic accents and tonalities of U.S. Negroes down South. And what is more, not only do they speak about downhome experience, which is to say human experience as perceived by downhome people, but they speak also in the terms, including the onomatopoeia, of downhome phenomena.

So much so that what may once have been West African drum talk has in effect at any rate long since become the locomotive talk of the old steam-driven railroad trains as heard by downhome blackfolk on farms, in work camps, and on the outskirts of southern towns. Not that blues musicians in general are or ever were—or need be—as consciously involved with railroad onomatopoeia as the old-time harmonica players who were Leadbelly's forerunners seem so often to have been. But even so there is more than enough preoccupation with railroad imagery in blues titles, not to mention blues lyrics, to establish the no less mythological than pragmatic role of the old steam-driven locomotive as a fundamental element of immediate significance in the experience and hence the imagination of the so-called black southerners.

Also, as an actual phenomenon of crucial historical significance the old steam-driven railroad train with its heroic beat, its ceremonial bell, and heraldic as well as narrative whistle goes all the way back not only to the legendary times of John Henry and the steel-driving times that were the heyday of nationwide railroad construction, but also to the ante-bellum period of the mostly metaphorical Underground Railroad that the Fugitive Slaves took from the House of Bondage to the Promised Land of Freedom.

The influence of the old smoke-chugging railroad-train engine on the sound of blues music may or may not have been as great as that of the downhome church, but both have been definitive, and sometimes it is hard to say which is the source of what. Item: As used in blues orchestrations one call-and-response sequence may have derived directly from the solo call of the minister and the ensemble response of the congregation in the church service; but another, say as in Louis Armstrong's recording of *Wolverine Blues* (Ace of Hearts AH 7), may well have come from the solo call of the train whistle and the ensemble response of the pumping pistons and rumbling boxcars; and there is a good chance that there are times when a little of both exists in each. Likewise, in church music, cymbals sound as Biblical as tambourines and timbrels, but what they are most likely to suggest when played by blues musicians is the keen percussive explosions of locomotive steam.

Similarly, some of the great variety of bell-like piano sounds that so many blues musicians, piano players in particular, like to play around with may sometimes be stylizations of church bells ringing for Sunday Morning Service, sending tidings, tolling for the dead, and so on; most often they seem to be train bells. The bell-like piano chorus that Count Basie plays against the steady four/four of the bass fiddle, guitar, and cymbals in *One O'Clock Jump* is far more suggestive of the arrival and departure bell of a train pulling into or out of a station than of church bells of any kind.

And the same is essentially the case with train whistles. The influence of church music on blues music is sometimes very direct indeed. Not only do many blues musicians begin as church musicians, but, as is well known, many blues compositions are only secular adaptations of church tunes. Yet as much church-organ influence as may be heard in numberless blues-ensemble passages, the tonal coloration of most of Count Basie's ensemble passages (as on *9:20 Special*, Epic LN 1117) sounds much more like a sophisticated extension of the train-whistle stylizations that have long been the stock in trade of so many downhome harmonica players and guitar players than like church hymns, anthems, spirituals, and gospel music.

But then what with all the gospel trains and glory-bound specials and expresses and all the concern about passengers getting on board and on the right track in church music long before blues music as such came into existence, many of the stylizations of locomotive sounds may have come into the tonal vocabulary of blues musicians by way of the church in the first place rather than directly from the everyday world. Thus for one listener Duke Ellington's *Way Low* (Columbia Archives Series C 3L 39) begins with a church moan while for another it sounds like an orchestrated train whistle; both are at least consistent with the idiom.

Nor does the association in either case lead to the implication that blues music is primarily programmatic. It is not. Onomatopoeia is only a point of departure for the idiomatic play and interplay of what is essentially dance-beat-oriented percussion and incantation. Once voiced or played, even the most literal imitation of the sound of the most familiar everyday phenomenon becomes an element of musical stylization and convention. Thus the railroad sounds in such Ellington compositions as *Daybreak Express* (RCA Victor LVP 506), *Happy Go Lucky Local* (Allegro 1591 and Pima DC 01 and 02) and *The Old Circus Train Turn Around Blues* (Verve V40722) remain unmistakable. But even so, Ellington's unique nuances aside, what all the whistles, steam-driven pistons, bells, and echoes add up to is the long-since-traditional sound of blues-idiom dance-hall music. And, except in novelty numbers like Fletcher Henderson's *Alabamy Bound* (Columbia C 4L 19), musicians approach it not as a matter of railroad mimicry, but in terms of form and craft. Indeed, much goes to show that what musicians are always most likely to be mimicking (and sometimes extending and refining and sometimes counterstating) are the sounds of other musicians who have performed the same or similar compositions.

Thus for all the use Duke Ellington had already made of railroad onomatopoeia in his own compositions over the years, what his version of *9:20 Special* (Swing Treasury 105) mimics, elaborates, and extends is not the sound of an actual train but rather the melody, the KC 4/4 beat, the ensemble choruses and solos with which Earle Warren and the Count Basie Orchestra had already stylized the sound of what may have been the original *9:20 Special*—or may have been still another composition derived from other locomotive sounds that nobody now remembers as such. Anyway, what Ellington's own bell-ringing piano fingers play around with are the already abstract bell-like piano choruses of Count Basie, and the same holds for the ensemble passages. The train-whistle-like sonorities are still very much there for those who have ears for that sort of thing, indeed they may be even more obvious, especially in such woodwind passages as follow the first piano bridge. Nevertheless, the musicians are most likely to have approached the whole thing not as another version of a train, a somewhat slower train; but rather as an Ellington takeoff on a Basie jump number, to be played more like a mellow bounce than as an all-out hard-driving stomp.

Such is the stuff of which blues musicianship is made. It is not a matter of having the blues and giving direct personal release to the raw emotion brought on by suffering. It is a matter of mastering the elements of craft required by the idiom. It is a matter of idiomatic orientation and of the refinement of auditory sensibility in terms of idiomatic nuance. It is a far greater matter of convention, and hence tradition, than of impulse.

It is thus also far more a matter of imitation and variation and counterstatement than of originality. It is not so much what blues musicians bring out of themselves on the spur of the moment as what they do with existing conventions. Sometimes they follow them by extending that which they like or accept, and sometimes by counterstating that which they reject. Which is what W. C. Handy did to folk blues at a certain point. Which is what Bessie Smith seems to have done to Ma Rainey's singing style. It is clearly what Louis Armstrong did to what King Oliver and Bunk Johnson had already done to the trumpet style of Buddy Bolden himself. Count Basie extended the Harlem Stride extension of the ragtime piano in the very process of stripping it down for use as an element of Kansas City riff-style orchestration. The unchallenged supremacy of Duke Ellington is not based on pure invention but on the fact that his oeuvre represents the most comprehensive assimilation, counterstatement, and elaboration of most, if not all, of the elements of blues musicianship.

It was not so much what Charlie Parker did on impulse that made him the formidable soloist and influential revolutionary stylist that he was, it was what he did in response to already existing procedures. His own widely quoted account of his evolution provides a concrete example of the dynamics of acceptance, rejection, and counterstatement, as it operates in the process of innovation:

> Now, I had been getting bored with the stereotyped changes that were being used all the time at that time, and I kept thinking there's bound to be something else. I could hear it sometimes, but I couldn't play it.
>
> Well, that night I was working over *Cherokee*, and as I did, I found that by using the higher intervals of a chord as a melody line and backing them with appropriately related changes, I could play the things I had been hearing.

Such is the nature of the blues-idiom tradition of stylization that what he played begins by being a most elegant extension of some of the innovations of Buster Smith and Lester Young heard in Kansas City back during the days of his apprenticeship.

As for the ritualistic significance of the essential playfulness involved in blues musicianship, it is in effect the very process of improvisation, elaboration, variation, extension, and refinement (or of just plain fooling around, for that matter) that makes sport of, and hence serves to put the blue demons of gloom and ultimate despair to flight. Much has been made of the personal anguish of Charlie Parker, perhaps even more than has been made of the tribulations of Bessie Smith, and indeed there is always some unmistakable evidence of the blues as such somewhere in all of his music, but they are always at bay somewhere in the background, never in the foreground, for there is probably no species of gloomy demon yet known to man that can tolerate the playful and sometimes insouciant and sometimes raucous elegance of the likes of Charlie Parker performing *Ko-Ko* (Savoy MG 12014), *Parker's Mood* (Savoy MG 12009), *Ornithology* and *Yardbird Suite* (Baronet Records B 105), or *Now Is the Time* (Savoy MG 12001) or jamming on *Sweet Georgia Brown* (Milestone MSP 9035). And when the clip gets too fast for most dance couples, as it does on the famous break on *Night in Tunisia*, all they have to do is hold on to each other and listen as Parker makes the notes dance.

EIGHT

Swinging the Blues

ONCE THEY STARTED MAKING phonograph records of it you could hear it almost any time of the day on almost any day of the week and almost anywhere that was far enough away from the church. Because not only did there seem to be at least one phonograph in almost every neighborhood from the very outset, but it was also as if that was the music that phonograph records were all about in the first place, which, incidentally, is also why the Victrola and the Gramophone, which were also called the graphonola and the talking machine, began by being condemned in so many Sunday Morning Sermons as the diabolical apparatus of the Devil's agents of wickedness.

Back before the first phonograph records there were the singing guitar strummers and pickers (and sometimes some harmonica blowers also) who used to play strolling (in half-time or deliberately out of time) along the street and while stashed on certain busy corners or sitting on certain store-front benches; and sometimes when not working in the honky-tonks until the wee hours of the morning like the piano players, they also used to play in certain yards and on certain porches in the summer twilight, and by certain firesides in the wintertime. And sometimes there also used to be one if not several on that part of the picnic grounds and in that part of the baseball field where the moonshine drinkers and gamblers and the sports and the fancy women usually gathered enjoying their own good time between the innings as much as the game itself.

Sometimes the dance orchestras, which were called social bands and ragtime bands and jazz bands but never blues bands or orchestras, also used to play at picnics and at baseball games, especially when it was also a holiday such as the Fourth of July or Labor Day, and afterwards at the dances in all the big ballrooms as well as all the honky-tonks. Because there were ballroom dances to celebrate every holiday of the year in addition to all the other special social occasions not sponsored by the church.

471

There were also the traveling minstrels and the vaudeville shows in those days. They used to stop and play the villages and small towns en route to the next big city theater for the next weekend. And sometimes when they pulled in early enough they also used to send the orchestra around on a truck, with the upright piano jangling and tinkling behind the driver's cabin, the slide trombone tiger-ragging out through the tailgate opening, with the woodwinds doubling in the background and the trumpet climbing up and up and away, echoing across the rooftops and steeples and all the way out beyond the trees to the hills and the outlying regions. Sometimes there was also the singer whose picture was on the advance placards pasted up all over town, especially if it was somebody like, say, Ma Rainey, Ida Cox, Bessie, Clara, Mamie, or Trixie Smith, but singers were mostly to be seen and anticipated, while the barker spieled the come-on through a megaphone.

The old downhome ragtime and barrelhouse piano players used to play (and more often than not, also sing) at night, because except for late Saturday afternoon and late Sunday afternoon that was when most people used to go to the honky-tonks during the week. So, when you were either not yet old enough to be allowed out that late, or you were too good a church member ever to be caught in such places, you heard the piano players mostly in the distance. But sometimes when business was good enough some of them also used to play during weekday afternoons and you could hear them from the street.

But the best time for honky-tonk piano players and blues singers back in those days was always Saturday night. Because the downhome workweek being what it was, that was when most people were out for a good time, and along with all the good barbecue and fried chicken, seafood, and all the whiskey and all the cigars and cigarettes and shaving lotions and hair pomade and perfume and powder, almost everywhere you went there was also music for dancing, and it went on and on into the night and sometimes until daybreak Sunday morning.

So if what you were looking for was the kind of cozy rocking, cozy stomping, downhome good time that goes with the best low-down dirty mean back-alley blues music, there was no time like Saturday night and no place like the honky-tonks, which were also called jook joints and jook houses, when the right singers plus the right piano players (or guitar players) were on hand. But one thing about the honky-tonks was that they featured mostly what was essentially the familiar blues music all the time, much the same, come to think of it, as the Sunday Morning Service retained the traditional chants, moans, hymn-book hymns, anthems, spirituals, and gospel ballads over the years, new compositions being not so much a matter of experiment and innovation as of contribution in kind.

Another thing about the honky-tonks was the big risk you were always running just by being anywhere near them. There was no admission fee; but not only were they forever being raided, broken up either by the county sheriff and his deputies or by the city police, there was also no telling when somebody was going to start another knock-down drag-out rumpus, or there would be another cutting scrape, or the bullets would start flying again. Because the music always added up to a good-time atmosphere. But not for everybody. For some, acceleration of the festivities only aggravated their torment, especially when the object of their passion was there having a good time with somebody else. What with the piano thumping and ringing and the singer walking it and talking it like an evangelist at a revival meeting, somebody was always getting *besides* himself and somebody else was forever getting maimed for life or killed right on the spot.

Saturday night was also the best time to hear the dance bands in such ballrooms as the Elks' Lodge, the Masonic Temple, Odd Fellows' Hall, the Casino, the Pavillion, and the like, where the pay dances and the private invitational socials were held. That was when you could find not only most of the local bands playing somewhere, but as often as not also a territory band or two. And that was also when the long-range traveling bands advertised on the placards were most likely to be booked for, although when they were famous enough and there was notice far enough in advance they were booked for any night their itinerary permitted.

The next best time for all the local bands, nearby territory bands, and also the road bands was on Friday nights. Because during nine months of the year, that was when most of the school-sponsored public dances were scheduled in the big ballrooms, as were also such annual dress-up and costume balls as did not fall on such holidays as Halloween, Saint Valentine's Day, Mardi Gras, Fourth of July, and Labor Day.

Also, the ballroom dances were where you used to hear the ballad singers as well as the blues singers (who were sometimes both), with the ballroom orchestras almost always playing some of the current popular hit tunes and some of their own arrangements and compositions as well as some of the usual everyday twelve-bar blues. Because there were always some dancers who wanted to do all of the latest steps plus all the standard ballroom steps, including at least one waltz, as well as some honky-tonk back-alley shuffling and rolling if the occasion permitted.

Then along with all the phonograph records, there were also the radio networks broadcasting dance music as well as popular songs and concert music day and night, and in no time at all there were more blues-oriented dance bands on the road than ever before. Because whatever else it was used for it was always mostly dance music. Even when it was being performed as an act in a variety show on a vaudeville stage, the most immediate and customary response consisted of such foot tapping, hand clapping, body rocking, and hip rolling as came as close to total dance movement as the facilities and the occasion would allow. Nor was the response likely to be anything except more of the same when the most compelling lyrics were being delivered by Ma Rainey or Bessie Smith, whose every stage gesture, by the way, was also as much dance movement as anything else.

Because such dance steps as consisted of bumping and bouncing, dragging and stomping, hopping and jumping, rocking and rolling, shaking and shouting, and the like, were (and are) precisely what all the percussive incantation was (and still is) all about in the first place; and obviously such movements add up to a good time regardless of the lyrics. Purification and celebration/affirmation without a doubt. But not because the participants proceed in such terms. So far as they are concerned they are out for a good time, which of course is not only reason enough but turns out to be the same thing in any case. And besides, aren't the most functional rituals precisely those that have long since become the most casual conventional and customary procedures?

All the same, it is the symbolical and ceremonial aspects of honky-tonk and ballroom dancing that downhome churchfolk object to first of all. They condemn all the good-time slow dragging, belly rubbing, hip grinding, flirtatious strutting, shouting, and stomping expressly because they regard such movements as not only sinful acts, but sinful ceremony to boot, which they seem to be clearly convinced is even worse. Indeed the impression of honky-tonk dancing that downhome churchfolk have given over the years is that it amounts to the breaking of all the Ten Commandments together.

Nothing therefore is more misleading than the standard dictionary emphasis on gloomy lyrics, the so-called blue notes, and slow tempo—as if blues music were originally composed to be performed as concert music, if not at a prayer meeting or at a convention of beggars. But just as the downhome church elders know better, so do the dance-hall patrons, not to mention working musicians, to whom *it don't mean a thing if it ain't got that swing* was a basic everyday operating principle long before the so-called Swing Era.

What W. C. Handy once wrote about the first performance of one of the great standards contains a typical account of the practical concerns of a working blues composer. "When *The St. Louis Blues* was written," he reports in his autobiography,

> the tango was in vogue. I tricked the dancers by arranging a tango introduction, breaking abruptly into a low-down blues. My eyes swept the floor anxiously, then suddenly I saw the lightning strike. The dancers seemed electrified. Something within them came suddenly to life. An instinct that wanted so much to live, to fling its arms and to spread joy, took them by their heels. By this I was convinced that my new song was accepted.

About the words, Handy, who was his own lyricist, had already written that he had

> decided to use Negro phraseology and dialect. I felt then, as I feel now, that this often implies more than well-chosen English can briefly express. My plot centered around the wail of a love-sick woman for her lost man, but in the telling of it I resorted to the humorous spirit of the bygone coon songs. I used the folk blues three-line stanza that created the twelve-measure strain.

He traces the germinal idea for his composition back to one night when he heard a drunken woman stumbling along a dimly lighted street in St. Louis mumbling, "My man's got a heart like a rock cast in the sea." He remembers the key of G as having been derived from someone whom he had heard giving the figure calls for a dance known as the Kentucky breakdown in a voice like a Presiding Elder preaching at a revival meeting. Then he goes on to say:

> My aim would be to combine ragtime syncopation with a real melody in the spiritual tradition. There was something in the Tango I wanted too. The dancers had convinced me that there was something racial in their response to this rhythm and I had used it in a disguised form in *The Memphis Blues*. Indeed the very word "tango" as I now know, was derived from the African "tangura," and signified this same tom-tom beat. This would figure in my introduction as well as in the middle strain.

Handy, who in 1912 had published *The Memphis Blues*, which he says caused people to dance in the streets in 1909, was recalling 1914. Jelly Roll Morton, the influence of whose musicianship has been infinitely greater than Handy's, says he called a composition he wrote in 1905 in tribute to Porter King, a fellow honky-tonk piano player, *The King Porter Stomp* because it made people stomp their feet. Freddie Keppard's direction to the musicians playing with him was always the same: "Let me hear the feet. Let me hear the feet."

And already before Handy or Morton or Bunk Johnson, Freddie Keppard, and King Oliver, there was the heyday of Buddy Bolden, whose dance-beat orientation went all the way back to the last days of the ancestral dances in Congo Square. The only existing photograph of him shows him and his sextet in a standard band pose for camera, with him holding his cornet chest-high. But the image that always comes first to mind is of him as the Pied Piper of New Orleans dancers; which is also how Jelly Roll Morton, who was there, recollects him:

> I remember we'd be hanging around some corner, wouldn't know that there was going to be a dance out at Lincoln Park. Then we'd hear old Buddy's trumpet coming on and we'd all start. Any time it was quiet at night at Lincoln Park because

maybe the affair hadn't been so well publicized, Buddy Bolden would publicize it! He'd turn his trumpet around toward the city and blow his blues, calling his children home, as he used to say.

The old saying which Duke Ellington turned into a popular tune (and also into a catch phrase for a generation in the bargain) was not so much a statement of fact as a declaration of working principles. *Music* which is not sufficiently dance-beat oriented is not likely to be received with very much enthusiasm by the patrons of downhome honky-tonks, uptown cabarets, and the ballrooms and casinos across the nation. Music can be sweet (and low and ever so slow), or it can be hot (and also fortissimo and up up-tempo) so long as it has the idiomatic rhythmic emphasis that generates the dance-step response. In other words, the incantation must be so percussion oriented that it disposes the listeners to bump and bounce, to slow-drag and steady shuffle, to grind, hop, jump, kick, rock, roll, shout, stomp, and otherwise swing the blues away.

Ellington, who at the time was well on the way to become the outstanding arranger/composer and maestro of the idiom, but was anything but pontifical about anything, was probably only declaring his own definitive aesthetic position, which he never abandoned. Even such extended recital pieces as *Black, Brown and Beige* (RCA Victor LPM 1715), *Such Sweet Thunder* (Columbia CL 1033), *A Tone Parallel to Harlem* [*Harlem*] (RCA Victor LJM 1002), *Suite Thursday* (Columbia CS 8397), are dance-beat oriented; and so are his *Sacred Concerts* (RCA Victor LSP 3582; Fantasy 8407/8; RCA Victor APL 1-0785), which were oratorios written to be performed not in a Holy Roller Church down home but in such all but totally restrained precincts of the Sunday Morning Service as Grace Cathedral, in San Francisco; Fifth Avenue Presbyterian Church and St. John the Divine, in New York; the Church of Saint Sulpice, in Paris; and Coventry Cathedral and Westminster Abbey, in England. Indeed, some thirty-odd years after *It Don't Mean a Thing if It Ain't Got That Swing*, Ellington was to say: "We've done things with the symphony orchestras and our major effort has been to make the symphony orchestra swing, which everybody says can't be done, but I think we managed to do it very well."

But, despite the very strong likelihood that Ellington was mainly speaking of his own conception of blues music, the old saying which he set to music was also a very appropriate motto for the aesthetic point of view that Louis Armstrong, Promethean bringer of syncopated lightning from the Land of the Titans that he was, seems to have taken for granted from the very outset, and to which musicians across the nation (including Ellington himself) were converted in multitudes as if by a spellbinding evangelist. Thus it was also as if Ellington, whose music embodies among other things the most comprehensive synthesis of Armstrong's innovations, was declaring that for most intents and purposes the Armstrong Principle was universal.

NINE

Kansas City Four/Four
and the Velocity of Celebration

NOWHERE ELSE in the nation and at no other time have
blues musicians ever been more firmly dedicated to the
proposition that it don't mean a thing if it ain't got that swing
than in Kansas City in the early 1930s. Nor was the result of the
dedication of this group of journeymen and apprentices to remain primarily a matter of local interest for very long. In no time
at all riffing traditional blues choruses in medium- or up-tempo in
a steady pulsing Kansas City Four/Four beat was picked up by
musicians elsewhere as if it had been in the public domain all
along, and was soon to become and remain the fail-safe tactic
used by blues musicians across the nation on all occasions for
calling Buddy Bolden's Children home to the good-time down-
home ambiance of the Saturday Night Function.

Sometimes when Jo Jones (né Jonathan David), who was
there from Birmingham, Alabama, by way of the entertainment circuit, remembers how things were in Kansas City back
in those days, it is as if the whole town was one big music
workshop. Some places never closed, he has told more than
one interviewer, "You could be sleeping one morning at six
A.M., and a traveling band would come into town for a few
hours, and they would wake you up to make a couple of hours'
session with them until eight in the morning. You never knew
what time in the morning someone would knock on your door
and say they were jamming down the street."

Mary Lou Williams, who was also there (from Pittsburgh
and also by way of the meandering route of the road musician)
remembers things in much the same way. When she arrived to
join her husband, John Williams, a reedman in Andy Kirk's
band at the Pla-Mor Ballroom, she found music all over town
and musicians from everywhere, and there was also plenty of
fine barbecue and seafood. There was always somewhere to go
and hear music, and in addition to the regular cabarets and
ballrooms, there were jam sessions all the time; and sometimes
as many as twelve bands would take turns playing during the

annual big shindig sponsored by the local musician's union. And along with such unforgettable piano players as Sammy Price, Pete Johnson, Clyde Hart, and the then young Count Basie, she also found three women, Julia Lee, who achieved a measure of national recognition as a singer as well; one she remembers only as Oceola; and another known as Countess Margaret.

Count Basie was there from Red Bank, New Jersey, by way of the vaudeville route. Andy Kirk was there from Denver, Colorado, by way of Texas and Oklahoma with The Clouds of Joy (once T. Holder's then his). Walter Page was there from Gallatin, Missouri, by way of Oklahoma City and the Blue Devils Orchestra, Hot Lips Page and Buster Smith were there from Texas by way of Oklahoma City and the same Blue Devils. And so was Lester Young, from Mississippi and Louisiana, by way of the Southwest minstrel, circus, and medicine-show circuit plus the territorial bands, including the Blue Devils.

Very much there already, and long since a part of what getting there was all about for the others was Bennie Moten, whose orchestra (which already had a reputation that extended beyond the region) was later to include a number of Blue Devils and after his sudden death would become the nucleus of the great Count Basie Orchestra. Also already there during that time were the bands of George E. Lee, Clarence Love, and Chauncey Downs (known as the Rinky Dinks).

There were such ballrooms as the Pla-Mor, the Fairyland Park, the Frog Hop in nearby St. Joseph; and such fabulous night spots as the Cherry Blossom, the Reno Club, from which the new Count Basie Orchestra was to be heard on radio in 1936; and Piney Brown's Sunset Club at 12th Street and Highland, where Pete Johnson used to play piano and Big Joe Turner used to shout the blues and serve drinks at the same time. There was also Piney Brown's Subway Club, at 18th and Vine, where so many newcomers got their first local exposure, and also where ambitious youngsters got a chance to sit in with the established professionals, which was also the way it was at the Yellow Front Saloon when it was run by Ellis (The Chief) Burton as if as much for the benefit of the musicians as for the entertainment of the paying customers.

It was a good-time town where a lot of people went out to eat and drink and socialize every night. So there were big

bands as well as combos, quartets, trios, and accompanied soloists working somewhere all during the week as well as Fridays
and Saturdays and holidays; and when on special occasions the
big ballrooms and outdoor pavilions used to sponsor a battle
of the bands as an added feature, the excitement, anticipation,
and partisanship would be all but indistinguishable from that
generated by a championship boxing match or baseball game.

The band to beat back in the old days was always the one led
by Bennie Moten, who because of his emphasis on high-level
musicianship and all-round classiness was sometimes called the
Duke Ellington of the West. Members of the old Blue Devils
Orchestra brag about winning so many battles against so many
other bands that Bennie Moten not only would not do battle
with them, but as a matter of historical fact, hired away most
of their best members, beginning with Count Basie, Eddie
Durham, Jimmy Rushing, Hot Lips Page, and eventually including Walter Page and Buster Smith. Members of The
Rockets still tell about how after leaving Moten upon the arrival of so many Blue Devils they later got the best of him in
the annual battle of the bands.

The Kansas City jam sessions, whose influence on most
contemporary blues musicianship has been far more direct
than, say, the old New Orleans street parades, were already a
matter of legend and myth even then. Most often mentioned
are the ones at the Sunset, the Subway, the Reno, and the
Cherry Blossom. But as almost everybody who was there remembers it now, since there was a piano (and as often as not, a
set of drums also) in almost every joint, there was no telling
when or where the next one would get going. Nor was there
ever any telling when one would break up. It was quite common for musicians to improvise on one number for more than
an hour at such times, and sometimes the session would run
well into the next day—as happened the time Coleman Hawkins came to town with the Fletcher Henderson Orchestra and
got hung up at the Cherry Blossom with Herschel Evans, Ben
Webster, Dick Wilson, and Herman Wadler, among others,
including Lester Young, who was not only to achieve a status
as tenor saxophonist comparable to that of Hawkins himself,
theretofore the undisputed master, but was also to be considered an innovator of perhaps even greater significance.

Sometimes these sessions turned into battles royal or "cutting" contests with the soloists trying to outdo each other; and sometimes they also served as showcases for new talent; but mostly the musicians just wanted to play for the sheer enjoyment of playing. Many musicians used to drop in to such places as the Sunset or the Subway on the way home from their regular engagements and end up jamming for nothing (except treats) the rest of the night. Because that was also where you could try out some of your own new ideas, and of course, it was absolutely the best way to keep current with the latest innovations. The number of Kansas City arrangements and compositions derived from jam sessions is incalculable.

Nor was the Kansas City jam session any less dance-beat oriented for being an experimental laboratory. Thus as much as the instrumental dueling at such sessions was to become a matter of storybook romance, what Kansas City musicians are most widely celebrated for is the drive with which they swing the blues and anything else in all tempos. Whatever they play becomes good-time music because they always maintain the velocity of celebration. Nothing's too fast or too slow to swing, runs Count Basie's correlative to the Armstrong/Ellington Principle: and in addition to the output of Basie's own orchestras over the years, there are also the collected works of Charlie Parker, perhaps the most workshop-oriented of all Kansas City apprentices, to bear him out in spite of all the undanceable European concert-oriented pretentiousness that has been perpetrated by self-styled disciples while using his name in vain. What you hear when you listen to Charlie Parker as a Kansas City innovator is not a theorist dead set on turning dance music into concert music. What you hear is a brilliant protégé of Buster Smith and admirer of Lester Young adding a new dimension of elegance to the Kansas City drive, which is to say to the velocity of celebration. Whether you listen to *Ko-Ko, Warming Up a Riff* (Savoy MG 12014); *Parker's Mood, Billie's Bounce* (Savoy MG 12009); *Charlie Parker with Strings* (Columbia 33 CX 10081 England); *KC Blues* (Verve V6-8409) or just anything chosen at random, the evidence is the same: Kansas City apprentice-become-master that he was, Charlie Parker was out to swing not less but more. Sometimes he tangled up your feet but that was when he sometimes made your insides dance as never before. At his best he could make your insides cut all the steps that your feet could not cut anyway.

Sometimes, as the traditional choreography of Saturday Night Function makes manifest, you get rid of the blues by jumping them, stomping them, swinging them (as a sack of rubbish), and so on. The special drive of Kansas City music is in this sense a device for herding or even stampeding the blues away. In any case the Kansas City drummer not only maintains that ever steady yet always flexible transcontinental locomotivelike drive of the KC 4/4, he also behaves for all the world like a whip-cracking trail driver. And so do Kansas City brass ensembles on occasion also bark and yap and snap precisely as if in pursuit of some invisible quarry, with the piano player sicking them on.

Similarly, as is altogether consistent with the characteristic velocity of affirmation and celebration that seems so inherent in the KC 4/4, the Kansas City blues singer, whose archetypes are Jimmy Rushing and Big Joe Turner, shouts the blues away and shouts a church-rocking-stomping-jumping-shimmying good time into being in the process. Obviously the shout-style vocal suggests the whistle of a transcontinental locomotive highballing it across the great plains. Also, whether or not another western workaday source of stylization for the Kansas City shout is the traditional whooping and hollering of the range rider and the trail driver, there is no question about whether or not Jimmy Rushing and Big Joe Turner rode herd on the blue devils, spurring on the instrumental accompaniment as if from the saddle atop a quarter horse the while.

But as far as that goes, sometimes it is also as if each Kansas City musician were riding the blues as if astride a bucking bronco. And come to think of it, wasn't there something of the rodeo about the Kansas City jam session from the outset? The competition among the participants was as incidental to the challenge of the music itself as the competition among cowboys for rodeo prizes was to the elemental contest between man and the wild animal.

About the evolution of the Kansas City Four/Four, Jo Jones, who as the drummer in the Count Basie Orchestra from the mid-thirties through the early forties was largely responsible for extending it into the national domain, has said: "When Bennie Moten's two beat one and three rhythm and the two and four of Walter Page's Blue Devils came together in the Basie band, there was an even flow one-two-three-four." (Walter Page himself playing what came to be known as walking string bass, with Eddie Durham and later Freddie Green chording on rhythm guitar, provided the anchor for the Basie rhythm section, as Jo Jones mostly subdued his snare and bass except to accentuate, and rode his high-hat cymbal as if whispering. Meanwhile there was also the also and the so forth and so on of talking drums plus tinkling and singing bells in Count Basie's own nothing-if-not-percussive piano.)

The Four/Four is a definitive element of the Kansas City process of stylization, and so is the use of jam-session-like riff choruses as a basic structural device. As is well known, many of the most enduring Kansas City compositions, which are essentially a sequence of such choruses (some alternating with solos, some used as background for solos, and some in call-and-response exchanges between solo and ensembles) began as head, or improvised, arrangements of jam-session renditions. Indeed, sometimes all the arranger/composer had to do was routine the order and limit the duration and number of exchanges.

Take *One O'Clock Jump*. Buster Smith says: "We were fooling around at the club and Basie was playing along in F. That was his favorite key. He hollered to me that he was going to switch to D Flat and for me to 'set' something. I started playing that opening reed riff [from *Six or Seven Times*] on alto. Lips Page jumped in with the trumpet part without any trouble and Dan Minor thought up the trombone part. That was it—a 'head.'"

Most of the early compositions that make up the now classic Basie repertory seem to have begun as head arrangements. As Dicky Wells, who was featured in the trombone section from 1938 to 1949, told Stanley Dance in *Night People*:

> Basie would start out and vamp a little, set a tempo and call out "that's it!" He'd set a rhythm for the saxes first, and Earle Warren in Buster Smith's old alto seat would pick that up and lead the saxes. Then he'd set one for the bones and we'd pick that up. Now it's our rhythm against theirs. The third rhythm would be for the trumpets and they'd start fanning with their

derbies. [Derbies were very effective with brass sections then, and it's too bad they're so little used now. Derby men like Lips Page, Sidney De Paris, and Harry Edison could always make your insides dance.] The solos would fall in between the ensembles, but that's how the piece would begin, and that's how Basie put his tunes together.

What Wells, who was not a Kansas City apprentice, by the way, goes on to say a few pages later, obviously has as much to do with Kansas City as with Count Basie nevertheless:

> Basie really began to get a book together when Ed Durham was in the band. Basie and Ed would lock up in a room with a little jug, and Basie would play the ideas and Ed would voice them. . . . After Durham left Basie began to buy different arrangements from the outside. Even so Basie always played a big part, because he would cut out what he didn't like, what wasn't Western style, just as he does today, until he got it swinging. . . . He always believed in making people's feet pat. . . . And he had that feeling for tempo. He'd start the band off, maybe fool around with the rhythm section for thirty-two bars, until he got it right. . . .

Eddie Durham, the guitarist-trombonist-arranger/composer, who was there from Texas back in the good old days of perpetual high times, and whose *Out the Window*, *Time Out*, and *Topsy* (Decca DXSB 7170) are almost always included in listings of the Best of Count Basie, says:

> Basie was always full of ideas, but you couldn't get him to stay still long enough to get them down. We'd be working together, him playing and me writing, and after a few bars he'd start getting restless. He just wanted to play it. And after he got famous he didn't care about writing at all anymore. I used to try to tell him they ought to get somebody to write up all that good stuff we'd been playing all that time, and he'd just say, "Aw, hell, they won't voice it right."

Incidentally, the context of the performance is the primary consideration underlying the length of riff-chorus compositions. They often begin with a vamp, and they usually end with an outchorus or tag; but the number of ensembles and solos in the main body of both the traditional twelve-bar blues and thirty-two-bar pop forms vary in accordance with the situation.

In a jam session they may run on indefinitely, as in the old Mary Lou Williams story about dropping members of the Andy Kirk band off at the Sunset on the way from their regular nightly nine to twelve engagement at the Pla-Mor, and going on home to bathe and change clothes and coming back to find Pete Johnson still riffing the same tune, with some of the musicians from Kirk's band now participating in relays. Sometimes the main reason Kansas City musicians recall the time the local saxophone players jumped Coleman Hawkins is to tell about how Ben Webster had to go and get Mary Lou Williams out of bed at 4 A.M. the next morning because they had worn out all of the available piano players. Jo Jones said it was not at all unusual for a number to be jammed for an hour and a half in those days.

The duration of a ballroom rendition for the customary turn around the dance floor tends to be approximately three minutes, which is also the length of the standard thirty-two-bar popular song, which was also the length of standard phono records. Perhaps as a result—but for whatever reason—even though most 33⅓ RPM recordings contain almost forty-five minutes of music (twenty-plus minutes per side), they tend to be albums or collections in which most of the items are less than ten minutes in duration. Not that Kansas City arranger/composers have failed to take advantage of the LP, but even so what they have mostly done is to extend the old three-minute composition much the same as it was always extended in the jam session. Sometimes they simply increase the duration of each solo. Sometimes they add new riff choruses, and sometimes they merely increase the number of repetitions of the same riffs. On some occasions the outchorus may be extended into an encore, or indeed several encores, depending on how many times the leader says *One more time.*

But whatever the circumstances of the performance, and whatever the duration of any given selection, Kansas City music seems always to have been nothing if not something to pat your feet by. And such has been the influence that it has exercised on contemporary sensibilities that not only has it now come to seem to be the most natural and irrepressible musical expression of down-to-earth merriment in the world, but also, whether the occasion is a ballroom dance, a night-club show, a concert recital, a jam session, or a record party in a living room, as soon as the Four/Four begins (sometimes along with the vamp and sometimes after it and sometimes before it) and the first riff chorus gets going, the atmosphere changes so instantaneously that it is as if a Master of the Revels had suddenly interrupted the proceedings to command: "*Say now, hey now, that's all right about all that other carrying on and stuff, I say let the good times roll!*"

TEN

The Blues as Dance Music

SOMETIMES you get the impression that many of the articles
and books about blues music were written by people who
assume that the very best thing that could happen to it would
be for it to cease being dance-hall music and become concert-
hall music. Over the years most of these writers themselves
have been show-biz-oriented entertainment-page reporters and
reviewers, whose contact with the workaday environment of
blues musicians is somewhat similar to that of the movie reporter and reviewer with the world of movie actors. So much
so in fact that many have spent a considerable amount of time
grinding out movie-fan-magazine–type articles on the personal
lives of the more prominent performers, whom they glamorize
and condescend to at the same time.

Many also overlard their copy with downhome and uptown
slang expressions, such as *dig* for *understand* and *appreciate*,
bad for *excellent*, *taking care of business* for *performing in an
outstanding manner*, and so on, as if to prove that their contact
with the idiom is that of a very hip which is to say sophisticated
insider. But sometimes the results are even more exasperating
than ludicrous. Item: The use of the word *funky* to mean
earthy and *soulful*. The insider's traditional use is synonymous
with foul body odor and connotes the pungent smell of sweat-
saturated clothes and unwashed bodies, undeodorized armpits,
improperly wiped backsides, urine-stained and fart-polluted
undergarments. To the ever-so-hip reporter *funky* seems to
suggest earthy people-to-people euphoria. To the insider it
suggests asphyxiation. As in a version of Jelly Roll Morton's
Buddy Bolden's Blues:

> *I thought I heard Buddy Bolden say*
> *Nasty, dirty, funky butt take him away.*
> *I thought I heard Buddy Bolden shout*
> *Open up the window and let the bad air out.*

But with all their pseudo-inside wordplay, all the gratuitous
redundancies about jazz which is to say blues music being an

488

art form indigenous to the United States, and indeed with all their ever ready lip-service to the element of swing as a definitive factor of the idiom, when these very same reporter/reviewers give their evaluations of actual performances, whether live or on records, it is almost always as if they were writing about the concert music of Europe. They condone as well as condemn on assumptions that are essentially those of the European Academy. Not that they themselves seem to be basically hostile to any of the indispensable elements of the idiom. On the contrary, they seem to be personally fascinated and delighted by them. But even so they almost always write as if about concert-hall music rather than dance music.

Some have even written that blues musicians should not have to play in honky-tonks, dance halls, night clubs, variety shows, popular festivals, and the like. As if downright oblivious to the literal source as well as the intrinsic nature and function of the idiom, some have gone so far as to represent the experience of playing in Storyville, or the dives and dance halls of Memphis, Chicago, Kansas City, and Harlem as a most outrageous form of injustice! There are those who even as they used to declare Duke Ellington to be the greatest of American composers immediately began wringing their hands and shaking their heads over what struck them as being the cruel state of affairs that forced him to spend most of his time on the road with his orchestra playing in night clubs, ballrooms, and theaters. The fact that Duke Ellington had already become Ellington the Composer by writing music for such places long before his first Carnegie Hall concert seems to have escaped them at such moments, as did the fact that as important as formal concerts came to be to Ellington, he never expressed any desire to take his orchestra off the circuit. As he said one night during an intermission in a dance at the Propeller Club at Tuskegee to a young literary type who was concerned about an article that had reported him (Ellington) as having said that he continued to write dance music mainly to win more people over to his longer concert pieces:

Don't pay any attention to those guys, sweetie. When you get so goddamn important you can't play places like this anymore you might as well give it up, because you're finished. We

try to play everything. We're always very happy when they ask
us to play proms, weddings, country clubs, ballparks. You see,
this way we get to have most of the fun, because the dancers
are not just sitting there watching; they're having a ball.

There is nothing at all ironic about *Stomping at the Savoy*
and *Moten Swing* being written by musicians for whom the
Saturday Night Function was as much a part of what life is all
about as is the Sunday Morning Service. Nor does there seem
to be any compelling reason why the audiences for whom such
music was written and performed in the first place should not
continue to be able to enjoy it in its natural setting simply because another audience now exists in the concert hall.

Not that the function of the concert hall is not also fundamental. It provides a showcase for the new and serves as a
permanent gallery, so to speak, for the enduring. Moreover, as
in the case of the great masterpieces of European church
music, it affords opportunities for the music to be heard on its
own apart from its role as an element in a ritual, in other words
as a work of art per se. Thus the concert-hall recital at its best
is in a very real sense also an indispensable extension of the
dance hall. It can serve as a sort of finger-snapping, foot-tapping
annex auditorium, where the repertory includes not only the
new and the perennial but also such classics as, say, *Grandpa's
Spells*, *Sugar Foot Stomp*, and *Potato Head Blues*, that some
dancers may be too fad-conditioned or otherwise preoccupied
to request. Also, inasmuch as all occasions and circumstances
seem to generate musical responses sooner or later, there is
nothing intrinsically inauthentic about blues music which is
composed specifically for concert recital.

But then the phonograph record has served as the blues
musician's equivalent to the concert hall almost from the outset. It has been in effect his concert hall without walls, his
musée imaginaire, his comprehensive anthology, and also his
sacred repository and official archive. Many blues-idiom composers use the recorded performance as the authorized score.
Jo Jones and Eddie Durham have said that the first written
arrangement of Count Basie's *One O'Clock Jump* was copied
from the record by Buck Clayton (Decca DXSB 7170). Historians and critics of the idiom also use the recorded performance

as the official score. What Martin Williams, for example, refers to in his discussion of Jelly Roll Morton, Duke Ellington, and Thelonious Monk as outstanding composers is not their collected scores but their recorded performances. Williams's book *The Jazz Tradition* is based primarily on recorded performances, and the same is true of Gunther Schuller's *Early Jazz.*

Nor is that all. For much goes to show that it may have been precisely the phonograph record (along with radio) that in effect required the more ambitious blues musicians to satisfy the concert-oriented listeners and Bacchanalian revelers at the very same time; long before the first formal concerts. Even as Chick Webb kept them stomping at the Savoy Ballroom on Lenox Avenue in Harlem, and Earl Hines kept them shuffling at the Grand Terrace on the South Side in Chicago, their orchestras were also playing what to all intents and purposes was a finger-snapping, foot-tapping concert for listeners huddled around radios all over the nation. (Not a few dance parties all over the nation were also geared to the radio, but that is another story.) Moreover most of the program was either already available on records or soon would be. When any of the orchestras that had made recordings of merit went on tour, musicians found other musicians and laymen alike in almost every town who were not only as familiar with their styles as with the mannerisms of a favorite athlete but also could recite their solos note for note.

Anytime a band pulled into town early enough before the engagement it was always the same story no matter where it was: *"Hey, here's that Goddamn Lester, man. Goddamn. What say Lester? This my man, cousin.* Dogging Around, *man, you know that record? That's my record. Right after old Count gets through cutting his little old diamond, here come my natural boy: Doo dooby dooby dooby daba doodadoo. . . . Say what you drinking Lester? You want something to eat? You can't spend no money in this town, Lester. You know that, don't you?*

"Man, here that bad Mr. Johnny Hodges. Man, here the Rabbit, in person all the way from the Cotton Club in the Heart of Harlem. Hey, Johnny, you know that thing you did called Squatty Roo? *Man I played that record and some cats around here started to give up blowing. Then they borrowed my record and like to wore it out. You got them working, Johnny."*

Louis Armstrong had so many musicians working like that

on his records in so many places that people used to say all he
had to do to play a dance in any town of any size was just turn
up with his horn, because all he needed was a couple of hours
and he could round up enough local musicians who knew his
records note for note to make up any kind of band he wanted
to work with for the occasion. They also used to like to tell
about how sometimes when the people got there and saw all
the hometown musicians on the bandstand they started grumbling, and then old Louis would thread it all together with his
trumpet as if with a golden needle and everybody would settle
down and have a good time. Whether that part was true or not
the way they used to like to tell it, you could see old Louis
with his trumpet case and his manager with a briefcase, and
maybe a piano player with a folder full of music, being met at
the local train station in the middle of the afternoon by the
hometown promoter, who already had all the musicians waiting for him at the dance hall. Then, as they used to tell it, all
old Louis would do was sit off to one side on the bandstand
stripping and cleaning his horn piece by piece while the piano
player held the audition and ran through a quick rehearsal.
That was all it usually took, because what happened was that
they spent the whole dance playing for old Louis, while the
rest of the local musicians (along with a number of radio and
record fans and hipsters) clustered around the stage in what
Count Basie has referred to as the bandstand audience and
which is the ballroom equivalent of the traditional Second
Line that dances and prances along beside the marching bands
in the New Orleans street parades.

In other words, although it may not have been possible for
the masterpieces of Mozart, Bach, and Beethoven to have
been composed had not music been released from the restrictions of its secondary role as an element in a ritual to become
an independent art form as such, it does not follow that the
concert hall is therefore indispensable to the extension, elaboration, and ultimate refinement of the intrinsic possibilities of
blues music. For one thing, the great body of European Art
Music was already in existence and already a part of the heritage of blues musicians. It was already there to be played with,
and blues musicians did just that, as they did with everything
else in earshot that struck their fancy. And the dancers loved it.

But what is at issue is the primordial cultural conditioning of the people for whom blues music was created in the first place. They are dance-beat-oriented people. They refine all movement in the direction of dance-beat elegance. Their work movements become dance movements and so do their play movements; and so, indeed, do all the movements they use every day, including the way they walk, stand, turn, wave, shake hands, reach, or make any gesture at all. So, if the overwhelming preponderance of their most talented musicians has been almost exclusively preoccupied with the composition and performance of dance music, it is altogether consistent with their most fundamental conceptions of and responses to existence itself.

And besides, as little as has been made of it by students of culture, not to mention assessors and technicians of social well-being, the quality of dance music may actually be of far greater fundamental significance than that of concert music anyway. Dance, after all, not only antedates music, but is also probably the most specific source of music and most of the other art forms as well. It is not by chance that poetry, for instance, is measured in feet, and that drama was originally mainly a combination of poetry and choreography performed not on a stage but in the orchestra, in other words, a dancing place! Furthermore, dance, according to impressive anthropological data, seems to have been the first means by which human consciousness objectified, symbolized, and stylized its perceptions, conceptions, and feelings. Thus the very evidence which suggests that the pragmatic function of concert music is to represent the dancing of attitudes also serves to reinforce the notion that dance is indispensable.

Reporters and reviewers who assume that their role is to determine how well blues music measures up to standards based on principles formulated from the special conceptions and techniques of European concert-hall music are misguided not only as to the most pragmatic function of criticism but as to the fundamental nature of art as well. For art is always a matter of idiomatic stylization, it transcends both time and place. Thus criticism, the most elementary obligation of which is to increase the accessibility of aesthetic presentation, is primarily a matter of coming to terms with such special peculiarities as may be involved in a given process of stylization.

What counts in a work of art, which after all must achieve such universality as it can through the particulars of the experience most native to it, is not the degree to which it conforms to theories, formulas, and rules that are best regarded as being, like Aristotle's *Poetics*, generalizations after the fact, but how adequately it fulfills the requirements of the circumstances for which it was created. When, as in the case of the masterpieces of Renaissance painting and Baroque music, great art goes beyond its original imperatives, it does so by extending the implications of its response to its original circumstances—as happened with the entertainments William Shakespeare concocted (in much the same manner as a blues-idiom arranger/composer, by the way) for the diversion of the patrons of the Globe Theatre. The source of the three unities in the drama of Ancient Greece is not Aristotle's abstractions about form and propriety but rather the vernacular circumstances of play production during the time of Aeschylus, Sophocles, and Euripides approximately a hundred years earlier!

Such being the nature of the creative process, the most fundamental prerequisite for mediating between the work of art and the audience, spectators, or readers, as the case may be, is not reverence for the so-called classics but rather an understanding of what is being stylized plus an accurate insight into how it is being stylized. Each masterwork of art, it must be remembered, is always first of all a comprehensive synthesis of all the aspects of its idiom. Thus to ignore its idiomatic roots is to miss the essential nature of its statement, and art is nothing if not stylized statement. Indeed it is precisely the stylization that is the statement. In short, no matter how much reviewers know about the classics of European music or any other music, they should presume to interpret and evaluate the work of blues musicians only when their familiarity with the special syntax of the blues convention is such that they are able to discern the relative emphasis each musician under consideration places on the definitive component of the idiom that is his actual frame of reference.

Not that the masterworks of the great European composers are not a fundamental part of all American musical sensibilities.

Not that they are not also indispensable to the reporter's over-all perception of context and universal significance. Nevertheless it is primarily in terms of his vernacular, which is to say, the actual working frame of reference, that a blues musician's sense of proportion must be judged.

ELEVEN

Folk Art and Fine Art

So far as some people are concerned, to be sure, the only authentic blues music is that which is made up and performed by folk musicians. As such people see it, the elaborations, extensions, and refinements of the professional musicians are not the means by which the idiomatic is given the more inclusive range, greater precision of nuance, and more universal impact of fine art. What it all adds up to in their opinion is a basic violation of the priceless integrity of folk art.

Sometimes such people seem to have as many academic pieties about the inherent merits of folk music as some others seem to have about the intrinsic superiority of the music of the European recital hall. Few hesitate to declare, if only by implication, that folk art is the most valid, reliable, and comprehensive representation of actuality—as opposed to the distortions inherent in the artificialities of fine art. And yet in the case of blues music, it so happens that their own firsthand contact with the actualities of the experience being stylized is often extremely limited, to say the least. Nevertheless, they seem to regard themselves as being fully qualified somehow to reject the professional blues musician's preoccupation with craft and refinement out of hand. *Because in their view it can only result in pretension and decadence.*

But the assumption that folk expression is the unalloyed product of a direct stimulus/response interaction with natural environmental forces is fallacious. Folk expression is nothing if not conventional in the most fundamental sense of the word. Far from being spontaneous, as is so often supposed, it is formal. It is of its very nature traditional. The exact opposite of unadulterated invention growing out of the creative ingenuity of individuals uninhibited by regulations and unencumbered by the whims of fashion, it conforms to rigorously restrictive local, regional, which is to say provincial, ground rules that have been so completely established and accepted as to require little if any enforcement as such beyond initiation and apprenticeship instruction.

Perhaps what makes folk responses seem so natural and so free of ceremonial formality is the fact that they have long since become deeply ingrained habits! In any case the most distinctive feature of folk expression whether in the crafts or the arts is not its inherent orientation toward innovation but rather its all but total reliance on custom. The folk craftsman as artist is not primarily concerned with turning out something never before seen or heard of. He is concerned with doing what is expected of him, with showing how well he can do what he has been taught to do, with maintaining standards. Thus his subjects, themes, and his procedures are always those that are customary to his locality or province—even when the raw materials are not. Indeed he even clings to as many of the old ways as possible long after he has been trans-planted to a new setting of radically different circumstances and requirements!

The seldom questioned assumption that folk creativity is the primal source or wellspring of sophisticated art and technology is also misleading. Being inherently conservative or traditional, folk expression is necessarily imitative and thus not primordial in any intrinsic sense at all but *derivative*. Moreover what it imitates and is itself derived from is such sophisticated art and technology as it has been able to come by through the process of corruption and vulgarization, or in a word, popularization. Folkways are always the old ways. Folklore is the old lore. Folk music is the old-time music. In other words, folk expression is old sophisticated technology, wisdom, and art, only now it is assumed to be indigenous to unsophisticated craftsmen, sages, and artists.

So actually it seems far more accurate to say that folk crafts, folk arts, and folklore are the source of much that in the natu-ral process of things becomes the object of interest of sophisti-cated craftsmen and artists and in consequence is *reprocessed* or re-refined into sophisticated technology and art. Even as hap-pens when some old hand-me-down folk ditty strikes the fancy of a sophisticated blues arranger/composer. Even as avant-garde artists appropriate a piece of commercial artwork that is a watered-down version of something copied from a sophisti-cated artist in the first place. The point, of course, is not the process of historical evolution of the dynamics of assimilation and feedback through which sophistication itself first came into being. What is at issue is whether folk expression is as pure a wellspring as it is so often taken for granted as being, and the evidence suggests only that it is one functional source among other functional sources—which include other sophisticated arts and crafts. After all, the creative process also involves counter-statement and extension.

Indeed, one very practical way to become properly oriented to the definitive characteristics of the work of any individual artist in any field is to approach it in terms of that which the artist is trying to counterstate as well as that which he is trying to extend. For the identity of each individual artist consists mainly of that unique combination of what he accepts among all the existing examples of stylization and is trying to extend, elaborate, and refine and maybe even transcend (as if to say: Yes, yes, yes, and also and also) on the one hand, and what he rejects as inadequate and misleading on the other and tries to counterstate with his own output (as if to say No, no, no; this is the way I see it, hear it, feel it).

Incidentally, sophisticated blues musicians extend, refine, and counterstate pop music, especially the thirty-two-bar show tune, in precisely the same manner as they do the traditional folk-type blues strain. Indeed, as the endless list of outstanding blues-idiom compositions derived from the songs of Jerome Kern, Irving Berlin, George Gershwin, Cole Porter, Harold Arlen, Vincent Youmans, and Walter Donaldson, among others, so clearly indicates, blues musicians proceed as if the Broadway musical were in fact a major source of relatively crude but fascinating folk materials!

As for those inclined to take exception to the notion that folk craftsmen and artists are lacking in imagination and inventiveness, perhaps they have forgotten what folk expression is really like. To begin with, it is predictable not experimental. In truth, it places no premium on newness as such. It is as far as is possible the same old stuff time and again. The same old-time tunes played (except for mistakes) the same old way, preferably on the same old instruments; the same old jokes and yarns and riddles and catches; the same old quilt patterns and needlework and pottery and straw baskets, and so on. Moreover those who do not adhere are far less likely to be applauded for being imaginative and inventive as derided for being ignorant and without talent and taste. It is the individual genius who deviates, experiments, and riffs. Folk craftsmen and artists conform. They do not accept the new until it has been well established. It is very obvious once you think about it: *Invention comes from people of special talent and genius, not from those who are circumscribed by routine.*

Nor should folk expression be confused with primitive, aboriginal, or savage arts and crafts. Folk arts and crafts are naïve. Primitive arts and crafts are sophisticated. They are not the crude imitation, corruption, vulgarization, or popularization of a more sophisticated stylization. They represent the very highest refinement of the rituals and technologies of a given culture. Also, no matter how relatively uncivilized or even utterly savage a given aboriginal culture may be, its art is the work of thoroughly trained professionals whose outlook being tribal-wide or kingdom-wide is anything but provincial in the sense that is characteristic of folk expression.

It may be that the only folk expression in many so-called primitive cultures exists at the level of children's play. The articles of carving and weaving for sale to tourists in contemporary African countries are of course another matter. They are not primitive; they are folk and pseudo-folk imitations of primitive carving and weaving. In any case it is also fallacious to assume that the origins of such Afro-American folkways, arts, and lore as may in fact have been derived directly from specific and clearly delineated African antecedents are folk origins.

There are also those who assume that folk simplicity represents a deliberate, down-to-earth, self-confident rejection of over-refinement and decadence. But once again the orthodox conformist is somehow made out to be a rebel. Once again the naïveté of the unsophisticated is represented as being a higher form of sophistication. It is no such thing. The truth is that folk artists are far more likely to be overimpressed and intimidated by fanciness than repelled by it. Indeed nobody seems more vulnerable to pretentiousness, decadence, and even perversion. Who buys all the dime-store junk, all the tacky clothes and gaudy furniture? Who supports the pulp magazines, the grade-B movies, and the freak shows? Any two-bit city slicker knows that the homespun suckers head for the section of town where the clip joints are. Only the overenthusiastic partisans of folk art seem not to suspect that such ridicule as provincials heap on the highfalutin is likely to come from uneasiness rather than any feeling of condescending superiority.

It is the nonfolk folk-art enthusiast, not the folk artist himself, who seems to dismiss most virtuosity as being tantamount to decadence and sterility. Folk artists almost always seem not only fascinated but overwhelmed by it—and only too eager to acquire and display as much of it as their limited technique will enable them to come by. Nor should it be forgotten that in the process many become top-level professionals who, when they look back, describe it all as a matter of personal improvement.

On the other hand all that is required for most professional blues musicians to play at the level of folk competence is less technical precision. Being for the most part a product of the very same folk experience as the folk artist they have always enjoyed comparable sensitivity to provincial nuances. In a sense all they have to do is relax into the proper fuzziness of articulation. Certainly it is not a matter of the folk artist being less artificial. It is all a matter of stylization. Perhaps the folk artist seems less artificial, but the fact is that he simply sticks to the old familiar modes of stylization, and the result is that customary artificiality which is taken for granted as the natural way, but which is no less artificial withal. The stylizations of Leadbelly, Blind Lemon Jefferson, Tampa Red, Leroy Carr, Lonnie Johnson, Muddy Waters, and Lightnin' Hopkins are not less artificial than those of, say, Floyd Smith, Charlie Christian, Otis Spann, and George Benson, only less sophisticated.

Still, many of the partisans of folk expression who also admire Bessie Smith, for instance, seem to do so not because they esteem her as the great professional that she was (whose stylistic innovations represent the very highest level of idiomatic refinement) but rather because they regard her as a natural phenomenon with a deeply stirring voice that was a great vehicle of honest expression precisely because it struck them as being untrained and hence unstylized. Perhaps they assume that her music is necessarily as crude as her diction so often was. It is not. Moreover, far from restricting herself to the limitations of her diction, she almost always worked with the most sophisticated professionals available in the idiom. Such accompanists as Clarence Williams, Fletcher Henderson, James P. Johnson, Porter Grainger, Louis Armstrong, Joe Smith, Buster Bailey, Don Redman, and Coleman Hawkins could hardly be considered folk musicians by any standard.

But after all what really seems to underlie most of the notions of those who prefer folk art to fine art are the same old essentially sentimental assumptions that make for pastoral literature (and for political theories about noble savages). Thus, much the same as pastoral poetry presents its rustics as being on better terms with life than courtiers because they are closer to nature, so would promoters of folk art as the true art have you believe that a provincial musical sensibility is somehow a greater endowment than a more cosmopolitan sensibility plus a greater mastery of technique. It absolutely is not. It limits not only what folk artists can do but also what they can perceive and imagine in the first place.

On the other hand, all too often the professional blues musician's involvement with elaboration, extension, and refinement does indeed get out of control and degenerate into pretentious display and a mindless pursuit of novelty for its own sake—or in the name of some sophomoric conception of progress. In fact, those who shift their primary orientation from the ballroom to the concert hall (giving up the immediate response of the dancers for that of the reviewer!) seem especially vulnerable to such decadence and pretentiousness.

No less pretentious, however, are those pseudo-folk blues musicians whose experiences are no longer those that gave rise to the traditional folk-blues folk song, but who limit themselves to traditional folk modes even as they address themselves to the problems of the New York Stock Exchange, the proper way to conduct international relations, space technology, and the like, for the edification of chic patrons of avant-garde night clubs, sometimes while performing on electronic instruments that are nothing if not as *dernier cri* as the limousines and jetliners they travel around in for the most part.

There is much to be said for such blues music as is indeed

folk song. But however much there is to say about the authentic earthiness of Blind Lemon Jefferson and Leadbelly, for instance, without whose best output no collection of twentieth-century American music should be considered truly representative, there is a good deal more to be said for the no less authentic extensions and refinements that have resulted from the playful options taken by such consecrated professionals as Jelly Roll Morton, Louis Armstrong, Bessie Smith, Lester Young, Charlie Parker, and Duke Ellington. Because the point is that unless the idiom is not only robust and earthy enough but also refined enough with a range comprehensive enough to reflect the subtleties and complexities of contemporary experience, it is not likely to be a very effective counteragent of the blues or any other demons, devils, or dragons.

The preeminent embodiment of the blues musician as artist was Duke Ellington, who, in the course of fulfilling the role of entertainer, not only came to address himself to the basic imperatives of music as a fine art but also achieved the most comprehensive synthesis, extension, and refinement to date of all the elements of blues musicianship. Indeed so all-inclusive was Ellington's synthesis that it amounts to a special vocabulary and syntax of orchestration.

But then as Ernest Hemingway wrote in *Death in the Afternoon* about bull fighting, regarding it not as a folk spectacle but a fine art practiced by individuals who were by exclusive devotion and training the most sophisticated professionals:

> All art is only done by the individual. The individual is all you ever have and all schools only serve to classify their members as failures. *The individual, the great artist when he comes, uses everything that has been discovered or known about his art up to that point, being able to accept or reject in a time so short it seems that the knowledge was born with him, rather than that he takes instantly what it takes the ordinary man a lifetime to know, and then the great artist goes beyond what has been done or known and makes something of his own.*

Those who regard Ellington as the most representative American composer have good reason. Not unlike Emerson, Melville, Whitman, Twain, Hemingway, and Faulkner in literature, he quite obviously has converted more of the actual texture and vitality of American life into first-rate universally appealing music than anybody else. Moreover he has done so in terms of such vernacular devices of blues musicianship as vamps, riffs, breaks, fills, call-and-response sequences, idiomatic syncopation, downhome folk timbres, drum-oriented horns, strings, and so on. By comparison the sonorities, not to mention the devices of Charles Ives, Walter Piston, Virgil Thomson, Aaron Copland, Roger Sessions, John Cage, and Elliott Carter, for example, seem if not downright European, at least as European as American. In any case the Ellington canon, which consists mainly of three-minute dance pieces, is by far the most comprehensive orchestration of the actual sound and beat of life in the United States ever accomplished by a single composer. *Mainstem, Harlem Airshaft, Echoes of Harlem, Across the Track Blues, Sepia Panorama,* and *Showboat Shuffle* are only a random few of an endless flow of matchless evocations of the spirit of place in America. Nor is any other American composer responsible for instrumental extensions of American voice and speech that are more significant than those that are so immediately manifest in *Mood Indigo, Harmony in Harlem, In a Jam, Ko-Ko, Concerto for Cootie,* and *Rockabye River.* Even when Ellington addresses himself to natural phenomenon, as in *Lightnin'* and *Dusk,* or to such universal rituals as the chase, as in *Cotton Tail,* or is just playing with instrumental possibilities, as in *Boy Meets Horn* and *Riding on a Blue Note,* his voice and accent are uniquely American.

TWELVE

The Blues as Statement

O RDINARILY BLUES MUSICIANS do not show very much
conscious involvement with the philosophical implications of what they play. Most often their primary musical concerns seem to be those of the artisan. Accordingly, what they
almost always seem to give most of their attention to are the
practical details of the specific convention of stylization in terms
of which they perform. Thus shoptalk as well as arguments
about such professional matters as the characteristics and peculiarities of musical instruments and accessories, fundamentals
of and innovations in technique, the merits and shortcomings
of various systems of execution and exercise manuals, keynote
preferences, the eccentricities of arrangers and the idiosyncra-
sies of other musicians, especially those they admire, are quite
commonplace among them. But beyond that it is mostly as if
they expect the music to speak for itself.

Those who respond to questions (seldom asked by other
musicians) about their involvement with some currently fashionable, though not necessarily popular, stylistic movement, do
so for the most part only with vague, superficial, hand-me-down
generalities about progress, changing with the times, giving the
public something new, making a new contribution, or about
finding themselves. Even when some of those who aligned
themselves with bop, cool, and the special extensions of John
Coltrane and Ornette Coleman, for example, used to claim
that the new music represented a new and even revolutionary
message, they never really addressed themselves to the content
of the new message, or the old one either for that matter. Indeed
what they say about the significance of Charlie Parker, Dizzy
Gillespie, Miles Davis, and John Coltrane, among others, including Thelonious Monk, Ornette Coleman, and John Lewis,
almost always suggests that they are either far more interested
in the social, economic, and political status of the blues musician than in his fundamental function, or that they may confuse
the two.

In any case, not very many blues musicians seem to bother

themselves very much about the fundamental personal and social function of percussive incantation, purification and fertility rituals, and ceremonies of affirmation. But such rituals and ceremonies are precisely what their work is very much about even so. Not only do most perform in special ceremonial costumes of one sort or another to begin with, for example, and not only are the bandstand procedures and manners of honky-tonk piano players, street-corner harmonica and guitar players, night-club and vaudeville entertainers, members of cocktail-lounge combos and dance-band sidemen alike always likely to be as ceremonial as functional; but so more often than not are their attire and deportment in most other situations.

Indeed, the off-duty blues musician tends to remain in character much as does the Minister of the Gospel, and as he makes the rounds he also receives a special deference from the Saturday Night Revelers equivalent to that given off-duty ministers by Sunday Morning Worshipers. The ever-so-casual speech, dress, and movements of Lester Young, for instance, having a sip and a chat with friends or fans in a gin mill in the middle of a midweek afternoon were no less stylized and ceremonial than the traditional formalities of the rhetoric, vestments, and bearing of a member of any priesthood. Nor are the most casual-seeming recording-studio procedures any less a matter of ritual. Most of the slouching about, the jive talk, the joking, and even the nonchalance is as deliberately stylized as is most of the stage business on the bandstand during a performance for a regular audience.

Nor are any of the blues musician's role-defining mannerisms, whether on- or off-stage, likely to be lost on the apprentices. An outstanding case in point is Louis Armstrong, Promethean Culture Hero that he was. In spite of all the uneasiness that some of the minstrel-show aspects of his stage routine caused among socially conscious U.S. Negroes, the extent of his influence on the speech, professional mannerisms, and grooming of blues musicians everywhere is comparable to that which he has had on their instrumental and vocal technique. Much of the ritual jive talk and many of the ceremonial gestures used by most sophisticated blues musicians (and dandyish hangers-on, also known as hipsters) are derived directly from Armstrong during his heyday back in the late twenties and the thirties. It was Armstrong who started musicians referring to themselves as cats and to their control and stamina as their chops (originally the brass player's lips), and to playing well as getting away (and hence, being gone!). It was also Louis Armstrong who popularized such ritualized greetings as What you say, Gates; Well, what you know, Jim; Well, lay it on me, Cousin, Hoss, Home, etc.; Well, give me some skin, man, and endless riffs thereon, with which sophisticated blues musicians still salute each other (sometimes also along with a mumbo-jumbo hand-shaking, palm-slapping, or finger-touching routine) precisely as if they belong to the same very special fraternal order, which of course they do.

At one point in a series of interviews with one Tom Davin, published in *The Jazz Review* in 1959 and 1960, James P. Johnson, one of the most formidable of the Harlem Stride piano players, goes to some lengths to show how fundamental to the blues musician's apprenticeship as a performer was what in effect was a consciousness of his ritual status and his skill at role playing. He begins by telling about how when Willie (The Lion) Smith, who was a sharp dresser and a fine dancer as well as one of the most fearsome piano players in town, walked into a place, his every move was a picture. Johnson in response to a question then goes on to say, "Yes, every move we made was studied, practiced, and developed just like it was a complicated piano piece." Then he not only describes a typical entrance routine but goes into the most minute detail about costuming, including material, the cut, shoes, hats, jewelry, prices, tailors, and hair preparations.

When he was a young fellow, he continues, he was

> very much impressed with such manners. . . . You had to have an attitude, a style of behaving that was your personal, professional trade-mark. . . . The older Clef Club musicians were artists at this kind of acting. The club was the place to go study these glamorous characters. I got a lot of my style from ticklers like Floyd Keppard, who I knew in Jersey City, Dan Avery, Bob Hawkins, Lester Wilson, Freddie Tunstall, Kid Sneeze, Abba Labba, Willie Smith, and many others. . . .
>
> I've seen Jelly Roll Morton, who had a great attitude, approach a piano. He would take his overcoat off. It had a special lining that would catch everybody's eye. So he would turn it

inside out and, instead of folding it, he would lay it lengthwise along the top of the upright piano. He would do this very slowly, very carefully, and very solemnly as if that coat was worth a fortune and had to be handled very tenderly.

Then he'd take a big silk handkerchief, shake it out to show it off properly, and dust off the stool. He'd sit down then, hit his special chord (every tickler had his special chord, like a signal), and he'd be gone!

Every tickler kept these attitudes even when he was socializing at parties or just visiting. They were his professional personality and prepared the audience for the artistic performance to come.

Not all blues musicians place such obvious emphasis on costume and role playing, needless to say. Some proceed for the most part as if they regard music as simply another means of earning a living much the same as any other means of livelihood, and some give the impression that they play mainly because it happens to be the thing for which they have the best technical qualifications. And yet even so, not only do they dress, act, and talk more like other blues musicians than like anybody else, but some of their most casual references to the most routine matters of performance are likely to reflect a functional awareness of their involvement with ritual and role fulfillment:

"Man, if they ain't patting their feet, you ain't swinging and ain't nothing happening, because they spending their money to have a good time, and that's your job. . . .

"People look at you sitting up there and they kinda expect you to be dressed kinda special, you know what I mean? You don't have to overdo it with all that old jive-time monkey stuff. You know what I mean. I'm talking about they come in somewhere they might try to tear the joint up before it's over but they still like to come in there and see some kind of special decorations and all that, because it might be the same old thing every night to you but you got to remember it's always a special occasion with them. That's why most bands wear uniforms. Like baseball teams. Because a baseball game is a special event. And when a band has its own uniform it also looks more professional.

"You know how old Count used to come on like Gang Busters, with the rhythm already up here and the brass up there

and the reeds solid in there. And then he might let the alto
or one of the trumpets do a quick get-away and then tickle
things up himself on the piano and then sic them two bad assed
tenors, old Herschel and old Lester on you and goddamn!
Sometimes we do that too. That's how we used to hit when the
man wanted to get the house warmed up and cutting from the
gitgo. Sometimes we might do a whole set like that, and then
a set to settle them down, and then we might bring on a girl
or maybe a guy or maybe both and do some pop ballads, some
sweet and some on some real snappy arrangements with the
band jiving and signifying and shouting and carrying on in the
background. Then after a while we always bring on the main
blues singer, like when old Count used to call Jimmy Rushing.
Old Duke's main blues singer was always old Johnny Hodges
on that alto, even when he had Herb Jeffries. From then on we
got them grooving until wrap-up time, when we ride on out
like till we meet again."

On the other hand there are also those who place primary
emphasis on costumes and stage business. Back during the
time when the so-called bop and so-called cool movements
were being publicized as the living (which is to say ultimate)
end of all blues stylization and hence the only possible route to
true hipness or in-ness, some used to dress the part of being
appropriately *modern* and *progressive* by wearing a beret and
heavy-frame glasses like Dizzy Gillespie, the then current pace-
setter on trumpet. Many, perhaps many more, used to act the
part by aping the self-centered bandstand mannerisms of Charlie
Parker, the veritable touchstone of the movement, who seems
to have struck them as being so totally wrapped up in the esoteric ramifications of what he was expressing with such overwhelming elegance that nothing else in the world mattered
anymore, not even the paying customers.

Which of course was not the case at all with Parker himself,
who, true to his Kansas City upbringing, was, with all his individuality and in spite of all his personal problems, nothing if
not a sensational crowd pleaser. Nevertheless such was the
primacy of role playing among some of his self-styled followers
that sometimes it was as if the only audience beyond themselves that counted was other musicians, whom they were not
nearly so interested in entertaining as impressing and being
one-up on. Not that they really wanted to be left alone. No

blues-idiom musicians were ever so recital oriented. They wanted audiences that would give them their undivided attention, not dancers out to have their own good time.

But thus did they become involved in another ritual altogether. For the ceremony they are concerned with is not a matter of dance-beat-oriented incantation leading to celebration. They proceed as if playing music were a sacred act of self-expression that can only be defiled by such Dionysian revelry as characterizes the Saturday Night Function, and thus should be restricted to Amen Corner witnesses, and to journalists who (despite their own incurable squareness) will give it maximum publicity in the national and international media and thus reemphasize its exclusiveness and gain new converts at the same time.

What it all represents is an attitude toward the nature of human experience (and the alternatives of human adjustment) that is both elemental and comprehensive. It is a statement about confronting the complexities inherent in the human situation and about improvising or experimenting or riffing or otherwise playing with (or even gambling with) such possibilities as are also inherent in the obstacles, the disjunctures, and the jeopardy. It is also a statement about perseverance and about resilience and thus also about the maintenance of equilibrium despite precarious circumstances and about achieving elegance in the very process of coping with the rudiments of subsistence.

It is thus the musical equivalent of the epic, which Kenneth Burke in *Attitudes Toward History* categorizes as a Frame of Acceptance as opposed to a Frame of Rejection. Burke is discussing poetic statements in terms of whether they represent a disposition to accept the universe with all its problems or to protest against it, and in the category of Acceptance he also includes tragedy, comedy, humor, and the ode. What is accepted, of course, is not the status quo nor any notion of being without potentiality nor even the spirit of the time; what is accepted is the all too obvious fact that human existence is almost always a matter of endeavor and hence also a matter of heroic action.

In the category of Rejection, which he characterizes as representing a negative emphasis while also pointing out that the differentiation cannot be absolute, Burke places the plaint or elegy, satire, burlesque (plus such related forms as polemic and caricature), the grotesque (which he says "focuses in mysticism"), and the didactic, which today is usually called propaganda. At bottom, what is rejected by such statements of lamentation, protestation, and exaggeration is the very existence of the circumstances that make heroic endeavor necessary. Not that most of the lamentation and protestation may not be in interest of better times, but what is featured all the same almost always turns out to be the despicable, the forlorn, the dissipated, and the down and out.

The trouble, however, is that when you get down to details rituals of self-expression are beyond criticism. Anything goes because it is all a matter of the innermost truth of the performer's being. Thus if his musicianship seems lacking in any way, it is not because he is working in an idiom with which the listener is unfamiliar but which has a different set of requirements, but rather because it is the best of all possible ways to express what the musician in question is all about! The self-portrait (and/or the personal signature) that emerges from the music of Jelly Roll Morton, King Oliver, Bessie Smith, Louis Armstrong, Duke Ellington, Lester Young, and Charlie Parker is not primarily a matter of such egotistical self-documentation but rather of the distinction with which they fulfilled inherited roles in the traditional ritual of blues confrontation and purgation, and of life affirmation and continuity through improvisation. Incidentally, the revolutionary nature of their innovations and syntheses was not nearly so much a matter of a quest for newness for the sake of change as of the modifications necessary in order to maintain the definitive essentials of the idiom.

In one sense Charlie Parker's widely imitated innovations did indeed represent a radical counterstatement of certain aspects of the blues convention that had been so overworked that he had come to regard them as the same old thing. But for all that, Parker, unlike so many of his so-called progressive but often only pretentious followers, was not looking for ways to stop blues from swinging; he was looking for ways to make it swing even more, and sometimes when he really got going he achieved an effect that was both flippantly humorous and soulfully lyrical at the same time. On balance, Parker, it is true, must be considered as having been more of a jam-session musician than a dance-hall musician as such; but for him the jam session was not primarily an experimental workshop; it was to remain essentially the same old multidimensional good-time after-hours gathering it had always been. The experimental innovations were mainly a matter of having something special to strut your stuff with when your turn came to solo on the riff-solo-riff merry-go-round.

Nor should the overall personal and social implications of the blues statement be confused with the flamboyant costumes and overstylized mannerisms of the so-called hipsters (erstwhile hip cats and hep cats), the dandies, fops, and swells of the idiom. After all, the hipster's behavior is the same as that of the dilettante, who lives the "literary life" but only dabbles in literature as such. He knows all the right names, and like the *flaneur* of the art galleries he is also nothing if not up to date on what is in vogue as of tomorrow. In a sense he is also like the sedentary spectator whose concerns are completely circumscribed by the world of his favorite sport. Costuming himself and sounding off as if he *belongs* are about the extent of his involvement.

In any case the hipster's application of the disposition to riff with elegance is usually limited to jiving and woofing on his street-corner hangout and to shucking and stuffing along the mainstem, as if the night club, the ballroom, the music hall, and the bars that the performers, gamblers, and the sporting crowd frequent were what life itself were all about. Indeed some hipsters, not unlike some churchgoers, are so preoccupied with the trappings and procedures of the ceremonial occasion per se that their involvement amounts to idolatry. They misconstrue the symbol and the ritual reenactment as the thing itself.

There are those who regard blues music as a statement of rejection because to them it represents the very opposite of heroism. To many it represents only the anguished outcry of the victim, displaying his or her wounds and saying that it is all a lowdown dirty shame. To some, such purification as is involved is not of the atmosphere (which is indeed a matter of epic heroism) but of the individual, whose action is an effort not to contend but to "let it all hang out"; which, however, removes blues music from the realm of ritual and art and makes it a form of psychological therapy (although there is a literary analogy even so: the tear-jerker, the penny dreadful, the pulp confession story, which is almost always the sad saga of a victim). But thus also is blues music mistaken for that of the torch singer.

Blues music, however, is neither negative nor sentimental. It counterstates the torch singer's sob story, sometimes as if with the snap of two fingers! What the customary blues-idiom dance movement reflects is a disposition to encounter obstacle after obstacle as a matter of course. Such jive expressions as *getting with it* and *taking care of business* are references to heroic action. Indeed the improvisation on the break, which is required of blues-idiom musicians and dancers alike, is precisely what epic heroism is based on. In all events, such blues-idiom dance gesture is in effect an exercise in heroic action, and each selection on a dance program is, in a sense, a rehearsal for another of a never-ending sequence of escapades *as is suggested by the very fact that each not so much begins and ends as continues: And one and two and three and four and another one and a two and a three and a four and also and also and also* from vamp to outchorus to the next vamp.

Epilogue

*T*HE MAIN THING *that it is always about is the also and also of dragging, driving, jumping, kicking, swinging, or otherwise stomping away the blues as such and having a good time not only as a result but also in the meanwhile. Which is also why whatever else hearing it makes you remember you also remember being somewhere among people wearing fine clothes and eating and laughing and talking and shucking and stuffing and jiving and conniving and making love. So sometimes it is also about the also and also of signifying and qualifying. Because sometimes, especially when you are still only a very young beginner standing at the edge of the dance floor getting yourself together to go over to where the girls (whose prerogative it is to say no) stand waiting to be approached and asked, it is also as if the orchestra were woofing at you. Back in the heyday of big dance halls like the Savoy, when the orchestra used to break into, say,* Big John Special *(Fletcher Henderson, Decca DL 9228) or, say,* Cavernism *(Earl Hines, Decca DL 9221) or* Second Balcony Jump *(Earl Hines, Bandstand Records 7115) or* Wolverine Blues *(Louis Armstrong, Ace of Hearts AH 7) or* Miss Thing *(Count Basie, Columbia G 31224) or* Panassié Stomp *or* Shorty George, *Every Tub* or *Dogging Around* (Count Basie, Decca DXSB 7170) or, say, *Cotton Tail* (Duke Ellington, RCA Victor LPM 1364), *Johnny Come Lately* (Duke Ellington, RCA Victor LPV 541), *Rockabye River, erstwhile* Hop Skip Jump *(Duke Ellington, RCA Victor LPM 6009) it was as if you were being challenged (in a voice not unlike the rhapsodized thunder of a steam-snorting bluesteel express train highballing it hell for leather) to test your readiness, willingness, and nimbleness by escorting a girl of your choice around and up and down and across and crisscross the ballroom floor as if into and back again from the region of blue devils with all her finery intact, as if who else if not you were the storybook prince, as if whoever if not she were the fairytale princess.*

Not that anybody has ever actually qualified once and for all. When the storybook hero is reported to have lived happily ever after his triumph over the dragon, it is not to be assumed that he is able to retire but rather that what he has been through should

513

make him more insightful, more skillful, more resilient, and
hence better prepared to cope with eventualities. Because there
will always be other dragons, which after all are as much a part
of the nature of things as is bad weather.

Nor has anybody ever been able to get rid of the blues forever
either. You can only drive them away and keep them at bay for
the time being. Because they are always there, as if always waiting
and watching. So retirement is out of the question. But even so
old pro that you have become, sometimes all you have to hear is the
also and also of the drummer signifying on the high-hat cymbal,
even in the distance (and it is as if it were the also and also of
time itself whispering red alert as if in blue italics), and all you
have to do to keep them in their proper place, which is deep in the
dozens, is to pat your feet and snap your fingers.

THE BLUE DEVILS OF NADA

*A Contemporary American Approach
to Aesthetic Statement*

For Mozelle and Michele

CONTENTS

Prologue

Q

Black fiction stems from a largely realistic tradition. Your novel,
Train Whistle Guitar, *and recent nonfiction books are written in
a lyrical, indeed musical style. Do you consider this a departure
from the realist tradition?*

A

I am searching for an adequate metaphor or "objective correlative" for my conception of contemporary actuality. Realism,
regardless of academic definitions, is essentially only a literary
device among other literary or narrative devices—no less than
naturalism, fantasy, surrealism, and so on. Yes, in a sense I
suppose you can say that many writers from my ethnic background have relied on "realistic" devices. But it seems to me
that they have mostly been preoccupied with the literal document as agitprop journalism, so much so that for all the realistic
details to make the reader feel that all this really happens, their
stories seldom rise above the level of one-dimensional patently
partisan social case histories. The Afro-U.S. tradition of idiomatic storytelling on the other hand (not unlike others elsewhere) is largely concerned with the exploits of epic heroes
who are involved with the complexities of human motives and
with the contradictions of human nature and with the ultimate
inscrutability of nature as such.

Q

*In line with that, I wonder if there are any other novelists today
doing the same kind of innovative fiction—and nonfiction—that
you are doing, imbuing jazz rhythms into fiction and prose?*

A

There is Ellison of course, and there are others that I like for one
reason or another, but as of now, aside from the outstanding

exception of Leon Forrest, I'm unaware of any others who share either Ellison's or my involvement with the blues as a literary device. Over the years there has been a tendency to confuse the blues with folk expression, but where the hell did all those writers get the idea that folk, which is to say peasant or provincial, art (or artlessness), is adequate to the complexities of black experience in contemporary America? Louis Armstrong knew better than that and so did Jelly Roll Morton, King Oliver, and Duke Ellington—as did Charlie Parker, Dizzy Gillespie, Miles Davis, and Thelonious Monk, all of whom extended, elaborated and refined that folk stuff as far as talent and craft enabled them.

Q

I've long felt that the English epic poem, which grew into the novel, was in many ways an extension of the ballad. In America there doesn't seem to be much of a musical underpinning to our literature—I guess because our literature was borrowed, historically speaking, from England. Do you think many critics today are receptive to, or aware of, the changes going on in black fiction?

A

I'm not so sure that the English novel is as directly derived from the epic and the ballad as you suggest. Perhaps some influence of poetry was inevitable, but a much more obvious source seems to have been the old practices of diary and journal keeping and letter writing. Nor do I think American literature was borrowed from English literature. It is rather an extension of English language and literature. Also, I don't know how far you can take that musical underpinnings business. What about Melville and Mark Twain? It seems to me that the oral tradition out of which they worked had musical underpinnings. Man, those old New England preachers were not only musical as hell but they were also a major source of the down-home pulpit style and manner. There are Afro elements in most down-home things to be sure; but what they represent is an Afro dimension or Afro accent, which sometimes adds up to an idiom—but an idiom within an existing tradition or convention. (As with basketball, if you get what I mean. The game is from the Northeast, but idiomatically it is more and more an extension of down-home and uptown choreography.) But back to your point, James Joyce's work was obviously influenced by Irish poetry and music, but Gertrude Stein was not less preoccupied with the music inherent in language as such.

Critics? Man, most critics feel that unless brownskin U.S. writers are pissing and moaning about injustice they have nothing to say. In any case it seems that they find it much easier to praise such writers for being angry (which requires no talent, not to mention genius) than for being innovative or insightful.

Q

I am fascinated with the influence of Hemingway on your work. In one article you say that his heroes are blues heroes, which makes a lot of sense. But your style and his are quite different. In what stylistic sense, if any, has he influenced you?

A

Hemingway writes a prose that strikes you as being realistic, and it is indeed more accurate than most reportage, but it is at the same time the very essence of ritual. His cadence is that of process and of ritual reenactment as well. As casual as it seems, his style achieves its realistic effect through what amounts to incantation.

Q

Lastly, and I hope you won't horse-laugh when I say this, but would you consider yourself a romantic?

A

I most certainly do not regard myself as being romantic in any undergraduate academic sense that suggests Byron, Shelley,

Keats, and Wordsworth. On the other hand, take a look at *The Hero and the Blues*. Look at the very last paragraph. In view of what we now think we know about the physical nature of the universe, anybody who thinks of human life as a story is romantic. The thing to avoid is sentimentality. To struggle against the odds, to continue in the face of adversity is romantic, which is to say heroic. To protest the existence of dragons (or even hooded or unhooded Grand Dragons for that matter) is not only sentimental but naïve, it seems to me.

After all, on the one hand there is always the threat of entropy (the tendency of all phenomena to become random), but on the other there is also human consciousness, to which modality is ineluctable, for even chaos is "perceived" as particles and/or waves! In any case, art is a species of deliberate modality derived from reenactment through ritual and play. Thus, the creative act is an effort to give enduring shape or pattern and meaning to perpetual-seeming flux of ongoing experience.

Interview with Jason Berry
in Southern Booklore *magazine, 1977*

Addendum 1995:
The objective of the following observations on the nature of the creative process is to suggest (as does The Hero and the Blues*) that the affirmative disposition toward the harsh actualities of human existence that is characteristic of the fully orchestrated blues statement can be used as a basis upon which (and/or a frame of reference within which) a contemporary storybook heroism may be defined.*

PART I

The Intent of the Artist

Regional Particulars
and Universal Implications

As a very ambitious writer who would like to create fiction that will be of major interest not only as American literature but also as a part of contemporary writing in the world at large, I must say I am not primarily concerned with recording what it is like or what it means to be a Southerner or even a down-home grandson of slaves. My concerns are more fundamentally existential, which is perhaps to say epical, if by epic we mean to suggest an account of a hero involved with elemental problems of survival rather than with social issues as such. In any case, my stories are really about what it means to be human. They are concerned with what Susanne K. Langer calls the life of human feeling.

Which is most certainly not to say that I am not at all or even only a little concerned with being a Southerner, for it is precisely by processing the raw materials of my southern experience into universal aesthetic statement that I am most likely to come to terms with my humanity as such. The condition of man is always a matter of the specific texture of existence in a given place, time, and circumstance.

But the point is that the regional particulars—the idiomatic details, the down-home conventions, the provincial customs and folkways—must be *processed* into artistic statement, *stylized* into significance.

Art, as André Malraux points out in *The Voices of Silence*, is the means by which form is rendered into style. And art is also, as Kenneth Burke has said, fundamental living equipment for our existence as human beings. What these two notions suggest to me is a concern with the quality of human consciousness. Which might also be said to be the basic concern not only of education, whether formal or informal, but also of religion and of all ceremonial occasions including holidays, red-letter days, and pastimes as well.

Applied to literature, this becomes, for me at any rate, a concern with the adequate image, by which I mean the image of the hero or effective protagonist, that personification of human endeavor, if you will, which most accurately reflects the complexities and possibilities of contemporary circumstances or indeed any predicament, and also suggests its richest possibilities. Perhaps one could say that an indispensable function of such an image is either to inform or remind us of these possibilities.

As for a working definition of adequacy, why not measure it in terms of its statistical validity, reliability, and comprehensiveness? It must yield a solid deduction. It must work time and again, and it must have broad applicability. It must work in the world at large; otherwise it has to be rejected as too exclusive, too narrow, or, to get back to the theme, too provincial. Too southern. Of some down-home significance, perhaps; if you like that sort of thing. But not of very much immediate use elsewhere.

So, yes, it is precisely the regional particulars that the storyteller as full-fledged artist processes or stylizes. But it is the universal statement he should be striving for. Beneath the idiomatic surface of your old down-home stomping ground, with all of the ever-so-evocative local color you work so hard to get just right, is the common ground of mankind in general.

The storyteller either says or implies as follows: *Once upon a time in a place far away or nearby or right on this very spot or wherever, where people did things this way or that or however, there was whoever who was in whichever situation (to wit, et cetera) and who did whatsoever. Once upon a time. But perhaps also time after time after time and so on up to this time and this very day. So take note.*

In other words as a serious writer and also as an engaging and entertaining storyteller, you are always concerned with what Kenneth Burke calls the *representative anecdote*, which I take to be that little tale or tidbit of gossip, that little incident that is in effect definitive in that it reflects, suggests, or embodies a basic attitude toward experience.

Ever mindful of the guidelines suggested by Malcolm Cowley in *The Literary Situation*, you approach your anecdotal tidbit not as a symbolic action per se, but rather by treating a basic southern occasion as a basic American occasion, which is in turn a basic contemporary occasion, and thus a basic human occasion. According to Cowley: "*If it isn't real, it isn't a symbol. If it isn't a story, it isn't a myth. If a character doesn't live, he can't be an archetype. . . ."*

Another definition. Art is the ultimate extension, elaboration, and refinement of the rituals that reenact the primary survival techniques (and hence reinforce the basic orientation toward experience) of a given people in a given time, place, and circumstance much the same as holiday commemorations are meant to do.

It is the process of extension, elaboration, and refinement that creates the work of art. It is the *playful* process of extension, elaboration, and refinement that gives rise to the options out of which comes the elegance that is the essence of artistic statement. Such playfulness can give an aesthetic dimension to the most pragmatic of actions.

It is indeed precisely play and playfulness that are indispensable to the creative process. Play in the sense of competition. Play in the sense of chance-taking. Play in the sense of make-believe and play also in the sense of vertigo or getting high. Play also in the direction of simple amusement as in children's games, and play in the direction of gratuitous difficulty as in increasing the number of jacks you can catch or the higher distance you can jump, and as in the wordplay in *Finnegans Wake* or soundplay in a Bach fugue.

Incidentally, implicit in the matter of playful option-taking extension, elaboration, and refinement is the matter of the function of criticism in the arts. For wherever there is extension, elaboration, and refinement, there is the possibility of overextension, overelaboration, and overrefinement, and as likely as not, attenuation.

Perhaps the very first function of criticism is to mediate between the work of art and the uninitiated reader, viewer, or listener. As mediator, the critic decodes and explains the elements of the game of stylization and makes the aesthetic statement more accessible. Then, having indicated what is being stylized and how it is being stylized, the critic may also give a "professional observer's" opinion as to how effectively it has been stylized and perhaps to what personal and social end. In doing all of this, criticism proceeds in terms of taste, which is to say a highly or specially developed sense of the optimum proportion of the basic elements involved and of the relative suitability of the processing. But all of that is a very special story in itself.

To get back to the matter of the representative anecdote. My primary vernacular, regional, or indigenous, or yes, down-home source is the fully orchestrated blues statement, which I regard and have attempted to define and promote as a highly pragmatic and indeed a fundamental device for confrontation, improvisation, and existential affirmation: a strategy for ac-knowledging the fact that life is a lowdown dirty shame and for improvising or riffing on the exigencies of the predicament. What is that all about if not continuity in the face of adversity? Which brings us all to the matter of heroic action and the writer to the matter of the heroic image.

I don't know of a more valid, reliable, comprehensive, or sophisticated frame of reference for defining and recounting heroic action than is provided by the blues idiom, which I submit enables the narrator to deal with tragedy, comedy, melodrama, and farce simultaneously. Obviously I do not hear the blues as a simple lamentation by one who has not loved very wisely and not at all well; and certainly not as any species of political torch song. I hear the music counterstating what-ever tale of woe (or worse) the lyrics might present for con-frontation as part and parcel of the human condition.

The ancient Greek playwrights, remember, addressed them-selves to tragic happenings in one form, dealt with comic confusions and resolutions in another (*even on other days*), and for satiric and farcical matters they used still other forms. I as-sociate melodrama with medieval romance. The great Elizabe-than tragedies, to be sure, did come to include comic relief sequences as a matter of course.

But the fully orchestrated blues statement is something else again. Even as the lyrics wail and quaver a tale of woe, the music may indicate the negative mood suggested by the dread-ful, or in any case regrettable, details, but even so there will also be tantalizing sensuality in the woodwinds, mockery and insouciance among the trumpets, bawdiness from the trom-bones, a totally captivating, even if sometimes somewhat am-bivalent elegance in the ensembles and in the interplay of the solos and ensembles, plus a beat that is likely to be as affirma-tive as the ongoing human pulse itself.

There is much to be said about the literary implications of this aspect of my down-home heritage, and I have written not only in direct terms of it in *South to a Very Old Place*, *The Spyglass Tree*, and *Train Whistle Guitar*, but also in no uncertain terms about it in *The Hero and the Blues* and in *Stomping the Blues*, both of which may be read as being among other things books about literary terminology and as attempts at a functional definition of improvisation as heroic action, as a way of responding to traumatic situations creatively.

So I will reiterate only in passing that (1) blues lyrics should not be confused with torch songs, which wail the heart-on-sleeve frustrations and yearnings of those rejected or discarded ones who still love not wisely and not at all well; and (2) that the improvisation that is the ancestral imperative of blues procedure is completely consistent with and appropriate to those of the frontiersman, the fugitive slave, and the picaresque hero, the survival of each of whom depended largely on an ability to operate on dynamics equivalent to those of the vamp, the riff, and most certainly the break, which jazz musicians regard as the Moment of Truth, or that disjuncture that should bring out your personal best.

The point of all this is that your representative anecdote also provides your representative man, your *hombre de época*, your all-purpose protagonist, whose personal best is exemplary. Incidentally, speaking of the South as such as a locus of motives, as a context for heroic action, I read fellow Southerner William Faulkner's great novel *The Sound and the Fury* as a story about the absence of truly heroic action. Neither poor Benjy, sad Quentin, nor mean Jason can riff or solo on the break, or set a personal pace for a truly swinging ensemble. They are all stuck with stock tunes that only add up to sound and fury, signifying a big mess.

But for all the restrictions that you inherited as a Southerner during the days of my coming of age as an apprentice in literature, being a Southerner did not automatically mean that my mind, my interests, and my aspirations were limited to things southern; moreover, it is not at all unsouthern to read a lot. In any event, it was in a down-home library that I discovered the Joseph in Thomas Mann's *Joseph and His Brothers*, *Young Joseph*, *Joseph in Egypt*, and *Joseph the Provider*, who as I have suggested in *The Hero and the Blues* is a hero whose playful creativity is his stock in trade, and also the salvation of his people.

My attempt to suggest an image of the hero as improviser is Scooter, the first-person narrator of *Train Whistle Guitar*, *The Spyglass Tree*, and *The Seven League Boots*, in which I try to make the literary equivalent of an Ellington orchestration of a little blue steel and patent leather down-home saying that goes: *my name is Jack the Rabbit and my home is in the briar patch*, which for me is only an upbeat way of saying: "*woke up this morning* [with the] *blues all around my bed*" . . . which means that Scooter could also say: *I live in a land menaced by dragons and even Grand Dragons, and that's why I have to be as nimble in brain as in body—or else!—and must either find or forge my own magic sword and be heroic or nobody.*

All of this is nothing if not down-home stuff. Which brings us to our out chorus: it is precisely such southern "roots" that will dispose and also condition my protagonist to function in terms of the rootlessness that is the basic predicament of all humankind in the contemporary world at large.

PART II

Two All-American Artists
First-Person Singular

Duke Ellington Vamping Till Ready

THE PERSONAL RECOLLECTIONS and reflections that Duke Ellington has left in *Music Is My Mistress* were programmed or routined into acts rather than orchestrated into a literary equivalent of, say, *Reminiscin' in Tempo*. So the overall effect is somewhat like that of an all-star variety show, including special guest appearances. But formal structure aside, time and again the actual narration as such becomes so suggestive of Ellington's unique speaking voice and conversational mannerism that you find yourself all but literally backstage looking on and listening in as he recalls people, places, times, circumstances, and events somewhat as if nudged into nostalgia by old friends or some very lucky interviewer.

Not that backstage is ever altogether offstage. But then Duke Ellington himself was never very far from the footlights for very long either. Nor did he ever show or express any overwhelming need to be. What he always needed was listeners, even at rehearsals. And audiences were as essential to his recording sessions as was the accustomed excellence of the studio equipment. After all from him, in whom the instrumentalist, composer, and conductor were so totally and inextricably interrelated, performing music was absolutely indispensable to writing it. Not only was there almost always a keyboard instrument of some kind in his dressing room whenever space permitted, such was also the case with his hotel suites and even his hospital rooms. And he was forever noodling and doodling and jotting and dotting no matter who else was there or what else was going on.

In any case, among the anecdotes, vignettes, plugs, takeoffs, put-ons, whatnots, and what-if-nots in *Music Is My Mistress* there are also some that even seem not so much written as jive-riffed into the microphone *onstage between numbers*. Nor are they thereby any less representative than the rest. Ellington was mostly himself no matter where he was. Indeed, the man behind the legend, as the interviews published several years ago by Stanley Dance in *The World of Duke Ellington* bear out, was if anything even more of a legendary figure to his closest associates than to his millions of worshipful admirers all over the world.

As for his mike spiel, what with the orchestra there in the background, he was (for most intents and purposes) quite possibly as much at home on the job as he was ever likely to be lounging in an armchair by a fireside on a rainy night.

Which is not to say that he was ever given to making public such private (but by no means secret) personal involvements as his schedule permitted. References in *Music Is My Mistress* to his adult family life, for instance, are oblique at best: "I took him [arranger Billy Strayhorn] to 381 Edgecombe Avenue and said, 'This is my home, and this is your home. I'm leaving for Europe in a few days, but you stay here with my son Mercer and my sister Ruth. They will take good care of you.'" So much for that. Mention of previous and subsequent adult addresses is less than oblique. And while there indeed was, as he says he discovered very early, always a pretty girl standing down at the bass clef end of the piano, the only "love interest" discussed concerns music. No kissing and telling for him, or perhaps there was too much kissing for telling. But then the title of his book may have been intended as a statement of precisely the delimitation he wanted.

But even so, *Music Is My Mistress* is an authentic autobiographical document that is strong at precisely those points where so many other books by and about so-called black Americans are so often so exasperatingly weak.

Seldom are such books concerned with making anything more than a political statement of some kind or other, mostly polemical. Rarely do they reflect very much personal involvement with the textures of everyday actuality as such. On the contrary, most often they are likely to leave the impression that every dimension of black experience is directly restricted if not inevitably crippled, by all-pervading (and always sinister) political forces.

More often than not it is as if all of the downright conspicuous orientation to style in general and stylish clothes in particular, all of the manifest love of good cooking and festive music and dancing and communal good times (both secular and sacred), all of the notorious linguistic exuberance, humor, and outrageous nonsense, not to mention all of the preoccupation with love and lovemaking (that blues lyrics are so full of)—it is as if none of these things, otherwise considered to be so characteristic of the so-black American's lifestyle, is of any basic significance whatever once a so-called black American becomes the subject of biographical contemplation.

Actually, most biographies and autobiographies of so-called U.S. black folks tend to read like case histories or monographs written to illustrate some very special (and often very narrow) political theory, or ideology of blackness, or to promote some special political program. Such writing serves a very useful purpose, to be sure. But the approach does tend to oversimplify character, situation, and motive in the interest of social and political issues as such, and in the process human beings at best become sociopolitical abstractions. At worst they are reduced to clichés.

The *Narrative of the Life of Frederick Douglass, an American Slave, Written by Himself*, is as much a classic of nineteenth-century American prose as are the works of Emerson, Longfellow, Hawthorne, Thoreau, Lowell, Holmes, and the rest. Moreover, the story it outlines is nothing less than an unsurpassed representative anecdote (or epic or basic metaphor) of the American ideal of self-realization through the resistance to tyranny. But still it is more of an autobiographical *political* essay than a full-scale comprehensive autobiography. And so were Douglass's *My Bondage and My Freedom* and the *Life and Times of Frederick Douglass.*

Booker T. Washington's *Up from Slavery* is another case in point. It is an autobiographical essay on post-Reconstruction education that is far more concerned with promoting the Hampton-Tuskegee emphasis on normal, agricultural, and trades courses as a basic means of black uplift than with the story of Booker T. Washington himself. And the same is true of Washington's *The Story of My Life and Work* and *My Larger Education.*

In the "Apology" for *Dusk of Dawn*, which he called an essay toward an autobiography of a race [*sic!*] concept, W. E. B. Du Bois flatly states that because midway through the writing he realized he was approaching his seventieth birthday "It threatened . . . to become mere biography. But in my own experience, autobiographies have had little lure; repeatedly they assume too much or too little; too much in dreaming that one's own life has greatly influenced the world; too little in the reticences, repressions, and distortions which come because men do not dare to be absolutely frank." And then curiously, he adds, "My life had its significance and its only deep significance because it was part of a problem. . . ." As if people involved with problems have not always been as great a preoccupation of biography as of fiction and dreams. Still, in *Dusk of Dawn* and in his *Autobiography* there is much richly textured autobiographical writing.

But all told, perhaps the most noteworthy exception to the general run of one-dimensional biographical writing by so-called black Americans is James Weldon Johnson's *Along This Way*. Johnson, who not only wrote the lyrics to "Lift Every Voice and Sing" (The Negro National Anthem) but was also the first executive secretary of the NAACP, was actively involved with problems of civil rights as few have been. But *Along This Way* is not political propaganda. It is a full-scale personal record of a marvelous American who was, among other things, also a professional music hall entertainer, poet, lawyer, diplomat, editor of anthologies of poetry and spirituals, and novelist. Indeed, for historical perspective, comprehensive grasp of circumstance, and sensitivity to the texture of life as such, it may well be the very best autobiographical treatment to date of the experience of a descendant of U.S. slaves.

None of which is to imply that *Music Is My Mistress* is comparable in overall literary merit to *Along This Way*. The two, however, do share basic virtues so often absent from so many autobiographical monographs geared primarily to political statement. To begin with, Ellington, like Johnson, always regarded himself not as a political theory but as a flesh-and-blood human being, a person of capability with many possibilities. Like Johnson he remembers his parents, for instance, not as if they were mostly social problems in urgent need of white liberal compassion, but rather as good-looking, affectionate, prideful, and authoritative adults who expected one to grow up and amount to something. Nor did his black elders treat him as if he were born under a curse. He was always somebody special. "Edward, you are blessed," his mother, who certainly knew the facts of life, told him. That he didn't have anything to worry about. And he believed her, and storybook Duke-designate that he already was, he went out and forged a magnificent sword and conquered the world.

In other words, as is entirely consistent for one whose all-pervading commitment is to an art form, the frame of reference of Ellington's most basic functional conceptions and definitions of himself and his purposes is not political but metaphorical. For all its concrete details including such specifics as employment and budgets, his is the fairy-tale world of heroic encounters and endeavors, where obstacles are regarded not as occasions for welfare-oriented protests, but as a challenge to one's creativity. Thus, the eight "acts" of *Music Is My Mistress* consist mostly of a recounting of the initiation rituals of the apprentice, the trials and contests of the journeyman, and the offerings of the full-fledged craftsman-practitioner. Then comes some modest (and some tongue-in-cheek) words of wisdom and advice from the long since venerable Old Pro, followed by a listing of ceremonial honors and awards and finally a catalog of his good works and exploits.

Such day-to-day actualities were no less the symbolic terms and underlying rituals of Ellington's existence. And to be sure, all of the key *felidae* (as he calls them) in his cast of characters were blue steel fables in the flesh. Which is also why, the dynamics of aesthetic feedback being what they are, references no matter how offhand to James P. Johnson, Willie "the Lion" Smith, Will Marion Cook, Will Vodery, Sidney Bechet, Louis Armstrong, and Fletcher Henderson, among others, are absolutely indispensable sources of insight. Even the sketches of the personalities of the musicians in his orchestra over the years—plus what he includes about Irving Mills, the agent who promoted him into the big time—provide more understanding of the structure as well as the content of Ellington's music than is ever likely to be derived from any examination of deep-seated anxieties resulting from political oppression, or ever likely to be revealed by even the most exhaustive confession of long-hidden personal hangups.

Moreover, although far too many students of history seem far too oversubscribed to the methodology of psychiatric case surveys to realize it these days, in making references to people who struck him as being literally *fabulous*, Ellington is also addressing himself to precisely those basic rituals and myths that all truly serious scholars must discover in order to come to comprehensive terms with the definitive forces that motivate the effort and achievement (or lead to the failures) and shape the lifestyle of the person who is the subject of any biographical study. After all, what the comprehensive, valid, and reliable biography or history must always add up to for all its entirely proper preoccupation with specific fact, is fiction. The subject's vital statistics are such and such and his doings and accomplishments are already a matter of public record and widespread acclaim. *But what is his story?* What, in other words, is his functional mythology, his personal frame of reference?

That Duke Ellington had no intention whatsoever of writing a conventional autobiography on the scale of James Weldon Johnson's *Along This Way*, or even on the lesser scale of W. C. Handy's useful but somewhat stilted *Father of the Blues*, need hardly be argued. Nevertheless, in *Music Is My Mistress*, along with all of the firsthand information and expert but seldom pontifical observations, he has left future biographers and historians the literary equivalent of some of the indispensable piano vamps he used to sit noodling, doodling, and riffing until the ensembles and soloists were ready for the downbeat. He has, that is to say, improvised a prelude, an overture, an introduction that establishes the key, the tempo, mood, direction, and overall treatment for those who wish to deal with his life in his own personal terms, for those who wish to come to terms with what he was really about rather than what they think he should have been about.

As for the biographical or autobiographical social science monograph, its shortcomings are inherent not so much in its methodology as such (aside, of course, from the fact that it cannot be *scientific* enough) but rather in the all too obvious assumption that generalizations, findings, and conclusions drawn from measurable fact are *not fiction*. But aren't all formulations necessarily fabrications? In all events, what finally matters most about both formula and metaphor is the extent of their functional immediacy or comprehensive applicability.

As for those historical research specialists who set out to replace the legendary, the fabulous, or the mythical with scientific
fact, what they end up with are all too often only stereotypes
derived from social science assumptions—which, of course, is
to say social science fiction.

Comping for Count Basie

I N AUTOBIOGRAPHY as in fiction, nothing has more to do with what the story is really about than the voice of the narrator. So the main thing was to get his voice on the page. Everything else came after that. Incidents mean only as much as the way they are told makes them mean. If you couldn't help him sound like himself in print, you'd probably be better off working on a book *about* Count Basie rather than one *by* Count Basie about himself.

Obviously it is the voice of the narrator that establishes not only the physical point of view including the relative sharpness or vagueness of focus and the limits of the field of vision, but also the listening post, which determines the reader's distance from the alarums and excursions if any, and also whether what is being said is heard verbatim or at second remove—and how much is to be heard in either case.

It is also the storyteller's voice that creates the overall atmosphere as well as the specific mood for each situation and sequence of action. The on-the-page equivalent of vocal cadence, tone, and timbre, together with vocabulary, syntax, and imagery determines just *how* whatever is being recollected and recounted is to be taken. Whether the narrator is deadpan or scowling or smiling or laughing or has his tongue in his cheek makes all the difference in the world. The tone of voice may not only represent a sense of life that is not otherwise stated, it may also of its very nature counterstate or cancel out any direct assertion or avowal.

Unlike the narrator of stories in the third person who can either maintain one position and one voice or shift position and voice source at will, the autobiographer speaks in his own voice at all times. Even when the conversation with and between others is quoted as if with total recall, it is still only an approximation. It is, in fact, the narrator mimicking others with his own voice barely disguised, and indeed what really counts is the impression he wishes to convey. Sometimes he may go so far as to put words and phrases that are obviously his own into the mouths of others to create a desired effect. But after all, this is only a storytelling device that has been employed since the days of talking animals during the age of fables and that also permits the ever-so-earthy peasant language of the aristocrats in most folk tales.

Third-person dialogue, on the other hand, can almost always be taken as literal transcription. Moreover, such is also the convention of third-person narration that the degree of intimacy and omniscience the storyteller chooses enables him to represent and indeed give voice to as many memory banks and individual streams of consciousness and to reveal as many private thoughts, anxieties, fears, wishes, confusions, and even motives as suit his purpose.

Even when fiction is narrated in the first person there are many more options than the autobiographer has. You may be an outsider with only a spectator's view of things. Or you may be personally involved in the action to some small or large degree. Or you may exist at the very center of all the action with everything happening around you and to you.

As autobiographer, you have only one position and that is at the center of everything that matters. Even though you may represent yourself as being only a passive witness to the times, you still occupy what Henry James called the "commanding center." Yours is the central informing intelligence, the comprehensive or overall sensibility that determines the operative frame of reference. And so it is that the autobiographer's voice is the vector of the basic sense of life, attitude toward experience, and hence the value system that everything in the story represents.

And so it is also that the limitations of the autobiographer's awareness are ultimately also an important part of what his story is about. Inferences may also be drawn from deliberate omissions. After all, since what is at stake is not a matter of *guilt* but of *attitude*, there is no literary Fifth Amendment. Language, as Kenneth Burke once said, is symbolic action, the dancing of an attitude. So, under certain conditions, is silence. In the context of a discourse, ellipses, omission, and silence are also *verbal actions* and as such also represent the dancing of an attitude.

But the point is that it is always the storyteller's story

because it is his voice that is the vector, even when he is anonymous, as when he is working in terms of the third person and seems totally concerned with depicting *somebody else* as the compositional center if not the protagonist. It is still his voice that provides the emotional as well as the physical context in terms of which everything else is defined.

II

And yet as literary craftsman, the cowriter of an as-told-to autobiography is also present on every page. Never as a partner in a duet, to be sure, but he is there nonetheless! Actually, his role is very much the same as that of the piano accompanist who comes on stage with the solo vocalist or instrumentalist. Once the performance gets under way, it is as if the very best accompanists are neither seen nor heard.

Even as the accompanist vamps till the soloist is ready, what he plays is like so many bars of preparatory silence. And the same is almost as true of his obbligatos and fills. Everything he plays is specifically designed to enhance the presence and the unique traits of the featured soloist, not to divert attention from him in any degree whatsoever. Nor does such background support compromise the integrity and authenticity of the solo as solo statement. Few soloists perform a cappella. Many singers accompany themselves on the piano, and perhaps even more do so on guitar.

Sometimes the accompanist, for all his unobtrusiveness, actually leads and prompts the soloist. Sometimes he only follows, perhaps most often as if he were whispering yes, yes, yes; and then, and then, and then; go on, go on, go on; amen, so be it. Even when he engages in call-and-response exchanges, it is always as if the soloist is carrying on a dialogue with someone who is either absent or totally imaginary. But always the accompanist is there to keep the melodic line and its frame of reference intact and the soloist in key, in tune, and in time.

For all that, however, it is only at the *end* of the performance when the bows, if any, are being taken that the accompanist shares a brief moment with the soloist in the spotlight. And yet two of the most prominent and influential contemporary American musicians, both of whom were easily identifiable by their piano styles, were also two of the very best comp artists who ever did it. One was Duke Ellington, and the other was Count Basie himself.

III

Count Basie's conception of the role of the literary craftsman (and research assistant) as cowriter of an as-told-to autobiography was just about everything you could want it to be. All-time exemplary bandleader and performing artist as improviser that he always was to his very fingertips, he was completely aware and appreciative of the fact that what he was involved in was an act of composition. He knew very well that getting his voice down on the page was not simply a matter of making a literal transcription of his recollections and then tidying them up for the printer.

As for dictating sequences and anecdotes into a tape recorder, very few people seem able to do that in their most natural or characteristic cadence, syntax, and tone of voice. More often than not, they become so self-conscious and spend so much time choosing words, revising their phrases, and measuring their statements that they not only interrupt the normal flow of discourse, but even lose the train of thought from time to time and have to begin again, and again, only to end up sounding stilted at best. Not that there are not those who do manage to maintain a steady on-mike flow. But more often than not, they sound more like overstylized media types than like the individuals they project otherwise. Indeed, in such instances their words are only likely to become on-the-page equivalents of masks and costumes. In any case, Basie knew that the microphone patter that he used on stage and in interviews with entertainment page reporters would not do for the kind of book he had in mind.

In point of fact, a small Sony tape recorder with a tiny clip-on microphone was used at every working session over a period of six years, and transcriptions were made from most of them. But the trick was to get him to respond to questions, not by speaking into the microphone, but to you in a casual person-to-person conversational tone and tempo. And that meant getting him in the frame of mind that made him try to take you back into his past with him, much the same as he was soon to do when he took you to Kansas City and later on to Red Bank, New Jersey. Then instead of addressing himself to abstract issues as such, he would simply become anecdotal and evoke people and details about places and days and nights and ongoing actions and relationships. Once he got an anecdote going, the I said, he said, she said particulars tended to fall into place with no effort at all.

The whole procedure worked as smoothly as it did because it was not really a new approach to composition for Basie. After all, he had been collaborating with staff arrangers and freelancers as well for almost fifty years. Also entirely in line with his definitive orientation to improvisation, he had his own functional conception of dictation. For him it was mostly a matter of feeding suggestions and instructions directly from the keyboard to band members during rehearsals, or perhaps as often as not during an actual performance. In either circumstance, it was only sometimes that his statements were repeated literally. And other times they were to be complemented—perhaps as often as not through counterstatement.

So he was already all set to utilize the services of a cowriter as the literary equivalent of the piano accompanist or comp artist who would supply him with chordal structures and progressions in the form of documentary notes, press clippings, photographs, recordings, and data from various colleagues over the years. But at the same time you were also to be his staff arranger and copyist who would prepare tentative score sheets that the two of you would rework and polish together, as if rehearsing the band.

Which made you Count Basie's literary Count Basie and also Count Basie's literary extension of such legendary arrangers as Eddie Durham, Buck Clayton, Buster Harding, Jimmy Mundy, Andy Gibson, Ernie Wilkins, Frank Foster, Frank Wess, and Thad Jones all rolled into one. No mean task or honor for you, but everyday stuff for him. And when he realized that you, for your part, already conceived your own writing in terms of vamps, choruses, riffs, call-and-response patterns, breaks, chases, and so on to outchoruses and tags, all he could do was point his finger at you as if at a sideman and say, "You got it." Which became "You got it, Mister Bateman" after you began addressing him by his nickname in the Gonzelle White troupe, only to have him turn it back on you. "Where the hell are we, Mister Bateman? How did I get off on this, Mister Bateman? Get me out of here, Mister Bateman. Stop pointing and just get us out of here, Mister Bateman. Hell, you the one with the dates, Mister Bateman, you tell me when I was supposed to do whatever it was, and I'll tell you what I remember about it."

Not only did he appreciate the fact that getting the voice on the page, with all of its distinctively personal inflections, was the *sine qua non* of an autobiography, he also understood that once there, it also had to function as a series of paragraphs and chapters in a book. And what he wanted was the kind of book that made you see and hear as you read. Indeed, he really wanted a book that would unfold like a movie script, with long and medium camera shots and closeups, with montage and flashback sequences, and all the rest, including panning, zooming, cutting to, crosscutting, fading in, and fading out, among others.

IV

Very much in line with the many recapitulations and revisions required by an as-told-to autobiography was the fact that being a performing artist, Basie was as used to regular rehearsals as he was to improvisation. So you could count on taking him back over some details time after time until the replay turned out to be a statement that he was willing to release to the public. As should surprise no one, he was no more inclined to release raw material as a writer than he was given to doing so as a musician.

He did not think that unguarded or loose expression represented one's true, honest, and material self. It represented one as careless, unorganized, and confused. As far as he was concerned, you should always get yourself together before you made any kind of presentation to others. Nor was this unusual for a bandleader. Very rarely do any musicians worthy of the name ever presume to play, or even rehearse, anything without first tuning up their instruments and getting in key, if only to get deliberately out of key. In any case, as fresh and impromptu as the best Basie bands always sounded, they were always well drilled. Even the widely celebrated unwritten, informal, or head arrangements were worked up during rehearsal and also reworked during subsequent rehearsals. Although many riff patterns and ensemble figures also came into being during actual performances, those that became a part of the repertory were reworked and refined in rehearsal after rehearsal. Such arrangements were called "heads" mainly because the band had memorized them long before they were copied out on the score sheets.

As relaxed and as basically geared to improvisation as Basie's bands always were, his musicians always looked and sounded well rehearsed and together. Nor was there ever any ring-around-the-collar sloppiness about their appearance. Their uniforms were sharp, and their deportment on the bandstand was beyond reproach. There was always room to hang loose and swing, but careful preparation was as characteristic of the Basie approach to performance as were the unexpected accents, on-the-spot obbligatos and extended vamps, solos, and out-choruses. One more time, indeed.

v

Even when it is offered as an entirely unprepossessing personal record of one's own life, undertaken with great reluctance, an autobiography is still of its very nature an exercise in exemplification, concerned with the narrator's sense of endeavor, fulfillment, and failure. As such it is really a species of *fiction*. It is a story with an explicit or implicit moral.

Sometimes it may be structured in terms of a dramatic plot (one thing *leading* to another) that enfolds on the dynamics of tragedy, comedy, melodrama, or farce. Or, as is perhaps just as often the case, its story line may be only a simple matter of one thing *following* another as in the genre of the picaresque novel, that literary extension of the logbook, diary, and journal (and perhaps also the rogue's deposition!). In either case, it is a story and as such it takes people and events from the context of vital statistics and the facts of everyday life into the realm of legend, myth, fairy tale, and fable (which, by the way, also has the effect of transforming the profane into the sacred).

It is the stuff of legend, myth, fairy tale, and fable, not the concrete facts per se, that accounts for the widespread interest in such classics of autobiographical writing as the *Confessions of Jean-Jacques Rousseau*, *The Autobiography of Benjamin Franklin*, *Narrative of the Life of Frederick Douglass, an American Slave, Written by Himself*, and *The Education of Henry Adams* (written in the third person!) that persist from generation to generation. Not that factual precision is unimportant, but rather that such books are read not nearly so much for the information per se as for the story.

But the autobiography is also a form of history even so. Being a personal record of one's own life, it is of its very nature an exercise in chronological documentation, which, however skimpy the details, is obviously intended to convey historical data. Thus it is in itself a historical document that may be the object of scholarly investigation, and its usefulness as such depends on its accuracy and its scope, both of which may be limited in some degree (but not necessarily compromised) by the author's inevitable subjectivity.

Whatever its limitations, however, the autobiography is still an indispensable form of historical documentation. So, along with all considerations based on the assumption that style functions as statement in autobiography, much the same as it does in fiction, there is also the matter of content as such: what is included and to what purpose and what is omitted either by design or through oversight. After all, whatever the story line of an autobiography is, the book itself is made up of factual details about real people involved in actual events.

VI

What Basie had in mind was a book giving his own account of some of the highlights of some of the things he had been involved in during the course of his career as a musician and bandleader over the years, including a few incidents thrown in for laughs. As far as he was concerned, there were no axes to grind, no special ideological points to make, and no old scores to settle. He did not even express any overall urge to set the record straight. He simply dealt with longstanding misrepresentations and misinterpretations as they came up in the normal sequence of putting the book together.

That was the way he put it for the cowriter at the very outset of the collaboration, and not only was it justification enough for undertaking an autobiography at any time, it was also precisely what was most urgently needed. Not a gossip or sensation-oriented show biz confession, which, as far as he was concerned, was out of the question anyway.

What was needed was the first book-length treatment of the Count Basie story by anybody at all. Because although he had never suffered for lack of publicity and promotion, but had been one of the most famous men of his time for nearly five decades, with a musical signature that is to this day still perhaps almost as instantly identifiable in international circles as the national anthem, there had at that time been only one book about him. It was titled *Count Basie and His Orchestra* and was written by an Englishman named Raymond Horricks, but it was mostly about the personnel of this orchestra over the years, with only a thirty-four-page sketch of Basie himself. *The World of Count Basie* by Stanley Dance didn't come out until Basie's own project was under way, and it, too, was mostly about members of the band.

Moreover, the personality sketches that had appeared as features in various journalistic publications were, for the most part, either based on very brief entertainment reporter interviews usually given on the go or backstage, and almost always off the cuff, or they were derived from secondary source materials, including other articles and unverified eyewitness and hearsay accounts.

Anyway, what he wanted the cowriter to help him put together was a book giving his own version of what struck him as the key elements and turning points of his life. And he was very aware of the fact that once released it would become the prime source (as likely to be double-checked as taken at face value) and point of departure for more detailed monographic studies and attempts at full-scale biographical undertakings as well.

The most obvious model for what he had in mind was the souvenir booklet that record companies sometimes include in deluxe boxed sets. It would contain more information about his childhood in Red Bank and Asbury Park, his apprenticeship in Harlem, and on the entertainment circuits, and also more about his years as a Kansas City journeyman than had ever been published anywhere before. In addition, it would also provide the most comprehensive running account of the band's extensive travels over the years, because he wanted future readers to realize that the band did not spend most of its time in theaters and dance halls in places like Harlem or the Chicago South Side, but was not only a national but also an international institution.

Also, instead of a formal discography as an appendix, he decided to treat the performance and reworking of key items in the band's repertory as the integral part of the main action of the narrative that it indeed was. When he thought of the book as a bound volume, he visualized it as standing on the record shelf at one end of the Basie collection with a complete discography by experts like Jorgen Jepsen or Chris Sheridan at the other.

VII

Most of the outstanding omissions from *Good Morning Blues* were intentional. Naturally there were also some that are due to faulty memory, but there were some lapses that were also deliberate. As Freddie Green pointed out to the cowriter early on, Basie was a much more reliable source of historical particulars than most of the self-styled experts. But he was also the type of person who would pretend not to know something, just to find out what somebody else knew. He was never one for showing that he knew more about anything than somebody else. But when he said, "Is that where that happened? Boy, my memory is gone! I thought that was out in Washington," anytime he said something like that, you'd better recheck your sources!

Sometimes he would say, "Let's skip that because I might not have it right, and I don't want anybody saying, 'See there, he don't know what he's talking about.'" But in writing about Kansas City, for instance, he just simply had no intention of going on record with everything he had seen or heard about the workings of the Pendergast machine, the business interests and invisible associates of Ellis Burton and Piney Brown, or the political connections of Bennie Moten. About the Reno

Club, for instance, he said, "Goddammit, somebody is always asking me to paint them a detailed picture of everything that went down in there, and name names. But why the hell should I get into that? My business in there was music, and that didn't have a damn thing to do with naming names and meddling around in somebody else's gig. Hell, ask them about it, not me. If they make a movie and show some other stuff, that's okay as long as it's true. But I don't want it in my book. Don't care how true it is. You don't have to go around talking about other folks' business just because what you're saying is true."

On the matter of the tells-all confession memoir, Count Basie was no less insightful than Somerset Maugham, for instance, who in *The Summing Up* said: "I have no desire to lay bare my heart, and I put limits to the intimacy I wish the reader to enter upon with me. There are matters on which I am content to maintain my privacy. No one can tell the whole truth about himself. It is not only vanity that has prevented those who have tried to reveal themselves to the world from telling the truth; it is direction of interest. . . ."

There was also Basie's unimpeachable sense of propriety. Never a blabbermouth, once he became a public figure he was not only extremely concerned with not becoming embroiled in controversy of any kind, he was also always very much alert to the untold damage a mean or even a careless word from him could do to other people's reputations and careers. Nor did he recognize any statute of limitations on promises made in the course of tipping on the q.t.

If the story he has chosen to tell is thereby made short on scandalous self-exposé, it is also short on outrageous self-inflation. If it is short on explanation, it is also short on false claims and pretentiousness. It is obviously a success story. But he does not presume to have a formula. And if it is short on advice, it is also short on condescension and pontification. If it also is short on the usual protest and polemics that are so predictable in the personal accounts of so many other so-called black Americans, it is also short on gratuitous (and politically naïve) self-degradation and the rhetoric of sackcloth and ashes or phony despair.

Behind all of that super cool, laid-back understatement, Old Base was mostly having himself a ball, and in his daily contacts with white people over the past forty-five years, he was much less concerned with keeping from being done in by hostile ones than with keeping from being bored to utter exhaustion by worshipful ones (*saying Bill this and Bill that in no time at all, curiously oblivious to the fact that true intimates were calling him Base*). He did not presume to speak for other so-called black Americans; instead, he set them an impeccable example of how to carry yourself in a way that always commands respect, as well as admiration, and even awe.

VIII

In the case of *Good Morning Blues*, some key answers to very basic and entirely appropriate questions about the influence of the cowriter, whether insidious, thinly disguised, or obvious, on both form and content, are already a matter of public record. There was *Stomping the Blues*. There was the essay titled "Duke Ellington Vamping Till Ready." There was *The Omni-Americans*, and there was also *The Hero and the Blues*.

The invitation to collaborate with Count Basie on his memoirs was a signal honor indeed, but it was also a great responsibility, which was accepted not only because the subject matter as such was so interesting, but also because it fell so neatly into the context of section nine of *Stomping the Blues*. So much so that it was like working on an elaborate representative anecdote as an extension of "Kansas City Four/Four and the Velocity of Celebration" to be called "For Instance Count Basie and His Orchestra."

There were also the notions about the special shortcomings of so much so-called black American biographical documentation as expressed in "Duke Ellington Vamping Till Ready." (See page 533.)

None of which should come as any surprise to anybody already familiar with *The Omni-Americans*. For one of the most obvious concerns of that book is that any image of "black" experience that is geared to the standard materialist assumptions about human fulfillment underlying most of the so-called findings of American social science technicians is very likely to fall into the trap of reinforcing the folklore of white supremacy and the fakelore of black pathology.

The Hero and the Blues, a book about the nature and

function of the heroic image in fiction, is based on the assumption that endeavor, whether in quest, in conquest, or defense, is what storytelling is really about. Accordingly, it rejects protest and elects to view the eternal necessity to struggle not only as the natural condition of mankind but also as a form of antagonistic cooperation without which there is no achievement and fulfillment, no heroic action, no romance.

There were also specific assumptions about the Basie project. One was that in addition to providing useful documentation of Count Basie's successful career as a bandleader it would of its very nature also be in effect a natural history of the very distinctive Basie style. As little interest as he himself ever had in analyzing and explaining *how* and *why* he played the way he did, as a casual account of what he was doing from time to time in place after place, his book would also be a story of his musical evolution. For example, when he went west on the vaudeville circuit, he used the striding left hand of an eastern ragtime piano player, but when he came back home from the stomp-oriented West, the *stride* hand had somehow been all but replaced by the *walking* bass of Walter Page.

Another of the cowriter's very personal assumptions was derived from a discussion about the refinement of aesthetic statement in "The Style of the Mythical Age," by Hermann Broch, published as the Introduction to Rachel Bespaloff's *On the Iliad.* In a passage about expressing the essential and nothing but the essential as in childhood before entering the cluttered world of subjective problems, and in old age after leaving the cluttered behind, Broch goes on to discuss the style of old age, which he described as being not so much the product of maturity as "the reaching of a new level of expression, such as old Titian's discovery of the all-penetrating light which dissolves the human flesh and the human soul to a higher quality, or such as the finding by Rembrandt and Goya, both at the height of their manhood, of the metaphysical surface which underlies the visible in man and thing and which nevertheless can be painted; or such as *The Art of the Fugue* which Bach in his old age dictated without having a concrete instrument in mind"—and so on. There he defines it as "a kind of *abstractism in which expression relies less and less on the vocabulary, which finally becomes reduced to a few prime symbols, and instead relies more and more on the syntax . . ."*!

Count Basie himself had no particular concern with such observations, but to the cowriter they were as directly applicable to the evolution of the quintessential style of understatement that Basie, not unlike Ernest Hemingway in literature, not only achieved and received universal recognition for, but did so at a relatively early stage of his career. Indeed, so far as the public at large was concerned, it was as if both had expressed themselves that way all along.

Another pet notion of the cowriter was that the distillation and refinement achieved by the all-powerful yet laid-back and understated Basie style were analogous not only to the seemingly purely pragmatic but nothing if not poetic and indeed ritualistic prose of Ernest Hemingway, but also to the visual simplifications of Henri Matisse, especially but not exclusively during the late years when Matisse settled on the cutouts as if to echo Hokusai, the great Japanese master who, at ninety and at the peak of his mastery, said, according to Broch, "Now at last I begin to learn how one draws a line."

There was (or so the cowriter liked to think) also a noteworthy resemblance between the music of Count Basie and the paintings of Matisse during the years of their apprenticeship. There were the tinkling, sparkling, and cascading notes and the fancy runs and finger-busting figures of young Basie during his Harlem stride or eastern ragtime phase, culminating in the *Prince of Wails*, recorded with Bennie Moten's orchestra in 1932. Just as there was, or rather had already been, the mosaic density sometimes of brush strokes and sometimes of detail, that characterized many of the early Van Gogh and Pointillist-influenced Matisse paintings, such as *Luxe, Calme, et Volupté* (1904–5), *The Open Window*, *The Moorish Screen*, and the various odalisques in which, as John Russell has said, he aimed "to fill the entire surface of the canvas with a unified decorative pattern and to achieve ever more exciting interactions of color." Also: Behind Basie there was the all-pervading influence of Louis Armstrong, much the same as there was old Cézanne for Matisse.

Naturally, the analogy does not apply to all particulars. Analogies seldom, if ever, do. Nevertheless, two more: Both men foreshadowed their mature reliance on syntax in much of their earlier work, but neither seems to have realized at the time that the subsequent development and refinement of their craft would take them back in the direction of their early efforts, not away from them. Young Matisse seems to have regarded his simplifications not as distillations, but as preliminary sketches and studies—and as such they were really throwaways. Basie regarded his purely functional vamps, riffs, and obbligatos as the stock in trade of the comp artist, which made them throwaways in the theatrical sense of the throwaway line!

But the point here is not that either old master was ever dead set on eliminating all density from all of the later work on the basis of some rigid principle. It is rather that such density as is so obviously there is even more obviously less a matter of vocabulary and detail than of syntax. In Matisse's *Tabac Royal* (1942), *The Egyptian Curtain* (1948), *The Parakeet and the Siren* (1952), and *Ivy in Flower* (1953), the density is based on fewer colors, less color nuance, and less detailing than in *The Moorish Screen* (1921), *Decorative Figure on an Ornamental Background* (1927), or *Odalisque in Red Pantaloons* (1922).

As a performing maestro, Basie, who thought in terms of perennials as well as new productions, always included items from every period of his repertory with no noticeable preference for the less complex ones. However, when earlier recordings of such vintage items as *Jumping at the Woodside* (1937) and *9:20 Special* (1941), for example, are compared with later ones, even when the sidemen are obviously geared to a rococolike density, strongly influenced, no doubt, by Charlie Parker, the overall statement is still more a matter of basic blues idiom syntax than of lush additions to the vocabulary. Indeed, against the unison and ensemble backgrounds so typical of the later-day Basie arrangements, the effect of the high-speed note solos is not unlike that of Matisse's use of decorative figures against the flat backgrounds in such final cutouts as *The Sorrow of the King* (1952) and *Large Decoration with Masks* (1953).

Anybody who has hung out with him knows very well that Count Basie had no concern whatsoever with such juxtapositions and speculations. He regarded them as being academic at best and a bit too highfalutin in any case. The suggestion that Matisse's reproductions be used as Basie album covers struck him as being very nice and appropriately contemporary. But so far as the rest: "Okay. I see what you mean, but that's you saying that now, not me."

Matisse, on the other hand, was highly conscious of musical parallels in his painting. He was theorizing in terms of "harmonies and dissonances of color" as long ago as 1908, and in 1946 he spoke of black as "taking a more and more important part in color orchestration, comparable to that of the double-bass as a solo instrument." And, of course, over the years there were *Harmony in Blue*, which became *Harmony in Red*, *Music, Dance, Joy of Life, Piano Lesson, Music Lover*, and so on. Then in fruitful old age there was the book of twenty prints (from cutouts) that represented "crystallizations of memories of the circus, of popular tales, or of travel," which he called *Jazz* because they were composed on unspecified principles of improvisation, but which resemble no other jazz in existence more than that of Count Basie's band in general and Count Basie's piano in particular.

One of the best possible models for keeping all of these and other personal assumptions and opinions under control was Count Basie himself. As universally popular as his uniquely individualistic piano style made him, few soloists, vocal or instrumental, ever sounded more like they had all of their own special attributes and nuances under more effective control than when they had him in there doing what he did in his own special way in the background, usually unattended by most of the audience.

But even so there is finally no getting around the fact that regardless of how self-effacing certain accompanists might seem to be, what they do has a crucial and even definitive influence on the manner as well as the substance of the performance of any soloist. Thus no matter how distinctively individual your personal identity remains, when, say, Duke Ellington supplies the accompaniment, you are very apt to sound even more rather than less like yourself than ever, to be sure, but at the same time your voice becomes Ellington music. And when you perform with Count Basie the chances are that you are going to sound very much like yourself on a Basie beat.

The implications of this aspect of the as-told-to autobiography for oral history projects in general should be obvious enough. After all, such projects are hardly ever initiated by the subjects, who as a matter of fact are seldom if ever in a position to exercise any basic control over context, theme, direction, emphasis, or nuance. Indeed, far from having any definitive editorial prerogatives, many do not actually know what use will be made of the data their interviews produce.

Such was certainly not the case with Count Basie and *Good Morning Blues*. In the first place, he himself initiated the project in his own good time. Then he chose an accompanist who met criteria that he himself had established. Moreover, in doing so he enjoyed the same position of unassailable authority that gave such headliners as Billy Eckstine, Sarah Vaughan, Ella Fitzgerald, Tony Bennett, and Frank Sinatra the option of having themselves showcased by Ellington, Basie, Nelson Riddle, some pickup combo, or an anonymous studio aggregation.

In any case, it was not for nothing that for all of his widely celebrated gracious deportment toward the press corps throughout his long career Basie was nevertheless one of the most reluctant and reticent of interviewees. He was admittedly extremely sensitive to and wary of the crucial influence that the reporter's frame of reference and editorial slant could have on what was to be printed as an objective rendering of verbatim quotations, and he dreaded the misrepresentation and destructive distortions that were so often the result.

Then there was also his longstanding suspicion that reporters were mostly concerned about getting credit for some sensational revelation, regardless of who was embarrassed or hurt in the process. In addition, there was also the matter of sharing idiomatic experiences with an insider rather than having to explain routine details to someone who, however curious and genuinely sympathetic, is nevertheless an outsider. Obviously this is not a matter of "for your ears only," but rather of "for your ears first," with everybody else getting the benefit of the more relaxed, natural, and revealing discourse. That storytellers do better with some audiences than with others should surprise no one.

When Basie asked prospective as-told-to collaborators what kind of book they thought his story would make, he already knew that he himself wanted a literary equivalent to the "class act" that his no less refined than down-to-earth orchestras always were. He also knew that he did not want to become involved with anybody who was going to try to maneuver him into reducing the chronicle of his career as one of the most successful of American musicians to a polemic about racism. He wasn't one to brag about his achievements, which were considerable; but he didn't stand for any putdowns either. The condescending rhetoric of do-gooders turned him off.

He was all for including anecdotes for laughs and for humor in general and especially for jokes on himself. But as for publicizing delicate indiscretions of no fundamental significance to his development as a musician, he felt that any man well into his seventies who did that was only putting tarnish on his own trophies and graffiti on his own monument.

PART III

The Armstrong Continuum

The Twentieth-Century American Herald

LOUIS ARMSTRONG claimed that he was born on the Fourth of July in 1900. True or not, such a birth date was not only appropriate to the status he achieved as a twentieth-century American legend, but it is entirely consistent with the crucial role he came to play as the quintessential embodiment of the spirit of his native land as it is expressed in contemporary music.

Moreover, if as some researchers now report, the date given by Armstrong was a personal choice rather than a documented fact, the symbolism of the choice may well suggest that Armstrong was not unaware of the fact that he was in effect a culture hero (not unlike, say, Prometheus), the bringer of indispensable existential equipment for the survival of humanity.

In any case, what the elegant innovations of his trumpet and vocal improvisations added up to was the American musical equivalent of "*emblems for a pioneer people who require resilience as a prime trait.*"

Nor, given the transitional nature of life in the twentieth-century world at large, is such resiliency or ability to maintain equilibrium through swinging and improvising any less an imperative for experiment-oriented people in the contemporary world elsewhere.

Whether he was born on July 4, 1900, or on August 4, 1901, as recorded in military conscription records of 1918, Louis Armstrong was destined to make music that is if anything even more representative of American affirmation and promise in the face of adversity than the festive reiterations of the most elaborate display of any Fourth of July fireworks. And it is received as such around the globe. Indeed, during the years following World War II, the sound of Ambassador Satchmo came to have more worldwide appeal than the image of Yankee Doodle Dandy ever did, not to mention the poster image of Uncle Sam, who by then had become synonymous with Uncle Sugar.

Generally acknowledged or not, much goes to show that it was

*through Louis Armstrong's definitive influence on jazz that the
United States has registered its strongest impact on contemporary
aesthetic procedure.*

Yes, it was an American named Louis Armstrong, not such
justly celebrated avant-garde Europeans as Igor Stravinsky, Béla
Bartók, Georges Auric, Darius Milhaud, Louis Durey, Paul Hindemith, Arthur Honegger, Francis Poulenc, Germaine Tailleferre,
or any of the heirs of the theories of Rimsky-Korsakov, Erik
Satie, and Nadia Boulanger, whose music matched the innovations of such twentieth-century sensibilities as are represented in
the visual art of Picasso, Braque, and Matisse, for instance, or in
literature by Joyce, Proust, Mann, Malraux, Hemingway, Eliot,
and Faulkner, or in architecture by the skyscraper, the Bauhaus,
Frank Lloyd Wright, Le Corbusier, and Mies van der Rohe.

Louis Armstrong, yes, Louis Armstrong from back o' town
New Orleans, Louisiana, whose American apprenticeship during
the first two decades of the twentieth century made him the
intimate beneficiary of ragtime and stride, the shift from the
popularity of the 3/4 waltz beat of the operetta to the 4/4 of
the fox trot, the one-step, the two-step, the drag, the stomp,
the Afro-U.S. emphasis on percussion and on syncopation, the
break, stop time, and so on.

On the other hand, by the way, in spite of all the unmistakable clues so readily available to them on ballroom floors and
vaudeville stages across the nation, none of the most publicized
twentieth-century American choreographers has yet risen to
the challenge of Armstrong's trumpet affirmations. Nor do
their productions share his universal appeal and acclaim, as
might be the case if they did. Why choreographers of all people
did not rise to the challenge is perhaps a very special American
story in itself.

"All this life I have now," the mature and long since world-
famous Armstrong told Richard Meryman in an interview, most
of which was printed as a memoir in *Life* magazine of April 15,
1966, "I didn't suggest it. I would say it was all wished on me.
Over the years, you find you can't stay no longer where you are,
you must go on a little higher now, and that's the way it all came
about. I couldn't get away from what's happened to me."

"But man," he went on to say, "I sure had a ball there growin' up in New Orleans as a kid. We were poor and everything like that, but music was all around you. Music kept you rolling."

He also told Meryman that he had spent about a year and a half in the Colored Waifs' Home (that has become such a famous part of accounts of his childhood) and that he never did go back to school. "I was about the fifth grade—and I regret that to a hell of an extent. But I had to take care of Mama and I was the only one to put somethin' in the pot. And at that time I didn't need school . . . I had the Horn."

In all events, what he also told the editors of *True* magazine when they published his memoir of Storyville in November of 1947, makes it clear enough that, whatever social science technicians might think, his hometown was not a God-awful place in which he grew up wishing to get out of: "*Every time I close my eyes blowing my trumpet, I look right into the heart of good old New Orleans.*"

About all of which he went on to say in the opening paragraph of the Meryman interview, "*I'm always wondering if it would have been best in my life if I'd stayed like I was in New Orleans, having a ball. I was very much contented just to be around and play with the old-timers. And the money I made—I lived off of it. I wonder if I would have enjoyed that better than all this big mucky-muck traveling all over the world. . . .*"

What Armstrong told Meryman and the editors of *True* magazine was not social welfare or civil rights propaganda to wring the condescending hearts and shallow pockets of self-styled do-gooders and patron saints of socioeconomic uplift, but the very stuff not only of legendary adventure and romance, but also of the world of epic achievement in terms of which national character is described.

As for those who are either critical of or defensive about the close interrelationship of jazz and the goings-on in Storyville in the New Orleans of Armstrong's childhood, let them remember not only what a disreputable place the Globe Theatre and environs was during the heyday of Shakespeare, Marlowe, and Jonson, but also that the great classic dramas of Aeschylus, Sophocles, and Euripides were not written for the approval of college professors but for the entertainment of revelers during the festival of Dionysus, the god of wine, whose celebration was as noted for sexual indulgence and food as for drunkenness.

"When I got to the station in Chicago I couldn't see Joe Oliver anywhere. I saw a million people, but not Mr. Joe, and I didn't give a damn who else was there. I'd never seen a city that big. All those tall buildings. I thought they were universities. I said, no, this is the wrong city. I was just fixin' to take the next train back home—standin' there in my box-back suit, padded shoulders, double-breasted, wide-legged pants. . . ."

So said the long since legendary Louis Armstrong in the Meryman interview. But even so, he never was the young man from the provinces come to seek his fortune in the big city by hook, crook, or whatever, such as was depicted by Balzac in *Le Père Goriot* and *Lost Illusions*, for instance. *He had come to Chicago because he had been asked to join his New Orleans mentor, then playing at one of the choice spots in town.*

As impressed as he undoubtedly was by the size of Chicago, then the second largest city in the United States, he was no hayseed from the sticks; he was a very promising young journeyman from New Orleans, a city of revelry, widely celebrated for the international flavor of its sophistication; and long before he had enough free time on his hands to wander around and be overwhelmed by Chicago, he himself was not only well on his way to becoming one of its most dazzling elements, but was also being invited to join the even more famous Fletcher Henderson Orchestra, then playing at the Roseland Ballroom at Fifty-second Street and Broadway, a choice midtown venue in the even greater city of New York.

Not that Chicago was not a world-class metropolis to be sure. It was not only the railroad center of the nation, but also the major U.S. port city on the Great Lakes outlet to transoceanic trade. And along with its exclusive position as the capital of the meatpacking and distribution industries, it was also the major regional focal point of the vast midwestern agricultural, manufacturing, and mail order enterprises.

Also, when you thought of the great city that Chicago had become at the time Armstrong arrived, you realized that by then it had not only surpassed Boston and Philadelphia, for instance, in its cosmopolitan outlook, but was also well on its way as a possible contender for New York's position as the nation's cultural capital. Certainly its architects had become pacesetters. Its newspapers were more powerful than most elsewhere, and its output of phonograph records and radio broadcasts was second only to New York's.

Nor as busy as he was kept could Armstrong not have known about and have been impressed by the fact that in addition to the sensationally popular jazz spots on the South Side, there was also the *Chicago Defender*, one of the two top black weekly newspapers (the other being the *Pittsburgh Courier*), with the largest nationwide circulation.

When Armstrong arrived in New York to join the Fletcher Henderson Orchestra, he felt some twinges of the old momentary uncertainty of his first night in Chicago. But not for long. Indeed, before the end of his very first rehearsal, his cornet was already inspiring other sidemen and the arranger as well to expand their approaches to music. And among many other New York–based musicians who heard him, either in person or on record, his impact seems to have been no less instantaneous and even more widespread.

In addition to the several dozen records on which he played with the Henderson Orchestra (most of which are generally thought to owe such lasting interest as they have mainly to his contributions, although he's featured on none), he also made a noteworthy impression as a member of recording studio groups backing the great blues singer Bessie Smith, among others.

But as Max Jones and John Chilton point out in *Louis: The Louis Armstrong Story, 1900–1971*, there were also his studio dates with another group: "Of more consequence to students of music—and probably to Armstrong himself, since they reverted to the spontaneous type of jazz-making he loved and excelled at—were the quintet sides he cut with Clarence Williams's Blue Five and similarly constituted group known as The Red Onion Jazz Babies, after a New Orleans dive named the Red Onion. In spite of the acoustic recording which muffled the tone of Armstrong's cornet, these tracks give a clear enough presentation of his authority and expressiveness as both solo and lead player."

It is also in *Louis*, the best Armstrong biography to date,

that Jones and Chilton make the following summary and assessment of Armstrong's initial New York experience: "*In his
first New York stay Armstrong scored a success only with musicians and those dancers and music fans who bothered to note who
was playing what. He commented once that five years after his
visit Broadway finally accepted him. The experience, however,
had been vastly worthwhile for him professionally. In the year
with Henderson he gained confidence, improved his knowledge of
reading and interpreting a score, learned many new tricks of
showmanship, and picked up ideas from dozens of musicians he
heard and in some cases recorded with.*"

Of Armstrong's second stay in Chicago, Jones and Chilton go
on to write: "*New York was the last of Louis's universities. There
were still finer points of the music game to be mastered, and he
was as eager as ever to learn them, but he returned to Chicago a
marvelous and mature all-around musician. Once back he
launched himself on a variety of enterprises which established him
as the jazz sensation of the city. A long series of recordings by his
Hot Five and Hot Seven, the first made under his own name,
carried his reputation beyond the United States to wherever Jazz
records were sold. They were soon to be rated by connoisseurs in
many parts of the world as the most advanced of all performances
in the rough-and-ready or gutbucket style. To this day they are
recognized as absolute classics of their field. In the opinion of
thousands of collectors they have never been bettered.*"

Dan Morgenstern, in an essay entitled "Louis Armstrong
and the Development and Diffusion of Jazz" in *Louis Armstrong: A Cultural Legacy*, writes: "*The more room Armstrong
gave himself on these records the better were the results, and with such
masterpieces as 'Big Butter and Egg Man,' 'Wild Man Blues,'
'Potato Head Blues,' and 'Hotter Than That,' the revolutionary
young Armstrong is clearly displayed. With solos such as these, he
created a vocabulary of phrases that would echo in the music for
decades, even unto this day—in the work not only of such older
players as Ruby Braff (b. 1927) but also Wynton Marsalis (b. 1961)
and other young neo-traditionalists (or post-modernists). Armstrong now proceeds with utter fearlessness and freedom, crossing bar
lines, extending the working range of the horn, mastering breaks
and stop time and other rhythmic devices, and creating lovely*

melodies and phrases that linger in the mind and stir the emotions. Hundreds upon hundreds of musicians, not only in America but wherever jazz records were sold, studied these solos, learning them note for note—to sing if not to play, for the technical demands, not to mention the rhythmic and harmonic ones, were well beyond the capacity of most. In 1927 the Chicago music publisher Melrose put out a book of Armstrong solos and breaks.

"Armstrong's phraseology now began to enter the mainstream of jazz; it would remain a cornerstone at least until the advent of bebop—and a close analysis of Charlie Parker's vocabulary will show that he, too, was steeped in Armstrong, willy-nilly."

In a reminiscence written especially for Chilton and Jones, Armstrong himself accounts for a significant transition in his development during his return to Chicago: "I changed from the cornet to trumpet while I was with Erskine Tate at the Vendôme; Jimmy Tate (Erskine's brother) played trumpet, and they figured that it would be better if I did, too. We played some difficult shows with that orchestra, good for reading, you'd suddenly get the call to turn back five pages in the overture or something like that. I never tried to be a virtuoso or the greatest; I just wanted to be good. I learned a lot playing under the direction of Erskine Tate, we played all kinds of music. I really did sharpen up on my reading there. We played the scores for the silent movies and a big overture when the curtain would rise at the end of the film. I got a solo on stage, and my big thing was *Cavalleria Rusticana*. That always stayed with me, sometimes I used to warm up with snatches from it."

The memoir edited by Meryman also sketches other moves (many suggested by his wife, Lil, King Oliver's piano player, whom he had married before going to New York) that led to his spectacular success in Chicago, including making the Hot Five and Hot Seven records. And then he also says: *"Toward the end in Chicago it was tough, as Lil and I went along through the years, she didn't dig me—and I picked up a gal named Alpha. . . . eventually I married her. My last job in Chicago was at the Savoy Ballroom with Carroll Dickerson's band, and every time payday come around, oh, oh, another hard-luck story. I figured it was time to go to New York."*

There was a quick trip to New York for a two-day guest shot with Luis Russell's band in March of 1929. But Armstrong's second stand there began in the third week of May, when he was invited to rejoin Fletcher Henderson to rehearse for a spot in Vincent Youmans' ill-fated musical *Great Day*; and on his own he took Dickerson and his orchestra along with him and picked up a two-night engagement at the Savoy Ballroom, followed by a four-month stand at Connie's Inn beginning in June. It was during this time that in addition to fronting Dickerson's orchestra he began doubling in the musical *Hot Chocolates*, backed by an orchestra led by one Leroy Smith in which he was featured on Fats Waller's and Andy Razaf's *Ain't Misbehavin'*.

Armstrong went out to the Pacific Coast for the first time in July 1930 because he had been offered a spot as soloist with a band, soon to be led by Les Hite, playing at Frank Sebastian's Cotton Club in Culver City, a favorite hangout of Hollywood personalities. It was a very successful engagement, but he returned to Chicago in March 1931. Meanwhile, however, his recordings of new popular tunes had already begun to make him a major stylistic influence on singers of mainstream popular song. Indeed, as Rudy Vallee, one of the most celebrated conventional dance band leaders of the decade, was to say in 1936: *"That Armstrong's delightful, delicious sense of distortion of lyrics and melody had made its influence felt upon popular singers of our own day cannot be denied. Mr. Bing Crosby, the late Russ Columbo, Mildred Bailey, and many others have adopted, probably unconsciously, the style of Louis Armstrong. Compare a record by Crosby, in which he departs from the 'straight' form of the melody and lyric and then listen to an Armstrong record and discover whence must have come some of his ideas of 'swinging.' Armstrong antedated them all and I think most artists who attempt something other than the straight melody and lyric as written, who in other words attempt to 'swing' would admit, if they were honest with themselves and with their public, that they have been definitely influenced by the style of this master of swing improvisation."*

Moreover, the fact that Armstrong began including pop

tunes in his repertory not only led other jazz groups to do so because it was in vogue, but also to use either the most sophisticated show tunes as if they were only other folk ditties to be extended, elaborated, and refined into jazz.

It was not until he came back to Chicago from California in 1931 that Armstrong, with the aid of second trumpet man Zilner Randolph, organized his first full band. This was a group he took on tours through Illinois, Kentucky, Ohio, and West Virginia, to the Graystone Ballroom in Detroit, and then down to New Orleans for his first homecoming after seven years, and for a three-month residency in the swank Suburban Gardens. Then between September 1931 and March 1932 his tours with the band included Dallas, Oklahoma City, Houston, Memphis, St. Louis, Columbus, Cincinnati, Cleveland, Philadelphia, and Baltimore before he disbanded.

He returned to California for a second stand as featured soloist in Sebastian's Cotton Club in April 1932, but stayed only until early in July and sailed for England.

By one of Armstrong's own accounts, he made his first trip to England and France in the summer of 1932 not because he had bookings to fill there but as a vacation and as a chance to do some sightseeing. Others have said that he also did so in order to escape from personal problems and business complications for the time being. Along with him went Alpha Smith, his third wife-to-be and his manager. But he took no musicians and left none on alert in case any engagements turned up.

Whatever his reason for making it, the trip actually turned out to be mostly a series of concerts in response to the astonishingly great enthusiasm his recordings had stimulated abroad. So, for a two-week stint at the London Palladium, a group of jazz musicians were brought over from Paris, and for tours that included the Glasgow Empire, the Nottingham Palais, York, Liverpool, and Buckingham he used a group of British jazzmen.

It so happened that he did not get around to his vacation until he crossed over from England to Paris for a short stay that fall before returning to New York on November 2, the day, incidentally, that Franklin D. Roosevelt was elected president.

Meanwhile, however, Armstrong had not only achieved a deeper appreciation of the significance of the beachhead that he had only just discovered that his records had established but had also become personally aware of the fact that his music and musicianship were taken to be a much more serious matter by intellectuals abroad than by their counterparts in the United States, where it was regarded as entertainment rather than so-called serious (i.e., classical) music. Indeed, in the United States more than sixty years later, the regular music critics leave jazz to entertainment page reporters who are regarded as specialists in pop music.

Not that Armstrong was ever to concern himself about the general cultural significance of his efforts, which were generally directed toward being as good a musician as he could become. But in the process, he took jazz from the level of popular entertainment and into the realm of a fine art that requires a level of consummate professional musicianship unexcelled anywhere in the world.

The crucial factor involved in distinguishing between fine art and folk art and between fine art and pop art, it should be remembered, is not the raw material or subject matter as such. It is rather the quality of the extension, elaboration, and refinement involved in the creative process, the process, to reiterate yet again, that transforms or stylizes raw, direct experience into aesthetic statement. In other words, it was Armstrong's phenomenal technical mastery of his instrument coupled with the unique emotional range of his sensibility and the elegance of his imagination that gave his renditions the range, subtlety, and profundity that placed his best performances in the category of fine art.

On his second trip to Europe, which began in midsummer 1933, Armstrong played in the Holborn Empire in London in August and then toured Denmark, Sweden, Norway, and Holland and came back to England that December. Then he was booked for engagements in England until April, following which he moved to Paris for a vacation before playing two concerts at Salle Pleyel and setting out for a tour that included Belgium, Holland, Italy, and Switzerland as well as other cities in France. In *Swing That Music*, he (and/or his ghostwriter) wrote: *"Just as I was about getting homesick again and ready to take my boat, a European impresario named N. J. Canneti asked me if I could tour the Continent and I decided I might as well since he had most everything arranged. . . . At Torino, we played before the Crown Princess of Italy. I remember we spent New Year's Eve 1935 in Lausanne. We went over the Alps into Switzerland by bus and that was a very thrilling thing to me. . . .*

"When that trip ended up in Paris, I packed up and took my boat back to America. It seemed I had been gone ten years when we landed in New York, and I was glad to be back home."

European response to Armstrong and his music included some embarrassingly provincial emphases on black exotica to be sure, but after all there was that downright worshipful fascination with the Josephine Baker phenomenon (which, much goes to suggest, was far more a matter of their own concoction than of her show biz self-promotion ingenuity).

But for all that, there were European musicians, reporters, and insightful students of the implications of twentieth-century aesthetic theories and innovations, who made Armstrong aware, as he never seems to have been before, of the fact that the music that his absolutely astonishing musicianship was now playing such an indispensable role in developing and disseminating was to be taken as something with profound implications far beyond its delightfully hypnotic and kinetic appeal as popular entertainment.

With the publication of *Made in America* (republished in paperback as *The Arts in Modern American Civilization*), John A. Kouwenhoven was to make much of the aesthetic and pragmatic significance of products resulting from the interaction and synthesis of the "learned" conventions, traditions, and implements imported mainly from Europe with improvised or homespun solutions and devices evolved from or inspired by frontier situations indigenous to the United States.

Some thirty-odd years earlier, Armstrong's impact on jazz musicianship had already placed in the international domain exemplary evidence of a magnificent achievement of the crucial and definitive learned/vernacular interaction that Kouwenhoven was to write about in *Made in America* and again in *Beer Can by the Highway.*

Before Kouwenhoven, the all too prevalent attitude among those regarded as the most sophisticated American students of and commentators on twentieth-century morals and manners led them to regard jazz as an exciting and amusing novelty, an obviously transitory popular art, and the term Jazz Age was widely used as a synonym for the post–Eighteenth Amendment or Prohibition decade also known as the Roaring Twenties, the lifestyle of which was characterized by the behavior of the so-called flaming youths whose symbolic setting was the speakeasy and whose personification of post-Victorian and postwar "liberated" morality was the cigarette-smoking, cocktail-sipping, bobbed-hair-sporting flapper, who zipped about town and out to fun country in the new widely available fancy automobiles of the postwar manufacturing boom.

To the popular culture theorists the new musical phenomenon called jazz was only a postwar boom-time fad, and perhaps most continued to regard as unworthy of the serious attention and assessment they were giving post-Cubist collage painting and even Art Deco. And for the most part such continued to be their attitude even as jazz continued to develop and to increase its international prestige during the very unfrivolous Depression and war years of the 1930s and the 1940s.

Nor did the intelligentsia of the so-called Harlem Renaissance of the teens and twenties seem to have had any special insight into or appreciation of the profound universal, existential implications of Armstrong's pied piper influence, which was tantamount to a major aesthetic continuum. Not that they didn't think that jazz was wonderful. On the contrary, to them it was (or so it seems) mostly just a lot of fun (some of which many feared was also questionable). So it was thus more a part of the world of entertainment and sometimes dangerous amusement than something they regarded as being serious enough to be a part of the rarefied world of the fine arts.

In any case, as serious students of the role of their people in contemporary culture (or cultivated society), the music they seemed to have identified most closely with consisted mainly of folk songs, work chants, field hollers, spirituals, jubilee songs, and the conservatory-oriented compositions and arrangements of "certified" composers and arrangers such as Harry T. Burleigh, R. Nathaniel Dett, J. Rosamond Johnson, and William Grant Still, among others. They celebrated the concert hall triumphs of singers such as Roland Hayes and Paul Robeson but not the far greater impact of the singing of Ma Rainey, Bessie Smith, and the likes of Louis Armstrong.

Back in Chicago after his second European tour and a stopover in New York, Armstrong began what was to become a lifelong relationship with a local entertainment business insider named Joe Glazer by engaging him as his manager.

Then after a debut in Indianapolis with another orchestra organized and supervised for him by Zilner Randolph, Armstrong hit the road on a tour that took him through the Midwest back down into the South and New Orleans once more and also included dates in Pittsburgh, Detroit, Washington, and New York, where he broke the attendance record at the Apollo Theatre in Harlem before disbanding in September.

In late October of 1935, fronting Luis Russell's band again, Armstrong opened at Connie's Inn in Harlem once more and stayed until February 1936. Then there were ballroom club and theater bookings (plus a film part in Hollywood) that kept him crisscrossing the country until he returned to Chicago for Christmas.

After being hospitalized in Chicago at the beginning of the following year, he hit the road again, and in April he began a series of radio broadcasts (as suggested by Rudy Vallee) for the top-rated Fleischmann's Yeast program. Later on, after dates in major cities in the East and Midwest, he made another tour through the South and by October was back out on the Pacific Coast for more film work as well as band bookings.

By this time such was the pervasive influence of devices derived from Armstrong's instrumental and vocal innovations, not only on other jazz musicians but also on the popular music of standard songwriters, that the decade of the 1930s was already being called the Swing Era. In fact, the impact was so strong that the general public still seems to be unable to distinguish between Swing Era bands who played music that qualifies as fine art, and excellent jazz-influenced conventional ballroom bands, a confusion not made less difficult by the fact that in following Armstrong's lead, so many jazz bands came to include so much pop fare in their repertory. But of course, in all matters of fine art the distinguishing

factors are range, precision, profundity, and the idiomatic subtlety of the rendition.

Armstrong continued to lead full ballroom-size dance orchestras throughout the thirties and went on doing so until
mid-1947, after which he initiated the Louis Armstrong All-
Stars, a sextet consisting of trumpet, clarinet, trombone, piano,
bass, and drums, the type of combo he was to lead for the rest
of his career.

Meanwhile, in 1942 he divorced his third wife and married
Lucille Wilson, a dancer with whom he was to spend the rest
of his life. Also during the war years, in addition to his
boom-time schedule of ballroom tours and posh nightclubs
and first-run theater stands, he also played an endless number
of U.S. Savings Bonds rallies, troop morale concerts, and
dances, and made numerous V-disk transcriptions for broadcast in worldwide overseas combat zones.

Also between 1936 and 1969 he appeared in at least thirty-
two soundies, cartoons, and movies.

Many conventional jazz journalists give the impression that
by the late 1940s the so-called Swing Era had been succeeded
by a post–World War II jazz stylistic emphasis known as
be-bop, and modern jazz [*sic!*]. But in point of fact for all the
promotion of it as the postwar new thing, and in spite of its
undeniably chic appeal to and influence on a great number of
young musicians, bop never achieved the widespread appeal
and universal impact that swing as such enjoyed. Dizzy Gillespie became the most influential trumpet player since the arrival
of Armstrong, and the influence of Charlie Parker's alto on all
instruments was also comparable to Armstrong's. Ironically, however, the so-called bop years were also a period characterized
by a very enthusiastic revival of interest in the New Orleans of
Armstrong's earlier years.

But even as bop boosters like Leonard Feather, for instance,
tried to write such revival enthusiasm off as the reactionary
hostility of those they referred to as "moldy figs," jazz musicians of all persuasions were beginning to express their long-
standing reverence for Armstrong by referring to him as Pops
(as in "old father, old artificer, stand me now and ever in good
stead"). To this day jazz musicians prefer Pops to Satchmo.

In any case, Armstrong's popular appeal was far from being

diminished by bop competition. On the contrary, while the typical venue of bop groups was to remain the small club in a number of the larger cities, Armstrong's audiences filled the largest theaters, concert halls, and stadiums around the globe.

The worldwide acclaim for Armstrong's genius and the unsurpassed sense of earthy well-being that his music generated everywhere he went seems to have meant very little if anything to spokespersons in the ever so dicty circles of the neo-Victorian watchdogs of proper black decorum. To them, apparently, there was no such thing as a genius who sometimes doubled as a court jester. In their view Louis Armstrong was only a very popular "entertainer" anyway. But even so, he owed it to "his people" to project an image of progressive if not militant uplift.

Ironically, offstage Armstrong in his heyday was not only a preeminent influence in sartorial matters but also a major source of the fashionable speech of the most elegant and sophisticated "men about town" from border to border and coast to coast. Nor at any time after he became a public figure was his offstage presence any less awe-inspiring than that of the sparkling tongue-in-cheek regal bearing of Duke Ellington or the laid-back banker-calm Count Basie. People from the boss-man down to the hired help became downright reverential when they approached him in person. No matter how informal the situation was, this sometime court jester was always given the deference of royalty.

And he was such a genuinely nice and unpetty person, always generous with cash handouts, supportive of worthy causes, and thoughtful of old friends. *But don't make him mad. And don't try to boss him around or try to pull any one-upmanship on him. He preferred merrymaking to conflict but could be devastating when crossed. He publicly rebuked one president of the United States over civil rights and angrily refused an invitation from another to be honored at the White House.*

As for his response to caricatures of himself in the media (mostly early on) and misguided attacks by the ever sensitive brotherhood of proper black behavior in front of white folks, what must not be forgotten is the fact that along with his incredible orientation to elegance and soaring magnificence, Louis Armstrong was also endowed with an irrepressible sense of humor and merriment, not to mention an acute awareness and profound appreciation of the ridiculous, the absurd, and the downright outrageous. After all, he did get away with addressing the king of England as Rex as he dedicated "I'll Be Glad When You're Dead, You Rascal, You" to him; and he caused no offense when he referred to devoted music fans among the British aristocracy as Lord (or Lady) Dishrag!

In all events, as his long career of continuous creativity goes to show, Armstrong, like most other truly great achievers, was one who took most things in stride—as if his music would counterstate and counteract caricatures, stereotypes, and stupid misperceptions and misinterpretations as well, much the same as it had the derisive nickname of Dippermouth, Dipper, and Dip early on, and Satchelmouth and Satchmo forever afterward.

On the other hand, as for himself, Armstrong never seems to have been given to causing embarrassment to others. And perhaps best of all there was nothing at all pretentious about him. When he made mistakes, he made corrections, not excuses. No wonder vicious satire and hostile caricatures didn't ever really work against him. There was nothing pompous to deflate. Indeed, did anybody set out to ridicule him without ending up having a ball imitating him?

After all, what Louis Armstrong did was mug *back* at the blues, saying Yeeeeah as in Oh, yeah??? or in Oh, Yeah!!! And then go on and riff all of that flashy-fingered elegance out into the atmosphere as if there were no such thing as the blues!

Armstrong's music made him a globetrotting goodwill ambassador for the irrepressible idealism of his native land because it was such an irresistible expression of what so many people elsewhere think of as being the American outlook on human possibility.

But long before he became Ambassador Satchmo to the world at large, there was the absolutely fundamental existential response that such music stimulated among people within the continental limits of the United States. All of the ever-resilient and elegantly improvised ballroom choreography was nothing if not the dancing of a definitively American attitude. It was an idiomatic representation of an American outlook on possibility and thus also was an indigenous American reenactment of affirmation in the face of the ever-impending instability inherent in the nature of things.

When Armstrong used to say, "They all know I'm there in the cause of happiness," nobody seems ever to have been inclined to insist otherwise. Because nothing was ever more obvious than the fact that he had come to town not to complain about the presence of the blues but to blow them away and hold them at bay—always with more subtlety and elegance than power, as overwhelmingly powerful as all of those astonishing high C's always were.

Nor, conditioned as he so profoundly had been by the ambivalence of those New Orleans funeral corteges he grew up marching in, was happiness ever a simple matter of thoughtless frivolity. To him, it was a hard-earned and extremely fragile thing indeed. After all, the blues were only at bay; they can never be blown entirely away once and for all. But (it should be remembered) such is the nature and function of art that it can foil them time and again. Hence standards, masterworks, and the classics that add up to the canon.

When Louis Armstrong, whatever the exact date of his birth, used to say that he and jazz music grew up together, not only could he have gone on to point out that he and jazz music had helped each other grow up, but he could also have added that being born in the first decade of the twentieth century, he and the automobile and the airplane and the movies and phonograph records and radio and television, not to mention the theory of relativity, subatomic physics, space technology, automation, and so on.

In fact, Armstrong's trumpet, symbolizing as it does the very spirit of the exploration and readjustment that are so indispensable for survival in such unstable times, qualifies him as the herald of the age that may not end with 1999.

PART IV

The Ellington Synthesis

The Vernacular Imperative

A PANTHEON, as you probably already know even if you don't remember your elementary Latin because you never studied any to begin with, is a sacred place dedicated to all of the gods, whether of a tribal community, a city-state, or an empire of one sort or another.

The original of such consecrated places was a domed circular temple created in honor of all of the gods of ancient Rome by the Emperor Hadrian, and the idea has long since been adopted and adapted and institutionalized for secular purposes. Indeed, much goes to show that pantheons are now used for the express purpose of giving a sacred dimension to the secular.

Thus public buildings commemorating and dedicated to the great citizens of a nation are now also regarded as pantheons. Such buildings may or may not contain tombs, statues, busts, and various other memorabilia. In all events there is also a world-famous public edifice in Paris that honors the most outstanding rulers and citizens of France that is also known as the Pantheon: Panthéon Français.

Sometimes, as common usage makes clear enough, a pantheon is not an actual temple of any sort but rather a metaphorical place. In this sense it refers to all of the gods, heroes, and outstanding champions and achievers of a particular people or nation (or even an organization or line of endeavor) taken collectively as if existing somewhere in an imaginary place, say not unlike Olympus, if you will, which was not so much a mountain as it was a metaphor. But then as for the gods themselves of pre-Roman-Greek antiquity, certainly it was not their physical presence but their spiritual presence (always in the disguise of a human being) that counted.

In one sense the National Museum of American History and also the Smithsonian Institution as a whole is a temple. In effect, it enshrines and deifies and even idolizes human beings. At the same time, however, it is nothing if not a secular place, obviously concerned to a very great extent with the nuts and bolts of works and days in factories, fields, and offices, with weather vanes and windmills and so to airfoils and beyond. To

581

many Americans, the very word *Smithsonian* is synonymous with the natural history of U.S. science, technology, and industry.

And yet, as a repository of indigenous and vernacular artifacts and memorabilia, the Smithsonian also serves, intentionally or not, the very express purpose of providing compelling documentary evidence that a very functional and, in fact, indispensable metaphorical American pantheon really does exist (even as the constellation of Roman gods [some adapted from the Greeks, some not] was already in existence, and Hadrian already regarded himself as their beneficiary long before he caused a temple to be consecrated to them).

And why not? Certainly much goes to show that such metaphorical or godlike national forces or influences and also inspirations have as much to do with the quality of American works and days and pastimes and notions of self-fulfillment as any other environmental factors, so to speak. In any case, to be in the national pantheon is to have a place of definitive influence among the aggregate forces that determine the fate of a people, for even as such forces shape rituals, customs, and traditions, which is to say, the way things are done, they modify expectations, define values, and, in effect, set the direction of endeavors.

So much for the nature and function of pantheons. But still, an extremely important thing always to keep clearly in mind about a position in the metaphorical pantheon with all of its godlike influence is that even in the most democratic of republics, it is not a matter of election campaigns. You must earn your own way in as gods and heroes have always had to do, through the intrinsic merit of what you do and how you do it, and as a result of the undeniability, the depth and scope, and the durability of its impact.

And, of course, that is exactly what Duke Ellington had done. He, whose name has for so many years been a proper noun, became a very uncommon common noun and in consequence a transitive and intransitive active voice verb as well, has been brought into these hallowing halls and archives precisely because he already existed and was already exercising so much, yes, Olympian influence *out there*, as if already *up* there where he has been awe-inspiring, emulated, and as yet never quite successfully ripped off.

Yes, you earn your own way into the national pantheon by fulfilling in an exemplary manner the basic national imperatives as they apply to your particular line of endeavor. That is the *sine qua non* and in the arts this becomes the *vernacular imperative to process (which is to say to stylize) the raw native materials, experiences, and the idiomatic particulars of everyday life into aesthetic (which is to say elegant) statements of universal relevance and appeal.*

Nor should such a requirement be confused with nationalism as the term is generally used in art history and criticism, for it has nothing to do with flag-waving, chauvinism, and Fourth of July jingoism. What makes it ancestral is a longtime underlying assumption that there are traits that are basic to and definitive of American character and thus a uniquely American outlook or attitude toward experiences that makes for a native value system and lifestyle.

To Constance Rourke, the author of *American Humor*, a study of the national character, and *The Roots of American Culture*, what characterizes American sensibility and conduct and distinguishes it from that of people elsewhere may be portrayed as a composite image consisting of the legendary Yankee peddler with his shrewdness and ingenuity, the equally legendary backwoodsmen, the Indian-modified gamecock of the wilderness with his ever eager disposition to adventure and exploration, his skill at improvisation and innovation and thus his adaptability, and the no less legendary and by no means invisible, even if not readily acknowledged Negro, with his blues-stomping Afropercussive banjos and fiddles and his tambos and bones and fifes and triangles plus his sense of humor and "his improvised melodies and verses to match all the occasions of the day," who, says Constance Rourke, "became a dominant figure in spite of his condition [of servitude]."

In *Made in America* (the arts in contemporary American civilization), John A. Kouwenhoven, also the author of *The Beer Can by the Highway: What's American About America*, documents what amounts to still another very closely entwined ancestral source for an indigenous American aesthetic. He relates numerous examples of how vernacular procedures evolved from the modification of established technologies and conventional ideas and customs and learned traditions from Europe and elsewhere as a result of frontier situations and also as a result of the rugged American orientation toward freedom of enterprise in the general as well as the economic sense of the word.

No other music has ever been more directly or more obviously derivative of or compatible with or more comprehensively representative of all of this than is the body of fully orchestrated blues idiom statements that make up the collected works of Duke Ellington. Moreover, no American artist working in any medium whatsoever in any generation has ever fulfilled the vernacular imperatives more completely and consistently. Not even Walt Whitman or Mark Twain, among the most illustrious of his literary ancestors.

Among his contemporaries, Ellington's place in music is equivalent to that of Hemingway and Faulkner in literature and Frank Lloyd Wright in architecture whose buildings were already swinging (or, in any case, appropriately resilient!) long before the one that survived the earthquake in Tokyo. Oh, yes, and there is Alexander Calder, whose stabiles no less than his mobiles were constructed as if on the Ellingtonian principle of it don't mean a thing if it ain't got that swing.

As for contemporary musicians, Ellington is the quintessential American composer not only because he was always mostly concerned with the actualities of life in an American landscape, but also because he was able to process it into such fine art and to such international effect. When Aaron Copland was asked a few years ago why he abandoned the style of his *Variations*, the *Short Symphony*, and *Statements* to do things like *El Salón México*, he replied in part that he became aware "that not only I but most composers I was familiar with were writing music that lacked appeal to a wide audience. It occurred to me that we could write music that would be true to ourselves and yet have a wider potential audience. The easiest way to do that would be to combine your music with ballet action on stage, or perhaps write it as background to a film, or *any other form than just pure concert music*."

All-purpose, ever-pragmatic, workaday bandleader and performer as well as arranger and composer that he always was, Ellington knew all along that such indigenous workaday requirements as were very specific to phonograph recording sessions, radio broadcasts, and moving picture soundtracks were key factors that were of far more crucial importance to the form as well as the content of his music than were any of the essentially academic pieties about the conventions of European music of whatever merit.

Such also were the American musical actualities or stateside facts of a native-born musician's everyday life that he operated in terms of that when Ellington, playing in Paris in 1933, was asked about Rimsky-Korsakov's *Treatise on Harmony* by one of his numerous and very enthusiastic admirers, among whom were the likes of Auric, Durey, Honegger, Milhaud, Poulenc, and Tailleferre, and he replied that he hadn't read it and didn't intend to, he could have added the obvious. The output of Fletcher Henderson, Don Redman, Fats Waller, Jimmy Mundy, and others soon to be joined by Edgar Sampson, Sy Oliver, and Eddie Durham and Count Basie, was what he had to contend with, not any European theories per se.

In any case, what an Ellington arrangement or composition represents is not even a free or even a deliberately iconoclastic appropriation of any European convention, but rather the extension, elaboration, and refinement of the basic twelve-bar (and less frequently the eight-, four-, and sixteen-bar) blues idiom statement of the old strolling and streetcorner folk musician with his train whistle guitar and harmonica and also of his sometimes less folksy honky-tonk keyboard colleague.

No wonder his music always sounds so unmistakably American, for the blues idiom statement (with its dead metaphors from locomotive onomatopoeia, among other things) is not only primarily concerned with indigenous raw material, it is even more preoccupied with its own vocabulary, grammar, and syntax.

Unlike other excellent American composers, whose music is no less involved with the everyday stuff of American life but who work it up mainly by using devices that so often make it sound like the work of irreverent Europeans, or perhaps the admirers and imitators of irreverent Europeans, or maybe just as children of Nadia Boulanger, Ellington proceeded not in terms of the convention of exposition, development, and recapitulation, but almost always in terms of vamps (when not coming on like gangbusters), riffs, breaks, choruses of various kinds, such as ensemble, solo, call and response, through chases and bar tradings to outchoruses and tags. Then there was all of that idiomatic timbre, harmony, those un-ofay minors and various dimensions of locomotive onomatopoeia. Not to mention all of that inimitable rhythm, tempo, and syncopation, all in the spirit of unrepressible improvisation to achieve, if not grace, at least a tentative equilibrium under the pressure of all tempos and unforeseeable but not unanticipated disjunctures.

But in the end, to say that Duke Ellington's achievements have earned him a place in the national pantheon should imply much more than that he has gained a place of honor for himself as an artist and as a person and has thereby set an example that will be an inspiration to other musicians and also to all people who have high horizons of aspiration, especially those from his own social background.

That is all well and good. The late great expert in international relations Ralph Bunche said more than once that Ellington had always been one of his most important role models, and there are others in many other walks of life who have been saying the same thing for generations.

But as important as the effect of Ellington's achievement has been in the area of career development, even more importance must be given to the legacy that the music itself embodies. It was created for the express purpose of becoming an integral—nay, indispensable—element of the nation's most basic equipment for everyday existence. Call it conditioning equipment, for it provides the very best of all contemporary soundtracks for the nation's workaday activities and its fun and games as well.

And in doing so, it also provides all Americans with a comprehensive score to which the tragedy, comedy, melodrama, and farce of the ongoing, even if mostly picaresque, episodes of their individual stories can be choreographed. Indeed, it is also here for the carefully deliberated purpose of inspiring each individual to choreograph his or her own solos and every couple its duets.

Nor should the implications of Ellington's ensemble writing as an all-American approach to harmony be overlooked.

Storiella Americana as She Is Swyung;
or, The Blues as Representative Anecdote

IT IS A COINCIDENCE both appropriate and profoundly symbolic that the quintessential American composer was born, grew to young manhood, came to his vocation, and began his apprenticeship in the capital city of the nation. Such achievement as his is hardly predictable, to be sure. But in this instance it is easy enough to account for, because it is so consistent with uniquely local environmental factors that conditioned the outlook, direction, and scope of his ambition and development.

As little as has been made of it, there is in point of historical fact, much to suggest that circumstances in Washington during the first two decades of the century made it just the place to dispose a bright-eyed and ambitious young brownskin musician to become the composer who has indeed achieved the most comprehensive and sophisticated as well as the most widely infectious synthesis of the nation's richly diverse musical resources, both indigenous and imported.

Duke Ellington (*né* Edward Kennedy Ellington, a.k.a. Ellington and Duke), whose collected works represent far and away the most definitive musical stylization of life in the United States, was born in the house of his maternal grandparents on Twentieth Street on the twenty-ninth of April 1899, and shortly thereafter was taken by his parents, James Edward and Daisy Kennedy Ellington, to their own residence in Ward Place off New Hampshire Avenue, about midway between Dupont Circle on Massachusetts Avenue and Washington Circle on Pennsylvania Avenue.

This was less than ten blocks from the White House of William McKinley, who was assassinated when Ellington was two years old. From then, until Ellington was ten it was the White House of Theodore Roosevelt, who was followed by four status quo ante years of William Howard Taft. From the time Ellington was fourteen until he was twenty-two, it was not only the White House but also very much the sharply segregated Washington of Woodrow Wilson.

The Washington of McKinley is said to have provided much more government employment for black citizens than any previous administration. But even so, post-Reconstruction disfranchisement continued apace, for McKinley's commitment was not to the implementation of the Thirteenth, Fourteenth, and Fifteenth Amendments, but to conciliation of the erstwhile Confederate states. Moreover, his capital city was also the seat of an American expansionism that was all too consistent with the underlying assumptions of the folklore of white supremacy and fakelore of black pathology.

Then there was the Washington of Theodore Roosevelt, whose admiration for the down-home Horatio Algerism of Booker T. Washington, the founder of Tuskegee and author of the best-selling autobiography *Up from Slavery*, was widely publicized, as was his defense of his appointment of William D. Crum as collector of the Port of Charleston. In point of fact Roosevelt's attitude toward black American aspirations was not only inconsistent and undependable, it was at times indistinguishable from that of those who were frankly opposed to anything except a subservient status for Negroes. The obvious immediate effect of his wrong-headed and high-handed over-reaction in meting out dishonorable discharges to black soldiers allegedly involved in the so-called Brownsville Raid of 1906, was to embolden whites who advocated terrorism as a means of keeping black people from full citizenship, something against which Roosevelt spoke neither loudly nor softly and against which he seems to have carried no stick of any size.

During the administration of Taft, Washington was the city of a president who in his inaugural address announced that he would not appoint Negroes to any position where they were not wanted by white people. On one of his better days Roosevelt had once written that he would not close the door of hope to any American citizen. But to aspiring black Americans and white reactionaries alike Taft's statement seemed like official capitulation to the forces of white supremacy, not all of them in the South.

During Ellington's adolescence and young manhood his hometown was the Washington of the downright evil forces of Woodrow Wilson, whose campaign promises to black voters were forgotten as soon as he was inaugurated. Once in office, it was as if he had never expressed his "warmest wish to see justice done to the colored people in every matter, and not mere grudging justice, but justice executed with liberality and cordial good feeling. . . . I want to assure them that should I become president of the United States they may count on me for absolute fair dealing, for everything by which I could assist in advancing the interest of their race in the United States."

But whereas his predecessors had been, on balance, perhaps more indifferent to black aspirations than intolerant of gradual improvement, Wilson's two administrations turned out to be downright hostile. In less than three months he signed an executive order segregating dining and toilet facilities in federal service buildings whose black employees were already being rapidly reduced in number and significance. And this was only the beginning. During the next eight years every effort was made to turn the nation's capital into a typical peckerwood town with a climate of white supremacy. "I have recently spent several days in Washington," Booker Washington wrote to Oswald Garrison Villard in a letter (10 August 1913) that he knew was going to be passed on to Wilson, "and I have never seen the colored people so discouraged and bitter as they were at that time."

As inevitable as a direct effect of all this was on his daily life, Ellington did not grow up thinking of himself as downtrodden. On the contrary, as far back as he could remember he was treated as though he were a special child, and he never seems to have doubted his mother when she told him as she did time and again that he didn't have anything to worry about because he was blessed.

His father, who was a butler, then a caterer, and then a blueprint technician at the navy yard, was not only a good provider, but a man who saw to it that his family lived in good houses, in good neighborhoods (no slum dweller, he), and Ellington said that he "kept our house loaded with the best food obtainable and because he was a caterer we had the primest steaks and the finest terrapin." Ellington added, "He spent money and lived like a man who had money and he raised his family as though he were a millionaire. The best had to be carefully examined to make sure it was good enough for my mother."

No, James Ellington's outlook was neither negative nor provincial. Nor was young Edward's. Indeed, such were his horizons of aspiration even as a child that when at the age of about eight a slightly older playmate nicknamed him Duke, he accepted it as if it were his natural due, and so did his family and everybody else in Washington who knew him, and in time so did the world at large, including the royal family of England and the ever so proletarian bureaucrats and workers of the Soviet Union.

(Apropos of the personal vanity that this readiness to define himself in aristocratic terms may suggest to some pseudo-egalitarians, let it be said that Ellington was always more charming than vain and not at all arrogant. The fact of the matter is that you would be hard put to find anybody who was ever more discerning and appreciative of other people's assets and as eager to develop and showcase them. His ability to utilize and feature specific nuances was one of the trademarks of his genius as a composer. And no other bandleader ever put up with so many exasperating personal faults in his sidemen just to have them on hand to supply shadings that perhaps most of his audiences would never have missed. What other bandleader always had so many *homegrown* superstars on hand at the same time?)

But to continue the chronology. What Ellington himself always emphasized when recounting the advantages of his coming of age in Washington was that he was born and raised among people to whom quality mattered and who required your personal best no less as a general principle than as a natural reaction to the folklore of white supremacy. In neither case would they accept excuses for failure. You either had what it took or you didn't, as somebody from less promising circumstances than yours would prove only too soon.

Not that Ellington would ever deny or ameliorate any of the atrocities perpetuated by the Wilson crowd between 1913 and 1921. He took them for granted much the same as the fairy tale princes and dukes of derring-do take the existence of the dragon (grand or not) for granted. Also like the fairy tale hero that he was by way of becoming, he seems to have been far too preoccupied with getting help to forge his magic sword (or magic means) to spend much time complaining about the injustice of the existence of the dragon. *Dispatching the dragon,*

after all, as devastating as dragons are, has always been only in-
cidental to gaining the ultimate boon to which the dragon denies
you access.

According to Ellington himself, the hometown he grew up
in was an exciting and challenging place of apprenticeship, in
which there were many people of his kind to admire, learn
from, and measure up to. As early on as the eighth grade there
was Miss Boston. "She taught us that proper speech and good
manners were our first obligations because as representative of
the Negro race we were to command respect for our people.
This being an all-colored school, Negro History was crammed
into the curriculum so that we would know our people all the
way back."

The mainstem hangout for the young man about town was
Frank Holliday's poolroom next to the Howard Theatre on T
Street between Sixth and Seventh. "Guys from all walks of life
seemed to converge there: schoolkids over and under sixteen;
college students and graduates, some starting out in law and
medicine and science; and lots of Pullman porters and dining
car waiters. These last had much to say about the places they'd
been. The names of the cities would be very impressive. You
would hear them say, 'I just left Chicago, or last night I was in
Cleveland.'" You could do a lot of listening in the poolroom,
where the talk "always sounded as if the prime authorities on
every subject had been assembled there. Baseball, football,
basketball, boxing, wrestling, racing, medicine, law, politics,
everything was discussed with authority."

Then when he really began to focus his ambitions on the
piano and music, there was a whole galaxy of virtuosi and
theorists not only at Holliday's but all over town, and they
were always willing to repeat and explain things. Among them
were Lester Dishman with his great left hand, Clarence Bowser,
a top ear man; Phil Wird from the Howard Theatre; Louis
Thomas, Sticky Mack, Blind Johnny, Gertie Wells, Caroline
Thornton, and the Man with a Thousand Fingers.

But most especially there was Louis Brown, who played
chromatic thirds faster than most of the greats could play
chromatic singles, and his left hand could reach an eleventh in
any key. There was also Doc Perry, to whose house the young
apprentice used to go as often as possible and "sit in a glow of

enchantment until he'd pause and explain some passage. He never charged me a dime and he served food and drink during the whole thing."

There was also Henry Grant, a conservatory-trained teacher who directed the Dunbar High School Orchestra. He volunteered to give the promising young Ellington (a student at Armstrong High School, not Dunbar) private lessons in harmony, and was much impressed with his talent for melody and unusual harmonic nuances *and also with his indefatigable devotion to the mastery of fundamentals.* Hence the incomparable precision that was characteristic of all Ellington bands over the years!

As no true storyteller whether of fiction or the most precisely documented fact should ever forget—such as the indispensable function of the dynamics of antagonistic cooperation (or antithesis and synthesis, or competition or contention) in perhaps all achievement—there is neither irony nor mystery in the fact that Washington during the vicious years of Wilson and his diehard Confederates was also the base of operations for Kelly Miller, dean of the College of Arts and Science at Howard (1907–19) and author of numerous essays on race relations, advocate of courses on the American Negro and on Africa, militant spokesman and pamphleteer, most notably of *As to the Leopard's Spots: An Open Letter to Thomas Dixon* (1905) and the widely distributed *The Disgrace of Democracy: An Open Letter to President Woodrow Wilson.*

It was likewise the Washington of Carter G. Woodson, with his B.A. and M.A. from Chicago and his Ph.D. from Harvard and his background of work and study in the Philippines, Asia, North Africa, and Europe, who taught French, Spanish, English, and history at the M Street School and at Dunbar and was later principal of Armstrong High School, and who was also cofounder of the Association for the Study of Negro Life and History from its beginning until his death in 1950.

And along with Miller and Woodson there was also Alain Locke from Philadelphia by way of Harvard and the Oxford of Rhodes scholars, who as a professor of arts and philosophy was especially concerned with making Howard a culture center for the development of black intellectuals and artists.

The national fallout of all of this (add to it *the work* of W E. B. Du Bois) was such that by 1925 Locke could edit an anthology of poems, stories, plays, and essays by black contributors and call it *The New Negro* and introduce it by saying, "In the last decade something beyond the watch and guard of statistics has happened in the life of the American Negro, and the three *norns* that have traditionally presided over the Negro problem have a changeling in their laps. The sociologist, the philanthropist, the Race-leader are not unaware of the New Negro, but they are at a loss to account for him. . . ."

It was during this ten-year period, which included World War I, that Ellington came of age and left Washington for New York.

But a word about usage. The emphasis that Miller, Woodson, and Locke place on race consciousness and even race pride should not be confused with the shrill, chauvinistic, pseudo-separatism of the so-called Garvey Movement. As Arthur Schomburg, who knew very well how easy it was for such matters to degenerate into "puerile controversy and petty braggadocio," was to write in "The Negro Digs Up His Past" for Locke's anthology, race studies "legitimately compatible with scientific method and aim were being undertaken not only to correct certain omissions and not merely that we may not wrongfully be deprived of the spiritual nourishment of our cultural past, *but also that the full story of human collaboration and interdependence may be told and realized.*" And Locke himself wrote, "If after absorbing the new content of American life and experience, and after assimilating new patterns of art, the original (Afro-American) artistic endowment can be sufficiently augmented to express itself with equal power in more complex pattern and substance, then the Negro may well become what some have predicted, *the artist of American life.*" If not Ellington and Armstrong in music, who else?

Ellington's all-American outlook was a direct result not of Howard University but of the Howard Theatre and Frank Holliday's poolroom cosmopolitans, but the fallout from Professors Miller and Locke and from Woodson was there all the same. After all, his impact was not only citywide but also, like that of Du Bois, nationwide.

In all events, when the group of ambitious young musicians
with whom Ellington went to New York in 1923 proudly advertised themselves as the Washingtonians they were not pre-
senting themselves as a provincial novelty but rather as a band
of sophisticated young men who were ready to get on with it,
because they had grown up in the capital city checking out the
best in the nation at the Howard Theatre, which, it should be
remembered, was on the same T.O.B.A. circuit as the Lincoln
and the Lafayette in Harlem. (There was no Savoy yet, no
Cotton Club, no Apollo.) New York was a bigger league, to be
sure, but the Washingtonians seem to have had no doubts that
they were ready to make the most of the breaks. And they were
right. In less than four years Ellington composed and recorded
East Saint Louis Toodle-oo, *Birmingham Breakdown*, *Washington Wobble*, *Harlem River Quiver*, *New Orleans Low-Down*,
Chicago Stomp Down (note the regional diversity), and also
Black and Tan Fantasie and *Creole Love Call.*

Nor was he to encounter any musical authority in cosmopolitan New York that was more crucial to his development as a
composer than that of Will Marion Cook, another Washingto-
nian. Cook, who was born in 1869, had been sent out to Oberlin
to study violin at the age of thirteen and on to Berlin (with the
encouragement and aid of the venerable Frederick Douglass) to
be a pupil of Joseph Joachim, the greatest music master of the
day, and had also studied composition in New York under
Dvořák, who had been brought over from Bohemia in 1893 to
head up an American conservatory and to encourage Americans
to create a national music based on indigenous sources.

Cook, who had given up the violin to concentrate on composition and conducting, had become passionately committed to
exploring and developing the possibilities of the Afro-American
vernacular and had written the score for Paul Laurence Dunbar's
Clorindy, or the Origin of the Cakewalk in 1898, such musical
comedies as *Bandanna Land*, *Abyssinia*, and *In Dahomey* for
the famous vaudeville team of Williams and Walker. He had also
organized, directed, and toured with various jazz bands, most
notably the Southern Syncopated Orchestra of some forty-one
pieces, which he took to Europe in 1919. When he returned to
New York, he became a pioneer arranger and conductor of radio

music, leading a hundred-piece Clef Club Orchestra in some of the earliest live broadcasts.

Not only was Ellington, who had named his son Mercer after Cook's son Will Mercer, very much impressed and personally influenced by all of this, but he was especially taken by the fact that Cook, with all of his formal training and all his strictness about technical precision, also insisted, as James Weldon Johnson wrote, "that the Negro in music and on the stage ought to be a Negro, a genuine Negro; he declared that the Negro should eschew 'white' patterns, and not employ his efforts in doing what the white artist could always do as weil, generally better." According to Ellington, Cook's advice was "first you find the logical way, and when you find it, avoid it, and let your inner self break through and guide you. Don't try to be anybody else but yourself."

Not the least of what Cook's advice may have done for young Ellington was to free him to compose in terms of what he liked about such stride or eastern ragtime masters as James P. Johnson, Willie "the Lion" Smith, and Luckey Roberts, such New Orleans pacesetters as Louis Armstrong, Sidney Bechet, King Oliver, and Jelly Roll Morton, and such special in-house talents as Charlie Irvis and Bubber Miley among others, including Johnny Hodges, Harry Carney, Jimmy Blanton, Ben Webster, and Ray Nance, who became stars even as they became Ellington "dimensions."

What Ellington went on beyond Will Marion Cook and everybody else to achieve was a steady flow of incomparable twentieth-century American music that is mostly the result of the extension, elaboration, and refinement of the traditional twelve-bar blues chorus and the standard thirty-two-bar pop song form. *And in doing so he has also fulfilled the ancestral aesthetic imperative to process folk melodies, and the music of popular entertainment as well as that of church ceremonies into a truly indigenous fine art of not only nationwide but universal significance, by using devices of stylization that are as vernacular as the idiomatic particulars of the subject matter itself.* It is not a matter of working folk and pop materials into established or classic European forms but of extending, elaborating, and refining (which is to say ragging, jazzing, and riffing and even jamming) the idiomatic into fine art. *Skyscrapers, not Gothic cathedrals. And as historians need not be reminded, barbarians eventually produce their own principles of stylization and standards of criticism.*

Moreover, what Ellington's fully conjugated blues statement adds up to is a definitive American Storiella as she is *swyung*, which is to say, a musical equivalent to what Kenneth Burke calls the representative anecdote, the effect of which is to summarize a basic attitude toward experience; or a given outlook on life.

For many U.S. citizens, the representative anecdote would be any tale, tall or otherwise, or indeed any narrative tidbit or joke or even folk or popular saying or cliché that has to do with a self-made and free-spirited individual, or any variation on the Horatio Alger rags to riches, steerage to boardroom, log cabin to White House motif. Among the so-called Founding Fathers, Benjamin Franklin's career qualifies him as a veritable prototype of the picaresque Alger hero and two other classic examples are the *Narrative of the Life of Frederick Douglass, an American Slave, written by Himself*; and Booker T. Washington's *Up from Slavery.*

Everybody knows that even now there are people all over the world dreaming of the United States in the ever-so-materialistic image and patterns of Horatio Alger. Others, however, see definitive American characteristics in terms that are no less pragmatic but are more comprehensively existential. In their view, the anecdotes most fundamentally representative are those that symbolize (1) affirmation in the face of adversity, and (2) improvisation in situations of disruption and discontinuity.

To this end, nobody other than Ellington as yet has made more deliberate or effective use of basic devices of blues idiom statement, beginning with the very beat of the ongoing, upbeat locomotive onomatopoeia (the chugging and driving pistons, the sometimes signifying, sometimes shouting steam whistles, the always somewhat ambivalent arrival and departure bells) that may be as downright programmatic as in the old guitar and harmonica folk blues but that also function as the dead metaphoric basis of the denotative language of common everyday discourse. The obviously programmatic but always playfully syncopated pistons, bells, and whistles of *Daybreak*

Express, Happy Go Lucky Local, and *The Old Circus Train Turn Around Blues* become as dead metaphors in *Harlem Airshaft* and *Mainstem.* Incidentally, Ellington's use of locomotive ono-matopoeia is resonant not only of metaphorical underground railroad but also the metaphysical gospel train.

As for the idiomatic devices that are basic to the structure of most Ellington compositions, there are the blues (mostly of twelve bars) and/or the popular song choruses (mostly of thirty-two bars), a series or sequence of which add up to a vernacular sonata form known as *the instrumental,* which is also made up of such special features as the *vamp* or improvised introduction or lead-in, the *riff* or repetition phrase, and the *break* or tem-porary interruption of the established cadence and which usu-ally requires a *fill.*

An excellent instance of the break as both structural device and statement is *C-Jam Blues,* which is also a perfect example of how Ellington used the jam session, which consists of an informal sequence of improvised choruses as the overall frame for a precisely controlled but still flexible instrumental compo-sition. In an elementary sense it is as playful as a children's ring game or dance, and yet it is also a basic way of ordering a dis-course, not unlike, say, that jam session of a social contract known as the Constitution with its neat piano vamp of a pre-amble followed by a sequence of articles and amendments. The point here, of course, is not one of direct derivation but of cultural consistency and perhaps a case could be made for oc-cupational psychosis.

Nor is the break just another mechanical structural device. It is of its very nature, as dancers never forget, what the basic message comes down to: *grace under pressure, creativity in an emergency, continuity in the face of disjuncture.* It is on the break that you are required to improvise, to do your thing, to establish your identity, to write your signature on the epider-mis of actuality which is to say entropy. The break is the musi-cal equivalent to the storybook hero's moment of truth. It is jeopardy as challenge and opportunity, and what it requires is the elegant insouciance that Hemingway admired in bullfight-ers. Representative anecdote indeed. Talking about the Amer-ican frontier Storiella as she is riffed!

As for any question of extended forms, so dear to the

reactionary hearts of so many old-line academics, the number of choruses in a jazz composition is determined by the occasion, as is the number of floors in a given skyscraper, depends on the anticipated use and/or the budget! Once there was the three-minute phonograph record, then came the radio sound bite for voiceover, and suitelike sequence of bites that make a movie soundtrack, and now there is the hour-plus LP. Ellington took them all in stride.

The quintessential composer should be so called because he is the one who provides that fifth essence, beyond earth, air, water, and fire, that substance of the heavenly bodies that is latent in all things, that spirit, nay that soul which is the magic means that somehow makes life in a given time and place meaningful and thus purposeful.

Indeed, the fifth essence may well be nothing less than the ultimate boon that the storybook quest is usually, if not always, about. If so, then the golden fleece of the composer's quest is the musical equivalent to the representative or definitive anecdote. *The assumption here is that art is indispensable to human existence.*

Duke Ellington is the quintessential American composer because it is his body of work more than any other that adds up to the most specific, comprehensive, universally appealing musical complement to what Constance Rourke, author of *American Humor: A Study of the National Character*, had in mind when she referred to "emblems for a pioneer people who require resilience as a prime trait." Nor can it be said too often that at its best an Ellington performance sounds as if it knows the truth about all the other music in the world and is looking for something better. Not even the Constitution represents a more intrinsically American statement and achievement than that.

Armstrong and Ellington
Stomping the Blues in Paris

I N THE MIDDLE of that October now already almost long enough ago to be remembered as once upon a time, Louis Armstrong and Duke Ellington, two of the most widely celebrated American musicians who ever lived, went to Paris to work on a moving picture for United Artists of Hollywood.

The title of the moving picture, which was to costar Paul Newman, Sidney Poitier, Diahann Carroll, and Joanne Woodward, was *Paris Blues*. The producer was Sam Shaw, also a very well known still photographer, and his director was Martin Ritt. The script, which was an adaptation of a novel by one Harold Flender, was written by Flender, Ted Allen, and others. The executive producer was Ian Woodner.

Armstrong had agreed to perform several instrumental selections on camera in the role of a world-famous trumpet player, obviously based on the living legend that he himself had long since become for great numbers of people in all walks and stations of life at every point of the compass. Appropriately enough, Armstrong, who even then was barnstorming the major European capitals on a concert tour with his all-star sextet, came to Paris not only for the filming of his sequences in the movie, but also to fulfill an already sold-out engagement at the Palais de Chaillot. None of the musicians in the sextet, which included Barney Bigard and Trummy Young, was used in the film, however. Nor was any footage of the concert acquired for use on the soundtrack.

No stranger to movie sets, Armstrong, like Ellington, had been involved with Hollywood for almost thirty years. In addition to having made numerous musical short features over a period dating back to the beginning of sound stages, he had played often brief but always memorable parts in such full-length productions as *Pennies from Heaven*, *Going Places*, *A Midsummer Night's Dream*, *Cabin in the Sky*, *New Orleans*, *Glory Alley*, *High Society*, and *The Beat Generation*.

Ellington, who within the past year or so had not only

written the signature music for *The Asphalt Jungle*, a very popular weekly television series, but also created the outstanding background music for Otto Preminger's production of *Anatomy of a Murder*, starring James Stewart, Lee Remick, and Ben Gazzara, had been commissioned to compose and conduct an original score. He was also to provide new arrangements for his *Mood Indigo* and *Sophisticated Lady* and for Billy Strayhorn's *Take the A Train*.

The script did not call for him to perform on camera either as a piano player or orchestra leader. The agreement, however, did stipulate that he would record some parts of the score for the soundtrack with his orchestra. Other segments were to be played by locally recruited groups made up of French musicians and American musicians then living and working in Paris. Two especially selected American instrumentalists were used to supply the sound for the trombone and saxophone performances represented on camera by Paul Newman and Sidney Poitier, respectively. *Anatomy of a Murder* was Ellington's first assignment as the composer of a full-length score, but he had made his screen debut as a composer and also a leader and performer in a musical short titled *Black and Tan* more than three decades earlier. He also played one of his own compositions called *Ring Dem Bells* in *Check and Double Check*, a full-length Amos and Andy feature made in Hollywood the following year; and the year after that he was back in Hollywood to appear in *Murder at the Vanities* and Mae West's *Belle of the Nineties*. There were spots in *A Day at the Races*, *Cabin in the Sky*, and *Reveille with Beverly*. Other short musical features following *Black and Tan* had included *A Bundle of Blues*, *Black Jamboree*, *Dancers in the Dark*, and *Symphony in Swing*.

II

Paris Blues was not a major production. It was, alas, only a routinely slick Hollywood adaptation of a story line about two American couples in Paris that was only a pop concoction in the first place. But the music is quite another matter. It is easily the most enduring element of the whole undertaking.

Old hands at turning popfare and even the lowest pulpfare into fine art, and no doubt also out of a deeply ingrained habit of performing at the same level of enthusiasm and authenticity in an obscure roadside joint or dance hall as in the grand ballrooms and auditoriums, Ellington and Armstrong proceeded as if they had simply been provided yet another occasion to play the kind of marvelous good-time music that keeps the blues at bay in the very process of acknowledging that they are ever present.

Paris Blues opens with a trumpet note that is the exact duplication of a European locomotive whistle. It turns out to be the introduction to *Take the A Train*, Ellington's theme, written, however, not by Ellington himself but by Billy Strayhorn, his protégé, assistant, and arranger.

The actual A train, a subway on the Eighth Avenue Independent Line in New York City, had no such whistle, to be sure. But even so, as Ellington's theme it becomes yet another extension, elaboration, and refinement of the traditional downhome railroad sounds that are so unmistakable in the guitars and harmonicas of the old folk blues musicians. Moreover, in the original recording, Ellington's piano intro rings the departure bell; the calling woodwinds and responding brass shout as if in an all-aboard announcement of destination, as the 4/4 percussion thumps onward, and in this case, homeward.

Most other blues-oriented musicians seem to use the basic railroad onomatopoeia of the folk blues guitar player as unconsciously as they proceed in terms of such idiomatic devices as, say, vamps, riffs, breaks (and pickups), eight-, twelve-, and sixteen-bar choruses and call-and-response patterns, among other things, including the syncopation and special nuances in timbre. To them the stylized sounds of locomotive whistles, bells, pistons, steam, and so on seem long since to have become such natural or conventional elements of their musical grammar, syntax, and vocabulary that they are for the most part as unnoticeable as if they were only so many dead metaphors that go to make up the denotative verbalization of everyday discourse. But not only did Ellington almost always proceed with an awareness of the folk derivation of the blues idiom expression comparable to that of an etymologist, he also had a very special attachment to trains and railroads per se as subject matter. And yet his *Daybreak Express*, which is if anything even more precise in programmatic detail than

Honegger's *Pacific 231*, is no less abstract in its purely musical cacophony and dissonant voicing. *Happy Go Lucky Local* is no less literal, no less abstract, nor any less symbolic than the trains in the traditional folk blues lyrics, in the spiritual and in Afro-American folklore that reaches all the way back to the underground railroad of the antebellum South.

He created two new trains for *Paris Blues.* One, *Wild Man Moore*, brings Armstrong into Gare St. Lazare; and the other is the boat train that pulls out of Gare St. Lazare, separating the lovers at the end of the story. The first comes in on a festive beat that is also suggestive of a New Orleans Mardi Gras parade. As for the other one, at another point in the story is the also and also of the blues in Paris more evident than in the sound of the departing locomotive (which Ellington scored in terms of the rattle and clatter specific to European railroads).

Everything in the outchorus up to the last somewhat un-European shout of the departing whistle is every bit as heart-rending as any of the old folk guitar blues lyrics about train number so-and-so done took my baby away from me. But even so, as the ongoing percussion gains momentum and heads for the *banlieue* and the open country and the transatlantic steamer, the atmosphere of lamentation and yearning is overridden by suggestions of continuity and expectation.

Ellington's train compositions following *Paris Blues* include *The Old Circus Train Turn Around Blues*; *LOCO MADI*, which was the final section of the *U WIS* [University of Wisconsin] *Suite*; and a one-minute, fifty-eight-second gem called *Track 360*, which features drummer Sam Woodyard.

III

No composer ever approached an assignment to do a background score better prepared and more habitually disposed to represent the spirit of place, time, and circumstance in music than was Ellington when he came to Paris that autumn.

He had written *A Tone Parallel to Harlem*, a concert piece commissioned by Arturo Toscanini for the NBC Symphony Orchestra some ten years earlier. But long before that there were such standard Ellington dance-hall and nightclub numbers as *Harlem Speaks, Echoes of Harlem, Uptown Downbeat,*

Harmony in Harlem, *I'm Slappin' Seventh Avenue with the Sole of My Shoe*, and *Harlem Airshaft*, that were also unexcelled evocations and celebrations of life in uptown Manhattan. Nor was the cacophonous hustle and bustle of midtown Manhattan, with its urgent horns and motors and neon lights and twinkling skyline, ever more compellingly rendered in than in *Mainstem*, his special arrangement of a finger-snapping, foot-tapping tone parallel to Broadway.

Harlem Airshaft, incidentally, provides a handy example of how stylized railroad sounds function as the musical equivalent of dead metaphors. The train whistles, bells, chomping drive rods, hissing steam, and much of the rest are all there as surely as they are there in the obviously down-home rural atmosphere of *Happy Go Lucky Local*. But not as such. They are simply a part of the language (ensemble choruses, solos, call-and-response patterns, riffs, breaks, and so on) now used to tell the story at hand. But then, as Ellington was perhaps even less likely to forget than the traditional folk blues guitar player, the old whistle-blowing engineers (and their bell-ringing fireman) were bearers of tidings and tellers of tales, tall and otherwise, in the first place. It is entirely consistent with the nature of the idiom that the main strains of the trombone player's work in progress in the film becomes a train's sound in the final scene in Gare St. Lazare, for by so doing it suggests, however fleetingly, the end of yet another blues tale told by a train whistle.

Ellington's extensions, elaborations, and refinements of the basic idiomatic particulars of blues idiom vocabulary, grammar, and syntax were not attempts to go beyond the form, but rather were efforts to take it as far as it would go. He was one on whom very little, if anything, was ever lost, and whatever became a meaningful part of his personal experience was likely sooner or later to be processed into music—Ellington music, dance music that was also all-purpose music.

He was neither a folk nor a provincial musician on the one hand, nor was he a pretentious one on the other. When his first performances in England and France back during the early thirties moved critics to hail him as a contemporary master and to discuss his work in context with such highly regarded composers as Debussy, Ravel, Ibert, and Delius, he was surprised, delighted, and even flattered, but the overall effect was to expand his functional frame of reference. Even as it increased his awareness of deeper and broader implications of what he was doing, it also encouraged him to proceed in *and on* his own terms, which he had evolved from King Oliver, Jelly Roll Morton, Sidney Bechet, and Armstrong, among others, with a good deal of help from such immediate forerunners as Luckey Roberts, James P. Johnson, Willie "the Lion" Smith, and crucial advice from Will Marion Cook, whose Southern Syncopated Orchestra toured Europe following World War I, and Will Vodery, musical director for Ziegfeld and bandmaster for General Pershing in postwar Germany and musical director of Cotton Club shows.

Unlike the American musician played by Paul Newman in *Paris Blues*, whose great ambition is to write a composition that measures up to the standards of a French critic, Ellington was not nearly so impressed by Auric, Durey, Honegger, Milhaud, Poulenc, and Tailleferre (also known as *Les Six*) as they, to the consternation of ever so avant-garde U.S. critics, quite frankly were by him. Not that he was not deeply touched by such serious and prestigious admiration, but he took it all, and Paris as well, in his stride, and returned home no less preoccupied with, or excited by, the challenges of the nightclub, dance hall, and theater circuit and the likes of Fletcher Henderson, Fats Waller, Don Redman and McKinney's Cotton Pickers, Chick Webb, Earl Hines, Jimmie Lunceford, and Art Tatum, with Count Basie in the wings.

IV

In its original and literal sense, the expression "the second line" refers to all those music lovers who go along with the parade through the streets of New Orleans as if they can't bear to go in the opposite direction from a bass drum. Sometimes they dance and prance along the sidewalks; and sometimes, when there is room enough, they share a side of the street itself. Armstrong once remembered them as "guys just following the parade, one suspender down, all raggedy, no coat, enjoying the music. 'Course they had their little flasks, but when the parade stopped to get a taste in a bar, the second line held the horses or the instruments for the band. . . ." Over the years their outrageous costumes, which sometimes included the umbrella regardless of the weather, their high jinks and irrepressibly high spirits and earthy cavorting have become as much a part of the marvelous tradition of the New Orleans street parade as the legendary bands themselves.

But in another sense, the second line refers specifically to those totally dedicated young New Orleans musicians who used to march along beside one special band to be near that particular and very special instrumentalist whose style and manner they preferred above all others, that master musician who was not only their model but also their household god. For quite a number of trombone players, for example, it was Kid Ory. For some reedmen, it was Johnny Dodds or Sidney Bechet. For Armstrong, it was Joe Oliver, the star of the Onward Brass Band—"he was the nearest thing to Buddy Bolden to me. When he went into a bar to yackety with the guys— he didn't drink—or when he'd be parading and not blowing, I'd hold his horn so all he had to do was wipe his brow and walk."

So in a third sense, the second line is an idiomatic reference to an apprenticeship to any given master. Obviously, the source of the image is the parade. But perhaps from the very outset, it also applied to musicians who did not play in marching bands. Piano players, for instance, had their second liners, as did banjo players, trap drummers, and so on. If Tony Jackson or Jelly Roll Morton was your model, it was not a question of marching, to be sure, but when as a devoted but underage youngster you sneaked into the honky-tonk, hid yourself as close to the piano as you could get, or, as was perhaps often the case, hung around outside listening from the sidewalk and the back alleys, you were in Jackson's or Morton's second line nonetheless. Banjo and guitar players did the same for, say, Johnny St. Cyr as did string bass players for Pops Foster. After all, the brass and woodwind apprentices also spent far more time in the second line outside the honky-tonks and dance halls than they spent in parades.

By further extension, the second line image also suggests a deliberate choice of mentors, role models, functionals and hence *true* fathers (and what the poet W. H. Auden once referred to as the real ancestors), ancestral imperatives, or mission in life. Not only did Armstrong almost always refer to King Oliver as *Papa Joe*, he always addressed him as such. Then he, in turn, came to be called Pops by instrumentalists of all kinds and vocalists as well as all over the world. Everywhere he went he was greeted in effect as the culture hero (bringer of fundamental equipment for living) that in fact he was.

Among those in the second line upon his rearrival at Gare St. Lazare that October was none other than Ellington himself, who was to pay him permanent tribute some nine years later with *A Portrait of Louis Armstrong*, Part III of his *New Orleans Suite*, the sixth segment of which is appropriately titled "The Second Line." Incidentally, there is much in his early work to suggest that although Ellington did not grow up marching alongside your Joe Oliver in the Onward Brass Band, somewhere along the way he did spend a significant amount of time in the metaphorical second line of King Oliver's Creole Jazz Band, among others, nonetheless.

v

What almost always seemed to count for most in Armstrong's estimation was not the architectural splendors or even the historical grandeur of a place, but the quality and quantity of the fun to be found there, whether upon arrival or in due course, as in some unheard-of, out-of-the-way stop on a tour of one-night stands.

But then he never seems to have been one of your wide-eyed and ever-so-eager young men from the provinces come to seek fame and fortune in the great metropolis anyway . . . not even when he arrived in Chicago as a twenty-two-year-old journeyman from New Orleans. He had been sent for by King Oliver, the master himself; and he took the great city by storm long before he had time to be dazzled by it. He went to New York at the insistence of Fletcher Henderson, another maestro of national standing, and his impact on older and younger musicians alike was hardly less than that of the Pied Piper on the children of Hamelin. Not only was the reception the same everywhere he went, but his phonograph recordings had made him a great celebrity in all of the cities of Europe years before he set foot in London and Paris at the age of thirty-three.

It was as if Armstrong had been born knowing that the blues was nothing if not good-time music. Certainly he was conditioned from infancy by postfuneral music that celebrated life in the very face of the finality of death. In any case, even before he began his apprenticeship in Storyville, the Mardi Gras fêtes, the dance halls, and the riverboats, he was already proceeding as if the basic social and, yes, existential function of the blues musician was to conjure up or otherwise generate an atmosphere of revelry, jubilation, and earthly well-being, and so also of affirmation and celebration. Nor was any of the exuberant slapstick and mockery of Armstrong the Entertainer any less a means of dispelling gloom and putting banality to riot than was the incredible elegance of his scintillating trumpet.

Armstrong enjoyed being in Paris not only because of the high critical esteem in which he was held there, but because it was a good-time town, not unlike the New Orleans of his youth. As for the Parisians, they knew that whenever he rolled into town (always as if atop the Glad Wagon), the blues would be held at bay (stone frozen in place not unlike the gargoyles at Notre Dame), at least for the time being.

VI

An Ellington composition is the product of a musician who was an extraordinary embodiment, if not archetype, of the artist as playful improviser. It is in overall shape, and specific detail as well, the happy consequence of a very imaginative and highly skillful playfulness that achieves that measure of elegance that can take even the most functional activity to that special level of stylization known as fine art.

Not that the basic dynamics of the Ellington method were unique. On the contrary, the skillful playfulness so characteristic of blues idiom musicians like Ellington the Orchestrator and Armstrong the Soloist may well be the indispensable condition of the creative process as such. For in painting, literature, dance, drama, or music, it is precisely through ever more skillful playfulness or playful skill that literal reproduction (representation, reenactment, even onomatopoeia) is subordinated to considerations of design and ornamentation, and that the raw material of everyday experience is processed into aesthetic statement.

In the case of Ellington, such play was also likely to be a matter of *interplay*, not only with the musicians on hand, as in a jam session, but also (on occasion) as if in an ongoing dialogue with the also and also of the entire idiom. "This is my this year's stuff," he could have well said to Armstrong as they rehearsed *Wild Man Moore* and *Battle Royal*, "that I got from your that year's stuff that you got from King Oliver's Buddy Bolden stuff back when."

Ellington's *Echoes of Harlem*, *Boy Meets Horn*, *Are You Sticking?*, *Warm Valley*, and *Concerto for Cootie* were not derived from the European concerto form but from playing around with the orchestral implications of the solo emphasis that Armstrong had brought into the forefront of the idiom even before his landmark performances on *Potato Head Blues* and *West End Blues*. Ellington's solo showcase compositions retain all of the spontaneity of a jam session while providing a consistently richer and more precise context. Showcase indeed.

VII

Those critics who presume to make fundamental distinctions between pure music and programmatic or descriptive music also tend to consign programmatic music to a lower order of aesthetic endeavor and achievement. But to Ellington, who was no less a performer and maestro than a composer, such categories were more academic than pragmatic. Along with all of their details evocative of uptown Manhattan, in *Echoes of Harlem* and *Harlem Airshaft*, for instance, were also idiomatic concertos for trumpet star Cootie Williams, and they were written to be played in dance halls and nightclubs far more often than in vaudeville theaters, not to mention concert halls.

Nor was *Wild Man Moore*, with all of its locomotive beat and terminal station atmosphere, any less a functional concerto than was *Battle Royal*, with its purely musical jam session-like play and interplay on the progression of *I Got Rhythm*. In *Wild Man Moore* the legendary trumpetmaster engages in a solo/ensemble call-and-response exchange with disciples assembled to greet him at the train station. In *Battle Royal* he playfully invades a nightclub and precipitates a musical free-for-all, in and out of which he soars as if from a perch somewhere on Mount Olympus.

The concertolike structure of Ellington's compositions provided precisely what was needed to feature Armstrong in both episodes of the film. But when the same two numbers were used sometime later in a recording session with Ellington's orchestra combined with Count Basie's, neither was performed as a concerto. Both were used as a framework for a series of purely musical exchanges by outstanding soloists from each orchestra.

Ellington's scenic numbers for the soundtrack were *Birdie Jungle*, *Autumnal Suite*, *Nite*, and *Paris Stairs*, all of which are as playful and artful as they are atmospheric. *Birdie Jungle* has a tongue-in-cheek dance beat. *Autumnal Suite* gives the signature strain a cozy medium tempo statement. *Paris Stairs* is a waltz for what in effect is the *pas de quatre* that the two couples' movements add up to during an afternoon outing.

Guitar Amour, which is used in the film as a number performed in a Paris nightclub, perhaps inevitably evokes memories of the late Django Reinhardt, the widely admired French Gypsy guitar player who made several records with some of Ellington's musicians during the orchestra's second visit to Paris in the spring before the outbreak of World War II and who also made a brief concert tour with Ellington in the United States shortly after the war. In point of fact, while he was in Paris working on the film, Ellington was not only in contact with Reinhardt's cousin, also a guitar player, he also playfully voiced phrases from his work in progress. In the film, however, the role of the Gypsy guitarist is played by Serge Reggiani, who in real life is an outstanding guitar player and also a very popular singer.

On the set, Ellington not only double-checked the suitability of the music for each episode but also, as was his usual practice, carefully voiced special passages for the instrumentalists, including Aaron Bridges, who played piano on camera, and the celebrated French drummer Moustache. Ellington seldom finished scoring his music until he had heard it played back not only on the appropriate instrument, but also by the individual musician he had in mind. With him it was always more a matter of getting it ear-perfect rather than note-perfect.

VIII

When the sequences in which Armstrong appeared had been filmed, he and his all-star sextet went on to the next stop on his heavily booked European concert tour. Ellington remained in Paris until all of the major work on the scenes shot on location there were finished. Then, having also done background music for another production, *Turcaret*, a classic French play by Lesage last performed in 1709, he came back to New York to complete the parts of the score that he had agreed to record for the soundtrack and also for a United Artists record album (UAL 4092) with his own orchestra.

What he actually did, of course, was to play each composition into the desired shape and texture during rehearsal. It was not a matter of drilling the musicians on each passage until each section of the orchestra could play its assignments in the new score to his complete satisfaction, as was the case with most other composers. It was rather a way of continuing the process of creation and orchestration that he had begun on the piano some time before. Each musician was provided with a score, to be sure, which each could read and play expertly at sight if necessary. But Ellington, who was always as sensitive to his sidemen's musical personalities as a choreographer is to the special qualities of each dancer's body in motion, always preferred to leave himself free to take advantage of the options that opened up during rehearsal and also during the performance itself.

As others have said, the whole orchestra was no less a personal instrument to Ellington than was the piano. In a sense, the same is obviously true of all conductors, but not in the same way and to the same extent as with Ellington. The control he exercised from the piano as a performing composer as well as conductor using the comp was much more complete than even a Toscanini could achieve with a baton. He not only set tempos, moods, and voicing as if the various sections of the orchestra were physical extensions of the keyboard, but he also inserted riffs and dictated phrasings, shadings, and even revisions.

He actually played the orchestra from the piano. His control was such that the voicing, phrasings, the interplay of soloist with ensemble and of soloists with each other, and the overall sound and inimitable beat usually seemed so organic that the precision of the musicianship was often likely to be obscured by the very effect it created. Nor was this achieved at the expense of the individuality of his musicians. The invention of the idiomatic concerto was only his most obvious device for showcasing their distinctive identities. The individuality, spontaneity, and inventiveness were no less intact and in evidence on such tightly constructed three-minute compositions as in *Harmony in Harlem*, *C-Jam Blues*, and *Mainstem*, in which each solo participant fulfills a role that is as immediately distinguishable as is a character in a story.

The remarkable evolution from excellent but not yet exceptional musicians into world-famous musical identities of such unmistakable and indelibly Ellingtonian sidemen as Johnny Hodges, Cootie Williams, Barney Bigard, Harry Carney, Lawrence Brown, "Tricky Sam" Nanton, Rex Stewart, Jimmy Blanton, Ben Webster, Ray Nance, and others, including Cat Anderson, Paul Gonsalves, and Jimmy Hamilton, should make it quite clear that the Ellington process did not reduce musicians to robots. It brought the very best they had in them. Indeed, in almost every instance, the musician found himself being featured before he himself realized that he had something special to offer beyond recent improvement in his craftsmanship.

The inspiration, no less than the discipline that came from working alongside Ellington the performing composer, conditioned his sidemen to use their solo space to make meaningful statements as if in the context of a discussion rather than as simply a chance to display their extraordinary technical virtuosity per se, as is often the case in jam sessions and in bands that use arrangements that are closer to jam session routines than to composition.

Not that such displays (which to be done well require every bit as much improvisational resourcefulness as technical facility) were not also a part of the Ellington repertoire. After all, he did work primarily in the world of show biz and entertainment that included the floor show, the vaudeville stage, the minstrel and specialty acts predating the *commedia dell'arte*.

So when the occasion called for it, he seldom hesitated to

parade his superb lineup of soloists across the stage as if they were so many dazzling musical acrobats, jugglers, and tumblers. But even as Ellington the Entertainer waved them into the spotlight like an ever-charming ringmaster, Ellington the ever-alert composer often sat at the piano during the next rehearsal and said, "Hey, how does that little thing you did during the second show last night go? Like this? How about this and then this?" But then, sometimes the same thing would happen to a purely technical run overheard as the musicians were warming up backstage. Sometimes he would simply play it and call out the name of the musician he was quoting and then go on playing around with it as a point of departure of a jam session, to which other members of the orchestra made contributions sometimes at his specific prompting and sometimes gratuitously, but always because by one means or another he stimulated them into participation.

Nor did his use of such material in a carefully wrought composition preclude its further use as a gimmick to display intensity as such, as in the case of *Wild Man Moore* and *Battle Royal*, used on the soundtrack of *Paris Blues* on the one hand and in his joint recording session (Columbia CL 1715) with the Count Basie orchestra on the other. Both approaches were acceptable forms of making music, which is nothing if not a form of play in the first place. Some play, no matter how artful and elegant, is primarily for sheer entertainment. Another kind adds up to an extension, elaboration, and refinement of the rituals that reenact the basic technologies of survival of a given people in a given time, place, and circumstance. This, of course, is the primordial function of fine art, which attenuates into banality and sterility when overextended, overelaborated, and overrefined.

IX

The blues-idiom soundtrack for every day goings-on in the United States (and by extension, the contemporary world) that the work of Armstrong and Ellington over the years adds up to is the musical approximation of the representative anecdote in literature. Indeed its special use of the break, for instance, not only reflects but embodies an attitude toward disjuncture that is no less affirmative than that of the explorers, frontiersmen, and early settlers facing the unknown. Nor is the processing of mundane onomatopoeia, workaday cacophonies and pop inanities, among other things, into no less elegant than soulful melodic and orchestral statement adequate to the emotional needs of the times, entirely unrelated to the miraculous erection of storybook castles or great American metropolitan areas—or, for that matter, the orchestration of a veritable jam session of dissonant colonial voices into a constitutional democracy. *E pluribus unum*, human nature permitting.

Moreover, the Armstrong/Ellington soundtrack not only provides the context but also prompts the choreography to condition any Dramatis Personae to the ongoing and yet somehow also ever recurring ride cymbal *also and also and so on* of contemporary actuality through resilience and evermore refined but never overrefined improvisation.

PART V

The Visual Equivalent to Blues Composition

Bearden Plays Bearden

As STRIKING as the figurative and thematic dimensions of most of the paintings and collages of Romare Bearden so often are, the specific forms as such—however suggestive of persons, places, and things and even of situations and events, actual or mythological—are by his own carefully considered account always far more a matter of on-the-spot improvisation or impromptu invention not unlike that of the jazz musician than of representation such as is the stock in trade of the portrait painter, the illustrator, and the landscape artist of, say, the Hudson River School.

Not that there is ever anything casual, random, or merely incidental about his choice of subject matter. Except for his completely nonobjective works of the late 1950s and early '60s, the raw materials he processes into aesthetic statement either come directly from or in some way allude to or otherwise reflect historic, geographic, or idiomatic particulars of Afro-American experience. Nor is it at all unusual for works in any given one-man exhibition to be so closely and deliberately interrelated in subject matter as well as style as to constitute a series, or even a sequence, that is undeniably not only narrative and anecdotal in nature but also intentionally so.

But even when a series or sequence comes as close to illustration as the twenty collages in the exhibition titled *Odysseus*, the images as such, for all their evocation of characters and episodes of a long-established and well-known story line, were seldom preconceived. More often than not they began simply as neutral shapes with contours that were simply what they happened to be. What each original shape eventually became was always determined only as each collage evolved.

Sometimes, as in the case of the autobiographical suite of twenty-eight collages titled *Profile/Part I: The Twenties*, the theme of childhood recollection was agreed upon in advance. But even so, the specific reminiscences that now seem so integral to each picture actually came only after each composition began to click into focus as an aesthetic statement. It was, he reports, more a matter of saying this looks like a garden, so why not Miss Maudell Sleet's garden, rather than saying now I'm going to re-create Miss Maudell's garden.

Of course, once such a painting is completed an artist can say any number of interesting and essentially literary things about it (as Bearden has done on request on not a few occasions). But although sometimes he may talk as if about an illustration, what he is referring to is a painting, a system of organized forms; and in the process of pulling it together he was far more concerned with such aesthetic elements as decorative and ornamental effect than with narrative or dramatic impact. Indeed, as charming as such remarks can be, the picture as a painting would not be changed one bit if he called Maudell Sleet Miss Emily Ellison and reminisced about how after her husband died she used to bury her savings in an Alaga syrup bucket. In the case of *Farewell Eugene*, Bearden tells a touching and informative anecdote about a boyhood friend in Pittsburgh and about how Eugene, who taught him how to draw, used to make pictures of houses in which the interior activities could be seen from the street. *But the painting does not tell that story at all!*

Each of his paintings is evolved out of what the juxtaposition of the raw materials at hand brings to mind as he plays around with them in much the same as, say, Duke Ellington in search of a tune or in the process of working up an arrangement or composing a fully orchestrated blues sonata begins by playing around with chords, phrases, trial runs, and potential riff patterns on the keyboard. The exact imitation of nature is irrelevant to the aesthetic statement Bearden wishes the picture to make. That statement, however, is altogether dependent upon the ornamental and decorative quality achieved.

"You have to begin somewhere," he has said. "So you put something down. Then you put something else with it, and then you see how that works, and maybe you try something else and so on, and the picture grows in that way. One thing leads to another, and you take the options as they come, or as you are able to perceive them as you proceed. The fact that each medium has its own special technical requirements doesn't really make any fundamental difference. My point is that my overall approach to composition is essentially the same whether I'm working with the special problems and possibilities of the collage, or with oils, watercolors, or tempera. As a matter of fact I often use more than one medium in the same picture."

"Once you get going," he has also said, "all sorts of things begin to open up. Sometimes something just seems to fall into place, like the piano keys that every now and then just seem to be right where your fingers happen to come down. But there are also all those times you have to keep trying something over and over and then when you finally get it right you wonder what took you so long. And of course there are also times when you have to give it up and try something else. But sometimes it turns out just great as the beginning of another, totally different picture. By the way, this sort of thing is much more likely to have to do with how something fits into the design or ornamental structure of the painting than with its suitability as subject matter."

Nor is Bearden unaware of the relationship of his procedures to those of jazz musicianship. He is conscious not only of beginning by vamping as if till ready for the downbeat and the first chorus of each composition, but also of hitting upon and playing around with details of both color and form as if with visual riff phrases. Nor is he any less aware of working in terms of relating sololike structural elements to ensembles, sometimes as call-and-response patterns, sometimes as in jam session leapfrog sequences and sometimes as in full band interplay of section tonalities (trumpets with or against trombones, reeds, or piano, and so on).

That he learned to work in his own way with the separations between colors and with the different values of a given color by studying the expressive use of interval in the piano style of Earl Hines is a matter of record. And he has also said that his application of what he learned from Hines led him to appreciate the visual possibilities of Ellington's absolutely fantastic use of blues timbres, down-home onomatopoeia, urban dissonance, and cacophony in numbers such as *Daybreak Express* and *Harlem Airshaft*; to Chick Webb's accentuations on *Stomping at the Savoy*; to rhythmic extensions of Count Basie's deceptively simple abbreviations of ragtime and Harlem stride; to the instantly captivating distortions and disjunctures of Thelonious Monk, and in due course also to the realization that his basic orientation to aesthetic statement had been conditioned by the blues idiom in general and jazz musicianship in particular all along.

Nor was anything more consistent with his background as an Afro-American who came of age between 1914 and 1935. His background in point of historical fact is hardly distinguishable from that of the great majority of the outstanding blues idiom musicians of his generation and of the preceding generation as well. He spent his early years in the bosom of the church, as the old folks in the pews used to say, down home in Mecklenburg County, on the outskirts of Charlotte, North Carolina; and in a transplanted down-home neighborhood in Pittsburgh, Pennsylvania, where he, exactly like those destined to grow up to become leaders and members of the great orchestras that conquered the world for American music, heard and absorbed the spirituals, the traditional hymns, gospel songs, and amen corner moans in context and conjunction with the prayers, sermons, shouts, testifying shuffles, and struts that make up the service or ritual that gave rise to them in the first place. As he also imitated and in some instances choreographed for playground purposes the work chants, railroad rhymes, and field hollers that, along with the music of the kitchen, the washplace, the fire circle, the street corner, the honky-tonks and the dance halls, were the secular complements to church music.

Not even the New Orleans of young Louis Armstrong himself during the first and second decades, or the Kansas City of young Charlie Parker during the 1930s, was dominated more definitively by music and musicians than was the Harlem that was Bearden's briar patch and stamping ground as a schoolboy and young adult. He spent his puberty and adolescence in the very Heart of Harlem, as the incurably square ofay radio announcers back during that time, which was the heyday of the uptown cabarets, used to say. The legendary rent party sessions, for instance, were regular, though informal, neighborhood events that were so much a part of his childhood awareness that he took them for granted much the same as if they were church suppers and socials, or even sandlot baseball games.

Such celebrated stride time piano players as James P. Johnson, Willie "the Lion" Smith, and Luckey Roberts, among others, were not only immediately recognizable as everyday figures on the sidewalks of the neighborhood, but were in most instances also instantly identifiable by the personal nuances that were their signatures as artists. Fats Waller, as a matter of fact, was a very close friend of Bearden's family. And so among many others was Flournoy Miller of the famous Miller and Lyles vaudeville team, whose reputation was comparable to that of Williams and Walker, and Sissle and Blake. The performers working in such smash hit Broadway revues of the period as *Shuffle Along*, *Chocolate Dandies*, *Hot Chocolates*, and *Lew Leslie's Blackbirds* were inseparable parts of the musical life of the neighborhood.

As were such headliners from the Columbia, Keith, and T.O.B.A. circuits and/or the world of phonograph records as Ethel Waters, Alberta Hunter, Mamie Smith, Lucille Hegamin, Perry Bradford, John Bubbles, and so many others. The stage entrance to the Lafayette Theatre was just across the street from the Bearden apartment on 131st Street. The main entrance was around the corner, on Seventh Avenue. The Lincoln Theatre was only a few blocks away, on 135th Street off Lenox Avenue. Before Florence Mills, the star of *Blackbirds*, became the sensation of Broadway and London, she had established her reputation at the Lincoln as well as the Lafayette; and when she died suddenly at the very peak of her triumph, all Harlem grieved as if for a most darling member of the household, and as the funeral procession slowly wound its way through the streets, young Bearden was among the hundred and fifty thousand mourners who are said to have lined the streets while thousands more waved farewell from windows and rooftops, and he also remembers that people came back from the burial talking about how one airplane flew over the ceremony and released a flock of blackbirds and another came scattering roses.

When the Savoy Ballroom opened at 140th Street on Lenox Avenue, about ten blocks away Bearden was not quite twelve years old. But even before that, the patterns of sound coming from such not faraway spots as the Renaissance Casino, Smalls Paradise, and the Nest Club were no less a part of the local atmosphere than were the voices of the woofers and jive shooters and tall tale tellers and signifiers in the various neighborhood lunch counters, poolrooms, and barbershops.

Then almost as if overnight the big orchestras of Fletcher Henderson, Duke Ellington, Chick Webb, Cab Calloway, Charlie Johnson, Claude Hopkins, Jimmie Lunceford, McKinney's Cotton Pickers, and the Savoy Sultans had either evolved on the scene, or had come to Harlem from elsewhere. Thus, during the time of the now-epical battles of the great bands and jam sessions, Bearden was a very curious, gregarious, and devilishly mannish adolescent of good standing in most social circles in Harlem; and not only was impeccable musical taste an absolute requirement for growing up hip, urbane, or streetwise, but so was the ability to stylize your actions—indeed, your whole being—in terms of the most sophisticated extensions and refinements of jazz music and dance.

"Regardless of how good you might be at whatever else you did," he has said more than once, "you also had to get with the music. The clothes you wore, the way you talked (and I don't mean just jive talk), the way you stood (we used to say stashed) when you were just hanging out, the way you drove an automobile or even just sat in it, everything you did was, you might say, geared to groove. The fabulous old Harlem Renaissance basketball team, like the Globetrotters that succeeded them, came right out of all that music at the Renaissance Casino." Nor were the Globetrotters unrelated to the fox trotters at the Savoy Ballroom. Incidentally, when Ellington's *It Don't Mean a Thing if It Ain't Got That Swing* came out, Bearden was eighteen and very much the fly cat about town and on campus as well.

II

But obviously he did not learn to paint by listening to music. He learned to paint by looking at and responding to many paintings. Even when he listens to music on the radio while at work in his studio, his specific objectives and procedures are exclusively those of a painter, and accordingly his efforts are best understood and most fully appreciated in terms of and in the context of the works of the visual artists, not the musicians he admires and attempts to extend, elaborate, and otherwise refine, and those he rejects either in part or on the whole, and so ignores or feels compelled to counterstate.

Each painting, that is to say, is a visual statement that is a reference or allusion to another or other paintings, to which in effect it either says yes and also and also and perhaps also; or it says no or not necessarily or on the other hand or not as far as I for one am concerned. Not that musicians don't do exactly the same thing. Ellington's unique voicings, for example, began by saying yes in some instances and no in others to King Oliver, Jelly Roll Morton, Fletcher Henderson, and even the likes of Paul Whiteman and the saw fiddle Tin Pan Alley extensions of George Gershwin. Such, after all, are the dynamics of the creative process. But the point is that as visual artists, painters must proceed in terms of existing *visual* statements. It is precisely thus that they participate in the ongoing dialogue that makes their métier what it continues to be.

Indeed, as should surprise no one, it was a painter who made Bearden realize, as only a painter could have, that elements of blues idiom musicianship could be applied to visual composition. During the days when he was still a young journeyman, so to speak, he used to visit the studio of Stuart Davis, an American master of post-Cubist persuasion, who had studied in Paris, and in the course of discussions about the approaches of Picasso, Matisse, Braque, and Juan Gris, among others, Davis, who had a large collection of jazz records, kept coming back to the music of Earl Hines and kept trying to make him see visual devices in terms of the way Hines did things on the piano. Davis, who was no less deeply involved with native U.S. techniques, raw materials, and attitudes than with avant-garde experimentation, also told him that the subject matter of painting includes the materials of expression.

But his friendship with Davis, who, by the way, was not native to the blues idiom, came not at the beginning of Bearden's career as an artist, but (as stated above) a few years later. It was not what motivated him to become a painter. It was rather advice from an older and more accomplished fellow professional, and it gave him new insight into, and eventually a greater facility with, the ideas and techniques he had already acquired in the normal course of his apprenticeship to visual expression. As his earliest works show, he was already trying to process raw material from the blues territory, as it were, into art long before he met Davis. What Davis said made him realize that the jazz aesthetic itself was applicable to visual statement.

At the outset of his career as a serious painter, there was George Grosz at the Art Students League. "It was during my period with Grosz," he has written, "under whom I began studying several months after graduating from New York University, that I began to regard myself as a painter rather than a cartoonist. The drawings of Grosz on the theme of the human situation in post–World War I Germany made me realize the artistic possibilities of American Negro subject matter. It was also Grosz who led me to study composition through the analysis of Brueghel and the great Dutch masters, who in the process of refining my draftsmanship initiated me into the magic world of Ingres, Dürer, Holbein, and Poussin."

His apprenticeship at the league also put him in an environment where his fellow students and his instructors lived in terms of visual art much the same as so many of the people among whom he had grown up in Harlem lived with, by, and for music. It was through them and their dialogues, debates, enthusiasms, and put-downs that he was to come to know and frequent the great midtown galleries and museums and also the small galleries and certain ateliers in Greenwich Village as young jazz musicians used to know and frequent the Harlem nightclubs, dance halls, practice rooms and showcase theaters. Young painters at the league and at parties shared their excitements over the ongoing explorations and achievements of Picasso, Matisse, Braque, Klee, and so on to Hans Hofmann with the same sense of direct involvement, even if not quite with the same degree of sophistication, as he was used to hearing in uptown hangouts where musicians registered their responses to the latest output of Armstrong, Ellington, Lunceford, and Basie, or discussed the basis of their personal sense of identification with Art Tatum or Teddy Wilson, Lester Young, or Coleman Hawkins, and so on.

In college (majoring in mathematics) he had drawn cartoons influenced at first by E. Simms Campbell, Ollie Harrington, and Miguel Covarrubias, and then also by Daumier, Forain, and Käthe Kollwitz. His initial attempts at serious painting began with tempera. Then came watercolor and then oil. About which he has written as follows: "My temperas had been composed in closed forms, and the coloring was mostly earthy browns, blues, and greens. When I started working with watercolor, however, I found myself using bright color patterns and bold, black lines to delineate semiabstract shapes. I never worked long on a painting with this method or made many corrections. I had not yet learned that modern painting progresses through cumulative destructions and new beginnings.

"When I started to paint in oil, I simply wanted to extend what I had done in watercolor. To do so, I had the initial sketch enlarged as a photostat, traced it onto a gessoed panel, and with a thinned color completed the oil as if it were indeed a watercolor."

Then he goes on: "Later I read Delacroix's *Journal* and felt that I, too, could profit by systematically copying the masters of the past and of the present. Not wanting to work in museums, I again used photostats, enlarging photographs of works by Giotto, Duccio, Veronese, Grünewald, Rembrandt, de Hooch, Manet, and Matisse. I made reasonably free copies of each work by substituting my own choice of colors for those of these artists, except for those of Manet and Matisse, when I was guided by color reproductions."

Still later, after he began to play with pigments as such "in marks and patches distorting natural colors and natural objects as well," and found out that tracks of color tended to fragment his composition, he went back to the Dutch masters once more. To Vermeer and Pieter de Hooch in particular, he says, and then adds that it was then that he "came to some understanding of the way these painters controlled their big shapes, even when elements of different size and scale were included within these large shapes. I was also studying at the same time the techniques which enable the classical painters to organize their areas, for example: the device of the open corner to allow the observer a starting point in encompassing the entire painting; the subtle ways of shifting balance and emphasis; and the use of voids, or negative areas, as sections of 'pacivity' also perhaps 'sections of reduced tension' and as a means of projecting the big shapes.

"As a result, I began to paint more thinly, often on natural linen, where I left sections of the canvas unpainted so that the linen itself had the function of a color. Then in a transition toward what turned out to be my present style, I painted broad areas of color on various thicknesses of rice paper and glued these papers on canvas, usually in several layers. I tore sections of the paper away, always attempting to tear upward and across on the picture plane until some motif engaged me. When this happened, I added more papers and painted additional colored areas to complete the painting."

Such in brief is Bearden's natural history as a painter; and appropriately—nay, inevitably—it reflects his personal involvement with the so-called Museum Without Walls, that imaginary collection or world anthology of art reproductions that enables a contemporary artist to proceed as if the art of all the ages in the world at large were coexistent (as indeed it is in the truly contemporary sensibility). Moreover, by the same token it reveals the specific nature of his personal dialogue or argument with the ongoing tradition of visual expression. Each statement of his own intentions as an artist coincidentally affirms some elements in the work of some painters and counter-states some elements in others, even sometimes not only in the same painter, but in a given painting.

The juxtaposition of paintings in Bearden's purely functional museum does not make any concessions to differences between historical periods. Only the aesthetic statement is relevant: "Some observers have noted that the apparent visual basis of my current (1969) work, the use of overlapping planes and of flat space, is similar to Cubism. In actual practice, however, I find myself as deeply involved with methods derived from de Hooch and Vermeer, as well as the other masters of flat painting, including the classic Japanese portrait artists and the pre-Renaissance Sienese masters, such as Duccio and Lorenzetti. What I like most about the Cubism of Picasso, Braque, and Léger is its primary emphasis on the essentials of structure. Nevertheless, I also find that for me the Cubism of these masters leads to an overcrowding of the pictorial space. This accounts for the high surface of the frontal planes, so prevalent even in some of the most successful early works of the Cubists. In fact, such exceptions as the collage drawings of Picasso in which emptier areas are emphasized only point up what is otherwise typical. Much of the agitation in Juan Gris's *Guitar and Flowers*, for instance, is the result of the violent diagonal twist of his planes away from the stabilizing rectangle of the surface. Even the early Cubism of Mondrian, who was in many ways a descendant of de Hooch and Vermeer, contains a number of small bricklike rectangular shapes, which strike me as being more a concession to the manner of the time than essential to his austere conception of space and structure." Still it is the Cubists who provide the contemporary context for his work. The Cubists, far from painting cubes or cubicals, are nothing if not flat-surface painters.

Other specifics of his museum dialogue, as it were, are spelled out with textbooklike precision and classroom-type demonstration in *The Painter's Mind: A Study of the Relations of Structure and Space in Painting*, which he wrote in collaboration with his longtime friend and colleague, the late Carl Holty, onetime member of the famous Creative Abstraction group in pre–World War II Paris, who also taught at the Art Students League. *The Painter's Mind* is a treatise on flat painting beyond everything else. In it, outstanding examples from the whole worldwide museum that is the heritage of all present-day painters are in effect reinterpreted in light of the twentieth-century emphasis on flat-surface painting as opposed to the lifelike representation and nineteenth-century misconceptions of the classical ideal and Renaissance perspective.

It was Bearden's early orientation to flat painting that led to his special interest in Stuart Davis. Indeed, it was in the very process of discussing decoration, ornamentation, and design as the primary objectives of contemporary painting that Davis, whose preoccupations were no less vernacular than avant-garde, began talking about Earl Hines and about how his own use of color intervals had been influenced by the way Hines used space as statement in building structures of sound on the piano. "Earl Hines' hot piano and Negro jazz in general," he once wrote, "were among the things which have made me want to paint, outside of other paintings." Remembering all the way back to the epoch-making Armory Show of 1913, in which he was represented by five watercolors, Davis also wrote, "I was enormously excited by the show, and responded particularly to Gauguin, van Gogh, and Matisse, because broad generalization of form and the non-imitative use of color were already practices within my experience. I also sensed an objective order in these works which I felt was lacking in my own. It gave me the kind of excitement I got from the numerical precision of the Negro piano players in the Negro saloons, and I resolved that I would quite definitely have to become a 'modern' painter."

At first Bearden didn't really know what to make of the fact that Davis, who had a large record collection to be sure, so often insisted on making a connection between painting and jazz. He had already had to endure more than his share of pseudo sophisticated ofays showing off how hip they were to the uptown jive, and there was always another one of those perhaps well-intentioned but boring do-gooders determined to talk about something you know about so as to make you feel comfortable in the great white world outside of Harlem. But as Davis went on to clarify his conception of the role jazz played in *predetermining an analogous dynamics in design*, Bearden was able to see just how fundamental all of Davis's points about jazz were. He was talking about how one was *disposed*, or rather predisposed, to process *any raw material* into aesthetic statement.

What Davis made him realize as never before was the workaday relationship of all of his formal training and apprenticeship, of all the abstract formulations and theoretical concerns to his basic idiomatic conditioning. "And from then on," he said, "I was on my way. I don't mean to imply that I knew where I was going. But the more I just played around with visual notions as if I were improvising like a jazz musician, the more I realized what I wanted to do as a painter, and how I wanted to do it.

"I must say I was not just impressed but also deeply moved by the fact that Stu Davis, who so far as I was concerned was one of the best American painters around, felt that it was so crucially important and worked so long and deliberately to acquire something that, as he pointed out, I had inherited from my Afro-American environment as a matter of course. I had gone to him to find out more about the avant-garde, and he kept trying to make me appreciate the fact that so far as he was concerned the aesthetic conventions of Harlem musicians to which so many of my habitual responses were geared, were just as avant-garde as Picasso, Braque, Matisse, Mondrian, and all the rest. By the way, jazz, especially boogie-woogie, was the main thing Mondrian wanted to talk to Davis about during the several times they met."

III

The Painter's Mind is in a very real sense a book about how to see the aesthetic statement in pictures in spite of the subject matter, or in any case, whatever the subject matter, and also in spite of, or whatever the stylistic convention. It is a book about structure and space with primary emphasis on design, decoration, and ornamentation as the indispensable fundamentals of visual expression. It does not discuss color, which as charcoal drawings and sketches and as black-and-white reproductions show, is a *dispensable* fundamental; but the implication is that color, like form, is to be used not in imitation of nature, but for decorative, ornamental, and design values.

According to *The Painter's Mind*, perspective and illusion are not essentials, only conventions, while structure is always necessary in any work of art. "Many things are revealed to us as we look at a work of art with its multiplicity of images. Not all who look will see the same thing; some people, for instance, will be pleased by a particular image, others depressed—each according to his temperament, his imagination, and his spiritual needs. But whatever the image, the only reality present is structure. There is no face, no ship, no landscape, no real depth. These are illusions; the structure that purports them is not."

Such contentions are entirely consistent with Bearden's orientation to flat painting, the use he makes of Byzantine painting and African art, his deliberate violations of scale, and his arbitrary use of color. (Obviously, his use of jet black as a color for human beings is not meant to be naturalistic.) Perhaps not so obvious is the fact that even when black functions as a symbolic reference to so-called black people of Africa and the United States, it is not the reference that is of paramount importance but the design: how the black shape works with other shapes and colors. Moreover, black may or may not say Afro, but inevitably says silhouette, and almost always has the effect of a cutout in a collage, perhaps the flattest of flat painting.

Everything in *The Painter's Mind* is predicated upon the definitive assumption of twentieth-century artists that the painter should dominate his subject matter rather than be dominated by it. His talent is not at the service of description. What counts is how what is said is said. It is a process of stylization. Even when the examples under discussion are such classic classical representations of religious subject matter as Duccio's *The Marys at the Sepulchre* or Giotto's *The Resurrection*, or Tintoretto's *The Baptism*, or Rembrandt's *Bathsheba*, what the authors concern themselves with are the particularities of technique that enable each master to make the painting his individual aesthetic statement beyond all else.

Only about his complete nonfigurative works, however, is Bearden likely to go so far as to say what Georges Braque, for instance, once said about the subordination of subject matter: "When you ask me whether a particular form in one of my paintings depicts a woman's head, a fish, a vase, a bird, or all four at once, I cannot give a categorical answer, for this 'metaphoric' confusion is fundamental to the poetry. . . . It is all the same to me whether a form represents a different thing to different people or many things at the same time, or even nothing at all; it might be no more than an accident or a 'rhyme'—a pictorial 'rhyme,' by the way, can have all sorts of unexpected consequences, can change the whole meaning of a picture—such as I sometimes like to incorporate in my compositions."

Indeed, Bearden is convinced that Braque's statement is clearly an exaggeration. The subjects in a Braque painting are more denotative than his declaration would lead you to expect. Whatever else they may be, any layman can see that his still lifes are made from tables, bottles, glasses, musical instruments, and so on. Bearden feels that Braque is closer to actual practice when he goes on to say: "Objects do not exist for me except insofar as a rapport exists between them and between them and myself. In other words it is not the objects that matter to me but what is in between them; it is this in-between that is the real subject of my pictures."

In practice, Bearden's position is closer to what Stuart Davis seems to have had in mind when in reference to one of his paintings done in 1924–25 he said that they were based on "a generalization of form in which the subject matter was conceived as a series of planes, and the planes as geometrical shapes—a valid view of the structure of any subject—these geometrical shapes were arranged in direct relationship to the canvas as a flat surface." In some paintings, Davis goes on to say, "the large forms were established on the flat-surface principle, but the minor features were still imitative."

It is generally accepted that twentieth-century painting does not have to tell a story and does not have to depict anything. Its figures can be shapes that mean nothing. Nevertheless, Braque's declarations seem to be somewhat modified, if not contradicted by his use of such titles as *Bottle and Glass, Man with Guitar, Bottle of Rum, Violin and Pipe, Still Life with Guitar, Painter and Model.* It is no doubt true that these are only shapes that tell no story. It is also true that no very special meaning is attached to these objects per se, that, in effect, they have been neutralized so that they exist primarily as elements in a picture not concerned with factual description. But it is likely to be less true that it would have made no difference to Braque if viewers saw cats and dogs instead of bottles and glasses and two generals instead of the painter and his model—although Braque could have made pretty much the same pictorial statement with two generals. Perhaps it is more to the point to say that bottles, glasses, guitars, violins, pipes, and even painters and models were not used to record, suggest, or symbolize anything about liquids, music, tobacco, and so on, rather only because they were ordinary, familiar three-dimensional objects, and as such could be used to emphasize the fact that the painter is working in terms of flatness and not perspective. Similarly, when letters are used in a Léger or Davis painting, whatever they may or may not spell, they function as two-dimensional ornamental shapes, and they also serve to keep the surface as flat as, say, a Mondrian.

But all the same, Bearden, who is nothing if not an exponent of the flat surface, sees no reason why his pictures should not tell a story so long as the narration and depiction do not get in the way of the painting as such. In his view, a painting does not have to say anything either literal or symbolic, but it can if it wishes. Of course, it must always avoid unintentional counter-statement or detrimental empathy. On the other hand, there can be no question of any violation of scale, perspective, or nonrealistic color destroying the illusion in a flat painting, since description is always subordinate to design.

Bearden is convinced that doctrinaire artists who would rigorously exclude all descriptive elements from all of their work are placing unnecessary restrictions on themselves. He sees no reason why aesthetic statement cannot be multidimensional. Certainly there is no inherent reason why a mural, for example, cannot be narrative without compromising its function as an ornament. Bearden, who has done both figurative and nonfigurative murals for interior as well as exterior walls, claims that he is aware of a preference only after the composition of a given project is already under way.

In any case, although the figurative shapes in his painting are almost always a matter of improvisation, and are completely subordinate to the most fundamental requirements of design, decoration, and ornament, once they come into existence as realistic objects, even as they fulfill their indispensable function as elements in the composition they acquire powers of sugges-tion and illusion that may be very strong indeed. Sometimes they stimulate associations with concrete objects, places, and events, and sometimes they become symbolic evocations by the same token. In other words, unlike Braque's neutralized bottles, glasses, guitars, painters, and models, Bearden's flat-surface musicians, train cutouts, his rural and urban landscapes with their farmers and apartment dwellers are not only meant to be taken as representations of very specific examples of real-ity, they may be deliberately symbolic at the same time, as in the case of *Carolina Shout*, for instance. What the figures sug-gest is an ecstatic high point in a down-home church service. At the same time, however, the title, made famous by a Harlem Stride piano composition, implies that the movements and gestures are not unrelated to the dance hall, the jook joint, the honky-tonks, and the barrelhouse. So even as the figures evoke the Sunday morning service, there are also overtones of the Sat-urday night function referred to in *Mecklenberg County Satur-day Night*.

The evocations and associations in Bearden's works are indeed so strong, and so deliberately and specifically and idiomatically either down-home rural or up-north urban, that perhaps it is not too much to say that his preoccupation with imagery from a special American context, which he uses in much the same way as Picasso, and especially Miró, uses Spanish imagery, is surpassed only by his commitment to the aesthetic process that will give his painting the "quality of a flat surface decorated by hand"—and also gives him the option to use any raw material whatever, or no identifiable subject matter at all.

But the fact is that once his arbitrary shapes and photo cutout details become figures in paintings, what they suggest very often reflects some aspect of the idiomatic particulars of Afro-American life. In other words, in spite of the obvious fact that he does not work primarily in terms of illusion, the trains, for example, that are present in so many of his pictures are meant to be taken as real-life railroad trains. As such, however, they connote as well as denote, as do the locomotives in the old guitar and harmonica folk blues. And as do those in Ellington's *Daybreak Express, Way Low, Happy Go Lucky Local, The Old Circus Train Turn Around Blues, Loco Madi*, and so on and on inbound and outbound. They are also not only the northbound limiteds and specials that down-home folks used to take or dream of taking up the country or the southbound ones bringing tidings and/or visiting relatives, or "my baby back to me," but are sometimes also symbolic of the totally imaginary vehicles in the spirituals and of the ever so metaphorical, but no less boardable, underground railroad of the fugitive slaves.

Perhaps the most distinctive, if not the definitive feature of Bearden's treatment of the figurative elements in his paintings is the pronounced emphasis that is almost always given to the ceremonial dimension of each scene and event. Even in his portraits, whether of individuals, couples, or groups, the people not only seem to pose for the occasion exactly as folks used to get themselves up to watch the birdie for the photographer of yesteryear, with his view camera on a tripod, his black cloth, and rubber-ball plunger. They also seem posed not only for the occasion, but also as if for some special occasion. There are few candid shots. Even when, as in the series of black-and-white *Projections* (1964), there are unmistakable evocations of newsprint and movies, it is the choreographic movement of the old silent films that comes to mind (along with the old newspaper *stills*), not the documentary Technicolor of *National Geographic* magazine.

Nor is there any contradiction between the compelling impact and hence importance of Bearden's subject matter as such, and the assessment of what is relevant and irrelevant in visual art given in *The Painter's Mind*. For, as should be obvious enough to anyone with even a slight familiarity with Byzantine, Romanesque, and African art, it is precisely by working primarily in terms of ornamentation and decoration that he generates the strong ceremonial and ritualistic associations that some reviewers refer to as mythic overtones. The ornamental emphasis also frees the evocative dimension of his work from sentimentality and provincialism. Compared to the ceremonial dignity of Bearden's radiant still lifes, Degas's great "snapshots" of ballet dancers, for example, look almost as genre as Millet's peasants. By contrast, not only are Bearden's North Carolina cotton pickers anything but genre, his folk and jazz musicians are depicted with a ritual formality that suggests characters in a ballet.

The ornamental and ritual emphasis also serves to counterstate the pathetic (as it does in the case of the agony in the highly stylized representations of the Crucifixion). As is to be expected of an artist who began as a political cartoonist and remains an enthusiastic admirer of Grosz, Goya, Daumier, Forain, and Kollwitz, Bearden sometimes, especially in his urbanscapes, creates configurations that may be taken as social commentary. But even so, the overall impact of *The Block, The Street, Evening Lenox Avenue, The Dove, Rocket to the Moon*, and *Black Manhattan*, for example, is, as he intended, much closer to such Ellington tone parallels and celebrations as *Uptown Downbeat, Echoes of Harlem, I'm Slappin' Seventh Avenue with the Sole of My Shoe, Drop Me Off in Harlem*, and *Harlem Airshaft* than to any of the Welfare Department tear-jerk rhetoric so habitual among so many mostly cynical spokesmen (and persons!) and so readily accepted and repeated by the world's champion one-upmen (and persons!) become do-gooders.

Incidentally, having grown up in close contact with such prominent Afro-heritage figures of the so-called Harlem Renaissance, New Negro movement as Arthur Schomburg, Langston Hughes, Countee Cullen, Claude McKay, and Aaron Douglas, Bearden has always had a special interest in African art. But it was not until he began working in terms of the assumptions underlying *The Painter's Mind* that he discovered the pragmatic aesthetic relevance of African art—along with that of Byzantine, Japanese, and Chinese art—to Cubist and post-Cubist painting. Before that he, like so many other U.S. Negro artists, attempted to identify with African art racially, or in any case politically (and also in its entirety), only to have his images come out looking exactly as if they were derived from the Mexican images of Diego Rivera and Miguel Covarrubias, and from one Winold Reiss, to whom as a matter of fact they were infinitely closer in spirit, and intention as well, than to Ife, Dogon, Fon, Senufo, or Benin.

He learned to apply certain devices of stylization appropriated from African art but, needless to say, he could not use African devices as if he were an African, because, for all his ancestral bloodlines, he could not be idiomatically African, not being native to African experience. He could not be idiomatically Spanish, Dutch, or French either. He could only be idiomatically American, and most specifically, blues idiom American. And that, it just so happens, is quite enough, because as a twentieth-century American he not only can but also must synthesize everything in the world as a matter of course—and feed it back to the world at large as a matter of course.

In all events, Bearden has made it clear that his actual use of African art is based on aesthetic, not political, and certainly not racial considerations. Accordingly, the very strong African-like elements in his work are derived not nearly so directly from the African artifacts on display in the Schomburg library in his old neighborhood as from such Cubist adaptations as, say, Picasso's *Demoiselles d'Avignon*. Moreover, it is on Picasso's terms, as it were (not to mention prices), that Bearden clearly intends his own appropriations to be judged.

IV

Of far more fundamental significance than any question of how much of the art of ancestral Africa is discernible in the work of Romare Bearden is the blues idiom. It is the aesthetics of jazz musicianship that has conditioned him to approach the creative process as a form of play and thus disposes him to trust his work to the intuitions that arise in the course of creating it, which, in turn, also enables him to make the most of the fact that the primary emphasis of contemporary painting is on design, decoration, and ornamentation.

It is also his blues idiom orientation to vamping and riffing and otherwise improvising (as classic African artists were forbidden by custom to do but as frontier Americans were required by circumstances to do) that leads him to dominate his subject matter precisely as the jazz musician does. Any musical subject matter whatsoever is only raw material to be processed into King Oliver music or Jelly Roll Morton music or Louis Armstrong music. A traditional twelve-bar blues progression becomes *Parker's Mood*. A thirty-two-bar popular standard titled *Please Don't Talk About Me When I'm Gone* is transformed by Thelonious Monk into *Four in One* as if it were only a folk ditty.

Nor is such domination merely in the interest of a romantic proclamation of individuality per se. Far from being egotistical in any conventional sense, it is rather a matter of just such free enterprise as is to be expected in an open and ever-changing society, as opposed to closed ones that are rigidly restricted by tribal taboos, or by despotic rulers. But even more than that, it represents the artist's participation in an ongoing dialogue with tradition and his never-ending struggle in the void. What it is mainly concerned with is not so much the individual as with human existence as experienced by an individual. At any rate, when the blues-oriented listener hears only a few bars of music on the radio or a phonograph and says Ole Louis or says Ole Duke or says Ole Count or says That's Yardbird or That's Monk or That's Miles or says I hear you Trane or I hear you Ornette, he has said it all. Moreover, he has spoken with the same sophisticated awareness of art as a playful process of stylization as that which qualifies the art critic to take only a glance at a picture and say: a Picasso or say a Matisse or say a de Kooning, Motherwell, Hans Hofmann, and so on. He is identifying the essence of the musical statement not by subject matter and title but by how it is played, as the art critic does with a picture when he tells how it is put together simply by acknowledging the name of the artist.

Whatever Ellington played became Ellington, as whatever Picasso painted became a Picasso beyond all else. And the same is true—and has been for some time now—of Romare Bearden. When one looks at his paintings one sees more than the subject matter. Ultimately it is not only Bearden's North Carolina or Bearden's Harlem or Bearden's musicians or Bearden's *Odysseus*, but also a Bearden stylization of an attitude toward human existence, a Bearden statement/counterstatement and thus that which stands for Bearden himself, and hence a Bearden (*which, incidentally, one is probably much more likely to see in real life after rather than before seeing in a frame*).

And what finally is a Bearden if not design or ornament or decoration for a wall, where it hangs not primarily as a record but as an emblem or badge or shield or flag or banner or pennant, or even as a battle standard and existential guidon. And of what is it emblematic if not that in terms of which the fundamental rituals of the blues idiom condition one to survive (with one's humanity, including one's sense of humor, intact, to be sure). What indeed if not flexibility become elegant improvisation not only under the pressure of all tempos and not only in the response of all disjunctures, but also in the face of ever-impending nothingness. Yes, it is precisely in doing this that a Bearden wall ornament functions as a totemistic device and talisman for keeping the blues at bay, if only intermittently.

PART VI

The Storyteller as Blues Singer

Ernest Hemingway Swinging the Blues and Taking Nothing

E RNEST HEMINGWAY was a man of active goodwill. He was also a man of practical action. He was, that is to say, a man whose personal commitment to what he once referred to as "society, democracy, and the other things" always went beyond parlor games and the light picketing stage. He was indeed a man well aware of his fundamental involvement in the welfare of mankind, and his response to the issues and movements of his time is not only a matter of biographical fact; it is also reflected in everything he wrote. But the much-quoted Hemingway statement about writers being forged in injustice was never intended as an argument for the literature of sociopolitical protest.

Hemingway never separated the world of fiction from the everyday actualities of life around him, but neither did he confuse the ends and means of aesthetics with those of politics. "The hardest thing in the world to do," he once declared and repeated in substance time and again, "is write straight honest prose on human beings. First you have to know the subject; then you have to know how to write. Both take a lifetime to learn and anybody is cheating who takes politics as a way out. It is too easy."

He believed that all the outs were too easy and that the thing itself was extremely hard to do. "But you have to do it," he went on, "and every time you do it, those human beings and that subject are done and your field is that much more limited." He was, as will be seen, always very much preoccupied with all of the things that affect the art of serious fiction, especially those that make it so everlastingly difficult.

He considered some of these things in *Death in the Afternoon*, continued with others in *Green Hills of Africa*, and *A Moveable Feast* is in part a review of some of the key working principles of his early apprenticeship. He also wrote a number of articles and letters on the subject. As a matter of fact, quite a bit of Hemingway's nonfiction is basically concerned with the aesthetics of narration.

In "Old Newsman Writes," a correspondence-article that he did for *Esquire* in 1934 during the heyday of the "social consciousness" movement in U.S. literature, he was specifically apprehensive about the writer's involvement with politics as such. A writer, he was convinced, could make himself a nice career by espousing a political cause and working for it, making a profession of believing in it, and if it won he would be very well placed. All politics, he said, is a matter of working hard without reward, or with a living wage for a time, in hope of booty later. "A man can be a Fascist or a Communist and if his outfit gets in he can get to be an ambassador or have a million copies of his books printed by the government or any of the other rewards the boys dream about."

Twenty-four years later, when George Plimpton, interviewing him for the *Paris Review* series on the art of fiction, asked him to what extent he thought a writer should concern himself with the sociopolitical problems of his times, he replied that everyone had his own conscience and that there should be no rules about how a conscience should function. "All you can be sure about a political-minded writer," he went on, "is that if his work should last you will have to skip the politics when you read it." He then added that many so-called politically enlisted writers change their politics frequently and that this is very exciting to them and to their politicoliterary reviews. "Sometimes they even have to rewrite their viewpoints—and in a hurry. Perhaps it can be respected as a form of the pursuit of happiness."

As the old newsman he had applied the same principle to Tolstoy and *War and Peace* in the *Esquire* article. Read it, he suggested, "and see how you will have to skip the big Political Thought passages that he undoubtedly thought were the best thing in the book when he wrote it, because they are no longer true or important, if they ever were more than topical; and see how true and lasting and important the people and the action are."

He had also had a few things to say about politicoliterary criticism in the *Esquire* article. "Of course, the boys would be wishing you luck," he said sarcastically; "but don't let them suck you in to start writing about the proletariat, if you don't come from the proletariat, just to please the recently politically enlightened critics. In a little while these critics will be something else. I've seen them be a lot of things and none of them was pretty. Write about what you know and write truly and tell them where they can place it. They are all really very newly converted and very frightened, really, and when Moscow tells them what I'm telling you, then they will believe it."

He then went on to say that books should be about the people you know, that you love and hate, not about the people you study up about. True writing about such things, he always insisted, would automatically have all the economic implications a book could hold. No serious writer, he was convinced, could ever allow himself to be deceived about what a book should be because of what is currently fashionable. Books, good books, at any rate, were always about what you really feel rather than what you are supposed to feel, and have been taught to feel.

He accused "recently enlightened" and "converted" writers of abandoning their trade and entering politics because they wanted to do something where they could have friends and well-wishers, and be a part of a company engaged in doing something instead of working a lifetime at something that will only be worth doing if one does it better than it has been done before—and for which, he might have added, there are no guarantees. He never withdrew this accusation, and as for converted critics, he rejected their laudations as well as their damnations, along with their sincerity. "Not a one will wish you luck," he quipped, "or hope that you will keep on writing unless you have political affiliations in which case these will rally around and speak of you and Homer, Balzac, Zola, and Link Steffens. You are as well off without these reviews."

On one occasion he spoke of declining enlistments (such as those under which Frederic Henry in *A Farewell to Arms* had served time for society, while quite young) and making oneself responsible only to oneself—exchanging "the pleasant comforting stench of comrades" for the feeling that comes when one writes well and truly of something and knows objectively that one has done so "in spite of those who do not like the subject and say it is all a fake." The same feeling comes, he went on, when one does something that people do not consider a serious occupation and yet one knows, in oneself, that it is as important and has always been as important as all the things that are in fashion.

The man who made these statements, it should be remembered, did not lack any concern for the plight of his fellowmen. He did not wish to live in an Ivory Tower indulging in Art for Art's sake. It is true, of course, that he did have a consuming interest in sports, that he spent a lot of time fishing and hunting, but his participation in such activities was neither frivolous nor decadent. It was not only a universally recommended form of healthful recreation but was, as such stories as "Big Two-Hearted River" and "The Short Happy Life of Francis Macomber," among others, indicate, quite obviously a highly rewarding extension of his profound preoccupation with the basic disciplines of human existence. Nor was there anything at all even questionable about his very special but completely serious enthusiasm for bullfights. He did not regard the bullfight as a form of casual amusement but as a ritual drama that had direct relevance to his personal sense of life and to the form as well as the content of his fiction. Violent death was for him neither a matter of cold-blooded indifference nor of degenerate fascination. It was something he wanted to write about because he had come to believe that it had fundamental literary significance; and his response to it in bullfighting was entirely consistent with long-established notions of epic poetry and tragic fiction and drama. Violence is not indispensable to literature, to be sure, but no one can deny that without it the tragic heroism in *Medea* and *Macbeth* and the epic heroism of the *Iliad*, the *Nibelungenlied*, and *Beowulf* would be something else altogether.

It is also true that in *Death in the Afternoon* Hemingway advises writers to let those who want to save the world do so "if you can get to see it clear and as a whole." But then there is also good reason to assume that the implication is that those who do not "see and hear and learn and understand" are not likely to be the ones to save it anyway. He was not referring to saving the earth from interplanetary disaster but those who join crusades. He was referring once more to writers who enlist, and he was to spell out some of his misgivings about them in "Old Newsman Writes." But the author of *A Farewell to*

Arms already knew that more confusion and destruction than salvation frequently came from people who were too busy saving the world to find out what it was about. That, few will deny, is reason enough to admonish writers to stick to the task of writing as well as possible.

Perhaps those who found evidence in *To Have and Have Not* that Hemingway had changed or was changing his mind about the role of the writer in society were more impressed by some of his personal political gestures than by what was actually in the novel itself. It is true that Harry Morgan, the protagonist of *To Have and Have Not*, comes to realize that one man alone does not have a very good chance the way things are. It was not at all difficult to hear overtones of social consciousness in his dying words to that effect in the 1930s. But it is Richard Gordon the novelist, not Harry Morgan, who is the writer in the story. Morgan is a smuggler. Richard Gordon is not at all the product of Hemingway's alleged hard-boiled anti-intellectualism that so many critics have made him out to be. What he really represents is Hemingway's response to literary opportunism and corruption. He writes "social consciousness" novels, of course, but he himself is really a "middle class" social climber, a slick literary opportunist who is not only ignorant of the people whose cause his books are supposed to serve, but he also has no real artistic integrity and is even deficient in personal competence. His "enlistment," as his wife makes clear, is part and parcel of his personal corruption. It is exactly the sort of thing the "old newsman" had in mind when he spoke of those who take the easy way out of the difficulties inherent in writing straight honest prose on human beings.

The scene, the world, the dramatic context of the action in *To Have and Have Not* is obviously and quite intentionally political. It is in a very literal sense a story about life in the United States during the Depression of the 1930s; and it is written in terms of, that is to say, in *the terms* of such political problems as unemployment, crime, socioeconomic exploitation, and revolution. But those who overemphasize Harry Morgan's conversion to the brotherhood of man while overlooking the implications of Richard Gordon's personal corruption seem to be more concerned with making political applications of fictional materials than with Hemingway's total fictional statement. Hemingway was not opposed to interpretations that indicated the political implications of his work, but he himself seems always to have been concerned with human problems that go beyond political issues as such.

It is true that he was already actively engaged in the Spanish Civil War even before *To Have and Have Not* reached the bookstores, but it should also be remembered that while this "novel about the Depression" was still in progress, he wrote "The Short Happy Life of Francis Macomber" and "The Snows of Kilimanjaro," two of his best short stories, both of which are extensions of the nonpolitical themes underlying the Richard Gordon episodes. Both are about personal corruption in the sophisticated world of money and leisure. Richard Gordon, whose fascination for this world (into which Francis Macomber was born) is his undoing, is deficient in personal and artistic integrity, in personal competence, and in moral and physical courage. Francis Macomber, a rich playboy who lives the life that both Richard Gordon and the writer in "The Snows of Kilimanjaro" ruin themselves to become a part of, does not until a few happy minutes before his wife kills him have that which is required to fulfill his manhood—and the role of the hero. He is, that is to say, a *have* who *has not*. One could also say that the writer in "The Snows of Kilimanjaro" compromises his talent *to get* only to find that he *has got* nothing.

Indeed, one can reverse the point of view and read *To Have and Have Not* as an extension of the themes in "The Short Happy Life of Francis Macomber" and "The Snows of Kilimanjaro," which, after all, are more fully realized as works of art. In this context Harry Morgan becomes the figure on the positive side of a coin, the negative side of which is a composite of Richard Gordon, Francis Macomber, and the writer in "The Snows of Kilimanjaro," whose name is also Harry. But in either case the double plot of *To Have and Have Not* suggests the dynamics of pastoral at least as strongly as it suggests those of revolutionary agitation. Either way one looks at the juxtaposition of episodes, Harry Morgan, the lowly fisherman, is the common man who personifies essential virtue and nobility, whereas Richard Gordon and those of higher social status are embodiments of human shortcomings. Harry may be poor, the pastoral poet might say, but he is the better man and he leads a better life, which from one political point of view might well indicate the need for revolution because society is upside down. But from another it could be regarded as the irony of fate: The have-nots really *have* while the haves have *not*!

William Empson refers to pastoral as being a puzzling form that looks proletarian but is not. In *Some Versions of Pastoral*, he also points out that the essential trick of this genre is to imply a beautiful relation between rich and poor. But then he goes on to observe that the pastoral poet is traditionally class-conscious *but not conscious of a class struggle as such* (emphasis added). "Pastoral is a queerer business," he says, "but I think permanent and not dependent on a system of class exploitation. Any socialist state with an intelligentsia at the capital that felt itself more cultivated than the farmers could produce it." Empson also believes that good proletarian art is usually "covert pastoral." And then he makes another observation, which should help to clear up much of the confusion that surrounds most committed, enlisted, or "social consciousness" writing. "To produce a pure proletarian art," he says, "the artist must be at one with the worker; this is impossible, not for political reasons, but because *the artist never is at one with any public*" (emphasis added).

What the writer wants to be one with is the great enduring traditions of literature. This holds as true for a writer like André Malraux, whose raw material is the very stuff of social consciousness, as it does for Ernest Hemingway, who never stopped insisting that the writer's primary job was to see and learn and write. Earlier, in *Some Versions of Pastoral*, Empson had already used Malraux as an example of the writer who had avoided the usual traps of proletarian literature. The heroes of *Man's Fate* "are communists," he begins, "and are trying to get something done, but they are very frankly out of touch with the proletariat; it is from this that they get their pathos and dignity and the book its freedom from propaganda."

When *Man's Hope*, the first major literary effort to come out of the Spanish Civil War, was published, *Time* magazine reported that Malraux had written it on the battlefield. "Between battles," a caption under his picture in the cover feature review-article ran, "impassioned prose." The article called the novel a new kind of book, one that combines vivid journalistic observation with extraordinary imaginative flights. "Largely written in Spain between July and November 1936, it was turned out diary fashion while Malraux was leading the Loyalist Air Force. After flights over Franco's territory, he shut himself up in Madrid's Hotel Florida, wrote in five- or six-hour spurts, making few corrections."

Hemingway, as is well known, wrote the play *The Fifth Column* in the same hotel in 1937 under similar conditions. Hotel Florida was struck by more than thirty high-explosive shells while composition was in progress. "So if it is not a good play perhaps that is what is the matter with it," he said. "If it is a good play, perhaps those thirty some shells helped write it. When you went to the front at its closest it was fifteen hundred yards from the hotel, the play was always slipped inside the inner fold of a rolled-up mattress. When you came back and found the room and the play intact you were always pleased."

The Fifth Column was the work of a man of action *in* action. But not even *The Fifth Column*, for all its newsprint atmosphere of immediacy, was turned out as agitation propaganda, impassioned, calculated, or any other kind. Hemingway was willing to risk his life for the cause but he did not deliberately compromise his aesthetic principles for political ends. What he wrote in the Introduction to the play when it was published in *The Fifth Column and the First Forty-nine Stories* is entirely consistent with what the old newsman had written about art and politics: "Some fanatical defenders of the Spanish Republic, and fanatics do not make good friends for a cause, will criticize the play because it admits that fifth column members were shot. They will also say and have said, that it does not present the nobility and dignity of the cause of the Spanish people. It does not attempt to. It will take many plays and novels to do that, and the best ones will be written after the war is over. It was," he said, "only a play about counterespionage in Madrid," and it had the defects of having been written in wartime, "and if it has a moral it is that people who work for certain organizations have very little time for home life."

The Fifth Column did have political relevance, of course, and given the subject matter, it was immediate relevance at that; but this in itself could never have been enough for a man who was always trying to write prose that would have five dimensions. And besides, it should never be forgotten that Hemingway was both clearly and finally convinced that political immediacy as such was an element that would always fall away and leave a story flat. *The Fifth Column* was not a very successful work by any yardstick. But if it had to stand on its political relevance it would probably be of very little significance whatsoever. As it is, however, it at least stands as an interesting finger exercise in preparation for the major novel that followed.

There was also immediate political relevance in *For Whom the Bell Tolls*, but Hemingway was also very much concerned about the relevance of the color, contours, and textures of the terrain and the smell and taste of food and drink and so on, none of which does political relevance any harm. After all, he believed that one should always write as well as possible, and besides, there is no law that has ever required a writer to work harder to describe the chronological development of a worthy cause, a good crop, or a conversion of a sinner than he would to describe anything else—say, the sheen on a freshly hooked trout or the beads of sweat on a chilled bottle of Pouilly-Fuissé.

The military material in *For Whom the Bell Tolls* is so accurately rendered that much of it was actually used by the U.S. Army in courses in the tactics of guerrilla warfare. But so far as Hemingway the novelist was concerned, it had to be written that way because it was that kind of story. There were political issues and military materials because these things had been completely assimilated as natural personal involvements and were ordinary elements in his literary imagination. As for the operational accuracy of his rendition, which, it should be remembered, was equally true of the fishing, hunting, prizefighting, and bullfighting sequences in any of his other stories, that was no doubt one of the dimensions he was referring to when he talked of going beyond the tricks of journalism.

For Whom the Bell Tolls was a work of art. As far as the specific political and economic elements in the story are concerned, nobody ever had to remind Ernest Hemingway that there things should not be left out. He had been talking and writing about that sort of thing ever since he had started trying to write fiction. Everything you know should be there, he began insisting in Paris in the 1920s, and never stopped.

Sometimes it showed and sometimes it didn't. But it was there like the underwater seven-eighths of the iceberg, sustaining the one-eighth one sees. His was a never-ending effort to comprehend the world in all of its complexity so that anything he wrote well enough about would represent life as a whole. He also liked to say that one could leave out the things one knew enough about. But he always went on to say that these things would be there anyway. And he did not mean to imply that they would be there by chance either. But the relative proportion of elements or of emphasis in a work of art is determined not by political significance as such but by the writer's sense of form.

Political significance is inherent in all stories. Political details, however, are something else. Like all other details, they were included in *For Whom the Bell Tolls* or omitted from it, on the principle of the iceberg. "Anything you know," Hemingway assumed, beginning back in the days of his apprenticeship and was still maintaining in the *Paris Review* interview in 1958, "you can eliminate and it only strengthens your iceberg. It is the part that does not show. If a writer omits something because he does not know it then there is a hole in the story." On the other hand, that which was omitted on the principle of the iceberg, he wrote in *A Moveable Feast*, could actually "make people feel something more than they understand." To which he added, "But they will understand the same way they always do in painting."

It is the "enlisted" writer who insists that the political significance be spelled out in no uncertain terms. But it is often in the very process of doing just this that such a writer is most likely to leave out other things, the omission of which can only make his fiction essentially thin, hollow, of limited interest and application—and all too ephemeral, no matter what initial impact it makes. Some writers leave out almost everything that does not serve their immediate political purpose. Many consider complexity of circumstances and motives to be precious indulgences that can wait until a better world has been achieved. There are those who do not hesitate to suppress details that run counter to, or do not contribute directly to, the social doctrines and objectives to which they are currently committed.

Beyond all political considerations, immediate or otherwise, the man who had not been able to make *Death in the Afternoon* enough of a book and who had declared in *Green Hills of Africa* that carrying prose as far as it would go was the most important thing a writer could do, wanted *For Whom the Bell Tolls* to contain as much of his sense of life as possible, "the good and the bad, the ecstasy, the remorse and sorrow, the people and the places and how the weather was." The awareness of the involvement in mankind and of one's possibilities for self-fulfillment and grandeur were also elements in that sense of life, as was one's consciousness, whether sharp or intuitive, of the relativity and ultimate absurdity of actuality and the objectivity and finality of death.

The writer's problem does not change, he had told the Marxist-oriented Second American Writers' Congress on a trip to New York after two active months in Spanish combat zones. "It was always how to write truly and having found out what is true to project it in such a way it becomes part of the experience of the person who reads it." Several years earlier he had expressed the same point of view as the old newsman, and in "Monologue to the Maestro" he had outlined his working assumptions and procedures; and his sample list of required reading had encompassed the entire range of prose fiction. Among the standards that he suggested to young writers to aim at were *Tom Jones* and *Joseph Andrews*; *The Charterhouse of Parma* and *The Red and the Black*; *Sentimental Education* and *Madame Bovary*; *War and Peace* and *Anna Karenina*; *A Portrait of the Artist as a Young Man* and *Ulysses*; *The Brothers Karamazov*, *Buddenbrooks*, *Huckleberry Finn*, *The Turn of the Screw*, *The American*, *Mr. Midshipman Easy*, and *Peter Simple*. His list of writers also included Turgenev, Maupassant, Kipling, Stephen Crane, W. H. Hudson, and Conrad. And to the objection that reading so many great books might discourage the apprentice, Hemingway replied that if such were the case he ought to be discouraged, that unless he runs against the clock like a miler "he will never know what he is capable of attaining."

What he was obviously trying to attain when he wrote *For Whom the Bell Tolls* was that which the best works of fiction always add up to: a representative image of life in the contemporary world. It was a story about an American engaged in guerrilla operations among Spanish partisans of the Loyalist cause; but to the extent that Hemingway was successful, his efforts to tell how it really was make it infinitely more important as a commentary on the predicament of man than as the document of the Spanish Civil War that some had expected in spite of the speech at the Second Writers' Congress. Hemingway had not intended to write a melodrama about the salvation of mankind through enlightened comradeship. His sense of life was not dialectical but dramatic, and what he wrote in this instance was tragedy. The story begins with the hero aware of his involvement in mankind but in the end he dies, and his death is that separate peace that all men must make with the world and must find within themselves.

II

He almost always worked for a surface simplicity, but completely dedicated to the fundamental aims of literature as he was, Ernest Hemingway was never any less concerned than were, say, André Malraux and Thomas Mann with creating fiction that would reflect an image of man consistent with contemporary insights into the complexities of human experience. Malraux was stating his most definitive conception of the function of fiction and indeed of all artistic expression when he pointed out that *The Conquerors* was not only a story about political revolution but was first of all a presentation of the human situation. And, of course, Mann makes it quite obvious that such a presentation is the basic objective of *The Magic Mountain*. No less mistakable, however, are the implications of the title, the tone, and the content of *In Our Time*; and when Hemingway insists that the adequately informed and accurately rendered *part* can be made to represent the *whole*, he is (as with his remarks about the iceberg principle of omission) not only reiterating the same objective but is also reconciling (for himself, at any rate) the comprehensive scope of his aspirations with the frequently misunderstood simplicity of his procedure.

What Malraux and Mann express in terms of general cultural and political considerations, Hemingway seems to have preferred to approach as the problems involved in the development of the individual writer as artist. Thus in *The Voices of Silence* and *The Metamorphosis of the Gods* Malraux has elaborated a comprehensive theory of all art as a revolt against man's destiny of nothingness. What lies before us is everything and nothing, and what is the past except everything and nothing. Likewise the political essays that Mann collected in *Order of the Day* along with the literary opinions in *Essays of Three Decades* add up to his definition of the New Humanism, a whole theory of human nature and conduct. On the other hand, in such books as *Death in the Afternoon, Green Hills of Africa*, and *A Moveable Feast* and in such magazine articles as "Old Newsman Writes" and "Monologue to the Maestro" Hemingway articulates his assumption about the craft of fiction only in terms that relate to the background conditioning and orientation of the individual writer, his literary aims, his competence as craftsman, and his imagination.

Nevertheless, Hemingway's notions about the significance of disorientation and isolation in the lives of individual writers have essentially the same philosophical implications as the cataclysmic and apocalyptic images of man's absurdity that enable Malraux to proclaim that art is man's means of humanizing the world. Hemingway and Malraux, differences in emphasis notwithstanding, are also in remarkable agreement with the process that Mann almost always associates with human refinement. *Buddenbrooks* in the end turns out to be a story about the emergence of artistic sensitivity against the breakdown of an erstwhile solid family. *The Magic Mountain* goes to great lengths to show how disease makes Hans Castorp a more complete man; and predictably the mistreatments and dislocations that Joseph suffers in *Joseph and His Brothers* are the specific means by which he improves his perspective on the contradictory elements of human brotherhood.

When George Plimpton asked about the remark he had once made about great writing and injustice, Hemingway replied that a writer without a sense of justice and injustice would be better off editing the yearbook of a school for exceptional children than writing novels. "The most essential gift for a good writer," he then went on to say, "is a built-in shockproof shit detector. This is the writer's radar and all great writers have used it."

He had made the original statement about writers and injustice in *Green Hills of Africa*. At one point during a dull stretch on safari, after reading in *Sevastopol*, an early novel by Tolstoy, he had begun ruminating about the importance of the experience of war on the development of writers like Tolstoy and Stendhal, and the influence of the revolution and the Commune on Flaubert and had not only decided that war, especially civil war, was an irreplaceable experience for a writer, but also that "writers are forged in injustice as a sword is forged." He had also suggested that the experience of prison in Siberia had made Dostoevsky, who was already a good writer, a better one, and then he had speculated about the effect such an experience might have on a writer like Thomas Wolfe.

Indeed, what Hemingway had to say about Wolfe is of its very nature a refutation of those who would quote his statement about writers and injustice out of context and then accuse him of not reflecting enough concern about injustice. Hemingway's basic assumption is not that the experience of injustice makes for political commitment, but that the realization that human life is contradictory and mysterious should make for aesthetic discipline. What he wondered was if sending Wolfe to Siberia or to the Dry Tortugas would "give him the necessary shock to cut the overflow of words and give him a sense of proportion."

He said nothing that implies that writers should be turned into weapons or instruments of social reform because of injustice. When he says forged as a sword is forged he is referring to the tempering of metal. The sensibility of the writer must be prepared to withstand the shocks and distortions inherent in human existence even as the blade must hold its edge in the clang and clash of battle. Metal that has been properly forged will hold up. The literary sensibility that has been exposed to human existence in the raw, so to speak, will maintain the sharp edge of its artistic integrity when confronted with complexity.

Hemingway did not express any concern at all about Wolfe's social and political affiliations. He didn't even mention them. What he was concerned about was Wolfe's prose. What bothered him was Wolfe's lack of an adequate sense of proportion, his lack of discipline, his overuse of words. He did not wonder if rugged blood and guts experience in Siberia or the Dry Tortugas would make him a better man and citizen; he wondered if it would make him a better novelist. A writer, he had already said in *Death in the Afternoon*, must always pay a certain nominal percentage in experience to be able to understand and assimilate what he inherits and what he must in turn use as his own point of departure. It is clear enough that he doubted that Wolfe had paid the minimum percentage in the sort of personal experience that builds in the required shockproof detector which is the serious writer's protection against sentimentality, among other things. *Look Homeward, Angel* and *Of Time and the River* make that all too obvious. The overflow of words that Hemingway wanted to cut was a rhetoric based not on hardheaded insight but on enthusiasm, and on academic sentimentality. "Didn't Hemingway say this in effect," wrote F. Scott Fitzgerald in his notebook, "if Tom Wolfe ever learns to separate what he gets from books from what he gets from life, he will be an original." The point is well taken, but the statement in *Green Hills of Africa* indicates that Hemingway was not so much concerned about Wolfe's originality as with his verbal sobriety. As was Wright Morris in *The Territory Ahead*.

"What we have," Morris complains after quoting one of Wolfe's outbursts, "is a man with his eyes closed, his pores open, whipping himself into a state of intoxication with what is left of another man's observations. The rhetorical flow, lyrical in intent, is unable to keep up with the flow of the emotion, the verbal surge of clichés, of scenic props." Instead of Whitman's closely and lovingly observed artifacts, Wolfe, Morris continues, produces "a river of clichés, nouns, and soaring adjectives. He may be in love with life but he woos her with books, and looks through another man's eyes and uses another man's language." "The presence of raw material, real raw, bleeding life—the one thing that Wolfe believed he got his big hands on—is precisely what is absent from his work. He begins and he ends with raw-material clichés."

The misgivings that Hemingway had about the effects of undigested reading and that have often been mistaken along with his interest in the so-called manly arts, as an indication of anti-intellectualism, was already very much in evidence as early as the time of *The Sun Also Rises*. In a very fundamental sense

most of Robert Cohn's troubles in that story grow out of the
stubbornness with which he clings to ideas he has gotten only
from books. "He had been reading W. H. Hudson," Jake
Barnes, the narrator, relates, "that sounds like an innocent occupation but Cohn had read and reread *The Purple Land. The
Purple Land* is a very sinister book if read too late in life. It
recounts the splendid imaginary amorous adventures of a perfect English gentleman in an intensely romantic land, the
scenery of which is very well described. For a man to take it at
thirty-five as a guidebook to what life holds is about as safe as
it would be for a man of the same age to enter Wall Street direct from a French convent, equipped with a complete set of
the more practical Alger books. Cohn, I believe, took every
word of *The Purple Land* as literally as though it had been an
R. G. Dun report. You understand me, he made some reservations, but on the whole the book to him was sound."

Robert Cohn, significantly enough, was also a writer. The
implications, however, are as personal and practical as they are
aesthetic. They are also obvious. Cohn, like Thomas Wolfe
(who was to come later, of course), did not have a built-in detector to spot the stuff and nonsense. He was thus likely to be
more enthusiastic than informed, more bookishly romantic
than really and truly reliable. When at one point he persists in
his Hudson-inspired fantasy about going to South America,
Jake Barnes tries to shift his attention to British East Africa.
When he refuses to budge, Jake tells him, "that's because you
never read a book about it. Go read a book all full of love affairs with the beautiful shiny black princesses."

Perhaps at least a large measure if not most of the essentially
academic confusion about his apparent resistance to intellectual elaboration is a result of the failure to realize that Hemingway himself was nothing if not intellectual. All serious
writers are inevitably intellectuals. They write for people who
like books, not for people who think books are unimportant.
No matter how much they may wish to save the world, they
really write not for "the people" but for "the readers." Many
for whom fiction is the primary mode of expression, however,
are frequently more functional intellectuals than nominal
ones—and would not have it otherwise.

Hemingway was one of these. He was first of all an image-maker and storyteller, and those who accuse him of not being sufficiently intellectual obviously ignore the specific nature of his intellectual commitment. But even so, they must concede that most of his nonfiction could only have been addressed primarily to other intellectuals, since they could hardly believe that the passages on the art of fiction in *Death in the Afternoon*, *Green Hills of Africa*, and the *Esquire* articles were written for the edification of big-game hunters, bullfighting fans, and *Esquire* hipsters. But then perhaps they also ignore or dismiss his nonfiction altogether. And yet, volume aside, not even Thomas Mann has left a more careful documentation of his intellectual position, and few writers since Henry James have written so much to explain their literary point of view.

The reply that he addressed to Aldous Huxley, who had accused him of writing as if he were ashamed of being thought of as intelligent and cultured, is a basic statement of what was actually Hemingway's longstanding working conception of the fiction writer as intellectual. A good writer, he wrote in *Death in the Afternoon*, should know as much as possible. "A great enough writer seems to be born with knowledge, but he really is not; he has only been born with the ability to learn in a quicker ratio to the passage of time than other men and without conscious application, and with an intelligence to accept or reject what is already presented as knowledge." But he was firmly convinced that a writer who made people in his stories talk about such things as painting, music, letters, and science when they wouldn't naturally do so or who did so himself to display his knowledge or used fine but unnecessary phrases was "spoiling his work for egotism."

But in spite of all the unmistakable clues that Hemingway provided, some of his most incisive observations are frequently misconstrued as obvious evidences of his *anti-intellectualism*. Nevertheless, few philosophical analyses of the modern temper reflect a more profound sense of responsibility than the "nothing sacred" recollections in which the narrator-protagonist of *A Farewell to Arms* registers his reactions to easy sentiment, enthusiastic lip service, and high-sounding abstractions. "I was always embarrassed by the words, sacred, glorious, and sacrifice and the expression, in vain," says Frederic Henry, remembering a wartime comrade whom he describes as being patriotic. "We had heard them sometimes standing in the rain almost out of earshot, so that only the shouted words came through, and had read them, on proclamations that were slapped up by bill posters over the other proclamations. Now for a long time, and I had seen nothing sacred, and the things that were glorious had no glory and the sacrifices were like the stockyards at Chicago if nothing was done with the meat except to bury it. There were many words that you could not stand to hear and finally only the names of places had dignity. Certain numbers were the same way and certain dates and these with the names of the places were all you could say and have them mean anything. Abstract words such as glory, honor, courage, or hallow were obscene beside the concrete names of the villages, the numbers of roads, the names of rivers, the numbers of regiments, and the dates."

What the built-in automatic shockproof stuff and nonsense detector was spotting and rejecting in this instance was not the Gettysburg Address itself, of course, but rather the cynical exploitation of its realism by enlistment propaganda technicians, who slapped posters over other posters. *A Farewell to Arms* is among other things a story about a young man who serves time for a great cause, becomes disenchanted, and declines further idealistic enlistment. It is a drama about his discovery of the bewildering absurdity of the human condition. The contradictions of human nature would seem to be bad enough, but on top of that, natural accidents turn out to be very natural indeed. It is, in this sense, also the story about a man who thinks he has enlisted to become a hero in a melodrama only to discover that he has always been involved in *the* eternal tragedy, who is a hero because he is not quite defeated and is wiser and therefore better prepared to confront future adventures, whose latent stuff-and-nonsense detector has been activated and calibrated and better secured to help him withstand the inevitable shocks to come.

The words that Lincoln spoke at Gettysburg were motivated by a profound sense of human life as a tragic struggle and by a commitment to that struggle in full awareness of human weakness. Lincoln, the embattled commander in chief, was talking about the realization of human possibilities through courage and hope. Reduced to platitudes and slogans, his words, as Hemingway's hero heard them several generations later in Italy, were being used to mislead naïve crusaders to expect melodramatic miracles in situations in which epic tenacity and endurance were hardly enough to keep hope itself alive. It was the overeager enlistee, not the cause, whom Hemingway was rejecting when he declared his willingness elsewhere to let those who want to save the world do so. There never was a time when he himself refused or did not volunteer to fight for the possibility of human freedom as defined by Lincoln at Gettysburg. But neither was there ever to be another time in which he would oversimplify the issues, the circumstances, and minimize the natural exasperations that are part and parcel of the best intentions in the world.

He was also to write that he "could only care about people a few at a time." But in view of his lifelong performance in the field, those who misinterpret this as a callous expression of a hard-boiled antisocial point of view can do so only by ignoring the fundamental complexity, to say nothing of the honesty involved. Nor does it contradict his status as a lifelong man of active good will. People love themselves and those intimates they hold most dear, they like their friends, hate their enemies and are more or less indifferent to the rest of mankind, until circumstances (and suddenly enlightened self-interest) force them to cooperate to ward off some common danger or to come by some benefit that cannot be secured in any other way. People who are forever protesting their love of mankind are seldom taken at their word by mankind, not even by their closest relatives, who, knowing them as they do, are likely to find them downright incredible. They themselves never expect to be taken at their word by bank clerks and policemen, for instance, who incidentally spend quite a lot of time protecting mankind whether they love it or not.

But if Hemingway's idealism was rugged, he was not given to easy and superficial cynicism either. His commitments remained firm because they were based on realistic estimates of the situation in the first place. Perhaps, as with all combat intelligence reports, the most immediate social value of his writing is to be found in its unflinching accuracy. In person, however, for all his shockproof calibration, he represented the kind of heartwarming support all movements are not only lucky to have but also cannot sustain themselves without.

Hemingway's goodwill is steadfast. But, as with Malraux and Mann, so was his artistic integrity. Nor was it ever an integrity kept carefully away from exposure. In the preface to *The Fifth Column and the First Forty-nine Stories*, he extended the image of the sword being forged. "In going where you have to go and doing what you have to do and seeing what you have to see, you dull and blunt the instrument you write with. But I would rather have it bent and dulled and know I had to put it to the grindstone again and hammer it into shape and put a whetstone to it and know I had something to write about, than have it bright and shining and nothing to say, or smooth and well-oiled in the closet, but unused."

He was not always successful. No writer ever was. That was another fact of life. "Am trying to be a good boy," he remarked twenty-some years later, in another context, "but it is a difficult trade. What you win in Boston you lose in Chicago." But he never stopped trying, and most of his nonfiction represents a never-ending effort to keep the fundamentals in focus. The old newsman in "Old Newsman Writes" editorialized about the literary risks involved in fulfilling one's political obligations. The monologist in "Monologue to the Maestro" was trying to spell out the essentials of good craftsmanship in everyday working terms, and twenty-three years later the interviewee was spelling out the very same essentials for a latter-day "maestro" from the *Paris Review*. The defender in "Defense of Dirty Words" counseled accuracy with details and advised against moral condescension and false propriety. And so on it always went. The huntsman stalking kudu in *Green Hills of Africa* was also seeking prose with five dimensions. The aficionado did not go to the arena to have "publishable ecstasies" about death in the afternoon, for even as he responded to the bullfighter's grace under pressure, the writer was working on the perpetual problem of how to render the actual thing that produced the emotion he was experiencing.

There was his conception of what straight honest prose on human beings was, and he tried to maintain what he once called "an absolute conscience as unchanging as the standard meter in

Paris, to prevent faking." He was not always successful at that, either, of course. But the built-in radar was always on red alert against easy outs and was constantly feeding back useful information about life as well as letters. "Really good writing very scarce always," he wrote in response to a *Time* magazine inquiry about the literary state of the nation in the late summer of 1947. "When comes in quantities everybody very very lucky." He was somewhat flippant as he sometimes was when he did not want to sound like a bloody owl, but he was never really kidding about these matters. As for his achievement, that was a matter of talent and luck, and he had no delusions about that either. "Madame," he said to the little old lady in *Death in the Afternoon* who was disappointed because "A Natural History of the Dead" was not like *Snowbound*, "I'm wrong again. We aim so high and we miss the mark." But that was never any reason for him to stop hunting the green hills, nor was it enough to make him stop fishing the Gulf Stream—or trying to write fiction that would have five-dimensional accuracy.

And yet—as Ernest Hemingway was no less aware than were André Malraux and Thomas Mann—the bard, the gleeman, the scop, the minstrel have always agitated and propagandized for the cardinal virtues and against the deadly vices. The great ones, however, as Mann came to realize and as Malraux seems to have been born knowing, have always gone against official policies on excellence and evil whenever in their considered opinion such policies were in conflict with the deepest, richest, and most comprehensive interests of human existence, even in the process of extolling official feats at functions of state.

Indeed, the very existence of the great epics suggests that long before constitutional provisions for freedom of the press, the ancients were aware, as contemporary totalitarians—whether of the right or the left—apparently are not, that fundamental human ideals and aspirations are best served not by routinizing the writer's subject matter and prescribing his areas of emphasis but by giving attention to the implications of his ambiguities—if only as even tyrants give ear to the wisdom of fools.

The great epics, the heroes of which always represent personal qualities that are unconventional but that are recommended for nationwide emulation, also suggest that while dissent and protest are perfectly natural and often inevitable

concerns of the writer, they are still only incidental to his ultimate ceremonial function, *celebration*. For even as bards, gleemen, and scops chanted in praise of heroic achievement, were
they not at the very same time updating the heroic context and
the ongoing necessity for heroic endeavor?

III

When Ernest Hemingway declared that all bad writers were in
love with the epic, he was not expressing disdain for epic heroism. Nor was he repudiating the epic as a fundamental category
of literary expression. He was objecting to overwritten journalism and pointing out that the injection of *false* epic qualities
into such writing did not transform it into literature. He was
condemning pretentious elaborations and fake mysticism. Thus
he was reemphasizing his preference for the clear-cut statement, or, as he puts it elsewhere, "straight honest prose on
human beings."

He was also expressing once again his definitive conviction
that the universal in art is achieved through the particular.
What he wanted to create was a prose style that would have
five dimensions, and his extraordinary artistic discipline was
always geared to that aspiration. But his actual procedure was
based on the assumption that the adequately informed and
accurately rendered incident becomes the representative anecdote with epic as well as economic, political, and all the other
implications fiction is capable of communicating. Moreover,
he was equally convinced that the suggestiveness of such communication was always enhanced when certain obvious details
were omitted on what he called "the principle of the iceberg"
—a procedure that may not have had as much to do with the
deliberate use of the device of understatement as such as with
the scrupulous avoidance of overstatement.

Perhaps his practice of omitting that which, like the unseen
seven-eighths of the iceberg, is already implicit (and need only
be suggested anyway) also accounts for his characteristic
avoidance of summaries. Perhaps he assumed that details were
supposed not only to speak for themselves but also add up in
such a way as to make generalizations unnecessary. At any rate,
he seems never to have been so much concerned with abstract

definitions of literature as a fine art as with the functional requirements of the process by which raw experience is transformed into style. In articles such as "Old Newsman Writes" and
"Monologue to the Maestro," in numerous interviews, and in
such books as *Death in the Afternoon*, *Green Hills of Africa*,
and *A Moveable Feast*, almost every observation he made about
art was specifically and immediately applicable to his special
conception of the mechanics of stylization.

Kenneth Burke has described literature as symbolic action
and has defined symbolic action as "the dancing of an attitude." Hemingway might well have employed the same concept if only to insist that the writer see to it that the dance be
consistent with the music of actuality. Indeed, it was for the
express purpose of protecting the writer against any involvement with inauthentic choreography that Hemingway required
the writer to develop a built-in shockproof stuff and nonsense
detector. (Incidentally, the remarks he made in *Death in the
Afternoon* about the "bedside mysticism of such a book as
Virgin Spain" indicate that he was also alert to the fact that
bad choreography only adds up to unintentional farce.)

Hemingway seems never to have consciously affiliated himself with any literary movement. The obviously ambitious and
completely sincere young apprentice in *A Moveable Feast* assimilated whatever he could from Gertrude Stein, Ezra Pound,
James Joyce, and every other source available to him in Paris
during the 1920s; but whenever he sat down to write he seems
always to have been entirely on his own. "All art," he was to
contend in *Death in the Afternoon*, "is only done by the individual. The individual is all you ever have and all schools only
serve to classify their members as failures." Nevertheless, the
working principles he evolved in the process of coming to
terms with his own individual technical problems as an artist
(not unlike those that emerge from the no less personally oriented prefaces of Henry James) are as valid for other writers as
for himself.

Indeed, what they add up to is a fundamental contribution
to the poetics of contemporary fiction. Much if not most of
the so-called Hemingway influence, however, almost always
seems to be based on certain obvious aspects of his fiction itself
rather than on the principles that underlie it. The principles

acknowledge tradition and provide for influence, but of their very nature they preclude imitation in favor of individuality. Hemingway himself, it should be remembered, preferred to regard the Hemingway influence as "only a certain clarification of the language"; and what he had to say about imitation was entirely consistent with his misgivings about schools and movements in art. "Anybody can write like somebody else," he wrote in "Notes on Life and Letters," another of the articles he did for *Esquire*, "but it takes a long time to get to write like yourself and then what they pay off on is having something to say."

Perhaps the most fundamental Hemingway principle, and certainly a good one for any serious craftsman to begin with, is the one that requires writers to know what they really feel rather than what they are supposed to feel or have been taught to feel. This distinction, as simple and as obvious as it sounds, is extremely difficult. Nevertheless, it is indispensable to the writer who is working for an accurate projection of what really happens in action, who is trying to record the sequence of motion and fact that stimulates his emotional response to an experience and is therefore for him the essential truth of that experience.

Some writers violate the stimulus-reaction principle as a matter of course because they are committed to the objectives of social and political agitation and propaganda. Such writers almost always manipulate stimulus-response patterns to present a specific case for a given sociopolitical program. Thus if they are engaged in promoting racial integration in the United States, for example, they systematically reduce stimulus-response sequences to oppressor-oppressed formulas and deliberately overemphasize all effects in terms of victimization in order to show the inhumanity of segregation. Sometimes such writers become so overzealous in the interest of a cause that they actually change virtues into shortcomings in order to blame them on oppression. On the other hand, writers defending segregation manipulate the stimulus-response pattern to show how "existing" shortcomings (regardless of what caused them) make some Americans unfit for integration. In order to prove that so-called blacks are unqualified to exercise their inherent

rights as native citizens, these writers show that they are incapable of making the "normal" response to "normal" stimuli. But
then, many pro-civil rights-writers also present the stimulus-
response pattern as abnormal, in order to promote the need
for rehabilitation programs!

Writers who become overimpressed with research data from
the behavioral sciences almost always seem to assume that they
already know what normal stimulus-response patterns are.
They seem to have convinced themselves that there is a scientific key to human conduct and that this key will enable them to
write more accurate fiction based on more reliable information
about human nature. What they forget, however, is that categories and formulations do not necessarily add up to dependable information and more precise insights. Somehow or other
they also seem to overlook the fact that the description of
stimulus and response in the novels of Henry James, Edith
Wharton, and Joseph Conrad remain for the most part valid,
while hardly any scientific treatise on the nature of human nature and conduct written during the same period can be read
today without fundamental reservations. Not only is this the
case, but the scientist himself would be the first to insist on
such reservations—in light of his subsequent "findings." It was
never necessary for Thomas Mann to revise *Buddenbrooks*, for
example, but Sigmund Freud was forever revising and supple-
menting basic assumptions underlying earlier "findings."

Indeed, it is precisely that fiction that is based most directly
on scientific "information" about human nature that seems to
date or "go bad afterward" most rapidly. Perhaps one reason
for this is the fact that such information is always based on
some assumed absolute, whereas any practical approach to
human nature should probably be relative. Writers who forget
this also seem to forget this even more crucial fact: As necessary and as natural as scientific procedure is, and as indispensable as scientific information is, so far as the creative process
is concerned such information is only raw material for the
imagination—real toads for Miss Marianne Moore's imaginary
garden, as it were.

On the other hand, those writers whose primary discipline is
literature are also aware of still another fundamental fact:

Science, no matter how richly human or even humanitarian its ultimate goals, *dehumanizes* experience in the very process of coming to terms with it. Whereas literature, by direct contrast, always humanizes or dramatizes experiences. Literature is always concerned with how things feel to the human being. Such, as a matter of fact, is an objective of all art. "A work of art," writes Susanne K. Langer, "expresses a conception of life, emotion, inward reality. But it is neither confessional nor a frozen tantrum; it is a developed metaphor, a nondiscursive symbol that articulates what is verbally ineffable—the logic of consciousness itself."

Thus when Hemingway begins with the problem of knowing and describing what one really feels, he is concerning himself with the most fundamental of all literary requirements. And when he renders the beads of sweat on a cold pitcher of beer in a darkened room in Valencia, or the shooting of six cabinet ministers in a rain-puddled courtyard in the early morning, or the dust rising and powdering the leaves of trees as the troops march by a house in a village that looks across the river and the plains to the mountains, he is proceeding on the firm, even if unstated, assumption that what he is writing is art to the extent that it communicates the essence of subjective experience.

There is, for whatever the juxtaposition may be worth, no essential difference at all between Susanne Langer's definition of art in *Problems of Art* and what Hemingway had already said about the nature of literature some twenty-two years earlier in "Old Newsman Writes." Hemingway's observations were written for *Esquire* magazine. Miss Langer's were originally part of a series of lectures dealing with the pivotal concepts in the philosophy of art. "A work of art," she stated, "is an expressive form created for our perception through sense or imagination, and what it expresses is human feeling."

She then went on to point out that feeling as she uses it includes "everything that can be felt, from physical pain and comfort, excitement and repose, to the most complex emotions, intellectual tensions, or the steady feeling-tones of a conscious human life." What Hemingway had already told *Esquire* readers was a pivotal concept in the philosophy of the art of fiction. "All good books," he wrote, "are alike in that they

are truer than if they had really happened," and after one finished reading one, "you will feel that all that happened to you
and afterward it all belongs to you; the good and the bad, the
ecstasy, the remorse and sorrow, the people and the places and
how the weather was. If you can get so you can give that to
people, then you are a writer."

Thus did he reveal the roles of his poetics. Thus did he state
his functional definition of literature; and if its relationship to
the prefaces of Henry James seems far-fetched, its affinities
with Joseph Conrad, for whose resurrection Hemingway once
declared his willingness to make sacrifice of a ground and
powdered T. S. Eliot, does not. Moreover, Conrad is perhaps
the best possible evidence that Hemingway's principles do not
restrict other writers to Hemingway's personal style.

"My task which I am trying to achieve," wrote Conrad some
two years before Hemingway was born, "is by the power of
the written word to make you hear, to make you feel—it is
above all to make you see. That and no more, and that is everything. If I succeed, you shall find there according to your deserts: encouragement, consolation, fear, charm—all you demand
—and, perhaps, also that glimpse of truth for which you have
forgotten to ask."

Another Hemingway working principle, closely related to the
first, applies to the material the writer uses. It requires the
writer to utilize the things he is really involved with and knows
and cares about. "Books," he said, "should be about the people you know, that you love and hate, not about the people
you study up about." Nor should the serious writer ever be
misled about what a book should be because of what is currently in fashion.

Hemingway was convinced that the writer who develops
sufficient insight into his own firsthand experience and achieves
sufficient accuracy in describing it can create stories about it
that will represent the whole of human experience. By this he
did not in any way imply that the writer should limit himself to
the knowledge at hand or even to the knowledge of the experience at hand. Nobody ever knew any better than he that the
writer has to learn to see the world as a whole before he can
make his part represent that whole; but he always warned the

writer not to show off his knowledge as such, and even insisted that the writer could leave out things precisely because he knew enough about them.

Perhaps some writers violate the principle of materials selection simply because they are overambitious, or perhaps they just simply do not know their own limitations. Many, however, are guilty of the fallacy of subject matter significance. These assume that some things are inherently more significant than others. As a matter of fact, some things obviously are, but, as matter for fiction, the importance or significance of things, places, events, and people depends on the quality of the writing. Most people would probably concede that coronations and presidential inaugurations are more important events than the crowning of a homecoming queen or the installation of a president of a campus fraternity. Nevertheless, an incompetent writer can turn an insignificant story even about suicide, while a good writer can create a masterpiece about a bauble. The blisses of the commonplace no more nor less than the thunder of peasants in revolt become exciting or dull depending upon the writer's insight, his sensibility, and his craft.

But perhaps along with its other misconceptions the subject matter significance fallacy confuses subject matter and theme at the very outset. On the other hand, the primary application of Hemingway's principle of selection is not to theme but to raw material. In this connection, Hemingway's basic assumption is that whatever his theme, the writer will have a better chance of realizing it if he works with the raw material he has a real feeling for and with which he is intimately familiar.

The writer works in terms of his raw material. That is to say, whatever his story is, he creates it out of or in the terms of some experience that presumably interests him, just as the painter composes his pictures in the terms of that which becomes his model, as it were, whether that model be a person, countryside, or skyline, an event or some trifling object that strikes his fancy. Georges Braque, for example, was forever painting still lifes that included tables and bottles. Matisse painted odalisques for years on end, and at one time Picasso painted picture after picture that included a musical instrument, while during another period there were sea urchins in almost every picture, and so on. Hemingway, as has been noted, frequently worked in terms of sports. There has always been a great deal of misunderstanding among some critics about the fact that he also worked in terms of war experience; but nothing seems to have caused more pretentious confusion than his use of raw material from sporting activities. This has even caused some to express doubts about his sincerity and among most Marx-Freud intellectuals the official word seems to be that he is not only frivolous but also unadult.

And yet it is all but impossible to imagine any of these same critics and intellectuals questioning the fact that Goya used the raw materials of war and bullfighting. Nor do they reject Degas for all his dancing girls or Toulouse-Lautrec because he haunted nightspots, whorehouses, and sporting events and used such material in his pictures. Serious writers should be able to see the snobbishness of superficial critics and shortcut intellectuals for what it really is, and should also realize that such superficiality in matters of art also betrays something else: Many intellectuals do not really know very much about just plain ordinary everyday life in the first place. And besides, it is seldom those who belong to the intellectual establishment who are forever protesting their commitment to the high-minded, the classy, the dignified, profound, and educational anyway. It is almost always the newcomer, the ambitious peasant, the pretentious son of a shopkeeper, the status seeker who learned or read or heard about it all in books at school.

Certainly no writer who has even the slightest contact with, or appreciation for, brownskin folks from down home can afford to allow himself to be misled by "intellectuals" whose own firsthand experience outside the world of books is so limited that they are unaware of the fundamental importance of sports in human society. Indeed, Hemingway's lifelong involvement in sports is in itself a good enough reason for so-called black writers to take him seriously, what with all the raw material all around them. Perhaps through Hemingway they will someday come to realize that their traditional involvement with figures such as Jack Johnson, Joe Gans, Sam Langford, Sugar Ray Robinson, Jesse Owens, Jackie Robinson, Willie Mays, Jimmy Brown, and Michael Jordan, with hunting and fishing and so on, has as much literary significance as anything else has.

Moreover, those who still insist that the subject matter or raw material itself must have profound philosophical implications to begin with, have only to realize that in spite of the three hundred years in which so-called black Americans have been the victims of human slavery, oppression, and unrelenting foul play, the so-called black athlete has displayed a sense of fair play and has achieved a reputation for sportsmanship that will stand beside that of any gentleman to the manner or manor born. Intellectuals will look long and hard before they find a more compelling manifestation of the transcendent dignity and nobility of man than that.

Still another fundamental working principle is involved when Hemingway maintains that fictional experience is not described but is made up. This does not contradict his requirement for descriptive accuracy. A story is invented, created, not recorded or simply reported. The writer makes it up, *but he must make it up the way things actually happen in life*. In other words, gardens in fiction are as imaginary as they are in Marianne Moore's poetry, but the toads that inhabit them must be every bit as believable as she required her metaphorical toads to be.

Nor did Hemingway ever confuse the writer's quest for the fable in the flesh with the detection and revelation of some traditional figure already existing beneath the surface obscurity of the carpet of human experience. The fable, he seems to have known from the very beginning, is that which the writer himself fabricates out of his sense of flesh-and-blood actuality. It is not something that the writer is supposed to find because he has been taught it is there. It is that which he makes of what he really and truly does find. The act of fiction is an art of configuration.

"If it was reporting," Hemingway wrote in "Monologue to the Maestro," "they would not remember it. When you describe something that has happened that day the timeliness makes people see it in their own imaginations. A month later that element of time is gone and your account would be flat and they would not see it in their minds or remember it. But if you make it up instead of describe it you can make it round and whole and solid and give it life. You create it for good or bad. It is made, not described."

Sometimes he referred to it as inventing from knowledge. "If a man is making a story up," he said also in "Monologue to the Maestro," "it will be true in proportion to the amount of knowledge of life that he has and how conscientious he is; so that when he makes something up it is as it would truly be. If he doesn't know how many people work in their minds and actions his luck may save him for a while, or he may write fantasy. But if he continues to write about what he does not know about he will find himself faking. After he fakes a few times he cannot write honestly anymore."

When "the maestro" wanted to know how the imagination fitted into the creative process, Hemingway told him that nobody knows anything about it except that it is what one gets for nothing. "It is the one thing besides honesty that a good writer must have," he went on. "The more he learns from experience the more truly he can imagine; if he gets so he can imagine truly enough people will think that the things he relates all really happened and that he is just reporting."

Perhaps blues-oriented writers will relate some of Hemingway's other notions about the process of literary creation to what they themselves have already learned about the improvisation from musicians. It should be easy enough for them to see a practical connection between what Hemingway once said about making up stories and what Duke Ellington, for instance, does when he begins a phrase or two and ends up with *C-Jam Blues* or *Mainstem*. Referring to *The Old Man and the Sea*, Hemingway told Robert Manning, "I knew two or three things about the situation but I didn't know the story. . . . I didn't even know if that fish was going to bite for the old man when it started smelling around the bait. I had to write on inventing out of knowledge." He rejected everything that was not or could not be completely true. "I didn't know what was going to happen for sure in *For Whom the Bell Tolls* or *Farewell to Arms*. I was inventing."

In the 1958 interview for the *Paris Review* series on the art of fiction, Hemingway reiterated and expanded some of the notions he had expressed in "Monologue to the Maestro" in 1935. When George Plimpton asked about changes in conception, theme, plot, and character, Hemingway replied, "Sometimes you know the story. Sometimes you make it up as you go along and have no idea how it will come out. Everything changes as it moves. That is what makes the movement which makes the story. Sometimes the movement is so slow it does not seem to be moving. But there is always change and always movement."

And then at the end of the interview, when Plimpton asked him why the creative writer was concerned with representation of fact rather than fact itself, Hemingway echoed "Old Newsman Writes" as well as "Monologue to the Maestro." "Why be puzzled by that?" he began. "From things that have happened and from things as they exist and from all things that you know and all those you cannot know, you make something through your invention that is not a representation but a whole new thing truer than anything true and alive and you make it alive. That is why you write and for no other reason that you know of." And then he concluded as if winking at the whole thing, "But what about all the reasons that no one knows?"

Unlike William Faulkner, who frequently wrote about racial interrelationship, Ernest Hemingway for the most part seems to have concerned himself with Negroes as subject matter even in *Green Hills of Africa*, only in passing, so to speak. Also, whereas Faulkner, who was always deliberately and sometimes fiercely southern, worked with raw material that involved the so-called black people of his immediate region of the United States, Hemingway, as one hardly needs to point out, wrote about Africans of various tribes and nations and Cuban Negroes as well as U.S. "black" people both northern and southern. He was never any less vernacular for being as cosmopolitan as he was, however, and U.S. "black" writers will find his work, whatever its raw material, no less relevant than that of Faulkner to the fundamental problems involved in the forging of Americans and the making of American literature.

Sometimes Faulkner wrote as if he were really an ambivalent self-searching Mississippi mulatto who was officially "white" because he grew up in the home of his "white" relatives but who always either knew or had reason to believe that he was kith and kin to some of the Negroes around him—some of whom had fundamental human qualities that he not only admired but found largely missing in many of the white people he knew. His intimacy with his "black mammy" and the Negro playmates of his childhood seems to have been far too complex for him to refer to himself as an honorary Negro, as Kenneth Tynan reports that Hemingway did one night in a bar in Havana, but although he often wrote as if he regarded himself as being an honorary confederate colonel, he also wrote as if he had been as much influenced by his listening to some Mississippi Uncle Remus lying and signifying as by what he had learned from books and from listening to the planters and lawyers and businessmen and rednecks in the mansions, in the courthouse square, and at the crossroads stores.

It was Ernest Hemingway the Midwesterner-become-cosmopolitan, however, not William Faulkner the race-oriented Mississippian, who wrote fiction that always expresses essentially the same fundamental sense of life as that which underlies the spirit of the blues. Hemingway, needless to say, did not write in terms of the blues, but what he wrote was the literary equivalent to blues music. Much of what Faulkner wrote not only includes blues idiom, wit, and wisdom; in some instances it also appears to be conscious extensions of Negro folklore. But as richly interwoven with Negro idiom as his highly distinctive rhetoric so frequently is, and as close to the feeling of some Negro spirituals as he comes from time to time, the fundamental sense of life that his fiction represents is always more closely related to the conventional Greco-Roman tradition of tragedy, comedy, and farce—of destiny, the fateful curse, doom, of honor, hubris, and outrage than to the blues tradition of pragmatic American existentialism.

Hemingway, for all his honorary Negrohood, wrote far more about Spanish bullfighters than about "black" U.S. athletes and next to nothing about "black" U.S. musicians. Nevertheless, not only was his sense of actuality closer to the blues tradition than to anything in Spain (except Goya, perhaps), his celebrated prose style, which has direct historical connections with Kansas City, also has astonishing even if incidental similarities to—and aesthetic affinities with—the instrumental blues style of the Kansas City jazz musicians.

The simple, direct, concrete declarative statements that are so characteristic of Hemingway's essentially coordinate prose style create a descriptive and narrative pace and precision, the

affirmative effect of which is actually comparable to that created by the steady but infinitely elastic and inclusive 4/4
rhythm of the now classic Kansas City blues score. There is no
one-to-one relationship between music and prose composition,
to be sure; and in this instance far more significant than any
question of direct influence, whether through derivation, imitation, or even adaption, is the implied affinity of sensibilities.

Whatever the reason, which could have as much to do with
being midwestern as with anything else, it was as if the editors
under whom Hemingway worked as an apprentice on the
Kansas City Star and the Kansas City Negro bandleaders, arrangers, and sidemen somehow or other represented two different aspects of the same fundamental orientation toward
communication. Had young Count Basie, for instance, gone
to work as a reporter for the *Star*, he would have found that its
style sheet for prose writers was in complete agreement with
his own basic conception of making statements on the piano.
"Use short sentences," the very first rule ran. "Use short first
paragraphs. Use vigorous English. Be positive, not negative."

Perhaps it is enough to say that by the 1930s Kansas City
musicians had evolved a style of blues orchestration that was
grounded on principles of brevity, vigor, and positive accentuation equivalent to those that Hemingway had picked up at
the *Kansas City Star* in 1917; and that Kansas City sidemen
such as Lester Young, Jo Jones, and Buck Clayton were if
anything even more scrupulous about clichés, about being
florid on the one hand or becoming mechanical on the other,
than were the editors of the *Star*; and that, in any case, the
fiction of Ernest Hemingway, by the very nature of its emotional authenticity, its stylized precision, its flesh-and-blood
concreteness, and the somehow relaxed intensity of its immediacy, qualifies not only as the blues but as classic Kansas City
blues.

So much having been implied, however, perhaps it is also
permissible to add (if only to provoke those with overprecious
literary taste) that the resemblance between Hemingway and a
Kansas City musician such as Count Basie (who, incidentally,
like the well-known man of letters Edmund Wilson was born
in Red Bank, New Jersey) becomes more striking and sugges-

tive on closer juxtaposition. Not only do both work primarily with blues material, which they usually turn into solidly pulsating no-nonsense celebrations of human existence in all its complexity, both also have a clean-cut surface simplicity that belies the multiple dimensions beneath and that actually seems more casual or natural than slice-of-life realism. Both are also lyric, but neither is given to oversentimentality and neither can tolerate elaborate structural embellishments. Indeed, the traditional Basie method of blues orchestration and the Hemingway system of omitting known details on what he referred to as the principle of the iceberg are one and the same, nor is that all: Count Basie's piano solo riffs, which are his instantly recognized trademark, resemble nothing in the world any more than they do the neatly stripped precision of a typical Hemingway passage of quoted dialogue.

And, incidentally, even more obvious in his dialogue sequences than elsewhere is the Hemingway equivalent to the Kansas City riff. In all probability, Hemingway actually derived his technique of repeating key words and phrases from the early experiments of Gertrude Stein, but what he achieved in the process of assimilating and refining (also influenced by Ring Lardner) was a very special rhetorical device not only for stating and repeating themes but also for playing and improvising on and around them as a Kansas City musician might do.

Thomas Mann sometimes spoke of themes in his fiction in terms of a "dialectic orchestration" that was based on the principles of sonata composition, and sometimes he also employed a prose version of the Wagnerian leitmotif. Similarly, Hemingway, who frequently spoke about what he had learned about writing description from his visits to art museums, also on at least two occasions spoke of his deliberate use of musical technique. "I should think," he said in his *Paris Review* interview, "what one learns from composers and from the study of harmony and counterpoint would be obvious." And elsewhere he told Lillian Ross of *The New Yorker* that he had used the word "and" consciously over and over in the first paragraphs of *A Farewell to Arms* "the way Mr. Johann Sebastian Bach used a note in music when he was emitting counterpoint."

But even as the reference to Bach is in itself somewhat more like jazz than like German, so perhaps is Hemingway's actual use of musical forms. Moreover, in spite of the traditional U.S. provincial overemphasis on European taste in U.S. music programs, Hemingway's ear, like that of most other U.S. writers, including Henry James, was more indigenously American than impressively classical. His fine literary ear for the music in the Spanish language, for instance, was obviously more American than Iberian. What he heard in Spain was almost always translated into comprehensive American in *For Whom the Bell Tolls* as Italian was translated in *A Farewell to Arms* and *Across the River and into the Trees*. At any rate, when Jake Barnes and others in *The Sun Also Rises* repeat words such as enjoy, joke, utilize, fiesta, irony, and pity, to name only a few, they actually play conversational riffs with them; and when Jake as narrator states, repeats, and rhymes hot with bright with sharply white in the same paragraph near the very end of the book, he plays nonconversational riffs. The narrator of *Death in the Afternoon* (Hemingway himself) organizes the entire final chapter or outchorus sequence of that book on a series of riffs. He begins with, "If I could have made this enough of a book," and improvises for seventeen paragraphs, playing with should have, would have, could have, should, would, could, if it were more of a book it would have, among others, such as "There is nothing in this book about . . . nor does it tell." Then he ends with "no, it is not enough of a book, but still there were a few things to be said. There were a few practical things to be said."

IV

Many intellectuals reject the image of man that the fiction of Ernest Hemingway represents. Some flatly dismiss the typical Hemingway hero as an inauthentic projection of little more than boyhood fantasy. Others, who accuse him of operating within a system of values so codelike that it amounts to a cult, insist that his involvements are so extremely circumscribed that his fiction has very little connection with the ordinary everyday obligations of human society, that he is not a hero but a zero.

A typical expression of this point of view is an article that Delmore Schwartz, a very intellectual New York poet, wrote for *The Southern Review* following the publication of *To Have and Have Not.* "There is a definite code," Schwartz declares, "by which characters are judged and by which they judge each other and which often produces the basis of the conversation. It is important to recognize that the code is relevant, and only relevant, to a definite period of time and to a special region of society. Courage, honesty, and skill are important rules of the code, but it is these human attributes as determined by a specific historical context. To be admirable, from the standpoint of this morality, is to admit defeat, to be a good sportsman, to accept pain without outcry, to adhere strictly to the rules of the game, and to play the game with great skill. To be repugnant and contemptible is to violate any of these requirements. It is a sportsmanlike morality, or equally, the morality of sportsmanship. It extends its requirements into the region of manners and carriage, and one must speak in clipped tones, avoid pretentious phrases, condense emotions into a few expletives or deliberately suppress it—noble, to borrow a pun from William Carlos Williams, equals no bull."

Several pages later Schwartz assesses *To Have and Have Not* as "a stupid and foolish book, a disgrace to a good writer, a book which should never have been printed." His own article, however, can hardly be regarded as a credit to a responsible intellectual. Hemingway's fiction has absolutely nothing to do with *requiring* people to speak in clipped tones or to condense emotion into a few expletives; not even the specific guidelines that he suggested to other writers make any such requirements, and of course nobody actually recommends pretentious phrases. Hemingway, it is true, did write about a world that requires heroic action. It may be said to be a world of tragic and epic action. But nowhere has it ever been reduced to any definite code by which characters are judged and by which they judge each other. It would be not only irresponsible but downright ridiculous to imply that Nick Adams, for instance, who figures in a number of Hemingway's most important short stories, is being initiated into a cult that is based on the belief that life is a game to be played by the rules of the sportsman or that Hemingway seeks to give the impression that Nick will be among the blessed if he can only master some "definite code" of conduct.

Wouldn't it be far more accurate to say that Nick's various initiations have to do with the fact that Hemingway seems convinced that life is extremely complex for everybody, initiated or not, that things are never necessarily as they seem, and that the best equipment is none too good? Can even the most casual reader of *A Farewell to Arms* seriously contend that the disastrous outcome of that story was in any way related to the fact that the hero and/or heroine did not measure up to some definite code?

Nevertheless, Schwartz, whose misreadings of Hemingway may have often been equaled but have seldom been surpassed, persists. "Examples," he asserts, "are in fact, too plentiful. Cohen [*sic!*] in *The Sun Also Rises* is a prime example of one character who violates the code again and again. He does not play the game, he discusses his emotions at great length, he does not admit defeat with the lady whom he loves, and when he is hurt, he lets everyone know about it. Thus he must be one of the damned." Nonsense. Almost everybody else in the book may be damned, but Robert Cohn's main problem is that he is a bloody bore.

None of Hemingway's critics ever suggest any reasons why anybody should be expected to put up with Cohn's eternal whining about his personal affairs—least of all why, given his own disabilities, Jake Barnes should. And yet Jake is Cohn's most patient friend. There is something to be said for that; and there is also something to be said for the fact that Jake, who has far greater personal troubles than Cohn, never burdens his friends with them. What can anybody do to help Jake? On the other hand, there is very little evidence that Cohn ever really is considerate of anybody but himself.

It is extremely difficult to believe that anybody prefers, accepts, or willingly endures people who are repugnant, contemptible, and unsportsmanlike, who have no courage, honesty or skill, and who complain all the time and try to evade the responsibility for everything. And yet young Saul Bellow, for example, did seem to be recommending the point of view expressed by the central figure of his early novel *Dangling Man*. Bellow's hero could hardly be referring to anybody other than Hemingway in the following statement from the opening section of that book: "Today, the code of the athlete, of the tough boy—an American inheritance, I believe, from the English gentleman—that curious mixture of striving, asceticism, and vigor, the origins of which some trace back to Alexander the Great—is stronger than ever. Do you have feelings? There are correct and incorrect ways of indicating them. Do you have an inner life? It is nobody's business but your own. Do you have emotions? Strangle them. To a degree, everybody obeys this code. And it does admit of a limited kind of candor, a close-mouthed straightforwardness. But for the truest candor, it has an inhibiting effect. Most serious matters are closed to the hard-boiled. They are unpracticed in introspection, and therefore badly equipped to deal with opponents whom they cannot shoot like big game or outdo in daring.

"If you have difficulties, grapple with them silently, goes one of their commandments. To hell with that. I intend to talk about mine, and if I had as many mouths as Siva has arms and kept them going all the time, I still could not do myself justice."

The dangling man refuses to feel that any of this represents self-indulgence. Nor does he seem to mind in the least that he may be imposing all of it on other people without so much as a by your leave, as it were. He proceeds as if he has an inalienable right to do so, never even pausing to ask himself why the hell anybody else should give one good goddamn about what happens to him. The dangler seems to be satisfied with the case he makes, and perhaps he is also satisfied with his compensations. But let him look to his manners, since (as Thomas Mann demonstrates so well in *Joseph and His Brothers*) it is not only the sheerest folly but sometimes downright dangerous to expect other people to love you more than they love themselves, there *are* correct and incorrect ways of indicating your feelings. There are wise and there are foolhardy ways of doing so. Etiquette, after all, goes far beyond being nice because it is pretty. It is always a matter of refined self-interest, even at the table. There is such a thing as altruism, to be sure, but nobody has the right to *demand* it of anybody else.

The dangling man makes much of the fact that he is keeping a journal; and he is forever talking about the blue ribbon books he is reading, and he engages in deliberately profound postgraduate debates with himself. Most serious matters, he scoffs, are closed to the hard-boiled, who, he contends, are unpracticed in introspection. But what he overhastily overshoots is the very real possibility that the closemouthed may well be much more given to introspection than the blabbermouth. And furthermore, his journal does not back up his claim to superiority. What his essentially academic notes reveal about his dangling life is not more introspective than what one gets from Jake Barnes or Frederic Henry. The dangler may be considerably more bookish and theoretical about himself and life in Chicago. But Jake and Frederic exercise infinitely more poetic sensitivity in dealing with themselves and life in France and Spain and wartime Italy. *The Sun Also Rises* and *A Farewell to Arms* being first-person narratives qualify as introspective journals, too. Moreover, not only are they memoirs and confessions by virtue of the specific stylistic convention employed, but also Hemingway made every effort to keep the tone and imagery consistent with the narrators' sensibilities. Indeed, in each case the rhetoric is a significant part of the first-person hero's characterization.

The facts just simply do not support those intellectuals who charge Hemingway with being preoccupied with the hard-boiled nonreflective hero anyway. Nick Adams is definitely not hard-boiled by any standards—except, of course, those of bookworms and incurable cowards (and there are such people), but they hardly count in such matters. Nick is constantly being hurt, shocked, scandalized, and even numbed by what he has to undergo and witness. His response to experience is not at all that of the tough guy, but of someone of delicate sensitivity and poetic imagination. As much as he represents anything else, and as much as it has been ignored, Nick is Ernest Hemingway's portrait of the artist as a very sensitive young man; nor does this separate him from Jake, Frederic, or Robert Jordan.

It is not really accurate to describe any of Hemingway's protagonists as hard-boiled, except Harry Morgan in *To Have and Have Not*. Perhaps Harry, the writer in "The Snows of Kilimanjaro," does come close. He is dying of gangrene, and feels that he has compromised his talent, is undeniably hard, bitter, and cruel. But even so, the flashbacks show him to be far too much involved with loneliness and introspection and far too concerned about the nuances of literary expression to qualify as hard-boiled. As a matter of fact, it is extremely difficult for any of Hemingway's writer-characters to qualify. As for Hemingway himself, what's a big fat tough guy doing carrying on like that about landscapes and architecture and paintings and fine food and vintage wines and all, in *Death in the Afternoon* and *Green Hills of Africa*? And as if that were not enough, what's he doing honing his phrases like that?

As for Harry Morgan, the smuggler in *To Have and Have Not*, as rugged as he is, there is much more to be said for him as an example of Hemingway's descriptive consistency than offended intellectuals can use against him as a member of the cult of the hard-boiled. To begin with, he has to be tough in the line of work he has been forced into—and as things turn out, he is not actually tough enough! And he is not a typical Hemingway hero anyway. It is easy enough to imagine Nick Adams becoming Frederic Henry, Jake Barnes, Robert Jordan, and even Harry the writer, but not Harry Morgan. There is perhaps still much of Nick in beat-up old Colonel Richard Cantwell in *Across the River and into the Trees*, but hardly any in Harry Morgan, although Nick would have been happy to be his friend and go fishing with him and would have been fascinated by his practical skill, his ruggedness, and his courage, and would never have made the mistake that Richard Gordon, the writer of the left-wing intellectual novels, made about Harry's wife, Marie.

It would be perfectly natural for Nick Adams to go to Spain to see the bullfights and the great art museums and write *Death in the Afternoon*. He would like the Spanish people not because they were hard-boiled (because they're not) but because they have great dignity and style in the face of death and are serious about life, but not sad and not cold, and liking them, he would become a sincere student of their language and literature. He would celebrate their food and wine and the national glories of their country because he always was lyrical about things like that. Given the chance, the boy from "Big Two-Hearted River" would also go on safari (although hysterically afraid of snakes) and write *Green Hills of Africa*. He could not possibly regard the bullfight and big-game hunting as preoccupations that preclude introspection and intellectual seriousness because *Death in the Afternoon* and *Green Hills of*

Africa are as intellectual and even scholarly as they are anything else.

But then Nick the writer (not unlike Flaubert, Henry James, Proust, and Joyce) would rather be identified as a novelist than as an intellectual anyway. And as for that special breed of self-righteous intellectual whose humanity somehow aligns them with the Miura bull against the man, and who complain because the fish can't hook fishermen and the wild animals can't shoot back at the huntsman, an essentially nice fellow like Nick would brush questions of their insanity aside and simply regard them as library tough guys whose strong-arm tactics are probably mostly verbal.

For his own part, Nick would not hesitate to claim that hunting, fishing, and his interest in the bullfights not only enhance his life and his feeling for life but also his feeling for fiction —and could always point to stories like "The Undefeated," "Now I Lay Me," and "The Short Happy Life of Francis Macomber" to prove it. Nick Adams may or may not have dictated "Remembering Shooting-Flying" to Ernest Hemingway. Either could have written the following passage: "When you have loved three things all your life, from the earliest you can remember, to fish, to shoot, and, later, to read; and when, all your life, the necessity to write has been your master, you learn to remember and, when you think back you remember more fishing and shooting and reading than anything else and that is a pleasure."

But finally, in all the intellectual epithet-slinging and chicken-house forensics, the most specific and perhaps the most significant statement Hemingway himself ever permitted any of his characters to make on the subject of being hard-boiled never seems to get mentioned—not even in passing. The nada passages from "A Clean, Well-Lighted Place" and the insomniac theme in "Now I Lay Me" are often referred to (and usually misinterpreted as the obverse side of the "cult of sensation"). But nobody ever seems to remember what Jake Barnes says about his own conduct in *The Sun Also Rises*. Jake does not go around begging for sympathy, like Robert Cohn, but sometimes lies awake at night thinking about himself and CRIES (!): "It is awfully easy to be hard-boiled about everything in the daytime," he says, "but at night it is another thing."

Even Malcolm Cowley, one of the first intellectuals to regard Hemingway as a haunted and nocturnal writer in the tradition of Poe, Hawthorne, and Melville, seems either to have overlooked or, worse still, underestimated the significance of Jake's self-revelation. But Cowley's oversight notwithstanding, no statement or gesture in any of Hemingway's fiction (or nonfiction) seems more indicative of Hemingway's own sensibilities or is a more fundamental clue to the conduct of any of his characters, rugged, tender, or insomniac. In one statement, Jake, who knows what bullfighters are like without their costumes, reveals the all-too-human knight without his shining armor and in so doing defines the essential nature of Hemingway's conception of heroic action. The Hemingway hero is not as hard as nails and fearless. He is a man who can pull himself together and press on (through the night as well as the daylight) in spite, or even because of, his fears and weaknesses.

Jake, who also knows that the sun will rise again and again and assumes the earth will abide with or without him, has already accepted the dreadful conditions of his existence. He does not submit to them, however. Nor does he simply struggle with them. It is not for nothing that he admires the bullfighter's grace and dignity. He makes the most of his restrictions. And in the process, as Hemingway makes very clear, he goes beyond them. Jake the cripple is a more admirable man and certainly a far less anxious one than Robert Cohn, who, when he is not wailing about his bad luck, uses his excellent if somewhat bull-like physical endowments as if a man can be more powerful than a dragon—as if might makes right after all.

Perhaps in spite of themselves, some intellectuals are frequently more interested in substantiating their own theories than in coming to terms with actuality. If so—and the evidence that Thurman Arnold offers in *Symbols of Government* and *The Folklore of Capitalism* is as sobering as it is convincing—then many will go right on accusing Hemingway of being head shaman of a cult of hard-boiled primitivism and zeroism. But even the most zealous defenders of the pieties of civilization against the forces of regression will be hard put to find any truly viable textual evidence to prove that Ernest Hemingway ever preferred the charges of a nine-hundred-pound Miura bull to the capework, the footwork, and the calmly and exquisitely executed faenas of an always vulnerable but seldom desperate man!

Many who agree with Malcolm Cowley's contention that Hemingway was a haunted and nocturnal writer whose images are symbols of an interior world do so apparently because they are already convinced that the interior world involved is itself the inherent source of the code of hard-boiled conduct they find so utterly deplorable. They almost always describe it as a world devoid of intellectual and spiritual insight and purpose and therefore doomed to an endless round of pointless violence relieved only by equally endless and pointless rounds of physical self-indulgence. In other words, they concede that Hemingway was haunted and then either state or smugly imply that his nightmare only reflects his own personal limitations. This puts all self-dedicated intellectuals one up on Ernest Hemingway for cocktail party purposes, of course, but the validity of the Hemingway image of life remains inseparable from the undeniable impact his fiction has always had on most readers, even the outright hostile ones.

There are also intellectuals who regard Hemingway as a writer whose images are symbols of man as victim, as if the people in his fiction have already been maimed by world-withering dragon flames and now numbly subsist in a nightmarelike domain of ruins imprisoned by an invincible reign of dragon terror. Those who focus from this point of view emphasize the prevalence of violence in all his work. They elaborate the implications of Jake's wound, Frederic's star-crossed romance, the "casual" brutality and perversion surrounding Nick Adams, and so on. They generalize, usually in terms Marxian, Freudian, or Spenglerian, about the oppressive condition of man "in our times" and the absence of human values in the modern world; and then somehow or other they, too, seem to blame it all on Hemingway's own shortcomings.

Even those who praise him for his reportorial objectivity and accuracy seem compelled to accuse Hemingway of a fundamental failure of sensibility. Indeed, many intellectuals, including those who acknowledge the fact that his style represents a highly sophisticated literary achievement, seem to have convinced themselves that his fiction is inadequate because his ideas are not as complex and as significant as their own. They express condescending opinions time and again about his "preoccupation" with violence and physical sensation, as if there would actually be less violence to be involved in (or to be haunted about) and less need for the gratification of physical appetite if only his intellectual interests were more elevated and more comprehensive!

What with all the gory deeds in Homer, Aeschylus, Sophocles, Euripides, Virgil, Dante, and Shakespeare and all the blood-stained pages in the *Charterhouse of Parma*, *The Brothers Karamazov*, *War and Peace*, *Great Expectations*, *Sentimental Education*, and *Moby-Dick*, one can only question the sincerity of anybody who implies in any way that peril, violence, and ruin are abnormal and even extraordinary preoccupations for literature. It would seem that anybody with even a minimum familiarity with epics and fairy tales would know better than that; and yet it is precisely the implication (or even insinuation) most intellectuals make when they encounter such things in the fiction of Ernest Hemingway.

But, except when matters involve so-called black Americans of course, at no time do U.S. intellectuals become more confused about fundamentals or more ensnarled in pretension and nonsense than when they express their reactions to the relish with which Hemingway wrote about "the pleasures of sensual experience." Intellectuals who normally insist on the keenest appreciation of the most subtle nuances in works of art somehow or other suddenly find it highly questionable that Hemingway created characters who can enjoy the firsthand experience of natural phenomena and life itself. Some accuse him outright of being insensitive to higher cultural values and of reducing human life to the aboriginal level of animal-like gratification of physical appetite. Others regard him as decadent and consider his enthusiasm for the sensual as a clear-cut manifestation of his pathological condition. His involvement with actual things and people, for them, strangely enough, becomes an escape from reality—a sinking into nature, a desperate compensation for something else. They never indicate what else.

Even the most intramural of anti-Hemingway intellectuals must know that savoring vintage wines and delicately blended foods has nothing at all to do with primitive behavior and is indeed the very opposite of desperation. Hemingway's heroes do not slake their thirst at any and every pond, nor do they tear at their food with murderous claws, and nothing could be more contrary to desperation than the way they hunt and fish. Contemporary American literary intellectuals, no matter how conditioned by Marx-Freud clichés, surely must realize that the terrain, the waters, the vegetation, and other life forms of the earth, in addition to the sustenance they provide, can also give delight that is sufficient unto itself simply by being there—and that sexual bliss is at least as worthy of celebration as political concepts, scientific discoveries, or a Bach fugue, and no less relevant to the well-being of mankind. And yet it is not at all uncommon for intellectuals who reject Hemingway to imply that there are human involvements, values, and benefits for which these things are only desperate substitutes!

When these same intellectuals read about the delights of physical existence in the well-established academic classics, however, their response seems to be quite different. They do not seem to find the celebration of physical gratification questionable at all when they read *Gargantua and Pantagruel*, *War and Peace*, *Tom Jones*, *Wilhelm Meister*, or *Buddenbrooks*. Nor do they ever seem to find it necessary to accuse the great poets of wishing to return mankind to savagery because some of their poems are odes to the elements and some rhapsodize the vigor and simplicity of buxom country wenches. Those who admire Thoreau, for example, become blissful and sentimental, with never a thought of compensation, at the mere mention of *Walden* and *A Week on the Concord and Merrimack Rivers*.

Hemingway, on the other hand, was for his part always ambivalent about nature. He knew too much about its complexity to become oversentimental about it. "An Alpine Idyll" is a definitive and unmistakable representation of this essential ambivalence. It shows that a holiday in the mountains is good for the two foreign skiers but that permanent residence there has had a shockingly opposite effect on a local peasant. The skiers are returning to the workaday world brown, healthy, and "glad there are other things beside skiing." The snowbound peasant, however, has become as brutally inhuman as nature itself. All winter long, every time he has gone to the barn, he has hung the lantern in the mouth of his wife's frozen corpse (which he has propped against the wall). The implications are clear enough. An idyllic landscape is as complicated as any other. Those who think of it only as a place of escape obviously do not know what is going on there. In the opening scene, at the very moment that it is impossible for the two skiers to realize that anybody can be dead on such a beautiful morning, they are witnessing the peasant relieving the sexton at the graveside —"spreading the earth as evenly as a man spreading manure in a garden."

Unlike Thoreau at Walden Pond, but very much like Jake and Bill at Burguette, Nick Adams is only a man on vacation at Big Two-Hearted River, a man taking time out for recreation. He is a man doing something that he happens to like to do very much. Thoreau, on the other hand, was a man trying to prove a point. He went into the (nearby) woods to get away from the complexity of society. His two-year residence in the thickets was part experiment and part protest demonstration and he spent most of that time reading, puttering about, theorizing, behaving for all the world like a decadent intellectual dabbling in petit trianon primitivism. Thoreau was a Harvard boy playing scout games—as if the whole country had already been settled and overcivilized. In 1845!

Nick Adams does not spend his time speculating and theorizing about man and nature. He is lucky enough to be where he wants to be and doing something he enjoys very much and he has put the need to think and write behind him for the time being. At no time, however, is it even remotely implied that he wants to make freshwater fishing a way of life. As with skiing in "Cross-Country Snow," it is something he likes to do when means and circumstances permit. He neither confuses it with other things nor tries to substitute it for them. He regrets the fact that a companion on a similar outing a long time ago, having come into wealth, has apparently become too involved with other things; but nowhere does Nick himself ever reject or even complain about "other things." He clearly does not agree with Bill in "The Three-Day Blow" that marriage ruins men; nor can it be said that he concurs when George in "Cross-Country Snow" laments that life is hell because Nick's becoming a father is going to curtail their skiing. Not only does Nick (in one story or another) accept social responsibility, including military service, he is also, without ever making too much self-certifying noise about it, an incurable book lover. In "Big Two-Hearted River," for example, as soon as he catches his first two trout and stops to eat his sandwiches, he begins wishing for something to read.

Books are also a part of the fun for the huntsman and fisherman in *The Sun Also Rises*, *Green Hills of Africa*, and "The Three-Day Blow." Of course, none of these characters works at his books while on holiday. He enjoys them. The huntsman in *Green Hills of Africa* whose main objective is to write as well as he can and to learn as he goes along, who feels that he must write a certain amount in order to enjoy the rest of his life, flatly states that he likes hunting kudu in Africa as much as he likes going to see the pictures in the Prado in Madrid. "One is as necessary as the other," he says when asked if one were not better than the other; and then he adds: "There are other things, too."

It was Thoreau, not Hemingway, who seemed to forget that there are other things. "I went to the woods," Thoreau declared in *Walden*, "because I wished to live deliberately, to confront only the essential facts of life, and see if I could not learn what it had to teach, and not, when I came to die, discover that I had not lived." As much as Hemingway liked the woods, he always knew that the essential facts of human life also include many things that people do in families, communities, cities, and nations. Jake Barnes, for instance, could have had fun at Walden Pond for a while. The fishing trip to Burguette is evidence of this. But extended residence on the outskirts of Concord can hardly be suggested as a solution to his problems. One can only wonder what Thoreau would have made of Jake's predicament; and one must also wonder what advice he would have given young men, like the one in "God Rest You Merry, Gentlemen," who wants to be castrated because he does not know that what he keeps feeling is an essential part of life. Hemingway could have told him that monks and pet cats feel the same thing.

Hemingway regarded the gratification of physical appetite as a fundamental and indispensable dimension of human fulfillment, but, his detractors notwithstanding, he never suggested that sensual experience was the only reality. If he had really believed that, he probably would have written guidebooks, if anything—certainly not novels and short stories as highly polished and as subtle as he could possibly make them.

Nor did he ever imply that the sensual is anti-intellectual. Quite the contrary. It is a part of the intellectual. It is as much a part of civilization as anything else. What he said about drinking, for instance, has nothing at all to do with "sinking into nature." "Wine," he wrote in *Death in the Afternoon*, a book about refinement and style, "is one of the most civilized things in the world and one of the natural things of the world that has been brought to the greatest perfection, and it offers a greater range for enjoyment and appreciation than, possibly, any other purely sensory thing which may be purchased. One can learn about wines and pursue the education of one's palate with great enjoyment all of a lifetime, the palate becoming more educated and capable of appreciation and you have constantly increasing enjoyment and appreciation of wine even though the kidneys may weaken, the big toe become painful, the finger joints stiffen, until finally, just when you love it the most you are finally forbidden wine entirely. Just as the eye, which is only a good healthy instrument to start with becomes, even though it is no longer so strong and is weakened and worn by excess, capable of transmitting constantly greater enjoyment to the brain because of knowledge or ability to see that it has acquired. Our bodies all wear out in some way and we die, and I would rather have a palate that will give me the pleasure of enjoying completely a Château Margaux or a Haut-Brion, even though excesses indulged in the acquiring of it has brought a liver that will not allow me to drink Richebourg, Croton, or Chambertin, than to have the corrugated iron internals of my boyhood when all red wines were bitter except port and drinking was the process of getting down enough of anything to make you feel reckless. The thing of course is to avoid having to give up wine entirely just as, with the eye, it is to avoid going blind. But there seems to be much luck in all these things and no man can avoid death by honest effort or say what use any part of his body will bear until he tries it."

Nor do any of the sentiments of the huntsman who wrote

"Remembering Shooting-Flying" have anything at all to do with despair. They are the sentiments of a man who knows something about having a good time. The woodcock, he says at one point, is easy to hit because he has a soft owl-like flight and you also get two chances at him. "But what a bird to eat flambé with armagnac cooked in its own juice and butter, a little mustard added to make the sauce, with two strips of bacon and pommes soufflé and Croton, Pommard, Beaune, or Chambertin to drink."

Many birds were fine to shoot and wonderful to eat. "There were lots of partridges outside of Constantinople and we used to have them roasted and start the meal with a bowl of caviar, the kind you never will be able to afford again, pale gray, the grains as big as a buckshot and a little vodka with it, and then the partridges, not overdone, so that when you cut them there was the juice, drinking Caucasus burgundy and serving French fried potatoes with them and then a salad with Roquefort dressing and another bottle of what was the number of that wine? They all had numbers. Sixty-one I think it was." There were also other birds in other places but none to beat the sand grouse, the lesser bustard, and the teal for pan, griddle, or oven.

"I think they were all made to shoot," he concludes, "because if they were not why did they give them that whirr of wings that moves you suddenly more than any love of country? Why did they make them all so good to eat and why did they make the ones with silent flight like woodcock, snipe, and lesser bustard, better eating than the rest?

"Why does the curlew have that voice, and who thought up the plover's call, which takes the place of noise of wings, to give us that catharsis wing shooting has given men since they stopped flying hawks and took to fowling pieces? I think that they were made to shoot and some of us were made to shoot them and if that is not so well, never say we did not tell you that we liked it."

Nor did his all-consuming enjoyment of terrain ever turn him away from the glories of landscape painting. The two things always enhanced each other. As did his enthusiasm for bullfighting and his appreciation of Goya. Nothing ever turned Hemingway away from painting or any other art. His reading enhanced his living and his writing; and his living enhanced his reading and his writing. "For we have been there in books and out of books—and where we go, if we are any good, there you can go as we have been."

Sooner or later everything comes around to his commitment to art. "A country finally erodes," he wrote in *Green Hills of Africa*, "and the dust blows away, the people all die and none of them were of any importance permanently except those who practised the arts, and these now wish to cease their work because it is too lonely, too hard to do, and is not fashionable. A thousand years makes economics silly and a work of art endures forever, but it is very difficult to do and now it is not fashionable."

The sentiments of a typical Hemingway hero, like those of Hemingway himself, are almost always those of a man involved with the *refinement* of experience. It is inaccurate to define any of his actions in terms of desperation, and downright ridiculous to classify them as escapism and substitution. It is also misleading to define them as the actions of a man in search of value in a naturalistic world. Nick Adams, Frederic Henry, Harry Morgan, Harry the writer, and Robert Jordan certainly are not looking for something to live for; they all proceed on the pragmatic values they already have. "I didn't care what it was all about," says Jake Barnes, "all I wanted to know was how to live in it. Maybe if you found out how to live in it you learned from that what it was all about."

But apparently once certain kinds of intellectuals have convinced themselves that the Hemingway hero is a man in despair because he cannot discover the essential meaning and values in a world of violence and chaos, they no doubt find it natural enough to think in terms of frustration and compensation and assume that anyone having fun must be a member of a cult devoted to hedonism. It is not at all difficult to see how this neat but hasty and pretentious and not unfatuous assumption could lead them to insist that there is a Hemingway code and to complain that it represents a fundamental evasion of intellectual responsibility.

The Hemingway hero, in point of fact, however, is not evasive at all. On the contrary, he is almost always a man who functions in terms of confrontation. He is too persistently pragmatic to be evasive and too thoroughly individualistic ever to be confined to a cult. He is a man of form, discipline, and courage, of course; but his behavior is much too realistic and far too flexible to conform to any conventional code of conduct. Nor does his rejection of the speculations, theories, and rationalizations of most contemporary intellectuals make him either nonintellectual or anti-intellectual. If anything, it indicates that he is all too intellectual. Nonintellectuals do not take issue with intellectuals. When they do not ignore them, they are likely to be overimpressed by them. Perhaps because they do not understand them. Hemingway not only understood the issues but was also convinced that only fiction was complex enough to deal with them.

No one can seriously accuse the Hemingway hero of not using his head. With the exception of Harry Morgan, the typical Hemingway hero is almost always not only a thinking man but also a reading man and frequently a writing man. He does not indulge in academic abstractions and intellectualized clichés and slogans but neither does he rely on tribal instinct, superstition, magic, or hand-me-down rules of thumb. He proceeds on concrete information, his discipline being that of the empiricist who responds in terms of what he personally knows and feels rather than what somebody else has decided he should know and feel. His movements, even in moments of crisis, are seldom desperate because, like those of the bullfighter, the huntsman, the fisherman, the soldier, and, yes, the scientist, they are based on his objective, practical, and operational estimate of the situation. Robert Penn Warren once wrote that the Hemingway hero was becoming aware of nada. Perhaps one might add that he is someone who has the blues (is bedeviled by blue devils) because, like Ecclesiastes, he has confronted the absurdity of human existence and knows that each moment and each experience count.

Blues-oriented writers should find it easy enough to recognize the pragmatic hero of the fiction of Ernest Hemingway as a man whose personal tradition of confrontation, discipline, and self-realization is in many essentials very much like their own. Ralph Ellison, in fact, has already done so. Indeed, for Ellison, everything Hemingway wrote "was imbued with a spirit beyond the tragic with which I could feel at home, for it was close to the feeling of the blues, which are, perhaps, as close as Americans can come to expressing the spirit of tragedy."

When Ellison on another occasion pointed out that the blues "express both the agony of life and the possibility of conquering it through sheer toughness of spirit," he was only reminding his idiomatic relatives of something that he knew very well they had every reason in the world to have known all their lives. He was, that is to say, articulating something that most live in terms of though they may never stop to think about it—or ever be able to define it. As a matter of fact, there are those who live in terms of the blues tradition and then not only accept but also repeat and even propagate clichés of outsiders whose firsthand contact with and information about the idiom even at its best tend to be extremely limited and often are actually questionable.

One such writer was Richard Wright. Ellison, who had a profound awareness of the process by which the blues move beyond the painful facts of life in the very act of acknowledging their existence, noted that the lyrical prose in Wright's autobiography "evokes the paradoxical, almost surreal image of a black boy singing lustily as he probes his own grievous wound." Wright himself, however, seemed to ignore the lustiness of the blues idiom in music as well as the traditional toughness of spirit exemplified by so-called black American spirit. Nor is this undeniable toughness to be confused with being hard-boiled. William Faulkner, for example, thought of it in terms of human endurance and celebrated it precisely because its humanity was seemingly unvanquishable!

It was as if Wright heard only the words and did not respond to the music at all. But the words, as magnificently poetic as they can sometimes be, are only a part of the statement of the blues pattern. The spirit of the music is something else again. The lyrics almost always have tragic implications. They tell of disappointments, defeat, disaster, death, of trials, tribulations, mistreatments, losses, separations, frustrations, and miseries. The music, however, does not create an atmosphere of unrelieved suffering, wailing, wall lamentation, chest-beating, and gnashing of teeth by any means. There is always an element of regret and sobering sadness that life should be this way, to be sure, but the most characteristic ambiance generated by the sound and beat of blues music as such is not despondency but earthiness and a sense of well-being. The verbal response to a blues vamp, whether in a ramshackle honky-tonk or a swanky midtown New York nightspot, is not "Alas" or "Alack" but rather some expression equivalent to "Hey now" or "Yeah now" or "Lord, am I born to die." At such a time "Lord, have mercy" means "Lord, enable me to endure the good time that this music is already generating." Indeed, once the music gets going, the words may be mumbled, jumbled, or scatted.

Incidentally, this intermingling of tragic and comic elements in the blues is often as complex and as outrageously robust as the tragicomic texture of Elizabethan drama. Gilbert Murray points out that "the peculiar characteristic of classical Greek drama is the sharp and untransgressed division between tragedy and comedy. The two styles are separate and never combined. No classical author is known to have written in both."

Not only did Elizabethan playmakers write in both, they often combined the two in the same script, alternating serious passages with comic or comic-relief passages. *In a fully orchestrated blues statement, it is not at all unusual for the two so-called elements to be so casually (and naturally) combined as to express tragic and comic dimensions of experience simultaneously!*

Sometimes, as in the now-classic Kansas City–style shout, stomp, shuffle, and jump, the very beat of the music actually belies or in effect even denies the words. Even as the singer spills out his tale of woe, the music in the background not only swings, stomps, jumps, and shouts irrepressibly, but often has comic capers and even mocking laughter among the trumpets, insistent bawdiness among the trombones, and at times the moaning and groaning in the reed section becomes almost unbearably seductive! Sometimes, as a matter of fact, the singer's own movements suggest dionysian revelry more than anything else.

Moreover, those conditioned by the idiom have always used the blues as *good-time music*. Social welfare–oriented technicians seem to regard the blues as an expression of despair. But in Sunday sermons, down-home and down-home-derived preachers of all denominations have traditionally (and knowingly) referred to it as music of worldly and devilish temptation.

The female singer of blues, for instance, is never regarded as an old witch, a sad Cassandra, or a foreboding old hag from a Greek chorus. She is not primarily the bearer of bad or sad tidings at all; on the contrary, she is one of the queens of the earth. She is the big mama, the great consort, the all-embracing female principle, and even when she is not personally good-looking in any conventional sense, she is still responded to as a highly desirable woman. When such blues dive divas as Ma Rainey, Bessie Smith, and Dinah Washington complained that they were laughing to keep from crying and had empty beds, there were always men in the audience who eagerly offered to comfort them—the offers implying that the men had heroic qualifications, it being fully understood at the outset that Big Mama has an empty bed not because there is none who is willing but because by her standards a good man is always hard to find.

As for the male blues singer, his role is almost always that of the combination of dashing sweet man and ever-ready stud male that women stand in line to touch as he passes. Even as a singer such as the Falstaffian Jimmy Rushing used to kid himself publicly about being five by five, as wide as he was tall, the women in his audiences responded as if he were the most irresistible phallic figure in the world.

But just as there are those who continue to insist that the good-time elements in the world of Ernest Hemingway are only manifestations of despair or even dehumanization, nevertheless there are many who are all too easily convinced, mostly by psychopolitical theories, that down-home and down-home-derived folks who find enjoyment in the blues can only be running away from the frustrations of oppression and regressing to sensual abandon as a means of escape, or else are just simply too completely victimized to realize what the obvious facts of life actually are and therefore doing jungle dances in a fool's juvenile paradise.

Most so-called black Americans know only too well that this is nonsense, and so does anybody else who knows the difference between what art reflects or is compounded of and what it expresses—or anybody who has ever really listened to music and felt the natural need to dance to it. And so should U.S. "black" writers. Nor should these writers fail to note the similarities between the indictments that U.S. intellectuals bring against Hemingway and the smug but provincial assumptions that allow them to condescend to so-called black expression as if most other U.S. expression were endlessly fructifying. It is not. And what is more, only a minimum understanding of rat race dynamics is required to enable such writers to see the cultural deprivation and intellectual bankruptcy, not to mention the all too obvious personal fear of physical inadequacy, behind such pretension. For one thing, those who condemn sensual gratification, whether in response to elements in the fiction of Ernest Hemingway or in the blues idiom in music, are never quite able to free themselves of envy. For another, they almost always overstate their charges in ways that are not only spiteful but that also betray an appalling disregard for simple ordinary everyday facts.

Only a willful obtuseness or something worse would allow anybody who has read the descriptions in the first chapter of *To Have and Have Not* to charge that even Harry Morgan represents any playing down of sensibility. And anybody who introduces even the sleeping bag sequences in *For Whom the Bell Tolls* as evidence that Hemingway was out to reduce the world to the gratification of the sex urge would be as intellectually irresponsible as those who describe so-called black Americans as childlike simple creatures of sensual abandon. An outsider—say, a blonde from the jet set—who comes into a down-home-style hall and pulls off her shoes, lets her hair down, and begins stomping and shaking and jerking and grinding in the spirit of personal release, liberation, and abandon, does not represent freedom; she represents chaos, and only an outsider would do it. Only an outsider could be so irresponsible to the music. Insiders know that the music and dance, like all other artistic expression, require a commitment to form. As is the case with all other artistic expression, they achieve freedom not by giving in to the emotions but through self-control and refinement of technique. Swinging the blues and swinging *to* the blues, however free they may seem to the uninitiated listener and onlooker, are never acts of wild abandon; they are triumphs of technical refinement and are among the most sophisticated things a human being can do.

U.S. "black" folks dancing to the blues, in no matter what tempo, would be no more likely to disregard the music and give themselves over to their physical and emotional urges, cravings, drives, and impulses than a Hemingway bullfighter (or any other kind) would start stabbing and hacking away as soon as the bull entered the ring or a huntsman would start banging and thrashing away at anything and everything as soon as he heard a rustle in the brush.

But nothing exposes the confusion of so-called white U.S. social critics and pundits more than the astonishing but well-known fact that these same antisensual intellectuals far more often than not may be numbered among the most dedicated dialecticians of the so-called Sex Revolution, the most esoteric apologists from the cult of psychedelic experience, and the time-honored literary champions of universal freedom of the por-nographic press!

It should also be easy for so-called black U.S. writers to spot the intellectual one-sidedness involved in the self-therapeutic concern that most people express about the effect of slavery and oppression. Somehow or other most people seem always to assume that oppression dehumanizes the oppressed more than it does the oppressor. But not only do such people over-look the unmistakable implication of antagonistic cooperation, it is as if they also deliberately ignore the most obvious fact of all: The oppressor who is already so dehumanized at the very outset that he can regard fellow human beings as chattels be-comes even more dehumanized in the all-consuming process of maintaining an inhuman system. The violation of the hu-manity of others becomes for him a full-time occupation, a preoccupation, and a way of life!

The oppressed, on the other hand, are not necessarily dehu-manized because their humanity is being violated by others. In-deed, there is evidence that the effect is quite the opposite. At the outbreak of the Civil War, for instance, it was an oppressed "victim" such as Frederick Douglass who upheld what was noblest in the American ideal of civilization, not a full-fledged citizen such as Robert E. Lee. Douglass was not dehumanized by suffering. Lee, however, was all too dehumanized by privi-lege. So far as Douglass was concerned there was no choice but to be for freedom and the nobility of all mankind, while Lee apparently felt that there was a choice, and for all his fine sentiments about civilization he gave his considerable support to those committed to legalizing human bondage even at the expense of seceding from the Union.

Nor should it be overlooked that even as these words are being written, oppressed Americans who are defining their political and economic aspirations in terms of human rights and values, are being resisted, obstructed, and even violently opposed at every turn by people who, far from having been *humanized* by freedom, seem to have become so *dehumanized* by being a part of a system that oppresses other people that they actually place the value and security of *property* above the welfare and fulfillment of *human beings* without even thinking twice about it. It should surprise no one that such people substitute statistics for wisdom and compassion, confuse human beings with machines, and assume that human behavior, including artistic expression, is mechanical and predictable. Human beings, however, unlike machines, may give high-octane performance on low-octane fuel and often give low-octane performance on the highest-octane fuel in the world. Deprived machines always gasp in desperation and run down; deprived human beings, on the other hand, may become immensely creative. But perhaps the catch in this is the fact that it is not really possible to deprive human beings as one deprives a mechanical device. After all, a human being can always wish and dream, and he can never be reduced to zero. Not as long as he is potentially capable of defining himself in terms of his own aspirations.

As for the blues statement, regardless of what it reflects, what it *expresses* is a sense of life that is affirmative. The blues lyrics reflect that which they confront, of course, which includes the absurd, the unfortunate, and the catastrophic; but they also reflect the person making the confrontation, his self-control, his sense of structure and style; and they express, among other things, his sense of humor as well as his sense of ambiguity and his sense of possibility. Thus the very existence of the blues tradition is irrefutable evidence that those who evolved it respond to the vicissitudes of the human condition not with hysterics and desperation, but through the wisdom of poetry informed by pragmatic insight.

V

Kenneth Tynan, the British journalist, drama critic, and aficionado who was with him at the time, reports that when Ernest Hemingway referred to himself as being an honorary Negro one night in Havana he did so "with a good deal of pride." Hemingway was responding to a performance by a trio of Cuban Negro musicians who had just serenaded him with a special song, repeated a Mau Mau chant he had taught them, and rendered a Spanish lament for which he had written the lyrics. There is reason to assume that his remark and the pride that Tynan noted, however, also included Negroes he had known elsewhere.

On another and far more impressive occasion he had already recalled with what was undoubtedly a very special satisfaction another honor, one that U.S. Negroes had bestowed upon him. The incident in Havana occurred in 1959. In 1954, at one point during all the excitement that went with being awarded the highest of all prizes for literary achievement, he found time to tell Robert Manning, then a feature writer for *Time* magazine, about how a Key West Negro announcing him as referee for a boxing match had introduced him as the world-famous millionaire, sportsman, and playboy. "Playboy," he chuckled, knowing exactly what the so-called black American connotation had to be, "was the greatest title they could give a man. How can the Nobel Prize move a man who has heard plaudits like that?"

In Venice earlier that same year Hemingway, perhaps as a straight-faced gag and perhaps not, told A. E. Hotchner, his sometime traveling companion and self-styled Boswell, about how during the trip to Africa from which he was returning, he had attained an admirable position in a Wakamba tribe during the temporary absence of his American wife by taking unto himself an eighteen-year-old African bride and in keeping with local custom had inherited her seventeen-year-old widowed sister, who became their bedmate. He showed Hotchner pictures of the bride and later in Aix-en-Provence told him she expected a child by him to be born in September. "Before I left I gave a herd of goats to my bride's family," he went on. "Most overgoated family in Africa. Feels good to have an African son."

Hotchner, who was never quite certain which of Hemingway's stories to believe anyway, seems inclined to regard this one as more fabrication than fact. But the implications are the same either way. With a writer like Hemingway, facts must always become fiction anyway; and, as Hotchner would probably be the first to admit, it is the fiction that perhaps best represents Hemingway's sense of significance. It was not with the incidents he reported but with the ones he made up that he expressed his most profound sense of actuality.

Indeed, if there seems to be something faintly familiar about the remark that Hemingway made to Tynan in Havana, it may well be due to the fact that both the statement and the circumstances are somewhat similar to an incident in one of his finest works of fiction. At one point in *The Sun Also Rises* there is a brief but easy exchange between Brett Ashley, dancing with Jake Barnes in a Paris nightclub, and a friendly Negro drummer that is loaded with "honorary Negro" implications and possibilities. Jake looks on and makes no comment, but Brett feels the need to account for the intimacy. "He's a great friend of mine," she says. "Damn good drummer."

Ad Francis, the belligerent prizefighter in "The Battler," is also an honorary Negro of sorts. He travels around the country with Bugs, his realistic and uniquely compassionate Negro friend, who looks after him (and his spending money) as if they were members of the same family. Ad Francis is an honorary Negro in precisely the sense that Benjy in William Faulkner's *The Sound and the Fury* is not. Luster, as much as Faulkner admires his humanity, takes care of Benjy because it is his assigned task to do so. There is something about Ad Francis, however, even in his punch-drunk state, that qualifies him for acceptance.

One fundamental clue to what is involved in Hemingway's conception of his honorary Negro status (as well as his honorary Spanish, French, and Italian status) is an observation he made during his first visit to Africa. "*They had that attitude that makes brothers,*" he wrote of one beautiful group of Masai warriors in *Green Hills of Africa,* "*that unexpressed but instant and complete acceptance that you must be Masai wherever it is you come from. That attitude you only get from the best of the English, the best of the Hungarians, and the very best Spaniards, the thing that used to be the most clever distinction of nobility when there was nobility. It is an ignorant attitude and the people who have it do not survive, but very few pleasanter things ever happen to you than the encountering of it.*" (Italics added.)

There are other clues in *To Have and Have Not.* Hemingway, like most people almost everywhere, also responded to the Negro idiom of motion, an orientation to African-derived dance rhythms that most Negroes everywhere seem to retain, which makes for an ease and coordination of body movement that is not only efficient and practical but also beautiful to behold. Some people have always confused such emphasis on rhythm with psychopolitical theories of race, while others regard it as unmistakable evidence of primitivism. Actually, it is fundamentally a cultural (or environmental), not a racial phenomenon and not necessarily an evolutionary one. There are non-African primitives who are as awkward as some Europeans.

It should not be at all difficult for anybody who has even a casual knowledge of the history of the slave system in the United States to realize that the traditional U.S. Negro idiom in music and dance, for instance, retains a strong African rhythmic emphasis not simply because the Negroes are born that way, but because the slaves, although forbidden African drums and rituals, were not only permitted but also encouraged to sing and dance. The slave masters rather enjoyed the African rhythmic emphasis (as they did the unusual timbres and harmonics) so long as there were no disturbing overtones of tribal communication and revolt—and besides, they were probably only too happy to note that the dance rhythms were also work rhythms that increased time and motion efficiency.

Harry Morgan, the rugged but ill-fated hero of *To Have and Have Not,* is hardly the kind of white Southerner who would refer to himself as being an honorary Negro. His response to the practical application of dance-oriented Negro coordination, however, is no less significant for being somewhat tainted. Moreover, in some ways he is less tainted with racism than, say, the average northern white journalist, intellectual, or even philanthropist. He can even see a "black" man killing "white" men in a gun battle in Havana and not only make no sentimental identification with the white men because of race or color but also can admire the "black" man's courage and cool efficiency as frankly as some "white" sportswriters came to admire the boxing skill of a Joe Louis and a Sugar Ray Robinson. When Harry, watching the Negro empty a submachine gun and switch to a shotgun while still under fire, says, "Some nigger," he is expressing his (and no doubt Hemingway's) profound appreciation for any man, whoever he may be, who can perform under pressure with grace and style. Back on his deep-sea fishing boat later on, when his client questions the extra expense of taking a "black" man to bait the hooks, Harry explains that the man can do it faster than he himself can under pressure. "When the big fish run you'll see," he tells him. Racial, primitive, or cultural—it is apparently all the same to him. He accepts the fact and shows no concern at all about the whys and wherefores.

He does indulge his curiosity about another very special implication of dance-oriented movement, however. He notices that his hook-baiting expert comes on board sleepy every morning and concludes that he has "been on a rhumba every night." Nor is this the extent of his curiosity or his involvement. One night while he and his buxom, passionate, and devoted wife, Marie, are making love and she suddenly expresses curiosity about what it is like with a "black" woman, it turns out that he has already known, presumably from personal experience, that it is "like nurse shark."

Since "black" men could hardly regard making love with a "black" woman as being anything like tangling with any kind of shark, Harry Morgan would seem to be deliberately disqualifying himself as an honorary Negro in that category. Not that there is the slightest evidence that he needs to be one. He and the ever-passionate Marie seem to do better than all right for themselves as things are.

Nevertheless, Harry Morgan provides important clues to at least some of what was no doubt involved when Hemingway referred to himself as being an honorary Negro. Morgan's appreciation for Negroes is fundamentally practical. It is never really exotic in spite of his language, and along with it there is a genuine feeling of human identification that enables him to respond with fraternal compassion when a "black" person behaves in a way that is somewhat less than admirable. Obviously, he hired Wesley for the rum-smuggling trip (which turned out so badly) because he needed someone special with him on a difficult mission; but when Wesley becomes bitter and irascible after being shot in the leg while they were being chased by the revenue agents, Harry, whose own wound is much more serious, not only remains considerate but even responds with humor when Wesley threatens to cut his heart out. "Not with no whetstone," he says, looking at the object in the Negro's hand. "Take it easy, Wesley."

But perhaps one clue to what being an honorary Negro meant to Hemingway, who once described a group of Senegalese soldiers as being too tall to stare, and once advised his brother not to trust anybody with a southern accent unless he was Negro, is the account that Harry Morgan gives of the departure of the hook-baiting expert.

"So Johnson gave the nigger a dollar and two Cuban twenty-cent pieces.

"'What's this for?' the nigger asks me, showing me the coins.

"'A tip,' I told him in Spanish. 'You're through. He gives you that.'

"'Don't come tomorrow?'

"'No.'

"The nigger gets his ball of twine he used for tying baits and his dark glasses, puts on his straw hat, and goes without saying good-bye. *He was a nigger that never thought much of any of us.*" (Italics added.)

There is much in the fiction of F. Scott Fitzgerald for all contemporary U.S. writers to admire and study. *The Great Gatsby, Tender Is the Night*, perhaps *The Beautiful and Damned*, and certainly some of his short stories, including "May Day," "The Diamond as Big as the Ritz," and "The Rich Boy," represent an indispensable dimension of life in America. No other U.S. writer has made a more compelling literary statement about the dynamics and the implications of the U.S. rat race for material success and social status than Fitzgerald did with the story of Jay Gatsby, for instance; and perhaps even "black" intellectuals will, on close study, concede that confidence man Gatsby, *né* James Gatz, is as significant and as fundamental a personification of the eternal U.S. problem of self-identity as is Joe Christmas, the race-confused "mulatto" in William Faulkner's *Light in August*.

These same "black" intellectuals, however, will find very little that has any functional or even suggestive affinity with any distinctive aspect of the blues idiom, either in subject matter, selection, point of view, or aesthetic approach in the fiction of the writer most often mentioned as typifying the so-called Jazz Age. They will look in vain even in *Tales of the Jazz Age* for anything remotely resembling either the spirit of the blues or the jazz sensibility. What they will find in his best work is outstanding twentieth-century fiction written by an ambitious, genuinely talented, but essentially naïve although intelligent American who, very much like so many others among all the sad young white men of his generation, obviously confused the blues and jazz with razzmatazz, hotcha, and hot diggity dog.

Fitzgerald was (among other reasons) always too busy trying to be a 100 percent "white" and naughtily successful darling of high society ever to have even kidded about being an honorary black man, even in a nightmare. Nor is it likely that he would have been able to qualify as one had he wanted to. Nor would any obstacles have been more difficult for him to overcome than the fact that the very aspects of riches and power that seem to have held such great fascination for him would have been regarded by "black" certifiers as being dull and unsophisticated. Indeed, Hemingway was well on his way to honorary blackness when he replied to Fitzgerald's starry-eyed claim that the very rich were different from other people by saying, "Yes, they have more money." Riffed with the inside information of a blues musician! Spoken like one who really knows something about what "black" doormen, headwaiters, bell captains, and chauffeurs are actually thinking behind those stylized masks of stylized smiles and stylized dignity and concern. "Man, they can have the difference. Just give me that checkbook."

It was Hemingway, not Fitzgerald, who saw what one sees

when one looks beyond the clichés about the blues. What Fitzgerald saw was essentially what a good conventional musician sees in the great metropolis; and what he wrote might well have been written by a truly gifted but essentially conventional small-town boy who has become "urbane" by way of an Ivy League campus, which he uses for family background as a young nobleman might use his ancestral manor.

Almost any black, brown, or beige chauffeur, doorman, bellboy, waiter, or Pullman porter of any experience at all would be able to spot the eager "young man from the provinces" beneath the Brooks Brothers veneer of Fitzgerald at first sight. Perhaps such a "black" person would also be inclined to smile somewhat complacently at the ofay quality of some of Hemingway's physical involvements. But even so, far from dismissing Hemingway as being unsophisticated, he would probably recognize him at once as a man from beyond the horizon, a very special man from whom he might be able to learn a thing or two and thus extend the dimensions of his own experience.

Hemingway, who evolved his own highly individual style and wrote only in his own personal terms, qualifies as an honorary blues musician precisely because he was always writing blues stories without ever trying to do so. What he was always trying to do, as he says over and over again, was write as accurately as possible about how he really felt about the things he really knew. It was only through the process of trying to write straight honest prose on human beings that he came to represent in fiction that fundamental aspect of the contemporary U.S. sensibility that the blues express in music.

Questions of derivation and adaptation aside, U.S. writers and intellectuals who think in terms of the blues idiom (and tradition) will find that a typical Hemingway situation is not only the archetypal situation of contemporary man but also a blues situation. The Hemingway hero is a blues hero, or a man with blues insights and responses. His conflicts and complications have blues ambiguities, and his resolutions, like those in blues problems, are always based on a confrontation and acknowledgment of the fundamental facts of life without illusion, facts that are sometimes as incomprehensibly absurd as they are ugly.

Blues-oriented readers can come to immediate and personal terms with the central statement in almost any Hemingway story simply by giving the title a blues twist or by playing verbal improvisations on the key characters or circumstances. *In Our Time*, for example, is composed of a series of thematically interrelated stories and vamplike and rifflike sketches, bridges, or interludes, the mood of which suggests *Blues in Our Time*, *Blues for Our Time*, or even *Blues Panorama*. And of course it is easy enough to read *The Sun Also Rises* as *Jake's Empty Bed Blues*, *Blues for Lady Brett*, *The Postwar Blues*, *Lost Generation Blues*, or even *Rocks in My Bed*. As for *A Farewell to Arms*, the hero gets *The Volunteer Blues* or *Crusader's Blues*, the *Empty Talk Blues* or *Nothing Sacred Blues*, *The Getaway Blues*, *Separate Peace Blues*, or *Hors de Combat Blues*, and ends up with the *Cold in Hand Blues*.

Among the short stories in a book that might as well have been called *Blues for Men Without Women* are *Blues in Another Country*, *The Fifty-Grand Blues*, *White Elephant Blues*, and *Ten Indians Blues*; and "Now I Lay Me" reads like nothing so much as *Now I Lay Me Blues* or *Blues After Midnight*. Nor should the *Undefeated* or *The No-Comeback Blues* be overlooked; and "The Killers," after all, is not the story of an actual murder. What the two cold-blooded gunmen actually do is give Nick Adams *The Cold-Blooded Blues*. They make him realize not only the fact of death, but also, and perhaps even worse, the cheapness of life. What really horrifies Nick is the fact that the intended victim is as resigned as the gunmen are casual, and in the outchorus, the story riffs on what might be called *The Blues to Be Gone* or *No Hiding Place Blues*:

"'I'm going to get out of this town,' Nick said.

"'Yes,' said George. 'That's a good thing to do.'

"'I can't stand to think about him waiting in the room and knowing he's going to get it. It's too damned awful.'

"'Well,' said George, 'you better not think about it.'"

But no statement by any contemporary U.S. writer extends the literary and philosophical implications of the blues further or gives them a more profound complexity than the inscription that Hemingway composed for *Winner Take Nothing*. At one juncture in *Death in the Afternoon* he had already written: "All stories, if continued far enough, end in death, and he is no true-story teller who would keep that from you." But as if that were not blues-confrontation disposition enough, and as if to reemphasize the significance of the title inscription to *The Sun Also Rises*, he wrote:

Unlike all other forms of lutte or combat the conditions are that the Winner shall take Nothing; neither his ease, nor his pleasure, nor any notions of glory; nor if he win far enough, shall there be any reward within himself.

To which he could easily have added a refrain he is reported as using in conversation many years later: "How do you like it now, gentlemen?" Now, that is, that you have found out that the blues go with winning as well as losing. Instead, he wrote and included a story that might have been called *The Clean, Well-Lighted Blues*, *Blues for Nothing*, or even *Blues About Being and Nothingness*, a story about an old man and a waiter who are in good health and have no apparent social, economic, or political difficulties but who have trouble sleeping nights because they are lonely and because they have become aware of the ultimate void that underlies human existence. "Some lived in it and never felt it," Hemingway had the waiter conclude, and then goes on, "but he knew it all was *nada y pues nada y nada y pues nada.*"

Nothing and then nothing and nothing and then (and perhaps even for) nothing. Or as the epigraph to *The Sun Also Rises* suggests so strongly: All is vanity. What profit hath man of all his labor wherein he laboreth under the sun? Or to put the whole matter of blues statement in still another way: In Jake Barnes, Hemingway has created a hero whose predicament is such that what he must acknowledge every day is the fact that he "woke up this morning blues all around my bed." Maybe he doesn't stomp, jump, or swing the blues. Nonetheless he is blues idiom hero enough to look at the world and say "Good morning, blues. Blues, how do you do?" And make the best of a terrible situation.

It is easy enough to write sincere and urgent propaganda about the necessity of food, clothing, shelter, freedom, and justice. Being for such things is only a matter of being in favor of adequate political structures. Not that bringing such structures into actual being is by any means simple; but as eternally complex as social, economic, and political problems always are, there are others that are not only far more difficult but also more fundamental and even more urgent. Most essential of all are problems that are directly involved in the affirmation and justification of human life as such. "There is but one truly serious philosophical problem," wrote Albert Camus in the opening paragraph of *The Myth of Sisyphus*, "and that is suicide. Judging whether life is or is not worth living amounts to answering the fundamental question of philosophy. All the rest . . . comes afterward."

Nobody was ever more firmly dedicated to the accurate definition of the eternal condition of man than was Ernest Hemingway. And certainly no twentieth-century U.S. writer ever stated the fundamental issues of human existence more comprehensively. Perhaps the most influential contemporary American statement of these issues is found in *The Waste Land* and "The Hollow Men." But in these two unsettling poems, T. S. Eliot implies that the problems of nada are somehow peculiar to contemporary life and that it is essentially a problem of the renewal of lost connections and energies. The title of *The Waste Land* and the crucial image of the Fisher King clearly establish the fact that Eliot assumes that "things ain't what they used to be," that evil days have fallen upon a once prosperous kingdom of once blessed people. And one hastens to concede that his observations, which are not at all like the assumptions of revolutionary politicians, are valid as far as they go. Eliot does not, however, confront the allegation that even in the best of times in the most fruitful lands the winner shall take nothing.

Hemingway did not hesitate to make the confrontation nor has anybody ever insisted more firmly than he that the immediate functional value of the evidence for affirmation never be compromised. It was all very well for William Faulkner to declare in a speech on a happy occasion that man would not only endure but would prevail, but what Hemingway always wanted to know was how man would prevail and on what terms.

He did not assume that any of the answers to the riddle of human existence would be comprehensive, or that they could ever be reduced to a code. His fiction indicates that he proceeded on the assumption that wisdom would be found in bits and pieces through trials and error from the arts and in experience itself and that he tried to shape his insights not into codes but into the rich, suggestive ambiguity of literature. Assuming, as he obviously did, that art was nothing if not the most basic equipment for living, Hemingway would probably have said of his collected works what he said of *Death in the Afternoon*—that they were not enough but that they represented at least some of the things that he felt had to be said. "These fragments," he may have added, playing another one of his riffs on T. S. Eliot, "I have shored not only 'against my ruins,' but also against my *ruin*."

The experience in which, according to Hemingway, writers are forged as a sword is forged involves more than anything else the confrontation of human existence in the raw. Nothing seems to have impressed Hemingway more than the fact that Tolstoy, Dostoevsky, Stendhal, and Flaubert had been firsthand witnesses to human behavior in the very worst circumstances and still found amid all the inhumanity enough evidence to enable them to write about human existence in terms that are not only affirmative and not only viable but that also suggest delight and magnificence.

What all contemporary U.S. writers can never afford to forget (no matter how strong the pressure to become engagé) is the fact that no social or political responsibility is greater than that which comes with the realization that there is more earthly chaos and human confusion than there is form and that he who creates forms and images creates the very basis of human values, defines accurately or not what is good and what is not, and in doing so exercises immeasurable influence on the direction of human aspiration and effort. Not even the commander in chief of a revolutionary army assumes a greater responsibility to mankind. After all, revolutionary commanders, no less than agitprop writers, are essentially errand boys. Seldom are they engaged to help establish a social order based on their own conception of what life is about!

Epilogue

O NCE THE WRITER *accepts the obligation which comes with knowledge of the chaos which underlies all human life, he must also accept another. He must presume to go beyond established categories. As with the self-elected dragon slayer who would save his fellow citizens, he must choose his own weapons and proceed as a one-man expeditionary force into the unsafe territory of the outlying regions.*

As with all self-designated Sphinx-confronters he will use all the relevant scholarly advice and tutorial assistance he can get, of course, but in the Ordeal itself he must take his chances with his own improvisations. Not only because established categories (conventional conceptions and clichés) are a part of the problem itself but also because, as Ernest Hemingway presumed, the only admissible answers to the questions asked by the Sphinx are those, however fragmentary, which one really knows, not those one is supposed to know because they are taught in the great Universities.

And yet James Joyce, for example, was not really being presumptuous at all when he wrote about a group of inhabitants of the grimy ghettos of Dublin, Ireland, in Homeric terms (whoever Homer was and however much he did or did not presume when he wrote in epic terms about the Reconstruction Problems of a Selected Number of Greek Veterans of the Trojan War). Joyce was being a very practical literary craftsman. He took such fragments as an Irish writer of his intellectual background and sensibility could scrape together and forge into an urgently needed device with which to encounter the actualities of his existence. What Joyce, like all other writers, presumed, no doubt, was that he could "signify" about the nature of time, place, and personality and by so doing could make life more interesting not only for himself but also for those who read him.

Conventional categories and hand-me-down reverence aside, it is only natural for contemporary U.S. writers to proceed as if Ralph Waldo Emerson, for all his New England stiffness, would have been moved by Louis Armstrong and would have acknowledged him as a Representative American Artist, a poet whose melodies "ascend and leap and pierce into the deeps of infinite time."

Perhaps it is also presumptuous, but it is no less natural for contemporary U.S. writers to assume that Jack Johnson—who in his conception of the potential of U.S. citizens would have conceded nothing to Abe Lincoln and could have had only contempt for sad Woodrow Wilson—was himself an American Work of Art to compare with anything in the major phase of Henry James; that Jelly Roll Morton and Fats Waller would have done better than hold their own with Mark Twain, jive artist become fine artist. Nor is it at all outrageous to assume that Walt Whitman would have been bewitched by the infinite flexibility of the Kansas City 4/4 beat of Count Basie or should have been. Or that Herman Melville having made what he made of the crew of the Pequod may have gained new dimensions and resonances from a world tour with the Duke Ellington Orchestra.

FROM THE BRIARPATCH FILE

On Context, Procedure, and American Identity

To Mozelle and Michele

CONTENTS

Part I

The Briarpatch

Antagonistic Cooperation in Alabama

IN THE REMARKS I MADE on April 16, 1983, at the University of Alabama in Tuscaloosa, where I was a participant in a symposium on "The American South: Distinctiveness and Its Limitations," I began by stating that as a writer of fiction which I hoped would be read as serious literary statement of universal appeal above all else, my primary concern was not with recording, reporting, or documenting sociopolitical data as such about the South.

But then I went on to point out that the universally appealing in art, which is to say aesthetic statement, is always achieved through the extension, elaboration, and refinement of the local details and idiomatic particulars that impinge most intimately on one's everyday existence. So the point was not that I was not at all concerned with writing about the South, but rather that I have always been more interested in ultimate metaphors about the South than in social science surveys about it. Because whereas sociopolitical reports in effect give circumstances which amount to predicament all of the advantages over incentive and ambition, the metaphor may be employed as a pragmatic device that functions as our most basic equipment for living, by which of course I mean self-fulfillment.

The metaphor represents how we *feel* about whatever facts and figures are used to describe or define the concrete circumstances of our existence wherever we are. And how we *feel* adds up to our *outlook* or *horizon of aspiration*, which is the source of our incentive or lack of incentive.

In brief, how I felt about the socioeconomic and political circumstances in the Alabama in which I grew up during the 1920s and the 1930s added up to me thinking of myself as having to be as the ever nimble and ever resourceful mythological Alabama jackrabbit in the no less actual than mythological Alabama briarpatch. Thus I have never thought of myself as a victim or a villain. I was always, *but always*, the fairy tale hero who would marry the fairy tale princess.

All of which is also why I've written so much about the blues (and about jazz, which is the fully orchestrated blues statement).

To me, blues music has never been the misery music that the ever so benevolent social-science-survey-oriented do-gooders and uplifters of the downtrodden seem to think it is. To me it has always been good-time music, music that inspires you to stomp away low-down blue feelings and stomp in an atmosphere of earthy well-being and affirmation and celebration of the sheer fact of existence.

Yes, the ever so blue lyrics are indeed about problems, troubles, disappointment, defeat, loss, and unhappiness. But the music, with its locomotive beat and onomatopoeia, not only counterstates and counteracts the complaint that life itself is such a low-down dirty shame, it also goes on to transform the atmosphere (of the juke joint, honky-tonk, or even the rent party) from that of a purification ritual to a fertility ritual! A juke joint, honky-tonk, or any blues dive is a good-time place, and I've never seen, heard, or heard of a blues musician who was not primarily interested in making the good times roll.

Anyway, to me blues music is an aesthetic device of confrontation and improvisation, an existential device or vehicle for coping with the ever-changing fortunes of human existence, in a word *entropy*, the tendency of everything to become formless. Which is also to say that such music is a device for confronting and acknowledging the harsh fact that the human situation (*the human situation as such*) is always awesome and all too often awful. The blues lyric never lets you forget that.

And yet the blues statement is neither a matter of commiseration nor of protestation as such. According to Kenneth Burke's book *Attitudes Toward History*, aesthetic statement falls into one or the other of two rhetorical frames of reference. On the one hand, there is a frame of *rejection* within which the basic statement is that life should not be a matter of tribulation. Hence the plaint, the complaint, the protestation, the grotesque, the burlesque, the satire, the caricature, the elegy, and so on. But on the other hand there is the frame of *acceptance* of the obvious fact that life is always a struggle against destructive forces and elements whether seen or unseen. Thus the aesthetic statement takes the form of the ode, the hymn of praise, the epic, the tragedy (of noble defeat), the comedy (of insightful resolution), the melodrama (of resolution through effective engineering); and then there is farce, which is where I place the blues and jazz because such music presents life as a matter of perpetual readjustment and improvisation.

Such is the context within which I place my blues-derived literary statement. When Scooter, the protagonist of *Train Whistle Guitar*, *The Spyglass Tree*, and *The Seven League Boots*, says "My name is Jack the Rabbit because I was bred and born and brought up in the briarpatch," he is speaking in terms of the idiomatic particulars of a brownskin boy from Alabama, but his actions should add up to the anecdotes that represent the basic ancestral American outlook on what life is all about.

As a frame of acceptance the blues as literary statement also functions in terms of the dynamics of *antagonistic cooperation*! In a blues composition or anecdote, a key structural device is the *break*, a cessation of the established rhythm and tempo which jazz musicians regard and respond to not as a detrimental or trauma-inducing disruption not unlike the abrupt intrusion of the villain or some other personification of disaster, but rather as an opportunity to exercise their personal best.

What makes the Alabama jackrabbit so nimble, so resilient, so elegantly resourceful? The briarpatch!

Context and Definition

AT MOBILE COUNTY TRAINING SCHOOL on the outskirts of Mobile, Alabama, where I was a high school junior in the spring of 1934, you had to compose, memorize, and deliver an essay in the annual juniors' oratorical contest, a major event of the commencement season, of greater importance and only slightly less popular than the annual junior-senior prom. It was an occasion when next year's seniors not only showed their promise but also began their competition for college scholarship grants, without which during those stark days of the Depression many of the most promising among us would not have been able to go to college.

It was while collecting materials in preparation for my oration that I came across a poem by one Langston Hughes. It was in an anthology of writings from the so-called Harlem Renaissance entitled *The New Negro*, edited by Alain Locke. The poem was called "Youth," and not only did I memorize it and use it as the outchorus for my statement, I also appropriated the title of Alain Locke's anthology as the theme and title of my presentation.

Well, Langston's poem didn't win the juniors' oratorical contest for me. But along with Locke's theme it did lead the sponsors to choose me as the lead-off speaker, which meant that faculty support for my college scholarship grant status was already very strong indeed.

I can't say that Langston Hughes or anybody else from the so-called Harlem Renaissance as such inspired me to be a writer. Once I got to college and became involved with literature as existential equipment for living rather than as academic exercises and ceremonial-recitation fluff stuff, nothing in *The New Negro* struck me as being in the same league as such world-class twentieth-century writers as James Joyce, Thomas

Originally written upon receiving the Langston Hughes Medal at City College, New York, in 1997, pages 722–23 were expanded to the present statement in response to receiving the Clarence Cason Medal for Distinguished Nonfiction Writing at the University of Alabama in 2001.

Mann, Marcel Proust, André Malraux, Ernest Hemingway, William Faulkner, T. S. Eliot, W. B. Yeats, and Ezra Pound, among others. Which is to say there was nothing from my idiomatic American context in literature that was comparable to what Jack Johnson, Joe Gans, Sam Langford, and the up-and-coming young Joe Louis represented as world-class prizefighters, or Eddie Tolan, Ralph Metcalfe, and Jesse Owens as Olympic-class track stars; nor was there any question in my mind that segregation kept Satchel Paige and Josh Gibson from being unsurpassed in the world of baseball. And that Louis Armstrong and Duke Ellington represented the very best that America had to offer in music went without saying. In other words, segregation was no excuse.

The point here is that, taking my cue from the world-class aesthetic, sophistication, and profundity of Armstrong, Jelly Roll Morton, Ellington, Basie, Lester Young, Dizzy Gillespie, Charlie Parker, and other definitive masters of what I refer to as the blues idiom (the ultimate extension, elaboration, and refinement of which is jazz), I decided that I would try to produce a literary equivalent of the world-class fine art music that they had processed from the idiomatic particulars of my most immediate and intimate American context.

You, of course, know that the ambition to produce world-class literature involves the matter of processing or stylizing idiomatic folk and pop particulars, which is to say extending, elaborating, and refining folk and pop material up to the level of fine art. Thus the jazz musicians that I am forever referring to were indispensable to me as an apprentice writer because what they did was develop the technique and sophistication necessary to transform folk and pop music into aesthetic statement that qualified as fine art and that has had the universal appeal, impact, profundity, and endurance of fine art.

As for my personal existential and literary point of view, the main thing is not some putative subtext that some academics seek out as if the writer has either hidden it or really doesn't know that it is there. The indispensable thing is the rhetorical context, the basic frame of reference that conditions the nature of the aesthetic statement that one's stylization of actuality adds up to.

My basic working assumption is that all literary statements

fall into one or the other of two categories or frames of reference that represent two opposite attitudes toward experience
or the circumstances of human existence: (1) the frame of acceptance or (2) the frame of rejection. These attitudes condition literary responses.

In other words, you can either accept the harsh facts of life
and do what you can to counteract or ameliorate them, such as
what has been done to counteract bad weather. Or you can cry
and shiver and feel sorry for yourself. Thus, on the one hand
you have the literary image-statement of the questing and
conquesting storybook hero who is still a hero and merits celebration even when he fails. Hence the epic, tragedy, comedy,
melodrama, and farce. Whereas on the other hand what you
have is the lamenting, protesting, perpetually pissed-off rebel
who *rejects* the all too obvious fact that life is not always fair,
weatherwise or otherwise, and who sees himself not as a potential self-made hero but as a victim of foul play!

All of my books are about the basis and possibilities of heroic
action that are endemic to life in the United States in our time.
That is why the name of my storybook hero in *Train Whistle
Guitar*, *The Spyglass Tree*, and *The Seven League Boots* is Scooter
and why he refers to himself as Jack the Rabbit and says that he
was bred, born, and raised in the briarpatch and realizes that
his possibilities of survival, not to mention achievement, are
predicated on his perpetual nimbleness, which means that he
must always be ready to swing as if he were a competent jazz
musician in the ever unpredictable circumstances of a jam session and also always be ready to riff or improvise on the break.

In the early-twentieth-century Viennese mythology of Sigmund Freud and others, the break may well have been regarded as a sudden disruption in the established cadence, the
effect of which was very likely to be shocking, traumatic, and
even disabling. In American legend, however, although the
break is a matter of jeopardy, it is also regarded as a matter of
opportunity. In the blues idiom it is also the moment of truth
and of proof!

And now, one more bit of signifying about Scooter as Brer
Rabbit in the complexities of the contemporary American
briarpatch. The one thing that faked Brer Rabbit out was a
phony image of his people! What I see when I look at social

science surveys and profiles of "my people" (which is to say, my idiomatic American relatives) is a bunch of social science fiction tar babies!

Down-home boy that I am, I have never been so unhip, so unbelievably square, as to mistake a tar baby for the me I think I should be, certainly not because some social science head-counting racial one-upman decides that a tar baby stands for all rabbits.

My rabbit, it turns out, is not literally the same as the one that old Uncle Remus used to tell the little bright-eyed boy over in Georgia about. My rabbit is the Alabama jackrabbit version of the one that Duke Ellington had in mind when he orchestrated the concerto for tenor saxophone entitled "Cotton Tail."

When I graduated from Tuskegee in 1939, it was as if the sound-track of the world of adult adventure that I was finally entering on my own authority was Count Basie's "Doggin' Around," a Kansas City 4/4 stomp number that may well have been a variation on an earlier shout tune entitled "Messin' Around" ("All over Town!") recorded by Trixie Smith and Freddie Keppard back in the 1920s. What was so profoundly impressive to me about this particular version of it was the elegant ease of each solo instrumentalist, who not only coped with the pressure of the band's up-tempo environment but also established and maintained his own distinctive individuality at the same time. Every time I remember the challenges of the uncertainties I faced that summer after college as I waited to find out what my first job offer was going to be, I also remember that old ten-inch, 78-rpm recording on the other side of which was a very melancholy instrumental torch tune entitled "Blue and Sentimental." I wondered if I would ever be able to respond to the pressures and requirements of the twentieth-century world at large as if dancing to Count Basie's "Doggin' Around."

That was in 1939. Then in 1940 came Duke Ellington's "Cotton Tail." I had been personalizing Ellington's music since 1927 when I was eleven years old, and my most intimate play-mate and I realized that we could do our notorious, sporty limp walk to Ellington's "Birmingham Breakdown" with the same sneaky cuteness with which we were already doing it to old Jelly Roll Morton's "Kansas City Stomp."

Between elementary school and college there were Ellington's "Rockin' in Rhythm," "It Don't Mean a Thing if It Ain't Got That Swing," "Daybreak Express," and "Harlem Speaks." And among those from that next four years that have meant most to me were "Diminuendo and Crescendo in Blue," "Tootin' Through the Roof," "Chatterbox," "Braggin' in Brass," "Boy Meets Horn," and "Ridin' on a Blue Note."

Count Basie's "Doggin' Around" provided me with the soundtrack that I needed for 1939. But it was Ellington's "Cotton Tail" that was a specific source for the metaphor of the nimble-or-nothing Alabama jackrabbit in the briarpatch, evoking tell-me-tale times around the fireplace in that shotgun-style quarters house on the outskirts of Mobile down off the Gulf Coast that was to become the idiomatic basis for my literary approach to American character, procedure, and heroic achievement.

In her *American Humor: A Study of the National Character*, Constance Rourke, a number of whose essays on the same subject were published posthumously as *The Roots of American Culture*, wrote about the ingenious Yankee, the adventurous frontiersman, and the adaptable Negro as a definitive mythic trio that provided *emblems for a pioneer people who require resilience as a prime trait*, resilience that is geared to spontaneous exploration, experimentation, inventiveness, and perpetual readjustment.

The challenge for me, as an apprentice of literature as a fine art, has been how to process local and regional folk or peasant (including illiterate) material beyond the limitations of the provincial and beyond the platitudes of pop fare and achieve the universal appeal and status of fine art. This requires the most reliable insight into the nature of human nature, the most basic appreciation of the complexity of our national imperatives, and the most refined mastery of the means of literary composition available.

What the valid, reliable, and comprehensive literary image should add up to is that which Kenneth Burke in *Attitudes Toward History* called the representative anecdote, a symbolic representation of survival and achievement. So far, what I've been able to do with the image of the Alabama jackrabbit in the briarpatch is to be found in *Train Whistle Guitar, The*

Spyglass Tree, and *The Seven League Boots*, which have no less to do with the rituals underlying the adventures of Tom Sawyer and Huckleberry Finn, for instance, than with "Doggin' Around," "Cotton Tail," or "C-Jam Blues." In fact, Scooter may even be thought of as Huck Finn's friend Jim's great-grandson.

Academic Lead Sheet

WHAT I HAVE PREPARED for this extremely important occasion is not a formal address, but rather an outline for some not quite solemn but altogether ceremonial remarks, to which I hope you will respond as if to such ever so avuncular advice as comes from the fire circle of the elders of your tribe, among whom I must say I am more than somewhat astonished to find myself.

Or if you prefer a somewhat less anthropological and more idiomatic analogy, I would be no less pleased to have you respond as your grandparents did to what they heard and overheard from the grownups around the firesides in the old down-home cabins of yesteryear during those evenings when so much hard-bought wisdom was imparted along with the very stuff of such ambition as brings us all here today.

And, to be sure, there is always all of that ever so offhand signifying that I myself was so privileged to grow up hearing and overhearing in the barbershops and on the general merchandise store stoop benches during the days of my coming of age on the outskirts of Mobile, Alabama. Such barbershops and storefront benches as were the hangouts of such legendary uncles as Uncle Bud, Uncle Doc, Uncle Ned, and Uncle Remus, among others.

In other words, the brief notes that I have jotted down for this talk are not an outline for formal pontification but are somewhat like a minimal lead sheet for a bit of riff style signifying such as may be associated with what comes from the piano in a jazz performance. Not such consummate statements as come from such fabulous keyboard soloists as, say, Art Tatum, Teddy Wilson, Earl Hines, and Bud Powell, to be sure, but rather from such suggestive vamping and comping as were used by such peerless keyboard masters as Duke Ellington and Count Basie to provide the contexts within which individual

This essay is based on an address given on January 20, 1978, at the Howard University Honors Convocation.

sidemen in their orchestras not only established but also developed their individual identities.

Nor, by the way, did even such super soloists as Johnny Hodges, Ben Webster, Cootie Williams, Lester Young, Dicky Wells, and Harry Edison misconstrue Ellington's and Basie's background setups as launching pads for ego trips. On the contrary, each of their most distinctive individual solos represented an indispensable dimension of the overall ensemble statement.

In other words, I come before you on this occasion as a sort of academic equivalent to a vamping and comping piano player in what amounts to an intellectual jam session in which your responses are no less real for not being heard. Indeed I hope that the solos, ensembles, arrangements, and orchestrations that my contextual vamps, comp chords, and progressions suggest will speak or sing or swing louder than any actual vocal or instrumental voicings ever can.

End of vamp. First chorus: This is the occasion on which the school officials celebrate the good students, the successful students. We are assembled here today to acknowledge and celebrate pupils whom special members of the faculty have selected as those whose academic performance qualifies them to be candidates to take on the indispensable responsibilities of being the elite of the generation now coming of age. Elite. Yes, elite. And again elite. Don't allow yourselves to be faked out by epithets. If elitism bothers you, substitute the word specialist and get on with the mission.

Can any group, based on whatever distinction, even survive, let alone develop and fulfill itself (to say nothing of transcending itself), without the benefit of its own elite corps of highly competent and dedicated intellectual, professional, and technical specialists? Obviously such an elite was what W. E. B. Du Bois had in mind when he advocated the development of what he called the Talented Tenth. Nor were Booker T. Washington's agricultural, technical, and normal school missionaries expected to add up to anything less than an even larger elite corps that was to include the big moneymakers.

The function of the elite is to provide the rest of society with equipment for living which is commensurate with the complexity and possibilities of the time in which they live. You have to be specialists in order to do that. And we hope that at least some of you are also geniuses. And you know something? If all the students of this institution were assembled here because they have grade point averages that qualify them as outstanding achievers, that would not be enough.

Indeed if all Americans were fully educated, technologically proficient, and productive, mankind in the world at large would still be in trouble. Perhaps it would be somewhat better off, to be sure, but the need for a continuous input of dedicated special achievers would be no less urgent.

And yet there are those who give a very strong impression that dropouts and self-reformed or cult-redeemed ex-cons who opt for the authority and responsibility of the elite can contend successfully with outstanding graduates from such world-class centers of precision and comprehensiveness as Heidelberg, Oxford, Cambridge, the Sorbonne, Harvard, Yale, Princeton, MIT, Caltech, and so on.

But certainly nobody on this campus is going to fall for such an unhip line of jive. Certainly everybody in this academic gathering knows enough about what "street smarts" is about —to know that street hip is not about such mathematical calculations as add up to space technology or computer science. Nor does the jive lingo of the street-corner hangout add up to the linguistic prerequisite to understanding anthropology, archaeology, or even the plain old ancient, medieval, and modern history and geopolitics underlying foreign policy. And so forth and so on, you get the point.

That was about leadership. But what kind of leadership? The big thing these days seems to be revolutionary leadership. So a quick segue to another matter that our most promising students should be alert to. Everywhere you go these days you find a significant number of students who seem to want to be regarded as revolutionary above everything else. But many confuse revolution with rebellion. Which is sometimes only a matter of rejecting or even destroying established procedures and institutions. But the primary concern of revolution is not destruction but the creation of better procedures and institutions. All too often being a rebel means only that you're against something. Whereas being a revolutionary should mean that you are *against* something because you are *for* something better. Indeed, primarily because you're for something better.

But the special fireside-and-barbershop-derived piano riff on revolutionary leadership that I wish to suggest is that, in contrast to many of the news media and storybook revolutionary heroes who often began with the problem of rejecting the conventional values of their forebears, the good American student from our ethnic and idiomatic background has only to try to prepare to become the living answer to the old folks' prayers.

The rebellion part, as rugged as it may get to be from time to time, is only incidental. It is the revolutionary change that counts. And all we have to do in order to contribute our part to achieving that is what our American, repeat American, grandparents and great-grandparents wanted their heirs to do. Everybody on this campus is the descendant of forebears who hoped and prayed that you would be outstanding students. What could be more subversive in the United States! And yet all that even the most activist of our antebellum ancestors wanted was the fulfillment of the promise inherent in the Constitution of the United States of America.

Which brings us back to the function of the elite. My concern here is not with the certified professions, the doctors, lawyers, scientists, engineers, and so on. My immediate concern is with the intellectuals and the artists. For it is they who provide the context for the so-called spokesmen and civic leaders (self- or otherwise elected). The function of the artist is to create images or the musical equivalents thereof that are commensurate with the complexities and the possibilities of life in our time. Whereas the intellectual or so-called thinking person has a responsibility to formulate questions, issues, and definitions that adequately reflect the problems of the times and thus form a basis that adequate specialized technicians can build on.

So our intellectuals must try to be sure that they are defining problems and issues in the most comprehensive terms. The intellectual's very first step should represent an effort to approach life in universal terms. Sentimental provincialism is out! Your ambition should be to become as cosmopolitan as possible. Now, you reach the universal or the cosmopolitan through the particular. So obviously you do not have to abandon your idiomatic roots. Indeed the more you dig down into yourself and deal with your personal problems against the richest possible background (and thus in the broadest context), the more universal the implications of your most casual personal gesture is likely to become.

I submit that as a responsible intellectual you proceed in terms of extension (as well as elaboration and refinement) and also counterstatement. You extend, elaborate, and refine that which you test and judge to be adequate, the objective being to give it its greatest precision and effectiveness. On the other hand, you counterstate that which you judge to be inadequate, unproductive, or counterproductive or which violates your sense of life in some way. Here, incidentally, is where the element of protest comes in.

You reject that which is unproductive or counterproductive. But you don't reduce everything to rejection and rebellion, because the whole idea of life, which is to say the process of living or continuing to exist, is affirmation. The whole idea of education is to find the terms and meanings that make fruitful continuity possible.

Protest is something that you must always be extremely careful about, because it can degenerate so easily into the self-righteousness of those who regard themselves as victims rather than people of potential and thus become more emotional than insightful and corrective. Militant rhetoric is not enough. And besides, it doesn't require the high grade point average that the truly qualified leader must earn. What with the news media being as they are these days, any street-corner jive artist can bring it off.

So where do I myself as a writer fit into all of this? Well, speaking of the need for the most comprehensive frame of reference that a literary intellectual and would-be pragmatic image-maker might suggest for coming to terms with the imperatives of the human proposition in a contemporary world, the most impressive device I've come across so far is very idiomatic indeed. It is the blues idiom, which I have come to regard as being the basic part of the existential equipment that we Americans inherited from our captive ancestors.

Many people seem to think that all the slaves left us was a

legacy of misery. I don't agree. They also endowed us with an attitude toward life that the blues idiom embodies. Which is in essence a disposition of affirmation of continuity in the face of adversity. The basic dynamics of the blues idiom are predicated upon confrontation or acknowledgment of the harsh facts of life. The fact that not only is one's personal plight sometimes pretty awful and unpromising, but also that life itself often looks like a low-down dirty shame that shouldn't happen to any creature imaginable. The blues require you to confront chaos as a fact of life and improvise on the exigencies of the situation, however dire, on the opportunities or the options that are also always there.

I've come to believe that the blues idiom provides the basis for a more comprehensive context for literary statement than any of the masterpieces in the anthology of world literature. As I have pointed out in my book *The Hero and the Blues*, it is a context which enables one to deal with the tragic, comic, melodramatic, and farcical dimensions of existence simultaneously. In the fully orchestrated blues statement, even as the tragic tale of woe (and blues lyrics are almost always negative) is being spieled by the soloist, it is being counterstated by the instruments—and not just with determination, but sometimes with bawdiness, sometimes insouciance, sometimes just devilishly, sometimes with nonsense or just plain old foolishness, but also always with a lot of elegance.

Because it turns out that a definitive characteristic of the descendants of American slaves is an orientation to elegance, the disposition (in the face of all of the misery and uncertainty in the universe) to refine all of human action in a direction of dance-beat elegance. I submit that there is nothing that anybody in the world has ever done that is more civilized or sophisticated than to dance elegantly, which is to state with your total physical being an affirmative attitude toward the sheer fact of existence. Talking about getting with it. Swinging the blues is something *else*!

So now for an outchorus of sorts. It seems to me that the legacy that I refer to as the blues idiom offers many crucial opportunities for good students who would really deal with the problems not only of one special group of people in contemporary America but of mankind in the world at large. One little example: you all know about that big concept of disjuncture as being trauma-producing and disintegrating that is so basic to contemporary psychology and psychiatry (or what I call Viennese mythology)! Well, in the blues idiom no less is made of the necessity to establish a form, a rhythm, a cadence, and a meaningful direction, the absence of which makes for that discombobulation that is precisely the effect also known as being blue or having the blues.

But in a blues performance there is also a very deliberate and indispensable disjuncture which, however, is not regarded as a crisis. It is called a break, and it has a double meaning. It is a disruption but it is also an opportunity. It is a moment of high jeopardy to be sure. But it is at the very same time a moment of truth, the moment in which your response defines your personal quality and identity.

The break is the very thing that every American worthy of the name is supposed to make preparations to take advantage of. And what that requires is precisely the same orientation to such ongoing improvisation as sustained the early American explorers, pioneers, frontiersmen, and homesteaders. In a word, perpetual creativity!

Or to put it another way, a musical break peculiar to the blues is a stylization or aesthetic statement that represents a basic American attitude toward experience or outlook on life. To this end it not only conditions one to regard disjuncture as a normal expectation but also should develop the resilience that facilitates improvisation. Incidentally, the disposition and proficiency required of the improvising blues musician and that required for scientific experimentation is not as different as many people might think.

There is a problem of disjuncture and there is also the problem of the rootlessness that is such an obvious and widespread result of twentieth-century technological innovations. Homesteads, for example, do not mean what they used to mean. Bulldozers wipe them out in no time at all. Homesteads, hometowns, and many other traditional landmarks as well.

As rootless as the pioneers or even the captive Africans were, contemporary mankind in the world at large may well be in a predicament that is basically worse. Naming all of your ethnic ancestors all the way back to Ham or even Adam and Eve is not likely to do very much to help you cope with contemporary instability nearly so well as a blues-conditioned disposition to remain perpetually resilient and alert to the ongoing need for improvisation.

The ancestors that are likely to be most useful to students in our time are those to whom, regardless of their ethnicity, honor students are required to relate themselves in the established courses in the great universities. I submit that the greatest challenge to the good student of our time is to learn as much as you can from the documented experiential data that has come down to us through the ages and then continue to look for something better.

PART II

The Creative Process

Art as Such

THE FOLLOWING REMARKS are based on the assumption that there is no such thing as *applied* art. Art does what it does on its own terms or it is not art. Art should not be confused with propaganda, advertisement, ideology, or hype of any kind. These remarks are concerned with the primordial nature and function of aesthetic endeavor, and thus they are about what any work of art can reasonably be expected to represent.

Nor should this be confused with the old so-called ivory tower notion of art for art's sake. On the contrary, the primary emphasis here is on art, which is to say aesthetic statement, as fundamental equipment for existence on human terms. The primary concern of art is not with beauty per se, as many people seem to think, but with the quality of human consciousness.

Thus these remarks are geared to a very pragmatic conception and approach to art. So are all of the books that I have published as a student of cultural dynamics and as an apprentice of the creative process. And so are the two works in progress. Naturally I hope that what follows will add up to a useful reiteration of essential definitions and the indispensable objectives that are crucial to all decisions about artistic undertakings of any kind.

I also hope you will agree that a conference of artists, arts administrators, board members of arts organizations, educators, public officials, and other interested people is a most appropriate audience for the review and reiteration I have in mind. After all, who, for instance, could possibly be more disturbed by the threat that the pressure to be politically correct represents to the ambitions of serious artists who accept the challenge that the great world classics embody?

Nor, by the way, does it help matters in the least that the

Keynote address at the Alabama State Council on the Arts Statewide Arts Conference at Perdido Beach, February 17, 1994.

pressure and restrictions of political correctness are being exerted in the guise of well-intentioned permissiveness in the interests of what our current crop of do-gooders think of as the empowerment of the downtrodden. Why should anybody's efforts to equate inaccuracy and mediocrity with excellence be indulged?

I submit that such questions are directly related to the policies, proposals, requests, and programs that councils on the arts have to consider every day. In any case, I hope you will agree that a review of fundamental definitions and assumptions is always useful, even to master craftsmen.

Not that I really expect to do justice to the issue in the format of an after-dinner talk. After all, I usually deal with such matters in semester-length university seminars. But you can always supplement what I am saying here by reading *The Hero and the Blues*, which is about literature, and *Stomping the Blues*, which is about music, and also *The Omni-Americans*, which is about the inadequacy of images based on social science theory and categories rather than precise insight and hard-earned wisdom.

In any case, point one: Art as such is a means by which the raw materials of human experience are processed into aesthetic statement. In this instance, to process is to stylize. So the work of art is stylization become statement, *aesthetic statement*. That is the objective of the creative process. And one assumes that it is also the sole objective of all grants from councils on the arts, since grants for other kinds of statements are funded by other councils and agencies.

What a work of art represents, which is to say re-*presents*, presents again, reenacts, reproduces, recalls, is not actuality per se, no matter how vivid the evocation of concrete detail, but rather how the artist feels about something. Indeed literal facts and figures are only incidental to a work of art. After all, given adequate stylization, fantasy and deliberate distortion will work just as well. Let us not forget that fables and fairy tales are as believable as naturalistic novels, precisely documented movies, and news-oriented television.

According to Susanne K. Langer, what art as such really records is the life of human feeling, how it feels to be a human being in this or that situation. Hence the feeling tones represented by tragedy, melodrama, and farce. And Kenneth Burke suggests that art is really a stylization of a basic attitude toward human existence. Hence expressive forms that condition people to accept the necessity for persistent struggle, on the one hand, and forms on the other hand that lament and protest human predicament. Incidentally, those who accept the necessity for struggle are also given to forms for the celebration of courage before danger, gallantry in defeat, and also forms for rejoicing in victory.

Another definition. Works of art are the product of an elegant extension, elaboration, and refinement of rituals that re-enact the basic (and thus definitive) survival technology of people in a given time, place, and circumstance. Which is why the main concern of art is the quality of human consciousness. Thus, it is also fundamental existential equipment in that it not only provides emblems of a basic attitude toward experience but also conditions and disposes people to behave in accordance with a given lifestyle (or survival technology!).

Which brings us to a brief natural history of aesthetic statement as such. First there is ritual, the ceremonial reenactment of the basic survival technology. Rituals enable anthropologists to define the basic occupations and security measures and thus also the characteristic orientation, mindset, or *preoccupations* of any given social configuration, whether tribal, regional, or national. Primal rituals include ceremonial reenactments of hunting, fishing, sowing, tilling, and harvesting, and warfare as well as continuity through purification and fertility.

Ritual reenactment supervised by a priesthood becomes religion, which also generates its own specific internal ceremonies of devotion and propitiation, which I mention only in passing along with magic, which is another kind of ceremonial reenactment.

In addition to religion and magic there is also the no less aboriginal matter of *playful* reenactment, which we refer to as recreation, and which indeed is literally a matter of re-creation, re-presentation, and re-producing. Thus the essential character or disposition of a nation as well as a tribe may be discerned in its games and toys.

But the key point of this brief natural history is that it is from the playful reenactment of primal ritual that art as such is most directly derived. I submit that not to understand this is to miss the very basis of aesthetic evaluation and critical judgment.

As you know, some play activities are restricted by rules and regulations, and some are also supervised by umpires and referees and judges, and some are not. But you also know, even the most closed codified play activity permits personal options from which not only individual expression but also individual improvisation, stylization, and elegance emerge. And it is the extension, elaboration, and refinement of such option-taking that adds up to the aesthetic statement that is a work of art. Which is to say, a product of elegant artifice.

A few more words about the role of play in the creative process. There are, according to Roger Caillois in *Man, Play, and Games*, four categories of play activity and two directions of playful effort. The categories are competition, chance, make-believe, and vertigo. And playful effort may be just a matter of fooling around, on the one hand, or a matter of gratuitously increasing the difficulty of execution on the other. This aspect of playful reenactment is obviously a key source of the extension, elaboration, and refinement that adds up to works of art.

So now a few words about the relative level of sophistication of technique and sensibility involved in the creative process. What this results in are three levels of achievement: folk art, pop fare, and fine art.

Folk art should not be confused with primitive art, although some visual arts commentaries refer to it as modern primitive. *To the extent that primitive artifacts are perceived as art rather than as ceremonial fetishes, they are neither folk art nor pop fare but fine art, because they are the handiwork of the most sophisticated skill in the culture of their origin.*

Folk art is the output of the least refined skill and the least precise information and the least subtle sensibility in a culture that is also capable of producing pop fare and fine art. It may be genuine and also deeply moving, but even so it is also likely to have a more limited range of appeal than pop fare or fine art. Which is not to say that it is emotionally less authentic than pop fare. It is, on the contrary, a more honest representation than pop fare, which is, after all, often given to gimmickry, cliché, cheap sentimentality, and downright vulgarity.

Yet the range and skill involved in pop-level stylization are such that it may include elements that are not only crude but also illiterate, along with devices expertly appropriated from the most highly calibrated levels of fine art. A major shortcoming of pop fare is shallowness and the rapidity with which most of it goes out of fashion.

Which brings us to fine art. Being the ultimate extension, elaboration, and refinement of the most representative images, anecdotes, and soundtracks, it may be sometimes less immediately accessible than folk art in its native province or pop fare in the world at large. But is it not precisely the function of courses in art appreciation to make fine art accessible? The very first obligation of critical briefings and reviews is to mediate between the uninitiated audiences, viewers, or readers and the work of art.

The purpose of reviewing these distinctions in degrees of sophistication involved in stylization is to remind you of the role that taste plays in all aesthetic matters. How can you make any truly useful decision about the arts if you are deficient in your perception of nuance or indifferent to propriety? Now, I am very keenly aware of the fact that many of our fellow Americans become somewhat uneasy, if not embarrassingly defensive, at the mere mention of aesthetic taste.

But taste in the arts is pretty much the same as it is in the kitchen and the dining room. It is the sense of the optimum proportion and processing of the ingredients required by a given recipe. In the arts taste begins with your sensitivity to the nuances of a given process of stylization being such that you would not confuse folk art, pop fare, and fine art. Each has its place. But it is fine art from which come the masterpieces that add up to the classic examples that make up the universal anthology, the worldwide repertory, the museum without walls that underlies our most comprehensive conception of human potential or indeed the human proposition.

If any of this sounds the least bit elitist to any of you, ask yourself if you really prefer anything but the most competent craftsmen, doctors, dentists, lawyers, teachers, or even servants, etc. Most people obviously prefer all-star quality over mediocrity in sports. Why not in the arts?

Riffing at Mrs. Jack's Place

EYE OF THE BEHOLDER. Eye of the beholder. Eye of the beholder, indeed. And never forget that point of view is synonymous with angle of vision, which also involves depth of field and sharpness of focus.

And as Mrs. Isabella Stewart Gardner obviously assumed, so is perception geared to apperception, that process of understanding and appreciation through which the newly observed qualities of an object are related to past experience. For certainly she was concerned with the background of the beholder: what the observer brings to the object on view, that which makes for the context of the onlooker's interaction with it.

Incidentally, there is convincing evidence that Mrs. Gardner was concerned not only with what her collection could add to the background that her fellow Americans would bring to the certified masterworks of Europe, she was also providing levels of aesthetic excellence by which Americans could measure their own efforts to create fine art from the raw materials of their native environment.

In other words, for all the intimidation it may have evoked from many upper-class, middle-class, and lower-class Bostonians alike, this Venetian palace was not built to insulate an ever so effete Mrs. Gardner from the crude actualities of everyday life in the still ever so frontierlike ruggedness of the United States at the turn of the century. For certainly hard-bargaining, hands-on Mrs. Jack Gardner was too hip not to know that the now magnificent Italians of the now hallowed Renaissance were themselves products of the extension, elaboration, and refinement of the barbarians of Europe of the Dark and Middle Ages.

Which is not to imply that she herself was as keenly, profoundly, and comprehensively aware of the dynamics of the evolution of a national character and its stylization in the fine arts as Constance Rourke (author of *American Humor: A Study of the National Character*, 1931) was to become within less than a decade of Mrs. Gardner's demise. But it most certainly is meant to insist that she was a very fundamental part of the natural history suggested by Constance Rourke, as well as John A. Kouwenhoven's notion of the effects of the interaction of imported learned traditions or practices with vernacular or homespun methods in the context of the pragmatic improvisation required of a pioneer people such as Americans still are.

Van Wyck Brooks pointed out that for all her discriminating taste and her unimpeachable collection, Mrs. Jack saw "Giorgione's finest points as she saw the virtues of Whistler and Sargent who blazed like meteors over the world of fashion. But she did not see the Yankee Giorgiones," by whom he meant Maurice Prendergast, Winslow Homer, and Albert Ryder. But even so, Fenway Court, like the Boston Museum of Fine Arts, the Metropolitan Museum of Art in New York, and countless others, has always been and continues to be an indispensable element in the development of the high level of aesthetic sensibility that American artists have achieved in the twentieth century.

Because for all its palatial walls of thoroughly convincing Old World patina on which hang some of the finest European art in the Western Hemisphere, Mrs. Jack's Eyetalian Palace also functions as a part of what has been called the museum without walls, what in effect is an imaginary universal museum that all the art in the world adds up to, a sort of visual equivalent of a *bibliothèque pléiade*, a worldwide anthology of literature. The creative impulse, after all, as André Malraux has pointed out, is at least as much a response to other aesthetic statements as it is to raw experience. In other words, art derives from other art.

Along with the obvious implications of all this for the specialist in the arts, there is also the no less obvious fact that twentieth-century innovations in and refinements of communication and transportation facilities have made even the most sedentary Americans nothing less than citizens of the world at large in spite of themselves. Indeed, the world at large impinges on the sensibilities of average Americans as it does on no other general populace elsewhere on the contemporary globe. Nor should the fact that this impingement includes an ever-increasing influx of immigrants from pretty nearly everywhere be overlooked.

Because of all of this, it is not only possible but also

obviously necessary for a contemporary American's conception of aesthetic statement to be more and more comprehensive, even more and certainly no less comprehensive than that of the most sophisticated elite of the British and French empires in their heyday. The characterization of "heiress of all the ages" that Henry James applied to the heroine of *Daisy Miller*, Milly Theale of *The Wings of the Dove*, and Maggie Verver of *The Golden Bowl* not only applied to his friend Mrs. Isabella Stewart Gardner as well but to all contemporary Americans.

And now for a few hard-driving choruses about the nature and function of aesthetic statement as such, which after all is what is really under consideration here. For what is artistic creation if not the means by which raw or actual experience is processed, by which is meant stylized, into aesthetic statement? An aesthetic statement which in effect is an *elegant* statement is precisely what all works of art are intended to be. Thus painting and sculpture are visual statements even as literature is verbal statement, and a piece of music is statement made with sound and rhythm, and so on. In any case, art appreciation is a matter of decoding the stylized statement, which is made in the terminology peculiar to the medium in which the artist works.

Also it should be remembered that a statement may be either denotative or connotative. A denotative statement is meant to be taken literally. Its aim is a precise representation of actuality. The ultimate in denotation is scientific terminology. A connotative statement is primarily evocative and may actually be deliberately ambiguous, figuratively symbolic, ironic, hyperbolic, and so on, in a word, poetic.

Furthermore, art, being stylized statement, is of its very nature connotative rather than denotative; hence figures of speech and devices of sound in literary statement and devices of rhythm, melody, harmony, and tone color in music, and so on. In all events, the primary objective of aesthetic statement is not literal documentation as such, but rather the equivalent of the representative anecdote in literature. It is thus a record not of facts as such, but of the emotional response of a given sensibility. It is a stylized statement of an emotional response to an experience which in itself may be either real or imagined. Which is why we look at a visual statement and identify it as a

Botticelli, Bellini, or Raphael, or call a literary statement Shakespeare, Goethe, Thomas Mann, James, Joyce, Hemingway, Faulkner, and so on. And a piece of music as Bach, Mozart, Beethoven, Stravinsky, Armstrong, Basie, Ellington, or Charlie Parker.

On the other hand, the more denotative the statement, which is to say the more literal the documentation, the greater the risk that the result will belong to the category of genre rather than becoming a representative anecdote and thus a vehicle for conveying such profound insights into the universal ambiguities and contradictions of the human situation as do totally unrealistic fables and fairy tales. Genre is about what something is like and thus may even be a stylization of the obvious and may actually be intended as a commonplace illustration.

The representative anecdote, on the other hand, is about possible implications and thus may be deliberately ambiguous, which is to say multidimensional, as stylized statements that qualify as fine art always turn out to be.

So now a few words about fine art as such. The process of stylization, or, as André Malraux would say, the creative act, proceeds on one of three levels of technological sophistication. As a result there is folk art, there is popular art fare, and there is fine art, which represent three different levels of extension, elaboration, and refinement of the basic and indeed the definitive rituals of the social or cultural configuration that is its context.

Folk art is a product of the no less serious or humorous, no less authentic but least informed and crudest aesthetic sensibility of a given social or cultural entity that is capable of producing a more widely appealing popular art that is technically more accomplished and better informed although it may also employ peasant-level naïveté and crudeness along with ever so chic devices consciously derived from fine art. Incidentally, folk art should not be confused with primitive art, as many critics and historians did for many years. For to the extent that the stylization of primitive, aboriginal, or downright primordial artifacts are viewed as art, they are not folk art but fine art because they are the product not of the lowest but rather of the most highly developed skills of stylization produced by the culture of their origin. Indeed fine art is precisely the ultimate extension, elaboration, and refinement of the fundamental rituals underlying the lifestyle survival techniques of the people, whether tribe or nation, by whom it is created.

And now for the outchorus plus a tag.

Much goes to show that the worldwide museum without walls that includes not only Fenway Court and the Boston Museum of Fine Arts across the way but the Metropolitan Museum of New York and the British Museum and the Louvre across the Atlantic, among all the rest; not only museums and galleries but also all of the art books and reproductions available here and elsewhere exist to inspire through the eye of the beholder an ever keener appreciation plus an ongoing demand for the very highest level of fine art.

Which also means multidimensional representative anecdotes, not simply the annals of the activities and incidents of a specific time and place. That would amount to provincialism even if it were the stylization of typical activities of a great metropolis. The great masterworks are about the human proposition as such, the struggle of human consciousness against chaos, the void, entropy. Yes, stylization is yet another way, the more elegant the better, of contending with entropy, of stomping the blues, which is to say, of keeping the blue devils of nada at bay.

Made in America:
The Achievement of Duke Ellington

O**N THE EVE** of the New York premiere of his Symphony no. 9 in E Minor, *From the New World*, in 1893, Antonín Dvořák stated in an interview that he was "now satisfied that the future music of this country must be founded upon what are called the Negro melodies. They must be the real foundation of any serious and original school of composition to be developed in the United States."

Dvořák had been brought over to New York from Bohemia in 1892 by one Mrs. Jeannette Thurber, the wife of a wealthy New York grocer, to help establish a national conservatory of music of America, the objective of which was to develop American composers who would follow the example of what Dvořák had done with the Slavonic folk materials of Bohemia and create music from indigenous American sources that would qualify as fine art worthy of being performed in the great concert halls along with the classics in the European canon.

What Dvořák did not point out, however, was the fact that for folk material to become a truly native fine art, it had to be extended, elaborated, and refined through the employment of devices that were also indigenous. What he either left out or failed to emphasize was the indispensable dynamics of the vernacular imperative. Those "Negro melodies" he referred to were the product not only of native folk material as such but also of a native or homegrown process, the employment of certain musical devices that were also native, if only through frontier modification of imported procedures.

Nor did Dvořák provide any example of what an original school of American composition would sound like. Certainly his *New World* Symphony was not American music. It was European music about America. It was American raw material or subject matter developed in terms of European conventions of composition. Not that any American idiom would, should, or even could be altogether different from European convention. It would be European-derived music significantly modified by conventions evolved in the Western Hemisphere.

Dvořák had heard Negro spirituals and other Negro melodies as well as the popular plantation-derived airs in the repertory of Stephen Foster to be sure, and on a visit out to Spillville, Iowa, he was impressed by various Indian melodies and chants. Moreover, between 1892 and 1894 he could also have heard ragtime tunes and cakewalk instrumentals—and perhaps also some of the new music for the fox-trot, the one-step, etc., that was beginning to replace the primacy of the waltz as the rage of popular music. Surely the composer of *Slavonic Dances* should not have missed anything so basic as that to a truly American music. Nor is it irrelevant to wonder what was or would have been his reaction to a musical element so uniquely American as syncopation.

In all events, he had returned to Europe in 1894, and he died in 1904, four years before W. C. Handy's codification of the blues put its basic structural devices in the public domain of the popular music that was to be extended, elaborated, and refined into jazz. But even so, Dvořák was prophetic enough to have declared that "in the Negro melodies of America I discover all that is needed for a great and noble school of music. They are pathetic, tender, passionate, melancholy, solemn, religious, bold, merry, gay, or what you will. It is music that suits itself to any mood or any purpose. There is nothing in the whole range of composition that cannot be supplied with themes from this source."

Among the American conservatory-oriented composers who took Dvořák's advice was William Arms Fisher, who published a book of Negro spirituals and also made an arrangement of a spiritual-derived melody from Dvořák's *New World* Symphony entitled "Going Home," which became a very popular semiclassic concert piece during the 1920s and 1930s. Another Dvořák protégé was Rubin Goldmark, who became an instructor at Mrs. Thurber's conservatory and later became the head of the Department of Composition at Juilliard from 1924 until his death in 1936. One of his best-known compositions was *A Negro Rhapsody*, and among his students at one time was George Gershwin, the composer of *Rhapsody in Blue*, Concerto in F, *An American in Paris*, and *Porgy and Bess*, who also studied with a legendary Harlem stride-style piano player and composer named Luckey Roberts. Incidentally, Gershwin's pre–*Porgy and Bess* attempt to compose a Negro folk opera was called *135th Street*, a street in Harlem.

With the exception of Gershwin, such Dvořák-inspired efforts, however, did not lead to music that was significantly more peculiar to the United States than was Dvořák's own. The subject matter was indigenous, to be sure, but the process of stylization was hardly less European than his. Indeed it was as if American musical training was primarily geared to putting American subject matter into the European canon. The concert hall status of the traditional Negro spirituals and gospel and jubilee songs was obviously enhanced by Dvořák's enthusiastic admiration, but alas even they were often Europeanized by conservatory-trained musicians. After all, European conventions of stylization were precisely what American musical training was all about.

And yet within less than a generation of Dvořák's sojourn at the American conservatory there was American music that Europeans recognized as such and that had a universal appeal that was downright infectious. And it was clearly the employment of indigenous devices of stylization that led ever so sophisticated European musicians and theorists not only to admire it but also to place it in the context of avant-garde innovation rather than of the homespun or the primitive.

Obviously the keyboard skill, nay, virtuosity, required to play the ragtime piano music of Scott Joplin, for instance, was not only beyond the level of primitive and folk musicians but also beyond the precision of conservatory-trained musicians in America and Europe alike, who were very hard put indeed to reproduce the subtleties of its idiomatic nuances even after careful study and rehearsal of the scores, and the piano rolls of American musicians.

On the other hand, in the American musical context in which Duke Ellington grew up and formulated his vocational and professional objectives, the technical nuances of ragtime or Harlem stride piano were among the earliest challenges one had to learn to cope with, and as for the "Negro melodies" that so captivated Dvořák, they were as much a part of his everyday musical environment as were the idioms of everyday discourse.

Duke Ellington, né Edward Kennedy Ellington, the musician who was to become the composer who would process or

stylize, which is to say extend, elaborate, and refine, more indigenous American raw material into universally appealing fine
art by means of idiomatic devices than any other, was born in
Washington, D.C., on April 29, 1899, six years after Dvořák's
pronouncement preliminary to the premiere of the *New World*
Symphony.

So in addition to the intricacies of ragtime keyboard technique as such, Ellington's musical context from the very outset
of his apprenticeship (circa 1914) was one in which primary
emphasis was placed on coming to terms with the vernacular
music of New Orleans, the blues, vaudeville show tunes and
novelties, and popular dance melodies. After all, the audiences
he was hoping to please were not in the great concert, recital,
and philharmonic halls. They were in the vaudeville and variety
show theaters, dance halls, at parties, parlor socials, honky-tonks,
after-hour joints, and dives. Moreover, Ellington always used to
point out that while some of his mentors were conservatory-
trained, others who were no less formidable played by ear, and
that he was strongly influenced by both.

Such was the nature of the immediate context of the beginning of the natural history of the sensibility of the musician
whose idiomatic approach to composition would produce the
largest body of works that amount to the musical equivalent of
the representative verbal or literary anecdotes about the national character and attitudes toward life in the United States
during the formative years of the twentieth century. By contrast, in most of the works of the most publicized of American
concert-hall-oriented composers even such idiomatic subject
matter as life in Appalachia, on the Mexican border, the world
of the rodeo, or New York's Central Park, the Louisiana bay-
ous, and the Great Plains tend to sound more like European
avant-garde experimentation than the extension, elaboration,
and refinement of American vernacular experience that has
achieved the stylistic level of fine art. Nor does any of it amount
to a significant or influential U.S. export. In any case, Ellington's music was to win a sophisticated international following
even as he began to receive national recognition as a star in the
area of popular entertainment in the United States.

But back to the context. As socially and politically reactionary as was the Washington of Ellington's early years of appren-

ticeship, it was not provincial in matters of entertainment and the arts. It was not as cosmopolitan as New York, to be sure, but even so it reflected much of the New Yorker's taste, perhaps to an extent comparable to that of a suburb of Manhattan. In fact, many Washingtonians were hardly, or only slightly, less regular patrons of New York cultural events than were residents of the five boroughs. Also, the quality of public education was such that even graduates of the outstanding segregated schools were academically qualified to satisfy the requirements of Ivy League and other elite northern colleges and universities, generally considered to be the best in the nation.

Ellington, whose academic performance in visual art qualified him for a scholarship to Pratt Institute in New York, did not graduate from high school, dropping out in his senior year to seek his fortune as a piano player in a local dance band. And yet although he never took any courses of any kind at Washington's nationally renowned Howard University, he never seemed less formally educated than those who did. Moreover, the urbane deportment of his sidemen was no less impressive than that of those in the Jimmie Lunceford Orchestra, which actually began as a student band at Fisk University, a very prestigious undergraduate liberal arts college in Nashville, Tennessee. Nor was his orientation to technical precision ever at issue. On the contrary, his band is said to have impressed other musicians as being very thoroughly rehearsed from the outset.

In all events, he never seemed to regard himself as "a young man from the provinces." And no wonder. When he and those who would become the nucleus of his great world-famous orchestra decided to go to New York and seek their fortune in the big time, they had not only heard but in a number of instances had also made personal and professional contact with such headline Manhattan-based musicians as James P. Johnson, Luckey Roberts, Eubie Blake, Fletcher Henderson, and Fats Waller, among others. After all, Washington's Howard Theater, which was more relevant to Ellington's destiny than Howard University, was not only the nearest thing in the nation to such New York T.O.B.A.-type (Theatre Owners Booking Association) circuit theaters as the Lincoln and the Lafayette, it was also the showcase for Washington's formally trained elite's cultural events.

Nor should it be forgotten that when Ellington and his musicians presented themselves to New York as the Washingtonians, they seemed to have had no fear of being mistaken for a bunch of hayseeds. Even Sonny Greer, the Manhattan-wise drummer from Long Branch, New Jersey, who had left a road show to join them several years before, seems to have had no objection to reentering the New York scene as one of the Washingtonians.

The immediate impact of Ellington on New York was not comparable to that which King Oliver, Louis Armstrong, Freddie Keppard, and other musicians from New Orleans had on the city of Chicago, but in a matter of four years he was well on his way to a prominent status in the city, the nation, and the world. Unlike the musicians from New Orleans who arrived in Chicago bringing a style of music that was not only revolutionary but immediately captivating, Ellington and his fellow musicians had come to New York to qualify as big-time professionals.

To which end, when he and his group of mostly Washingtonians that he was leading in the Hollywood Club in midtown Manhattan on Forty-ninth Street between Broadway and Seventh Avenue were booked into the plush Cotton Club nightspot uptown on Lenox Avenue at 142nd Street near the Savoy Ballroom in 1927, he had been in New York since 1923, during which time he had played in a significant variety of theaters and nightspots, including the Lafayette Theatre, Barron Wilkins' Exclusive Club, and other uptown venues, and had also made regular rounds of the legendary rent-party sessions frequented by such topflight Harlem stride virtuoso keyboard ticklers as James P. Johnson, Luckey Roberts, Willie "the Lion" Smith, the Beetle, the Lamb, Fats Waller, and others. And there were also the tours he and his group had made in New England during which they had been enthusiastically received on the circuits played by such well-established orchestras as those of Paul Whiteman, Vincent Lopez, Coon-Sanders, and Mal Hallett.

Meanwhile he had also begun to apply himself to becoming a professional writer of popular songs, and by the spring of 1925 had written the music for a revue called *Chocolate Kiddies*, the production of which featured a band led by Sam Wooding, who took it on a European tour beginning in May 1925. Also in 1924 he had begun making recordings, and by the time he began his tenure at the Cotton Club he had already recorded such enduring Ellingtonia as "East St. Louis Toodle-Oo," "Birmingham Breakdown," "Creole Love Call," and "Black and Tan Fantasy."

All of which also adds up to the definitive working context (including the competition for bookings and recording dates and sales) of the natural history of the kind of composer that Duke Ellington was to become. In New York as in the Washington of his early apprenticeship, his approach to music was not predicated on the requirements of conservatory-oriented composers of what Americans refer to as the serious music of the concert halls. It was rather the product of the immediate and daily response to and interaction with the vernacular aesthetics of the world of popular entertainment *that ranged all the way from folk-based minstrel fare through the wide variety of popular and novelty songs and the most elaborate production numbers of the more sophisticated nightclubs, hotel ballrooms, and music halls.*

Nor should it be forgotten that as a musician who was no less a performing artist than a composer, Ellington possessed a sense of context that was absolutely inseparable from his awareness of the nature of his daily and perpetual competition. Thus obviously his evolution was more directly and profoundly influenced by the approach to musical statement in the procedures involved in the output of his competition than by any established principles of formal conservatory training. In fact, in his workaday milieu many of the legitimate approaches to tone, execution, structure, and so on were often more likely to be frowned upon and derided than admired and praised.

Not that Ellington or any other major jazz musician ever hesitated to employ any conventional or so-called classical or legitimate devices that suited their needs. After all, inasmuch as the overwhelming majority of the most influential jazz musicians are musically literate, their elementary exercise books, whatever their instrument, were precisely the same as for all other formally trained musicians. The definitive idiomatic approaches and modifications of procedure were evolved and developed (extended, elaborated, and refined) as required.

Such are the dynamics of the vernacular imperative to process indigenous material into aesthetic statement through the use of technical devices that are also peculiar to native procedure.

No wonder, then, that Ellington as an arranger and composer of indigenous American folk and pop music was far more directly and profoundly influenced by the output of King Oliver, Louis Armstrong, Sidney Bechet, Fletcher Henderson, and Don Redman, and by his early and indelible identification with such stride-time piano players and composers as James P. Johnson, Luckey Roberts, Willie "the Lion" Smith, and others, including such music show master craftsmen as Will Vodery, than by such highly celebrated contemporary concert hall revolutionaries as Igor Stravinsky, Béla Bartók, Claude Debussy, Erik Satie, and Maurice Ravel, or the theories of Nadia Boulanger.

Such were the background factors and workaday circumstances and incentives that actually enabled Ellington to fulfill the aspiration that led Mrs. Jeannette Thurber to bring Antonín Dvořák to the United States to head an American conservatory back in 1892. Nor should the fact that Ellington's achievement was recognized by European critics before their counterparts in the United States come as any surprise either, inasmuch as it reflects the reason Mrs. Thurber sent for Dvořák in the first place.

When Ellington made his first trip abroad in 1933, such items as "East St. Louis Toodle-Oo," "Mood Indigo," "Lightnin' Louie," "Creole Love Call," and "Rockin' in Rhythm," among others, created for performance in nightclubs, dance halls, popular stage shows, popular music records, and radio broadcasts, had gained him the status of a new celebrity in the American world of popular entertainment, but he was of little or no concern to "regular" music critics and theorists in America. In Europe, however, his musicianship was regarded as a matter for serious analysis not only as quintessential American music but also as it related to contemporary European music on its own terms.

In England, for example, as Barry Ulanov reports in his biography of Ellington, Constant Lambert wrote: *"The orchestration of nearly all the numbers shows an intensely musical instinct and after hearing what Ellington can do with fourteen players in pieces like 'Jive Stomp' and 'Mood Indigo' the average modern composer who splashes about with eighty players in the Respighi manner must feel chastened. All this is clearly apparent to anyone who visits the Palladium, but what may not be so apparent is that Ellington is no mere band leader and arranger, but a composer of uncommon merit, probably the first composer of real character to come out of America."*

The European trip, during which it became quite obvious to Ellington that his approach to music was a matter of serious attention and even admiration and emulation by such highly regarded concert hall composers as Auric, Durey, Hindemith, Honegger, Poulenc, and Tailleferre, came about almost ten years before his band made its debut at Carnegie Hall in January 1943. There had been concert performances on several American college campuses during the mid 1930s, but the Carnegie Hall concert symbolized the achievement of the ultimate level of musical prestige in the United States.

Ellington, who is said to have declined an invitation to participate in the "From Spirituals to Swing" extravaganza of American folk and entertainment circuit music staged in 1938–39 by a jazz enthusiast and booster named John Hammond, certainly seems to have regarded his performance of a program of his own arrangements and compositions there as a very special historic achievement not only for his personal career but also for the idiom of American music that he represented.

So for the occasion, in addition to the premiere of *Black, Brown, and Beige*, a forty-five-minute tone parallel to the history of American Negroes, composed specifically for concert performance, the program also included such already unmistakably Ellington items as "Black and Tan Fantasy," "Rockin' in Rhythm," "Portrait of Bert Williams," "Portrait of Bojangles," "Ko-Ko," "Jack the Bear," "Cotton Tail," "Boy Meets Horn," "Don't Get Around Much Anymore," and "Mood Indigo," among others.

In contrast to generally enthusiastic approval from reporters and reviewers in the realm of popular music, the so-called regular music critics, unlike a significant number of their European counterparts, tended to be condescending and dismissive, especially of *Black, Brown, and Beige*. Said one, "Such a form of composition is entirely out of Ellington's ken." As for the other selections, they were approached as if their brevity were more important than their musical content. Conspicuously absent from all the condescension, however, was any evidence of any practical understanding and appreciation of the dynamics of the evolution of national cultural identity in the arts comparable to that to be found in Constance Rourke's *American Humor: A Study of the National Character* (1931) and her posthumous *The Roots of American Culture* (1942); or in John A. Kouwenhoven's *Made in America: The Arts in Modern Civilization* (1948) and his *The Beer Can by the Highway: Essays on What's American About America* (1961).

But not only was the Carnegie Hall concert a commercial success that turned out to be the first of a series of annual "Ellington at Carnegie Hall" concerts, some previewed or repeated in comparable prestigious auditoriums in Chicago and Boston, it can also be said to have played a crucial role in making a significant number of Americans aware of the fact that a form of American music had achieved the status of fine art of universal appeal through the extension, elaboration, and refinement of folk and pop fare by means of such vernacular devices of stylization as vamps, riffs, blues choruses, pop song choruses, breaks, fills, call-and-response sequences (solo to ensemble, solo to solo, ensemble to ensemble), turn-arounds, substitutions, among others, including idiomatic timbres, harmonies, elementary-level onomatopoeia (especially of the pre-diesel and electric locomotives), plus a combination of individual sensibility and skill at on-the-spot improvisation required for effective participation in a jam session.

Between the first Carnegie Hall concert in 1943 and his death in 1974 at the age of seventy-five, Ellington had gone on to compose, perform, and record such extended works, among others, as *The Deep South Suite*, *The Liberian Suite*, *A Tone Parallel to Harlem*, *A Tonal Group* ("Rhapsoditty," "Fuguea-ditty," "Jam-a-ditty"), *The Tattooed Bride*, *Night Creature*, *Such Sweet Thunder*, *Toot Suite* ("Red Shoes," "Red Carpet," "Red Garter," "Ready Go"), *Anatomy of a Murder*, *The River*, *The Goutelas Suite*, *Afro-Eurasian Eclipse*, *New Orleans Suite*, and *The University of Wisconsin Suite*.

Shorter but no less important works such as "Mainstem," "Cotton Tail," "Someone," "Idiom '59," "Opus 69," "Let the Zoomers Drool," "Track 360," "Satin Doll," "Laying on Mellow," "In a Mellow Tone," "Sepia Panorama," "C-Jam Blues," "B.P.," "Volupté," "The Purple Gazelle," "Afro-Bossa," "Black Swan," and others not only outnumber those of any other jazz arranger/ composer but also exceed them all in variety. And there are enough vocal vehicles such as "Sophisticated Lady," "Solitude," "I Let a Song Go out of My Heart," "I Got It Bad," "Rocks in My Bed," "I'm Just a Lucky So and So," "Everything but You," "Prelude to a Kiss" to qualify him as an outstanding songwriter.

When Lincoln Center for the Performing Arts, which includes the New York Philharmonic Orchestra, the Metropolitan Opera, the New York City Ballet, and the Juilliard School, inaugurated its first year-round program of "Jazz at Lincoln Center," Duke Ellington's music was the definitive source of its approach to jazz composition, and his orchestra was the comprehensive model upon which the now internationally admired Lincoln Center Jazz Repertory Orchestra is based.

Such is the context within which "Jazz at Lincoln Center" elected to take the leading role that it played in the yearlong worldwide centennial birthday celebration of Duke Ellington in 1999. During which repeated most honorable mention should also have been made of Mrs. Jeannette Thurber, who, according to an article by J. E. Vacha in the September 1992 issue of *American Heritage* entitled "Dvořák in America," "didn't merely endorse her director's theories [about the importance of 'Negro melodies' in American music], she backed him up with concrete action." The same article that carried Dvořák's interview also announced her decision to open the national conservatory to black students. Tuition would be waived for the most gifted.

Two who achieved historic distinction were Harry T. Burleigh and Will Marion Cook. Burleigh, who became an outstanding singer (and who incidentally served as soloist at St. George's Episcopal Church from 1894 to 1946 and concurrently at Temple Emanu-El from 1900 to 1925), is most widely celebrated for his choral arrangements of such "classic" Negro spirituals as "Deep River," "My Lord What a Morning," "There

Is a Balm in Gilead," "Were You There," "Every Time I Feel the Spirit," and "Joshua Fit the Battle of Jericho."

Will Marion Cook, who had been an outstanding young violinist at the Oberlin Conservatory and at the Berlin Hochschule, was primarily interested in composition at the National Conservatory, and he went on to collaborate with poet Paul Laurence Dunbar on *Clorindy; or, The Origin of the Cakewalk*, a musical comedy sketch, and to write a number of other musicals on his own and with other collaborators. He also served as musical director for the legendary Williams and Walker Variety Show Company. But perhaps his most celebrated undertaking was his organization and direction of the Southern Syncopated Orchestra, which he took on a highly successful national tour in 1918 and then took to England and high acclaim in 1919.

It was Will Marion Cook (also from Washington, by the way) who was Ellington's most direct connection to Dvořák and Mrs. Jeannette Thurber. Not only did Ellington already admire him enough by 1919 to name his son Mercer Ellington after Cook's son Mercer Cook, he also sought him out in New York and began an informal mentor-and-protégé relationship that lasted until Cook's death in 1944. Incidentally, for all of his own highly impressive formal training, Cook's technical advice to Ellington was entirely consistent with the dynamics of the vernacular imperative. *Don't be restricted by the established rules. Proceed in terms of what is most natural to your own individual sensibility.* Obviously, the devices most natural to Ellington's personal (*which is to say idiomatic*) sensibility were those of ragtime, the blues, and the pop song chorus. Which suggests that as enthusiastic about American folk music as Dvořák was, he may have mistaken the vernacular devices peculiar to European musical convention for universal principles of composition. Ellington did not.

PART III

Memos for a Memoir

Me and Old Duke

BACK IN 1927, when I was eleven years old and in the fifth grade at Mobile County Training School on the outskirts of Mobile, Alabama, some twenty-plus years before Kenneth Burke's notion of art as basic equipment for living became a fundamental element in my concept of the pragmatic function of aesthetic statement, I was already trying to project myself as the storybook heroic me that I wanted to be by doing a syncopated sporty limp-walk to the patent leather avenue beat of Duke Ellington's then very current "Birmingham Breakdown."

There were also highly stylized facial expressions, gestures, postures, and other choreographic movements that went with "Mood Indigo," "Black and Tan Fantasy," and "Creole Love Call," all of which were also elements in the texture of the troposphere of that part of my preteen childhood. But "Birmingham Breakdown" (along with old Jelly Roll Morton's "Kansas City Stomp" and Fletcher Henderson's "Stampede") functioned as my personal soundtrack some years before Vitaphone movies came into being.

In junior high school there was Ellington's recording of "Diga Diga Doo," a novelty vocal that some of my classmates and I sometimes used as a cute little takeoff jive ditty on Talladega College, which, along with Morehouse College in Atlanta and Fisk University in Nashville, was a choice liberal arts college, scholarship grants to which we as honor students were already competing with each other for upon graduation. The Ellington swagger perennial from that period was "Rockin' in Rhythm."

Along with the advanced courses and grade point average competition of senior high school, plus all of the ritual challenges of full-fledged adolescence, which, by the way, included cosmopolitan standards of sartorial elegance set by the latest fashions in *Esquire*, a new men's magazine, came "It Don't Mean a Thing if It Ain't Got That Swing," "Sophisticated Lady," "Solitude," and "Delta Serenade." Although "Stormy Weather," "Cocktails for Two," and "(Everybody's) Truckin'" were not Ellington compositions, it was Ellington's arrangements and recordings that established them as radio hits and stash-swagger-fare for hip cats.

When "Caravan" came out I was in college, and that was also the year that T. E. Lawrence (of Arabia) published *Seven Pillars of Wisdom*, which eventually led me to Charles Doughty's *Travels in Arabia Deserta* and to Sir Richard Burton's *Personal Narrative of a Pilgrimage to El-Madinah & Meccah*. The dance step that used to go with "Caravan" and other ballroom exotica was the camel walk, which for a while was right out there with "Truckin'" and was no less intricate than the Suzy Q. Then came "I Let a Song Go out of My Heart" with an instrumental version that was no less popular than the lyric.

I was also in college when "Echoes of Harlem" came out, and along with "Diminuendo and Crescendo in Blue" it was to come to represent an aesthetic statement that was more in line with my evolving sensibility and artistic aspiration than anything I had come across in *The New Negro*, Alain Locke's anthology of the so-called Harlem Renaissance.

The world I graduated into from college in 1939 was that of Count Basie's "Doggin' Around" and "Blue and Sentimental." But in 1940 came Ellington's "Cotton Tail," a musical stylization of the elegantly nimble rabbit in the briarpatch, which for me was to become the musical equivalent of a representative literary anecdote. *For example, the blues as such may be approached as the ever nimble rabbit copes with the jam-session-like challenges of the briarpatch.* Hence the name Scooter for the protagonist of *Train Whistle Guitar*, *The Spyglass Tree*, *The Seven League Boots*, and the book now in progress.

When I came to New York the first time, "Echoes of Harlem," "Uptown Downbeat," "I'm Slappin' Seventh Avenue with the Sole of My Shoe," "Harlem Airshaft," and the then new "Take the A Train" had as much to do with my preconceptions and anticipations of the idiomatic texture of life in uptown Manhattan as Hollywood movies and the WPA guidebook had to do with my expectations of the great metropolis as a whole.

It was on my second visit to New York that I picked up on "Mainstem," Ellington's tone parallel to Broadway, which did for midtown Manhattan what "Harlem Airshaft" had done and still does for the special ambience of New York City above 110th Street. And as "Sepia Panorama" does for the brownskin area of every large city in the United States that I have ever visited. After all, as the old barbershop saying goes, "Nobody ever knew more about what to do with all that old chitlin circuit stuff than old Duke."

When, as a young college teacher attending graduate school at NYU, I finally met Ellington and began going to his rehearsals and recording sessions, I felt, and still feel, that what I was doing was as relevant to my career as a writer as meeting Ernest Hemingway, Thomas Mann, James Joyce, T. S. Eliot, André Malraux, William Faulkner, and W. H. Auden would have been. Incidentally, it was from Mann's application of devices of German music to prose fiction that led me to explore the existential implications of the blues and also to try to make literary applications of the devices of jazz orchestration.

In time, my personal contact with Ellington became such that he sponsored a party that his sister Ruth gave at 333 Riverside Drive at 106th Street (now renamed Duke Ellington Boulevard) when my second book, *South to a Very Old Place*, was published. And his blurb on the jacket of *Train Whistle Guitar*, my first novel, is not only the most flattering I've ever received but is also the one most often quoted in profiles and platform introductions.

But even before that, there was the fall term that I spent at Colgate University as O'Connor Professor of Literature, which was in itself an unforgettable high point in my early literary career. What made it an all but incredible time for me, however, were two other surprises. Even as I was still finding my way around the campus, the *New Yorker* magazine published a long and enthusiastic review by Robert Coles of my first book, *The Omni-Americans*. And shortly thereafter Duke Ellington himself, en route to Los Angeles where he and Ella Fitzgerald were booked into the Coconut Grove, called and said, "Hey, Albert [pronounced French style], since you have no classes between late Thursday afternoon and early next Tuesday afternoon, why not let me have our office set up a weekend round-trip flight out to L.A. I'd like to talk to you about this book that Stanley Dance and I are trying to put together."

On the flight to California, the big thrill for me was not that

I was on my way to Hollywood. As an Air Force Captain assigned to duty at Long Beach Municipal Airport from 1958 to 1961, I had not only become used to driving from my residence in Compton into downtown Los Angeles and out to Hollywood to attend art exhibitions, musical entertainment and sports events as often as several times a week, I had also become a regular backstage visitor during concerts, club dates and dances every time the Ellington Band came to town. So I had also begun to go to rehearsals and recording sessions including those that produced the Ellington-Strayhorn version of *The Nutcracker Suite*.

No, the big thrill for me as I boarded the flight to Los Angeles Airport was the fact that my invitation was a follow up on a very flattering compliment that Duke had paid me two years earlier. On October 20, 1968, he had played one of his sacred concerts at Metropolitan AME church on 135th Street off Lenox Avenue, only three blocks from my apartment in Harlem. When I arrived early enough to go "backstage" to the pastor's office and study, which Duke was using as his dressing room, he introduced me to Ralph Bunche, the great United Nations diplomat. Bunche was scheduled to present Duke with a commemorative Duke Ellington postage stamp being issued by Togoland. When Duke called me over to meet Bunche, Duke told him that I was a new writer whose magazine articles were well worth checking out. "He's gone, man," he said as he turned to start dressing to go on stage, "he's already way out there."

As Bunche and I shook hands, he said "Duke's recommendation is certification enough for me." He told me about how when he, who was not a musician, was coming of age, Duke Ellington became one of his most influential role models, a development that pleased his father very much because his father thought that Ellington's cosmopolitan deportment was entirely consistent with the universality of his music.

Nor was that all. There was also the all too recent fact that when Duke's sister Ruth called from the office with specific information about transportation and lodging, she said that he had seen the very enthusiastic review of *The Omni-Americans* in *Newsweek*, which also included a snapshot of me sitting beside Duke at the Newport Jazz Festival of 1961. Duke had said "It's because of cats like that I'm going to have to amount to something one of these days." I would have been just thrilled en route to meet him at a roadhouse anywhere on the chitlin' circuit.

Me and Old Uncle Billy
and the American Mythosphere

THERE WAS NOTHING at all avuncular about the impression he made on me when I began reading him during the first term of my freshman year at Tuskegee in the fall of 1935. At that time he, along with Ernest Hemingway, John Dos Passos, F. Scott Fitzgerald, Sherwood Anderson, Gertrude Stein, and James Joyce, and also such poets as T. S. Eliot, Ezra Pound, Archibald MacLeish, Carl Sandburg, Robert Frost, and Edwin Arlington Robinson, and such playwrights as Eugene O'Neill, Maxwell Anderson, Robert E. Sherwood, and Clifford Odets of Broadway and William Butler Yeats and John Millington Synge of the Abbey Theatre, was very much a part of what the current literary news and commentaries in newspapers and magazines in the periodicals room of the Hollis Burke Frissell Library were about.

At the time my main literary interest was drama, and the book that led me to anthologies and surveys of world literature was *The Theatre: Three Thousand Years of Drama, Acting and Stagecraft* by Sheldon Cheney, who was also the author of *A Primer of Modern Art*, from which by that next spring I had become familiar with such aesthetic terms as Impressionism, Post-Impressionism, Cubism, Futurism, Expressionism, Dadaism, Surrealism, and so on, including Vorticism and Constructivism.

By which time, because of such weekly magazines as the *Saturday Review of Literature*, the *New York Times Book Review*, the *New York Herald Tribune Book World*, the *New Republic*, and the *Nation*, none of which had been available to me in high school, I was already spending more of my extracurricular reading time on contemporary fiction, poetry, and critical theory than on drama and stagecraft, although I was also keeping current on what was happening on the Broadway stage and on the screen and radio.

Come to think of it, although I was not really aware of it at the time, the shift of my primary reading interests from drama to prose fiction probably had already begun between mid-

768

September and mid-November. In any case, along with Ernest Hemingway, who was writing about Florida and Cuba in sequences from *To Have and Have Not* (and also correspondence dispatch observations about the craft of fiction as such) in current issues of *Esquire* magazine, there was also one William Faulkner, whom I still remember as if it all happened yesterday. Because I will always remember the faded red print on the blue and beige binding of the Jonathan Cape–Harrison Smith edition of *These 13* that was right there on the tilted display tray at your elbow on the checkout counter in the main reading room on the second floor of the Hollis Burke Frissell Library.

So it all began with "Dry September," "Red Leaves," "That Evening Sun," "A Rose for Emily," "A Justice," and "Hair." Then came the blue-embossed sun-bleached-meadowland-beige-bound Harrison Smith–Robert Haas edition of *Light in August*, with Joe Christmas and Lena Grove and Byron Bunch and Joe Brown and Lucas Burch and Reverend Gail Hightower, Old Man McEachern, Old Doc Hines, Miss Joanna Burden, and the sheriff, plus Percy Grimm to be sure.

Then came *Absalom, Absalom!* hot off the press in 1936. *Soldiers' Pay, Mosquitoes, Sartoris, The Sound and the Fury, As I Lay Dying*, and *Sanctuary* were not available at Tuskegee at that time. John Gerald Hamilton, my favorite classmate of all times, had already read *Sanctuary* back in Detroit, his hometown, where he had also seen a movie version entitled *The Story of Temple Drake*. I don't remember him saying anything about any of the others, so I assume that he had not yet read any of them either, because I can't imagine him not saying anything about the stylistic innovations that Faulkner employed in the Benjy and Quentin sections of *The Sound and the Fury*, and I still think about how much fun it would have been to have him there with his input on the decoding of those first 222 pages. What with him already checked out as he alone among the undergraduates I knew was on such contemporary writers as James Joyce and Marcel Proust and such stylistic innovations in narration as the stream of consciousness, the fourth dimension, free association, imagism, symbolism, and so on.

Which, of course, is why both *Light in August* and *Absalom, Absalom!* were so much easier going for him than for me. But

I was no less captivated even so. And I still think of both (which I reread immediately) as belonging as much to me as to anybody. Incidentally, the fact that the current reviews of *Absalom, Absalom!* were hardly laudatory had no negative effect on our enthusiasm whatsoever. Both novels were like tunes you keep humming to yourself because you like them for yourself regardless of what anybody else thinks.

Hamilton was back up north when *The Unvanquished* arrived in 1938. So I made what I made of the Civil War and Reconstruction escapades of Bayard Sartoris and Ringo on my own. But there was something about the curiosity that the two of them shared and the running-mate games they played that reminded me time and again of how things were when he was there. Young Bayard Sartoris was no Huck Finn to be sure. Although in some ways he and Ringo were personally closer than Huck and Jim (who, after all, was an adult, not Huck's age peer). And I had serious doubts about the naïveté of Ringo's devotion to the Confederacy. But Faulkner's rendering of Ringo's competitive curiosity and self-confident ingenuity are not condescending, and his account of Ringo's efforts to conceive the concrete image of a functioning railroad train, something he not only has never heard of before Bayard comes back from a trip and tells him about one but has nothing to compare it with, is as profoundly insightful as it is hilarious.

And yet, as far as I know, Faulkner never got around to coming to terms with an emancipated and reconstructed Ringo. There was the formidable Lucas Beauchamp of *Go Down, Moses* and *Intruder in the Dust* to be sure, and several others not unlike him who exemplify the traditional orientation to the dignified bearing and noble aspirations of their "high-class" white relatives in the Edmonds, McCaslin, and Sartoris families. But what about the ex-slaves, mulatto or not, who became leaders, teachers, professionals, and businessmen? The Reconstruction was not a farce, nor was it mostly a disaster perpetrated by corrupt carpetbaggers. In spite of the widespread hostility and all of the horrendous acts of terrorism by the likes of Nathan Bedford Forrest and others, the transition from freedom from slavery to responsible U.S. citizenship and unimpeachable patriotism is unexcelled by any other stories of the making of any other Americans.

The last Faulkner novel I read before graduating from Tuskegee in 1939 was *The Wild Palms*, in which the nightmarish Old
Man River flood story came across very effectively in spite of
the way it was seemingly arbitrarily interwoven with the totally
different narrative sequences of the Harry Wilbourne–Charlotte
Rittenmeyer fiasco, the implications of which became richer
later on when I eventually got around to reading Faulkner's
New Orleans–based equivalent to the influential 1920s *Waste
Land*–oriented efforts of the poet T. S. Eliot, the novelist F. Scott
Fitzgerald, and others in such books as *Soldiers' Pay*, *Mosquitoes*, *Pylon*, and *New Orleans Sketches*. Then very belatedly
there was also *Sartoris* (*Flags in the Dust*) for all its benchmark
status in the Yoknapatawpha chronicles.

William Faulkner's stylization of the idiomatic particulars of
the Deep South is very much a part of what impressed me
about his fiction from the very outset. Moreover, even then it
was not simply a matter of regional or provincial atmosphere
or local color, not as such. Even then there was something
about it that had the effect of transforming all too familiar everyday down-home environmental and demographic details
into the stuff of poetry, the stuff that the so-called avant-garde
poetry of T. S. Eliot, Ezra Pound, e. e. cummings, Marianne
Moore, and Robinson Jeffers, among others, was made of.

For me, the "mot juste" prose of Ernest Hemingway's *In Our
Time* and *The Sun Also Rises* was also the stuff of such poetic
endeavor. But whereas the poetry of Hemingway's prose struck
me as being all-American in a Walt Whitmanesque sense (also
with overtones of syndicated wire service vernacular to be sure),
Faulkner's Southerners' linguistic southernness, not unlike the
unmistakably Irish idiom of James Joyce's *Dubliners*, was no less
potentially international in its avant-garde chicness and already no
less immediate in the universality of its implications. (*For me, at
any rate, what André Malraux made of* Sanctuary *recalls what
Baudelaire and the French made of Poe!*) Stylization could make
small-town down-home stuff, even Mississippi small-town down-
home stuff, as universal as anything from anywhere else.

*Also, when I think of the near-symphonic orchestral convolu-
tion of some of Faulkner's prose as compared with the streamlined
precision of Ernest Hemingway's* Kansas City Star–*disciplined*

4/4-like incantation, it is as if Faulkner were a not-quite-not-Thomas-Sutpen Mississippi planter and occasional-riverboat-to-New-Orleans dandy and sometime gentleman rider-huntsman who inhabits a haunted antebellum mansion on what is left of a vast plantation inherited from ancestors whose accruals were derived directly from owning and exploiting human slaves. Some of them very close relatives indeed. A prop-laden stage set for costume drama with ever so historical resonances.

Whereas for me, it was as if Hemingway's style was that of some species of an all-American sportsman in leotards on a clean, well-lighted, starkly symbolic, multilevel stage set for ritual sketches. And of course much goes to show that it is the ritual sketch that the costume drama, however elaborate, must add up to. Which well may be as good a reason as any why "The Bear" in Go Down, Moses *may be regarded as a crucial if not definitive Faulkner achievement.*

No, there was nothing about the impression that William Faulkner made on me during those early years that was as yet avuncular. But even so, he had become Old Faulkner almost as fast as Little Louis Armstrong had become Old Louis and the handsome young Duke Ellington had become Old Duke. That was because at a very early age he had his own way of doing what he did that commanded the serious attention and respect not only of his peers but also of his elders as well. Indeed what it meant was that he was already on his way to becoming an elder himself. Because there was something about the way that he did what he did that left you more bemused and/or astonished and impressed than aghast and outraged. In any case, I submit that he had already become Old Faulkner early on because it was already so obvious that he was headed for the status of the legendary and, who knows, perhaps eventually the status of a classic.

As an undergraduate I associated the idiomatic particulars of Faulkner's role as a regional elder in the arts with what I regarded as a post-Confederate southern small-town seed store, feed store, courthouse square sensibility. Not that I had any firsthand experience of such places. I had grown up hearing fireside tales, tall and otherwise, about such potentially explosive southern small towns as Atmore, Bay Minette, Flomaton, and so on in Alabama. But Magazine Point, where I spent the

first nineteen years of my life, was a small suburb of the international seaport city of Mobile, whose downtown municipal
and business center we were directly connected to by a trolley
car ride of only a matter of perhaps thirty minutes or less and a
shortcut walk of less than an hour. So the small courthouse
square Macon County seat of Tuskegee was actually my very
first ongoing contact with a small courthouse square town
with a Confederate statue like Faulkner's town of Jefferson. So
Jefferson was just as real as Tuskegee town, and the town of
Tuskegee was just as much a part of a storybook world as
Faulkner's Jefferson.

In all events, when as a graduate whose literary context by
that time included Thomas Mann, André Malraux, James Joyce,
Marcel Proust, Arthur Koestler, Ignazio Silone, and Franz
Kafka, among others, and such poets as Auden, Spender, and
C. Day-Lewis, I came back around to reading Faulkner when
The Hamlet and then *Go Down, Moses* were published, my image
of the idiomatic dimension of him as a Deep South elder became
that of a book-oriented corn-whiskey-drinking cracker-barrel lie
swapper and hot-stove yarn spinner, whose cosmopolitan literary awareness was as natural to him as was his comprehensive
courthouse square awareness of local, regional, national, and
global affairs. None of which seemed to have very much if anything to do with drawing room chic but was clearly of a piece
with the nuts-and-bolts stuff of local politics and ever so confidential inside gossip. And thus perhaps not a little to do with
the motives underlying narrative action.

It was when he became more and more involved with the
Snopes people and the Varners that I realized that, along with
everything else that had made him Old Faulkner, there was
also something that made him Old Uncle Billy as far as I was
personally concerned. My having grown up in the Deep South
as I had, he was my own personal very special big-house equivalent to and literary extension of my traditional brownskin
fireside, barbershop, and storefront loafers rest-bench Uncles
Bud, Doc, Ned, Pete, and Remus (with pipe sometimes alternating with cigar).

Because just as it was as if old Uncles Bud, Doc, Ned, Pete,
and Remus existed to make you aware of attitudes, acts, and
implications that you were not yet old enough to come by on

your own for all your ever alert and even ingenious curiosity, so were old Uncle Billy's books there to pull you aside and provide you with inside insights not readily available to you as an everyday matter of course, because you were neither white nor a personal servant.

So the quest for universality in aesthetic statement being what it is, and despite his avowed but ambivalent desire for anonymity, Old Faulkner became and still is my very own idiomatic old Uncle Billy. Not for all intents and purposes to be sure, but for quite a few even so. In all events, anywhere his concerns and curiosity took him I could go also, and so can you. For such is indeed the nature and function of literary artistic endeavor in the human scheme of things.

Thus what William Faulkner's avuncular status with me comes down to is precisely the role of the literary artist in the contemporary American mythosphere, a term I am appropriating from my friend Alexander Eliot. In other words, there is the physical atmosphere of planet Earth which is said to extend some six hundred miles out into space in all directions and consists of the troposphere in which we live, and beyond which is the stratosphere, beyond which are the mesosphere, the ionosphere, and exosphere.

The mythosphere is that nonphysical but no less actual and indispensable dimension of the troposphere in which and in terms of which human consciousness exists, and as we all know, the primary concern of all artistic endeavor is the quality of human consciousness, whether our conception of things is truly functional, as functional as a *point or moral* of the classic fables and fairy tales. But that is quite a story in itself. Let me just say that I assume that the role of the serious literary artist is to provide mythic prefigurations that are adequate to the complexities and possibilities of the circumstances in which we live. In other words, to the storyteller actuality is a combination of facts, figures, and legend. The goal of the serious storyteller is to fabricate a truly fictional legend, one that meets the so-called scientific tests of validity, reliability, and comprehensiveness. Is its applicability predictable? Are the storyteller's anecdotes truly representative? Does his "once upon a time" instances and episodes imply time and again? I have found that in old Uncle Billy's case they mostly do.

PART IV

Book Reviews

The HNIC Who He

MANY WHITE PEOPLE may always seem only too eager to seize upon any explanation that traces the Negro Revolution to some single source of motivation. But when you come right down to it nobody in the United States is actually convinced that when you have heard one Negro you have heard them all—any more than anybody has ever really believed that once you have seen one you have seen them all. Nevertheless, somebody who knows very well that there is no single spokesman for anybody else is forever asking somebody to tell him who speaks for the Negro!

When somebody approaches and says, "Take me to your leader," a Negro is faced with the same problem as other Americans. All anybody has to do is glance at the headlines or switch on the television to find out that there are not only a lot of different Negroes to be spoken for but also a lot of different ones who are not about to let anybody else speak for them.

No one can deny that the resulting confusion is often exasperating. But neither can any responsible American dispute the fact that such diversity, *although it sometimes becomes downright chaotic*, is a normal and inevitable outcome of the freedom of speech. Hence, not only do Negroes have as much right to dissent from each other as from Whitey, they are as likely to do so in any case. Moreover, as Harold Cruse obviously assumed when he undertook *The Crisis of the Negro Intellectual*, the only realistic thing to do is come to practical terms with it.

Such, at any rate, is the indispensable requirement that this book fulfills. Indeed, in the process of establishing what is by all odds the most imaginatively documented and politically sophisticated working perspective on the built-in contradictions and disjunctions of the Negro Revolution up to now, he has written the most urgently needed if not the most important book of the year.

There will be some quibbling over details, to be sure, and certainly there are going to be a number of furious people with exposed and tingling backsides. But they had better get it all together before they lash back at Harold Cruse. Many Negro writers either shirk or shuck on intellectual matters. Not him. He takes care of business. But let us hope that a great number of general readers and intellectuals as well will be quick to realize that *The Crisis of the Negro Intellectual* adds a long-overdue dimension to the national dialogue on the nature and implications of racial and cultural pluralism.

Most other Negro writers still rely on the same old easy devices that make white people feel so deliciously defensive and guilty—only because they also make them feel so powerful. Cruse, who is as thoroughly checked out on militant protest as the next black brother, expresses his often brilliant insights into the political and cultural implications of Negro experience on the highest level of intellectual abstraction, against the broadest and richest historical background, and always with a practical eye on the possibilities of implementation.

Also unlike most other Negro writers, who almost always allow fatherly white spokesmen to set up the same old context within which Negro aspirations will be interpreted and considered, Cruse establishes his own frame of reference. He makes his own historical and ideological assessments and reevaluations and derives his own point of view. Thus his working conception of cultural black nationalism does not fit into any of the oversimplified categories now being popularized by mass media.

In consequence, his carefully documented observations on the development of Harlem as culture capital, on the differences between U.S. Negroes and West Indian Negroes, on Negroes and Jews, Negroes and left-wingers, and so on, should make truly concerned Americans realize just how little useful information most of the reporters and social science experts have been able to give them about the so-called Negro community.

The Burden of Race, edited by Gilbert Osofsky, the author of *Harlem: The Making of a Ghetto*, is a compilation of documents and short articles that expose once more the horrors of white racism and black victimization. Given a publisher's contract, any fairly competent Negro college librarian could get one up in a couple of weeks. The minute someone other than a Negro has the same batch of clippings done up as a book, however, he is immediately accepted by the Do-good Foundations as having qualified as a scholarly authority, panelist, and consultant on black miseries.

The titles and commentaries of *The Burden of Race* only reiterate what Osofsky's first book had made clear enough: he has no business being promoted into black experthood for the simple reason that he has nothing significant to say about Negro experience. Negroes already have enough burdens without being saddled with any more cliché-nourished, Stanley M. Elkins–oriented theorists who insist on confusing them with Jews.

No one is likely to accuse Budd Schulberg of trying to become the Great White Jewish Father and Spokesman for Watts. But the voices he has chosen for audition in *From the Ashes* make it only too clear that the writers' workshop he set up there after the riot of 1965 is based on the same old sentimental liberal conception of the making of the wailing-wall spokesman. The establishment of Douglass House as an experiment in vocational education proves that Schulberg cares about giving the downtrodden a break. But the quality of the writing in *From the Ashes* does not indicate that he either cares or even knows as much about developing first-rate writers. No white coach bent on finding first-rate Negro athletes would ever allow himself to be faked so far out of position.

Most of the sketches, stories, verses, and various works in progress that Schulberg has so generously included in this anthology are not only pretty dull but also embarrassingly square. Not because any of the writers lack the necessary intelligence or potential but because they are so woefully "not yet with" what big-league literature is really all about. Evidently Schulberg has failed to tell them that they're writing not like John Coltrane and after, but like way before Dixieland. Schulberg became so turned-on caring about people and encouraging them to tell it like it nitty-gritty is that he forgot that writing is an artistic process. It involves the creation of significant form, which is always derived from some other form. Thus, no matter how much suffering, injustice, or anything else young writers have personally undergone, what their writing is likely to begin reflecting is not the pulsating actuality of raw experience but rather what they have been able to make of their *reading* experience.

Had Schulberg not forgotten about the writers he had wor-shiped and imitated in the process of finding himself as a writer, he might have noticed that Watts musicians, who are not any better off economically or socially, are infinitely more sophisticated about great musicians and the world of music at large than his writers seem to be about literature.

This acknowledged, Schulberg may also have realized some-thing else: young people who really and truly aspire to be seri-ous writers are hooked on books as musicians are hooked on records and painters are hooked on museums. They just simply do not stand around waiting for some best-selling novelist to suffer an attack of brotherhood fever and come out and start corralling them in from the sidewalks. Poverty does not kill young writers any faster in Watts than in Paris or in Greenwich Village—and it doesn't force them to be any farther out of things than it forces musicians to be. Item: No other young musicians anywhere in the world were up any tighter with what was happening in their chosen profession than were Charlie Mingus, Buddy Collette, and Chico Hamilton when they came out of Watts.

Perhaps it is through just such a realization that Schulberg may still find the clue to a more effective workshop. He might do well to begin with another conception of poetic license. Freedom of expression does not come from ignoring great books but from reading as many as possible and thus increas-ing one's range of awareness. Writers do not discover them-selves by studying their own belly buttons but by realizing what they like and dislike about other writers. Aspiring Negro writers must be made aware of the mainstream of contempo-rary expression if only to reject it.

But the chances are that once they really dig the literary scene, black writers will begin playing the same highly imagi-native improvisations on the works of James Joyce, Thomas Mann, Proust, Malraux, Hemingway, Faulkner, T. S. Eliot, Auden, Dylan Thomas, and Robert Lowell that the Harlem Globetrotters play with "the white man's" basketball, and Willie Mays plays with "the white man's" baseball, and Sugar Ray used to play with "the white man's" boxing gloves and Jim Brown with "the white man's" pigskin. Nor should the current emphasis on "black consciousness" be allowed to obscure the fact that neither Lester Young nor Charlie Parker compromised his blackness because he played "the white man's" saxophone. As for the integrity and the potential of Negro writers, anybody who begins by assuming that they won't learn to play their own riffs of *Finnegans Wake* just simply has never really listened to them talk.

Stokely Carmichael often sounds much more like a black prince making decrees for a nation of gullible black subjects than like one black spokesman among many others. Perhaps that's why white image-makers have always confused his rise with the Return of Emperor Jones. In any case, when he appears on television (sometimes in costume) chanting rhymes and slogans, white people have been only too quick to regard him as a part of show biz. Not many will mistake *Black Power* for entertainment.

The polemic which he has written with Charles V. Hamilton of Roosevelt University is not only serious, it is furious. It states his case for black radical political action; and it is a stimulating and useful political manifesto in spite of his same old bewildering reliance on undigested theories and superficial oversimplification. If only black activists would get off that Instant Mass Psychiatry kick! If only they would do more homework in general culture and remember the richness of their actual experience with black complexity and become less glib with fancy jargon. If activists really concur with the current social science conjectures about black emasculation and self-hatred, they cannot possibly believe that Negroes are now ready for revolt. But Negroes are ready. And they didn't get that way overnight.

There are any number of techniques that black revolutionaries can use to undermine the symbols of white authority. But instead of exposing and ridiculing the personal weaknesses and insecurities of white individuals and the hysteria of white masses, most Negro spokesmen almost always spend most of their time inflating the efficiency of the White Power Structure while reinforcing all of the clichés of black wretchedness. A short seminar on white pathology with a few old insightful black headwaiters, bellboys, maids, and Pullman porters might be as useful to black insurgence as the hypotheses of Marx, Freud, and Frantz Fanon.

But then the fact that Carmichael literally cringes when white people describe Negroes as lazy, shiftless, apathetic good-timers shows how taken in by "white middle-class values" he still is. If not, why not insist that black laziness and shiftlessness have been forms of subversive resistance since slavery; that black apathy really represents a profound rejection of the white "rat race," and that black good times only go to show what wonderful human beings U.S. Negroes are in spite of white brutality.

Black Power zings with urgent black concern about black welfare. But for all their repeated references to black consciousness, Carmichael and Hamilton, unlike the author of *The Crisis of the Negro Intellectual*, often sound like white do-gooders speaking through black masks. So much so that you get the uneasy feeling that in spite of themselves they might be confusing human dignity with white middle-class norms and suburban respectability. But their observations on white political double-dealings and black social imperatives may just prove to be enough to take care of the business they really have in mind. After all, U.S. Negroes often turn the flimsiest pop tunes into some of the richest music in the world.

Soul Brothers Abroad

THE TYPICAL IMMIGRANT arriving in New York can hardly wait to be naturalized. His fantasies about being in the United States almost always include playing an active role as a full-fledged citizen. Seldom is there a comparable eagerness for such commitment to an alien land on the part of Americans who settle elsewhere. The vast majority never give up their American citizenship; and among those who do, only a few ever become as integrated into civic activities as they were in the United States. In truth, the stateside internationalist often seems more involved with the fortunes of France and Italy than most Americans who have lived in Paris and Rome for decades.

Most of those whose observations Ernest Dunbar records in *The Black Expatriates*, a book of interviews with U.S. Negroes living in Europe and Africa, conform to the pattern of their fellow countrymen abroad. But as anyone could guess, there are also some significant differences. One is the ostensible reason for living abroad. All of the Negroes interviewed cite racism in America. White expatriates, of course, rarely give racism as a reason for exile—although the psyches of most whites are terribly scarred by the role, active or passive, they play in the exploitation of black Americans.

On the other hand, hardly any Negroes have departed in disgust at the emptiness of American materialism. Unlike the white expatriate, who is forever reiterating his renunciation of a system which was trying to shrink him to a meaningless cipher, the Negro émigré—even the artist—always seems resentful precisely because he was spurned by the selfsame system. What everybody in *The Black Expatriates* seems most concerned about is not the furious banality of the rat race back home, but how to become an acknowledged part of it.

In his introduction, Dunbar claims that for many Negroes the resolution of "problems of identity" and the "battle for integration" are complicated by black "rejection of some of the dominant values of white America." Granted. But the only "white" value his interviewees complain about is preferential treatment. Otherwise, time and again they carry on as if there would be no problem of identity or anything else if Negroes were accepted by white Americans.

In spite of all the unmistakable evidence in the arts (not to mention psychiatric case histories) and all the social chaos and political bankruptcy, most of Dunbar's black expatriates seem downright oblivious to the fact that white Americans are having infinitely more trouble identifying themselves than Negroes have ever had. The widely admired and imitated U.S. Negro idiom in music, dance, social deportment, and even food either means that there is a U.S. Negro cultural tradition —and hence context for identity—or it means nothing! Significantly, the black exiles' nostalgia for down-home cooking (not hot dogs and hamburgers) remains strong.

The people in *The Black Expatriates* know very well who they are and what they want, but they confuse self-realization with mass-media publicity. (A rich and famous white musician, for example, does not automatically have more *identity* than an obscure Negro whose material he has appropriated.) Nevertheless, as a book about how to become more American by going overseas, *The Black Expatriates* makes interesting reading.

And so does *Where To, Black Man?*, which has drawn from a diary Ed Smith kept during his two years in Ghana with the Peace Corps. A Negro from Alabama by way of Chicago and elsewhere, Smith is not an expatriate. He is an active idealist with keen literary as well as journalistic insight. Thus his book is, among other things, a much needed antidote for some of the racist nonsense currently fashionable among "African bag" hipsters. "No," he writes of Ghana, "I shouldn't think that the Afro-American has much call to feel secure here: I'll bet when the axe of Africanization falls, white *and* black outsiders will find their wings clipped."

Freedom Bound U.S.A.

T HOSE NEGROES and those ever so liberal, completely compassionate, but very white friends of the Negro who are so
readily convinced that they must look beyond the shores of the
United States to find a great and honorable tradition of Negro
heroism are obviously unacquainted with the extraordinary
studies in Americana which have been made by Henrietta
Buckmaster, the author of *Freedom Bound*. This is unfortunate, for Miss Buckmaster's work contains indispensable information about the *actual* history of Negroes in this nation, a
subject about which most present-day liberals and those very
special Negroes they befriend seem to know so little that one
can only wonder what they really know and truly *understand*
about the nation itself. It is extremely difficult to believe that
they could possibly understand very much that is of fundamental significance. For since there never was a time when
freedom was not a basic issue in the United States, there never
was a time since 1619 when Negroes were not a basic issue.

One also wonders where their conception of heroism comes
from in the first place. They insist that they are searching for a
heritage of honor and pride and courage and devotion to
human dignity and freedom. But when they also persist in ignoring so much of the flesh-and-blood history all around them
at home and go chasing off to beat the Herskovitsian under-
brush along some African riverbank, their very procedure de-
stroys that which they claim they are seeking, and besides,
nothing that they might find in Africa could possibly be as
significant as what they have overlooked in Dismal Swamp,
Virginia.

There are homegrown Negroes who are the very embodiment of all that has ever qualified anybody for heroism. They
are in fact beyond number. They are found in every section of
the country. And they always have been there.

The very first American to shed his blood in defense of liberty at the battle of Bunker Hill was Crispus Attucks, a Negro,
who fell before the British foe on the first assault. Most very
white patriots seem never to have heard of him. On the other

hand, every U.S. schoolchild, very white, very black, brown, and beige, not only remembers but reveres Patrick Henry for merely *saying*, "Give me liberty or give me death!" It is enough to make one wonder just how much of this national hero business is really kid stuff after all.

Crispus Attucks was only one of scores of Negroes, freedmen and slaves alike, known to have served with great distinction during the Revolution even while the "problem" of their enlistment was still being debated in the Continental Congress. (It is also forgotten that white men could substitute Negroes to do their military service, and did. But that is a whole story in itself, and there is still another story in the scores of slaves who deserted to the British, who promised them freedom.) During the War of 1812 thousands fought again after having been promised emancipation for doing so. This promise, by the way, which had also been made during the Revolutionary War, was generally forgotten as soon as the war was over. Forgotten? The legal protection of slavery was made tighter! And after each war many Negroes who had been granted freedom for military service were pressed back into bondage.

But even during the days of the middle passage there were *Amistad*s and Cinqués; and during the two hundred years of slavery there were more than three hundred known slave uprisings large and small. There just simply never was a time when U.S. Negroes were not performing daring feats in quest of freedom.

And as for the fugitive slave—and there were thousands upon thousands of him—what other national figures does one place above him man for man? Who at Jamestown? Who on the *Mayflower*? Who at Valley Forge? Who at Vicksburg or Gettysburg? What mythological heroes? What fairy tale heroes, even?

There is no need to minimize the justly celebrated exploits of the backwoodsman, the keel boatman, and the prairie schoonermen (among whom, incidentally, there were also Negroes, and not unusually), but given the difference in circumstances, equipment, and, above all, *motives*, these exploits become relatively *safe*. When one sets them beside the breathtaking adventures of the runaway slave beating his way south to Florida, to the West and the Indians, to faraway Canada,

God knows how, through swamp and town alike, to freedom. Daniel Boone has been immortalized for finding his way through the wilderness to Tennessee, but remember *nobody* was chasing him. The fugitive slave not only qualifies as a national hero, he was an epic hero if ever there was one, and he came a dime a dozen. But so far the very laws which were enacted against him have been his only official tribute.

And yet all of this will come as incredible news to most very patriotic Americans. And among them will be found a staggering number of "good" teachers from the very best white schools. That every stripe of bigot will manifest this exasperating ignorance is to be expected, but so will an astonishing number of people of demonstrated goodwill. One had not thought segregation had undone so much in so many ways.

None of this (information), however, and none of its implications will come as a surprise to Henrietta Buckmaster, who is not one of those overtime friends of the Negro and the ghetto Indian, thank goodness. She is, more fundamentally, a friend of freedom, a friend of the rights of man, and therefore not only a friend but also a champion of the American Republic as the last best hope on earth. She is also a friend of journalistic accuracy and academic responsibility.

A number of years ago she made the shocking discovery that "nine out of ten" U.S. historians were guilty of ignoring, omitting, distorting, and even suppressing information about the Negro, and set about putting the record straight. The research involved was exciting enough in itself. The world she discovered "*was the very essence of adventure and romance.*"

The first result of her findings was a superbly rendered popular account of the Underground Railroad and the growth of the abolition movement which was published in 1941. It was called *Let My People Go* and has already become something of a classic on that subject. This book alone resurrected enough heroes Negro and white to fill a special national pantheon.

And speaking of representative men, it is Frederick Douglass, an ex-slave, who by any and all standards of essential worth to the nation deserves a place near Lincoln as the finest example of a nineteenth-century American, not Robert E. Lee. Schoolchildren should be told the truth. Robert E. Lee was a *Confederate* general. He fought *against* the Union. He was a *traitor.* His armies did their very best to *defend human slavery.* This was *bad.* He was *very* bad. He was *un-American.* Frederick Douglass was all-American. He championed the rights of all men. This is what the United States stands for, not the lost cause of special privilege. How utterly confusing all the hypocrisy and subversive sentimentality about Robert E. Lee must be to newly arrived immigrants and *their* children! Or is this just the sort of thing which makes European refugees realize that the simple oath of allegiance puts them one up on all native-born U.S. Negroes in so many ways?

Freedom Bound is Henrietta Buckmaster's current book. It is a relatively brief but fairly comprehensive and vividly documented summary of events immediately following the Civil War, and again she has had to set the record straight. For the image of U.S. Negroes during this critical era has not only been misrepresented, it has been defiled. In fact, no other period in U.S. history has been more systematically falsified to justify racism, segregation, and the political doctrine of white supremacy.

Consequently the average American, even today, still thinks of the Reconstruction as having been ill advised if not downright sinister and even degenerate at its very inception. This same sometimes well-meaning American is also likely to *concede* that the Reconstruction program was at any rate foredoomed by completely unscrupulous Yankee carpetbaggers and thoroughly corrupt local scalawags who used totally and inherently unfit Negroes to add insult to injury as they plundered the prostrate but gallant South.

The facts are otherwise. Never in history has a defeated enemy received such *generosity* from the victors. Those who had tried to destroy the Union were back in the Union with an incredible amount of power and privilege in six weeks' time and were allowed to continue the old fight by all means short of formal declaration of war! As for the Reconstruction program itself, it was designed to convert the freedman *and the poor white* into productive citizens. Property confiscated toward this end, it should be remembered, had already been *won* in the battle. *After all, the owners could have been shot as traitors.*

As for the Negro politician of that day, *Freedom Bound* cites instance after instance to show that not only was he as well qualified as the general run of his white colleagues in many ways, his credentials were outstanding. And at any rate, the measures which he supported were not only worthwhile but also in the best interests of the nation at large. Ironically enough, one has only to indicate the key role the Negro politician (and voter) played in bringing *universal suffrage*, *public education*, and *public health services* to the South, an indispensable role which he played consciously.

But then heroism, when it is tragic heroism—which is certainly what this was—always involves irony. On the other hand, it is not only ironic but downright ludicrous when present-day white northern liberals who never heard of the nearly two hundred thousand Negroes who fought in the Union army, to say nothing of the work many of the veterans did with the Freedman's Bureaus, presume to teach U.S. Negroes self-respect. In thick accents yet, *mamma mia, nein*, comrade! How many white American voters have ever faced the threats of overwhelming terror the Negro voters braved during the Reconstruction? Thousands of unintimidated Negroes were murdered, ambushed, massacred on their way to and from polling places during one seven-year period.

The Reconstruction was not a golden age. Not by any means. It failed. But not only can current civil rights leaders look with frank pride at the statute of the remarkable predecessors in whose great footsteps they follow, they should aspire to be as bold. They should hope to have visions as broad. They should seek to maintain as much integrity under fire.

The nineteenth-century U.S. Negro leader did not take his cues from tax-exempt charitable organizations. He welcomed assistance of course. But he also insisted on his own definitions and he never ceased to *demand* his rights. He had traveled the Underground Railroad, had been through the Civil War; he knew very well what all of the shooting was about, and he had never really regarded the United States as being the white world, even during slavery. He thought of it as a land of incomparable opportunity for *free* men, and he was right.

Neither did he waste very much of his time on any nonsense about Negritude and the whole complex continent of Africa. He was much too busy with such immediate things as the everyday bread-and-butter matters of U.S. citizenship for that. Few freedmen went back to Africa after emancipation. Far more came back "home" from Canada. Most were here to stay and had always known it, and many among them were actively engaged to run things. Hiram Revels, for instance, became U.S. senator from Mississippi, filling the seat vacated by Jefferson Davis. James Rapier and Jerimiah Haralson went to Congress from Alabama, and in Washington they met many Negro politicians from other states. There were Negroes elected to the legislatures in most southern states, and in South Carolina, Mississippi, and Louisiana they became lieutenant governors. P. B. S. Pinchback became governor of Louisiana for a short time. And so on and on it went.

These men were seldom faked off-balance by disguised theories of race or ideology. It took betrayal on a national scale and wholesale terrorism and outright murder unparalleled in U.S. history to reduce them to second-class citizenship. They were never reduced to second-class men. In a very special sense the last of these men were still around until Jack Johnson died in an automobile accident in 1946.

Somebody is forever and ever reminding U.S. Negroes that they need allies. Perhaps they do, although the reminder is itself obscenely racist in its implications. All causes need allies. Genuine allies. But U.S. Negroes most emphatically do not need a bunch of misinformed, misdirected, self-indulgent white creeps and silly billies fouling up the atmosphere with a lot of nitwit definitions and generalizations from Marx and Freud without the slightest awareness of the basic issues, the political realities, or the actual historical context of the struggle itself.

U.S. Negroes certainly do need more white "allies" who will take the time to study and try to understand what *American Negroes* are all about, who can identify with their glories and therefore truly empathize with their defeats. They can use many more people like Henrietta Buckmaster. But then she is not really so very white as she is a responsible and very much engaged fellow citizen, and after all, the nation needs her freedom-based heroes as much as Negroes do.

The Good Old Boys Down Yonder

To some people the special breed of ever so colorful white Southerners that Paul Hemphill recommends as the good old boys are likely to be nobody but the same old too-familiar hateful-eyed, razor-backed, lynch-mob-prone, willfully backward, hysterically insecure, but undeniably gritty peckerwoods, hillbillies, crackers, rednecks, Hoosiers, and swamp crawlers once thought to be the primary antagonists of civil rights. To others they will no doubt suggest nothing so much as William Faulkner's brass-stealing, barn-burning, horse-trading, manure-tracking, but no less shrewd than persistent Snopeses of *The Hamlet*, *The Town*, and *The Mansion*. Indeed, in Hemphill's own words, they represent a "mean, half-educated, vengeful, regressive" side of the South, and the world could very well do without it.

But for Hemphill, who grew up as one of them (or, perhaps more precisely, as the son of one of them), they also represent something "distinctive and good," a spirit and a style that gives him a "sense of place" that eludes him in such unsavory whereabouts as New York and the Philadelphia of Grace Kelly (of Monaco?). As good old Louis Armstrong once did about the blues, he allows as how if you don't already know what a good old boy is, you never will. But it is easy enough to see that he is talking about a special kind of self-styled and even wrongheaded personal integrity that he for one associates with hard-drinking, hell-raising, chance-taking truck drivers, good old sheriffs(!), baseball bums, country singers, and stock car racers, among others, whose motto is probably: "Hang in there, old buddy."

Paul Hemphill himself is a journalist from Alabama by way of Georgia, the *Atlanta Journal*, and the Harvard of Nieman Fellows. He is also the author of *The Nashville Sound*, a book about country music. *The Good Old Boys* is a collection of newspaper and magazine articles about the South in the late 1950s and early 1970s, and he says it is intended more or less as an epitaph.

To be sure. Even as he reconciles himself to the inevitability

791

of the extensive changes that have brought better housing, food, education, and race relations to the South, his mood becomes elegiac: "The Good Old Boys are out in the suburbs now, living in identical houses and shopping at the Kmart and listening to Glen Campbell (Roy Acuff and Ernest Tubb are too tacky now) and hiding their racism behind code words. They have forfeited their style and their spirit, traded it all in on a color TV and Styrofoam beams for the den, and I find them about as exciting as reformed alcoholics."

In other words, as full of a "sense of place" as he becomes when he remembers the South from elsewhere, and for all his folk-hero-worshipful protestations, when Hemphill actually gets down to cases he finds very little left to celebrate. The good old boys, like the good old days during which they came into being, are something else southern that is mostly gone with the wind: "No more tent revivalists blowing through town like rainmakers," he laments at another point. "No more fat-bellied sheriffs fleecing the Yankees out on U.S. 1. No more Crackers double-parking in front of the Grand Ole Opry House and coming out later with a contract. No more Governors with the audacity to tell the multitude that they have three friends: 'God, Sears & Roebuck and Eugene Talmadge.'" And so on. No more fooling the Feds and so on.

Still, nostalgia for the good-old-time good times is hardly the definitive characteristic of the childhood and family experiences he recalls with so much feeling in "Me and My Old Man." Nor can his attitude toward his father be called idolatrous. It is now very pleasant to remember some of the long highway trips they made in the truck together and baseball games and fantasies they shared. But the fact is his old man (who was a family maverick to begin with) was a hell of a problem to come to terms with. Indeed, it was not until Hemphill came back from his year at Harvard and decided to overlook his father's racial hang-ups, among other things, that he finally found his present appreciation for his father's "involvement in and passion for life, his willingness to take on the world if necessary," and his disposition to hang in there, win, lose, or draw.

Nor does Hemphill recount his misadventures as a Class D

baseball novice to commemorate any days of youthful glory. They were miserable days of very thin hope and great anguish and disappointment. Furthermore, what everybody else down there in Class D was about above everything else was making it the hell out of there and into the big leagues, which was strictly up north in those days. And most would never come as close as the failed "bonus babies" dug up for "What Ever Happened to Whatsisname?" On the other hand, Bob Suffridge, the all-time all-American from Tennessee, has had some absolutely splendid days at the very summit of national acclaim. But if he is an example of a good ole poor white boy hanging with it, Hemphill better forget it. As for such contemporary marvels as mortician Ray Ligon of the Death Hilton, Judge Roy Hofheinz of the Houston Astrodome, the Georgia "folk" movie moguls, such new-style evangelists as Oral Roberts and Mike Gilchrist, and the new best-selling hillbilly singers, and so on and on and on, are they to be more admired than puzzled over?

The Good Old Boys is not nearly so free of old-time rebel-hooping sentimentality as was Marshall Frady's *Wallace* of several years ago. Nevertheless, as a result of treating poor white Southerners as colorful, and even legendary—but still flesh-and-blood human beings—Hemphill gets much closer to the actual texture of circumstances in the South today than do the so-called findings of survey technicians, the validity, reliability, and comprehensiveness of whose methodology is supposed to go without saying, but whose obligatory social relevance somehow always seems to lead them to downgrade intrinsic human values and potentialities in favor of welfare statistics. Anyway, anybody who thinks you have to be well-to-do and politically powerful *before* you can be colorful or fabulous not only knows nothing at all of Southerners but very little about human nature.

But perhaps best of all, Paul Hemphill himself (who sometimes thinks of himself as a failed baseball player but is clearly a big-league journalist, and is also the true hero of *The Good Old Boys*) may just turn out to be one of a new breed of pretty good old boys who in the end are likely to be of far more worth to the best interests of the nation at large than any except a few of those from the good old days. Already—or so his sober ambivalence toward his father seems to indicate—he is one who is beyond embracing, or in any case defending, all of the worst shortcomings of the South because he prefers to live there. It's almost enough to raise your outrage tolerance level for square dancing and Grand Ole Opry music.

The "Reconstruction" of
Robert Penn Warren

ROBERT PENN WARREN, a white Anglo-Saxon Protestant Southerner, a onetime apologist for segregation, a long-time colleague of the old agrarian romantics, and a sometime friend of countless white supremacists and even Dixiecrats, has written a new book which is perhaps the very best inside report on the Negro civil rights movement by anyone so far. In spite of several ridiculous flaws, which are much more characteristic of certain New York indoor intellectuals than of a worldly, realistic, and thoughtful son of a hardheaded old Kentucky dirt farmer, *Who Speaks for the Negro?* deserves the widest possible circulation.

The title is misleading. This is not only a book about current U.S. Negro leaders and spokesmen. It is really a book about the fundamentals of citizenship which the author, a top-flight novelist, poet, and critic, compiled from a series of taped interviews and interspersed with his own reactions and commentary. It is also by far the most comprehensive treatment of the complex issues in the civil rights controversy on record. For the most part it is also the most objective. But even when it is most personal its accuracy is seldom compromised. Indeed it achieves its greatest reliability through the very frankness with which it indulges in introspection.

It is as if Jack Burden, the self-searching southern reporter/press agent, the narrator of *All the King's Men*, Warren's prize-winning novel of some fourteen years ago, had finally gone back into the newspaper business. At the end of the sequence of sordid and sanguinary events which climaxed that hard-boiled story about power politics in a southern state, Burden holed up in one of those beautiful but haunted antebellum mansions finishing a book about one of his Confederate ancestors. He had always had a very special personal urge to come to terms with the past. In fact, the book he was working on had actually started out as a dissertation for a Ph.D. in *history*. But even as he wrote he knew very well that soon now he would "*go out of the house and go into the convulsion of the world, out of history into history and the awful responsibility of Time.*"

It was inevitable that this responsibility, awful or magnificent, would require a truly serious and sensitive Southerner to confront the all too obvious fact that Negroes are a major force which determines much if not most of the convulsion in his immediate region of the world. Most Southerners, sensitive or not, come to realize this in some way or other sooner or later. Too many other Americans never do. In the special case of Jack Burden, his very sense of history would eventually lead him to realize that his destiny has always been inextricably entangled with that of the Negroes all around him.

At any rate, in *Who Speaks for the Negro?* Robert Penn Warren himself turns out to be just the sort of all-American star reporter/commentator one had hoped his training and experience had prepared Jack Burden to become. As a matter of fact, few present-day newsmen can touch him. The writing is much more than first-rate journalism. At its best it has many of the finest qualities of good fiction: strong narrative progression, carefully observed and rendered detail, roundness and mystery of character, a mature awareness of the enigmatic complexity of human motives, and a fine sense of the texture of human life itself.

Warren is always at his best when he works within the framework of the novelist. He is least reliable when he allows himself to be sucked in by the all too neat theories of this or that social science. Then he sounds like a reading room intellectual. He wastes entirely too much time, for instance, fumbling around with Stanley M. Elkins's classroom theories about Samboism (*sic!*). When he sits listening to Charles Evers telling about the heroic past between himself and his martyred brother Medgar, the novelist in him spots the almost too pat rhetorical dynamics even as he accepts the truth of what is being said. Not so, however, when some postulating head-shrinker wraps *his* rhetoric about Sambo archetypes in the jargon of psychiatry. He also lets the cocktail party theorists fake him into making glib speculations which would reduce music, dance, sports, and even robust sexuality into questionable assets. Do these writers ever wonder how they sound to Negroes? Negroes think all of these things are wonderful. They are not the least bit interested in giving them up. They want to add other things to them.

A most remarkable quality of Warren the interviewer, on the other hand, is his unique lack of condescension. Unlike most U.S. newsmen, he accepts his people for what they are, tries to understand them, records their opinions as faithfully as possible whether he agrees with them or not, never presumes, never attempts to browbeat. Thus his subjects come through as highly significant human beings engaged in a very serious controversy, and his book is a highly dependable source of firsthand historical highlights of this domestic crisis over the last ten years.

The Negro leaders and spokesmen Warren visited on his zigzag trips to most of the key locations directly involved in the civil rights struggle represent all of the organizations and all the walks of U.S. Negro life. They themselves range from folk types to intellectuals. All are dedicated. All have a great awareness of the moral issues involved, and the overwhelming majority have a responsible and realistic sense of their own power. Those who have been physically brutalized, jailed, terrorized remain even more steadfast. Not only are most of them very articulate, many have held their own in the highest councils of the nation, and Warren respects their achievements, their courage, and their intelligence.

There is, however, far too much academic pretentiousness among them. Almost everybody takes the stance of a social scientist of some kind, as if one's own sense of life is not valid unless it conforms to the going terminology. This sometimes causes some to talk a lot of pedantic nonsense which their very existence and their very actions belie. None, for example, seem more cocksure than those who insist that they have been oppressed and degraded to the point of self-hatred. None are more racist and Afro-nationalist than those who complain loudest about being *forced* into a *ghetto*!

There are significant statements of policy and outlook by Martin Luther King Jr., Adam Clayton Powell, Roy Wilkins of the NAACP, Whitney Young of the Urban League, James Farmer of CORE, James Foreman of SNCC, Robert Moses and Aaron Henry of the Mississippi Freedom Democrats, and the late Malcolm X, among others. There are also the theories of Bayard Rustin, the organizer, and Kenneth Clark, the child psychologist and self-styled ghetto expert, and there are the polemics of best-selling civil rights author James Baldwin, whom Warren calls "the voice himself."

Richest in intellectual resonance are Warren's exchanges with Ralph Ellison, whose *Shadow and Act* speaks not only for Negroes but for the United States and for contemporary man. Ellison is as solidly grounded in social science as most specialists who work at it full time. But first-rate novelist and man of letters that he is, his insights always extend beyond the standard assumptions. Thus he discusses integration, for instance, but in terms of the basic pluralism of U.S. life. And when he examines the actual nature of the experience of Negroes during slavery and under oppression he is always aware of the Negro's own conception of himself. This enables him to reveal the background to that power of character, that courage and tenacity, that sense of timing, and that discipline before provocation and violence which sustains the flesh-and-blood heroism one witnesses in the movement in confrontation after confrontation.

Robert Penn Warren, still the professional Southerner in spite of himself, sitting in his New England study with his fresh travel memories, notes and tape recorder, and the voices of Yankees outside his window, has gone a long way from Pondy Woods and such smug provincialisms as "Nigger, your breed ain't metaphysical." He had gone a great distance when he wrote *Segregation*, his account of the inner conflict in the South in 1956; and was a bit farther on when he wrote *The Legacy of the Civil War*.

Like most Americans, he still has a long way to go. But like an increasing number of Southerners, among them Lyndon B. Johnson of Texas and Ralph McGill of Georgia, he is much farther along than many damn Yankees, including some black ones, who thought they were there already.

Louis Armstrong in His Own Words

THERE CAME A TIME when Louis Armstrong decided that his importance as a musician and his status as a worldwide American entertainer and "ambassador of goodwill" were such that he should produce his own personal documentation of his career. The first of those efforts was published in 1936, when Armstrong himself was not yet thirty-six years old. Its title was *Swing That Music*. No collaborator, editor, or ghostwriter was identified, not even when the book was reissued fifty-seven years later. Most of the personal information may well have come directly from Armstrong or was presumably approved by him, but not even the inscription in the book comes across as a credible approximation of either his voice on the page or his point of view. It runs as follows: *"To the memory of the Original 'Dixieland Five,' to 'King' Oliver, to 'Bix' Beiderbecke and Eddie Lang, now gone, and those other pioneers of a quarter of a century past, known and unknown, who created and carried to the world a native American music, who created swing. And, finally, to the young musicians of today who will carry it on."*

The grateful list of specific names is not intended to be comprehensive, of course; but given the restricted nature of social relations in New Orleans when he was growing up there, did Armstrong himself really think of the Original Dixieland Five as being more crucial to his conception of music than the legend of Buddy Bolden, who came before King Oliver? And what about Mr. Peter Davis, who as bandmaster at the Waifs' Home turned him into a cornet player in the first place? And what about the definitive influence of the blues and of ragtime piano players including Tony Jackson and also of old Jelly Roll Morton, whose "King Porter Stomp" dates back to 1903? And what about the impact of Armstrong's parade and funeral cortege "second-line" apprenticeship upon his art, or his Mississippi riverboat experience as a member of Fate Marable's crackshot band on the *Dixie Belle*, which took him all the way up north for the first time.

Swing That Music covers the chronology of Armstrong's career up to 1936, and it includes just about all of the highlights and significant transitions up to that point, except his trouble with Chicago and New York gangster owners of nightclubs and with his manager Johnny Collins in England. But the book reads more like it was written for him than by him or even with him, except for occasional interviews and consultations. It is hard to imagine him at one of those C-SPAN book events fielding questions about the career of the Original Dixieland Band. It is impossible to imagine him as the author of this representative passage: "They [Sidney Bechet, soprano sax, and Ed Atkins, trombone] actually got to London ahead of the Dixieland, which arrived about the end of 1917, and those boys took old London by storm. Nobody there had ever heard anything like it. Later on Bachet [*sic*] toured the Continent with Jim Europe's band."

Armstrong's second book-length autobiographical publication, *Satchmo: My Life in New Orleans*, appeared in 1954. It comes across as an "as told to" memoir, though once again no collaborator is listed. It obviously went through many revisings and polishings, but it comes closer to representing Armstrong's voice in its language as well as its recollections and perceptions and attitudes. Of course, the accurate representation of one's voice on the page should not be confused with verbatim transcription of one's voice in person or on the stage.

As any competent student of literary composition should know, the more natural and casual a voice sounds in print, the more likely it is to have been edited time and again. It is not a matter of making a record of things, memories, opinions, and notions as they come to mind. It is a matter of composition. Effective stream-of-consciousness narration is the product of verbal precision, not just jotting things down as they come to mind or through free association. It requires as much unity, coherence, and emphasis as any other form of effective communication. As Count Basie made a point of telling his "as told to" collaborator at the outset of the recorded interviews that were to be used as the raw-material basis for *Good Morning Blues*, the most likely effect that the publication of the literal transcriptions would create was the impression that he didn't know what he was talking about, that he was fumbling around because he didn't have himself together yet.

If it is properly done, the "as told to" autobiography represents how the subject *wants* his story told. To achieve this end, he enlists a competent and empathetic craftsman to make him sound like he thinks his voice should come across on the page. Unless he is completely illiterate he realizes that producing a book is a matter of *writing*, not just talking and gesturing. You may imagine that the reader can hear your voice and see the gestures and the action as you remember them, *but he can do so only if it is all effectively rendered by the words as written.*

Satchmo takes the Armstrong story only up to his arrival in Chicago in 1923 to join King Oliver's band, then playing at the Lincoln Gardens at Thirty-first Street and Cottage Grove Avenue. A sequel to *Satchmo*, much of which is said to have been a part of the original manuscript, was planned but it is also said to have been suppressed by Joe Glaser, Armstrong's longtime manager, because it included numerous references to Armstrong's passion for marijuana, and his numerous questionable friends, and his troubles with unsavory or even criminal producers as well as law enforcement agencies that Glaser felt would be extremely damaging to Armstrong's universally popular public image. After all, by 1950 he had come to be regarded as a worldwide American "ambassador of goodwill," a bona fide national treasure.

Still, Armstrong is said to have continued to work on the manuscript for years; but no book-length drafts of it have turned up, in spite of claims by friends that he read parts of it to them from time to time. Now a new miscellany of selected writings has appeared, as *Louis Armstrong: In His Own Words.* It includes a 28-page selection labeled "The Armstrong Story," dated 1954, which recounts the years in Chicago from his arrival through 1924 and includes his marriage to his second wife, Lil Hardin, a piano player, who also had become a member of King Oliver's band. There is also a short biographical summary labeled "The Goffin Notebooks," which was prepared sometime around 1944 for Robert Goffin, the Belgian jazz critic and historian who was writing *Horn of Plenty*, the first biography of Armstrong.

These notes begin with entries about his life in New Orleans in 1918, and they include anecdotes about his first years in Chicago; his time in New York with the Fletcher Henderson Orchestra; his return to Chicago and stints with his wife Lil's band, with Erskine Tate's Vendome Orchestra, Carroll Dickerson's Orchestra; his affair with Alpha Smith (she was to become his third wife); his return to New York, where he played at Connie's Inn and in Connie's *Hot Chocolates* musical on Broadway; and his trip out to California and Frank Sebastian's Cotton Club in Culver City. The text concludes with Armstrong's return to Chicago in 1931 and his troubles with gangster club owners about bookings:

> Then this 'Guy said—"I am 'Frankie Foster." At 'first—I 'still didn't 'pay it any 'Attention—to 'that extent. 'Anyway—*Then* it 'dawned on me what he said—And I 'turned in 'Cold 'Sweats as I 'Back 'Cap'd—'Mugg'd—And took a 'double look'—As I said to him—"What you say your 'name wuz?: By this time he had his Big 'Pistol—Pulling it out—As he said—"My name is 'Frankie Foster." And he said he was sent over to my place (Show Boat) to see that I 'Catch the first train out to 'New York. I 'still try to make it appear that he ain't 'Frightening me.' I said—"New York? 'Why—that's 'News to me. Mr. Collins didn't tell me anything about it.'" Frankie Foster (a bad "sommitch") said, "Oh, yes.'—'you're going to 'New York to work at 'Connie's Inn. And you're 'leaving 'tomorrow morning." Then He Flashed his Big Ol' Pistol and 'Aimed it 'Straight at 'me. With my 'eyes as 'big as 'Saucers and 'frightened too I said—" *Well* 'Maybe I '*AM* 'going to 'New York." "Ooh 'God." Then 'Frankie Foster said—"O.K. The 'Telephone 'Receiver is 'Down waiting for you to come and 'say you'll be there. Now—'you and 'me are going to the 'telephone booth and you'll 'talk." By this time—'Anything he 'ordered of me was 'alright—because it's no trouble at all for a 'Gangster to 'pull the 'Trigger—'especially when they have you 'Cornered and you 'Disobey them." "Soooo" we went to the 'phone (with a gun in my side) and sure enough, someone said hello, a familiar voice too—yes sir—I know that voice if I heard it a Hundred years from now. The first words he said to me was—'When are you gonna open here?' I turned and look 'direct into Frankie Foster's face—and said 'Tomorrow AM.'

Armstrong wrote by ear. He did not write as one was taught to write in grade school, with pencil, pen, and blackboard chalk. Somehow the idea or the anecdote that he has in mind comes across, but it reads more like a very rough first draft, rougher even than a hurriedly dashed-off letter of gossip or a postcard from foreign parts. His grammar and his punctuation are hit-and-miss when they are not just eccentric.

Now, one can often get away with playing music by ear when it is not being recorded, but writing is another matter, its mistakes are not forgotten because they are still there to confuse us. The fact is that old Gates did not make that typewriter sing like his horn. He did not write as masterfully as he sang or as he spoke his instantly and universally infectious jive talk.

The new collection, edited by Thomas Brothers, includes also "The Satchmo Story," from early 1959, which Armstrong also labeled "The Satchmo Story, Second Edition" (by which it is possible that Armstrong really meant the Satchmo Story, volume two). Here Armstrong discusses the origins of his life-long involvement with marijuana. He began to use the drug when he came back to Chicago from his first stay in New York. Armstrong regarded marijuana as a healthful herb that should not be classified as an illegal narcotic drug, and he continued to use it and to celebrate it, even though it got him into trouble with the authorities during a sensationally successful engagement in Culver City,

> where I was blowing like mad at the Frank Sebastian's Cotton Club—upsetting all the movie stars. . . . They would pack that great big fine place every night. . . .
>
> The first time that I smoked Marijuana (or) Gage as they so beautifully calls' it some time [he wrote] was a couple of years after I had left Fletcher Henderson's Orchestra—playing at the Roseland in New York. . . . And returned to Chicago. . . . It was actually in Chicago when I first picked up my first stick of gage. . . . And I'm telling you, I had myself a Ball. . . . The days when I first found out about gage—there weren't any law against it. . . . New York weren't 'up on it—when I first went there. . . . Of course 'I wasn't 'either at the time. . . . I probably wouldn't have paid any attention to it either. . . . But to me—I being a great observer of life, I happen to notice the white young musicians coming every night to this swell night club where I was playing—and although they had just finished their jobs, they still looked fresh neat and very contented. . . . And they would really enjoy my trumpet playing with the highest

enthusiasm that any human being could do for another. . . . I just came up from the South, I was just thrilled with the closeness and warmth of these great musicians, performers, etc. . . .

 . . . And they would praise me, which sounded to me like they were swinging a tune. . . . Beautiful. . . . So it wasn't any problem when I went places with them. . . . After all this knowing each other and when they'd 'Light up, why—during the conversation, of whom ever be sitting around the room,—and at the same time—somebody or everybody would be 'blasting like Heavenly,'—out of a clear skies a *stick of gage* would touch the palm of my hand—or the tip of my finger. . . .

Armstrong names no names, not even Mezz Mezzrow, the Chicago saxophone and clarinet player who was his main supplier for years, not only in Chicago but also in New York, where, as Mezzrow wrote in his own as-told-to memoir *Really the Blues*, "Louis and I were running together all the time, and we togged so sharp we got to be known as the Esquires of Harlem." Mezzrow himself was eventually done in by hard drugs, but his appreciation of Armstrong was as profound as it was worshipful: *"Everyday, soon as I woke up about 4 in the P.M., I would jump up to Louis' apartment and most of the time catch him in the shower. That man really enjoyed his bath and shave. I would sit there watching him handle his razor, sliding it along with such rhythm and grace you could feel each individual hair being cut, and I'd think it was just like the way he fingered the valves of his horn, in fact, just like he did everything. When he slid his fingertips over the buttons, delicate as an embroiderer and still so masculine, the tones took wing as though they sprang from his fingers instead of his lips. The way he shaved put me in mind of the time Louis was blowing and I brushed up against him by accident, and goddamn if I didn't feel his whole body vibrating like one of those electric testing machines in the penny arcade that tell how many volts your frame can stand. Louis really blew with every dancing molecule in his body. He did everything like that, graceful and easy but still full of power and drive. He was a dynamo with a slight slouch."* About Mezzrow and music, Armstrong once remarked that "Mezz could explain every little iota of meaning in jazz, every little beat of the drum, riff on the piano, the changes in the blues and every little phrase he thought would benefit those Austin high school lads." (The latter were among his most enthusiastic fans and emulators in Chicago in the 1920s.)

Armstrong is said to have continued to smoke marijuana while serving out his suspended sentence in California, and he never stopped, recommending it to friends and admirers and sometimes providing it to members of his band for certain sessions because he thought it would improve their performance. "First place it's a thousand times better than whisky. . . . It's an Assistant—a friend a nice cheap joke if you want to call it that. . . . Good (very good) for Asthma—Relaxes your nerves. . . . Great for cleanderness. . . . Much different than a dope fiend. . . . A dope addict, from what I noticed by watching a lot of different 'cats' whom I used to light up with but got so carried away they felt they could get a much bigger kick by jugging themselves in the ass with a needle—Heroin—Cocaine—etc.—or some other ungodly shit. . . . Which would not ever phase a man like myself, who've always had a sane mind from the day I was born. . . ."

In an article in the December 1951 issue of *Esquire*, also reprinted in Brothers's volume, Armstrong discusses certain selections from the epoch-making Hot Five and Hot Seven recording sessions in Chicago during the period of 1926–27, the recordings that announced Armstrong's preeminence as a definitive jazz innovator. In the arts, the actual avant-garde (as opposed to the theoretical one) always makes itself known by its real impact, its actual influence, rather than by declarations of intent and stirring, abstract manifestos. When the Hot Five and Hot Seven recordings were issued, Armstrong, who never produced a manifesto in his life, became the very embodiment of the avant-garde artist. The Hot Five and Hot Seven recordings amounted to a musical revolution.

Armstrong's solos became the model for the jazz solo on all instruments; and the impact of these sessions on jazz arrangement and orchestration amounted to the beginnings of an American approach to the concerto, or showcase, for solo instruments. The Hot Five and Hot Seven combos existed only as recording studio groups; they never played for a live audience in a club, a dance hall, or a theater. Still, their output became the model for a truly indigenous American chamber music—the actual venue for American chamber music being the rent party and other parlor socials, the honky-tonk, the juke joint, the neighborhood bar and grill, the gin mill, the cocktail lounge, the small nightclub, and the like.

In an "editor's note," *Esquire* provided an appropriate introduction to Armstrong's reflections: *"Mr. Satchmo Louis Armstrong couldn't be expected to write about Jazz of the Twenties in the usual way simply because he is a very unusual personality. Herewith, recording by recording—eighteen of them—Satchmo tells his own jazz story as it really happened; the people, the places, the inspirations. As always, he says what he has to say with freshness, originality and meaning—the way he would say it on his horn."* Of course, the whole piece also reads as if it has been carefully and respectfully copyedited (perhaps from a transcription) as it should have been.

Armstrong talks about the pieces as the recordings are played for him, and his observations are not technical or academic. He does not offer musical theory; but what he says amounts to a natural history of the processes involved in the creation of these masterpieces. These sessions are not only a celebration of the improvisation that is an indispensable element of the New Orleans music that produced Armstrong; they are also an extension, an elaboration, and a refinement of it, as Armstrong goes beyond King Oliver while giving him credit for setting the standards that he is still trying to reach.

The result, again, caused a revolution in American musical taste and musical practice comparable to the effect that the innovations of Picasso and Braque had on contemporary visual art, and that the poetry of Eliot and the prose of Hemingway had on contemporary literature. In the music of the Hot Fives and Hot Sevens, the "barbaric yawp" of Whitman's energetic pioneers acquires the syncopated elegance of the blues. It is not at all far-fetched to imagine that Emerson would have discerned in the extraordinary solos of Armstrong's omni-American trumpet "melodies of the poet [that] ascend and leap and pierce into the deeps of infinite time." If only the great American Transcendentalists had heard "Potato Head Blues"! And what could announce the arrival of the genuinely American more truthfully than "West End Blues"?

In his comments about the Hot Fives and the Hot Sevens in *Esquire*, the achievement that Armstrong is most happy to acknowledge is the fact that the pieces were played well, and are still a pleasure to hear. In these remarks he is concerned not with innovation, but with authenticity. What pleases him most about the Hot Fives and Hot Sevens is that the New Orleans musicians with whom he recorded in Chicago—Kid Ory, trombone; Johnny Dodds, clarinet and alto; Johnny St. Cyr, banjo; Zutty Singleton, drums; Baby Dodds, drums; and his wife Lil Hardin, who had worked with King Oliver's band—played together better than he had expected, and his expectations always were high.

For some reason, the present volume does not include an auto-biographical sequence about Armstrong's experiences in and around Storyville, the legendary red-light district in New Orleans, that was published in November 1947 in *True* magazine. The magazine observed about this little memoir that "although his manuscript contains many minor mistakes in grammar and punctuation, we, as editors, believe it contains some of the finest writing we have ever seen." It is indeed a highly effective sequence which at its best reminds one of some of the old outrageous yarns that used to get spun and respun and challenged and sometimes topped and even transfigured during those old pre-radio and pre-TV down-home fireside, barroom, and barbershop whiskey-sipping, lie-swapping sessions. Here is a typical passage: "Two of the biggest funerals I've ever seen in New Orleans were Clerk Wade and Henry Zeno. . . . Of course Clerk was killed by one of his whores when he was standing at the bar in (25) and she came in to ask him to take her back and he shun'd her and he abused her lightly in front of the other Pimps. . . . She stood back and pulled out a shiny pistol and emptied it into his body. . . . Clerk died right there on the spot. . . . The district was very sad about it for days and days. . . . The day 'Clerk was buried—I never saw so many girls crying over one man in my whole life. . . . All the pimps turned out also all the prostitutes —colored and white. . . . Some of the Pimps were Pallbearers. . . . He was so famous until even the respectable people of the city—the churches were all sad over his death. . . . The woman who killed him pleaded guilty and told the judge she 'supported him and 'hustled for him and gave him every nickle she could rake and scrape. . . . She was Aquited. . . ."

Armstrong's reminiscences here (as elsewhere) are no less a

product of this old idiomatic down-home practice—it is really a kind of aesthetic form—than are some of the poems of Langston Hughes or the fiction of Ralph Ellison. When Ellison finished *Invisible Man* in 1951, he wrote to a friend and literary colleague at Tuskegee that his editor was "having a time deciding what kind of novel it is, and I can't help him. For me it's just a big fat old Negro lie, meant to be told during cotton picking time over a water bucket full of corn [whiskey], with the dipper passing back and forth at a good fast clip so that no one, not even the narrator himself will realize how utterly preposterous the lie really is."

Such lie-swapping may best be delivered in a highly idiomatic rhetoric, including the crudest forms of dialect. In print, though, these mischievous narratives will not be enhanced by illiterate imprecision. After all, publishers hire editors to correct such rawness. Talking is one thing and writing is another, even when the subject is the same. In terms of sense and coherence, what is the average reader to make of the following?

> I was still married to 'Lil Armstrong—she was also out in California with me the whole time I was out there. Also the man she 'claimed she had him 'travel with her from New York everywhere she would go to '*Massage* her '*Hips*.—Keeping them from getting too 'large—'UMP—She sure must have thought I was a *Damn fool 'Sho Nuff*.' As if I didn't know her 'Hips are sure to '*Ignite*' from the 'Friction.'—Later on, I found out that this 'Guy' and 'Lil had been "Going together and 'he'd been 'Spending my 'money for years.
>
> So while I was out at the 'Cotton Club out in 'Culver City—'Alpha came out there too. The 'Lord Must have sent her out there to me.—As 'surprised as I were, that she came—I was 'Glad to see her also. 'Alpha said she 'love me so, she happen to be thinking 'strongly 'about me in 'Chicago. And after she had finished doing her 'Show out in 'Cicero Ill., which she was a chorus girl on 'Al Capone's Night Club—'Lucky Millender was the 'Producer. 'Alpha said she was so 'Blue from 'thinking about me, and 'missed me so "terribly much," that she 'Boarded a 'Train for 'California. And before she *knew* it—she wuz in 'California she gotten 'Scared—'lost her 'nerve—and thought that I'd get 'sore with her for 'coming 'way out there. But I was so 'glad to see her again, which I hadn't for 'months and 'months. I just couldn't help but say to her—"Now that you are 'out

here you might as well 'stay and I'll find you a 'room"—which I 'did. So after 'Lil and her 'sweet 'Daddy return home from 'California in my 'Car, I sent for 'Alpha to come back home in 'Chicago. Alpha's 'mother Mrs. 'Smith was still staying in that old 'Shabby Apartment at '33rd and 'Cottage Grove Avenue. So since I was back with 'Lil,' Alpha went back 'home and lived with her 'Mother.—

Alas, for all the attention that Armstrong himself called to his serious and ongoing commitment to writing his own story, and to his constant use of his typewriter and dictionary, both of which he took along with him on all of his travels, there is very little evidence in any of his published writings that he ever grasped the importance of, say, a junior high school level of competence in the fundamentals of grammar, syntax, and meaning. Surely they are just as indispensable to the writing of even the simplest narratives as the rudimentary technical elements that he spent so much time practicing and mastering in order to play his music.

Armstrong had much to say over the years about musicians he admired and imitated, but the only mention of a writer that comes to mind is a somewhat questionable reference to Mark Twain in *Swing That Music*. And there is no impressive evidence in any of Armstrong's writing to suggest that Twain's prose motivated Armstrong to master the typewriter as King Oliver and other New Orleans jazz musicians had inspired him to master the cornet and the trumpet.

If he had only realized that right there, along with all of those fly threads in *Esquire* that all of those big-city sharp cats were checking out in the 1930s, was Hemingway, and that he was swinging a lot of American prose like Armstrong himself was swinging the blues and pop song choruses, and was trying to put other writers hip to how it was done, just as King Oliver and other New Orleans musicians tried to clue him in on swinging the trumpet: "Listen," Hemingway wrote in a dialogue entitled "Monologue to the Maestro" in *Esquire*, October 1935, "when you start to write you get all the kick and the reader gets none. So you might as well use a typewriter because it's much easier and you enjoy it that much more. After you learn to write, your whole object is to convey every sensation, sight, feeling, place and emotion to the reader. To do this you have to work over what you write. If you write with a pencil, you get three different sights at it to see if the reader is getting what you want him to. First, when you read it over; then when it is typed you get another chance to improve it. That is .333, which is a damn good average for a hitter. It also keeps it fluid longer so that you can better it easier."

The irresistibly elegant good taste that is always there in Armstrong's music is just simply not very often there in his "writing." For instance, nothing that ever came out of his horn was as downright embarrassingly corny as the oft-repeated phrases, "red beans and ricely yours," "Pluto waterly yours," and "Swiss Crissly yours," with which he used to conclude his letters. In the language of music, by contrast, Armstrong was perfectly immune to banality and cliché. When he began featuring current popular songs and show tunes as a regular part of his repertory, for instance, his rendition of conventional lyrics had an influence on popular vocalists that was comparable to that which his trumpet stylizations had on most jazz instrumentalists and arranger/composers. In the introduction to the original edition of *Swing That Music*, Rudy Vallee observed: "That Armstrong's delightful, delicious sense of distortion of lyrics has made its influence felt upon popular singers of our own day cannot be denied. Mr. Bing Crosby, the late Russ Columbo, Mildred Bailey, and many others have adopted, probably unconsciously, the style of Louis Armstrong."

The painfully obvious shortcomings of his writing take nothing away from his achievements as a musician, of course. Nor do the numerous instances of factual imprecision disqualify *In His Own Words* as a useful historical document. The excellent editorial commentaries by Thomas Brothers, the author of *Chromatic Beauty in the Late Medieval Chanson*, provide a great scholarly service. While this collection of miscellaneous autobiographical pieces can hardly be said to add up to a truly significant literary achievement, the evocative effect of some of its narrative lines and its anecdotes is considerable.

Indeed, Armstrong's character sketches are instantly credible, and not without literary merit:

I'll never forget the first time Soldier boy took me out to the Club, where I first heard that band play, I almost jump out of my skin. . . . The little slick headed drummer (with his hair—gassed to kill) and he kept it slick and shiny. . . . A fly would have slipped and broke his neck immediately. . . . And that's for sure. . . . Konks were the things in those days. . . . I can remember that time when I joined Smack Henderson (Fletcher's pet name) I spent the whole day having my hair gassed—so I could make a big hit when I left Chicago to joint Fletcher Henderson's band.

Speaking of Konkilines (hairdo). As far back as I can remember, —this cute little drummer in Elkins' band and Arthur Bryson, our once great dancer—were the only two guys whom I admired the way they kept their hair looking so pretty all the times. . . . [S]o you had to be real hipped and *be sharp—feel sharp—and stay sharp*. . . . And that's just what this cute little drummer playing in Elkins band did. . . . His smile was infectious (I think—that expresses what I mean). When this little 'Cat would be drummin smiling while twirling his drumsticks he never missed—he was perfect at it. Smiling with his chops stretching from ear to ear. . . . I couldn't stand it. . . . I just let out a yell and a scream. . . . It was too much. . . . Folks—that little drummer was Lionel Hampton. . . .

Brothers's book broaches also another aspect of Armstrong's life, and a far-reaching one. It begins with a section labeled "Louis Armstrong + the Jewish Family in New Orleans, La., the Year of 1907." This text was written by Louis Armstrong in his bed at Beth Israel Hospital in New York on March 31, 1969. It is a memoir of his experiences, at the age of seven, in 1907, with the Karnofskys in New Orleans, where Armstrong was born.

In this manuscript, Armstrong expresses his gratitude to one Dr. Gary Zucker, whose treatment pulled him twice through intensive care. The expert and tender ministrations that he received at Beth Israel put him in mind of the warm, caring relationship he had enjoyed with the Karnofsky family, for whom he worked when he was a boy. Hearing Dr. Zucker singing "Russian Lullaby," he writes: "This is the song that I sang when I was *seven* years old—with the *Karnofsky family* when I was working with them, every night at their house when Mother Karnofsky would rock the Baby David to sleep. Then I would go home—across the track, cross town to *May-Ann* and *Mama Lucy*, my mother and sister." And a few paragraphs later, he goes on to say: "I had a long time admiration for the Jewish People. Especially with their long time of courage, taking So Much Abuse for so long. I was only *Seven* years old but I could easily see all the *ungodly treatment* that the White Folks were handing the poor *Jewish* family whom I worked for. . . . Even '*my race*,' the Negroes, the way I saw it, they were having a little *better* Break than the *Jewish* people, with jobs a plenty around. Of course, we can understand all the situations and handicaps that was going on, but to me we were better off than the Jewish people. But we didn't do anything about it. We were lazy and *still are*."

And he adds that "we never did try to get together and show younger Negroes such as myself to try and even to show that he has ambitions and with just a little encouragement—I could have done something worthwhile. But *instead* we did nothing but let the young *up*starts know that they were young and simple, and that was that."

This flatly contradicts what he wrote in *Satchmo: My Life in New Orleans* about Mr. Peter Davis, the bandmaster at the Colored Waifs' Home for Boys, who made him a cornet player as well as a student bandleader. "The first day we paraded through my old neighborhood," Armstrong there recalled, "everybody was gathered on the sidewalk to see us pass. All the whores, pimps, gamblers, thieves and beggars were waiting for the band because they knew that Dipper, May-Ann's son, would be in it. But they never dreamed that I would be playing the cornet, blowing as good as I did. They ran right up to Mama, who was sleeping after a night job, so she could see me go by. Then they asked Mr. Davis if they could give me some money. He nodded his head with approval, not thinking the money would amount to very much. But he didn't know that sporting crowd. Those sports gave me so much I had to borrow the hats of several of the boys to hold it all, I took in enough to buy new instruments for everybody who played in the band." It is curious that there is no mention of the Karnofsky family during the Waifs' Home period.

Armstrong's late celebration of his relationship with the Karnofsky family is very affecting. But I must add that it is not a very unusual or surprising story about Jewish Americans and their black employees. I recall that in Mobile, Alabama, in the

1920s and 1930s, one had schoolmates whose Jewish employers encouraged them, and even insisted that they go to high school, and also continued to employ them during the summer breaks if they went on to college; and some of those benefactors were said to patronize their former employees who became doctors and dentists.

Many of Armstrong's outbursts are overly sentimental, obsequious, ill tempered, wrongheaded, and glibly misinformed. Still, not unlike the soliloquies in a play, they serve the indispensable biographical function of complicating the protagonist's character, by providing concrete evidence in his own words that this man whose charm was legendary, and whose lifelong motto was "I'm always there in the cause of happiness," also had his hang-ups.

The editor rightly does not allow this special dimension of Armstrong's complexity to go unremarked. In his introduction to the book's first section, Brothers notes that "there are references to '*over Educated fools*' who condemn the '*White* Folks *Nigger*.' To them, Armstrong sharply retorts: 'Believe it—the White Folks did *everything that's decent for me*. I wish that I can *boast* these *same* words for Niggers. I think that I have always done *great* things about *uplifting* my *race* (the Negroes, *of course*) but I *wasn't appreciated*.'" And Brothers wisely comments: "The document may be read, in part, as a commentary on the change in audience that sectionalizes Armstrong's long career: during his apprenticeship in New Orleans and during the first great peak of his career, in the 1920s in Chicago, he played almost exclusively for blacks; the last decades of his career found him playing almost exclusively for whites, while many African Americans resented the cultural role in which he seemed to thrive."

In any case how could Armstrong ever forget how obvious and enduring his influence on those education-oriented Negroes who went to high school and college in the 1930s was and still is! They not only studied and memorized his music, they also admired and emulated his personal deportment (the neatness symbolized by his clean white handkerchiefs) and the elegance of his up-to-date but unfaddish tailor-made wardrobe. They may have rated Duke Ellington's diction as classier, but Ole Louie's was the jive talk you also had to be able to lay on them if you wanted to be a hip man about town, a cat whose life was geared to swinging (and if you weren't, no use licking your chops!).

When the musicians of that generation came into prominence, the overwhelming majority of them always acknowledged their indebtedness to him. And when he clowned before predominantly "white" audiences as he never did before "black" audiences, they didn't go around ridiculing him. Some may have shaken their heads or rolled their eyes in bewilderment and exasperation—as Ralph Ellison, whose admiration of Armstrong's musical tone and inventiveness was second to none, used to say, "Man, sometimes Ole Louie shows his ass instead of his genius"—but they always referred to him, and always addressed him, as Pops. And so do their children and grandchildren.

Still, in sharp contrast to the ease with which he seemed to combine the role of musical genius and court jester or minstrel clown and refer to himself as Satchel Mouth, Satchmo, Satch, Dipper Mouth, Dipper, Dip, Mo Mouth and Gate Mouth, Armstrong did not take kindly to condescension. Not even Lucille, his fourth and (according to him) most wonderful wife, could get away with rubbing him the wrong way status-wise: "By, Sweets having that baby for me," he wrote to Joe Glaser on August 2, 1953, "gave Lucille the best ass whipping of her life. As nice + sweet + as wonderful as she is she still has a sense of *Airs* that I've never particularly cared for—Being raised around people who were, just plain human beings, and loved (at least) respect for each other. And not the Attitude that you're just a musician or low trumpet player, Smokes, Reefers, etc. That I'm more than you type, which is all *Bullsh——t.* Which Goes to show, that I Can tolerate Anything, as long as it doesn't interfere with my trumpet."

The primary emphasis in *Louis Armstrong: In His Own Words* is where it should be, on the wonderful fact that nothing was ever more important to Armstrong than blowing that horn. Certainly not the accumulation of great wealth, and not fame either, which he feared would restrict his freedom just to be himself and spend his time doing what he wanted to do, hanging out with friends wherever he happened to be, making the rounds, dropping in on neighborhood bars, nightspots, informal parties, sitting in with bands and joining jam sessions whenever he was moved, requested, or simply welcome to do so: ". . . you see; I've always been a happy go lucky type of sort of fellow in this way—I never tried in no way to ever be *real real* filthy rich like some people do and after they do they die just the same.—

"But Mary-Ann had already 'hipped to what was happening in this healthful wide beautiful world. . . . So, by me doing that (even before I heard of gage) I was always the happiest young trumpet player that anyone ever wanted to meet. . . . From this first time I picked up my trumpet, or the one that was out to the Orphanage, I was a popular youngster. . . . Success has always been—mine. . . ."

The wide range of autobiographical documentation that Brothers has included in this volume makes it a very significant source for the study of Louis Armstrong. Meanwhile, for those in search of an Armstrong memoir that transcends the obvious limitations of the most provincial dimensions of the idiomatic and yet retains the entirely convincing flavor of his voice much the same as his music does, there remains "Louis Armstrong: A Self-Portrait," the interview by Richard Meryman that was published as the cover story in the April 15, 1966, issue of *Life* magazine and was slightly expanded and republished as a small and handsome volume (with illustrations) by the Eakins Press, New York. It is still unsurpassed. Meryman used expertly crafted questions, and he repeated them shrewdly, and then shaped Armstrong's various answers into a fine, uninterrupted narrative. In the Armstrong centennial that is upon us, surely Armstrong's only successful exercise in as-told-to autobiography should be made available again.

If getting the voice on the page is the objective, consider the Armstrong-Meryman vamp: "I'm always wondering if it would have been best in my life if I'd stayed like I was in New Orleans, having a ball. I was very much contented just to be around and play with the old timers. And the money I made—I lived off of it. I wonder if I would have enjoyed that better than all this big mucky-muck traveling all over the world—which is nice, meeting all those people, being high on the horse, all *grandioso*. All this life I have now—I didn't suggest it. I would say it was all wished on me. Over the years you find you can't stay no longer where you are, you must go on a little higher now—and that's the way it all came about. I couldn't get away from what's happened to me."

And here is the outchorus: "I've had some great ovations in my time. When people do that they must feel *something* within themselves. I mean you don't go around waking people up to the effect of saying, 'You know, this music is art.' But, it's got to be art because the world has recognized our music from New Orleans, else it would have been dead today. But I always let the other fellow talk about art. 'Cause when we was doing it, we was just glad to be working up on that stage. So for me to be still on earth to hear that word, sounds pretty good. I'm just grateful for every little iota.

"Some cats wants pats on the back, and they wants you to kneel down 'cause they did this and did that and they are so and so. But I still feel I'm just an ordinary human being trying to enjoy the work I live. It's something to know you still can make that call when the man say, 'All on.' That's enough won-derment for me. . . ."

And not for him only.

PART V

Commentary

Manhattan in the Twenties

IT WAS DURING the ten-year period beginning in November 1918 that New York City not only consolidated its status as undisputed culture capital of the United States, and indeed of the Western Hemisphere, but also accelerated its irrepressible momentum of urban influence and prestige that led to the unrivaled global preeminence it enjoys today.

Already long gone were the pre-world-class days of the Philadelphia and Boston of the Revolutionary War era and the Boston of what is sometimes called the period of the flowering of New England and sometimes the American Renaissance. Also preliminary to the war there had been the New York of Herman Melville and Walt Whitman, to which came Mark Twain to spend his final years. Nor was the identity and sensibility of Henry James in any of his phases ever anything other than that of a cosmopolitan or, in all events, international New Yorker, a Manhattanite abroad.

And now came the postwar decade of the Roaring Twenties, with its deluxe sedans and sporty roadsters and increasingly available flivvers and jitneys, with the newly ratified Eighteenth Amendment issuing in the Prohibition Era with its bootleg liquor and heyday of gangster-affiliated speakeasy nightspots, a time also known as that of the newly liberated post-Victorian generation of flaming youth, with its cocktail-sipping, cigarette-flourishing, bobbed-hair, and short-skirt-flaunting flappers swishing about with their ever so debonair playboy and/or sugar daddy escorts.

Such, in fact, was the seemingly undauntable exuberance of the new lifestyle that came with postwar prosperity that the decade was already being referred to as the Jazz Age as early on as 1922. Young F. Scott Fitzgerald, a novelist from the Midwest by way of Princeton, who, along with Ernest Hemingway and William Faulkner, was to become one of the most celebrated American writers of the twentieth century, published a collection of fiction entitled *Tales of the Jazz Age* that year. He had published *This Side of Paradise*, his first novel, in 1920; *Flappers and Philosophers*, another collection of stories, including "Bernice Bobs Her Hair," in 1921. *The Beautiful and*

Damned, a second novel, was also published, in 1922. *The Great Gatsby*, his masterpiece, came in 1925. President Warren G. Harding referred to the postwar period as a "return to normalcy [*sic!*]"; Fitzgerald called it "the greatest, gaudiest spree in history."

Jazz, ragtime, and blues-derived syncopated music from uptown Manhattan was the new rage of smart-set revelers in speakeasies and ballrooms alike. It did not originate in Harlem, to be sure. New Orleans claims that distinction, and Chicago claims a significant role in its development and dissemination (after all, it was from Chicago that New York summoned Louis Armstrong in 1924 and again in 1929), but even so, what with the dominant role that Tin Pan Alley had come to play in the business of publishing, recording, and distributing popular music by 1910, New York was to become in effect the national center for the refinement of all American popular music and has remained the major venue of jazz ever since.

Incidentally, Tin Pan Alley was simply a part of the economic, financial, and commercial foundation for New York's 1920s boom and comprehensive cultural development that had been established as long ago as the so-called gilded age of the accumulation of the great American fortunes, the benefits from which the cultural institutions and enterprises of no other city could challenge. Its art museums, collections, galleries, and auctions, and its popular amusement and recreational facilities, already outstripped all other cities of the nation, as did its opera, philharmonic, and recital patronage. And as for drama, Broadway was not only already ahead of what other cities had to offer, it was actually the national theater district of the United States.

Along with all this there was also the largest concentration of publishers of books and magazines, distributing the most extensive range of subject matter available anywhere in the nation. Thus, such was the cultural clout of New York by the middle of the decade that for all that has been made of the protestations and declarations of those postwar arts and letters exiles, expatriates, and refugees fleeing what they regarded as the uninspiring if not withering barrenness of America, those who became successful while abroad could hardly deny the all too obvious fact that their achievement was completely predicated on aesthetic value judgments and investments made not by Europeans but by the New York cultural establishment.

Indeed, it was as if the European arts and letters elite didn't even realize that the expatriates were over there among them. In any case, it is quite obvious that none of the U.S. writers, painters, composers, or even architects received any attention or had any impact on the Europeans comparable to that of James Reese Europe's Hellfighters Band from uptown Manhattan's 369th Infantry during the war. Or the response that Will Marion Cook's Southern Syncopated Orchestra from uptown Manhattan received during its European tour in 1919.

Meanwhile uptown Manhattan had already had its own post-Reconstruction consciousness-raising phenomenon known as the Harlem Renaissance or New Negro movement under way since 1915. *The New Negro*, an anthology of fiction, poetry, and commentary representing its point of view, was published in 1925.

At this time Paul Whiteman, a white leader of an all-white thirty-plus-piece light classic and popular music orchestra, was called "the king of jazz." But actually the most authentic jazz in midtown Manhattan was being played in the Roseland Ballroom by the orchestra of uptown musicians led by Fletcher Henderson that Louis Armstrong had come from Chicago in 1924 to join for a while.

Paul Whiteman's orchestra was a much bigger hit to be sure, and his recordings and radio broadcasts made him one of the top celebrities of the period. At the same time, however, Broadway audiences that were so enthusiastic about such Harlem-generated Broadway musicals as *Shuffle Along*, *Running Wild*, and *Chocolate Dandies* were becoming part of the uptown nightlife scene in ever-increasing numbers, in response to which such instantly legendary uptown spots as Connie's Inn, the Nest, and Smalls Paradise came into being. And by 1926 there was also the Savoy Ballroom, the uptown counterpart of midtown's Roseland Ballroom.

Not that midtown entertainment was short on exciting attractions. Even before the highly visible show biz support of playboy mayor Jimmy Walker, who was elected in 1924, such popular annual variety shows as the *Ziegfeld Follies* that dated back to the previous decade (when Vernon and Irene Castle were doing the cakewalk, the fox-trot, and other ballroom steps to the syncopated music of Jim Europe's prewar dance band) came into their heyday and were followed by *George White's Scandals* and *Earl Carroll's Vanities*. Then there was also the more tightly constructed musical comedy establishing itself and replacing the operetta in the process.

Still, it was uptown music and dance that was to provide the decade's most felicitous symbols. Nothing evokes the twenties of the speakeasies, roadsters, flappers, and underlying mood of *The Great Gatsby* more movingly than the shimmy, the break-down, the black bottom, and above all the Charleston, the dance, as well as James P. Johnson's stride piano, the elegant fun of which was a joyous counteragent to the pervasive banal-ity suggested by T. S. Eliot's *The Waste Land*, the most presti-gious literary statement of the times.

Nor should it be forgotten that it was during this decade that such uptown musical devices and conventions as the twelve-bar blues chorus, the thirty-two-bar pop song chorus, the break, and syncopation, among others, had produced Je-rome Kern, George Gershwin, Vincent Youmans, Harold Arlen, Vernon Duke, and Cole Porter, among others, who followed the lead of Ben Harney, Shelton Brooks, W. C. Handy, and Irving Berlin and conquered the world for Ameri-can popular song.

In sports, prewar New York had had the legendary John J. McGraw, manager of the highly competitive New York Giants National League baseball team whose home park (the Polo Grounds) was up at Coogan's Bluff and whose fabulous super-star was a pitcher named Christy Mathewson. With the postwar boom came the American League New York Yankees, whose superstar was an ex-pitcher named Babe Ruth, who hit more home runs than anybody ever had, or would for years after-ward, and drew such large crowds that Yankee Stadium became a national sports landmark.

The postwar boom was still very much in evidence in 1927. The Chrysler and Empire State Buildings, for years the two tallest skyscrapers in the world, were already in the works, and such was the outlook in the entertainment business, for in-stance, that a new, almost immediately famous nightspot called the Cotton Club opened only a few short blocks away from the Savoy Ballroom on Lenox Avenue in Harlem and soon began broadcasting the music of Duke Ellington and his orchestra via a coast-to-coast radio network, music which (like the performances of Louis Armstrong) was to make Ellington one of the two American musicians who have achieved the most spectacular international admiration in the twentieth century.

Such indeed was the worldwide status of New York City in the autumn of 1927 that when Charles Lindbergh accomplished the most sensational feat of the decade with his solo transatlantic flight, his ticker-tape-blizzard welcome parade in New York was regarded everywhere as the ultimate tribute of the contemporary world at large, nothing less than the triumphal celebrations of Imperial Rome, Napoleonic Paris, and post-Waterloo London. Incidentally, even as the lindy hop, an uptown, up-tempo dance step, continued this celebration on into and even beyond the next decade, it not only became the swing era equivalent of what the Charleston had been for the Jazz Age and thus an extremely useful and widely popular counteragent to the gloomy prospects of the Depression years, it also helped to generate as well as symbolize the energy, high morale, and ever ready improvisation that the nation needed for World War II.

The growth of New York over the last one hundred years has been such that some urbanologists now argue that it has not only established itself as a five-borough metropolis but, for many intents and purposes, has also come to function as a five-city megalopolis that includes the northeastern seaboard urban areas of Washington, Baltimore, Philadelphia, and Boston.

Part VI

Conversations

The Blue Steel, Rawhide, Patent Leather
Implications of Fairy Tales

*A*T THE RIPE AGE OF EIGHTY-ONE, *Albert Murray is at once the patriarch of a growing number of spirited, independent-minded intellectuals and—in the on-target words of Mark Feeney's recent* Boston Globe *profile—"as close to a classic nineteenth-century man of letters as one might find in this country today." I very much wanted to talk with him while I was working in New York City recently, and I fell into a piece of luck. Murray agreed to a meeting because he had seen an article of mine about his most recent books—*The Blue Devils of Nada *(1996), a work of cultural criticism, and* The Seven League Boots, *the third in a series of autobiographical novels chronicling the life of a brown-skinned Alabamian named Scooter—and, with a few caveats here and there, liked what I had to say. He greeted me at the door of his Harlem apartment looking dapper (he sported a pale green velour sweatshirt with Lincoln Center Jazz Orchestra logo, sleeveless pale yellow pullover poking out at the neck, and khaki trousers). A man who had graduated from Tuskegee in the late thirties, he struck me as an aging preppy—with, alas, the emphasis on aging, because a recent back operation has forced him to use a walking stick, making him more homebound than he was only a few years ago.*

My plans for a stroll with Murray through the Harlem streets obviously had to be scrapped, but that turned out to be no loss: it soon became clear that Murray lived more intimately with his books and CD collection, with his bulging folders of papers and assorted scraps of a long career at the writing desk, than he did in the rhythms of his neighborhood. On his coffee table were recent books about Picasso, Cézanne, and Corot, along with Thomas Cahill's How the Irish Saved Civilization, *Simon Schama's* Landscape and Memory *and* Thirteen Ways of Looking at a Black Man, *a recent collection of profiles (one on Murray himself) by Harvard professor/celebrity Henry Louis Gates Jr.*

Recently presented with a lifetime achievement award from the National Book Critics Circle, Albert Murray is the author of three novels (the earlier Scooter novels were Train Whistle Guitar, *1974, and* The Spyglass Tree, *1991) and numerous works of cultural criticism, including* The Omni-Americans: New Perspectives on Black Experience and American Culture *(1970) and* South to a Very Old Place *(1971), an account of Murray's travels through the region of his birth. He is also the author of* The Hero and the Blues *(1973) and* Stomping the Blues *(1976), a study of what the blues is—and is not.*

Born in 1916 in Nokomis, Alabama, Murray grew up in Magazine Point, a slip of a townlet outside Mobile. He attended Tuskegee Institute (where Ralph Ellison was an upperclassman), graduated in 1939, and returned to teach there in 1940. A stint in the Air Force during World War II was followed, courtesy of the G.I. Bill, with an M.A. earned at New York University, study in Paris, and eventually a return to the Air Force in 1951. Murray taught courses in geopolitics in the Air Force ROTC program at Tuskegee, served in Morocco during the revolution, and was later stationed in California and Massachusetts. He retired in 1962; that's when he moved to New York City and began his full-time literary career.

Those are, as it were, the public facts; what speaks more importantly, however, are the years he spent reading his way through the library. When he began publishing articles in magazines such as Life *and the* New Leader *in the mid-sixties—and when the best of them were collected in* The Omni-Americans—*it was clear that Murray's long period of preparation had paid off. He knew as much about modern literature and modern art as any Ivy League professor. Better yet, he could apply his principles to the rhythms of jazz and to the larger patterns of American culture in ways that were as original as they were often unsettling. More conventional critics of race and identity simply didn't quite know what to make of him. They still don't.*

Meanwhile Murray continues his intellectual pursuits with a gusto that belies his years and the ravages of arthritis. His gravelly voice moves easily from the erudite high to the low-down, frequently punctuated by an infectious laughter when he figures that he's scored a particularly telling point.

The following interview was conducted in Murray's spacious book-lined Harlem apartment on the fourth and the twenty-sixth of February 1997.

SANFORD PINSKER: *I'd like to begin with a question that Charlie Rose recently posed to Alfred Kazin during a "conversation" at*

New York's 92nd Street Y—namely, "What led you to a life of letters?" Kazin obviously didn't think much of this as an ice-breaker and made his annoyance palpable when he snapped back: "I have no idea." What followed was a long, tense evening. So I realize that I'm taking something of a risk in prompting you to think about your beginnings as a literary person and the forma-tive influences that mattered greatly at the time.

ALBERT MURRAY: Well, as a matter of fact I do have some idea of the elements that led me to a career as an all-purpose literary intellectual. It started in my freshman year at college. I was impressed by two people: my English teacher, Morteza Drexel Sprague, and a student named John Gerald Hamilton. As I remember it, Mr. Sprague made an assignment in which we were to write a personal essay modeled on William Saroyan's "Myself upon the Earth," a section from his book *The Daring Young Man on the Flying Trapeze.* He told us to use that as a free-flowing model to see what we could do in terms of pre-senting ourselves in words. I don't remember what *I* did, but Hamilton did a thing called "Myself and Tyrannosaurus Rex upon the Earth." He was writing about his pipe, you see. Saroyan was writing about his typewriter and about learning to be a writer —not minding that he was living in a garret or often going hungry. But finally he had to eat, so he hocked his typewriter and splurged his money. After a while, though, he sobered up from all the eating and began to miss his typewriter. As best I can remember, it's a piece that ends, "This morning I got it back and this is what I've written." Hamilton could take off on that, but I had never experienced this kind of free-flowing prose which is personal and poetic and had a rhythm and, best of all, *sang.*

Well, I got into contact with Hamilton and found out that he was reading all sorts of things, classical as well as contempo-rary. He knew, for example, about Don Marquis—all this un-capitalized prose that looked like poetry—and lots of other stuff as well. Shortly afterward, Mr. Sprague gave us a reading list. And right there my courses became secondary. I got my assignments out of the way quickly so I could read the books in the library. And it turned out that Tuskegee had a very good library. All the stuff you read about in the magazines was available in the New Books section. As you walked toward the circulation desk, you could see the book jackets on the bulletin board. There was Faulkner's *Absalom, Absalom!* during my second year at college, and I'd see *These 13* and *Light in August* in the display racks, and I'd say to myself, "You've *got* to read those!"

So I started reading and then I noticed that Mr. Sprague was teaching a course in the novel for upperclassmen and that Ralph Ellison and a bunch of people were taking it. Well, I was curious about that and figured I'd better prepare to take it. And the first novel I read in college was *Tom Jones*. That continued ever since—reading classics as well as contemporary authors.

I was also terribly interested in the periodicals room—book reviews and what was happening generally. But I guess it was the literary anthologies and historical surveys that grabbed my attention the most. In fact, the first books I checked out of the library at Tuskegee were not assigned ones, but rather things like *The Golden Thread* by Philo M. Buck, *A Treasury of the Theatre* by Burns Mantle, or Sheldon Cheney's *The Theatre: Three Thousand Years of Drama, Acting and Stagecraft*. These made me cosmopolitan because they took me all the way back not only to Greek ritual and myth but also to Indian plays, Noh plays, all that. You see, I wanted to know about the literature of the world, and I began during my freshman year.

But I'm told that you were a pretty good storyteller even before you arrived at Tuskegee.

That's true. I also had a good memory. In high school I was involved with the theater and could remember my lines for act one by the time we had our first rehearsal. And when we got to act two, I knew my lines, but also everybody else's lines for act one. I continued acting in the little theater at Tuskegee, but now I had the benefit of all the reading I was doing in the history of world theater. All that's where, years after, stuff like *commedia dell'arte* began to dovetail with jazz.

That's what I want to get to—how the various aspects of your education contributed to your unified theory of American culture and identity.

Well, you were interested in jazz and blues as a matter of course. It was all around me. The same thing became true for Hollywood films and lots of other things. But it was putting them together that was the real trick. I suspect that my ability to understand the theater, and to know almost instinctively that the key to learning a part—and, later, to help others learn their parts—was an appreciation of the *story* being told. The same thing is probably true for the mythic stories that a culture tells, or tries to tell. Anyway, in college I began reading theater critics like Brooks Atkinson and John Mason Brown, the New York newspapers which were in the library, and lots of magazines like *Theatre Arts Monthly* and *Stage*. I read Stark Young's book on the theater. We had all of it at Tuskegee, and it did wonders for my imagination and my sense of what the world was about.

You make Tuskegee Institute sound like an exciting intellectual place.

For me, it *was*.

How, then, do you account for the fact that Ralph Ellison apparently didn't find it so exciting—at least if we rely on the portrait of his college days presented in Invisible Man?

He's a different personality. If you compare Scooter's college days with those of *Invisible Man*, you wouldn't think that they attended the same school. But you've got to remember that I wasn't concerned about the goddamn administration; I was concerned about what was in the library and what I was going to get out of this time I had in college. What positions the administration had I didn't know, and I didn't care to know. All I knew was that a teacher was going to come into the class and I wanted to be ready for him. I did not feel I was mature enough to make decisions about administrative matters. I had mostly contempt for the students who went off half-cocked in protests about some administrative ruling. I wasn't about to get kicked out of school over some protest rally. Man, I just barely got to school in the first place. I didn't have money enough to get home for Christmas, and I wasn't about to be an activist. I was there to get my education. I could just see it—because I was already a novelist in my mind—on the goddamn bus to Mobile by myself and all the people at home saying, "Albert Murray's back. They kicked him out of Tuskegee because he was up there running around with some of these other students and they're jumping the administration. What makes them think they know more about running a college than the teachers? What are they doing up there? That Murray guy can't even pay his way!" And they'd be right too. Man, I had to win scholarships every year.

Can we connect what you've just said with my sense that the phrase "protest literature" is a contradiction in terms?

I agree. Look, protest literature is a form of discourse all right, but only a genius can make it work by going beyond what it's designed to do. At its best, I suppose that protest literature could be close to the function of very important satire—in terms of dynamics. You know, spoofing something that is really out there at the time. And if you're good enough, it'll go beyond that. But it's got to go beyond *that* in order to be literature. Otherwise it's just campaign sloganeering, it seems to me. If you're interested in the human predicament and human possibilities on the earth, you're concerned with something more fundamental than a structure that might change in two, four, or six years, depending on who gets into office.

What I came to realize when I started studying Marxism was that it doesn't matter so much whatever form of government we have, it will be run by *politicians*. As for myself, I didn't even want to be president of the class. I didn't want to be president of the student body. And when I began teaching, I certainly didn't want to be the dean. I just wanted my tweed jacket, my contrasting slacks, and my books—and to be better-looking than Ronald Colman or Robert Donat.

Am I right in thinking that Ralph Ellison's mythic sense of what Tuskegee was and your own myth of college come to pretty much the same thing—namely, that all experience is finally shaped by some mythic story or other?

Absolutely. But remember that my memory of Tuskegee is mythic, too, and no less mythic than Ralph's was. What my sensibility attached itself to and gave emphasis to, and what his gave emphasis to, may have differed, but we became friends and never had any clashes about how he saw Tuskegee.

He had certain criticisms which always struck me more as matters of implication rather than documentation, and as such, I could accept the validity of his statements. But I was not concerned with those implications. I was concerned with the protagonist himself and what he could do. And I perceived no obstructions of the nature that some people think he saw.

Now, when you did the Scooter novels, how aware were you of the Bildungsroman *tradition, and perhaps even of specific books that served you as models?*

The Scooter books were definitely part of that. The Stephen from James Joyce's *A Portrait of the Artist as a Young Man*, a novel I knew well, as I knew Goethe's *Wilhelm Meister*. And certainly Thomas Mann's *Joseph*. All finally, I suppose—all heroes of all fiction. Odysseus, for example. At one point in *Seven League Boots*, we see Scooter as Ulysses, but at another point he's Telemachus. The same thing is true when Scooter is involved with Jewel Templeton. Sometimes she seems to be Athena, but at other times she's Circe. But she's the type of Circe that Ulysses came in contact with, and she tells him the way to get home.

What you've just described—namely, the way that your characters can be protean, can change shapes and identities, can be plastic, or perhaps elastic, strikes me as very similar to the rhythms of jazz.

I think so.

And what I really want to get to is the way improvisation in jazz music can become a structural foundation for prose.

Right.

Well, I'm glad you agree, but could you be more specific about how this business works?

In what way?

Well, think of the writers who have tried to reproduce jazz rhythms in their prose—Jack Kerouac, for example, in On the Road—*and why they make a botch of it. It looks much easier than it in fact is.*

If I can claim anything about my own work, it is this: I was immersed in, and influenced by, the twentieth-century literary sensibility. There's Eliot and Pound, and the fallout from Yeats. There's Kafka and Mann, and all of that. That's my context. That's my conception of what prose is. I know where Hemingway was coming from, and he pulled more of it together for me than anybody. Faulkner was playing some other stuff—doing Coleman Hawkins, don't you see. Then there was Proust and all of that. But at the same time I'm reading these guys I'm also listening to Louis and Duke and Kansas City jazz and coming to terms with that too. So it's all part of the same thing with me. It's not an artificial exercise, but an integrated one. When a sentence sounds right to me, it's probably some variation of the Kansas City 4/4, and when it has the right rhythm, it's getting close to what Hemingway and e. e. cummings did, and even to guys like Sandburg and Vachel Lindsay. In fact, I think of the whole Louis Untermeyer anthologies of modern British and American poetry when paragraphs came out sounding right. And don't let me forget to mention Auden, because nobody loves Auden more than me. Man, I'm an Auden man from way back. Couldn't write the blues, but he could write everything else.

> [*At this point Murray began reciting long passages of Auden from memory and sending me scrambling to the top of his bookshelf for other examples from "the Auden section." As I threw down volume after volume, Murray would quickly find the particular poem he had in mind and continue our impromptu afternoon poetry reading. He had first editions of Auden's books, arranged chronologically, as well as equally impressive collections of Joyce, Hemingway, Eliot, Proust, Malraux, and Mann.*]

The way it works, I pick up whatever the other guy's music is—in this case, Auden's—and then I play a tune too. To me, you can write more poetry in prose than if you restrict yourself to certain verse forms.

Does all this—the books, the poetry, the art on your walls—seem very far from the Mobile of your childhood?

Not really, because I was already dreaming my dream of the world when I was in Mobile. Ralph used to say that we were southern gentlemen, men of letters—you know, reading the best books, seeing the best art in reproductions or the originals. I mean, these other guys had some abstract bullshit that had to do with civil rights or some other kind of political context. I live in a *literary* context. I know the realities of that other stuff, but my whole thing is to process it into literary statement. So I always thought in terms of heroic action, of *conquering* the world. I was not interested in "escape," I was interested in *conquest.* That's a different thing altogether. It's just like the old Kenneth Burke distinction between frames of rejection and frames of acceptance. I thought, "This is a rough place, I'm going to have to be a hero." Or you could say, "This is a rough place, and it shouldn't be that way—why me?" But the result of the latter position is that you spend all your time bellyaching about the fact that it's rough. So you've got to do this, and then you've got to do that. But the way I figured it, if I couldn't go to the University of Alabama, I'd go to a university in New York or someplace else. Besides, the Big Ten and the Ivy League were indeed bigger leagues. Meanwhile I knew what was happening at Sewanee, at Vanderbilt, and at the *Southern Review* being published at Louisiana State University. You see what I mean? All that was part of it.

But having said all this, do you really want to claim that growing up in the Jim Crow South had no effect on you whatsoever?

I was *beating* that. I was better than that. I wasn't their conception of me, I was *my* conception of me. And my conception of me came from the great books of the world. That's what I thought of human possibility, not what some dumb-assed white guy thought a colored guy should be doing and feeling. Do you see what I'm saying? So I was not impressed with certain things as achievements that they thought of as achievements.

There's a wonderful line in Saul Bellow's The Adventures of Augie March *where a character says about Augie: "He has opposition in him." Could the same thing be said of you—namely, that you are filled with opposition or counterstatement?*

Well, maybe. But it depends on the nature of the counterstatement. Actually, Ralph said something similar to this in his essay responding to Irving Howe—you know, when he talks about being much wider than the narrow box of social protest that Howe wanted to put him in. I could agree with that. But I wasn't doing that consciously to make a counterstatement, but simply because the opportunity was there. And my butt was *not* being kicked on the campus at Tuskegee. I was in a castle-like situation, and I was doing what you do in a castle. Because it was all a fairy tale, and if you can't make it a fairy tale it doesn't come to anything. The blue steel, rawhide, patent leather implications of fairy tales—*that*'s what my writing is about. Fables and fairy tales. If you turn that into literature or see the fairy tale beneath, no matter how rough the surface is, down underneath is the other thing. Nothing is more brutal than a fairy tale. You got the wolf, you got the trials and tribulations —you always have something brutal and threatening in a fairy tale. But you've got to translate the quotidian into metaphor. Why not metaphors of heroism?

I take it that this links up with what you said earlier about creating a mythic self.

My perception is that whatever self you create is mythical. The downtrodden, that's a myth. The heroic, that's a myth too.

In this sense, was Constance Rourke's discussion of American mythic types in her book on American humor a particularly important book for you?

Well, that came about later. I already had it when I read Mann's essay on "Freud and the Future." That was part of three lectures that he gave at the New School in 1938. The other two were on Goethe and Wagner.

[*At this point Murray sent me to his bookshelves again, where I retrieved a copy of Mann's pamphlet "What I Believe" and encountered Murray's marginalia: "This was the first thing that I read by Thomas Mann. I read it in* The Nation, *December 10, 1938. I was then a senior at Tuskegee. It marked a definite turning point in my thinking."*]

What about some of the other writers who mattered to you—Hemingway, for example?

Always. Hemingway and Mann—then you get to the others.

To change gears for just a moment, could you talk a bit about the way jazz musicians fit into the wide reading we've been talking about so far?

Well, I can only talk about my perception of it. I had all this in me for a long time—a reverence for the jazz musician as artist along with my reading of literature as a college student—but what I needed to do was get it into focus. And I had as much trouble with this as anybody else because jazz was popular and this and that, but usually not taken with much seriousness. You had to be much more sophisticated than I was to make certain distinctions. Now, people were always making these distinctions when it came to Duke, but that was more difficult when it came to Louis Armstrong. There, the mask of the entertainer kept getting in the way.

Ralph used to talk about the necessity of putting a frame around art to separate it from actuality. So you had to have this, and he thought about Louis's mask as the comedian as functioning very much as this frame. After all, art is *not* reality; it represents a stylization of reality, and that's what Louis was about. He could reach all sorts of insights with that trumpet of his—and then relieve you of that with his final "Oooooh, yeeah." Once you begin to take this seriously, you begin then to see the dynamics in different terms.

With Duke, though, what I see is a portrait of absolute elegance.

Right. But don't you see: that's a frame too.

It's usually the case that writers are more interested in what they're working on than in what they published many years ago. So if you'll permit me, what are you working on now?

Well, I just finished a lecture that I'm going to give at the Gardner museum. It's called "The Eye of the Beholder." Structurally, I play around with jazz forms. It starts with a vamp—and I tell them that it's a vamp—and then a riff on and on to the outchorus. That's the structure. There's a light irony in the fact that I'm giving this lecture in a museum that houses some of the finest masterpieces of European art, but for all that, Mrs. Gardner's place is a part of a universal "museum without walls"; and this functions to provide models of excellence for efforts on the part of Americans to process the raw elements of their culture into aesthetic statements. And that's pure Murray, out of André Malraux.

As you probably know, playwright August Wilson debated Robert Brustein at Town Hall just a few weeks ago, and one of the things he kept insisting upon was the importance of the African blood coursing through his veins. Afrocentrism retains a considerable grip on the imaginations of many blacks, and I wondered what you thought about this. They often claim, for example, that anything Western or Eurocentric must be rejected out of hand.

Well, would you want to send a guy to Africa to learn how to deal with elevators and skyscrapers? Of course not. Nor would you go over there to learn about hydraulics. You can't argue that there's such a thing as "African hydraulics." Or any other kind of hydraulics. So if you're into hydraulics, you've got to deal with people who deal with hydraulics. This is the sort of argument I sometimes use to get people to back away from an impossibly stupid provincialism.

Would you say much the same thing about many of the people connected with the Harlem Renaissance? That is, were they also rather provincial, afraid to stick their toes in the big cultural waters of modern art?

I first became acquainted with Alain Locke's *The New Negro* in the middle thirties, when I was a junior at the Mobile County Training School, the local high school. You were required to deliver an oration for the juniors' annual oratorical contest, and the Locke essay was an important influence on my speech. Indeed, much of my presentation was a paraphrase of his central arguments.

So I was very much aware of the Harlem Renaissance when I was in the eleventh grade. But when I got to Tuskegee Institute and discovered their fine library, Louis Untermeyer's anthologies wiped out all that stuff for me. Here was modern British poetry and modern American poetry at its best: Pound, Eliot, Frost, all them cats. And I thought, "This is what contemporary poetry is." The other stuff is nice in the sense that we see people trying to stylize the idiomatic particulars of any experience, but as for what I came to regard as big-league writing, this was sandlot stuff. All the way.

But even more important, these guys missed the real avant-garde in America—which was Louis Armstrong. The whole change in American aesthetics was jazz. That was the vehicle through which America has made the greatest aesthetic impact on the world at large—and these guys in the Harlem Renaissance didn't know that. Sure, they knew Armstrong was a hit, but they plain missed the connection between jazz and aesthetics. Duke Ellington is a similar story. So, later on, when Ralph and I began talking about these cultural connections, too many black writers were still too stuck in rebellion and power to pay much attention.

What was so good about jazz, of course, was that it was universal—and that's where the real revolution in sensibility was taking place. There was King Oliver in the 1920s, and then there were the great bands of the 1930s that had a definitive impact on many people outside the tradition—including, for instance, a Jewish guy named Benny Goodman, who had no objection whatsoever to being called "the king of swing." And he's playing with all these chitlin-eatin', pork-chop-eatin' Negroes who need that stuff to play the blues—and the point is that what they're doing is bigger than all that. It's universal. It's the dynamics, I'm talking about the impact it made on the American sensibility. Which is why I get so tired of people who point out that Goodman made more money, blah, blah, blah, because that's not the issue. The issue is the universality of the music, which is nothing if not a Negro idiom.

The formula you talk about in The Hero and the Blues *is "No dragon, no hero." Has the black aesthetic movement been one of these dragons?*

I suppose, but on a deeper level the dragon is a personification of chaos, of entropy. So we're back to the symbols of an aesthetic. The guys you're talking about are antiform. Art is about form, winning form in the face of chaos. That's why I extend the blues to mean all that. But you've got to be careful here, because somebody might think I'm talking about a physical confrontation, and I'm not. That's being too literal about the "dragon" and conjures up images of the medieval romance or something like that. Because the kind of dragons I'm talking about can come in all sorts of subtle shapes. Ultimately this stuff is particles and waves, but even *that* is formal, because a particle is something you can conceive of, and a wave is something with a pattern. Whereas entropy is without a pattern . . . you see? So these various aspects of disorder, disruption, destruction— the dragon is just one symbol for that, which is why I play around with the twist on dragons and Grand Dragons.

Suppose just for argument's sake that I take a hard black separatist line on what you've been talking about, and say: "Look, Murray, all your ideas about form and chaos betray Western ideas about art."

Of course, I'm a Western man.

But what if I insist that this is inauthentic.

What makes it inauthentic?

Because you're black.

But that's racism, and the ultimate stupidity about racism is that race is not a scientific term. Race, to all people who use the term correctly, is a matter of a few easily observed physiological characteristics: the color of your skin, the texture of your hair, and the shape of a few extremities, and all that. *But there is no scientific correlation between those physical features and behavior. The only correlation comes from the conditioning of the consciousness—and that is not the same thing as race.* Consciousness and race just don't correlate. There *is* no scientific way of doing that.

So when people try to argue about the physiological by way of genetics, I respond by pointing out that all tests must be scientific if they're going to be valid. That means that evidence is required, and not only that, but it must meet the tests of statistics: validity, reliability, and comprehensiveness. Now, if you can't put these tests on the correlation between blue eyes or thick lips or anything else physiological and behavior, then you're out of business because you're outside the realm of science.

But the kind of people you were talking about earlier, those racists on the other side of the coin, don't care about scientific validity, much less about how one operates in a Newtonian, let alone a post-Newtonian, world. They just don't care, which means that they simply express their prejudices. But so far as getting to the truth of things, those people have no idea what the function of literature is. They don't separate campaign propaganda from literary statement. The existential implications of a literary statement is something they're just not concerned about. The only dragon for them is white prejudice.

But, to me, this seems terribly limiting on them, even limiting in terms of their art.

That's right, and that's why I don't like it. That's why I counterstate it.

Meanwhile the black aesthetic movement—then and now—seems to get lots of media attention and often lavish overpraise from reviewers and critics who ought to know better.

Well, you've already referred to the general cultural dynamics. But when Ralph and I were kids and a Negro got up and tried to pull this kind of shit, white folks would laugh at him and say, "Yeah, you'll never be educated." Nowadays it's politically incorrect to ridicule such stupidity. But I suspect many see such stupidity for what it is, even so.

But the real problem with all this is that it wipes out the greatest fact of a present epoch, which I think of as, say, being two thousand years old. And what I mean is Eurocentrism and my sense that the *real* diaspora is not the dispersal of the Jews from their Holy Land, but rather the dispersal of European information around the globe—which, by the way, the Europeans invented. There was no globe until they invented it. It was nowhere in human consciousness until circumnavigation of the globe—Columbus and all those cats—put it into European consciousness. Smart as the Japanese were or Indians or whoever were, it was the Europeans who said, "Hey, you're here [*pointing in one direction*] and we're here [*pointing in another*]; this we're going to call the Pacific Ocean and this the Atlantic. Add it all up and what we have is the globe . . . you get what I'm saying? Everybody should know this before finishing high school. Greenwich mean time *means* that it's Tuesday here in New York and either Monday or Wednesday in other time zones, and you can't get around that. It's a fact—or, in any case, an established convention.

What this comes to, when you boil it down, is that the world's very idea of itself is what defines this epoch. So the great diaspora is a dissemination of European insights and the synthesis of things and ideas they brought back to Europe from their travels: tea from China, corn from America, and so forth. As good as the Egyptians were two thousand years before this, they didn't make the synthesis that the Europeans did—simply because they didn't have a broad enough concept of the earth and thus of "man-kind." What I'm playing with is what Malraux meant when he talked about a "museum without walls." Now we live in terms of *all* art, do you see what I mean? All art. That's what Malraux meant when he talked about a museum without walls, but not what people in colleges mean when they talk about multiculturalism these days. That kills me.

That reminds me of Henry Louis Gates Jr.'s new Dictionary of Global Culture, *which the* New York Times *reviewed last Sunday.*

I saw that.

Well, let me tell you something that the reviewer didn't *point out —namely, that you'll find 300-word entries for Richard Wright, Langston Hughes, Zora Neale Hurston, Ralph Ellison, Toni Morrison, and even Alice Walker, but not a single word about a writer you might have heard of—Saul Bellow.*

But the most obvious point they miss comes out of what I'm saying. It is the nature of Eurocentrism to be inclusive. The trouble with these people is that they always jump up and down on some small point and miss the general dynamics involved. When I went to college in the middle thirties, how many great universities offered courses in Chinese or Japanese? Sure, you could always go somewhere and study Hebrew because of the vector that came in on—the Puritans, Jonathan Edwards, Cotton Mather, all that. But my point is that now you can go to a small college like Washington and Lee—where I was a guest professor a few years ago—and study Japanese. The dynamics involved with this are that these things come as they're needed, which is when this stuff starts impinging on European consciousness. So the need for what you must know is constantly being expanded—not because of morality or fair play or anything like that, but because of pragmatism. And that's the trouble: guys like Gates turn *need* into multicultural pieties and what people presumably "need" to know. It reminds me of the old story Clifton Fadiman liked to tell about the little girl who wrote a book report that went like this: "This book tells me more about mushrooms [or butterflies or penguins or something] than I need to know."

From what I read about it, Gates's dictionary is likely to tell me more than I need to know about all sorts of things. As a student of contemporary literature I don't need to know very much about Alice Walker, for example, but I think I would get caught with my pants down if I didn't know anything at all about Bellow. I don't think you can get through the forties or the fifties and sixties in American literature and not know anything about Bellow. On the other hand, we may not have missed much by not knowing about all the female black writers from the nineteenth century that Gates brought to our attention. The headnotes are all right, I guess, because anybody who does want to read the authors can go over to the Schomburg Library and look them up. My feeling, though, is that some things you just don't want to bother with. There's no real need for it.

It's like some people who get all worked up about the fact that there are so many black athletes dominating the games of football or basketball or whatever, but very few blacks in the front offices of these sports. They feel that this is terribly wrong, but I think they miss the whole point. I said, "Hey, do you think the New York Yankees came into being because there were so many great baseball players in New York City? No, it's because some businessman decided to *build* a baseball team. He invested in this thing." It's the same thing with basketball teams. Somebody had to know the economics, the business of such things, and then go do it successfully. So when people go on and on about the "conspiracy" against black athletes, they just don't understand the cultural dynamics of how things work.

Take the great department store builders, for example. Many of them started out with pushcarts, and then some of the luckier ones moved into small stores. What they all had to do, though, was learn about finance, legal protection, bookkeeping, and all the other stuff that goes with merchandising. The big department stores like I. Magnin and Saks were the result of a long evolution. And you just can't shortcut this natural history by citing injustices and shouting "conspiracy" if things don't change overnight. There was no conspiracy. How many of the great sports venues and organizations were built by white superstars?

Still, conspiracy theory has the wonderful appeal of simplicity.

Sure it does, but it doesn't hold a candle to understanding the way cultural dynamics really work. Look, we can go on about this, but here's something else I think you might be even more interested in. [*Murray holds out a one-inch sheaf of manuscript pages.*] These are the letters Ralph Ellison sent me during the period between 1950 and 1960. My agent is going to get in touch with the Ellison estate about them, and if we can come to terms, I'll edit them and write a short introduction. The letters are filled with good talk about aesthetics and national identity, and because they shed some interesting light on the making of *Invisible Man*, I think they will be a major addition to Ellison's collected work. Would you like to hear some sections?

Needless to say, I did, and I spent the rest of a long afternoon drinking single-malt Scotch while Murray flipped through the correspondence, stopping to read particular passages or whole letters he found interesting. Here is one example, from a letter Ellison, then in Rome, wrote to Murray, who was stationed in Morocco on June 2, 1957:

> Human anguish is human anguish, love love; the difference between Shakespeare and lesser artists is eloquence. And when Beethoven writes it, it's still the same anguish, only expressed in a different medium by an artist of comparable eloquence.
>
> Which reminds me that here, way late, I've discovered Louis [Armstrong] singing "Mack the Knife." Shakespeare invented Caliban, or changed himself into him. Who the hell dreamed up Louis? Some of the bop boys consider him Caliban, but if he is, he is a mask for a lyric poet who is much greater than most now writing.

I left—hours later than I had intended—high not on the Scotch but on Ellison's words and Murray's passionate intelligence.

An All-Purpose, All-American
Literary Intellectual

This interview was conducted by Charles H. Rowell by telephone on January 28, 1997, between Charlottesville, Virginia, and New York City.

ROWELL: *I want to start at the very beginning: Nokomis, Alabama. What does that little Alabama town have to do with you now—Albert Murray, novelist, essayist, educator? Actually, I should also include Mobile. These places and the experiences you had there, one could argue, went into the making of you as person and as writer.*

MURRAY: Well, I was born in Nokomis, Alabama. But I know nothing about it, because my parents moved to Mobile shortly after I was born. The people who became my parents—who received me from my mother—moved to Mobile. This was during the buildup for the world war in Europe. So this must have been about 1917 when they moved. I was born in 1916. I grew up on the outskirts of Mobile, in a place called Magazine Point, which I fictionalized as Gasoline Point. What this place has to do with my writing should be obvious in *Train Whistle Guitar*. I don't think I could explain it any better than it is depicted in the novel—except, of course, for the specific technical things about writing. But there is the consciousness about place and learning, and then there is the whole business of what to do about them in terms of creating a literary text. It's all related. And I take it with me everywhere I go—whatever I remember from there. If you look at my fiction—there are three novels so far, and I'm working on a fourth—you'll always find flashbacks to Scooter's earliest consciousness. And Scooter is a fictional representation of my consciousness. *He is not, of course, a documentary image of me; rather he is a literary device for dealing with my consciousness.*

Your Tuskegee Institute (now Tuskegee University) experience was obviously very important to your consciousness too.

846

Well, that's just a matter of refinement; that's just college—I mean you go to high school and then to college, a higher level of abstraction, a higher level of intellectual insight. Then, too, in college there are more facilities to deal with and broader contacts; there you deal with more of the world. That's why the second book in the series is called *The Spyglass Tree*, which means that it's an extension of the chinaberry tree in the front yard of the house in Gasoline Point. And Miss Lexine Metcalf's classroom, with its bulletin board and its maps and so forth of the world, serves to expand Scooter's consciousness beyond what he could see from his favorite place in the chinaberry tree. So when he's in college and he thinks of his room, his dormitory room, it's like a medieval castle, like a garret in Paris, or all the places where you go to look out, to learn, to expand your consciousness of the world. And it always goes back to this earlier thing. As a writer, you're trying to put together what is called a *Bildungsroman*—that is, an education story, a coming-of-age story, a story about how a person's consciousness develops. That's what it's all about, and those various contexts are extensions of the original contexts. You see what I mean. Scooter doesn't stay on the ground in Gasoline Point: he gets up in this tree and looks out over an expanse of the land; he expands his awareness of what's around him. When he goes to school, he encounters maps and globes and sand tables and other languages and geography. Scooter is very much interested in all of these, especially geography. As a writer, then, you try to find poetic images for the expansion of consciousness and the deepening and enrichment of insight. You have to have something concrete, because you deal with these big abstract questions in terms of idiomatic particulars (that is, concrete details) that you actually experience. These things, I hope, are quite obvious in my work.

Many Americans of my generation and after have looked at Tuskegee with a narrow vision—that is, we have viewed it not as what it actually is: not only as an academic center where one can receive a technical or industrial education but also as a university where one can receive a liberal arts education. I am certainly reminded of your autobiographical nonfiction prose in which you

refer to your experiences as a student at Tuskegee. There you en-
countered extraordinary professors of literature, and there you
read far into European and North American literatures. We
have misread Tuskegee as an academic institution.

Well, for a long time Tuskegee was basically a normal and industrial school, basically a school designed to meet the problems of the freedmen after the Reconstruction period. Tuskegee's
intention at that time was to prepare people to be American
citizens, and at that time they were primarily assisted in agri-
culture and the trades and education—that is, elementary education and stuff like that. But as Tuskegee developed, it became
such a powerful and important institution that the facilities
expanded and they added a great library.

Tuskegee was not particularly interested in what I was
doing. There were some teachers who had come there from a
liberal arts education. But their primary emphasis was not
on liberal arts; it was on education—that is, an emphasis on
teaching and school administration, on the trades, on various
industrial arts, and on scientific farming, stuff like that. But by
the time I got there, it was a college and it also had a musical
conservatory. That's why Ralph Ellison was already there when
I got there. We turned out to be people who were very much
interested in liberal arts. You would think that we had gone to
liberal arts schools like Talladega or Fisk or Morehouse, or
Howard or places like that. But it turns out that I don't know
many people who went to those schools whose books are more
involved with the various dimensions of literature as our books
are. You see what I mean? But it was because he and I had the
same type of curiosity and because Tuskegee had great facilities. Tuskegee had a wonderful library; that was the thing that
was so great for us. But you didn't score any social points or
any other kind of points with the students at Tuskegee by
being good at literature and the arts. They were interested in
money and power and general progress, like the civil rights
movement people. Like most of the people I know, they were
interested in owning property or having money, being successful, going into administrative jobs, and some, eventually, into
politics. It seems to me that they're about the same as they
were. Of course, if you became a *famous* writer or something

like that, then they'd think you must be making a lot of money and that you're powerful, and they think that's important. But if you become a serious writer and you try to deal with problems which literature deals with, they don't line up behind you, as if you were their spokesman. They'd much rather go and hear a famous singer, pop or classical, or go and celebrate a famous athlete or some other icon of material success. And that's just as true of the liberal arts colleges as it is of the Big Ten–type colleges. I think of Tuskegee as being more like the Big Ten–type school without the strong liberal arts programs that Big Ten schools also have.

Were you reading texts at Tuskegee that you return to now?

I have them right here on my wall. You've seen them; you've been to my home. I bought them as soon as I could afford them. I mean I was a college boy, not just a generic Reconstruction Negro. I wanted to be a writer. I found out that I wanted to be an intellectual. I wanted to deal with the problems of the world in terms of literary images and in terms of philosophical concepts—but not in terms of running a business or holding an office or being a lawyer or something like that. Just like another who might want to become a preacher—he wants to save people's souls. In a way, a writer is closer to that than he was to being an engineer. The writer is trying to get people's heads straight, trying to get to the poetic dimensions of life, trying to make people conscious of those dimensions, and trying to make his ideas and art available to them. So if you're interested in literature, it seems to me that's what you're interested in: how people think and how they look at the world and how rich their experiences can become, how many dimensions they can see in events and in things. And if you had a good librarian like they had at Tuskegee by the time I got there, you had a great collection of books.

I was already the type of person, from the third grade on, who thought of books and bulletin boards as windows on the world. That's Scooter's relationship to Miss Lexine Metcalf, his third grade teacher, which is where geography started. That's what she meant to him. And I'm trying to make it obvious that at each stage of his development, when other people come into his consciousness, they are like Miss Lexine Metcalf; they are other dimensions and extensions of her. That should take the reader back to either Odysseus or Telemachus. Miss Lexine Metcalf becomes somebody like Athena. She's giving instructions, as if from Mount Olympus. You should be able to see these different images in various stages. That's what the contemporary literary statement should do. After all, these books that I'm writing are being composed after Proust, after Thomas Mann, after James Joyce, after André Malraux, after Ernest Hemingway, after William Faulkner, and they should reflect that. Then there is all that other stuff you read in school: naturally it's after Shakespeare, after Goethe, after Balzac, after Dumas, all these people, after Tolstoy. You're supposed to have all of that as part of your literary sensibility.

You said that at some point you knew that you wanted to be a writer, an intellectual. When did you realize that? What did that mean to you then?

Well, I guess I didn't *fully* realize it until I was well into college at some point. I had been interested in the theater and in drama, and when I got to college, I started reading books on the history of the theater. I also read anthologies of world literature which I had never seen before. When I read comprehensive anthologies of world drama, my first thought was that maybe I could write plays like this. I was first interested in acting and directing, and then I became interested in writing plays. The first creative things I wrote were little theater pieces. But I had read some stuff as a freshman that later on I realized had been sort of crucial in focusing on the type of approach to writing that I came to have. And one thing we read as freshmen was called "Myself upon the Earth," a short story, a personal memoir type of narrative by William Saroyan, and it turned out to be a part of a book called *The Daring Young Man on the Flying Trapeze*. I have that book still. When I got enough money to buy it, you know, years later, I bought it. Many of the books I have go back to that period of my life. At Tuskegee, the many magazines in the periodicals room of the library I had never seen before in my high school library, and I didn't use the big downtown Mobile library. There was a

Colored Branch of the Mobile Public Library, but I didn't use it very much, except for materials for special assignments I couldn't find at the school library, because we didn't have the capacity for that kind of research. But when I got to college and saw the great periodicals room with all those magazines, I discovered the *New Republic, The Nation, North American Review, Atlantic, Harper's,* the *New York Times Book Review,* the *Herald Tribune Book Review.* Then there were a lot of newspapers from major cities all over the country; they were all there in the library at Tuskegee. It was just terrific to me. When I visited other colleges, I didn't see that they had better libraries. For example, I had the opportunity to visit Talladega College, which is a very fine liberal arts school, but I discovered that the college did not have as big a library as Tuskegee. (I always went to the libraries when I visited other colleges or universities.) Well, Tuskegee had more. There were better facilities generally and certainly a larger campus. Have you ever been to Tuskegee?

Oh, but of course. I grew up in Auburn; my father's farm is only fifteen minutes from Tuskegee. By the way, I was admitted to the undergraduate school when I graduated from high school.

Oh yes. That's right.

As you talk about your earlier background in Mobile and Tuskegee, I think of my own in Auburn, Alabama, where, before I went to college, I read many Shakespeare plays—such as Macbeth, Hamlet, Julius Caesar, *and* Twelfth Night. *Of course, I did not understand the plays as I do now. In high school we also read Charles Dickens and George Eliot and Whitman and Hawthorne and Poe and numerous other British and American writers. But I did not come to Homer and the Greek playwrights until much later.*

Well, me too. But I was reading anthologies and histories of world literature. I remember a book called *The Golden Thread* by a Stanford University professor named Philo Buck. It gave you a whole picture of world literature. There was another book which, as soon as I got some money to spare, I bought. I still have it. It was one of the very first books I bought. It is by a man named Sheldon Cheney, and is entitled *The Theatre: Three Thousand Years of Drama, Acting and Stagecraft*. It deals with the world theater. So unlike these people who were just doing classwork for a specific course they were taking, I was much more interested in trying to come to terms with all this stuff. I read that book, and I checked the other books out. You could recheck these books out because not many other people were checking them out.

And I had a buddy who was like a roommate, not an actual roommate. John Gerald Hamilton is his name. He was from Detroit. He had read so many more books than I because he had gone to a high school in Detroit where there were good facilities. So his picture of the world of literature and of world history was broad. In school, I had read H. G. Wells's history of the world, which gave me a fairly comprehensive view that had started developing back when I began studying geography back in the third grade. But at Tuskegee I saw other more advanced and more comprehensive books. I was challenged by them. I realized that they were some of the books one should read, and that the courses I took were just *elementary* steps in that direction. So in addition to doing my assignments, I read other books. And it turned out that I was more interested in reading those books than in the assignments. I would get the assignments out of the way so I could really read about the things I wanted to know about. And I would read the magazines. I was coming across magazine articles, and I was coming across theater pieces in *Stage* magazine and *Theatre Arts Monthly*. The magazines I read took me back and forth over different periods in theater history. I read discussions of plays, and I also got information on what was being performed onstage in Paris and on Broadway and in little theaters. I had a big opportunity to expand my consciousness, and I tried to make the most of it.

When did you come to read William Faulkner and André Malraux and Mark Twain?

Well, Twain: I read *Tom Sawyer* and stuff like that in high school. In college, I also got Twain in our survey courses in

American literature. On the bulletin board in the main reading room of the Tuskegee library, they would put up the book jackets of current acquisitions, and they would put up worthwhile books in little racks on the circulation counter. These displays stimulated our interests in books. I especially remember seeing *These 13* by William Faulkner at the circulation desk that first term, and I turned through it. It looked good. Later I saw *Light in August* there. By the next year I saw *Absalom, Absalom!* That is, its book jacket was on display among the new books. When I read "Dry September" and "A Rose for Emily" in *These 13*, I realized that this stuff was good. Meanwhile I was reading *Esquire*, which most hip guys checked out for the latest men's fashions in those days. But Ernest Hemingway was also writing for *Esquire* in those days. And so was John Dos Passos. Then you also saw little things by F. Scott Fitzgerald in *Esquire*. Hemingway was writing *To Have and Have Not*, and some of it had been coming out serially in *Esquire*. I had read part of *Green Hills of Africa* in *Scribner's*. Anyway, the magazines and the book reviews really put you in the world of literature, where I have been living ever since. I remember Malcolm Cowley and Edmund Wilson as regular book reviewers of that time. Freda Kirchwey was reviewing at *The Nation*, and there were various people reviewing for the *New York Times* and the *Saturday Review of Literature*.

I also read the southern writers. I was reading T. S. Stribling and people like that, and a few other Alabama writers. Then one of the big things that hit when I was a freshman was *Gone with the Wind*. Meanwhile my English instructor, Mr. Sprague, who happened to be Ralph Ellison's English instructor too (but Ralph was a couple of years ahead of me), taught our sections of the freshman and sophomore English courses, the required composition and literature survey courses. In these courses, Mr. Sprague gave us a list of one hundred great books that a well-read person should know about. Mr. Sprague, who was a Hamilton College graduate, had done graduate work at Howard and Chicago. He was a big favorite right off, as you can see from reading *South to a Very Old Place*. I have accounted for all of this in the three novels, as well as in the "Tuskegee" section in *South to a Very Old Place*.

What was important to you about Ernest Hemingway?

His use of twentieth-century English appeals to me much the same as the beat and pulse of the music of Louis Armstrong and Duke Ellington. It was great; I had taste, I guess. It was great. Of course, I could see that Faulkner was doing something different, and that was a challenge too. When I learned about other contemporary writers, I realized what was special about the apparent simplicity of Hemingway's English and how this fitted in with other contemporary writers. I was reading James Joyce and Thomas Mann. So when I got to T. S. Eliot, I saw how he was related to James Joyce. I also read Ezra Pound and e. e. cummings. I was reading Louis Unter-meyer's anthologies of modern American and British poetry. I was also high on cummings, Eliot, Pound, and Archibald Mac-Leish, and even Carl Sandburg; I was reading all of them.

It turned out that Ralph Ellison was doing something very similar to what I was doing. I didn't know any of the upper-classmen well. But I would see his name on the checkout forms in library books, and I also knew that he was taking a course on the novel. He and some other people whom I still remember were taking a course on the novel under Mr. Sprague, who was my freshman English teacher. They were doing all English novels, and I have copies of some of them right here. So I also read *Tom Jones* when I was a freshman. That was a great book to read with all those digressions and the stuff on comedy, and then I was reading the current books. My favorite of the pop-ular books was not *Gone with the Wind*. It was the current best-seller, but the big best-seller just before that was *Anthony Adverse*, a novel by Hervey Allen. I thought that was a terrific novel. Later on, I also realized that it was sort of like a Bal-zacian novel. It was a historical novel; it had to do with the slave trade and the establishment of colonies and plantations in the New World.

But while I was keeping up with what I was reading in the literary magazines and books, I was also aware of what was happening among the upperclassmen. I was also trying to fig-ure out who at Tuskegee was the kind of college student I really wanted to be like. I looked at these upperclassmen, and I picked out Ralph Ellison. Although he was taking music, I always associated him with books. The Ralph I knew was standing with books in his arms, with novels by Samuel Richardson and Laurence Sterne, all the way up to Thomas Hardy. I have said this somewhere else: when I hear somebody say *Jude the Obscure*, I always think of Ralph because I remember when the upperclassmen were reading Hardy in Mr. Sprague's class. I was looking forward to the time I would become an upperclassman and take that course. I was also interested in athletics, in what, for example, was going on in football practice. But books won out. Not that I gave up sports.

For the first time I want to confess something to you. You have already referred to South to a Very Old Place. *My confession is this: sometimes I go to that book to remind myself of who I am as a Southerner. Will you talk about the genealogy of* South to a Very Old Place?

How do you mean?

How did that book come into being? What occasioned it? How did you come to write it?

Well, it started out as an assignment from *Harper's* magazine. It comes after *The Omni-Americans*. Then I wrote *The Hero and the Blues* because I had been pulling my thoughts together about the nature of literature—that is, what writing involves. Then I was invited to give lectures in a very important series at the University of Missouri (at Columbia), and I used half of the manuscript to create three lectures which were somewhat like the Norton Lectures at Harvard. You would get a book out of it. So I pulled this material out of the larger manuscript and wrote what in effect is my approach to a theory of American literature with the blues idiom as a frame of reference for defining heroic action.

But to get back to *South to a Very Old Place*: after working on what became *The Omni-Americans*, I got this assignment from *Harper's* magazine to participate in a series which they called "Going Home in America." Somebody was going home in the Midwest, somebody going home in the East, somebody going home in the Far West. So the editor, who is a friend named Willie Morris, decided to give me an assignment. Instead of going to Mobile, I decided to go south, with Mobile included in it, Mobile being a point of return back north. When I got to Mobile, I thought of myself as on the way back to New York, but I did go a bit farther south, to New Orleans. As the piece grew, I decided that I was not going to write a civil rights report or anything like that; I would write a book about coming to terms with yourself, with myself upon the earth, as it were, in dealing with how I came to have the outlook and the sensibility I have. So I made *South to a Very Old Place* a book about that. In certain places in the book, you get a poetry—rather than ordinary concrete details—that informs the narrator's sensibility, because it is through that sensibility that the reader discovers how the narrator feels about things that he's going through, and what he makes of it when he records it. All of these make the story. And that's how it happened. When he got to a certain place, he zoomed in, and he realized you can really make something out of that moment, other than just a journalistic report. And then I realized that I was writing a book, but at times I really forgot about the assignment, although I used the outlines of it, because I would say, "Well, I'll go south and stop in North Carolina, stop in Georgia, and then go by Tuskegee, go to Mobile, go to New Orleans, go to Greenville, Mississippi, and then stop in Memphis," and that would be a swing through the South. But it would not be the kind of book V. S. Naipaul was to write in *A Turn in the South*, which is really a report on the South; he merely went there and made a report of a trip through the South. But in *South to a Very Old Place* I tried to make a poem, a novel, a drama—a literary statement—about being a Southerner; that's what I was writing. And I am very pleased with the way it came out. I read parts of it to audiences at colleges, universities, and other places—and I give a lot of readings at various other places too. There are often requests for me to read from *South to a Very Old Place* and *Train Whistle Guitar*. But at public readings, I don't like to deal with the abstract ideas you find in *The Hero and the Blues*, *Stomping the Blues*, and *The Blue Devils of Nada*. By the way, once you get the whole Scooter cycle or saga of novels, it will be as if *South to a Very Old Place* is a sort of extended epilogue to whatever the last volume about Scooter is about. It is from the type of literary sensibility operating in *South to a Very Old Place* that stories in the Scooter saga come.

Scooter is still in process. Are there other volumes coming?

At least another one, I hope. So it's just a matter of what I can deal with at another stage, which is what else you can invent in order to deal with other dimensions of his sensibility. That's what that is. Volume one is *Train Whistle Guitar*, and that's like an evocation to adventure. That's what Luzana Cholly represents, the call to adventure, the call to heroic action, the call to the world at large. Then there's the preparation for Scooter in *The Spyglass Tree*, which has two parts, one being benchmarks and the other being the briarpatch. And then there is *The Seven League Boots*, in which you have an apprentice, a journeyman, and the craftsman. The title is a reference to a fairy tale about Puss in Boots. By putting on these boots he can make a stride of seven leagues; he can make longer strides. See the fairy tales of Charles Perrault, the Frenchman. These literary references are not to show off; they are functional things as in Eliot and Pound and Joyce. Well, when you see the title of the novel, *The Seven League Boots*, you think Scooter is going to run right to a castle, but when you open the book you see a quotation from Franz Kafka which says, "The castle hill was hidden, veiled in mist and darkness, nor was there a glimmer of light to show that a castle was there." It certainly does not mean that the seven league boots are going to solve all of Scooter's problems. It means that when he comes down out of the spyglass tree he has a better stride. In fact he's playing a goddamned bass fiddle, and he's playing what is equivalent to a stride. He's keeping time. He's a novice at this thing; he's only an apprentice with a part-time job. There is nothing that says that Scooter came into the world to be a bass fiddle player. But because he is a very bright young man, a very good college student, a Phi Beta Kappa sort of guy, he could certainly learn the bass fiddle, which Hortense Hightower has given him so he can listen to everything while keeping time.

Music, as well as literary texts, informs your prose fiction and nonfiction prose.

Music is style; it's form. What you're dealing with is chaos, you're dealing with nada, you're dealing with entropy, and that's what makes the blues central to my work. The blues puts a form on you and enables you to cope with entropy.

I'm talking about art, man. But what is art? Art is a means by which your experience is processed into aesthetic statement. That's true of painting, that's true of literature, it's true of music, it's true of sculpture, it's true of everything you're dealing with when you're ultimately trying to make an elegant statement. Another definition of art, of course, is this: it is the ultimate extension, elaboration, and refinement of the rituals which encapsulate the basic survival techniques of a given cultural configuration. So that if you went back to the primordial level of society and human consciousness, and you went back to hunting societies and fishing societies or something like that, and if you looked at what they do for a living (if they survived by hunting, or fishing, or finding and picking berries or whatever), you'd find that there are games and there are ceremonies. All of these, you would discover, are reenactments or forms of reenactments of their survival technology of hunting, fishing, and so forth. The ultimate extension, elaboration, and refinement of these rituals is art. So you're always dealing with something that's fundamental if you're dealing with art.

We are not talking about just ripping off something or imitating somebody else. We are talking about coming to terms with yourself, with your consciousness. That's what Scooter is about. In the very first book, he tries to name himself. He says, "My name is Jack the Rabbit because I was bred and born and brought up in the briarpatch," which means that he has to be nimble or nothing. He's got to be resilient. In other words, he's got to be a swinger. He's got to be able to improvise on the break. He's got to do all this. That's the same thing in the blues and in jazz. That's what it is. All that stuff is interrelated, and it is so obvious because this is right there. That's why societies produce people with special minds and imaginations to make other people aware of what they really live in terms of.

Can't you see that is what I think my function is, my function as a writer?

There are other people who think their function as a writer is to get white people to like black people, to get desegregated, or all those important but relatively superficial things. But the sociopolitical problems of the moment are always relatively superficial to what your ultimate involvement of life is. If you reduce life to social and political problems, you will never really be as profound about the meaning of human existence as you are when you're in church. By the way, until Martin Luther King and those other civil rights leaders came along, church folks were mainly concerned with the saving of their souls. Their concerns were not material but metaphysical. I was never in a church where the preacher preached about God and white folks, or prayed to God to tell white folks to stop segregating them. That's not what those ministers preached about. They didn't act like politicians. To the artist, material matters are ultimately as superficial as they were to those old sackcloth-and-ashes prophets of yore. But that is not to say that is not important; it is important. What the preacher, who is not a politician, tries to do is tell his congregation to watch what they're doing on earth in order to get themselves ready for the afterlife. Basically that's what you do on Sunday; you try to get your soul ready for the afterlife. Serious literature or any type of art fundamentally deals with the same thing: one's basic conception of life—that is, the quality of consciousness that you live in terms of. Conventional religion is concerned with eternal salvation in the afterlife. Secular art is concerned with salvation on earth, a salvation, however, that is not primarily concerned with material matters.

In your society, in your lifestyle which is based on your survival technique, there are these things that you have to come to terms with in order to have a satisfactory existence. That's how music, painting, and other art forms, for example, come into existence in a particular idiom. In the idiom I grew up in, music played a big role. Music actually functioned to enable people to survive. It is about what is around you.

For example, there is in blues music a certain rhythmic beat that's like the old down-home train drivers, whistles, and bells which add up to locomotive onomatopoeia. So-called black people in this country came from Africa, and they had a disposition to make percussive music that was dance-oriented. But they could not continue to play African music, because their requirements were no longer African or no longer a matter of an African existence. So they didn't play African music, but they had the disposition to play the drum, but they were not playing African music. They were playing American music, what became American music. They were imitating a train, something American, not African. They weren't playing for a chief or a bunch of barefooted or sandal-clad people jumping around because the chief wanted to see somebody dance. That's not what they were doing. If they played music, they expected people to come to hear them on their own and to buy a drink or a ticket, to come in and listen and dance. That's a different thing altogether from the old rituals of their African ancestors. But the percussive nature and the sound of the music came out of the locomotive of their everyday environment.

If you want really to study the locomotive as a student of culture would study it, as an artist would study it, you would see that the image of the train—or the idea or notion of the train—was deeply embedded in the consciousness of these particular Americans. That is, if they went to church they talked and sang about "gettin' on board." When they wanted to be free, they talked about the "Underground Railroad," which made the train a political metaphor. In church, the train was a metaphysical metaphor. All these images—that's poetry. So when you hear music from a blues guitar player, what do you hear? It's a train whistle guitar—just as I said it was. So that's where the music comes from.

The music is a basic part of the ritual that enabled people to survive in whatever predicament they found themselves. We might be talking about a primordial tribe or another group of people here or there. Whatever the case, people would evolve something equivalent to what I am trying to establish in my writing as something symbolic of American behavior. Improvisation, frontier exploration, resilience—these are basic elements of American behavior. One of my favorite quotations from Constance Rourke about our objective is this: "to provide emblems for a pioneer people who require resilience as a prime trait." You can't get a better definition of swinging than that. Resilience. So art symbolizes lifestyles. Dance is an art. How do they dance? They know that there is a formalized dance, but they dance a loose, resilient, improvisational dance. That's American behavior. That's why I say there is a quintessential American music. We're talking about that group of Americans who synthesize the American experience in a way that really represents the American attitude toward experience. The frontiersman, the early settler—the spirit of that is what is in jazz. But if you can't get people to study you as literature, then they miss the point, like missing the point of *The Seven League Boots.* You don't know that there's no castle there. So then why the seven league boots? It at least increases your stride. How do you like that? [*Laughter.*] You have a better chance of getting somewhere, wherever it is. [*Laughter.*] But Scooter doesn't know where he's going yet, does he?

As you speak, I hear a merging of two separate genres—that is, the novel and the essay or nonfiction prose. In you as artist, these two meet via imperatives I hear through ritual and through music, for example. There is no separation of the sensibilities here. I see the same sensibility.

Separate genre? Come on, Charles. Do you get two separate genres in *A Portrait of the Artist as a Young Man* or in *Ulysses* or *Finnegans Wake?* Do you get it in *The Magic Mountain?* Do you get it in *Joseph and His Brothers?* Do you get it in Proust? Let's not make genres where they're not. That's the kind of crap Skip Gates implied about *The Seven League Boots* in his *New Yorker* profile of me. What the hell has he been reading? Everything in *The Spyglass Tree* and in *The Seven League Boots* is justified by the character's schoolboy sensibility. It's no stiff-ass stuff like some of what your friends write, where they have a character stand up, in effect, and speechify about civil rights. That's artificial to me. Scooter and his old roommate were *schoolboys,* and they read a lot of books. Sounding bookish is as much a part of what they were as sounding hep on occasion. So that doesn't intrude on the story; that's what the story is about, isn't it? It's like what you said earlier. You said you're taken back to the south when you read *South to a Very Old Place.*

The author is trying to write a poem really, and the language is trying to swing as hard as it can. But the narrator can discuss books. That is entirely consistent with me. I can't sit on the phone in this abstract interview without talking about Proust and Joyce and Mann and Hemingway. We don't separate ideas as such from other dimensions of fictional statement like that. We are talking about a *contemporary* novel. Right? You can't read a book as old as Goethe's *Faust* and say that he's discussing some deep stuff, so this is not a play. No. It is a play. That's what the play is doing. What he says is entirely consistent with the personality of the character. When Faust needs to bring something in at a given point, he does so. Well, when Scooter gets a letter from an old roommate, we know he's going to get a lecture almost like a college professor. He's as much like a college professor as a college student, because he's a genius.

What you are saying demonstrates something I remember from one of your other books, in which you say that "all statements are counterstatements."

Yes, of course. A counterstatement means that you're disagreeing with something that has already been said. So somebody's got an assumption about something, and you are counterstating —that is, an assumption or an implied assumption with which you would disagree. So what I was doing just then was counterstating an assumption which you expressed. You said, "I see the merging of two different genres." And I said, "No. No. No." I jumped right on that. You can separate them, but in fiction you can't subtract abstract ideas presented as abstract ideas. Otherwise you're going to wipe out Henry James, Balzac, Flaubert, and a host of novelists. How are you going to read *Crime and Punishment*, *The Possessed*, or *The Brothers Karamazov*? They are constantly explaining things. Where is the novel that doesn't do that? And besides, there are two obvious useful reasons for attributing your sources: (1) it broadens the intellectual context; and (2) it prevents people from mistaking somebody else's ideas for your own. But, alas, I must admit that I do know a lot of people who are either intimidated, threatened, or in any case challenged by references to books they have not read or heard of. I refuse to restrict my writing to their limitations. As for myself, when I hear references to books with which I'm not familiar, I look them up.

Actually, Al, I read Train Whistle Guitar *as a counterstatement about a southern boy coming of age. It sounds as if you are revising or rewriting. Rewriting the South.*

Yes. That's true. Why did I write *The Omni-Americans*? To counterstate the use of sociological concepts to provide images of human behavior, particularly brownskin American behavior. You see what I mean? You're not going to get an adequate image of black Americans that way. You can't play poker against a Negro by just reading about Negro behavior in those surveys. You can't even play football against them if you believe what you read in those surveys. And you'd never hire a Negro football player. [*Laughter.*] Would you? Especially if they play white people, because, according to these social science assessments, they would feel so inferior that the white boys run all over them. Wouldn't they? [*Laughter.*] White boys can hardly buy a job on many erstwhile white teams in many places nowadays. [*Laughter.*] When I look at college football and basketball on television now and see the University of Virginia playing the University of North Carolina, it looks like Hampton is playing Tuskegee, or like South Carolina State is playing Alabama A&M. [*Laughter.*] You can even go to a college up in the hills and you find the same thing. Another way to speak about my writing as counterstatement is to say that I'm trying to make a more adequate image that reflects the *actuality* of somebody's life. I can't come up and look at people who have so much fun just walking, who have such a sense of humor, who bring so much elegance to anything that they get involved in (regardless of the relative crudeness of their taste, their orientation is to elegance)—I cannot look at these people and say that they had downtrodden spirits.

The Hero and the Blues seems to be more than a counterstatement. It seems to be something else.

I was trying to suggest an approach, a blueprint. I was talking to a guy yesterday. Somebody from Washington was here interviewing me. (As I told you earlier, I've been having a string of interviews lately.) What I pointed out—and the point I'd like for you to get—is that a lot of people, now that they've grown up a little bit intellectually or, at least, academically, are saying admiring or concurring things about *The Omni-Americans*. You remember that Skip Gates in his *New Yorker* profile made it a big deal. To my profound and furious disappointment, however, he didn't say a damned word about *South to a Very Old Place*, a literary statement that was nominated for a National Book Award. I was trying like hell to make it a piece of literature. He didn't even mention it. So that probably means that he was more oriented to race relations and stuff like that than to the existential problems of life, of being an individual, of who you are at three o'clock in the morning. Anyway, I think *South to a Very Old Place* should be a very useful way of coming to terms with my nine books. Look at *The Omni-Americans* and look at that stuff that I disagreed with. So I counterstated it—whether it's so-called black people making it or so-called white people making it. I am never going to accept anybody's argument about Negroes having self-hatred. I'm never going up to anybody thinking I can pull something on them because they hate themselves. Would you do that? Can you imagine saying, "I'm gonna go on over and get that guy's old lady, because he ain't got no self-respect anyway. He hates himself." [*Sustained laughter.*] What you actually hear is this: "This guy is a college teacher. He's an army officer. He earns all that money, and he thinks he's better than I am. I'll kill that son of a bitch. Who does he think he is?" That's the way the Negroes I know talk and act. [*Laughter.*] You think all these guys are going to fall out because "the great genius Albert Murray is here." No! They'll turn around and ask, "*Who is he?!!! What does he think he's doing?* Man, I remember when he was a little raggedy-butt boy and couldn't keep his nose clean. I remember when he was going over there to Mobile County Training School." That's the way they talk. I want them in my books because they inhabit my America. Do you know that line in *South to a Very Old Place* about how you might get kicked out of a liquor store "by looking at the wine too long"? "Who the hell is he?" "He's a wino, man. Get him out of here." "Man, all this good whiskey here, and he's looking at wine."

Such a cat might be ignorant as hell, but he is not guilty of self-hatred. So my images of people like him are a counter-statement of the social science fiction image of devastation that so many brownskin spokesmen and academics seem to have been taken in by.

In *The Omni-Americans*, I tried to convince people that they were on the wrong track to identity. As for myself, I don't like being called "black American," because it so often implies *less American*. And I absolutely despise being called "African-American." I am not an African. I am an American. And I still can't believe my ears when I hear educated people calling themselves a **minority**-something, by the way, which unedu-cated people never do. All of my values and aspirations are geared to the assumption that freedom as defined by the American social contract is my birthright. Man, ain't nothing African about that kind of birthright. Ain't nothing Chinese or Japanese or Italian or Austrian or Iranian or Jordanian and so on either. Otherwise we wouldn't have had all those people from Europe and elsewhere migrating over here and messing up the promises of the Reconstruction. At any rate, I did what I could. I kicked these guys' butts here and there for the stupid definitions of themselves they were putting out there. And now they are doing the same thing over and over. What I was doing is writing affirmation, not protest. What I did in *The Omni-Americans* was to lay out what I thought the problem was and how it was being misdefined.

All of my other books are about what the possibilities are. For example, in *South to a Very Old Place* you have an image of what it was really like to be a southern boy growing up. Then how could a Negro in all those circumstances you've read about in sociology become an all-purpose, all-American liter-ary intellectual? How could he have an affirmative attitude toward this or that? How could he have nice-looking clothes, a good-looking wife, and a lot of admirers? How could he have those? Let this writer assure you that it's a perfectly natural American expectation for this down-home boy. In *Train Whis-tle Guitar*, you see, we move from one stage of Scooter's life to another stage of his life. Some reviewers of *The Seven League Boots* complained that "Scooter never met a woman that didn't want to go to bed with him." That's not true. It's not a primary thing of Scooter's life anyway. Sex is just a part of it. In Scooter's experience as a road band musician, sex is a very casual part if not an occupational hazard in the world of entertainment. But even so, in the overall saga, as I relate it, each sexual encounter turns out to be mostly a matter of a *rite de passage*. All of the nonfiction books are about how to write. They are not concerned about what Kenneth Clark thinks or about what Richard Wright, James Baldwin, and all those guys were dealing with. I was searching for a way to write affirmative books. Then I wrote *The Hero of the Blues*. I wanted to create affirmative images that would make people wish they could be that way. Not the victim, not the villain. I have never seen myself as a criminal. I could see myself as becoming a Robin Hood, but never a Bigger Thomas.

Then after that we get into *Train Whistle Guitar* and that sense of adventure, that sense of what I call, in the outchorus to *South to a Very Old Place*, "the adventuresomeness of the brown-skinned hometown boy in us all." Man, that's turning that stuff all the way around. Isn't it? That's what you can do as you develop literary skill—you can constantly signify on all those different levels. That's what I tried to do in *Train Whistle Guitar*. You have the issue of adventure, the sense of adventure, but these boys are not ready for adventure. So Luzana Cholly, the guy they admire as an epic hero, brings them back. Scooter realizes that he has to go through Miss Metcalf. Going through Miss Metcalf means that he has to go to college. When he gets to college, there is Hortense Hightower, who is obviously more interested in his potential than in his body and from whom he earns a bass fiddle. He knows not to make any mannish mistakes with her, just as he never got fresh with Miss Lexine Metcalf. So when he gets out there on the road with the band, he is supposed to be pretty hep. He is accused of having made one little false move at that party where the rich girl picks him up. And the guys kid him because he didn't touch her for an expensive gift. That's a little joke they're playing on him, telling him that hepcats don't shack up with horseback-riding, sailboat-sailing rich girls with hot pants just for fun.

You speak of the blues. Will you talk about how the blues impulse is played out in other arenas of American life?

Well, what a case of the blues represents is chaos, entropy, futility, depression, defeat, contention—all of that. Now, to survive you got to have an affirmative attitude toward your possibilities rather than an attitude of defeatism and lamentation. When many people outside the functional context of the blues idiom think about the blues, they want to think in such negative terms. They want to say that these are Negroes who came out of slavery and are inferior citizens, and that when they sing the blues, they're just bemoaning their sorry state in life. You know better than that. [*Laughter.*] Folks go to the juke joints to hit on something; otherwise they might just as well sing the blues in church. This they never do. All those illegitimate children come from the Dionysian dimension of the blues—that is, they come from stomping away the blues. In other words, the juke joint is a temple where this rite takes place. You start out by chasing the blues away or stomping the blues away or snapping or swinging or bopping or riffing the blues away. That's a purification ritual. Then at some point you cross that line, and it becomes a fertility ritual. There is nothing more aphrodisiac than the blues. You don't get on your knees and pray when you hear the blues. When you get on your knees and blues is playing, there is no lamentation. [*Sustained laughter.*] You're involved in a fertility ritual, even if it's a mock fertility ritual. You're still going through the motions that are part of a fertility ritual. And what could be more affirmative than a fertility ritual?

When you really look at the nature of a blues statement, you see what the whole thing involves. You discover that it is a music of affirmation; it is not a music of commiseration. It's out of that affirmation that you get all of that elegance. And on the break you get all of those elegant movements and rhythms. With the break the musicians go to town, and then later they pick up where the cadence stopped. Nobody can be exposed to that without responding affirmatively. That kind of musical statement is a basic existential affirmation. And the musicians counterstate their problems; they counterstate the depression, despair, despondency, melancholia, and so forth. Blues music is a ritualistic counterstatement. That is what all of those self-styled victims who go in for protest rhetoric do just like every-body else, and yet they go out and write or talk as if it were all just the opposite. I'm looking at what they really do instead of what they say in their pitches for welfare handouts.

It seems to me then that one of the main points of your writing has been to reveal to us Americans who we are.

Right, exactly.

That is, in your books you've been trying to explain to us who we are.

Right. Identity—that's one of the things I talk about, one of the most basic. Reread *The Seven League Boots* and you discover that this book, which began with *Train Whistle Guitar* and the question of Scooter's personal identity, is about the larger context of his American identity.

OTHER WRITINGS

"The Problem" Is Not Just Black and White

THE SO-CALLED NEGRO REVOLUTION, which is largely a belated white awareness of the discontent that has been there all along, has now begun to produce an outpouring of books by whites and Negroes. Each book purports to explain, and even to solve, "the problem." Each in its own way attempts to move the great dialogue over discrimination out of the ruts in which it has become wedged. But as "the problem" varies for each individual, so each writer is hampered by the preconceptions and limitations he brings to it.

Nowhere do the smug assumptions which underlie the ideas of white supremacy work more insidiously than among the so-called American liberals, the self-styled "friends of the Negro." Their methods are rooted in the jargon of social science, their judgments based on tricky statistics, their proposed solutions basically materialistic—and seldom if ever do they stop to consider Negroes as people. Instead, these authors' good intentions become so enmeshed in misinformation and guesswork that their books wind up preaching the same false generalities as white supremacists. The only difference is that their attitude is condescending rather than malevolent.

The two current examples of these attitudes are Nat Hentoff and Charles Silberman. Hentoff is a jazz journalist who also writes promotion notes for record liners and hires out as a jazz expert. *The New Equality* is his report on the Negro revolution. It is more speculation than fact or understanding, and Hentoff's sense of the nuances of everyday life among Negroes is every bit as unreliable as his ear for the Negro idiom in music. On the one hand he makes pretensions to scientific scholarship. On the other he is given to extremely personal opinions.

Hentoff makes greater claims to inside information about U.S. Negro life than most Southerners do. His chapter on the mystery of blackness (whatever that is) is a case in point. It cites "authorities" but it is all really a statement of Hentoff's own anxious conjectures about Negro sex life. Silberman doesn't claim the same cozy familiarity with his subjects— instead, he takes the loftier, daddy-knows-best attitude which types him for Negroes as more a self-righteous missionary than a liberal. *Crisis in Black and White* purports to reveal incisive truths that will offend both blacks and whites.

It turns out that Silberman's truth about the Negroes is that they really are as God-awful as the segregationists have been saying all along but they are not inherently that way. He catalogues a lot of back-fence gossip, borrows a half-baked theory about concentration camp Jews to explain the Negro slave's "servile attitude," and then falls back on the catch-all patronizing apologia that "society" is responsible for the shortcomings of the Negro. But when he acknowledges that Negroes "have 'looser morals'" than white folks he only shows that Negro maids and bellboys know more about white morals than he does, and certainly Negro mothers of mulattoes know more about the white man's "sense of family."

Even a trained minority-group specialist like Harvard University's Oscar Handlin falls prey to condescending generalities. In *Fire-Bell in the Night* he describes the fundamental American aspiration to "create a free nation out of a population of diverse origins" as "breath-taking," and states that this is at the heart of "the problem." Southern senators would agree with him, but most Americans would place more emphasis on making this aspiration a reality. Handlin's book gives the impression that he is more concerned about moderation than about freedom. A good thing there were no minority group specialists during the Revolutionary War.

Interestingly enough, the best and most straightforward account of the integration struggle is *Ten Years of Prelude*, written by a white Southerner who claims no special knowledge of Negroes. Benjamin Muse, a member of the Southern Regional Council, displays a commitment to freedom which allows him to identify more closely with Negroes than most Northern liberals, who talk in proprietary fashion about *the white world* and *white schools* as much as the reactionary.

Another Southerner, Bradford Daniel, a freelance journalist from Fort Worth, has compiled in *Black, White, and Gray* an excellent civil rights source book containing the opinions of liberals, moderates, reactionaries, and those who are just downright confused but go on writing anyway. Among the most confused contributors are James Baldwin, who even brings the problem of homosexuality into the issue of oppression, and Norman Podhoretz, a Brooklyn liberal gone sinister, who confesses fear and hatred of Negroes, proposes miscegenation, and *then* starts worrying about his womenfolk. Far less confused is Ronnie Dugger, a white Southerner whose confession of his personal struggle to practice his beliefs about equality is neither fashionable, safe, nor profitable—but it is thoroughly honest and responsible.

Those who expect any special insights from Simeon Booker, a Negro who is Washington bureau chief for *Ebony* magazine, will not find them in *Black Man's America*, which is just another political report about the new mood of Negro militancy. Booker, like most other reporters, Baldwinizes too much about the Negro's new liberation from fear of the white man. But he has his facts backward: what the Negro has always been concerned about is the white man's sometime hysterical fear of *him*, a fear that expresses itself all too often in terms of lynch mobs, police brutality, racist juries, unconstitutional state laws, and fanatical defiance of federal authority. By not challenging the white man's control until the time was ripe, the Negro has been wiser than the American Indian, who tried to meet white brutality head-on and was all but annihilated in the process. Today the Black Muslims pretend that frightening white people is something new, but then they are not looking for a route to integration. In fact, they also pretend they want to be sent to a reservation!

If most whites who write about Negroes are too strongly influenced by social science and superficial do-goodism, too many Negro spokesmen and writers such as Booker overestimate the practical value of moral outcry. They are forever pleading their cases in such naively overstated terms of degradation and desperation that they often seem to be promoting the completely ridiculous idea that Negroes (unlike other people) must be well-housed, well-fed, and loved by all their diverse neighbors *before* they can become ambitious, creative, or interested in anything more than civil rights. But nowhere in U.S. life has there ever been a richer mixture of vitality and elegance than in the Negro idiom, whether in sports, speech, dance, or everyday style and manner; and nowhere in any of the contemporary arts is there a more life-affirming spirit and culturally sophisticated style than in U.S. Negro music. All of the fatuous nonsense about the white world and minority groups has too long obscured the fact that although the mainstream of American political and economic control has always been predominantly white Anglo-Saxon Protestant, the mainstream of American culture and character has always been something else again. But nowhere in *Black Man's America* or in most of these other books is there an appreciation or even awareness of this.

Perhaps the most significant "message" in *Why We Can't Wait*, Martin Luther King Jr.'s personal report on the Battle of Birmingham, 1963, is that U.S. Negroes, whose great-grandparents were slaves, today think and act more like true descendants of the founding fathers of this nation than do most Americans who snobbishly trace their actual blood lines back to the American Revolution. Whatever shortcomings the technique of nonviolence may have, those who truly understand the strategy and the courage involved will recognize King as not only a worthy namesake of the German Martin Luther and a canny, home-grown disciple of the Hindu Gandhi, but also the uncompromising descendant of ragtag, bobtail Colonel George Washington at Valley Forge.

Those *Blues for Mister Charlie* militants who sneer at the techniques of nonviolence should take a second look at its effectiveness under fire. For when the chips are down, nuclear spitball–commander Malcolm X, for all his loud-mouthed empty-handed threats, won't be able to muster one medium weapons-carrier load of hand grenades. Whereas Martin Luther King, as all Southern governors are well aware, is like to have the backing of the entire might of the U.S. military. For the threat of violence which hangs over the Negro revolution has never been a matter of 20 million U.S. Negroes against 160 million U.S. "Others." It is a matter of the basic national commitment to defend freedom against all enemies, foreign and domestic.

1964

U.S. Negroes and U.S. Jews: No Cause for Alarm

AMERICAN NEGROES are not and never have been anti-Semitic. They never have wished that all Jews in the world were either dead or in concentration camps. They do not wish to send all U.S. Jewish immigrants back to where they came from. They do not think Jews should still be restricted to the ghetto. And they most certainly are not involved in any plans to evacuate all U.S. Jews to Israel. Nevertheless U.S. Negroes do resent the way some U.S. Jews behave toward all Negroes, and many will go right on disliking certain Jews no matter how many charges of anti-Semitism are made against them.

But the overwhelming majority of U.S. Negroes are firmly convinced that the great majority of U.S. Jews not only wish all Negroes well but have demonstrated their good will in circumstance after circumstance. Seldom if ever do U.S. Negroes single out U.S. Jews as being special enemies. They are much more likely to assume that even those Jews who are actually indifferent, are really their special friends. Many Southern Negro civil rights workers, for example, hasten to explain that Southern Jews do not help the Movement more only because of the fear of Southern white reprisals—but that these Jews like all others are their undercover allies.

No Negroes anywhere in the United States need any prompting to acknowledge the numerous ways in which they have benefited from Jewish philanthropy. As a matter of fact, many Negroes have the impression that most philanthropic foundations are Jewish. The name Julius Rosenwald, for instance, has had more meaning for thousands of Southern Negro school children than the name Peabody or Horace Mann. Every day Negroes see other Negroes whose achievements were aided by Jewish money and encouragements.

Nor are Negroes unmindful of the fact that Jews play key roles in the NAACP, CORE, the Urban League, and SNCC, four of the most powerful civil rights organizations. In many ways, indeed, the NAACP is really a Jewish organization for Negroes. Roy Wilkins, the executive secretary, is a Negro, but

Jack Greenberg, the successor to Thurgood Marshall as chief legal counsel, Herbert Hill, the chief labor agitator, and June Shagaloff, the chief school desegregation strategist, are all very efficient and dedicated Jews. Martin Luther King's Southern Christian Leadership Council also receives strong Jewish support. Negroes will long remember those sixteen courageous Rabbis rallying to King in St. Augustine, Florida, a few years ago, and they remember the many Jews among the thousands who rallied to him again in Selma.

But Negroes also know that there are very real causes for the resentments they have against some Jews. They know very well what economic and social atrocities these particular Jews have committed and continue to commit against Negroes. Unfortunately, there are Negroes who mistrust many Jews because of the unforgiveable things which only some Jews are guilty of doing. But then it is also an ironic fact that most Negroes do not show any special concern at all about the very specific role a number of Jews now play in complicating one of the U.S. Negro's most fundamental problems.

Nothing has ever given U.S. Negroes more trouble than other people's theories, conjectures, and misdefinitions. Slavery and segregation were always explained away with theories. *And for some time now Jewish Intellectuals, by persisting in misrepresenting and misinterpreting the rituals and motives of U.S. Negro life in terms of clichés and values peculiar to the Jewish tradition, have been propagating and "documenting" a new theory of Negro inferiority.*

Cultural variation is the norm of life in the United States. Thus pizza is not Negro, bagels are not Italian, and neither chitterlings nor jazz is Jewish but any New Yorker can have any, all, or none of these things and still be a good U.S. citizen. Jewish Intellectuals, however, in far too many instances, establish their own norms of U.S. behavior and then not only do they condemn U.S. Negro life as sub-human for not conforming, they are actually insisting that official programs be instituted to bring Negroes into line.

It is as if such Intellectuals unequivocally refuse to acknowledge the most obvious thing about U.S. Negro cultural expression. Negroes have always been making choices among the many things available to them as Americans, accepting, rejecting—and modifying much of what they accept. U.S. Negro music is an excellent example of this acceptance–rejection–modification process of assimilation. It represents all the music played in the United States and it sounds as it does because that is the way Negroes feel all other music really should sound. Negro soldiers are another example. They march swinging that way because they feel that is really the way U.S. soldiers should strut. It is a mistake either arrogant or stupid to assume that in spite of all those great Negro cooks and waiters in most of the great restaurants through the country, Negroes still eat hog maws because they don't knows about caviar or cannot afford it. If they can afford all of those finely tuned Cadillacs they can afford a little dab of caviar every now and then if they really want it.

Few Jewish Intellectuals seem to have any real understanding of culture in this sense and yet there are probably more articles and books on U.S. Negro life being written by Jews than by all other Americans together. In fact it sometimes seems as if Negro Matters, as the saying goes, have been turned over to the supervision of Jews. There are actually more self-appointed Jewish Negro experts than Negro Negro experts. Indeed, on close inspection most Negro Negro experts turn out to be trained, supervised, or subsidized by Jewish Negro experts and benefactors. At any rate the Marx-Freud clichés most Negro Negro experts so glibly gab do not corroborate Jewish intellectualizations, they only echo them.

Most Negro Negro experts, unlike Negro barbershop philosophers, seem to overlook the fact that Jewish Negro experts play down their own cultural differences from other U.S. whites, play up their own whiteness, but play down Negro Anglo-Saxon Christian racial and cultural kinship and play up color differences as if most U.S. Negroes were not only jet black but also recently arrived natives from Africa.

None of this is to imply that U.S. Negroes should not avail themselves of the infinite riches of the great Jewish Intellectual tradition. One does wish, however, that their own conclusions reflected the kind of vernacular assimilation of various influences as do the blues. And after all Jews have more to offer besides Marx and Freud.

Given the obvious but for the most part confused good intentions of most Jewish Negro experts, none of this is quite enough to become anti-Semitic about. But as more and more Negroes become more intimately involved with books and mass media, they are almost certain to express more and more displeasure at all the misinformation Jewish Negro experts are spreading about them. At the present time, however, they simply shrug and say all white writers lie about Negro life for one reason or the other. Perhaps this is not entirely accurate but neither is it anti-Semitic.

Not even the most extreme Negro hate groups or race rhetoricians have expressed, announced, or even betrayed any plans which can be called anti-Semitic. If the truth were known, those black nationalist leaders are really hoping some generous Jewish millionaire will buy them that fifty-first state they are forever claiming they want. But then maybe not. If a group of nice Jewish philanthropists got together and offered one-way tickets to Africa for all Black Nationals there would probably be a whole lot of black anti-Semitism overnight.

But not even the Black Muslims are anti-Semitic. They make much of their identification with the Arab world, but they show no practical interest at all in the unrelenting conflict between the Arabs and the Jews. As a matter of fact, Nasser would be horrified by the pro-Jewish theories of some of the Black Muslim stalwarts: Jews are not white devils; they are the black man's brothers, sabotaging the white devils from within. When Hitler was killing Jews he was really warming up to get to Negroes. Everybody knows what the Germans really wanted was Africa! "Solomon was a black man, brother," they insist learnedly, "and the Queen of Sheba was a black woman like Cleopatra, black and beautiful, brother."

II

Some U.S. Jews seem to regard any complaint against any Jew as evidence of deep anti-Semitism. Others seem to interpret any specific reference to Jews as such as anti-Semitic. This is unfortunate, and it is also as great a waste of time as all the name-changing that some Jews are given to. So far as U.S. Negroes are concerned, it should be obvious to all other Americans that since Negroes themselves are always singled out and always identified as Negroes, they find it perfectly natural to specify Italian grocers, Irish policemen, Chinese laundrymen, and so on, insofar as they are able to recognize them (so many white people look alike). So if a lot of Harlem merchants are Jews, they are obviously Jews to Negroes and that is that, whether they are good ones or bad ones.

However, the frankly admitted resentment that U.S. Negroes feel toward many Jews is exactly the same as that which they feel for gentile whites. The violent hatred which Negroes express against Jewish Harlem slumlords is the same as that which they feel for all other loathsome Harlem slumlords, nor are black ones excepted. In fact more often than not Negroes confuse Jewish slumlords with Southern gentile landlords. Thus the vilest epithet that U.S. Negroes use against Jews is not "You Jew!" but "You Southern cracker, you redneck, you peckerwood!" This does not make anything any nicer, of course, but it certainly doesn't make it anti-Semitic either.

Perhaps such an expression as "Jewish pawnbroker" sounds like a stereotype to people who deal primarily with abstractions but a Jewish pawnbroker is a very harsh and specific detail of actual existence to those people who have to deal with him year after year. Jewish Intellectuals might as well stop trying to tell Harlem and Watts Negroes how they should react to all those crooked Jewish pawnbrokers, merchants, and slumlords. The Negroes involved know more about these particular Jews than all the Jewish together are likely to know. Harlem Negroes know how to react to Jewish crooks just as they know how to react to all the good Jewish teachers and social workers among them (and they know that some of these are more opportunistic than anything else too). Negroes have their own ways of telling a good Jew from a bad one and they do not need anybody else's.

And anyway, if U.S. Negroes were actually anti-Semitic, accusing them of anti-Semitism would not change them any more than accusing Southern segregationists of racism changes anything. Imagine James Baldwin, a veritable Savonarola to guilty Northern liberals, pointing his finger at a Ku Klux Klansman and saying "Whiteman, you are a dirty bigot!" Almost everybody was calling the Nazi anti-Semitic but the Nazis only admitted it and went right on and wiped out more than six million Jews. And when they finally stopped, it was not because they could no longer bear being thought of as anti-Semitic.

Negroes find it absolutely astonishing that so many Jews for all their revulsion to epithets do not seem to realize that when they express displeasure with other people by charging them with being anti-Semites they themselves are indulging in the lowest form of irresponsible name calling. And of course Negroes know only too well that some Jews use such charges as a device to avoid criticism and to excuse individual shortcomings. Most Negroes know that old trick only too well because they have been using it themselves for years.

More than astonishing is the fact that for all the unquestionable Jewish goodwill for The Negro Cause, Norman Podhoretz, the editor of *Commentary* magazine, perhaps the best-known Jewish publication, is a self-confessed Negro-hater. Most Negroes have never heard of *Commentary* to be sure, but the response of the few who did read Podhoretz's obscene article "My Negro Problem—and Ours" were not anti-Jewish but anti-jerk —like that of a nice Jewish girl on *The New Yorker* named Renata Adler. Perhaps other Jewish intellectuals expressed their embarrassment at Podhoretz's sloppiness in private letters to their personal Negro friends. Everybody however knows that the venerable Max Lerner thinks that the Jewish Ku Klux Klansman who committed suicide upon being exposed last year was just a crazy mixed-up kid—but after all the Klan is anti-Semitic.

When Podhoretz asks himself in print if he wants his daughter to marry a Negro (or perhaps The Negro), most U.S. Negroes would not think he was a Jew at all. They would be absolutely certain that he was a southern redneck. Podhoretz, like many other Northern squares, obviously does not know what happens when one Negro sees another with a white woman. If she is pretty that speaks for itself. If she is not, her money and power speak for her. If she is neither pretty nor rich and powerful the whole thing is regarded as a joke—but the joke does not exclude the very real possibility that the two might just simply like each other very much.

III

Negroes pick and choose among U.S. Jews just as they have always been doing with all other people. There may be a few nervous fund-oriented Social Science Negroes who pretend that all Jews are ever so nice, but there are many other Negroes who have every reason in the world not to think so, and some don't mind saying as much. If this makes anybody resign from interracial organizations these Negroes couldn't care less. Nobody in the world can intimidate these particular U.S. citizens (first class or second) by accusing them of anti-Semitism in such a way as to imply that Jews are going to cut off the handouts.

Jewish friends of the Negroish Cause, who are so quick to remind Negroes of all the help the Jewish are giving "you people," should realize that such tactlessness turns gratitude into immediate resentment, cold hostility, and dark suspicion. Negroes, who after all think that nothing less than equality is good enough for anybody, will be appreciative but they are not likely to be over impressed with what so many rich and powerful Jews are doing for them since they are still stuck with most of the problems they have always had.

Parents of young Jews among all those other well-meaning young men and women who have been going South to work in the civil rights movement might as well realize the facts of life also. Good intentions are warmly received. Literacy is roundly appreciated as far as it goes. Naïveté is duly noted and often excused. But white condescension and presumption are blackly resented. It should also be realized that when these eager youngsters go rushing off somewhere else because "the new thing" is opposition to Viet Nam, Southern Negroes are relieved to have them out but philosophical about the additional complications these kids brought with them. They only wonder how Martin Luther King came to follow them. But some Negroes, it should be noted, are already beginning to complain that too many Jewish rehabilitation experts don't seem to be able to handle their own problems, personal or otherwise. And yet maybe all the current concern and hysteria about black anti-Semitism will serve some immediately useful purpose after all. Maybe it will stop a lot of self-esteemed white Americans from wasting their time on academic nonsense about Negro self-hatred and self-rejection, and direct their attention to some of the source of the deep-seated resentment and boiling hatred Negroes feel toward other people. The Negro Revolution after all did not grow out of self-hatred.

All native-born many-generation U.S. Negroes (who represent service in every war this nation has ever fought and are
still regarded as second-class citizens) bitterly resent any white
immigrant who comes into the United States on a preferential
quota allocation, cashes in on the color system, gets himself
straight financially, moves out of the slums into an exclusive
residential area, and then not only opposes integration but
expresses contempt for Negroes because they are not doing
enough for themselves and proudly cites his own progress to
imply that Negroes are inherently inferior to other Americans.

There are thousands of Jews who are guilty of such arrogance and racism, but New York Negroes still express a very
special disgust for those Jews who just narrowly escaped the
gas ovens and arrived in New York and immediately began
complaining about having Negroes in *their* neighborhood and
in *their* buildings.

Any nice NAACP Negro who says he is happy that these
particular Jews made it to safety over here is not to be trusted.
Since Negroes violently resent all segregationists no matter how
subtle, it is ridiculous to expect them to make any special exception for Nathan Glazer because he is Jewish. Glazer, a Social
Scientist of course and an ethnicist (*sic!*) at that, maintains essentially that the United States is an Open Society only in that it
allows many ethnic groups to co-exist with a minimum of conflict. He apparently sincerely thinks he is being realistic about
this but he is in fact actually apologizing for it. He even goes so
far as to claim that U.S. Negroes (which he does not recognize
as a group except in matters of civil rights agitation) are mainly
struggling to integrate into a society that doesn't even exist, that
they are struggling to integrate with all white people whereas
white people are not really integrated with each other! But then
this is the same unmelted-pot Glazer who gleefully reports that
Jews are overrunning state and Protestant schools, and that they
force the New York *public* schools to close on Yom Kippur and
Rosh Hashanah because the great majority of the principals and
50 percent of the teachers are Jews. Glazer can emphasize ethnic
distinctions all he wants to but it is preposterous to tell Negro
Civil Rights workers that all those Anglos, Irishmen, Italians,
Jews, and Poles and so on intermingling in all those *public* offices, *public* hospitals, *public* housing areas do not exist. Negroes

can see very well that they do exist and can only wonder why it is assumed that all those thick foreign accents are so much better than cotton-picking English. Negroes will go along with a Jew who objects to Sammy Davis pushing his way into a private family circle during Seder, but a Jew trying to intellectualize Negroes out of the U.S. mainstream by pretending that it doesn't exist is obviously too busy concocting a theory of segregation to notice all those Negro domestics going in and out of all those restricted areas. Some of those servants become intellectuals too.

But Negroes do not want to deport Glazer to Israel. They would like to deport him and his ethnicity to Mississippi to give him a chance to indulge his respect for "the group pattern of American life." It is Glazer's non-Jewish friend Patrick Moynihan Negroes would like to ship beyond the melting pot to Israel.

IV

Far from being anti-Semitic, U.S. Negroes are among the most many generation pro-Semitic people anywhere in the world. Most native-born U.S. Negroes may well be part-white Anglo-Saxons and overwhelmingly Christian. They have also *traditionally* identified themselves with Jews. As for religious *differences* they simply regard the Jewish Church as another Protestant denomination. (Negroes by the way have never thought Jesus Christ was Italian.)

It is not for nothing that U.S. Negroes have been referring to themselves as the Hebrew Children, the Children of Abraham and of Israel, all these years. And when they sing about Moses and Joshua and crossing Jordan and the promised land of Canaan, it is sincerity not irony which always comes through. The Negro spirituals, incidentally, are downright ecumenical. And as little as the culture experts seem to have noted it, there are probably more Jews (orthodox, reformed, and Marx-Freud) going in and out of Negro churches these days than have ever been inside any Christian churches anywhere at anytime in the history of the world. Nor should it be overlooked that Andrew Goodman and Michael Schwerner were murdered while investigating the destruction of a *Christian* church.

But it is also possible that some of the bitter disappointment which many Negroes experience in their personal relations with some Jews grows out of their traditional sense of brotherhood with good Jews. After all very little real estate and very few businesses in Harlem or Watts are owned or managed by righteous Old Testament Hebrew prophets. And as a matter of fact all of those neighborhood-school Jews in New York look and act as much like Philistines and Pharaoh Egyptians as anybody in Bogalusa.

Good and bad Jews alike seem overwhelmingly anti–Adam Clayton Powell. Negroes, who have always been puzzled by this, become apprehensive and suspicious when they realize that many more Jews seem to be out to get Powell than ever seemed to be out to get anybody in the Ku Klux Klan. Powell, it is true, forced Jewish merchants to begin integrating stores in Harlem twenty some years ago but he never has been anti-Semitic. He is anti–white presumption and condescension. To some Negroes it seems that other people would rather see Powell back out on the picket line than sitting as chairman of the powerful Congressional Committee on Education and Welfare.

Even most good U.S. Jews seem unable to accept Powell as the hardheaded, thoroughly professional U.S. politician U.S. Negroes know and *want* him to be. Negro voters in Harlem think he is good for them and Negro non-voters in Alabama think he is good for *them* also.

Jewish friends-of-the-cause can no longer afford to ignore this. Nor can they presume to write it off as Negro naïveté. Negro political power is already a force to be reckoned with in every key area in the nation, and it is growing and becoming conscious of its potential every day. Future Negro leaders, therefore, are not very likely to be social workers operating on good will but politicians negotiating in terms of the realities of power. Such leaders are obviously going to be much more like Powell, Russell Long, Herman Talmadge, and Everett Dirksen than like James Farmer or Whitney Young.

Nor is there anything in this for Jews or anybody else to become alarmed or hysterical about. There will be fewer Jews speaking for the Negro no doubt because there will be more Negroes speaking for themselves. But the thrust of Negro politics is not toward ethnic blocs and polarities but toward *integration* based on common interests. Southern Negro voters will support senior southern politicians on the basis of their promises and performances just as New York Negroes support Jake Javits and Bobby Kennedy. There will be sharp differences of opinion on many issues from time to time but they will be between equals, and Negroes have always regarded that sort of thing as a fact of family life.

When U.S. Negroes, who have always had to pick and choose very carefully among people, say that some of their best friends are Jewish they really mean it. Negroes feel that good Jews are those who act as if the United States is not only the Promised Land for Jews but for all other U.S. citizens as well.

Bad Jews on the other hand couldn't care less about other people. Them, Negroes feel, everybody can do without. Most people could also do without so many Marx-Freud experts who substitute color struggle for class struggle and then explain the effects of color-class exploitation with makeshift Freudian speculations. Negroes would certainly be better off without any of the Hollywood Jews who produced movies which not only ennobled the Confederate cause but helped to promote the notions of white supremacy by degrading the image of Negroes before all the world. Negro musicians can do without so many crooked Jewish booking agents but they thrive on enthusiastic Jewish appreciation. They never needed Gershwin or Goodman; and Bernstein they could take or leave; but all U.S. music was enriched by the late Noah Greenberg, and nobody should ever be without at least one Isaac Stern. There will never be a time when serious U.S. Negro writers, artists, and educators should be without Meyer Schapiro and Moses Hadas; and no books show more American grain than those of Matthew Josephson and Harold Rosenberg. Some Negroes say Norman Podhoretz has all the earmarks of a frustrated Klansman but they are only kidding and would be the first to welcome his editorial assistance on *Ebony* magazine—but not in matters of literary taste. For that they would prefer Alfred Kazin or the Stanleys Kauffmann and Edgar Hyman.

One could go on and on naming Jewish Americans who are indispensable to Negroes precisely because they mean so much to the nation at large. Arthur Goldberg and Abe Fortas, for instance, are good for Negroes for exactly the same reasons that they are good for Lyndon Johnson and everybody else. The so-called Negro cause is always best served not by specialized sentimentality for the downtrodden but by a hardheaded sense of responsibility toward the ideals and interests of the United States as the last best hope of Earth.

1966

"Soul": Thirty-two Meanings
Not in Your Dictionary

*I*N RECENT MONTHS *a new word (or, rather, an old word with new meanings) has been appearing with increasing frequency in novels, news stories, and conversations. To help dictionary editors, here is a full definition they can clip and file.*

Soul (sōl), *n.* [U.S.] **1.** Of, pertaining to, indigenous to, associated with U.S. Negroes, i.e., native-born black, brown-skinned, mulatto U.S. citizens of full or partial, direct or remote African descent. **2.** U.S. Negro style, especially as reflecting the folk idiom of Southern Negroes. **3.** Style or any stylistic element or device characterized by features with roots in the folkways of Negroes in the South, i.e., down South, *viz.* DOWN HOME. **4.** Anything expressive of down-home roots. **5.** Hence also: earthiness, often as in down-home church services, but also secular, as in work songs, blues, chants, hollers, epithets, and exclamations, but not restricted (as by hung-up white hippies) to obscenity, profanity, and pseudo-dialect. **6.** Any unpretentious-seeming Negro behavior. **7.** But also sophistication, as in any Negro stylization in which references and meanings are *signified* (by gesture and innuendo) rather than stated outright in conventional terms familiar to whites. **8.** Hence, anything that makes Negroes laugh but that puzzles most whites present. **9.** Any black-oriented behavior or any black behavior in the interest of a black cause. **10.** Any word or statement suggesting resentment or rejection of white folks. **11.** Any aesthetic projection expressive of black American experience. **12.** The U.S. Negro accent as when introduced into anything not Negro; e.g., as where Negro dance rhythms are added to pop and "classical" music and to military drill, etc. **13.** [currently] Any provincial or countrified behavior acceptable to Northern city Negroes. **14.** Anything that becomes a fad in Harlem. **15.** Any quality considered positive and assumed to be Negro by U.S. Negroes. **16.** Anything assimilated by U.S. Negroes. (African robes and ornaments do not become *soul threads* until worn by U.S. Negro dandies.) **17.** Any Negro "thing" imitated by white people. Probable derivation *soulful* (*adj.*, with feeling), as in a soulful performance or interpretation, especially of music and dance, but as adapted by U.S. Negroes and applied specifically to the rendition of nuances of music and subtleties of dance movements expressive of U.S. Negro life style. **18.** Hence *adj.*, authentic, as from deeply felt human passion expressive of innermost being as opposed to artificial or phony. **19.** Expression which reflects knowledgeability earned through profoundly personal involvement. **20.** Black mother-wit as opposed to white theory. **21.** The ability to *riff*, i.e., to improvise or take care of business in the Negro idiom. **22.** Hence *v. intr., tr.*, to employ elements of the down-home style. [Man, the splibs were *souling* then, and them honkies for*got* it.] [If you can't soul it, you might as well hang it up, bro.] **23.** Also a likely *var.* of SOUL, *syn.* spirit, essence, core, heart embodiment. Hence anything expressive of fundamental human (i.e., Negro) sentiment. **24.** Hence by implication the human dimension as defined by Negroes. **25.** Also (*vulgate*) the nitty-gritty of any thing, being, or state of being. Also construed as being from the soul, as synonymous with the heart or core of beings as opposed to *from the head*; in the terminology of jazz, however, *from the head* indicates the opposite of playing or singing from a written score. In this sense *from the head* means from the depths of the soul. **26.** Also any U.S. Negro, male or female, as in a soul, the souls, etc. [There were three souls and a gang of charlies out there, and I mean up tight, man; and the brothers fit to do their thing.] From *soul brother* and *soul sister*, frequently shortened to *brother* and *sister*, and *bro* or *brer* as in traditional church parlance but currently less frequently to *sis*. In black nationalist-internationalist political jargon all black people are soul brothers, but in strict usage only those whose heritage includes spirituals and blues-and-gospel are so designated. Those from the West Indian–Calypso–Afro-Latin backgrounds, for example, are somewhat more like soul cousins, except on certain political issues. Black African continentals are soul relatives by virtue of a common dance-beat-oriented ancestry, but those who speak English with a colonial *British* or *French* accent can hardly be said to speak soul, an indispensable prerequisite for acceptance into the inner sanctum of stone soulhood. (Stokely is a CLOSE CUZ; Rap is a STONE BRO.)

27. Also down-home recipe cooking, as in *soul food, soul feast, soul table* (but not SOUL BREAD, which is money). Sometimes construed as food for the soul but more often the traditional food of soul people. Hence a down-home menu or any item therefrom, including but not limited to the following when prepared from down-home recipes: black-eyed peas (also with rice, *viz.* BUCKET GEORGE), red beans with rice, collards, corn bread, cracklin bread, hoe cakes, cornmeal dumplings in turnip and mustard greens; chicken, southern fried, also baked with highly spiced corn meal and onion stuffing, also with dumplings; chitlins, crab gumbo, catfish, fish head stew; grits-eggs-and-streak-o-lean; molasses and flap jacks, molasses with bacon grease and biscuits, buttermilk with crumbled corn bread; pork ad infinitum: pigs' feet, tails, ears, head (hog's); rabbit, fried or stewed; possum or coon with yams, sweet potato pie and pone, jelly layer cake, etc. **28.** Also the U.S. Negro idiom in music. **29.** But in the argot of contemporary disk jockeys and record promotion copy, secularized gospel music commercialized originally for the Negro pop music trade. **30.** The beautiful sonorities of such singers as Ray Charles, James Brown, Jackie Wilson, and Aretha Franklin; (when redolent) of such church sisters as Sister Rosetta Tharpe, Clara Ward, and Mahalia Jackson, among others. **31.** Its current vogue among the young Afro-Brillo civil rights militants and separatists notwithstanding, soul is still music which goes with the robust Negro genre of rawhide-beneath-patent-leather elegance. **32.** Hence a musical equivalent to processed hair-dos, conks and stocking caps, weekend wigs, colorful high-sheen fabrics and show-biz fashions. Soul music is almost always misrepresented in the folklore of white supremacy as being a manifestation of the culture of the poverty of culture. Which only goes to show who souls and who freaks out.

1968

"Stone": Definition and Usage

Stone (stōn) [U.S. uptown Manhattan and similar locations elsewhere, from down home] **1.** *adj.*, Complete, total, absolute, characteristic, consummate, exemplary. **2.** *adv.*, Altogether, downright, outright, out and out, thoroughly, utterly. **3.** *v. intr.*, To perform excellently, to do (your thing) forever [Man, I ain't shucking, I'm I mean stoning, baby].

Mostly, *stone* is descriptive of the state or condition of completeness of a thing, being, or state of being; or the ultimate or definitive degree of any condition, state, style, or manner of being or of any given circumstance or relationship. Also the supreme level of achievement or fulfillment. Hence the state of being IN SOLID, as of sitting solid in a given situation. The uppermost state of innermost solidity; ergo, suggestive of the solidarity, stability, and security of status, even as of a fortified position, and in consequence unassailable, impregnable, inviolate.

Also, as of a solid or firm foundation and hence (apparently) neither shakeable nor shake-upable and certainly not yet shook. Thus to all intents and purposes, unquestionable, indubitable, incontestable, and by implication imperturbable. Thus also the state of being without sweat, i.e., anxious effort, as with NO SWEAT, NO STRAIN, NO PAIN.

As in the case of most other words in the U.S. down-home-become-up-here lexicon, the soul status of *stone* is determined not so much by its origin as by its usage, which must be tasteful. The English word *stone*, according to Skeat and others, goes at least as far back as Anglo-Saxon. In sooth, such ofay expressions as STONE BLIND, STONE BROKE, STONE DEAF, etc., were old hat ages before tricorns (George III was clearly convinced that George Washington was stone crazy). As with soul music, dance, food, and so on, it is the idiomatic nuance which socks it.

The most constant element in the stoniness of any being or given state or manner of being has, of course, always been constancy itself. And yet there did come a time when to be solid (as in such obsolete phrases as SOLID SENDER and expressions like SOLID, MAN; SOLID, JACK; SOLID, DAD) was to be the epitome of a swinger, i.e., a highly sophisticated, riff-style improviser. But then to swing is also to groove (easily or deeply), and be groovy is to be nothing if not foxy, though there never was or could be a solid fox. There can only be a stone fox.

In this sense, however, *stone* becomes an exclusive female attribute. A male, i.e., STUD, may because of his suavity be THE FOX, THE OLD FOX, a NATURAL FOX, or a NATURAL-BORN FOX, but hardly a stone fox, which is the superlative category of female togetherness. In addition to being strikingly good-looking, a stone fox also maintains not only her cool but also her idiomatic "something else," no matter what the scene. A classic example of stone foxiness is Lena (who is earthy but never kittenish), in haute couture, riffing up-tempo at the Waldorf. Meanwhile, elsewhere, the stoniest of stone foxes are capable not only of sporting Afro-Brillo coiffures, though resembling H. Rap Brown not at all, but also of perpetrating more social upheaval just by doing their own natural-activist thing than any Molotov cocktail ever—which is, whatever the context, stone for days and perhaps for all ages.

1969

Two Nations? Only Two?

W HAT IS TO BE MADE of the fact that so little has been made of the fact that between 1954 and 1994 the cities listed in the next paragraph, plus numerous smaller municipalities and townships, have elected and re-elected "black" mayors, many of whom have been succeeded by other "black" mayors? And hardly any have been replaced by an all too obvious white backlash.

The cities are Atlanta, Baltimore, Birmingham, Camden, Charlotte, Chicago, Cleveland, Dayton, Denver, Detroit, Hartford, Kansas City (Missouri), Los Angeles, Memphis, Newark, New Haven, New Orleans, Newport News, New York, Oakland, Philadelphia, Richmond, Roanoke, Rochester (New York), St. Louis, Seattle, Tallahassee, and Washington, D.C.

There is, to be sure, much to be said for taking such incredibly revolutionary changes in stride as if they were not really remarkable at all but rather only a normal eventuality in the open society that the United States is at last becoming. Just look at how casually sportsfandom, that great representative cross section of national attitudes, has come to accept the superstar status (supersalaries, windfall endorsement contracts, and all) of an undeniably impressive number of their "black" fellow countrymen in baseball, pro football, and basketball during the past twenty-five years.

Perhaps there is something to be said for the benign neglect that Daniel Moynihan had in mind after all. It is certainly preferable to the crocodile tears of condescending do-gooders like one Andrew Hacker, whose book *Two Nations* is an exasperatingly obvious example of how American social science survey "findings" function as the folklore of white supremacy.

According to Hacker, race relations in the United States seem to be as god-awful as ever—if not worse—since in Hacker's view self-improvement in conduct and proficiency has not made "black" U.S. citizens more *acceptable* to "white" folks.

Contribution to "How Have We Changed? 1954–1994," a symposium feature in the fortieth-anniversary number of *American Heritage* magazine (December 1994).

On the other hand, Hacker explains away the election of all those black mayors by saying that "black candidates who gain white support come from middle class backgrounds and display middle class demeanor." *So do most white candidates from upper- and lower-class backgrounds alike.* Moreover, lower-class voters obviously prefer middle-class efficiency to upper-class "classiness" or lower-class anything. Middle-class efficiency with the common touch is the ticket in American politics. After all, aren't politicians elected to improve things? Black politicians certainly are. So what the hell is Hacker implying? Lower-class people who are content to remain lower-class don't vote. Nor did black Americans fight against school segregation in order to remain lower-class. Could it be that the professor doesn't know that revolution is a middle-class, not a lower-class, thing?

Two nations black and white, separate, hostile, unequal, Hacker proclaims with his title. Two nations? Only two? What about the Asians, Mexicans, Puerto Ricans, Cubans, and other not very white U.S. citizens from Latin America and elsewhere? And as of this morning the Anti-Defamation League was still very much in the business of fighting domestic anti-Semitism. Nor does it become anything other than American by doing so. Nor have the passports held by black passengers become null and void during the last twenty-five years.

One thing that does not seem to have changed very much during the last twenty-five years is the pessimism of white academic experts on black prospects. Two nations? Who thinks the Democratic Party would have been better off without Ron Brown as chairman during the last election? Probably not President Clinton! Two nations?

1994

Bearden in Theory and Ritual

*T*HIS INTERVIEW *was conducted on July 15, 1996, at Albert Murray's New York apartment, in what he has referred to as the "Center of the Universe," overlooking the street scene that inspired Romare Bearden's* The Block. *Murray and Bearden first met in Paris in the early 1950s and renewed their friendship a decade later after they had both returned to New York City. Friends and intellectual comrades, they visited museums together and shared books, music, and ideas. Fascinated by the idea of André Malraux's "museum without walls" and the persistence of rituals in all cultures, they translated the raw materials of their Southern experiences into "universal aesthetic statements." As Murray stated, "The condition of man is always a matter of the specific texture of existence in a given place, time, and circumstance." This interview deals with the issues that pervaded the thought and art of these two men.*

GAIL GELBURD: *You have frequently stated that ritual is the basis of art. How would you incorporate ritual into a definition of art?*

ALBERT MURRAY: One fundamental definition of art is that it's a means by which the raw materials of human existence are processed, which is to say *stylized* into aesthetic statement; the work of art is the aesthetic statement. It's a form of communication. If you decode the statement, and that's what you're trying to do in terms of understanding art, you would know what the painting was saying. But it's not a verbal statement, a report as such, it's a visual statement which may be more concerned with connotation than with denotation.

So we begin with raw experiences and end up with aesthetic experiences.

Contribution to Gail Gelburd and Thelma Golden's catalog for *Romare Bearden in Black-and-White: Photomontage Projections 1964*, an exhibit on view at the Whitney Museum of America Art, New York, January 16–March 20, 1997.

Another more anthropological definition is that art is an elegant extension, elaboration, and refinement of the rituals which re-enact survival technology. When you look at a painting, what you see is a stylization, but it is also a visual or plastic re-enactment of a ritual, and a ritual is a ceremonial re-enactment of some aspect of the basic survival techniques of a given cultural configuration, which may be an aboriginal tribe or a very highly developed nation, a subcontinent, or even a whole continent.

And that's why art exists in all cultures, because we all need to survive. The arts reflect that primordial need. How does the need evolve and in what form was it first present?

It seems that the art form which develops earliest in most cultures as a unique art form is dance. For example, various studies of aboriginal cultures show that dance was the most highly developed art form. Think of mimicry. It turns out that one of the last to become an independent art is music! You could go to a play in ancient Greece or Rome, containing fully developed dance and poetry, whereas it seems that music was just a matter of strumming in the background. There were no concerts or recitals or extended forms of music as we know it. Music was not separated as an art form until Europe came into being. And that was really just the day before yesterday!

How then did people remember, express themselves, and survive before the arts and develop the memory that went into the arts?

They developed it through rituals. A hunting society would re-enact the survival technique of hunting. This technique could be throwing a spear, making a sling of bows and arrows, or making a trap—we're talking about primordial man and those people didn't even know the sun was going to rise the next day!

So art became a record of the method of survival and part of the natural history of human memory?

You've got to have that before you have a recorded way of doing it, so the first step involves what was to become formal education. Education is the most obvious as well as the most comprehensive survival technique. The mind had to be conditioned so that you could do what was required to survive in whatever environment you had.

And how was it decided who led the development of these rituals?

Anthropologically speaking, this must have come even before the birth of the gods. But let's not get into that. Ritual re-enactment supervised by a priesthood becomes religion, which also generates its own specific internal ceremonies of devotion and propitiation, which I mention only in passing, along with magic, which is another kind of ceremonial re-enactment. In addition to religion and magic there is also the no less aboriginal matter of playful re-enactment, which we refer to as recreation, and which indeed is literally a matter of re-creation, re-presentation, and re-producing. Thus the essential character or disposition of a nation as well as a tribe may be discerned in its games and toys. But the key point of this brief natural history is that it is from the playful re-enactment of primal ritual that art as such is most directly derived. The role of play in the creative process is that it permits the personal options from which individual expression, improvisation, stylization, and elegance emerge. It is from the playful re-enactment of primal ritual that art is most directly derived.

It is the continuity and repetition of the process that matter, the re-creation, the re-presentation of life.

That's a much better term than "imitation of life," as Plato described art. That might not have been what he meant, that just might have been the best translation of what Plato said. And then it stuck. But for me a better term would be my term—re-enactment. One contemporary term would be "occupational psychosis," or another could be "mindset."

So being an artist is an occupational mindset.

No. No! Don't jump to the artist yet! Re-enactment is a means of developing an occupational mindset. There was no formula or book . . . you couldn't give the artist a guide. That was eons away. But you can do something to establish procedure. Whether the quarry is a fish, or a rabbit, or whatever, he'll know what to do. He's got a mindset.

A mindset, then, is the primitive person or someone today re-enacting over and over the basic occupational rituals?

Rituals enable anthropologists to define the basic occupations and mindset or preoccupations of any given social configuration, whether tribal or national. Back when humans were breaking open mussels on rocks, they were doing that primordial thing; the birds do that—they didn't get beyond it! They still drop mussels on rocks! We were at that stage once too; but we went beyond it. The main concern of survival technology is human continuity. It is also the fundamental existential equipment in that it not only provides emblems of a basic attitude toward experience but also conditions and disposes people to behave in accordance with a given lifestyle. Human consciousness or knowledge is part of what comprises your environment. My environment is also all of this [*pointing to his giant wall of books*], it's you [*pointing to us*], it's out there [*pointing outside to Harlem and beyond*]. A guy comes up and wants to see *Harlem*, I don't care about just that out there, it's also all of this [*again pointing to his books*] plus that, so my conception of what's out there is quite different from his, because I've got Dickens, Malraux, Hemingway, Joyce, and Veblen, plus the sociology, plus entertainment pleasures, plus the stuff we're bootlegging from other cultures from all over the world.

And all that then comes into your writing, and all that came into Romy's painting—all the pieces come together, making the ritual prevail as a sophisticated aesthetic statement.

It's sophisticated because ritual is universal as opposed to provincial, which is to say that when you look at particular details in his painting, you see the universal implications. Romy's art is not the product of a folk sensibility, and folk art, incidentally, should also not be confused with primitive art. Primitive art is fine art in that it is the product of the ultimate extension, elaboration, and refinement. Folk art is crude by comparison. Now this jumps forward to a great "Bearden achievement": his very special awareness of the ritualistic dimension of stylization saved him from genre, from being just provincial. The ritual dimension takes him beyond his province.

So he takes the genre, the raw material, and imbues it with ritual, to make it universal, and yet it is derived from a specific place and time. The ritual visualizes the metaphor. It is, as you said before, the playful ritual re-enactment that leads to the production of what we call art.

Some play activities are restricted by rules and regulations and some are also supervised by umpires, referees, and judges, and some are not. But as you also know, even the most closely codified play activity permits personal options from which not only individual expression but also individual improvisation, stylization, and elegance emerge. When you turn the raw experience into a style, the style becomes the statement. And it is the extension, elaboration, and refinement of such option-taking that add up to the aesthetic statement that is a work of art. Which is to say, a product of elegant artifice. This is how you go from ritual to art. A playful re-enactment is specifically a game of extension, elaboration, and refinement. There are, according to Roger Caillois in *Man, Play, and Games,* four categories of play activity and two directions of playful effort. The categories are competition, chance, make-believe, and vertigo.

Vertigo?

You forgot about vertigo, didn't you? Just spin around! Remember seesawing! or swinging! You got high! Once you get into art, you are into vertigo! exhilaration!

Yes, of course, now you experience the art, the play.

Play can be in two different directions in various combinations, one is gamboling, that's playing or fooling around; and the other could be called "gratuitous difficulty." In a game of jacks, the player bounces the ball and picks up one jack, then a bounce and two jacks, then the player becomes interested in making the game more difficult—so he throws the ball up one time and slaps one time, steadily increasing the difficulty, and the interest of the game. This can also be seen in a musical composition when a composer first tries a tune in one key, then in other keys. That can take you all the way from a simple melody to a Bach fugue!

You mean how a composer creates a melody, responds with a variation of that melody, and then another, to create the fugue?

Why is the composer doing that? Because it is difficult! You look down there at the piano and you don't know where your fingers go! You look at it, then you realize you've got to slow it way down and put this finger over here and there and this finger has got to go here. But we're into art now! Now, when you get up to that level remember what we're talking about: play. So play involves extension, elaboration, refinement. And anytime you start messing around with extension, elaboration, and refinement you're also vulnerable to over-extension, over-elaboration, and over-refinement! Which leads to dilution, attenuation, decadence, and, alas, effeteness! Hence the function of critical assessment along with critical mediation.

The two sides of human consciousness, the refinement versus the over-refinement.

Stylization is the basis of human consciousness, the basis of history, which is always about patterns, design!

There must have been lively discussions with Romy and others.

My three most sophisticated friends were [Ralph] Ellison, Bearden, and Duke [Ellington]—but Duke was older. Romy, Ralph, and I were all about the same age, within two years of each other, whereas Duke was the age of my father. But he had the sophistication of a genius who could make his connections fast *and* who could explain them. Romy was capable of a lot of explanation and mathematical logic. We spent so much time together going to galleries and museums and bookstores. So that's why we were so close over a long period of time. I had ongoing conversations with him about the conceptions that he was going to stylize.

Did the literary and iconographic references come just from art history? Where were the concepts of baptism, Paradise, and the conjure woman from?

Now, remember, as Duke Ellington pointed out, there are many more churches in Harlem than nightclubs! Bearden would remember some minister that he liked and he would remember certain sermons like "The Sun Do Move." After he did *Sermons: The Walls of Jericho*, I wrote the title *Sermons: In That Number*, from [*singing*] "Lord I wanna be one in that number . . ."

From "When the Saints Come Marching In."

Sometimes Romy would come up with one sermon and even would start talking about it as if it already were a series. But Romy had certain sermons he would remember from time to time and he would do a number of paintings based on them. Sometimes his photomontage pieces projected a series that he never completed. Other times what started out as a series ended up as only a photomontage.

That explains the repetition of themes, which began in the 1964 photomontages, and continued throughout his career. Those ritu- als and sermons he heard, saw, and discussed were in fact the raw materials of existence that Bearden stylized into his aesthetic statement, into his art.

1997

Three Omni-American Artists

To my delight, this book is remarkably free of social science findings and studies and speculations about race relations. Its fundamental concern is with the development of an American aesthetic sensibility. The author, William Zinsser, wants to find out how that sensibility was formed, and that leads him to approach Dwike Mitchell and Willie Ruff as artists. He isn't thrown off by issues of politics and justice and injustice. What he's after is how an American personality develops. There's something about these two musicians that attracted him to them. He wants to know: Where did they come from and how did they get to be where they were when I encountered them? What enables them to play music that I admire so much?

John A. Kouwenhoven, in his book *Made in America*, talks about what's particularly American about American culture. He suggests that it's a mixture of learned traditions imported by emigrants from Europe with native or frontier forms, which together create the vernacular. That combination in turn gets refined, beyond folk, beyond pop, into the most comprehensive forms of fine art. You can find the twelve-bar blues stanza of a Mississippi delta guitarist, for example, elaborated into an American sonata form known as the jazz instrumental in Duke Ellington's "Harlem Airshaft." The process has nothing to do with social status. It's a matter of how artists develop a growing mastery of their medium.

In *Mitchell & Ruff*, Zinsser never loses sight of that process. He focuses on why Dwike Mitchell plays the piano as he does, and why Willie Ruff plays the bass and the French horn as he does. He discovers that their music is a fusion of what was imported to this country and what evolved here. Everything he learns about the life of the two musicians reaffirms that dynamic. Mitchell realizes as a young man that the piano is his destiny. The more he learns about it, the more he wants to

Foreword to *Mitchell & Ruff: An American Profile in Jazz*, by William Zinsser (Philadelphia: Paul Dry Books, 2000).

learn about it. He wants to know what a piano is, and what has been done with it, and therefore what *he* can do with it—what he can say with the piano about his experience. He can say more if he knows what other people have done with piano keys, so there's everything possible to be learned. His whole life becomes a search for what will make him a better artist. The same is true of Willie Ruff. He goes wherever he needs to go to learn what he wants to know next: to Yale to study with Paul Hindemith, to Africa to study the drum language of the Pygmies, to St. Mark's Church in Venice to listen for "a distant sound."

Zinsser stays focused on that double search. He goes down to Florida and Alabama, where Mitchell and Ruff grew up—which is a long way from his own hometown of New York. But he doesn't confuse what he finds with exotica. He never forgets that he's dealing with American character and how it gets shaped into art. Being a down-home boy myself, from Alabama, I feel a connection between Mitchell and Ruff's early years and my own early years as I describe them in my novel *Train Whistle Guitar*. The novel is about a little boy growing up on the outskirts of Mobile, listening to the guitar players and juke-joint piano players and becoming a serious schoolboy. I was that schoolboy, developing literary and intellectual interests at an early age and going on to win scholarships, right through college. Mitchell and Ruff did it in a different way. I did it through literature and music, but they achieved the same level of sophistication in their chosen métier. Their way was more improvisational—their first conservatory was an Air Force base in Ohio—but for all three of us it was the same picaresque fairy tale.

The similarity really hit me when Dwike Mitchell talks about how he was made to play the piano in the Baptist church when he was a small boy in Florida and how the minister would preach about how everyone would be damned and go to hell. What he says is very close to what I say about Sunday mornings in *Train Whistle Guitar*: "The sermons used to be so full not only of ugly prophecies and warnings but also outright threats of divine vengeance on hypocrites that when people all around you began stomping and clapping and shouting you couldn't tell whether they were doing so because they were being visited by the Holy Ghost or because being grown folks and therefore accountable for their trespasses they were even more terrified of the dreadful wrath of God than you were (whose sins after all were all still being charged against your parents)."

The point is that I feel a close personal identification with Zinsser's portrayal of Mitchell and Ruff, not just because I'm from the South, but because his book is an excellent natural history of the development of our sensibility as indigenous American artists. The book has nothing to do with race relations as such. Zinsser has an omni-American sensibility—it's neither white nor black. That sensibility is also at the heart of my work. I never think of myself as an "African-American." As Willie Ruff says to the old monsignor in St. Mark's Church, it's a word I don't use.

Mitchell & Ruff is the literary equivalent of a jazz piece. It's composed, it has themes, and it develops those themes. Zinsser's prose tries to get as close as possible to the rhythms these two men use in their music. To me the *ur*-father of jazz in prose is Ernest Hemingway. Hemingway swings; his prose is as precise as it is lyrical. What he did is exactly what Count Basie thought you should do when playing music: Don't use frills or curlicues; get a good solid rhythm; make it swing. That's what Zinsser does. He tells his story with a directness and a simplicity that add up to the kind of elegance that the higher physicists admire.

Zinsser sees Mitchell and Ruff just about as I would see them. That impressed me, because he's a Yankee, working in a context he's not as intimate with as I am. Ordinarily when people enter an unfamiliar situation there are two common reactions. One is insecurity, which results in xenophobia: fear, or hostility, or condescension. The other is to see the situation as exotic, or weird, or dangerous, and to find it fascinating—as all those people did who used to go slumming in Harlem. But here's a man who identifies with Mitchell and Ruff because their story is universal, and he's sensitive to the local conventions that an outsider needs to penetrate in order to tell that story. He doesn't allow anything to get in the way of the relationship—the kinship—of these two men from the South.

So what you've got in *Mitchell & Ruff* is not only a profile of two people but, in effect, a profile of three people: Dwike

Mitchell and Willie Ruff and William Zinsser. I'm completely comfortable with Zinsser's take on the down-home neighborhoods he visited. He never got deflected from what he wrote this book to find out: how these two men forged their American identity as artists. It pleases me that he chose to move into this context and that he wrote about it so well.

2000

Jazz: Notes Toward a Definition

JAZZ MUSIC, as is also the case with the old down-home spirituals, gospel and jubilee songs, jumps, shouts, and moans, is
essentially an American vernacular or idiomatic modification of
musical conventions imported from Europe, beginning back
during the time of the early settlers of the original colonies.

Specifically, jazz as such began as a secular dance music that
evolved from ragtime piano music, brass-band music, and the
guitar, vocal, harmonica, barroom, honky-tonk, and juke-joint
music called the blues, which generates an atmosphere of groovy
delight and festive well-being in the very process of recounting
a tale of woe. As any church member will testify, generating a
Dionysian atmosphere is precisely what honky-tonks, juke joints,
barrooms, and gin mills are all about.

In any case, the jazz musician's blues should not be confused
with the torch singer's lament, which is a matter of wearing
one's heart on one's sleeve because one has loved unwisely and
not well and has become not the one and only, but the lonely,
"ain't these tears in these eyes telling you." In this sense, Billie
Holiday's famous recording "Strange Fruit" is not blues music.
It is a political torch song, a lament about unrequited patriotic
love. We have loved and fought and died for this country for
all these many years, the song asserts, because it has been our
official homeland for this many generations, and now just look
at what some of these other folks think they have a right to do
to somebody because they want to think that they are better
than them.

Actually, "Strange Fruit" is not even written in any of the
established blues stanzas. "The St. Louis Blues," by contrast, is
also about unrequited love, but it is written in the most widely
used blues form, the twelve-bar blues chorus. And what it inspires, whether in up-tempo or in slow drag, regardless of the
words, is not regret and despair, but elegance and good-time
movement. (For a jazz musician's inflection of a famous torch
song, listen to Roy Eldridge's rendition of "After You've Gone"
of 1937, and also the Jazz at the Philharmonic version of 1946,

featuring Mel Powell, Charlie Parker, Howard McGhee, Lester Young, and others.)

Ironically, as little as it has been noticed, it is the pale-skinned or so-called white European, not the dark-skinned Africans, the brown-skinned inhabitants of the Middle East, the so-called yellow-skinned Asians, or the so-called red-skinned people of the Americas, and so on, who describe their moods in terms of changes of the color of their skin (mainly of their faces!), which have traditionally been described as becoming red with embarrassment, green with envy, gray with concern, dullness, or "the blahs" of boredom, and blue with sorrow and self-pity. Hence the blue devils of torment or torment by blue demons, as in the case of delirium tremens. (Blue skies are another matter altogether.)

There was a time between the 1890s and the early 1920s when ragging a tune and jazzing a tune added up to just about the same kind of musical statement. Did the word "jazz" win out because "jazzing" sounded more Dionysian than "ragging"? After all, legendary accounts of early jazz in New Orleans place great emphasis on its connection with the red-light district of Storyville. According to *Webster's Collegiate Dictionary*, jazz is "a Creole word meaning to speed up, applied to syncopated music, of American Negro, and probably of African origin; a type of American music, characterized by melodious themes, subtly syncopated rhythms, and varied orchestral coloring."

But neither the earthy ambivalence of the blues nor the elegant syncopation of ragtime is indigenous to New Orleans. It was in Memphis that W. C. Handy, who was from Alabama, codified and put the old down-home blues stanza (which he first heard in Mississippi) into the public domain of American popular music, as Scott Joplin from Texas had done for ragtime in Sedalia, Missouri, a few years earlier. Perhaps the most obvious—if not the most definitive—characteristic of early New Orleans jazz was its special emphasis on polyphony and improvisation, though it was Kansas City jazz that was to become known and celebrated for the subtle syncopation of its swinging 4/4 stomps, jumps, and shouts.

Even so, there was a small group in New Orleans in 1908 that was sometimes known as the original Creole Jass Band.

Also King Oliver, after moving to Chicago following the closing of Storyville, once led a group called the Original Creole
Jazz Band, and at another time he led one called the Dixie
Syncopators. Most ballroom or dancehall bands outside of
New Orleans continued to bill themselves as "syncopated orchestras" until the early 1920s. By the mid-1930s, they were
advertised as swing bands as well as jazz bands. But by then
jazz had become the generic term for an American secular
dance music with its own style, variations, and repertory.

II

A jazz tune, melody, or composition is usually based on either
a traditional twelve-bar, eight-bar, or four-bar blues chorus or
on the thirty-two-bar chorus of the American popular song. In
either case, the overall structure is a series of choruses, which
may be preceded by an improvised vamp instead of a conventional prelude or overture, and it is climaxed with an out-chorus
that may or may not be followed by a coda, the jazz term for
which is a tag.

Duke Ellington's "Ko-Ko" is in effect a blues-obbligato minus
the original twelve-bar melody. "Moten Swing," by Count
Basie and Eddie Durham for Bennie Moten's Kansas City Or-
chestra, is in effect an obbligato minus the thirty-two-bar
chorus of the original melody of the pop song "You're Driving
Me Crazy." Thelonious Monk's obbligato treatment of "Please
Don't Talk About Me When I'm Gone" became "Four in
One," his version of "Sweet Georgia Brown" became "Bright
Mississippi," and "Straighten Up and Fly Right" became
"Epistrophy." Thus did Charlie Parker's recording of "Orni-
thology" come from "How High the Moon," and Dizzy
Gillespie's "Groovin' High" from "Whispering." And so on it
goes, with the jazz musician treating even the most sophisti-
cated popular standards as if they were folk ditties.

The improvisational nature of jazz musicianship is such that
a truly competent performer must be prepared to function as
an on-the-spot composer who is expected to contribute to the
orchestration in progress, not simply to execute the score as it
is written and rehearsed. In fact, the "score" or lead sheet may
often turn out to be "dictated" verbally or instrumentally

rather than written. There is much to suggest that it is this special aspect of jazz musicianship as it is exercised, developed, and refined in informal jam sessions that accounts for the rapid rate at which jazz (which was perhaps never really a folk art!) moved from the level of a popular art around the beginning of the twentieth century to the precision and the sophistication of a fine art by the mid-1930s. Nor should the matter of aesthetic refinement and existential depth be confused with social status: it is the innovating artist, regardless of his or her formal training and certification, who actually creates that which the so-called critical establishment evaluates and values after the fact.

III

The dance-oriented percussive emphasis of jazz was derived from West Africa along with the various tribal natives imported during the years of the North Atlantic slave trade, although very little African music as such continued to be performed by them in North America. Not only were ancestral African rituals generally forbidden, but also, as a rule, the local slave population was almost always so diverse in language and in tribal culture that the erstwhile Africans could not communicate with one another in their native tongues anyway. Moreover, they were inevitably more preoccupied with practical techniques of coping and surviving on harsh local terms than with preserving procedures, relics, and talismans from their past environments, however sentimental they may have been.

In any case, there are grounds to believe that the definitive percussive emphasis in jazz is owed finally to trains—that it is more a matter of an aesthetic involvement with American railroad locomotive onomatopoeia than with transmitting tribal messages. Messages to whom? About what? After all, slave owners were always on the alert and were notoriously preemptive about Africans' talking drums. But it is the locomotive onomatopoeia that is so characteristic of down-home guitar, harmonica, and honky-tonk piano folk blues: its employment as an elementary local color or atmospheric device should be obvious as soon as you listen seriously to the music.

Trains, train whistles, and train bells came to suggest all

kinds of possibilities and aspirations. There were the meta-physical trains in the sermons and songs of the Christian church, which incidentally the captive West Africans seem to have embraced with fervent enthusiasm largely on their own. There were the metaphorical trains of the underground railroad escape routes from bondage to freedom, the likes of which existed nowhere other than America. And there were also those actual north-to-freedom locomotives running on railroad tracks that captive West Africans had been used to help lay and maintain, inventing section-gang spike driving and track alignment rhythms and chants even as other slave workers invented field chants, woodsman's calls, swamp hollers, and so on. Moreover, it is not very likely that any creatures anywhere in West Africa were more impressive than these man-made, man-controlled mechanical creatures that also had voices, personalities, and even names and numbers.

Incidentally, in many instances, especially in down-home folk blues, the syncopating locomotive onomatopoeia is very literal, and the music (that is, the sonority) as such as well as the rhythm and the beat is in effect as programmatic as it is in Honegger's *Pacific 231* or Duke Ellington's "Track 360," or as in such novelty popular features as "Alabama Bound," "California, Here I Come," and "Chattanooga Choo Choo," all of which employ programmatic devices in much the same way as, say, Prokofiev did in *Peter and the Wolf*.

But time passes, and over the years the refinement of loco-motive onomatopoeia as a definitive device of jazz sonority as well as rhythm has been such that the locomotive elements now function in the way that dead metaphors function in conventional discourse. In Ellington's "Harlem Airshaft," the blues locomotive sounds are still there, but now they represent a storyland panorama of people in a given area of a great metropolis. The locomotive onomatopoeia is also still there in Ellington's "Mainstem," but there it evokes the sights, the tempo, and the sounds of Broadway, including the special glitter of midtown Manhattan and Times Square. A very popular early "swing era" example of Ellington's programmatic use of locomotive onomatopoeia is his rendition of the old ragtime showcase novelty tune "Tiger Rag" as "Daybreak Express."

Fletcher Henderson's arrangement of "Shanghai Shuffle,"

by contrast, and his orchestra's recording of Benny Carter's arrangement of "Limehouse Blues" are excellent examples of musical dead metaphors. The syncopation is definitive, but it is no longer about locomotives as such. It is about a dance tempo. But then there is Ellington's three-part *Uwis Suite*, written near the end of his life, as a tribute to the University of Wisconsin while the band was in residence on campus. The first part is an instrumental prom chant of deluxe-hotel-ballroom-type music that goes nicely with fraternity and sorority functions, groovy and up-tempo plus off-beat by turns. The second part is a tongue-in-cheek polka to charm the Midwesterners and the outsiders alike. And then comes the third part, which at first sounds for all the world like an old down-home juke-joint bump-and-grind stomp, but turns out to be "Loco Madi," a fine onomatopoeic account of the band's train trip—from, say, Chicago up to Madison and the University of Wisconsin. Incidentally, in this instance the locomotive onomatopoeia is somewhat less obviously programmatic than in its use in the "Happy Go Lucky Local" section of Ellington's "Deep South Suite," where, as in "Daybreak Express," the train itself is the subject. Here it suggests how the composer feels about his destination, the happiness with which he anticipates his arrival.

Whether it is a dead metaphor or a thematic program, the syncopating locomotive onomatopoeia is precisely what provides the velocity of celebration that drives the jubilee songs, shouts, jumps, and ever so elegant stomps and grinds, shakes and shimmies and wobbles, on festive occasions. There is also reason to believe that locomotive onomatopoeia may be the most direct source of that definitive emphasis on syncopation that distinguishes jazz percussion from the West African percussion from which it was derived, and also from the Afro-Caribbean percussion to which it is so closely related.

The juke joint, the honky-tonk, and the ballroom also represent one more thing, anthropologically speaking: a ceremonial context for the male-with-female-duet dance flirtation and embrace, upon which the zoological survival of the human species has always been predicated. The Latin American influence on this aspect of jazz as dance music is quite obvious. (The African dancing most familiar to Americans tends to be ensemble or choral dancing that suggests military preparation for aggression or defense.)

Although jazz music for such dancing is generally regarded as secular, neither the music nor the dance movements (which may be ceremonial re-enactments of primordial purification and fertility rituals) are totally forbidden at religious feast day celebrations. They are excluded from church ceremonies as such, but not from such sacred but extramural church-based celebrations as public Christmas and Easter season dances and post-church wedding receptions. And the relationship of male-female duet dances to rituals of season changes and of planting, cultivation, harvesting, storing, and preserving should not require elaboration.

Jazz music has come to be internationally recognized as something like the musical equivalent of Constance Rourke's idea of American humor: an emblem for a pioneer people who require resilience as a prime trait. Jazz is also the musical equivalent of what Kenneth Burke called representative anecdotes. By its very nature, jazz typifies the national dynamics or natural history of exploration, discovery, and improvisation; and the ever so tentative settlement of what might become a great metropolis, a pit stop, or a ghost town of lost chords. As the musical equivalent of representative anecdotes, not only do jazz performances make people around the globe feel that they know what the texture of life in the United States is like, they also make a significant number of those people want to become American. (I wonder how many immigrants to America the performances of Louis Armstrong were responsible for.) How appropriate then that what amounts to a national shrine to exploration and improvisation is now being inaugurated as a world-class jazz performance venue at Columbus Circle by an institution bearing the name of Abraham Lincoln. So let the trail blaze on and on, and the riffs, too, those elegantly improvised tidbits that inevitably turn back into solo opportunities!

2004

CHRONOLOGY

NOTE ON THE TEXTS

NOTES

INDEX

Chronology

1916   Born on May 12 in Nokomis, Alabama, to sixteen-year-old Sudie Graham, at the home of one of her relatives. Graham (b. circa 1900), a Nokomis-area native living in Tuskegee, Alabama, will in the fall enter the teacher training program at Tuskegee Institute. Father, John Lee Young (b. circa 1895), is one of a middle-class black family in Tuskegee; he had met Graham the year before, when she worked as an assistant in his aunt's real estate firm. To protect her educational prospects and the Young family name, Graham gives the infant to Hugh and Mattie Murray (b. circa 1868 and 1882, respectively), a childless couple of her family's acquaintance, who legally adopt him as Albert Lee Murray. Hugh Murray, who appears Caucasian in a photograph and will be remembered by his adopted son as resembling William Faulkner, is identified as black ("B") on the U.S. Census. He is illiterate and works in a lumberyard. Mattie Murray, who is black and literate, is a homemaker. By year's end the family will move to Magazine Point, Alabama, a suburb three miles north of Mobile and about forty-five miles southwest of Nokomis. Murray will remember Magazine Point as a rough, poor black neighborhood alive with music and "rife with juke joints." Adjacent African Hill or Africatown is home to the survivors (and descendants of survivors) of the schooner *Clotilde*, one of the last U.S. ships to import slaves from Africa, in 1859. (Scooter, the protagonist-narrator of Murray's semi-autobiographical novel *Train Whistle Guitar*, recalls the rivalry between the neighborhoods as follows: "When somebody from up there used to call us them old sawmill quarters niggers, section gang niggers and foggy bottom niggers who didn't come from anywhere but from looking up a mule's ass back on the old plantations back in slavery times, all I thought was that they were trying to get even because we were also not only closer to all the best places for hunting both land game and water game, but we also had a baseball team that was in the same class as those from Chickasaw and Whistler and Maysville and Bayou La Batre and Biloxi.") The hulk of the *Clotilde*, which was scuttled then burned by her legally embattled owner, can still be seen at the mouth of Chickasaw (Chickasawbogue) Creek throughout Murray's childhood. Murray's neighborhood was rezoned for industrial use and razed in midcentury, but nearby neighborhoods retain the look, the winding streets, as well as the shotgun-style house in which Murray grew up.

1920   Appears in U.S. Census of 1920 as the son (not adopted) of Hugh and Mattie Murray. By this time the Murrays are also raising three other children, aged ten to eighteen (and all with the last name Leatherwood), whom they list as "adopted."

1927   Works intermittently as a gofer during construction of the Cochrane Bridge, spanning the Mobile River. (Will later recall twice meeting Zora Neale Hurston, once while she was collecting folklore from workmen during the construction of the bridge, and again while she was interviewing community elder Cudjo Lewis, one of the last survivors of the *Clotilde*. In Murray's first novel, *Train Whistle Guitar*, Lewis is the model for Unka Jo Jo.) Adoptive father Hugh Murray manages semipro baseball teams, some featuring Mobile native Satchel Paige (a model for Gator Gus in *Train Whistle Guitar*). Murray closely follows the 1927 New York Yankees via newspapers; recalls it as a watershed moment in personal literacy, a realization that he is able to read more than what he is assigned in elementary school. In fall begins fifth grade at Mobile County Training School, which he will attend through 1935.

1930   Sudie Graham, who had moved to Mobile years earlier to be near Murray and whom he calls his auntie (Miss Tee in *Train Whistle Guitar*), marries and has a son, Murray's half-brother James Burke. (Burke, who will have a career in the military, writes to Murray in 2002, "I remember the auntie bit, but she *always* told me you were my *brother*.")

1931–35 As student in high school program of Mobile County Training School, participates in theatrical productions, playing Aubrey Piper in *The Show-Off*, a comedy by George Kelly, and Thea Dugger in *Bad Man*, a Harlem Renaissance "folk play" by Randolph Edmonds. Appears in Negro History Week pageants, one time performing a juba dance to "Juba," from R. Nathaniel Dett's piano suite *In the Bottoms* (1913). Excels in French and Latin. Paints.

Plays baseball and basketball. In sophomore year is voted best all-around student by the faculty.

1935   In January travels to Tuskegee Institute for a regional high school basketball tournament. There, through arrangements made by Sudie Graham Burke, meets for the first time his biological father, John Young. (Young is now a foreman at the institute's power plant, where he has worked since returning from World War I, and the father of Murray's eleven-year-old half-sister, Rowena Young.) Graduates from Mobile County Training School and is granted full-tuition scholarship to Tuskegee. Picks cotton for a week ("It seemed heroic to me") to earn the bus fare to Tuskegee, 205 miles from Magazine Point. Matriculates at Tuskegee, where he lives with Young and his family.

1935–39   Studies education at Tuskegee. Takes four years of ROTC training. Studies military science and tactics under Benjamin O. Davis Sr. (the first black general in the U.S. Army) during his freshman year, and under Benjamin O. Davis Jr. during his senior year. Joins Alpha Phi Alpha fraternity. Becomes president of Tuskegee chapter of Alpha Kappa Mu honor society. Works in the power plant with John Young during the summers. Also works as a cook in the veterans' hospital in Tuskegee. Mentored in modern literature by English department chairman Morteza Drexel ("Mort") Sprague, a charismatic teacher still only in his twenties. Reads James Joyce, T. S. Eliot, Hemingway, Faulkner, Edna St. Vincent Millay, e. e. cummings, Wallace Stevens, W. H. Auden, William Saroyan, Charles and Mary Beard, Sigrid Undset, Romain Rolland, Kenneth Burke, and many others. Notices that many of the books he has been borrowing from the library have also been checked out by upperclassman Ralph Ellison, a clerk at the library's circulation desk and a fellow protégé of Sprague. (Ellison and Murray have a few brief conversations in the library but will not become friends until the 1940s in New York City.) In junior year writes one-act play, *Odds and Ends*, which is staged by Tuskegee's Little Theater on the evening of April 28, 1938. The setting is a shoe store in Mobile and the play has seven characters, none played by Murray. (Only a program survives.) Pays close attention to contemporary theater through periodicals and anthologies. After reading Thomas Mann's essay "The Coming Humanism" in *The Nation* (December 10, 1938), seeks out the author's *The Coming Victory of Democracy* and *Joseph* novels.

1939   Graduates from Tuskegee with B.S. in education. Reads Joyce's *Finnegans Wake* when it appears in the spring. Takes job as principal of Damascus Junior High School in Damascus, Georgia (population 477). When he misses a bus connection en route to Damascus and is stranded at night in Columbus, Georgia, a fellow black traveler points him to Ma Rainey's house. Rainey lets him sleep on her couch. (He will write about this episode, and of Rainey's kindness, in *South to a Very Old Place*.) Reading includes Kierkegaard, Sir James George Frazer, Virginia Woolf, and John Dewey.

1940   Position in Damascus proves disappointing. In the 1940 Census is listed as again living in Mobile with Hugh and Mattie Murray. In summer begins graduate coursework in education at the University of Michigan, likely his first trip outside the South. Reading includes Marx and Nietzsche. Studies Thomas Mann's work in depth. Returns to Tuskegee in the fall to teach in the night school and direct the Little Theater company.

1941   On May 31 marries Mozelle Menefee (b. 1920), who grew up in Tuskegee and has just completed her sophomore year at the Institute. Postpones honeymoon, and spends summer doing graduate coursework on theories of reading instruction at the University of Chicago and at Northwestern University. Returns to Tuskegee in the fall. Begins to develop two signatures, one for official documents, with a circular A, the other for writing his name in books, with a stylized, pointy A. Will maintain this system, with few exceptions, for the rest of this life.

1942   Teaches English at Tuskegee and directs the Little Theater company. In summer takes honeymoon trip to New York with Mozelle; they stay at Hotel Theresa in Harlem, then the hotel of choice for black show business and sports figures. Renews acquaintance with Ralph Ellison.

1943   On January 5 enlists in U.S. Army Air Corps, and reports for duty one week later. Sent to Utah for basic training. Attends Army Administration School at Atlanta University from March through May. Mozelle graduates from Tuskegee in the spring. Murray attends Officers Candidate

School in Miami Beach, Florida, from September through January 1944. Commissioned second lieutenant. Daughter, Michele Alberita Murray, born on October 3.

1944   Transferred in January to Tuskegee Army Air Field and soon becomes assistant training coordinator for the Tuskegee Airmen. Studies War Department Pamphlet 20-6, *Command of Negro Troops*, published in February. Reading includes Kafka, Arthur Koestler, Anaïs Nin, and the autobiography of Giambattista Vico. Enjoys discussing Faulkner's work with Colonel Noel F. Parrish, commander of Tuskegee Army Air Field.

1945   In April takes training-instructor course in San Antonio, Texas. Promoted to training coordinator at Tuskegee Army Air Field on June 25. On August 2 is transferred to Army Air Force Camouflage School in Buckley, Colorado. (He will later say that this transfer had something to do with plans for an Allied invasion of Japan, and that he had expected to end up in the Pacific theater.) Promoted to first lieutenant on August 8. Japan surrenders on August 14. Camouflage School ends on August 18. Returns to Tuskegee Army Air Field. Mozelle begins teaching career in Alabama public schools.

1946   On January 4, through arrangements made by an army buddy related to Ellington band member Harry Carney, has backstage meeting with Duke Ellington after fourth annual concert at Carnegie Hall. In October applies to remain on active duty during demobilization of the U.S. armed forces then under way. Application is denied. On November 13 the Army determines Murray's position to be redundant. Instructed to use sixty days of accrued leave time before being demobilized.

1947   Officially placed on reserve duty on January 14. Returns to Tuskegee Institute as instructor of freshman and sophomore English. In the fall enters the master of arts program in English at New York University. Lives at 147 Bainbridge Street in Bedford-Stuyvesant, Brooklyn, with Mozelle and Michele. Takes courses with Margaret Schlauch (Chaucer) and Oscar Cargill (American literature). Pursues active social life in Greenwich Village. Forms friendships with Maya Deren, Joseph Campbell, Seymour Krim, and Anaïs Nin. Spends his days studying, writing, and researching at the Forty-second Street branch of the New York Public Library. Frequently meets Ellison for lunch. (Ellison is working on *Invisible Man* in an office on loan from Francis Steegmuller at Forty-ninth and Fifth Avenue.) After classes at NYU, Murray goes sometimes to the Fifty-second Street nightclubs to hear Charlie Parker, Dizzy Gillespie, and other jazz musicians, and sometimes to Ellison's Harlem apartment to listen to him read from *Invisible Man*. Attends New Year's Eve party at Ellison's. Reading includes Constance Rourke and art historian Heinrich Zimmer.

1948   Writes master's thesis, "*The Waste Land* and *The Sun Also Rises*: A Comparative Study." Returns to Tuskegee in the fall and begins two-year stint of teaching. Master's thesis approved in October.

1949   Works on a semi-autobiographical novel concerning the childhood and adolescence of Scooter, a poor Alabama-born "jack rabbit raised in the briarpatch" who, with the help of several larger-than-life mentors, passes all the tests of life to become, successively, an accomplished student, a jazz musician, and a writer.

1950   Begins ten-year correspondence with Ralph Ellison (which he will coedit, annotate, and in the year 2000 publish as *Trading Twelves: The Selected Letters of Ralph Ellison and Albert Murray*). Ellison reports on the progress of *Invisible Man*—"the goddamnedest experience of my life"—and encourages Murray to complete his *Bildungsroman*. In late spring sails to Paris to study French at the Sorbonne courtesy of the G.I. Bill. Receives $300 grant for the trip from Tuskegee, equivalent to five weeks' salary before taxes. Stops first in Lisbon, Genoa, and Venice. Arrives in Paris in mid-June and stays at the Hotel Londres. Meets and forms friendships with James Baldwin, Jean Hélion and Pegeen Guggenheim, René Liebowitz, and H. J. "Kappy" Kaplan, a diplomatic attaché and Paris correspondent for *Partisan Review*, whose apartment is a social and cultural center. Meets Sidney Bechet. Meets painter Romare Bearden, who will become a close friend and intellectual comrade. Reconnects with Duke Ellington. Meets Ollie Stewart, foreign correspondent of the *Baltimore Afro-American*, who will devote half of his July 1 "Report from Europe" column to Murray's residence in Paris and his novel-in-progress. Worries about being recalled to active duty when Korean War begins on June 25. Writes to Mozelle for news of war preparation at Tuskegee. Kaplan takes his family to the United States for the summer in late June or early July, and Murray moves into his apartment at 132 boulevard du Montparnasse, one floor above Henri Matisse. (Murray will recall catching glimpses of Matisse at work from the open elevator.) In August visits Antibes with Baldwin, whom he teaches how to swim. Leaves Paris on August 29. Returns to Tuskegee via Montreal and New York.

1951   Recalled to active duty in U.S. Air Force on June 6. Assigned to Tuskegee Institute as assistant professor of air science and tactics and teaches courses in geopolitics as well. Takes course at Air University at Maxwell Air Force Base in Montgomery, Alabama. Buys lot number three on Hudson Street at the intersection of Bibb Street in Tuskegee. Hires architect Bill Mann, an old friend from Tuskegee, to design a house. Completes first draft of semi-autobiographical narrative, provisionally titled "Jack the Bear," that will eventually yield the novels *Train Whistle Guitar* (1974) and *The Spyglass Tree* (1991). Sends manuscript to Ellison late in the year. Interviews Duke Ellington on local radio show.

1952   Ellison provides detailed feedback on manuscript in February letter. Murray follows reviews of *Invisible Man* closely when Random House publishes novel in the spring. Receives mixed criticism of "Jack the Bear" from Ellison's editor, Albert Erskine, who feels that Murray is under the spell of Faulkner. Reads André Malraux on art.

1953   Takes course for Air Force instructors at Ohio State University. Visits Cuba and returns home with conga and bongo drums, which he takes up playing. Submits novel, now retitled "The Briarpatch," to Arabel J. Porter, editor of *New World Writing*, a recently launched "paperback magazine" published by New American Library. Porter fashions a section of "The Briarpatch" into a short story, "The Luzana Cholly Kick," and, in October, publishes it in issue number four. In a biographical note preceding the story, Murray writes: "We all learn from Mann, Joyce, Hemingway, Eliot, and the rest, but I'm also trying to learn to write in terms of the tradition I grew up in, the Negro tradition of blues, stomps, ragtime, jumps, and swing. After all, very few writers have done as much with American experience as Jelly Roll Morton, Count Basie, and Duke Ellington." Writes to Porter that being included in the anthology (which also included Jorge Luis Borges, Gore Vidal, Nadine Gordimer, Shelby Foote, Robert Motherwell, and others) was like being "in the World Series in your first season in organized baseball" and "just about the best thing that could happen to an apprentice."

1954 Promoted to captain in the U.S. Air Force on March 11. Helps arrange for Ellison to speak at Tuskegee.

1955 Construction of house in Tuskegee begins in April. The Murrays will never live in it. In August Murray is transferred to Nouasseur Air Base, just outside Casablanca, Morocco. Lives first in Casablanca and then on the base. Buys Leica M3 camera for $244 in the fall. Begins discussing photography with Ellison, who had worked as a professional photographer in the late 1940s.

1956 Serves as chief of military training at Nouasseur. Tuskegee house completed in March and rented out. Rent covers mortgage and yields a small profit (rent collection overseen by local bank). At the request of the U.S. Information Service, begins lecturing (in French) on jazz at various Moroccan venues, including the Maison d'Amérique in Casablanca and the U.S. embassy in Rabat. Receives commendations from American diplomats and superior officers. Visits Greece in May. In the summer drives with Mozelle and Michele from Spain to Italy. They then travel through Europe with Ellison (then in residence at the American Academy in Rome) and his wife, Fanny.

1957 Vice President Richard Nixon visits Nouasseur in March. Murray writes to Ellison about the surprisingly large number of blacks in Nixon's entourage. Murray writes memo to Air Force superiors in April: "I am particularly interested in working in a position involving international relations, perhaps in conjunction with an Attaché, Mission, or Advisory Group type assignment." Suffers mild heart attack on May 18. Recuperates at base hospital. Visits West Germany in June and the Netherlands in October. Returns to duty on November 20.

1958 Visits West Germany in January. In April is transferred to Air Reserve Flying Center at Long Beach (California) Municipal Airport and is placed in charge of personnel. In July buys home at 1515 West 166th Street, Compton, for $13,500.

1959   In the spring is reassigned by Air Force from position as personnel specialist to that of supply officer. Writes ardent letter to superiors protesting his new assignment as beneath his level of training, established skill set, and previous achievements. Also argues that reassignment violates established protocol, as he was not briefed ahead of time. Letter is either ignored or not acted upon. Takes three-month supply management course for Air Force officers in Amarillo, Texas. Becomes officer accountable for air base property in Long Beach.

1960   In June photographs Duke Ellington's recording sessions at the famed Radio Recorders studio in West Hollywood. Travels in summer throughout California.

1961   In January, as base accountable officer, signs documents closing the Air Reserve Flying Center in Long Beach. Begins new assignment at Headquarters Air Base Wing, Air Force Systems Command, at Hanscom Field in Bedford, Massachusetts, twenty miles northwest of Boston. Placed in charge of Materiel Control Office, becoming responsible for sixty-four aircraft, some experimental. Lives in base officers' quarters while Mozelle and Michele stay in Compton so that Michele can finish high school there. Promoted to major "as a Reserve of the Air Force" on March 11. Quickly becomes a friend of Charlie Davidson, proprietor of the Andover Shop in Cambridge and a tailor, jazz buff, reader, and raconteur. (The Murrays and the Davidsons will become lifelong friends, attending the Newport Jazz Festival and sometimes vacationing together.) Begins attending Alpha Phi Alpha gatherings around Boston. In June sells home in Compton for $15,525. Moves with Mozelle and Michele to 54 High Road in Bedford following Michele's graduation. Becomes chief of logistic branch at Hanscom on September 16. Michele enters Juilliard in the fall to study dance and lives with Ralph and Fanny Ellison in New York City.

1962   Sells house in Tuskegee on March 19 for $9,500. (Cost of lot and construction was $11,500, but probably realizes a small profit after seven years of rent collections and tax deductions.) Approaching fifth anniversary of heart attack, receives extensive physical examination at Hanscom from May 1 to 4. On May 15 a panel of Air Force physicians at Andrews Air Force Base, in Washington, D.C., determines that he be assigned early retirement due to arteriosclerotic heart disease. Glowing report of physician at Hanscom emphasizes Murray's otherwise excellent health, and notes that Murray has never been prescribed cardiovascular drugs, perhaps to leave the door open for an appeal. The doctor writes, toward the end of a long report, "Patient is a well-developed, well-nourished, middle-aged man who appears neither acutely nor chronically ill and who is in no acute distress. . . . At the present time I do not think he has any symptoms due to heart disease." Yet Murray accepts early retirement. Retires on June 29, with the permanent grade of major. Will live another fifty-one years and never suffer further heart problems. Stands five foot eight and weighs 168 pounds. Letter of appreciation from his commanding officer states that Murray is "the prototype of the military man whose leadership qualities, devoted service, military bearing, and desirable personal qualities motivate our younger personnel to emulation." Moves to New York and rents apartment 8P at 45 West 132nd Street in the Lenox Terrace Apartments complex in Harlem, a middle- and upper-middle-class residential development whose residents have included many distinguished Harlem professionals and politicians, such as Congressman Charles Rangel, New York governor David Patterson, and Manhattan borough president Percy Sutton. The enclave of six large buildings between Lenox Avenue and Fifth Avenue is less than a decade old when the Murrays move in. Their eighth-floor corner apartment has two bedrooms, one and a half bathrooms, a balcony, and spectacular views of Harlem and midtown. The Murrays will live here for the rest of their lives. Renews friendship with Romare Bearden in Manhattan. (The view from Murray's balcony of the west side of Lenox Avenue between 132nd and 133rd Streets will be Bearden's vantage point for his giant collage "The Block" [1971], which will be acquired by the Metropolitan Museum of Art in 1978. Two photographs by Murray of that portion of Lenox Avenue, taken from his balcony circa 1971, are also part of the Metropolitan Museum of Art's permanent collection.) Tries to revive prospects of "The Briarpatch," unsuccessfully submitting it to editor Peter Davison at Atlantic Monthly Press.

1963   Works assiduously on an essay, begun years before, on what he calls the "blues idiom," that special character of art born of a determination to achieve "elegance in the face of adversity." The essay, called "The Hero and the Blues," will soon grow into a book-length manuscript. Mozelle begins teaching in New York City preschools.

1964   On January 20 enjoys stint as on-camera theater critic, reviewing three plays in an arts segment of *The World at Ten* on WNDT, New York. Publishes first work of nonfiction in July 3 issue of *Life*, an omnibus review of what the editors bill as "seven new works on the racial crisis." At Ellison's suggestion, begins reviewing books for *The New Leader*, a biweekly magazine of politics and opinion edited in New York by Myron Kolatch. Michele begins work as a professional dancer at the World's Fair in Queens.

1965   Ellison brings Murray on board as a credited consultant for three documentaries for educational television (WNET, New York). (Ellison, through his work with the Carnegie Commission, had been lobbying for the creation of a public television network.) Two are on jazz (*Jazz Goes Intellectual: Bop!*, featuring Dizzy Gillespie, and *Jazz: The Experimenters*, featuring Charles Mingus and Cecil Taylor) and the other is on Ellison himself (*Ralph Ellison: Work in Progress*). Murray serves as "technical consultant" and may have done some script work as well. Michele begins dancing with the Alvin Ailey Company. (She will work with other companies as well, including the Lar Lubovitch Company, before becoming a featured dancer with Ailey circa 1968.) Around this time begins tradition of throwing downhome-style New Year's Day parties—pigs' feet, black-eyed peas, collard greens, cornbread, bourbon—which will continue for several decades.

1966   During the New York City transit strike in January, Murray chauffeurs Michele and her dancer-colleagues from Harlem to the Clark Center in midtown for Ailey Company rehearsals. (He will abandon car ownership within the next few years.) In February is invited by editor Kirkpatrick Sale of *The New York Times Magazine* to write an essay on current and historical relationships between blacks and Jews. (Essay is rejected, with apologies from Sale.) In April speaks at the Peace Corps Training Center in Arecibo, Puerto Rico. Mozelle begins teaching in New York City public schools. "The Luzana Cholly Kick" (1953) is reprinted, under revised title "Train Whistle Guitar," in

John Henrik Clarke's landmark anthology *American Negro Short Stories*, published by Hill and Wang. Murray's essay on James Baldwin is a frequently cited highlight of *Anger, and Beyond: The Negro Writer in the United States*, a wide-ranging anthology of previously unpublished writings edited by Herbert Hill and published by Harper & Row. Mort Sprague dies, at age fifty-seven, at the end of the year. Sprague, to whom Ellison dedicated his essay collection *Shadow and Act* (1964), had been paying close attention to Murray's magazine work and writing to him about it.

1967   In April, begins two-year involvement with New York's Center for Urban Education (CUE), a public-education policy institute funded from 1964 to 1973 by the U.S. Office of Education. Contributes essays to CUE periodicals (*The Urban Review*, a bimonthly journal, and *The Center Forum*, a monthly newsletter) and works as researcher and consultant on several of CUE's multimedia educational initiatives. Writes draft of essay that will become Part I of his collection *The Omni-Americans*. Publishes negative review of William Styron's novel *The Confessions of Nat Turner* in December 4 issue of *The New Leader*.

1968   Interviews painters Charles Alston (Bearden's older cousin) and Hale Woodruff for the Smithsonian Institution's Archives of American Art oral history program. Teaches course at Columbia University School of Journalism. "Train Whistle Guitar" is revised for inclusion in Theodore L. Gross and James A. Emanuel's anthology *Dark Symphony: Negro Literature in America*, published by Free Press. Editor Angus Cameron at Knopf, responding to a proposal from Murray, says that he is interested in publishing a collection of his essays and reviews but disagrees with him on a few points. Meanwhile, two of CUE's top editors, David E. Outerbridge and Harris Dienstfrey, leave the institute to establish their own book-publishing firm. They admire Murray's work, and invite him to contribute to their list.

1969   Second excerpt from "The Briarpatch" is published in February issue of *Harper's* as "Stonewall Jackson's Waterloo." The magazine's editor, Willie Morris, then sends Murray on an assignment to assess the South, especially his native Alabama, in the wake of desegregation. This long nonfiction piece, part personal memoir, part interview-based journalism, will be Murray's chief project over the next two years. (Murray's interview subjects include Robert Penn Warren, C. Van Woodward, Walker Percy, and many Southern newspaper editors and reporters.) On March 3, Outerbridge and Dienstfrey make a formal offer to publish Murray's collection of essays *The Omni-Americans*. Murray, his discussions with Knopf having reached an impasse, accepts. In October acquires James Oliver Brown as literary agent.

1970   *The Omni-Americans* is published by Outerbridge and Dienstfrey in March. A Book-of-the-Month Club alternate selection, the collection is widely and enthusiastically reviewed. (Robert Coles, in *The New Yorker*, writes that Murray "speaks for himself [and] as a man who is proud of his people and their considerable achievements. . . . His purpose [here] is to set forth those achievements and to warn against America's 'experts,' especially what he calls 'social survey technicians,' [who] do not see the richness, the complexity of the black man's experience in America; they merely contribute to the caricatures that so many of us cannot get out of heads.") Takes two-week vacation with Mozelle to Sag Harbor, Long Island, in July. In August delivers first post-*Omni-Americans* lecture, "Beyond Separatism," to Brandeis University's Summer Adult Institute. Serves as O'Connor Professor of Literature at Colgate University in the fall. Duke Ellington, then in residency in Los Angeles, interviews Murray for job as co-author of his autobiography. (In the end Ellington will write *Music Is My Mistress* [1973] with longtime confidant Stanley Dance.)

1971   Brown sells book rights to *Harper's* article to Joyce Johnson, an editor at McGraw-Hill and an acquaintance of Murray since 1969. In March Willie Morris is fired from *Harper's* and magazine publication of the article, scheduled for the fall, is canceled. Murray serves as visiting professor of literature at the University of Massachusetts–Boston. "Train Whistle Guitar" is reprinted in his friend Toni Cade Bambara's anthology *Tales and Stories for Black Folks* and receives positive mention by Toni Morrison in *The New York Times*. Michele tours Soviet Union with Alvin Ailey Company. In November *South to a Very Old Place* is published by McGraw-Hill to excellent reviews.

(Robert R. Gross, in *Saturday Review*, writes that Murray, by intermingling "reminiscences of youth with engaging conversation, cultural criticism, and comments on his folk heritage," has created "a disciplined work of art: a reflective and elegant rendering of one man's coming to terms with his roots.") *The Omni-Americans* is reprinted in paperback by Avon Books.

1972 In January Ruth Ellington (Duke's sister and music publishing manager) throws book party for *South to a Very Old Place* at 333 Riverside Drive (which is also Duke's mailing address). In February accepts invitation from the University of Missouri–Columbia to deliver the Paul Anthony Brick Lectures for fall 1972. Revisits "The Hero and the Blues," his essay on the blues idiom, and begins adapting the material for a series of three hour-long lectures. *South to a Very Old Place* named a finalist for the National Book Award in the Arts and Letters category. Jack Valenti, formerly a top aide to President Johnson, writes to Murray regarding how much LBJ appreciated *South to a Very Old Place*, especially Murray's account of a conversation among elderly Alabamians about Johnson's civil rights policies. Receives Alumni Merit Award from Tuskegee. Speaks at Southern University, in Baton Rouge, Louisiana. Correspondents around this time include Michael Harper, James Alan McPherson, Ernest J. Gaines, Robert Bone, Martin Williams, and Leon Forrest. Spanish translation of *The Omni-Americans* is published by Editorial Letras in Mexico City. On October 7, 8, and 9, delivers Paul Anthony Brick Lectures at the University of Missouri.

1973 Serves as O'Connor Visiting Lecturer at Colgate University. Speaks at Yale University. Elected to executive committee of PEN. In spring Harvard undergraduate Lewis P. Jones III, editor of "Black Odyssey: A Search for Home," a special issue of the *Harvard Advocate*, invites Murray to contribute to the publication. Instead of an article, Murray suggests that the issue's chief theme, "the role and responsibilities of black artists operating in the larger American context," be the subject of a Harvard symposium and that the transcript be published in the *Advocate*. The symposium, moderated by Dean of Students Archie Epps and featuring Murray, Ellison, Harold Cruse, and Nathan I.

Huggins, marks the beginning of Murray's decades-long friendship with Jones, who will later have a career in law, banking, and finance. Brick Lectures published as *The Hero and the Blues* by the University of Missouri Press. (An unsigned review in *The New Yorker* says that "[Murray] is succinct, funny, and marvelously original in defining what a hero is in fiction and drama—his reading of *Oedipus* is a knockout, and his comparison of Mann's Joseph to American black heroes is eye-opening.")

1974   Elected to membership in the Century Association, an exclusive club of writers, artists, musicians, and patrons of the arts in midtown Manhattan. Quickly becomes a regular for lunch and an active participant in club affairs. (The club will remain an important part of his life through 2005.) At St. Peter's Evangelical Lutheran Church in Manhattan (famous for its ministry to the jazz world) serves on committee (along with Ruth Ellington, Phoebe Jacobs, Stanley Dance, and others) that organizes seventy-fifth-birthday concert for Duke Ellington on April 29. (Ellington will die on May 24.) In early May *Train Whistle Guitar*, a novel of childhood fashioned from the first half of "The Briarpatch," is published by McGraw-Hill. The book, which will later that year win the Lillian Smith Award for Fiction from the Southern Regional Council, is well and widely reviewed. (John Edgar Wideman, writing in *The New York Times Book Review*, says that "the only way to appreciate the music of Murray's prose is to immerse yourself in long passages of dialogue and monologue, the lyric descriptions of countryside and fireside, which are nothing so much as the riffs and choruses of a blues artist translated into speech and action. . . . [They tell us] the truth about black experience just as resolutely as the runaway, star-climbing notes of a Charlie Parker solo.") At the invitation of Martin Williams, teaches at Smithsonian Institute in Music Criticism, where Gary Giddins is among his students. Is a regular at Upper East Side restaurant Elaine's. Speaks at public schools in Sacramento. Receives contract from McGraw-Hill for sequel to *Train Whistle Guitar*.

1975   Receives honorary doctorate from Colgate University. Social circle at this time includes Mary Hemingway, Robert Penn Warren, Sidney Offit, Herbert Mitgang, Drew

Middleton, John Chancellor, Matt Clark, John Hammond, Romare Bearden, and Ralph Ellison. Michele, no longer with the Alvin Ailey Company, teaches courses on dance and movement for actors at Howard University.

1976   In October *Stomping the Blues* is published by McGraw-Hill. An idiosyncratic study in the history, aesthetics, rituals, and anthropology of jazz, focusing on its black derivation and affirmative disposition, the book is widely reviewed in both the mainstream and the music press. (Greil Marcus, writing in *Rolling Stone*, explains that for Murray blues music "is not involved with self-pity or resignation . . . but with affirmation and the act of creation. . . . *Stomping the Blues* is anything but the last word on the blues. It is, though, the best word anyone has offered in a long time.") For book party, McGraw-Hill throws a "Kansas City Jam Session" at its building on Sixth Avenue in midtown Manhattan, featuring jazz legends Budd Johnson, Eddie Durham, Buck Clayton, Oliver Jackson, Mary Lou Williams, Bill Pemberton, and Doc Cheatham. Murray's students and acolytes around this time include Gary Giddins, Henry Louis Gates Jr., Charlayne Hunter-Gault, and Stanley Crouch. Murray writes catalogue essay for Bearden's exhibition *Of the Blues* at Cordier & Ekstrom Gallery in New York.

1977   Jason Berry's essay "Musical Literature," the first long-form critical appraisal of Murray's oeuvre, appears in the January 15 issue of *The Nation*. Travels to West Germany in June for the United States Information Agency, speaking at the Free University of Berlin, the University of Bonn, and the University of Bremen. *Stomping the Blues* wins ASCAP/Deems Taylor Award for Music Criticism. Approached by Willard Alexander, longtime booking agent for Count Basie, to act as Basie's co-writer on an as-told-to autobiography. Agrees. Travels with Basie on and off through 1983. Repeatedly interviews old acquaintance Jo Jones, the drummer for the Basie band during its first decade, originally for background for the Basie book and then for a possible book on Jones's life. Exhaustively corroborates Basie's memories by interviewing band-mates, including Eddie Durham, Budd Johnson, Dan Minor, and Buck Clayton, and by checking Basie's memories against newspaper stories and publicity materials. Is "Special Guest Speaker" at conference of African and African American Folklorists at Indiana University–Bloomington. Speaks at the Studio Museum in Harlem.

1978   In spring is writer-in-residence at Emory University, where Mike Sager, who will become a prominent journalist, is among his students. Befriends literary scholar and biographer Richard Ellmann, also teaching at Emory. Conducts several long interviews with Jo Jones in the summer and fall. Writes wall labels for Bearden's *Profiles* series, on view at Cordier & Ekstrom. Presents lectures at Morehouse College and Howard University. Attends concert at the White House celebrating the twenty-fifth anniversary of the Newport Jazz Festival. Speaks at Long Island University's C. W. Post campus on several occasions throughout the 1978–79 school year under auspices of the political science department. In December, filmmaker Nelson E. Breen records joint conversation of Murray, Bearden, Alvin Ailey, and James Baldwin for the documentary *Bearden Plays Bearden* (1980).

1979   Smithsonian interview with Hale Woodruff (1968) is published in the catalogue to Woodruff's exhibition at the Studio Museum in Harlem. Herbert Mitgang interviews Murray about his collaboration with Count Basie for his Book Ends column in *The New York Times* on November 18. Murray tells Mitgang: "My job is to help him get his voice right so readers will say 'I know that's Count Basie talking; what did Albert Murray do to get his name on the book?'"

1980   Begins teaching creative writing at Barnard College as an adjunct associate professor. (He will continue on and off through 1983.) Declines Nathan I. Huggins's offer of a teaching position at Harvard University. Stanley Crouch's laudatory essay "Albert Murray's Gourmet Chitlins" appears in the March 3 issue of the *Village Voice*. Works with photographer and movie producer Sam Shaw on *Paris Blues*, a book based on Shaw's 1961 film of that title. (The book, commissioned by a French publisher but never realized, was to include photographs by Shaw, collages and other artworks by Bearden, and a text by Murray.) Writes catalogue essay for Bearden retrospective *Romare Bearden:*

1970–1980 at the Mint Museum in Charlotte, North Carolina. Travels to Charlotte for the exhibition's opening. Appears in documentary *Bearden Plays Bearden,* several scenes of which are filmed on the balcony of Murray's apartment.

1981   Delivers lecture on Bearden at the Brooklyn Museum in October; a concert by Teddy Wilson follows Murray's presentation. Introduced by Stanley Crouch to nineteen-year-old Juilliard student Wynton Marsalis, a composer and trumpeter who will become Murray's most famous protégé.

1982   Serves as Colgate Professor of Humanities at Colgate in the fall, teaching junior-level course on regional writing and senior-level course titled "Implications of the Blues Idiom in Contemporary American Literature." Attends an "All-Star Jazz Program" at the White House on December 4. Fires his literary agent, James Oliver Brown. *Stomping the Blues* reprinted by Vintage a few months after Nelson George's lament, in the *Village Voice,* that it had fallen out of print.

1983   Increases frequency of interviews with Count Basie. Makes several trips to Basie's home in Freeport, Bahamas. Speaks at Drew University. *The Omni-Americans* reprinted by Vintage. Speaks at the Jane Globus Seminar at Baruch College. Serves as judge of the Robert F. Kennedy Book Awards.

1984   Count Basie dies on April 26, just months after he and Murray had completed the first draft of his autobiography, *Good Morning Blues.* Speaks at Swarthmore College.

1985   Signs contract with Random House for *Good Morning Blues.* (Andrew Wylie, who represents him in the deal, will remain his agent for the rest of his life.) Book acquired by editor Erroll McDonald, who will publish all of Murray's future work, usually under Random's Pantheon imprint. Collaborates with saxophonist David Murray (no relation) on musical stage adaptation of *Train Whistle Guitar.* (Producer Joseph Papp of the New York Shakespeare Festival shows serious interest in this work-in-progress, but the musical is never realized.) In July Murray conducts his last interview with Jo Jones, who dies, at age seventy-three, on September 3. Speaks at Harvard University in November.

1986   *Good Morning Blues: The Autobiography of Count Basie as told to Albert Murray* is published in early January. (By March Random House will sell twelve thousand copies.) Black-tie book party for a thousand people at the Palladium in New York on January 17 is covered by national news media. Conducts long interview with Dizzy Gillespie, a truncated version of which appears in *Interview Magazine* for April. Murray is included in a fashion photo shoot in *New York* magazine. Receives award from literary journal *Callaloo*, which in December hosts a tribute to Murray at the convention of the Modern Language Association, featuring readings by Elizabeth Alexander, Thulani Davis, and Melvin Dixon. Joins board of directors of American Composers Orchestra, and will serve until 1989. Appears in "Black on White," episode five of Robert MacNeil's PBS documentary *The Story of English.*

1987   With Wynton Marsalis, Gordon Davis, and Stanley Crouch, Murray serves on committee that proposes the establishment of a classic jazz program at New York's Lincoln Center for the Performing Arts. (He will work closely with Crouch and Marsalis over the next several years on developing the project.) Delivers lecture to the Peter Rushton Seminars on Modern Literature at the University of Virginia. Speaks at Ohio University. German translation of *Good Morning Blues* published by Econ Verlag. Speaks at Dayton Art Institute, with concert by David Murray following presentation. Appears in documentary *Long Shadows: The Legacy of the American Civil War.* Interviewed twice at his apartment by V. S. Naipaul, in the spring and the fall. Helps make arrangements for Naipaul's visit to Tuskegee for his book *A Turn in the South* (1989). Mozelle retires from teaching in June.

1988   Romare Bearden dies on March 12, at age seventy-six. Murray becomes involved in creation of Romare Bearden Foundation. French translation of *Good Morning Blues* published by Éditions Filipacchi.

1989   On June 17, in honor of Murray's work with Central Pennsylvania Friends of Jazz, "Albert Murray Day" proclaimed in Harrisburg by Governor Bob Casey Sr. Speaks at the New School for Social Research alongside Wynton Marsalis and jazz composer/arranger David Berger. Paperback edition of *Train Whistle Guitar* issued by Northeastern

University Press with a new introduction by Robert G. O'Meally. Paperback rights to *The Omni-Americans* and *Stomping the Blues* licensed by Wylie to Da Capo Press.

1990   Appears in documentary *Lady Day: The Many Faces of Billie Holiday*. In spring spends two weeks at Dillard University, in New Orleans, as United Negro College Fund Distinguished Scholar. In October takes long vacation with Mozelle and Michele to England and France, traveling from London to Paris to the Côte d'Azur, visiting friends along the way.

1991   Group of friends throws surprise party for the Murrays on their fiftieth wedding anniversary. Second novel, *The Spyglass Tree*, originally under contract with McGraw-Hill, is published by Pantheon in the fall. A sequel to *Train Whistle Guitar*, it continues the adventures of Scooter, now a student at a black college based on the Tuskegee of the 1930s. Novel is well received by critics, including Michiko Kakutani, who writes in *The New York Times* that "the book, as a whole, works beautifully . . . Like all good *Bildungsromane*, it leaves the reader with a vivid portrait of a young man and his struggles to come to terms with his receding past and his beckoning future." In December receives Directors Emeriti Award from Lincoln Center for outstanding service to the institution in a volunteer capacity. Writes script for and appears in British television documentary *Count Basie: Swingin' the Blues. South to a Very Old Place* reprinted in paperback by Vintage.

1992   On his birthday has conversation with Wynton Marsalis onstage at Lincoln Center. Endures operation on back and neck, after which he will walk with a cane for several years, later with a walker. Speaks at the Center for American Culture Studies at Columbia University. Writes captions for photographer Ming Smith's book *A Ming Breakfast: Grits and Scrambled Moments.*

1993   Serves as Du Pont Visiting Professor at Washington and Lee University in the fall. Appears as commentator, with blues scholar Robert Palmer, in documentary *Bluesland: A Portrait in American Music.*

1994   Attends eightieth birthday dinner for Ellison on March 1 at Le Perigord in New York. Ellison dies on April 16 after a brief illness. In April Murray is interviewed at his apartment by Wynton Marsalis, and in July is interviewed by Robert G. O'Meally for the Smithsonian's Jazz Oral History Project. (These wide-ranging discussions will appear, along with a much longer version of the 1986 interview with Gillespie, in *Murray Talks Music* [2016], edited by Paul Devlin.)

1995 *South to a Very Old Place* republished in hardcover by Modern Library. *The Hero and the Blues* reprinted in paperback by Vintage. Paperback edition of *Good Morning Blues* issued by Da Capo.

1996 In February Pantheon publishes two new books to an avalanche of attention: a third Scooter novel, *The Seven League Boots*, and an essay collection, *The Blue Devils of Nada*. (In the daily *New York Times*, Richard Bernstein calls the novel "a prose poem full of character and wisdom" in which Scooter, now a young man, "becomes part of a famous jazz band, travels the country, conquers Hollywood, goes to France, and is loved by several glamorous women, all the while reflecting on history and mythology, on Odysseus and Telemachus . . . and above all on the folks back in Alabama who sent him into the world to do great things." Charles Johnson, praising Murray's "wise and authoritative essays" in the Sunday *Book Review*, writes: "What deserves very close appraisal in *The Blue Devils of Nada* is Mr. Murray's acute awareness of how the 'on-going dialogue with tradition' across cultures, races, and countries forms the basis for the works—especially American ones—deservedly enshrined in the pantheon of world-class masterpieces.") Murray is profiled in February 22 issue of *Newsweek*. Receives National Book Critics Circle's Ivan Sandrof Award for outstanding contribution to American arts and letters. Profile by Henry Louis Gates Jr., titled "King of Cats," appears in April 8 issue of *The New Yorker*. Murray participates in "An International Celebration of Southern Literature" at Agnes Scott College in June, a "Literary Olympiad" event affiliated with the Olympic Games in Atlanta. Receives honorary doctorate from Spring Hill College in Mobile. Speaks at Cornell University at invitation of Cornell's president. Interviewed by Brian Lamb on C-SPAN's *Booknotes* program and by Charlie Rose on his PBS talk show. Gives a reading, combined with a performance by Wynton Marsalis, at PEN/

Faulkner event at the Folger Shakespeare Library in Washington, D.C., in November. In December speaks at MLA convention in Washington as part of panel celebrating release of *The Norton Anthology of African American Literature*, which includes an excerpt from *Train Whistle Guitar*. Jazz at Lincoln Center becomes full constituent of Lincoln Center for the Performing Arts, and is now on par with the New York Philharmonic, Metropolitan Opera, and New York City Ballet. Murray will be an active board member through mid-2005.

1997   In January elected to membership in the American Academy of Arts and Letters. Receives lifetime achievement award from the Anisfield-Wolf Book Awards "for important contributions to our understanding of racism and our appreciation of the rich diversity of human cultures." *Conversations with Albert Murray*, a collection of new and selected interviews edited by Roberta S. Maguire, published by the University Press of Mississippi. Delivers lecture in "Eye of the Beholder" series at the Isabella Stewart Gardner Museum in Boston. Receives honorary doctorate from Hamilton College, alma mater of his Tuskegee mentor Morteza Drexel Sprague. Speaks at Vassar and at Yale. Reads from his fiction at the Unterberg Poetry Center of the 92nd Street Y with John Edgar Wideman. Reads at twenty-fourth annual Faulkner and Yoknapatawpha Conference at the University of Mississippi. Appears on cover of *The New York Times Magazine* for March 9 alongside George Plimpton, Geoffrey Beene, Ed Koch, Allen Ginsberg, Cynthia Ozick, Eartha Kitt, Brooke Astor, Uta Hagen, and others under the headline "Funny, We Don't Feel Old."

1998   Participates in tribute to Ellison at the 92nd Street Y along with Saul Bellow, James Alan McPherson, John F. Callahan, and R. W. B. Lewis. Elected to membership in the American Academy of Arts and Sciences. Serves on literature awards committee of the American Academy of Arts and Letters with William Weaver, Charles Simic, Robert Stone, Reynolds Price, Anne Tyler, and Anthony Hecht. Receives inaugural Harper Lee Award from Alabama Writers' Forum. *Train Whistle Guitar* is reprinted by Vintage. Two lectures from the 1980s appear in Robert G. O'Meally's compendious reader *The Jazz Cadence of American Culture* from Columbia University Press.

1999   Receives honorary doctorate from Tuskegee University (formerly Tuskegee Institute), to which he and Mozelle have maintained many connections over the past six decades. On June 18 participates in reading from Ellison's posthumous novel *Juneteenth* along with Toni Morrison and Peter Matthiessen at Barnes & Noble bookstore on Seventeenth Street in Manhattan. Speaks at Ellison symposium at CUNY Graduate Center at the invitation of Morris Dickstein. Jazz at Lincoln Center staff presents him with an enormous birthday card thanking him for being its "resident scholar and guru of the blues." Presents lectures at Iowa Writers' Workshop at the invitation of James Alan McPherson. Italian translation of *Stomping the Blues* published by Cooperativa Libraria Universitaria Editrice Bologna.

2000   *Trading Twelves: The Selected Letters of Ralph Ellison and Albert Murray* published by Modern Library. Receives honorary doctorate from Stony Brook University, Long Island, New York. Good friends around this time include Paul Resika, Bernard Holland, Matt and Phyllis Clark, Sidney and Dr. Avodah Offit, and John Hollander and Natalie Charkow. Favorite restaurants include Daniel and Bistro du Nord. Delivers keynote address to Ralph Ellison–Albert Murray Symposium at Dallas Institute of Humanities and Culture.

2001   Appears in Ken Burns's documentary *Jazz* and in the University of Alabama/Alabama Public Television's *Coat of Many Colors: A Tapestry of Alabama Artists*. Speaks at University of North Carolina–Chapel Hill in February. In March receives Clarence Cason Award from the School of Journalism at the University of Alabama–Tuscaloosa. Paul Devlin, an undergraduate at St. John's University in Queens, New York, sends letter to Murray expressing interest in his work. Murray and Devlin meet on March 28, beginning what will become a close friendship. (Devlin will quickly become the latest of Murray's many intellectual apprentices, as well as his chauffeur and all-around assistant.) In May buys diamond and platinum ring for Mozelle from Tiffany & Co., a gift for their sixtieth wedding anniversary. On 9/11 Mozelle is in Rhode Island visiting friends as the attacks on New York and Washington unfold. (Murray is especially shocked by the attack on the Pentagon, calling it unthinkable from the perspective of a retired officer.) Appears in "Giants of Jazz" photo shoot in

October issue of *Talk* magazine, alongside several musical legends and up-and-coming performers. *Talk* feature also includes a philosophical statement by Murray in response to 9/11. Pantheon publishes two new books in November: a volume of new and previously uncollected essays, *From the Briarpatch File*, and a collection of poems, *Conjugations and Reiterations*. Real estate developer Jack Rudin throws grand book party for Murray at the Four Seasons restaurant in the Seagram Building in Manhattan on December 5, with performance by Wynton Marsalis.

2002   Participates in Mobile's tricentennial celebration. Attends exhibition opening for painter Richard Mayhew in New York and renews old friendship with him. Maintains demanding schedule of working on fourth and final Scooter novel and judging student essays for Jazz at Lincoln Center's "Essentially Ellington" band competition. *Good Morning Blues* is reprinted by Da Capo with a new introduction by Dan Morgenstern.

2003   Receives award for literary achievement from the Alabama Council on the Arts in Montgomery in May. Visits Tuskegee for the last time. Loans one of several works he owns by Romare Bearden, the 1985 monotype *Celebrations: Trumpet Spot, Wynton*, to the National Gallery of Art's major retrospective traveling exhibition *The Art of Romare Bearden*, and attends the show's opening in Washington in September. Speaks at St. John's University on September 30. It will be his last lecture at a college or university.

2004   Attends numerous events throughout the fall celebrating the opening of the new home for Jazz at Lincoln Center in the Time Warner Center at Columbus Circle. Attends black-tie gala at Columbia University for Basie's centennial. *The Art of Romare Bearden* travels to the Whitney in New York and Murray appears on a panel to mark the exhibition's opening on October 14. "Jazz: Notes Toward a Definition" published in the *New Republic* in October. It is the last piece of his nonfiction published during his lifetime. Attends book party for Dan Morgenstern's *Living with Jazz: A Reader* at Rutgers–Newark in November. With novel *The Magic Keys* delivered to Pantheon, begins to imagine a work focusing on several minor characters in the Scooter saga.

2005   Spends long afternoon in the Bearden retrospective at the Whitney in January. Excerpt from *Train Whistle Guitar* centering on Jack Johnson is read in Ken Burns's documentary on the boxer, *Unforgivable Blackness*. Interviewed on Bearden at the Metropolitan Museum of Art in February. Falls from chair at home on May 15 or 16 and injures his head, possibly sustaining a concussion. Refuses to go to the hospital, citing several important events on his calendar. *The Magic Keys* published on May 17 to generally warm reviews. Extraordinarily heavy traffic the following evening delays his arrival for Q&A with John Edgar Wideman at New York's Housing Works Bookstore, but even after an hour's wait the capacity crowd does not thin out. Private publication party held in the rare book room at the Strand Bookstore on May 19, with performance by a combo featuring Wycliffe Gordon, Kengo Nakamura, and Aaron Diehl, followed by a public Q&A and book signing. Pleased by review of new novel in the May issue of *Harper's*, in which John Leonard calls it "less kiss-kiss bang-bang . . . than elegy, reverie, memory book, and musical score, as well as thank-you note to the entire sustaining community of black America." (Leonard describes the Manhattan sections, which include an *a clef* rendering of Ralph Ellison, as "the creation myth of the postwar black intelligentsia.") By mid-June it becomes almost impossible for Murray to stand up without assistance. For past few years he has been able to walk short distances but has used a wheelchair for excursions in public places such as airports, museums, and Lincoln Center. Severe back pain becomes worse. Begins to lose control of legs in late June. In July, at Mozelle's insistence, is admitted to Lenox Hill Hospital in Manhattan for battery of tests; remains in hospital through late August. Upon discharge is attended by nurses twenty-four hours a day and will be for the rest of his life. Makes rebound toward the end of the year, regaining energy and liveliness missing since his fall in May. Reads newspapers every morning at kitchen table. Assigns power of attorney and executorship of his estate to Lewis P. Jones III, his good friend since the *Harvard Advocate* symposium of 1973. (Jones will oversee the Murray family's personal affairs and finances as their attorney-in-fact and executor.)

2006   Enjoys cheerful, crowded ninetieth-birthday party at his apartment on afternoon of May 12, and receives numerous visitors over the course of birthday weekend. Encourages

Paul Devlin to listen to his 1977–85 interviews with Jo Jones to see if they might be turned into a book.

2007 Awarded W. E. B. Du Bois Medal from Du Bois Institute at Harvard University. Henry Louis Gates Jr. bestows medal at a packed-house ceremony in Murray's apartment on afternoon of June 3. In hospital again from mid-December through January 2008.

2008 In January Auburn University hosts "Albert Murray and the Aesthetic Imagination of a Nation," the first symposium on his work alone. Italian translation of *Good Morning Blues* published by Minimum Fax.

2009 In final public appearance (and his first since 2005), receives Ed Bradley Award for Leadership from Jazz at Lincoln Center at concert portion of its fall gala in November. Receives standing ovation from sold-out concert audience. His hearing, which has been worsening for years, is now almost completely gone. Visitors must talk into a microphone attached to a headset, speak almost at a shout, or write questions and comments on paper to be understood.

2010 Photographed by Jake Chessum for photo essay "Nine Over 90" in September 26 issue of *New York* magazine. Fellow nonagenarians profiled in the essay include Robert Morgenthau, Carmen Herrera, Elliott Carter, George Avakian, Ruth Gruber, Andy Rooney, Zelda Kaplan, and Hugh Carey. Enjoys the attention and commotion of the elaborate photo shoot in his apartment. Papers from the Auburn symposium, along with other articles and interviews, published as a book by the University of Alabama Press in June.

2011 Commemorates seventieth wedding anniversary with a small party at home. *Rifftide: The Life and Opinions of Papa Jo Jones*, as told to Albert Murray, is published by University of Minnesota Press in September. (The book, edited by Paul Devlin, is well-received: in the *New York Times Book Review*, Colin Fleming writes that it is "the kind of book that delights jazz fans: the straight-talking, defiantly espousing firsthand record. Anyone interested in authenticity of voice is going to be on the verge of fist-pumping the air throughout, or else exclaiming, 'You tell it like it is, baby,' as if partaking in a call-and-response with the book.") In October becomes Director Emeritus of

Jazz at Lincoln Center. The board's citation honors him as "Jazz at Lincoln Center's guiding spirit, shaping its values with the lessons of jazz and providing the pedagogical foundation for all its programs." Continues to receive visitors, but decline is noticeable. Talks of Mobile often. Mozelle, too, begins to need around-the-clock nursing care.

2012   Selection of five works from Murray's art collection (three by Bearden, two by Norman Lewis) exhibited at D.C. Moore Gallery in New York; the show, with wall text by Paul Devlin, runs from January 6 through February 4. In June receives lifetime achievement award from the Jazz Journalists Association.

2013   Strength and energy, declining for some time, fade rapidly in the late spring. Loses what had been a handshake with a vise-like grip. Eats less and less, and then stops completely for a period in May. Makes modest rebound through June and July, but stops eating again in August. Dies in his sleep at home on the evening of August 18, at age of ninety-seven. Cremated. He is survived by Mozelle, his wife of seventy-two years, and by their daughter, Michele, now sixty-nine. (Mozelle will die in her sleep at home on July 3, 2015.) Wynton Marsalis and Jazz at Lincoln Center host memorial service on September 13. About five hundred people attend the midday event in the Appel Room, facing Columbus Circle, with an overflow crowd of approximately one hundred watching on screens in an adjacent room. In November Henry Louis Gates Jr. delivers a tribute at the American Academy of Arts and Letters. "This was Albert Murray's century," he remarks; "we just lived in it. And as we keep on living, we will never forget what he meant to our American story or the music animating it with a soul force he taught us to hear."

Note on the Texts

This volume presents a selection from the nonfiction writings that Albert Murray published from 1964, when he was forty-eight years old, to 2004, when he was eighty-eight. It includes the texts of six books, *The Omni-Americans* (1970), *South to a Very Old Place* (1971), *The Hero and the Blues* (1973), *Stomping the Blues* (1976), *The Blue Devils of Nada* (1996), and *From the Briarpatch File* (2001). It also includes, under the rubric "Other Writings," eight pieces that Murray wrote for books and periodicals but did not collect during his lifetime.

THE OMNI-AMERICANS

In June 1962 Captain Albert Murray, diagnosed by military doctors with arteriosclerosis, voluntarily retired from the U.S. Air Force with the grade of major. Upon completing his final assignment, at Hanscom Field in Bedford, Massachusetts, he moved with his family to Harlem to start a long-deferred career as a full-time writer. A sometime college instructor in literature, Murray had received an M.A. in English from New York University in 1948 and was, in 1962, the author of "The Briarpatch," a semi-autobiographical fiction manuscript that would eventually yield the novels *Train Whistle Guitar* (1974) and *The Spyglass Tree* (1991). He had also begun a long essay on "the blues tradition in modern fiction" that ten years later would provide the basis of *The Hero and the Blues* (1973). In Harlem Murray continued working on these projects, but also, through introductions arranged by his close friend Ralph Ellison, began soliciting book-review assignments from Ellison's editorial acquaintances at *Life*, *The New Leader*, and other publications.

By early 1967 he had published a dozen or so reviews, mostly of novels by contemporary black writers or of works of social science examining black life in America. That April he was invited by Nelson W. Aldrich Jr., editor of *The Urban Review*, to write a piece on Harlem for the journal. In this and subsequent assignments from *The Urban Review*'s parent organization, a New York–based education policy institute called the Center for Urban Education (CUE), Murray began to treat at length certain ideas about urban black culture and American life that placed his book reviews in a larger intellectual and aesthetic context. "When I got into these [CUE] pieces," Murray said in an interview with Louis Edwards in 1994, "I realized I was writing on a theme, the theme of identity. [America is] a mulatto culture. . . . You can't be American unless you're part *us*, and you can't be American unless you're part *them*. . . . I knew I was writing a book. . . . It *had* to be a book. . . . I wanted to deal with the richest possible context . . . all these other things which I was dealing with at the time—jazz, literature, style."

By 1968 Murray was pitching a proposal for a volume of articles and reviews, then called "The All-Americans," to various New York trade publishers. Later that year, two of CUE's top editors, David E. Outerbridge and Harris Dienstfrey, left CUE to start their own small book-publishing firm, and invited Murray to contribute to their list. Murray delivered the manuscript of *The Omni-Americans* to Outerbridge and Dienstfrey, New York, in the summer of 1969 and completed correcting the page proofs the following November.

Most of the pieces collected in *The Omni-Americans* had previously appeared in books and periodicals. The history of their composition and publication is given below.

Much of the essay "The Omni-Americans" was developed, at the request of Herbert Hill, labor director of the NAACP, for the unrealized volume "Revolt of the Powerless: The Negro in the North," a collection of original essays that Hill, under contract with Random House, commissioned from more than a dozen black writers from 1963 to 1969. An abridged version of the essay first appeared, as "The Omni-Americans," in *The Urban Review* 3.6 (June 1969), 38–45.

"Image and Unlikeness in Harlem" was commissioned by *The Urban Review* to accompany a suite of contemporary black-and-white photographs by Fred W. McDarrah. The text and photographs were published, as "Image and Likeness in Harlem," in *The Urban Review* 2.2 (June 1967), 12–17.

"Oneupmanship in Colorful America" first appeared, as "Another Name for Another Game," in *The Center Forum* (a newsletter of the Center for Urban Education) 2.4 (October 5, 1967), 8.

"The Illusive Black Middle Class" grew out of research done by Murray in early 1968 for "The Subculture of Suburbia in Crisis," a multimedia education initiative of the Center for Urban Education. It first appeared in *The Omni-Americans* (1970), 86–96.

"Claude Brown's Soul for White Folks" first appeared, as "Social Science Fiction in Harlem," in *The New Leader* 49.6 (January 17, 1966), 56–59.

"Gordon Parks Out of Focus" first appeared, as "Out of Focus," in *The New Leader* 49.10 (May 9, 1966), 18–20.

"Who That Say, What Dat, Every Time Us Do That?" grew out of research done by Murray in early 1968 for "The Role of the News Media in the Urban Crisis," a multimedia education initiative of the Center for Urban Education. It first appeared in *The Omni-Americans* (1970), 113–20.

"Star-Crossed Melodrama" first appeared, as "Star-Crossed Activists," in *Book Week* 4.19 (January 15, 1967), 6, 16.

"Warren Miller and His Blackface Vaudeville" first appeared, as "White Man's Harlem: The Novels of Warren Miller," in *The New Leader* 47.25 (December 7, 1964), 28–30.

"William Styron and His Troublesome Property" first appeared, as "A Troublesome Property," in *The New Leader* 50.24 (December 4, 1967), 18–21.

"James Baldwin, Protest Fiction, and the Blues Tradition" first appeared, as "Something Different, Something More," in Herbert Hill, editor, *Anger, and Beyond: The Negro Writer in the United States* (New York: Harper & Row, [February] 1966), 112–37.

"A Short History of Black Self-Consciousness" first appeared in *The Omni-Americans* (1970), 171–80.

"The Role of the Pre-American Past" first appeared, as "African Culture and Black Identity," in *Interplay: The Magazine of International Affairs* 3.6 (February 1970), 12–14.

"Black Pride in Mobile, Alabama" first appeared, as "Whose Dues for Good Black News? (Some Notes from a Journey to Mobile)," in *The Center Forum* 3.5 (March 1969), 22–24.

"Black Studies and the Aims of Education" first appeared in *The Omni-Americans* (1970), 203–17.

The epilogue, "Situation Normal: All Fouled Up," was written in October 1966 at the invitation of William Phillips, editor of *Partisan Review*, for the quarterly's symposium feature "What's Happening in America." The questions posed by the editors of *Partisan Review* to Murray and to other public intellectuals and social critics are enumerated in the note at 185.3–5. Murray's response ran long, and despite his efforts to shorten it in page proof, it was not among the sixteen that the editors published in their Winter 1967 number. It first appeared in *The Omni-Americans* (1970), 221–27.

The Omni-Americans was published, in hardcover, by Outerbridge and Dienstfrey, New York, in March 1970. The first edition bore the subtitle "New Perspectives on Black Experience and American Culture," but reprint editions, beginning with the Vintage Books paperback of 1983, bore Murray's preferred subtitle, "Some Alternatives to the Folklore of White Supremacy." Except for adoption of the revised subtitle, the text of the Outerbridge and Dienstfrey edition of *The Omni-Americans* is used here.

SOUTH TO A VERY OLD PLACE

In the late 1960s, through the agency of Ralph Ellison, Murray met Willie Morris, an editor who had joined *Harper's* in 1963 and had become the magazine's editor-in-chief in 1967. After accepting Murray's short story "Stonewall Jackson's Waterloo" (published in the issue for February 1969), Morris asked Murray to revisit the scene of his Southern childhood and to record his impressions for the ongoing *Harper's* series "Going Home in America."

Morris's original idea was that Murray, an Alabama native who lived in Harlem, would return to his old neighborhood in Mobile to see how things had (and had not) changed in the forty-odd years since he was a boy there. But Murray was interested in writing something more than just a personal reminiscence: he asked to revisit Mobile—as well his alma mater, Tuskegee Institute—and record what he saw and heard there within the context of the aesthetic he had developed in *The Omni-Americans*. He also wanted to open up his personal story to include critical commentary on the "new" desegregated South solicited during personal visits with certain contemporary Southern writers—novelists, historians, and newspaper journalists—in Greensboro, Atlanta, New Orleans, Greenville, and Memphis, and at Yale University. Murray, with Morris's permission, pursued his assignment "not as a reporter as such and even less as an ultra gung-ho black black spokesman but rather as a Remus-derived, book-oriented downhome boy."

In March 1971, while Murray was preparing the final version of his sixty-four-thousand-word article, Willie Morris was fired from *Harper's*, the "Going Home in America" series was suspended, and Murray's story was canceled by the publishers. By that time, however, Joyce Johnson, a senior editor at McGraw-Hill Book Company and an acquaintance of Murray's since 1969, had acquired the rights for publication in book form.

South to a Very Old Place was published, in hardcover, by McGraw-Hill, New York, in November 1971. When, in 1995, the book was republished, in hardcover, in Random House's Modern Library, Murray made a single change in the text: at 200.5, he substituted "ellington-conjugated" for "ellington-orchestrated." Also, in his personal copy of the first McGraw-Hill edition Murray noted several errors in his transcription and formatting of Langston Hughes's poem "Youth," errors that persisted in all printings during Murray's lifetime but that are here corrected on page 221. Except for adoption of these changes, the text of the McGraw-Hill edition of *South to a Very Old Place* is used here.

In early February 1972, Murray received a letter from J. Donald Crowley, a professor of American literature at the University of Missouri–Columbia, inviting him to be the university's ninth Paul Anthony Brick Lecturer. Crowley, the chairman of that year's Brick Lecturer Selection Committee, explained that the lectureship, established in 1960, had been made possible by a bequest from a Missouri-based philanthropist to help the university foster a "science of ethics." He also explained that, according to terms of the bequest, each Brick Lecturer was charged to define the *science of ethics* for a general audience and to define it broadly, "including ethics not merely in the technical and philosophical sense but also in its relations to literature, society, religion, and other phases of contemporary culture." Crowley then elaborated on the terms of the university's offer, namely that (1) three roughly hour-long lectures were to be delivered on campus in the fall of 1972, and (2) publication of the lectures (should both Murray and the university find it desirable) was to follow in the next year, under the auspices of the University of Missouri Press. Murray, who was then again working on his essay on "the blues tradition in modern fiction," accepted Crowley's invitation and immediately began adapting his material to the requirements of a three-part lecture series.

The text of *The Hero and the Blues* is based on the Paul Anthony Brick Lectures that Murray delivered at the University of Missouri–Columbia on October 7, 8, and 9, 1972. Thomas Lloyd, director of the University of Missouri Press, attended the lectures and secured the book rights later the same month. Murray's manuscript was edited for publication by Carolyn F. Dickinson, an associate professor of English at the university as well as an editor for the press.

The Hero and the Blues was published, in hardcover, by the University of Missouri Press, Columbia, in December 1973. (An excerpt from "The Dynamics of Heroic Action" had appeared before publication as "The Literary Implications of the Blues: The Hero as Improviser," in *Quadrant* [Sydney, Australia] 16.6 ["USA 1973" number, November–December 1972], 34–38. An excerpt from "The Blues and the Fable in the Flesh" had also appeared, as "Riffing and the Creative Process," in *American Journal* 1.1 [December 1, 1972], 29–32.) Murray did not revise the text for reprint editions. The text of the University of Missouri Press edition of *The Hero and the Blues* is used here.

STOMPING THE BLUES

Following the critical success of *South to a Very Old Place* (which was a finalist for the 1972 National Book Award in the Arts and Letters category), McGraw-Hill offered Murray a two-book contract for his novel *Train Whistle Guitar* (1974) and an "Untitled Book on Africa." By 1974 he had abandoned the notion of an African project for a work he called "The Blues as Background." The manuscript, ultimately titled *Stomping the Blues*, was accepted by McGraw-Hill in early spring of 1975.

McGraw-Hill, concerned that an essay-length meditation on "the blues as such and the blues as art" would not find a wide general audience, convinced Murray that the book would benefit from an ambitious art program, both to lend visual interest to the text and to double the book's page count. Murray's editor, Joyce Johnson, enlisted Harris Lewine (b. 1929), a former art director of McGraw-Hill, to research and design a visual component for *Stomping the Blues*. Lewine was well-known in the world of jazz and blues as the art director of several distinguished music-related art books and scores of record-album sleeves and multidisc packages. Lewine's art program for *Stomping the Blues* consisted of some 150 jazz photographs and again as many facsimiles of concert posters, sheet-music covers, and labels from vintage 78s. The selection of imagery, each item of which was approved by Murray, complemented but was not keyed to Murray's text. All of the images, arranged to fit full-page units or double-page spreads, were printed in black and white, and most of the units were accompanied by captions by Murray, written to fit Lewine's design specifications, down to exact character counts. None of the images are reproduced here, but certain of Murray's captions are, when apposite, included among the notes on pages 995 to 999.

Stomping the Blues, by Albert Murray—"Produced and Art Directed by Harris Lewine"—was published, in hardcover, by McGraw-Hill, New York, in October 1976. The first printing was issued with an errata slip correcting an editorial error in chapter 9 (the second paragraph on page 484 of the present volume, beginning with the words "Take *One O'Clock Jump*"). When the book was printed in 1978 by Quartet Books (London) from the original McGraw-Hill film, Murray took the opportunity to patch the paragraph, using a wording somewhat different from that on the McGraw-Hill errata slip. The text of the first edition of *Stomping the Blues* is used here, but with the adoption of the revised paragraph from the Quartet printing mentioned above. In addition, the editors have inserted, on pages 509 and 511, two section breaks that Murray marked in his personal copy of the book. Due to design and space limitations, these section breaks could not be accommodated in the McGraw-Hill printing.

THE BLUE DEVILS OF NADA

In the fifteen years that followed *Stomping the Blues*, Murray focused on cowriting the memoirs of pianist-composer-bandleader Count Basie (*Good Morning Blues*, 1986) and on completing his second novel (*The Spyglass Tree*, 1991). These years were also rich in short-term teaching assignments and in invitations to write and to speak about music, art, and literature. By the end of 1994 Murray had begun selecting and revising the lectures, speeches, reviews, and short nonfiction pieces he had written since 1970 for his first such collection since *The Omni-Americans*. In the early months of 1995 Murray submitted *The Blue Devils of Nada* to Erroll McDonald, his editor at Random House and Pantheon Books since *Good Morning Blues*.

Most of the pieces collected in *The Blue Devils of Nada* had previously appeared in books and periodicals. The history of their composition and publication is given below.

The Prologue first appeared, as "Booklore Interview: Albert Murray Talks the Blues, by Jason Berry," in *Southern Booklore: A Quarterly Book Review* 1.2 (Spring 1977), 12–13.

"Regional Particulars and Universal Implications" is based on a paper presented at the symposium "The American South: Distinctiveness and Its Limits" at the University of Alabama, Tuscaloosa, on April 16, 1983. It first appeared, as "Regional Particulars and Universal Statement in Southern Writing," in *Callaloo* 2.1 (Winter 1989), 3–6.

"Duke Ellington Vamping Till Ready" first appeared, as "Duke Ellington Vamps 'Til Ready," in *The Village Voice* 21.26 (June 28, 1976), 66–67.

"Comping for Count Basie" is based on "Comping for Count Basie: The Orchestration of *Good Morning Blues*," a lecture delivered at the Peter Rushton Seminars in Modern Literature, University of Virginia, Charlottesville, on March 18, 1987. It first appeared in Werner Sollors, editor, *The Invention of Ethnicity* (New York & Oxford: Oxford University Press, [March] 1989), 209–25.

"The Twentieth-Century American Herald" first appeared, as "The Armstrong Continuum," in the sixteen-page program for the concert-and-lecture series *The Armstrong Continuum: The American Genius of Twentieth-Century Music* (New York: Jazz at Lincoln Center, December 14–19, 1994), 9–13.

"The Vernacular Imperative" is based on Murray's keynote address for the symposium "The Ellington Legacy at the Smithsonian," delivered at the National Museum of American History, Smithsonian Institution, Washington, D.C., on April 27, 1989. The essay first appeared, as "The Vernacular Imperative: Duke Ellington's Place in the National Pantheon," in *Callaloo* 14.4 (Autumn 1991), 771–75.

"Storiella Americana as She Is Swyung; or, The Blues as Representative Anecdote" is based on "Duke Ellington and the Culture of Washington, D.C.," the opening-night address at the annual meeting of the Organization of American Historians, Washington Hilton Hotel, Washington, D.C., on March 22, 1990. It first appeared, as "Storiella Americana as She Is Swyung: Duke Ellington, the Culture of Washington, D.C., and the Blues as Representative Anecdote," in *Conjunctions* 16 (Spring 1991), 209–19.

"Armstrong and Ellington Stomping the Blues in Paris" was written in 1980 as the text for a Franco-American book project, later abandoned, that Murray sometimes called "Paris Blues," sometimes "Jazz Suite." The project, commissioned by the Société Française de Promotion Artistique, Paris, was occasioned by the twentieth anniversary of Martin Ritt's black-and-white United Artists feature *Paris Blues* (1961), for which Duke Ellington and Billy Strayhorn wrote the score and in which Louis Armstrong played a supporting dramatic role. The book was to have been illustrated with on-the-set black-and-white photographs by the film's coproducer Sam Shaw, and with drawings, etchings, and fourteen color collages by Romare Bearden based on and incorporating imagery from Shaw's photographs. Murray's text was to have been published both in English and in French translation. (Sample page spreads from the book, based on Bearden's layouts, were created by Florio Design, New York, for *Paris Blues Revisited: Romare Bearden, Albert Murray, Sam Shaw*, an exhibition organized by Robert G. O'Meally, C. Daniel Dawson, and Diedra Harris-Kelley, on view in the Peter Jay Sharp Arcade of Frederick P. Rose Hall at Jazz at Lincoln Center, New York, from September 24, 2011, to July 27, 2012.) "Armstrong and Ellington Stomping the Blues in Paris" first appeared in *The Blue Devils of Nada* (1996), 97–113.

"Bearden Plays Bearden" first appeared, as "The Visual Equivalent of the Blues," in *Romare Bearden: 1970–1980*, the catalogue of an exhibition, organized by Jerald L. Melberg and Milton J. Bloch, on view at the Mint Museum, Charlotte, North Carolina, October 12, 1980–August 9, 1981 (Charlotte: Mint Museum, 1980), 17–28.

Much of the material in "Ernest Hemingway Swinging the Blues and Taking Nothing" was developed for, but not used in, the lectures that make up *The Hero and the Blues* (1973). Part of section V first appeared, in somewhat different form, as "The Storyteller as Blues Singer," in *American Journal* 1.5 (April 10, 1973), 14–17. The complete essay first appeared in *The Blue Devils of Nada* (1996), 143–226.

The Blue Devils of Nada: A Contemporary American Approach to Aesthetic Statement was published, in hardcover, by Pantheon Books, New York, in February 1996, in tandem with Murray's third novel, *The Seven League Boots*. The text of the Pantheon edition is used here.

FROM THE BRIARPATCH FILE

In early 2001, at the age of eighty-four, Murray sent Erroll McDonald his final collection of short nonfiction pieces. *From the Briarpatch File* contained speeches, essays, and occasional writings published since 1995 as well as, under the heading "Book Reviews," several previously uncollected pieces from the 1960s and '70s. It also contained two significant interviews published too late for inclusion in Roberta S. Maguire's volume *Conversations with Albert Murray* (Jackson: University Press of Mississippi, 1997).

Most of the pieces collected in *From the Briarpatch File* had previously appeared in books and periodicals. The history of their composition and publication is given below.

"Antagonistic Cooperation in Alabama" is based on remarks made upon receiving the Harper Lee Award from the Alabama Writers' Forum, at Alabama Southern Community College, Monroeville, Alabama, on May 29, 1998. It first appeared, as "Albert Murray's Remarks Upon Receiving the Harper Lee Award," in *First Draft: The Journal of the Alabama Writers' Forum* 5.2 (Summer 1998), 8–9.

"Context and Definition" is based on remarks made upon receiving the Clarence Cason Writing Award from the Department of Journalism at the University of Alabama, Tuscaloosa, on March 15, 2001. (As Murray states in the footnote on page 722, the opening paragraphs are adapted from remarks made upon receiving the Langston Hughes Medal from the City College of New York in November 1997.) It first appeared, as "The 'Alabama Jack Rabbit' Comes Home," in *The Tuscaloosa News* 183.84 (March 25, 2001), 8.

"Academic Lead Sheet" is based on a speech delivered at the Honors Convocation of the graduating class of Howard University, Washington, D.C., on January 20, 1978. It first appeared in *From the Briarpatch File* (2001), 14–23.

"Art as Such" is based on the keynote address delivered at the Statewide Arts Conference of the Alabama State Council on the Arts, Perdido Beach, Alabama, on February 17, 1994. It first appeared in *Alabama Arts* 13.1 (Spring 1994), 20–22.

"Riffing at Mrs. Jack's Place" is based on an "Eye of the Beholder" lecture delivered at the Isabella Stewart Gardner Museum, Fenway

Court, Boston, Massachusetts, on March 13, 1997. It first appeared in *From the Briarpatch File* (2001), 34–40.

"Made in America: The Achievement of Duke Ellington" first appeared, as "Ellington Hits 100," in *The Nation* 268.7 (February 4, 1999), 22–29.

"Old Duke and Me" first appeared, as an untitled contribution to a symposium feature, edited by Gary Giddins, called "Rockin' in Rhythm: Duke Ellington at 100," in *The Village Voice* 44.23 (June 15, 1999), 105.

"Me and Old Uncle Billy and the American Mythosphere" is based on a paper delivered at "Faulkner at 100," the twenty-fourth annual Faulkner and Yoknapatawpha Conference, at the University of Mississippi, Oxford, on July 29, 1997. It first appeared in Donald M. Kartiganer and Ann J. Abadie, editors, *Faulkner at 100: Retrospect and Prospect* (Jackson: University Press of Mississippi, [March] 2000), 238–43.

"Manhattan in the Twenties" first appeared, as "High-Stepping to an Uptown Beat," in "Then & Now: NYC 100" (a special section commemorating the centenary of the five-borough city), *The New York Times* 148.51,048 (January 25, 1998), Section TN, 10.

"The HNIC Who He" first appeared, as "The Illusive Black Image," in *Chicago Sun-Times Book Week* 1.10 (November 26, 1967), 4, 10.

"Soul Brothers Abroad" first appeared, as "Soul Brother Abroad," in *Book World* 2.20 (May 19, 1968), 10–11.

"Freedom Bound U.S.A." was written in the winter or spring of 1965, perhaps for *The New Leader*, but was not published. It first appeared in *From the Briarpatch File* (2001), 88–96.

"The Good Old Boys Down Yonder" first appeared, as "The Good Old Boys," in *The New York Times Book Review* 79.38 (September 22, 1974), 372, 374.

"The 'Reconstruction' of Robert Penn Warren" first appeared, as "Asking Questions, Searching Souls," in *The New Leader* 48.13 (June 21, 1965), 25–27.

"Louis Armstrong in His Own Words" first appeared, as "Jazz Lips," in *The New Republic* 222.21 (November 22, 1999), 29–35. In two passages here (at 801.13 [was planned, but it] and at 810.31 [provide]), the editors have restored matter from the *New Republic* version dropped from the first book version of the text.

"The Blue Steel, Rawhide, Patent Leather Implications of Fairy Tales" first appeared, as "'The Bluesteel, Rawhide, Patent-Leather Implications of Fairy Tales': A Conversation with Albert Murray, by Sanford Pinsker," in *The Georgia Review* 51.2 (Summer 1997), 204–21.

"An All-Purpose, All-American Literary Intellectual" first appeared, as "'An All-Purpose, All-American Literary Intellectual': An Interview with Albert Murray, by Charles H. Rowell," in *Callaloo* 20.2 (Spring 1997), 399–414.

From the Briarpatch File: On Context, Procedure, and American Identity was published, in hardcover, by Pantheon Books, New York, in November 2001, in tandem with Murray's collection of poetry, *Conjugation and Reiterations*. (A feature called "From *From the Briarpatch File*—Memos for a Memoir," comprising the complete texts of "Me and Old Duke" and "Me and Old Uncle Billy and the American Mythosphere," appeared in *Callaloo* 24.4 [Fall 2001], 1127–34, upon the book's publication.) Except as noted above, the text of the Pantheon edition is used here.

OTHER WRITINGS

Collected under the rubric "Other Writings" are eight pieces that Murray wrote for books and periodicals between 1964 and 2004 but did not collect during his lifetime.

"'The Problem' Is Not Just Black and White," Murray's first published nonfiction piece, appeared in *Life* 57.1 (July 3, 1964), 8, 17, 19. The text from *Life* is used here, but with paragraphing that follows Murray's fair-copy typescript of the piece, archived by the author as part of the as yet unprocessed "Albert Murray Papers: 1948–1996," housed at Houghton Library for the Hutchins Center for African and African American Research, Harvard University.

"U.S. Negroes and U.S. Jews: No Cause for Alarm" was commissioned by Kirkpatrick Sale of *The New York Times Magazine* in January or February 1966. The piece was not accepted for publication, and appears here for the first time. The source of the text is an undated, seventeen-page fair-copy typescript, titled "U.S. Negroes Pick and Choose Among U.S. Jews; They're Not Anti-Semitic," from Murray's personal files. It appears here, with the permission of Murray's executor, Lewis P. Jones III, under a title adapted by the editors from Murray's working draft of the same piece.

"'Soul': Thirty-two Meanings Not in Your Dictionary" first appeared in *Book World* 2.25 (June 23, 1968), 6. The text from *Book World* is used here, but with paragraphing that follows Murray's autograph manuscript of the piece, archived by the author as part of the as yet unprocessed "Albert Murray Papers: 1948–1996," housed at Houghton Library for the Hutchins Center for African and African American Research, Harvard University.

"'Stone': Definition and Usage" first appeared, as "Defining 'Stone,'" in *Book World* 3.16 (April 20, 1969), 6. The text from *Book World* is used here, under a title supplied by the editors.

"Two Nations? Only Two?" first appeared, as an untitled contribution to a symposium feature called "How Have We Changed? 1954–1994," in *American Heritage* 45.8 (fortieth-anniversary number, December 1994), 74. The text from *American Heritage* is used here, under a title supplied by the editors.

"Bearden in Theory and Ritual" first appeared, as "Bearden in Theory and Ritual: A Conversation with Albert Murray, by Gail Gelburd," in *Romare Bearden in Black-and-White: Photomontage Projections 1964*, the catalogue of an exhibition, organized by Gail Gelburd and Thelma Golden, on view at the Whitney Museum of American Art, New York, January 16–March 20, 1997 (New York: Whitney Museum/Harry N. Abrams, 1997), 53–60. The text from *Romare Bearden in Black-and-White* is used here.

"Three Omni-American Artists" first appeared as the untitled foreword to William Zinsser, *Mitchell & Ruff: An American Profile in Jazz* (Philadelphia: Paul Dry Books, 2000), vii–xi. (*Mitchell & Ruff* is the second, revised edition of Zinsser's *Willie & Dwike: An American Profile*, published by Harper & Row in 1984.) The foreword was reprinted, under its present title, in Paul Devlin, editor, *Murray Talks Music: Albert Murray on Jazz and Blues* (Minneapolis: University of Minnesota Press, 2016), 134–37. The text from *Murray Talks Music* is used here.

"Jazz: Notes Toward a Definition" was written to commemorate the opening of Frederick P. Rose Hall, Jazz at Lincoln Center's performance facility in the Time Warner Center, at Broadway and Sixtieth Street, New York, on October 18, 2004. Murray began work on the essay in January 2003 and read from an early draft as part of a talk at St. John's University in Queens, New York, on September 30, 2003. (A transcript of that talk appears in *Murray Talks Music*, 96–104.) Murray had hoped to place the essay, complemented by a photo-essay on the new JALC facilities, in *The New York Times Magazine*, but instead it appeared, without photographs and with reference to Lincoln Center omitted, in *The New Republic* 231.16 (October 18, 2004), 25–28. It was collected, with the sentence about Lincoln Center restored, in Paul Devlin, editor, *Murray Talks Music* (2016), 219–26. The text from *Murray Talks Music* is used here.

This volume presents the texts of the original printings chosen for inclusion but does not attempt to reproduce nontextual features of their typographical design. The texts are presented without change, except for the correction of typographical errors. Spelling, punctuation, and capitalization are often expressive features and are not altered, even when inconsistent or irregular. Errors in quoted material are not corrected, since they can reflect how Murray understood or read the quotations. The following is a list of typographical errors corrected, cited by page and line number: 8.35, mislead; 12.25, consciousness and; 17.2, *unim*; 27.7, *Change* is; 31.30, Steppin'; 41.5, sems; 41.8, desparately; 44.3, possibilities; 44.4–5, incidentaly; 44.20, clubs,; 47.14, exicted; 65.28, as Moynihan; 66.40, anti-sceptic; 76.8, wih the; 78.25, ante-bellem; 84.1, *Ramparts*'; 84.24, in not; 85.18, Mohammad; 85.20, Leroi; 86.26, guitar!'"; 93.9, that; 94.3, Paranasi.; 98.38, Parks', life; 99.14, Matthew; 99.24, Kaufman; 101.18, high fallutin'; 102.13, phoney; 102.37, mislead; 103.1, bibliographies and; 103.4, (and; 104.8, chauffers,; 104.9, cooks),; 107.9, ladies; 109.6, wtih; 110.24, ladies; 113.34 (and *passim*), Seige; 116.40–117.1, intanglements); 117.21, 1966),; 119.22, mislead; 122.14 (and *passim*), Hard Bought; 124.40, Greenwhich; 125.2, existentalists,; 125.31, *Gentlemen's*; 126.22, erectible; 126.24, traditions As; 128.6, essay,; 132.38, koolade.; 134.9, imaginary.); 136.13, ambitions.; 136.26, muscial; 140.33, *Charley*; 143.28, *Soldier's*; 151.11, "Koko"; 151.28, generation whose; 152.3, did) is; 155.14, forceably; 156.17, Tschombe,; 158.5, were; 158.40, soulfullness; 161.14, History which; 164.9, *Malcom*; 167.19, *Yearbook*;; 168.38, *the the*; 171.13 (and *passim*), Pritchard; 171.16, folk's; 172.22–23, development and; 181.25, *Goodbye Mr.*; 182.1, mislead; 185.3, *1967,*; 185.5, *in America?*"; 186.29, effects; 186.32–33, Morganthau,; 188.20, or; 193.22, continous; 194.1, is this; 197.36, Chophouse,; 198.6, Small's; 198.6, Schomberg; 202.37, *Thompson*; 204.23, *Leaksville*,; 206.14, Morrison; 208.3, Stacey; 214.26, Frank Hirsch; 215.25, Sutpens; 217.30, Beatty; 219.4, Jesse; 227.39–40, later: *A*; 229.24, Berdichev; 239.3, POSTION; 244.9 (and *passim*), Cleighorn; 247.23, Arnoud; 248.26, *Oh*; 249.26, Zachary; 250.20 and .30, Rosamund; 251.23, Talledega; 253.32, Communisits; 256.34, *Greens*; 258.16, *viciousness was*; 259.31, *Greens Forks*; 260.10, Detroit will; 261.30, Henningburg; 262.26, music probably; 263.5, Talledega,; 263.9, Columbia) will; 263.14–15, individuality he; 266.22, Baudelarian!; 266.25, pacesetters will; 267.30, wind'; 267.40, *The Case*; 269.34–35, McCaslins) also; 269.35, Colfield; 269.35, Sutpens; 272.12, *all) every*; 272.20, *Dr DuBois*; 273.33, Millender,; 275.28, Mistinguette:; 276.9, *tattersal*; 277.30, *moon!*); 280.22, Coleman; 286.33, Blackshear; 287.23 (and *passim*), Veleena; 288.10, a MCTS; 289.18, *newsstand) not*; 295.15, Stepinfetchit; 298.8, Wednesday (or; 298.38, nickle; 301.10, now,"; 306.36, say.; 312.4, saying.; 314.7, *reason*"; 317.32, Nunn-Busch; 324.38, Ponchartrain; 325.25, enthnocentrism; 325.32, Anglo-caucasian have; 326.35, Morehead?; 327.36, Chapell; 327.37, MacCarthy:; 334.22, Dancing,"; 336.33, Jenson; 338.11, technican; 339.3, Conner; 339.25, technician,; 339.27, *Hariet*; 343.22, *last as*; 378.2, Berens,; 383.17, Altimire; 387.37 (and *passim*), Suzanne; 389.14, aesthetic; 402.28, one self; 408.32 (and *passim*), Frederick; 417.16, *existence,*; 423.13, Fountain,; 436.19–20, *Roll Em, Pete*; 436.22, *Wagnall's*; 448.11, Rushing and; 451.24, repudiate and; 460.37, Greene,; 473.19, was their; 481.35 (and *passim*), Hershel; 484.6, Greene; 491.36, Squaty; 502.19, sythesis,; 503.20, significant those; 520.20, *fiction.*; 537.14, consists; 540.15, or second; 549.21, Freddy; 549.38, Benny; 553.27, Benny; 563.28, ring; 566.30, *Egg Man.*; 568.27, *Colombo,*; 569.9, Greystone; 570.32, Halborn; 571.31, devises; 573.14, Louis; 573.27, influences; 574.35. figs.,:"; 584.12, Whitman, Mark; 584.19, that his; 584.33, audience."; 584.36, *music.*; 586.1, call, and; 587.26, Wards; 591.34, Carolynne; 593.24, on the; 594.32, Lawrence; 594.34, *In Abyssinia,*; 595.19, Lucky; 600.28, *Belle of the Beverly.*; 602.7, *Wildman*; 604.6, Lucky; 609.13–14, has tongue-in-cheek; 612.21, ACL; 617.25, evocation characters; 620.29, 1930s was; 621.2, Lucky; 621.16, Hegemin,; 621.38, Small's; 622.4–5, Charley; 622.6, Sultons; 625.9, distructions; 628.18, roll; 631.3, on a; 635.7, Japanese and; 635.34, prices) that; 636.18, Thelonius; 645.18, and-intellectualism; 646.31, side, which; 647.14, capitol; 651.29–30, *American, Midshipman*; 653.12, to Maestro"; 660.18, is difficult; 661.14, *Snowbound.*; 680.1, hard-boiled who; 681.16, Barnes Robert; 693.24, Americans; 701.5, *Spanairds,*; 703.14, no clue; 704.3, *né* Joey; 719.2, 1988, 721.14, temp; 723.14, clue; 725.28, 72-rpm; 725.39, Jellyroll; 730.19, is gong; 744.36, less that; 745.7–8, "Giogione's; 745.10, Giogiones,"; 746.28, figuratively, symbolic; 746.29, in a word poetic.; 749.4 (and *passim*), Anton; 750.32, Ruben; 750.34, Julliard; 757.6, *merit probably*; 759.14, Julliard; 764.15–16, as to; 770.4, affect; 777.30, prospective; 780.11, not stuff; 788.28, prostate; 791.31, Neiman; 792.5, Glenn; 792.19, Old; 793.7, "Whatever"; 793.8–9, Sufferidge; 793.14, Hofheintz; 796.8, soon; 797.40, Malxolm; 800.10, Akins,; 803.9, spoke, his; 804.27, *fintertips*; 808.4, 1952,; 810.20–21, Vallee, observed:; 810.31, *Chanson*, a; 811.24, L.A.,; 811.27, is memoir; 811.41, *Lucy* my; 814.3, chops!); 820.32, publishers, of; 821.16, view was; 827.11, *(1995),*; 827.31, to Look; 835.32, *on your*; 836.11, abut; 842.22, school Greenwich; 850.3, Telemachas.; 864.34, Country; 866.5, road ban; 874.23, *Mr.*; 877.38, beside; 879.6, However the; 880.31, It she; 884.30, or its; 892.30, State; 909.24–25, as say; 909.25, Prokofiev, did; 911.6, is.

Notes

In the notes below, the reference numbers denote page and line of this volume (line counts include headings). No note is made for material included in standard desk-reference books. Biblical quotations are keyed to the King James Version. Quotations from Shakespeare are keyed to G. Blakemore Evans, editor, *The Riverside Shakespeare* (Boston: Houghton Mifflin, 1974). For further biographical detail than is contained in the chronology, see Roberta S. Maguire, editor, *Conversations with Albert Murray* (Jackson: University Press of Mississippi, 1997); Albert Murray and John F. Callahan, editors, *Trading Twelves: The Selected Letters of Ralph Ellison and Albert Murray* (New York: Modern Library, 2000); and Paul Devlin, editor, *Murray Talks Music: Albert Murray on Jazz and Blues* (Minneapolis: University of Minnesota Press, 2016). The tribute volume *Albert Murray and the Aesthetic Imagination of a Nation* (Tuscaloosa: A Pebble Hill Book/University of Alabama Press, 2010), edited by Barbara A. Baker, collects critical essays, biographical articles, interviews, and reminiscence, including "King of Cats" (1996), a *New Yorker* profile by Henry Louis Gates Jr.; "An Interview with Michele Murray" (2010), by Paul Devlin and Lauren Walsh; "Albert Murray and Visual Art" (2010), by Paul Devlin; "Albert Murray and Tuskegee Institute: Art as the Measure of Place," by Caroline Gebhard (2010); "Wynton Marsalis on Albert Murray," by Roberta S. Maguire (2001); and "At the Bar and on the Avenue with My Pal Al Murray" (2010), by Sidney Offit. See also Robert G. O'Meally's Smithsonian Jazz Oral History Project interview with Murray (1994); Kurt Thometz's interview with Murray (circa 2001) for Thometz's "Private Library/The Well-Dressed Bibliophile" series at colophon.com; Brian Lamb's interview with Murray (1996) for C-SPAN's *Booknotes* program, available at booknotes.org; and David A. Taylor, "Albert Murray's Magical Youth," in *Southern Cultures* 16.2 (Summer 2010).

Grateful acknowledgment is made to Dana Chandler, Harrietta Eaton, Gary Giddins, Diedra Harris-Kelley, Ida Hay, Joyce Johnson, Kristin Jones, Lewis P. Jones III, Harris Lewine, Michele Murray, Sidney Offit, Juanita Roberts, and Melissa Stevens for their assistance on this project.

THE OMNI-AMERICANS

3.1–7 The individual stands . . . intends to feed.] From Malraux's preface to his novel *Days of Wrath* (*Le Temps du mépris*, 1935), translated from the French by Haakon M. Chevalier (New York: Random House, 1936).

7.2–3   counter-statements] See *Counter-Statement* (1931), a work of rhetorical criticism by American literary theorist Kenneth Burke (1897–1993). In his introduction to the book, which is largely an essay on taste, style, and the effectiveness of persuasive prose, Burke writes: "We have chosen to call it *Counter-Statement* solely because . . . each principle it advocates is matched by an opposite principle flourishing and triumphant today. Heresies and orthodoxies will always be changing places, but whatever the minority view happens to be at any given time, one must consider it as 'counter.' Hence the title—which will not, we hope, suggest either an eagerness for the fray or a sense of defeat."

7.36–8.1   Gilbert Murray . . . *Greek Religion*] Murray (1866–1957) was Regius Professor of Greek at Oxford University from 1908 to 1936. *The Rise of the Greek Epic* (1907) is a study of Homer and his world, and *The Five Stages of Greek Religion* (1951) the third and final edition of a work first published in 1912.

8.31–32   *Report of the National Advisory Commission on Civil Disorders*] In July 1967, President Johnson appointed a commission (1) to examine the causes and consequences of race riots that since the summer of 1965 had erupted in several American cities, and (2) to recommend a national course of action to prevent further race riots. The commission, led by Illinois governor Otto Kerner, reported its findings in February 1968. They concluded that the nation was "moving toward two societies, one black, one white—separate and unequal," and warned that unless conditions were remedied, the country faced a "system of 'apartheid'" in most of its major cities.

10.16   dramatic sense of life] Murray alludes here to Dramatism, a poetic theory of "what people are doing and why they are doing it" developed by Kenneth Burke (see note 7.2–3) in his book *A Grammar of Motives* (1945). For Murray's discussion of Dramatism as a counter-statement to social science, see page 245 of the present volume.

12.7–8   folklore of white supremacy . . . fakelore of black pathology] Murray's terminology was influenced by that of American historian Marshall W. Fishwick (1923–2006), especially as used in the article "Folklore, Fakelore, and Poplore" (*Saturday Review*, August 26, 1967).

13.22   Professor "Clinkscales"] In his autobiography *Music Is My Mistress* (1973), Duke Ellington named one "Mrs. Clinkscales" as the best of his childhood piano teachers.

17.3   the prelude to *Joseph*] "The Descent into Hell" ("*Höllenfahrt*"), in *The Tales of Jacob* (*Die Geschichten Jakobs*, 1933), book one of the tetralogy *Joseph and His Brothers* (*Joseph und seine Brüder*, 1933–43), by Thomas Mann. Murray's quotations are from the English translation by H. T. Lowe Porter (New York: Knopf, 1934).

17.20–21   Lord Raglan . . . *The Hero*] Richard FitzRoy Somerset, Fourth Baron Raglan (1885–1964), a British soldier and writer, was the author of *The*

Hero (1936), a study in comparative literature and anthropology that cata-
logued themes and motifs of hero tales across cultures and centuries.

18.27 Constance Rourke] Writer and educator Constance Rourke (1885–
1941), a native of Ohio, was a pioneer in the fields of American studies, American folk art, and American popular culture. Her books include *American
Humor: A Study of the National Character* (1931) and the posthumous collection *The Roots of American Culture and Other Essays* (1942), edited by Van
Wyck Brooks. These two works were touchstones for Murray and are alluded
to throughout his nonfiction.

19.16–18 *homo Americanus . . . homo Europaeus*] Paul Valéry's essay
"Homo Europaeus" was published, in France, in 1922. In a 2003 interview
with Paul Devlin collected in *Murray Talks Music* (2016), Murray remarked
that "*The Omni-Americans* . . . had two definitive sources. During the war
I read a book called *The Heart of Europe* [Klaus Mann, ed., New York: L. B.
Fischer, 1943]. And in that anthology there was an essay by Paul Valéry called
'Homo Europaeus.' He said *Homo Europaeus* was Greek logic, Roman admin-
istration and law, and Judeo-Christian morality. A few years later I came across
a book by Constance Rourke, who is one of my patron saints. It was called
American Humor but it could have been called *Homo Americanus . . .*"

20.24–26 the arrival of a Dutch ship . . . in 1619] According to John Rolfe,
the secretary and recorder-general of Virginia (1614–19), the first Africans to
be sold into slavery in America were traded at the end of August 1619, when
"a Dutch man of Warr . . . arrived at Point-Comfort [Hampton, Virginia]
[with] 20 and odd Negroes." See Susan Myra Kingsbury, ed., *Records of the
Virginia Company, 1606–1626* (1909).

20.38–21.3 "The whites," . . . coastal trading centers."] See Benjamin
Quarles (1904–1996), *The Negro in the Making of America* (New York: Collier, 1964).

22.6–7 "a nobler, higher spirit . . . human form."] William H. Seward
(1801–1872), U.S. secretary of state (1861–69), in a testimonial to Tubman
solicited by Sarah H. Bradford for her biography *Harriet, the Moses of Her
People* (1868).

23.4–8 "that considering the condition . . . most meritorious man in the
United States."] It was through John Eaton (1829–1906), U.S. commissioner
of education during the Civil War, that Lincoln first met Frederick Douglass,
in Washington, D.C., on August 10, 1863. Eaton, in a letter of condolence to
Douglass's widow dated February 21, 1895, wrote that the president, upon
learning of his and Douglass's friendship in July 1863, paid Douglass the compliment that Murray quotes here. Eaton's letter was printed in Helen Douglass's tribute volume *In Memoriam: Frederick Douglass* (1897).

25.11 Negro pilots of the 332nd Fighter Group] The so-called Tuskegee
Airmen, all of whom were graduates of the Army Air Force pilot training

programs at Alabama's Moton Field and Tuskegee Army Airfield from 1941 to 1945.

26.21 HARYOU-Act Program] Harlem Youth Opportunities Unlimited (HARYOU), founded in 1962 by black psychiatrist Kenneth B. Clark (1914–2005), merged with Associated Community Teams (ACT), founded in 1963 by U.S. congressman Adam Clayton Powell Jr. (see note 82.27–28), to form HARYOU-ACT in 1964. The organization, dedicated to increasing educational and employment opportunities for Harlem youth, dissolved in 1968.

27.6 *Youth in the Ghetto*] Kenneth B. Clark's 664-page report was distributed for free by HARYOU in 1964–68. Its publication was subsidized by grants from President Johnson's Committee on Juvenile Delinquency and the Office of the Mayor of New York City.

27.14–15 Brimmer . . . Davis . . . Stokes . . . Johnson] Andrew Brimmer (1926–2012), first black governor of the Federal Reserve Board (1966–74); Benjamin O. Davis Jr. (1912–2002), first black general officer in the U.S. Air Force; Carl Stokes (1927–1996), Democratic mayor of Cleveland, Ohio (1968–71); John H. Johnson (1918–2005), publisher of *The Negro Digest, Ebony*, and *Jet*.

27.17–18 antagonistic cooperation] Term coined by American sociologist William Graham Sumner (1840–1910) in his book *Folkways* (1906). Antagonistic cooperation, writes Sumner, "consists in the combination of two persons or groups to satisfy a great common interest while minor antagonisms of interest which exist between them are suppressed." Murray appropriated Sumner's term as a non-Marxist way of talking about a *thesis* and an *antithesis* that yield a desirable *synthesis*.

28.34 Moynihan Report] Report (*The Negro Family: The Case for National Action*) by then Assistant Secretary of Labor Daniel Patrick Moynihan (1927–2003), issued in January 1965 by the Labor Department's Office of Planning and Policy. Among Moynihan's more controversial statements was that life among America's lower-class urban black families is a "tangle of pathology" at the center of which is "the weakness of the Negro family": "The family structure of lower class Negroes [with its absent fathers, single mothers, and illegitimate births] is highly unstable, and in many urban areas is approaching complete breakdown. . . . The Negro community has been forced into a matriarchal structure which . . . seriously retards the progress of the group as a whole and imposes a crushing burden on the Negro male and, in consequence, on a great number of Negro women as well." Moynihan concluded: "The policy of the United States is to bring the Negro American to full and equal sharing in the responsibilities and rewards of citizenship. To this end, the programs of the Federal government bearing on this objective shall be designed to have the effect . . . of enhancing the stability and resources of the Negro American family."

34.36 Organization Man] *The Organization Man*, by sociologist William

H. Whyte (New York: Simon & Schuster, 1956), was a best-selling analysis of postwar American business corporations, in which, the author argued, co-operation within a hierarchical organization was more prized than individual initiative and creativity.

35.1–2 Jack Lemmon and Tony Randall] Lemmon (1925–2001) and Randall (1920–2004) were American comic actors who, in the 1950s and '60s, were often typecast as henpecked husbands or neurotic, buttoned-down suburban "squares."

36.19–20 *An American Dilemma*] *An American Dilemma: The Negro Problem and Modern Democracy* (New York: Harper & Bros., 1944), best-selling two-volume study in World War II–era U.S. race relations by Gunnar Myrdal (1898–1987), Swedish sociologist and, later, Nobel Laureate in Economics.

38.32 Stanley M. Elkins] American historian (1925–2013) who, in his best-selling *Slavery* (Chicago: University of Chicago Press, 1959), posited the "Sambo" theory of black dependency upon the dominant white society, arguing that the institution of slavery had created a "totalitarian environment" that had infantilized blacks, robbing them of the ability to form positive relationships among themselves and with "mainstream" American culture. The book was controversial, and when, in 1969, a second, revised edition was released, it occasioned a collection of fourteen critical essays, *The Debate Over 'Slavery': Stanley Elkins and His Critics*, edited by Ann J. Lane (Urbana: University of Illinois Press, 1971).

38.35 *Dark Ghetto*] *Dark Ghetto: Dilemmas of Social Power*, by Kenneth B. Clark (New York: Harper & Row, 1965), grew out of Dr. Clark's experience as director of HARYOU (see note 26.21) and as an "involved observer" of ghetto life in Harlem. As the author writes in his introduction, the book's "emphasis on the pathologies of American ghettos"—that is, on "the delinquency, narcotics addiction, infant mortality, homicide, and suicide statistics"—"attempts to describe and interpret what happens to human beings who are confined to depressed areas and whose access to the normal channels of economic mobility and opportunity is blocked. . . . The truth about the dark ghetto is not merely a truth about Negroes; it reflects the deeper anguish and torment of the total human predicament."

38.39–40 Charles Evers . . . H. Rap Brown] Evers (b. 1922), brother of slain civil rights activist Medgar Evers (1925–1963), was the mayor of Fayette, Mississippi, from 1969 to 1981 and again from 1985 to 1989; Brown (b. 1943) was chairman of the Student Nonviolent Coordinating Committee (SNCC) in 1967–68 and, later, an outspoken member of the Black Panther Party.

39.27–28 *Black Rage*] Best-selling book (New York: Basic Books, 1968), by William H. Grier, M.D. (1926–2015), and Price M. Cobbs, M.D. (b. 1928), "two black psychiatrists," the jacket copy stated, "[who] reveal the full dimensions of the inner conflicts and the desperation of the black man's life in America."

40.33   Talcott Parsons] American sociologist (1902–1979) who created and headed Harvard's sociology department (1927–73). He and Kenneth B. Clark coedited *The Negro American* (1966), a volume of sociopsychological essays commissioned by the American Academy of Arts and Sciences.

48.24   patent-leather glossy coiffure to Brillo] James Brown switched from the conk to the so-called Afro hairstyle circa 1968.

49.28–29   shirt collar ad Anglo-Saxon and Gibson Girl images] Early-twentieth-century mass-culture images of American masculinity (as found in Arrow Collar advertisements created by J. C. Leyendecker [1874–1951]) and femininity (as found in magazine illustrations by Charles Dana Gibson [1867–1944]).

51.30   Kenneth Burke has equated stylization with strategy.] See *The Philosophy of Literary Form: Studies in Symbolic Action* (Baton Rouge: Louisiana State University Press, 1941).

53.20   *homo ludens*] *Homo Ludens* ("Man the Player," 1938), by Dutch cultural theorist Johan Huizinga (1872–1945), is a comparative study in the significance of games and athletic contests to human culture. *Homo Ludens: A Study of the Play Element in Culture*, translated from the German by R.F.C. Hull, was published in London in 1944.

54.19   *la condition humaine*] *La Condition humaine* ("The Human Condition," 1933), a novel by André Malraux concerning the failed 1927 communist revolution in Shanghai, was translated into English, by Haakon M. Chevalier, as *Man's Fate* (1934).

55.20–21   "emblems of a pioneer people . . . trait."] Constance Rourke, in *American Humor* (see note 18.27).

56.35   Guevara . . . Fanon] Che Guevara (1928–1967), Argentine-Cuban Marxist revolutionary and a theorist of guerilla warfare; Frantz Fanon (1925–1961), Afro-Caribbean psychiatrist, philosopher, and Marxist critic of colonialism whose books include *Black Skin, White Masks* (1952) and *The Wretched of the Earth* (1961).

57.1–2   Harold Cruse's *The Crisis of the Negro Intellectual*] For Murray's review of Cruse's book (1967), see pages 777–82 of the present volume.

58.32–34   *magnanimity of the black mammy . . .* worldly wit and wisdom of Uncle Remus] Throughout his writings Murray evokes "Aunt Hagar" and "Uncle Remus" as archetypal black elders who transmit life lessons, moral principles, and black folk culture to the children of the black and, especially, the white communities.

66.5   Bigger Thomas' response] Thomas is the twenty-year-old protagonist of *Native Son* (1940), a deterministic novel by Richard Wright (1908–1960) that suggests that Thomas's criminal nature is attributable mainly to his social environment, the slums of Chicago's South Side during the early 1930s.

66.33   As James Weldon Johnson noted] See "Harlem: The Culture Capital," by James Weldon Johnson (1871–1938), in Alain Locke, editor, *The New Negro* (1925).

68.21   Leontyne] Soprano Leontyne Price (b. 1927), who in 1961 became the first black American singer to join the Metropolitan Opera Company.

69.3   *An American Dilemma*] See note 36.19–20.

75.40   Reichianism] System of Austrian psychologist Wilhelm Reich (1897–1957), developed in such books as *The Mass Psychology of Fascism* (1933) and *The Sexual Revolution* (1936). Reich's mixture of far-left politics, sexual frankness, and mystical pseudoscience was embraced by the counterculture of the 1950s and '60s.

78.34   *From Slavery to Freedom*] The first edition of *From Slavery to Freedom: A History of American Negroes* was published in 1947, when John Hope Franklin (1915–2009) was a junior professor of history at Howard University. A standard work on its subject, the ninth edition was published posthumously in 2010.

79.25   *Life and Labor in the Old South*] Social and economic history of the antebellum South (1929) by Yale historian Ulrich Bonnell Phillips (1877–1934), a Georgia native educated at the University of Georgia and Columbia University.

81.15–16   Mays . . . Gibson, Big O . . . Simpson] In 1970, when Murray published *The Omni-Americans*, Willie Mays (b. 1931) was a power-hitting center fielder for the San Francisco Giants; Bob "Hoot" Gibson (b. 1935) a pitcher for the St. Louis Cardinals; Oscar "Big O" Robertson (b. 1938) a guard for basketball's Cincinnati Royals; and O. J. Simpson (b. 1947) the Heisman Trophy–winning running back for the Buffalo Bills.

81.18   Negro senator] In 1966 Edward W. Brooke III (1919–2015), then the Republican attorney general of Massachusetts (1963–67), became the first black person to be popularly elected to the U.S. Senate. He served from 1967 to 1979.

82.27–28   Adam Clayton Powell] New York Democrat Powell (1908–1972), a pastor of Harlem's Abyssinian Baptist Church (from 1937), served as a U.S. congressman from 1945 to 1971.

83.12–13   Farmer . . . Moses . . . McKissick . . . Carmichael] James Farmer Jr. (1920–1999), head of the Congress of Racial Equality (CORE) and an organizer of the Freedom Rides; Robert Parris Moses (b. 1935), leader of the Student Nonviolent Coordinating Committee (SNCC) and voting rights advocate; Floyd McKissick (1922–1991), civil rights lawyer and Farmer's successor at CORE; Stokely Carmichael (1941–1998), leader of both the American civil rights movement and the global Pan-African movement.

83.21–23   *Autobiography* . . . a magazine writer] *The Autobiography of*

Malcolm X was written by Malcolm X (1925–1965) with American journalist Alex Haley (1921–1992). Their collaboration began when Haley, then a staff writer for *Playboy*, interviewed Malcolm X for the magazine in 1963. The *Autobiography*, published mere months after Malcolm X's assassination, was one of the best-selling books of the late twentieth century.

83.38   Whitney Young] American civil rights leader (1921–1971) who, in 1961, after serving the organization since 1947, became executive director of the National Urban League.

83.40   Eldridge Cleaver] American political activist (1935–1998) who was a member of the Black Panther Party (1966–71) and the author of *Soul on Ice* (New York: Ramparts Press, 1968), a collection of memoirs and polemical essays written from Folsom State Prison, where in 1965–66 he served time for rape and attempted murder.

84.1   *Ramparts* magazine] Glossy magazine (1962–75) that, by the late 1960s, had evolved from a monthly of liberal Catholic opinion into a leading news organ of the American counterculture.

84.40   Claude (Manchild) Brown] Brown (1937–2002) was a juvenile delinquent from Harlem who, with guidance from a reform-school psychiatrist, entered Howard University and later studied law at Rutgers and Stanford. Murray's review of his memoir, *Manchild in the Promised Land* (1965), appears on pages 87–92 of the present volume.

85.20–22   Jones . . . Hooks . . . Anderson . . . Kilson . . . Epps] LeRoi Jones (1934–2014), later known as Amiri Baraka, cultural critic, poet, and playwright; Robert Hooks (b. 1937), actor, producer, director for stage and screen; Jervis Anderson (1932–2000), versatile staff writer at *The New Yorker*; Martin Kilson (b. 1931), professor of government at Harvard University; Archie Epps (1939–2003), longtime dean of students at Harvard University.

85.23   *Freedomways*] Quarterly journal (1961–85), founded by Louis E. Burnham and Edward Strong (both of the Southern Negro Youth Congress), that chronicled what the editors called the Negro Freedom Movement—not just the American civil rights movement but also the Pan-African, Négritude, and Black Arts movements.

85.35–36   Julian Bond] American civil rights leader (1940–2015). The son of academics, he was educated at Morehouse College, and in 1970, when Murray published *The Omni-Americans*, was known as the Atlanta-area leader of the Student Nonviolent Coordinating Committee (SNCC).

87.9   CLAUDE BROWN'S SOUL] See note 84.40.

87.24   earth dark womb!] See John Milton's poem "On the Death of a Fair Infant, Dying of a Cough" (circa 1625).

88.6–7   Smith . . . Robinson . . . Powell . . . Motley] Four prominent figures in twentieth-century Harlem: Willie "The Lion" Smith (1893–1973), stride pianist; Sugar Ray Robinson (1921–1989), prizefighter; Adam Clayton Powell Jr. (see note 82.27–28); Constance Baker Motley (1921–2005), the first black woman to serve as a federal judge (1966–86).

88.8–9   Lenox Terrace . . . Smalls Paradise . . . *Amsterdam News*] Postwar Harlem apartment complex (and, after 1962, Murray's place of residence); Harlem nightclub (1925–mid-1980s); and Harlem-based weekly paper (founded 1909).

90.1   J. William Fulbright] Arkansas Democrat (1905–1995) who served in the U.S. Senate (1945–74) and chaired its Foreign Relations Committee (1959–74). His book *The Arrogance of Power* (1966) was an indictment of America's Vietnam policy.

90.3   Mary McCarthy] American writer (1912–1989) whose novel *The Group* (1963) chronicled the adult lives of eight Vassar graduates from the 1930s through the early 1960s.

90.9–11   Mailer . . . Hentoff . . . Podhoretz . . . Wolfe] Novelist Norman Mailer (1923–2007) wrote a jacket blurb for Brown's book; jazz critic Nat Hentoff (b. 1925) reviewed it in *Book Week*; Norman Podhoretz (b. 1930), editor of *Commentary*, interviewed Brown on WNET Television's *Open Mind* program; and journalist Tom Wolfe (b. 1931) profiled Brown in *The New York Herald Tribune Magazine*.

91.4–12   Negroes like Duke Ellington, Louis Armstrong . . . how you get that way.] Cf. the following passage, deleted from "Something Different, Something More" (in Herbert Hill's anthology *Anger, and Beyond*, 1966) when Murray revised it, as "James Baldwin, Protest Fiction, and the Blues Tradition," for *The Omni-Americans*: "This music, far from being simply Afro-American (whatever that is, the continent of Africa being as vast and as varied as it is), is, like the U.S. Negro himself, All-American. This is why so many other American musicians, like Paul Whiteman, George Gershwin, Benny Goodman, Woody Herman, Gerry Mulligan, and all the rest, identify with it so eagerly. The white American musician (excluding hillbillies, of course) sounds most American when he sounds like an American Negro. Otherwise he sounds like a European."

92.20   GORDON PARKS] Parks was born in Fort Scott, Kansas, in 1912, and died at home in Manhattan in 2006. His memoir *A Choice of Weapons* (1966) was followed by three further volumes of autobiography: *To Smile in Autumn* (1979), *Voices in the Mirror* (1990), and *Half Past Autumn* (1998).

94.17   *The Learning Tree*] Parks's autobiographical first novel, concerning the lives of black adolescents in a segregated Kansas town of the 1930s, was published by Harper & Row in 1963. A feature film based on the book—written, produced, directed, and with music by Parks—was released in 1969, and in 1989 was selected for inclusion in the National Film Registry of the Library of Congress.

99.23–24 Mydans . . . Kauffman] Carl Mydans (1907–2004) and Mark Kauffman (1923–1974) were, like Parks, contract photographers for *Life* magazine.

100.3 NEW YORK NEWSPAPER PUNDIT] Baltimore native Murray Kempton (1917–1997), a columnist for several New York papers from the 1930s to the 1950s, wrote, in "To Be a Negro," a 1962 essay for the London *Spectator*, that "there is no Negro so alienated that he does not trust some white man somewhere for at least a limited distance down the road."

100.21 Amos and Andy and Lawyer Calhoun] Farcical characters created by blackface writers and actors for the radio series *Amos 'n' Andy* (1928–55).

103.19–20 Odetta . . . Joan Baez] Odetta (1930–2008), black folksinger, musician, and civil rights activist, and Joan Baez (b. 1941), white folksinger, musician, and social activist, shared record labels, festival dates, and campus and coffeehouse concert circuits throughout the 1960s.

105.13–14 Lemberg Center for the Study of Violence] Domestic policy institute, based at Brandeis University, that from 1965 to 1973 conducted research into the causes of social violence, particularly race riots.

106.33–34 "very essence of adventure and romance"] From *Freedom Bound*, a popular history of the Reconstruction era by the white independent scholar Henrietta Buckmaster (1909–1983), published by Macmillan in 1965. For Murray's review of *Freedom Bound*, see pages 785–90 of the present volume.

107.12 *Five Smooth Stones*] First novel (1966) by American writer Dorothy Fairbairn Tait (1905–1972), using the pseudonym "Ann Fairbairn." Tait was the longtime manager of New Orleans clarinetist George Lewis (1900–1968) and, under the name "Jay Allison Stuart," the author of his biography, *Call Him George* (1961).

109.23 *Mojo Hand*] First novel (1966) by California poet Jane Phillips (b. 1944), who also publishes under the name J. J. Phillips. A revised version of the novel, *Mojo Hand: An Orphic Tale*, was published in 1985 by City Miner Press, San Francisco.

110.10–11 Hi-de Hi-de Hi-de-ho] "Hi-De-Ho" (1934) was a trademark tune of singer and bandleader Cab Calloway (1907–1994).

111.7 WARREN MILLER] American writer Miller (1921–1966) was educated at the University of Iowa and then taught in the writing program there until his death, from lung cancer, at age forty-four. His novel *The Cool World* was published by Little, Brown, in 1959. A stage version, adapted by Robert Rossen and starring Billy Dee Williams, played for two nights at the Eugene O'Neill Theater, New York, in February 1960. A film version, produced by Frederick Wiseman and starring Hampton Clanton, was released in 1963.

111.22 U.S. white negro] See Norman Mailer's essay "The White Negro:

Superficial Reflections on the Hipster" (*Dissent*, Fall 1957), collected in *Advertisements for Myself* (1959). Mailer argues that white youth should embrace rebellion, hedonism, and hypersexuality, which he associated with blackness, in response to the existential threat of nuclear war.

113.38   Joel Chandler Harris] Atlanta-based journalist and folklorist (1848–1908) whose tales of Brer Rabbit, learned from slaves on Turnwold Plantation, near Eatonton, Georgia, were collected in *Uncle Remus: His Songs and His Sayings* (1880) and other volumes.

114.1   Cohen . . . Bradford] Octavus Roy Cohen (1891–1959), a white writer from South Carolina, contributed "downhome" tales in black dialect to *The Saturday Evening Post*. Roark Bradford (1896–1943), a professor of English at Tulane University, also wrote in blackface. His collection of tales *Ol' Man Adam an' His Chillun* (1928) was the inspiration for Marc Connelly's Pulitzer Prize–winning play *The Green Pastures* (1930).

114.12–13   Apollo Theatre . . . Markham] The Apollo (1934), on 125th Street, is Harlem's premier music hall. Black vaudevillian Dewey "Pigmeat" Markham (1904–1981) was the Apollo's unofficial house entertainer, appearing there more frequently than any other performer.

114.16   Father Divine] The Reverend M. J. Divine (circa 1876–1965) was founder and charismatic leader of the International Peace Mission Movement (1932–   ), a ministry whose tenets include racial equality, economic self-sufficiency, and the power of positive thinking.

115.39–40   *If you see dear Mrs. Equitone . . . careful these days.*] From "The Burial of the Dead," the first section of T. S. Eliot's poem *The Waste Land* (1922).

116.1   WILLIAM STYRON] Virginia-born writer (1925–2006) whose fourth novel, *The Confessions of Nat Turner* (1967), was awarded the Pulitzer Prize for Fiction. The controversy that the book occasioned culminated in *William Styron's Nat Turner: Ten Black Writers Respond* (Boston: Beacon Press, 1968), a collection of essays edited by John Henrik Clarke, and *The Nat Turner Rebellion: The Historical Event and the Modern Controversy* (New York: Harper & Row, 1971), edited by John B. Duff and Peter M. Mitchell.

117.19   Warren . . . Woodward . . . Clark] Three white intellectuals concerned with American race relations: poet, novelist, and critic Robert Penn Warren (1905–1989), whose nonfiction included *Segregation* (1956), *The Legacy of the Civil War* (1961), and *Who Speaks for the Negro?* (1965); historian and educator C. Vann Woodward (1908–1999), whose histories of Reconstruction and the New South culminated in *The Strange Career of Jim Crow* (1955); and civil rights lawyer Ramsey Clark (b. 1927), who as a justice official in the Johnson administration was architect of the Voting Rights Act of 1965 and the Civil Rights Act of 1968.

117.35   "room for many more."] Phrase from the chorus of the traditional

American spiritual "The Gospel Train": "Get on board, children, / There's room for many a more."

118.11–14 Well you can be milk-white . . . gaining ground] See "traditional song (circa 1831)" published by the folklorist Lawrence Gellert in his article "Two Songs About Nat Turner," *The Worker* (June 12, 1949).

118.23 Stanley M. Elkins') Sambo] See note 38.32.

118.27 neo-Reichean] See note 75.40.

119.24 Aptheker] American Marxist historian Herbert Aptheker (1915–2003) wrote about Nat Turner's rebellion in his study *American Negro Slave Revolts* (New York: Columbia University Press, 1943).

119.37 U. B. Phillips] See note 79.25.

120.26–34 "an event . . . with them always."] From Kenneth Stampp, *The Peculiar Institution: Slavery in the Antebellum South* (New York: Knopf, 1956). Murray's later quotes from Stampp are from the same volume.

122.4–5 author of Uncle Remus] See note 113.38.

122.14 "Freedom's a Hard-Bought Thing"] Short story (1940) by American writer Stephen Vincent Benét (1898–1943) evoking the inner life of Cue, an American slave, as he escapes to Canada via the Underground Railroad.

122.20–21 Schillinger exercises] Musical composition exercises developed by Russian-born music theorist Joseph Schillinger (1895–1943).

123.1 *James Baldwin*] American man of letters (1924–1987) whose works include the novels *Go Tell It on the Mountain* (1953) and *Another Country* (1962), the play *Blues for Mister Charlie* (1964), and several volumes of essays.

123.7 "Everybody's Protest Novel,"] Baldwin collected this essay, together with its sequel "Many Thousands Gone," in his book *Notes of a Native Son* (1955). Murray's quotes are from the book versions of these essays.

124.16 hero of . . . *Native Son*] See note 66.5.

124.20 *Uncle Tom's Children*] Collection of short stories (1938; expanded 1940) by Richard Wright (see note 66.5).

125.31–34 *Gentleman's Agreement . . . Sound and the Fury*] Laura Z. Hobson's *Gentleman's Agreement* (1947), an exploration of institutional anti-Semitism; James M. Cain's *The Postman Always Rings Twice* (1934), a noir novella of infidelity and murder; Sinclair Lewis's *Kingsblood Royal* (1947), an allegory of a prosperous white man who discovers he has a black ancestor; Chester Himes's *If He Hollers Let Him Go* (1945), a tale of racial politics and union organizing in Los Angeles; William Faulkner's *The Sound and the Fury* (1929), four views of the fall of a distinguished Mississippi family.

132.6 *negritude*] Négritude was an international literary movement (fl.

1930s–1960s) founded by Francophone African and Caribbean writers living in Paris in protest of French colonial rule. Its leaders—including Léopold Sédar Senghor, of Senegal, and Aimé Césaire, of Martinique—argued that black assimilation was a betrayal of black specialness, and that blacks everywhere should honor their connection to traditional African folkways as a balm against the soullessness of Western culture. The French intellectual Jean-Paul Sartre, in his 1948 essay "Orphée Noir" ("Black Orpheus"), called Négritude the necessary antithesis to colonialism that would one day result in the synthesis of racial equality.

132.18 "black arts"] The Black Arts movement of the 1960s and early '70s grew out of a populist American aesthetic in literature that reflected political ideas of the Black Power movement. It led directly to the creation of several black presses, periodicals, and theater companies, and indirectly to the establishment of black studies departments in colleges and universities.

133.16–22 Jean Genet . . . *The Blacks*] *The Blacks: A Clown Show* (*Les Nègres: Clownerie*, 1958), by the French writer Jean Genet (1910–1996), was, in its English translation by Bernard Frechtman, the longest-running off-Broadway drama of the 1960s. A farcical study in white racist attitudes, it featured an all-black cast, with some of the actors in "whiteface." It had its U.S. premiere at the St. Mark's Playhouse on May 4, 1961, and closed in 1964 after 1,408 performances. Sartre's study of the playwright, *Saint Genet*, was published in 1951. Its English translation (1963), by Frechtman, was reviewed by Susan Sontag (see "Sartre's *Saint Genet*," in *Against Interpretation and Other Essays*, 1966).

133.32 *The New Negro*] Anthology (1925) edited by Alain Locke (1885–1954) and published in New York by Albert and Charles Boni. Locke, a philosopher, writer, and professor at Howard University, commissioned and collected a group of stories, poems, and commentary that both articulated the aims and embodied the achievement of the Harlem Renaissance movement. Among the contributors were Countee Cullen, E. Francis Frazier, Langston Hughes, Zora Neale Hurston, James Weldon Johnson, Claude McKay, Kelly Miller, and Jean Toomer. Locke wrote five pieces for the volume, including the title essay.

134.11–12 ersatz tiger noises . . . boom boom and all.] See "Under the Bamboo Tree," song (1902) by J. Rosamond Johnson (1873–1954) with lyrics by his brother, James Weldon Johnson (see note 66.33), and Bob Cole (1868–1911). It was popularized by Judy Garland and Margaret O'Brien in the film *Meet Me in St. Louis* (1944).

135.30–32 Thus does the American . . . and Marxist environs.] Cf. the opening sentence of James Joyce's *Finnegans Wake* (1939): "riverrun, past Eve and Adam's, from swerve of shore to bend of bay, brings us by a commodius vicus of recirculation back to Howth Castle and Environs."

138.7 Ralph Ellison wrote an article] "Richard Wright's Blues," a review of *Black Boy* (1945), a memoir by Richard Wright, collected in Ellison's *Shadow and Act* (1964).

139.12 Nexø] Martin Andersen Nexø (1869–1954), Danish writer on under-
class themes.

140.26 address at the New School] According to Nat Hentoff, in his article
"Uninventing the Negro" (*Evergreen Review*, November 1965), Baldwin, as
the keynote speaker at the New School/Harlem Writers' Guild symposium
"The Negro Writer's Vision of America," said, in April 1965, that "my models
—my private models—are not Hemingway, not Faulkner, not Dos Passos, indeed not any American writer. I model myself on jazz musicians, dancers, a
couple of whores and a few junkies."

140.33 *Blues for Mister Charlie*] Baldwin's three-act play, based on events sur-
rounding the 1955 lynching of Mississippi teenager Emmett Till, opened in
New York on April 23, 1964, and was published later the same year by Dial
Press.

140.40 *An American Dilemma*] See note 36.19–20.

140.40 *Mark of Oppression*] Abram Kardiner and Lionel Ovesey, *The Mark
of Oppression: A Psychological Study of the American Negro* (New York: Norton,
1951).

141.3 sounds more like the reds than the blues.] In an earlier version of this
essay, published in Herbert Hill's anthology *Anger, and Beyond* (1966), this
paragraph ended with a parenthetical statement: "(Incidentally, when down-
home people used to speak of having the reds, the mean old reds, they meant
they were in a fighting mood, that they could see red. But being down-home
blues people, and Joe Louis people to boot, they did what they were going to
do and talked about it later, if at all.)"

149.3–4 they knighted Benny Goodman] The Benny Goodman Quartet
(white clarinetist Goodman, white drummer Gene Krupa, black vibraphonist
Lionel Hampton, and black pianist Teddy Wilson), which formed in 1937, was
the first high-profile integrated jazz group. A year earlier, Teddy Wilson had
joined Goodman's previously all-white big band.

149.29 *Black Power*] *Black Power: A Record of Reactions in a Land of Pathos*
(1954) is Richard Wright's nonfiction account of his visit to Ghana on the eve
of independence from Britain.

149.39–40 "Blue Print for Negro Writing."] Uncollected essay by Richard
Wright, published in *New Challenge* I (Fall 1937).

150.23 "How 'Bigger' Was Born,"] Essay by Richard Wright, dated March 3,
1940, published in *Saturday Review* (June 1, 1940). It appears as an appendix
in most reprint editions of *Native Son* (1940).

151.11 first concert at Carnegie Hall] On January 23, 1943.

152.22 Eldridge Cleaver] See note 83.40. After 1966 Cleaver was a staff
writer for *Ramparts* magazine (see note 84.1).

152.27–28 Rinehart and Ras the Exhorter] Characters, one a black hustler of fluid identity, the other a West Indian black separatist, in Ellison's *Invisible Man* (1952).

152.32 Norman Mailer] See note 111.22, on Mailer's essay "The White Negro."

153.2 Mickey Spillane] Prolific writer of "American noir" crime novels (1918–2006), some twenty of which feature the detective/antihero Mike Hammer.

153.32 "puerile controversy and petty braggadocio."] See "The Negro Digs Up His Past," by Arthur A. Schomburg (1874–1938), in Alain Locke, ed., *The New Negro* (1925). Schomburg was a pioneering collector of books and manuscripts of the African diaspora. Harlem's Schomburg Center for Research in Black Culture, a research library in the New York Public Library system, had its basis in his collection.

154.11–13 Woodson . . . Brawley . . . Wesley . . . Du Bois . . . Johnson . . . Quarles . . . Franklin] Carter G. Woodson (1875–1950), pioneering black historian, author of *The Negro in Our History* (1922), and founder, in 1915, of the Association of American Negro Life and History and, in 1926, of Negro History Week (later Black History Month); Benjamin Brawley (1882–1939), first dean of Morehouse College and author of *A Short History of the American Negro* (1921) and *Negro Builders and Heroes* (1937); Charles H. Wesley (1891–1987), author of some twenty works in black history; W. E. B. Du Bois (1868–1963), sociologist, historian, cofounder of the NAACP, editor of its journal *The Crisis*, and author of *The Souls of Black Folk* (1903); James Weldon Johnson (see note 66.33), whose historical works include *Black Manhattan* (1930); Benjamin Quarles (see note 20.38–21.3); and John Hope Franklin (see note 78.34).

156.17 Lumumba, Tshombe, or Nkrumah] Patrice Lumumba (1925–1961), short-lived prime minister of independent Congo (June–September 1960); Moïse Tshombe (1919–1969), one of his embattled successors (1964–65); and Kwame Nkrumah (1909–1972), first president of the Republic of Ghana (1960–66).

157.17 John A. Kouwenhoven] Professor of American studies and American literature (1910–1990), long associated with Barnard College, whose books on American culture—high, folk, and pop—include *Made in America: The Arts in Modern Civilization* (Garden City, N.Y.: Doubleday, 1948) and *The Beer Can by the Highway: Essays on What's American about America* (Doubleday, 1961). Kouwenhoven's work was a touchstone for Murray and is alluded to throughout his nonfiction.

161.12–13 Woodson and . . . Brawley] See note 154.11–13.

161.22–23 Logan . . . Franklin . . . Quarles] Rayford Logan (1897–1992), professor of history at Howard University and author of more than a dozen books; John Hope Franklin (see note 78.34); Benjamin Quarles (see note 20.38–21.3).

161.26–27 Du Bois . . . Frazier] W. E. B. Du Bois (see note 154.11–13); E. Franklin Frazier (1894–1962), American sociologist whose chief field of study was the urban black American family.

163.24 *Bull Connor and Al Lingo*] T. Eugene "Bull" Connor (1897–1973) was commissioner of public safety in Birmingham, Alabama, from 1937 to 1963. During the 1963 civil rights protests in his city, he approved the use of cattle prods, fire hoses, and attack dogs on the demonstrators. Connor's superior at this time was Albert J. Lingo (1910–1969), director of the Alabama Department of Public Safety (1963–65).

163.40–164.1 *high yallers . . . peola*] A "high yellow" is, in antebellum parlance, a mulatto with very light skin. A "peola," in 1930s Harlem slang, is a mulatto woman with skin so light as to be able to "pass" for white, after Peola Johnson, the heroine of Fannie Hurst's novel *Imitation of Life* (1933).

164.13 NOW] Neighborhood Organized Workers of Mobile, Alabama, was a civil rights and economic improvement organization (1966–75) founded by local activist Dorothy Parker Williams and educator David Jacobs.

167.17 Miller . . . Locke . . . Brown] Polymath Kelly Miller (1863–1939) was a mathematician, sociologist, writer, and teacher at Howard University; Alain Locke (see note 133.32); Sterling Brown (1901–1989) was a poet, folklorist, and literary critic.

167.18 Monroe N. Work] American sociologist (1866–1945) who edited several pioneering reference works, including the *Negro Year Book: An Annual Encyclopedia* (1912–45) and *A Bibliography of the Negro in Africa and America* (1928).

167.20–21 Ira De A. Reid] American sociologist and anthropologist (1901–1968) who published nine book-length academic studies, most of them documenting the lives of urban black workers.

167.21–22 Charles S. Johnson] American sociologist (1893–1956) and the first black president of Fisk University (1946–56).

167.39–40 Denmark Vesey and Nat Turner] American slaves Vesey (1767–1822) and Turner (1800–1831) each led a slave revolt that ended in his execution.

168.37 *Rockefeller*] Businessman Nelson Rockefeller (1908–1979) was governor of New York (1959–73) and, in 1960, '64, and '68, a Republican candidate for U.S. president. He was later vice president under Gerald Ford (1974–77).

169.1 *Wallace*] George Wallace (1919–1998), three-time governor of Alabama and, in 1968, an independent candidate for U.S. president.

171.2–3 rather be a lamp post in Harlem than the mayor of Mobile] Catchphrase in the Harlem of the 1920s, sometimes attributed to the poet Langston Hughes.

171.11 Benjamin F. Baker] Dr. Baker (d. 1953?) was the principal of Mobile County Training School (MCTS), Murray's junior high and high school, from 1926 to 1947. In 1950 he became the first principal of Mobile's Central High (see note 290.29).

171.12 Ella Grant] Ella Grant (d. 1937) was a master teacher at Meachem Elementary School, in the Mobile County Public School district. In 1944 the Prichard School, a Mobile district grade school, was rechristened the Ella Grant School in her honor.

177.15–24 "[Some black Americans . . . other resources."] Tom Mboya, "The American Negro Cannot Look to Africa for an Escape," in *The New York Times Magazine* (July 13, 1969). Mboya (1930–1969) was assassinated a week before his essay appeared.

179.28 Charles Houston] Prominent black lawyer (1895–1950) who was dean of Howard University Law School (1929–35) and special council to the NAACP (1935–50).

179.35–36 David Susskind's vaudeville hour] After a career as a theatrical producer, David Susskind (1920–1987) was the host of an hour-long New York–based talk show on NET/PBS television from 1958 to 1986.

181.25 *Goodbye, Mr. Chips*] Novel (1934) by English writer James Hilton (1900–1954) that sentimentally dramatizes the twilight years of a teacher of classics at a second-tier boys' school.

185.3–5 *In the fall of 1966 . . . "What's Happening in America."*] The symposium feature "What's Happening to America" was published in *Partisan Review* for Spring 1967. The editors sent to writers whom they invited to participate the following questionnaire, which was also published as a preface to the symposium:

> There is a good deal of anxiety about the direction of American life. In fact, there is reason to fear that America may be entering a moral and political crisis. If so, the crisis isn't to be explained by any single policy, however wrong or disastrous. There seems instead to be some more general failure or weakness in our national life. The deterioration in the quality of American life during the last few years has been made evident in several ways. The rhetoric through which issues are created and argued and which seemed during the Kennedy years to have some relation to the seriousness of the problems facing the country has become jingoistic and question-begging. The economy seems to be out of control. The civil rights movement has become more desperate as the government has become more cautious and the white population less sympathetic. U.S. foreign policy is becoming more and more indistinguishable from John Foster Dulles', if in fact it isn't even more an adjunct of our military power. Throughout the country, there is a sense of drift and frustration and confusion—and a growing sense of urgency.

Of course there are many people who don't think conditions are so bad, who regard the idea that we are in some kind of crisis as extremist, and who in any case feel sure that our problems can be solved within the terms of our current methods and policies.

To give the discussion some focus, we suggest the following questions. But you are free, of course, to approach the problem of what is happening to America in any way you choose.

1. *Does it matter who is in the White House? Or is there something in our system which would force any President to act as Johnson is acting?*
2. *How serious is the problem of inflation? The problem of poverty?*
3. *What is the meaning of the split between the Administration and the American intellectuals?*
4. *Is white America committed to granting equality to the American Negro?*
5. *Where do you think our foreign policies are likely to lead us?*
6. *What, in general, do you think is likely to happen in America?*
7. *Do you think any promise is to be found in the activities of young people today?*

Partisan Review published responses from Martin Duberman, Michael Harrington, Tom Hayden, Nat Hentoff, Robert Lowell, Harold Rosenberg, Susan Sontag, Diana Trilling, and eight other public intellectuals and social critics.

185.17–18 "not nostrums . . . but serenity."] Republican presidential candidate Warren G. Harding (1865–1923), in a campaign speech of May 14, 1920, promised American citizens a "return to normalcy" after World War I.

185.33–186.1 Elijah Muhammad . . . Mailer . . . Wallace . . . Buckley] Elijah Muhammad (1897–1975), leader of the Nation of Islam from 1934 until his death; Norman Mailer (see note 90.9–11); George Wallace (see note 169.1) and his wife, Lurleen Wallace (1926–1968), governor of Alabama from 1967 until her death; William F. Buckley Jr. (1925–2008), conservative talk-show host and founding editor of the weekly *National Review*.

186.25–26 *The Walnut Trees of Altenburg*] André Malraux's fragmentary final novel (*Les Noyers de l'Altenburg*, 1943), translated from the French by A. W. Fielding (London: John Lehmann, 1952).

186.31–33 Bundy . . . Katzenbach . . . Taylor . . . Jessup . . . Kennan . . . Morgenthau . . . Howe] McGeorge Bundy (1919–1996), American national security expert; Nicholas Katzenbach (1922–2012), U.S. attorney general (1964–66); General Maxwell Taylor (1901–1987), diplomat and chairman of the Joint Chiefs of Staff (1962–64); John K. Jessup (1907–1979), editorial-page writer for *Time* magazine (1944–66); George Kennan (1904–2005), Princeton professor and Cold War strategist; Hans Morgenthau (1904–1980),

German-born American writer on international politics; Irving Howe (1920–1993), socialist critic of American life and literature.

187.16–17   Moynihan Report] See note 28.34.

187.35–36   Norman Podhoretz] See note 90.9–11.

188.15   Senator William Fulbright] See note 90.1.

SOUTH TO A VERY OLD PLACE

193.1–5   (Stoop) . . . miscegenations.] From Book 1 of *Finnegans Wake* (New York: Viking, 1939).

193.8–18   But lo . . . my goal.] From "The Journey Downwards," part one of *Joseph in Egypt* (*Joseph in Ägypten*, 1936), book three of the tetralogy *Joseph and His Brothers* (*Joseph und seine Brüder*, 1933–43), translated from the German by H. T. Lowe-Porter (New York: Knopf, 1938).

193.21–22   The true ancestral line . . . one.] From "Journal of an Airman," part two of the long poem *The Orators: An English Study* (London: Faber & Faber, 1932).

197.10–11   IND Station at 125th Street] The Independent Subway System (today's A–G lines) was one of several New York City subway lines (IRT, BMT, BRT, etc.) operated by private companies prior to the unification of the system, in 1940, under the Metropolitan Transit Authority. Harlem's 125th Street Station (A–D lines) was opened in 1932.

197.35   Theresa Hotel] Thirteen-floor Harlem hotel (1912–67) that was the choice of black celebrities in the 1940s and 1950s. The Theresa, now called Theresa Towers, has been repurposed as an office building.

198.2–7   Lenox Terrace . . . Schomburg Library . . . Smalls Paradise] See notes 88.8–9 and 153.32.

198.38–39   *Powell . . . Bolden*] Adam Clayton Powell Jr. (see note 82.27–28); Buddy Bolden (1877–1931), New Orleans–style cornet player.

200.5–6   Billy Strayhorn's ellington-conjugated nostalgia] Strayhorn (1915–1967) wrote "Take the A Train" (1939), the signature tune of the Duke Ellington Orchestra.

201.16–17   *Robert Penn Warren and there is C. Vann Woodward*] See note 117.18. Warren taught drama and English at Yale from 1950 to 1973; Woodward taught American history at Yale from 1961 to 1977.

202.25   *Tom Mix*] American silent-movie actor (1880–1940) who, like Buck Jones, Fred Thomson, and Ken Maynard, was known for genre-defining cowboy roles.

203.5–6   *"You're right . . . live with them"*] Deacon speaks these words to

Quentin Compson in "June Second, 1910," the second section of Faulkner's *The Sound and the Fury* (1929).

203.32   *cut a hog*] Do something foolish that betrays one's "country" background.

204.29   "*ostrygods gagging fishygods*"] See Book 1 of *Finnegans Wake* (1939), by James Joyce.

205.1   L&N] Louisville & Nashville Railroad (1850–1982).

205.34–206.13   "The ironic thing . . . their country will be better for it. . . ."] C. Vann Woodward, "The North and the South of It," in *The American Scholar* (Autumn 1966).

206.14–15   Beard, Morison, Commager, Nevins] Leading American historians of the generation before Murray's: Charles A. Beard (1874–1948), Samuel Eliot Morison (1887–1976), Henry Steele Commager (1902–1998), and Allan Nevins (1890–1971), all of whom wrote on slavery, the Civil War, and Reconstruction.

206.15–16   Aptheker . . . Genovese . . . Franklin] Leading American historians of the South of Murray's generation: Herbert Aptheker (see note 119.24), Eugene D. Genovese (1930–2012), and John Hope Franklin (see note 78.34).

206.18–29   "I am prepared to maintain . . . beneath white skins. . . ."] C. Vann Woodward, "American History (White Man's Version) Needs an Infusion of Soul," *The New York Times Magazine* (April 20, 1969), collected, in a fuller version, as "Clio with Soul," in *The Future of the Past* (New York: Oxford University Press, 1989). This essay is based on Woodward's presidential address to the Organization of American Historians in April 1969.

206.39   Moynihan] See note 28.34.

207.28–33   Booker T. Washington . . . "Let down your bucket where are"?] On September 18, 1895, Booker T. Washington (1856–1915), founder and president of Tuskegee Institute (1881), spoke before a predominantly white audience at the Cotton States and International Exposition in Atlanta. His speech outlined what would become known as "The Atlanta Compromise," a proposition that Southern blacks would submit to white political rule only if Southern whites guaranteed them basic education and certain legal rights. The excerpt below is from the text of the speech printed in Washington's autobiography *Up From Slavery* (1901): "A ship lost at sea for many days suddenly sighted a friendly vessel. From the mast of the unfortunate vessel was seen a signal, 'Water, water; we die of thirst!' The answer from the friendly vessel at once came back, 'Cast down your bucket where you are.' The captain of the distressed vessel . . . cast down his bucket, and it came up full of fresh, sparkling water from the mouth of the Amazon River. To those of my race . . . who underestimate the importance of cultivating friendly relations with the Southern white man . . . I would say: 'Cast down your bucket where you are'—cast it down in making friends in every manly way of the people of all races by whom we are surrounded. To those of the white race who look to [European immigrants] for the prosperity of the South . . . I would repeat what I have said to my own race: 'Cast down your bucket where you are.' Cast it down among the eight millions of Negroes whose habits you know . . . Cast down your bucket among these people who have without strikes and labor wars tilled your fields, cleared your forests, builded your railroads and cities, brought forth treasures from the bowels of the earth, just to make possible this magnificent representation of the progress of the South."

208.10–17 "National myths, American myths . . . to conform."] C. Vann Woodward, *The Burden of Southern History*, revised edition (Baton Rouge: Louisiana State University Press, 1969).

208.20–27 "The separatists and nationalists . . . to be a Negro."] C. Vann Woodward, "Comment on Eugene D. Genovese, 'The Legacy of Slavery and the Roots of Black Nationalism,'" *Studies on the Left* (November–December 1966).

208.24–26 Blyden . . . Garvey] Edward Wilmot Blyden of St. Thomas (1832–1912), the nineteenth century's premier proponent of pan-Africanism, and Marcus Garvey of Jamaica (1887–1940), his twentieth-century successor.

209.3–5 "*instinctive fear . . . of abstraction.*"] Robert Penn Warren, in *Segregation: The Inner Conflict of the South* (New York: Random House, 1956).

209.16 Jug Hamilton] John Gerald Hamilton, a brilliant classmate of Murray's at Tuskegee and a model for the character T. Jerome Jefferson in Murray's fiction. For Murray's extended sketch of Hamilton, see pages 260–65 of the present volume.

209.27 *Ulrich B. Phillips*] See note 79.25.

209.29–30 *Sambo Elkins jive you once gave . . . blurb to*] Woodward provided the following endorsement of *Slavery* (see note 38.32): "Elkins' book on slavery opens up new ways of looking at an old subject and endows slavery with new significance for the present and new meaning for the past."

210.11 "by one of my colleagues, a Negro, here at Yale,"] John W. Blassingame (1940–2000), longtime chairman of the African American Studies Program at Yale University, was the author of *The Slave Community: Plantation Life in the Antebellum South* (New York: Oxford University Press, 1972). In 1973, he and theater professor Larry Neal invited Murray to speak at Yale.

212.6–8 *Calhoun . . . Murdock . . . Sarrett*] Three principal characters in Robert Penn Warren's second novel, *At Heaven's Gate* (1943).

212.6–11 *Boss's entourage in* All the King's Men *. . . Jack Burden*] *All the King's Men*, a Pulitzer Prize–winning novel by Robert Penn Warren (1946), is narrated by Jack Burden, who chronicles the rise of his onetime mentor Willie

("Boss") Stark from principled lawyer to charismatic, crowd-pleasing, and corrupt governor of an unnamed Southern state.

212.15–16 Battle House . . . Gomez Auditorium] Historic hotel (1852) and, during Murray's youth, a concert venue, both in downtown Mobile.

212.24 "Lift Every Voice"] Song ("Lift Every Voice and Sing," 1900) with words by James Weldon Johnson (see note 66.33) and music by his brother, J. Rosamond Johnson (see note 134.11–12). In 1919 the NAACP named the song "The Negro National Anthem."

212.25 Negro Builders and Heroes] Book by Benjamin Brawley (see note 154.11–13).

213.9 *Tailspin Tommy*] Syndicated comic strip about a daredevil pilot (1928–42).

213.10 *AT&N*] Alabama, Tennessee & Northern Railroad (1897–1971).

213.15–21 "By the way . . . after Auden).] The poem that Murray read to Warren is not among his published works.

213.34 Fugitive Poets] Group of Southern poets and critics that published the literary magazine *The Fugitive* at Vanderbilt University in the 1920s. Among the Fugitives were Warren, Allen Tate (1899–1979), Donald Davidson (1917–2003), and John Crowe Ransom (1888–1974).

214.4–5 Cue . . . "Freedom's a Hard-Bought Thing."] See note 122.14.

214.9 George Plimpton] American "participatory journalist" (1927–2003) who wrote accounts of his adventures "trying out" various highly skilled jobs, including pitcher for the major leagues (*Out of My League*, 1961) and quarterback for the Detroit Lions (*Paper Lion*, 1966).

214.14–17 "'We flee . . . Brahmins. . . .'"] Cf. John Crowe Ransom, in the editors' preface to the first number of *The Fugitive* (April 1922): "*The Fugitive* flees from nothing faster than the high-caste Brahmins of the Old South."

214.25–26 Starr brothers, Frank, Hirsch] Alfred Starr and his brother Milton, Sidney Hirsch, and Hirsch's brother-in-law James M. Frank were all Vanderbilt undergraduates and (except for M. Starr) contributors to *The Fugitive*.

214.33 *Stanley Edgar Hyman*] American literary critic (1919–1970) who, in the 1940s and '50s, taught at Bennington College alongside Kenneth Burke (see note 7.2–3). Like Murray, Hyman was a regular contributor to *The New Leader*, a collector of jazz records, and an expert on folklore, myth, and ritual.

214.35 *New Criticism*] Method of literary criticism advocated by Warren, Cleanth Brooks, William Empson, and others, and widely practiced in the United States after World War II. It advocated the "close reading" of literature and forswore the need to bring historical context into critical analyses, especially of poetry.

215.20   *Band of Angels*] Novel (1955) by Robert Penn Warren set during the Civil War. Its protagonist is the daughter of a slave woman and her white master.

215.21   *The Confessions of Nat Turner*] See pages 116–22 of the present volume.

215.29   Caroline Barr] Caroline "Callie" Barr (1840–1940) was William Faulkner's black "Mammy" throughout his childhood. He dedicated his book *Go Down, Moses* (1942) to her.

215.30   Dilsey] Strong black woman who takes care of the dysfunctional Compson family as well as her own family in Faulkner's *The Sound and the Fury* (1929).

216.11–17   "*when it is still not yet two o'clock . . . all in the balance.*"] See William Faulkner, *Intruder in the Dust* (1948).

216.29–30   not only to endure but to prevail] Cf. Faulkner's Nobel Prize acceptance speech, December 10, 1950: "I believe that man will not merely endure: he will prevail. He is immortal, not because he alone among creatures has an inexhaustible voice, but because he has a soul, a spirit capable of compassion and sacrifice and endurance . . ."

216.37–38   your piece in *I'll Take My Stand*] Warren's essay in *I'll Take My Stand: The South and the Agrarian Tradition*, by "Twelve Southerners" (New York: Harper & Bros., 1930), is titled "The Briar Patch." Warren later characterized this early piece, written when he was twenty-five, as "a defense of segregation" that he attempted to atone for twenty-five years later with his book *Segregation: The Inner Conflict of the South* (1956). "The Briarpatch" was also a working title for Murray's *ur*-novel of the 1950s, the manuscript that later yielded *Train Whistle Guitar* (1974) and *The Spyglass Tree* (1991).

217.26   Refectory] Dining hall of the Yale Divinity School.

217.30   Beattie Feathers . . . Vols] W. Beattie "Big Chief" Feathers (1909–1979) began his career as one of American football's greatest player-coaches as a halfback for the University of Tennessee Volunteers (1931–33).

218.5–6   *Literary Opinion in America*] Two-volume anthology (1937), edited by critic and academic Morton Dauwen Zabel (1902–1964), that, in the words of its subtitle, collected "Essays Illustrating the Status, Methods, and Problems of Criticism in the United States in the Twentieth Century."

218.36   Hollis Burke Frissell] Main library building (1932) of the Tuskegee Institute.

219.4–5   Blackmur . . . Fergusson . . . Weston . . . Burke] R. P. Blackmur (1904–1965), American poet, critic, and longtime professor at Princeton; Francis Fergusson (1904–1986), author of *The Idea of a Theater* (1947); Jessie

L. Weston (1850–1928), British medievalist and author of *From Ritual to Romance* (1920); Kenneth Burke (see note 7.2–3).

219.17–18   written testimony by you exists] See pages 795–98 of the present volume.

220.3–4   HAGAR-WIT . . . UNCLE WHAT-YOU-MAY-CALL-HIM] See note 58.32–34.

220.13   *hithering-and-thithering*] Cf. Book II of *Finnegans Wake* (1939): "hither-and-thithering waters of. Night!"

220.19   Jonathan Daniels] Daniels (1902–1981), a Rhodes scholar from UNC–Chapel Hill, was the longtime editor (and, after 1948, publisher) of the Raleigh *News and Observer*. From 1942 to 1947 he held several jobs in Washington, including personal aide and then press secretary to President Franklin D. Roosevelt. His books include *A Southerner Discovers the South* (1938), *A Southerner Discovers New England* (1940), and *White House Witness: 1942–45* (1975).

221.14–21   *We have to-morrow / / We march!*] "Youth," early poem by Langston Hughes, as it appeared in Alain Locke's anthology *The New Negro* (1925).

221.31–33   Montgomery *Advertiser* . . . Pittsburgh *Courier*] The *Advertiser* and the *Constitution* were left-leaning metropolitan dailies. The *Defender* and the *Courier* were among the nation's leading black weeklies. Ralph McGill (1898–1969), publisher of the *Constitution*, was a syndicated columnist known for his antisegregation activism.

221.36   Talmadge . . . Arnall] Eugene Talmadge (1884–1946), an opponent of desegregation and the New Deal, was Democratic governor of Georgia in 1933–37 and 1941–43. Former state attorney general Ellis Arnall (1907–1992), a liberal reformer, was Democratic governor in 1943–47.

221.38   *New Masses*] Monthly magazine of the American Communist Party, published in New York from 1926 to 1948.

222.4   Edwin Yoder] American journalist (b. 1934) and a Rhodes scholar from UNC–Chapel Hill. When Murray met him in 1970, he had been associate editor of the Greensboro *Daily News* since 1965. He would later win a Pulitzer Prize for his editorials for the *Washington Star* and write a syndicated column for the Washington Post Writers Group.

222.5   W. J. Cash] South Carolina–born writer and newspaperman (1900–1941) whose book *The Mind of the South* (1941) grew out of a series of essays written for Mencken's *American Mercury* in 1929–37. Contrary to Murray's statement, Cash was never associate editor of the Greensboro *Daily News*, but did serve in that role for the *Charlotte News* from 1937 until his death.

222.15–23   "we Southerners . . . day alone."] Jonathan Daniels, *A Southerner Discovers the South* (see note 220.19).

222.29 Joseefus] Josephus Daniels (1862–1948), father of Jonathan Daniels (see note 220.19), was a journalist and author, the majority owner and publisher of the Raleigh *News and Observer* (from 1894), and secretary of the Navy under Woodrow Wilson (1913–21). The *News and Observer* would remain in the Daniels family's hands through 1995.

223.31 Ma Rainey] Blues diva and theater owner (1886–1939). Her residence in Columbus, Georgia, is today the Ma Rainey House and Blues Museum.

225.9–10 Sissle and Blake] Noble Sissle (1889–1975) and Eubie Blake (1887–1983) were a songwriting team and creators of the Broadway musical revues *Shuffle Along* (1921) and *The Chocolate Dandies* (1924).

228.16–21 "fount of authority . . . age,"] See William Faulkner, "Funeral Sermon for Mammy Caroline Barr" (1940), in James B. Meriwether, ed., *William Faulkner: Essays, Speeches, and Public Letters* (New York: Random House, 1965).

229.19 *Commentary* or *Dissent*] In the 1960s, *Commentary* was a right-leaning monthly edited by Norman Podhoretz, and *Dissent* a left-leaning quarterly dominated by contributor Irving Howe.

229.23 Pat Moynihan] See note 28.34.

229.24 Levi Yitzchak of Berditchev] Prominent Hasidic rabbi (1740–1809) from Berditchev, Ukraine.

229.28 Compsons . . . Snopeses] Upper-class white Southerners and lower-class white Southerners in Faulkner's fiction.

229.33 Teachers College–plus–Bruno Bettelheim] Graduate School of Education at Columbia University; Austrian child psychologist (1903–1990).

230.26–27 Uncle Dipper] Nickname (along with Dippermouth, Satchelmouth, Satchmo) for Louis Armstrong.

231.39 Yoknapatawpha] Fictional Mississippi county in which several works by William Faulkner are set.

232.18 jack teagarden rejoinder] Teagarden (1905–1964) was a trombonist who frequently recorded with Louis Armstrong.

233.10–11 "trained incapacity,"] See Kenneth Burke, *Permanence and Change* (1935).

233.26–27 grammar of motives . . . dramatism] See note 7.2–3.

233.35–36 "W. J. Cash After a Quarter Century"] Essay by Edwin Yoder in *Harper's Magazine* (September 1965).

235.34 "*Boy, try to be one on whom nothing is lost.*"] Cf. "The Art of Fiction" (1884), essay by the novelist Henry James (1843–1916).

235.40 emperors of back-porch ice cream] See "The Emperor of Ice-Cream" (1922), poem by Wallace Stevens (1879–1955).

236.2–3 with a wooden spoon . . . beat the monkeys on the behind] See "The King of Harlem" (1929–30), poem by Federico García Lorca (1898–1936), translated from the Spanish by Stephen Spender and J. L. Gill (1947).

236.11 Sambo Fallacy] See note 38.32.

236.15 Minority-Group Psyche Fallacy] See, for example, the language of the *Brown v. Board of Education* decision: "Segregation of white and colored children in public schools has a detrimental effect upon the colored children. The impact is greater when it has the sanction of the law, for the policy of separating the races is usually interpreted as denoting the inferiority of the Negro group. A sense of inferiority affects the motivation of a child to learn. Segregation with the sanction of law, therefore, has a tendency to [retard] the educational and mental development of Negro children and to deprive them of some of the benefits they would receive in a racial[ly] integrated school system."

236.19 Self-Image Fallacy] See, for example, the psychological experiments of Kenneth B. Clark, who, in the 1940s through the 1960s, studied the effects of segregation on the self-esteem of low-income black students by studying their self-images in artwork and their preferences for white dolls over black dolls. "What was surprising," Clark later said, "was the degree to which children suffered from self-rejection, with its truncating effect on their personalities, and the earliness of the corrosive awareness of color."

237.25–30 *Gimme a good ole ghetto man / / Lordy Lord . . .*] A "contemporary" blues lyric of Murray's own invention.

239.11 *Willie Morris*] Morris (1934–1999), a Rhodes scholar from the University of Texas–Austin, was editor of *Harper's Magazine* from 1967 to 1971. Murray figures in his autobiographical memoir *North Toward Home* (Boston: Houghton Mifflin, 1967).

239.22 *"And Hodding Carter."*] W. Hodding Carter Jr. (1907–1972) was editor of the progressive *Delta Democrat-Times*, of Greenville, Mississippi, which he founded in 1939. His books include *The Lower Mississippi* (American Rivers series, 1942), *Where Main Street Meets the River* (memoir, 1953), *The Angry Scar: The Story of Reconstruction* (1959), and *First Person Rural* (collection, 1963).

239.28–29 *Frady . . . Watters . . . Cumming . . . Nelson*] Marshall Frady (1940–2004), magazine features writer, usually on Southern subjects, and author of *Wallace* (1968); Pat Watters (1927–1999), a reporter and editor for the *Atlanta Journal* (1952–63), then director of information for the Southern Regional Council (1963–74); Joe Cumming (b. 1926), Atlanta bureau chief of *Newsweek* (1961–79); Jack Nelson (1929–2009), who began his career at the

Atlanta Journal Constitution (1952–65), was Washington bureau chief for the *Los Angeles Times* (1965–75).

239.30–31   *John Corry . . . Ray Jenkins*] Corry (b. 1935), who spent most of his long career in journalism at *The New York Times*, was a contributing editor at *Harper's* in 1968–71; Jenkins (b. 1930) enjoyed a long career at the Montgomery *Advertiser-Journal* (1959–79), ending as executive editor.

239.31–33   *young Hodding . . . Halberstam . . . Percy . . . Foote*] W. Hodding Carter III (b. 1935) worked for his father's *Delta Democrat-Times* (1959–77) before serving in the Carter administration and enjoying a career in broadcast journalism; David Halberstam (1934–2007), a native New Yorker, began his reporting career on small papers in Mississippi and Tennessee (1955–62) and later covered the civil rights movement for *Harper's* and *The New York Times*; Catholic writer Walker Percy (see note 320.25) was the author of *The Moviegoer* (1961) and five later novels; novelist and historian Shelby Foote (see note 327.16) was the author of, among other works on the South, *The Civil War: A Narrative* (three volumes, 1958–74).

240.27–31   *"that implies impression . . . ensuance of existentiality."*] Cf. James Joyce, Book I of *Finnegans Wake* (1939).

244.7   Herren's] Lunch spot in downtown Atlanta (1934–87) and, in 1962, one of the first well-known Georgia restaurants to integrate.

244.9   Reese Cleghorn] From 1969 to 1971, Atlanta-based journalist Cleghorn (1930–2009) was project director for the Southern Regional Council and founding editor of its civil rights quarterly, *South Today* (1969–73).

244.12   Ralph McGill] See note 221.31–33.

244.13   Julian Bond . . . uncle J. Max] Educator and college administrator J. Max Bond (1902–1991), dean at Tuskegee in 1940–44, was the uncle of Julian Bond (see note 85.35–36).

244.20   Charles Evers] See note 38.39–40.

246.8   credibility gap] Media buzzword of the late 1960s describing the difference between what the U.S. government said it was doing, especially in matters of foreign policy, and what it was *actually* doing.

246.40   Tobacco Road] See note 267.38.

248.4   Algonquin or the Café de la Paix] *Beau monde* hotel restaurants in New York and Paris, respectively.

249.15   Eugene Patterson] Pulitzer Prize–winning editorial-page writer (1923–2013) who was an editor and executive at the *Atlanta Journal-Constitution* (1956–68) before joining the *Washington Post* as managing editor.

249.19–20   *newly elected member of the Tuskegee Board of Trustees*] McGill joined the board in 1949.

249.34   Henry W. Grady] Grady (1850–1889), an ardent proponent of Northern investment in what he hailed as "the new industrial South," was managing editor of the Atlanta *Constitution* throughout the 1880s.

250.8   Guy B. Johnson] American sociologist (1901–1991), a pillar of the Institute for Research in Social Science at the University of North Carolina.

250.18   "Lift Every Voice and Sing."] See note 212.24.

251.33   Frank Forbes] Franklin L. Forbes (1904–1972) was the athletics director at Morehouse College and coach of its basketball and football teams.

251.40   Benjamin Mays] Mays (1894–1983), a Baptist minister and civil rights activist, was president of Morehouse College from 1940 to 1967.

252.33   Charlayne Hunter and Hamilton Holmes] On January 9, 1961, Hunter (b. 1942), later known as journalist Charlayne Hunter-Gault, and Holmes (1941–1995) became the first blacks to register at the University of Georgia–Athens.

254.5–15   It is not at all surprising . . . from the summit.] Events of February 1968.

254.36–38   Malcolm X . . . "autobiography"] See note 83.21–23.

255.7–8   Lester Maddox] Defiantly segregationist Democratic politician (1915–2003) who was governor of Georgia from 1967 to 1971.

255.8   Hank Aaron] Mobile native Henry Louis "Hank" Aaron (b. 1932) was a power-hitting right fielder for the Milwaukee/Atlanta Braves from 1954 to 1974. (In 1972 Aaron's agents approached Murray about cowriting his autobiography.)

255.24–25   *Payton . . . Bancy and Tanny*] Julius "Bo" Payton was manager of the Mobile Black Shippers, of baseball's Negro National League, during Murray's youth. Walter "Bancy" Thomas and (presumably) "Tanny" were players on the Shippers' roster.

255.27–28   *Satchel Paige*] Pitcher (1906–1982) in both Negro League (1926–48) and Major League baseball (1948–65).

256.3   TRIANGULATION POINT THREE FIVE THREE NINE] Murray was a student at Tuskegee Institute from the fall of 1935 through the spring of 1939.

256.10–11   *Monkey Town to Skeegum-Geegum*] Montgomery to Tuskegee.

256.12   *Ray Jenkins*] See note 239.30–31.

256.20   *Air University*] Professional military educational institution at Maxwell Air Force Base in Montgomery, Alabama. Murray studied there in 1951.

259.36   THRILLED] Song (1935) by Harry Barris (1905–1962), words by Mort Greene (1912–1992).

259.37–40 *"the ashes on the floor / / . . . you used to do"*] From "The Little Things You Used to Do," song (1935) by Harry Warren (1893–1981), words by Al Dubin (1891–1945).

260.10 John Gerald Hamilton] See note 209.16.

261.28–40 Payne . . . Heningburg . . . Dr. Carver . . . Cap'n Neely . . . Cap'n "Now Now B-Buddy" Love] Faculty and staff at Tuskegee during Murray's college years: W. Henri Payne, professor of romance languages; Alphonse Heningburg, director of personnel, and his wife, Willa Mae Scales Heningburg, a popular faculty hostess; George Washington Carver, chairman of the Agricultural Department; Captain Alvin J. Neely, registrar and dean of men; Captain Walter J. Love, assistant professor of military science and tactics.

262.11 Lewis Mumford . . . Golden Day] *The Golden Day: A Study in American Experience and Culture* (1926), book on American transcendentalism by polymath Lewis Mumford (1895–1990).

262.28–30 *"You press the middle valve down / / and it comes out here."*] From "The Music Goes Round and Round," song (1935) by Edward Farley and Michael Riley, words by Red Hodgson.

262.37–39 Dad Moberly . . . Big Ben Stevenson] William "Dad" Moberly, later the coach of the semipro Detroit Pioneers, and Benjamin "Big Ben" Stevenson, a six-foot-two halfback who, in 1924–30, led the Tuskegee Golden Tigers to six Black College National Championships.

263.6–7 Talented Tenth] W. E. B. Du Bois (see note 154.11–13), in his 1903 essay "The Negro Problem," argued that it was the most talented 10 percent of African Americans that would lead the rest to success.

263.9 Sprague, Morteza Drexel] "Mort" Sprague (1909–1966), a native of Washington, D.C., was chairman of the English Department of Tuskegee Institute and later its head librarian. He held degrees from Hamilton College, Howard University, and Columbia University, and his lessons in modern literature had a shaping influence on Ellison and Murray. Ellison dedicated his essay collection *Shadow and Act* (1964) to him.

264.9 Cheney's *Primer*] American art and theater critic Sheldon Cheney (1886–1980) was the author of *A Primer of Modern Art* (New York: Boni & Liveright, 1924), a short history that enjoyed fourteen editions during its author's lifetime.

264.11 *Coronet*] Digest-sized general-interest monthly (1936–71) created by *Esquire*'s publisher David Smart.

264.33–34 Rockwell Kent's . . . *Candide*] American artist Kent (1882–1971) illustrated Voltaire's satire (1759) for Random House in 1928.

265.19 Shadow in *Winterset*] In the Hollywood crime drama *Winterset* (1936), based on the Maxwell Anderson play of 1935, the supporting role of

Shadow, a fall guy set up by his gangster boss, was played by British character actor Stanley Ridges (1890–1951).

265.30   College will not interfere with his education."] Cf. "I never let my schooling interfere with my education," a witticism coined by Canadian novelist Grant Allen (1848–1899) and often misattributed to Mark Twain.

265.31   *Seven Gothic Tales*] Collection of stories (1934) by Danish writer Isak Dinesen (1885–1962).

265.35–36   *Personae, The Waste Land*] Books of high-modernist poetry by Ezra Pound and T. S. Eliot, respectively.

265.38   *Roan Stallion*] Epic poem (1925) by American poet Robinson Jeffers (1887–1962).

265.39–40   free verse about . . . nothings."] Murray recited these lines by Ellison during a toast to the author at the eightieth-birthday party at Le Périgord, in New York, on March 1, 1994: "Life is nothing, / Death is nothing, / How beautiful these two nothings!" (See David Remnick, "Visible Man," *The New Yorker* [March 14, 1994].)

266.1   *Hound of Heaven*] Long "Christian mystic" poem (1893), mainly in blank verse, by British poet Francis Thomson (1859–1907).

266.7   Joyce locked up, with Radclyffe Hall] The Tuskegee library's copies of the novels *Ulysses* (1922), by James Joyce, and *The Well of Loneliness* (1928), by Radclyffe Hall, were, due to their sexual content, off limits to undergraduates.

266.14–17   desolate because sick of an old passion? . . . *Cynara*] Cf. "Non Sum Qualis Eram Bonae sub Regno Cynarae" (1894), by the English poet Ernest Dowson (1867–1900).

266.19   *Mais où sont les neiges d'antan?*] "Where are the snows of yesteryear?," from "Ballad de dames du temps jadis" ("Ballad of the Ladies of Times Past," circa 1460), poem by François Villon (circa 1431–1463).

266.27–28   *"How beautiful . . . daughter!"*] *How Beautiful with Shoes*, by Wilbur Daniel Steele, appeared in *Harper's Magazine* (August 1932).

266.38–39   *Anthony Adverse*] For Murray's thoughts about Hervey Allen's bestseller of 1936, see page 854 of the present volume.

267.2   Alexander House] The Alexander House, a Greek Revival–style plantation house built circa 1840, is now the president's residence at Tuskegee University.

267.25   where Teddy Roosevelt stayed] Roosevelt visited Tuskegee in October 1905 and March 1906.

267.38   *God's Little Acre* and *Tobacco Road*] "Southern gothic" novels, of 1933 and 1932, respectively, by Georgia native Erskine Caldwell (1903–1987).

269.8 "Monologue to the Maestro."] Essay on the craft of fiction, by Ernest Hemingway, published in *Esquire* (October 1935) and collected in William White, ed., *By-line: Ernest Hemingway—Selected Articles and Dispatches of Four Decades* (New York: Scribner's, 1967).

269.10–13 Peola . . . *Imitation of Life*] See note 163.40–164.1.

269.27 *rigoureusement*] French: strictly.

270.4 Mozelle] Mozelle Menefee (1920–2015) married Albert Murray on May 31, 1941, and remained his wife until his death.

270.5 Moketubbe] Chickasaw chieftain in the fiction of William Faulkner.

271.17 Warren Logan] Logan (1858–1942) was treasurer of Tuskegee Institute and the right hand of founder-president Booker T. Washington.

271.18 Von Rundstedt] Karl Rudolf Gard von Rundstedt (1875–1953), German field marshal during World War II.

271.23–24 Portia Pittman] Mrs. William Sidney Pittman (1883–1978), née Portia Marshall Washington, was the first child and only daughter of Booker T. Washington. An accomplished pianist, she was a music teacher at Tuskegee from 1928 to 1939, when she opened a private studio in her home near the campus.

275.2 Ken *magazine*] *Life*-sized illustrated biweekly magazine (1938–39) founded by Arnold Gingrich and David Smart, who had together founded *Esquire* in 1933. Ernest Hemingway contributed fourteen pieces during its brief run.

275.3 *Hans Castorp*] Protagonist of Thomas Mann's novel *The Magic Mountain* (*Der Zauberberg*, 1924).

275.5 *Miqué*] Michele Murray (b. 1943), daughter of Albert and Mozelle Murray.

275.10–11 *Alfred A. Knopf . . . Mrs. H. T. Lowe-Porter*] Thomas Mann's American publisher and English translator, respectively.

275.28 Mistinguett] Jeanne Florentine Bourgeois (1875–1951), French entertainer.

276.5–11 *Saxe Commins . . . down, down' . . ."*] This letter, dated April 9, 1953, is printed in full in John Callahan and Albert Murray, eds., *Trading Twelves: The Selected Letters of Ralph Ellison and Albert Murray* (New York: Modern Library, 2000). Commins (1892–1958) was editor-in-chief of Random House from 1933 until his death.

276.13 *Ras the Exhorter*] See note 152.27–28.

276.34 *Sam Eliot Morison*] See note 206.14–15.

277.25–26 *that crap old Norman Mailer wrote about us*] "Of a Fire on the

Moon," a three-article series on NASA's lunar program appearing in *Life* magazine from August 1969 to January 1970. The third installment, "A Dream of the Future's Face," contains Mailer's racist speculations that, because blacks are not oriented to understanding "numbers," they would resent "whitey" for having landed a man on the moon.

278.13 *Ideas and Forms*] Homer Andrew Watt and James B. Munn, eds., *Ideas and Forms in English and American Literature* (Chicago: Scott, Foresman, 1925).

281.6 *Battle House*] See note 212.15–16.

282.1 Gibson Girl–proper] See note 49.28–29.

282.13 Dave Patton] Mobile-area real estate investor and philanthropist (1879–1927).

285.7 *high-yaller*] See note 163.40–164.1.

287.23 Valena Withers] Valena McCants (b. 1925), née Withers, was an educator who, while a student at Tuskegee Institute, encountered Murray as a mentor figure who looked out for fellow-Mobilians. She taught civics to tenth graders at Mobile County Training School and was later the assistant to the president of Bishop State Community College and director of the BSCC Foundation.

287.26 Baker, Benjamin F.] See note 171.11.

287.39–40 Noble Beasley] Civil rights activist Noble "Bip" Beasley (1932–2014) was president of NOW (see note 164.13) from 1968 to 1973.

288.10 Henry Williams] Mobile native Henry C. Williams Sr. (1920–2008) was the founder, in 1946, of Williams Welding and Industrial Trade School. He was also a talented local historian, the chairman of the Progressive League of Africatown, and the author of such self-published monographs as *A History of the MCTS* (1977) and *Africatown U.S.A.: A Pictorial History* (1981).

288.26 *Clotilda*] The schooner *Clotilde* (or *Clotilda*) was one of the last U.S. ships to import slaves from Africa, bringing 160 captives from Dahomey to Mobile in the fall of 1859. Its hulk, which was scuttled then burned by its legally embattled owner, could be seen at the mouth of Chickasaw Creek throughout Murray's childhood. Many of the Africans brought over on the *Clotilde* settled in the Africatown and Magazine Point neighborhoods of Mobile.

290.29 Jonathan T. Gaines] Dr. J. T. Gaines (1908–1982), Murray's algebra teacher at Mobile County Training School, became principal of MCTS (1947–53) and then of Mobile's Central High School (1953–70). (In 1991 the campus of Central High School, closed in 1971, was given by the city of Mobile to Bishop State Community College, which renamed it the Gaines-Baker Central Campus in honor of Dr. Gaines and Benjamin F. Baker [see note 171.11].)

295.14 Hambone stuff] Vaudeville term for black-dialect comedy written and performed in blackface (see notes 100.21 and 114.1).

295.15–16 Stepin Fetchit and Willie Best and Mantan Moreland] Comic actors with personas based on black stereotypes who played supporting roles in the B movies of Murray's youth.

302.26–29 honor thy father . . . giveth thee] Exodus 20:12.

302.29 Elder Ravezee] The Reverend Ravezee Hargress Sr. (1919–1974) was an elder of the Emanuel African Methodist Episcopal Church, Mobile, Alabama.

302.31 Joyful Keeby] The Reverend Joiffu "Joyful" Keeby (1871–?), son of *Clotilde* survivor Oluoalo "Ossie" Keeby (circa 1841–1925?), was pastor of the Union Missionary Baptist Church, Mobile, Alabama.

302.36 *Crowtillie*] *Clotilde* (see note 288.26).

303.15–16 that's the Bible again.] What follows is a pastiche of Genesis 9:20–27, I Corinthians 13:4, and James 3:9.

306.8 old blue-eagle jive] New Deal programs of the National Recovery Act (NRA), whose symbol was a blue eagle.

308.18 Teddy Roosevelt . . . Bookety] Booker T. Washington was the Roosevelt family's private dinner guest on October 16, 1901.

308.33–34 Muscle Shoals and Three Point Two] In early 1933 President Franklin D. Roosevelt proposed that the New Deal's Tennessee Valley Authority be headquartered in Muscle Shoals, Alabama, but in the end it was established upriver, in Knoxville, Tennessee; later that year, nine months before the end of Prohibition, he signed the Cullen-Harrison Act, which permitted U.S. manufacture and sale of low-alcohol beer and wine (alcohol content not to exceed 3.2 percent of weight).

309.7–8 Johnson . . . got in there on a humble] Lyndon Johnson became president following John F. Kennedy's assassination. The speaker believes Johnson could not have become president through the electoral process.

309.35 creditability gap] See note 246.8.

310.19 Weaver] Robert C. Weaver (1907–1997), the first black person to hold a cabinet-level position, was the first secretary of housing and urban development (1966–68).

310.29–30 He got up there . . . we shall overcome] President Johnson, in his televised address to Congress on March 15, 1965, concerning recent events in Selma and the Voting Rights Act, said that we, all Americans, "must overcome the crippling legacy of bigotry and injustice. And we *shall* overcome."

310.33 Big Jim Folsom] James Folsom Sr. (1908–1987), an integrationist, was governor of Alabama in 1947–51 and 1955–59.

311.23–29 Send me old Thurgill Marshall . . . keep an eye on the money] Thurgood Marshall (1908–1993) was the first black justice on the U.S.

Supreme Court, and Andrew Brimmer (1926–2012) the first black governor of the Federal Reserve Board (1966–74).

312.34   young fess?] Young professor.

313.9   Scotchbug mess] Trial of the so-called Scottsboro boys, nine young Alabama blacks accused of the gang rape of two white women in 1931, a case that occupied the courts and the national headlines from 1931 to 1937.

315.29   plurabilities] Allusion to Anna Livia Plurabelle, the shape-shifting archetypal mother-figure of James Joyce's *Finnegans Wake*.

317.17   howard-johnsoning you] Howard Johnson's, a once ubiquitous chain of hotels and casual restaurants in the U.S. of the mid-twentieth century.

318.1–3   Jim Brown . . . Johnny Mack Brown] Cleveland Browns fullback Jim Brown (b. 1936) and Crimson Tide halfback Johnny "Mack" Brown (1904–1974) both had high-profile second careers as Hollywood leading men.

318.6   Admiral Semmes] Mobile hotel (1940) named in honor of Confederate navy officer Raphael Semmes (1809–1877), admiral of CCS *Alabama*. In 2014 it was renamed the Admiral Hotel.

320.13–14   *Charles . . . Harris . . . Benny . . . Lady Mary Jack the Bear*] Four urban legends of New Orleans: Robert Charles, "cop killer" who caused a race riot in 1900; Aaron Harris, cold-blooded murderer abetted by a voodoo woman; "Black Benny" Williams, bass drummer extraordinaire; Lady Mary Jack the Bear, a prostitute.

320.25   *Walker Percy*] Catholic writer Walker Percy (1916–1990) was, when Murray met him in 1969, the author of two acclaimed novels, *The Moviegoer* (1961, winner of the National Book Award) and *The Last Gentleman* (1966). Percy, who lived in Covington, Louisiana, near New Orleans, earned an M.D. at Columbia University (1941) with the aim of becoming a psychiatrist.

320.37   William Alexander Percy] Walker Percy's bachelor uncle (1885–1942) was a lawyer, a poet and book editor, and the author of *Lanterns on the Levee: Recollections of a Planter's Son* (1941), a best-selling memoir of his privileged youth in Greenville, Mississippi. When, in 1929, Walker and his two younger brothers were orphaned by their mother's suicide, William Percy became their ward.

322.30   Lucas Beauchamp or Sam Fathers] Characters in Faulkner's Yoknapatawpha fiction.

322.30–35   "*as one thinks . . . shows him how.*"] Letter by Percy to the editors of *Harper's Magazine* (May 1967) in response to "A Very Stern Discipline," an interview with Ellison that had appeared in *Harper's* for March 1967.

323.4   Gavin Stevens] Lawyer in Faulkner's Yoknapatawpha fiction.

323.6–9   "*Changing men's hearts . . . if they try.*"] Walker Percy, "The Fire

This Time," review-essay of seven nonfiction books about contemporary Mississippi, in *The New York Review of Books* (July 1, 1965).

326.10–11   interview in which he called himself a failed poet] Jean Stein, "William Faulkner: The Art of Fiction, No. 12," *The Paris Review* (Spring 1956).

326.17   *Nada*-Confrontation Hero] The Hemingway hero, like the old man drinking alone in the story "A Clean, Well-Lighted Place" or the old waiter who serves him, who confronts *nada* (Spanish for "nothingness" or spiritual emptiness) with a kind of existential courage.

326.19–20   Malraux-Pascal image of man's fate] Malraux, an admirer of Blaise Pascal, may have titled his novel *La Condition Humaine* (*Man's Fate*) after Pascal's *Pensée* number 434: "Imagine a number of men in chains, all under sentence of death, some of whom are each day butchered in the sight of the others; those remaining see their own condition in that of their fellows, and looking at each other with grief and despair await their turn. This is an image of the human condition." (Pascal, *Pensées* [1669], translated from the French by A. J. Krailsheimer [New York: Penguin Books, 1966].)

326.23–26   "history is something . . . divine providence."] C. Vann Woodward, *The Burden of Southern History*, revised edition (1969).

326.29   Mary Painter] Mary S. Garin-Painter (circa 1920–1991) was an American government analyst of postwar European economies. She was a close friend of James Baldwin, who dedicated his 1962 novel *Another Country* to her.

326.34–35   Agnes Moorehead] American actress Moorehead (1900–1974) memorably played the role of housekeeper to the reclusive owner of a Louisiana plantation house in the Hollywood thriller *Hush . . . Hush, Sweet Charlotte* (1964).

327.5   Akim Tamiroff] Russian-born actor (1899–1972) who played Jean Lafitte's right-hand man at the Battle of New Orleans in Cecil B. DeMille's *The Buccaneer* (1938).

327.10–11   Heston's Andy Jackson . . . Barrymore's Old Hickory] Andrew Jackson was played by Charlton Heston (1923–2008) in the 1958 remake of *The Buccaneer* (see above) and by Lionel Barrymore (1878–1954) in the film *The Gorgeous Hussy* (1936).

327.16   Shelby Foote] Greenville native Foote (1916–2005), a novelist and a historian of the Civil War, was a boyhood neighbor and lifelong friend of Walker Percy. (*The Correspondence of Shelby Foote and Walker Percy*, edited by Jay Tolson, was published by W. W. Norton in 1996.)

328.28–29   Sidney Poitier slapping . . . greenhouse incident] In the film *In the Heat of the Night* (1967), black Philadelphia homicide detective Virgil Tibbs, played by Sidney Poitier (b. 1927), reflexively slaps back when slapped across the face by the white owner of a Mississippi cotton plantation.

329.7   agenbite of . . . inwit] Poetic Old English term for conscience, revived by James Joyce in *Ulysses* (1922).

329.16   David L. Cohn] Prolific essayist on Southern topics (1894–1960) whose best-known book was *God Shakes Creation* (New York: Harper & Bros., 1935), a memoir of his Mississippi Delta youth. The book was later republished in an expanded edition under the title *Where I Was Born and Raised* (Boston: Houghton Mifflin, 1948).

331.9   Hodding Carter] Hodding Carter Jr. (see note 239.31–33).

332.5   young Hod) Hodding Carter III (see note 239.31–33).

332.10–12   Hepburn . . . Tracy . . . two-fisted editorship] Hollywood actors paired in several enduring films, including the newsroom comedy *Woman of the Year* (1942).

332.25   Brent . . . Generelley] Betty Brent, wife of Jesse Brent (1912–1982), founder and operator of Greenville-based Brent Towing Co., a major employer on Mississippi's inland waterways, and Bel Generelley, wife of L. Roger Generelley (1900–1974), founder of Valley Fertilizer Co., Greenville.

332.31   Willie] Willie Morris (see note 239.11).

333.21–22   Erskine . . . *Sanctuary*] Albert Erskine (1911–1993), a native of Memphis, was William Faulkner's editor at Random House. The most shocking scenes of Faulkner's novel *Sanctuary* (1931) are set in a Memphis whorehouse.

333.33–34   Handy . . . Boss Crump . . . St. Louis] "The Memphis Blues," published in 1912 by W. C. Handy (1873–1956), was subtitled "Mister Crump" in honor of Edward Hull Crump (1874–1954), mayor of Memphis from 1910 to 1915. Handy's "St. Louis Blues" was published in 1914.

335.28   Emperor Jones stuff] American murderer Brutus Jones, the black protagonist of Eugene O'Neill's play *The Emperor Jones* (1920), escapes from a jail and soon becomes the strongman of a small island in the West Indies.

337.13–14   Max Weber . . . use of power] In his essay "Politics as Vocation" ("Politik als Beruf," 1919), German sociologist Max Weber (1864–1920) defined power as one's ability to achieve goals despite the opposition of others. C. Wright Mills (1916–1962), of Columbia University, and Talcott Parsons (see note 40.33), of Harvard, were American sociologists deeply influenced by Weber.

337.21–22   Memphis Confrontation] The series of confrontations between Memphis police and the city's striking sanitation workers, some of which were mediated by Martin Luther King Jr., in the months preceding King's assassination, on the balcony of the Lorraine Hotel, on April 4, 1968.

339.3   Bull Connor] See note 163.24.

339.15–16   Big Daddy Moynihan's notorious monograph] See note 28.34.

341.17   Uncle Jack the Bear] Jack the Bear, apparently slow and lazy but actually quick-witted and able, is a trickster hero in African American oral tradition. ("Jack the Bear" was a working title for Murray's *ur*-novel of the 1950s, the manuscript that later yielded *Train Whistle Guitar* [1974] and *The Spyglass Tree* [1991].)

THE HERO AND THE BLUES

353.10–12   It was once stated . . . Leon Trotsky] See Delmore Schwartz (1913–1966), "Ernest Hemingway's Literary Situation," in *Southern Review* (Spring 1938).

356.25   Dynamic Image] See Susanne K. Langer (1895–1985), "The Dynamic Image: Some Philosophical Reflections on Dance," in *Dance Observer* (July 1956), collected in *Problems of Art: Ten Philosophical Lectures* (New York: Scribner's, 1957).

359.31–360.21   "Tragedy is the enactment . . . death is conquered."] From *The Classical Tradition in Poetry* (1927), by Gilbert Murray (see note 7.36–8.1), a book based on his Charles Eliot Norton Lectures at Harvard University in 1926–27.

365.3   THE REMARK which Ernest Hemingway made] "Writers are forged in injustice as a sword is forged": Ernest Hemingway, *Green Hills of Africa* (New York: Scribner's, 1935).

365.21   "Monologue to the Maestro"] Ernest Hemingway, "Monologue to the Maestro: A High Seas Letter" (see note 269.8).

365.23   *A Moveable Feast*] Posthumous memoir of Paris in the 1920s, by Ernest Hemingway (New York: Scribner's, 1964).

365.26   interview for *Paris Review*] George Plimpton, "Ernest Hemingway: The Art of Fiction, No. 21," *The Paris Review* (Spring 1958).

365.29   another interview] Unsigned books department interview, "Hemingway in the Afternoon," *Time* (August 4, 1947), collected in Matthew J. Bruccoli, ed., *Conversations with Ernest Hemingway* (Jackson: University Press of Mississippi, 1986).

369.17–18   *meaning* of his name] Oedipus is Greek for "Swollen Foot." When Oedipus was an infant only three days old, his parents received a prophecy that one day he would kill his father, and so they scarified the soles of his feet and abandoned him on a mountainside. Oedipus was marked for suffering, by the actions of his parents, from the very beginning of his life.

369.27–30   Shakespeare's Prince Hal . . . ruffians] Characters and events in Shakespeare's *Henry IV, Part One*.

369.36   *corridas*] Spanish: bullfights.

371.21–22 to paraphrase André Malraux] From the preface of *Days of Wrath* (see note 3.1–7): "It would be nice to think that the word *art* can make men aware of the greatness they do not recognize in themselves."

371.25–26 *Uncle Tom's Children* and *Native Son*] See notes 124.17–18 and 66.5.

373.31 NCO] Non-commissioned officer.

374.23 Stephen Dedalus] Protagonist of James Joyce's *A Portrait of the Artist as a Young Man* (1916) and a major character in *Ulysses* (1922).

375.4 *The Coming Victory of Democracy*] Lecture by Thomas Mann ("Vom kommenden Sieg der Demokratie," 1937) exhorting the free world to join forces against the Third Reich. An English version of the text, translated from the German by Agnes E. Meyer with Ernst Meyer, was delivered by Mann on a tour across the United States from February to May 1938. It was published as a small book by Knopf in the fall of 1938.

375.26 "the blisses of the commonplace"] Mann used the phrase "eine ganze keusche Seligkeit" in his long short story "Tonio Kröger" (1903). It was translated into English, by H. T. Lowe-Porter, as "bliss of the commonplace" when the story was published in *Death in Venice and Seven Other Stories* (New York: Knopf, 1936).

375.31–32 *The Reflections of a Non-Political Man*] Thomas Mann's *Betrachtungen eines Unpolitischen* (Berlin: Fischer, 1918), written in 1915–18, is an apology for Germany's conduct during World War I and a meditation on the artist's role in politics. The text, unavailable in English during Mann's lifetime (1875–1955), was translated by Walter D. Morris as *Reflections of a Nonpolitical Man* (New York: Ungar, 1983).

375.39–376.1 *Order of the Day*] Thomas Mann, *Order of the Day: Political Speeches and Essays of Two Decades*, translated from the German by H. T. Lowe-Porter with Agnes E. Meyer and Eric Sutton (New York: Knopf, 1942). This volume collects writings from 1923 to 1941, including "The Coming Victory of Democracy" (1937), "What I Believe" (1938), and "Culture and Politics" (1939).

377.36–37 *The Transposed Heads*] Thomas Mann, *The Transposed Heads: A Legend of India* (*Die vertauschten Köpfe: Eine indische Legende*, 1940), translated from the German by H. T. Lowe-Porter (New York: Knopf, 1941).

378.14–22 "and it will have the artist's attitude . . . cancel each other."] Thomas Mann, "The Coming Humanism," *The Nation* (December 10, 1938), collected, as "What I Believe," in *Order of the Day* (1942).

379.5 *Man's Hope*] André Malraux, *Man's Hope* (*L'Espoir*, 1937), a novel of the Spanish Civil War, translated from the French by Stuart Gilbert and Alastair Macdonald (1938).

382.8 *Voices of Silence*] André Malraux, *The Voices of Silence* (*Les Voix du Silence*, 1951), translated by Stuart Gilbert (Princeton: Princeton University

Press, 1953). The book originally appeared in English, in 1949–50, as *The Psychology of Art* (*Psychologie de l'art*, three volumes, 1947–49).

384.3–6   T. S. Eliot addressed himself . . . past] See "Tradition and the Individual Talent," *The Egoist* (December 1919), collected in *The Sacred Wood* (1920) and *Selected Essays* (1932).

384.7   "Freud and the Future,"] Lecture by Thomas Mann, delivered in Vienna on May 8, 1936, on the occasion of Freud's eightieth birthday, and again, in the English of H. T. Lowe-Porter, at the New School for Social Research, New York, in April 1937. Published in *The Saturday Review of Literature* (July 25, 1936) and collected in *Freud, Goethe, Wagner* (1937) and *Essays of Three Decades* (1947).

389.30–37   Maurice Grosser . . . ultimate reality."] *The Painter's Eye: On the Psychology and Techniques of Painting*, by the American figurative painter Maurice Grosser (1903–1986), was published by Rinehart & Co., New York, in 1951.

391.15   *Time* magazine inquiry] See note 365.29.

391.33   as he told George Plimpton] See note 365.26.

392.2–12   "No . . . so few plots to write about."] See Faulkner on Hawthorne (May 6, 1957), in Joseph Blotner and Frederick L. Gwynn, eds., *Faulkner in the University: Class Conferences at the University of Virginia, 1957–1958* (Charlottesville: University Press of Virginia, 1959).

392.38–393.2   "uses everything . . . something of his own."] Ernest Hemingway, *Death in the Afternoon* (1932).

395.33   Burbage] Richard Burbage (1567–1619), a member of the Globe Theater company, created many of Shakespeare's tragic roles, including Hamlet, Othello, Richard III, and Lear.

396.29   "objective correlative"] See T. S. Eliot, "Hamlet and His Problems," *The Athenaeum* (September 26, 1919), collected in *The Sacred Wood* (1920) and *Selected Essays* (1932).

396.32   *life of human feeling*] See Susanne K. Langer, *Mind: An Essay on Human Feeling*, Volume I (Baltimore: Johns Hopkins University Press, 1967).

399.31   Kenneth Burke has suggested] See *The Philosophy of Literary Form: Studies in Symbolic Action* (1941).

400.15   "The Secret Life of Walter Mitty"] Comic story by James Thurber, first published in *The New Yorker* (March 18, 1939) and collected in *My World and Welcome to It* (1942).

401.38   "How 'Bigger' Was Born"] See note 150.23.

403.5–6   *Chanson de Roland*, the *Nibelungenlied*] The French medieval epic

The Song of Roland, and the High Middle German epic *The Song of the Nibe-lungs* (the source for Wagner's *Ring* operas).

405.39–40   *nada*-confrontation hero] See note 326.17.

407.25   *Attitudes Toward History*] Kenneth Burke, *Attitudes Toward History* (New York: New Republic Books, 1937). For Murray's précis of the main argument of this book, see pages 509–10 of the present volume.

STOMPING THE BLUES

416.9   *When Jimmy Rushing sings*] On "Good Morning Blues" (by Count Basie and Eddie Durham) as recorded, in 1937, by Count Basie and His Orchestra (Decca 1446 A).

417.22   *the Wasteland episode*] See Jessie L. Weston, *From Ritual to Romance* (Cambridge: Cambridge University Press, 1920).

422.4   the old Savoy] In a caption to a photograph in the first edition of *Stomping the Blues*, Murray described the Savoy (1926–59) as "a world-renowned stomping place on Lenox Avenue at 140th Street. . . . The ballroom floor was a block long with a bandstand to accommodate the two orchestras that usually played alternating sets."

423.10–12   Madam Marie Laveau . . . Doctor Jim Alexander] Marie Laveau (1794–1881), legendary Creole practitioner of voodoo, and Dr. Jim Alexander (d. 1890), her rival and successor.

428.1   Satchmo the Jester] In a caption to a photograph in the first edition of *Stomping the Blues*, Murray wrote that "Satchmo the Jester was sometimes a source of embarrassment and confusion among some civil-rights spokesmen and black college students; but he always counter-stated his clowning with his trumpet, which was no laughing matter."

428.11–12   same spirit of parody holds true for . . . Louis Jordan] In a caption to a photograph in the first edition of *Stomping the Blues*, Murray wrote that "the element of frolicsome mockery in [Jordan's] verbal delivery is as obvious as is the downhome earthiness represented by the instrumental accompaniment."

436.13–14   "When my feet say dance . . . call the Blues."] From "Aunt Hagar's Blues," song (1920) by W. C. Handy, lyrics by J. Tim Brymn.

436.36–437.6   Well the blues jumped the rabbit . . . fifty years ago!] From "Rabbit Foot Blues," song (recorded 1926) by Blind Lemon Jefferson.

437.13   Hugues Panassié] French jazz critic and record producer (1912–1974) whose *Le Jazz Hot* (Paris: Éditions R-A Corrêa, 1934) was one of the first book-length studies of jazz music.

439.17   "We have something of the blue devils at times."] Thomas Jefferson, in a letter to Virginia politician Dr. Walter Jones, dated March 5, 1810. (See H. A. Washington, ed., *The Works of Thomas Jefferson*, volume 5, *Letters 1780–1826* [New York: Townsend MacCoun, 1884].)

441.15 Bessie Smith] In a caption to a photograph in the first edition of *Stomping the Blues*, Murray called Smith (1894–1937) "the most magnificent blues diva of them all." In another he wrote that "she was already a vaudeville prima donna with a considerable following before her first records were released. By the end of 1923 her popularity was that of a superstar."

443.12 *The Real Jazz*] Hugues Panassié, *The Real Jazz* (*La véritable musique de jazz*, 1942), translated from the French by Anne Sorelle Williams (New York: A. S. Barnes, 1960).

444.37–445.2 once W. C. Handy had arranged, scored and published . . . folk expression] In a caption to an illustration in the first edition of *Stomping the Blues*, Murray wrote: "Promotion copy sometimes represented W. C. Handy [see note 333.33–34] as the 'Father of the Blues' . . . Handy's own account does not back such a claim—although in fact he claimed credit for writing the first blues ever published, which he clearly pointed out was based on a form already in existence and already known as the blues. Handy did pioneer not only in the composition but in the publication of blues scores for professional musicians."

445.13–14 *Standard Dictionary of Folklore, Mythology, and Legend*] The entry on blues music in Jerome Fried and Maria Leach, eds., *Standard Dictionary of Folklore, Mythology, and Legend* (New York: Funk and Wagnalls, 1949), was written by American folklorist Theresa C. Brakeley (1912–2011).

450.25–26 Bessie Smith's slow drag version] In a caption to an illustration in the first edition of *Stomping the Blues*, Murray notes that Smith, in her "classic rendition" of *The St. Louis Blues* (Columbia 14064 D), sings "only the first verse and chorus of [Handy's] original [but] makes several alterations to the lyrics even so. Most notably she changes 'pack my *trunk* to make my git-away' to 'pack my *grip*' (*i.e.*, suitcase), which suggests that she intends to travel considerably lighter than Handy seems to have in mind. Incidentally, although the words, the slow tempo, and the ever so sorrowful harmonium accompaniment are all geared to lamentation, what her great and irrepressibly earthy voice expresses is a determination that is as undaunted as that of an empress of the earth itself."

451.9–10 (erstwhile *Mister Crump*)] See note 333.33–34.

454.32 Going to Chicago / Sorry but I can't take you] From "Going to Chicago Blues," song (circa 1941) by Count Basie and Jimmy Rushing.

461.4–5 it was as if Jo Jones only whispered the beat] In a caption to a photograph in the first edition of *Stomping the Blues*, Murray wrote that Jo Jones (1911–1985), "the most masterful, influential, and enduring of Kansas City percussionists, is as widely celebrated for the way he signifies with his

sticks and wire brushes as for the way he testifies, bears witness, exhorts, an-
notates, approves, or otherwise comments—not only with his sticks and his
foot pedals but also with his mallets and sometimes with his bare hands. Moreover, musicians and dancers alike almost always seem to respond as readily to
his most offhand insinuations as to his most forthright declarations and most
authoritative decrees."

462.22–23 tonal stylization derived from other performers.] In a caption to
a photograph in the first edition of *Stomping the Blues*, Murray elaborated on
this observation in a note on "one of the great vocal stylists," Billie Holiday
(1915–1959): "The great and lasting distinction of [Lady Day] is based not on
her highly publicized addiction to narcotics (a show-biz rather than a blues-
idiom phenomenon) but on her deliberate use of her voice as an Armstrong-
derived instrumental extension. . . . Time and again she used to say she
didn't think of herself as singing but as blowing a horn; and at her best she
achieved an emotional impact akin to Bessie Smith's, an elegant inventiveness
suggestive of Armstong's trumpet (and voice) plus that special intensity that
Lester Young could generate with cool understatement."

469.15–22 Now, I had been getting bored . . . I had been hearing] See
chapter 19, "The Experimenters," in Nat Shapiro and Nat Hentoff, eds., *Hear
Me Talkin' to Ya: The Story of Jazz as Told by the Men Who Made It* (New York:
Rinehart & Co., 1955).

474.27 Because such dance steps] In a caption to a photograph in the first
edition of *Stomping the Blues*, Murray made a clarifying point about the dance
steps: "In action performance jump music, as in *One O'Clock Jump*, is indistinguishable from a stomp, as in *Panassié Stomp*, or swing, as in *Moten Swing*.
The dance steps are different, of course, but even so one can jump to a stomp
and swing; stomp to a jump and swing; or swing to a jump and stomp."

475.21–30 "When *The St. Louis Blues* was written . . . was accepted] This
and subsequent quotes from W. C. Handy are from Handy's autobiography,
Father of the Blues, edited by Arna Bontemps (New York: Macmillan, 1941).

476.35–477.3 I remember we'd be hanging . . . used to say] Alan Lomax,
*Mister Jelly Roll: The Fortunes of Jelly Roll Morton, New Orleans Creole and
"Inventor of Jazz"* (New York: Duell, Sloan & Pearce, 1950).

477.35–39 "We've done things with the symphony orchestras . . . very
well."] Stanley Dance, "The Duke in India," *Saturday Review* (January 11,
1964).

479.22–27 "You could be sleeping one morning . . . street."] See chapter
17, "From Kansas City . . . ," in Nat Shapiro and Nat Hentoff, eds., *Hear Me
Talkin' to Ya: The Story of Jazz by the Men Who Made It* (New York: Rinehart
& Company, 1955).

480.28 the new Count Basie Orchestra] Murray means the Count Basie orchestra of 1936, as opposed to the short-lived Count Basie Orchestra of 1934, which disbanded in Little Rock, Arkansas, due to lack of money and bookings.

482.23–24   there are also the collected works of Charlie Parker] In a caption to a photograph in the first edition of *Stomping the Blues*, Murray wrote that "chances are that no real-life bird ever actually flew like Charlie the Yardbird. As magnificent as the most beautiful birds look against the sky, they mostly only flap and glide—whereas Parker cut figures with the dance-beat elegance of the pilots of the old 332nd Fighter Group."

484.1–4   "When Bennie Moten's two beat . . . one-two-three-four."] Cf. chapter 17, "From Kansas City . . . ," in Nat Shapiro and Nat Hentoff, eds., *Hear Me Talkin' to Ya* (1955).

484.23–30   "We were fooling around . . . a 'head.'"] Ross Russell, *Jazz Style in Kansas City and the Southwest* (Berkeley: University of California Press, 1971).

484.35–485.20   Basie would start out . . . until he got it right.] Dicky Wells, as told to Stanley Dance, *The Night People: Reminiscences of a Jazzman* (Boston: Crescendo, 1971).

488.31–34   *I thought I heard Buddy Bolden say // . . . bad air out.*] Jelly Roll Morton's lyrics are based on a bawdy folk song ("I Thought I Heard Somebody Say") that was well-known in black communities throughout the South.

491.5   *The Jazz Tradition*] Martin Williams (1924–1992), *The Jazz Tradition* (New York: Oxford University Press, 1969). Murray provided the following endorsement for the book's dust jacket: "Not only a serious, scholarly, and critically perceptive book on the blues idiom as an art form; it is, in effect, also a significant contribution to the literature of 'Black Consciousness.' . . . [Williams's] primary emphasis is on artistic creation and his standards are high. All students can learn much from his affirmative approach to Black experience."

491.6   *Early Jazz*] Gunther Schuller (1925–2015), *Early Jazz: Its Roots and Musical Development* (New York: Oxford University Press, 1968).

493.25–27   the first means by which human consciousness objectified . . . feelings] See Curt Sachs (1881–1959), *World History of the Dance* (*Eine Weltgeschichte des Tanzes*, 1933), translated from the German by Bessie Schönberg (New York: Norton, 1937).

504.25–26   John Coltrane and Ornette Coleman] In a caption to a photograph in the first edition of *Stomping the Blues*, Murray wrote: "John Coltrane . . . along with Ornette Coleman, became one of the most important innovators of the 1960s, is essentially a post–Charlie Parker instrumental extension of the traditional hard-driving blues shouter. Such Coltrane compositions as *Blue Train, Locomotion,* and *Traneing In* also represent post-bop avant-garde elaborations and refinements of traditional blues-idiom railroad onomato-poeia."

506.23–25 "Yes, every move we made . . . piano piece."] This and subse-quent quotes from James P. Johnson are drawn from Tom Davin, "Conversa-tions with James P. Johnson," *The Jazz Review* (August 1959), the third of a five-part series.

508.14 Old Duke's main blues singer . . . Johnny Hodges] In a caption to a photograph in the first edition of *Stomping the Blues*, Murray expanded this insight: "In some compositions Hodges functioned in effect as Ellington's instrumental extension of Bessie Smith."

THE BLUE DEVILS OF NADA

519.8–9 "objective correlative"] See note 396.29.

520.1 Leon Forrest] Chicago-born American writer (1937–1997) whose nov-els included *The Bloodworth Orphans* (1977).

521.17 *In one article*] "The Storyteller as Blues Singer," *American Journal* (April 10, 1973).

522.18 *Jason Berry*] New Orleans native Berry (b. 1949) is an investigative reporter and jazz journalist whose books include *Up from the Cradle of Jazz* (1986; revised and expanded 2009).

525.13–14 Susanne K. Langer . . . life of human feeling.] See note 396.32.

525.26 *The Voices of Silence*] See note 382.8.

525.28–29 Kenneth Burke . . . human beings.] See Kenneth Burke's essay "Literature as Equipment for Living" (*Direction*, April 1938), collected in *The Philosophy of Literary Form: Studies in Symbolic Action* (1941).

526.31 *representative anecdote*] See Kenneth Burke, "The Representative An-ecdote," in *A Grammar of Motives* (1945).

526.36 *The Literary Situation*] Collection of familiar essays (1954) on writ-ers, reviewers, English professors, publishers, and booksellers, and how they live and earn their livings—that is to say, on the culture of American letters at midcentury—by literary critic Malcolm Cowley (1898–1989).

527.10 *playful* process] Murray here gives a précis of *Le Jeux et les hommes* (1958) by the French polymath Roger Caillois (1913–1978), a book that en-larges on the studies of games and play begun by Johan Huizinga (see note 53.20). The book was translated into English as *Man, Play, and Games*, by Meyer Barash (New York: Free Press, 1961).

529.23 *hombre de época*] Spanish: "man of the epoch," concept derived by the Spanish philosopher José Ortega y Gasset (1883–1955) from Emerson's idea of the "representative man."

533.3   *Music Is My Mistress*] Autobiography of Duke Ellington (1899–1974), as told to Stanley Dance (Garden City, N.Y.: Doubleday, 1973).

533.36   *The World of Duke Ellington*] Collection of essays about, and oral histories of, Duke Ellington, written and compiled by English jazz critic Stanley Dance (1910–1999) and published by Charles Scribner's Sons, New York, in 1970.

535.39–536.6   "It threatened . . . part of a problem. . . ."] W. E. B. Du Bois (see note 154.11–13), *Dusk of Dawn: An Essay Toward an Autobiography of a Race Concept* (1940).

536.13–14   *Along This Way*] Autobiography of James Weldon Johnson (see note 66.33), published in 1933.

538.17–18   W. C. Handy's . . . *Father of the Blues*] See note 475.21–30.

540.1   *Comping for Count Basie*] In a caption to an illustration in the first edition of *Stomping the Blues*, Murray defined "comping" as "backing soloists with imaginative accompanimental chordal punctuations [usually] on the piano."

540.4   So the main thing was to get his voice on the page] Murray was co-writer of the "as-told-to" book *Good Morning Blues: The Autobiography of Count Basie* (New York: Random House, 1985).

541.23–24   "commanding center"] Term, popularized by R. P. Blackmur (see note 219.4–5), for the "narrative point of view" in a work of fiction, appropriated from a phrase by Henry James used in the short story "The Patagonia" (1909).

541.35   Language . . . is symbolic action] See Kenneth Burke, *The Philosophy of Literary Form: Studies in Symbolic Action* (1941).

548.14   *Count Basie and His Orchestra*] Book (subtitled "Its Music and Its Musicians") by the British jazz biographer Raymond Horricks (1933–2005), published in 1957 by Victor Gollancz (London) and Citadel Press (New York).

548.17–18   *The World of Count Basie*] Collection of essays and oral histories by Stanley Dance (New York: Scribner's, 1980) modeled on *The World of Duke Ellington* (see note 533.36).

549.15   Jorgen Jepsen or Chris Sheridan] Denmark's Jorgen Grunnet Jepsen (1927–1981) and his British counterpart Chris Sheridan (b. 1943) are among the leading discographers in jazz.

549.36   Pendergast machine] Political boss Tom Pendergast (1873–1945) controlled the Democratic Party machine in Kansas City, Missouri, from 1925 to 1939.

549.37   Burton . . . Brown] Ellis Burton, bootlegger and proprietor of the Yellow Front nightclub, and Piney Brown, gambler and proprietor of the

Sunset Club, were patron saints of Kansas City jazz musicians during the Pendergast era.

549.38–550.1   Reno Club] Kansas City nightclub, owned by Solomon "Papa Sol" Steibold, that employed the Basie Orchestra as its house band in 1935–36. It was there that John Hammond heard the band and signed them to a Decca recording contract.

550.13–19   "I have no desire . . . direction of interest. . . ."] W. Somerset Maugham (1874–1974), *The Summing Up* (1938), a personal memoir of 1890–1938.

550.27   tipping on the q.t.] Slang: indulging in clandestine dalliances. ("Tipping on the Q.T." is also the title of a tune recorded by Basie in 1952.)

552.23   "The Style of the Mythical Age,"] Hermann Broch (1886–1951), "The Style of the Mythical Age," introduction to Rachel Bespaloff, *On the Iliad* (Washington, D.C.: Pantheon, 1947).

553.33–35   "to fill the entire surface . . . interactions of color."] John Russell (1919–2008), *The World of Matisse, 1869–1954* (New York: Time-Life Books, 1969).

561.17–18   *"emblems for a pioneer people . . . trait."*] See note 55.20–21.

561.31   Ambassador Satchmo] During the postwar years, Armstrong toured extensively for the U.S. State Department. He also performed in Dave and Iola Brubeck's musical *The Real Ambassadors* (1962), which satirized the State Department's use of jazz in Cold War diplomacy.

562.33   Armstrong told Richard Meryman in an interview] Richard Meryman (1926–2015), "An Authentic American Genius: An Interview with Louis Armstrong," *Life* (April 15, 1966). The Meryman-Armstrong quotations in this piece are not from *Life* but from the expanded version of the interview published as *Louis Armstrong—A Self-Portrait: The Interview by Richard Meryman* (New York: Eakins Press, 1971).

563.12   what he told the editors of *True* magazine] Louis Armstrong, "Louis Armstrong, Who Tells You About Storyville, Where the Blues Were Born," *True: The Man's Magazine* (November 1947).

564.16–17   *his New Orleans mentor*] King Oliver (Joseph Nathan Oliver, 1885–1938).

565.29–30   *Louis: The Louis Armstrong Story, 1900–1971*] Biography by British jazz critic Max Jones (1917–1993) and British journalist and trumpet player John Chilton (1932–2016), with a preface by Armstrong (Boston: Little, Brown, 1971).

566.26   Dan Morgenstern, in an essay] Dan Morgenstern (b. 1929), "Louis Armstrong and the Development and Diffusion of Jazz," in Marc H. Miller, ed., *Louis Armstrong: A Cultural Legacy* (Seattle: University of Washington Press, 1994).

568.5   *Great Day*] American musical (1926) with songs by Vincent Youmans, words by Billy Rose and Edward Eliscu, and a book about antebellum life on a Louisiana cotton plantation. Though it closed after thirty-six performances, it yielded the enduring songs "(There's Gonna Be a) Great Day," "Without a Song," and "More Than You Know."

568.22–23   Rudy Vallee . . . was to say] Rudy Vallee, introduction to Louis Armstrong, *Swing That Music* (New York and London: Longmans, Green & Co., 1936).

572.37–39   Burleigh . . . Dett . . . Johnson . . . Still]   Black American composers of concert music: Harry T. Burleigh (1866–1949), a baritone, was a writer of vocal music and arranger of spirituals; R. Nathaniel Dett (1882–1943) was a pianist, composer, arranger, and choir director; J. Rosamond Johnson (see note 134.11–12) wrote orchestral music and operettas as well as show tunes and songs with his brother, James Weldon Johnson (see note 66.33); William Grant Still (1895–1978) was a composer-conductor of orchestral music whose works include five symphonies.

574.18   soundies] Three-minute musical films, produced exclusively for the Mills Novelty Company in 1939–47, for viewing on a coin-operated "video jukebox" called the Mills' Panoram.

574.38–39   "old father . . . good stead"] Stephen Dedalus, paying tribute to his spiritual father, Daedalus, in James Joyce's *A Portrait of the Artist as a Young Man* (1916).

575.31–33   *He publicly rebuked one president . . . refused an invitation from another*] Dwight D. Eisenhower and Richard Nixon, respectively.

577.4–5   "They all know I'm there in the cause of happiness,"] Armstrong said this to Meryman in his *Life* interview. Murray chose it as one of two epigraphs for his and Count Basie's *Good Morning Blues: The Autobiography of Count Basie.*

584.26   when Aaron Copland was asked] By Carol Oja, interviewer, in "Aaron Copland and Minna Lederman on American Music in the Thirties," *Institute for Studies in American Music Newsletter* (November 1979), a publication of Brooklyn College.

585.37   children of Nadia Boulanger] Boulanger (1887–1979) was an instructor in composition at the American Conservatory at Fontainebleau, France. Her "children" included many of twentieth-century America's leading composers, such as Aaron Copland, Virgil Thomson, Roy Harris, and Elliott Carter.

587.1–2   *Storiella Americana as She Is Swyung; or, The Blues as Representative Anecdote*] Murray alludes to James Joyce's *Storiella as She is Syung* (London:

Corvinus Press, 1937), an excerpt from what would be published two years later as *Finnegans Wake* (1939), and to Kenneth Burke's essay "The Representative Anecdote" (see note 526.31). The word "Storiella" is Italian for "comic anecdote."

588.15–16 William D. Crum] Black American public servant (1859–1912) whose appointment by President Theodore Roosevelt, in 1902, as customs collector of the Port of Charleston was bitterly contested in, yet in the end approved by, the South Carolina senate.

589.1–7 "warmest wish . . . race in the United States."] During the campaign of 1912, W. E. B. Du Bois, head of the NAACP, asked Democratic presidential candidate Woodrow Wilson for a statement supporting black civil rights. Three weeks before the election, Wilson obliged by way of a public letter to Alexander Walters, bishop of the African Zion Church of New York City and vice president of the NAACP, containing the words quoted here.

591.8–13 "she taught us . . . way back."] This quotation, and those from Duke Ellington that follow, are from *Music Is My Mistress*, by Duke Ellington, as told to Stanley Dance (see note 533.3).

592.19–35 Miller . . . Woodson . . . Locke] See notes 154.11–13 and 167.17.

593.1–2 *the work* of W. E. B. Du Bois] In other words, Du Bois was not a physical presence in Washington during those years.

593.4 call it *The New Negro* and introduce it] See note 133.32. Alain Locke's essay "The New Negro" opens the collection.

593.7 three *norns*] The three Norns, of Norse mythology, are analogous to the three Fates, or goddesses of destiny, of Greek mythology.

593.17 Garvey Movement] See note 208.24–26.

593.17–26 Arthur Schomburg . . . *told and realized.*"] See note 153.32.

594.7–9 Howard . . . T.O.B.A. . . . Lincoln . . . Lafayette] The Theater Owners' Booking Association (TOBA, 1920–circa 1935) was a vaudeville circuit for black performers working all-black venues. Among the largest of TOBA's venues were the Howard Theater (1910), in Washington, D.C., and the Lincoln (1915) and Lafayette (1912), in Harlem.

594.20 Will Marion Cook] Stage name of American composer-conductor William Mercer Cook (1869–1944), bandleader of the globetrotting Southern Syncopated Orchestra (1918–21). In *Music Is My Mistress*, Ellington refers to him as "Dad" Cook.

594.35 Williams and Walker] Bert Williams (1874–1922) and George Walker (1872–1911), immensely popular black vaudeville duo around whose comic and musical talents many Broadway revues were written.

595.8–12 "that the Negro in music . . . generally better."] James Weldon Johnson, *Along This Way* (see note 536.13–14).

599.3 MIDDLE of that October] Principal photography for *Paris Blues* was completed in France in the fall of 1960, and the film was given its premiere in the United States on September 27, 1961.

599.10 Sam Shaw] American photographer (1912–1999) known for his film-set portraits of Hollywood stars, especially Marilyn Monroe and Marlon Brando. Early in his career he shared studio space with Romare Bearden (see note 617.3), and through Bearden became a close friend of Murray. His work as film producer, which began with *Paris Blues*, included a fruitful decade-long collaboration with John Cassavetes (1970–80).

599.12 script, which was an adaptation of a novel] The source material for *Paris Blues* was a novel of the same title by American writer Harold Flender (1924–1975), published by Ballantine Books in 1957. It was given a story treatment by Lulla Adler Rosenfeld, and the screenplay was written by Jack Sher, Irene Kamp, Walter Bernstein, and the uncredited Ted Allen.

600.21 *Black and Tan*] RKO featurette (1929), written and directed by Dudley Murphy, starring Duke Ellington and Fredi Washington and featuring performances of "Cotton Club Stomp" and "Black and Tan Fantasy." It was added to the National Film Registry in 2015.

602.8–9 the other is the boat train] "A Return Reservation."

604.34–38 "guys just following the parade . . . instruments for the band. . . ."] This, and the other quotations from Louis Armstrong in this piece, are from Richard Meryman, *Louis Armstrong—A Self-Portrait* (1971).

605.39–40 W. H. Auden . . . real ancestors] See note 193.21–22.

610.11 (UAL 4092)] Duke Ellington, *Paris Blues: Original Sound Track* (1961), featuring Louis Armstrong.

612.21 (Columbia CL 1715)] Duke Ellington/Count Basie, *First Time! The Count Meets the Duke* (1961), featuring performances of "Battle Royal" and "Wild Man Moore."

617.3 Romare Bearden] American artist Bearden (1911–1988) is best known for his enigmatic modernist collages depicting "down-home" and urban black American experience. He also created political cartoons, watercolors, monotypes, drawings, and abstract expressionist works, and was a successful songwriter. He and Murray met in Paris in 1950 and became close friends after Murray moved to New York City in 1962.

617.18–19 any given one-man exhibition] This essay was written for the catalogue of *Romare Bearden: 1970–1980*, an exhibition organized by the Mint Museum, Charlotte, North Carolina, and on view at the Mint from October 12, 1980, to January 4, 1981.

617.24 *Odysseus*] Bearden's *Odysseus* exhibition was on view at Cordier & Ekstrom Gallery, New York, from April 27 to May 28, 1977. Some of the *Odysseus* pieces were later shown in the Mint Museum exhibition.

617.32 *Profile/Part I: The Twenties*] Exhibition on view at Cordier & Ekstrom, New York, from November 8 to December 16, 1978, with "picture titles and text reviewed and edited by Albert Murray."

618.2 Miss Maudell Sleet's Garden] *Maudell Sleet's Magic Garden* (collage on board, 1978) was included in both the *Profiles/Part I* exhibition and the Mint Museum's exhibition. The text for the picture in the *Profiles/Part I* exhibition is as follows: "I can still smell the flowers she used to give us and still taste the blackberries."

618.15–16 Alaga syrup] Brand of pure cane syrup made by the Alabama-Georgia Syrup Co., of Montgomery, Alabama.

618.32–619.17 "You have to begin somewhere . . . subject matter."] This long quotation, like most others from Bearden in this 1980 essay, is original to Murray's text. In the notes that follow, only quotes from sources published prior to 1980 are documented.

619.31–32 expressive use of interval in the piano style of Earl Hines] In a television interview with Charlayne Hunter-Gault (*The MacNeil/Lehrer Report*, June 26, 1987), Bearden said: "I listened for hours to the recordings of Earl Hines at the piano. Finally, I was able to block out the melody and concentrate on the silences between the notes. I found that this was very helpful to me in the transmutation of sound into colors and in the placement of objects in my paintings and collages . . . Jazz has shown me the ways of achieving artistic structures that are personal to me."

621.14–15 Columbia, Keith, and T.O.B.A.] The Columbia Amusements Co. and the Keith-Albee-Orpheum Corporation booked vaudeville and burlesque acts throughout the early twentieth century. For TOBA, see note 594.7–9.

621.18–20 Lafayette . . . Lincoln] See note 594.7–9.

621.22 Florence Mills] Black actress and entertainer known as "The Blackbird of Harlem" after her starring role in the Broadway revue *Lew Leslie's Blackbirds* (1926–27). She died in 1927, at the age of thirty-one, from tuberculosis.

624.5–15 "It was during my period with Grosz . . . Poussin."] See Romare Bearden, "Rectangular Structure in My Montage Paintings," *Leonardo* (January 1969). Murray's quotations from this article are freely adapted from Bearden's published text.

625.2–626.10 "My temperas . . . complete the painting."] Romare Bearden, "Rectangular Structure in My Montage Paintings" (see note above).

626.27–627.9 "Some observers . . . space and structure."] Romare Bearden, "Rectangular Structure in My Montage Paintings" (see note above).

627.15 *The Painter's Mind*] Romare Bearden and Carl Holty (1900–1973), *The Painter's Mind: A Study of the Relation of Structure and Space in Painting* (New York: Crown, 1969).

627.35–37 "Earl Hines' hot piano . . . other paintings."] Stuart Davis, "The Cube Root," *Art News* (February 1943).

627.40–628.8 "I was enormously excited by the show . . . become a 'modern' painter."] Stuart Davis, autobiographical statement for *Stuart Davis* (New York: American Artists Group, 1945), AAG Monographs, No. 6.

630.19–29 "When you ask me . . . compositions."] Georges Braque, in an interview with John Richardson ("The Power of Mystery") published in the *Observer* (UK), December 1, 1957, and revised by Richardson for his book on Braque in the Penguin Modern Painters series (1959).

630.36–40 "Objects do not exist . . . pictures."] Georges Braque, "The Power of Mystery" (see note above).

631.3–10 "a generalization of form . . . still imitative."] Stuart Davis, quoted in Eugene C. Goosen, *Stuart Davis* (New York: Braziller, 1959).

633.40 *Projections*] This exhibition, which was on view at Cordier & Ekstrom from October 6 to October 24, 1964, marked a major turning point in Bearden's career.

635.13 Winold Reiss] German-born black graphic artist (1886–1953) who provided the decorations for Alain Locke's anthology *The New Negro* (see note 133.32).

641.6 "society, democracy, and the other things"] Ernest Hemingway, *Green Hills of Africa* (1935).

641.18–28 "The hardest thing in the world to do . . . much more limited."] Ernest Hemingway, "Old Newsman Writes: A Letter from Cuba," *Esquire* (December 1934), collected in William White, ed., *By-line: Ernest Hemingway—Selected Articles and Dispatches of Four Decades* (New York: Scribner's, 1967).

642.3 "Old Newsman Writes,"] See above.

642.16–17 George Plimpton . . . *Paris Review* series] See note 365.26.

643.32 Link Steffens] Lincoln Steffens (1866–1936), politically committed New York City newspaper reporter and, after 1901, a "muckraking" journalist for *McClure's* magazine.

643.36–40 "the pleasant comforting stench . . . all a fake."] Ernest Hemingway, *Green Hills of Africa* (1935).

647.6 William Empson] English literary critic (1906–1984) and proponent of the New Criticism (see note 214.34) whose works include *Seven Types of Ambiguity* (1930) and *Some Versions of Pastoral* (1935).

647.37–38 *Time* magazine reported] Unsigned book review, "News from Spain," *Time* (November 7, 1938).

648.8–9 *The Fifth Column*] Play in three acts, first published, with an introduction, in Ernest Hemingway, *The Fifth Column and the First Forty-nine Stories* (New York: Scribner's, 1938).

651.6–8 "the good and the bad . . . weather was."] Ernest Hemingway, "Old Newsman Writes" (see note 641.18–28).

651.17–19 "It was always how . . . who reads it."] Speech to the Second American Writers' Congress, New York, June 4, 1937. Published as "Fascism Is a Lie," *New Masses* (June 22, 1937), collected in Matthew J. Bruccoli, ed., *Conversations with Ernest Hemingway* (1986).

651.35–36 "he will never know what he is capable of attaining."] Ernest Hemingway, "Monologue to the Maestro: A High Seas Letter" (*Esquire*, October 1935), collected in William White, ed., *By-line: Ernest Hemingway* (1967).

653.37–38 "The most essential gift . . . all great writers have used it."] George Plimpton, "Ernest Hemingway: The Art of Fiction, No. 21" (see note 365.26).

654.9 "writers are forged in injustice as a sword is forged."] See note 365.3.

655.15–18 "Didn't Hemingway say . . . original."] See Matthew Bruccoli, ed., *The Notebooks of F. Scott Fitzgerald* (New York: Harcourt Brace Jovanovich, 1978), entry 1045.

655.22–35 "What we have . . . raw-material clichés."] Wright Morris (1910–1998), *The Territory Ahead* (New York: Harcourt Brace & World, 1957).

656.5 *The Purple Land*] Novel set in nineteenth-century Uruguay (1885) by the English writer W. H. Hudson (1841–1922).

656.15 R. G. Dun report] Business-to-business credit report from R. G. Dun & Co., known since 1933 as Dun & Bradstreet.

659.15–16 "could only care about people a few at a time."] Ernest Hemingway, *Green Hills of Africa* (1935).

660.17–19 "Am trying . . . in Chicago."] Quoted by Lillian Ross (b. 1926) in her profile of Hemingway, "How Do You Like It Now, Gentlemen?" (*The New Yorker*, May 13, 1950), published as *Portrait of Hemingway* (New York: Simon & Schuster, 1961).

660.28–29 "Defense of Dirty Words"] Ernest Hemingway, "Defense of Dirty Words: A Cuban Letter," *Esquire* (September 1934).

660.40–661.1 "an absolute conscience . . . to prevent faking."] Ernest Hemingway, *Green Hills of Africa* (1935).

661.4–7 "Really good writing . . . very very lucky."] From "Hemingway in the Afternoon" (see note 365.29).

662.15–16 "straight honest prose on human beings."] Ernest Hemingway, "Monologue to the Maestro" (see note 641.18–28).

663.10–11 "the dancing of an attitude."] See the title essay in Kenneth Burke, *The Philosophy of Literary Form: Studies in Symbolic Action* (1941).

663.19 *Virgin Spain*] Waldo Frank (1889–1967), *Virgin Spain: Scenes from the Spiritual Drama of a Great People* (New York: Boni & Liveright, 1926).

664.4–5 "only a certain clarification of the language"] From "Hemingway in the Afternoon" (see note 365.29).

664.8 "Notes on Life and Letters."] Ernest Hemingway, "Notes on Life and Letters: Or, A Manuscript Found in a Bottle," *Esquire* (January 1935).

665.36–37 real toads . . . garden] See Marianne Moore (1887–1972), in the poem "Poetry" (1919), which contains the line "imaginary gardens with real toads in them."

666.6–11 "A work of art . . . consciousness itself."] Susanne K. Langer, *Problems of Art: Ten Philosophical Lectures* (1957).

667.15–22 "My task . . . to ask."] Joseph Conrad, "Author's Note on 'The Nigger of the *Narcissus*: A Tale of the Sea,'" *The New Review* (December 1897).

667.26–28 "Books . . . study up about."] Ernest Hemingway, "Old Newsman Writes" (see note 641.18–28).

671.27–34 "I knew two or three things . . . I was inventing."] Robert Manning (1920–2012), "Hemingway in Cuba," *The Atlantic Monthly* (August 1965), collected in *Conversations with Ernest Hemingway* (1986).

673.3–4 Kenneth Tynan reports] Kenneth Tynan (1927–1980), "A Visit to Havana," *Holiday* (February 1960), collected in *Conversations with Ernest Hemingway* (1986).

674.16 style sheet for prose writers] A 1925 version of the *Kansas City Star*'s style sheet is reproduced as a gatefold in Matthew J. Bruccoli, editor, *Ernest Hemingway, Cub Reporter: Kansas City Star Stories* (Pittsburgh: University of Pittsburgh Press, 1970).

675.35 Lillian Ross] See note 660.17–19.

677.2–19 "There is a definite code . . . equals no bull."] Delmore Schwartz, "Ernest Hemingway's Literary Situation" (see note 353.10–12).

683.1–4 Even Malcolm Cowley . . . underestimated] See Malcolm Cowley, "Hemingway at Midnight," *The New Republic* (August 14, 1944).

683.32 Thurman Arnold] Washington-based antitrust lawyer and iconoclastic political analyst (1891–1969) whose books include *The Symbols of Government* (1935) and *The Folklore of Capitalism* (1937).

690.1 "Remembering Shooting-Flying"] Ernest Hemingway, "Remembering Shooting-Flying: A Key West Letter," *Esquire* (February 1935), collected in *By-line: Ernest Hemingway* (1967).

691.2–4 "For we have been . . . as we have been."] Ernest Hemingway, *Green Hills of Africa* (1935).

692.28–29 Robert Penn Warren once wrote] See Robert Penn Warren, introduction to *A Farewell to Arms*, in the Scribner's Modern Standard Authors series (1949), collected as "Ernest Hemingway" in his *Selected Essays* (New York: Random House, 1958).

692.39–693.2 "was imbued . . . tragedy."] Ralph Ellison, "The World and the Jug (II)," *The New Leader* (February 3, 1964), collected in *Shadow and Act* (1964).

693.4–5 "express both the agony . . . toughness of spirit,"] Ralph Ellison, "Richard Wright's Blues" (see note 138.7).

694.13–16 "the peculiar characteristic . . . written in both."] From *The Classical Tradition in Poetry* (see note 359.30–360.21), by Gilbert Murray (see note 7.36–8.1).

699.7 "with a good deal of pride."] Kenneth Tynan, "A Visit to Havana" (see note 673.3–4).

699.24–28 "Playboy . . . plaudits like that?"] Robert Manning, "Hemingway in Cuba" (see note 671.27–34).

700.2–5 "Before I left . . . African son."] See A. E. Hotchner (b. 1920), *Papa Hemingway: A Personal Memoir* (New York: Random House, 1966), chapter 6, "The Riviera—1954."

703.16–17 once advised his brother] See Leicester Hemingway (1915–1982), *My Brother, Ernest Hemingway* (Cleveland and New York: World, 1962).

704.33 "Yes, they have more money."] This remark, sometimes said to have been part of the original manuscript of Hemingway's story "The Short Happy Life of Francis Macomber" (1936), is part of the oral history of American literature.

707.24 the epigraph] Ecclesiastes 1:4–7.

707.25 All is vanity] Ecclesiastes 1:2.

707.25–26 What profit hath man . . . under the sun?] Ecclesiastes 1:3.

708.33–34 would not only endure but would prevail] See note 216.29.

709.9–10 'against my ruins,'] From "What the Thunder Said," the fifth and final section of T. S. Eliot's poem *The Waste Land* (1922).

711.37 "*ascend and leap . . . infinite time.*"] Ralph Waldo Emerson, "The Poet," in *Essays, Second Series* (1844).

FROM THE BRIARPATCH FILE

722.17   "Youth,"] See page 221 for the complete text of Langston Hughes's poem (1925) as it appeared in *The New Negro* (see note 133.32).

724.3–4   frame of acceptance . . . rejection] See also Murray's discussion of Kenneth Burke's *Attitudes Toward History* on pages 509–10 of the present volume.

726.36–37   *Attitudes Toward History* . . . representative anecdote] See Kenneth Burke's *A Grammar of Motives* (1945), not his *Attitudes Toward History* (1937), for a definition of "representative anecdote." (See also note 526.31.)

729.32–34   Du Bois . . . Talented Tenth] See note 263.6–7.

740.38–39   Langer . . . life of human feeling] See note 396.32.

742.14   Roger Caillois in *Man, Play, and Games*] See note 527.10.

744.1   *Riffing at Mrs. Jack's Place*] Isabella Stewart Gardner (1840–1924), widely known as "Mrs. Jack" (after her husband, the shipping merchant John L. Gardner), was a major American art collector and arts patron. In 1896–1902 she supervised the creation of Fenway Court, a building on the model of a fifteenth-century Venetian palazzo, as both her principal residence and a museum for her collection of European and American masterpieces. The Isabella Stewart Gardner Museum, in Boston's Fenway section, has been open to the public since 1903.

744.2   EYE OF THE BEHOLDER] "Riffing at Mrs. Jack's Place" was Murray's contribution to a late 1990s lecture series, "The Eye of the Beholder," in which the Gardner Museum invited several public figures to speak "on a work or works in the permanent collection that illuminated [their] concerns or world view."

745.7–10   "Giorgione's finest points . . . Yankee Giorgiones,"] Van Wyck Brooks (1886–1963), *New England: Indian Summer 1865–1915* (New York: Dutton, 1940).

745.24   *bibliothèque pléiade*] Series of classic French texts, and of world literature in French translation, published by Gallimard (Paris) since its founding in 1931. The Bibliothèque de la Pléiade provided the model for The Library of America series.

745.25–26   as André Malraux has pointed out] In *The Voices of Silence* (see note 382.8).

749.5–9   "now satisfied . . . United States."] This and the other quotes from Dvořák used here are from James Creelman, "Dvořák on Negro Melodies," *New York Herald* (May 21, 1893). Murray's source was Eileen Southern, *The Music of Black Americans: A History*, third edition (New York: Norton, 1997).

749.11 Jeanette Thurber] American music patron (1850–1946) whose National Conservatory of Music of America flourished in New York City from 1884 to about 1920. Dvořák was the conservatory's director from the fall of 1892 to the spring of 1894.

750.15–16 W. C. Handy's codification of the blues] See note 333.33–34.

750.27–30 William Arms Fisher . . . "Going Home,"] American composer Fisher (1861–1948), a student of Dvořák at the National Conservatory of Music of America, wrote a text and choral setting for the theme of the second movement of the *New World* Symphony, published as "Goin' Home" (1922). His collection *Seventy Negro Spirituals* was published in 1926.

753.37–38 T.O.B.A. . . . Lincoln . . . Lafayette] See note 594.7–9.

756.37–38 biography of Ellington] Barry Ulanov, *Duke Ellington* (New York: Creative Age Press, 1946).

756.38–757.7 "*The orchestration . . . out of America.*"] Constant Lambert (1905–1951), "The Art of Duke Ellington" (review of a concert at the London Palladium), London *Sunday Referee* (June 25, 1933).

757.21 John Hammond] American music producer (1910–1987) who, as a concert promoter and a producer at Columbia Records, helped to desegregate the American music stage and to shape the twentieth century's folk, blues, jazz, and rock scenes.

757.38–39 "Such a form . . . Ellington's ken."] New York *Daily News* music critic Douglas Watt (1914–2009) reviewing *Black, Brown, and Beige*, which received its premiere at Carnegie Hall on January 23, 1943.

759.34 Burleigh . . . Cook] Harry T. Burleigh (see note 572.37–39) was the first black student accepted by Dvořák at the National Conservatory of Music of America, and Will Marion Cook (see note 594.20), recommended to Burleigh by Frederick Douglass, the second.

763.4–5 Kenneth Burke . . . basic equipment for living] See note 525.28–29.

765.21–22 his blurb on the jacket of *Train Whistle Guitar*] Ellington, in 1974, wrote: "Albert Murray is a man whose learning did not interfere with understanding. An authority on soul from the days of old, he is right on right back to back and commands respect. He doesn't have to look it up. He already knows. If you want to know, look him up. He is the unsquarest person I know."

765.30–31 *New Yorker* . . . Robert Coles] Robert Coles (b. 1929), "Human Nature Is Finer," *The New Yorker* (October 17, 1970).

765.38–39 this book that Stanley Dance and I are trying to put together."] *Music Is My Mistress* (see note 533.3).

766.20 Ralph Bunche] American diplomat (1903–1971), a key member of the U.N. team in the early postwar years, who received the 1950 Nobel Peace Prize for his work in the late 1940s on the Arab-Israeli truce in Palestine.

768.20 Sheldon Cheney] See note 264.9. *The Theatre* was published in 1929.

769.9 *These 13*] Short story collection by William Faulkner, published in 1931.

769.23 John Gerald Hamilton] See note 209.16.

771.33 *what André Malraux made of* Sanctuary] André Malraux's preface to *Sanctuaire*, the French translation of *Sanctuary* (Paris: Gallimard, 1933), first appeared in the *Nouvelle Revue Française* (November 1, 1933). It has been translated into English as "A Preface for Faulkner's *Sanctuary*," *Yale French Studies* (1952), and "A Preface to William Faulkner's *Sanctuary*," *Southern Review* (1974).

777.1 *The HNIC Who He*] This omnibus review considers four books: Harold Cruse, *The Crisis of the Negro Intellectual: A Historical Analysis of the Failure of Black Leadership* (New York: Morrow, 1967); Gilbert Osofsky, ed., *The Burden of Race: A Documentary History of Negro-White Relations in America* (New York: Harper & Row, 1967); Budd Schulberg, *From the Ashes: Voices of Watts* (New York: New American Library, 1967); and Stokely Carmichael and Charles V. Hamilton, *Black Power: The Politics of Liberation* (New York: Random House, 1967).

777.24 Harold Cruse] American social critic (1916–2005) and cofounder, with LeRoi Jones, of Harlem's Black Arts Repertory Theater. After the success of *The Crisis of the Negro Intellectual* he became a professor of African American studies at the University of Michigan (1968–c. 1985).

778.33 Gilbert Osofsky] American historian (1935–1974) and author of *Harlem: The Making of a Ghetto, 1890–1930* (1966). He was a professor of history at the University of Illinois–Chicago (1963–74).

779.8–9 Stanley M. Elkins] See note 38.32.

779.11 Budd Schulberg] American writer (1914–2009) known for his novels (*What Makes Sammy Run?*, 1941) and screenplays (*On the Waterfront*, 1954, and *A Face in the Crowd*, 1957).

781.7 Stokely Carmichael] See note 83.12–13.

781.16 Charles V. Hamilton] Professor of government and political science (b. 1929) who, after a number of short-term academic appoints, taught at Columbia University from 1969 to 1998.

781.40 Frantz Fanon] See note 56.35.

783.15 *The Black Expatriates*] Ernest Dunbar, *The Black Expatriates: A Study of American Negroes in Exile* (New York: Dutton, 1968). Dunbar (1928–2011) was senior editor of *Look* magazine from 1959 to 1971 and later a writer and editor for Exxon.

784.23 *Where To, Black Man?*] Ed Smith, *Where To, Black Man? An American Negro's African Diary* (Chicago: Quadrangle, 1967). Smith (b. 1937), a native of Birmingham, Alabama, was a Peace Corps volunteer in Ghana in 1962–63.

785.8 *Freedom Bound*] Henrietta Buckmaster, *Freedom Bound* (New York: Macmillan, 1965). See note 106.33–34.

785.18 since 1619] See note 20.24–26.

785.24 Herskovitsian] Referring to anthropologist Melville Herskovits (1895–1963), a specialist in the African diaspora.

789.39 Negritude] See note 132.6.

791.3 Paul Hemphill] Birmingham native Hemphill (1936–2009), a human-interest columnist for the *Atlanta Journal* from 1965 through the 1970s, collected his columns in *The Good Old Boys* (New York: Simon & Schuster, 1974) and *Too Old to Cry* (1981). His best-selling first book, *The Nashville Sound: Bright Lights and Country Music* (1970), was written while he was a Nieman Fellow at Harvard.

793.20 *Wallace*] Marshall Frady's biography *Wallace* (1968) was written during the Alabama governor's 1967 campaign as an independent candidate for U.S. president. See note 239.28–29.

795.12 *Who Speaks for the Negro?*] Robert Penn Warren, *Who Speaks for the Negro?* (New York: Random House, 1965). See notes 117.19 and 201.16–17.

796.29 Stanley M. Elkins's . . . Samboism] See note 38.32.

796.30 Charles Evers] See note 38.39–40.

797.35 significant statements] By Adam Clayton Powell Jr. (see note 82.27–28); Roy Wilkins (1901–1981), civil rights activist and head of the NAACP (1955–77); Whitney Young (see note 83.38); James Farmer (see note 83.12–13); James Foreman (1928–2005), executive secretary of SNCC (1961–65); Robert Parris Moses (see note 83.12–13); Aaron Henry (1922–1979), head of the Mississippi branch of the NAACP (1959–82).

798.1–3 Rustin . . . Clark . . . Baldwin] Bayard Rustin (1912–1987), civil rights activist, pacifist, and chief coordinator of the 1963 March on Washington; Kenneth B. Clark (see note 26.21 et seq.); James Baldwin (see note 123.1).

798.24–25 "Nigger, your breed ain't metaphysical."] From Warren's poem "Pondy Woods," published in *Thirty-Six Poems* (New York: The Alcestis Press, 1935) and reprinted in John Burt, ed., *The Collected Poems of Robert Penn Warren* (Baton Rouge: Louisiana State University Press, 1998).

798.31 Ralph McGill of Georgia] See note 221.31–33.

799.8 *Swing That Music*] See note 568.22–23.

800.16 *Satchmo: My Life in New Orleans*] Autobiography of Louis Armstrong (New York: Prentice-Hall, 1954).

801.27 *Louis Armstrong: In His Own Words*] Thomas Brothers, *Louis Armstrong in His Own Words: Selected Writings* (New York: Oxford University Press, 1999).

801.35 *Horn of Plenty*] Belgian critic Robert Goffin (1898–1984) published *Louis Armstrong, le roi du Jazz* in Paris in 1947. The U.S. version—*Horn of Plenty: The Story of Louis Armstrong*, translated from the French by James F. Bezou—was published by Allen, Towne & Heath, New York, in 1947.

804.12 Mezz Mezzrow] Chicago-based clarinetist (1899–1972) whose memoir *Really the Blues* (1946), cowritten with Bernard Wolfe (1915–1985), was a best-selling tell-all of drugs, race, and jazz music.

804.40 those Austin High School lads."] The Austin High School Gang was a group of white jazz enthusiasts in Chicago.

805.19 article in the December 1951 issue of *Esquire*] "Jazz on a High Note," by Louis Armstrong with Robert Riggs.

807.12–14 biographical sequence . . . in November 1947 in *True* magazine] See note 563.12.

808.4–5 a friend and literary colleague] Murray himself. See *Trading Twelves: The Selected Letters of Ralph Ellison and Albert Murray* (2000), letter from Ellison to Murray dated June 6, 1951.

814.23 "By, Sweets having that baby for me,"] Armstrong believed he had fathered a child by Lucille "Sweets" Preston and thought it to be a psychological blow to his wife, Lucille. Sharon Preston-Folta, daughter of Lucille Preston, auctioned off letters between her mother and Armstrong in 2012. Articles in *The New York Times* (December 13, 2012) and *The Times-Picayune* of greater New Orleans (December 7, 2012) covered the auction and addressed the question of Armstrong's paternity in some detail.

815.7 Mary-Ann] Armstrong refers to his mother variously as Mary-Ann, Mary Ann, and May-Ann.

820.3–4 "return to normalcy [*sic!*]"] See note 185.17–18.

821.8 James Reese Europe's Hellfighters Band] Europe (1881–1919), a native of Mobile, Alabama, was a lieutenant of the U.S. Army's 369th Infantry Regiment, known as the Harlem Hellfighters. He led the sixty-five-member Hellfighters Band, which helped introduce ragtime to France, from 1913 until his death, at age thirty-nine, in 1919.

821.10 Will Marion Cook] See note 594.20.

821.29–30 *Shuffle Along, Running Wild*, and *Chocolate Dandies*] See notes 225.9–10 and 621.22.

821.40–822.3 Castle . . . Europe's prewar dance band] Americans Vernon and Irene Castle were the premier ragtime dance duo of Broadway and silent film from 1911 until Vernon's death in 1918. During their year in France (1911–12) they headlined at the Café de Paris, the home of James Reese Europe's Clef Club Orchestra (1910–13).

827.5–6 *Feeney's* Boston Globe *profile*] Mark Feeney (b. 1957), "The Unsquarest Person Duke Ellington Ever Met," *The Boston Globe Magazine* (August 1, 1993), collected in Roberta S. Maguire, ed., *Conversations with Albert Murray* (1997).

827.10 an article of mine] Sanford Pinsker, "Albert Murray: The Black Intellectuals' Maverick Patriarch," *Virginia Quarterly Review* (Autumn 1996). Pinsker (b. 1941) is emeritus professor of the humanities at Franklin & Marshall College, Lancaster, Pennsylvania, where he taught for thirty-seven years.

829.11–12 Morteza Drexel Sprague . . . John Gerald Hamilton] See notes 263.8–9 and 209.16.

829.33 Don Marquis] American humorist (1878–1937) who, in 1927, created Archy the Cockroach for his column in the New York *Sun*. Archy, who could not operate the key shift of Marquis's typewriter, communicated with Marquis by jumping up and down on the keyboard, producing a kind of lowercase free verse.

830.18–19 *The Golden Thread* . . . *A Treasury of the Theatre* . . . *The Theatre*] Philo M. Buck Jr., ed., *The Golden Thread*, an annotated anthology of writings from classical Greece and Rome (New York: Macmillan, 1931); Burns Mantle and John Gassner, eds., *A Treasury of the Theatre: An Anthology of Great Plays from Aeschylus to Eugene O'Neill* (New York: Simon & Schuster, 1935); Sheldon Cheney, *The Theatre: Three Thousand Years of Drama, Acting, and Stagecraft* (New York and London: Longmans, Green & Co., 1929).

831.10 Atkinson . . . Brown] During Murray's undergraduate years (1935–39), Brooks Atkinson (1894–1984) was the chief drama critic of *The New York Times* and John Mason Brown (1900–1969) was his counterpart at the New York *Evening Post*.

831.12–13 Stark Young's book on the theater] Stark Young, *The Flower in Drama: A Book of Papers on the Theatre* (New York: Scribner's, 1923, expanded 1955). Young (1881–1963), a native of Mississippi, was theater critic for *The New Republic* from 1926 to 1947.

834.27 Couldn't write the blues] Among W. H. Auden's early works are such blues-inspired poems as "Funeral Blues" (1936) and "Roman Wall Blues" (1937).

835.18–19 frames of rejection and . . . acceptance] See Murray's discussion of Kenneth Burke's *Attitudes Toward History* on pages 509–10 of the present volume.

836.10–11   essay responding to Irving Howe] Ralph Ellison, "The World and the Jug" (see note 692.39–693.2).

837.2   "Freud and the Future."] See note 384.7.

837.6   *"What I Believe"*] See note 378.14–22. The essay was not published as a pamphlet; Murray's inscription appears on the first page of the essay in his copy of *Order of the Day* (1942): "This was the first thing that I read by Thomas Mann. I read it in *Nation*, December 10, 1938. (I was then a senior at Tuskegee.) It marked a definite 'turning point' in my thinking."

838.7   "The Eye of the Beholder."] Collected in *From the Briarpatch File* as "Riffing at Mrs. Jack's Place" (pages 744–48 of the present volume).

838.18–19   *Wilson debated . . . Brustein . . . a few weeks ago*] On June 26, 1996, in Princeton, New Jersey, playwright August Wilson (1945–2005) delivered the keynote speech at the biennial conference of the Theatre Communications Group. He lamented that America had almost no black theater companies and said that the practice of "colorblind casting"—or the casting of black actors in roles originally written for white actors—was "an aberrant idea . . . a tool of the Cultural Imperialists who view American culture, rooted in the icons of European culture, as beyond reproach in its perfection." He then named Robert Brustein (b. 1927), theater critic of *The New Republic*, artistic director of the American Repertory Theater in Cambridge, Massachusetts, and one of Wilson's harsher critics, "a sniper, a naysayer, and a cultural imperialist." When the speech was printed, as "The Ground on Which I Stand," in the September 1996 number of *American Theater* magazine, Brustein published a rejoinder, "Subsidized Separatism," in the October number. The controversy, which continued in the pages of *American Theater, The New Republic*, and the intellectual press, culminated in "On Cultural Power," a live debate between Wilson and Brustein, moderated by Anna Deavere Smith, at New York's Town Hall on January 27, 1997.

845.17   *Here is one example*] Ellison's letter is printed in full in *Trading Twelves: The Selected Letters of Ralph Ellison and Albert Murray* (2000).

846.3   *Charles H. Rowell*] Rowell, a poet and educator and the founding editor of *Callaloo: A Journal of African Diaspora Arts and Letters* (1976–), was born in Auburn, Alabama, in 1929. At the time of this interview he was a professor of English at the University of Virginia.

850.38–851.1   There was a Colored Branch] Following the separate-but-equal guidelines of *Plessy v. Ferguson* (1896), the "colored branch" of the Mobile Public Library (1903–61) was an exact replica of the white branch, but on a dramatically smaller scale. Today it is home to a museum of African American history.

851.33–852.2   *The Golden Thread . . . The Theatre*] See note 830.18–19.

852.11   John Gerald Hamilton] See note 209.16.

852.15–16   H. G. Wells's history of the world] *The Outline of History: or, The Whole Story of Man* (1919).

853.22   Freda Kirchwey] Kirchwey (1893–1976) was a book critic for, and then, from 1933 to 1955, the editor of, *The Nation*.

853.25   T. S. Stribling] Tennessee writer (1881–1965) remembered for a trilogy of social novels set in Alabama, one of which, *The Store*, was awarded the 1933 Pulitzer Prize for Fiction.

855.24–25   half of the manuscript] The other half, more or less, was a version of the essay "Ernest Hemingway: Swinging the Blues and Taking Nothing," pages 641–709 of the present volume.

856.1   Willie Morris] See note 239.11.

856.26–27   *A Turn in the South*] Naipaul (b. 1932) interviewed Murray for his book *A Turn in the South* (New York: Viking, 1989) and Murray helped to make arrangements for his trip to Tuskegee. In the book Naipaul presents a brief but closely observed profile of Murray and describes their meeting and conversations.

857.24–25   "The castle hill . . . castle was there."] Murray used this passage from Kafka's novel *The Castle* (*Das Schloss*, 1926) as the epigraph to *The Seven League Boots* (1996). The translation, from the German, is by Willa and Edwin Muir (New York: Knopf, 1941).

861.27–28   Skip Gates . . . *New Yorker* profile] Henry Louis Gates Jr., "King of Cats," *The New Yorker* (April 8, 1996).

862.17–18   "*all statements are counterstatements.*"] See page 7 of the present volume.

864.38   "by looking at the wine too long"?] See page 199 of the present volume.

866.10   what Kenneth Clark thinks] See note 26.21 et seq.

OTHER WRITINGS

871.1   "*The Problem" Is Not Just Black and White*] This omnibus review considers seven books: Nat Hentoff, *The New Equality* (New York: Viking, 1964); Charles E. Silberman, *Crisis in Black and White* (New York: Random House, 1964); Oscar Handlin, *Fire-Bell in the Night: The Crisis in Civil Rights* (Boston: Little, Brown, 1964); Benjamin Muse, *Ten Years of Prelude: The Story of Integration Since the Supreme Court's 1954 Decision* (New York: Viking, 1964); Bradford Daniel, ed., *Black, White, and Gray: Twenty-one Points of View on the Race Question* (New York: Sheed & Ward, 1964); Simeon Booker, *Black Man's America* (Englewood Cliffs, N.J.: Prentice-Hall, 1964); and Martin Luther King Jr., *Why We Can't Wait* (New York: Harper & Row, 1963).

871.22–23 Hentoff . . . Silberman] Nat Hentoff (b. 1925), for fifty years a jazz writer for *The Village Voice*, is also a social critic and the author of several novels and works of nonfiction. Economist Charles E. Silberman (1925–2011) wrote several books on economics, education, race, and social justice.

872.17 Oscar Handlin] American historian (1915–2011) whose book *The Uprooted: The Epic Story of the Great Migrations That Made the American People* won the Pulitzer Prize for History in 1952.

872.30 Benjamin Muse] Virginia-based Republican politician, journalist, and small-town newspaper publisher (1898–1986) who was a "gradualist" in his approach to desegregation.

872.35 Bradford Daniel] Roman Catholic poet and writer who was a longtime editor of *Sepia* magazine (1951–82) and the literary assistant to John Howard Griffin, author of *Black Like Me* (1961). Among the pieces collected in his *Black, White, and Gray* are Eve Auchincloss and Nancy Lynch, "Disturber of the Peace: An Interview with James Baldwin" (*Mademoiselle*, May 1963); Norman Podhoretz, "My Negro Problem—And Ours" (*Commentary*, February 1963); and Ronnie Dugger, "Confessions of a White Liberal" (*Commentary*, April 1964).

873.9 Simeon Booker] Chronicler of the civil rights movement (b. 1918) who was the Washington bureau chief for *Jet* magazine for fifty-one years.

874.10 *Why We Can't Wait*] King's book collects his "Letter from a Birmingham Jail" as well as his thoughts on John F. Kennedy's assassination.

874.23 *Blues for Mister Charlie* militants] See note 140.33.

875.28–31 Rosenwald . . . Peabody . . . Mann] American businessman Julius Rosenwald (1862–1932), a friend of Booker T. Washington and a major donor to the Tuskegee Institute, helped build schools for African Americans across the South. Endicott Peabody (1857–1944), an educational theorist, was founder and headmaster at the Groton School in Massachusetts, and Horace Mann (1796–1859), a U.S. congressman from Massachusetts, helped to create the nation's tax-supported public school system.

875.37–876.3 Wilkins . . . Greenberg . . . Hill . . . Shagaloff] Roy Wilkins (see note 797.35); Jack Greenberg (b. 1924) served under Thurgood Marshall at the NAACP Legal Defense Fund from 1949 to 1961 and litigated landmark civil rights cases, including *Brown v. Board of Education*; Herbert Hill (1924–2004) was labor director of the NAACP from 1951 to 1977; June Shagaloff Alexander (b. 1928) was education director of the NAACP from 1961 to 1972.

876.7 Rabbis rallying to King] Sixteen rabbis participated in a civil rights protest in St. Augustine, Florida, on June 18, 1964, and were subsequently jailed for a night. They wrote and cosigned a letter titled "Why We Went," which was printed in newspapers throughout the country.

880.11–18 Podhoretz . . . Adler] Norman Podhoretz's essay "My Negro Problem—And Ours" appeared in *Commentary* (February 1963) and was collected in Podhoretz's book *Doings and Undoings* (New York: Farrar, Straus, 1964). Renata Adler (b. 1937) wrote about Podhoretz's "well-intentioned but poorly reasoned essay" in "Polemic and the New Reviewers" (*The New Yorker*, July 4, 1964), collected in her book *Toward a Radical Middle* (New York: Random House, 1970).

880.20–23 Everybody however knows . . . Klan is anti-Semitic] On October 31, 1965, Daniel Burros, the twenty-eight-year-old Grand Dragon of the New York State Ku Klux Klan, took his own life after his Jewish upbringing, which he had gone to great lengths to hide from the Klan, was exposed by a *New York Times* reporter. Max Lerner (1902–1992), liberal opinion columnist for the *New York Post*, wrote a syndicated piece speculating about what he called Burros's Jewish "shame and self-hate" ("Suicide of Burros Sheds Light on Tensions of Our Times"), published on November 5, 1965.

882.21 Nathan Glazer] American sociologist (b. 1923) and a professor at Harvard University who, in 1966, when Murray drafted this article, had recently cowritten (with Daniel Patrick Moynihan; see note 28.34) *Beyond the Melting Pot: The Negroes, Puerto Ricans, Jews, Italians, and Irish of New York City* (1963) and *Negroes and Jews: The New Challenge of Pluralism* (1964).

883.36 Goodman and . . . Schwerner] Andrew Goodman (1943–1964) and Michael Schwerner (1939–1964), along with a black man, James Earl Chaney (1943–1964), were civil rights workers who were murdered in Philadelphia, Mississippi.

885.26 Noah Greenberg] Greenberg (1919–1966), New York choral director and proponent of early music, died shortly before this essay was commissioned.

885.29–31 Schapiro . . . Hadas . . . Josephson . . . Rosenberg] Meyer Schapiro (1904–1996), art historian; Moses Hadas (1900–1966), classical scholar and translator; Matthew Josephson (1899–1978), literary critic and historian of America's Gilded Age; Harold Rosenberg (1906–1978), art critic for *The New Yorker* and other publications.

885.36 the Stanleys] Stanley Kauffmann (1916–2013), longtime film critic for *The New Republic*, and Stanley Edgar Hyman (see note 214.33).

885.39 Goldberg . . . Fortas] In 1966, when this essay was written, Arthur Goldberg (1908–1990) was U.S. ambassador to the United Nations and Abe Fortas (1910–1982) an associate justice of the U.S. Supreme Court.

889.7 BUCKET GEORGE] Better known as Hoppin' John: black-eyed peas and rice, seasoned with onion, bacon, and spices.

889.12   streak-o-lean] Salt pork; the fatback cut of a pig.

890.27   Skeat] The Reverend Walter W. Skeat (1835–1912), compiler of *A Concise Etymological Dictionary of the English Language* (Oxford: Clarendon Press/Oxford University Press, 1879–82).

891.14   Lena (who is earthy but never kittenish)] Allusion to cabaret singers Lena Horne (1917–2010) and Eartha Kitt (1927–2008).

891.17   H. Rap Brown] See note 38.39–40.

892.27   Andrew Hacker . . . *Two Nations*] Hacker (b. 1929) is Professor Emeritus of Political Science at Queens College in New York. The title and subtitle of his book *Two Nations: Black and White, Separate, Hostile, Unequal* (New York: Ballantine Books, 1992) allude to the Kerner report of 1968 (see note 8.31–32).

894.13–14   *"The condition of man . . . place, time, and circumstance."*] See page 525 of the present volume.

894.17   GAIL GELBURD] Gelburd (b. 1954) is a painter and photographer, an independent curator of exhibitions, and a professor of museum studies and art history at Eastern Connecticut State University.

895.13–14   It seems that the art . . . art form is dance] See note 493.25–27.

896.27   "imitation of life,"] *Mimesis*: see Plato, *The Republic*, Book 10.

898.24–25   Roger Caillois in *Man, Play, and Games*] See note 527.10.

900.12   "The Sun Do Move."] Sermon by the Reverend John J. Jasper (1812–1901), a Baptist preacher in Richmond, Virginia, published in the *Richmond Dispatch* in 1882.

901.2   this book] Murray's essay is the foreword to *Mitchell & Ruff: An American Profile in Jazz* (2000), by freelance journalist and amateur jazz pianist William Zinsser (1922–2015), author of *On Writing Well* (1976). Ivory "Dwike" Mitchell Jr. (1930–2013), pianist, and Willie Ruff (b. 1931), bassist and French horn player, performed as the Mitchell-Ruff Duo from 1955 to 2011.

902.20   *Train Whistle Guitar*] Murray's first novel, published by McGraw-Hill, New York, in 1974.

905.19   "ain't these tears in these eyes telling you."] From "Am I Blue," song (1929) by Harry Akst, words by Grant Clarke.

911.29–32   How appropriate then . . . Abraham Lincoln] Murray alludes to Jazz at Lincoln Center's performance facilities in the Time Warner Center at Columbus Circle in Manhattan, which opened to the public on October 18, 2004, the date of this piece's publication in *The New Republic*.

Index

*This book is set in 10 point ITC Galliard, a face
designed for digital composition by Matthew Carter and based
on the sixteenth-century face Granjon. The paper is acid-free
lightweight opaque that will not turn yellow or brittle with age.
The binding is sewn, which allows the book to open easily and lie flat.
The binding board is covered in Brillianta, a woven rayon cloth
made by Van Heek–Scholco Textielfabrieken, Holland.
Composition by Dedicated Book Services.
Printing and binding by Edwards Brothers Malloy, Ann Arbor.
Designed by Bruce Campbell.*

THE LIBRARY OF AMERICA SERIES

The Library of America fosters appreciation of America's literary heritage by publishing, and keeping permanently in print, authoritative editions of America's best and most significant writing. An independent nonprofit organization, it was founded in 1979 with seed funding from the National Endowment for the Humanities and the Ford Foundation.